PUBLIC PAPERS OF THE PRESIDENTS
OF THE
UNITED STATES

PUBLIC PAPERS OF THE PRESIDENTS
OF THE
UNITED STATES

George Bush

1992–93

(IN TWO BOOKS)

BOOK II—AUGUST 1, 1992 TO JANUARY 20, 1993

UNITED STATES GOVERNMENT PRINTING OFFICE
WASHINGTON : 1993

Published by the
Office of the Federal Register
National Archives and Records Administration

For sale by the
Superintendent of Documents
U.S. Government Printing Office
Washington, DC 20402

Foreword

The six months between August 1992 and January 1993 should really be divided into two parts: The first part was the final stage of a long and difficult election campaign; the second saw both the orderly transfer of power to a new administration and several important economic and foreign policy developments.

We showed promising signs of economic growth as the Gross Domestic Product grew 3.4% in the third quarter, and 4.8% in the fourth quarter of 1992.

On October 7, I met with Prime Minister Mulroney of Canada and President Salinas of Mexico in San Antonio to initial the North American Free Trade Agreement, which I later signed on December 17. This historic agreement proposes to link North America, its 350 million people and its 6 trillion dollar market into the largest free trading block in the world. Currently, 2.1 million Americans owe their jobs to trade with Canada and Mexico. This number would continue to increase dramatically with the passing of NAFTA.

On December 8, I ordered the deployment of U.S. troops to Somalia for Operation Restore Hope. This historic humanitarian effort helped to secure the distribution of food and supplies to desperate and starving Somali villages. Over the New Year holiday, I visited our troops in Somalia and saw the dramatic success of the Operation, as literally thousands of Somalis a day were saved from imminent starvation.

I traveled to Russia on January 2 to sign the START II weapons treaty with Russian President Boris Yeltsin. This treaty eliminates the world's most threatening land-based missiles. START II, together with START I, greatly enhances strategic stability and will result in an overall reduction of approximately 75 percent in nuclear forces.

Much was accomplished during the last six months of our Administration. I am proud to have passed on to the next Administration a recovering economy and a United States strong and respected around the world.

George Bush

Preface

This book contains the papers and speeches of the 41st President of the United States that were issued by the Office of the Press Secretary during the period August 1, 1992–January 20, 1993. The material has been compiled and published by the Office of the Federal Register, National Archives and Records Administration.

The material is presented in chronological order, and the dates shown in the headings are the dates of the documents or events. In instances when the release date differs from the date of the document itself, that fact is shown in the textnote. Every effort has been made to ensure accuracy: Remarks are checked against a tape recording, and signed documents are checked against the original. Textnotes and cross references have been provided by the editors for purposes of identification or clarity. Speeches were delivered in Washington, DC, unless indicated. The times noted are local times. All materials that are printed full-text in the book have been indexed in the subject and name indexes, and listed in the document categories list.

The Public Papers of the Presidents series was begun in 1957 in response to a recommendation of the National Historical Publications Commission. An extensive compilation of messages and papers of the Presidents covering the period 1789 to 1897 was assembled by James D. Richardson and published under congressional authority between 1896 and 1899. Since then, various private compilations have been issued, but there was no uniform publication comparable to the Congressional Record or the United States Supreme Court Reports. Many Presidential papers could be found only in the form of mimeographed White House releases or as reported in the press. The Commission therefore recommended the establishment of an official series in which Presidential writings, addresses, and remarks of a public nature could be made available.

The Commission's recommendation was incorporated in regulations of the Administrative Committee of the Federal Register, issued under section 6 of the Federal Register Act (44 U.S.C. 1506), which may be found in title 1, part 10, of the Code of Federal Regulations.

A companion publication to the Public Papers series, the Weekly Compilation of Presidential Documents, was begun in 1965 to provide a broader range of Presidential materials on a more timely basis to meet the needs of the contemporary reader. Beginning with the administration of Jimmy Carter, the Public Papers series expanded its coverage to include all material as printed in the Weekly Compilation. That coverage provides a listing of the President's daily schedule and meetings, when announced, and other items of general interest issued by the Office of the Press Secretary. Also included are lists of the President's nominations submitted to the Senate, materials released by the Office of the Press Secretary that are not printed full-text in the book, acts approved by the President, and proclamations and Executive orders. This information appears in the appendixes at the end of the book.

Volumes covering the administrations of Presidents Hoover, Truman, Eisenhower, Kennedy, Johnson, Nixon, Ford, Carter, and Reagan are also available.

The Public Papers of the Presidents publication program is under the direction of Gwen H. Estep. The Chief Editor of this book was Karen Howard Ashlin.

White House liaison was provided by Marlin Fitzwater, Assistant to the President and Press Secretary. The frontispiece and photographs used in the portfolio were supplied by the White House Photo Office. The typography and design of the book were developed by the Government Printing Office under the direction of Michael F. DiMario, Acting Public Printer.

Martha L. Girard
Director of the Federal Register

Trudy Huskamp Peterson
Acting Archivist of the United States

Contents

Cabinet

Secretary of State.. James Addison Baker III
Lawrence S. Eagleburger
(acting, effective August 23)

Secretary of the Treasury............................... Nicholas F. Brady

Secretary of Defense....................................... Richard B. Cheney

Attorney General... William P. Barr

Secretary of the Interior................................. Manuel Lujan, Jr.

Secretary of Agriculture .... Edward R. Madigan

Secretary of Commerce.................................. Barbara Hackman Franklin

Secretary of Labor.. Lynn M. Martin

Secretary of Health and Human Services ... Louis W. Sullivan

Secretary of Housing and Urban
Development.. Jack Kemp

Secretary of Transportation .... Andrew H. Card, Jr.

Secretary of Energy... James D. Watkins

Secretary of Education .... Lamar Alexander

Secretary of Veterans Affairs......................... Edward J. Derwinski

Director of the Office of Management
and Budget... Richard G. Darman

United States Trade Representative............. Carla Anderson Hills

Administration of George Bush

1992–93

Remarks at a Fundraising Brunch for Rich Williamson in Rosemont, Illinois

August 2, 1992

Thank you all very, very much. What a wonderful welcome. And that makes me convinced that I'm going to win in November, too.

Let me thank Rich Williamson. And good morning and my respects to Jane, and of course, to Jim Edgar, who is just doing a superb job as Governor of this State. You ought to be very, very proud of him. Rich couldn't have a better man at his side than secretary of state George Ryan, longtime friend. I'm grateful also to the Lieutenant Governor, Bob Kustre, who was out there at the airport to say hello; and to the State's attorney, Jack O'Malley; my old friend Congressman Phil Crane, with us today. And if you want some heavy lifting done in the fundraising, get H. Clark involved. H., thank you very, very much for what you've done here. And also, I want to salute our State chairman, Al Jourdan. And national committeewoman Mary Jo Arndt is here today. I see she brought some of her family with her; that's good.

It's great to be back here in Chicago. I was half tempted to call the Mayor while I'm in town. My guess is that he was pretty upset by his party's recent gathering in New York. He thought Chicago had the nickname "the Windy City." [*Laughter*]

But this afternoon, I want to tell you a story about a young girl, poor in pocket but rich in hope, who left her German village to come to America. She came in search of something larger than herself, a future for her children and for their children. Here in Chicago, she married another immigrant. She took in laundry; he sold clothes. They lived in a tiny apartment and never gave up hope that their daughter would have a better future and their daughter's son an even better one.

That's how this country was born. And that's how it grew into the most proud, the most free nation on the face of the Earth. America became great through millions of stories like this, stories of men and women who left behind their homes in order to take a chance on a dream for their children here in the land of opportunity.

If that young woman I just told you about were here today, she would see how her sacrifice made the American dream come true for her grandson. She would see with pride that he stands here today, determined to make that dream come true for all of us, the sons and the daughters of Illinois, the whole country. Helen Salisbury would be proud to see the next Senator from Illinois, her grandson, Rich Williamson.

As he said, Rich and I go back a long way. Rich and his dog, Mac, knew Millie before she was a best-selling author. [*Laughter*] So I'm here out of friendship for a brilliant, dedicated leader. But I'm also here for what's good for the United States of America. I thought George Ryan put it very, very well when he spelled out what's at stake here because Rich's race and the race I'm involved in have a lot in common. If you really want to make a change in this country, let's change the institution that hasn't changed for 38 years and change control of the United States Congress. Rich can do a lot to help.

In the dog days of summer, it's very easy to be attracted to the new candidate, the one who says the things the polls say the people want to hear. But by the fall, the American people look more closely, and they ask this question: Who do we trust to change America? Who has the ideas to carry us forward to a better future?

Rich Williamson is a leader worthy of your trust. Just as we've changed the world, we now have the ideas to change America. Rich and I both believe that to lead a great

Nation you must first trust the people you lead.

Look at the two sides in this election, and the choice is very clear. On one side you have people advocating a Nation of the Government, by the Government, for the Government. Rich and I have a very different philosophy. We agree with another son of Illinois: America should be a Nation "of the people, by the people, and for the people."

Let me just take one issue today, discuss one issue to show the Grand Canyon of philosophy that separates the two sides in this election. It is one of the most pressing concerns that we face today: I'm talking about health care. Our health care system doesn't work today. We all know that. Thirty-four million Americans are without insurance. Millions more worry that they cannot afford the rising costs of health care.

What are we going to do about it? Well, the other side and I have both put forward plans; you can look them over. I invite comparison. The other plan offers health care reform. My plan offers health care reform. The other plan is printed on plain white bond paper, and my plan is printed on plain white bond paper. From there the differences are wider than an Illinois cornfield.

The other plan will dump 52 million Americans into a new Government bureaucracy, and my plan will help 90 million Americans afford private insurance to take care of their health care needs. The other plan would slap at least a 7-percent payroll tax on middle-income Americans, and my plan would provide tax relief to Americans to help them pay for their own health care. The other plan will cost America at least 700,000 jobs, and my plan helps small business afford health insurance so they can hire more people. The other plan will create lines at hospitals so long you'll think they were selling Bears tickets inside. [*Laughter*] My plan will allow you to get the care you need when you need it, and my plan will preserve the quality of health care in this country. The other plan is going to put bureaucrats in charge of setting health care prices, and my plan attacks the root causes of rising costs: faulty insurance,

too much paperwork, far too many frivolous lawsuits out there.

Understand what's at stake here. If the Governor of Arkansas is elected with a Democratic Congress and a new Democratic Senator from Illinois, within a year the Government will run health care in this country. Our health care system will combine the efficiency of the House post office with the compassion of the KGB. I am not going to let that happen.

Give me Rich Williamson in the Senate, and we will fight against those who put the Government first all the time. We'll fight for what works for America. We will fight for what's right for America. That's what this election is all about, not about change alone because change always happens. The question is, who do you trust to change America? On health care, taxes, education, and every other issue we face, Rich and I say the same thing: Let others listen to the polls; let others listen to the pols. Rich and I want to fight for what's right for the United States of America.

Rich touched on it, and he and I share a strong love of a certain proud American tradition, one that his kids, Ricky and Lisa, already shared with us today. I want to close by asking all of you to listen once again to these familiar words. I believe with all my heart that Americans must join and once again pledge allegiance to the finest vision of the United States of America: "one Nation under God, indivisible, with liberty and justice for all."

That is the country I love, the country Rich loves, the country you love. When I ask you to help that country by believing in this good man, working for him, and voting for him, I'm sure you'll answer in the words of the motto of this great city of Chicago: I will.

God bless you all. Thank you very, very much for this fantastic turnout and this wonderful support. Thank you very much.

Note: The President spoke at 12:15 p.m. at the Hyatt Regency O'Hare Hotel. In his remarks, he referred to Jane Williamson, wife of Rich Williamson, and H. Clark, master of ceremonies.

Remarks at the Northwest Republican Family Picnic in Elk Grove Village, Illinois
August 2, 1992

Thank you very much. Hey, you guys ready for a 45-minute speech, okay? Thank you very much. Thank you very much. Here is a man suggesting that we change control of the United States Congress. He is right. That's what some of this election is going to be about.

Let me salute the Governor, let me salute Governor Edgar and say what a great job he and the Lieutenant Governor and others are doing for this country. Let me tell you, it is absolutely essential that we get more support in the United States Senate. So vote for Rich Williamson here and send him to Washington.

Let me just say this—I won't talk but a second—we have indeed changed the world. Now I need your help in getting this country on the move, changing America for the values we all believe in. And we can do it.

I've never seen such a strange political year, but I'll tell you this: When that convention in Houston is over, I am going to come out and go after that opponent. He's been on my case for 6 months. We are going to define it, and we are going to win the election—6 months, 6 months of distorting the great Republican record. I'm going to take the case to the people, and we will win in November.

Thank you all very much. Thank you very, very much. Now go dry out.

Note: The President spoke at 1:25 p.m. at Ned Brown Preserve.

Remarks to Multitex Employees in Dalton, Georgia
August 3, 1992

We wanted to come down here and see the tremendous job that Dalton does in selling product all over the world. Don't tell me the United States can't compete when you see a place like this. We are number one. You know, the guy I'm running against called America the laughingstock, or said that we were ridiculed around the world. Let me tell you something: The United States is the leader of the entire world, the most respected country on the face of the Earth. So don't let these pessimists start downgrading our great country.

Now, here's my view. I love this political rally, but I've got a confession to make. I've said that until our convention in Houston I'm going to hold back a little bit. But I'll tell you something: I can't wait for that convention to be over. It's going to be strong. It's going to be good. And then I am going to set the record straight.

For 6 months the opposition has been distorting a good, solid world leadership record, and we're not going to let that stand. So to all you Georgians who believe you can accomplish things, who are demonstrating right here in Dalton to the rest of the world what the American worker can do: Stay in there and help me. We are going to win.

Thank you very, very much.

Note: The President spoke at 8:40 a.m. at the Multitex Corp.

Remarks to Shaw Industries Employees in Dalton
August 3, 1992

Thank you very, very much for that welcome back to Georgia, and Bob, thank you, sir. I don't know if I detected a note of relief on Anna Sue's face that this event, that I'm sure has taken everybody's time, is here at hand and about to end. But thank you for making us feel so welcome in this wonderful corner of Georgia.

I want to greet our other hosts, Bill Lusk and Norris Little, Carl Rollins of Shaw, and my Georgia political team here: Fred Cooper, my dear friend, and also another dear friend, Alec Poitevint, who are doing a great job for us.

I would like to single out one department in this magnificent, enormous facility, and I'm talking about the area rug department, who made a nice little souvenir for me to take home with my own name on it. I'll tell you, I can't think of a nicer, more personalized remembrance than that. So wherever you may be, thank you very, very much, and thank the computers that spelled my name right. [*Laughter*]

Now, it is great to be in Dalton. I came here—I want to be first in line for the Catamount tickets when they go on sale, and I've come here for another reason, too. America, our great country, is moving into a new age, and Dalton gives us a glimpse of the future. Dalton takes challenges and reinvents them as opportunities. With the flexibility of companies like this one, like Shaw, with the brainpower and grit of your chemists and your maintenance mechanics and your designers, Dalton shows America the face of the 21st century. Dalton shows the way.

In the history of your industry you find a parable of American progress. It starts simply, families selling hand-tufted bedspreads that they made themselves out on Highway 41, Peacock Alley. It continues with the sprawling factories that sprung up after the war, rolling their carpets into homes and offices in every corner of America. And it continues today with an industry retooled by high tech, a work force more highly skilled than ever before, and a mar-

ketplace as big as the entire world.

The story has important lessons, lessons about how America grows and prospers. This election year, these lessons could not be more timely. The question today is not, can America compete in the global economy. I know and you know that we can. The question is how: How do we stay number one? How do we create jobs for every American and create opportunities for our kids, our children, and our families?

Some people say, "Well, let the Government do it. Let the Government get in there." But Government does not create jobs; people do. Government does not provide opportunity; hard work does. Look around. This company, this industry was not built by some industrial planning congressional subcommittee in Washington, DC. It was born and built right here in Dalton, where the men and women take the risks and reap the rewards.

That's a lesson we shouldn't forget even given the hue and cry of this election year. When you get down to it, leadership is about trust. Trust runs both ways. You need a leader who you can trust, but you also need a leader who trusts in the American people, trusts you and not the Government to make the important decisions about your lives.

When you forget about this kind of trust, trusting people, you get some crazy ideas. I'll give you an example. These days the other side is pushing an idea that the way to fix this economy is to raise taxes by $150 billion. And at least half of that will fall on family farmers and small businesses. They call that change. I guess it makes sense because if the other side get in power, change is all you'll have left in your pocket. [*Laughter*]

Here's another crazy idea that's being pushed. They think they can fix health care by slapping you with at least a 7-percent payroll tax to finance a Government takeover scheme. Well, we'll have a health care system with the efficiency of the motor vehicles if we do that, the motor vehicles division, and also the KGB, the same compassion. As long as I am President, I am not going to let our medical system be socialized or nationalized. We have a plan that will provide insurance to all, those who need it, those who cannot afford it, and will protect the basic quality of American health care.

So trusting the people, it's an idea that applies to almost every issue in this election, especially when it comes to how we can compete in this whole new world global economy, how we can take on the new global competition head-on-head and win it.

Let me tell you how I learned about competing in the world. I'm a Texan, moved there in 1948, built a business there, raised my family there. Incidentally, I think it's a pretty good credential, for being President of the United States even, if you held a job in the private sector. I think that's good. In Texas I saw businesses and cities and towns rise up from those dusty plains, a place where you'd never expect it. The reason was that the whole world thirsted for what Texans had to offer, crude and cattle and cotton. We knew the more goods we sold outside our borders, the more jobs we created within them. I never forgot that lesson.

I saw it again when I went into public life. And yes, I was Ambassador up there at the United Nations and lived overseas in China—just talking to Bob Shaw about that—ran the CIA, and as Vice President, traveled around the world some. And every day I was outside of this country I learned again how important America was to the entire world and how important the world was to America. I'm talking about creating American jobs, about making this economy grow and prosper, and making sure our kids have an even better life than we've had.

I've seen this every day for 3½ years as President. I heard a certain southern Governor say the other day that this country was being ridiculed around the world. Well, I suspect—and I'm not going to name names quite yet—I suspect that he hasn't been around much. I'd like to have him walk the streets of Warsaw, as I did a few days ago, or Moscow or maybe sit down with Boris Yeltsin or Helmut Kohl or Miyazawa or a myriad of leaders south of our border. And they'd tell him what you

and I already know: The United States is the undisputed leader of the world. That did not happen by accident. It happened by leadership and by the sons and daughters of America doing what they had to do, from Iraq all the way across a major spectrum of other places. It's the spirit of the United States. To tear down this country, to stand there and try to make the American people think we're a second-rate power, they simply don't understand the greatness of the United States of America.

Here's one way we're going to demonstrate it: trade, exports, open up markets so you can sell the goods you make right here. I heard Bob Shaw talk about it, and he is 100 percent correct. The day is long gone when you could sell carpets and rugs in 50 States and leave it just there. These days, standing still means falling behind. It's a new world. Markets are opening up in Guadalajara and Jakarta and Santiago and Moscow. And I'm going to see to it that Americans get there first.

It's not going to be easy. This export business is not easy. If you want America to lead the world, you need somebody who understands; you need a leader who understands the territory, someone you can trust to hammer out a good deal around the negotiating table. But you need even more. You need a leader who trusts you and someone who knows that Americans are the most productive, the most competitive workers the world has ever seen. All you need is a chance to show your stuff. As long as I am President, I'm going to fight to see that you get the chance to sell these products anywhere around the world.

Let me give you one example. Some people look at the former Soviet Union and see 300 million former Communists over there. Well, we look at it, and we see 300 million future customers. Now, math was never my favorite subject, but I've done some computing on this one. Let's say there's 50 million homes—I don't know, give or take—50 million homes in the former Soviet Union; maybe 4.5 billion square yards of floor space, bare floor space. That's 4.5 billion square yards just waiting to be covered by your finest patterned berber. Of course, I'm factoring in kitchens and bathtubs, too. But I have faith in your sales force. They can sell anything, anyplace, anytime.

Another example: Since 1989—now, listen to this one—since 1989, exports, carpet exports to Mexico are up by 60 percent. That's pretty darn good. But here in Dalton, pretty good isn't good enough. We're going to build on that success. Right now we're hammering out a new free trade deal with Canada and Mexico. We call it the NAFTA. I'm sure you've read about it. Here's what it will do. It will create 300,000 American jobs by 1995 and one of the largest free trade areas in the world. Free trade opens up the road, and on the open road, American workers leave the competition in the dust. Or as my friend Arnold Schwarzenegger would say, *"Hasta la vista, baby!"* We are on the move, and we're going to keep it on the move.

Now, it may be hard to believe, but the other side looks at these barriers falling and they say, "Hold everything." They see these unbelievable opportunities, these vast markets to sell your goods, and they say, "Well, we'd better not try. The challenge is too great; the odds are too long." They just by implication say the Americans can't compete. They say these other countries are going to walk all over us. Well, let me tell you something. In a way they are going to walk all over us. They're going to walk all over carpet made right here in Dalton, Georgia.

This is the year—for 6 months we've been subjected to the darnedest pessimism about our great country that I have ever heard. Every time you turn on that television at night, somebody telling you what's wrong. Well, let me tell you what's right. They say that America can't compete. I say we can compete and that we'll win. They say, "Pull the blinds and lock the door; the American worker can't hack it anymore." I say the American worker can outthink, outwork, outcompete anyone, anytime, anywhere.

Here's a fact these pessimists better understand: Foreign trade supports the jobs of 153,000 Georgians, more than 7 million

Americans. Here's my pledge to you: I will not let anyone endanger a single one of those jobs by going protectionist and closing up trade.

Let the other side criticize and say our country is ridiculed, laughed at around the world. They ought to open their eyes. Let them worry and whine. I am going to fight for these open markets because that means more jobs in this country, right here in Dalton, Georgia, among others, every city and State of our country. Let them run this country down; let them carp on what's wrong with America. I'm going to do what's right. That's what leadership is, and that's what trust is.

I'd like to bring these pessimists down here to this part of Georgia. I'd like to bring them right here to see this town, this industry. They might discover they've got nothing to fear from American workers and that American workers have nothing to fear from competition. This is one work force that can beat the pants off any competition.

That is the lesson of Dalton. That's why I'm here. I want that lesson to reverberate all across our entire country. You didn't fear the future; you shaped it. Your industry didn't retreat from foreign markets; you went out and conquered them. And with leadership that trusts in you, you'll keep beating the pants off the competition.

You and I do not feel that we are the laughingstock of the world. We are the undisputed leader. So let's keep it just exactly that way in the future. Let's keep America number one.

Thank you. And may God bless our great country. Thank you very, very much.

Note: The President spoke at 8:58 a.m. in the Shaw Industries Distribution Center South. In his remarks, he referred to company officials Robert Shaw, president and chief executive officer, William Lusk, senior vice president and treasurer, Norris Little, senior vice president for operations, and Carl Rollins, vice president; Mr. Shaw's wife, Anna Sue; Fred Cooper, State chairman, Bush-Quayle '92; and Alec Poitevint, Georgia Republican Party chairman.

Remarks on Arrival in Jacksonville, Florida
August 3, 1992

The President. What a great rally. What a fantastic Jacksonville turnout. Thank you all very, very much. This is good for the soul.

Audience members. Four more years! Four more years! Four more years!

The President. Thank you so very, very much. Senator Mack, Connie, my friend, thank you for that warm introduction. Let me just tell you something that you must know well: When the going got tough in Desert Storm days, you could turn to Connie Mack for success, for trust, for conviction. He was right on the ball all the way. And he is right: If you really want to change America, change control of the United States Congress, and let us get this country moving.

I want to thank the Mayor for that warm introduction. I'll forgive him for being a Democrat; he's a good man, and—[*laughter*]—I was delighted to have him say those pleasant things. To Mark Little: Mark, you've got a great voice, you ought to go in radio. [*Laughter*] Thank you. Thank you very much for being here and getting this gang all fired up. When I say fired up, I'm talking literally. I saw you when I came by on Air Force One—a little warm out there. And may I salute Cliff Stearns and Craig James, both great Congressmen. And let me say this: Please elect Tillie Fowler and send her to the United States Congress. You want to change things; there's a good way to do it. And may I salute Minority Leaders Crenshaw and Lombard and our State Treasurer Gallagher and so many others that are here with us today. And to the kids, the Americakids that kept you entertained, my thanks to them and also to the Fletcher High School marching band and the Fletcher High School cheerleaders. Don't say I didn't mention them. And Mayor, thanks once again for your open-mindedness and your warm welcome to your city.

If you're like me, you're grabbing every spare moment you can to keep up with the great Olympic games in Barcelona. My favorite events have been in the swimming, for three reasons. Make that four. First, Martin Zubero. His backstroke was for Spain, but I bet his heart, with his hometown of Jacksonville. And also, your own Gregg Burgess, who took home the silver. We're proud of him.

Here's another guy I like, Pablo Morales, the guy who missed out. Remember, he missed out in '84; he didn't make the team in '88; then he came back this year to take the gold, and at the ripe old age of 27. I don't know why, but I kind of like a guy who proves that youth and inexperience are no match for maturity and determination.

The fourth one was Summer Sanders. How's that for the name of a swimmer. Summer was trailing halfway through the 200 meter butterfly, then came on strong to win at the finish. Came on strong to win at the finish, I like that. We are going to do exactly the same thing to these guys coming out of this so-called new team.

We've heard a lot of talk about change this year; the other side has put forth more heat than this Florida sunshine. But don't worry; let's see how they can take it. I am going to carry it back to them and take my case to you, the American people. They've had their day, 6 months of carping and griping and tearing down the United States, and that day is over. We're going to take the case to the American people.

The other side, they talk about change, but when you look at their position on the most radical change of all, limiting the tenure of Members of Congress, they quietly admit they're against the idea. That's change, just changing their tune. [*Laughter*]

The other side talks about change, but in a certain 7,000-word speech at a convention that I was happy to miss—[*laughter*]—they devoted just 141 words to defense of this country and to our foreign policy. Then when they finally get around to it, they propose $60 billion in defense cuts beyond which my national security experts tell me is responsible. They do not mention the fact that these reckless cuts will cost a million jobs across America, some right here in

Jacksonville. They dry up Mayport to look like a prune, and we are not going to do that. We've got to keep our country strong. You talk about that change; that's called changing the subject.

The other side talks about change. Look at the first two ideas of the economy. They propose—and Connie knows this, and he's fighting hard against it—they propose a $150 billion tax increase now, half of it paid by small businessmen and farmers, and then follow it up with a new payroll tax of at least 7 percent to pay for a Government-run health care scheme. That is change, but change is all you're going to have left in your pocket if you listen to them.

I stand for a change, and here it is, a new approach. Congress has a lower rate of turnover than the Soviet Politburo used to have—[laughter]—36 years with one party holding the power. I am fighting for term limits because the only way to break the deadlock in Washington is by clearing out a little deadwood on Capitol Hill.

I know when you have up there in some of these liberal communities, if you want people to do something that's politically appealing, yes, they want to gut the defense. But I am not going to let that happen. For the sake of our children and the economy, I am determined to keep the United States of America strong.

I don't believe the way to jump-start this economy is with a new tax-and-spend program. I trust you to spend your hard-earned dollars better than any bureaucrat can.

And so this election is not just about change. It's about something else, a flip side of change, and that is called trust. When you get right down to it, this election will be like every other. When you pull that curtain closed and cast your vote on November 3d, trust really does matter.

Many times in the White House, late at night, the telephone rings. Most times it's an aide checking up on the schedule. But sometimes it's another voice, more serious, more solemn, bringing news of a coup in a powerful foreign country, bringing word of Americans held against their will, bringing word of a bully threatening the peace halfway around the world. The American people need to know that the man who answers that phone has the experience, the

seasoning, and yes, the guts to make the right decision and to make the tough call. You want a leader you can trust. I have worked hard to prove that I am that man.

Audience members. Four more years! Four more years! Four more years!

The President. The bottom line is, that's trust in the traditional sense. That keeps America safe and strong. But that's part of the picture. And trust matters when you're looking to someone to build strength in the economy of this country, as Connie said, a better future. I stake my claim on a simple philosophy: To lead a great nation, you must trust the people that you lead. You look at every big issue we face, and you'll see a choice between those who put their faith in everyday Americans and those who put their faith in Government.

The other side says they want to put people first. But if you look at their ideas real close, the people they put first are all on the Government payroll. They remind me of the cartoon of a bus, maybe you saw it recently, two donkeys on board. The traffic above says, "Left lane closed; keep right for the next 4 months." And one donkey is whispering, "Don't worry, we'll just stay in this lane 'til November."

Well, I did not adopt my philosophy 4 months ago, nor did you. I adopted it, mine, more than four decades ago, when I first had a job and ran a business and tried to meet a payroll. That is a good credential for the President of the United States. I learned then not to put my trust in the Government but to put it in the people.

I trust parents, not the Government, to make the decisions that matter in life. I trust the parents, not the Government, to choose their children's schools, public, private, and religious. I trust parents, not the Government, to choose their children's child care. And when the other side says, "Government knows best," I say, "Parents know better." Parents know better than some bureaucrat way up there in Washington, DC.

I trust the people, not the Government, to decide where and when you get a doctor's help. We can control costs. We must and will—and I have a plan to do this— make insurance coverage more available to everybody that needs it without a Government takeover of health care in this country. Frankly, I think we need, Americans deserve a better health care system than one that's run with the efficiency of the department of motor vehicles and the compassion of the KGB. We do not want to go to a nationalized or a socialized plan.

I know that, look, this is a funny year. You live and die every time you turn on the news, you hear some new poll. Let me tell you something about that. I know that my stands are not popular in all places. But they don't come from the latest poll or a special interest. They come from principle. And I make you one promise in this campaign. Others can listen to the polls; others can pay attention to the pols. I am going to do my level-best to do what is right for the United States of America.

I am delighted to be with our son here, Jeb, today, my boy—[*laughter*]—my little boy. I just wish that Barbara were here. I think she's doing a first-class job for this country.

But let me just close with that in mind, with family in mind, with a few words right smack from the heart. We are blessed, Barbara and I, blessed to serve at a moment in history when so many of the old fears have been driven away, when so many new

hopes are within our reach. The changes that we've worked for have come to pass: the end of the cold war, the collapse of imperial communism, a new birth of freedom from Managua to Moscow, a new world of hope for ourselves and for our kids. The world we live in, let's face it, is a safer world, safer than it was a decade ago, a year ago, safer than it was 2 months ago when the children right here walked out of school and off into the summer. We have done so much to reduce the threat of nuclear war, and that is good for the world and good for the United States.

The bottom line is this: When we have done so much for the past 4 years, when we put our faith in the people, we can do anything we want. We have changed the world, and we will change America. We will not do what is easy or politically appealing. We will do what is right for the United States of America.

Thank you and God bless you all.

Note: The President spoke at 12:31 p.m. at Jacksonville Landing. In his remarks, he referred to Mayor Ed Austin of Jacksonville; Mark Little, master of ceremonies; Ander Crenshaw, Florida State Senate minority leader; and James Lombard, Florida State House of Representatives minority leader.

Message to the Congress Reporting on the National Emergency With Respect to Iraq
August 3, 1992

To the Congress of the United States:

I hereby report to the Congress on the developments since my last report of February 11, 1992, concerning the national emergency with respect to Iraq that was declared in Executive Order No. 12722 of August 2, 1990. This report is submitted pursuant to section 401(c) of the National Emergencies Act, 50 U.S.C. 1641(c), and section 204(c) of the International Emergency Economic Powers Act ("IEEPA"), 50 U.S.C. 1703(c).

Executive Order No. 12722 ordered the immediate blocking of all property and in-

terests in property of the Government of Iraq (including the Central Bank of Iraq) then or thereafter located in the United States or within the possession or control of a U.S. person. In that order, I also prohibited the importation into the United States of goods and services of Iraqi origin, as well as the exportation of goods, services, and technology from the United States to Iraq. I prohibited travel-related transactions and transportation transactions to or from Iraq and the performance of any contract in support of any industrial, commercial, or governmental project in Iraq. U.S. persons were also prohibited from granting or extending credit or loans to the Government of Iraq.

The foregoing prohibitions (as well as the blocking of Government of Iraq property) were continued and augmented on August 9, 1990, by Executive Order No. 12724 which I issued in order to align the sanctions imposed by the United States with United Nations Security Council Resolution 661 of August 6, 1990.

This report discusses only matters concerning the national emergency with respect to Iraq that was declared in Executive Order No. 12722 and matters relating to Executive Order No. 12724 ("the Executive orders"). The report covers events from February 2, 1992, through August 1, 1992.

1. The economic sanctions imposed on Iraq by the Executive orders are administered by the Treasury Department's Office of Foreign Assets Control ("FAC") under the Iraqi Sanctions Regulations, 31 CFR Part 575 ("ISR"). There have been no amendments of those regulations since my last report.

2. Investigations of possible violations of the Iraqi sanctions continue to be pursued and appropriate enforcement actions taken. These are intended to deter future activities in violation of the sanctions. Additional civil penalty notices were prepared during the reporting period for violations of the IEEPA and ISR with respect to transactions involving Iraq. Penalties were collected, principally from financial institutions which engaged in unauthorized, albeit apparently inadvertent, transactions with respect to Iraq.

3. Investigation also continues into the roles played by various individuals and firms outside of Iraq in Saddam Hussein's procurement network. These investigations may lead to additions to the FAC listing of individuals and organizations determined to be Specially Designated Nationals ("SDN's") of the Government of Iraq. In practice, an Iraqi SDN is a representative, agent, intermediary, or front (whether open or covert) of the Iraqi government that is located outside of Iraq. Iraqi SDN's are Saddam Hussein's principal instruments for doing business in third countries, and doing business with them is the same as doing business directly with the Government of Iraq.

The impact of being named an Iraqi SDN is considerable: all assets within U.S. jurisdiction of parties found to be Iraqi SDN's are blocked; all economic transactions with SDN's by U.S. persons are prohibited; and the SDN individual or organization is exposed as an agent of the Iraqi regime.

4. Since my last report, one case filed against the Government of Iraq has gone to judgment. *Centrifugal Casting Machine Co., Inc.* v. *American Bank and Trust Co., Banca Nazionale del Lavoro, Republic of Iraq, Machinery Trading Co., Baghdad, Iraq, Central Bank of Iraq, and Bank of Rafidain,* No. 91–5150 (10th Cir., decided June 11, 1992), arose out of a contract for the sale of goods by plaintiff to the State Machinery Co., an Iraqi governmental entity. In connection with the contract, the Iraqi defendants opened an irrevocable letter of credit in favor of Centrifugal, from which Centrifugal drew a 10 percent advance payment. Repayment of the advance payment in case of nonperformance by Centrifugal was guaranteed by a standby letter of credit. Performance did not occur due to the imposition of economic sanctions against Iraq in August 1990, and the United States claimed that an amount equal to the advance payment was blocked property. The district court ruled that the standby letter of credit had expired, that no U.S. party was liable to an Iraqi entity under the standby letter of credit, and that the advance payment funds were therefore not blocked property and could be distributed to U.S. persons. The court of appeals affirmed the ruling of the district court that there was no blocked Iraqi property interest in the advance payment funds, based on applicable principles of letter of credit law.

5. FAC has issued 288 specific licenses regarding transactions pertaining to Iraq or Iraqi assets. Since my last report, 71 specific licenses have been issued. Most of these licenses were issued for conducting procedural transactions such as filing of legal actions, and for legal representation; other licenses were issued pursuant to United Nations Security Council Resolutions 661, 666, and 687, to authorize the exportation to Iraq of donated medicine, medical supplies,

and food intended for humanitarian relief purposes. All of these licenses concern minor transactions of no economic benefit to the Government of Iraq.

To ensure compliance with the terms of the licenses which have been issued, stringent reporting requirements have been imposed that are closely monitored. Licensed accounts are regularly audited by FAC compliance personnel and deputized auditors from other regulatory agencies. FAC compliance personnel continue to work closely with both State and Federal bank regulatory and law enforcement agencies in conducting special audits of Iraqi accounts subject to the ISR.

6. The expenses incurred by the Federal Government in the 6-month period from February 2, 1992, through August 1, 1992, that are directly attributable to the exercise of powers and authorities conferred by the declaration of a national emergency with respect to Iraq are estimated at $2,476,000, most of which represents wage and salary costs for Federal personnel. Personnel costs were largely centered in the Department of the Treasury (particularly in FAC, the U.S. Customs Service, the Office of the Assistant Secretary for Enforcement, the Office of the Assistant Secretary for International Affairs, and the Office of the General Counsel), the Department of State (particularly the Bureau of Economic and Business Affairs and the Office of the Legal Adviser), the Department of Transportation (particularly the U.S. Coast Guard), and the Department of Commerce (particularly in the Bureau of Export Administration and the Office of the General Counsel).

7. The United States imposed economic sanctions on Iraq in response to Iraq's invasion and illegal occupation of Kuwait, a clear act of brutal aggression. The United States, together with the international community, is maintaining economic sanctions against Iraq because the Iraqi regime has failed to comply fully with United Nations Security Council resolutions calling for the elimination of Iraqi weapons of mass destruction, the demarcation of the Iraq-Kuwait border, the release of Kuwaiti and other prisoners, compensation for victims of Iraqi aggression, and the return of Kuwaiti assets stolen during its illegal occupation of Kuwait. The U.N. sanctions remain in place; the United States will continue to enforce those sanctions.

The Saddam Hussein regime continues to violate basic human rights by repressing the Iraqi civilian population and depriving it of humanitarian assistance. The United Nations Security Council passed resolutions that permit Iraq to sell $1.6 billion of oil under U.N. auspices to fund the provision of food, medicine, and other humanitarian supplies to the people of Iraq. Under the U.N. resolutions, the equitable distribution within Iraq of this assistance would be supervised and monitored by the United Nations and other international organizations. The Iraqi regime continues to refuse to accept these resolutions, and has thereby chosen to perpetuate the suffering of its civilian population.

The regime of Saddam Hussein continues to pose an unusual and extraordinary threat to the national security and foreign policy of the United States, as well as to regional peace and security. The United States will therefore continue to apply economic sanctions to deter Iraq from threatening peace and stability in the region, and I will continue to report periodically to the Congress on significant developments, pursuant to 50 U.S.C. 1703(c).

GEORGE BUSH

The White House,
August 3, 1992.

Statement by Press Secretary Fitzwater on the Decisions of Railway Labor Dispute Arbitrators
August 3, 1992

On July 30 and 31, 1992, the President received for his review the decisions of the arbitrators in three of the four remaining railway labor disputes that led to the nationwide shutdown of the Nation's railroads in late June. These decisions were rendered pursuant to the arbitration process the Congress established in legislation for resolving the disputes. The decisions become final and binding upon the parties unless the President disapproves them within 3 days following their receipt.

The President has decided that he will not disapprove any of the three decisions. The decisions submitted to the President were rendered in the arbitration of the dispute between the International Association of Machinists and the National Railway Carriers' Conference, the arbitration of the dispute between the International Association of Machinists and Amtrak, and the arbitration of the dispute between the Brotherhood of Locomotive Engineers and Amtrak.

The President is grateful to the arbitrators for their work in resolving these disputes.

Statement on Publication of Rules Allowing Parental Choice in Child Care
August 4, 1992

Today we are publishing rules that will allow parents to choose the kind of child care they believe is best for their children. Under these rules, parents receiving child care and development block grant funds will be able to decide what kind of child care their children receive, including care provided by relatives, neighbors, or church-based centers.

New grant programs now provide over $1.1 billion a year in vouchers and child care assistance that did not exist when I took office. Just as importantly, the child care legislation I initiated has expanded the earned income tax credit so that low-income working families receiving that help can decide how best to care for their children. Providing tax relief for low-income families who work is the best way to help these families end the cycle of poverty. Over the 5-year phase-in of the earned income tax credit expansion, low-income families will receive an additional $18 billion in refundable tax credits.

These rules reflect my commitment that we should trust parents to make the best decisions for their children.

Nomination of Edward S. Walker To Be United States Deputy Representative to the United Nations
August 4, 1992

The President today announced his intention to nominate Edward S. Walker, of Maryland, a career member of the Senior Foreign Service, class of Minister-Counselor, to be the Deputy Representative of the United States to the United Nations with the rank and status of Ambassador. He would succeed Alexander F. Watson.

Since 1989, Ambassador Walker has served as Ambassador to the United Arab Emirates. Prior to this, he served in several positions with the Department of State including Deputy Assistant Secretary of State for Near East and South Asian Affairs, 1988–89; Deputy Chief of Mission at the American Embassy in Riyadh, Saudi Arabia, 1985–88; participant in the senior training program at the Royal College of Defense Studies in London, 1984–85; executive assistant to the Deputy Secretary of State, 1982–84; special assistant to the Assistant Secretary of State for Near East and South Asia Bureau, 1981–82; and special assistant to the Personal Representative of the President for Middle East Negotiations, 1979–81.

Ambassador Walker graduated from Hamilton College (B.A., 1963) and Boston University (M.A., 1965). He was born June 13, 1940, in Abington, PA. He served in the U.S. Army, 1962–65. Ambassador Walker is married, has two children, and resides in Severna Park, MD.

Nomination of Roland Karl Kuchel To Be United States Ambassador to Haiti
August 4, 1992

The President today announced his intention to nominate Roland Karl Kuchel, of Florida, a career member of the Senior Foreign Service, class of Minister-Counselor, to be Ambassador of the United States of America to the Republic of Haiti. He would succeed Alvin P. Adams, Jr.

Mr. Kuchel currently serves as Acting Deputy Assistant Secretary for the Bureau of Personnel at the Department of State. Prior to this, he served in several positions at the State Department including Chief of the Senior Officer Division in the Office of Career Development and Assignments, Bureau of Personnel, 1990–91; Deputy Chief of Mission at the American Embassy in Stockholm, Sweden, 1986–90; Deputy Director and then Director of the Office of East European and Yugoslav Affairs, 1983–86; Deputy Chief of Mission at the American Embassy in Budapest, Hungary, 1980–83; and Deputy Chief of the Political Section at the American Embassy in Rome, Italy, 1976–80.

Mr. Kuchel graduated from Princeton University (A.B., 1961). He was born March 5, 1939, in Salem, MA. Mr. Kuchel is married, has three children, and resides in Washington, DC.

Nomination of Robert E. Wallace To Be an Assistant Secretary of Labor
August 4, 1992

The President today announced his intention to nominate Robert E. Wallace, of New Jersey, to be Assistant Secretary of Labor for Veterans' Employment and Training. He would succeed Thomas E. Collins III.

Since 1991, Mr. Wallace has served as the commander in chief of the Veterans of Foreign Wars. Prior to this, he served as senior vice commander in chief in 1990 and junior vice commander in chief in 1989. In addition, Mr. Wallace was appointed by Gov. Thomas Kean to the position of deputy commissioner and administrator for veterans affairs in New Jersey, 1988–90.

Mr. Wallace graduated from Rutgers University (B.S., 1976) and Fairleigh Dickinson University (M.A., 1978). Mr. Wallace served in the U.S. Marine Corps, 1967–69, and was the recipient of three Purple Hearts. He was born June 28, 1948. Mr. Wallace is married, has one child, and resides in Milton, NJ.

Remarks to the Knights of Columbus Supreme Council Convention in New York City
August 5, 1992

Thank you very, very much for that warm welcome. Thank you, ladies and gentlemen. Please be seated, and thank you all. May I salute Virgil Dechant, my friend of long standing, and thank him for that most generous welcome here. Your Eminence, Cardinal O'Connor, it is a great pleasure, an honor, sir, to see you again. May I salute Cardinal Baum, Cardinal Gagnon, Bishop Daily; another old friend, Ambassador Tom Melady, who is doing a superb job for our country, representing us at the Vatican; and the clergy and ladies and gentlemen. May I salute a man who used to be—whose house made him a neighbor, Archbishop Cacciavillan, from Washington, the Nuncio there, a good man, a good friend. Nice to see you. I'm glad you're here, sir.

I have only one regret, Virgil. My timing was such that I did not hear the fitting and warm and wonderful ovation that you gave Mother Teresa yesterday. I understand it was really fantastic.

A report came across my desk the other day. It stated that most people in the Western world "felt exceedingly gloomy about the future." It said that "institutions were decaying, well-meaning people were growing cynical." These are exact quotes.

My first thought was that's what happens when people spend too much time watching the evening news. [*Laughter*] I'm going to pay for that one tonight on that first 20 seconds. [*Laughter*] Just kidding, Dan. [*Laughter*]

No, but what I was reading was not a report about 1992. It was a history of public attitudes in Europe in 1492. Public moods are prone to change, of course. We know that the gloom of 1492 was not to last for long. It was dispelled by the achievement of a man of humble birth, a man of vision, of courage, a man named Christopher Columbus.

Now, I know that every speaker comes before you and says they identify with Columbus. But I really mean it. Think about it. The guy was faced with questions at home about whether his global efforts were worth a darn. Some critics wanted him to cut his voyage short. He even faced the threat of mutiny. [*Laughter*] And yet Columbus persevered and won; not a bad analogy in my view. So I know this isn't political. [*Laughter*] Now, I admit, Columbus also had to worry at the time about a lack of wind. I don't have that problem with Congress. [*Laughter*]

This year, as in Columbus' time, we hear a lot of talk about change. Sure, change is natural. But maybe a better word for the United States of America is renewal because the changes we need must be based on principles that never change.

I think my parents were like yours: They brought me up to understand that our fundamental moral standards were established by Almighty God. They taught me that if you have something for yourself, you should give half to a friend. They taught me to take the blame when things go wrong and share the credit when things go right. These ideas were supported by society.

Only recently—His Eminence and I were talking about, not in this detail, but talking about this subject just a few minutes ago—only recently in America have we seen the rise of legal theories and practices that reject our Judeo-Christian tradition. Cardinal O'Connor eloquently describes this as an "invasion of values." It's a deeply disturbing trend, and it is diametrically opposed to my idea of the kind of change that's good for our great country.

Last month, just 12 blocks from here, there was another convention. Now, I was very lucky, I did not—and this is the honest truth—I didn't hear any of the speeches. I was out fishing in Wyoming with Jim Baker. But I understand one of the speakers, known for his florid language, called me "the captain of the ship of state." I'm not sure he meant it as a compliment, but believe me, as a Navy man at a Knights of Columbus convention, the term suits me just fine. [*Laughter*]

I look at this office that you've entrusted with me as a lot of things, as more than managing the economy, more even than being Commander in Chief. I stake my claim to a simple belief: The President should set the moral tone for this Nation.

All around us, we see evidence that America's moral compass has gone awry. We seem to be moving away from the enduring idea of taking responsibility for our actions. Our city newspapers are filled with stories of drive-by shootings, the taking of human life made more horrible by the awful anonymity through which it is accomplished. Recently I read a story of a kid from a good neighborhood charged in a gun store robbery. He told the police who caught him, "It's not like I'm a criminal. I'm on the dean's list."

What is happening to America? As a nation, we face enormous challenges in education, crime, drugs. Yet each of them come back to the challenge of pointing our moral compass in the right direction. So I believe that a central issue of this election year should be, who do you trust to renew America's moral purpose? Who do you trust to fight for the ideas that will help rebuild our families and restore our fundamental values?

I believe, and I've tried hard on this, I believe I've earned your trust. I am committed to fighting for ideas that help repair this great Nation's moral fiber.

Welfare is one example. We all know that our welfare system has literally destroyed the concept of personal responsibility, tearing families apart, with no incentives for people to work and save and improve. I want something different. I have fought for a new welfare system that says "yes" to human potential.

Today, as we speak, we are granting waivers to States so they can change welfare rules, encourage families not to fall apart, not to live apart, but to stick together. States are saying to recipients, either you get training, or you don't get a check. Some States are even going so far as to make a very tough call of saying to parents, if you can't afford another child, don't expect the taxpayer to pick up the added costs. Now, these are tough choices. These are very tough choices, but they're all intended by the States to promote responsibility.

The other side says they agree with the ideas. But if you look close, some argue that ultimately the only solution to welfare is a guaranteed Government job for every recipient. I ask, is this any way to promote responsibility? If we guarantee everyone a Government job, how can we reward initiative? Our reforms may sound tough, but not as tough as a lifetime of despondency and despair, a lifetime that strips every recipient of his or her dignity. Let's give people hope. Let's give them opportunity.

Let's take a look at education. We know that to renew America, we literally must renew our schools. I happen to believe that competition can be the greatest force for change in our schools in an entire century.

The other side says they agree, almost. The "almost" is what troubles me. Remember how old Henry Ford used to tell his customers they could have any color Model T that they wanted, so long as it was black. [*Laughter*] Well, the other side says their ideal is that parents could choose any school for their kids, so long as it's run by the government.

If you'll excuse one blatantly political comment in which you'll have to concede has so far been a nonpartisan, almost, speech—[*laughter*]—my opponent won the teachers union endorsement by saying he's "unalterably opposed," those are his words, "unalterably opposed" to letting Catholic parents and other private school parents have a fair share of education benefits.

I believe that it's time to have the courage to fight for a different approach. Right now, if you want an alternative to public schools, you have to pay twice, first for tuition and again through taxes. A couple weeks ago I was in Philadelphia, hosted by Cardinal Bevilacqua. And a group of parents told me, "We want our kids to go to

Catholic school, but we just can't afford it." So my solution is something called the "GI bill" for kids. Like the original GI bill, my new approach offers scholarships or vouchers for students to take to any qualified school, not only public schools but Bible schools, yeshivas, Catholic parish schools. When it comes to schools, I say let the parents choose public, private, or religious.

What about promoting religion as a force for good in our society? I'm reminded of the story of a small boy who once began a prayer this way: "God bless Mother and Daddy, my brother, my sister. And God," he said, "do take care of yourself. If anything happens to You, we're all sunk." [*Laughter*] Maybe there's some doubts, but America is still the most religious nation on Earth. I want to strengthen our faith further.

Again, there are wide differences. Some think it's okay to hand out condoms in schools but oppose amending our Constitution to allow our kids to put their hands together to say a prayer. I disagree. I call again on the Congress to pass a constitutional amendment restoring voluntary prayer to our classrooms. The Senate opens its meeting with a prayer. The House of Representatives opens its meeting with a prayer. Nobody doubts that they both need it. [*Laughter*] But let's allow the faith of our fathers back into those schools.

And there's a national tragedy: More than a half a million abortions in this country every year. We know there's got to be a better way, human alternatives like adoptions and abstinence. Seven times I have ignored the polls and acted on what I believe is fundamental principle and vetoed, as Virgil very generously pointed out, abortion legislation. And I promise you again today, no matter the political price, and they tell me in this year that it's enormous, I am going to do what I think is right. I am going to stand on my conscience and let my conscience be my guide when it comes to matters of life. [*Applause*] Thank you very much.

Here's something else that bothers me. In some places, a 13-year-old girl cannot get her ears pierced without parental permission, without bringing her mother and father along. But some believe that the same girl should be able to get an abortion without parental consent. I think most Americans believe this idea is crazy, and I'm going to fight to see that that doesn't happen.

So these issues, they all come up in an election year. They'll be part of campaigns in the fall all across the country. Today I make the same appeal to you that I'll make to every voter. Look beneath the rhetoric. Take a look at the ideas to determine who has the courage to stand up for changes that are morally right for America. I'm going to take my case to the American people. And if you're looking to restore America's moral fiber, why buy synthetic when you can get real cotton? [*Laughter*]

But I do believe America needs a leader willing to do what's right, not merely what is politically popular at the moment. Nowhere is it more clear in the decisions a President must make every day to build real peace, to establish freedom and democracy, not the mere, simple absence of war.

Saint Ignatius said, "Work as though all depended upon yourself, and pray as though all depended on God." The practice of that motto conquered communism. Ceaseless prayer and tireless work halted the cold war and spared us from the catastrophe of a third world war. Believers behind the Iron Curtain defied persecution; believers in the West defied indifference.

Over four decades, our servicemen trained, our taxpayers paid $4 trillion to keep our defenses strong. As a consequence, the Iron Curtain is no more, and our kids no longer go to bed at night worrying about that dreadful specter of nuclear war. But while the Soviet bear is no more, there are still plenty of wolves in the woods. When we faced our first big challenge after the cold war, we didn't shrink. We stood up to Saddam's aggression and expelled him from Kuwait. We protected the people of Israel and Saudi Arabia. Now we've brought age-old adversaries to the peace table for the first time. His Holiness Pope John Paul has spent many days and nights at work and in prayer for peace in the Middle East. As long as I am President, I assure you I will do everything I can to bring about that peace that so many pray for.

And so, in conclusion, let me say this: This is the year of change, change, change. The election will all be about change because change really is the natural condition of our land. This isn't something new. I believe that now we've changed the world, we are poised and ready to change America, to make America even better. But we must keep something important in mind. Now that our moral values are victorious around the globe, we cannot and we will not abandon them at home.

We didn't stand together to see courageous moral values rise in Russia only to be ignored here at home. We did not sacrifice so that personal responsibility could triumph in totalitarian regimes, only to become passé here in this great Nation.

It's time to get back to some basic American values. So I am going to defend the principles for which you stand so firm. We will keep our sights on what's good in America. We will keep our focus on the potential in our families and, most of all, in our young people, in our kids. We'll keep a reliable compass. We'll put our ship of state in finest sailing trim, and as this Nation has so many times before, we will sail on to shining new horizons.

Thank you. May God bless you and our beloved country, the United States of America. Thank you very much.

Note: The President spoke at 11:04 a.m. at the Marriott Marquis Hotel. In his remarks, he referred to Virgil C. Dechant, Supreme Knight, Knights of Columbus; John Cardinal O'Connor, Archbishop of New York; William Cardinal Baum, Patrimony of the Holy See; Edouard Cardinal Gagnon, president, Pontifical Committee for International Eucharistic Congresses; Thomas Daily, Bishop of Brooklyn; Archbishop Agostino Cacciavillan, Papal Nuncio; Mother Teresa of Calcutta, founder and superior of the Missionaries of Charity; Dan Rather, CBS News; and Anthony Cardinal Bevilacqua, Archbishop of Philadelphia.

Remarks to the Disabled American Veterans National Convention in Reno, Nevada
August 5, 1992

Let me tell you that it is a great pleasure to renew old ties, greet new friends. And of course, I want to thank Cleveland Jordan for the introduction. He said he persuaded me to come. This man's tough; you get the arm up behind the back, twist the elbow here, and here I am. And I am very, very pleased. Sorry that I missed the other one, but delighted to be at your side and congratulate you on your service to this wonderful national organization.

Butch Joeckel greeted me earlier, the national adjutant; Jesse Brown, the national executive director of the DAV. And of course, I want to single out and salute a man who's helped me enormously, Ed Derwinski, our Secretary of Veterans Affairs. And may I also mention Robin Higgins. Cleve most appropriately mentioned Colonel Higgins, and I want to salute her here.

And thanks to all of you who represent America's disabled veterans, their families, their survivors; they're fully 1.4 million strong.

I was just asking Joe about the vintage of some of you all. And I must say, looking out at the audience, and I don't want to put everybody in this category, a lot come out of the same war that I was in. And I don't want to say that you're old guys or women, but nevertheless—[*laughter*]—you kind of make me feel at home here. So I'll leave it there.

But I also want to bring you best wishes from a great friend and fan of yours named Barbara. She and I were talking about coolness under fire. I told her, the more I'm criticized, the more I turn it into humor. You know her; she said, "The rate you're going, you'll soon be funnier than Johnny

Carson." [*Laughter*]

Last September, I was very honored to be with many here, but honored to attend your salute to the Persian Gulf veterans. Today, I'm proud to salute the American veteran. The American vet deserves safe streets, a sound economy, strong families, a world at peace. You believe, and I agree, America should serve those who served their country.

That's why my administration has not wavered in our commitment to you and your families. We must change our health care system in this Nation, and we will. But let me be clear: We will not change our commitment to the integrity of veterans health care. No program is going to change that.

If, in all this talk about change, Congress sends me legislation to dismantle the VA system, I will whip out my veto pen and knock down that Scud missile, that Scud missile that's aimed right at your very well-being. If you ask how many VA hospitals I'll close, I'll say not three, not two, not one. If anyone again suggests taxing your benefits, I'll say what I have said before: Don't take it from our veterans.

Now, I know you're concerned about having your voice heard as the Washington bureaucracy debates your health care future. So just yesterday I created a special panel there in the White House to guarantee your leadership's involvement. We will listen, and we will act to stand by those who stood up for America.

I am very proud of the progress that we've made together. Your leadership has sensitized all of us, brought the problems to us, worked cooperatively when there were difficulties. I can't tell you how much cooperation we've had. But they've never held back, saying we must do this, we must do that. They've been strong leaders.

We have created specialized centers. We funded new outpatient clinics and moved more resources into VA medical care, too. I also am proud of how we have built on these beginnings. Two years ago we passed the Americans with Disabilities Act. That is the most sweeping civil rights legislation since the sixties. And it will help the disabled enter the mainstream, and it's just about time that this country did that.

Three years ago, as Cleve mentioned, I was on my way to address this convention, your convention. You know what changed my plans. It concerned a husband, a father, an American hero. And again, with us today is the wife of Colonel Rich Higgins, Major Robin Higgins. On behalf of every American, let me just once again tell you I admire your courage from the bottom of my heart. We all do. We're very, very grateful to you.

Two years ago this week, I made a decision that I think every Commander in Chief, every President, dreads having to make: to send our men and women in the Armed Forces into harm's way. This one was at the beginning of Operation Desert Shield. No President, no father, no parent makes that decision lightly. But I acted because America must stand for freedom, and we must stand by those who preserve it.

I don't want to start telling war stories here because then I'd have to listen to you guys. [*Laughter*] And I don't have time. But let me tell you this: From my own experience, I learned firsthand what it means to know that America will never abandon its fighting men, whatever their fate. My family never had to face the agony of a phone call in the night or a knock on the door. Let me say to the families waiting still for their loved ones: We will not forget you.

I am pleased that the League of Families last week strongly supported our administration's efforts and commended my administration's programs. But though dramatic progress has been made, all are not accounted for. I will fight to make sure that America stands with you, the veterans, until the fate of every POW and MIA is known.

Over the last 3½ years, America's heroes have helped a war crumble in Berlin; from Kuwait to Panama, helped free those once enslaved. Our soldiers were not wounded in vain. You helped end the cold war. Those who served at whatever time in recent history helped end the cold war. And America won the cold war.

Having won, we worked with the republics of the former Soviet Union to reduce strategic nuclear arms. But President Yeltsin and I have agreed to go even further. You may remember my meeting with him a couple of months ago. We agreed to eliminate the most destabilizing of all those terrible multiwarheaded ICBM's, those great big—in their case, those SS–18's that have cast fear into the hearts of everybody. By that agreement we have reduced the threat of nuclear war. This is something that every family in America, every child in America is grateful for.

Let me make another point about that. Our victory in the cold war means that our defenses can be smaller. And so earlier this year, based on the recommendations, and I emphasize this point, based on the recommendations of Secretary Cheney and our distinguished Chairman of the Joint Chiefs, Colin Powell, I made some responsible cuts. I responsibly cut our long-range defense budget. But we cannot lose sight of the fact that for all the great gains that we have made for freedom, for all the peace of mind that we have secured for our children, the world remains a dangerous place.

The Soviet bear may be extinct, but there are still plenty of wolves in the world, renegade rulers, terrorists, outlaw regimes, Baghdad bullies. And as long as I am President I will not allow a madman to get a finger on the nuclear trigger. We will stay strong as the United States.

You know, today some have forgotten every hard-won lesson of this American century. I know you haven't. So some propose to cut our national defense, to cut $60 billion in defense beyond what our military experts deem responsible for the national security of this country.

Well, let me answer them: Yes, I know this is a political year. But the defense budget is more than a piggy bank for people who want to get busy beating swords into pork barrels, and we are not going to have that. I owe it to you, the veterans of this country, to be able to certify to you that we are keeping our national security at proper levels.

I know this fundamental truism, that to keep America safe, we have to keep America strong. That's why when the other side says "Let's ravage the Strategic Defense Initiative," I say, "Remember the lesson of Desert Storm." We will not leave the world defenseless against nuclear attacks. We will push forward with SDI.

Think for a moment about what a strong America has helped achieve. Think about the worries we once faced and the world we see today: not a Europe in flames, not a world at war, touched off by the death throes of the Soviet empire, but a world at peace, a new birth of freedom; not a Latin America consumed by revolution and resentment that has plagued that area for so long but a hemisphere moving toward free trade and free government; not a Middle East dominated by a dictator but a region where ancient enemies at long last are talking peace, sitting across from each other at the peace table, something that people thought was impossible to bring about. Our policies and your backing help make all of this possible.

So when the Sunday strategists say that I've spent too much time on foreign policy, let me just put it this way: I will never apologize for a single minute spent keeping America strong, safe, and free.

Well, where do we go next? Well, I think about our challenges. When I do that I'm reminded of a football story, a football story, a story about a freshman football player thrust into a close game, the close of a tie game, late there in the fourth quarter, with the ball on his own team's one-yard line. And the coach grabbed the quarterback and he said, "Don't take any chances. Just fall on the ball three times and then punt." Well, on the first snap, a huge hole opened up in the line and the quarterback scrambled all the way to the 50. The next snap, another huge hole, and down to the 25 he went. On the third play, the quarterback ran through an opening wider than the River Nile and fell just one yard short of a touchdown. The crowd was going crazy, screaming for victory, and the freshman took the fourth snap, stepped back, calmly punted the ball completely out of the stadium. [*Laughter*] And on the sideline the coach was tearing his hair out. He ran onto the field screaming. "What could you possibly be thinking?" And the freshman replied, "I was just thinking, you must be the dumbest coach in the entire world." [*Laughter*]

As the coach of the American foreign policy, or foreign policy coach, it would be the height of stupidity for me to suggest that we just ignore our foreign commitments, as some suggest now. And by the way, I'm tempted to say that now the world playing field is so competitive, I'm not sure we should trust to a team a rookie quarterback. But that's something else again. [*Laughter*]

Now, my point is, we can't punt out foreign concerns. We have important work to do. First we must do all we can to bolster the process of democracy, especially where democratic friends have replaced totalitarian enemies in Eastern Europe and in the former Soviet Union. I hope you will stand with me and urge Congress to act immediately to approve this "FREEDOM Support Act," to lend a helping hand to the former Soviet Union, take out an insurance policy on democracy. After World War I, we ignored the summons for help, and we paid dearly. We paid dearly for that. After World War II, we lent a helping hand, and our lives are richer for it. So let us not ignore the lesson of history. Let us act now to support freedom and free enterprise.

Our second challenge is not to turn our back on the world economy. Seventy percent of our economic growth the last 4 years has come from exports; 7.2 million American jobs are tied to trade. I will work to open foreign markets, to strengthen our schools so that we can compete, because what is true today will be true tomorrow: Give an American worker the chance, and he will beat the pants off of the competition.

Over the past 3½ years, America has changed the world, just as we're now ready to change America, building the kind of nation here many of you fought so valiantly for abroad.

Think of what you fought for, an America of better jobs and better schools and safer neighborhoods and equality for all, a land where our kids and grandkids would live in prosperity and peace. Think of what we can now achieve, an America which eclipses even its greatest triumphs. But I need your help.

Landing here in Reno this afternoon and being greeted by our very able Lieutenant Governor, Sue Wagner, who's here with us right now, I had an incredible treat. I was met by a Nevadan, a guy from Carson City named J.C. Crume, who has joined me here

at the convention today. I think he's here; he was trying to get on in. I met him—this is a little history—50 years ago, 1942. I was 18 years old. He was my first flight instructor at the naval air station there in Minneapolis, Minnesota. He took this scared 18-year-old kid and put me behind the stick of a Navy plane. And J.C.'s hair looked a little gray, but he told me that it wasn't age. It's the lingering effects of the terror he felt 50 years ago with this young kid sitting in the back seat. [*Laughter*] And very frank and honest guy that he is.

But more seriously, I did learn something from him and from my other soul mates and comrades in arms in the Navy. I learned about teamwork, and I learned about the importance of sticking together from Mr. Crume and all the other guys in the Navy. I learned to depend on my wingman for friendship, for support, and even for survival.

As you know, some of you may know this history, but after I left basic training, J.C.'s great instruction, I was assigned to the Pacific. One day, my plane was shot down, TBF flying over the island of Chi Chi Jima, just off the island, and parachuted into the water. When I was swimming in the middle of the Pacific, one of my wingmen pointed me to a liferaft that had fallen from the plane, while another wingman then helped keep the enemy at bay. They put boats out from this island of Chi Chi Jima.

After the Navy, I didn't wear my uniform every day, but believe me, friends have been part of every good fortune in my life, every good fortune. Now I'm about to embark on another political battle, and I know this is a nonpolitical convention, but I would be remiss if I did not express my thanks to those who have helped here and to those, regardless of party, who have done so much to strengthen, whatever our politics, strengthen support for the American veteran.

And I am saying, some things transcend politics. And I'm just saying to all of you, let's stay together. Let's stay together. Let's not the wingman peel off as we fight for the proper recognition of and support for the American veteran.

Thank you all very, very much. And may

God bless the United States of America.

Note: The President spoke at 5:02 p.m. in the Goldwyn Ballroom at the Reno Hilton Hotel. In his remarks, he referred to Cleveland Jordan, national commander, DAV;

Joseph C. Zengerle, national senior vice commander, DAV; and Maj. Robin Higgins, whose husband, Col. William R. Higgins, was killed while held hostage in Beirut, Lebanon.

Remarks to the American Legislative Exchange Council in Colorado Springs, Colorado
August 6, 1992

Thank you for that wonderfully warm ALEC welcome. And Fred Noye, thank you for that generous introduction. I want to thank the official host, the Mayor, Mayor Isaac, for his hospitality; recognize Sam Brunelli, of course, an old friend with us here who feels very comfortable here; Holly Coors, so well-known to all in ALEC; my dear friend and respected leader of faith, Jim Dobson here. Let me just say, Fred, you have done a wonderful job as chairman. I'm not pronouncing you dead yet; you have a few more months. But you've done a great chairman job. And I know that your shoes will be ably filled by Bill Raggio, over here, from the State of Nevada.

Bill flew in with us last night from Reno on Air Force One. And all the White House stationery and matchboxes from the plane are missing. But he swears there's no correlation whatsoever. [*Laughter*] But I was so honored that he came all the way up from the convention, took the puddle-jumpers all the way, to just represent ALEC on the ride down, fill me in on what a fantastic convention is underway right here in Colorado Springs.

Twenty years ago, when ALEC started, I see it that you were a lone voice in the conservative wilderness. Now you gather in these marvelous Colorado mountains at a time when the endangered species list is topped by that creature rarely spotted outside of the 202 area code; I'm talking, of course, about the unabashed, unreconstructed liberal. [*Laughter*]

But your energy and your ideas and your enthusiasm helped lead the ideological transformation of America. So it's an honor to be standing here as your guest, invited to speak to you today. I understand that, I think the figure is no fewer than six members of my Cabinet will speak here. I'm especially delighted that you've chosen to give the Thomas Jefferson Freedom Award, that coveted award, to the idea man of the conservative movement, Jack Kemp.

As you know, so far this election has been a little one-sided. For 9 months—and I'm not complaining; my day is coming—for 9 months, five other candidates, maybe it was six way back then, various sundry surrogates have aimed a firehose of criticism at me. I have been blamed for everything except that crazy scoring system that was used in the Olympic boxing competition. I shouldn't really go out on a limb like that because I haven't checked the AP wire and see how it went. [*Laughter*]

But I admit I've been a little slow to fight back. My opponent has mentioned my name about once every 5 seconds, not always in the most flattering light. I still haven't even said his name in full. I've referred occasionally to "my opponent," "the other guy," and even "the Governor of a certain State with a profitable chicken industry on the Mississippi River, located somewhere between Texas and Oklahoma." [*Laughter*]

Let me tell you why I have waited. As I listen to the American people, I get a sense of something you might pick up from your own constituents. People are sick of politics. I think they think this election year has gone on a little too long. You used to start on Labor Day. Labor Day isn't even at hand yet. They're tired of the charges and the countercharges. They want ideas, and they want action. They want to trust their leaders to turn the first into the second.

That's what I want to talk about this morning: ideas, action, and trust. Well, I don't want to get too partisan. I'm going to draw a few comparisons. Grant me a favor, though, and I'll save the "C" word for my convention in Houston. And then I'll just stick with the all-purpose title for today of "my opponent." But let me guarantee you one thing: When our convention is over—I am tired of being slugged by these people, and I will fight back. I am going to win this election. I will fight tough, but I will fight fair.

Which reminds me, remember the old story of the fierce gladiator? He'd killed every lion that they could throw up against him, every lion he'd faced. So one day the centurions went out, went to Carthage and found the meanest lion in the world. They'd buried the gladiator in the arena there in Rome, right up so just his head was sticking out, fill him with sand. The lion was released, charged him, making a deadly pass at the gladiator's head. And as he did, the gladiator reached up and took a very ferocious bite in a very sensitive place in the lion's anatomy. [*Laughter*] The lion howled in pain and ran for the exit, fled from the arena. And the lead centurion ran out, attacked the gladiator screaming, "Fight fair, damn it! Fight fair!" [*Laughter*]

Now, every time I tiptoe into the water with this guy, they start yelling, "Negative campaigning." I am going to fight back. And I will define his record as he's ill-defined mine. I will fight on the only battleground that really counts, and that is the battleground of ideas. And ideas matter.

If ever there was an organization that understood it, ideas matter, and ALEC knows. They know that. When Americans choose their leadership, they're choosing a direction. They're choosing a set of beliefs.

For the past quarter century, the tide has flowed our way for a very simple reason: The American people agree with our philosophy and with our ideas. If imitation is the sincerest form of flattery, the whole world is wearing those red ALEC blankets that I saw last night. For years your members, working in both political parties, have

been holding the line on Government spending. You've been resisting the Pavlovian impulse to raise taxes at every turn. And you're fighting to give parents the chance to choose their kids' schools and choose their day care. I am for this, and I hope you'll all support it.

This is the wave of the future. It will make the public schools better, the private schools better, and the religious schools better. When I got out of the service nobody said to me, "Here's the GI bill; you can only go to School A." They said, "Go to the school of your choice." That enhanced the great State universities and the private universities and those based on religious faith.

On many of the major issues of this campaign, my opponent and I have entirely different ideas. On education, on health care, on life, on defense, on prayer in school, for example, we are separated by a gulf as wide as the Grand Canyon. But on some issues, especially economic issues, I'm afraid we don't yet sound all that different.

Of course, unlike my great predecessor, I will have to confess I am not known for threatening Daniel Webster's place in oratorical history. I will confess, there have been other greater speakers. But to me, real eloquence, real eloquence, lies in action. So when it comes to ideas for fixing our economy, I say, look not just at what we say; look at what we are trying to do and have done.

Let me give you some examples. I firmly believe we must get a handle on this budget deficit before it strangles our future. My opponent supposedly agrees with me. He says in his speeches that Government takes too much of your money and gives you too little in return. And what do we do about it?

Well, I have fought for a freeze on domestic discretionary spending. I have fought for a cap, and this is the only way we're going to get the deficit down, a cap on mandatory Federal spending, with specific proposals for savings, and a responsible, I emphasize that word, a responsible reduction in defense spending consistent with our mission as the leader of the world and consistent with my oath to be responsible for the national security. I am not going to cut into the muscle of our defense and go back to a hollow army. So let's be clear on that.

I know everybody at ALEC likes light reading. Now here is a midsession review, and in it, it tells exactly and specifically how to get this budget deficit down. It's been sitting up and languishing in the Congress, who do not want to make the tough decisions that I have recommended year after year. I urge you all to go out to your nearest bookstore, hopefully getting it at a discount, and read this program. You'll be impressed because it is ALEC philosophy.

Now, my opponent has taken a very different approach. He has proposed over $200 billion of new spending and at least $150 billion in new taxes. And when it comes to any concern about the Federal budget deficit, his action sounds like John McLaughlin's sign-off every week, "Bye-bye." [*Laughter*]

Look, ultimately—you know this; the men and women of ALEC know this—I believe the only way to get the budget deficit under control, the major disciplinary tool, is a balanced budget amendment to the Constitution. You at ALEC have done for the amendment what Rush Limbaugh has done for the art of passionate communication.

Let me just single out one person, probably embarrass the daylights out of him, but I know of what David Halbrook, a former ALEC chairman, had done. A most respected Democrat, he has taken the lead on the balanced budget amendment. He has taken your message and mine all across this country, and we owe him a vote of gratitude. Thank you very, very much. I knew he'd be embarrassed. There he is. Don't give him equal time or he'll tell you how his town in Mississippi is the center of the universe. I don't have time for that. [*Laughter*]

No, but again, on this question of the balanced budget agreement, look at the rhetoric out there. My opponent agrees with me in principle. But at the moment of truth, when we finally got that amendment to the floor of the House this summer, he came out against it. The amendment fell short by 9 votes, after that liberal congressional leadership convinced 12 cosponsors, 12 people that had cosponsored the amendment, to

change their position at the last minute and to vote no.

Okay. We're going to keep fighting. But if we can't get a balanced budget amendment right now, at least give me a line-item veto like virtually every Governor in the United States has. But again, he says he favors the idea, this opponent, nameless opponent. But look at our actual proposals. In my budget this year—and again, I don't want to lift that heavy book up—I identified 246 Government programs—will you mind holding it up at the appropriate time? [*Laughter*] This is an all-purpose book, I'll tell you—246 that I would end and another 4,000 wasteful projects that I will also get rid of altogether. They're in there. They are defined.

Now, this list includes some big-ticket items as well as some smaller things like a vitally important Federal research program into the mating habits of the mink. Again on this issue, my opponent is singing the same tune, but the dance steps are different. When he released his economic plan—look at it, don't take my word for it—he searched and searched through thousands of Government programs and found only one that he would eliminate, Federal subsidies for honeybee farmers.

Now, I have gone head-to-head in this job day in and day out, regardless of the polls. And I'm going to continue to do what I think is right with some very powerful special interests: the NEA, the powerful teachers union; the labor bosses; the ACLU; the Ralph Naders of beltway fame. But I doubt anyone will get stung by taking on the honeybee industry. They're just not that tough. [*Laughter*]

What about mandatory spending? It's devouring more and more of our budget every year. About two-thirds of the budget the President doesn't get a shot at, I think we all know that. I propose it's time to roll up our sleeves and go after it. No matter what the political price, we owe it to the young people here today. My opponent nods his head in agreement saying, and here's a quote, "We need a Government that offers more empowerment and less entitlement." And all, again, I'm asking, and I'll be asking this all fall, is do the words match the action?

In my past three budgets, I have proposed the caps on mandatory spending, and I have submitted specific ideas for savings. The amounts aren't paltry: $72 billion in this year's budget, $47 billion last year, $119 billion in 1990. And what does the opposition offer? You can search the entire economic program and find one very tiny idea: reducing Medicare subsidies for the wealthy. That isn't a bad idea. In fact, I put it in my own budget. But keep in mind, it would reduce mandatory spending by one-tenth of one percent next year. This hardly qualifies as a profile in budget-cutting courage.

Do you see a pattern? Do you see a pattern here? Look at our most pressing economic challenge: how to create more jobs now. I have proposed a package that includes incentives for investment to create jobs, many incentives that ALEC has been so forcefully advocating; that help, that credit, for the first-time homebuyer so that that homebuyer can participate in the American dream; tax savings through juggling around the IRA's for families that are trying in these tough times to save.

My opponent copies you and me when he says that an expanding economy's the best policy of all. But first, he proposes the largest tax increase in American history, larger than what Mike Dukakis and Walter Mondale proposed together. Then he proposes at least a 7-percent payroll tax to finance a new Government-run health care scheme. Then his friends in the congressional leadership took my growth package and added a tax increase to it, and I took care of that with the veto pen. And as your able chairman said, that's the first time a President has done that.

So you have every right to say, "What's going on here? What's happening? What's really happening?"

As I peel through the details of our economic plans, I can't help but think of the words of another George—I'm not used to quoting him—George McGovern. George McGovern has never been what I would call a big friend or fan of mine. But you may recall during the New York convention, he called the other ticket, and I quote here, "a Trojan horse." He said, here's the

quote, exact quote, "They are really much more liberal than they appear. And they'll show it after they are elected." Well, I don't know if I ever have told you this before, but George McGovern is a very smart man. He is very intelligent. [*Laughter*]

But this is what worries me. As I compare the details of what we have to offer, the details, and I begin to wonder. Is all this talk of what they call a new covenant simply a coverup for some very old and tired ideas? The other side talks about changing the economy with new spending and taxes. But when they talk about change, that's all you're going to have left in your pockets when these guys get through with you. [*Laughter*] So please get the ALEC message around this country.

There's one other thing—and I say this with respect for the conservatives on both parties that are here—my opponent talks about change, but he refuses to even mention the one thing that hasn't changed in 36 years. I'm talking about the liberal leadership in the United States Congress. It's about time we changed that if we want to move this leadership forward.

So if you really want to clean out the deadlock in Washington, why not clean out that same liberal deadwood on that leadership that has fought me every inch of the way, scared to death that the American economy might just get a little bit better if they pass those incentives that I know would have helped this economy grow.

Now I'm hoping, and I really do, this may be George McGovern's Trojan horse will be a tiger when it comes to holding the line on taxes and spending. But I doubt it. I believe the voters need more proof than mere words. So today I have an idea to propose to the American people, a way to move away even in this fiercely partisan election year, a way to move away from partisanship, a way to get some of the ideas you fought for off the drawing board and into action, a way to get our economy moving today and keep it growing tomorrow, and most important, a way to do what is right for our country.

Today I issue a challenge to my opponent and to his close allies there in the congressional leadership: If you really agree with us that these ideas are important, why hold them hostage to a political campaign? If you really believe that tax cuts can create jobs, pass my growth package now. If you want to get a handle on Government spending, put a line-item veto on my desk right now and give me a chance to get this deficit under control. I'll start cutting right away. If you want to control mandatory spending, convince the Congress to adopt this proposed savings plan just next week. They don't have to wait. If you really want to reform health care, bring it up. Our plan is up there. It's a good one. Bring it up, and vote on it. If you really believe in a balanced budget amendment, let's call it up and vote for it again. And leave the pressure off of these Members, and let them vote their consciences, and let them do what's right for the American people. Send it to your States right now for ratification.

Now, the plan I've outlined today, a plan based on so many ideas that you've fit into the system, ALEC ideas, ALEC initiatives, is the strong, compelling action that our economy desperately needs. Quite frankly, I don't expect the other side to come forward and back their ideas, these pronouncements, back them with action. I think there's a Trojan horse lurking in the weeds,

ready to pull a fast one on the American people, and I simply am not going to let that happen.

In the next 4 months and for the next 4 years, I will accelerate our fight for these tax incentives and lowering the taxes, for budgetary discipline, for making the tough calls on runaway spending. I will put my case in words, but I will back my words with action. I will show the American people we must not return to a failed philosophy for America, no matter how neatly packaged it is today. It is time to continue moving forward, forward on a positive, conservative vision for our great Nation.

May I thank each and every member of ALEC. And may God bless the greatest, freest, fairest country on the face of the Earth, the United States of America. Thank you all very, very much.

Note: The President spoke at 9:12 a.m. at the Broadmoor Hotel International Center. In his remarks, he referred to ALEC officers Fred C. Noye, national chairman, Sam Brunelli, executive director, and William Raggio, incoming national chairman; Bob Isaac, Mayor of Colorado Springs; Holland H. Coors, who gave opening remarks at the meeting; and James Dobson, president, Focus on the Family.

Remarks on the Situation in Bosnia and an Exchange With Reporters in Colorado Springs
August 6, 1992

Bosnia

The President. A few remarks on the situation in Bosnia and the former Yugoslavia and what the United States, working with the international community, is doing to contain and defuse this escalating crisis.

Like all Americans, I am outraged and horrified at the terrible violence shattering the lives of innocent men, women, and children in Bosnia. The aggressors and extremists pursue a policy, a vile policy, of ethnic cleansing, deliberately murdering innocent civilians, driving others from their homes. Already the war has created over 2.2 mil-

lion refugees, roughly the population of greater Pittsburgh and Baltimore. This is, without a doubt, a true humanitarian nightmare.

Now, the war in Bosnia-Hercegovina and Croatia is a complex, convoluted conflict that grows out of age-old animosities. The blood of innocents is being spilled over century-old feuds. The lines between enemies and even friends are jumbled and fragmented. Let no one think there is an easy or a simple solution to this tragedy. The violence will not end overnight, whatever pressure and means the international community brings to bear. Blood feuds are very difficult to resolve. Any lasting solution will only be found with the active cooperation and participation of the parties themselves. Those who understand the nature of this conflict understand that an enduring solution cannot be imposed by force from outside on unwilling participants.

Defusing this crisis and preventing its spread will require patience and persistence by all members of the democratic community of nations and key international organizations. Bringing peace again to the Balkans will literally take years of work.

For months now we've been working with other members of the international community in pursuing a multifaceted and integrated strategy for defusing and containing the Baltic conflict. Let me explain the critical steps that we already have underway to help defuse and to contain this crisis.

First, we must continue to work to see that food and medicine get to the people of Sarajevo and elsewhere in Bosnia no matter what it takes. To this end I have directed the Secretary of State to press hard for quick passage of a United Nations Security Council resolution authorizing the use of all necessary measures to establish conditions necessary for and to facilitate the delivery of humanitarian assistance to Bosnia-Hercegovina. This resolution is critical; it is absolutely critical to our efforts to bring food and medicine to the people of Bosnia.

This resolution will authorize the international community to use force if necessary to deliver humanitarian relief supplies. My heartfelt hope is that that will not prove necessary. But the international community cannot stand by and allow innocent children, women, and men to be starved to death. You can be assured that should force prove necessary, I will do everything in my power to protect the lives of any American service men or women involved in this international mission of mercy.

To truly end the humanitarian nightmare we must stop ethnic cleansing and open any and all detention camps to international inspection. We will not rest until the international community has gained access to any and all detention camps.

Second, we must support the legitimate Governments of Slovenia, Croatia, and Bosnia-Hercegovina. To this end, I have decided that the United States will move now to full diplomatic relations with those Governments. I'll shortly submit to the Senate my nomination for Ambassadors to these posts.

Third, we must continue to isolate Serbia economically and politically until all the United Nations Security Council resolutions are fully implemented. We must continue to tighten economic sanctions on Serbia so that all understand that there is a real price to be paid for the Serbian Government's continued aggression. And the United States proposes that the international community place monitors in neighboring states to facilitate the work of those Governments to ensure strict compliance with the sanctions.

Fourth, we must engage in preventive diplomacy to preclude a widening of the conflict into Kosovo, Vojvodina, Sandzhak, or Macedonia. Therefore, the United States is proposing that the Conference on Security and Cooperation in Europe, CSCE, place continuous monitoring missions in these locations to provide an international presence and inhibit human rights abuses and violence.

Fifth, we must contain the conflict and prevent its spilling over into neighboring states like Albania, Hungary, Bulgaria, Romania, and Greece. To this end, the United States proposes that the international community again place civilian monitors, thereby reassuring these Governments of our concern for their welfare and inhibiting any aggression against them.

And sixth, we are consulting with our allies in NATO on all aspects of this crisis and how the NATO alliance might be of assistance to the United Nations.

Now, these steps represent an integrated strategy for defusing and containing this conflict. We've been working with the international community to advance our work on each of these and will continue to do so in the weeks ahead. It is through international cooperation, through the U.N., NATO, the EC, CSC, other institutions, that we will be able to help bring peace to that troubled region.

Thank you very, very much.

Q. Mr. President, are you mobilizing United States military personnel now to go there?

The President. The question is, are we mobilizing United States military personnel. The answer is no. The United States has military assets that are available. Indeed, I think everyone knows that we have had a significant presence not only in the Mediterranean but in the Adriatic. I am confident that we have what assets it takes to get the job done without any excessive moves on mobilization. We're not in that state anyway. I'm hoping that we will not have to use force.

Q. What about in the Middle East?

Q. How credible are the reports of death camps?

The President. Well, what I have done is task our intelligence community to use every asset available to see if we can confirm them. We know that there is horror in these detention camps. I cannot confirm on hard evidence some of the charges that have been made. It is absolutely essential, whatever is going on there, that there be open inspection and that humane treatment of the people in these concentration camps be guaranteed.

But in all honesty, I can't confirm to you some of the claims that there is, indeed, a genocidal process going on there.

Q. How far along is the process in determining that, sir? When do you think you'll have a determination?

The President. Well, I don't know. It's very difficult, as you know. The main thing we're doing is pressing through this United Nations action, through the Human Rights Commission, to get access to have visible guarantees as to what's going on.

Yes.

Q. Sir, when you see the vivid footage from Bosnia of innocent civilians being bombed and mortared and shelled from the hills, does it not make you want to send in U.S. air power to take out those emplacements?

The President. It makes me want to do whatever we have to do to stop the killing. I would only suggest that this is a very complicated military question, very, very complicated, indeed. We have probably—well, I know we have the best intelligence in the

world on this, and it is not an easy military problem even for our fantastic Air Force.

Q. Sir, if Serbia does not open the camps——

Iraq

Q. Mr. President, do you have a message to Saddam Hussein?

The President. Do I what?

Q. Do you have a message today for Saddam Hussein?

The President. A message for him?

Q. Yes, given his statement that U.N. inspectors will not be allowed in.

The President. Well, I think what he said, they would not be allowed into the ministries. I would say that the United Nations resolutions will be honored in full and he will comply with United Nations resolutions, and just leave it at that. I can't tell you what the inspection targets will be, but if they prove to be in the ministry, the United Nations has every right under international law to inspect. And we will help guarantee that right.

Q. Well, sir, are you getting a little fed up with this, I mean, with Saddam's playing games?

The President. I've been fed up with him for a long time.

Bosnia

Q. Sir, if the Serbians do not open the camps to inspectors, what would the next——

The President. Too hypothetical. We're going to get those camps opened the way I've said.

Q. Sir, are our allies in full support of using any necessary means?

The President. No, and one of the reasons that we're working hard in the United Nations: to be sure we're all together. This really does require international action. We've been working this problem for a long time at the United Nations, not a long time but several, a couple of weeks. I have to tell you there have been some differences. You asked the right question, but we've got to get them together. I think there's increasing concern on the part of our allies. So we are taking the lead in trying to get that done.

Q. Mr. President, if it is confirmed that there are death camps there, would the United States have a moral obligation to do whatever was necessary to stop that?

The President. Well, I feel a moral obligation to see that these camps are inspected. I feel a moral obligation to see, just on the evidence we have. So it—don't even need to go any further than that. I think all of the American people feel, and I'm sure it's true of other peoples around the world, feel that we must have access to these camps, and we must stop the killing, and we must stop this cleansing process. Leave out genocide for a minute. And genocide just compounds it and makes it even worse, if that is proven, certainly.

Q. But to do whatever is necessary, including the use of troops?

The President. Well, I've said that, but that's what our resolution would propose.

Thank you all very much. Thank you.

Note: The President spoke at 12:02 p.m. at Peterson Air Force Base prior to his departure for Washington, DC.

Statement on Executive Branch Revised Standards of Conduct
August 6, 1992

In the first Executive order of my Presidency, I established a Presidential Commission on Federal Ethics Law Reform to examine the ethics laws and regulations that govern the Federal work force. The Commission recommended that the Office of Government Ethics consolidate all executive branch standards of conduct regulations into a single set of regulations. By Executive Order 12674, issued April 12, 1989, I directed the Office of Government Ethics to develop a single comprehensive and understandable set of ethics regulations that would apply to all employees in the executive branch.

Tomorrow that enormous task will be completed. A single set of ethical standards will be published in the *Federal Register* and will replace over 100 different and often conflicting agency regulations. These new standards will be set forth in one place so that the public can examine them, so that those who do business with the Federal Government can easily understand them, and so that all executive branch employees will have a clear understanding of the rules governing them. The final rule addresses a broad range of ethical concerns including gifts from outside sources, financial interests, and circumstances presenting an appearance of impropriety. It also provides guidance to employees who are involved in activities outside their Government jobs or who are seeking other employment.

In the coming months, ethics officials in the departments and agencies throughout the executive branch will begin to brief the Federal work force on the new standards, another enormous endeavor. I want to reiterate my personal commitment to see that the standards set forth in these new regulations will be vigorously and conscientiously observed throughout the executive branch.

I am very grateful to the Office of Government Ethics and all the ethics officials in the Government for their work in developing these new standards.

Appointment of Charles A. Gillespie, Jr., as Special Assistant to the President for National Security Affairs
August 6, 1992

The President today announced the appointment of Charles A. Gillespie, Jr., as Special Assistant to the President for National Security Affairs. Mr. Gillespie, an experienced career diplomat, will be Senior Director for Latin America and the Caribbean at the National Security Council.

Mr. Gillespie was Ambassador to Chile from 1988 through 1991 and Ambassador to Colombia from 1985 to 1988. From 1983 to 1985, he was Deputy Assistant Secretary of State for the Caribbean and Deputy for Operations in the State Department's Inter-American Affairs Bureau. While in that position he was named Chief of Mission in Grenada as United States forces landed there in October 1983. Mr. Gillespie is a career minister in the U.S. Foreign Service, which he entered in 1965. His early assignments included Embassies at Manila, Jakarta, Brussels, Mexico City, Managua, and the U.S. mission to NATO.

Born in Long Beach, CA, Mr. Gillespie graduated from the University of California at Los Angeles. He served as a commissioned officer in the U.S. Army in Europe. He has done graduate work at Syracuse University's Maxwell School of Public Affairs and is a graduate of the National War College. Mr. Gillespie is married to Vivian Havens; they have two children.

The President's News Conference
August 7, 1992

The President. Let me comment on three subjects this morning, and then I'll be glad to take a few questions. We only have a short period of time because I'm going over to an event outside the White House.

The Economy

While I'm pleased that the unemployment rate declined by one-tenth of a percent in July, and it shows that about 200,000 new jobs were created in that month, I simply cannot be satisfied until every American that wants a job has one. We must work to ensure that economic growth is strong enough to bring unemployment down rapidly.

It's interesting that just that one-tenth percentage point resulted in that many jobs. Our household employment survey reported a drop in unemployed persons by 215,000, and the 198,000 new jobs that were created in July is the most since December of last year. Also, the number of people employed in May and June was revised upward by 80,000.

Some good precursors of stronger growth are definitely in place. For example, interest rates and inflation are at their lowest level in a generation, creating conditions for sustained growth. But there's also a restructuring underway of the management and operation of many of our larger companies. They're adjusting to a more competitive national and international environment.

As this takes place, it is crucial that we continue to expand our markets abroad, to accelerate our job training, and to reform our educational system so that tomorrow's work force is the most competitive in the world.

Bosnia

Now let me turn to the subject I talked a little about yesterday, the terrifying violence that's occurring in Bosnia. The pictures of the prisoners rounded up by the Serbian forces and being held in these detention camps are stark evidence of the need to deal with this problem effectively.

The world cannot shed its horror at the prospect of concentration camps. The shocking brutality of genocide in World War II in those concentration camps are burning memories for all of us. That can't happen again, and we will not rest until the international community has gained access to any and all detention camps.

As I said yesterday, let no one think there is an easy or simple solution for this tragedy. But we are taking the complex and strong steps necessary to bring humanitarian relief to the people of Bosnia and political resolution to the crisis in that country.

Iraq

Finally, we continue to work with the United Nations to monitor the situation in Iraq. We have great confidence in Mr. Ekeus and his inspection team as they pursue compliance with the United Nations resolutions. Once again, we're hearing the bluster of Saddam Hussein. He speaks of Kuwait as the 19th province, and he threatens not to allow inspection of his ministries. We will continue to demand full compliance with all resolutions, but we will speak with the measured confidence of a nation and a community of nations that is totally dedicated to seeing every single one of these United Nations resolutions fully enforced.

I have time for a few questions. And Helen [Helen Thomas, United Press International], you go ahead.

Bosnia

Q. Mr. President, if the international community, the U.N., NATO, et cetera, do not support you on the use of force, will you go it alone? Will you only use air and naval power, or will you use ground troops? In addition to the terrifying pictures, were you also pushed by Clinton and Thatcher into this stronger stance, which seems to be a change for you?

The President. Let me answer the last part of that question. I want to be sure I remember all the parts of it, but the last part of it is, absolutely no. This is not a political matter. This is a matter of humanitarian concern. I will not engage the other side on this particular issue. We're trying to handle it in a sound way with sound foreign

policy as the backbone to it. So that's the end of that one.

What was the first part now?

Q. Would the U.S. go it alone if it does not get the U.N. backing in NATO?

The President. Well, I'm confident we'll have the U.N. backing, so it's too hypothetical. You asked about the use of force. Everyone has been reluctant for a very understandable reason to use force. There's a lot of voices out there in the United States today that say, use force. But they don't have the responsibility for sending somebody else's son or somebody else's daughter into harm's way, and I do.

We are thinking it out very carefully. I do not want to see the United States bogged down in any way into some guerrilla warfare. We lived through that once. And yet, I have a lot of options available to me, and I will contemplate every one very seriously but in conjunction with the United Nations. And so we're going to continue to press for the resolutions that I hope will solve this problem.

Incidentally, there was a statement this morning by Yugoslavia's Prime Minister Panic, where he said that he will order the Serbs in Bosnia to close all detention camps or that their leaders must resign. Well, that's a move in the right direction. The diplomacy that's going on behind the scenes will all push towards that kind of resolution of the question. But we have a lot of options available to us, Helen.

Iraq

Q. Mr. President, on Iraq, we heard yesterday that they were going to prevent U.N. forces from entering other ministries. Have you been able to determine whether that's a real threat? And what are you prepared to do if, in fact, that's the case?

The President. Well, I think the answer is overall he is going to comply with the U.N. resolutions, and that is just going to happen. So I can't tell how much of this is bluster, how much on their part is determination to provoke confrontation. But they're going to comply with these resolutions. I'm absolutely certain of that.

Q. Are you going to do anything to speed up the timetable to force the inspections to go quicker than they are?

The President. No. I think we have great confidence in Dr. Ekeus. He is a very persistent individual. The timetable as I understand it, which I'm not at liberty to discuss, seems to me appropriate to get to the bottom of all this, fulfill all these inspections.

Secretary of State Baker

Q. What effect do these knotty foreign policy problems, Bosnia and Iraq, have on your flexibility in assigning Secretary of State Baker?

The President. Well, when I have something to say about what Secretary Baker might or might not do, I'll be sure to let everybody here know about it. But I have great confidence in him and in the Department on the diplomacy. There's no question about that, Brit [Brit Hume, ABC News]. It's very important that we handle not only this matter; we've got some others. We've got a very important visit coming up with the Prime Minister of Israel. And so I continue to rely heavily on the State Department, on the Secretary of State for substantive advice. But what lies ahead, or what might or might not—having read all the speculation that emanated from this newsroom a couple of weeks ago, I thought you told me that a deal had already been made. But he's still in his job, and I'm still relying heavily on him for sound advice and action over there.

Q. Deputy Secretary Eagleburger said a week or 10 days ago that he expected Secretary Baker to be on the job at State for a long time. Would you second that?

The President. But that counters what I think I read out of this newsroom. So——

Q. Well, we'll be glad to get authoritative advice by you, sir, on what's going on.

The President. ——I've got to sort it all out, and then I'll get back to you.

Foreign Policy and Domestic Politics

Q. Bill Clinton commended your statement yesterday on Bosnia. Yet Marlin Fitzwater said about a week ago that Bill Clinton had been reckless when Clinton called for the United States to urge the United Nations to authorize air strikes to get those relief shipments through. Do you regard Bill Clinton as reckless in Yugoslavia, the former Yugoslavia, or anyplace else in foreign policy?

The President. I'm going to keep on these foreign policy issues and try to keep them out of the political arena, the jockeying, the instant statement. I am confident that what we're doing is correct. I have no problem with his offering advice on these matters. But I am not going to get engaged in the political arena when we are trying to do something that really has a tremendous humanitarian aspect.

Q. But sir, you talk about defining yourself and Bill Clinton. On foreign policy, have you no disputes with him on any foreign policy?

The President. There will be plenty of time to define that, but not in the context of trying to do something that is very important. I have some responsibilities as a candidate, eventually when I become the nominee of this party, to just take the issues to him, to define his background, to tell it as it really is, and to fight for the programs and the issues that I believe in. So I've got all that to do.

But when it comes to a serious foreign policy initiative, I'm going to do my level-best to keep it out of the political arena. It is too very, very important that we conduct ourselves, whether it's in Iraq or whether it's in Bosnia, without kind of political leanings, and I'm going to do that. Therefore, I'm not going to answer questions that relate to his charge or trying to come back with some countercharge.

Presidential Campaign

Q. Mr. President, there was the flap this Monday about the memo, or the fax rather that was sent to news organizations from your campaign. And you subsequently denounced this or disavowed it and said you didn't want to get involved in the sleaze business, et cetera. There are many in your campaign that are quite happy with the impact that that fax had and seem to think that tactically this was quite beneficial and that you were able to distance yourself from this. Is that a pattern we should expect, or are you confident that this is now never going to happen again?

The President. The pattern you should expect is, after my being hounded and pounded for 9 months by my principles being ill-defined and what I stand for being ill-defined, you're going to see some hard-hitting attacks which are going to fairly define his positions. And that's what you should look for.

Q. What did you feel was unfair about the memo?

The President. I already said that I want to keep this campaign out of the sleaze business. Inasmuch as some interpreted the replay of Clinton's campaign manager's words as sleaze, I don't want any part of that.

Bosnia

Q. Mr. Bush, I know you've said that you hope there will be no need for any military use of force in Bosnia. But if it should come to that, does the resolution you want envision U.S. troops or aviators in some way being involved in that use of force? Could you specify——

The President. That is too hypothetical. We're working with the United Nations, and if we make a determination that force is necessary, we will do that after thorough discussion with our allies and with the United Nations Security Council participants.

Q. But surely, your allies are expecting some sort of indication of what your involvement——

The President. Well, we've already evidenced our willingness to be involved. We moved a carrier task force into the Adriatic. We have given support for humanitarian relief and will continue to do that. So I am not saying what we'll do or what we won't do, but whatever we do, I want to do it in conjunction with the international community.

Aid to Russia

Q. Mr. Bush, now that the IMF has approved some Russian assistance, the $1 billion loan in the World Bank, is the U.S. going to expedite any more financial assistance to Russia? Would you expect to offer them additional agricultural credit guarantees for the September-October period?

The President. Well, I have no plans on that; no recommendations have come to me on that. I do want to thank, though, both the Republican and Democratic leadership in the House for a very strong vote yesterday. I think it's a great boost for Yeltsin, who has our strong backing as he goes about his reforms under very difficult conditions. But no recommendations have come to me yet on further grain sales or anything.

The Economy

Q. Mr. President, as you noted in the unemployment numbers, figures are good but there's still a long way to go. Is it time now, do you think, to tell the American people that they probably won't start feeling good until maybe next year about the economy, but if they just hang on, it's coming? I mean, is this sort of a time——

The President. I'd just like to see them understand that there's some very strong signs here that are good. That doesn't mean there's no problems out there, but I think all they've heard are negative news about the economy, a lot of it because of the political process. If the other side can only win by things being bad, they're going to go out and point out all the things that are bad. All I'm saying is this is good news.

Now, you can help by putting a nice, positive interpretation on the fact that there are 200,000 more jobs created. And please do it because it's only fair that the American people understand that every once in a while something reasonably good happens. Interest rates are down, and inflation is down, and we are poised for a strong recovery. We've been growing, albeit anemically.

So it's important. I think your question is a good one because I think it is important that the American people understand the facts and try to separate out those facts from the political rhetoric that they've been handed for month after month about how horrible things are. Yes, conditions are not perfect. And yes, the economy has grown too slowly. But it has been anemically growing. Now this is fairly good news, you see.

Q. Let me just follow up, sir. Part of the problem has been expectations, that sometimes, as it's been said here, your own expectations were raised, along with everyone else. I'm just saying is it time now to say, "Okay, probably by November it may not look as good as you'd like it to, but hang on because it's cyclical, and it will get better, and we see signs." I mean, I'm asking you to put the spin on it.

The President. Well, I feel comfortable with that. [*Laughter*]

Mr. Fitzwater. Final question, please.

Presidential Campaign

Q. Mr. President, you mentioned that your principles have been ill-defined by your opponents in the campaign. As you know, there's been some talk even within your own party that a problem has been that you haven't gone forward and said what you really stand for, what you're going to fight for in a second term. Why do you think, after so many years in public life and 4 years as President, there are still these questions out there about what George Bush really stands for?

The President. I'm not sure I know the answer to that. But they'll sure know it by the time they go into the voting booth in November. They'll see the record. The record will be an accurate record, and it will be a positive record. I'm not going to permit the Democratic Party and the Democratic National Committee and the Democratic nominee to ill-define it.

So I can't answer as to why. Maybe some of the answer can be, you know, little seminars; we can discover that ex post facto. But now what I'm going to do is join the fray and go after him and define his record. And that's going to be fun. I'm looking forward to it. Then I'll contrast it with not only what have we done but what do I want to do.

I've not done that. I explained to them yesterday, I thought I had some obligations here as President to try to get some things through, even though the Congress has dug

in and made it very difficult to get something done. So I'll take that case to the American people. If you want to change an institution that hadn't changed in a long time, try on the Congress, the liberal Democratic control of the Congress. That will help. Then say, here's what the man is trying to do in education reform. Here's what he's been trying to do in welfare reform. Here's what he's been trying to do in enterprise zones. Here's what he's been trying to do, and it's been blocked by a hostile, highly political, liberal leadership in the Congress. So that hasn't been defined out there, and I've got to get that done.

This is the last. Yes, followup.

Q. If I could just follow up. I just wonder why you think even some within your own party make this charge about you not having articulated what you stand for. Even some of the people, you may support the programs that they're advocating, but they don't really believe you're going to fight for them.

The President. Well, I keep reading that in various journals and books, and it's not true. So what I have to do then is say, here's what a convention is about, here's what a campaign is about, and set the record straight and take the facts out there and let the American people make that determination themselves, not through some filters out there. That's the only way to take care of this problem which I think has existed.

Thank you all very much. We're off to the Guadalcanal memorial.

Note: The President's 137th news conference began at 10:05 a.m. in the Briefing Room at the White House. During the news conference the following people were referred to: Rolf Ekeus, Executive Director, United Nations Special Commission on Iraq, and Margaret Thatcher, former Prime Minister of the United Kingdom.

Remarks at a Ceremony in Arlington, Virginia, Commemorating the 50th Anniversary of the Landing on Guadalcanal
August 7, 1992

Thank you all very much. Thank you, Mr. Secretary, Senator Chafee, and the other Members of Congress that are with us who are veterans of Guadalcanal. May I salute the Chairman of the Joint Chiefs, General Colin Powell; Commandant of the Marines, Carl Mundy; General Sullivan, Commandant of the Army, is with us; the Acting Secretary of the Navy, Sean O'Keefe; distinguished Commandant of the Coast Guard, William Kime; and of course, the Medal of Honor recipient, Mitchell Paige, but most important, you marines. I would like to open—[*applause*]—I thought they had a little life left in them.

I'd like to open if I may with a story. It's a story of heroism, a story of courage, sacrifice. It's a story from Guadalcanal. Kenneth Bailey was commanding officer of Company C, 1st Marine Raider Battalion, when his men were called upon to defend Henderson Field during the Japanese assault, September 12th and 13th of 1942. The enemy had penetrated our main line of defense, their number superior to ours. Only a miracle, it seemed, could defend that airfield.

Major Bailey and his men provided the miracle, turning back the flank attack, then covering the withdrawal of our main force. In the fighting, Major Bailey sustained severe wounds to his head, and even so, for 10 hours he and his men engaged the enemy in vicious hand-to-hand combat. The attack was repulsed, and Henderson Field was secured. Major Bailey died 2 weeks later from machine-gun fire in yet another battle on Guadalcanal. He received the Congressional Medal of Honor for his gallantry on Bloody Ridge.

Major Bailey's story serves as a summation for thousands of other stories, tales that could be told by the brave men gathered here who survived the hell that was Guadalcanal. Secretary Cheney mentioned the lesson of those battles, and I'm struck, recounting Major Bailey's story, of one lesson in particular.

Kenneth Bailey was from Pawnee, Oklahoma, in a town of 2,000 near the Arkansas River in the north central part of the State. In the months and years before the great war in the Pacific, who could have predicted that a son from Pawnee, Oklahoma, or the sons of Raritan, New Jersey, or Sioux Falls, South Dakota, or Rutland, Vermont, who could have foretold that these young men from every corner of America would be called upon to defend freedom 6,000 miles away on an obscure Pacific island called Guadalcanal? It's safe to say that few, if any, had ever heard of the island. None could have predicted what would transpire there. But it was on Guadalcanal that the forces of freedom began their long march, a march that wouldn't end until 3 years later in Tokyo Bay on the deck of the U.S.S. *Missouri.*

No one can foretell when or where freedom will be challenged. That is one of the lessons of Guadalcanal. How many Americans in 1947 had heard of Inchon or Pusan or Chosen? How many of us 15 years later had heard of Da Nang or Khe Sahn? How few Americans in the summer of '90 had yet heard of Khafji or Safwan? Yet today, these names are indelibly part of the rollcall of honor, places where Americans made their stand and offered up their sweat and blood to a cause greater than themselves.

We honor the dead, not merely for their sake, but for our own sake as well. In commemoration and remembrance, we learn again that freedom, in the deepest sense, always hangs in the balance; that we earn it day by day in hot wars and cold; that its price, as Jefferson said, is eternal vigilance, an endlessly renewed dedication to keeping our great country strong, our defenses second to none, our leadership unquestioned and unchallenged.

There was a rhyme passed around during those dark 6 months that I'm sure many marines here today out front remember, 6 months, as the battle raged on, when freedom hung by the unbreakable thread of American bravery and resolve. Every marine who wasn't fighting on the island knew the lines, "Say a prayer for your pal on Guadalcanal."

This morning, in this place—and thank you, Pastor, for your loving invocation—this morning and in this place, we remember those words and the men who inspired them. With hearts full of pride and awe and thanksgiving, we once again say a prayer for those who fought and died in a place few had known of but which all of us will never forget.

May God bless them. May God bless you. And may God bless our great country, the United States of America. Thank you. Thank you very much.

Note: The President spoke at 11:11 a.m. at the Marine Corps War Memorial.

Statement on Signing the Pacific Yew Act
August 7, 1992

Today I am pleased to sign into law H.R. 3836, the "Pacific Yew Act." This Act ensures that Federal lands will be managed to provide for the sustainable harvest and long-term conservation of the Pacific yew. The bark of this tree is currently the only reliable source of taxol—an experimental drug used to treat cancer. By signing this bill into law today, we ensure that Pacific yew bark is made available to companies to produce a drug that has the potential to benefit thousands of patients.

It is very important that the collection of Pacific yew bark proceed with as little delay as possible, because taxol has shown very promising results in combating ovarian and breast cancer. In fact, the National Cancer Institute considers it to be the most important new cancer treatment drug discovered in the past decade. The Administration realizes the importance of taxol and is working to make sure that Pacific yew bark is available for taxol production.

The potential value of taxol for treating ovarian and other cancers was not known until 1989. By September 1991, 900,000 pounds of Pacific yew bark were collected on Federal lands. This quantity of bark will yield enough taxol to treat more than 12,000 patients, or about the same number of women who die from ovarian cancer each year.

As the demand for Pacific yew bark increases, we realize that we have to ensure a continuing supply of Pacific yew, while not threatening the resource's long-term existence. The Administration has already initiated a comprehensive Pacific yew management program involving the Forest Service, the Bureau of Land Management, other Federal agencies, local governments, and the private sector.

Our efforts have provided an opportunity for the Federal Government and private industry to work cooperatively for the public good. Additionally, our efforts to collect bark from the Pacific yew have brought in millions of dollars to local economies and provided numerous jobs in these local economies.

The Federal Government is already meeting many objectives of H.R. 3836. This Administration is committed to ensuring a continuous supply of yew bark to help cancer patients, while sustaining the Pacific yew for future generations. H.R. 3836 will help us do even more to meet this commitment.

GEORGE BUSH

The White House,
August 7, 1992.

Note: H.R. 3836, approved August 7, was assigned Public Law No. 102–335.

The President's News Conference in Kennebunkport, Maine
August 8, 1992

Bosnia

The President. Let me thank you all and just say that I've just met with Secretary Cheney, Deputy Secretary Eagleburger, Ambassador Watson from the United Nations mission, U.S. mission to the United Nations, and General Scowcroft. We are discussing, of course, the situation in Bosnia. We reviewed the situation in Bosnia but with a lot of emphasis on the United Nations. I'm delighted that Ambassador Watson could join us.

I'm pleased with the first indication from those controlling the detention camps that access will be given to the International Red Cross, the ICRC. We're determined that those camps must be submitted to inspection.

I've just spoken to the Secretary-General of the United Nations Boutros-Ghali about our concern of the camps. I had a chance to review with him in some detail the situation at the United Nations and with UN-PROFOR; that's the United Nations force there in Sarajevo. I thanked him for all of his efforts. The United Nations, of course, is playing a very constructive role.

I'm pleased that the Sarajevo airport is open once again and that the relief flights are able to go in. We are continuing to work with United Nations Security Council members on the substance of a resolution which would enhance our collective ability to deal with this situation. We're emphasizing the critical importance of early action to prevent the deterioration of the situation.

Having said all that, nothing is ruled in or out, and I will say that the object of providing humanitary assistance is our goal. Nothing has been ruled in or out to achieve that, and we have talked about a wide array of actions we can take in cooperation with our allies. The first and primary thing is to continue to work at the United Nations.

I must say that the Secretary-General did express some optimism about access to the camps, not just for the International Red Cross but also for the Office of the High Commissioner of Refugees which is, as we all know, a United Nations agency.

So we're updated on it, and I will try to keep the American people filled in as we go along on this, trying to help solve these tremendous humanitarian problems there.

I'd be glad to take a couple of questions, and I know they have to go back.

Q. There are reports now coming out of the U.N. that there is some agreement among the allies that NATO would be supplying air power and that the Western European Union would supply forces on the ground to protect those shipments of humanitarian aid. Is that the case?

The President. No, that is not the case. As I say, we are talking about all kinds of options, but there's no determination to that effect.

Q. Mr. President, Chancellor Kohl has suggested this firm blockade. I'm not sure how that would help get supplies through, but I wonder if you could give your reactions to that as well as to the belligerent talk coming from the people who represent themselves as the government of the Serbians threatening retaliation.

The President. When the United Nations takes a position and when countries join in, in terms of sanctions, it is in everybody's interest that those sanctions be fulfilled, that they be implemented. There have been some leaks in all of that, and we discussed Chancellor Kohl's call. No specific action taken, but again, it's highly complex. But we are determined to see that when the United Nations passes a resolution, it is implemented.

I did see a report of a rather reckless statement by a professed leader. Certainly no policy of the United States and I don't believe any policy of the United Nations will be affected by threatening statements of that nature.

Q. Mr. President, could you characterize the difference between Britain and France and the U.S. position on the use of force? And also, tell us if you were surprised at their characterization of your possible use of force as being politically motivated?

The President. No, I don't think we got a difference; I don't think anybody wants to go forward to use force. One thing I've reviewed today with Secretary Cheney and particularly with both Eagleburger and Cheney was the complexity. Larry Eagleburger's lived there for 7 years of his life. General Scowcroft has lived there, and Secretary Cheney has looked very carefully at all this.

So, it is highly complex. The American people must not be misled into thinking that there is some quick and easy military answer to this highly complex question. I don't believe, after talking to Ambassador Watson and—I did talk, as you know, I believe; I think we announced it yesterday—to Prime Minister Major, that there are wide differences between France, England, and the United States. There may be some differences.

But as in the past, as it was with Desert Storm and other resolutions, we worked those differences out. But I don't think it would help to categorize what they might be. But there are no fundamental differences in terms of rushing in to use force. If something I said or anybody has said implies we want to go in there with ground forces, something along those lines, please let me lay that to rest. Because you know, I don't care what the political pressures are, before one soldier or whatever it is, marine, is committed to battle, I'm going to know how that person gets out of there. We are not going to get bogged down in some guerrilla warfare. I owe it to the military not to make some rash decision based on politics.

So I'm glad you asked it because I will shoot it down right now. I don't care what the pressures are. If the Senate's going to pass a resolution, fine; let them pass it. But I have the responsibility not just to try to help solve this humanitarian problem but for the lives of young Americans. I take that responsibility very, very seriously.

Q. Sir, you apparently are for air strikes to free up these relief supplies. However, it's been said by the British and the French and others as the only way you can assure these convoys going in is to have ground forces there. The air strikes can't protect people who are being sniped at from road-ways and from mountains and hills. You talk about the difficulties. Can you explain some of the difficulties and how air strikes would be helpful?

The President. I'm not certain that the air strikes themselves would solve the problem, nor am I certain that putting ground forces into this situation, as it stands now, would solve the problem. Therein lies its complexity. This is a highly complex problem with all kinds of ethnic problems in there, all kinds of ancient rivalries. Our goal is to help solve the humanitarian problems. And John [John Cochran, NBC News], there isn't an easy formula. If there was, we would have put it into effect before now.

Q. What will the U.N. resolutions be that we want? Do you know yet?

The President. Well, we're working. I can't give you the exact details, but I referred to it the other day that we want to have authority to do whatever it takes to get in and solve this humanitarian question.

Presidential Campaign

Q. Mr. President, could I ask a non-Bosnian question? Your political director of your reelection campaign appears to want to keep alive whether or not there was an apology rendered for an attack-type press release on Governor Clinton. Is she off the reservation, or are you trying to have it both ways?

The President. No, she's not off the reservation. That matter, as far as I'm concerned, has been laid to rest. I don't know what you mean by she wants to keep it alive. I mean, we're going to have a hard-hitting campaign. Let me just repeat it, and I hope this will lay it to rest.

For 9 months, the other side has been hammering me. We put one toe in the water to fight back, and they start yelling "negative campaigning." We are going to hit them hard, legitimately, on issue differences and on their record. That's going to happen. We've got a very good bulldog doing that in Mary Matalin, and she's going to keep doing it. One little error in that because of interpretation, where we got across the line that I don't want to cross, and that is an area that I would term as a sleaze area. She understands it, and that's not going to happen again.

Q. Mr. President, you said in an interview that if Governor Clinton were elected President, he would return us to the economic problems of the late seventies.

The President. Yes.

Q. Are you prepared to tell the American people now that if you are reelected, that you will not raise their taxes?

The President. I'm prepared to say we don't need to raise taxes. We've got a plan up there that controls the growth of spending. We've got a plan to stimulate the economy. Absolutely. So I will go back to when the previous administration, Jimmy Carter administration left office, and I was talking about the "misery index" being right through the roof, unemployment and inflation right out there to almost a historic high. We don't want to return to what his program of tax and spend would get us into. So we're going to have a big difference on all that.

Bosnia

Q. Mr. President, back on the Bosnian situation. Margaret Thatcher said today that she felt the arms embargo against Bosnia should be lifted, that those people have a right to defend themselves and should have the arms to be able to do so. Would you favor lifting the arms embargo?

The President. I don't think the area needs more arms. I think it needs less arms. But we didn't go into that in detail. I don't know.

Do any of you want to address that question?

Deputy Secretary Eagleburger. They've got enough arms there already.

The President. Secretary Eagleburger backed up the President by saying there's enough arms there already. [*Laughter*] And I'm pleased to note that. But really, we've got to stop the killing some way. I don't know that it's enhanced by more and more arms.

Q. Sir, we don't know what you did today. We don't know what you decided today. We don't have a feel for what came out of the meeting.

The President. Stay tuned because you'll see this unfold at the United Nations.

Q. On that same subject, is it too imperti-

nent to say that we are here in order for you to show that you are on the case doing something, instead of relaxing?

The President. Well, I hope you'll say that because it's the truth. And I'm sure that these gentlemen could have had a lot more fun doing something else today. This is a serious matter. It's not a political matter. This is something that a Commander in Chief and a President has to deal with, and I plan to do it. And if informing the American people of just step by step is not good, well, I'm guilty. But I'm going to keep doing it. Nobody has to attend. Nobody has to attend. This is not political. I'm getting sniped at politically, but I will not make one decision based on American politics, election politics '92. Now, you can believe that or not, but that's the truth.

Intelligence Reports for Candidates

Q. Are you providing intelligence reports to Governor Clinton so that there's——

The President. We offered them, yes. I don't know how much they've accepted.

General Scowcroft. They have accepted, and we are working out arrangements.

The President. General Scowcroft said that it's been offered, I assume, to both challengers, and they have accepted it. But the details are being worked out.

Politics and Foreign Policy

Q. Is this the kind of crisis that you're better equipped to handle than Bill Clinton?

The President. Now, John, clearly you are hard of hearing because I said I don't want to put this into a political context. The lady standing next to you would kill me if I answered that question. So I'm not going to do it because she would then say, hey, they're playing—look, to suggest that because it's an election year, every decision you make has to be purely political, I think that's crazy.

I'm trying to conduct the foreign affairs and the national security affairs of this country with doing what's right and not be influenced by political criticism, political sniping, or political constructive suggestions. We've got a good team working this problem, and we're going to keep on working the problem and try to keep it out of the political arena.

We're talking about lives being lost this very minute. A lot of people are suggesting that, in my view, reckless uses of force, of American force. I don't do it that way. I haven't conducted myself that way in charge of our foreign policy and in charge of national security, and I'm not going to start now for election reasons. So please understand that.

Last one. Yes.

Intelligence Briefings

Q. Mr. President, Mr. Clinton has said he hoped he could work out the briefings. But he also said that in connection with a recommendation on Bosnia last week that he felt he knew all that he needed to know. Can you tell us if there is more to this matter than what's in the newspapers and whether a person who hasn't had the briefings really understands the situation?

The President. Well, I've found that there is always more—let me put it in my own personal terms. I learn a great deal from my daily briefings from the intelligence community and the CIA. I've taken them every single day. I remember when I first got the nomination as Vice President back in 1980, the Carter administration offered these briefings. I found them extraordinarily helpful. But I think they've been turned down. I'm not sure. But in 1984, I'm not sure these briefings took place because I believe the candidate didn't want them. I could be wrong on that, whether it was '84 or earlier. But look, I have no criticism. If he wants the briefings, fine. I can just tell you that I learn a great deal from them.

Q. But then he's operating on less than full information on the recommendations he's——

The President. I just find the briefings extraordinarily helpful. And when I have them, I have more information than I would have if I didn't.

Bosnia

Q. What similarities do you see to Vietnam, sir, in this situation?

The President. I don't see any yet. And I'm determined there won't be any——

Q. Sir, a question on Saddam Hussein.

The President. ——in terms of U.S. role, the U.S. role.

Q. You keep talking about not getting caught—you haven't actually said "quagmire" but used synonyms to that. I mean, is it the terrain, difficult terrain; you can't tell where the enemy is?

The President. The terrain is difficult. The finding of the opposition is difficult. You have a history in that area—you don't have to go very far back—go back to World War II and see a history of successful guerrilla fighting in the area. You have a terrain problem at Sarajevo that's similar; at the G–7 meeting, people were telling me Dien Bien Phu.

So I think there are parallels. But there isn't going to be a parallel as long as I make the decisions in terms of putting people in there and not clearly understanding the mission and not clearly understanding how that mission is achieved and then seeing those people come out with their honor intact, fully backed by the United States.

So it's highly complex in using that formula that I just spelled out and then applying that formula to the situation, that highly complex situation on the ground today in Yugoslavia.

Q. Ground troops is out of the question?

The President. I didn't say that. I just spelled out to you the formula that is going to be applied if ever any American force is used, air, ground, sea, whatever it is.

Q. Mr. President, you have a situation there where we see television pictures of buses full of orphans being shot up, the funerals of orphans that are killed in that attack being mortared, and the international community seems to be powerless to do anything. Why would it not be worthwhile to at least try threatening an ultimatum, threatening use of force to halt the bloodshed?

The President. The international community is working together to try to do something about it. And when we get through there, and not before we get through—but at the same time, we are grieved by the suffering in Somalia. I've been concerned about the eruptions of fighting in different parts of the world in addition to those, in other parts of the globe.

So all I'm saying is it's a very hard problem to solve, wave a wand and solve it. But we are concerned, and we're working hard to get this humanitarian aid in there and to also have access to these camps.

Q. You said you're continuing to seek substance for a resolution. Is there a particular hangup with our allies over the wording of a resolution?

The President. Well, I think there have been some differences that we were asked about earlier. But I'm satisfied that they will be resolved. Then of course, when you go into a U.N. resolution, it's not just the United States. If we are correct, and I think we are, that we should use the United Nations in this area, we have other countries. It's not simply the permanent members of the Security Council, although they obviously have a large say. If they're not together, all five countries, why, nothing's going to happen in the Security Council.

So there have been some nuances of differences. But there's no differences in terms of the purpose, in terms of the need to do what we need to do to fulfill this humanitarian mission. So there have been some, I think it's fair to say. Wouldn't you, Alex? Ambassador Watson filled us in on some of the detail. I just don't think it would be helpful to publicly go into these differences when we're trying to come to a satisfactory conclusion on a resolution.

Thank you all very much. Thank you.

Note: The President's 138th news conference began at 4:35 p.m. at his home on Walker's Point. In his remarks, he referred to Mary Matalin, deputy campaign manager for political operations, Bush-Quayle '92.

Remarks on the Arrival of Prime Minister Yitzhak Rabin of Israel in Kennebunkport
August 10, 1992

Q. Mr. Bush, will the Prime Minister get his loan guarantees?

The President. This is what we call a photo opportunity, and we're not going to take any questions now, but we'll have plenty of opportunity after we have discussions.

The only thing I want to say is that the welcome mat is out for Prime Minister Rabin. He has many friends in the United States, including the man he's standing next to, and we are looking forward to strengthening a relationship that is strong and will be even stronger. So that's all I care to say.

But welcome, Prime Minister. We're so pleased you're here.

The Prime Minister. Mr. President, first I would like to thank you for your kind invitation at this chapter of the life of Israel and no doubt of my own life as the new Prime Minister. My purpose, as it was stated before the elections, after the elections in Israel, that we would like on the one hand to give a chance, a real chance to the peace negotiations within the framework of the Madrid conference. We would like to change the order of our national priorities. We believe that the real problems are in the domestic field. In addition, to make a real effort to negotiate these seriously without endangering Israel's security, vital interests. And no doubt, we would like to make sure that there is a better and more intimate relationship between our two countries, our two peoples, and our two Governments. Let's hope that this visit will give a chance to at least make clear where we stand, what we can do together to achieve these goals.

The President. It's a good objective, and I agree with him. Anyway, welcome, once again. We're very pleased you came. Look forward to our meeting.

Well, we're off to have some meetings right now, as a matter of fact.

Q. By candlelight? We understand your power's out, Mr. Bush.

The President. Well, it's so beautiful out-doors, we might just meet outside.

Note: The President spoke at 10:23 a.m. at his home on Walker's Point.

Statement on the Middle East Peace Talks
August 10, 1992

We are pleased to announce that we have received positive responses from all the parties to the bilateral negotiations in the Arab-Israeli peace process to attend the sixth round of talks which will commence in Washington on August 24.

The United States and Russia, as cosponsors, welcome this opportunity for the parties to engage in substantive negotiations and to make real progress during this round.

The United States is prepared to continue to play its role as a driving force, catalyst, and honest broker to promote progress in these negotiations.

Nomination of Harry J. Gilmore To Be United States Ambassador to Armenia
August 10, 1992

The President today announced his intention to nominate Harry J. Gilmore, of Virginia, a career member of the Senior Foreign Service, class of Minister-Counselor, to be Ambassador of the United States to the Republic of Armenia.

Mr. Gilmore currently serves as Deputy Commandant for International Affairs at the U.S. Army War College. Prior to this, he served in several positions at the Department of State including principal officer at the U.S. Embassy Office in Berlin, 1990–91; U.S. Minister and Deputy Commandant at the U.S. Mission in Berlin, 1987–90; Deputy in the Office of Central European Affairs at the State Department; Deputy Chief of Mission at the American Embassy in Belgrade, Yugoslavia, 1981–85; Deputy Director for Eastern European and Yugoslav Affairs at the State Department; political officer and deputy principal officer at the American consulate general in Munich, 1975–78; and country officer for Yugoslavia at the Bureau of European Affairs at the Department of State, 1973–75.

Mr. Gilmore graduated from the University of Pittsburgh (B.A., 1960). He was born November 16, 1937, in McKeesport, PA. He is married, has three children, and resides in Carlisle, PA.

The President's News Conference With Prime Minister Yitzhak Rabin of Israel in Kennebunkport
August 11, 1992

The President. Well, I've just spent the best part of the past 24 hours with Prime Minister Rabin, and it has been a true pleasure for Barbara and me to spend this time with the Prime Minister and Mrs. Rabin. We've known them for many years. As a matter of fact, we're charter members of the former ambassadors club, and we could not be happier than to have them visit us here at Kennebunkport, this very special place for me and for my family.

Before I say some more about my hours of conversation with the Prime Minister, I want to take this opportunity to say a few things about the relationship between the United States and Israel. This is a relationship that goes back more than four decades to Israel's birth in 1948. This is a relationship that's been tested in times of peace and war, one capable not only of weathering differences but of accomplishing great things. This is a relationship based on a shared commitment to democracy and to common values, as well as the solid commitment to Israel's security, including its qualitative military edge. This is a special relationship. It is one that is built to endure.

Now, we reviewed a great many issues, often in considerable depth, and I want to begin with the peace process. I will let the Prime Minister, obviously, speak for himself, but I do not think he would object to my saying that we agree 100 percent that our goal goes beyond that of ending the state of war. What we seek is real peace, codified by treaties, characterized by reconciliation and openness, including trade and tourism. It must be a comprehensive peace on all fronts, grounded in U.N. Security Council Resolutions 242 and 338, born of direct negotiations.

Two weeks from now in Washington, representatives of Israel along with those of the Palestinians, Jordan, Syria, and Lebanon will resume direct negotiations launched in Madrid last October. I am optimistic that these talks are about to enter a new, more productive phase.

Prime Minister Rabin has persuaded me that Israel's new government is committed to making these talks succeed, and I call upon the Arab parties to respond in kind. The time has come to make peace, not simply to talk of it.

We also spent time discussing the region at large. It is tragic that so much of the history of the Middle East is measured by wars. It's a crime to waste so much of the area's resources, human and material alike, in preparing for wars or waging them. It is time these resources were committed to meeting the needs of people. We thus committed ourselves to work to stem the proliferation of conventional arms as well as

weapons of mass destruction. We agreed to work together on behalf of the multilateral process begun in Moscow earlier this year to promote progress between Israel and her neighbors on issues ranging from water, the environment, economic development, to refugees and security.

The Prime Minister and I focused as well on the international situation, and we agreed that the world must seize the historic opportunity created by reform in Russia and the other newly independent States. We agreed, too, that the world must act to bring to an end this humanitarian nightmare that now exists in what was Yugoslavia.

The Prime Minister and I also devoted a good deal of time to bilateral issues. Let me say that it's a source of considerable satisfaction to me to look back on all that has been accomplished just over the last few years. With the assistance of the United States, Israel has been able to take major strides in breaking out of its diplomatic isolation. Israel no longer is stigmatized so unfairly by a U.N. resolution equating Zionism with racism.

Literally hundreds of thousands of Jews from Ethiopia and from the former Soviet Union now make their homes in Israel; and this, more than anything else, is what the Jewish state is all about. In this regard, I am extremely pleased to announce that we were able to reach agreement on the basic principles to govern the granting of up to $10 billion in loan guarantees. I've long been committed to supporting Israel in the historic task of absorbing immigrants, and I'm delighted that the Prime Minister and I have agreed to an approach which will assist these new Israelis without frustrating the search for peace. We can thus pursue these two humanitarian goals at one and the same time.

I look forward to sitting down with the congressional leadership and recommending to them that Congress take swift action on authorizing up to $10 billion in loan guarantees to facilitate Israeli absorption of immigrants. Together with the economic reforms the new Israeli government is committed to, I am confident that these loan guarantees can make a considerable contribution, a critical contribution, to Israel's future. I would hope that other governments with the means to do so would also consider extending loan guarantees for this purpose.

I'd like to say one more thing about my time with the Prime Minister. The meetings were important for what we discussed, but they were also significant for the tone of the discussions. Our time together can best be described as a consultation between close friends and strategic partners, one characterized by trust, warmth, and a commitment to meeting these common challenges. This is strategic cooperation at its very best.

So again, let me just end these remarks by saying how much we've enjoyed having the Rabins visit us at our home here and now, speaking for all Americans, how much we hope the Prime Minister and his wife will be regular visitors to the United States of America.

Thank you, sir.

The Prime Minister. Thank you very much.

Mr. President, let me first thank you wholeheartedly for the kind and warm hospitality bestowed by Mrs. Bush and yourself on my wife and me, as well as our colleagues. It has been a real pleasure to spend with you, with Secretary Baker, General Scowcroft, and your other colleagues, this highly pleasant day. We really appreciate it.

I would also like to thank you for your kind words this morning. Our exchange of views here included a great number of subjects, both of a general character, dealing with international issues and concerns, specific bilateral matters. It was done in a constructive and friendly atmosphere for which we are grateful.

I would like to allude, first, to the human tragedy in Bosnia. We, the Jewish people, having suffered persecution throughout history, can never remain indifferent to such tragedies. The killing must stop. I know that the United States is now making great efforts towards a solution there. We, on our part, are trying to contribute as much as we can in humanitarian aid. Let us hope that those tortured people will find peace.

Mr. President, as you kindly indicated, the basis of the relationship between Israel and the United States is the unshakable foundation of shared values and hopes. Our joint commitment to democracy and to freedom stands as a permanent, solid rock on which a very special relationship is built.

This relationship, which has seen occasional, temporary differences—differences, views—include our strategic cooperation among other important links developed over many years. We have both reiterated our mutual desire to continue those links, facing the challenges that lie ahead.

Mr. President, we live through troubled times, reflected also in our region. We have supported since the beginning of the Gulf crisis the U.S. and your policy against Saddam Hussein's brutal aggression. The strong approach taken by the United States during the war greatly contributed to the regional sense of security and made a positive contribution to Israel's security as well.

We continue to support a determined policy towards still-existing dangers. We are committed together, Mr. President, to the pursuit of peace in our region. The new government in Israel which I'm privileged to head will do its utmost to promote the peacemaking efforts begun and cosponsored by the United States under the Madrid framework. This framework has been structured to a great extent on the basis of the Camp David accords and took into considerations many of Israel's desires.

On our part, we shall do our best to inject new momentum to the negotiations, both in the bilateral and the multilateral spheres. We shall do so as much as we can on a continued basis while, of course, scrupulously preserving Israel's security against all threats.

We will be glad to attend the coming round of the bilateral negotiations in Washington later this month and through much of the next months. We look forward to fruitful negotiations with the Jordanian-Palestinian delegation, as well as with the Syrian and the Lebanese delegation. It is our hope that our counterparts will share our good will and openness. The chances for a better, peaceful future are there. Let us all take the advantage of them. We also look forward to the multilateral negotiation starting anew in September.

Mr. President, I would like on behalf of my country to express to the United States and to you, personally, our gratitude for your support to the opening of the gates of the former Soviet Union and Ethiopia for the immigration of our brethren who so wished to their homeland, Israel. This role will not be forgotten.

In the same spirit, the U.S. has supported the idea of absorption of these immigrants, enabling them to achieve appropriate housing and employment and rebuild their lives. Your decision now to submit to the Congress a proposed legislation concerning the loan guarantees is a significant step in this direction.

We, on our part, are determined to improve our national economy towards more efficient and privatized system for this and other goals that must be achieved. We have also announced in the basic guidelines of our government a change in the national priorities towards this direction.

We shall also carry as much as possible of the burden, of the financial burden of the guarantees so as to lessen any cost to the American taxpayer. But your readiness to extend them following our discussions means a lot to me and to Israel. And again, thank you very much.

The President. Thank you, sir.

Now we'll be glad to take some questions.

Middle East Peace Talks

Q. Mr. President, can you now envision a time of real peace between Israel and its Arab neighbors? And to what extent has a new government in Israel contributed to this process?

The President. Well, I salute the Prime Minister. He has been very forthright, as he said here in his statement, about wanting to continue the peace negotiations, and absolutely, I think all of us should look optimistically about the chances for peace. There are always obstacles. But the fact that they are coming together across a table, the people that have had ancient enmity, is a very good sign. I think the approach of this new government which is saying, "Let's meet; let's talk," is exactly what it's going to take to achieve the kind of peace that everybody wants.

As you'll notice in my statement, I called

upon Arab governments to be forthcoming in the forthcoming talks. So yes, we are optimistic. We all know there are problems, but we must achieve it.

Q. When can we expect results, sir?

The President. Well, I think we just have to wait now and see how the talks go.

Would you like to comment on that question, sir?

The Prime Minister. Well, we are coming with open-minded—we believe that the negotiations, face-to-face, on the three delegations, the Jordanian-Palestinian, the Syrian, and the Lebanese, can be conducted, the purpose to achieve, when it comes to the Jordanian-Palestinian delegation, the interim arrangement for self-rule to the Palestinians.

The way it is described in principles in the letter of invitation to the Madrid conference, we are open-minded, we are interested to achieve. But in the Middle East, there is a saying that for war, one side is enough; for peace, you need two. We hope we'll have the second partner.

The President. We're going to try to alternate between U.S. and Israeli journalists, if that's all right.

Israel-U.S. Relations

Q. Mr. President, you spoke of a strategic partnership between the two countries. I was wondering if you could elaborate a bit and tell us if you believe Israel has strategic importance to the United States in the aftermath of the cold war.

The President. I do, and I think that when we talk about militarily qualitative edge, that is a longstanding position of the United States. We will continue to uphold it. Israel is a democracy surrounded by countries that aren't, and they have been loyal and staunch friends.

My responsibilities as for President of the United States and the security of this country relate to the fact that nobody knows where the next crisis could come. You rely on friends in a crisis. Israel is not only important as a friend, but they have demonstrated strategic reliability. So I don't care to elaborate any more, but I just would reemphasize the fact that it is not only historic friendship based on democracy, but it is in the interest of the United States. It is in our security interest to retain the kind of relationship we have militarily and every other way with Israel.

Palestinians

Q. To follow it up, after your discussions with Mr. Rabin, I assume you exchanged views on perhaps the shape of Palestinian self-rule. Would you say that you basically see eye-to-eye on how that should—the terms?

The President. Well, I'd say he made a very clear presentation about this. And I don't know, there might be some differences, but I think basically we recognize that as he approaches the peace table, that is the way to decide what happens. We're not going to prejudge or precondition from the United States standpoint.

Loan Guarantees for Israel

Q. It's been said that you had reached agreement on the basic principles for granting the loan guarantees. Does that mean that the agreement is less than final?

The President. No, I'm going to go forward. I'm going to keep it a little bit—I'm not going to go into a lot of detail right now. I think I owe it out of courtesy to the congressional leadership to go forward with recommended legislation. I will be doing that. I think we're set for this afternoon to do just that, and I think that will give us a chance to—so it's more than just a general agreement, but there's enough specifics here for me to recommend enthusiastically to the United States Congress and to the American people that this is in not only the interest of Israel, but it is in our interest.

Q. Well, what are those basic principles, sir, and how do they relate to this touchy question of settlements?

The President. Well, I've just touched on one of them, that we have a strategic ally. There's a broad humanitarian principle, and that is we would like to be helpful in settling those that have come home, those that have left Ethiopia, those that have left the former Soviet Union, and that's kind of the humanitarian aspect of it.

There's all kinds of implications. A strong Israel, an Israel that is better able to cope through the borrowings it's making, is in

our interest.

Q. Well, what about this basic question of settlements, sir, that's been so touchy between the two countries?

The President. I think that I would let Prime Minister Rabin's words speak, not just the words here but the words that he spoke during his campaign, and then the actions that he has taken. We see a very different approach to settlements, and we salute the Prime Minister. It was not an easy position, and I'm sure there are divisions in Israel on this position. But he took a lot of courage, and he has begun to implement that policy certainly to the satisfaction of the United States.

I would prefer you call on your traveling journalists so I don't overlook anybody, and then, well, if they ask me the question, I'll be glad to try to——

Israeli POW–MIA's

Q. Mr. President and Mr. Prime Minister, did you deal with the problem of the MIA's and POW's, the Israeli ones?

The President. We discussed it, and the Prime Minister just forcefully said to me, "Look, please do everything you can to account for whoever else might be held prisoner." And so he made the case, and I pledged to him to do whatever it is we can. We do not have great influence on solving that problem. We didn't have too much on solving the one where Americans were held. But as long as one prisoner is held, everybody should be outraged and try to do his level-best.

Jerusalem

Q. Mr. President, may I ask you please as to whether you are prepared to recognize a unified Jerusalem as the capital of the sovereign State of Israel and that you will move our Embassy to Jerusalem in your second term?

The President. Let me just say that our policy on Jerusalem remains unchanged. It must never be divided again, and its final status must be resolved through negotiation. And nothing in approach here changes that policy. That's the U.S. policy, and I will just stay with that and not go into anymore detail.

Politics and Foreign Policy

Q. Mr. President, do you feel that the positive tone of these talks and Prime Minister Rabin's warm words here will help in helping you win over American Jewish voters who were alienated by your remarks on September 12th and by the tensions in your relationship with former Prime Minister Shamir?

The President. Well, let me try to be clear on this one, just as I was the other day on Bosnia. We're not talking here about domestic United States politics, nor are we talking about domestic Israeli politics. We're talking about principle. We're talking about doing what is right. We're saluting the policy that we see as very forthcoming and very proper on the part of the Prime Minister and his new government.

So I'd like to try to leave it out of the American election process, and I would readily recognize that isn't easy. On anything you do, whether it's a foreign policy matter or a domestic matter, every question tries to hook it into domestic politics. But I'm going to finesse that because I think what we're talking about here is too important.

New York Post Allegations

Q. Mr. Bush, uncomfortable as the subject is, I would think it's one in which you feel a necessity to respond because you've said that family values, character, are likely to be important in the Presidential campaign. There is an extensive series of reports in today's New York Post alleging that a former U.S. Ambassador, a man now deceased, had told several persons that he arranged for a sexual tryst involving you and one of your female staffers in Geneva in 1984.

The President. I'm not going to take any sleazy questions like that from CNN. I am very disappointed that you would ask such a question of me, and I will not respond to it. I haven't responded in the past. I think it's—I'm outraged. But nevertheless, in this kind of screwy climate we're in, why, I expect it. But I don't like it, and I'm not going to respond other than to say it's a lie.

Israeli Policies

Q. Mr. President, what is the outstanding achievement you achieved during this 24-hour period with the President?

The Prime Minister. What?

Q. The most outstanding achievement, do you think, to the people of Israel.

The Prime Minister. Well, I believe that the first and the foremost importance of the visit is to try to establish relationship of trust and confidence. From the very beginning, from the visit of Secretary Baker to the region, I made it a point to put the facts, to put everything on the table to avoid in the future any misunderstanding because not stating exactly both our positions, sometimes they can bring differences of opinion. But the real issue is, even when there are differences of opinion, how to work together, Israel and the United States, to achieve our common goals, goals that we agree on.

In what I have said and described here was basically the policies of the new government of Israel. We want, first, to try our best within the framework of the Madrid conference to move in the peacemaking process, not in the peace process.

Second, we changed our national priorities from spending our own money, the Israeli taxpayer, on settlements that I define them in a certain way, and to take them and to shift them to cope with the real problems of Israel, unemployment, et cetera, in Israel.

Thirdly, not to take steps that in accordance to our opinion can interfere with the peace negotiations. These are our decision. We are going to bring about rezoning, reclassification of government assisting to building houses, absorption, that we'll really shift them to what we believe should be.

I presented the new policy to the President, to his colleagues, as I did to the people of Israel, as I did in the Knesset on the July 13 when I presented my government.

Q. Mr. President——

Israeli Settlements

Q. Prime Minister Rabin, during his campaign and after the election, distinguished between political settlements and the security settlements. After your long talks with Prime Minister Rabin, do you agree to that distinction?

The President. Well, we understand the position. All I will say is that I salute this change. We salute what the Prime Minister is trying to do. We understand his position. He understands our position. And obviously, we would not be going forward with this loan guarantee if we did not salute the change. So I'd just leave it right there.

Palestinians

Q. Mr. President, are you satisfied, generally, with the modalities of autonomy that Mr. Rabin has presented here?

The President. Modalities of the what?

Q. Autonomy for the Palestinians?

The Prime Minister. I didn't present modalities here. [*Laughter*]

Q. Did you talk about the autonomy?

The Prime Minister. Well, I described Israeli position. It was an exchange, first exchange between the President and me, on the issues that might be brought up in the coming bilateral negotiation and in the multilateral. It was in a form of consultation, not taking decisions. It was exchange of views, and I wouldn't go beyond that. The issues have to be solved, agreed on, between the parties to the conflict.

Q. Mr. President, are you going to ask——

Q. Why didn't you play tennis?

Q. Mr. President——

The President. I did the day before.

Secretary of State Baker

Q. Are you going to ask Secretary Baker to take a different job?

Q. Did you discuss Secretary Baker's imminent departure from the State Department? And I'd like to ask the Prime Minister what impact that will have on the peace talks.

The President. Susan [Susan Spencer, CBS News] is referring to a lot of domestic speculation that the press has written about with such certainty and finality that what she's saying is that Jim Baker will leave the State Department. What I've said—I'm just filling him in and then I'll answer your question—[*laughter*]—what I've said is that if anything happens in that regard, I'll be

sure to let them know. But the answer to your question is, that was not discussed with the Prime Minister.

Q. Does the Prime Minister feel that that would have a major impact on the peace talks?

The President. Nice try.

The Prime Minister. I don't deal with domestic political American or personal domestic American problems.

Q. Maybe one last question from the Israeli——

The President. This is the final question because Marlin is looking very nervous, and I know we've got some logistics problems here.

Middle East Peace Talks

Q. From both your opening statements, it seems like the onus now will be on the Arabs in the peace talks. My question to Mr. Rabin is: Do you expect this from the Americans? Do you expect them to put more pressure on the Arabs? And my question to Mr. Bush is: Are you actually going to do that?

The Prime Minister. I didn't ask anyone to put pressure on anyone. We exchanged views in a form of consultation about the options, but I didn't ask for any pressure, as I expect that no one on the other side will ask the United States to put pressure on Israel.

The President. One of the major accomplishments in the last few years is getting the parties across from each other at the peace table. That was not done through pressure. Peace will not be brought about through pressure. If the United States can be a catalyst for peace in the process, we want to be one. But no sovereign government is going to be pressured into reaching out and achieving peace, reaching out for and achieving peace. It just doesn't work that way.

In any event, thank you all very much.

The Prime Minister. Thank you.

Note: The President's 139th news conference began at 9:27 a.m. at his home on Walker's Point.

Remarks Congratulating the United States Olympic Team
August 11, 1992

These guys are fired up, listen. I am so sorry about the weather. We had a spectacular event planned out there. But it can't diminish this. May I salute Bill Hybl, the president of the committee, and of course, Arnold Schwarzenegger, who's Chairman of our Fitness Committee and led our official delegation over there to see you all magnificent athletes. And welcome to the White House. It's an honor to have this marvelous U.S. Olympic team right here. I didn't recognize you almost without Bob Costas as a voice-over.

But I want to welcome you to the White House and to extend this message: Whether you won a gold, silver, bronze, or simply gave your best, I believe that you all are winners in the eyes of your countrymen. You really set a great example.

The last couple of weeks we were completely caught up here at home by this Olympic spirit. Barbara asked me to help rearrange a couple of chairs upstairs. And I said, "What's the degree of difficulty?" [*Laughter*] But on and on it went, everybody reflecting the glory that you all helped bring to this country for 16 days, over 100 hours. You showed how competition lifts the human spirit and that now that spirit really lifts the American character. When I was a kid I read about the game being well worth the candle burned long into the night. Now I'm told your nights in Barcelona were long, but I'm betting that that candle is going to still last longer.

Each Olympics is one for the record books. This one was one for the history books. Our world has been remade since those Seoul Olympics, and we Americans, I think, can take pride in the fact we helped remake it. But in 1989 the wall came down in Berlin, and this summer more barriers tumbled there in Barcelona. This was an Olympics, this is why I say it's historic, without boycotts, without terrorism, without politics. And it's just exactly as it ought to be.

You all must have sensed it there in the village in meeting East and West Germans, black and white South Africans, North and South Koreans. One by one these old divisions gave way. The world watched as countries that didn't even exist in the last Olympics took their place on the field and the medal stand, too. Think of that. You know what it means to make America a winner, but think what it must mean to be the first athlete to bring a medal home to Latvia or Croatia. They, like you, made this an Olympics worthy of its name.

Today we honor here in the White House all of you, the fastest, the strongest of America's athletes. And here's what I like even more: You're among its most inspirational. With us today is Shannon Miller, back here in the front row, who overcame a bone chip in her elbow; Gail Devers overcoming Graves' disease; Charles Barkley overcoming his shyness. [*Laughter*] That brings me to Ron Karnaugh, who wore his deceased father's hat and made every father proud. And Oscar de la Hoya, he not only brought home the gold, he brought honor to his mom's memory. Each of them competed, competed to win for the wonderful family called America.

Ask diver Mark Lenzi what it takes to get the gold. He'll tell you about Dad's carpools or Mom's care packages, his favorite brownies, her special lasagna. Talk to Summer, Summer Sanders, one of swimming's new kids on the block, and she'll say that success—is she making signs—[*laughter*]—success comes down to the support of people around you. And let me add, I'm especially amazed by the synchronized swimmers. Maybe it's because I live in a city where it's tough to get any two people to agree on anything, say nothing to do it in tandem.

Family: Look at the Oden sisters, Kim and Elaina, volleyball's "sisters of smash." Then there's the men's wonderful bronze medalist volleyball team. It was sensational. I saw that last game. We've had a lot of athletes proudly represent the symbol of the bald eagle. They're the first ones that looked like bald eagles. [*Laughter*] From Trent Dimas and Chris Campbell and Janet

Evans, Carl Lewis, from Gigi and Mary Joe Fernandez to the woman Leora "Sam" Jones representing those who won not only medals but also our hearts, and look, this list goes on and on, on and on. Suffice to say that in Barcelona this Nation became your family. And why not? Sports are not abstract. Fitness is not abstract. These things mean something. Sports are flesh and blood. Americans see you, and then they relate to you.

Wrestler Bruce Baumgartner shows what I'm talking about. Watching him on TV, he's even stronger than I thought he was. Anytime he wants to come here, and weightlifting equipment isn't good enough, he's welcome to drop by and bench-press the Federal budget. [*Laughter*]

Eighteen days ago Bruce called his 2-year-old son, Bryan, in western Pennsylvania. That day was doubly special. It was the opening day of the Olympics, and it was the kid's birthday, too. But he doesn't know what a gold medal is yet. The kid doesn't know that, but his mother coached him to say, "Bring home the gold medal." Two years old. Last Thursday Bruce did exactly that. Now, he had a lot of company, for instance, the Dream Team which sent basketball soaring.

My good friend Arnold Schwarzenegger, who led this delegation to Barcelona, our official one, once starred in a movie where he uttered those famous words, we all remember them, "*Hasta la vista*, baby."

[*Laughter*] In Barcelona that's what all of you said to opponents and to couch potatoes. You inspired the mother who plays softball with her kids, the dad shooting hoops with his boys or girls, the family who knows that sports are ageless. Take Pablo Morales—front row, where is he, can't find him, but he's in there somewhere; whoops, there he is—the swimmer. He missed out in '84, didn't make the team in '88, then came back this year to earn a gold medal at the ripe old age of 27. That just goes to show, youth and inexperience are no match for maturity and determination.

This summer the entire world was barely a match for you all. In Barcelona you KO'd the opposition: 108, and I want to repeat this one for the cameras, 108 medals, the most ever since 1904 in a nonboycotted Olympics.

And you really paved the way magnificently for a knockout punch in Atlanta. I just can't wait until 1996. A proverb says, "On the day of victory, no one is tired." Today we celebrate Olympians, like America, who are victorious, refreshed, and free.

Thank you so very much for coming to the White House. May God bless this great country that you've made so very proud, the United States of America. Thank you all very, very much.

Note: The President spoke at 5:05 p.m. in the East Room at the White House. In his remarks, he referred to William Hybl, president of the U.S. Olympic Committee.

Message to the Congress Transmitting the Annual Report on Radiation Control for Health and Safety
August 11, 1992

To the Congress of the United States:

In accordance with section 540 of the Federal Food, Drug, and Cosmetic Act (21 U.S.C. 360qq) (previously section 360D of the Public Health Service Act), I am submitting the report of the Department of Health and Human Services regarding the administration of the Radiation Control for Health and Safety Act of 1968 during calendar year 1991.

The report recommends the repeal of section 540 of the Federal Food, Drug, and Cosmetic Act that requires the completion of this annual report. All the information found in this report is available to the Congress on a more immediate basis through Center technical reports, the Radiological Health Bulletin, and other publicly available sources. This annual report serves little useful purpose and diverts Agency resources from more productive activities.

GEORGE BUSH

The White House,
August 11, 1992.

Presidential Determination No. 92–38—Memorandum on Arms Exports to Zambia
August 11, 1992

Memorandum for the Secretary of State

Subject: Eligibility of Zambia to be Furnished Defense Articles and Services Under the Foreign Assistance Act of 1961 and the Arms Export Control Act

Pursuant to the authority vested in me by section 503(a) of the Foreign Assistance Act of 1961, as amended (22 U.S.C. 2311(a)), and section 3(a)(1) of the Arms Export Control Act (22 U.S.C. 2753(a)(1)), I hereby find

that the furnishing of defense articles and services to Zambia will strengthen the security of the United States and promote world peace.

You are directed to report this finding to the Congress and to publish it in the *Federal Register.*

GEORGE BUSH

[*Filed with the Office of the Federal Register, 3:08 p.m., August 24, 1992*]

Remarks Announcing the Completion of Negotiations on the North American Free Trade Agreement
August 12, 1992

Today marks the beginning of a new era on our continent, on the North American Continent. This morning the United States, Mexico, and Canada are announcing the completion of negotiations for a North American free trade agreement, NAFTA.

First, I want to express my deep appreciation to Ambassador Carla Hills, our United States Trade Representative, to Secretary Serra of Mexico, and to Minister Wilson of Canada for this outstanding achievement. Also standing next to me is Carla Hills' Deputy, my able friend Jules Katz, who had a very instrumental role in all these negotiations.

This historic trade agreement will further open markets in Mexico, Canada, and the United States. It will create jobs and generate economic growth in all three countries. Increased trade with North America will help our Nation prepare for the challenges

and opportunities of the next century.

The cold war is over. The principal challenge now facing the United States is to compete in a rapidly changing, expanding global marketplace. This agreement will level the North American playing field, allowing American companies to increase sales from Alaska to the Yucatan. By sweeping aside barriers, NAFTA will make our companies more competitive everywhere in the world. We've seen this happen with the U.S.-Canada Free Trade Agreement, and we'll see it even more with the NAFTA.

Open markets in Mexico and Canada mean more American jobs. Our Nation is the world's leading exporter, well ahead of Japan and Germany. Today over 7 million Americans are hard at work making products that will be sold around the world. Export-related jobs pay 17 percent more than the average U.S. wage. These jobs are the kind that our Nation needs to grow and prosper, the kind that showcase American talent and technology.

More than 600,000 Americans are now employed making products and selling them to Mexico, our fastest growing export market. We sold over $33 billion worth of goods to Mexico last year and are projected to sell $44 billion this year. In the last 5 years, as President Salinas has dismantled many longstanding Mexican trade and investment restrictions, our exports to Mexico have nearly tripled. In the last 5 years, let me repeat that, our exports to Mexico have nearly tripled. That's one-quarter of a million new American jobs. This agreement helps us lock in these gains and build on them.

Last year the Congress endorsed moving forward with NAFTA by extending the Fast Track procedures for congressional consideration and implementation of trade agreements. The rapid completion of the NAFTA talks shows how much can be accomplished when the executive branch and the Congress work together to do what is best for our Nation. And I'll work closely with the Congress for rapid implementation.

At the time Fast Track was extended, I outlined steps that we would take to address environmental and labor concerns. We've taken every promised step, and we are meeting or beating every commitment that I outlined. This is the first time a trade agreement has included stringent provisions to benefit the environment. The NAFTA maintains this Nation's high environmental, health, and safety standards. In fact, it goes even further and encourages all three countries to seek the highest possible standards.

The Environmental Protection Agency and its Mexican counterpart have already developed a comprehensive integrated border plan to clean up air, water, and hazardous wastes along the Rio Grande. These problems are serious, but they will be solved by environmental cooperation, increased trade, and higher levels of economic growth, not protectionism. Unfortunately, Congress has reduced the funding for our border plan in the appropriations process. I ask the Congress to fully fund these important environmental initiatives.

With NAFTA we're moving forward with our trade strategy. Trade is part of my long-term economic growth plan to create more opportunities for all Americans. In a changing world, we must give our workers the education and skills they need to compete and assistance and training to find good jobs. I've said many times: Level the playing field and the American worker can outthink, outproduce, and outwork anyone, anytime.

Today's historic agreement links our future with our past. Five centuries ago this very month, a man of courage and vision set sail from the Old World in search of new trade routes and opportunities. Christopher Columbus was an entrepreneur, and the journey he started 500 years ago continues to pay off abundantly today. By moving forward with the NAFTA, with the North American free trade agreement, we will replenish that investment, opening up new horizons of opportunity and enterprise in the New World.

So this is a good day for America, a good day for North America. Once again, I want to express my appreciation to Ambassador Hills and her extraordinarily able team, who have worked literally day and night for months to complete this negotiation phase of the agreement. It's good news, and as I understand it, the Ambassador will be having a briefing on the details of it in a few minutes from now.

Thank you all very much.

Note: The President spoke at 7:50 a.m. in the Rose Garden at the White House. In his remarks, he referred to Jaime Serra Puche, Mexican Secretary of Commerce and Industrial Development, and Michael Wilson, Canadian Minister of International Trade.

White House Fact Sheet: The North American Free Trade Agreement
August 12, 1992

The President today announced that the United States, Mexico, and Canada have completed negotiation of a North American free trade agreement (NAFTA). The NAFTA will phase out barriers to trade in goods and services in North America, eliminate barriers to investment, and strengthen the protection of intellectual property rights. As tariffs and other trade barriers are eliminated, the NAFTA will create a massive open market, over 360 million people and over $6 trillion in annual output.

Background

With sharp increases in global trade and investment flows, U.S. economic growth and job creation have become closely tied to our ability to compete internationally. Since 1986, U.S. exports have increased by almost 90 percent, reflecting our success in opening foreign markets and the competitiveness of American industry. In 1991, the U.S. exported over $422 billion of industrial and agricultural products and over $164 billion in services, making the United States the world's largest exporter, ahead of Germany and Japan. More than 7.5 million U.S. jobs are tied to merchandise exports, up from 5 million in 1986. Of these jobs, 2.1 million are supported by exports to Canada and Mexico.

For many years, Mexico used high tariffs and licensing restrictions in an effort to encourage industrial development and import substitution. Under President Salinas and his predecessor, President de la Madrid, the Mexican Government has opened its market and implemented sweeping economic reforms. In 1986, Mexico joined the General Agreement on Tariffs and Trade (GATT) and began reducing its tariffs and trade barriers.

As a result, bilateral trade has increased dramatically. From 1986 to 1991, U.S. exports to Mexico increased from $12.4 billion to $33.3 billion, twice as fast as U.S. exports to the rest of the world. U.S. agricultural exports rose 173 percent to $3 billion, consumer goods tripled to $3.4 billion, and exports of capital goods surged to $11.3 billion from $5 billion. U.S. exports to Mexico now support approximately 600,000 American jobs, while exports to Canada support 1.5 million.

Economic reforms have also been good for Mexico. Its inflation rate has dropped from over 100 percent in 1986 to under 20 percent in 1991, and its economy has grown at an average annual rate of 3.1 percent over the last 4 years, after stagnating during the 1980's.

In June 1990, Presidents Bush and Salinas endorsed the idea of a comprehensive U.S.-Mexico free trade agreement and directed their trade ministers to begin preparatory work. Canada joined the talks in February 1991, leading to the three-way negotiation known as NAFTA. Formal negotiations began in June 1991 after Congress extended through May 1993 the Fast Track procedures originally enacted in the Trade Act of 1974, authorizing the administration to submit the agreement with implementing legislation for an up-or-down vote.

The President's trade strategy, which is a key part of his overall economic growth plan, is designed to create new markets for American products and provide new opportunities for American companies and workers.

The NAFTA Agreement

The NAFTA will create a free trade area (FTA) comprising the U.S., Canada, and Mexico. Consistent with GATT rules, all tariffs will be eliminated within the FTA over a transition period. The NAFTA involves an ambitious effort to eliminate barriers to agricultural, manufacturing, and services trade, to remove investment restrictions, and to protect effectively intellectual property rights. In addition, the NAFTA marks the first time in the history of U.S. trade policy that environmental concerns have been directly addressed in a comprehensive trade agreement. Highlights of the NAFTA include:

Tariff Elimination. Approximately 65 percent of U.S. industrial and agricultural exports to Mexico will be eligible for duty-free treatment either immediately or within 5 years. Mexico's tariffs currently average 10 percent, which is 2½ times the average U.S. tariff.

Reduction of Motor Vehicle and Parts Tariffs. U.S. autos and light trucks will enjoy greater access to Mexico, which has the fastest growing major auto market in the world. With NAFTA, Mexican tariffs on vehicles and light trucks will immediately be cut in half. Within 5 years, duties on three-quarters of U.S. parts exports to Mexico will be eliminated, and Mexican "trade balancing" and "local content requirements" will be phased out over 10 years.

Auto Rule of Origin. Only vehicles with substantial North American parts and labor content will benefit from tariff cuts under NAFTA's strict rule of origin. NAFTA will require that autos contain 62.5 percent North American content, considerably more than the 50 percent required by the U.S.-Canada Free Trade Agreement. NAFTA contains tracing requirements so that individual parts can be identified to determine the North American content of major components and sub-assemblies, *e.g.* engines. This strict rule of origin is important in ensuring that the benefits of the NAFTA flow to firms that produce in North America.

Expanded Telecommunications Trade. NAFTA opens Mexico's $6 billion market for telecommunications equipment and services. It gives U.S. providers of voice mail or packet-switched services nondiscriminatory access to the Mexican public telephone network and eliminates all investment restrictions by July 1995.

Reduced Textiles and Apparel Barriers. Barriers to trade on $250 million (over 20 percent) of U.S. exports of textiles and apparel to Mexico will be eliminated immediately, with another $700 million freed from restrictions within 6 years. All North American trade restrictions will be eliminated within 10 years and tough rules of origin will ensure that benefits of trade liberalization accrue to North American producers.

Increased Trade in Agriculture. Mexico imported $3 billion worth of U.S. agricultural goods last year, making it our third-largest market. NAFTA will immediately eliminate Mexican import licenses, which covered 25 percent of U.S. agricultural exports last year, and will phase out remaining Mexican tariffs within 10 to 15 years.

Expanded Trade in Financial Services. Mexico's closed financial services markets will be opened, and U.S. banks and securities firms will be allowed to establish wholly owned subsidiaries. Transitional restrictions will be phased out by January 1, 2000.

New Opportunities in Insurance. U.S. firms will gain major new opportunities in the Mexican market. Firms with existing joint ventures will be permitted to obtain 100 percent ownership by 1996, and new entrants to the market can obtain a majority stake in Mexican firms by 1998. By the year 2000, all equity and market share restrictions will be eliminated, opening up completely what is now a $3.5 billion market.

Increased Investment. Mexican "domestic content" rules will be eliminated, permitting additional sourcing of U.S. inputs. And for the first time, U.S. firms operating in Mexico will receive the same treatment as Mexican-owned firms. Mexico has agreed to drop export performance requirements, which presently force companies to export as a condition of being allowed to invest.

Land Transportation. More than 90 percent of U.S. trade with Mexico is shipped by land, but U.S. truckers currently are denied the right to carry cargo or set up subsidiaries in Mexico, forcing them to "hand off" trailers to Mexican drivers and return home empty. NAFTA will permit U.S. trucking companies to carry international cargo to the Mexican States contiguous to the U.S. by 1995 and gives them cross-border access to all of Mexico by the end of 1999. U.S. railroads will be able to provide their services in Mexico, and U.S. companies can invest in and operate land-side port services. The combination of truck, rail, and port breakthroughs will help create an efficient intermodal North American transport system.

Protection of Intellectual Property Rights. NAFTA will provide a higher level of protection for intellectual property rights than any other bilateral or multilateral agreement. U.S. high technology, entertainment, and consumer goods producers that rely heavily on protection for their patents, copyrights, and trademarks will realize substantial gains under NAFTA. The agreement will also limit compulsory licensing, resolving an important concern with Canada.

The objective of NAFTA is to open markets. It is not designed to create a closed regional trading bloc and does not erect new barriers to non-participants. The NAFTA is fully consistent with GATT criteria for free trade agreements and with U.S. support for strengthening the multilateral trading system in the Uruguay round.

Economic Studies

At the request of the Office of the U.S. Trade Representative, the U.S. International Trade Commission surveyed and evaluated the various economic analyses of NAFTA. In May of this year, the USITC reported that:

> [T]here is a surprising degree of unanimity in the results regarding the aggregate effects of NAFTA. All three countries are expected to gain from a NAFTA.

These independent studies found that NAFTA would increase U.S. growth, jobs, and wages. They found that NAFTA would increase U.S. real GDP by up to 0.5 percent per year once it is fully implemented. They projected aggregate U.S. employment increases ranging from under 0.1 percent to 2.5 percent. The studies further project aggregate increases in U.S. real wages of between 0.1 percent to 0.3 percent.

U.S. exports to Mexico currently support over 600,000 American jobs. The Institute for International Economics recently estimated this figure will rise to over 1 million U.S. jobs by 1995 under NAFTA.

Environment, Labor, and Adjustment Issues

In a May 1, 1991, letter to the Congress, the President described actions that the administration would implement to address concerns regarding the impact of free trade on the environment, labor rights, and worker adjustment programs.

Environment. The administration has moved forward with a comprehensive bilateral environmental agenda to allay concerns that free trade could undermine U.S. environmental and food safety regulations or lead to environmental degradation on the U.S.-Mexico border. During the last year, substantial progress has been made. Highlights include the following:

—*Standards.* The NAFTA allows the U.S. to maintain its stringent environmental, health, and safety standards. It allows States and localities to enact tougher standards based on sound science. It encourages "upward harmonization" of national standards and regulations, and prohibits the lowering of standards to attract investment.

—*Integrated Border Plan.* In February 1992, EPA and its Mexican counterpart (SEDUSOL) completed a comprehensive plan for addressing air, soil, water, and hazardous waste problems in the border area. Agreement has been reached on measures to implement the first stage of the plan covering the period 1992 to 1994.

—*Border Infrastructure.* The President has proposed a 70-percent increase in the budget for border environmental projects to $241 million for FY 1993, including $75 million for the "colonias" (unincorporated communities on the U.S. side of the border that often lack effective sanitation services and running water) and over $120 million for border wastewater treatment plants.

—*Border Plan/FY 1993 Appropriations.* To date, in the FY 1993 appropriations process, the House of Representatives has refused to fund the $50 million EPA request for the colonias and cut the administration's $65 million request for a Tijuana-San Diego sewage treatment plant to $32 million. For its part, the Senate failed to fund $120 million of the requested funds for border wastewater treatment. The President has called upon Congress to reverse these cuts.

—*Environmental Conference.* On September 17, 1992, EPA Administrator

Reilly will host a trilateral meeting with the Canadian and Mexican environmental ministers in Washington, DC, to discuss environmental aspects of NAFTA.

Worker Rights. Mexico has a comprehensive labor law that provides workers with extensive legal rights. The economic benefits of the NAFTA will provide Mexico with resources to move forward with vigorous enforcement initiatives launched by the Salinas administration.

—*Labor Cooperation.* The U.S. Department of Labor has negotiated a 5-year Memorandum of Understanding (MOU) to strengthen bilateral cooperation with respect to occupational health and safety standards, child labor, labor statistics, worker rights, labor-management relations, and workplace training. Several joint MOU initiatives are now underway.

Safeguards. President Bush committed that NAFTA would contain measures to ease the transition for import-sensitive U.S. industries. For our sensitive sectors, tariffs will be phased out in 10 years, with particularly sensitive sectors having a transition of up to 15 years. In addition, NAFTA contains "safeguard" procedures that will allow the U.S. to reimpose tariffs in the event of injurious import surges.

Worker Adjustment. Dislocations in the U.S. are likely to be minimal, since U.S. trade barriers are already quite low. Nonetheless, during the Fast Track debate, the President promised that dislocated U.S. workers will receive timely, comprehensive, and effective services and retraining, whether through improvement or expansion of an existing program or creation of a new program. The administration has already begun consulting with the relevant congressional committees regarding adjustment services for displaced workers.

Next Steps

The timing of congressional consideration is governed by the Fast Track procedures, which require the President to notify the Congress of his intent to enter into the agreement at least 90 days before it is signed. Although today's announcement reflects the completion of negotiations, the draft text probably will not be finished until September, since further legal drafting and review are required to implement the understandings reached by the negotiators.

After the agreement is signed, legislation must be prepared to implement it, including any necessary changes to U.S. law. Under the Fast Track, the NAFTA will not go into effect until the Congress has approved the implementing legislation on an up-or-down vote. The approval process must occur within a specified time: 90 "session" days of Congress.

Message to the Senate Transmitting the Treaty on Open Skies
August 12, 1992

To the Senate of the United States:

I transmit herewith, for the advice and consent of the Senate to ratification, the Treaty on Open Skies. I believe that the Treaty on Open Skies is in the best interest of the United States. By engaging all participating States actively in cooperative observation, the Treaty on Open Skies will strengthen international stability. The Treaty also provides an important means of increasing mutual understanding of military forces and activities, thus easing tensions and strengthening confidence and security, not only in the area covered by the Treaty, but in other areas as well.

The Treaty includes twelve Annexes, which are integral parts thereof. The Treaty, together with the Annexes, was signed at Helsinki on March 24, 1992. I transmit also, for the information of the Senate, the Report of the Department of State on the Treaty.

In addition, I transmit herewith, for the information of the Senate, five documents associated with, but not part of, the Treaty that are relevant to the Senate's consideration of the Treaty: Decision Number One on the Distribution of Costs Arising Under the Treaty on Open Skies in accordance with Annex L, Section I, paragraph 9, dated June 29, 1992; Decision Number Two on Additional Non-Destructive-Testing Equipment To Be Used by the Observed Party in accordance with Annex F, Section I, paragraph 7, dated June 29, 1992; Decision Number Three on Methodology For Calculating the Minimum Height Above Ground Level at Which Each Optical Camera Installed on an Observation Aircraft May Be Operated During an Observation Flight in accordance with Annex D, Appendix 1, Section III, paragraph 2, dated June 29, 1992; Decision Number Four on Minimum Camera Specification For an Observation Aircraft of an Observed Party Exercising its Right To Provide an Observation Aircraft For an Observation Flight, dated June 29, 1992; and Decision Number Five on Responsibility For the Processing of Film Used During an Observation Flight in accordance with Article IX, Section II, paragraph 2, dated June 29, 1992. Except for Decision Number One on the Distribution of Costs, these Decisions are legally binding.

The Decision on the Distribution of Costs Arising Under the Open Skies Treaty in accordance with Annex L, Section I, paragraph 9 has not been adopted by the Open Skies Consultative Commission (the implementing body of the Treaty made up of representatives from each State Party and the body which adopted the above-mentioned Decisions). The Open Skies Consultative Commission will adopt this Decision during its next session, scheduled for September 1992, and it will have the same legally binding status as the other Decisions. The Open Skies Consultative Commission has endorsed the current draft text of the Decision; however, agreement could not be reached on the issue of navigation fees which a great majority of the States Parties—including the United States—believe should be waived. Pending resolution of this issue, some States Parties—including the United States—have reserved their position on other cost issues.

The Open Skies Treaty establishes a regime of unarmed aerial observation flights over the entire territory of its 25 signatories (North Atlantic Treaty Organization Allies, Eastern European members of the former Warsaw Pact, and Russia, Ukraine, Belarus, and Georgia). The Treaty is designed to enhance mutual understanding and confidence by giving all participants, regardless of size, a direct role in observing military or other activities of concern to them. Covering territory from Vancouver to Vladivostok, Open Skies is the widest-ranging international effort to date to promote openness and transparency of military forces and activities. The Treaty allows for consensus decisions to improve sensors, to adjust quotas, and to admit new participants in order to enhance its effectiveness. The Open Skies principles may be applicable to States in other regions of the world as well.

The Treaty's operative provisions focus on four subjects:

—*Territory:* The entire territory of all participants will be accessible to aerial observation. Whereas the former Soviet Union had insisted on closing areas for national security reasons, the Treaty provides that only flight safety considerations may restrict the conduct of observation flights.

—*Aircraft:* Unarmed fixed-wing aircraft provided by either the observing or observed Party can be used. All Open Skies aircraft and sensors must pass specified certification and inspection procedures to ensure that they meet the standards of the Treaty.

—*Sensors:* Open Skies aircraft may have video, panoramic and framing cameras for daylight photography, infra-red line scanners for a day/night capability, and synthetic aperture radar for a day/night all-weather capability. Photographic image quality will permit recognition of major military equipment, e.g., distinguishing a tank from a truck—allowing significant transparency of military forces and activities. Sensor categories and capabilities can be improved by agreement among the States Parties. All equipment used in Open Skies must be commercially available to all participants. Data collected from the flights will be immediately shared by the observing and observed Parties, and may also be obtained by other States Parties.

—*Quotas:* Loosely scaled to size, each State Party has agreed to an annual quota of observation flights it is willing to receive (42 for the United States and Russia/Belarus to 2–4 for the smallest States Parties). States Parties may conduct as many observation flights as they are willing to receive.

The Treaty establishes an Open Skies Consultative Commission, composed of rep-resentatives designated by each State Party, to meet in Vienna, to promote the objectives and to facilitate the implementation of the provisions of the Treaty.

Therefore, I urge the Senate to give early and favorable consideration to the Treaty and its related Annexes, and to give advice and consent to its ratification.

GEORGE BUSH

The White House,
August 12, 1992.

Nomination of Lois L. Evans To Be United States Representative to the Economic and Social Council of the United Nations
August 12, 1992

The President today announced his intention to nominate Lois L. Evans, of New York, to be the Representative of the United States of America on the Economic and Social Council of the United Nations, with the rank of Ambassador. She would succeed Jonathan Moore.

Currently Ms. Evans serves as president of Acquisition Specialists, Inc., 1975 to the present, as well as a consultant at Richard Kinser & Associates, 1991 to the present. Ms. Evans has also served as U.S. Representative to the 30th and the 31st sessions of the South Pacific Commission; member of the Advisory Committee at the Export-Import Bank of the United States, 1988–90; Chairman of the Federal Home Loan Bank of New York, 1986–88; Director of the Federal Home Loan Bank of New York, 1984–88; and Assistant Chief of Protocol of the United States of America with the Department of State's New York office, 1981–82.

Ms. Evans graduated from Barnard College (B.A., 1957). She was born December 1, 1934, in Boston, MA. Ms. Evans is married, has three children, and resides in New York, NY.

Nomination of John J. Maresca To Be Special Cyprus Coordinator
August 12, 1992

The President today announced his intention to nominate John J. Maresca, of Connecticut, a career member of the Senior Foreign Service, class of Minister-Counselor, for the rank of Ambassador during his tenure of service as Special Cyprus Coordinator.

Ambassador Maresca has served as Chairman of the U.S. Delegation to the Negotiations on Confidence and Security-Building Measures, 1989 to the present. Prior to this, he served as Deputy Assistant Secretary of Defense, 1986–88. From 1985 to 1986, he was a visiting fellow at the School of Foreign Service at Georgetown University. Ambassador Maresca has also served in several other positions with the State Department, including Deputy Chief of Mission at the U.S. Embassy in Paris, France, 1982–85; Director of the Office of Western European Affairs, 1980–82; and Deputy Political Counselor at the U.S. Embassy in Paris,

France, 1977–80.

Ambassador Maresca graduated from Yale University (B.A., 1959). He was born December 9, 1937, in Stresa, Italy. He also served in the U.S. Navy, 1959–65. Ambassador Maresca is married, has one child, and resides in Chevy Chase, MD.

Nomination of Brian C. Griffin To Be Chairman of the Administrative Conference of the United States
August 12, 1992

The President today announced his intention to nominate Brian C. Griffin, of Oklahoma, to be Chairman of the Administrative Conference of the United States for a term of 5 years. He would succeed Marshall Jordan Breger.

Since 1989, Mr. Griffin has served as Deputy Assistant Attorney General with the Tax Division at the Department of Justice. Prior to this, he served as a partner with the firm of Griffin & Griffin, 1979–80 and 1985–89. From 1980 to 1985, he served as executive vice president and general counsel for Petroleum Investments, Ltd.

Mr. Griffin graduated from Harvard University (B.A., 1974), Oxford University (B.A., 1976; M.A., 1983), University of Oklahoma (J.D., 1978), and Southern Methodist University (LL.M., 1989). He was born January 11, 1953, in Oklahoma City, OK. Mr. Griffin is married, has two children, and resides in Bethesda, MD.

Remarks on the Resignation of James A. Baker III as Secretary of State
August 13, 1992

I have a brief statement to make, and I'll be followed by Marlin taking some questions.

I've asked Secretary Baker to resign as Secretary of State to join me as Chief of Staff and Senior Counselor to the President, effective August 23d. He will help me build on what we started by developing an integrated second-term program of domestic, economic, and foreign policies.

This is a pivotal point in America's journey. In the world today, these three topics have become one issue. We must ensure that the United States is unquestionably safe and strong at home and abroad. I also want his counsel and assistance as I seek a mandate from the American people to put this program into action.

Secretary Baker has served our country with great energy, intelligence, and personal commitment over the past 12 years. I won't spend a long time listing his many successes, leaving that record to other statements and to history. But I do want to say a word about my friend.

I've known Jim Baker for 35 years. He is a committed trustee of the American public interest. I know Americans have been proud to see him on TV representing the United States abroad. I know they respect his many skills. I know that they trust his judgment. He's the sort of man you want on your team.

As Secretary of State, Jim Baker has appreciated the unique role and capabilities of American power. He's also understood and acted upon the exceptional appeal and calling of American ideals. He's been bold, quick, and tenacious, and he's achieved important things, willing to see new possibilities and patterns during an epic of revolutionary change. He acted while others were still struggling to comprehend, and he got things done.

He was central to our efforts to assemble an unparalleled U.N. coalition against Iraq. He's made great progress towards transforming victory on the battlefield into a broader peace between Israelis and Arabs. During his tenure we totally transformed our relationship with the Soviet Union, bringing the cold war to a peaceful end. He negotiated deep cuts in the nuclear weapons, conventional weapons as well. In so doing, he helped establish a vastly safer security structure on which to build a new Euro-Atlantic community and protection against the plague of proliferation. In helping to overcome the division of Europe, he helped lead the way for the unification of Germany. He helped silence the wars in Central America by building policies around democracy and the power of the ballot box.

From Tokyo to Toronto, Jim Baker is known for accomplishment. He knows about change, how to distinguish wise moves from foolish ones. He knows about America's Government having helped to develop and implement domestic, economic, and foreign policies. Perhaps most important, he knows our people are the source of our country's strength.

I make this move with full confidence that the State Department will remain under able leadership. Larry Eagleburger, a 30-year veteran of America's foreign policy, a man to whom I feel exceptionally close personally, will serve as Acting Secretary. He will do so with distinction.

I also want to say a word about Sam Skinner. I want to thank him for his dedicated service at the White House over the course of this turbulent year. He recognized right up front the contribution that Jim Baker can make here, given my longstanding personal relationship with Jim. He and I have actually discussed this matter for some time,

and he encouraged me to make this change. Sam and I have decided that he can best complement this move by assuming the position of general chairman of the Republican National Committee, and I will recommend to the RNC that this appointment be confirmed. Some may remember the Paul Laxalt role, close to the White House, very helpful at the committee, and that precedent is there.

He's been at my side, Sam Skinner has, in politics and Government, too, for over a decade. He served the public with extraordinary distinction in Illinois and is a respected and highly effective member of my Cabinet. Remember he was responsible, I'd give him a major part of the credit, for passing the historic transportation bill to modernize our National Highway System, a significant accomplishment.

I am personally appreciative of his willingness to assume this new assignment as we move into the general election campaign. I am convinced that this appointment will strengthen the Republican National Committee structure, and Sam will be able to work very closely with Rich Bond who will remain as chairman.

I recognize that many Americans today are anxious. Many have genuine concerns; others have doubts. But over the past 4 years Americans have accomplished results that once seemed beyond possibility. Now we'll focus our attention on the policies at home and abroad that will make the United States unrivaled on all fronts, economically secure for our children, and a safer and better place to live.

That's the end of the statement. Marlin will be able to flesh out some of the details for you. Thank you very much.

Note: The President spoke at 10:02 a.m. in the Briefing Room at the White House.

Letter Accepting the Resignation of James A. Baker III as Secretary of State
August 13, 1992

Dear Jim:

With this letter, I accept with deep appreciation your decision to resign as Secretary of State effective August 23, 1992; and I look forward, with great pleasure, to your joining me at the White House as Chief of Staff and Senior Counselor to the President.

Your service as Secretary of State has been superb. You have brought to foreign policy-making a rare combination of personal characteristics: substantive command, political sophistication, extraordinary negotiating skills, tireless dedication, personal integrity, and consistent grace. Applying these distinctive characteristics in yet one more public policy domain, you have again excelled.

With your outstanding leadership at State, Eastern Europe has been liberated. Germany has been peacefully and democratically unified, within NATO. The Soviet empire has disbanded; the captive nations have regained their independence; and Russia is becoming a democratic nation, seeking to transform itself into a market economy. You have successfully concluded negotiations that make the risk of super-power nuclear conflict a thing of the past. At the same time, you have turned U.S. strategy toward the new post-Cold War era by establishing a framework for continued U.S. engagement in Europe; and by advancing the global effort to stem the proliferation of weapons of mass destruction.

In addition, you deserve special credit for leading our successful negotiating efforts to stabilize areas of regional conflict: first, gaining international support for free elections in Nicaragua and a peace accord for El Salvador; second, organizing a U.N. coalition that effectively stopped and reversed Iraqi aggression in Kuwait; and finally, getting Arabs and Israelis to sit down together—in order that a stable Mideast peace might be won in the aftermath of the Gulf War.

The record is of genuinely historic proportions. I can well understand your reluctance to resign as Secretary of State.

Foreign policy will continue to demand vigilant and creative attention in the post-Cold War period and the team there at the Department of State under Acting Secretary Larry Eagleburger, working closely with the White House as you have done so well, is well qualified to handle any and all challenges. But America will not be able to fulfill her historic mission at home or abroad if our domestic leadership and performance are not strong and secure.

To help assure that America enjoys both domestic strength and security, I have asked you to join me in the White House. As a former Chief of Staff and Treasury Secretary, you bring extraordinary skills and experience to the policy challenges that lie immediately before us. It is imperative that we define appropriate new policies for a changing domestic environment—just as we have done for a radically transformed international environment. In so doing, we must attend to the connections between domestic and foreign policy, and between economic and security policy. At the same time, we must develop and implement more effective strategies for advancing our policies through the U.S. Congress.

For all of this, you are uniquely well-suited. I am profoundly grateful that you have agreed to yet another challenge of service. We have been friends and colleagues for a very long time. So again let me say: I appreciate your willingness to change assignments, and look forward to our working even more closely together.

Barbara and I know how difficult the demands of travel have been for you, Susan, Mary Bonner and the rest of the family. If there is any consolation in this new challenge, it may be that, although I will still call upon you in foreign policy, you will not have to travel so much in this new job!

Sincerely,

GEORGE BUSH

Dear Mr. President:

It is with pride and a sense of accomplishment that I submit my resignation to you as Secretary of State effective August 23. It is also with a sense of gratitude to you, Mr. President. Gratitude because you have placed great trust and confidence in me and do so again by asking me to work with you to build a safe, strong America at home and abroad. Gratitude, also, because you gave me the high honor of serving you to shape American foreign policy during a period of extraordinary and revolutionary change.

I have little doubt that when we look back on these last three years and seven months, we'll understand we've lived through a fundamental watershed in world politics. In this short period of time the strategic verities of the post-World War II era were shattered. The Cold War ended. The division of Europe was undone. The Soviet empire collapsed, and the Soviet Union dissolved.

Changing those verities created new hopes and new possibilities—and what was unthinkable before became achievable through very active and dynamic diplomacy that you mandated. Germany was unified in NATO, something we were told at the time was impossible. Central America has been transformed through a policy based on free elections and peaceful reconciliation of long-standing differences. A peaceful settlement has been developed for Cambodia. Iraqi aggression was defeated in Kuwait with an unprecedented coalition that would never have been possible in the bipolar world of the past. And, in the aftermath, in defeating Iraq and rescuing Kuwait, it became possible to break the historical taboo and produce Arab and Palestinian partners to talk peace with Israel.

Nothing was inevitable, and managing these historic transformations both to create new possibilities and to ensure a peaceful transition to a new, vastly safer world required very active American leadership. You provided it, Mr. President.

Working with Presidents Yeltsin, Kravchuk, and others, we managed to help shape a peaceful dissolution of the Soviet Union and empire; to ensure there would be no new nuclear states emerging from ᵗhe breakup of the USSR; to assure that tactical nuclear weapons would not fall into dangerous hands; and to negotiate ground-breaking START and CFE agreements that drastically reduce both nuclear and conventional arms.

On top of this, Mr. President, we were able to conclude the most far-reaching understanding on strategic arms reduction in history at your June Summit with President Yeltsin. We came into office with the US having 13,000 strategic nuclear arms and the Soviets about 11,000. Your agreement with President Yeltsin means we will slash those levels by over 75 percent by the year 2003. In addition, we will eliminate all MIRVed ICBMs, the most destabilizing strategic weapons.

There is still much to be done and new international challenges to deal with. The tragedy that is unfolding in the former Yugoslavia is a reminder of one of the new dangers in the world caused by the explosive mix of extremist nationalism and ethnicity in politics. As you have led the way in ending the Cold War, so too we must lead in building a new peace, developing the collective means to defuse these kinds of conflicts before they begin; contain those where they can't be defused; and employ peacekeepers and monitors to preserve ceasefires and ensure conditions for peacemaking. That's a tall order, and it will require American leadership. But it will be necessary if we are to mobilize the coalitions that can be useful and effective in dealing with a challenge we and others are sure to face in the years ahead.

Active American leadership will also be necessary as we continue our efforts to stop and undo the proliferation of nuclear, chemical, and biological weapons and the missiles that might deliver them. This will increasingly dominate the arms control agenda of the 1990's.

Of course, we will also have to continue accelerating our efforts to promote free markets and free trade and facilitate the work of American businesses and investors overseas. Free markets and free trade do not simply reflect our values, they promote our economic growth and well-being. The more we open markets to our goods and services internationally, the more we will expand economically and generate good jobs domestically. NAFTA can be a model for the future.

I look forward to supporting your efforts to more strongly integrate domestic and foreign policy and to build our strength here at home. Mr. President, we have been friends for 35 years, and I have always known you to finish the jobs you've begun. Work remains to be done and I look forward to helping you complete the job you started.

Sincerely,

JAMES A. BAKER III

Note: These letters were made available by the Office of the Press Secretary but were not issued as White House press releases.

Letter Accepting the Resignation of Samuel K. Skinner as Chief of Staff to the President
August 13, 1992

Dear Sam:

It is with deep regret but even more with pride in your many accomplishments that I accept your resignation as Chief of Staff. I am very pleased, at the same time, that you will serve as General Chairman of the Republican National Committee.

You have worked in every one of my campaigns since 1979, and you have served with great distinction in two demanding jobs in the last four years. As Secretary of Transportation, you developed the National Transportation Policy that will keep our Nation on the move well into the next century, obtained record levels of Federal funding for the aviation infrastructure, and strengthened mass transit programs. Under your leadership, the Coast Guard performed superbly in Operations Desert Storm and Desert Shield.

Your many accomplishments at the Department are crowned by one of our most significant legislative achievements—the Intermodal Surface Transportation Efficiency Act. That law establishes the National Highway System, builds partnerships between all levels of government and the private sector, and strengthens highway safety programs.

As Chief of Staff, you led the White House during a period of great change both at home and abroad. I deeply appreciate your loyalty in fighting for the programs that we know will change America for the better. This year, among many other accomplishments, we presented our Comprehensive Health Care Reform proposals, accelerated welfare reform in the States, and announced the "G.I. Bill for Children" to promote school choice for middle- and low-income families. We sent our economic growth agenda to Congress and worked to improve our economy, to ensure that every American who wants to work can have a productive job, and we concluded negotiations for a North American Free Trade Agreement. In foreign relations, President Yeltsin had a successful State Visit to Washington.

Throughout your distinguished career, both in your beloved Illinois and on the national scene, you have been known for your integrity and "can do" approach to problems. As a lawyer and public servant, you have brought your friendly style and deep devotion to the principles we share, and all of us at the White House are the richer for your tenure here.

I am deeply grateful for all your accomplishments on behalf of our Nation. Thank you for your service, dedication, and most of all your friendship to me and my entire family.

Barbara and I send our warmest wishes to you and Honey.

Most sincerely,

GEORGE BUSH

———————

Dear Mr. President:

It has been the greatest honor of my life to serve in your Administration as Secretary of Transportation and Chief of Staff. When I arrived from Chicago almost four years ago, I had a single aim: to faithfully serve you and this Nation. I am proud that, under your leadership, we have accomplished much. It has truly been an exhilarating and rewarding four years.

History will judge you to be one of the greatest Presidents this country has ever had. But it is vitally important that you be permitted to finish the work you have begun, here and around the world. I will do everything within my power to support your election to a second term.

I respectfully resign the office of Chief of Staff to the President of the United States effective August 23, 1992.

SAMUEL K. SKINNER

Note: These letters were made available by the Office of the Press Secretary but were not issued as White House press releases.

Excerpt of Remarks by Press Secretary Fitzwater Announcing White House Staff Appointments
August 13, 1992

I'd like to announce several additions to the White House staff. Margaret Tutwiler will return as Assistant to the President for Communications. Robert Zoellick will become Assistant to the President and Deputy Chief of Staff. Dennis Ross will become Assistant to the President for Policy Planning. Janet Mullins will become Assistant to the President for Political Affairs.

All of these Presidential appointments will become effective on August 23, 1992. In addition, Steve Provost, who is currently on the staff, will become Assistant to the President and chief speechwriter.

Note: Press Secretary Fitzwater made this announcement during his press briefing which began at 10:25 a.m.

Statement on the United Nations Security Council Vote on Humanitarian Aid to Bosnia
August 13, 1992

Last week the United States proposed that the U.N. Security Council authorize all measures necessary to see to it that humanitarian aid is delivered to the citizens of Bosnia. I welcome today's vote approving a resolution which does just that. The United States worked hard for this result. The international community has served notice that the innocent people caught in this conflict will not be denied the means to survive.

Our hope is to be able to maintain and broaden the relief effort through cooperation not only with our partners, the responsible relief agencies and the United Nations, but also with the parties to the conflict. I call on the authorities in Belgrade, the leadership of the Bosnian Serbs, and the Governments of Bosnia and Croatia to give their full cooperation to this effort. For all concerned, this is surely the preferred way of getting help to hundreds of thousands of victims.

The international community must be

able to reach people trapped by the fighting. All parties should facilitate immediate and safe access for international teams to visit cities and areas under siege in order to assess conditions and relief requirements. We expect full cooperation.

We have moved urgently to gain access to all camps, prisons, and detention centers, as today's U.N. resolution demands. As a result of the emergency meeting of the U.N. Human Rights Commission going on right now, we expect international inspectors to have unimpeded and continuous access to all possible camps or centers. Any brutality must be exposed and terminated, and the practitioners held personally accountable for their crimes. The U.N. Security Council has today also passed a resolution proposed by the United States to put war criminals on notice that they will be brought to justice. We seek and expect the full cooperation of all the parties in uncovering the facts, identifying those responsible, and bringing an end to acts of barbarism.

The United States has also taken action on the other initiatives I presented on August 6. Measures to inhibit a spillover of the conflict are moving ahead, and we are pressing for agreement in the Conference on Security and Cooperation in Europe on our proposal to put monitors in other parts of the former Yugoslavia to discourage human rights abuses and violence.

We are also tightening the economic sanctions imposed by the United Nations on Serbia. Those responsible for aggression are also responsible for the damage being done to the Serbian economy by the sanctions.

Finally, I am pleased at the strong bipartisan concern and support we have received as we grapple with this very complex, very agonizing, and very dangerous conflict. I would also like to praise those journalists who risk their lives in the cause of reporting this terrible conflict. We are all shocked and saddened to learn that one of the latest casualties is ABC producer David Kaplan.

Today's United Nations vote marks an important milestone in our response to this human tragedy. We will continue to work with the international community to end the violence and relieve the suffering.

Statement by Press Secretary Fitzwater on the Military Airlift for Humanitarian Aid to Somalia
August 13, 1992

The President has ordered the Department of Defense to offer a U.S. military airlift to transport a U.N. guard force and its associated equipment to Somalia. Authorized by U.N. Security Council Resolution 751, the force of 500 guards will help provide the security needed to deliver food and other relief supplies so desperately needed in Somalia. Now that the relevant Somali factions have agreed with the United Nations, the guards should be transported to Mogadishu as soon as possible.

This offer to the United Nations of airlift assistance is part of a broader U.S. effort to prevent suffering and starvation in Somalia. The total U.S. contribution to Somali relief to date has exceeded $76 million, and we will be intensifying our efforts in the days and weeks to come.

Statement by Press Secretary Fitzwater on the Chemical Weapons Convention
August 13, 1992

The President announced today strong United States support for the Chemical Weapons Convention completed at the Conference on Disarmament in Geneva, August 7. He said the United States is committed to signing the treaty as soon as it is open for signature, and he called on all other nations to make a similar pledge.

The treaty, concluded after years of intensive negotiations, calls for the total banning of chemical weapons worldwide. The United States has been committed to that goal since the beginning of the negotiations

and applauds the dedicated efforts of all who have helped to bring the talks to a successful conclusion. The United States firmly believes that removing the threat of these weapons of terror is now possible and will be achieved when all states join and abide by this treaty.

The United States underscores its intention of working actively to bring the Chemical Weapons Convention into force at the earliest possible date and believes that all responsible governments will join us in this pursuit.

Letter to Congressional Leaders Transmitting Proposed Legislation on Welfare Reform
August 13, 1992

Dear Mr. Speaker: (Dear Mr. President:)
Enclosed for the consideration of the Congress are four legislative proposals to promote work, provide flexibility, and encourage innovation in Federal public assistance programs. Enactment of these proposals is a necessary step to ending welfare being a way of life and accomplishing this task in a way that learns what works in making public assistance recipients self-sufficient.

Much has been accomplished during my Administration to transform welfare from a system of assistance to a ladder of opportunity. Much more can be accomplished. What we have done and what we have already asked you to do were reviewed in a paper my Administration released on July 31.

We must do more if we are to realize the call I made in my State of the Union address to you earlier this year to replace the assumptions of the welfare state. My objective for welfare reform is this: to create conditions that will enable recipients of public assistance to achieve self-sufficiency at the earliest possible moment. Achieving

this goal means a new commitment to work. To realize this commitment, I am proposing to remove obstacles and limitations that currently face States that want to make a commitment to work the center of what welfare means in that State. The "Welfare Employment and Flexibility Amendments of 1992" and the "Food Stamp Employment and Flexibility Amendments of 1992," forwarded with this letter, remove limits to work.

In the State of the Union address, I promised help for States that wanted to reform their welfare systems. The Federal Government would give expeditious consideration of State requests for waivers. Since that time, my Administration has approved six demonstration waiver projects for five States.

All six demonstrations involve the Aid to Families with Dependent Children (AFDC) program. But our public assistance program is broader than AFDC, and many individuals benefit from multiple programs. The "Food Stamp Employment and Flexibility Amendments of 1992" and the "Housing

Assistance Innovation Act of 1992" create the authority comparable to that available for AFDC to test new ideas in the food stamp and public housing programs.

And yet the program of assistance to low-income Americans offered by the Federal Government is far more extensive than AFDC, food stamps, and public housing. One effort to catalogue them all counted more than 150 programs. To allow States, localities, and community groups to pursue new ways for programs to function and interact, we propose the "Community Opportunity Pilot Project Act of 1992." This would allow five communities, competitively selected, to put into effect new ideas about how the streams of resources from the myriad Federal programs that reach a single community can be made to serve as an integrated effort to create opportunity for the low-income residents of that community they are intended to serve.

We must give new attention to personal responsibility, especially that of absent parents. All mothers and fathers have obligations to their children. Child support en-forcement holds absent parents responsible for financial support of their children. Under my Administration, the number of identified absent fathers has already increased dramatically—from 307,000 in 1988 to 462,000 in 1991—but the number is still too low. Thus our "Welfare Employment and Flexibility Amendments of 1992" proposes to strengthen the requirement that mothers receiving assistance identify the fathers of their children.

Progress has been made in making our welfare system an opportunity system, but this progress has been insufficient to the task at hand. Prompt enactment of the legislation I forward with this letter will add rungs to the ladder of self-sufficiency we offer to recipients of public assistance.

Sincerely,

GEORGE BUSH

Note: Identical letters were sent to Thomas S. Foley, Speaker of the House of Representatives, and Dan Quayle, President of the Senate.

White House Fact Sheet: The President's Welfare Reform Legislation
August 14, 1992

The President has transmitted to the Congress by letters to the President of the Senate and the Speaker of the House four legislative proposals to implement those parts of his welfare reform strategy requiring legislative changes. The President announced his plans for further welfare reform on July 31, 1992, in Riverside, CA.

The legislative proposals sent to the Congress today are the:
- "Welfare Employment and Flexibility Amendments of 1992" that would amend the Aid to Families with Dependent Children (AFDC) statute;
- "Food Stamp Employment and Flexibility Amendments of 1992," making similar changes to the Food Stamp Act;
- "Housing Assistance Innovation Act of 1992" that would allow innovation in

public and assisted housing programs on a basis similar to other welfare programs; and
- "Community Opportunity Pilot Project Act of 1992" that would authorize selection of five communities to redesign the delivery of Federal assistance to create increased opportunity in those communities.

The Problem

Flexibility. Federal public assistance programs are structured in fixed, categorical ways. This limits the ability of the State and local agencies administering Federal funds to meet local needs and conditions.

State and local officials seeking a greater role for work in welfare programs face unnecessary obstacles in implementing workfare with significant work requirements. Current law limits the number of hours each month that a recipient can be required to "work off" to the number of hours that results from dividing the amount of the AFDC benefit by the minimum wage ($4.25 nationally). A family household of $170 per month in AFDC would be limited to 10 hours per week. That family, however, may receive food stamps worth $210 per month and Medicaid that provides insurance coverage worth $300 per month, bringing the total value of assistance to $680 per month.

Also, Federal law limits the positions that can be used in workfare programs. Vacant positions in public or nonprofit agencies cannot be given to workfare participants. A public or nonprofit agency must create new positions to take on someone with a workfare obligation, either increasing the work done or dividing work among more workers.

Scope of Innovation. Since the President's State of the Union Address, in which he pledged Federal cooperation with State efforts to reform welfare programs through expeditious consideration of requests for waivers of Federal law or regulations, six waivers have been granted to five States. All relate to AFDC and Medicaid program changes. The degree of flexibility currently available in the AFDC and Medicaid programs does not exist for the food stamp, rental assistance, or public housing programs.

The President's Principles

The President's fundamental goal for welfare reform is to create a system that will enable welfare recipients to leave the system at the earliest possible time, as economically self-sufficient and responsible participants in their community.

The President's Legislative Proposals

The President's four legislative proposals to promote work, personal responsibility, and flexibility sent to the Congress today are:

1. "Welfare Employment and Flexibility Amendments of 1992"
The legislation would:
- Relax restrictions on the placement of

workfare participants in jobs. For example, a vacant real job could be assigned to a workfare participant; it would not be necessary to create a new position or find new work to be done;
- Allow States to determine maximum workfare obligations by aggregating the value of AFDC payments, food stamps, Federal housing assistance, and average Medicaid costs, up to a maximum of 40 hours per week. Current law allows only for inclusion of AFDC payments;
- Emphasize job search in welfare-to-work programs operating under the Job Opportunities and Basic Skills (JOBS) training program by removing limits on the period a person can continue to be asked to look for a job;
- Allow States to distribute AFDC benefits *after* work and training assignments have been completed; and
- Require that failure to provide promptly all information necessary to determine the father of a child would result in a partial loss of AFDC benefits for uncooperative mothers. AFDC payments are made because a parent, usually the father, is absent. The requirement in current law that a mother cooperate in identifying the father of her child, enforced by the potential for losing part of the welfare check, would be expanded to include all information necessary to determine who the father is.

2. "Food Stamp Employment and Flexibility Amendments of 1992"
The legislation would:
- Apply provisions in the "Welfare Employment and Flexibility Amendments of 1992" that remove limitations on work requirements to the food stamp program; and
- Expand waiver authority in the Food Stamp Act to make it comparable to that available for AFDC.

3. "Housing Assistance Innovation Act of 1992"
The legislation would:
- Provide waiver authority for public

housing agencies and resident management corporations so they could try new approaches to self-sufficiency and resident empowerment;

• Allow waivers of Davis-Bacon wage requirements for residents of public housing or subsidized housing and the homeless for projects that improve the housing and community in which they live and that increase their ability to get jobs; and

• Allow eviction of convicted felons from public housing without an administrative hearing where State eviction processes contain similar due process protections.

4. "Community Opportunity Pilot Project Act of 1992"

The legislation would:

• Create broad authority to waive program rules that govern the use of Federal funds to allow break-the-mold approaches to creating opportunity and promoting self-sufficiency;

• Provide authority to approve projects in five communities that would be selected after a nationwide competition;

• Allow proposals to come from States, local governments, and nonprofit organizations; and

• Evaluate the projects to determine their effect and the applicability of the projects' findings.

—For example, ideas that emerge from the effort to rebuild south central Los Angeles and the Atlanta Project could be implemented, even if they are not consistent with the rules that currently govern Federal funds flowing to those areas.

—A community could take Federal transportation, community development, food stamp, job training, and drug abuse treatment funds and devise a multiyear project for a group of youth that would provide them with drug treatment, transportation to jobs outside the community, and training for jobs the project would create in the home community. Compared to current law:

The project and all its uses of several categorical funding programs for different purposes could be approved; and

All necessary waivers could be granted in a single action, without application to multiple agencies.

Statement on the Summer Jobs Program for Disadvantaged Youth
August 14, 1992

I am pleased to announce that more than 265,000 disadvantaged youth already have jobs under the $500 million supplemental appropriation for the 1992 Summer Youth Employment and Training Program. More than 116,000 of these young people are employed in the 75 largest cities.

This is excellent news for our young people and our cities. It is a success story. We successfully urged the Congress to quickly appropriate the needed funds. Once the funds were appropriated, we moved quickly to get the money where it was needed to create the jobs.

The 265,000 jobs resulting from the supplemental appropriation bring the total number of jobs to date under the summer program to over 781,000 nationwide or 97 percent of the total expected.

Prior to the approval of the supplemental appropriation for the summer jobs program, over 516,000 disadvantaged youth would have had jobs, nearly 145,000 in the 75 largest cities and about 371,000 throughout the country.

Another 23,000 young people are expected to have summer jobs before the program ends. Of these, about 7,000 are likely to be in the 75 largest cities and 16,000 are expected in the rest of the Nation.

I commend the entire job training network, including the Department of Labor and the States and localities for putting the expanded summer program in place very quickly. On June 19, 1992, Governors and large city mayors were notified of their share of funds under the emergency aid bill. Official funding authorization was issued on June 24, 1992.

The summer jobs program is part of the Job Training Partnership Act (JTPA), admin-

istered by the Employment and Training Administration of the U.S. Department of Labor. JTPA, which began operating in 1983, has served more than 10 million adults and youth who face economic, social, and other barriers to employment.

White House Statement on the Forests for the Future Initiative
August 14, 1992

The White House yesterday launched implementation of the President's Forests for the Future initiative. The initiative will be directed by an interagency task force cochaired by William K. Reilly, Administrator of the EPA and former president of World Wildlife Fund and the Conservation Foundation, and C. Boyden Gray, Counsel to the President.

The Forests for the Future initiative, announced by the President on June 1 and advanced at the Rio Earth summit, is designed to stimulate effective actions for forest conservation and sustainable use. It follows from the President's call at the Houston economic summit in July 1990 for a global agreement to conserve forests, which led to the Statement of Forest Principles agreed to in Rio. It encourages the cooperative, joint actions which may help to achieve a global forest agreement, and it builds on the administration's actions to conserve U.S. forests, such as the America the Beautiful initiative and the new ecosystem approach adopted in June by the major Federal forest management Agencies.

Under the initiative, countries would form cooperative, action-oriented forest partnerships to conserve and sustainably use forests. Partnerships would be based on proposals made by interested countries using

effective and efficient approaches. To support such partnerships, the President is urging countries to double international forest assistance to a new international total of $2.7 billion per year. The President has committed an additional $150 million next year above already planned U.S. forest assistance and is working with other countries to gain their participation.

At its meeting yesterday, the task force emphasized the need to make progress as soon as possible by pursuing early forest partnerships with interested countries and by convening a partnership forum to share ideas on forest conservation and sustainable use. Forest partnerships will be the key to achieving meaningful conservation results and motivating additional participation in the initiative.

In addition to cochairs Reilly and Gray, the task force includes senior officials from the State Department, the Agency for International Development, the USDA Forest Service, the Bureau of Land Management, the Smithsonian Institution, the Office of Management and Budget, the Council on Environmental Quality, the Council of Economic Advisers, the Office of Science and Technology Policy, the Office of Policy Development, and the National Security Council.

Statement by Press Secretary Fitzwater on Additional Humanitarian Aid for Somalia
August 14, 1992

The growing suffering and mass death by starvation in Somalia is a major human tragedy. The United States Government and other international donors have already made significant contributions to alleviate this manmade famine. Because armed bands are stealing and hoarding food as well as attacking international relief workers, the primary challenge that the international community faces is the delivery of relief supplies.

The United States will take a leading role with other nations and international organizations to overcome the obstacles and ensure that food reaches those who so desperately need it.

On Thursday, we announced our offer to transport U.N. troops to enhance security for food deliveries in Mogadishu. Today, the President is announcing the following additional measures:

1. The Defense Department will begin as soon as possible emergency airlift operations to deliver food. We are asking the Kenyan Government to join us in supporting airlifts to northern Kenya for Somali refugees and drought-stricken Kenyans and to locations inside Somalia where there is sufficient security to support these relief operations. We are also examining other means of delivering food to Somalia.

2. Ambassador Perkins at the United Nations will begin immediate consultations to seek a Security Council resolution that would authorize the use of additional measures to ensure that humanitarian relief can be delivered.

3. We are also proposing that the United Nations convene a donors conference to include representatives of the major Somali factions so that their cooperation can be gained. Such cooperation would be the most important step to accelerate delivery of relief supplies and minimize security problems.

4. The President has also directed that an additional 145,000 tons of American food be made available for Somalia.

5. Finally, to ensure that all U.S. relief activities are properly coordinated, Andrew Natsios, Assistant Administrator of AID for Food and Humanitarian Assistance, has been appointed as Special Coordinator for Somali Relief.

The President calls upon other nations to join us in this urgent and important effort to alleviate starvation in Somalia.

Statement by Press Secretary Fitzwater on America's International Broadcasters
August 15, 1992

President Bush believes that one of the most effective weapons in the defeat of communism in Eastern Europe, the Soviet Union, and elsewhere has been the power of truth broadcast by America's international broadcasters: Voice of America, Radio Free Europe, Radio Liberty, and Radio and TV Marti. As democracy's victory is consolidated in the months and years to come, we will continue to need these broadcasts. The President intends to see that they remain active and effective.

These voices of freedom and democracy have a vital role to play in a post-cold-war world where dictatorship and repression continue. Indeed, they are also welcomed as a stimulus and an example in newly emerging democratic states that are developing their own free and independent media. For hundreds of millions in Europe, Asia, Africa, the Middle East, and especially in Cuba, these broadcasts are a beacon of hope that must continue to shine. The President is committed to keeping that

light shining brightly.

Remarks and an Exchange With Reporters on Iraq
August 16, 1992

The President. Well, there's currently a good deal of speculation about potential U.N. inspections and then possible military measures in Iraq and alleged political motivations. I'm not going to comment on today's speculative stories, except to say I saw quite a few inaccuracies.

From now on, some will accuse us of political opportunism for every move I make, and that's unfortunate. But it is not going to deter me from doing what is right, regardless of the political fallout. We're determined that U.N. Resolution 687 will be fully implemented. Now, this requires U.N. teams to inspect and destroy the Iraqi network of weapons of mass destruction: nuclear, chemical, biological, and missile.

I have total confidence in Rolf Ekeus of the United Nations and of the U.N. teams who have the responsibility for this mission. Let me make clear that what they elect to inspect and when they do these inspections is strictly their decision. The U.S. role is to provide support for their efforts.

Saddam Hussein needs to realize that the world will not ignore interference with these U.N. requirements. He cannot be allowed to dictate what can and cannot be inspected.

So let me underscore something which I think you all know. As President, whatever I decide has immediate consequences. But there will be no politics, and I will do what is right for the United States and in this case for the rest of the world.

I just wanted to get that statement out because I've read some ugly speculation. Thank you.

Q. Mr. President, if that leak came from a military source, isn't that a breach of security? Are you checking to determine whether that did in fact happen?

The President. Well, again, I don't want to confirm what leak we're talking about. But yes, there's been a clear breach of security.

Q. Mr. Bush, how do you feel about reading what the New York Times wrote today?

The President. Well, I don't like it. But I, unfortunately, have not grown accustomed to but am less shocked than I used to be by breaches of this nature. But in any event, I don't want to go further into what I like or don't like about it. But I must say I was shocked to read all this today.

Q. Mr. President, will you say what the situation is in order to clarify?

The President. No, I won't, because the U.N. makes these decisions. Dr. Ekeus makes these calls. He has our full confidence, and what he plans to do next is his business. That is not something that's done by the United States.

Q. Does the U.S. have a plan to strike the Iraqi ministry buildings if Saddam Hussein denies access?

The President. The United States has plans to be sure that Saddam Hussein does what he's supposed to do, and that is to comply with Resolution 687 and also 688, which refers to the brutalization of his own people.

Q. Even if he refuses to allow U.N. inspectors in during convention week or during the course of the campaign?

The President. The campaign and the convention have nothing to do with this. This is the national security interests of the United States. This is obligations to support the United Nations. So I'm glad you raised it, Randall [Randall Pinkston, CBS News]. But I will repeat it: I have responsibilities as President and responsibilities as Commander in Chief. I will go through with those responsibilities regardless of the politics. That is a very important point in all of this, and I hope I have demonstrated that enough to earn the trust of the American people when it comes to making this kind of decision. I do not make decisions involving military force lightly. I've been there myself. I know what it's like. I don't commit somebody else's son or daughter to battle or to any kind of combat unless it is the right thing to do, regardless of politics.

Q. Mr. President, has there been——

Q. ——Houston convention if there were a problem that demanded your attention during the week?

The President. If there was a problem that demanded my attention, I would. But I'm not sure. I can handle whatever comes up from wherever I am. We've got a great system of communications, and I think we demonstrated that during the Gulf war.

Last one.

Q. Mr. President, you don't seem to be denying this report. Am I right?

The President. What report?

Q. The report that was published today in the New York Times.

The President. Please repeat it for me, because I've read several different—what part of it?

Q. The part that there is some plan for the United States to sort of encourage Saddam Hussein to get involved in some kind of fight. I mean, there is some kind of contingency plan——

The President. I totally deny that.

Q. Not picking a fight——

The President. I totally deny that we're trying to pick a fight, and I totally deny we're trying to pick a fight for political purposes. If that was in the report, I really am angry about it. Didn't read it that carefully. But is he going to oblige; is he going to

follow through on these resolutions? I've stood right here and said that over and over again, and he has.

But if this is the argument, I can totally deny that.

Q. Are they going to go in on Monday, are the bombs——

The President. It is ugly, and it is uncalled for.

Q. Are the bombs going to start falling tomorrow? This was in the report as well, that something could happen tomorrow.

The President. I am not going to say what we are or are not going to do. Don't believe everything you read in these reports.

Q. I guess what people just want to know is, is there or is there not a game plan for air strikes if there's a problem with Iraq?

The President. I have said before, all options are open. That's all I'll say.

Q. What about consultations with the allies on a new enforcement plan? Have there been those kinds of consultations in recent days?

The President. We've been in constant touch with our allies, yes.

Q. Is your speech ready for Thursday night? It's not ready?

The President. It's not ready, no. [*Laughter*]

Note: The President spoke at 4:45 p.m. on the South Lawn at the White House upon his arrival from Camp David, MD. In his remarks, he referred to Rolf Ekeus, Executive Director, United Nations Special Commission on Iraq.

Statement on Signing the Thomas Jefferson Commemoration Commission Act
August 17, 1992

Today I am signing into law S. 959, the "Thomas Jefferson Commemoration Commission Act." This bill would establish the Thomas Jefferson Commemoration Commission, which would be responsible for planning and developing programs to commemorate the 250th anniversary of Jefferson's birth. In doing so, it is my understand-

ing that in light of the constitutional requirement that all executive functions be exercised by officers of the United States appointed in conformity with the Appointments Clause, *Buckley* v. *Valeo*, 424 U.S. 1 (1976), only those Commission members so appointed may exercise the executive authority granted in this bill. In addition, the

Archivist of the United States, the Secretary of the Interior, the Secretary of Education, the Chairman of the National Endowment for the Humanities, and the Librarian of Congress are members of the Commission who also are officers of the United States properly appointed for this purpose. Other members may directly participate only in the ceremonial or advisory functions of the Commission.

GEORGE BUSH

The White House,
August 17, 1992.

Note: S. 959, approved August 17, was assigned Public Law No. 102–343.

Letter to Congressional Leaders on the Determination Not To Prohibit Fish Imports From Certain Countries
August 17, 1992

Dear Mr. Speaker: (Dear Mr. President:)

Pursuant to section 8(b) of the Fishermen's Protective Act of 1967, as amended (22 U.S.C. 1978(b)), generally known as the Pelly Amendment, I am notifying you that on July 31, 1992, in accordance with section 101(a) of the Marine Mammal Protection Act (MMPA), the Secretary of Commerce certified to me that a ban on the importation of yellowfin tuna and yellowfin tuna products from Canada, Colombia, Malaysia, the Netherlands Antilles, Singapore, Spain, and the United Kingdom has been in effect since January 31, 1992. This ban is the result of an order issued by the U.S. District Court for the Northern District of California, which the Administration has appealed.

By the terms of the MMPA, such certification is deemed to be a certification for the purposes of the Pelly Amendment, which requires that I consider and, at my discretion, order the prohibition of imports into the United States of fish and fish products from the identified countries, to the extent that such prohibition is sanctioned by the General Agreement on Tariffs and Trade. The Pelly Amendment also requires that I report to the Congress any actions taken under this subsection and, if no import prohibitions have been ordered, the reasons for this action.

After thorough review, I have determined that sanctions against these nations will not be imposed at this time, particularly as the Administration pursues its appeal of the District Court order, and to allow implementation of an international dolphin conservation program in the eastern tropical Pacific Ocean.

Sincerely,

GEORGE BUSH

Note: Identical letters were sent to Thomas S. Foley, Speaker of the House of Representatives, and Dan Quayle, President of the Senate.

Letter to Congressional Leaders Transmitting Reports on Security Arrangements With Other Nations
August 17, 1992

Dear Mr. Chairman: (Dear Senator):
(Dear Congressman):

Pursuant to Section 1457 of the National Defense Authorization Act for Fiscal Year 1991 (Public Law 101–510), I have the honor to transmit reports, in both classified and unclassified form, on U.S. security arrangements with, and commitments to, other nations.

Sincerely,

GEORGE BUSH

Note: Identical letters were sent to Sam Nunn and John W. Warner, chairman and ranking minority member, Senate Committee on Armed Services; Claiborne Pell and Jesse A. Helms, chairman and ranking mi-nority member, Senate Committee on Foreign Relations; Les Aspin and William L. Dickinson, chairman and ranking minority member, House Committee on Armed Services; and Dante B. Fascell and William S. Broomfield, chairman and ranking minority member, House Committee on Foreign Affairs.

Presidential Determination No. 92–39—Memorandum on Assistance for Angolan Refugees
August 17, 1992

Memorandum for the Secretary of State

Subject: Determination Pursuant to Section 2(c)(1) of the Migration and Refugee Assistance Act of 1962, as Amended

Pursuant to section 2(c)(1) of the Migration and Refugee Assistance Act of 1962, as amended, 22 U.S.C. 2601(c)(1), I hereby determine that it is important to the national interest that up to $14,000,000 be made available from the U.S. Emergency Refugee and Migration Assistance Fund (the Fund) to meet the unexpected and urgent needs of Angolan refugees and returnees. These funds are to be contributed to the United Nations High Commissioner for Refugees in response to its appeal to assist Angolan refugees and returnees.

You are directed to inform the appropriate committees of the Congress of this determination and the obligation of funds under this authority and to publish this memorandum in the *Federal Register*.

GEORGE BUSH

[Filed with the Office of the Federal Register, 3:34 p.m., August 31, 1992]

Presidential Determination No. 92–40—Memorandum on Export-Import Bank Services for Albania
August 17, 1992

Memorandum for the Secretary of State

Subject: Determination under Subsection 2(b)(2)(D) of the Export-Import Bank Act of 1945, as amended—Albania

Pursuant to subsection 2(b)(2)(D) of the Export-Import Bank Act of 1945, as amended [12 U.S.C. 635(b)(2)(D)], I determine that it is in the national interest for the Export-Import Bank of the United States to guarantee, insure, extend credit, and participate in the extension of credit in connection with the purchase or lease of any product or service by, for use in, or for sale or lease to Albania.

You are authorized and directed to report this determination to the Congress and to publish it in the *Federal Register*.

GEORGE BUSH

[Filed with the Office of the Federal Register, 3:42 p.m., August 31, 1992]

Presidential Determination No. 92–41—Memorandum on Resumption of Foreign Air Cargo Service to Lebanon
August 17, 1992

Memorandum for the Secretary of Transportation

Subject: Resumption of Foreign Air Cargo Service to Lebanon

By virtue of the authority vested in me by section 1114(a) of the Federal Aviation Act of 1958, as amended ("the Act") (49 U.S.C. 1514), I hereby determine that the prohibition of all transportation services to Lebanon by Presidential Determination 85–14 of July 1, 1985, is hereby amended to permit the outward carriage of cargo to Lebanon by foreign carriers. All other pro-hibitions set forth in Presidential Determination 85–14, including the prohibition on U.S. air carriers flying into Lebanon, remain in effect.

You are directed to bring this determination immediately to the attention of all air carriers within the meaning of section 101(3) of the Act (49 U.S.C. 1301(3)).

You are further directed to publish this determination in the *Federal Register*.

GEORGE BUSH

[*Filed with the Office of the Federal Register, 10:38 a.m., August 20, 1992*]

Appointment of C. Dean McGrath, Jr., as Deputy Assistant to the President and Deputy Staff Secretary
August 17, 1992

The President today announced the appointment of C. Dean McGrath, Jr., as Deputy Assistant to the President and Deputy Staff Secretary.

Since 1991, Mr. McGrath has served as Counsel to the Director and General Counsel of the Peace Corps of the United States. Previously, Mr. McGrath served as the Acting General Counsel, Deputy General Counsel, and Associate General Counsel at the Department of Transportation, 1989–91; Special Counsel, Office of the Secretary of Defense, Department of Defense, 1989; and Associate Counsel to the President,

1986–89. Mr. McGrath began his career in public service as an attorney-advisor, Office of the General Counsel, Department of the Treasury. Mr. McGrath has also served as a Special Assistant U.S. Attorney, U.S. Attorney's Office, District of Columbia, 1981.

Mr. McGrath is a graduate of Duke University (B.A. with distinction in economics, 1975), the University of Nebraska College of Law (J.D., 1978), and the National War College (1985). He was born May 27, 1953, in Chicago, IL, and was raised in Grand Island, NE. He is married, has one son, and resides in Alexandria, VA.

Remarks to the Veterans of Foreign Wars National Convention in Indianapolis, Indiana
August 17, 1992

Thank you all so much. I'm proud to be back with you. This time I'll remember Pearl Harbor Day, too. [*Laughter*] May I salute Bob Wallace and thank him for that warm introduction; and salute Diane Wallace; say a special hello to a man who's doing a great job for this State and for our country in the Senate, Senator Dan Coats, and his lovely wife, Marcia, over here who flew out with us. I also want to salute our incoming chief, and I say "ours" because I am a member, a courageous leader in his own right, Jack Carney. Just had the pleasure of meeting with Jack and Joanne and the president of your ladies auxiliary who I also just met, Mary Sears, and Mary's husband, Sam. You've got a good first team.

There's two other true heroes I want to mention. If they haven't spoken, you're in for a treat. But General Jack Galvin is one of the greatest soldiers this country ever had. He just finished up as head of our NATO forces and did a superb job. And of course, next to him, or right down one from him, you all know Senator McCain, who gave many years of his life fighting for his country, spending several years in a prison camp, an outstanding Member of the United States Senate.

Bob Wallace invited me here. He said your members wanted to hear from a leader with charisma and popularity, whose words are revered from coast to coast. Unfortunately, Barbara wanted me to speak. But I'm delighted she's here with me.

Well, as you may know, I'm on my way to Houston to the Republican National Convention. When I saw the size of this crowd, I thought about giving a dress rehearsal of that Houston speech, complete with a few partisan political observations. But then I got to thinking about you guys. You don't need to hear a political speech. You've already sacrificed enough for your country. [*Laughter*] So instead, I'd like to talk a little bit about where our Nation has been and where we're headed together.

As we gather here today, the cold war is over. For more than 40 years, our GI Joes and Janes hit the ground and sucked the dust in faraway places like North Africa and Normandy, Pork Chop Hill and Ia Drang Valley. Back then, we called you heroes. Today, we call you winners. If anyone tells you that imperial communism fell on its own, tell them that you helped punch it in the gut and sent it tumbling back down the back stairs of history. Each of you who served, each of you, won the battle for humanity's heart and soul.

What a group we've put forth, these sons and daughters of Paterson and Peoria, you who wrote, some of you, "Kilroy was here" on the walls of the German stalags and left signs in the Iraqi desert that said, "I saw Elvis"—[*laughter*]—and you who sang "Don't Sit Under the Apple Tree" on the roads outside London and listened to the Beatles with Chris Noel and Adrian Cronauer in Saigon.

Goering, Hermann Goering, thought the American fighting forces were a pushover. We showed him. Kim Il-Söng in Korea thought he could take us. Wrong again. And Saddam Hussein miscalculated. He thought we'd grown soft over the years. He didn't think we'd commit our Armed Forces. He misread the will of the American people, and he didn't believe we would do what it would take to win. But our men and women showed him. To put it real simple: We kicked a little Baghdad bully.

Now I have a special word for those who served in Vietnam, and I know we have many here who did. That war was controversial. Many refused to serve. The Government didn't go all out to win. You were fighting with one hand tied behind your back, and still, you fought with courage and with valor.

But your Nation, when that war ended, never appropriately said thanks. Then 20 years later, America was called to fight again, and this time we did what was needed to win. We fought quickly; we fought with purpose. And when the Desert

Storm troops came home, a wondrous thing happened. America saluted, unanimously saluted, not just those heroes but our forgotten heroes, the men and women who served in Vietnam. The tribute was genuine. It was heartfelt, and it came from every corner of this Nation. And so, let me say this: It was long overdue. God bless those of you who served in that troubled war.

As we all know, in every encounter, from World War II to Desert Storm, for every one of us on the front lines, there were other Americans supporting us at home, fathers and mothers and sisters, brothers, neighbors, who said the prayers, sent the cookies, and watched the mailbox. Over the years, together we footed a bill of over $4 trillion to pay for all the tanks and ships and missiles. And so, let's not forget the unsung hero of the cold war, the American taxpayer.

Why did we do it? Why did we make the sacrifice? If you ask me, we shed our blood and spent our treasure because we believed enough in our American ideals to defend them. Today, those ideals, your ideals, are triumphant around the entire globe. In Germany, a wall has fallen. In Moscow, citizens troop to the polls. Think about this: In just the past 4 years, more people have taken the first breath of freedom than in any time in all of human history. You made history, and you should be proud of that. This is something major and important.

But there is a method to our unselfishness. Calvin Coolidge defined patriotism as "standing up for yourself by standing up for your country." We fought so our children don't have to fight.

Remember that awful movie of several years ago—some of you may well remember it; Barbara and I do—"The Day After"? It brought the horror of the aftermath of a nuclear explosion home to a small Kansas suburb. People gathered in churches and lecture halls to watch it in fear together. Some called it a documentary of the future. Today, it doesn't even belong in the science fiction bin of movie rental stores. Because of your sacrifice, the nuclear nightmare has receded, and our kids and our grandkids now sleep in the sweet sunshine of peace, no longer afraid of nuclear war. You helped

do that.

So this is the progress in which we take pride. It's the progress that you've brought to the world and to our children. And yet, the question today is: What do we do next? We can start by remembering something John Kennedy once said: "A nation reveals itself not only by the men and women it produces, but by the men and women it remembers."

I understand right in here what makes military service so special. Military service is the great leveler. My own Navy squadron included farm boys and city hustlers, athletes, bookworms, preacher's kids, Army brats. Together we experienced the tingling excitement of that sport of kings when I first went into the service, picking up cigarette butts. [*Laughter*] Now, later we felt the knots in our stomach from our first carrier landing and the heaviness in our hearts from spending our first Hanukkah or Christmas without our loved ones and the horrible, sickening feeling of watching our buddies go down in battle, never to return.

These memories are etched in my mind, as they are etched in yours. No matter that the cold war is over, no matter how places like Guadalcanal and Hamburger Hill recede in our memory, our Nation can never and must never forget. As long as I am President, I make this solemn promise: We will always stand by those who stood up for America.

That means keeping in mind a lesson that every soldier and sailor knows in his heart: Weakness tempts aggression. With the cold war over, I have put forth a responsible plan to cut defense spending, cut it to the level recommended by General Galvin's former colleagues, our true military experts. But in this political year, some will want to go further, a lot further. One plan offers to cut 4 times more than what our experts say is responsible.

Let me say this. In the sands of Kuwait, our sons and daughters showed that courage is hereditary, but courage will be of no use if fighter planes can only be found in museums and our ships are all in mothballs. When it comes to defending our country, my loyalty lies not with the Gallup polls but with our young people who must gallop in the way of danger. We simply must never go back to the hollow army of the late seventies. I stand with the marines, the soldiers, the sailors, the airmen, the guardsmen. We can never ask these men and women to stand in harm's way and then tie one arm behind their back. As long as I am Commander in Chief, I will stand for our Armed Forces, and I will keep the United States of America strong, so I can tell the American people our national security is second to none.

We owe you more than a strong America abroad. We owe you a strong America at home, an America that lives up to the dream that you defended, where you can get work, and protect your family's well-being. Just as you can't build a home without a hammer, you can't build a dream without a job. Some say the way to create jobs is with more taxes; I disagree. I have a plan to cut Government spending and use incentives to get this economy moving again. So far, being very candid, that plan is blocked by the Congress. But this fall, with your help, I intend to change all of that.

I have a special concern for those who are caught in the transition of our economy, for example, veterans who once worked the turrets of a tank and are now getting used to the keyboards of a high-tech economy. So I have advanced a national strategy to retrain our workers, especially those in the defense-related industries. I have asked our leader, Bob Wallace, to come to Washington and help lead that job training effort in the veterans community. I'm asking the Senate to confirm Bob as Assistant Secretary of Labor for Veterans' Employment and Training. And he will do a first-class job.

Assistant Secretary of Labor for Veterans' Employment and Training, that's just a fancy title that really means "Potomac pitbull for veterans' rights." [*Laughter*] If anyone tries to forget the vet, Bob and I are going to be there to clamp down on their arm.

Now, jobs is one priority; health care, another. Our health care system is broken today, and we all know it. Costs are rising too fast. Too many people can't get coverage. Some say it's time to throw up our arms and let the Government take it over. Well, I have a different plan, a way to get

at the real causes of skyrocketing costs, like faulty insurance programs, piles of paperwork, and way too many frivolous lawsuits. We're suing each other too much instead of caring for each other enough in this country.

But let me make a commitment to you this morning. I am proud of what we have accomplished together to strengthen our veterans health care system, proud of the specialized health care centers that we've created and the new outpatient clinics. I am proud of our new registry to track Persian Gulf veterans and, most especially, of the billion dollars more every year we've invested in your health care. Every inch of the way we have had sound advice from Bob Wallace and Larry Rivers and so many others with the VFW. But let me be very clear on a key point here. While we must change our health care system, we will not change our commitment to the integrity of veterans health care.

A couple weeks ago, I announced a new White House advisory panel, which will include a representative of the VFW. I want to make sure that when it comes to making health care changes, the veteran's voice comes through loud and clear. If Congress sends me legislation to dismantle the VA system, I will whip out that veto pen and knock down that Scud missile headed right for the well-being of every family represented here. If anyone again suggests taxing your benefits, I'll say what I've said many times before, "Keep your hands off the veterans."

Now, there's one more promise I'll make to you. It concerns those who are not with us today, the ones that John McCain knows so much about from his own life experience. I'm talking about the POW's and the MIA's.

As Bob mentioned, I did have my own experience with combat, nothing quite like John's or like many of yours. But after my plane was shot down on September 2, 1944, at 0732—I can't remember Pearl Harbor Day, but I can sure remember September 2d. [*Laughter*] But look, I remember floating around in the Pacific. Off in the distance I could see this Japanese-held island of Chichi Jima in the Bonin Islands. I remember worrying about whether anyone in my squadron would find me. Then I remember thinking: What if the other side does?

By the grace of God, along came a submarine, U.S., and by the grace of God, my family never had to face the agony of a late-night phone call or a knock on that door. But to those who do wait for the calls or knocks to bring news of loved ones, let me simply say, we will never forget you.

The search for answers about POW-MIA's is a question of justice, of oaths sworn and commitments kept. For 241 families, the uncertainty has already ended. I salute General Vessey, and I salute those in the Senate and those in the White House who have worked to this end. But there are still more answers to find. Without further progress, my administration will not move forward with Hanoi. We will not rest until we have received the fullest possible accounting of every POW–MIA.

In preparing for this visit today, I ran across a quote from Daniel Bennis, a disabled veteran from Hamel, Minnesota. Dan Bennis was asked why he went to war in the first place. He said, "I fought for the right to see my country in the splendor of all seasons." I fought for the right to see my country in the splendor of all seasons.

Well, Dan, America is a country of all seasons. But to me, America is a nation where one season dominates, the season of spring. Today, as we listen to all the talk of pessimism and lost potential, we may think that the cold winds of winter are blowing. But I sense a different wind, the American wind, the warm breeze of renewal and rebirth.

In our workplaces, our economy is being reborn as our companies retool for the new competition. In our schools, our students are being reborn as, for the first time in a century, we change the very way we learn. In our homes, our families are being reborn as we turn back to our moral foundations.

Some ridicule me. Some ridicule us when we talk about family values. But it's the family that teaches us right from wrong, teaches us discipline, respect for the law. As every vet knows, it's family that wiped the tears away when we cry. Strengthening the family is not something we ought to do; it is something we have to do.

Now, some take a look at all we must do as a nation and say, "Look, our challenges are too big, too daunting." I would remind them that America is still the only place where miracles not only happen, they happen every day.

This is the Nation that toppled the wall. This is the Nation that won the war. This is the Nation that produced you. None have been braver or sturdier. Through your courage, your valor, your sacrifice, you changed the course of human history. We have changed the world, and now we will change America because America is the land of the eternal spring.

Thank you very much. May God bless the VFW, and most of all, may God bless the greatest, freest country on the face of the Earth, the United States of America. Thank you very, very much.

Note: The President spoke at 11:02 a.m. at the Indiana Convention Center. In his remarks, he referred to Robert E. Wallace, commander in chief, VFW, and his wife, Diane; John M. Carney, senior vice commander in chief, VFW, and his wife, Joanne; Mary Sears, national president of the ladies auxiliary of the VFW, and her husband, Sam; Chris Noel, entertainer and recipient of the VFW commander in chief's Gold Medal of Merit; Adrian Cronauer, Armed Forces Network disc jockey during the Vietnam war; Larry W. Rivers, executive director, Washington, DC office, VFW; and Gen. John W. Vessey, U.S.A., ret., Special Presidential Emissary to Hanoi for POW–MIA Affairs.

Remarks at the Bush-Quayle Welcoming Rally at the Republican National Convention in Houston, Texas
August 17, 1992

The President. Thank you all very much. What a wonderful welcome home.

Audience members. Four more years! Four more years! Four more years!

The President. You got it.

Audience members. Four more years! Four more years! Four more years!

The President. Thank you all very much. Thank you so much. Let me just thank a couple of people at the beginning. First, let me thank Craig Fuller, who's done a great job as our convention chairman; Rich Bond, our national chairman; Jeanie Austin, our cochairman. And let me say this: What a wonderful welcome home. It is sure great to be back here in Texas, home again.

May I thank Ray Childress and Warren Moon, great heroes right here, and deservedly so, in Houston, for being with us; and of course, another friend who entertained us, and at least I got here in time to hear him, a great American and a great singer, Randy Travis. By golly, he was first-class.

I'm leaving out a lot of people, but one other person, my partner in a great adventure, with me every step of the way from west Texas to the White House, Barbara Bush.

Let me thank our great Governor, Carroll Campbell, who's given this Nation so much leadership as Governor of the State of South Carolina, and a special word, a special word about two very special friends of ours, Dan and Marilyn Quayle, the Vice President of the United States.

Four years ago, Dan Quayle and I teamed up. I told him then, speaking from some personal experience, that the job of Vice President was a real character-builder. [*Laughter*] And I was not exaggerating. But look, this guy stood there, and in the face of those unfair critics he has never wavered. He has never wavered. He simply told the truth, and let the chips fall where they may.

He said we need families to stick together and fathers to stick around, and he is right. He says what we need is an America that stands behind our law enforcement officers, and he is right about that. He also said we've got to take on those trial lawyers and all those who inundate this country with frivolous lawsuits, and he's right about that. Let that ABA turn off to the left; we are with the American people.

So when the establishment in Washington hears all this, they get all uptight about it, about him. They gripe about it. But folks in the real world understand, and they nod their head. He has been a super Vice President, and he will be for another 4 years.

Audience members. Four more years! Four more years! Four more years!

The President. I couldn't help but notice an interview that my opponent gave to the USA Today last week. It was absolutely incredible——

Audience members. Boo-o-o!

The President. You haven't heard it yet. [*Laughter*] He talked about how he's already planning his transition, figuring out who should be Deputy Assistant Under Secretary in every Washington Agency, even where he can get away from the White House for a day or two. I half expected when I went over to the Oval Office to find him over there measuring the drapes. [*Laughter*] Well, let me say, the first shot out of the barrel, I have a message for him: Put those drapes on hold. It is going to be curtain time for that ticket. And I mean it.

You know, for 9 months the other side has had a one-way conversation with the American people, and now it's our turn. They have called our great country a mockery and sounded the saxophone of change. And that sound sure sounds familiar. They say they want to shake up Washington, but they oppose limiting the terms of Congressmen. That's a change, just changing the subject.

They say they believe in a strong America, but they propose gutting the national defense of this country. That's called changing their tune. They say they want to put people first, but they are proposing the largest tax increase in the history of the

United States of America.

Audience members. Boo-o-o!

The President. I guess that's change, but by the time they're through, change is all you're going to have left in your pocket. We're not going to let that happen to the United States.

So don't kid yourself, America. We're not running against the Comeback Kids, we're running against the Karaoke Kids. They'll sing any tune, any tune they think will get them elected, say one thing in one place and then whisper something else in another. And we're not going to let them get away with it.

You know, I've never pretended to be much for words, but for me, eloquence is action. And for the next 78 days we're going to go out there to ask the American people a simple question: Who do you trust to do what's right for the United States of America? It's a question of trust.

Audience members. George Bush! George Bush! George Bush!

The President. Forty-four years ago, Barbara and I started out, out in west Texas, the Odessa-Midland area. I remember traveling across that country to Wink and Kermit and Notrees and Andrews, places where parents worried and watched when a kid crossed the street; the kind of towns that sent those kids halfway around the world, from the DMZ to Da Nang and to Desert Storm. Barbara and I loved the rhythms of west Texas. You remember the Friday night football and Saturday picnics and Sunday sermons. We raised a family and built a business, made friends that have lasted us an entire lifetime. We worked hard. But when the work was done, we sat around the table late at night, and we talked, talked about report cards—same thing you all do—schoolyard fights, small things, big dreams.

No matter what the other side says, America is still the land of dreams, dreams as vast and wide as those plains out there in west Texas. Our dream, our ideals, and our ideas have awakened dreams from Managua, to our south, all the way to Moscow. With faith in our people, we will reawaken those dreams right here in the United States of America.

My opponent wants to protect the jobs of the past. And I have a plan to create the jobs of the future so that the sons and daughters of steelworkers and linemen can build their dreams. My opponent wants to change our schools, oh, just a little bit. And I have a plan to revolutionize our schools so that our kids can do as well in the science labs and math room as they now do in the swimming pool and out there on the basketball courts.

My opponent, and Dan touched on this, ridicules or attacks me as we talk about family values. Well, let me tell you something: We are going to keep on trying to strengthen the American family, to make American families a lot more like the Waltons and a lot less like the Simpsons.

Now that I'm getting warmed up, let me tell you about another target that I'm going to get in the crosshairs. The Democratic leaders of the United States Congress don't like our ideas. They are the sultans of the status quo. They are the only people in America who could drive to work with a blindfold every morning because they've been going the same way, controlling that Congress for 38 years.

Audience members. Clean your House! Clean your House! Clean your House!

The President. You tell me about it. You're darn right. You talk about gridlock, we know where the gridlock is. It's under those leaders that control the Congress, both the Senate and the House, and we're going to change it. We are going to get the American people to change it.

I was very lucky; I didn't get to see the Democratic Convention. [*Laughter*] But up in Manhattan last month, you didn't see those congressional leaders. Finding them was like playing "Where's Waldo" in the Astrodome. They gave a new meaning to the word "closet liberal."

Don't kid yourselves. Look at where their support is coming from, that same ossified, entrenched, change-allergic support groups out there supporting the Democratic leaders of the Congress. We're going to make the American people understand it. I'm going to do what Harry Truman did. I am going to take that message to change the Congress all across this country.

I've held out my hand to those crazy

guys. I've held out my hand to them, only to have it bitten off, and I'm tired of it. We're going to change that Congress. And we are going to link that Clinton-Gore ticket right in close to those Democratic leaders. They are one and the same, and we're not going to let the American people forget that.

You hear a lot about these polls. Yes, they say it's going to be a tough fight. We know that. The truth is I get a little comfort from some of these polls. You know me. In politics I've always done better when I fight back, when I'm behind, because you have a certain freedom. It gives you a certain freedom. The other guy can do what the polls want. The other side can pay attention, changing this or changing that because of what the polls say. I'm going to roll up my sleeves and do what is right for the American people, and I don't care what the polls say. Do what's right for America. And I am a fighter, and I intend to fight for what's right for America.

Right next door there's a big building. They call it the eighth wonder of the world. Well, Houston, get ready for wonder number nine, the most stirring political comeback since Harry Truman gave them hell in 1948. It starts right now.

Audience members. Four more years! Four more years! Four more years!

The President. It all starts right here. You know, the Gatlin Brothers like to sing, "Houston means I'm one day closer to you." Well, no offense to Larry, but to me Houston means that we are one day closer to victory, one day closer to building a better and a brighter future for the people of this great country.

Barbara and I want to thank you for coming here. We want to thank you for this magnificent show of support. When history writes about this election, they're going to say it started right here when you fired up this President to take this message to the American people.

May God bless the United States of America. Thank you all very much.

Note: The President spoke at 5:35 p.m. at the Houston Astrodome. In his remarks, he referred to Houston Oilers football players Ray Childress and Warren Moon and country music entertainers Randy Travis and the Gatlin Brothers.

Remarks at an Antidrug Rally in Houston
August 18, 1992

Thank you very, very much. Speaking of goals, that's one of the reasons I'm back in Houston. Yesterday we got off to a pretty good start, I think.

But nevertheless let me salute first my friend Chuck Norris, friend of long standing, commend him on being what we call a Point of Light, reaching out to help others. What this program is about, kicking drugs out of school, it should have the support of all Americans. And I salute him for giving of his time so generously.

I salute these instructors. I salute these experts that we saw in action. I thank you all for this most wonderful presentation. May I also thank the school principal who is with us; our new, or not so new but our most distinguished superintendent of schools; and also our new police chief; all of them with us today. I don't know if you saw them when they came in. Maybe they'd stand up. Chief?

There's a message in all of this because we support our law enforcement officers who are trying to keep not only the schoolyards clean but preserve order in this wonderful city of ours. I salute our school superintendent who has led the way in making Houston a Houston 2000 educational community, not fearing to change. He's on the leadership edge of literally helping revolutionize education in this country, and I salute him for that. As for our principal, just hearing wonderful things about her and what she's done. May I express our appreciation for letting this marvelous group come in here today.

With them today is a man who is on the cutting edge of trying to change education. I'm not talking about just simply fine-tuning. We're talking about revolutionary change. And I'm talking about our Secretary of Education, our national Secretary, a former Governor, Lamar Alexander, who is really out in the lead for new American education. Lamar, would you stand up?

As you may know, we've set six educational goals for this Nation; got all across party politics, something that's never happened before. We did it, but we had with us the Democrat and the Republican Governors of the States. One of those goals was to have a learning place where people could learn without fear of crime, certainly without fear of drugs. And that's what this program is all about. We saw a little example today. I'm glad I was not in the last act on the receiving end; that guy looked pretty tough and pretty powerful.

But this is happening all across the country. We are beginning to make enormous headway on the war on drugs. And I want to finish that job. Sixty percent less use of cocaine among the teenagers in this country, that is dramatic progress in the last 3 years. Now we've got to keep it going. In schools like this, school superintendents like this, police chiefs like this, and then dedicated teachers and students like this, and then dedicated leaders like Chuck Norris come together to make this happen, not just for today and not just for Houston but for our country and for tomorrow as well.

So I am very pleased to be here. I have only one regret and that is that Barbara Bush, who had a school named after her in Houston—and she's still rubbing it in. But nevertheless—[*laughter*]—she is not here because she's out kind of nervously looking at the podium in the Astrodome, getting ready for her command performance tomorrow night. But she certainly joins in. I hope you know how committed she is to helping these kids be literate, helping them learn to read, helping the families in this country stay together so they can help the kids.

It's a great joy to be back in Houston. Yesterday was a wonderful day for me. These times have been a little complicated, as some of my friends from Washington know that are traveling with us. But you get here, and you feel something happening; you feel something positive. It wasn't just the political arena yesterday, where we got off to a great start, but it's programs like this. It's the grassroots of America, determined to make life better for these kids, that have me inspired.

So thank you all for what you're doing. And may God bless our great country.

Note: The President spoke at 10:20 a.m. at Hamilton Middle School. In his remarks, he referred to actor Chuck Norris; Diane B. Mutlet, principal of the school; Frank R. Petruzielo, Houston superintendent of schools; and Sam Nunchia, Houston chief of police.

Remarks at the Republican National Committee Gala Luncheon in Houston
August 19, 1992

The President. Lod Cook, thank you, sir. Thank you all for that warm welcome. Thank you so very much. Thank you, Lod. Please be seated. Let me just single out at the beginning of these remarks Lod Cook, who does so much, not just for the party and for candidates but who's certainly done so much for Barbara and for me. Every-thing he touches works out, and I couldn't be more pleased to be at his side through this luncheon. This gives me an opportunity to thank him and all of you who made this luncheon quite clearly a tremendous success. I think this bodes well for what lies ahead.

I want to single out a couple of people. I

thought that Boy Scout color guard was great, and so was the Boys Choir and the Houston Chorus; take great pride in them. Reverend Claude Payne is, as Lod said, Barbara and my home parish minister at St. Martin's Church here, and we're just delighted to be with him.

I want to single out, of course, a man that did a great job firing up the troops last night, getting our message of hope and opportunity across the country, our distinguished keynoter, Phil Gramm. He did a superb job last night. We've got a lot, but let me just also add Rich Bond, who came in in this national committee, grabbed ahold of it, taking our message out there. He is a feisty devil, and he's doing a first-class job, too. And so, really, this then, with this dramatic entrance, is the first of our whistlestop tour. I think the train sure beats the hell out of the bus, frankly.

I want to just salute the Vice President and Marilyn. Dan Quayle has served with great distinction. He's taken on a lot of substantive tasks and done them well. He's done his job with dignity and honor, and he's taken the best shots the other side can fire. If you ask me, he's given better than he's got. His head is up; he's ready to charge. And I am proud and honored to have him at my side in the convention and the days that lie ahead.

Now, I know the excitement's building. Each hour we get closer to the moment everyone's waiting for, packed house at the Astrodome, nationwide TV audience. I'd be less than honest if I didn't tell you I've got a few butterflies. But I'll tell you, you're going to love Barbara's speech. [*Laughter*] But after she's through, then I get my turn tomorrow. I want to spell out where I'm going to take this country with your help over the next 4 years. But first, just a little bit about why we're here in Houston.

Some of you may have read an interview by my opponent, the one he gave to the USA Today last week. It was absolutely incredible. He talked about how he's already planning the transition, figuring out who should be Deputy Assistant Under Secretary in every Washington agency, even where he will go to get away from the White House. Heck, I've expected to come forward Friday morning and find somebody

measuring the drapes in the Oval Office.

This guy got a problem up here? Are they with the press corps?

I can't hear you. Please speak up. This is a crazy year, when they have credentials for the——

Audience members. What about AIDS? What about AIDS? What about AIDS?

Audience members. Four more years! Four more years! Four more years!

The President. As I was saying—that guy—hey, listen, for those of you who haven't been around my line of work lately, this is normal. Don't get worried. [*Laughter*] Don't get worried.

But let me just say this. I saw a demonstration out there on the television the other day, and let me be clear where I stand: Everybody has a right to protest, but I have a right to stand with our law enforcement people who have to put these protests in the proper perspective. Thank you, to those from the sheriff's office.

Audience members. What about AIDS? What about AIDS? What about AIDS?

The President. May I address myself to the gentleman's question? Our administration last year spent $4.3 billion on AIDS. That is 10 times as much for a person sick with AIDS as we spend on cancer. This year, we've asked for $4.9 billion, the highest research and prevention program in the world. We have the best scientists working on the problem. My heart is full of compassion, and we are doing what we can to get to the bottom of that.

Now, does anybody else have something they would like to say while we're all standing?

Audience members. What about AIDS? What about AIDS? What about AIDS?

Audience members. Four more years! Four more years! Four more years!

The President. Thank you very much.

Anybody else like to be heard up here, because I have one or two things only that I want to say. I was telling you how my opponent gave an interview to the USA Today, and he talked about planning his transition and picking out who's going to be the Deputy Assistant Under Secretary in each Washington agency, where he'll go to get away from the White House. I expected to go to the Oval Office on Thursday to find him there in the Oval Office measuring the drapes. But I have a message: Put the drapes on hold, for pretty soon for you it is going to be curtains. We are going to take this to the American people.

This week, right here in Houston, we began this conversation with the American people, talking about the issues that shape the world, about the values that are close to home. I'm talking about jobs and family and faith and about neighborhoods free from crime and about a world free from fear.

If you listen to the other side tell it, you're for them if you're for change. But this election is not just about change, because change has a flip side, and that is called trust. When you get right down to it, the election is going to be like every other. When you pull that curtain closed and cast your vote on November 3d, trust matters. The American people are going to say, I trust President George Bush because he's made the tough decisions and he's conducted himself with honor and decency in that office.

You know, I used this example the other day, that when a phone rings in the middle of the night at the White House, when a crisis comes half a world away, the American people do want to know that their leader has the experience, the background, and the guts to do the right thing. I am proud of the changes that we've made together. I am proud of our total victory in the cold war, proud that in the past 4 years more people have taken the first breath of freedom than at any time in human history. That is major change. That is significant in terms of world peace.

But the job is not finished. There are plenty of wolves. The Soviet bear may be extinct, but there are plenty of wolves out there. As long as I am President, no madman will get his finger on the nuclear trigger. As long as I am Commander in Chief, America will remain safe and strong. I owe that to the American people.

Electing our leader who will protect our Nation means trust in the traditional sense. But that's just part of the picture. Each election is a referendum on the future and what we want it to look like. I stake my claim on a very simple philosophy: To lead a great nation, you must first trust the people that you lead.

And think about this fact: Nearly one out of every two delegates in Manhattan at that convention was on a government payroll. That's just not true in Houston. We are the party of real people: the preacher, the payroll meeter, the wage earner, the entrepreneur, the veteran, and yes, the volunteer, God bless them. And look at every big issue we face. You'll see a choice, a choice between we who put our faith in everyday Americans and they who put their faith in a big, unresponsive Government.

If you haven't heard by now what that Government-first crowd has planned, let me just give you a couple of examples. First, they're calling for over $200 billion in new spending and another $150 billion in new taxes. Now, they're going to come back at me and say, "Wait a minute, we're the new breed. We're no Walter Mondale, or we're no Michael Dukakis." And they may be right. I don't want to be unfair to Mr. Mondale or Dukakis—[*laughter*]—$150 billion in new taxes is more than the two of them ever dreamed of offering the United States of America.

But I think we'd all agree that we trust the people, not the Government, to create the jobs and get this economy moving. You heard Phil Gramm talk about it. You saw that film showing what we've tried to do, blocked, blocked by that Congress.

Let me just say another thing: We trust the parents, not the Government, to make the decisions that matter in life. We trust parents, not the Government, to choose their children's schools, public, private, or parochial. We fought for and we got a child care bill, where the parents choose the children's child care. And when the other side says Government knows best, I say parents know better. Parents know better than some bureaucrat in Washington, DC, or some subcommittee chairman out there that's been there for 38 years and is mandating everybody in this country how to behave.

We trust the people, not a new Government bureaucracy, to fix our health care system. We've got a good proposal that provides health insurance to the poorest of the poor and still provides the quality of medical care that would be decimated if we turn to the Government to do it all.

Well, you know that we've tried to get things through Congress. Now I'm going to take this fight to every corner of the Nation and make the case not just to reelect me, not just to reelect the Bush-Quayle ticket but to give Congress back to the people. You heard it here today: The House has remained under the same control since Khrushchev ruled the Kremlin and since Castro's coup in Cuba. And today, the status quo is under siege. The only way to break the deadlock in Washington is to clear out the deadwood on Capitol Hill. I'm going to do what Harry Truman did, take that case to the American people for a November decision.

Now, let me close with just a few words to my friends here in Houston and others from across this country. We've been talking about it, and for Barbara and me this week is bound to have a very special meaning. This is our last big convention, last time, you might say, around the track. It is great to come back home to Texas, come home to where it really began for us in a political sense.

I remember back in 1948 traveling out there when Bar and I were living in Odessa and then in Midland, traveling out across the plains to towns like Wink and Notrees and Andrews and Kermit and Crane, towns where parents worried and watched when the kid crossed the street; towns that sent their kids halfway around the world to fight for freedom, to the DMZ or to Da Nang or, yes, to Desert Storm. I remember the rhythms of that part of our country, the rhythms of west Texas: Friday night football, Saturday night picnics, the Sunday sermon. Barbara and I raised a family, built a business, and we made friends. We shared the small triumphs and the sorrows. As my good friend Dan Jenkins—you remember Dan the Hornfrog Man, the T.C.U. writer— he put it this way, "We lived life its own self." I remember, when the work was done, how we sat around the table late at night, and we talked: report cards, schoolyard fights, small things, big dreams.

I was not born in Texas, but in Texas 48 years ago, whatever it was, 44 years ago, I came of age. The lessons that Barbara and I learned here are the lessons that we have tried to live by. The friends that we made here and throughout our lives are the friends who are in this room, some from Texas, some elsewhere, every one of whom we owe a vote of gratitude to, the friends who have stood by us when times are great and when times are tough.

Now we are about to embark on the fight of our life and the fight to keep the American dream alive but keeping faith in people. I look forward to this fight. I can feel it. I can feel it building in my blood. One thing that is the most comfort is that through good times and bad, I have had you at my side. And we want to thank you for this fantastic show of support.

May God bless this great Nation of ours. Thank you for our many blessings, and may God bless the United States of America. Thank you very, very much. Thank you all. Thank you so very much.

Note: The President spoke at 2 p.m. at the George R. Brown Center. In his remarks, he referred to Lodwrick M. Cook, chairman of the luncheon, and Senator Phil Gramm of Texas.

Statement by Press Secretary Fitzwater on Possible Changes in the Cabinet
August 19, 1992

President Bush yesterday commented in a PBS interview that there would undoubtedly be changes in the Cabinet in the second term. He said this would be a normal situation historically, and he did not refer to any specific individual. The President believes his Cabinet is doing an excellent job.

The President called Jack Kemp, Secretary of Housing and Urban Development, this morning to congratulate him on his speech to the convention and to express his concern about Jack being singled out by the Houston Post this morning as departing from the Cabinet. The President assured Jack that he was referring only to the routine departure of Cabinet members that historically occurs in a second term.

Nomination of James Michael Reum To Be a Member of the Securities and Exchange Commission
August 19, 1992

The President today announced his intention to nominate James Michael Reum, of Illinois, to be a member of the Securities and Exchange Commission for the term expiring June 5, 1997. He would succeed Edward H. Fleischman.

Since 1979, Mr. Reum has served as a partner in the law firm of Hopkins & Sutter in Chicago, IL. He has also served as associate Republican counsel for the Committee on the Judiciary in the U.S. House of Representatives, 1974. From 1973 to 1974 and 1974 to 1978, he served as a corporate lawyer with the firm of Davis Polk & Wardwell.

Mr. Reum graduated from Harvard College (B.A., 1968) and Harvard Law School (J.D., 1972). He also served in the U.S. Army Reserves/National Guard, 1969–75. He was born November 1, 1946, in Oak Park, IL. Mr. Reum currently resides in Chicago, IL.

Remarks at a Prayer Breakfast in Houston
August 20, 1992

Thank you very much, Mary Lou. For heaven sakes, that was just wonderful, and thank you for that wonderful introduction.

Let me repeat what I said last week to the 1992——

[*At this point, audience members interrupted the President's remarks.*]

I apologize to those who have put together this ecumenical, lovely prayer breakfast, but you just can't control things like this. I hope you understand. I certainly do.

I was saying that I salute Mary Lou and thank her. Let me repeat what I said last week to the 1992 summer Olympic team when they came to the White House. Whether they won a gold, silver, or bronze medal, or simply gave their best, they are all heroes in the eyes of each American.

I also want to salute my friend and running mate, Vice President Dan Quayle.

Ninfa said it all; my friend Ninfa said it all: first-class.

May I salute the Mayor. And fellow Texans and Americans, I'm delighted to address this ecumenical prayer breakfast on this great occasion. You see, breakfast speeches are always my favorite. I figure it's the one meal where broccoli is never served. [*Laughter*]

Let me first salute that marvelous choir behind us. Think of it: a 40-piece orchestra; 85 singers from the Houston Children's Choir, too; our adult choir, members of 40 area congregations, 1,200 voices; and then, of course, there was Alan Green, football player, "A" student, Rice graduate, and magnificent musician. Believe me, as one who works in the divisive world of politics, it's amazing to hear that many voices raised in unison on anything.

As you know, we meet on a special day.

Tonight I give my acceptance speech. If it catches fire, it might give a whole new meaning to the story of the "burning bush." [*Laughter*] The only problem is I have a funny feeling that Barbara and Marilyn Quayle raised the high bar quite a bit for me.

But anyway, as we meet today, deep in the heart of Texas, we meet deep in the heart of the most religious nation on Earth, too. I'm usually not much for polls, but here's a Gallup poll that makes sense to me. According to this survey, 7 in 10 Americans believe in life after death; 8 in 10, that God works miracles; 9 in 10 pray; and more than 90 percent believe in God. To which I say, thank God for the United States of America.

I'm delighted that Jim Baker's here, fellow Houstonian, and Susan. As he knows and as our Vice President knows and the other members of our Cabinet who I see out here know, we open every Cabinet meeting with a prayer. And it's going to be that way as long as I am President.

Today we've got difficult times, but we Americans have much to thank God for. Yes, challenges face us: good schools and safe streets, sound economy—all the problems that Bob Lanier works with as Mayor of our great city—and a world at peace. But we will meet and master them as Americans always have, not by running America down but by using God's gifts to lift America up.

Thomas Jefferson, Ronald Reagan's friend—[*laughter*]—he phrased the first gift best. "The God who gave us life," he said, "gave us liberty at the same time." Today God's gift of liberty is remaking the entire globe. In Berlin, like Jericho, the walls come tumbling down. In Barcelona, just ask Mary Lou, this summer the games were held without boycotts, without terrorism, without politics. That's exactly as it should be.

On that score, all of us have Olympic heroes; mine, Pablo Morales. Pablo, he's the swimmer who missed out in 1984, didn't make the team in '88, then came back this year to earn a gold medal at the ripe old age of 27. Now, let that be a lesson: Youth and inexperience are no match for maturity and determination.

Over the past 3½ years, bayonets have been no match for the righteousness of God. Look at Bulgaria, where at last people wish Merry Christmas to each other without fear of being labeled religious. Look to Russia, where a cathedral once called the All Union Museum of Religion and Atheism now houses God's apostles, or the former East Germany, where Bible studies are like bluebonnets in the spring, they're busting out all over. In a season of thanksgiving the world says grace. By God's providence, the cold war is over, and America's views prevailed.

I remember when, 10 years ago, one of God's great soldiers went to Eastern Europe and the Soviet Union. Returning to America, Billy Graham predicted that freedom would outlast tyranny. He felt that religion was alive way back then. The doubters said, "He's been tricked." But Dr. Graham knew something they didn't. He knew the chains of oppression forged by men were no match for the keys to salvation forged by God.

I talked about this with Billy, Barbara and I did, just, well, it was a year ago in January when we invited him to stay at the White House the night before our troops started Desert Storm. I thought a lot that night about thousands of people praying in churches, about our own home parish right here, Jim's and mine, St. Martin's. I see our bishop over here, and welcome, sir. St. Martin's parish, with its prayer books and its crosses and handmade Christmas cards made in Sunday schools for our troops in the Gulf. It's true of every parish represented at this wonderful ecumenical service. It is absolutely true of all religions.

We prayed for the troops themselves, the finest sons and daughters any nation could ever have. I know how a second gift of God's, family, can lift America. I can no more imagine a life without family than I can a universe without love. Last night—here she is—you saw Barbara on television. I'll let her explain why family matters so much. I thought she did a first-class job of that last night. But here's her quote. "At the end of your life," she said, "you will never forget not having passed one more test, not winning one more verdict, nor closing one more deal. You will regret time not spent with a husband, a child, a friend, or a parent."

Barbara knows that kids, quoting Art Linkletter, say not only the funniest but the most insightful things, especially about religion. Once a Sunday school teacher started talking about the story of Jonah and the whale, and she asked what the story showed. A small boy raised his hand. "I know," he said. "People make whales sick." [*Laughter*]

Well, each of us turns to God daily to make lives well, and we act through the third and greatest of God's gifts, prayer. If Congress can spend time debating Vanna White's appearance on the Home Shopping Network, surely Congress can find time to pass an amendment allowing voluntary prayer in our classrooms. So let's do what we can to bring the faith of our fathers back to our schools.

You know, I've been President for 3½ years now. More than ever, I believe with all my heart that one cannot be President of our great country without a belief in God, without the truth that comes on one's knees. For me, prayer has always been important but quite personal. You know us Episcopalians. [*Laughter*] And yet, it has sustained me at every point of my life: as a boy, when religious reading was part of our home life; as a teenager, when I memorized the Navy Hymn. Or how 48 years ago, aboard the submarine *Finback* after being shot down in the war, I went up topside one night on the deck, on the conning tower, and stood watch and looked out at the dark. The sky was clear. The stars were brilliant like a blizzard of fireflies in the night. There was a calm inner peace. Halfway around the world in the war zone, there was a calm inner peace: God's therapy.

This month I got a letter from a little girl, age 11, Joy Vaughn. Oh, I love getting the mail at the White House, but this one was special. She lives in Mesa, Arizona, and one of her brothers is a missionary. She wrote, "I just wanted to tell you that I am praying for you." And then she added, "God is in charge."

So Barbara and I have concluded, as every family that's been privileged to live in the White House I'm sure has concluded, that you cannot be President without believing in God. We say our prayers every night. When we sit in that historic family dining room on the second floor of the White House, we say the blessing before our meals. Today I ask for your prayers, not for the campaign that we're in but prayers asking God to give those of us in leadership positions and give me as President the strength to do what is right, the courage to lead this, the greatest nation on the face of the Earth, the United States of America, one Nation under God.

Thank you, and may God bless our great country.

Note: The President spoke at 9:30 a.m. at the University of Houston. In his remarks, he referred to Mary Lou Retton, 1984 Olympic gold medalist; Ninfa Laurenzo, Houston business leader; and evangelist Billy Graham.

Statement by Press Secretary Fitzwater on the Decision of the Railway Labor Dispute Arbitrator
August 20, 1992

On August 18, 1992, the President received for his review the decision of the arbitrator in the one remaining railway labor dispute associated with the shutdown of the Nation's railroads in late June. This decision was rendered pursuant to the arbitration process established by the Congress and concerns the dispute between the National Railroad Passenger Corporation (Amtrak) and the American Train Dispatchers Association. The decision becomes final and binding upon the parties unless the President disapproves it within 3 days following its receipt.

The President has decided that he will not disapprove this decision. The President is grateful to the arbitrator for his work in resolving this dispute.

Remarks Accepting the Presidential Nomination at the Republican National Convention in Houston
August 20, 1992

The President. Thank you all very much. Thank you, thank you very much. And I am proud to receive and I am honored to accept your nomination for President of the United States.

May I thank my dear friend and our great leader, Bob Dole, for that wonderful introduction.

Let me say this: This nomination's not for me alone. It is for the ideas, principles, and values that we stand for.

My job has been made easier by a leader who's taken a lot of unfair criticism with grace and humor, the Vice President of the United States, Dan Quayle. And I am very grateful to him.

I want to talk tonight about the sharp choice that I intend to offer Americans this fall, a choice between different agendas, different directions, and yes, a choice about the character of the man you want to lead this Nation. I know that Americans have many questions about our economy, about our country's future, even questions about me. I'll answer them tonight.

First, I feel great. And I am heartened by the polls, the ones that say that I look better in my jogging shorts than the Governor of Arkansas.

Four years ago, I spoke about missions for my life and for our country. I spoke of one urgent mission, defending our security and promoting the American ideal abroad.

Just pause for a moment to reflect on what we've done. Germany is united, and a slab of the Berlin Wall sits right outside this Astrodome. Arabs and Israelis now sit face to face and talk peace, and every hostage held in Lebanon is free. The conflict in El Salvador is over, and free elections brought democracy to Nicaragua. Black and white South Africans cheered each other at the Olympics. The Soviet Union can only be found in history books. The captive nations of Eastern Europe and the Baltics are captive no more. And today on the rural streets of Poland, merchants sell cans of air labeled "the last breath of communism."

If I had stood before you 4 years ago and described this as the world we would help to build, you would have said, "George Bush, you must have been smoking something, and you must have inhaled."

This convention is the first at which an American President can say the cold war is over, and freedom finished first.

Audience members. U.S.A.! U.S.A.! U.S.A.!

The President. We have a lot to be proud of, a lot. Some want to rewrite history, want to skip over the struggle, claim the outcome was inevitable. And while the U.S. postwar strategy was largely bipartisan, the fact remains that the liberal McGovern wing of the other party, including my opponent, consistently made the wrong choices. In the seventies, they wanted a hollow army. We wanted a strong fighting force. In the eighties—and you remember this one—in the eighties, they wanted a nuclear freeze, and we insisted on peace through strength. From Angola to Central America, they said, "Let's negotiate, deliberate, procrastinate." We said, "Just stand up for freedom." Now the cold war is over, and they claim, "Hey, we were with you all the way."

Audience members. Boo-o-o!

The President. You know, their behavior reminds me of the old con man's advice to the new kid. He said, "Son, if you're being run out of town, just get out in front and make it look like a parade."

Well, make no mistake: The demise of communism wasn't a sure thing. It took the strong leadership of Presidents from both parties, including Republicans like Richard Nixon and Gerald Ford and Ronald Reagan.

Without their vision and the support of the American people, the Soviet Union would be a strong superpower today, and we'd be facing a nuclear threat tonight.

My opponents say I spend too much time on foreign policy, as if it didn't matter that schoolchildren once hid under their desks in drills to prepare for nuclear war. I saw the chance to rid our children's dreams of the nuclear nightmare, and I did. Over the past 4 years, more people have breathed the fresh air of freedom than in all of human history. I saw a chance to help, and I did. These were the two defining opportunities not of a year, not of a decade, but of an entire span of human history. I seized those opportunities for our kids and our grandkids, and I make no apologies for that.

Now, the Soviet bear may be gone, but there are still wolves in the woods. We saw that when Saddam Hussein invaded Kuwait. The Mideast might have become a nuclear powder keg, our energy supplies held hostage. So we did what was right and what was necessary. We destroyed a threat, freed a people, and locked a tyrant in the prison of his own country.

What about the leader of the Arkansas National Guard, the man who hopes to be Commander in Chief? Well, I bit the bullet, and he bit his nails. Listen to this now. Two days after Congress followed my lead, my opponent said this, and I quote directly: "I guess I would have voted with the majority if it was a close vote. But I agree with the arguments the minority made." Now, sounds to me like his policy can be summed up by a road sign he's probably seen on his bus tour, "Slippery When Wet."

Look, this is serious business. Think about the impact of our foreign policy failures the last time the Democrats controlled both ends of Pennsylvania Avenue: gas lines, grain embargoes, American hostages blindfolded.

There will be more foreign policy challenges like Kuwait in the next 4 years, terrorists and aggressors to stand up to, dangerous weapons to be controlled and destroyed. Freedom's fight is not finished. I look forward to being the first President to visit a free, democratic Cuba. Who will lead the world in the face of these challenges? Not my opponent. In his acceptance speech he devoted just 65 seconds to telling us about the world.

Then he said that America was, and I quote again—I want to be fair and factual—I quote, being "ridiculed" everywhere. Well, tell that to the people around the world, for whom America is still a dream. Tell that to leaders around the world, from whom America commands respect. Ridiculed? Tell that to the men and women of Desert Storm.

Audience members. U.S.A.! U.S.A.! U.S.A.!

The President. Let me just make an aside comment here because of what you've been reading in the paper. This is a political year, but there's a lot of danger in the world. You can be sure I will never let politics interfere with a foreign policy decision. Forget the election; I will do right, what is right for the national security of the United States of America, and that is a pledge from my heart.

Fifty years ago this summer, I was 18 years of age. I see some young people in the audience tonight, and I remember how I felt in those days. I believed deeply in this country, and we were faced with a world war. So I made a decision to go off and fight a battle much different from political battles.

I was scared, but I was willing. I was young, but I was ready. I had barely lived when I began to watch men die. I began to see the special place of America in the world. I began to see, even then, that the world would become a much smaller place, and faraway places could become more and more like America.

Fifty years later, after change of almost Biblical proportions, we know that when freedom grows, America grows. Just as a strong America means a safer world, we have learned that a safer world means a stronger America.

This election is about change. But that's not unusual, because the American revolution is never ending. Today, the pace of change is accelerating. We face new opportunities and new challenges. The question is: Who do you trust to make change work for you?

Audience members. George Bush! George Bush! George Bush!

The President. My opponent says America is a nation in decline. Of our economy, he says we are somewhere on the list beneath Germany, heading south toward Sri Lanka. Well, don't let anyone tell you that America is second-rate, especially somebody running for President.

Maybe he hasn't heard that we are still the world's largest economy. No other nation sells more outside its borders. The Germans, the British, the Japanese can't touch the productivity of you, the American worker and the American farmer. My opponent won't mention that. He won't remind you that interest rates are the lowest they've been in 20 years, and millions of Americans have refinanced their homes. You just won't hear that inflation, the thief of the middle class, has been locked in a maximum security prison.

You don't hear much about this good news because the media also tends to focus only on the bad. When the Berlin Wall fell, I half expected to see a headline, "Wall Falls, Three Border Guards Lose Jobs." [*Laughter*] And underneath, it probably says, "Clinton Blames Bush." [*Laughter*]

You don't hear a lot about progress in America. So let me tell you about some good things we've done together.

Just two weeks ago, all three nations of North America agreed to trade freely from Manitoba to Mexico. This will bring good jobs to Main Street, U.S.A.

We passed the Americans with Disabilities Act, bringing 43 million people into the economic mainstream. I must say, it's about time.

Our children will breathe easier because of our new clean air pact.

We are rebuilding our roads, providing jobs for more than half a million Americans.

We passed a child care law, and we took a stand for family values by saying that when it comes to raising children, Government doesn't know best; parents know best.

I have fought against prejudice and anti-Semitism all my life. I am proud that we strengthened our civil rights laws, and we did it without resorting to quotas.

One more thing of vital importance to all: Today, cocaine use has fallen by 60 percent among young people. To the teenagers, the parents, and the volunteers who are helping us battle the scourge of drugs in America, we say, thank you; thank you from the bottom of our hearts.

Do I want to do more? You bet. Nothing hurts me more than to meet with soldiers home from the Persian Gulf who can't find a job or workers who have a job but worry that the next day will bring a pink slip. And what about parents who scrape and struggle to send their kids to college, only to find them back living at home because they can't get work.

The world is in transition, and we are feeling that transition in our homes. The defining challenge of the nineties is to win the economic competition, to win the peace. We must be a military superpower, an economic superpower, and an export superpower.

In this election, you'll hear two versions of how to do this. Theirs is to look inward and protect what we already have. Ours is to look forward, to open new markets, prepare our people to compete, to restore our social fabric, to save and invest so we can win.

We believe that now that the world looks more like America, it's time for America to look more like herself. And so we offer a philosophy that puts faith in the individual, not the bureaucracy; a philosophy that empowers people to do their best, so America can be at its best. In a world that is safer and freer, this is how we will build an America that is stronger, safer, and more secure.

We start with a simple fact: Government is too big and spends too much.

I have asked Congress to put a lid on mandatory spending, except Social Security. I've proposed doing away with over 200 programs and 4,000 wasteful projects and to freeze all other spending.

The gridlock Democrat Congress said no.

Audience members. Boo–o–o!

The President. So, beginning tonight, I will enforce the spending freeze on my own. If Congress sends me a bill spending more than I asked for in my budget, I will veto it fast, veto it fast, faster than copies of Millie's book sold.

Now, Congress won't cut spending, but refuses to give the President the power to eliminate pork-barrel projects that waste your money. Forty-three Governors have that power. So I ask you, the American people: Give me a Congress that will give me the line-item veto.

Let me tell you about a recent battle fought with the Congress, a battle in which I was aided by Bob Michel and his troops, and Bob Dole and his. This spring, I worked day and night to get two-thirds of the House Members to approve a balanced budget amendment to the Constitution. We almost had it, but we lost by just nine votes. Now, listen how. Just before the vote, the liberal leaders of the Congress convinced 12 Members who cosponsored the bill to switch sides and vote no. Keep in mind, they voted against a bill they had already put their names on. Something fishy is going on.

And look at my opponent on this issue. Look at my opponent. He says he's for balanced budgets. But he came out against the amendment. He's like that on a lot of issues, first on one side, then the other. He's been spotted in more places than Elvis Presley.

After all these years, Congress has become pretty creative at finding ways to waste your money. So we need to be just as creative at finding ways to stop them. I have a brandnew idea. Taxpayers should be given the right to check a box on their tax returns so that up to 10 percent of their payments can go for one purpose alone: to reduce the national debt.

But we also need to make sure that Congress doesn't just turn around and borrow more money to spend more money. So I will require that for every tax dollar set aside to cut the debt, the ceilings on spending will be cut by an equal amount. That way, we will cut both debt and spending and take a whack out of the budget deficit.

My feelings about big government come from my experience; I spent half my adult life in the private sector. My opponent has a different experience; he's been in government nearly all his life. His passion to expand government knows no bounds.

He's already proposed, and listen to this carefully, he has already proposed $220 billion in new spending, along with the biggest tax increase in history, $150 billion. And that's just to start.

Audience members. Boo-o-o!

The President. He says he wants to tax the rich. But folks, he defines rich as anyone who has a job. [*Laughter*]

You've heard of the separations of powers. Well, my opponent practices a different theory: the power of separations. Government has the power to separate you from your wallet. [*Laughter*]

Now let me say this: When it comes to taxes, I've learned the hard way. There's an old saying, "Good judgment comes from experience, and experience comes from bad judgment." Two years ago, I made a bad call on the Democrats tax increase. I underestimated Congress' addiction to taxes. With my back against the wall, I agreed to a hard bargain: One tax increase one time in return for the toughest spending limits ever.

Well, it was a mistake to go along with the Democratic tax increase, and I admit it. But here's the question for the American people. Who do you trust in this election? The candidate who's raised taxes one time and regrets it, or the other candidate who raised taxes and fees 128 times and enjoyed it every time?

Audience members. Viva Bush! Viva Bush! Viva Bush!

The President. Thank you very much.

Audience members. Hit 'em again! Hit 'em again, harder, harder! Hit 'em again! Hit 'em again, harder, harder!

The President. When the new Congress convenes next January, I will propose to further reduce taxes across the board, provided we pay for these cuts with specific spending reductions that I consider appropriate, so that we do not increase the deficit. I will also continue to fight to increase the personal exemption and to create jobs by winning a cut in capital gains taxes.

That will especially help small businesses. You know, they create—small businesses—they create two-thirds of the new jobs in America. But my opponent's plan for small business is clear, present, and dangerous. Beside new income taxes, his plan will lead to a new payroll tax to pay for a Government takeover of health care and another new tax to pay for training. That is just the beginning.

If he gets his way, hardware stores across America will have a new sign up, "Closed for despair." I guess you'd say his plan really is "Elvis economics." America will be checking into the "Heartbreak Hotel."

I believe that small business needs relief from taxation, regulation, and litigation. And thus, I will extend for one year the freeze on paperwork and unnecessary Federal regulation that I imposed last winter. There is no reason that Federal regulations should live longer than my friend George Burns. I will issue an order to get rid of any rule whose time has come and gone.

I see something happening in our towns and in our neighborhoods. Sharp lawyers are running wild. Doctors are afraid to practice medicine, and some moms and pops won't even coach Little League any more. We must sue each other less and care for each other more. I am fighting to reform our legal system, to put an end to crazy lawsuits. If that means climbing into the ring with the trial lawyers, well, let me just say, round one starts tonight.

After all, my opponent's campaign is being backed by practically every trial lawyer who ever wore a tasselled loafer. He's not in the ring with them; he's in the tank.

There are other things we need to do to get our economy up to speed, prepare our kids for the next century. We must have new incentives for research and new training for workers. Small businesses need capital and credit, and defense workers need new jobs. I have a plan to provide affordable health care for every American, controlling costs by cutting paperwork and lawsuits and expanding coverage to the poorest of the poor.

We do not need my opponent's plan for a massive Government takeover of health care, which would ration care and deny you the right to choose a doctor. Who wants health care with a system with the efficiency of the House post office and the compassion of the KGB?

What about our schools? What about our schools? My opponent and I both want to change the way our kids learn. He wants to change our schools a little bit, and I want to change them a lot. Take the issue of whether parents should be able to choose the best

school for their kids. My opponent says that's okay, as long as the school is run by government. And I say every parent and child should have a real choice of schools, public, private, or religious.

So we have a clear choice to fix our problems. Do we turn to the tattered blanket of bureaucracy that other nations are tossing away? Or do we give our people the freedom and incentives to build security for themselves?

Here's what I'm fighting for: Open markets for American products; lower Government spending; tax relief; opportunities for small business; legal and health reform; job training; and new schools built on competition, ready for the 21st century.

Now, okay, why are these proposals not in effect today? Only one reason: the gridlock Democratic Congress.

Audience members. Clean your House! Clean your House! Clean your House!

The President. A very good idea, a very good idea.

Now, I know Americans are tired of the blame game, tired of people in Washington acting like they're candidates for the next episode of "American Gladiators." I don't like it, either. Neither should you. But the truth is the truth. Our policies have not failed. They haven't even been tried.

Americans want jobs, and on January 28th, I put before Congress a plan to create jobs. If it'd been passed back then, 500,000 more Americans would be at work right now. But in a Nation that demands action, Congress has become the master of inaction.

It wasn't always this way. I heard President Ford tonight. I served in Congress 22 years ago, under him. And back then, we cooperated. We didn't get personal. We put the people above everything else. Heck, we didn't even own blow dryers back in those days.

At my first Inauguration, I said that people didn't send us to bicker. I extended my hand, and I think the American people know this, I extended my hand to the congressional leaders, the Democratic leaders, and they bit it.

The House leadership has not changed in 38 years. It is a body caught in a hopelessly tangled web of PAC's, perks, privileges, partnership, and paralysis. Every day, Congress puts politics ahead of principle and above progress.

Now, let me give you just one example: February 20th, 1991. It was at the height of the Gulf war. On that very same day, I asked American pilots to risk their lives to fly missions over Baghdad. I also wanted to strengthen our economic security for the future. So that very same day, I introduced a new domestic energy strategy which would cut our dependence on foreign oil by 7 million barrels a day.

How many days did it take to win the Gulf war? Forty-three. How many did it take Congress to pass a national energy strategy? Five hundred and thirty-two, and still counting. I have ridden stationary bikes that can move faster than the United States House of Representatives and the United States Senate, controlled by the Democrat leadership.

Audience members. Hit 'em again! Hit 'em again, harder, harder! Hit 'em again! Hit 'em again, harder, harder!

The President. Okay. All right. You wait. I'm fixing to.

Where does my opponent stand with Congress? Well, up in New York at their convention, they kept the congressional leaders away from the podium, hid them away. They didn't want America to hear from the people who really make the decisions. They hid them for a very good reason, because the American people would recognize a dangerous combination: a rubber-check Congress and a rubber-stamp President.

Governor Clinton and Congress know that you've caught on to their lingo. They know when they say "spending," you say "uh-oh." So now they have a new word, "investment." They want to "invest" $220 billion more of your money, but I want you to keep it.

Governor Clinton and Congress want to put through the largest tax increase in history, but I will not let that happen. Governor Clinton and Congress don't want kids to have the option of praying in school, but I do. Clinton and Congress don't want to close legal loopholes and keep criminals behind bars, but I will. Clinton and Congress will stock the judiciary with liberal judges who write laws they can't get approved by the voters.

Governor Clinton even says that Mario Cuomo belongs on the Supreme Court. [*Laughter*] Wait a minute, though. No, wait. Maybe not a bad idea. If you believe in judicial restraint, you probably ought to be happy. After all, the good Governor of New York can't make up his mind between chocolate and vanilla at Baskin Robbins. He's there, we won't have another court decision for 35 years, and maybe that's all right, too.

Are my opponent and Congress really in cahoots? Look at one important question: Should we limit the terms of Congress?

Audience members. Yes.

The President. Governor Clinton says no. Congress says no. I say yes.

We tried this—look, we tried this once before, combining the Democratic Governor of a small southern State with a very liberal Vice President and a Democratic Congress. America does not need Carter II. We do not want to take America back to those days of malaise. But Americans want to know: Where's proof that we will have better days in Washington?

I'll give you 150 reasons. That's how many Members of Congress are expected to leave Washington this year. Some are tainted by scandal; the voters have bounced them the way they bounced their own checks. But others are good Members, Republican and Democrat, and they agree with me. The place just doesn't work anymore.

One hundred-fifty new Members, from both parties, will be coming to Washington this fall. Every one will have a fresh view of America's future.

I pledge today to the American people, immediately after this election, I will meet with every one of these Members, before they get attacked by the PAC's, overwhelmed by their staffs, and cornered by some camera crew. I will lay out my case for change, change that matters, real change that makes a difference, change that is right for America.

You see, there is a yearning in America, a feeling that maybe it's time to get back to our roots. Sure we must change, but some values are timeless. I believe in families that stick together, fathers who stick around. I happen to believe very deeply in the worth of each individual human being, born or unborn. I believe in teaching our kids the difference between what's wrong and what's right, teaching them respect for hard work and to love their neighbors. I believe that America will always have a special place in God's heart, as long as He has a special place in ours. Maybe that's why I've always believed that patriotism is not just another point of view.

There are times in every young person's life when God introduces you to yourself. I remember such a time. It was back many years ago, when I stood watch at 4 a.m. up on the bridge of a submarine, the United States *Finback*, U.S.S. *Finback*. And I would stand there and look out on the blackness of the sky, broken only by the sparkling stars above. And I would think about friends I lost, a country I loved, and about a girl named Barbara. I remember those nights as clearly as any in my life.

You know, you can see things from up there that other people don't see. You can see storm clouds rise and then disappear, the first hint of the sun over the horizon, and the first outline of the shore far away.

Now, I know that Americans are uneasy today. There is anxious talk around our kitchen tables. But from where I stand, I see not America's sunset but a sunrise.

The world changes for which we've sacrificed for a generation have finally come to pass, and with them a rare and unprecedented opportunity to pass the sweet cup of prosperity around our American table.

Are we up to it? I know we are. As I travel our land, I meet veterans who once worked the turrets of a tank and can now master the keyboards of high-tech economy. I see teachers blessed with the incredible American capacity for innovation who are teaching our children a new way to learn for a new century. I meet parents, some working two jobs with hectic schedules, who still find new ways to teach old

values to steady their kids in a turbulent world.

I take heart from what is happening in America, not from those who profess a new passion for government but from those with an old and enduring faith in the human potential, those who understand that the genius of America is our capacity for rebirth and renewal. America is the land where the sun is always peeking over the horizon.

Tonight I appeal to that unyielding, undying, undeniable American spirit. I ask you to consider, now that the entire world is moving our way, why would we want to go back their way? I ask not just for your support for my agenda but for your commitment to renew and rebuild our Nation by shaking up the one institution that has withstood change for over four decades. Join me in rolling away the roadblock at the other end of Pennsylvania Avenue, so that in the next 4 years, we will match our accomplishments outside by building a stronger, safer, more secure America inside.

Forty-four years ago in another age of uncertainty a different President embarked on a similar mission. His name was Harry S Truman. As he stood before his party to accept their nomination, Harry Truman knew the freedom I know this evening, the freedom to talk about what's right for America, and let the chips fall where they may.

Harry Truman said this: This is more than a political call to arms. Give me your help, not to win votes alone, but to win this new crusade and keep America safe and secure for its own people.

Well, tonight I say to you: Join me in our new crusade, to reap the rewards of our global victory, to win the peace, so that we may make America safer and stronger for all our people.

May God bless you, and may God bless the United States of America. Thank you very much.

Note: The President spoke at 9:20 p.m. at the Houston Astrodome.

Remarks to the Republican National Committee in Houston
August 21, 1992

I think the Republican National Committee, under Rich Bond and Jeanie Austin's leadership, put on the best convention that we've ever had. It was first-class. Bill Harris was to be here. But Craig Fuller and so many others were intimately involved in all of this. It was a complex organizing job. It was done in a wonderfully imaginative way. I think that the convention gives us now a great lift as we take the battle to the opposition, but more importantly, take this positive message to the American people. I first wanted to come over here and say thanks. No longer will we tell Rich to cool his jets. We'll simply suggest that he keep doing what he's doing.

Let me just mention another item of business which I hope you all agree with me on, and that is I've recommended, as you know, Sam Skinner to be general chairman, the same role that Paul Laxalt had. We thought long and hard about that, but Sam has earned my confidence through superior performance, not just in the trenches politically where he and I have been shoulder to shoulder for a long, long time, out in Illinois particularly, but more recently as Secretary of Transportation. One of the major accomplishments of this administration, and you're going to hear more and more about this as the campaign goes on, is an innovative, creative, job-creating national transportation bill. No one deserves more credit for that major national accomplishment than Sam Skinner.

So when Jim Baker came back, I wanted to keep Sam suited up, out front, working for the cause. He and Rich will do a superb job there at the committee. He is good, and I know he's most enjoyable to work with, so I strongly recommend that.

Barbara and I just came from another event. When I saw what our local law enforcement people went through at this convention to keep the peace and to give everybody their rights, and I mean those that were inside the hall as well as those out, we decided that we wanted to go over and thank the police officers. So we went over there just now, had a representation of the full 3,000 police officers that serve this city that Barbara and I love so much.

As I was walking down the rope line, one of the press reporters inquired, "Well, what about the tax plan?" I said, "Well, it's fairly simple." You see, I do believe, as I said last night, that the Government is taxing too much and spending too much. So I mentioned something like that. I said, "Well, it's a very easy plan. What you do is you tax people less, and the Government spends less." "Well, how is it going to work?" And I said, "Well, it's going to work because it benefits the taxpayers." There was a follow-on question, as always happens, and the police officers standing there, certainly not the highest tax brackets of all, were saying, "Hey, we're taxpayers. We're taxpayers. It will help us."

I think that we've got a good message now to take to the American people. It's been there one way or another. I thought when Dan Quayle put it in perspective in what I felt was an outstanding speech by him last night, incidentally. I was sitting behind the podium, and I watched the reactions of various people in the audience that they focused in on. Not just that part of his speech but the whole thing resonated very well, indeed.

We came down here to Houston with more dire predictions, more gloom-and-doom negativism than I've ever seen in my long, long time in the political arena or, indeed, in the private arena. I think, first thanks to the work of the organizers of the convention, then thanks to the speeches and the presentations at the forums of so many of our party leaders and so many just plain grassroots Republicans, a lot of that is turning around.

Now I've got a big job on my shoulders; Barbara does; Dan and Marilyn do. But I just want to say one thing: I really am ready for this challenge. We've got so much at stake. As I tried to say last night, it isn't just a question of my winning an election. That really is coincidental to who can do the best job for the country. We're going to take this out there to the American people not just on the financial issues but on the questions of values. And then in the final analysis, as I touched on last night, it's going to be a question of trust.

I, for 6 months, have been letting Bill Clinton define me, erroneously, I might add, to the American people. Perhaps I miscalculated, because I said, look, it's more important to try to get something done. It's more important to keep working with Congress to get some incentives that will put people back to work or to pass a strong anticrime bill or to get our energy bill that we talked about last night out or to try to make some steps on passing our health care reform bill. I really felt that it was more important to get that done.

The Congress stalled and did nothing. So, as I told you last night, I'm going to link the Gore-Clinton, G–C, to the gridlocked Congress. G–C, put them right together. Put them right in there, and don't let them come apart.

The reason it will work is because it's true. It's true. The American people, if they don't understand it yet, will understand it when I get through, because it's factual. It is accurate. That one institution, the House of Representatives, that hasn't changed for 38 years, is now going to have not just a one-way street, which they've been pounding me on, every one of those leaders up there; I'm going to take it to them. And I'll go into a congressional district, and I'll do exactly what Harry Truman did. I'll go into a congressional district, and I'll say, "You have the worst Congressman that you know. You think he's a nice guy, but he's terrible because here's what he's doing on a crime bill or energy or education, health reform, or whatever it is." We're going to single them out because they, each one of those liberal Democrats in Congress, have been singling me out and singling the Vice President out for the last 3½ years and smiling when I go up there to the Congress.

They say Clinton has a good reaction squad. We're going to give him plenty to react to, every single minute. Let them try to sever that umbilical cord. Let them sever the umbilical cord between the people that are blocking legal reform: Congress, Bill Clinton, and Gore. Let them try to sever it. They're not going to be able to do it because they can't.

The American people don't yet have that in focus. When we're through with the next 70-some days or whatever it is, I guarantee you they will. Then in the final analysis, as I say, I think that people are going to go into that voting booth, and I hope that they're going to say that this President has upheld the public trust. I hope they're going to say, "Look, we may not agree on this issue or that. He might have done a better job on this phase of our agenda or that, but he has demonstrated that he has our trust. He has treated the White House and the Presidency with a certain respect and dignity. He has had a clean administration, free of scandal, and he stands with us on these fundamental values." And that's what I want the people to say.

And if we are—well, put it this way, when we are successful, we'll be accompanied by a lot of new people to town, these new Congressmen. It's going to happen anyway. We'll get out, and we'll try again. We'll say: You've been out to the American people, and you've been elected. And you wouldn't have been elected if you didn't listen to them this year, because this is a strange political year. And I wouldn't be standing here now with 4 more years to go if I hadn't listened to the American people and touched a chord representing what they believe.

So let's try again to get something done for every family in America. I know it will work. It will work especially if all of you, whatever organizations you represent, whether it's the RNC or Huda Jones' marvelous group in the Federation or the Young Republicans or the College Republicans, the State parties which are so vital. We have the State leadership here, of course, members of the RNC. If we bring all of this together, under Rich Bond and Jeanie Austin's able leadership, I know we can get the job done.

Thank you all very, very much for what you're doing.

Note: The President spoke at 8:05 a.m. at the Hyatt Regency Hotel. In his remarks, he referred to Rich Bond, chairman, and Jeanie Austin, cochairman, Republican National Committee; William D. Harris, convention manager; Craig Fuller, Bush-Quayle convention chairman; Paul Laxalt, former general chairman, Republican National Committee; and Huda Jones, president, National Federation of Republican Women.

Remarks at a Bush-Quayle Rally in Gulfport, Mississippi
August 21, 1992

The President. Wow. Thank you very, very much. This is good for the soul.

Audience members. Four more years! Four more years! Four more years!

The President. Thank you, thank you. Thank you so very much. Thank you for this warm Mississippi welcome. It is great to be back in Gulfport, great to be back in Fordice, Lott, Cochran, and Bush-Quayle country. Thank you very, very much.

This is our first stop after Houston, the first step into the future. We're here to kick off a crusade to bring back values and to build a stronger, more secure America.

We're grateful to be here with your Mayor and our Lieutenant Governor, Eddie Briggs. And may I single out my dear friend, a man of real values, a man of real talent, Ricky Scaggs.

You talk about southern hospitality, let me thank all the Republican leadership, those who greeted us on the ground, all of you who worked on this fantastic rally, and those who came with me on Air Force One. This is, as I say, our first step out of Houston, on to the election. I am delighted to be back here in this place which has sound family values, great tradition, and believes in a strong America.

I understand that since my last visit, Biloxi is something of the Monte Carlo of the gulf coast. Well, my pastor may be listening, so I want to say I never was much of a gambler. But let me offer a little sporting advice: Don't bet against us in November. We are going to win this election.

Now, let me put something in perspective. You've been reading about some of these crazy reports about my health. Well, let me say I am blessed with good health, blessed with good health. Last night I laid out an agenda for America, and the reaction has been very positive. If those overnight polls are any barometer, the American people agree with me that I do look better in my jogging shorts than Bill Clinton.

You know, last night we answered some questions for the American people. One of them is, "Well, why spend any time anymore on foreign policy?" Well, remember the days when some of these schoolchildren, or when some of you all were schoolchildren, hiding under the desks in drills to prepare for nuclear war. Well, I saw a chance to rid our children's dreams of the nuclear nightmare. And I did it, with the help of many others before me.

Seriously, do you know that over the past 4 years, more people have breathed the fresh air of freedom than in all of human history? We saw a chance to help, and we did it. And understand something: These were the two defining opportunities, not of a year, not of a decade but of an entire span of human history. We can all take great pride in that.

And yes, now that we have made the world safer and more secure, it's time to build a safer and more secure America. Here in Gulfport, you understand how the world has become linked, interconnected. The challenge before America today is to bring together foreign policy, economic policy, and national security policy to make a difference in your home.

So this election isn't simply, as the opposition, as that new twin ticket says, simply about change. It's about who do you trust to make the change work for you. That is the question.

And our opponents, my opponent is——

Audience members. George Bush! George

Bush! George Bush!

The President. Look, creating jobs is the number one issue. My opponent has laid out his plan; it is clear, present, and dangerous. Here's the way it starts out: $220 billion in new, what he calls, investment. When he says investment, watch out for your wallet. Investing $220 billion of your money, that is not investment.

It goes on with the largest tax increase in history. Right up front, right up front before he's had to govern at all, he says tax them $150 billion more. No, we are not going to have that.

Along with it, a massive scheme to have Government take over the health care system. We have a program to make health insurance available to the poorest of the poor, to everybody, but not to get the Government tell you who your doctor can be.

I was talking to Thad Cochran and Trent, the Governor coming down here. And my opponent, we all agree, seems to like to compare himself to Elvis Presley. [*Laughter*] Well, my apologies to the King, but to me, the Governor of Arkansas' plan really does sound like Elvis economics. Because the time he is finished, American workers will all be checking into the Heartbreak Hotel. And I think we ought to treat those Clinton-Gore ideas the way Elvis would: Return to sender. Return him to Arkansas. Send them back to Arkansas and Tennessee.

We offer a different way to create jobs and get the economy moving. And last night I proposed a brandnew idea—some of you may have heard it—to let you, the taxpayer, check a box on your tax return to vote up to 10 percent of your taxes to go for nothing but reducing the Federal deficit. And then for every check, we have to reduce Federal spending by that much.

There's something else that I want to do, and every place I go in America people are saying, "Please get it done." I'm talking about this: A lot of sharp lawyers are wreaking havoc in middle America. Doctors sometimes, maybe it's true here in Biloxi, scared to practice medicine; some parents afraid to even coach Little League. The bottom line is we are suing each other too much and caring for each other too little.

We have been, with the help of Trent and the help of Thad, we've been trying to go to toe with that Democratic liberal Congress to take on the trial lawyers and take on their new hero, incidentally, the Governor of Arkansas. I am keeping on fighting to put an end to these outrageous lawsuits that raise everybody's costs and scare people half to death.

We've got other ideas we're fighting for: To open markets for our products—I saw a sign here about agriculture. Our farmers can compete with and outhustle anybody in the world if we give them a chance. Open markets for our products, not protection. Make health care more affordable without a Government takeover of medicine. Improve our schools so our kids can get the education they need to succeed, and tell the union to start thinking new ideas. Let's help these kids.

Now the fundamental: In order to get all these ideas and more into action, I need your help. I need you to change the U.S. Congress, to clean House. Clean the House. Exactly, exactly.

Audience members. Clean the House! Clean the House! Clean the House!

The President. We've got two guys here today that are trying to do just that, Paul Harvey and Clyde Whitaker, so help them out. I might say, if we had more like Trent Lott and Thad Cochran, we wouldn't have this problem of a Congress that obstructs everything we're trying to do.

You know, let me be very candid with you, Congress is an institution in gridlock. The liberal Democratic leadership has been in charge—it's hard for these young people to believe—but has been in charge of the House of Representatives for 38 straight years. The gridlocked Democratic Congress has blocked my jobs program, blocked my education program, and blocked the progress of the people of Gulfport, Mississippi. They are caught in a knot of PAC's and perks and privileges and paralysis.

Let me give you one example: It took us, with the help of many sons and daughters of Mississippi, 43 days, 43 days to win the Gulf war, while Congress has taken 533 days, and still counting, to give us a national energy policy to cut our dependence on foreign oil. That is gridlock. That is congressional gridlock. As I said, I've ridden stationary bikes that can move faster than the U.S. Congress.

Make no mistake about it: We are not going to let the Clinton-Gore ticket fool the American people. The Clinton-Gore ticket and the gridlocked Congress are totally interlocked. One is C–G, and the other is G–C: Clinton-Gore, gridlocked Congress. But don't let them try to separate themselves from each other. They are one and the same, even though they tried to hide the leaders away at their Madison Square convention.

Now, let me give you one example of what I'm talking about. When Saddam Hussein invaded Kuwait, I turned to the American people—and no area of our country responded better than the people of Mississippi—I turned to the American people and asked for their support, and of course, to our young men and women, for sacrifice, before the Middle East became a nuclear powder keg threatening us all. Mississippi responded, and you made America proud. But many of the liberal Democrats in Congress stood against us.

As I said last night, what about the leader of the Arkansas National Guard, the man who hopes to be Commander in Chief? Let me repeat it for you. Two days after Congress voted to follow my lead, my opponent said this, and I want to be fair about it, so I'll give you the exact quotation: "I guess I would have voted with the majority if it was a close vote, but I agree with the arguments the minority made." What kind of message would that send to a man like Saddam Hussein?

You talk about wishy-washy indecision that is offered up by both my opponent and the gridlocked Congress; they are one and the same. So if you want to see this country go forward with optimism, first send Bill Clinton back to Arkansas, but just as important, help me shake up that gridlocked Congress and get rid of them.

Speaking for this district, you can do it by electing a seasoned leader, General Paul Harvey, to represent you in the Congress. I told the general I was going to make a joke about his providing "the rest of the story." But I'm sure you heard this kind of kidding. I'm sure he's heard it about 3,000 times every day.

Our crusade, and it is one, will not be easy. And I know that. But I'm absolutely certain that in November we will prevail. Two weeks ago, they were totally writing off the Bush-Quayle ticket, all those smart talking heads on television. We are going to take it to the American people. We're going to the people with our message.

For 9 months the Governor of Arkansas has been distorting my record. I don't care what the polls say, I'm going to take this case to the American people like Truman did, go against the Congress, go against the opponent, say what I'm for.

God bless the United States of America. We are going to win this race. Thank you all.

Note: The President spoke at 12:25 p.m. in Jones Park. In his remarks, he referred to Gov. Kirk Fordice; Senators Trent Lott and Thad Cochran; Ken Combs, Mayor of Gulfport; and entertainer Ricky Scaggs.

Remarks at a Bush-Quayle Rally in Branson, Missouri
August 21, 1992

The President. Thank you all very much. Thank you so much. What a wonderful welcome back to the Ozarks. Thank you very, very much. May I just salute our great Governor, John Ashcroft, thanking him for all he's done to strengthen the American family and to bring decency and honor to

the governorship of this State. He has been superb. I'm glad that all the entertainers, these marvelous stars who stand for grassroots America, are with us today. They are friends, and we honor them. And I know why you came here, just to hear them. So thank you very, very much.

May I tell you, perhaps it sounds a little bit prejudiced, but I think Barbara Bush is doing a first-class job as First Lady of this land. If you ask Barbara, she'll tell you that my favorite kind of music is a two-way tie between country and western. So, for me to visit Branson is really a dream come true. America loves country music because, I believe, country music really loves America. It's a great pleasure to be here.

Let me talk just briefly this afternoon about the choice that we face this fall. I might even mention a couple of country songs along the way. This is my second stop after our great Republican Convention in Houston that ended yesterday. Now we've got 70-some days left——

Audience members. Four more years! Four more years! Four more years!

The President. ——70-some days left to take our message of hope for a safer and stronger and more prosperous America to every voter. I will take on the Governor of Arkansas. I will define him. And we will win.

You know, last week he gave an interview, Governor Clinton did, where he sounded as if he was getting ready to measure the drapes in the Oval Office. Well, I've got news for you. Not so fast. I believe that, come November 3d, my opponent and his saxophone will be playing that old Buck Owens classic, "It's Crying Time."

You know, last night I had a chance to have some straight talk with the American people. One of the questions I wanted to answer was why, with all the challenges at home, foreign policy is important. Look, remember back to those days when the kids, and some of you were there then, had to climb under your desks to practice nuclear war drills? I saw the chance to rid our children's dreams of the nuclear nightmare. I did it, and I am proud of it. And the American people supported me. If that Clinton-Gore ticket doesn't understand it, I believe the American people do. That our kids can now sleep in the sunshine of peace is good for the American family, good for the entire world.

Do you remember Garth Brooks' song "One Dream Per Customer"? Well, to me, that's not a bad description of our great country because freedom means that every citizen can have their dream. In the past 4 years, more people around the world were able to have their first dream of freedom than at any time in human history. With your help and the help of the American people that kept America strong, we got that done.

If the opposition doesn't think that's important, let them go to ethnic America. Let them talk to people whose families still live there or families that came here for the first time. Let them discuss that. Let those Clinton-Gore people hear from the American people that freedom is important. And I am glad I had a hand in bringing it about.

There's another side of all of this. There's another side of a more peaceful world. And that means that this new freedom brings new demands for American products, all American products. That means jobs for the American people.

Now, my opponent's ideas, they are clear, present, and dangerous. He says he's converted, he's not a liberal. But right out of the block, he offers $220 billion in new Government spending, that's true, and then $150 billion in new taxes, the largest tax increase in history. And he calls that investment. He wants to invest your money in Government spending, and I'm not going to let it happen.

When you peel away all his nice-sounding rhetoric about the plan he's got, the impact of his plan can be summed up by a song by my old friend Loretta Lynn, "When the Tingle Becomes a Chill."

I propose a dramatically different way to create new jobs. I believe that we get a change in Congress, we can do it this way: Cut the Government spending and then cut the taxes. Get it down. Get Government further out of the lives of the people. And the Congress, that gridlocked Congress, has failed. Last night I promised a new idea to let you, the taxpayer, check your income tax form to designate up to 10 percent of your taxes for one purpose: reduce the deficit. And then, to the degree you check it, put lids on so we have to reduce the spending to go with that deficit reduction.

They get on me about spending. Look, I've sent up to the Congress proposals to eliminate over 200 Government programs and 4,000 projects, and I've asked for a freeze on discretionary spending. That gridlocked Congress has refused to go along. So today I say, let's give the American people the freedom to do what Congress has refused to do and been unable to do for 38 years under that liberal Democrat control.

As I say, I want to go further. As we cut the spending, I believe we can cut those taxes and give families more money to pay their bills and businesses more incentives to hire new workers. The Congress linked in to Bill Clinton say no, and I say yes. That's the way to bring prosperity back to the United States of America.

We have other priorities.

Audience members. We want Bush! We want Bush! We want Bush!

The President. We have other priorities. Let me tell you about health care. My opponent has a plan that would lead to a back-door Government takeover of our health care system and would slap a tax on the already overburdened small-business man and small-business woman in this country. I want to unfetter small business, not stick a new tax on them.

I have a different approach to health care, the plan I've got to the Congress that the gridlockers refuse to move on. What it says is: Make insurance available to all, the poorest of the poor and everybody else. Get these costs under control. Do something about these malpractice lawsuits. But do not turn the health care over to the Government; would run it like they ran the post office and the bank.

We've got a great plan to renew our schools, and God bless the teachers that are out here today. We also have another plan, and that is put the lid on some of these crazy lawsuits that are costing our economy hundreds of millions of dollars, scaring coaches out of the Little League, scaring doctors out of the medical profession. Suing each other too much and caring for each too little, and I want to change it.

You might ask, why haven't you done that as President? I'll tell you. We've had proposal after proposal up on Capitol Hill to do it, to change the law. And the gridlocked Congress doesn't dare think about it because they are in the pocket of the trial lawyers association. That's the fact. That is

the fact, and I'm going to keep telling the American people that: Blocked by the gridlocked Democrat-controlled Congress. Remember that. You're going to hear a lot about it for 74 days.

All right, let me give you another example. I mentioned it last night. On the day I sent the planes over Baghdad—God bless those men and women of Desert Storm—on that day I sent a new energy program to the Congress. It took 43 days to win the Gulf war, but it has taken 533 days, and still counting, to get Congress to send a national energy program down to the White House. That is too long. The Congress is in gridlock. They don't dare move. Too many——

Audience members. Clean the House! Clean the House! Clean the House!

The President. That's it: Clean the House, clean the House. That is the expression. That's it. All right, I'm going to be saying that from now on, too. This is exactly right. That is the problem: 38 years the Democrats have controlled the House. You ought to be able to just make a mistake and get a change in one time. They've never done it. Throw them out with their PAC's, their privileges, and their perks, and give us a chance.

Tomorrow, Branson, I understand, is hosting the fifth Oldtime Fiddle Contest. I wouldn't be surprised to see all the liberal leaders of the Congress there, signed up, participating as a team, fiddling while America gets burned by their inaction. But make no mistake about it, that Clinton-Gore ticket are locked, they are interlocked with the gridlocked Congress. I'm not going to let the American people forget that. We've got to change the Congress and send Bill Clinton back to live happily after across the Ozark Lake.

So I've got two messages, two messages. First, for the opponent: Follow that old Elvis Presley song "Return to Sender." Return him over here across the lake. And then, you may have guessed it, break up the gridlocked Congress. Kick the liberals out of Washington. Give me a Congress that will cut the spending and cut the taxes and do what is right to get our great country moving again.

You know, the thing that got me the most

about this Governor across the way is when he said we were ridiculed around the world. We are not. We are the most respected nation in the world. Let him tell that to the leaders there, and they'll tell him he's wrong. If he wants to say we're ridiculed, let him tell that to the men and women that fought in Desert Storm and see what happens to him.

So yes, I am proud to say we have changed the world. Now we've got to move this country forward. My good friend Randy Travis put it this way: "There is no stopping us now." Thank you for this hospitality. Thank you for this fantastic welcome.

Let me put it this way. Here's the way it's going to be from now on out. Do you remember the son of Missouri, Harry Truman? He was a big underdog, and he fought back. He wrapped another Governor challenging him right around that do-nothing Congress. I'm going to do the same thing with the Governor of Arkansas, wrap him to the gridlocked Congress, take my message of peace and a stronger America to the American people, and win this election, not for me but for the American people.

Thank you very, very much. Thank you. Great rally.

Note: The President spoke at 4:36 p.m. at Silver Dollar City. In his remarks, he referred to entertainer Randy Travis.

Remarks to the Community in Woodstock, Georgia
August 22, 1992

The President. Thank you very much. You know, this reminds me of a great country song, "If you want to see a rainbow, you've got to take a little rain." And we're going to show the American people a rainbow.

May I salute Mayor Rogers and thank my friend of long standing, and I hope your next Senator, Paul Coverdell, for that introduction; salute our leader, Newt Gingrich, who helps us so much in Washington; members of the city council here; the cheerleaders and bands from Cherokee and Etoyah and Sequoia High Schools; and Daron Norwood, the Spirit of Atlanta; and of course, Dr. Johnny Hunt, who I'm told is not only a spiritual leader here, but that First Baptist Church here in Woodstock stands for family, family values, one Nation under God. Jane Hancock and Audra Dinsmore and Johnny Isaacson, thank you all. And of course, I'm glad to be standing here with one of Woodstock's own, my friend Orlando Wilson, who is a good—if anybody likes bass fishing, they know all about this guy. Now, Fred Cooper, my chairman, and Alec Poitevint, our leaders, thank you all.

It's great to be here in Cherokee County, the land of the free and the home of the Warriors. Okay, and let's not forget the Chiefs and the Eagles. Frankly, it's great to be out of that DC mode and out on the campaign trail, taking our case to the American people. We are going to give them something to talk about down at Dean's Store here in Woodstock.

So I want to talk briefly—and the skies have cleared now, I'm glad to say—about the sharp choice, the clear, sharp choice that we're going to offer every American. It's a choice between different agendas, different directions for our great country, and it's a choice about the character of the man that you want to lead this Nation for another 4 years.

They say this election is about change. Well, they're right. But let's not forget the things that must guide change are the things that never change: our belief in a strong defense, in strong families, and in leaving the world a better and more prosperous place for the young kids here today. That's what this election is about.

Think for a minute about the world we've already seen, a world of change: the Berlin Wall down; millions of people around the world took the first breath of freedom; and America, her ideals and her strengths intact, won the cold war. That is good for every American.

I can't come to Georgia without saluting one other thing. Thanks for the contribution that this State made to that wonderful victory of Desert Storm. It is something strong about the American spirit.

All this change didn't come about by accident. The world changed because we, the American people, stayed true to our unchanging principles. My opponents—let them say this—they say I spent too much time on national security and foreign policy. Well, let me tell you, when I took office I saw a chance to help finish off imperial communism, and I did it with your help. Perhaps even more important, I saw a chance to help rid our children's dreams of the nuclear nightmare, to help them live in a safer world. And I did that with your help, and that is good. So let the Clinton-Gore ticket understand one thing: I am not going to apologize for one minute for having spent time making the world a place of peace for all the children in this country.

For 40 years this was a change that Americans fought and died for. Now it offers us a defining challenge of the nineties, to take advantage of our victory around the world and then to build a stronger and more prosperous Nation right here at home.

So for these next 73 days I'm going to ask the American people: Who do you trust to bring it all home, foreign policy, security policy, and economic policy? Who do you trust?

Audience members. Bush! Bush! Bush!

The President. So I came here to Georgia today to ask the good people of this patriotic State to give me your support based on my experience, my ideas, and my character. I will not let you down.

Here we go. Let me spell out the differences. Okay, we're going to start it right here, right now in Woodstock. I believe our Government is too big, and it spends too much of your money. I believe the deficit is a dark cloud on the future of these young people. You know it, and I know it.

Clinton does not know it, and Gore does not know it. Hey, listen, you listen to these guys and you think the deficit is a big game of the "Wheel of Fortune." You know that one? They want to buy three vowels: I, O,

U. That's not good enough for the American taxpayer.

In Houston 2 nights ago, I announced a freeze on Government spending, and let me repeat it right here. If Congress sends me a bill spending one penny more than I requested, I will veto it faster than a spinner bait after Orlando's lure. We're going right after it. For the past 3 years, past 3 years, we've endorsed and proposed significant cuts in Federal spending. But that gridlock liberal Democratic-controlled Congress has chosen to direct your taxpayer dollars to their favorite projects. If they need more help curing the pork addiction, I'll say as I said the other night, let's give the taxpayers the power to dedicate up to 10 percent of their tax dollars to the deficit. If Congress won't cut that spending, the people of America will. It's just that clear.

And yes, we must cut spending. With a new Congress cutting that spending, I'll propose a tax cut to give you more of the money to pay the bills, to give the businesses the incentives to create the new jobs that this economy so desperately needs, and we will do more to jump-start the economy.

Frankly, it's the small business people that are hurting. They're the ones that create the jobs. I want to give small business a shot in the arm. Small businesses, they create two-thirds of the jobs in this country. You take places like the Cost Plus on South Main Street or Morgan's Hardware. If we're going to get this country moving, small business needs relief from taxation, these awful lawsuits, and from regulation. And we are going to give it to them.

Now, let me tell you this: the Governor of Arkansas, the commander of the Arkansas National Guard, he wants a different kind of change.

Audience members. Boo-o-o!

The President. Now, wait a minute. This is a fact. He has actually proposed already, isn't even in there yet, and he's proposed raising Government spending by $220 billion and raising taxes, the biggest increase in history, by $150 billion. We cannot have that.

Audience members. Boo-o-o!

The President. You think those guys only

know one word, change. They talk about it. Well, that's change all right; that's about all you'll have left in your pocket when they get through with you. Yes, we want change, but it's also a question of trust. Look at every big issue we face, and you're going to see a choice between the people who put their faith in everyday Americans and those who put their faith in the Government.

I trust you, the families and the parents, to make the decisions that matter in life. I trust the parents, not the Government, to choose their children's schools, private, public, or religious. Very, very candidly, the Congress opens a meeting with a prayer. I think the schoolchildren ought to have a voluntary prayer in schools. You could argue that Congress needs it more, but I think everybody ought to have that option. I trust the parents, not the Government, to choose the children's child care. It's better to have parents do it than have some subcommittee in Washington tell you how to look after your kids.

Frankly, it all sums up to this: I think the Government is already big enough, and they tax people too much. It's that simple. If you want fewer lawsuits and fewer regulations and more opportunity for small business, vote for me.

I wonder about the Governor of Arkansas. I wonder why it is that whenever he's faced with any problem, his solution is always to put Government first. But you know, it's not so surprising. When you spent more of your life in government, like he has, government is all you know anything about. I've got my belief in trust, about limited Government from working out in the oilfields of west Texas, from trying to build a business and trying to meet a payroll. That's where I learned how jobs are created. That's where I learned this: In this country, the Government works for the people, not the other way around.

But Bill Clinton isn't the only one who's forgotten that lesson, if he ever knew it. There's a whole party of his colleagues up there on Capitol Hill who have spent their lives on the Government payroll. They, that liberal Democratic gridlock, has been controlled by one party for 38 years, 38 years. I call them the gridlocked Congress. I'm going to remind the American people: 38

years. Clean the House, clean the House, clean the House. You have to do it; we ought to do it.

Audience members. Clean the House! Clean the House! Clean the House!

The President. Let me just put it parenthetically, the last thing this country needs is a rubber-check Congress and a rubber-stamp President. We don't need it, and we're not going to have it.

I think the American people know this, that I've tried to work with these people. You remember when I said, "We didn't come here to bicker. We came here to do something for the people"? I held out my hand, and that liberal Democrat-controlled Congress bit it off. Now I'm going to take that case to the American people and say, change the Congress.

Every American knows the truth that Congress has become corrupt and conceited and confused, a body of these PAC's and privileges and partisanship and paralysis. They can't run a tiny bank. They can't run a tiny post office. And yet, they're running your lives. We've got to change it.

You know, Harry Truman took it this way. He went out across the country. He got in his sights the Congress, took his case to the people, and then he linked his opponent right into those sights. Well, let me tell you this. I'm going to do the same thing.

I am for Paul Coverdell, and here's why. He was willing to stand up and think anew. As Truman did, he's willing to single out those who talk one way and vote another. The thing in this Senate race is this: I stand for a balanced budget amendment; Wyche Fowler is against it. I stand for the line-item veto; Wyche Fowler is against it. I stand for those who stood at Desert Storm, and he opposed me. Now we want a change. That is the fact. It's fine to talk one way in downtown Woodstock and vote differently in Washington, but we cannot have that anymore.

You know, I know this race is long, know it; read all these polls about being behind. But yes, I really believe and have a confidence that we will win. We're going to win, not because of a victory for me but because we trust the American people. We win because our ideas are strong, and we win because we understand the American way. We'll win also because I think we've got a great First Lady who stands for the family and family values.

So you tell Governor Clinton and that gridlocked Congress: If you can't run with the big dogs, stay under the porch. We're coming after them.

Thank you very, very much. May God bless the greatest, freest country on the face of the Earth. And thank you for this fantastic rally. Thank you so very much.

Note: The President spoke at 1:06 p.m. on Main Street. In his remarks, he referred to entertainer Daron Norwood; Jane Hancock, who sang the national anthem; Audra Dinsmore, who sang "I'm Proud To Be an American"; Johnny Isaacson, Republican candidate for Georgia State Senate in the 21st district; Fred Cooper, Georgia Bush-Quayle chairman; Alec Poitevint, Georgia Republican Party chairman; and Senator Wyche Fowler, Jr.

Remarks at the Pride in Alabama Rally in Hoover, Alabama
August 22, 1992

The President. Roll up your sleeves; we're going to work. Thank you very much. Thank you very, very much. Thank you so very much for that welcome. I reminded them over in a little rainstorm in a rally in Georgia of a country song, "If you're going to see a rainbow, you've got to stand a little rain." And you've sure done it. Thank you.

We are going to have a rainbow. We are going to win this election for the American people. May I thank Emory Folmar; and of course, my good friend Governor Guy Hunt, your Governor, I support him all the way; single out two Members of the United States Congress, Sonny Callahan and Bill Dickinson, old friends, both doing a great job; my fishing pal Ray Scott, Sportsman of the Year for Alabama.

Let me say this magic city is a wonderful place to start a magic campaign. I've got a feeling this fall we're going to use that magic to make some Democrats disappear, disappear from the Presidency, disappear from the House. There's a very important battle going on this fall, big battle this fall: two fiercely determined rivals locked in gridlock, locked in combat. And I'm not just sure whether this thing's going to be won by the War Eagles or by the Crimson Tide, but nevertheless, that's your business.

Hey, I did like it, though, when George Archer won the Senior PGA Tournament around here. I would have loved those big headlines, "George comes on strong, pulls off big win." Help me do that in the fall, because we are coming on strong, and we're taking our case to the American people. We're bypassing those talk shows and going to you, the American people, saying, "Give us your support."

The reason we'll win is we're talking about entirely different directions for this country, different agenda. It's a choice about the character of the person you want to lead this Nation and the direction you want us to go. I believe I am the person to have that support.

All the other side does is talk about change, change, change. But the thing that must guide change are things that never change. We believe in a strong defense, in strong families, in leaving the world a better place for our children.

Think for a minute, just think for one minute about the world of change that we've seen the last 4 years: the Berlin Wall down; millions of people took their fresh first breath of freedom; and America, her strength and ideals intact, won the cold war. And you, the taxpayers, helped get that job done. These changes are not accidental. The world changed because America remained true to her unchanging principles. So when Governor Clinton says we're ridiculed around the world, he is disconnected. We are respected around the world.

My opponent said I spent too much time on national security and standing up against aggression, too much time on foreign policy. Let me tell you something. When I took office I saw the chance to help finish off imperial communism, and I did it with the help of the American people. I saw the chance to help rid our children's dreams of the nuclear nightmare, to help them live in a safer world. I did it with your help, and I am proud of it. And that is important. So let them criticize and carp. I will never apologize for one single minute that I have met trying to make this world a more peaceful place for all the young people here today.

The challenge now: to build a more prosperous and secure nation right here at home. And so for these next 73 days I'm going to ask the American people: Who do you trust to bring it all home?

Audience members. Bush! Bush! Bush!

The President. Bring it home, foreign policy, security policy, and economic policy, so that it can make a difference to you right here in these neighborhoods, right here in Alabama. I ask for your support based on my experience, my ideas, and my character. Let me say this. I share Alabama's commitment to family values, and we will never forget: We are one Nation under God, one Nation under God.

So we start right now, right here. I do believe here's a principle with which I differ from my opponent, the Governor of Arkansas. I believe our Government is too big, and it spends too much of your money. I believe the deficit is a dark cloud on our children's future. You know it, and I know it. And I put forward a program to do something about it.

If the Congress sends me any bill spending one penny more than I requested, I will veto it fast, right on the spot, faster than the sales of Millie's book. I've repeatedly proposed cuts in the Federal spending to deflate the deficit. This year alone, I called for the elimination of 200 specific programs and 4,000 wasteful projects, and this gridlocked Congress has said no and diverted your money to pork barrel projects. So here's the proposal: If Congress needs more help curing its addiction, I say let's give the American people a chance. Give the people the power to dedicate up to 10 percent of their tax dollars directly to the deficit. If Congress won't cut the deficit, the American people will. Give the people that power.

Let me repeat what I said at our convention. As we get these appropriate spending reductions, I will propose a tax cut to give you more money to pay your bills, businesses more incentives to create the jobs that this economy needs. We've got to do both: lower spending and lower taxes.

One other thing, one other point: We've got to give the small businesses a shot in the arm around here. They're the ones that create two-thirds of America's jobs. Think of them right here in the mall, McMillan's or Norton's Florist, right here in this area. If we're going to get this economy moving, small business needs relief from taxation, from regulation, and yes, from these crazy lawsuits that are killing us off.

These lawsuits are costing our economy billions of dollars each year, and we're fighting now to reform our legal system. As a Nation, very candidly, we need to sue each other less and care for each other more. About 460 days ago, May 15th, 1991, I sent my first plan to control these outrageous lawsuits up to the Congress. It is still sitting there, blocked by Congressmen beholden to that powerful lawyers' lobby, gridlocked in this liberal Democrat-controlled Congress. I say: Let's change the Congress. Let's clean House.

Audience members. Clean the House! Clean the House! Clean the House!

The President. Very true. Elect these guys. I'm coming to them in just a minute. Let me just remind you, I hate to ruin a wonderful day like this, but let me remind you what Governor Clinton wants.

Audience members. Boo-o-o!

The President. He's gotten the fever. He's gotten that liberal Democratic fever, and he's not even there yet. He wants to raise Government spending, he's already proposed this, by $220 billion. He wants to raise taxes, the biggest increase in history, by $150 billion. And to that, I say: No way, Governor. No way.

They talk about change. The only thing you'll have left in your pocket, if this guy gets in, is change, I'll tell you that. They always want to put Government first. That's not so surprising. When you've spent most of your life in Government, Government is pretty much all you see. I spent half my adult life, thank heavens, in the private sector. I earned my belief in limited Government from working out, having a job, holding a job, working in the oilfields, building a business, and meeting a payroll. That is a good credential for anybody that wants to be President of the United States of America.

I learned what all of you have learned and some are now learning. That's where I learned how jobs are created, that you can't have employees without employers. That's where I learned in this country that Government works for the people, not the other way around.

But in all fairness—we've got to be fair in this election—Governor Clinton is not the only one who has forgotten that lesson, if he ever knew it. There's a whole party of his colleagues right up there on Capitol Hill in Washington, DC, who have spent their entire lives on the Government payroll. I call them the gridlocked Democratic liberal-controlled Congress, and I don't believe the Governor can stand up to them. The last thing we need is a rubber-check Congress and a rubber-stamp President. We don't need that.

And look, I've tried to work with this Congress. You all remember at the Inaugural Address I said, "People didn't send us here to bicker, they sent us here to get something done." I held out my hand, and these old mossbacks bit it off. Enough! We've got to change the Congress.

So we're talking clean House. We need Spencer Bachus here for the Sixth District. We need Terry Everett for the Second District, Don Sledge for the Third, Mickey Strickland for the Fourth, Terry Smith for the Fifth, and Kervin Jones for the Seventh. And then we can clean House.

While we're at it, the Senate needs a little work. Those liberals that control that Senate are blocking me every inch of the way. Give us Richard Sellers for the Senate. Make change. Make change.

Look, I know this and you know it: Americans are tired of the blame game, sick of all the excuses, tired of these people up there acting like they're the candidates for the next episode of "American Gladiators". But

I'll tell you this: I am tired of it, too. Every American knows the truth. Congress—look at the post office, look at the bank—they have become corrupt, conceited, confused, a body of these PAC's, perks, privileges, partisanship, and paralysis. We must change the Congress with which Bill Clinton is interlocked.

You ask him when he comes south. He talks about change. What about changing the one institution whose control hasn't changed in 38 years, since he was 7 years old? The Congress. They have a lower rate of turnover than the Soviet Politburo.

So it's time to say, "Enough is enough." If you want to get rid of that deadlock, give me some new faces in that Congress and watch this country move forward. There is so much to do: a balanced budget amendment, locking this line-item veto into place so we can cut that spending. Give the parents some choice in the schools that their kids attend—private, public, or religious. Give us that kind of a positive change.

I know this is a long race and that some have counted us out. Oh boy, are we having some problems with the national media. They don't know good news when they see it. They are going to know change when they see it. And we're going to win this in the final analysis on this basis because I trust the American people, and I hope I have earned the trust of the American people.

When I think of the great patriotism shown by this wonderful State of Alabama and I think of those men and women that served in Desert Storm and I think of the opposition I had in the Congress, I say let's change it. So if we're faced with a problem again, we can solve it just as quick as we did Desert Storm in spite of that opposition.

So, my message is this—after once again saying thanks. I can't tell you what this does for the spirit, this, the largest rally, as Emory told me, he's ever seen around here.

Audience members. Four more years! Four more years! Four more years!

The President. So you tell the opposition we stand for family values. And the best evidence of this, standing right here with me today, is Barbara Bush, who does so much for literacy in this country.

Audience members. Barbara! Barbara! Barbara!

The President. You tell them we stand for family and faith and one Nation under God. And then go tell the gridlocked Congress and Governor Clinton: If you can't run with the big dogs, stay under the porch.

Thank you all very much.

Note: The President spoke at 2:55 p.m. at the Riverchase Galleria shopping mall. In his remarks, he referred to Emory Fowler, Mayor of Montgomery. A tape was not available for verification of the content of these remarks.

Remarks at the National Affairs Briefing in Dallas, Texas
August 22, 1992

Thank you very much. Hey, listen, this is a nonpolitical gathering. Thank you. Life is not fair. For me to get up here after Dr. Adrian Rogers, one of the great religious leaders of this country, it just doesn't seem fair. Adrian, thank you, sir, for that introduction. I mean, seven standing ovations in the introduction, my heavens, what's going on here? [*Laughter*]

But I am so pleased to be here. I have great respect for the man that did the introducing and so many here with us tonight. I'd like to recognize a true fighter for the American family. I heard him when Barbara and I were standing in the wings; we heard him. I'm talking about one of this Nation's truly great and, I would say, spiritual Governors, Governor John Ashcroft from Missouri. He gets it on his own and also from his wonderful dad that is so well known to, I'm sure, many people here.

Thanks to Denee Varnum for that singing and the First Baptist Church choir and orchestra for that assist on "The Battle Hymn of the Republic." May I salute—I think Congressmen Sam Johnson of Dallas and Dick Armey of a neighboring district are here with us tonight, both doing a superb job.

Of course, another old friend for Barbara and me, now doing a superb job for this city, Mayor Steve Bartlett. You're lucky to have him. You Dallas folks are lucky to have him as your leader.

In my line of work, loyalty and friendship really count, and I want to single out Dr. Jerry Falwell, who is with us tonight, because he sure fits that description as far as the Bush family goes. I'm sorry that I

missed Dr. E.V. Hill. I was with him in his church in South Central out there in Los Angeles. I understand he just wowed them here tonight. But here's a real man of the cloth and a man I respect enormously. I wish he were here now.

Of course, special thanks to our organizer and wonderfully dedicated chairman, Ed McAteer; a man who I was sitting next to, he and I go back many, many years out here in Texas, and he was reminding me of a meeting we had some 36 years ago out in west Texas, Ed Drake, chairman of the national NAB. Or is he the local chairman? Which are you? Local chairman, all right. And Dr. Jack Graham, the chairman of the ministerial committee.

Let me just say it's a pleasure to be here. I've got a very difficult assignment. I plan to fulfill it to the letter. I was told that this is a nonpolitical event. We're just coming off of a fantastic campaign swing, so I'm going to cool it down, though, and talk about things that I think are near and dear to our hearts.

You see, we meet tonight at a time of great change. It's exciting change; makes me wish I were about 40 years younger at times. In both the world and our Nation this change is exciting. Changes are taking place, and they literally defy the imagination. I remember 10 years ago when one of God's great soldiers, a friend to all here, I'm sure, visited Europe and the Soviet Union. Returning to America, Dr. Billy Graham predicted that freedom would outlast tyranny. He'd sensed something as he traveled across that monolithic Communist empire.

The doubters said he'd been tricked. But Dr. Graham, Billy, knew something they didn't. He knew the chains of oppression forged by men were no match for the keys to salvation forged by God.

Over the past 3½ years, bayonets have been no match for the righteousness of God. Now, look to Bulgaria, where at last people wish Merry Christmas not only in the privacy of their homes but in public, in the streets. Look to Russia, where a cathedral that was called the All Union Museum of Religion and Atheism now houses God's apostles, or the former East Germany, where Bible studies are like bluebonnets in Texas in the spring, they're busting out all over.

In a season of thanksgiving the world says grace. And by God's providence the cold war is over, and freedom finished first. Because of the changes that have been wrought outside our Nation, our children and our grandchildren now sleep in the sweet sunshine of peace. And now it is our challenge, it is our sacred challenge, to build for them a nation that is as secure from the inside as it is safe from the outside.

I met not long ago with some of the mayors of our great cities in this country. It was the directors or the executive board of the National League of Cities. I asked what was the root of the ills with which they are afflicted in these cities, problems like crime, drug abuse, unemployment. They could have complained of the lack of Government money, but they didn't. They could have complained at the lack of Government programs, but they didn't. These mayors, including those from the other party, liberal, conservative, Republican, Democrat, large city, small city, said that all their problems could be traced to the breakdown of the American family. I would simply add to that, an erosion of traditional moral and religious values on which our very Nation was founded.

Some want us to get away from that. Some want us to get off of that theme, get away from that. I simply cannot do it. It is too fundamental. Leave out the election. It is fundamental that we restore and strengthen the American family.

Now, this week you saw a very charismatic, dynamic, insightful Bush family member appear on television and talk to the Nation. I'm speaking, of course, of our First Lady, Barbara. By the way, I recall the Book of Proverbs said that "Grandchildren are the crown of the aged." Well, while I wouldn't quite put myself up there with the aged yet—some will, but I don't put myself there—I must tell you I felt like I was wearing a crown the other night when I listened to one of our grandkids, George P., speak to this Nation. This is a family night here, and I hope you'll understand how emotional Barbara and I felt when we saw this little guy get up. I asked him ahead of time, "Are you scared?" Oh, no, no, he wasn't scared at all. But he carried it off well, and he spoke from the heart.

Then yesterday, we were over in Gulfport, Mississippi, and then at this marvelous country music town of Branson, Missouri, and we saw a sign, "George P. in 2024. Viva Bush." It's wonderful, this politics. But you know, in a tough political year—it's been pretty tough, let's face it, and all the criticism, but it all subsides. It all gets into proper perspective when you see your own grandkid up there and can take pride in what your family does.

You know, Barbara in her speech said something I remember. She said, "To us, family means putting your arms around each other and being there." Now, those are truly words of insight and wisdom. When I speak of family values, of restoring a little moral and religious fiber to our Nation's diet, my opponents accuse me of mouthing slogans. But it is no slogan that America remains the most resolutely religious nation on God's great Earth. It is no slogan to say that America will always occupy a special place in God's heart. But that is true only as long as we keep Him in a special place in our hearts. So I believe that now that the world has become more like America, it is time for America to become more like herself. That means strengthening the American family, and yes, it means increasing our faith in God.

Government policy can make a difference. That's why I fought for changes—some that Steve was generous enough to talk about—in our welfare laws to encourage families to stay together, fathers to stick around, children to be able to save a little money when their mother's on welfare so they can get themselves educated. We've got to change the way the old welfare system has worked.

When Congress was considering a new law giving parents help with child care, I fought to make sure that parents would be able to choose the child care provider of their choice. I fought especially hard, and we were successful on this one, to allow care provided in religious settings. We had to fight, but we won that fight. You see, when it comes to deciding who should care for children when parents are working, I believe Government doesn't know best; parents know best. Parents should choose.

The same is true of education. I have spoken often of roots and wings. Wings, of course, are the subjects our children learn, math, science, English, that allow them to make their way in our complex world economy. But just as important are the roots, the moral values taught around the kitchen table or in our churches, and yes, as Dr. Rogers said, I believe, in our schools. For without roots our children will never fly in a moral and good direction.

Many parents want their children to attend religious schools, but they simply can't afford it. So I am fighting for a "GI bill" for children. It will give Federal money to working parents so that they can choose the best school for their children. The choice should include all schools, public, private, and religious.

I happen to believe that just as we fix our economy and improve our schools, we've got to strengthen our moral foundation. If I could make one political comment, I was struck by the fact that the other party took words to put together their platform but left out three simple letters, G–O–D. As you may have heard, Governor Casey of Pennsylvania was also shut out of the convention because he wanted to talk about the rights of the unborn. At least he's in good company. My party's platform is different. We are proud to celebrate our country's Judeo-Christian heritage unrivaled in the world. [*Applause*]

While you're still standing may I say, as I said, I happen to believe that all human life

is precious, born or unborn. I think it's ridiculous that a 13-year-old girl here in Dallas has to get her mother's permission to get her ears pierced in a mall but can get an abortion without telling her mom and dad. That doesn't make sense to me. I don't believe it makes sense to most Americans.

Something's wrong when kids can get birth control in school but can't say a prayer in school. If Congress can debate the merits of Vanna White appearing on the Home Shopping Network, surely Congress can find enough time to pass an amendment to allow our kids to thank God. So I call on the Congress again, and I'll keep calling on them to pass a constitutional amendment allowing voluntary prayer. Let us bring the faith of our fathers back to schools.

These are the kinds of issues that I care about and, certainly, I know you care about. So I'm not going to be dissuaded by the critics who call family values a cliche, who say that family values have no place in our national debate. I will ignore those who would rather not talk about a moral revival in America because I believe it is as important as any other challenge that we face.

Barbara and I have crisscrossed the country today, started out in Missouri, went to Georgia, spent our afternoon in Birmingham, Alabama, where a crowd of 20,000 people were kind enough to wait in the rain to see us. As we came out on the stage, singer Lee Greenwood was just beginning that marvelous anthem you know, a beautiful version of the song "I'm Proud To Be an American."

As I looked over the crowd, the rain was pouring down, falling, and I saw a little girl with blond ringlets perched upon her dad's shoulders. She had a little ball cap on her head, an American flag in one hand. As Lee Greenwood began to sing she began to wave the flag, and I looked and in her other hand she had scrawled a sign. All the rain had smudged the ink, but I could still make out the words "I love America. America loves God."

That little girl will grow up in a world filled with miracle medicines, a world where all the volumes of all the books in the Library of Congress will be able to be stored on one tiny little disk. While scientific progress is good, it is my fervent hope that she will also come of age in a nation where family is always first and where the Creator is worshipped above all else. That is what has made America the greatest nation on God's Earth. It is our faith which will guarantee that the Sun never sets on our Nation.

I'm just delighted to have been with you. Thank you for inviting us. And may God bless this most wondrous land on the face of the Earth, the United States of America. Thank you very, very much.

Note: The President spoke at 9:25 p.m. at the Dallas Convention Center. In his remarks, he referred to Adrian Rogers, pastor, Bellevue Baptist Church, Memphis, TN; evangelists Jerry Falwell and Billy Graham; Edward V. Hill, pastor, Mount Zion Missionary Baptist Church, Los Angeles, CA; and National Affairs Briefing officers Ed McAteer, national chairman, Ed Drake, Dallas steering committee chairman, and Jack Graham, ministerial committee chairman.

Remarks to the Community in Springfield, Illinois
August 23, 1992

The President. Thank you, thank you. Thank you, Jim Edgar. You in Illinois are lucky to have Jim Edgar and Brenda here in Springfield, I'll tell you. And of course, I'm very pleased that Illinois' own Ed Madigan is our Secretary of Agriculture. He understands it, and he's doing a great job. May I salute Bob Kustra, the Lieutenant Governor, and his wife, Kathy; an old friend of mine, the secretary of state, George Ryan, and Lura Lynn. George has been at my side through a lot of political battles, and I'm very grateful to him.

May I salute a good Member of Congress; if we had more like him we wouldn't need to clean House. I'm talking about Representative Thomas Ewing here. And two others that I want to single out because as we talk about change, real change to help this country, we've got to change the Clinton-Gore gridlock Congress. We've got to change it. And in Rich Williamson running for the Senate, we have a man that can do just exactly that. He's with you on the values. He's with us on taxing less and spending less. He's with us on the fundamentals, and we must have him in the United States Senate. And I want to see John Shimkus elected from the 20th District.

I am going to do what Harry Truman did in this campaign. No, it's not give 'em hell, but they're going to think it's hell when I get through with them. But here's what it is. Look, I'll tell you why I'm going to do it this way. For months, I've held out my hand to the Congress only to have it bitten off. And now I am starting right here in Illinois. The Congressman from this district voted against us on Desert Storm. He tried to bring legal papers against me. He is against the balanced budget amendment. And I want John Shimkus to replace him in the United States Congress.

We've had it. We've had it with this gridlocked Congress. The American people have told Barbara and me, "Here are our values." And they've said, agreed with me in the election, "Here's want we want to do." And it hasn't worked because the Congress blocks us at every turn. You've got to turn out these—no matter how nice they are, how kind they talk about the farmer when they come back here, look at the record. Don't let them talk one way in Illinois and vote differently in Washington, DC.

And let me just say it is really great to be back in Springfield. Lincoln, you recall, Abraham that is, said of this, he said, "To this place and the kindness of these people I owe everything." I think he had good taste in political parties. I think he had great taste in hometowns.

And as you know, until Houston I stayed out of the actual political arena. I stayed out of it because I was trying to get some things done to bring tax relief, incentives for the first-time homebuyer, investment tax allowance, reduction in capital gains, trying to get those done for the farmer and for the American people. But I felt like one of those corndogs at the fair, skewered by the Democratic opposition for 9 months. And that's changing; it changed as of Houston, and it's going to change for every single of the remaining 73 days.

You know, we've had dramatic change. I see these kids here. And you do not hear a word about this from the Democratic Convention. Don't you think it's a wonderful thing that these young kids go to bed at night without the same fear of nuclear war that the generations precedent had? This is big. This is important.

So we've got our priorities. And one of them affects every single Illinois farmer: We must open markets abroad. We will get a GATT agreement. We've gotten a NAFTA agreement. And we cannot go for protection. One fact: One-third of the corn and soybeans grown in Illinois head for markets outside the United States. And if we can get that playing field level, if we get access to foreign markets, it means bonanza for the farmers in this country. They can outproduce anybody, outhustle them, outwork them. And so, open trade, free trade without apology is what I believe in and the case I'm taking to the American people.

Illinois farmers and workers feel that the Government takes too much and gives too little. And so, when next year Congress comes back in, I pledge a dramatic new effort to slash Federal spending and then get these taxes down.

Listen to the opponents on this one. It's wonderful new——

Audience members. Clean House! Clean 'House! Clean House!

The President. Yes, as soon as we get a Congress in that will do it. And I want to cut spending and taxes. And he accuses me of fearmongering? He's wrong. Capital gains is one right there. That's a good place to start. Get the income taxes down. And if you'll excuse me one political comment, I have a message for Governor Clinton:

Americans aren't afraid of cutting spending and lowering taxes. They fear most of all a rubber-stamp President that will rubber-stamp this spendthrift Congress. So there. We're not going to let that nightmare happen.

You know, I think that you all understand perhaps as well as any in America—certainly is true in rural America—the values, what we're talking about when we talk about family values. And here we learn that the family is there to teach us right from wrong, to lend a helping hand to a neighbor, respect for the law, hold out your hand to help somebody else, wipe a tear away when something goes wrong. Now, Barbara and I try to impart these values to our kids and grandkids. And I have great respect for what she has done, helping with literacy, helping other Americans to have a better life.

You know, today the American family is under attack. And we've got to defend it because it is the foundation of our nature. And that is why when we cut Government spending, I will fight for an increase in the personal income tax exemption so more Americans can afford to build and strengthen their families.

We're going to reform the welfare program to encourage families to stick together and have fathers stick around and do what they ought to do.

I see the signs out here of the teachers; God bless those people that teach our young people. And we have proposed the most far-reaching reform in American education in a century, and with a new Congress we will get it passed. We need to reform education, support the teachers, and be sure these kids can grow up in a competitive world number one.

I'll give you another idea why I want to change this Congress. I mentioned it in Houston. We are suing each other too much and caring for each other too little. And we have been trying for 3 years to reform the legal liability laws so that you don't have these excessive suits that drive doctors out of medicine, drive Little League coaches out of Little League. Locked in that gridlocked Congress by Bill Clinton and the liberal leadership in Washington. We've got to change it. We have got to change that gridlocked Congress. We've got to clean House.

Let me just say in conclusion: Two years ago I made, I think, the toughest decision that a President can make, and that is to send America's sons and daughters into battle. The sons and daughters of Illinois and every other State fought against aggression, fought to keep a people free, fought to prevent the Mideast from becoming a nuclear powder keg. Now they have come home. And this election, like every other, is about making an America that they can be proud of, an America we all can be proud of: good jobs, safe streets, and strong families. And so I ask for your support, not to change for the sake of change but to change America to make it more secure, more safe, more promising to every young person here today.

May God bless you all. And thank you for this fantastic rally. I am so proud to be back. Four more!

Note: The President spoke at 1:07 p.m. at the Illinois State Fairgrounds. In his remarks, he referred to Jim Edgar, Governor of Illinois, and his wife, Brenda.

Remarks on Disaster Assistance for Florida Following Hurricane Andrew
August 24, 1992

I just very briefly want to express my heartfelt concern to the people of Florida on this devastating storm. Apparently it's one of the worst, probably the worst in six decades. We've already gotten two FEMA teams, that's the Government emergency teams, down there in Florida. I will be declaring today that Florida is a disaster area. There will be 27 agencies of the Government then ready to help in any way that the Federal Government can help.

But I will be in touch during the day to see that everything runs smoothly and that we do everything we can to help the people down there. Apparently it was a very bad storm, a storm that kept the evaluation teams from sizing it up up until now, but I expect that'll change during the day. But it's a serious matter, and my heart goes out to the people in Florida.

Note: The President spoke at 8:06 a.m. on the South Lawn at the White House prior to his departure for Union, NJ.

Remarks at Lincoln Technical Institute in Union, New Jersey
August 24, 1992

The President. Thank you very much, Secretary Martin. Let me just salute our great Secretary of Labor and thank her very much for her introduction. Salute the former Governor of this State, Tom Kean. The working man and woman never had a better friend than Tom Kean. Mattie Rinaldo, he and I go back a long time. He's the Congressman from this area, doing a superb job. If we had more like him, we wouldn't have a gridlocked Congress. And I want to thank Pat Santangelo for the tour, and also Senator Don DiFrancesco and all the students and faculty here. This has been an inspiring visit.

Now, let me tell you why I've come to Lincoln Tech. I'm here today because of what will take place 71 days from now, because of the decision you're going to be making on November 3d. And that's going to set the course of this Nation. The defining challenge of the 1990's is to win the economic competition and to win the peace.

America's got to be—and is, a military superpower—an economic superpower, though, and an export superpower. Now, in this election you're going to hear two very different versions of how we go about this. Theirs is to look inward and protect what we've got. And ours is to look forward to open new markets, to create incentives, to restore our social fabric, and to prepare our people to compete so that we can win. And that's what this is all about here today.

I want to talk about the last of those challenges, the new ways to prepare our American workers to compete. We know the world economy is changing. And America must change with it. As President, we worked to create new jobs, open new markets all the way from Moscow to Mexico. And that means new American jobs from Union, New Jersey, all the way out to California.

Right now, one in every six Americans' manufacturing job is tied directly to exports. And that doesn't count the economic ripple effect created when those workers pay the mortgage, buy a car, or feed the kids. Since 1988, three-fifths of all of our economic growth has come from people in other countries buying what's made in the United States of America, the good products made right here in New Jersey.

Now, the jobs in these new export industries demand workers with higher skills than the old economy. And workers must realize what you know here at Lincoln: During the course of a career you may develop as many as five or six skills or proficiencies, putting a premium on flexibility, long-life learning. Now, these principles are reflected in a new commitment to job training. This is a new national commitment to job training that I'm unveiling today, a program that is bold. It is innovative, and it is loyal only to the future and to the needs of the American workers.

Now, earlier this year we introduced a program called Job Training 2000, a comprehensive program to streamline this crazy quilt of over 100 different Federal jobs programs. Now that we've designed that effective structure for delivering job training, I want to expand on our efforts. If our Nation is to succeed in this world economy, we cannot afford to waste the talent of one single worker. And that means we need better training for young people first coming into the work force, better retraining for workers that are changing careers, and better training and assistance for workers who lose their jobs.

You start with this new initiative. We call it the Youth Training Corps. The program is aimed at young people, primarily in our inner cities, kids with talent, kids with ambition, but with no outlets for their abilities other than a life of drugs and crime. Right now we have a great program called the conservation centers, which takes these kids to job training centers, often in rural areas, puts them to work, for example, helping rebuild the parks or recreation and community facilities. But at the same time these kids learn a skill, find out how to manage their finances, and get counseling about how to break away from the temptations of the mean streets that they once hung out on.

Now, we're going to build on those conservation centers, add 25 new centers with positions for 43,000 new trainees. And to staff these centers we will give hiring priority to former members of our Armed Forces, people with the proven leadership skills—these people, they've demonstrated that they can lead—proven leadership skills, the drive, and the discipline that breeds success.

Now, we need to expand our existing efforts to teach high school kids about their opportunities in life, provide them strong role models, and encourage a sense of personal responsibility and discipline. And so also today I am also doubling the size of our Junior ROTC program. It is in almost 1,500 schools today; we're going to expand it to 2,900 schools. And with $50 million a year in new funding, another 150,000 kids will get the benefit of what has been a great program that boosts high school competition, high school completion rates, reduces drug use, raises self-esteem, and gets these kids firmly on the right track.

Now, I will also urge the Congress to expand my youth apprenticeship program. This one's aimed at high school juniors and seniors who may be in danger of dropping out. And the program combines classroom instruction with structured work programs. And when students finish, they not only have a diploma, they have a certificate saying they've developed a skill and can get a job. Right now this program is working as a demonstration project in six States. It ought to be expanded. If I have my way, it will be expanded to all 50 States.

Another part of this: We'll also do more for troubled kids, and we'll connect our efforts to get the young people off of drugs with the skills that help them get a clean start. We are going to expand drug treatment to reach an additional 28,000 kids a year. We're going to tie successful drug treatment to job training. I call it Treat and Train. It will guarantee these kids a place in our job training program the moment they finish rehabilitation.

So helping young people is a part of the picture. But if we want to compete, we've got to help older workers obtain new skills. These are people caught in the transition of our economy, eager to earn new skills so they can get new jobs and protect their standard of living. And that's why I'm announcing today a dramatic new departure in job training for Americans in the middle of their careers.

The key concept here is something I call skill grants. These are vouchers worth up to $3,000 per person that can be used toward training programs of their choice. And these vouchers can go not simply to those that are unemployed but to those who worry the next pink slip may be coming their way, to help defense workers retool, to help workers in declining industries sharpen the skills that they'll need to stay one step ahead. What Pell grants have done to open up opportunities for our younger kids, skill grants will do for experienced workers in need of new skills.

The program will focus on the needs of what we call dislocated workers, people in industries that are changing because of global competition. Twelve days ago I announced the North American free trade agreement to open new economic opportunities for American products from the Yukon to Yucatan. In the 1990's that agreement will create millions of new American jobs, but near-term may also mean dislocations in some industries. And thus, I've as-

sured the Congress that I'd work with them to ease the transition for the workers in the NAFTA. Today's plan will meet that commitment.

My plan sets aside up to, I think it's $670 million per year for the Secretary of Labor to pump into areas that might be negatively affected by NAFTA. This funding is more than enough to ensure that any and every affected worker gets the kind of training he or she needs. And more important, they'll have a choice, get them into programs that they want to be in, not shoehorned into some training program that just happens to have openings.

Now, that's our approach to job training. And it rests on the proposition that we should empower people with skills instead of empowering bureaucracies with people. Just a quick political word here: My opponent agrees with this in principle, but when you get to the details we really do have a vast philosophical difference. I believe we can pay for this new job training offensive without raising taxes on people or increasing overall Government spending.

We've got to make the tough calls. This is a priority. We've got to make the tough calls, set the budget priorities. This entire proposal, and yes, it's going to cost money, but it will be funded under the budget caps. And I will project these in more detail as we move into the next budget cycle.

My opponent is different. He sees job training as a tax raiser, and he wants to tax workers to pay for their own training and tax small businesses—this is the one that's the worst——

Audience members. Boo-o-o!

The President. ——taxing small businesses around the country 1.5 percent. That is 1.5 that will come out of your paycheck, and it's on top of the new income and other payroll taxes he's proposing. Think of what this is going to do to small business, which has created over two-thirds of the new jobs in the past decade. So let me say this to my opponent: There is no point in training people for jobs if your plan is going to be in the process of destroying jobs.

And there's another difference between our two approaches. My opponent says he'll do more to help defense workers coping with the post-cold-war economic realities. What he won't tell you, though, is this: We sent forward a prudent defense budget. Because of what we've accomplished around the world, because the world is more peaceful, we are able to reduce spending. But he sent forward a program that plans $60 billion in additional cuts in defense beyond what the experts say is responsible. And that not only will damage the national defense, it will throw one million more defense-related industry employees out of work and on to the unemployment rolls. And I'm not going to have it, on two counts: adding to the unemployment, but fundamentally I must protect the national security of the United States.

Once these workers have lost those jobs, high-paid, high-tech jobs, the other side will step in with some, you know, kind of a make-work program. Someone ought to ask the workers whether they would rather have their high-tech jobs and good training for another high-tech industry, or some short-term Government make-work job. I vote for the former. We can do it. We can get everybody engaged in high-tech jobs with this retraining approach.

Now, the big point I want to make here in this working State is higher spending and higher taxes will not do any favors to the American worker. According to one congressional analysis, it could cost America almost 3 million jobs, this tax-and-spend approach. And my opponent's whole approach reminds me of the guy with the head cold. The doctor wants to amputate his leg. And to the patient it sounds a little odd, you know, a little radical. To the doctor it's logical: If your cold settles in your lungs, you'll get pneumonia; if you get pneumonia, your circulation will go; if your circulation goes, you'll get gangrene. So just to be safe,

better take off the leg. [*Laughter*]

Well, that ain't it. That's not going to get the job done. We need a new approach and one that doesn't cripple the economy and then offer workers a crutch, one that helps people keep the jobs they have, creates the new jobs that they demand, and one that helps America retool for the challenges of a new century, for the challenges of your lifetime.

I like the spirit here at Lincoln. The people at Lincoln, students and faculty, seem to understand that training for jobs that exist and moving people up the ladder is the goal that we all ought to share. It's certainly one I do. And I appreciate this visit very much.

You know, I put forward this approach. I'm going to fight for it in the campaign, fight for it with what I hope is a new, non-gridlocked Congress—that is fouling up everything in this country. And so I appreciate very much what you all have shown me here today. I wish each and every student at this wonderful institution Godspeed and good luck. And I'll tell you, I will do my level-best to hold the line on the taxes and to hold the line on the spending and create new jobs through this kind of new job training approach.

Thank you all, and God bless you. May God bless you all. And let me say this: I know things have been tough, but we are the United States of America. We can overcome our problems and continue to lead in the world. Thank you very much.

Note: The President spoke at 10:05 a.m. in the main automotive shop area. In his remarks, he referred to P.J. Santangelo, Lincoln Technical Institute president and chief executive officer, and Donald T. DiFrancesco, New Jersey State Senate president.

Excerpts of a Statement by Press Secretary Fitzwater on Disaster Assistance for Florida Following Hurricane Andrew
August 24, 1992

The President has ordered Federal assistance to the State of Florida to help in the disaster relief efforts going on there. He has just signed the declaration declaring three counties, Dade, Broward, and Monroe, as eligible for disaster assistance. We probably will have other counties come in later.

The President talked to the Governor this morning by telephone and expressed that he wanted to make sure he knew that he would have the full support of the Federal Government in this effort.

We will be going to Florida within an hour or two. We will probably step up the pace of this event a little bit and depart here at around 3 p.m. to 3:20 p.m. for Florida.

Wallace Stickney, who is the head of the FEMA, Federal Emergency Management Agency, and Senator Connie Mack will be joining us, and we will fly to Opa Locka, Florida, arriving there probably a couple of hours after we depart here.

———

We don't have very much information at the moment. The initial damage estimates, the requests for assistance cover about $50 million, but the initial reports of damage could go as high as $6 billion to $8 billion.

So this is just the beginning, but we want to get on the scene quickly and start making available funds for housing particularly and for cleanup and for other emergency needs.

Note: Press Secretary Fitzwater spoke to reporters at 2 p.m. in Warsaw Park Hall in Ansonia, CT. The statement also provided schedule and departure information for the press.

Remarks to the Chamber of Commerce in Ansonia, Connecticut
August 24, 1992

The President. Thank you very, very much. Michael, thank you and all the others at the Chamber. Thank you for that introduction. Let me just explain what Michael was talking about. There has been this hurricane down in Florida, and so we leave right from here to go down to Newark, take the plane, and head on down to look at that damage and express our concerns to the people there.

But I am just delighted to be here. A warm reception coming into town. I want to thank David Rifkin and especially the Mayor Thomas Hallihan. Let me also mention an old friend and a good man, Gary Franks, who's the Congressman here. I am so indebted to him. And another that you all know so well in this valley, John Rowland, he's a great man, and I want to see him do more. I was touched by the Reverend Father Weiss' invocation. And I want to ask today that we now take a little political look ahead to the fall.

I'll tell you something. I came out of that Houston convention, and the whole spirit around this country is different. I am determined to win this election, and I'm determined to do it fair and square. If I hadn't been fired up when I walked in here, the Company, that great music, would have got it going, I'll tell you. That was fantastic. I don't even know where they are.

But anyway, we're looking ahead to a great classic that takes place this fall. I'm not talking about Ansonia versus Derby— [*laughter*]—I'm talking about the November 3d contest. That does have a lot to do with the direction of this country and also the new century beyond.

I heard my grandson speak at our convention, and I was so very proud of that young kid. It just reminded me on a very personal basis of what the Reverend Father was talking about and the job that lies ahead of us, to make life better for all.

Now, we have witnessed, as I pointed out down there, a world of change from Managua to Moscow. Millions of men and women now turn towards freedom. They're celebrating a new birth of freedom. I believe people right here in the valley, many of whom came here from other countries, many of whose family came here, understand what I'm talking about when I say this Nation can take pride in the freedom of others. Many right in this room, because of family, not just because of freedom and democracy, because of family, prayed for this day of freedom to come to Eastern Europe, to Russia, to the countries south of our border. We've witnessed this remarkable change, and this miracle has come true.

So now the challenge for this country is to bring that spirit home from Warsaw, Poland, to Warsaw Park and to focus this great Nation on the mission ahead. We have literally changed the world with the help of the taxpayer, Presidents that preceded me, fighting men and women that have served this great country with distinction. We've changed the world, and now we must change America for the better.

Our challenge quite simply is to win the global economic challenge, to win the peace, be a military superpower, an economic superpower, an export superpower. In this election you're going to hear two very different visions of how to do this. Theirs is to turn inward and protect; and ours is to look outward and open new markets and prepare our people to compete, to restore social fabric, to save and invest. When I'm talking about investment, I don't mean more taxpayer money going into Government investment. I mean more private investment, small business investment.

I don't want to get too personal in this wonderful area that I understand has some wonderfully smart Democrats, because I need you guys in the fall. But let me say this, that my opponent has spent most of his adult life in government, and that's pretty much, I think, all he knows about. But his idea about creating jobs is to have Government jobs, public payroll jobs. And I come at things a different way. I spent, I computed it the other day, half of my adult life in government service, one kind or another, and half in the private sector. Long before I was in the public sector, I worked for a living out in the oilfields of west Texas, built a company, and did what many here has in small or larger operations, I met a payroll. I took risks, and I made it work. I happen to think having held a job is not a bad qualification even for President of the United States of America.

Look, the world economy is changing, and we've got to be in the lead of that change. Think of the economic changes you've seen right here in Ansonia, from moving from that brass and copper age in the mills along the Naugatuck to the new corporate headquarters in the industrial parks across the valley. Right now one in every six American manufacturing jobs is tied directly to exports. That doesn't count the economic ripple effect created when those workers pay mortgages or buy a car or feed the kids.

Since '88, since 1988, three-fifths of the economic growth has come from people in other countries buying what we do best, the products we make right here in America. We are the best manufacturers in the world, and don't let anybody tell you, don't you let that gloomy opposition tell you we can't compete or say that we're a nation in decline. We are not.

As President, I'm working now to create jobs, new markets, markets in Moscow, markets in Mexico City that mean new American jobs. I am convinced that the answer is not to build a wall around our economy, not to put the Government in charge but to use the Government to help you literally go back to work in this country. That's what I want to tell you, how I'm going to do it.

Here are some of what we stand for: open markets for American products. Here's one we have a big difference on: lower Government spending and tax relief, not spend and tax; tax relief and less Federal Government spending. And the other one is opportunities for small business. We've got to do better getting the regulatory burden off the back of these mom-and-pop, these small operators. We're going to keep doing it until we get that job done.

You know my feeling about too many lawsuits in this country. I've been fighting to change that, blocked by this gridlocked Congress. We sue each other too much. We care for each other too little. We've got to break the back of those that are breaking this country with these damn lawsuits.

Audience members. Clean House! Clean House! Clean House!

The President. I'll get to that. New schools—and I know we've got some teachers here, and God bless them. But I'll tell you something. We need new schools to back up these teachers, new ideas. Our whole program, America 2000, is a good program to literally revolutionize how we bring our kids into the next century. It's exciting program. I might say, we've got to win this fight on narcotics. Teenage use of cocaine is down, but we've just begun to fight. We've got to win it, clean out these schoolyards.

You know, a big difference is, a big one, I do believe that they're too big in Government and spend too much. Last week I offered an idea to get the deficit down. We'll give you a special box—I believe that people should have it—a special box on that tax return to check so that up to 10 percent of your income tax can go for one purpose, and that is to reduce the budget deficit. If Congress doesn't like it—all these editorials that you read around here on some of these sophisticated journals don't like it—but the Congress has failed to do it. So let's get the people a chance to check that box, and then we have to live with it.

Then there's something that's very important to the valley that I talked about today in Union, New Jersey, a dramatic new approach to job training: To help young people find that first job, a program we call the Youth Training Corps, to get inner-city kids off the mean streets and get them a second chance to build the skills they need to succeed. For older workers who have lost their job or worry that next pay envelope may have a pink slip, we've developed a new concept called skill grants, vouchers worth $3,000 to be used towards the training program of their choice. Our plan is based on empowering people to get the kind of training they want, not empowering the bureaucracies to hire more people. That is a very different approach than the approach the others are taking toward job training.

The Governor of Arkansas says he's all for free enterprise. Then he proposes right out of the box the largest tax increase in history, much of it on the back of small business. I learned the hard way, holding out my hand to that gridlocked Congress, and they

bit it off. Once you make one mistake you don't make it again. I am not going to go forward and go with this program of spending and taxes.

We've literally proposed, and it's before Congress right now, eliminating over 200 programs and 4,000 projects. It's there; it's put down in detail. It's before this gridlocked Congress. We've got to do something about changing the Congress. If we had more people like Gary Franks, we wouldn't have a gridlock problem. But the Congress has been controlled, they have been controlled by the same party for 38 years. Everything else has changed in the country; not the House of Representatives. Help me change the House. Clean it. Clean the House.

My opponent says he's for fiscal responsibility. He's against a balanced budget amendment. Says he's for a line-item veto, but the gridlocked Congress refuses to give it to the President. I stand for something different. I want to see us cut that Federal spending with the help of a new Congress, get the taxes down so we can get the economy stimulated and let people keep a little more of what they earn. It's a big philosophical difference between the Bush-Quayle ticket on the one hand and Clinton-Gore on the other. Look at it. It is fundamentally different.

Now, in this campaign, we've got to call it as we see it. This year I believe the choice is very clear. We've got two different, fundamentally different approaches. I believe in the Government. You get all this talk: Government, Government, of the Government, by the Government, for the Government. That's not going to get the job done. We are fighting against that because we happen to believe still that the power should flow from the people, so it's of the people, by the people, and for the people. Really, what's at stake here is the future of this country.

We're in choppy waters. I heard the Reverend. I know it. People that are hurting and can't find jobs when they need it. I'll tell you another area we've got a big difference: on the defense spending. I have cut defense, but we're not going to cut into the muscle of the defense. The other side wants to take $60 billion more than Colin Powell and Cheney tell me is the right level. We still have a tough world out there. We must still be strong. While you're thinking about it, we don't needlessly need to throw another million defense workers out of work by cutting back on defense below the levels needed for national security.

Let me just tell you, I wish Barbara Bush were here. This would be great for her morale. This would be great for her spirits.

But I'll tell you something. I want to be serious about this one point. When I drove in here today—and I've been here as some of you know many, many times. My dad was a Senator from this State, and we grew up down the way. Leave out the politics for just a minute. When I came in here this morning, a lot of the people out there were waving. I'm sure they were not for me. They were there because I am privileged to be the President of the United States of America.

But you sense something else out there along the highway. You sense this community feeling and this feeling of family. I want to tell you something. The cynics, the liberal theoreticians, they can ridicule me all they want when I talk about family values. But this one transcends Democrat. It transcends Republican. It gets to the heart of what our community is about. The community has been diminished by the decimation and sometimes the decline of the American family.

I saw it today, that family spirit is still strong. And I just want to pledge to you, I am not going to get off talking about that because we must find ways—whether it's welfare reform, whether it's making the fathers that run away stay there, whether it's helping, as Barbara does, hold someone in the arms to demonstrate the compassion and love we feel for our fellow man—we've got to find ways to strengthen the American family. It is not demagoguery. It's fundamental to America.

She and I will continue to try to do our level-best to set a level of decency and honor and, hopefully, trust there in the Oval Office and there in the White House.

Thank you very much for this wonderful reception. May God bless the Naugatuck Valley, and may God bless the United States of America.

Note: The President spoke at 2:05 p.m. in Warsaw Park Hall. In his remarks, he referred to Michael Pacowta, president, and David Rifkin, chairman, Greater Valley Chamber of Commerce; former Representative John Rowland; and Father Robert Weiss, pastor, St. Joseph's Church.

White House Fact Sheet: Worker Adjustment Initiative
August 24, 1992

The President today announced a new, comprehensive $10 billion worker adjustment initiative to assure that American workers have the training and skills they need for employment security today and into the next century.

The President's proposal features:

Universal coverage. All dislocated workers would have access to basic transition assistance and training support.

Skill grants. Vouchers of up to $3,000 would be available to help meet the costs of providing new skills and training for dislocated workers.

$10 billion in Federal funding. The plan almost triples the resources currently devoted to skill training and worker adjustment—to $2 billion a year in each of the next 5 years. This level of funding is sufficient to ensure that workers anticipated to need these adjustment services will have access to those services.

The Problem

Three related developments have created the need for a flexible, adaptable, well-trained, and highly-skilled workforce in the United States.

First, world trade is expanding and promises to continue to expand during the coming decade. The United States has been at the forefront of this effort through the Uruguay round GATT negotiations and the North American free trade agreement. Expanding trade brings with it great opportunities for exports and job creation. But, it also brings with it the need for adjustment as nations concentrate on what they do best.

Second, the pace of technological change has accelerated. Computers and innovations in production technology have sharply increased manufacturing productivity. Technological advances are reducing the need for certain skills and increasing the need for others.

Third, the end of the cold war provides the U.S. with an historic opportunity to re-evaluate and revise its national security requirements. This development inevitably involves redeploying resources, including human resources, from the defense to the civilian economy.

These changes create new opportunities; they also involve adjustments. Adult workers who lose their jobs need the training and skills that will allow them to adjust and adapt in a dynamic economy, to make the transition to new industries and occupations, and to compete successfully in the global marketplace.

The problem and the challenge is how best to facilitate the development of a dynamic, well-trained workforce that will keep the U.S. globally competitive.

The President's Proposal

In January, the President announced a comprehensive, streamlined Federal job training system that provides "one-stop shopping" for job training services in every community. This structure is designed to meet the Nation's workforce needs into the next century.

Building on this plan, the President proposes to complete the restructuring of Federal job training programs by replacing the current dislocated worker adjustment programs under the Economic Dislocation and Worker Adjustment Assistance (EDWAA) and Trade Adjustment Assistance (TAA) Acts with a new $2 billion a year comprehensive retraining and transition assistance program.

The Department of Labor's new Advancing Skills through Education and Training Services (ASETS) program will assist all dislocated workers, including those who may change jobs or careers as a result of the North American free trade agreement (NAFTA), as well as other workers in changing industries who need training in new skills.

The President's proposal would serve: workers who have lost their jobs, workers who have been notified their jobs are being terminated, and workers employed in industries experiencing significant changes and work force adjustments who fear job loss in the future.

Dislocated workers would be eligible to receive three types of assistance: transition assistance, to help them find and secure new employment. This includes: skills assessment, counseling, job search assistance and job referral services; training assistance, in the form of skill grants, for those workers who want and need retraining and skills development; transition income support, where necessary, for workers completing retraining.

Program Funding

The President's program would be funded at $10 billion over the next 5 years—$2 billion annually—and structured as a capped mandatory program to ensure continuity of funding. At this funding level, an estimated 1.2 million workers could be served annually. Two-thirds of the total annual funding ($1.3 billion) would be allocated to the States. These funds would more than triple the resources now available to States through EDWAA to respond to dislocations. States would provide basic transition assistance service and skill grants for training to dislocated workers regardless of the cause of dislocation, including trade and NAFTA-related employment changes, defense adjustments, etc. One-third of the total annual funding ($670 million) would be retained by the Secretary of Labor for discretionary allocation for uses of national priority. At least $335 million a year would be reserved specifically to respond to

NAFTA-related dislocations. The balance would be reserved to respond to multi-state and industry-wide dislocations (e.g., defense-related layoffs and environmental impacts). This triples the existing funding for these programs. If NAFTA-related dislocations require more funding, the Secretary may shift the allocation to as high as the full $670 million per annum. Likewise, if NAFTA dislocations require less, as is likely to be the case, the Secretary may shift those resources to other priority dislocations.

Transition Assistance

Every dislocated worker would be eligible to receive basic transition assistance, including: an assessment of their current skills, counseling, help in résumé preparation and interviewing skills, job search assistance and job referral services.

Skill Grants for Training

In addition to basic transition assistance, many dislocated workers may need to develop additional skills or upgrade their current skills. The President's proposal would provide dislocated workers with a skill grant in the form of a voucher. Grants would be awarded in amounts up to $3,000 per year. Workers would be eligible for the grants for up to 2 years. The grant could be redeemed at any qualified college, junior college, community college or public or private trade school or training institution. Workers would have the freedom and flexibility to choose the type of training that would best meet their needs and aspirations.

Funding priority for individuals applying for the skill grants would be: (1) currently dislocated workers; (2) soon-to-be dislocated workers; (3) workers employed in industries experiencing significant work force adjustments who fear future dislocations.

Transition Income Maintenance

Dislocated workers who enter training early in their unemployment, have exhausted their unemployment insurance benefits, and need income support to complete their training will be eligible to receive transitional income maintenance.

White House Fact Sheet: Youth Skills Initiative
August 24, 1992

The President announced today his Youth Skills Initiative, a new strategy to prepare our Nation's non-college-bound youth for success in the rapidly changing workplace. The President's Youth Skills Initiative consists of four major elements:

Youth Training Corps (YTC). A new residential and nonresidential training program for economically and socially disadvantaged youth;

Treat and Train. A comprehensive youth drug treatment program that will tie rehabilitation together with the Youth Training Corps to ensure that rehabilitated kids get the training needed for a new start in life;

National Youth Apprenticeship Program. A comprehensive school-to-work transition training program for high school juniors and seniors.

Junior Reserve Officer Training Corps (JROTC). Doubling the size of the existing voluntary instructional program for high school students that emphasizes self-discipline, family and social values, citizenship, and personal responsibility.

The Problem

Put simply, the United States needs an increasingly better trained and skilled workforce for the remainder of this decade and the next century. International competition, the expansion of new and complex technologies into the workplace, and a dynamic labor market require a well-trained and highly-skilled work force. One of our greatest challenges in creating such a work force is to facilitate the transition from school to work for non-college-bound youth.

Of the students enrolled in the 11th and 12th grades this fall, approximately 40 percent will not immediately go to college. Of those who do attend, half will fail to complete their first year. Moreover, roughly one-fifth of American high school students either drop out or do not complete high school graduation requirements on schedule.

These young Americans need to acquire the vocational training and workplace skills that will allow them to compete successfully in the job marketplace.

The President's Proposal

In January, the President announced a comprehensive initiative to streamline the Federal job training system designed to implement "one-stop shopping" for job training in every community. Building upon this concept, the President has proposed a comprehensive plan to expand and improve job training for non-college-bound youth.

The President's Youth Skills Initiative consists of four major elements:

Youth Training Corps (YTC)

The Youth Training Corps will provide economically and socially disadvantaged youth with intensive vocational training and workplace skills. This training will be combined with community service and conservation work in rural areas and on public lands.

The Youth Training Corps will create 25 new YTC centers patterned after the Job Corps' 30 existing Civilian Conservation Corps (CCC) centers to create a total of 55 residential YTC centers nationwide.

These residential centers, located primarily in rural areas, will utilize converted Department of Defense facilities, where appropriate.

Hiring preference for YTC staff will be given to individuals leaving military service. This will allow the YTC to take advantage of the military's high level of leadership and training expertise.

The President's proposal will add 29,600 new training slots that will help 43,000 additional kids each year. Of these additional slots: 16,600 slots will be residential, located at the 25 new YTC centers; 13,000 slots will be non-residential, located at existing Job Corps centers.

The President's proposals will serve an additional 43,000 disadvantaged youths

(ages 16 to 21) annually. This will bring the total number of youths served annually by both the YTC and Job Corps to 113,000: 18,700 additional youths would be served at the 25 new YTC centers; 24,300 additional youths would be served on a non-residential basis at new or existing centers.

The YTC will utilize an expanded Job Corps model, relying on a combination of remedial education, technical training, life-skills training, counseling, and other support services.

The YTC participants will spend an average of 7 months as a resident at the Youth Training Corps center and receive both applied learning experiences and basic job training. Participants will work to help improve parks, recreation, or community facilities, and public/low-income housing.

The YTC would have an initial, start-up cost of $200 million (FY 1994 and FY 1995), expanding to $385 million per year when fully in place.

Treat and Train Program

This initiative will strengthen existing youth drug treatment programs and complement the Youth Training Corps. The President's proposal will fund 10,000 new drug treatment slots at intensive drug rehabilitation centers. Two-thirds of the new slots will be residential. Participants stay in the residential centers an average 9 months. One-third of the new slots will be out-patient. The President's proposal will serve an additional 28,000 youths annually, increasing the number of youth served by Federally-funded treatment by roughly 30 percent. Successfully completing the treatment program will give participants priority status for admission to the Youth Training Corps (YTC). The program will cost $150 million per year beginning in FY 1994.

National Youth Apprenticeship Program

This initiative will substantially expand the President's "National Youth Apprenticeship Act of 1992," which was initiated in January as a component of the Job Training 2000 proposal and transmitted to the Congress in May. This plan is a comprehensive, voluntary program for high school juniors and seniors that combines classroom instruction with a structured, paid, work experience program. The Department of Labor will provide community organization funding, planning, and curriculum design using the current six-State demonstration program as a model to expand the program to all 50 States. Students who successfully complete the program receive a high school diploma and a widely-recognized certificate of skill competency. Students will also have the opportunity to continue training at the post-secondary level. The Targeted Jobs Tax Credit will be available to employers to cover participating students that meet current TJTC economically disadvantaged eligibility criteria. The National Youth Apprenticeship program will cost $100 million per year beginning in FY 1994. The TJTC expansion will cost an estimated $10 million in FY 1994 and $160 million over 5 years.

Junior Reserve Officer Training Corps (JROTC)

This initiative will more than double the size of the present JROTC program, a very successful and popular partnership between the military services and the public and private schools. JROTC emphasizes self-discipline, values, citizenship, personal responsibility, and staying in school among high school students, and provides an alternative to drugs and gangs. The President's proposal will add 1,500 new JROTC units to the present 1,482 units, and will include as many as 225,000 more high school students. The program will emphasize increasing the number of inner city high school JROTC programs initially, but plans call for JROTC to be made available to every high school across the country that requests it and qualifies. The goal is to establish 2,900 units by 1994. JROTC is a low-cost education program that provides those who participate in it with positive incentives to stay in school. Well-trained, highly motivated former military personnel serve as instructors. This initiative will provide job opportunities for highly qualified personnel retiring from military service. The Department of Defense will help local school systems absorb some of the costs for the new inner-city school JROTC programs.

Appointment of Robert B. Zoellick as Deputy Chief of Staff to the President
August 24, 1992

The President today announced the appointment of Robert B. Zoellick, of the District of Columbia, to be Deputy Chief of Staff to the President.

Since 1991, Mr. Zoellick has served as Under Secretary of State for Economic and Agricultural Affairs and also as Counselor of the Department of State since 1989. Prior to this, Mr. Zoellick served on the State Department transition, 1988–89. Mr. Zoellick also has served in several capacities at the Department of the Treasury: Counselor to the Secretary of the Treasury and Executive Secretary, 1988; Executive Secretary and Special Advisor to the Secretary, 1986–87; Deputy Assistant Secretary for Financial Institutions Policy, 1985–86; Acting Deputy Assistant Secretary for Financial Institutions

Policy, 1985–86; and Special Assistant to the Deputy Secretary, 1985. In addition, Mr. Zoellick has served as a law clerk for the U.S. Court of Appeals for the District of Columbia Circuit, 1982–83; as a staff assistant in the Office of the Assistant Attorney General in the Criminal Division at the Department of Justice, 1978–79; and as a research assistant for the Council on Wage and Price Stability in the Executive Office of the President, 1975–76.

Mr. Zoellick graduated from Swarthmore College (B.A., 1975), Harvard University's Kennedy School of Government (M.P.P., 1981), and Harvard Law School (J.D., 1981). He was born July 25, 1953, in Evergreen Park, IL. Mr. Zoellick is married and resides in Washington, DC.

Appointment of Margaret DeBardeleben Tutwiler as Assistant to the President for Communications
August 24, 1992

The President today announced the appointment of Margaret DeBardeleben Tutwiler as Assistant to the President for Communications.

Since 1989, Miss Tutwiler has served as Assistant Secretary of State for Public Affairs and Department Spokesman. Prior to this, Miss Tutwiler served as deputy to the chairman of the Bush-Quayle '88 campaign and as Assistant Secretary for Public Affairs and Public Liaison at the U.S. Department of the Treasury, 1985–88. Prior to her work at Treasury, Miss Tutwiler was a member of President Reagan's senior White House staff, serving as Deputy Assistant to the President for Political Affairs, 1984–85. Following President Reagans' reelection in 1984, Miss Tutwiler was Director of Public Liaison for the 50th American Presidential Inaugural; and from 1980 to 1984, Special Assistant to the President and Executive Assistant to the Chief of Staff. In 1985, Miss Tutwiler served as a member of the U.S.

delegation to the 1985 World Conference to Review and Appraise the Achievements of the United Nations Decade for Women in Nairobi, Kenya. She was also a member of the American Center for International Leadership's delegation from the United States to the Soviet Union in October of 1986.

Miss Tutwiler was the public affairs representative for the National Association of Manufacturers in Alabama and Mississippi before joining Ambassador George Bush's Presidential campaign as director of scheduling in 1978. Following the Republican Convention in 1980, she continued as director of scheduling for Vice Presidential candidate Bush. She began her political career in 1974 with the Alabama Republican Party and from 1975 to 1976 worked for President Gerald Ford's reelection campaign.

Born in Birmingham, AL, on December 28, 1950, Miss Tutwiler attended Finch College and graduated from the University of Alabama in 1973.

Appointment of Janet G. Mullins as Assistant to the President for Political Affairs
August 24, 1992

The President today announced the appointment of Janet G. Mullins as Assistant to the President for Political Affairs.

Since 1989, Ms. Mullins has served as Assistant Secretary of State for Legislative Affairs. Prior to this appointment, she served as director of congressional affairs for the Presidential transition. She served in Kentucky State government as special assistant to the deputy secretary of commerce, specializing in international and agricultural trade. From 1979 to 1982, Ms. Mullins was legislative director and chief of staff for Senator Bob Packwood of Oregon. In 1984, she managed the successful Senate campaign of Mitch McConnell of Kentucky. Ms.

Mullins was the first woman to run a statewide Senate campaign in Kentucky. She went on to serve as chief of staff for Senator McConnell from 1985 to 1987. In 1987, Ms. Mullins was named executive director of the Fund for America's Future, then-Vice President Bush's political action committee. She joined the Bush campaign in September of 1987, serving as national field director for the Bush primary campaign. During the general election, she was deputy national political director and media director.

Ms. Mullins received her B.A. in political science at the University of Louisville and studied international economics at American University in Washington, DC. She was born September 7, 1949, in Louisville, KY, and has one daughter.

Appointment of Dennis B. Ross as Assistant to the President for Policy Planning
August 24, 1992

The President today announced the appointment of Dennis B. Ross as Assistant to the President for Policy Planning.

Since 1989, Mr. Ross has been Director of the Policy Planning Staff of the Department of State. In that position he played a major role in formulating and implementing U.S. policy toward the former Soviet Union and the Middle East peace process. Prior to becoming Director, Mr. Ross served as the senior foreign policy adviser to the George Bush campaign and the head of national security affairs during the Presidential transition. He was the Director of Near East and South Asian Affairs on the National Security Council staff from May 1986 to July 1988. From 1984 to 1986, he was outside the Government in the academic world, serving as the executive director of the Berkeley-Stanford program on Soviet international behavior. In the early 1980's, he held positions in both the State and Defense Departments, serving first as a member of the policy planning staff with responsibility for Middle Eastern issues. Later, from 1982 to 1984, he was the Deputy Director of the Office of Net Assessment in the Pentagon, working principally on Soviet, Middle Eastern, and broad military balance issues.

Mr. Ross did his undergraduate and graduate studies at UCLA, wrote a doctoral dissertation on Soviet decisionmaking, and has published extensively on Soviet and Middle Eastern policy questions. He was born on November 26, 1948, in San Francisco, CA. Mr. Ross is married and has three children.

Nomination of Randall Harvey Erben To Be an Assistant Secretary of Housing and Urban Development
August 24, 1992

The President today announced his intention to nominate Randall Harvey Erben, of Texas, to be an Assistant Secretary of Housing and Urban Development for Community Planning and Development. He would succeed Skirma Anna Kondratas.

Currently Mr. Erben serves as Deputy Assistant Secretary for Community Planning and Development at the Department of Housing and Urban Development. Prior to this, he served as director of the State of Texas Office of State-Federal Relations, 1989–91; assistant secretary of state for the State of Texas, 1987–89; and a member and shareholder with the law firm of Foster, Lewis, Langley, Gardner & Banack, Inc., 1981–87.

Mr. Erben graduated from Princeton University (A.B., 1978) and the University of Texas School of Law (J.D., 1981). He was born August 23, 1956, in San Antonio, TX. Mr. Erben is married and currently resides in Bethesda, MD.

Remarks to the American Legion National Convention in Chicago, Illinois
August 25, 1992

Thank you very, very much. And may I salute our Governor who is with me; our Secretary, Ed Derwinski; Governor Edgar here. And thank you, Dom, for that introduction. He put a lot of emphasis on that "paid up" member. [*Laughter*] You've had a great leader here, and I know you're going to have another great one. But I just salute Dom for all he's stood for. And let me also mention Sparky Gierke who is serving with the same devotion he served those here at the Legion, serving in the administration.

A lot happens in a week. A week ago, I could have laid claim to being the second most charismatic member of the Bush family. But after my grandson got up there, George P., at our convention in Houston, I guess I'm now the second most charismatic George Bush. Things are not going well here. [*Laughter*] So anyway, I mention this only because I know how Legionnaires feel about family. And I hope you'll excuse me if I say I was very proud of both Barbara and that grandson.

You know, I very much appreciate even the invitation to speak here this morning. If you'll allow me just to divert a minute because of something that is happening in the country. I was in south Florida last evening. And while I was stunned by the incredible physical destruction that I witnessed on this hurricane, you can't help but be impressed by the way Americans pull together in times of crisis. We are at our best when times are tough.

South Florida has been declared a Federal disaster area, and you should know that there are, what, 27 Federal Agencies, including our military services, pulling together to assist all Floridians in their time of need. I know I speak for all veterans on this one and all Americans when I say that our prayers are with the people of south Florida and also the Louisiana coast being threatened, the people also of south Louisiana who stand in Andrew's path at this very moment. No matter where the victims live,

we as a nation will do absolutely everything we can to help these good people recover.

I want to start this morning by saying that the bond we share links us, whether we served in the South Pacific or South Vietnam or whether we stood watch along that 38th parallel or braved the sands of Desert Storm. Just as you answered your country's call, so too America should serve those who served their country.

The specialized health care centers we've created, the new outpatient clinics, the billion dollars more we've invested in veterans health care every year, each is a sign of the debt we owe America's veterans, of the investment we make in the men and women who wear this country's uniform. Just yesterday I announced an innovative new job training program that will help all Americans including servicemen leaving the military, defense workers retooling for the new challenges of this civilian economy, or older veterans seeking better jobs and a new beginning. Frankly, the debt we owe is one we can never pay in full, but we need to do our utmost, just as America's vets gave their all when they were called. You have my commitment, as a proud member of the American Legion, post 77 member for life, that we will protect these programs that preserve your well-being. We owe it to the veterans.

I was a little negligent in my introductory remarks because sitting over my right shoulder here, albeit a Democrat—this is a nonpartisan meeting, so I—you're showing the flag here—is Sonny Montgomery, one of the great friends the veterans have ever had, I'll tell you, Congressman Montgomery of Mississippi.

Now, I know that today I'll not have your attention all to myself. Two hours from now, you're going to hear maybe a different message. But I respect the American Legion's tradition of nonpartisanship. It's been that way, and I'm determined it will remain that way today. I wouldn't give a partisan speech to this group. You've already sacrificed enough for your country. [*Laughter*] So bear with me because I want to make a few serious comments. I want to talk to you this morning about the world we knew, about the new world we're now forging.

Fifty years ago this summer, America's at war. At the age of 18, I went off to fight. Like many of you, I was scared, but I was willing. And I was young, but I was ready. Like so many of you, I had barely lived when I began to watch men die.

My own experience was in my mind during Operation Just Cause, when we freed Panama and jailed Noriega, and then again two Augusts ago, when I had to make a tough call, a call that only the Commander in Chief makes: the difficult decision to send young men and women into harm's way. As President, with that experience behind me and mindful of the trust, everyone who would serve, my sense of duty was magnified a thousand times.

And when I faced that decision, the American Legion never wavered. You were there with solid support, no vacillation. You supported our men and women 100 percent. And I will always be grateful to you. Your leaders went there. Your leaders went and showed the Legion flag and gave those young men and women the strong support, bringing with them messages from home from the families. It was a wonderful way that the American Legion supported those who were actually in the field. Whether they were regular Army or the magnificent National Guardsmen that were called to serve, whoever it was, the Legion backed them up. I want to thank you for that support over the years. If you had not been there in the past to help fight for a strong defense, our soldiers would not have been prepared; they would not have been equipped to fight to keep us free.

And when the calm came after Desert Storm, when our troops came home to a hero's welcome, the outpouring of love and honor was a grateful Nation's way of saying thanks. But it was something more. It was a reaching out, a warm embrace, a welcome home to all who wear the uniform, including the unsung heroes of another war, those who till that moment had not been recognized, a long-overdue recognition of gratitude to the veterans of the Vietnam war.

And the country rallied behind them and at long last gave them their proper honor.

Now, some of you may remember this. Four years ago, I met with you as Vice President: September 7th, a day that will live in infamy. [*Laughter*] Okay, I wanted to say it before you did. What does it take to live something down with this crowd? [*Laughter*] Since then, we've seen a world of change. What if I'd said then, that day, that by the end of my first term a wall would fall in Berlin; that we would have agreed to cut nuclear weapons by a full 75 percent, including the elimination of all those MIRV'd ICBM's, the most destabilizing strategic weapons? Because we did, our children sleep safer. What if I'd said that the Soviet regime that once claimed that history was on its side would be found only in the history books, and that the "dominoes" would fall in democracy's direction? What if I told you 4 years ago that the cold war would be over, that the West would win without a shot being fired? You'd say it was a miracle. But a miracle we did more than pray for: a miracle that Americans worked for, fought for, died for. Because the truth of the matter is, communism didn't just fall, you helped push it.

There are many heroes of the cold war, men and women whose courage and sacrifice turned the tide toward freedom: the brave people of Eastern Europe, who kept faith when freedom was a distant dream; the people in this country who gathered in taverns and restaurants in Cleveland and Pittsburgh and Detroit and, yes, right here in Chicago, to keep the hope of the captive nations alive, even when the fashionable few mocked their devotion as futile. The honor roll must also include men of moral courage like Pope John Paul II; like President Ronald Reagan, who called the Soviet Union an "evil empire"—which it was—and called for the Berlin Wall to be torn down, and it was.

Most of all, the tribute must include the American people, who paid the price in more ways than we can measure to win freedom's great victory. And especially you, you who slogged through the mud, sailed the seas, flew headlong into fire: This was truly your finest hour. And there is one hero America must never forget, and that is the hero who has not yet come home. And I pledge to every American family awaiting word of its loved ones: We will demand the fullest possible accounting for every POW and MIA. And we will not have normal relations with Hanoi until we are satisfied on that count.

I am very proud of our accomplishments, thankful that I've been able to give the order so many Presidents longed to give, for many of our nuclear forces to stand down, stand down from alert. And yet, in spite of freedom's great gains, I know that our world today is more uncertain, more unpredictable than the world we've left behind. The Soviet bear may be extinct, but there are still plenty of wolves in the woods, renegade rulers, outlaw regimes, madmen we simply cannot allow to get a finger on the nuclear trigger. You have my word: This President will never allow a lone wolf to endanger the security of the United States of America.

Foreign policy is not a footnote, a loose end that we wrap up and then safely forget. It requires steady, experienced leadership. Think back not too long ago to the time of gas lines and grain embargoes. In Teheran, Americans were held hostage. In Moscow, America was seen as weak and uncertain. This is a lesson we ignore at our own peril. Now those days are gone, but our strength in the future, like any great nation, rests on our eternal vigilance. We need to speak up for the military muscle that gives meaning to America's moral leadership. We need to say even now that the cold war is over: America is safe as long as America stays strong. You see, the world is still a dangerous place, and if America does not lead, who will?

Take Iraq as a test case for the most difficult security challenges we are likely to face in the future. We tried peaceful means to bring Iraq into the family of nations. Given the dangerous neighbors, given the vital interests at stake, it was right to try. Had we not made those efforts, had we not exhausted every peaceful means, we would never have been able to build the unprecedented United Nations coalition that stopped a tyrant in his tracks and rolled him back to Baghdad.

Now, let's also get straight what was at stake: A madman with missiles and chemical weapons stood on the brink of a chokehold on much of the world's energy supplies, threatening to overrun our allies. We destroyed that threat, liberated Kuwait, and locked up a tyrant in the prison of his own country. We know now Saddam Hussein was developing the weapons to destroy Israel. Tens of millions of deaths of Arabs or Israelis would not matter to this killer. The Middle East could well have become a nuclear apocalypse. That is what was at stake.

Now, some who were faint-hearted and stood in the way of crushing Saddam's aggression now have the gall to say, "You stopped the war too soon." Some also say that General Norman Schwarzkopf wanted to march into Baghdad and "get" Saddam. False! I'll never forget—this is a true story and history has it recorded on film—sitting in the Oval Office on February 27, 1991, our troops having performed so magnificently in the field. And with me in the room was General Scowcroft and the Secretary of Defense, Dick Cheney, the Chairman of the Joint Chiefs of Staff, Colin Powell. They recommended to me, as President who has the responsibility for this, that we stop the slaughter; our mission was accomplished. I asked, are you sure that our field commanders feel this way? They both said yes. But to double-check, Colin Powell got up from the couch in our office—you all have seen pictures of it—walked over to the desk that you see pictures of, reached into the front right-hand corner of the desk, and there was a secure telephone; picked up that secure phone and got General Schwarzkopf on the line in my presence. And General Powell looked up at me after he had talked to Schwarzkopf, and he said, "Mission accomplished. Stop the killing."

And it was right. We are not in the slaughter business. We were in the business of crushing aggression. And we did it. And I don't like this historical revision. We did the right thing; we did the compassionate thing in the end as well. If we'd continued, hundreds of thousands of American troops would be on the ground in Iraq today attempting to pull warring factions together or bogged down in some guerrilla warfare.

Whether in Korea or in Lebanon, history shows us the danger of losing sight of our objectives. Liberators can easily become occupiers. A Commander in Chief has to know not only when his objectives have been reached but when to consolidate his gains.

And one other thing let me say right here. I feel on me the obligation to every family of every single man or woman serving in the Armed Forces. And I am not going to commit our ground forces to a war until I know what the mission is, how that mission will be achieved, and how those forces will come out, their honor intact, victory in hand. We've seen too many combat situations where we asked those kids to fight with one hand behind their back. Not as long as I am Commander in Chief.

Instead of playing the world's policeman, we worked with the United Nations to destroy Iraq's remaining weapons of mass destruction, to keep Iraq under control. Through an embargo, through tight control over oil exports and U.N. inspections, we are putting the lid on Saddam. And believe me, he is going to live up to each and every one of those U.N. resolutions. I am determined to see that, and I will.

As you know, today a whole new world of hope is dawning in the Middle East. This very week, as Arab and Israeli sit down together in Washington, DC, we are winning the peace. And that was made possible by the sacrifice of those involved in Desert Storm.

There will be other regional conflicts. There will be other Saddam Husseins. Look around the world. Look at the threats we face: terrorism, the terrible drug cartels, regional conflicts as the breakup of empire gives vent to ancient hatreds, the spread of nuclear and chemical weapons. From Qadhafi in Libya to Kim Il-sŏng in North Korea, the threats on our horizon could look a lot like the threat we turned back in Iraq.

Take the threat of chemical weapons. I really get emotional about chemical weapons when I see these young people here today and think of the horror that they can wreak. During Desert Storm, the danger from chemical weapons did not materialize. In the next conflict, it might. Our task is

clear: There must never be a next time. For me, banning chemical weapons has been a priority since the day 8 years ago when I went to Geneva on instructions from President Reagan to present our draft convention. In the next few days, we expect the completed convention to be presented in Geneva. And it is my hope, it is my aim that before this year is out, the nations of the world will unite to ban chemical weapons, to banish this scourge from the face of the Earth.

Now, our work in the world did not end with our victory in the cold war. Our task is to guard against the crises that haven't yet even caught fire, the wars that are waiting to happen, the threats that will come upon us with little or no warning. I make this promise: As long as I am President, our services will remain the best trained, the best equipped, the best led fighting forces in the entire world. That is the way we guarantee the peace.

I hope that I've earned your trust to meet those challenges and to stand up for America's interests and these ideals that all veterans share. I hope I've earned your trust to bring together foreign policy and security policy and economic policy so that it can make a difference in your hometown, your neighborhood, your life. Because the military challenges we're bound to face are only a part of the future.

The end of the cold war means new opportunities, new opportunities for global prosperity, for new markets for American goods. From Moscow to Managua, free market reform is now sweeping away the dead hand of state socialism. Capitalism is recognized the world over as the engine of prosperity and social progress. And nations are reorganizing themselves to unleash the limitless potential of the individual.

Now, governments can go two ways: They can help foster free enterprise, or they can put obstacles in its path. There is no question what course we must take. The U.S. will remain a forceful advocate for free and fair trade. In the 21st century, America must be not only a military superpower but an economic superpower, an export superpower. I won't wade into all the statistics that point in this direction, but I will tell you this: Every additional billion dollars of exports stamped "Made in America" means 20,000 new American jobs. Last year alone, America was the world's number one exporter. We sold a record $422 billion worth of goods. That's a lot of paychecks for the American people.

But the promise of new prosperity must not blind us to new challenges. It's an economic fact of life that many of our key security partners are now our toughest economic competitors. Nations that lack the confidence to compete will be tempted to seek refuge behind the walls of protectionism. We didn't end the cold war to make the world safe for trade wars. We must fight the protectionist impulse here at home, and we must work with our partners for trade that is free, fair, and open. We're making progress by forging a new North American free trade agreement to open new markets from Manitoba to Mexico. And we're pushing hard to complete a strengthened global trade agreement.

My strategy would go further. The U.S. must build a new network of trade agreements with Eastern Europe's new democracies, with the new nations of the old Soviet Union, with our neighbors to our south, to the south in Latin America, with the dynamic economies of the Pacific as well. If we are to sustain our status as an export superpower, we must not allow ourselves to be tied down to one trade bloc. Our domestic market, the largest market in the world, gives us leverage. I intend to use it for good by strengthening America's global reach as a complement to our security presence. America must maintain a strong presence in markets across the Atlantic and the Pacific.

The key is an agenda that fully integrates our domestic, economic, and foreign policies. In our world today, these three topics have become one issue. You're going to ask, you ought to ask, all right, what are we going to do to get ready for the game? Well, fair question. Here's my answer: We

must build on the fundamentals of lower tax rates, limits on Government spending, less redtape and regulation, and more trade and more competition to generate the growth that means more opportunity and more jobs. And I think that in the nineties, Government can add to this growth program by building opportunity and hope for individuals, empowering families and communities.

I'd like to close with the words of a President from the other party, John F. Kennedy. On a sentry box in Gibraltar, he found scrawled these words. I'd like to read them to you:

God and the Soldier all men adore

In time of trouble and no more

For when war is over, and all things righted

God is neglected—and the soldier slighted.

Just as we must never forget our God, we must never forget you who put your lives on the line for freedom. Sure, that means supporting the programs, the policies, the principles that keep us strong. But it also means building an America of which you can be proud, an America worthy of the blood we shed and the friends that we lost. It means building an America which is safer, stronger, and more secure, an America in which every coast guardsman, every soldier, every sailor, every airman, every marine, every guardsman can say, "This is the dream that I fought for."

Thank you very much for your warm welcome, for your love of our country. And may God bless the United States of America, the greatest, freest country on the face of the Earth. Thank you all.

Note: The President spoke at 10:15 a.m. at the Sheraton Chicago Hotel. In his remarks, he referred to Dominic D. DiFrancesco, national commander of the American Legion, and Herman F. (Sparky) Gierke, judge on the U.S. Court of Military Appeals and former national commander of the Legion.

Remarks at a Bush-Quayle Rally in Canton, Michigan
August 25, 1992

The President. Thank you all very much for that warm welcome. May I salute all the party leaders here, especially the great Governor of Michigan, John Engler. He's doing a first-class job. May I thank the band, the Catholic High School band, the Motown band, Canton VFW colorguard; Susan Heintz and all those that have been out here making this program possible. Thank you very, very much.

You know, this town proves what we all know in our hearts. America's best days are ahead of us. Last Thursday at our great convention in Houston, I laid out a central challenge to our Nation to win the global economic competition, to win the peace. America must be a military superpower, an economic superpower, and an export superpower.

I differ with the Governor of Arkansas. He wants to turn inward and protect. I want to look outward and expand markets, expand American jobs. Let me just touch on what Governor Engler said because it affects the life of everybody in the automobile industry and everybody who's connected with the automobile industry.

Governor Clinton's record on the environment, to be charitable, is a little less than stellar. Listen to his own chairman of the Arkansas Pollution Control and Ecology Commission who said that the Arkansas laws are so lenient that "if California was operating on the laws of Arkansas, you'd have to wear a gas mask." How is that for the laws in Arkansas on the environment? Now, is it any wonder that they rank dead last in the Nation in policies to protect the environment, according to a study by the Institute of Southern Studies. The good people of Arkansas deserve better than that. And we don't need that kind of record running the environmental policies of the United States Government.

Remember what I said down there in Houston, slippery when wet? Well, listen to this one. Listen to this one. He's gone all the way over from that lousy record now to becoming bright green. He's turned that bright. And if Clinton has his way, Michigan auto workers are going to be turning green with illness. Here's why.

In a speech in Drexel University on April 22, Governor Clinton talked about a more ambitious Federal regulation that he supports involving the fuel standards for cars. He said this, and this is an exact quote: "In my administration we will accelerate our progress toward fuel-efficient cars and seek to raise the average goal for automakers to 40 miles per gallon by the year 2000, 45 miles by the year 2020." Now, that is not me, that is Governor Clinton talking.

You might ask what would happen if we did that. Well, according to the National Highway Traffic Safety Administration, fatalities and injuries will increase. But the worst thing is we will throw American autoworkers out of their jobs, and I'm not going to have that. The Motor Vehicle Manufacturers Association in Michigan alone said that 40,000 workers would go from the assembly line to the unemployment line if we go from those ridiculous standards.

We've got to fight against that kind of extremism. Those 40,000 will be joined by 700,000 workers put out there by the payroll tax that Governor Clinton is suggesting for his backdoor Government takeover of our health care system. You know, he says he likes to put people first. He doesn't mention that it's first out there on the unemployment line. We're trying to get people off of that. His tax-and-spend policies will put people out there. We don't want that.

I normally don't speak much about his running mate, Senator Gore of Tennessee, but he's written this famous book now that Governor Clinton talks about. On page 325 of the book, he makes an interesting comparison. He says that the automobile industry, and I quote right here, quotation, "poses a mortal threat to the security of every nation, that is more deadly than that of any military enemy we're ever again likely to confront." That is Clinton's running mate talking about the auto industry that means so much to our country. And one page later he calls for the "elimination of the internal combustion engine." What kind of people are we dealing with here? [*Laughter*]

Well, it would be funny if it weren't so serious, if one out of six jobs in America today weren't in some way tied to the car industry, and if this philosophy of tax and spend, regulate and regulate wasn't going to make it impossible for us to win the economic competition. Now, look, we have a sound and positive and strong environmental record. I fought for and won the first meaningful revision to the Clean Air Act, and we got that done in spite of that gridlocked Congress.

Audience members. Clean the House! Clean the House! Clean the House!

The President. I'll be there. Just a minute. I've got more to say about that one, and I love saying it because it's true. Now, wait a minute, I'll be there in a second.

Environment: We have expanded our parks and wildlife refuges. We've curtailed drilling in the environmental sensitive area of California and New England. We've enforced our environmental laws so we've collected record amounts of fines. I have been criticized by some in big business and by environmentalists. But I believe that somewhere you can find a reasonable formula where you protect jobs and still clean up the environment. That's what we've got to do.

So when that Clinton-Gore bus goes off the left side of the highway onto the shoulder, we've got to guard against that, too.

Here's what I want to do to lift the burden from the small businessman, the mom-and-pop operations, and others: Put a freeze on unnecessary Federal regulation. We're regulating ourselves to death.

You didn't hear much about this in the Clinton-Gore convention, but I'll tell you something. The Federal deficit is threatening the very future of these children here today, these young ones. So I am fighting for a line-item veto, a balanced budget amendment to the Constitution. You know who says no to all this: the gridlocked Congress, the Clinton-Gore gridlocked Congress.

So last week, last week—the editorial writers don't like this one; the sophisticated elitists don't like it—but let me tell you something, I unveiled an idea last week that the American people like, and it says this. You have the right to check off on your tax return using up to 10 percent of your income tax for one purpose, if you want to, and that is to reduce the budget deficit. It's a good idea. If Congress can't do it, let the American people have a shot at it. The editorial writers and Congress, they call it a gimmick. But I think the American people want the power to say to Congress, "If you won't cut the deficit, we'll get the job done for you."

Yesterday, we unveiled a new program to help people that need to transition into new jobs. Because we've been successful in war and peace, because we've changed the world, we have been able to reduce defense spending. Now, that's cost people some jobs. So now we've got a new training program to help those people find work, find work, jobs, productive jobs in this country. So we're talking about skill grants, giving workers in certain industries $3,000 to go out and buy training on their own. The philosophy isn't to empower the bureaucrats but empower the people so you can stay ahead of the economic change.

Heavens knows, we've got to reform our welfare system, get people to work and to learn and avoid the indignity of welfare. So later today I'm going to be signing a welfare waiver giving Michigan the authority to experiment with welfare programs that keep families together and get people off the dole and into jobs.

And one other thing. My opponent is supported by this trial lawyers group. I want to break the back of those who are suing us too much and caring for ourselves too little, caring for us too little. These reckless lawsuits are keeping doctors from practicing medicine, keeping people out away from coaching Little League, and we've got to stop it. I've tried for 3 straight years. Now change that Congress, and help me stop it.

Audience members. Clean the House! Clean the House! Clean the House!

The President. All right, I'll give you an example. That's a great idea. Now I'll give you an example. We know that our schools have to improve. If we're going to compete, they've got to improve. I believe competition can be a force for good in education, just as it's been a force for greatness in American industry. Earlier this year I sent a proposal to Capitol Hill, a "GI bill" for kids to give States and localities the flexibility to allow parents, not government, to choose the schools their kids attend, public, private, or religious.

A few weeks ago this came before the gridlocked Congress, a brandnew proposal, and they killed it. Why did this great idea fail? It failed, according to news reports, because the Democratic leadership did not want to give me credit for a new idea in education. Now, that is not progress. That is gridlock, and they are doing it to the taxpayer in this country.

Let me be a little more specific. I'm a little tired of Congressmen that talk one way in Michigan and vote different in Washington. I'll give you an example. One of those Democratic leaders that blocked this new proposal in education is named Congressman Ford, Bill Ford. He has stood against school choice and just about every education reform I have put forward. And what's worse, Governor of Arkansas agrees with him.

Audience members. Boo-o-o!

The President. Want parents to have real choice in where to send their kids to school? The Governor and Congressman Ford say no. I say yes.

You want to stand up to a Baghdad bully like Saddam Hussein? Governor Clinton waffled. Congressman Ford said, "No way." I say yes.

You want a balanced budget amendment that disciplines both the Congress and the executive branch? Governor Clinton and Congressman Ford say no. And I say yes.

Do you want to limit the terms of Congressmen? Governor Clinton and Congressman Ford say no. And I say yes. It's about time. The President's term is limited. Let's limit this gridlocked Congress and get them out of there.

The key issue—clean that House! You're right. The key issue is, do you want to try to cut Federal spending and give Americans relief from higher taxes? Well, Governor Clinton and Congressman Ford, linked together, say no. And I say yes.

Governor Clinton refers to himself as Elvis. Well, let me tell you something. [*Laughter*] He does. We're playing an old Elvis Presley song, "Return to Sender," return to Arkansas. As we get that done in November, as we get that done in November, let's take Congressman Ford and others like him that talk one way at home, vote different in Washington, that whole leadership of the gridlocked Congress, and do what those brooms say: Clean House!

Audience members. Clean the House! Clean the House! Clean the House!

The President. Get them out of there. We have been trying and trying to move this country forward, blocked by this gridlocked Congress. And I am tired of it.

While we're at it, let's send Charles Vincent, Dick Chrysler, Megan O'Neill, John Gordon, Frank Beaumont, Nick Smith, and don't forget Joe Knollenberg and John Pappageorge. Get them in there. In this district, replace that leader that talks one way and votes another. Send Bob Geake to Washington, and get this country moving.

You know, the other day we were in Alabama, a crowd of about 20,000 people in the rain. Lee Greenwood, you know, that great singer, was with us. And as he started to sing "I'm Proud To Be an American," I looked out in the crowd and saw a little girl, couldn't be more than 4 or 5, perched on her dad's shoulders waving a little American flag and singing. This election is about that little girl, and all the kids in this crowd, all the kids across America. Do we want them to grow up in an America that is stronger, safer, and secure, more secure? You bet we do. With my ideas and a new Congress, we can make it happen. We are the United States of America. We are going to make it happen.

May God bless Michigan, and may God bless our great country.

Note: The President spoke at 2:40 p.m. in Canton Township Heritage Park. In his remarks, he referred to Susan Heintz, master of ceremonies for the rally.

Statement on Michigan Welfare Reform
August 25, 1992

I am pleased we are approving today Michigan's request for welfare waivers. This will allow Michigan to initiate a system of incentives for welfare recipients that strengthens families and encourages greater self-sufficiency.

Families will be strengthened by encouraging employment and stability. Two-parent families will receive assistance as long as they meet a financial needs test. Currently one parent must have worked for a limited time in order for the family to receive welfare. Additional amounts of earnings will also be allowed before welfare payments are reduced, and the earnings of children will not be counted in determining whether the family can receive welfare.

Child support collections will be pursued aggressively. Noncustodial parents who are not fulfilling their financial responsibility may participate in activities leading to self-sufficiency such as completing high school, being involved in job training, or participating in community services.

Self-sufficiency will also be encouraged by requiring all welfare recipients to participate in some type of productive effort for at least 20 hours each week. These efforts can include working, job training, education, or participation in community service.

These and other reforms will allow Michigan to change their welfare program to give all those Americans in need a chance to discard long-term dependency for a life of renewed purpose and dignity.

Presidential Determination No. 92–42—Memorandum on Assistance for Refugees of the Former Yugoslavia
August 25, 1992

Memorandum for the Secretary of State

Subject: Determination Pursuant to Section 2(c)(1) of the Migration and Refugee Assistance Act of 1962, as Amended

Pursuant to section 2(c)(1) of the Migration and Refugee Assistance Act of 1962, as amended, 22 U.S.C. 2601(c)(1), I hereby determine that it is important to the national interest that up to $12,000,000 be made available from the U.S. Emergency Refugee and Migration Assistance Fund (the Fund) to meet the unexpected and urgent needs of refugees, conflict victims, and displaced persons from the former Yugoslavia. These funds will provide U.S. contributions to the United Nations High Commissioner for Refugees (UNHCR), the International Committee of the Red Cross (ICRC), and the United Nations Children's Fund (UNICEF) in support of their emergency assistance efforts.

You are directed to inform the appropriate committees of the Congress of this determination and the obligation of funds under this authority and to publish this memorandum in the *Federal Register*.

GEORGE BUSH

[*Filed with the Office of the Federal Register, 3:51 p.m., August 31, 1992*]

Presidential Determination No. 92–43—Memorandum on Assistance for Refugees in Africa
August 25, 1992

Memorandum for the Secretary of State

Subject: Determination Pursuant to Section 2(c)(1) of the Migration and Refugee Assistance Act of 1962, as Amended

Pursuant to section 2(c)(1) of the Migration and Refugee Assistance Act of 1962, as amended, 22 U.S.C. 2601(c)(1), I hereby determine that is important to the national interest that up to $15,200,000 be made available from the U.S. Emergency Refugee and Migration Assistance Fund (the Fund) to meet the unexpected and urgent needs of refugees, conflict victims, and displaced persons in Africa. These funds will be used for U.S. contributions in response to the appeals issued by the United Nations Special Emergency Program for the Horn of Africa (SEPHA) and by the International Committee of the Red Cross (ICRC) for its programs in Somalia and Mozambique.

You are directed to inform the appropriate committees of the Congress of this determination and the obligation of funds under this authority and to publish this memorandum in the *Federal Register*.

GEORGE BUSH

[*Filed with the Office of the Federal Register, 3:52 p.m., August 31, 1992*]

Presidential Determination No. 92–44—Memorandum on Arms Exports to the Organization of African Unity
August 25, 1992

Memorandum for the Secretary of State

Subject: Eligibility of the Organization of African Unity (OAU) to be Furnished Defense Articles and Services Under the Foreign Assistance Act and the Arms Export Control Act

Pursuant to the authority vested in me by section 503(a) of the Foreign Assistance Act of 1961, as amended (22 U.S.C. 2311(a)), and section 3(a)(1) of the Arms Export Control Act, as amended (22 U.S.C. 2753(a)(1)), I hereby find that the furnishing of defense articles and services to the Organization of African Unity will strengthen the security of the United States and promote world peace.

You are directed to report this finding to the Congress and to publish it in the *Federal Register*.

GEORGE BUSH

[*Filed with the Office of the Federal Register, 4:05 p.m., August 31, 1992*]

Letter to Congressional Leaders on Trade With Republics of the Former Yugoslavia
August 25, 1992

Dear Mr. Speaker: (Dear Mr. President:)

I am writing to inform you of my intent to add each of the former republics of the Socialist Federal Republic of Yugoslavia, other than Serbia and Montenegro, to the list of beneficiaries under the Generalized

System of Preferences (GSP). The GSP program offers duty-free access to the U.S. market and is authorized by the Trade Act of 1974.

I have carefully considered the criteria identified in sections 501 and 502 of the Trade Act of 1974. In light of these criteria, and particularly the Balkan nations' ongoing political and economic reforms, I have determined that it is appropriate to extend GSP benefits to the former republics of the Socialist Federal Republic of Yugoslavia, other than Serbia and Montenegro.

This notice is submitted in accordance with section 502(a)(1) of the Trade Act of 1974.

Sincerely,

GEORGE BUSH

Note: Identical letters were sent to Thomas S. Foley, Speaker of the House of Representatives, and Dan Quayle, President of the Senate. This letter was released by the Office of the Press Secretary on August 26. The related proclamation is listed in Appendix E at the end of this volume.

Remarks on Hurricane Andrew and the Situation in Iraq and an Exchange With Reporters
August 26, 1992

The President. First this morning, I want to express our continued concern and support for the people of Florida and Louisiana as they recover from this dreadful hurricane, Hurricane Andrew. I want to go to Louisiana as soon as possible today to communicate this directly to the people of that State, and I'm clearing my schedule to do just that.

As we saw in Florida 2 days ago, the destruction from this storm goes beyond anything we've known in recent years. It will test the resources of all volunteer organizations, private sector help, and State, local, and Federal governments. Damage is in the billions of dollars, and deaths already in double digits. Literally millions of American citizens today find themselves in the midst of personal devastation.

We're committing all the resources available to assist in this recovery. But just in terms of the number of people affected, our country must pull together to help. We've directed the military to provide over 2,000 MRE's, meals, to the people of Florida, and public health medical teams are there on the ground. Federal Emergency Management Centers are established in Florida and Louisiana, and they will focus all of the Government's assets on this problem.

Finally, I'm establishing a high-level task force under the direction of the Secretary of Transportation Andy Card to coordinate Federal efforts. We're making available today $10 million to create 5,000 short-term jobs for Floridians to clean up and restore public services in the aftermath of the hurricane. This grant will be dispersed by the Florida Governor's office and may be used to employ workers left without jobs from the hurricane.

Governor Chiles has worked very closely with Federal authorities, and we are both pleased by the initial response. He said so himself, and certainly I feel that way.

During my trip to Louisiana today we will be assessing similar needs in that State. In addition, we will be asking the private sector of our country to help in every way possible. As I said earlier, this disaster threatens to overwhelm the resources of all public and private institutions, so we must all chip in and help.

Now I want to turn to the situation in Iraq. In recent weeks and months we have heard and seen new evidence of harsh repression by the government of Saddam Hussein against the men, women, and children of Iraq. What emerges from eyewitness accounts, as well as from the detailed August 11th testimony before the United Nations Security Council of U.N. human rights envoy Max van der Stoel, is further graphic proof of Saddam's brutality.

We now know of Saddam's use of helicopters and, beginning this spring, fixed-wing aircraft to bomb and strafe civilians and villages there in the south, his execution last month of merchants in Baghdad, and his gradual tightening of the economic blockade against the people of the north. These reports are further confirmation that the Government of Iraq is failing to meet its obligations under United Nations Security Council Resolution 688.

This resolution, passed in April of 1991, demands that Saddam Hussein end repression of the Iraqi people. By denying access to U.N. human rights monitors and other observers, Saddam has sought to prevent the world from learning of his brutality. It is time to ensure the world does know.

Therefore, the United States and its coalition partners have today informed the Iraqi Government that 24 hours from now coalition aircraft, including those of the United States, will begin flying surveillance missions in southern Iraq, south of the 32 degrees north latitude, to monitor the situation there. This will provide coverage of the areas where a majority of the most significant recent violations of Resolution 688 have taken place.

The coalition is also informing Iraq's Government that in order to facilitate these monitoring efforts it is establishing a no-fly zone for all Iraqi fixed- and rotary-wing aircraft. This new prohibition will also go into effect in 24 hours over this same area. It will remain in effect until the coalition determines that it is no longer required.

It will be similar to the no-fly zone the coalition imposed on northern Iraq more than a year ago. I want to emphasize that these actions are designed to enhance our ability to monitor developments in southern Iraq. These actions are consistent with longstanding U.S. policy toward Iraq. We seek Iraq's compliance, not its partition.

The United States continues to support Iraq's territorial unity and bears no ill will towards its people. We continue to look forward to working with a new leadership in Baghdad, one that does not brutally suppress its own people and violate the most basic norms of humanity. Until that day no one should doubt our readiness to respond decisively to Iraq's failure to respect the no-fly zone.

Moreover, the United States and our coalition partners are prepared to consider additional steps should Saddam continue to violate this or other U.N. resolutions.

Now, Ed Djerejian is going to brief on the details. There will be a briefing on the military aspects of this—I believe it's over at the Pentagon—as soon as we're finished.

Yes, I'll take two or three questions. Then I must run.

Bosnia

Q. Mr. President, are you planning similar action to save the people of Bosnia who are also being slaughtered?

The President. We are in close consultation on Bosnia. As you know, the conference is going on right now. Acting Secretary Eagleburger is there, and we are discussing a wide array of things regarding Bosnia. I have expressed my concerns about use of U.S. force, certainly ground forces, in that area. But there's a lot of consultation going on right now, and I hope that that conference can come forth with productive answers that will encourage the people in that area to find peaceful means of solving these questions. The conference is off, I'm told by Secretary Eagleburger, to a pretty good start.

Iraq

Q. Mr. President, obviously, these violations to which you refer have been going on for some time. So the question naturally arises as to why this action now and not before, or not later.

The President. Well, one peg is the report from this U.N. official, Mr. van der Stoel, and I think that gets things in focus. Then the other side of it is we've had rather intensive consultations on this to be sure that we are operating in the coalition. I still think that's very important.

Q. How concerned are you that Saddam Hussein's regime may retaliate against U.N. inspectors on the ground?

The President. Well, they've already taken some steps there. That is a matter of concern because I think that just further antagonizes, properly so, the United Nations against them. But whether there's any steps, I don't know that he'd be foolish enough to take any steps as it relates to this no-fly zone.

Q. Mr. President, what if the Iraqis keep their planes on the ground, yet continue to suppress the Shiites with ground forces? What does this coalition do in that case?

The President. Well, we are not—that's hypothetical, and I just hope that that doesn't occur. But quite obviously, we would be extraordinarily concerned about that because that would be in violation of 688, as this use of these planes is. So we just have to wait and see what further action might be taken.

Iran-Contra Investigation

Q. Mr. President, yesterday in proceedings involving the Iran-*contra* trial of Caspar Weinberger, there was a memo released, a memo from then-Secretary of State Shultz concerning a telephone conversation he had with Cap Weinberger. It appeared to indicate that you knew about the diversion of arms sales, monies to Iran, to the *contras*, before the time that you acknowledge. Could you address that, sir?

The President. No, I don't know about that. I've told very openly everything I have to say about it. I don't know about that memo. I find nothing—I see no reason to contradict myself at all. I think what I've done is give the facts as I've seen them. I saw a story on it, and to be honest with you, I didn't read it.

Q. Do you know what they're talking about——

The President. No.

Q. ——this conversation that they had?

The President. No.

Tax Cuts

Q. Mr. President, we haven't had a chance to talk to you since your convention address in which you proposed tax cuts. Will you be specifying which tax cuts you're talking about and how you plan to pay for it? And if you don't, how do you expect the American people to—are they supposed to take this on faith?

The President. Well, I think what we're talking about here is a fundamental difference. And the difference is going to be whether you think you can—whether people can have lower taxes to pay and less spending, or the opposition says they want to raise taxes and raise spending. Much more important than the detail of it, which I would obviously have to support in the budget, would be the philosophy: Which approach are you taking?

We already have specific spending cuts recommended up there in the Congress, and so how specific I'll be, I'm not sure. I've already made specific recommendations on cutting taxes that have been up before the Congress. Whether I elaborate on that or not, I'm not sure. Right now my goal is to make sure people know the fundamental difference. One side wants to raise taxes and raise Government spending. My view is that we must cut taxes and cut Government spending. So I want to keep it in that perspective and not get all bogged down in a lot of detail.

Iraq

Q. How dire will the consequences be if Iraq is partitioned into three parts? Does the United States support that partition?

The President. No. And as I said in my statement, we do not.

Q. Sir, it seems one reason we didn't defend the Shiites after the war was we were concerned about this partition. Now have you had a different read on the Shiites? We hear stories about the Shiites not being considered a threat; in fact, they're more Iranian—rather, more Iraqi than they are pro-Iranian and Shiite. Is that true? Is that your latest intelligence read on them? Are you concerned that you're now doing this solely in a political year that this simply is going to look funny to the American people?

The President. Well, do you think it looks funny to the British people, the French people, the Saudi people? The answer is no. I'm not concerned about that in the least. I don't think the other side will try to put a political spin on this. We're talking about something that's very serious here. General Scowcroft notified Governor Clinton of what it is we're doing. I'm not worried about the politics of it at all.

On the separation, I'd like to leave that

question to Ed to answer as to whether these Shiites are pro-Iran. They're Iraqi, and we do not want to see the partition of Iraq.

Yes, John [John Mashek, Boston Globe]. This is the last question.

Presidential Campaign

Q. Mr. President, since the convention, another development is that the Democrats are saying that you've replaced patriotism of 1988 with love of God and family values in '92. Are those code words this year?

The President. Well, I was very pleased with something. I noticed that Governor Clinton was proclaiming there at the American Legion his pride in the fact that they had passed in Arkansas an anti-flag-burning resolution. That was in the litany of things he talked to the American Legion about. I think that's very good. So I don't think that one side is more patriotic than the other.

I'm going to continue to talk about the values that I think are very, very important. But I don't think we can say one—what was the rest of your question?

Q. Well, that both the love of God and family values are code words, that the Democrats aren't as strong as the Republi-

cans on those two issues.

The President. Well, I think we'll just say what we're for and let them reply as to what they're for. I noticed a rather vigorous response. I didn't hear—the press didn't ask me about it, but when Governor Cuomo equated us with Nazis, front page of one of the New York papers 2 days ago, it was—you know, we're in a funny year when people can say those things. So they've got their hot shooters out there; we've got some. What I'm trying to do is spell out what I think is fundamental. We're not going to stop talking about family values. If they want to talk about that, that's fine.

Q. Is Chief of Staff Baker prepared now to agree to three Presidential debates with Governor Clinton?

The President. I suggest, John, that you address that to—I was going to see whether to punt that ball into Baker's end zone—[*laughter*]—but I think the answer to your question, though, is no. But we'll see. We'll see. We haven't discussed it.

Note: The President spoke at 10:48 a.m. in the Briefing Room at the White House. In his remarks, he referred to Edward P. Djerejian, Assistant Secretary of State for Near Eastern and South Asian Affairs.

Statement on Signing Legislation Extending Terms of Members of the United States Sentencing Commission
August 26, 1992

Today I am signing into law S. 1963, which permits Members of the United States Sentencing Commission whose terms have expired to continue to serve until either a successor takes office or the next session of the Congress ends.

The legislation does not specify whether it would apply to the current Members of the Commission. Were the Act read to apply to the current Members, it would appear to violate the Appointments Clause of the Constitution by, in effect, permitting the Members to extend the terms of the office to which they were appointed by the President and confirmed by the Senate. Ac-

cordingly, I sign this legislation based on my understanding that it applies only to appointments made after the date of enactment of the Act, so as not to infringe on my constitutional appointment authority. This is in keeping with the well-settled obligation to construe ambiguous statutory provisions to avoid constitutional questions.

I note that this interpretation of the Act is supported by the fact that the Senate deleted from the Act a provision that would have expressly applied it to current Members of the Commission.

GEORGE BUSH

The White House,
August 26, 1992.

Note: S. 1963, approved August 26, was assigned Public Law No. 102–349.

Statement on Signing the Marsh-Billings National Historical Park Establishment Act
August 26, 1992

Today I am pleased to sign into law S. 2079, the "Marsh-Billings National Historical Park Establishment Act."

S. 2079 will establish the Marsh-Billings National Historical Park in Vermont with the purpose of interpreting the history of conservation. This site includes the boyhood home of George Perkins Marsh. In 1864 Marsh published the first book on conservation, called *Man and Nature.* He warned that not providing for the proper protection of forest cover would lead to the pollution of streams and rivers, the loss of soil, wildlife, and plants, and the ability to farm the land.

The Marsh home was later purchased by Frederick Billings, an attorney and railroad magnate who began a scientific farm on this site, and reforested the land. It has been owned for the last 60 years by Laurance and Mary Rockefeller.

This National Historical Park will include the mansion and 550 acres of hillside that were replanted by Frederick Billings. The legislation will also provide for cooperation with the historic Frederick Billings Farm and Museum, and allow the National Park Service to interpret for the public the beginnings and the evolution of the conservation movement.

Conservation principles, first articulated by Marsh and practiced by Billings, have also been primary themes of my Administration. Just as Frederick Billings replanted trees over a century ago on the 550 acres of hillside, my Administration has set a goal to plant one billion trees per year across America.

Since 1989, I have proposed an America the Beautiful initiative which has doubled funding for national parks, forests, wildlife refuges, and other public lands, and tripled funding to States for outdoor recreation. Nearly 20 national park units and 60 wildlife refuges have either been created or significantly expanded. In total, over 1.5 million acres have been made available for the use and enjoyment of present and future generations.

The Nation owes a debt of gratitude to Laurance and Mary Rockefeller, who are donating their home as the first national park in Vermont. I salute the Rockefeller family's long-standing support for the protection of America's natural and cultural wonders and their close relationship with the National Park System. They have provided substantial support to the Virgin Islands National Park and Grand Teton National Park in Wyoming. All Americans will benefit from their generosity.

I welcome the Marsh-Billings National Historical Park as the next worthy addition to the National Park System.

GEORGE BUSH

The White House,
August 26, 1992.

Note: S. 2079, approved August 26, was assigned Public Law No. 102–350.

Statement on Signing Legislation Granting Most-Favored-Nation Trade Status to Albania
August 26, 1992

Today I am signing into law H.J. Res. 507, approving the extension of nondiscriminatory treatment (most-favored-nation status) to the Republic of Albania.

The United States Government fully supports this resolution granting most-favored-nation (MFN) status to the Republic of Albania. The bilateral trade agreement between the United States and Albania, of which MFN is a key element, was transmitted to the Congress during Albanian President Berisha's visit to Washington in June and marks an historic point in Albanian-American relations.

Albania elected its first post-communist government in free and fair elections held in March of this year after decades of self-imposed isolation. Since then the country has been struggling to convert to a free market economy. The extension of MFN status to Albania could provide an impetus to Albania's faltering economy and help the country's difficult transition from a command economy to a free market.

The United States now enjoys a close, cooperative relationship with the Government of Albania, a government that is firmly committed to democracy and the free market.

We hope that with our assistance, and that of its other friends, Albania can transform itself from an underdeveloped, closed, centralized society to a democratic country with a free market. A freer and more prosperous Albania can also be a stabilizing force in the volatile Balkan region.

GEORGE BUSH

The White House,
August 26, 1992.

Note: H.J. Res. 507, approved August 26, was assigned Public Law No. 102–363.

Letter to Congressional Leaders Reporting a Budget Deferral
August 26, 1992

Dear Mr. Speaker: (Dear Mr. President:)

In accordance with the Congressional Budget and Impoundment Control Act of 1974, I herewith report one deferral of budget authority, totaling $17.6 million. Including this deferral, funds withheld in FY 1992 now total $5.8 billion.

The deferral affects the Agency for International Development. The details of this deferral are contained in the attached report.

Sincerely,

GEORGE BUSH

Note: Identical letters were sent to Thomas S. Foley, Speaker of the House of Representatives, and Dan Quayle, President of the Senate. The report detailing the deferral was published in the Federal Register on September 3.

Memorandum on Administrative Dismissal of Employees Affected by Hurricane Andrew
August 26, 1992

Memorandum for the Heads of Executive Departments and Agencies

Subject: Administrative Dismissal of Employees Affected by Hurricane Andrew

Our hearts go out to the thousands of Americans in South Florida and along the Gulf Coast who have suffered tragic losses at the hands of Hurricane Andrew. Many parts of the Federal Government have been mobilized to respond to this disaster and to begin a massive effort to recover from the ravages of this storm.

As part of this effort, I request heads of executive departments and agencies who have Federal civilian employees in the geographic areas designated as disaster areas because of Hurricane Andrew to use their discretion under OPM and agency regulations and where appropriate excuse from duty, without charge to leave or loss of pay, any such employee who is faced with a personal emergency because of the storm and who can be spared from his or her usual responsibilities. This policy should also be applied to any employee who is needed for emergency law enforcement, relief, or clean-up efforts authorized by Federal, State, or local officials having jurisdiction.

GEORGE BUSH

Remarks to Public Safety Equipment Employees in St. Louis, Missouri
August 27, 1992

Thank you all. I know, anything to get out of work. [*Laughter*] Steve, thank you, thank you very much for that kind and genuine introduction. Let me thank some other members of the host committee: Mike Latta, one of the founders, Ed Ryan, Andrew Smith. And of course, I'm very, very pleased that my dear friend and your great Governor, John Ashcroft, could be with us this morning. He's done a superb job for this State, and I'm proud to be at his side once again.

This is really great. Look at the equipment you have here, lightbars, beacons. You've given a new meaning to "a thousand points of light." [*Laughter*]

Over the past 3½ years we've seen a world transformed, as Steve mentioned in his introduction. And yes, the cold war is over. And now the defining challenge of the nineties is to win the competition of this new global economy, to win the peace. Our goal is simple and profound: We must be a military superpower, an economic superpower, and an export superpower.

In this election, you're going to hear two versions of how to do this. My opponent's answer is to turn inward, to protect what we already have from the challenges of this new world. My approach is to look forward, to look out, to open new markets, prepare our people to compete, to restore our social fabric, and to save and invest so that we can win.

I've come to St. Louis today, you'll be happy to know, not to have a political rally but really to deliver a serious message to the people in this factory, the people in Missouri, and the people in the country. I want to point out the sharp difference between Governor Clinton and me on the crucial issues of investment and open trade. My policies encourage both because my experience in business and foreign affairs has shown me that trade and investment create jobs.

In contrast, my opponent and, regrettably, the Democratic Congress want to tax both trade and investment. But common sense tells us that if you tax something you get less of it. Taxes stifle growth and chase away business and destroy jobs.

I know that the other side has lots of slogans and policy buzzwords that sound appealing when you first hear them, but America cannot afford them. There's a difference between soundbites and sound policy. Talk is cheap until you get the bill.

The reason I'm so pleased to be here is because PSE is an example of where I believe this whole country should go and how we should get there. Not so long ago, companies like PSE could be satisfied with a national market, sell your goods in the 50 States, leave it at that.

That's no longer good enough. So a few years ago, you decided to take on the world. I'm told that now 35 percent or about a third of what you make is sold outside the borders of the United States and in 48 different countries. Today your lightbars and sirens help save lives not only on the streets of Detroit and Peoria but in Israel, Hong Kong, and Spain. I was told that when the Kuwaitis, their country freed, went back in, that your products helped lead the way and keep the peace.

You know, your story is a parable for our Nation's economic future. You've taken the challenges of foreign competition and re-shaped them as opportunities, made your name literally a standard of excellence. You should be very, very proud of that, every single person that works here.

I don't want to bore you with life history, but let me tell you how I first learned about competing in the world. I learned my economics in the oilfields of west Texas, painting rigs, and then for a while I drove tens of thousands of miles through the fields in Texas and New Mexico and then California and back to Texas. All around me in those days I saw towns and businesses start from nothing, for a simple reason: The world wanted what Texas had to offer, cotton, cattle, crude.

Later on, when I started my own business, I shopped for investors on the west coast and the east coast, but I couldn't stop there. I traveled the world. We had a tiny company, smaller than PSE by far. And that little company exported our services, and I

think success, to Japan, to Brunei, to South America, and to the Middle East. We created American jobs in the process.

Now, I tried to build on that experience when I got involved in foreign relations. And I saw again how important America is to the world and how important the world is to America, not just for national security in the traditional sense but for economic security, for our own economic security, for creating jobs right here at home.

We've held steady to this vision for 3 years now, and we have made solid progress. As we knock down trade barriers, American companies are rushing to meet the demand all around the world. More and more people are buying American. Since I took office, exports have increased by one-third. America is the greatest exporter in the entire world, greatest one the world has ever seen, $422 billion of exports last year alone.

Let me bring that right into the shop here in St. Louis, bring it close to home. In Missouri, exports are up 37 percent over the last 3 years, $3.8 billion worth of goods shipped to 151 countries around the world. It looks like the Show Me State is showing the world.

Now these numbers are impressive, but when you dig behind them, get in behind the math, you find the real benefit of the new world economy, and in a word, it is jobs. Here in Missouri, 150,000 jobs are supported by foreign trade. Across the country, more than 7 million Americans owe their jobs to exports.

Everyone recognizes, everyone now, that the world is moving at a faster clip, but I see something more: It's moving our way. Right now we're building on the export success of the last 3 years. Two weeks ago we entered into an era, a new era, I'd say, of open trade. Along with Mexico and Canada, we concluded talks on the North American free trade agreement, called NAFTA, knocking down tariffs and creating one of the largest free-trade areas in the world, an integrated economy worth more than $6 trillion.

Here in Missouri, you already export $2 billion worth of goods to Mexico and Canada. That's a lot of paychecks, but our new agreement will create even more American jobs and make us even stronger in the race with our European and Asian competitors.

NAFTA is a solid agreement. But right now, before the ink is even dry, the Democratic leadership in the Congress is calling for us to slap a tariff on any new trade that comes from NAFTA. Now, you've got to— this is complicated, but just think about it for a minute. After long and tough negotiations with our closest trading partners, we've agreed to end tariffs. The protectionist Democrats say, "Okay, fine. But first you have to put on a new tariff."

In other words, they think the way to eliminate trade barriers is build a new trade barrier. And they call this new tariff a transaction tax. It'll make it more expensive for businesses like yours to compete in the world economy. And it will discourage the creation of new jobs for your neighbors and, most important, for you. It turns the agreement on its head. They may think that's good politics, but it is, frankly, lousy policy.

Now, you might ask, what about Governor Clinton on this, where does he stand? Just last week, he was asked about our new trade agreement, and he hemmed and hawed. At last he said, and I quote, "When I have a definitive opinion, I'll say so." I hope nobody's planning to hold their breath on this one. [*Laughter*] I know politics. And I guess as a candidate you can be on both sides of every question. But as a President, you cannot. You have to make the tough decisions. And you shouldn't be on both sides of each issue.

Governor Clinton can fudge all he wants, but the difference couldn't be clearer. The difference is based on two very different views of our future. My opponents see us knock down trade barriers, and they say, "Hold everything." They see us open new markets for American goods, and they say, "Wait a minute. Maybe we can't compete. Maybe the American worker can't cut it. So let's pull down the blinds, lock the doors, and hope the world goes away."

Let me tell them something you already know in this plant. The American worker doesn't have to hide from anybody. Americans can outwork, outthink, outcompete anybody, anywhere, anytime. And that's

what we're trying to do, expand these markets. That's something everyone in the world seems to understand, everybody but the protectionist Democrats.

Over the last decade, we have literally seen a boom in foreign investment in the United States, even when things are very, very tough at home. We've seen a boom in that, businesses from all over the world coming here, setting up shop from Portland, Oregon, to Portland, Maine. These investors follow a simple logic: If you want the best science and universities in the world, if you want the best workers in the world, you have to come to the United States of America. And the result has been jobs. One out of every ten manufacturing workers in the United States works for a company supported by foreign investment. That's the bottom line: jobs for Americans, a growing economic pie for everyone.

Now, here's one issue Governor Clinton does not fudge. He's proposed to increase taxes on foreign investment in the United States, even though those companies employ a total of 4½ million American workers. Governor Clinton says his tax increase will crack down on foreign companies. But that crackdown is more like an eviction notice. When those companies pack their bags, they'll take those jobs with them. I'm not going to let that happen.

We've got to open markets. We've got to encourage investment here, encourage investment abroad, create new markets for the American worker.

All I ask is that you just travel around this State. Go to New Madrid, talk to the 1,200 employees at Noranda Aluminum, or to Joplin, talk to the 425 employees at Atlas Powder. Go to any of the 244 foreign-owned companies that employ 60,000 workers, 60,000 Missouri workers right here. And I don't think you're going to find any of those Missourians complaining about foreign investment. If Governor Clinton's tax hike had been in effect these past few years, those companies simply would not be here, and those jobs wouldn't have been created for the citizens of Missouri. And it's not just Missouri. Whether it's the Nissan plant in Smyrna, Tennessee, or the Honda plant in Marysville, Ohio, Governor Clinton's tax increase would be felt in every region of every State in this country.

And he could use a lesson in international relations. If he raises this tax, our foreign competitors are going to say, what's good for the goose is good for the gander. His tax hike is like a gilded invitation sent to foreign governments where U.S. companies do business. And the invitation reads: Please retaliate. You do not want these governments abroad to retaliate against Code 3, against your wonderful products, because of tariff policies or tax policies in the United States.

His tax would not only destroy jobs and reduce investment here, it would do the same throughout the global economy, causing a worldwide contraction. I don't have to ask you to go back to the history books, but there was an occasion when that happened, right before the Great Depression. And we're fighting our way out of a tough recession now, and we don't need to throw more Americans out of work. So look carefully at this taxing.

Those are the facts about Governor Clinton's tax: It will literally destroy jobs, discourage investment, and it threatens to start an economic war just as markets the world over are opening up to American products.

We should ask why, given all this, Governor Clinton would ever propose such a tax in the first place. Well, I have a hunch. Today change is accelerating, and change breeds a certain uneasiness, skepticism, even fear. And by attacking the bogeymen of foreign investors, Governor Clinton hopes to exploit the darker impulses of this uncertain age: fear of the future, fear of the unknown, fear of foreigners.

Now, I know his reputation for opportunism, as the kind of guy who will say anything, do anything for political gain. But he should understand what's at stake here. And if he doesn't understand it, let me tell him. Those are American jobs he's playing politics with. Those are American workers he's putting at risk. The American people simply won't buy it. The proudest people on Earth have never stooped to fearmongers before, and we must not stoop now to fearmongers.

In talking about our future in the global economy, I mentioned, touched on my own experience because I want you to understand why I believe what I do about America's ability to compete. I've, with a lot of help, built a business, and I've dealt with foreign nations. I know how to bring it together. I know what it takes to make America secure and strong at home and abroad.

So, you see, your vote will make a difference this year, not only in the Presidential election. When you look at your candidates for Congress, I'd like you to ask them something. Ask them where they stand on keeping America an export superpower, on our new trade agreement, and on Governor Clinton's new taxes on investment and jobs. Please listen to the answers very carefully. Don't let them talk any longer—talk one way in Missouri and another way back in Washington, DC.

And this is important. Please follow up. Some of them will do more flip-flops than Ozzie Smith out there. [*Laughter*] I'll give you an example. Earlier this summer we lost a close battle in Congress for a constitutional amendment to balance the Federal budget, to discipline the Congress and discipline the executive branch. One of St. Louis' Representatives, Joan Kelly Horn, signed up—this is going to be hard for you to believe—signed up as a cosponsor, one of the leaders of, a cosponsor of the amendment to cause us to have to balance the budget. She signed up in April. And then when it came to the vote, she flipped. She voted against the very same amendment that she had cosponsored.

Enough is enough. This fall ask her about that balanced budget amendment, and vote for Jim Talent, her opponent. And I know Mack Holekamp supports the balanced budget amendment, too. Vote for him. We need to make people do in Washington what they tell you in Missouri they're going to do.

Well, anyway, those are the kind of choices we face this year, a choice between the patrons of the past and the architects of the future. I believe we can shape our future not by taxing trade but by opening markets, not by scaring off investment but by using it to create jobs for ourselves and our kids.

I have great faith in America's future because I have faith in the American people and in the American worker. It is the same faith that brought me out to Texas more than 40 years ago, the same faith that brought me into public life, the same faith that has led me to fight for these open markets, because I know that no challenge is too great for the hearts and the minds of America.

And lastly, do not listen to the pessimists who tell you that the United States of America is in decline. We are at the sunrise, not the sunset. And if we pursue these opening of markets, we will demonstrate to the entire world once again why everybody looks to America: peace, security, strength, freedom, democracy, and an ability to outwork anybody, anywhere, anytime.

Thank you all very, very much. And God bless you.

Note: The President spoke at 9:10 a.m. on the shop floor at Public Safety Equipment, Inc. In his remarks, he referred to PSE officials Stephen Rose, engineer; Michael D. Latta, president; Edward F. Ryan, vice president, marketing; and Andrew G. Smith, vice president, engineering; and Ozzie Smith, St. Louis Cardinals baseball player.

Remarks to a Bush-Quayle Rally in Cincinnati, Ohio
August 27, 1992

The President. Thank you very much. Hey, George Voinovich, thank you very, very much. Thank you. Last time I was at a rally at this marvelous park, Johnny Bench and I rode in on a fire engine, and it started to rain. Now the sun is out, and things are looking good.

I want to thank George Voinovich, all our other great leaders here. I want to thank Ronnie McDowell for that musical number and mention those Olympians that were here, Mike McMurray and Joe Hudepohl and Tim Austin, thanking them for being with us and for what they did for the United States of America in Barcelona. Also, a special thanks to my friend Johnny Bench, everybody's hero.

These athletes, these competitors know something about competition, and this year's campaign is about one question: how America can win the economic competition and win the peace. I believe I am the person to lead us to do just that.

You know, you can't build a home without a hammer; you can't build a dream without a job. So you need to know which candidate has a plan to fulfill your dreams. I believe I have the plan that works for America. My plan starts with the idea that the deficit, the big spending deficit, is a dark cloud hovering over the future of these kids. The Federal Government spends too much of your hard-earned money. Help me put an end to that.

I have asked Congress to take over 4,000 specific projects, 250 Federal programs and send them the way of the pet rocks and the mood rings. And they refuse to act.

Here's another idea. So far, Congress has said no to my efforts to cut spending. So last week I put forth a new idea. If they can't do it, I want to give you, the taxpayer, the power to take up to 10 percent of your tax return, earmark it for one purpose only: reduce the dangerous Federal deficit. If you can check off for America, I believe we will finally get the big spenders up there in Washington in check.

You might say, "How do we create jobs in America?" Well, unlike my opponent, I spent half my life in the private sector, trying to meet a payroll like many of you out here. I happen to believe that having held a job in the private sector is a good qualification for President of the United States or for anything else.

I know this, that taxes stifle growth and they stop job creation. So with a new Congress, and we're going to have a new one, we will cut spending, and then we'll cut

1439

taxes. They want to increase spending and increase taxes, and that is the big difference.

Another thing: I want to get rid of all those crazy lawsuits. If you fall off a stepladder today, a lawyer will be there to catch you before you hit the ground. My opponent doesn't believe this is a problem, nor does the gridlocked Congress. I've got to dig out my coat now because I want to read you something here. Earlier this year, the head of the Arkansas Trial Lawyers Association, a guy named David Williams, wrote a letter of endorsement for Bill Clinton. He said, and I quote directly, "I can never remember an occasion where he failed to do the right thing where we trial lawyers are concerned."

Well, I don't want to do the right thing for the trial lawyers, I want to do the right thing for the American people. We've got to sue each other less and take care of each other more.

Audience members. Four more years! Four more years! Four more years!

The President. You know, we've got to have—there are too many families that wonder whether they're going to be able to pay their medical bills. We've got a good, strong health care reform program. The Clinton program is to go the way, the same old way the liberal Democrats do: put your fate in the hands of Government. I believe that we control costs, extend coverage, insurance coverage, to the poorest of the poor without putting your health care under the control of those same people who brought us the House post office and the House bank.

Audience members. Clean the House! Clean the House! Clean the House!

The President. Right. You know, listen, this is really fact here, Governor Clinton's health care plan would lead to a new health care tax on those who can afford it the least, the small business. I believe small business needs capital, needs incentive, needs relief from regulation. What small business doesn't need is the Excedrin headache of Governor Clinton's new taxes.

Here's some of the other things I'm fighting for: Job training, to lend a helping hand to workers that are caught in the transition of our economy. I want to revolutionize the

way we teach our children, giving many American parents a new freedom, the freedom to choose where your kids go to school, public, private, or religious; make the public schools greater and make the private schools like St. Xavier's right here greater. I want to reform our welfare system to encourage families to stick together and fathers to stick around.

Some people don't like it when I talk about family values. Well, they'd better get used to it because let me tell you something, let me tell you something that everybody in Cincinnati knows, and that is that the family is the foundation of America. All our other successes are worthless if we fail at home. We need to strengthen the American family if we are going make America stronger and more secure.

So we've got a wide array of issues we're talking about here. You might ask, well, where does my opponent stand on the issues? Well, good question, very good. As this campaign gets underway, it's getting harder and harder to tell. He's turning up in more places than Elvis Presley. You just can't tell. [*Laughter*]

Take the question of whether to stand up to Saddam Hussein, the most important foreign policy decision that a President had to make, certainly the most important one that I had to make. Two days after Congress followed my lead, let me quote you what my opponent said. I want to be fair about this. Here's the quote directly: "I guess I would have voted with the majority if it was a close vote. But I agree with the arguments the minority made."

Now, in the Oval Office, when you have to make life and death decisions you cannot have it both ways, not when people's lives are at stake. You have to make the tough call, whether it's popular or not. I hope I have earned the trust of the American people.

Audience members. Four more years! Four more years! Four more years!

The President. Listen, the big problem is the economy. In his acceptance speech, Governor Clinton insists that Government takes too much and gives too little in return. But then he proposes, and this is factual, $220 billion in new spending, plus the largest tax increase in history, $150 billion.

I say, and you say, let's go the other way. Let's cut spending, and let's cut taxes.

I'm just getting wound up here. Let me give you one more example, though, one more example because it affects a lot of lives here in the State of Ohio. A few months ago, Governor Clinton said he wanted to raise fuel efficiency standards, they're called CAFE standards, for cars to 45 miles per gallon. It sounds like a great idea, but scientists will tell you it is impractical. It will cost lives, and most important, it will throw 30,000 Ohioans out of work.

Governor Clinton finally figured this out. So last Friday he sang a different tune, keeps shifting ground. He said, and I quote, "I never said that I didn't think there was more than one way to do it, or that we shouldn't be flexible in the way we approach it." Now, you talk about back-pedaling. The Bengals could use him in their secondary, for heaven sakes. This is crazy. It is strange.

So I ask the American people, is there a pattern going on here? Will Governor Clinton say anything to anybody? America cannot afford in a President double-speak, double-talk, double-time. Please elect me to keep the integrity and honor of that White House.

I see some of these signs out here. Hey, this is great. I see some of these signs out here; I'm reminded of a story, reminded of a story about the farmer and the certain farm animal. The animal was so slippery that it kept slipping out of its pen. One day the farmer went looking for it, followed the animal's track all over creation. When the farmer returned, his wife asked if he knew where the animal was. The farmer said, "Yes, ma'am, I found him. He's on both sides of the fence." [*Laughter*]

Now, in this campaign you're going to find me on just one just side, the side of the American family, the American taxpayer. But it's not just enough electing a President; I need some help. The gridlock Congress has been run by the same entrenched, ossified, change-allergic leadership for 38 years. The one institution that hasn't changed in this country is the Democrat-controlled House of Representatives. And it

is time.

Audience members. Clean the House! Clean the House! Clean the House!

The President. It is time to take a broom and clean the House. You can start right here by giving me Mike DeWine for the U.S. Senate. Change the Senate; get him elected. Do what the people of Ohio want done: Have somebody in Washington that will vote the same way there that he talks in Ohio. Send Mike DeWine to the Senate. We need to clean the House, so give me Steve Grote to the first district seat right here in Washington; send him up there from the first district.

Sending Mike and Steve to Washington and then fighting side-by-side with Bill Gradison and John Boehner and Bob McEwen, we will break the gridlocked Congress, and we will get this country moving again. We will fight for a balanced budget amendment and a line-item veto and for this tax check-off. If you change the Congress, we can get that job done for the American people. We will fight to lower spending and taxes. We will fight to stop these crazy lawsuits. We will fight for you so that, together, we can build a stronger and a more secure America.

The last point is this: We've been through a lot in the world. These young people here go to sleep at night with a lot less fear of nuclear war. That is something good. That is something wonderful for every family. But make no question about it, when you hear the other side talking about that we're ridiculed abroad, don't believe it. We are the most respected nation on the face of the Earth, and we're there because we made the tough decisions. We stood up against what was wrong and fought for what was right. Now I ask you to help me and give me 4 more years to continue to lead this country.

May God bless the United States of America. Thank you all very, very much. Thank you.

Note: The President spoke at 1:42 p.m. in Fountain Square. In his remarks, he referred to Gov. George Voinovich of Ohio; Mike McMurray, Cincinnati disc jockey; and Johnny Bench, former Cincinnati Reds baseball player.

Remarks to Findlay Machine and Tool Employees in Findlay, Ohio
August 27, 1992

The President. Thank you very, very much. Thank you, Mike. If we had more Congressmen like Mike Oxley and had Mike DeWine in the Senate, everybody wouldn't be yelling at me, "Clean House!" everyplace I go.

And thanks to all of you especially for that warm welcome. I salute our Lieutenant Governor, Mike DeWine. Thanks to the Mayor, Mayor Keith Romick. And let me also thank our hosts, Joe Kirk—[*applause*]—you better clap for Joe Kirk. [*Laughter*] Now, as well as the local celebrities providing the music; band was fantastic, that Findlay High School Band over there. I'm also pleased that two men with whom I served in Congress, who no longer are there—Del Latta is here and Jack Betts, both outstanding Members of the United States Congress.

And as Mike Oxley said, this is a return engagement. It's great to be here in Findlay, Flag City, U.S.A. I couldn't count every one of the 319 flags that I'm told you fly around here, but let me assure Jim Woodward, every flag I did see looked great to me.

It is a time of great pride for our flag and for the freedoms that it represents. And yes, the cold war is over, and freedom finished first. Now, the defining challenge of the nineties is to win the competition of the new global economy. Our goal is simple; it is straightforward: In the 21st century, America must be not only a military superpower but an economic superpower and particularly an export superpower.

In this election, you'll hear two versions of how to do this. My opponent's answer is to look inward, to pretend we can protect what we already have. And ours is to look forward, to open new markets, prepare our people to compete, restore the social fabric, to save and invest so that we can win for everybody in the United States of America.

You know, already Findlay is rising to the challenge. When I was here 4 years ago, this spot where we're standing was a forest. Today, Tall Timbers is a testament to the transforming power of the international economy, a living, working blueprint for how America can compete. And you are showing the rest of our country, you're showing the rest of America, that in the new global economy America can earn a gold medal. And that's exactly what we're doing right here in Findlay today.

What do the economists say about this new economy? Well, I realize that economists are not always the most admired profession. My own economic advisers tell the story about a business leader who traveled to New York City for a conference. In the Grand Central Station, he was confronted by a bum in tattered clothes. And the bum said, "Hey, can you give me 10 bucks for a cup of coffee?" The businessman said, "Ten bucks! That sounds a little steep." And the bum replied, "Haven't you heard? The dollar is weakening. The M1 money supply has been loosened too quickly, and that could set off an inflationary spiral, driving up the cost of consumer goods." The businessman looked at this guy, and he said, "You're pretty smart. Why aren't you an economist?" And the bum glared back, "Buddy, I still have some pride." [*Laughter*]

Someone will probably tell me that the shop next door is the American Economics Association. But nevertheless, I know that economists can be confusing sometimes. But when it comes to the value of foreign trade, they all agree: Foreign trade creates American jobs. Right now, one out of every seven Ohio manufacturing jobs is tied to foreign trade. Whether it's toothpaste from Procter and Gamble or the M–1A2 tank built in Lima for sale to Saudi Arabia, exports equal paychecks for the people of Ohio.

That's why I want to talk today about a dangerous idea embraced by my opponent, a new tax increase that he's taken to heart. And I'm not talking about the $150 billion tax increase that he wants in new income taxes. I'm not talking about the new payroll tax that he will need to pay for a Government takeover of health care or the training tax he wants to chain to our economy or the carbon tax he wants to put on your cars. I'm talking about a new idea, a tax on foreign companies doing business in the United States.

Some might say, "What's wrong with that? At least the one tax that American workers won't have to pay." Well, you should care, and here's why. You'll feel the effect up and down these loading docks, starting with the seven companies right here in Tall Timbers. Because these companies may be foreign owned, but the jobs are American jobs. I know that our economy is struggling right now, and a lot of people are hurting in this country. The economy's struggling to accelerate right now. And I don't want to see anyone take these jobs away from you, the American worker.

Look at this one, look at FMT, an American-owned company, selling what it makes here in the U.S. But Joe here, Joe Kirk, tells me FMT sells to a number of companies that are American based but foreign owned, sells to those. And if my opponent had his way and your customers get hit by his tax, when they start to cut back, when they cancel orders, you'll get hurt. We need to do better by the American worker. We need a policy that creates jobs, not a tax machine that spits out pink slips.

Now, here's what I have to offer: a coherent plan, one that sees that in today's world foreign policy, domestic policy, and economic policy are three sides of a single issue; a strategy that reaches out to the world in a way that makes a difference right here in Findlay, in your neighborhoods and in your lives. We must build on the fundamentals of lower tax rates, limits on Government spending, less redtape and regulation, and more trade, more competition to generate the growth that means more opportunity and thus more jobs.

It begins with an aggressive strategy to open new markets, so that "Made in America" is understood in any language from Lima, Ohio, to Lima, Peru, and beyond. Some will say that the American worker isn't up to it. And I say: Look, give our workers a level playing field, and they will outperform any worker in the world, anyplace, anywhere, anytime.

I learned this myself. Thank God I spent some time in the private sector. Half my adult life was in the private sector, and half in public service. But I learned this part in a very personal way 35 years ago when I started and headed a small drilling company, service company, a tiny company. But we sold our services in Japan, in Brunei, in the South Pacific, sold them over in the Middle East, sold them in Venezuela and Trinidad. And I learned something from all that. I learned you don't have to be a big company to export. I learned that our crews, our workers could compete, hold their own with workers, do better than workers anywhere in the rest of the world. And I learned that when we export, we really help the American economy. That is firsthand experience that a young businessman learned, and as President I feel even more strongly about it. We cannot go to protection and higher taxes. We must go to more exports and more competition.

I also believe in a very simple philosophy: The Government is too big, and it spends too much of your money. So far, this gridlocked Congress has resisted many of my attempts to cut the budget deficit. So last week I unveiled at Houston there a new idea: Why not give you, the taxpayer, the right to earmark up to 10 percent of your tax return and have it go for one purpose alone, to reduce the budget deficit? Let's get the deficit down and lift the burden of debt from the children's shoulders around here. Lift that burden of debt by getting the deficit down.

Once we have runaway spending under control, we need to cut taxes across the board to give businesses incentives to grow and create new jobs for America. I've been accused of being one of those who thinks every day is the Fourth of July. Well, that's a lot better than my opponent. He thinks every day is April 15th. That's going to be the big issue in this campaign. That's going to be the big issue. It's time to take the bull's-eye off the back of the American taxpayer.

I have a small concern about small business, a special concern about that. They create two-thirds of the new jobs in our economy, small businesses. And I have a plan to give small businesses relief from taxation, regulation, and litigation.

You may have read the story, and this is true, about the fellow up in New York who threw himself in front of a subway train and then sued for damages, and he was awarded $650,000. Doctors are afraid to practice medicine; some moms and dads won't coach Little League. And my opponent and the trial lawyers of America eye each other with "goo-goo eyes" like Boris and Natasha in those old Bullwinkle cartoons. And I want to stand up to the trial bar and reform our legal system. As a nation, here it is, we ought to sue each other less, and we ought to care for each other more. And we've got to do something about these lawsuits.

Audience members. Four more years! Four more years! Four more years!

The President. Time and again, I have sent proposals up to that gridlocked Congress to do something to put some caps on these lawsuits. And time and again, the gridlocked Congress has said no because they are in the pocket of the trial lawyers association. Give me new Members of Congress, and let us change that for the American people.

I have other priorities, and they're your priorities: To control health care costs, we've got to do something about health care in this country, but control the costs without a backdoor Government takeover. We need more job training for workers caught in the transition of our economy. And I have a plan, a good one, to create new schools for a new century—we call it America 2000—and with new ideas like using competition to make schools more accountable to you, the taxpayers and the parents. Give the parents a choice as to whether to send this kid to private, public, or religious school.

If you agree with these ideas, then I ask you a favor. Help me make this reform agenda a reality. Come November 3d, send me a Congress I can work with, and give the existing Democratic leadership a pink slip to get on home and go about their business.

Congress today has become a gridlocked Congress, the only institution that has not changed in 38 years. Presidents come and go; Senators come and go. The Senate has changed control. The House of Representatives has not changed control in 38 years,

and they spend their time debating, incredibly, important issues like Vanna White and the "Wheel of Fortune"—[*laughter*]—while neglecting the business of the Nation.

Now, next year, there are going to be an estimated 150 new Members of Congress, at least, and they're going to come to Washington. We then have a real opportunity to break the gridlock. As you look at the various candidates, ask them the tough questions: Are you for free and fair trade? Are you against the kind of business tax that will cost American jobs? Do you want to get the deficit down and the economy moving? And send me a Congress that will do what's right for America. I want to see the line-item veto. I want a balanced budget amendment for this Constitution.

Don't you believe for one minute what the opponents say when they say we are a nation in decline, we are a nation not respected around the world. I've been to many places around the world, and if one thing is clear, it is we are the undisputed, respected leader not just of the free world but of other countries that are striving for the freedom and democracy we sometimes take for granted.

Since this is Flag City, let me close with a flag story. During the Gulf war, I received a letter from the Mayor of Stantonsburg, North Carolina. He told me about watching two little girls about 10 years old walking across the school yard. One day, they went across. He was watching, and they were pulling their mom's laundry on a wagon. As the girls passed the pole in front of the town hall, they looked up and saw the United States flag flapping in the wind. Unaware that anyone was watching, these two little girls stopped, placed their hands over their hearts, and pledged allegiance to the flag. One little girl said simply, "It's important to do this, you know, because of the war and all."

Well, this election, like all elections, is about that little girl, and all the kids in Findlay, in Lima, and all the kids in America. If we do what is right today, we can take advantage of the opportunity of our global victory. We can build a land where they will be safe and strong and secure, where they can climb the flagpole of opportunity and put their hands over their hearts with pride, knowing that in their land the sun is always just peeking out over the horizon.

I'm delighted to have been back in Findlay. Thank you once again for this warm welcome, and may God bless the United States of America. Thank you very much.

Note: The President spoke at 5:15 p.m. at Findlay Machine and Tool, Inc., in Tall Timbers Industrial Park. In his remarks, he referred to Joe Kirk, company president, and Jim Woodward, chairman, Adopt a Flag Committee in Findlay, OH.

Remarks in Toledo, Ohio, on Additional Disaster Assistance for Florida Following Hurricane Andrew
August 27, 1992

The President. I want to make a brief statement on the hurricane situation in south Florida. I've been on the phone with Secretary Card; with the White House, of course; and with Governor Chiles, the Governor of Florida. Secretary Card is the head of this Federal task force that is responding to the aftermath of Hurricane Andrew, and I talked to both him and Governor Chiles about what more needs to be done.

I've directed the Federal troops to be immediately alerted and begin to provide additional emergency assistance to the victims of the disaster. We are going to fulfill the request of the Governor for Federal participation by the military. And then we will be doing a lot more because, as these reports have come in today, the damage is far more widespread than even we had feared. We directed the Department of Defense to supply comprehensive assistance to the affected areas, including mobile tents, food, water, field kitchens. I've also directed them to supply whatever transportation is necessary, including aircraft and helicopters, to fulfill that vital mission.

The damage has created tragedy for millions of Floridians. Some are estimating it may be the worst national disaster this country has seen, natural disaster. And on behalf of every American, of course, let me just express profound concern to those residents of Florida.

But the military is moving, and there's meetings right now to further enhance this mobilization. So help is on the way. It will be a major effort because the National Guard in Florida, according to the Governor, has been fully mobilized now. I think we saw half the troops mobilized as of yesterday, but even that, with a lot of troops, have not been able to handle this job. So the Federal Government is not only prepared to assist but is in this instance very eager to assist. So that will be underway, and relief will be forthcoming very, very soon.

Q. Mr. President, what will the role of the troops be? Is there a problem of looting there?

The President. No, I think the Florida Guard has done a good job in the security aspects. And I think these troops and these facilities will be used for sanitation, for feeding, for housing, tents, for example, and to bring that kind of relief to the people.

Thank you all very, very much.

Q. Do you want to talk about politics a little bit?

The President. I'd better not right now.

Note: The President spoke at 5:40 p.m. at the Toledo Express Airport prior to his departure for Washington, DC.

The President's News Conference on the Aftermath of Hurricane Andrew
August 28, 1992

The President. I have with me several of the key leaders at the Pentagon who are working on this humanitarian problem. And our military resources are responding promptly and massively to the hurricane disaster.

At least 7,000 Federal troops are on station or en route to deliver services to Floridians who are the victims of this horrible disaster. That amounts to a full brigade. Another 1,000 Marines are going to Opa Locka to help, if necessary.

Two tent cities with sanitation facilities which can house 5,000 people will arrive in Florida this afternoon from Guantanamo. General Reimer, with me today, and Secretary Atwood tell me that the Department of Defense has already delivered nearly 200,000 meals. In addition, another 200,000 would be delivered today and tomorrow. Also, 20 mobile kitchen trailers, which are each capable of feeding 300 personnel every 2 hours, will serve food around the clock. The Department of the Navy is providing shelter for up to 5,000 personnel.

In addition, the Army is sending up to 1,250 tents, 25,000 cots, and 50,000 blankets. The military is sending a full medical brigade and seven special medical teams to deal with the health problems. Ten thousand gallons of bottled water arrive today. Contracts have been let for 6 million more gallons of water, Generators are being supplied for electricity support in relief centers. In addition, the Army Corps of Engineers is on the ground to help with the removal of debris that will allow people to move around.

The United States Department of Agriculture has just distributed over 100,000 food packages. In addition, 7,000 cases of food from the Red Cross and other agencies have been sent to Florida shelters.

Finally, with the respect to the maintenance of public order and security, functions now the responsibility of State and local officials in Florida, I have made very clear to Governor Chiles both yesterday and today that I am willing to send more Federal troops and federalize the National Guard in Florida if he wants us to. We will commit all Federal military resources necessary to help the people in Florida. I've just talked to Governor Chiles, and I think we are in agreement on all of this.

As far as Louisiana goes, problems for some families are terrible. The size, the scope of the disaster is not near as great. But the military is helping there as well. There are MRE's on the ground. The generator sets are there. And I've been trying to contact Governor Edwards, with whom I visited the area the other day, to be sure that we are giving him the proper support for the people of Louisiana.

So things are moving, and the big thing is to get this job done for the people. It is a cooperative effort between private agencies, between local, State, and the Federal government. I am very, very proud of the way the military has responded here.

State and Federal Cooperation

Q. Mr. President, how do you respond to criticism that you did not act fast enough or you didn't respond to the needs——

The President. Well, I think the reason—I would simply say this: First place, I'm not going to participate in the blame game, nor is Governor Chiles. What we're trying to do is help people. It doesn't do any good to go into "who shot John." I can tell you this, that this large a military movement would not have taken place if there was not very early planning and cooperation by the military, and we have responded. I think the Governor would agree that when he asked for this massive movement of force, it was only within a few hours that we responded to that.

So I think much more important than when something took place or didn't take place is the feeling we must convey of total cooperation. I'm satisfied that we responded properly, and I'm very confident that the military have conducted their mission so far with beautiful planning, now excellent execution. I'm also satisfied that they will do whatever it takes to go the extra mile to help the people of Florida. And that's all I'm going to say about that.

Q. Was Chiles slow to ask for Federal troops?

The President. I'm not going to say that. I just expressed myself on this subject. I think we've responded. I think he would agree that when he asked for a massive amount of force yesterday, it's on the way. There were some things he asked about that we were not able to do, but as he said down there, and I will say here, we are having excellent cooperation between the Governor's office, the State of Florida, and the Federal Government. He said it, and I say it. I'm not going to change my mind on that. He's working——

Q. Weren't you ready to send troops in there sooner?

The President. ——very, very hard to coordinate. He's got a very difficult job down there.

Q. Weren't troops ready to move sooner than that at Bragg, though, and elsewhere?

The President. I've already said when we were asked to move, we moved these massive numbers of forces.

Q. But they were ready to move sooner if asked, weren't they?

The President. I'm not going to go into that because I don't—what you seem to be interested in is kind of assigning blame or something. That is not what's at stake here, and I don't want to participate in that.

There was some unit that we couldn't— what was it?

Mr. Heldstab. One air battalion.

Mr. Reimer. Air battalion.

The President. ——engineer, and what was the reason for that?

Mr. Heldstab. They had already been on their 2-week active duty and were unable to be involuntarily recalled.

The President. There was one battalion he wanted to have—this was before yesterday's request—and we were not able to do it because those people had served. It was a reserve unit. They had served, and under the law we're not able to mobilize them. But perhaps that's what's causing some of the concern.

But the Governor and I are looking at this, I think, the same. I'm not going to— you can ask him. But we want to give full cooperation to what's happening there. You just turn on the set, and you can see these planes rolling in there. That's the main thing. Look forward, try to help, and try to wipe out these little differences that some people want to talk about. I want to dwell on how we're going to help the people in Florida.

Q. Mr. President, does the Federal Government have the lead role in this right now?

The President. The Federal Government has a leading role in the humanitarian relief. It does not have a role in the security right now. That's in the hands of the State, and it's been entrusted largely to the National Guard, which is under the control of the Governor because it has not been federalized.

Q. Mr. President, is the magnitude of this disaster going to require additional Federal funds?

The President. Well, if it does, we will have to acquire additional Federal funds. I have not had an estimate on that yet.

President's Schedule

Q. Mr. President, what are your plans for this weekend? And since you were able to manage the crisis involving the Soviet coup and the prewar plans last year, why did you decide to scrub your trip to Kennebunkport?

The President. Well, I think I'll be having meetings here over the weekend. I'll be down here either tomorrow or Sunday for a report from the people on the ground down there. I don't want to pull them out of there right now, but I think it is very important that the coordination go forward. We've talked here about the military. We have a lot of civilian agencies, 27 of them to be exact, that are involved in all of this. Our staff here under Jim Baker have been actively involved almost 'round the clock. But I think it's important that all of these agencies know that the President is going to be on top of this.

Q. Was there a political consideration in not going to Kennebunkport, sir?

The President. No political consideration. I'd very much would like to be there and regret not going. But I've got my responsibilities here, and I think I can do that from here. Then I'm going to be at Camp David. We've got excellent communications; it's almost like being in your office here. But I'll just do what I've got to do.

Q. Mr. President, did Jim Baker or anyone say it wouldn't look right, sir?

Disaster Planning

Q. Mr. President, you mentioned that what happened last night and this morning was the result of considerable planning that had been done by the military. When did that planning actually begin, sir, and how closely did you stay on top of it on the days that followed your visit to Florida?

Secretary Atwood. On Sunday we activated the Army to make plans. This was before the hurricane struck.

The President. Sunday the planning began, and they activated the planning before the hurricane struck. They were giving me reports on what possibly we would use in terms of assets.

Q. Mr. President, were you in contact with Governor Chiles as soon as that plan was developed to be sure that he understood it and could right then, that the second he asked for Federal assistance these troops would be in there?

The President. I think I said that publicly when I was in Florida on Tuesday—was it Tuesday I was down there? But when I was there he was standing right next to me, and we did talk about that, yes.

I think we've had a good, cooperative relationship. I heard some local officials who were somewhat, well, not somewhat, quite critical. But I understand that. These people have been up all night. They've been worried about their constituency. In this case it was a commissioner. They're wondering how their people are going to get fed. So I can understand tempers flaring. But I don't want to contribute to that. We want to move forward here.

Q. Mr. President, part of the problem also that they were saying was that there was, as you were saying earlier, a lack of coordination, and also they were saying perhaps some redtape. Is there anything more the White House can do to eliminate some of the redtape to get the aid going quicker?

The President. Well, any time you have this massive an operation I suppose, as the young major I heard on the television right now, he said, "Well, there's a glitch from time to time, but it's overwhelmed by the fact that so much good is happening." But we've got good, competent people trying to work out the coordination between the agencies. Andy Card, our Secretary of Transportation, has my full confidence, and he's on the spot working with the other Federal officials and with the Governor's people. So if there are any difficulties or redtape, we want to cut right through it.

Q. Were you disappointed—*[inaudible]*—early response, sir?

The President. No. I don't know what area they've not responded in. Listen, if anybody can do the job better, why, we'll be pushing them to do it better.

Louisiana

Q. To clear up the situation in Louisiana, Mr. President, is it your expectation that no Federal troops will be necessary there?

The President. Well, I gather that's the case right now. But we made clear to Governor Edwards that if more was required, please let us know. I think we had assurance on that. I didn't talk to him. I've been trying to get hold of him. But one of our White House officials talked to him, and I think that was his last, latest judgment on it.

I've got time for one more question.

State and Federal Cooperation

Q. Mr. President, yesterday you said the reason you were sending in the military is because the size of the disaster is so much larger than originally anticipated. Sir, why didn't we know sooner that hundreds of thousands of people have been left homeless?

The President. I think one of the reasons is you've got a lot of isolated areas. Secondly, I don't know that there was a large discrepancy in numbers of people that are out of their homes. But as I said, yesterday we received the request for massive numbers of troops, and yesterday we responded within several hours. I think that will be

Governor Chiles' understanding, too.

But look, if any Federal official is trying to blame a State official, I want it to stop. If any State official is trying to blame the Federal official or local official, that's not constructive. I know it makes very good, wonderful debate, but it doesn't help anything. What we're trying to do is work together here. I am determined that from the Federal Government's standpoint we give maximum cooperation to local and State officials. And that's the way it's going to be.

There is no point getting into blame and this "who shot John" thing that I know everybody's fascinated with. I don't want that, and I don't want one single Federal official trying to be in the blame-assigning business. I've given you the facts here today. I think Governor Chiles will understand that those are the facts. The important thing is to help the people.

This military of ours, these men standing behind me and those that work for them, are doing a first-rate job in responding to the order. The order is to get down there and help people, and it's a wonderful thing. I think the people of Florida when they see this, see the magnitude of this operation, will be very, very grateful. We all should be grateful that we can have this kind of response.

Thank you all very much.

Note: The President's 140th news conference began at 12:10 p.m. in the Rose Garden at the White House, following a meeting with Deputy Secretary of Defense Donald J. Atwood, Jr.; Lt. Gen. Dennis J. Reimer, USA, Deputy Chief of Staff for Operations and Plans; and Maj. Gen. John Heldstab, USA, Director of Operations, Readiness and Mobilizations.

Nomination of Alvin P. Adams, Jr., To Be United States Ambassador to Peru
August 28, 1992

The President today announced his intention to nominate Alvin P. Adams, Jr., of Virginia, a career member of the Senior Foreign Service, class of Minister-Counselor, to be Ambassador of the United States of America to the Republic of Peru.

Since 1989, Ambassador Adams has served as Ambassador to the Republic of Haiti at the American Embassy in Port-au-Prince. He has also served in several other positions at the Department of State including: Associate Coordinator for Counter-Terrorism, 1987–89; detailed to Ryder Systems, Inc., 1986; Ambassador to the Republic of Djibouti, 1983–1985; Deputy Executive Sec-

retary at the State Department, 1981–83; Director of the Secretariat Staff, 1981; Special Assistant for Legislative and Public Affairs at the Bureau of Economic and Business Affairs, 1979–81; and Deputy Director of the Office of Business Practices at the Bureau of Economic and Business Affairs, 1977–79.

Ambassador Adams graduated from Yale University (B.A., 1964) and Vanderbilt University (LL.B., 1967). He was born August 29, 1942, in New York, NY. Ambassador Adams is married, has one child, and resides in Alexandria, VA.

Statement by Press Secretary Fitzwater on the London Conference on the Former Yugoslavia
August 28, 1992

The President met this morning with Acting Secretary of State Lawrence Eagle-

burger to discuss the results of the London conference on the former Yugoslavia.

The conference has given us a better foundation to defuse, contain, and bring to an end the conflict in former Yugoslavia. It has established a new, permanent negotiating forum, cochaired by the United Nations and the European Community, in Geneva. The United States has offered $3 million to help with startup costs of the conference.

The conference developed an international plan of action to deal with this crisis. As a result, the international community is taking a number of concrete actions to provide humanitarian relief, increase pressure on the aggressors, and contain the conflict. These include a massive humanitarian relief effort for this winter; a strengthening of the sanctions regime by introducing international monitors in neighboring states; and the placing of human rights monitors as well as "early warning" monitors in neighboring states and regions.

The conference also made progress with the parties themselves. The leader of the Bosnian Serbs has agreed to consolidate heavy weapons under international control and the Government of Bosnia has agreed to rejoin the negotiating process.

The causes of this conflict are complex; it will not be ended overnight. We thank Prime Minister Major and Secretary-General Boutros-Ghali for organizing and running this conference, which has succeeded in galvanizing international action to alleviate the humanitarian nightmare in Bosnia, to support the negotiating process, to punish the aggressors, and to quarantine the conflict.

Remarks and an Exchange With Reporters on Disaster Relief Efforts
August 29, 1992

The President. Let me just bring you all up to date. Yesterday I talked to the Governor of Guam, Governor Ada. His main problem there is getting that airport to function, getting generators in to get water going for the people. The military have responded superbly here. And those problems, thank heavens, are less extensive than the problems in Florida or Louisiana. But nevertheless, there are a lot of people hurting there, and we're trying to help them in every way possible.

I talked to Governor Edwards of Louisiana yesterday. He expressed his appreciation for the Federal support. I've just had a briefing from General Sullivan as to what the military have done. And of course, if their pockets need additional support, we're prepared to give additional support. But again, that one is a little further along now. It's getting into the reconstruction phase of things.

As to Florida, General Sullivan and Andy Card and Wally Stickney, who's the head of FEMA, have briefed us; Admiral Jeremiah of the Joint Chiefs and, of course, Secretary Atwood helping out along the way.

First, I think the cooperation from the military has been absolutely outstanding. We've just reviewed the status of the Federal, State, and then the local efforts in Florida to help the people in the aftermath of Andrew. The mobilization I ordered of nearly 7,000 Federal troops in addition to the 5,000 National Guardsmen is well underway. Significant progress is being made in delivering food, water, shelter, and other basic necessities to the people of the region.

I am today ordering an additional 5,000 military troops be sent in order to increase existing services such as the provision of food, kitchens, tents, and delivery of shelter-related items. We're also sending more medical units with doctors who are capable of advising and treating patients in the area.

I'm also augmenting our current effort in the following way: I'm making available nearly $300 million to help the delivery of services by FEMA, by the Federal Emergency Management Agency, and the Small Business Administration—$300 million. Furthermore, I intend to submit a supplemental appropriations request as soon as Congress returns in whatever amount necessary to respond to the human needs on the ground in Florida and Louisiana and, if need be, in Guam.

I want to emphasize that we intend to respond to this crisis on a human level, block by block, right out there where these people live. People have lost their homes and their possessions, and we want to reach out to people so they don't have to leave what few possessions they have and leave the familiar surroundings that they have lived in.

We've made it known again today to Governor Chiles that I am prepared to federalize the National Guard at any time. I repeat that offer now. The Governor, city managers, and other local officials are doing an excellent job at reaching out to help their citizens. This is a time for all of us to pull together.

I also want to announce an agreement that's been reached today with the State of Florida to provide an additional $127.2 million in emergency food stamps for the people of Dade County. I've received a full report today on our military and our civilian efforts to help. I am satisfied that everyone is dedicated to pulling out all of the stops to help the people of Florida recover from this enormous disaster.

I am grateful to the men on the ground, men and women of the military who are performing with the same excellence that this country's come to expect. And I am grateful to Andy Card and Wally Stickney for what they're doing. It's a massive problem of coordination and distribution, but I am determined that we will get on top of it and that we will see these problems solved. It's not easy. But we're moving with a lot of effort here, a lot of people, to get the job done.

Q. Mr. President, do you as President bear some responsibility for the delay in Federal help?

The President. We're not talking about delay. The military was ready to move instantly, hot planning right from the very beginning. And there's no point going back trying to dig up difficulty between one government agency or another. I said that yesterday, and I'll repeat it today. What I'd like to see is somebody tell what exactly is happening down there and what people are

trying to do.

Q. Governor Clinton suggested, sir, that the Federal response should be looked into to see how it could be improved, said that he's not criticizing you but thinks that it should be looked into. What's your response to that?

The President. Well, I don't respond to Governor Clinton on these matters. We have a national emergency here, and we're trying to get this job done. And I have full confidence in the people that are trying to get the job done.

I don't take that as critical. If there are ways to improve what we're doing, fine. But this isn't a business of second-guessing; it's a business of trying to help people. And that's what we're about here. Again, I salute those who are involved. Andy Card had hardly any sleep down there working with these local officials. Governor Chiles is being as cooperative as he possibly can; same with the Senators down there, one Democrat and one Republican, trying to help us, Senator Graham, Senator Mack.

And so I look for the positive things in a matter of this nature. We're not going around trying to find blame or make some politics out of a national disaster.

Q. Do you have even a ballpark idea of how much additional money might be needed?

The President. I don't think we have any estimates on that. Director Darman is here, who has the total view in mind. But we haven't—unless Wally, did you want to——

Director Stickney. No, sir, I think it's too early.

Q. Mr. President, any response to Clinton's suggestion or charge that you're distorting his tax record and his claim——

The President. No. We're talking about something that's very serious business here, and I'm going to keep on this subject. I want the American people to understand what we're trying to do to solve this big problem, Federal, State, and local governments working together. And it's a very impressive effort. I think the people of this community who have been heartbroken and scared, wondering where their meals are coming from, are now seeing—and certainly those that are not seeing will see—

that this is a magnificent response, local, State, and Federal, with an awful lot of credit to the U.S. military who once again have performed admirably.

Those who want to dramatically cut the military, they ought to take another look when it comes to being prepared to do things of this nature.

Q. Sir, do you think your handling of this will be viewed in any way by the electorate down in Florida in a particular way?

The President. Look, may I tell you something? This may be hard for you to believe: I am thinking about what's good for the people here. I don't even think about the politics of it. We're trying to help people.

I see a bunch of people running around interviewing people who have been thrown out of their homes by a natural disaster, saying how do the politics work. Good heavens, isn't there any honor here? Can't we help people without having somebody try to put a political interpretation on it? I mean, heaven sakes, we have people that are hurting out there. And then to try to cast it politically, I'm sorry, I just simply find that a little bit outrageous.

And it's happening all over Florida, I'm told today by the local head of one of these communities, Homestead, that's been hit so badly. He said he's just shocked by it. That's the way it is. That's the way it is.

Q. ——Mr. President, from your responding much quicker, at least going down there quicker than you went to South Carolina or California?

The President. I think we've responded properly, and I think history will show that.

Note: The President spoke at 4:13 p.m. in the Cabinet Room at the White House. In his remarks, he referred to Gen. Gordon Sullivan, Army Chief of Staff in charge of the Federal forces involved in the recovery efforts in Florida.

Remarks on Hurricane Andrew Disaster Relief
August 30, 1992

The President. Let me simply say that this meeting is just a follow-on meeting. The Secretaries and Administrators here are able to help the victims of the hurricane, and I'm going to hear from them, each of them, as to what their Departments can do. We'll figure out how to follow up.

Over the weekend I was in touch with the manager of Homestead, city manager Alex Muxo; talked to the director of public safety of Dade County, Fred Taylor, and to Otis Wallace, one of the top officials in Florida City; and then General Sullivan called in with a good report as to what they're doing. And I must say I think progress is being made. And now we need to follow up with our Agencies and Departments in every way that we possibly can to assist the victims of this storm.

I might say for the benefit of the reporters here, as far as we're concerned, cooperation between the State and Federal is good. I've talked with General Sullivan about the coordination between the Guard and the regular Army, and he felt that that's in good shape, as did the director of public safety of Dade County. So I think real progress is being made, but there's still an awful lot of human suffering there. And what we all are going to try to do is continue to move forward as fast as we can to help alleviate that.

Q. Mr. President, some people have suggested that additional funding is going to be essential to help the people of southern Florida. Are you prepared to ask Congress now for additional funding?

The President. Yes. I think I made that statement the other day, that we are prepared. As soon as we get the estimates that are pouring in every day, why, we will go forward.

Q. Do you have any idea how much you'll be asking for?

The President. I don't have it now.

Note: The President spoke at 11:05 a.m. in the Cabinet Room at the White House. In his remarks, he referred to Gen. Gordon Sullivan, Army Chief of Staff in charge of the Federal forces involved in the recovery efforts in Florida.

Presidential Determination No. 92–45—Memorandum on Extension of the Exercise of Certain Authorities Under the Trading With the Enemy Act
August 28, 1992

Memorandum for the Secretary of State, the Secretary of the Treasury

Subject: Extension of the Exercise of Certain Authorities Under the Trading With the Enemy Act

Under section 101(b) of Public Law 95–223 (91 Stat. 1625; 50 U.S.C. App. 5(b) note), and a previous determination made by me on September 13, 1991 (56 FR 48415), the exercise of certain authorities under the Trading With the Enemy Act is scheduled to terminate on September 14, 1992.

I hereby determine that the extension for one year of the exercise of those authorities with respect to the applicable countries is in the national interest of the United States.

Therefore, pursuant to the authority vested in me by section 101(b) of Public Law 95–223, I extend for one year, until September 14, 1993, the exercise of those authorities with respect to countries affected by:

(1) the Foreign Assets Control Regulations, 31 CFR Part 500;

(2) the Transaction Control Regulations, 31 CFR Part 505;

(3) the Cuban Assets Control Regulations, 31 CFR Part 515; and

(4) the Foreign Funds Control Regulations, 31 CFR Part 520.

The Secretary of the Treasury is directed to publish this determination in the *Federal Register.*

GEORGE BUSH

[*Filed with the Office of the Federal Register, 3:45 p.m., September 16, 1992*]

Note: This memorandum was released by the Office of the Press Secretary on August 31.

Statement on the Russia-United States Agreement on the Disposition of Uranium From Nuclear Weapons
August 31, 1992

Over the past year the United States and the former Soviet Union have agreed to cut their strategic nuclear arsenals by two-thirds and to eliminate most of their tactical nuclear weapons, including all ground-launched systems. As a result of these dramatic reductions, thousands of nuclear warheads are being dismantled in Russia and the United States. The United States and Russia are cooperating closely to help ensure the safe and secure transport, storage, and dismantlement of former Soviet nuclear weapons.

I am pleased to announce that the Russian Federation and the United States have now also initialed an agreement to ensure that highly enriched uranium from dismantled nuclear weapons will be used only for peaceful purposes. Our two Governments have initialed an agreement, which we expect to sign quickly, providing for the conversion of this material into civilian reactor fuel. We have also agreed to establish measures to ensure that the nonproliferation, physical security, material accounting and control, and environmental requirements covering this material are fully met.

Under the agreement, the United States and Russia would seek within the next 12 months to conclude an implementing contract establishing the terms of the purchase of weapons-grade uranium by the U.S. Department of Energy and the dilution of that material to reactor-grade uranium for sale as commercial reactor fuel. The contract would also provide for the participation of the U.S. private sector and the use by the

Russian Federation of a portion of the proceeds to increase the safety of nuclear reactors in the former Soviet Union.

Abroad, this agreement will help ensure that nuclear weapons-grade material does not fall into the wrong hands, while providing funds to promote economic reforms and the transition to a market-based economy. At home, this agreement will secure long-term supplies of less expensive fuel for U.S. nuclear power stations to the benefit of American consumers, with no adverse impact on American jobs. Thus, this U.S.-Russian agreement illustrates how foreign policy accomplishments can promote our domestic economic well-being while making the world a safer place to live.

Remarks on Hurricane Andrew Recovery Efforts
August 31, 1992

The President. Let me just make a brief statement because it's been a very busy day regarding the hurricane and trying to help the victims thereof. I met today with the homebuilders, the volunteer organizations, a lot of the Federal officials. And at this meeting we're going to be talking with representatives of the insurance companies and small business.

We are exploring the medium and longer term needs of the hurricane aftermath. This has got to be a long-term commitment, as I'm sure everyone here knows. And it's going to take months, literally, to rebuild these communities. In many ways the hardest work is yet to come. And these will be the times that test this commitment, to guarantee to the victims of this terrible tragedy that we're with them for the long haul.

I want to make one special plea here today. I'd ask the full support of the news media on this one, and that is an appeal for all Americans to give generously to these volunteer organizations who served so valiantly in south Florida and in Louisiana. Today we've talked about the complexities of the problems ahead, from building codes and check cashing to getting the kids back

in school. But the cooperative spirit has been fantastic, as I'm sure Pat Saiki knows, who is head of our Small Business Administration. I just would strongly urge the American people to participate in any way they can by supporting these volunteer organizations. I'll tell you more about that, but they are doing a superb job. And they need the support of everybody.

And so thank you all very much for being here. I want to shift here and get from you the size of the insurance problem that's facing the people there, how we can help, the Federal Government can help. I'll be glad to tell you about our Federal efforts in which I have great confidence. The military has moved in. They're doing very well. But the volunteers, I'll tell you, it's really the best in the American spirit, what's happening there.

Q. Mr. President, do you plan to go back to Florida and——

The President. Oh, I will, yes. Let me simply say that I'll—leaving at 5:45 in the morning to go back down there, going to Florida. At 5:45 Barbara and I will leave. Secretary Cheney will be joining me. We will have a chance to talk to the top civilian and military and some of the volunteer leaders. And then we'll fly over to Louisiana, touch base there, and be back here tomorrow evening.

Note: The President spoke at 4:25 p.m. in the Roosevelt Room at the White House.

Remarks and an Exchange With Reporters on Disaster Relief Efforts in Homestead, Florida
September 1, 1992

The President. Let me, at the outset of these remarks, say how much I appreciate the cooperative spirit here, the Governor of Florida, the Mayor and the city manager of Homestead, and the other cities here that are represented. And all are pitching in. I am so proud of what our military is doing. And God bless the volunteers, those who are giving of themselves to help others. It is a moving and a wonderful message that's going forth to the whole country, whether it's from the military, from State officials, from local officials, or from the volunteers, the propensity of one American to help another. That's the message that I get loud and clear.

Last week I was here in south Florida, and then I returned to Washington and issued the orders to help people get back on their feet. We're in this for the long haul. We won't leave until the job is done. That's why I'm here this morning with Secretary Cheney, the Secretary of Defense. And I'm proud to be at the side of our two Senators from Florida who have been working day and night along with the Governor trying to help the people of this State.

Today I'm announcing that we are committed to rebuilding Homestead Air Force Base to show our commitment to south Florida. Homestead is very important to our military. It helps combat the cocaine trade. It provides air defense. And it will be rebuilt.

Now, I don't underestimate our task in south Florida, particularly after being back here today. And to ease the financial burden, today I am authorizing under the Stafford Act full Federal reimbursement for 100 percent of all eligible public assistance, including projects such as debris removal, to eliminate immediate threats to public

health and safety, and repair and reconstruction of nonprofit facilities. After the State has committed an amount equal to, what was it, $10 per capita—but this authorization is the maximum that we can do, and I am very proud that we're doing this. Temporary housing and mortgage assistance crisis counseling, disaster unemployment assistance will continue to be 100 percent federally funded where permitted under the law. And although some cost sharing is involved, the Federal assistance that I have authorized today represents an extraordinary and very appropriate response to this human tragedy.

However, the real heroes of Hurricane Andrew have been and will continue to be the people, the people of south Florida. They offer great hope for tomorrow. And to help coordinate the private sector response to Hurricane Andrew, I've asked Alvah Chapman, a very respected Florida leader and businessman, to serve as the private sector liaison to work with Secretary Card, to work with the Governor, to work with the Federal task force to ensure the most effective recovery effort possible.

Also, as I said yesterday, I want to commend and thank in the strongest terms possible the great effort of these private volunteer agencies who have responded so quickly and so well to the crisis. God bless the volunteers. I know, and I say this confidently, that these volunteers can count on the continued support of the American people in their ongoing work in meeting the critical needs of the people of south Florida. We are going to succeed. We will succeed because the people of south Florida, because of their spirit.

I've seen many examples of this just since I've been here, but let me just mention Isa

Haydem who owns a Days Inn in Homestead. Isa fired up his commercial-sized outdoor grill, cooked steaks, shrimp, and scallops, food donated by the local restaurants. And last Wednesday they fed 2,500 people during the day. And at night they fed almost 300, most of whom are police out there working their hearts out to keep order.

Well, it's heroes like this, and there are many other such examples, which make Alex Muxo, the Homestead city manager, say, "It's never gone. There's always tomorrow." Well, I agree. And we, working cooperatively with everybody, will rebuild south Florida. The spirit's still here. The spirit is still intact.

And may God bless the people that have been hurt. We're here to help. Thank you all very, very much. A great crowd. I did not mention the Congressmen here, Congresswoman Ileana Ros-Lehtinen and, of course, my old friend Dante Fascell, who represents this area. He's been the conscience here, getting in touch with us on things that we could do, including this matching of funds situation. So I salute him and Ileana.

Q. Mr. President, how long is the long haul in your estimation, sir?

The President. Whatever it takes. Whatever it takes.

Q. Years, perhaps?

The President. I'd have to defer to the experts on that. But amazing progress has been made. Out of the rubble you can see tent cities springing up. You can see medical units staffed by volunteers, former military guys and other—down here pitching, right in this very facility. So it's happening all over the place. And, again, I don't think you can know the answer to the question to how long until we actually can measure not only the Federal response and the State and local response but the response of the volunteer sector, which I'm convinced will be overwhelming. It already has started. Look what the Red Cross and these ministries are doing. It is unbelievable. And that spirit is going to move it along very, very fast.

Q. Mr. President, Governor Clinton says that once the dust settles that there should be an investigation——

The President. Well, look, let me say this,

Jim: I'm not even going to take any political questions. I have tried, and I know the Governor has, these Senators have, Congressmen standing with me have, try to keep it out of the political arena. And I have no comment whatsoever, simply to say we're here to help, and I really mean that. This is nothing to do with partisanship. It has everything to do with helping the families, some of whom are standing right here today. And we're going to try to keep it that way.

Q. Well, in a nonpartisan spirit, then, is there going to be an investigation into the Federal response, sir?

The President. I am very proud of the Federal response. And I think the Governor has been very gracious in his comments, certainly the others have. And let me express my total confidence in the Federal response and in the response particularly of the military, be it the Guard under the State, be it the military that comes under Secretary Cheney and General Powell's command. They've moved fast; they're here in large numbers. But they're here with hearts that are reaching out to the people, and that's what matters.

Q. Mr. President, does your 100-percent reimbursement mean that there will be billions of dollars in Federal aid?

The President. Yes, it does mean that. Well, I don't know, we have to wait and see what the estimates are.

Q. Andy Card——

The President. Well, he's an expert, and he has my full confidence. And I salute Andy Card, Secretary of Transportation. He's pulled off of his duties and responsibilities there, and he's taken on a massive job of coordination. He deserves great support and certainly the thanks of the President. I know we all feel that way about what he's doing.

Q. If you had a message specifically for young people of the community, what would it be?

The President. It would be, have hope. We're going to get these schools open again, working with the State and local officials. I talked to the State superintendent, to the Miami superintendent of schools today. He demonstrates a determination and a spirit that just really moved me. I called him from the plane coming down here. And I'll tell you, with that kind of spirit and then the cooperation from these officials, local, State, and Federal, why, we're going to get the job done.

But my message to these kids would be, look, you've had a tough time, and you lost a lot of stuff, a lot of toys, a lot of—you've seen your mothers and dads hurt, but you're going to bounce back. You're living in America. And the American spirit is going to lift you up. And that's the answer.

Last one.

Q. Mr. President, a lot of people, they're afraid to use the tents because they're concerned about security of their homes. And do you have anything you can say to encourage them?

The President. Yes, I would encourage them to use these tent cities. If they don't want to stay there all night long, they ought to go there, get medical attention, get showers, use the sanitary facilities there, get the food that's there. But I've talked to Governor Chiles about this. He has expressed his confidence not only in the National Guard, who has the security function and will be patrolling, but all of us have expressed our support for the local law enforcement people. I think it's a tribute to the spirit of Florida and the people of Florida that the acts of violence have been far less than predicted. We would, of course, condemn any violence, any taking advantage of one's neighbor. But nevertheless, I think that my message to them would be, use the facilities that exist.

I met a family right across the way here, literally less than a block from here. They needed medical attention for a child. And

they were asking, "We need medical attention. Where can we get help?" Here are these fantastic volunteers, right here, less than a block away, who stand ready to help in whatever the ailment, whatever the illness.

And so I think the city officials, the Mayor, the city manager are doing what they can now to get the message out. The Army has distributed, I think it's 10,000 radios. Those will be in the communities. And over those radios will be broadcast: What's available? How do you get your insurance? How do you get your Social Security check? Where do you go for medical attention? And once that communication networks gets going, say nothing of word of mouth, then I think these people will be beautifully served.

Some are scared to leave their homes. And I would simply say to them, trust in the security that's being provided in the neighborhoods. You don't have to be gone for all the time. If you feel more comfortable in your home or what's left of it, go, take the kid and go and leave somebody else in the house, and then come back. But soon that confidence will build, because these military people that have set up the camps, these private sector people, the Red Cross and others that have set up these facilities really have the spirit that will give the people the reassurance they need.

And it'll take care of itself, but we need to get the message out. And we're going to continue to try to do that.

Thank you all very, very much.

Note: The President spoke at 10 a.m. to community members at Homestead Middle School.

Statement by Press Secretary Fitzwater on Naming Alvah Chapman as Florida Disaster Relief Adviser
September 1, 1992

President Bush today asked Alvah Chapman, of Miami, FL, to work with Secretary of Transportation Andrew Card and the Federal Task Force on Hurricane Andrew as an adviser on private sector resources and relief efforts in south Florida. Mr. Chapman is director and chairman of the executive committee of Knight-Ridder, Inc., a newspaper chain that includes the Miami Herald and other Florida newspapers. As a resident of Florida for almost 40 years, he has been a leader in many community service endeavors. Mr. Chapman will help address the needs of the people in south Florida and marshal private sector resources in the local community.

White House Statement on Additional Disaster Relief for Florida
September 1, 1992

The President today announced that he has amended his August 24, 1992, declaration of a major disaster in the State of Florida to waive State and local cost sharing requirements, where permitted to do so by law, and to allow reimbursement of 100 percent of eligible public assistance costs exceeding $10 per capita.

This additional relief provided by the President is consistent with a request made by Gov. Lawton Chiles. It was taken in response to the unprecedented damage and destruction caused by Hurricane Andrew. By waiving customary State and local cost sharing requirements, the President can provide maximum Federal assistance to the people of Florida whose lives have been so severely disrupted by this disaster.

This waiver applies to all authorized public assistance. It will provide additional help to the State in its efforts to remove debris from the disaster areas, eliminate immediate threats to public health and safety, and carry out emergency work to save lives. Assistance for temporary housing, crisis counseling, and disaster unemployment will continue to be 100 percent federally funded where allowed under the law.

Note: The amended disaster declaration was attached to this release.

White House Statement on Additional Disaster Relief for Florida Schools
September 1, 1992

The President today called Octavio Visiedo, superintendent of schools for Dade County, FL, to inform him that $40 million will be immediately available to hard-hit Florida schools. The funds will be used to provide transportation to schools and new portable classrooms and to cover extraordinary operating costs.

Hurricane Andrew destroyed or severely damaged 15 percent of the 297 Dade County schools, creating transportation needs for 40,000 more children than expected. It is anticipated that with the additional assistance all children in Dade County will be able to return to school on September 14.

Other aid to be provided by the Department of Education will help students affected by the disaster. This aid includes: additional Federal grant and loan money to college, university, and trade school students; new funds for supplemental grants and campus-based loans to all institutions that enroll students affected by the disaster; and sensitivity in accommodating students' financial needs in general.

Nomination of Nancy A. Nord To Be a Commissioner of the Consumer Product Safety Commission
September 1, 1992

The President today announced his intention to nominate Nancy A. Nord, of the District of Columbia, to be a Commissioner of the Consumer Product Safety Commission for a term of 7 years from October 27, 1992.

Currently Ms. Nord serves as a senior consultant and attorney with Jellinek, Schwartz and Connolly, an environmental consulting firm in Washington, DC. She has also served as executive director of the Republican National Lawyers Association, 1991–92. She has also served as the executive director of the American Corporate Counsel Association, 1982–90; General Counsel for the Council on Environmental Quality, 1981–82; and associate minority counsel for the Energy and Commerce Committee in the U.S. House of Representatives, 1975–81.

Ms. Nord graduated from the University of Nebraska (B.A., 1968) and George Washington University (J.D., 1971). She was born September 14, 1946, in Sioux Falls, SD. Ms. Nord is married, has one child, and resides in Washington, DC.

Address to the Nation on Hurricane Andrew Disaster Relief
September 1, 1992

Good evening, everyone. Eight days ago the people of south Florida and Louisiana were confronted by perhaps the most destructive natural disaster in our history. Tonight I want to report to the Nation on the aftermath of Hurricane Andrew and the effort required to help Andrew's survivors back on their feet.

In the past week I've twice visited Louisiana and Florida. And in Florida, where the storm was strongest, up to a quarter million people have lost their homes, many huddled beneath the busted timbers of what was once a living room or a kitchen. There's no running water, no electricity. Little children are left without even a toy to play with.

In the aftermath of Hurricane Andrew, a relief effort has risen, unprecedented in size and impact. And tonight as we speak, almost 20,000 troops are on the ground assisting in everything from providing meals to erecting tent cities. Basic human needs, food, water, shelter, and medical assistance, are being provided.

In Florida, a curfew is in place, and the National Guard and local police patrol the streets. It's a tribute to these officers and to the people of this region that looting has been kept to a minimum. Social Security checks are being delivered on time. Financial help is being made available to families who have lost their homes and their jobs.

This relief effort has generated incredible cooperation. My thanks go to so many people who slept so little the past 8 days, to State and local government officials, Federal Agencies, private charities, and the heroic men and women of the United States military. Most especially, my appreciation goes out to the volunteers. When we arrived in Florida, some of the first people we met were from South Carolina, victims of Hurricane Hugo who had spent the night driving so they could help others through their ordeal. We met doctors and firefighters spending sleepless vacations lending a helping hand. Through the eloquence of their action, I've been reminded that America will always be a nation of neighbors.

Although the relief effort is well underway, urgent needs still exist. And so tonight I make a special appeal to the generous spirit of the American people. People in Florida and Louisiana want to stay in their homes. They're in desperate need of rolls of plastic to cover open roofs, lumber to board up walls, and cots to sleep on. They also need diapers, baby formula, and other infant supplies. And fresh volunteers are needed to staff medical facilities or help with the cleanup.

Right now, America's churches and charities are mobilizing to meet these needs. And I encourage all Americans to pitch in, in any way you can. If you don't know where to turn and you want to help right now, please call the American Red Cross at 1–800–842–2200. 1–800–842–2200.

Once our relief effort is complete, we will accelerate the process of recovery. Already today we announced plans to rebuild Homestead Air Force Base, the linchpin of the economy in devastated areas. And a distinguished Florida business leader, Alvah Chapman, has agreed to head a national private sector effort to help rebuild south Florida. It's called "We Will Rebuild." This effort has my strong support and the support of Florida Governor Chiles. All of us are in this for the long haul. If you want to be a part of this effort, please write We Will

Rebuild. And the address is Post Office Box 010790, Miami, Florida, and the ZIP Code is 33131.

In the past 8 days we've seen on our TV screens real tears, real sorrow, real hurt. Livelihoods have been destroyed. Lives, even young lives, have been tragically lost. But already in Florida and Louisiana, we're talking not just of relief but of recovery. This is a tribute to what is inside us. And yes, Andrew blew a whirlwind of devastation. But he could never extinguish the American spirit, a spirit of compassion and sacrifice and endurance. We have seen that spirit in action the past 8 days. And with this spirit and your enduring commitment, our neighbors in south Florida and Louisiana will recover.

Thank you for your generosity. And our prayers are with all who stood in Andrew's path. Good night.

Note: The President spoke at 9 p.m. from the Oval Office at the White House. The address was broadcast live on nationwide television.

Teleconference Remarks to the America 2000 Satellite Town Meeting
September 1, 1992

The President. Lamar, I'm here.

Secretary Alexander. Well, terrific.

The President. Delighted to be here. And I'm delighted you're willing to take this phone call from this very interested participant from the White House.

Secretary Alexander. We're honored that you'd take the time to call. We know you've had a very busy day.

The President. Well, let me just make a couple of comments butting into this wonderful program. But first a compliment, and then I do want to ask one question. But my compliments to the more than 2,500 communities out there who are working together on these national education goals.

When the Governors and I established the goals at Charlottesville at that education summit, we hoped to set a new direction

for education in our country. But we also knew that the goals would not make much difference unless they were adopted community by community. And so I guess the way to say it is we had high hopes at Charlottesville. But I don't think any one of us envisioned anything quite like this, over 2,500 different communities working together on the goals at one time by satellite. I really just want to say that I hope you will all stick with it, join the town meeting every month, and become an America 2000 community, if you're not in there already.

There are no quick fixes. The change we're talking about is really fundamental. It is really enormous, literally reinventing education. And that'll require what we call the break-the-mold schools, higher standards and certainly better tests, getting government off the teachers' backs, and then giving families more choice in schools and academic programs. There's nothing more important than creating the best schools in the world for our children, and this is the way to do it.

So my compliments to all assembled for what you're doing. My compliments also to the U.S. Chamber and all the local chambers of commerce out there who are involved in these community efforts, and then, of course, to the wonderful Wal-Mart associates who are participating. I do know firsthand how important education was to Sam Walton. And he would be glad, he would be thrilled that you were participating tonight. So, congratulations.

Now for my question, and I want to place it to Len Sirotzki of Bensenville, Illinois. And I suspect that almost all of the participating communities have this question in mind because I've challenged each one of them to create a break-the-mold school. And now Len, if you're there, you've turned your entire community into a break-the-mold site. And my question is, how did you get started and how is it working out?

Mr. Sirotzki. Mr. President, thank you for asking that question. It certainly is wonderful of you to join us this evening. The way we started, very simply put, was that we started. I think that the number one message to communities everywhere is to start, and don't wait for some perfect time that may never come. But we looked for individual persons who were willing to go beyond personal agenda for the benefit of the community, all of the families in the community, and I mean all of them, not only school-aged children. And I think all of us want better communities, but they will not come about magically. It's going to take a very, very long-term commitment, and there will be a great deal of pain, bringing about the kinds of changes that are needed.

But we have five different taxing bodies representing all the wonderful people of Bensenville who are working together. And I know that I can speak for all of the people in Bensenville in saying that whatever it is that we do that is of interest to others, we would be more than happy to share, because that's the kind of place Bensenville is.

The President. Well, thank you, Len, very

much. And I know everybody's experience can be helpful to the other fellow. And this experience in Bensenville, I appreciate your sharing it with us. And let me just say here in conclusion, it's been a long day. In fact, it's been a very emotional day for me. I've been out surveying the aftermath of Hurricane Andrew in Florida and over in Louisiana. And let me just say that one of our participants tonight, I believe, is Connie Jones. She's the principal of Three Oaks Elementary School at Fort Myers. And she got her school turned into a shelter, taking in those who were stricken by the hurricane. May I just say at the end of this emotional day that I salute Connie and all the others across this great country of ours who reach out to help their neighbors. It's a marvelous thing when you see the spirit of the people in the areas that have been hit by this storm. But we see it every day in communities across the country as they face adversity.

So, congratulations to all, and I am proud, Lamar, that this America 2000 effort continues to be bipartisan. And look, we all know that we're in an unusual political season. But let me just say I am determined to do my part, as I know Lamar is and as I know everyone out there is, to keep this effort out of partisan politics and just in the arena of helping people. All the Governors, Democrats as well as Republicans, are a part of all of this, and it's been that way from the very beginning. And I just wanted to assure every participant that I'm determined to keep it that way.

So, thanks for what you're doing. God bless you all, and good night. And thanks, Lamar.

Secretary Alexander. Thank you for taking time to call. I know that was exciting for everybody that participated.

The President. Well, keep up the great work, to you and all involved. Goodbye.

Note: The President spoke at 9:25 p.m. via satellite from the Oval Office at the White House. In his remarks, he referred to Len Sirotzki, project director, Bensenville Community Design Project, who was with Secretary of Education Lamar Alexander in the U.S. Chamber of Commerce television studio in Washington, DC.

Remarks to the Community in Humboldt, South Dakota
September 2, 1992

Please be seated. And let me just say how very pleased I am to be back in this State. Today I want to give a rather serious speech. I'm glad you all have seats, don't have to stand through this epic. But first of all, I want to thank George Mickelson, the Governor. You've got a great Governor. He's a great friend of agriculture and a great friend of George and Barbara Bush.

And I hope you'll excuse us for being a little tardy in getting here because Sue and Jeff Kapperman have just introduced us to one of the largest and nicest families I believe I've ever met back there. There's a representative group of them standing up against that fence; I cannot guarantee it's all of them.

But in any event, we're just very pleased to be here. I want to say that it's fun seeing the kids and visiting the farm here and coming to Montrose and Humboldt. It's special because with us on the plane today, Air Force One, coming out was Larry Pressler, who's here someplace. Went right by his own home farm, I believe. We salute him and thank him for his support there in Washington. And I can get a little feel, coming back here, for what Money magazine was talking about when they named Sioux Falls the best place to live in America. That's pretty high praise.

I also want to salute another public servant and one who has been at my side for a long time, the Lieutenant Governor, Walt Miller. I think he's here with us, Walter Miller; anyway, an old friend. And Mayor White greeted us. I thank him for that. Senator Shanard is here, Don Jarrett of the South Dakota Wheat Commission, and two people that I plan on seeing in Washington. I've known Charlene Haar. She's a good woman and a good, active campaigner. And I salute her, for the United States Senate, and also John Timmer, running for the congressional seat here. I'd back him. We've got to make a change in this gridlocked Congress. And of course, I'd be remiss if I didn't single out another guy that's been at my side in politics, your former Governor,

Bill Janklow. I thank him and also Don Peterson, out there helping with the Republican election effort this year, so many people doing so much for what I think is good, sound government.

I'm told that Jeff is a Democrat. But looking around at this setting, even I can't hold that against him. [*Laughter*] And I must say that I am very, very grateful to him and to his family for letting this mob, including you guys out here, hit this beautiful place of his. It's something very special about talking about agriculture in a setting that's so down-to-earth and so wonderfully family oriented. Jeff and Sue, as family farmers, represent something very important about this State and, I would say, also very important about this country. Agricultural families represent the heart of South Dakota's economy.

So I came out here today to rural America to talk with you about how I have been fighting and will continue to fight for the economic security of American farmers through a program that is based on opening markets abroad and then helping you export and grow more, keeping the Government off your back as best we can, and being there to help you get back on your feet when disaster strikes.

I plan to speak mainly today about wheat and about disaster assistance, but let me just say to America's corn growers—I noticed the cornfields as we came in—that I am a strong supporter of ethanol. We have worked hard to see ethanol demand go to new heights through everything from tax credits to research and new programs for clean fuels. And we're working now on a very difficult legal problem facing the White House: to make sure that ethanol plays a leading role in America's drive for cleaner air and America's drive for greater markets, diverse markets for the corn growers of this country. And we're going to whip that problem.

We now enjoy an unparalleled reign of free markets and free people around the globe, an unprecedented opportunity for growth. When I think of my Presidency, I must say I look at these kids, and I think we are very lucky that in the last 3 years we've been able to reduce the threat of nuclear war that has scared every family half to death in this country.

Today, when I talk to Boris Yeltsin, the Russian President—and I talked to him just last week—we don't talk about nuclear weapons. We talk about how much grain we can provide to Russian consumers and how we can solidify his democracy, his freedom, his reforms. We also talk about the biggest swords-into-plowshares agreement ever, one that will return that Russian bomb-grade material, uranium, into fuel for the peaceful generation of electric power right here in America.

The American people are universally respected as the most generous and innovative on Earth. American products, whether it is a pair of blue jeans spun from Texas cotton or a bushel of wheat from here in South Dakota, are in demand everywhere. The challenge before us, then, is to seize this moment. Our challenge now is to win the economic competition, literally to win the peace. In the 1990's, we must be a military superpower, an economic superpower, and an export superpower.

In 2 months, you're going to be asked to choose between two completely different versions of how to win this global economic competition. One vision is to turn inward, to try to protect what we have, to put up walls around America. Mine is to look forward, to open new markets to American exports, to prepare our work force to compete, to keep the social fabric of this country strong, and to save and invest in those things that will help us win.

The best example that I can cite of our forward-looking approach is the work we've done to open new markets for American agriculture. In the last 4 years, we have signed 11 bilateral agreements with 10 countries to open up new markets for American farm exports. We signed agreements to increase beef exports to Japan and Korea, now the third largest market for U.S. beef. We've made inroads throughout Asia, which now accounts for 38 percent of American agricultural exports, 38 percent going to Asia. And just last month, we concluded the North American free trade agreement, which will boost our $3 billion worth of agricultural exports to Mexico.

One in every three acres planted in this country produces crops for export. That may be hard for some to realize, but that's a lot of export. One in every three goes to exports. U.S. agricultural exports support over a million jobs. And just since 1989, our agricultural trade has reduced our overall trade deficit by almost $69 billion. You are doing the Lord's work.

Make no mistake, if the other side puts up walls around America, whether they're high tariff walls or high tax walls, the first loser is going to be the American farmer. Now, let me drive this point home. Seventy-six percent of South Dakota's wheat is exported, 76 percent of it. Agriculture contributes $13.2 billion to South Dakota's economy, 3 times more than any other industry. We were talking about it with the Governor coming in here. And if Governor Clinton gets infected with that antitrade strain from the protectionist crowd he's running around with, it will be the American farmer that catches pneumonia, and South Dakota is going to get mighty sick.

Where does the Governor stand on free trade, on our historic free trade agreement with Mexico? He won't say, says nothing about all of that right now, is studying it, taking another look. The newspapers reported in Washington this morning—I don't like to read those papers very much, but I do from time to time—and they reported this morning that one of the most powerful labor bosses in the country, Lane Kirkland, said that they decided to, the unions decided to let Governor Clinton off the hook on this one until after the election. They'll let him be on both sides of this free trade agreement now.

Big labor made it clear that they are vehemently opposed to this free trade agreement, mind you. And one labor source said, and this is a quote: "There have been private conversations with the candidate, and he remains receptive to us." I have found as President you cannot be on both sides of every issue. You've got to take a position and say what you think is right, whether some people like it or some people don't.

This was in the paper today. Here's another quote from them: "Labor does not plan to push Clinton for specific public commitments that might prove politically embarrassing to his candidacy." I think you're entitled to know, not just as voters but as people that are doing the Lord's work out in the field, you're entitled to know where a person stands on something as fundamental as a free trade agreement that's going to open up more markets for your products.

You cannot be on every side of every issue. He's stuck riding the fence so hard he's got saddle sores. I might say "straddle sores". [*Laughter*] But don't kid yourselves. The money, the manpower, and the support for his campaign comes from the opponents of free trade. And after the election, they'll call in that anti-free-trade IOU, and then you'd better watch out. American agricultural exports and job-creating exports of every kind will be the victims.

I don't believe that this double-speak means one thing except double-trouble. The Congress is going to take this vacillation as weakness, and the vital national economic interest will lose out to congressional logrolling, back-scratching, and business-as-usual.

Over 7.5 million jobs, American jobs, are tied to merchandise exports. We can create hundreds of thousands of additional new jobs with a free trade agreement. And we cannot afford a President who will put these jobs at risk. That's why I fought very hard to reach a new agreement under the GATT, the General Agreement on Tariffs and Trade. USDA, Ag Department, estimates that a successful GATT agreement will add over a billion dollars a year to farm income, a billion dollars a year. And it will do something else. It will force our competitors, especially in the European Community, to reduce their excessive export subsidies in agriculture. We want free trade, but we must insist on fair trade. To help us reach good agreements, I've been using a strategy that won us military security: peace through strength, no unilateral disarmament.

Our export enhancement program—you all refer to it as EEP—have enabled us to help farmers fight for market share against the EC's subsidized exports. Since 1989, we have doubled the number of EEP initiatives. We've nearly tripled the value of EEP bonuses. Just since the beginning of this year, we've awarded $914 million worth of EEP bonuses, leading to sales of over $3 billion under the EEP program: wheat to Algeria, Egypt, the Philippines; veg oil to Morocco and Turkey; a pork EEP to the former Soviet Union. In total, our EEP's have helped us fight back against European subsidies and sell almost $10 billion worth of commodities to 93 countries during these past 4 years.

But now we need to do more. The fact is that the prices farmers are receiving are too low today. To get the prices up, we must expand demand, and that means an aggressive export policy. Today I am announcing a broadside of EEP initiatives to sell over one billion bushels or 30 million metric tons of U.S. wheat, with a market value of over $3 billion, to 28 countries around the world. This is the largest quantity of wheat ever made available under the EEP program at one time.

There is no question that in a world of open trade, the U.S. would be the premier supplier of wheat to world markets. That's why we are committed to reducing subsidies worldwide. But my announcement today should leave no doubt. With heavy EC subsidies continuing, this EEP program is vital, and we will use it as necessary. I am putting foreign governments on notice to that effect right here today in South Dakota.

That's why I am also taking a second step today to show that we're in this competition for the long haul. Two years ago, I worked with Congress to include two so-called GATT triggers in our law. They were a warning to other nations that we would counter their subsidized exports if they would not agree to negotiated cuts. The date of the first trigger has passed. So today we are acting to protect the American farmer. We will increase programs to promote agricultural exports by $1 billion. The law said we would do this in 1994 and 1995. I am announcing that we will increase these programs beginning now. And my support for wheat is the first step.

Let me make this comment to those

friends of ours overseas also. Let me be clear: This action is aimed at those who subsidize, not at those, such as Australia and others, who do not subsidize.

Today's wheat EEP initiatives will give farmers, exporters, and buyers more certainty about market opportunities. We want to help growers plan, and we want to strengthen America's reputation as a reliable supplier. The other side's approach to trade is to create barriers here, right here in this country, that increase prices, dull our competitive edge, and hurt our growth. The usual strategy is to propose production controls. My approach is to help our farmers take the battle to the competition; offense, not defense. My strategy is to outproduce our competition and beat their socks off in the marketplace.

But as every farmer here knows, to win in the marketplace we must also take steps today that will make us more competitive tomorrow. So another part of my agricultural program is to help farmers keep pace by developing new techniques through our national research initiative for fighting pests and disease, for understanding human nutrition, for growing more. We're increasing research in biotechnology and into new uses of ag products from cleaner fuels to printer's ink to biodegradable plastics. The initiatives that we are pushing will help strengthen prices, boost farm income, and create jobs. That's why farm income over the past 3 years has averaged a higher level than at any time in American history. And more of that income is coming from the market, instead of from the Government, than at any time in decades.

But even so, 1992 has been a difficult year in parts for rural America. Last fall's drought, followed by a freeze in late May, severely weakened the winter wheat crop in Kansas and right here in South Dakota and elsewhere. Weather has hit farmers from Nebraska to New York, California to the Cotton Belt. And now this Louisiana sugarcane has been damaged by the winds of Hurricane Andrew. Barbara and I saw some of that devastation yesterday there in Jeanerette, Louisiana.

For some farmers, these disasters come on the heels of losses in 1990 and 1991. Late last year, I signed a bill to provide about $1 billion in disaster assistance for the 1990 and 1991 crops. Today I would like to announce the next step. I am releasing an additional $755 million in disaster assistance funds. A minimum of $100 million is set aside for crops planted in 1991 for harvest in 1992, such as winter wheat. American farmers need help. With this action, this disaster relief action, you will get it.

Now, I know that this $755 million is not going to solve every problem. We will begin signups for winter wheat next Tuesday, other crops shortly thereafter. We can't prevent an early freeze, and I know that this amount may not be enough to pay the full amount of every loss. But these funds will help keep farmers on their feet so that bankers will work with you and next season's crop can be planted.

We've worked hard over the past several years to reduce farm debt. Debt is way down; equity is up; balance sheets are stronger. Today's announcement will help secure those gains to advance the economic security of the American farmer. If additional disaster funds is needed, we will go to bat with the Congress to secure them.

You see, an economic strategy based on competition is not an abandonment of governmental responsibility. Sometimes when disaster strikes, the Federal Government is uniquely equipped to help. We've seen that this week in Florida and Louisiana in the aftermath of the hurricane. That's one reason I went down to Florida and Louisiana again yesterday, to see the progress and the problems with my own eyes. And we're going to stay with the people of Florida and Louisiana until we get that job done.

Now getting the job done in agriculture means Government should get out of the way of the producers when intervention will hurt our competitiveness. Take the subject of regulation. My opponents want to take the world's safest food supply, tie it up with more regulation, and make it more expensive for the consumer. We want to work to make our food supply safe and affordable without this extremism, without this hysteria.

Take the subject of taxation. My opponent says that Government takes too much of your money in taxes. But they want to take more of it, $150 billion already proposed in new taxes, new taxes on small business to pay for Government health and mandatory training. I want to cut the taxes, cut them across the board, reduce the burden particularly on small business. Small business is overregulated and overtaxed.

Take the subject of spending, which is absolutely critical, Federal spending. They want to use those no taxes to add $220 billion in new spending. And Newsweek magazine pointed out this week that Governor Clinton failed even to put a price tag on his four biggest programs. The real cost of his spending binge, said Newsweek, "is arguably at least three times higher than that." That's the quote from Newsweek.

And remember, we tried this recipe of higher taxes and higher spending before. We went down the path of foreign policy inexperience. We tried the combination of a Democratic-controlled Congress and a Democratic President, and you remember the results. We had back-to-back years of double-digit inflation. And farmers were devastated. We had interest rates at 21.5 percent. And farmers were devastated. We had grain embargoes—nobody here forgets that—we had grain embargoes and food as a foreign policy weapon. And farmers were devastated.

In this political year it is easy to be fooled. The new kid on the block shows up with a new set of lyrics, but it is the same old song. Wouldn't it be ironic if now, at the exact moment of America's triumph around the world, we were to turn backwards, to turn inward?

Not far from here, on the way into Humboldt, there's a sign that calls this a small town with a big heart. Well, now that the entire world is turning our way, toward open markets, less bureaucracy, less regulation, more freedom, more competition, we Americans must not and cannot lose heart.

We've learned this: Freedom works. Opportunity awaits those who dare to reach for it. Competition brings out the best in our people, especially those here working in the soil, those farmers that know how to really get out there and do the hard work. If we remember these home truths, there is no telling what we can accomplish, for America's finest hour is yet to come.

The opposition tells you that we're not respected abroad. They tell you that we're in decline. We are not a declining nation. We've had enormously difficult economic problems; so has the entire world, caught up in a global recession. But we are the United States of America. And if we follow these policies, we can outcompete, outhustle, outwork anybody on the face of the Earth.

I wish I were this guy's age over here. It's going to be an exciting time ahead. And the American farmer is going to lead the way. Thank you all very, very much. And may God bless our great country. Thank you.

Note: The President spoke at 10:05 a.m. at the Kapperman farm. In his remarks, he referred to George Shanard, South Dakota State Senate majority leader, and Don Peterson, South Dakota Republican Party chairman.

Remarks to Shallowater Co-op Gin Company Employees in Shallowater, Texas
September 2, 1992

The President. Thank you all very much. Hey, let me tell you something. In case you don't know it, we finally have a first-class, great secretary of agriculture in Texas that understands the farmer in Rick Perry. And I was very, very proud of him at that Houston convention when he got up there and told it as it is, making all Texans proud, making people across the country understand that we know about agriculture and we know about the American spirit. Rick, thank you very much for that introduction.

And let me salute the Future Farmers that are with us today. Also, you know I'm having a little feud with the liberal grid-locked Congress. If we had more Congress-men like Larry Combest, we wouldn't have a gridlocked Congress. And may I thank Mayor Moe Dozier and, of course, Sonny Lupton, the one-footed glider pilot who has made us feel so much at home here, turned the facilities of this great place over to us. And I'm very, very grateful to him. May I say hello to Carye Gruben, the 1992 South Plains Maid of Cotton. You should be very proud to be represented by her. And special thanks to Randy Kennedy, who has worked so hard on this event, and Jane Anne Stinnett, both of them and so many more.

Our convention in Houston was so successful that I just had to get back in Texas for another major event. But unfortunately, I won't be able to stay to see the Raiders open it up tomorrow with Oklahoma. But go Texas Tech!

A little bit of reminiscing: Barbara and I moved down into Odessa in 1948, and then we lived in Midland, Odessa-Midland for 12 years. And I've driven every mile between Lubbock County and Ector and Midland County, into Dawson County and Howard County and—[applause]—I thought we might have a few from around there. But I'll tell you, on a day like this, you can't help but feel you're glad to be back. This is beautiful, and I'm very grateful to all for this fantastic turnout.

I remember when west Texas was dry. I remember picking out the Lubbock tumbleweeds out of one of those evapora-tive air conditioners in our little house in Odessa. No more, I'll tell you. But when I lived in—one more reminiscent that some of you football fans, older ones, might re-member. We had a touch football team in Midland. And we played against the Lub-bock team made up of Glen Davis, Mel Kutnow and Bobby Lane. Now, how do you like that for Lubbock excellence? We lost.

Now, I came back here to Texas today to the heart of this wonderful part of rural America to talk about the farm and to talk about the future of the farmer. Let me be very clear right up front: I am for opening up world markets, for increasing exports, for keeping the Government off your back at home, and being there to help you get back on your feet when disaster strikes.

The challenge for agricultural America is to win this economic competition and to win the peace. And out here in Texas we know this: We must be a military superpow-er, we must be an economic superpower, and we must be an export superpower. That means looking forward and getting ready to compete. Make no mistake, Ameri-ca's farmer can compete with anybody, any-where around the world, provided that playing field is level, provided we get an even shot at world trade. I've fought to open new markets for American agricul-ture: Texas beef to Asia, Midwest grain to Russia, and just last month we concluded a North American free trade agreement with Mexico. That means new markets, and that means jobs for Americans. Open up trade.

You all know this, but I want to share it with the rest of the country here today. American products, from blue jeans spun from Texas high-plains cotton to bushels of wheat from Haskell County, are in demand everywhere. In fact, one in every three acres planted in this country produces crops for export. Exports are up, and that is good for the growth of the American economy. If it hadn't been for exports, we'd really be in deep trouble. Thank you for exporting our goods and services abroad.

This fall we've got a choice. Rick, I appre-ciate what you said, that I do stand with American agriculture. This fall we've got a real clear choice, an important choice be-cause it's going to mean the economic health of American farmers all across the country. And if our opponents in this year's election put up these walls around America, whether they're high tariff walls or high tax walls, the first losers will be American agri-culture and American jobs.

And let me make this point. You know that Texas is America's number one export-er of cotton, and the State of Texas ranks among the top 10 exporters in 14 different major crops. And if Governor Clinton gets infected with that antitrade strain from the protectionist crowd he's running around with, the big labor guys, it's going to be Texas that catches pneumonia. And we cannot have that.

One of the big union heads in Washington today was quoted in a Washington paper as saying, "Well, we're not going to get Clinton to take a position on the free trade agreement. We'll get that all worked out after the election." They're trying to get it worked out for protection, and that's going to hurt jobs in west Texas. And we cannot have it. He's got to commit. When you're President you can't sit on the fence—"Well, on the one hand it's this way, and on the one hand another." You've got to say, I'm for it or against it. I am for opening markets abroad. I am for free trade.

Audience members. Four more years! Four more years! Four more years!

The President. I hope the west Texas farmer knows this because you're in this fight with us. We are fighting for a successful conclusion of the GATT round. That's the General Agreement on Tariffs and Trade. A GATT agreement will force our competitors, especially those in the European Community, to cut their massive export subsidies on agriculture. And we want free trade, but I am going to insist on fair trade.

To help us reach these good agreements we're going to be using the same strategy that won the U.S. military security: peace through strength, no unilateral disarmament. And we've used this export enhancement program, we call it EEP, to fight for market share against the EC subsidized exports. And since 1989, we have doubled the number of EEP initiatives and tripled the value of these EEP bonuses, selling almost $10 billion of commodities to 93 countries. But now we need to do more. The fact is that farm prices, the ones you all are getting are too low today. And to get those prices where they belong, we must expand demand. That means an even more aggressive export policy. And so today I am announcing the largest EEP initiative in history, to sell over one billion bushels, or over 30 million metric tons of wheat, with a market value of over $3 billion, to 28 countries around the world. The wheat farmers have to lead the way from up in the Panhandle. We're committed to reducing subsidies worldwide, but my announcement ought to leave no doubt. With heavy EC subsidies continuing, this export program is vital, and we will use it as necessary.

Now, to keep running, work in the global marketplace, we've got to get ready to compete. So we've expanded research in everything from alternative uses of agricultural products to biotechnology. And right here in Texas, a new kind of cotton called B.T. cotton looks and feels like regular cotton, but protects itself from bugs by producing its own insecticide. And we will always work to make sure of this: American products are the highest quality products in the entire world.

I know you've had it tough here with these excessive rains, but I'll tell you one thing: Over the past 3 years agricultural income has averaged a higher level than at any time in American history. But even so, 1992 has been a tough year for rural America. And last fall's extreme drought—Sonny and I were talking about it, and Randy, inside—followed up by a freeze in late May, hurt the winter wheat crop from Kansas to the Texas Panhandle. And you know the Cotton Belt, what's happened: You saw a freeze in '91 followed by a wet spring that prevented many acres from being planted at all. And for some farmers, these disasters come on the heels of losses last year and the year before.

Last fall I signed a bill, and Rick referred to it, I believe, to provide almost $1 billion in disaster assistance for '90 and '91 crops. And today I want to announce the next step. I am today releasing an additional $755 million in disaster assistance funds to help tackle these emergencies which have stricken the American farmer. American farmers need help, and with this action you'll get it. I know that that $755 million will not solve every problem. We will begin signups for winter wheat next Tuesday, other crops shortly thereafter. We can't prevent an early freeze, but these funds will help keep farmers on their feet so that the bankers will work with you and the next season's crops can be planted. And if additional disaster funds are needed, we will secure them.

You know, when people are hurting in this country, whether it's from a hurricane in south Florida or losing a tremendous sugar crop over in Louisiana, the Government must help. We must help in disasters of the magnitude that you've suffered right here in cotton country. And sometimes Government can help by just simply getting out of the way and letting Americans do what they do best, roll up their sleeves and get the job done.

Take the subject of regulation. My opponents want to regulate the world's safest food supply and drive up its costs. Yes, I'm for food safety, but let's also protect the consumer from the bureaucrats. Let's have less regulation out of the United States Congress.

And now let me get to a subject that I really want to warm up to. Take the subject of taxes. The difference here is simple. Already, and he hasn't even started yet, my opponent wants to raise them by $150 billion. And I want to cut them across the board. I made one mistake; I'm not going to make another. He's already said $150 billion. No, we're not going to have that.

And if any area understands what I'm about to say it's west Texas, with the values we have. Government spending: the choice is clear. They want to spend—already, his own proposal—want to spend $220 billion more. And I want to cut spending, keep the growth on mandatory programs. And I need your help. Ask Congress to pass my plan for a check-off for America. If the Congress can't do it, give the taxpayer the right to check his tax return and force all of us to get that deficit down. I mentioned that in Houston, but I'll mention it again. We're mortgaging the future of these Future Farmers here, and we've got to stop it. I want a balanced budget amendment to the Constitution, and I want a Congress that will pass it. Help me. We can get that done. And while we're at it, give me what 43 Governors have, a line-item veto. If they can't do it, give me a shot. Give me a chance.

Now, let me just say this in conclusion. We tried the other side's recipe of higher taxes and higher spending before. We went down that path of foreign policy inexperience. We tried that combination in the late seventies of a Congress controlled by the liberal Democrats and a liberal Democratic President. And you remember what the results were. We had back-to-back years of double-digit inflation. Farmers were devastated. We had grain embargoes. We had interest rates at 21.5 percent. Farmers, totally devastated. We had grain embargoes that just kind of fizzled out, but nevertheless hurt every grain grower in the whole United States. Farmers were devastated. So let's not try that again. We cannot afford a rubber-check Congress and a rubber-stamp President. Do not take a chance on that and go back to those misery index days.

So in this political year it's easy to be fooled. And the new kid on the block always shows up with new lines, the same old song. Here in west Texas you know all about the choice between the latest synthetic fiber and real cotton. And I don't pretend to have the stretch of spandex; I don't understand all of that. But I do know this: Some ideas and values and concepts are timeless. Freedom works. Opportunity awaits those who dare to reach for it. Competition brings out the best in the American people, brings it out. So if we remember those home truths and remember the strengths that we get from the families that are all here today, there is no telling what we can accomplish. The other side says that we're a country in decline. Don't you believe it for one single minute. We are number one, the most respected country anywhere in the world.

So coming back to west Texas is good for the soul. Thank you for this fantastic, fantastic welcome back. I ask for your support. We have changed the world. We have brought dramatic reduction in nuclear weapons. We won a magnificent victory with the sons and daughters of Lubbock County there in Desert Storm. And now help me bring this new prosperity to the United States of America. We can get the job done.

Thank you all very much. And may God bless our great country.

Note: The President spoke at 1:48 p.m. at Shallowater Co-op Gin Co. In his remarks, he referred to Rick Perry, Texas commissioner of agriculture; Sonny Lupton, president, Shallowater Co-op Gin Board; Randy Kennedy, manager, Shallowater Co-op Gin Co.; and Jane Anne Stinnett, regional chairman, Bush-Quayle '92.

Remarks to General Dynamics Employees in Fort Worth, Texas
September 2, 1992

Thank you all very much for that welcome. And Bill Anders, thank you, Bill. It's a great pleasure to be introduced by Bill Anders, a friend of long standing. And it's great to be back here, back home in Texas, the home of Jose Canseco. [*Laughter*] I think we're all in the wrong line of work, don't you? I'll tell you.

But let me thank Jim Mellor here. I'm glad to be back here with him. He reminded me that I flew the simulator when I was here last time. He was gracious enough, given the circumstances, not to remind me that the simulator obviously had a failure because it crashed with me at the helm there. [*Laughter*] But it was pilot error, I'm afraid. And let me also thank our two Congressmen here today, Pete Geren, Joe Barton. Mayor Granger is with us, the Mayor of Fort Worth. And look at this hardware. I guess they had General Dynamics in mind when they said, don't mess with Texas.

With all the Air Force types here, the true heroes of Desert Storm, I hate to bore you with war stories. But 48 years ago to this very day, September 2, 1944, I was shot down while on a bombing raid flying off our carrier over the island of Chichi Jima. I think if I'd only had F–16's, things might have been a lot different, a lot different. In all seriousness, I can't blame the plane I was flying. It was the best torpedo bomber ever to land on a carrier. I did learn, though, from that combat experience something that I think everybody here knows and has contributed to: Give our pilots the best, and then fight to win. Don't tie their hands behind their backs. And that's exactly what they did over there in Desert Storm.

I am very pleased to be here this afternoon, even for a brief visit. I wanted to come to General Dynamics to personally make a statement that concerns all of you, your families, and this wonderful community. I'm announcing this afternoon that I will authorize the sale to Taiwan of 150 F–16 AB aircraft, made right here in Fort Worth. We're proud to do this. This F–16 is an example of what only America and Americans can do. Only American technology, only American skill could have produced this flawless piece of craftsmanship which is sought all around the world.

Throughout this century, the marvels of American defense have saved lives, kept the peace, and defended American values. The world has seen the F–16 in action. Over the skies of Desert Storm the F–16 continued America's tradition of military excellence in more than 13,000 combat sorties. At this very moment planes like these may well be flying over Iraq to guarantee that the bully of Baghdad, Saddam Hussein, will not brutalize his own people by striking at them from the skies.

This sale of F–16's to Taiwan will help maintain peace and stability in an area of great concern to us, the Asia-Pacific region, in conformity with our law. In the last few years, after decades of confrontation, great strides have been made in reducing tensions between Taipei and Beijing. During this period, the United States has provided Taiwan with sufficient defensive capabilities to sustain the confidence it needs to reduce these tensions. That same sense of security has underpinned Taiwan's dramatic evolution toward democracy.

My decision today does not change the commitment of this administration and its predecessors to the three communiques with the People's Republic of China. We keep our word: our one-China policy, our recognition of the P.R.C. as the sole legitimate government of China. I've always stressed that the importance of the 1982 communique on arms sales to Taiwan lies in its promotion of common political goals: peace and stability in the area through mutual restraint.

Your airplane, this great airplane, and this sale also sends a larger message to the American people as we consider how we're going to win the global economic competition. The weapons of defense that the world saw perform so brilliantly in Desert Storm were conceived by American research scientists, designed by American engineers, crafted by the best workers in the world, the American working men and women. They were guided and operated by the young men and women of our volunteer Armed Forces, the very generation that will lead America into the next century.

My message is simple: No nation can defeat us when we set our minds to a task. Now we've got to turn those same energies and genius to the challenge at home, to secure our economic base, to ensure that the high-wage, high-tech jobs of the future are made in America. The country that dropped missiles down smokestacks, that created a technological miracle like the F–16 can and will create the products the world needs in the new era of economic competition. The country that produced the most disciplined and high-skilled fighting force in history can and will find a way to utilize the talents of all of our young people.

America's role as a military superpower was not preordained. It took the ingenuity of our workers, the creativity of our scientists, and the experience of our business leaders. Now we must maintain our lead as the world's economic superpower and export superpower. And it will require the same magical combination of ingenuity and creativity and experienced leadership, the same magical combination that you've created right here at General Dynamics.

Let me make one final point, one final point. Though the world is a much more peaceful place today, I will continue to fight for a strong defense budget. We cannot take a chance. We cannot take a chance.

Some are already proposing defense cuts far beyond the levels that our military experts feel are reasonable. I've had sound budget levels recommended to me by Colin Powell, by all the Joint Chiefs of Staff, by the Secretary of Defense. And now some in this political year want to slash defense budgets, slash the muscle of our defense. I do not want to see us go back to the days of the hollow Army or the return of an Air Force less strong than our needs require. And not only would some of the cuts proposed in this election year cut into the real muscle of our defense, they would needlessly throw defense workers out of work. And I will not have that.

Thank you very, very much for this welcome. And let me say it is a great pleasure to be able to support this sale. It is a great pleasure to come here and to salute you, the finest workers in the world. Thank you all. And may God bless our great country. Thank you very much. Thank you.

Note: The President spoke at 5:11 p.m. at the General Dynamics facility at Carswell Air Force Base. In his remarks, he referred to William A. Anders, chief executive officer, and James R. Mellor, president, General Dynamics; and Jose Canseco, Texas Rangers baseball player.

Appointment of Frederick H. Grubbe as Deputy Director of the Office of Consumer Affairs
September 2, 1992

The President today appointed Frederick H. Grubbe to be Deputy Director of the Office of Consumer Affairs at the Department of Health and Human Services. He would succeed Clayton S. Fong.

Since 1989, Mr. Grubbe has served at the Department of Transportation in positions including: Deputy Administrator of the National Highway Traffic Safety Administration, 1991 to the present, and Special Assistant to the Secretary for Personnel and Organization Management, and White House liaison, 1989–91. From 1988 to 1989, he served in the Office of the President-elect, in the Office of Presidential Personnel.

Mr. Grubbe graduated from Northern Illinois University (B.A., 1984). He was born May 14, 1961, in Oak Park, IL. Mr. Grubbe is married and currently resides in Alexandria, VA.

Statement on Expediting Small Business Administration Loans for Hurricane Andrew Victims
September 3, 1992

I have just met with Administrator Saiki who informed me that the Small Business Administration has responded to my request to expedite their loan process so that victims of Hurricane Andrew can swiftly receive disaster loan checks. SBA loans that typically require 30 to 60 days will now be processed in just 7 days.

I have also asked the IRS to be on site so that they can provide tax information to the loan applicants whose tax records have been lost or destroyed as a result of the hurricane. Treasury Department officials will also be there to cut the checks immedi-

ately. Today Pat Saiki will depart to Florida and Louisiana to deliver the first disaster loan checks. By the time they are finished, the SBA will have made thousands of loans to businesses and homeowners who are resolved to rebuild their neighborhoods, repair their communities, and get on with their lives.

The SBA is ready to help homeowners and renters qualify for low-interest, long-term loans to rebuild or repair their homes as well as their businesses. Like the rest of the Federal Government, the SBA is in for the long haul.

Letter to Congressional Leaders Transmitting Proposed Legislation on Nevada Public Lands Wilderness Designation
September 3, 1992

Dear Mr. Speaker: (Dear Mr. President:)
I am pleased to submit for congressional consideration and passage the "Nevada Public Lands Wilderness Act".

The Federal Land Policy and Management Act of 1976 (FLPMA), (43 U.S.C. 1701, *et seq.*), directs the Secretary of the Interior to review the wilderness potential of the public lands.

The review of the areas identified in Nevada and Lassen County, California, began immediately after the enactment of FLPMA and has now been completed. Approximately 5.2 million acres of public lands in 110 areas in Nevada and Lassen County, California, met the minimum wilderness criteria and were designated as wilderness study areas (WSAs). These WSAs were studied and analyzed during the review process and the results documented in 17 environmental impact statements and eight instant study area reports.

Based on the studies and reviews of the WSAs, the Secretary of the Interior is recommending that all or part of 52 of the WSAs, totaling 1,892,041 acres of public

lands, be designated as part of the National Wilderness Preservation System.

I concur with the Secretary of the Interior's recommendations and am pleased to recommend designation of the 52 areas (totaling 1,892,041 acres) identified in the enclosed draft legislation as additions to the National Wilderness Preservation System.

The proposed additions represent the diversity of wilderness values in the State of Nevada and Lassen County, California. They range from the Black Rock Desert and the canyons of the Humboldt and Owyhee Rivers, to the ancient bristlecone pines in central Nevada, to the Mojave Desert in southern Nevada and its Joshua trees and desert tortoises. These areas span a wide variety of Nevada landforms, ecosystems, and other natural systems and features. Their inclusion in the wilderness system will improve the geographic distribution of wilderness areas in Nevada and Lassen County, California, and will complement existing areas of congressionally designated wilderness. They will provide new and outstanding opportunities for solitude and unconfined recreation.

The enclosed draft legislation provides that designation as wilderness shall not constitute a reservation of water or water rights for wilderness purposes. This is consistent with the fact that the Congress did not establish a Federal reserved water right for wilderness purposes. The Administration has established the policy that, where it is necessary to obtain water rights for wilderness purposes in a specific wilderness area, water rights would be sought from the State by filing under State water laws. Furthermore, it is the policy of the Administration that the designation of wilderness areas should not interfere with the use of water rights, State water administration, or the use of a State's interstate water allocation.

The draft legislation also provides for access to wilderness areas by Indian people for traditional cultural and religious purposes. Access by the general public may be limited in order to protect the privacy of religious cultural activities taking place in specific wilderness areas. In addition, to the fullest extent practicable, the Department of the Interior will coordinate with the Department of Defense to minimize the impact of any overflights during these religious cultural activities.

I further concur with the Secretary of the Interior that all or part of 106 of the WSAs encompassing 3,277,546 acres are not suitable for preservation as wilderness.

Also enclosed are a letter and report from the Secretary of the Interior concerning the WSAs discussed above and a section-by-section analysis of the draft legislation. I urge the Congress to act expeditiously and favorably on the proposed legislation so that the natural resources of these WSAs in Nevada and Lassen County, California, may be protected and preserved.

Sincerely,

GEORGE BUSH

Note: Identical letters were sent to Thomas S. Foley, Speaker of the House of Representatives, and Dan Quayle, President of the Senate.

Statement by Press Secretary Fitzwater on Capital Gains Tax Regulations
September 3, 1992

In response to a request from the White House, the Department of Justice's Office of Legal Counsel has rendered a formal opinion on the issue of "indexing." We are disappointed that the opinion concludes that neither the President nor the Treasury Secretary nor the Commissioner of the IRS has the authority to act to revise the IRS regulations in a way that would index for inflation the cost of assets bought and sold in capital gains transactions.

The President believes that such indexing of cost would be sound economic policy and would be sound as a matter of fairness. Accordingly, he has instructed the Treasury Department to add to his legislative program a provision that would provide the taxpayer with the option of indexing cost when determining income subject to gain.

Remarks to the Community in Fredericksburg, Virginia
September 4, 1992

The President. Thank you, Dori, very much. And thank all of you for this great welcome to this marvelous town. And may I salute two Members of Congress with me, Congressman George Allen, a good man, and to Herb Bateman, another great Congressman. Two State delegates that you all know well, Bill Howell and Bobby Orrock, they're with us today. And I want to thank your Mayor of 16 years, Lawrence Davies, who greeted us at the airport. You've got a lot to be proud of here. And I know that there are six Olympians from this area, two gold medal winners, and I salute all of them.

I told Barbara I was coming down to a hardware store this morning. [*Laughter*] She told me I'd better come back with the tools to fix Millie's doghouse or else I'd be in one myself.

But here we are in Fredericksburg to talk about small business. I'm going to ask you to bear with me because some of these points are serious points about the future of this country. And we want to drive home the fact that businesses like the one I just visited, Fredericksburg Hardware, and Goolrick's here do more than sell doorknobs and drywall, hairnets and lipsticks. Small business generates the hope and the pride and the jobs that hold America together.

America's economy is working its way through a period of profound change. Many of the larger companies have retrenched and restructured. And I know those changes have been difficult for many working Americans. But American small businesses, they've shown the staying power, creating new products by the thousands and new jobs by the hundreds of thousands. And we are grateful to every small-business man and woman in this country. It is critical that we concentrate on the importance of small business to our economy. Because today, the defining challenge of the nineties is to reinvigorate our national economy so that we can win, we can win the competition in this whole new global economy.

In this election, you're going to hear two very different versions of how to do this. My opponent's answer is to turn inward, to pretend that we can protect what we have. And ours is to look forward, to open new markets, to prepare our people to compete, to restore the social fabric of this country, and to save and invest, so that we can win. And that's why we've placed small business at the heart of our agenda for America's economic future. Small businesses employ over half our work force, create two-thirds of new American jobs. And they're the hothouse for innovation, risk-taking, and new ideas, the powerful locomotive that will take our economy right down the tracks, full steam ahead into the 21st century. I am optimistic about this country.

When it comes to renewing the American economy, my loyalty lies with small business. I've actually held a job in the private sector, something my opponent has not done, half my life in the private sector and half in public life. And I started a small business, built it from the ground up, know what it is to go out and work with partners and employees. And I know what it's like to sweat out a tough deal, to shop for credit, to try your darnedest to meet the next payroll—and even if I got ulcers to prove it. I believe that meeting a payroll is a good qualification for President of the United States of America.

Now let me tell you what must be done to help small businesses here and across the country. We've got to give business the relief from excessive Government regulation. We need to increase access to credit and investment. And while Governor Clinton wants to raise taxes and has already proposed it, I want to cut the taxes on small business. And I need a change in Congress to get that done.

I was out in western Michigan the other day, talking to a group of people and small business leaders. I met a guy who runs an asphalt paving company. And he said, "Mr. President, when regulation doesn't make sense, it's the worker who pays with his job." And we are tackling this problem head-on. In January, I ordered a freeze on Federal regulations. The business men and women have enough to worry about without Washington double-checking their every move.

Regulation, less of it. But without the burden of overregulation, businesses can't grow without capital. The credit crunch has hit our small businesses hard. And that's why we've been working with bankers and regulators to ease that crunch. We have the SBA, the Small Business Administration, working double-time to help these credit-starved businesses. And this year, we have increased by more than 30 percent the general business loan guarantees offered through the Small Business Administration, more than $6 billion going to men and women with good ideas who want to turn those ideas into jobs. That's the kind of help Government should be giving these businesses.

I've also been trying to work with that gridlocked Congress to provide even more credit relief.

Audience members. Clean the House! Clean the House! Clean the House!

The President. That's a good idea. And this morning, you're going to see the result. We've come here to Fredericksburg to sign a new piece of legislation. Typical of us—the Washington—it's got the name "the Small Business Credit and Business Opportunity Enhancement Act." But it's going to loosen up credit even more for deserving small businesses. Not only does it increase the levels of SBA loans, it creates new ways of bringing investment to small business owners. It reaches out to women and minority entrepreneurs who want to get started. I've always believed that the best economic program is a job. And this bill gives more Americans the tools to create a job.

Now, we're talking about regulation and credit. All that is good. But it won't do it if we cannot help take the monkey, that tax monkey, off the backs of small business. I am for lower taxes. He is for higher taxes. Already we've taken a number of steps to streamline the ways small businesses pay their taxes. One example: Right now, small businesses have to file payroll taxes twice a week. And that's a waste. I've proposed we change it to once a month, so business men

and women can get back to the business of running their businesses.

Now, the Clinton-Gore tax-and-spend ticket doesn't understand that taxing capital investment is bad. None of our industrial competitors taxes capital gains at our punitive rates. Almost half of all new businesses literally begin at home, when enterprisers convert their own nest eggs into capital. And it is time to reward this initiative. It is time to make us competitive with businesses around the world. It is time to cut that tax on capital gains so these small businesses can thrive.

That's my agenda for small businesses: three obstacles, three concrete steps to clear those obstacles out of the way. Now let me just get into the politics here. Where does Governor Clinton stand on small business? It's a strange coincidence, but his plan has three parts, too: tax, tax, and tax.

Audience members. Boo-o-o!

The President. I see small business as the backbone of the American economy, and he sees it as a golden-egg-laying goose that ought to pay more in taxes.

Audience members. Boo-o-o!

The President. And he starts with a big idea. Here it is, you heard the proposal right from him: Mr. Clinton says that he wants $220 billion in new Government spending.

Audience members. Boo-o-o!

The President. We don't need $220 billion in new Government spending. [*Applause*] You're right. And how will he pay for it? Nobody knows for sure, but he's already advocating at least another $150 billion in new taxes. And now he says he wants to soak the rich, raise taxes on the top 2 percent. What he won't tell you is this: Two out of every three business people hit by that tax increase are small businesses or family farmers. And these folks aren't millionaires; they are mom-and-pop operators. And we don't need to tax them any more. The Governor offers—you know that program—he offers the small business a reverse version of the "Lifestyles of the Rich and Famous." You may not live like a millionaire, but you can be taxed like one if you listen to Clinton and Gore. It is strange.

Health care: He's also backing a health

care plan called "play or pay." I was just in here in the hardware store, talking to the people there about the escalating costs of health care. His plan will leave small businesses with two options: one, cut workers' wages to pay for mandated health care, or two, fire some workers and use the savings to cover the rest. And according to an independent Urban Institute study, the plan will lead to a 7-percent payroll tax for those businesses who don't play the Government's game. And another estimate says the tax will cost this country 700,000 jobs. We cannot afford to lose these jobs.

So that's his plan. It's out there in black and white, $150 billion in new taxes, a new Government health care plan leading to a new payroll tax of 7 percent, not to mention a new training tax. Then you throw in an irresponsible slashing of our defense budget, and it all adds up to 2.6 million, 2.6 million jobs lost. And we cannot have that.

The differences between the Governor and me are based on two very different philosophies. Look again at the health care issue. This is of critical importance to small business. Over the past 2 years, 83 percent of small business owners have seen their health care costs increase. And at the same time, too many Americans are without coverage, or they're worried about losing the coverage they have.

And so let's go right down the line. My health care reform will give tax breaks and credits to make health care more affordable, so that 30 million people who can't get health care insurance will be safe and will have health care in the private sector. He prefers taxes. He says, let's raise taxes and compel people to participate. And I say, let's give tax incentives and encourage people to do what's right.

And I want to use the force of competition—the force that's in action all along Main Street here—the force of competition to keep these medical costs down. He wants to put the Government in the business of setting health care prices. That will not work. I want to go after the root causes of health care. And he won't because the special interests won't let him.

Now, let me tell you one that's important here. I'll give you an example. Last year alone, legal costs inflated our doctors' bills

by $20 billion dollars. And so we've targeted these malpractice insurance for reform, as one way to keep costs down. I don't think you should have to hire a lawyer when you want to see a doctor. But Governor Clinton stands against malpractice reform. And there is a simple reason. The trial lawyers of America, the same fat cats who are getting rich off those malpractice lawsuits, are his staunchest supporters. Here's what one Arkansas trial lawyer wrote about him, trying to raise money for the Clinton campaign: "I can never remember an occasion where he failed to do what was right where we trial lawyers are concerned." Small businesses are drowning in litigation, and Governor Clinton wants to throw them a firehose. Well, help me get Congress to put an end to frivolous lawsuits. We'd be a lot better off if we sued each other less and cared for each other more in this country. I have had proposals up before this gridlocked Congress for 3 years in a row. And now you've got a man who wants to run for President that says he doesn't want to do anything about malpractice. Let's change that Congress. Help me get this malpractice under control.

From taxes to regulators to health care to the litigation explosion, the election is a contest between two very different views of business and of how our economy works. And here is the bottom line. He talks a good game, but his policies threaten to tax and spend and regulate you right out of business. Small business should not be the big Government's piggy bank. We are trying to do what is right for the average family, right for the man and woman that are out there holding a job, working for a living. Reform welfare, help in every way we can to help the families in this country.

Audience members. Four more years! Four more years! Four more years!

The President. Let me tell you something. I was in a hardware store, and Mr. Janney said something to me. He said, "You see my grandchildren here?" He said, "I am very happy that they're going to grow up, thanks to you and your administration, in a world that has less fear of nuclear weapons, an administration that bit the bullet and did what was right in Desert Storm." Now, give us your support, and let's do what's right for the small-business man and woman in this country.

May God bless you. May God bless all of you, and thank you very, very much. Thank you very much. Thank you all.

Audience members. Four more years! Four more years! Four more years!

The President. Now, if you've never seen legislation signed, watch this one, because I'm now going to sign the Small Business Credit and Business Opportunity Enhancement Act of 1992, an example of what we can do to put small business first.

[*At this point, the President signed the bill.*]

Thank you all for coming.

Note: The President spoke at 11 a.m. at Goolrick's Pharmacy. In his remarks, he referred to Dori Eglevsky, president, Fredericksburg Chamber of Commerce, and H.M. Janney, owner/operator of Fredericksburg Hardware. H.R. 4111, approved September 4, was assigned Public Law No. 102–366.

Statement on Signing the Small Business Credit and Business Opportunity Enhancement Act of 1992
September 4, 1992

Today I am signing into law H.R. 4111, the "Small Business Credit and Business Opportunity Enhancement Act of 1992." The Act will provide a major stimulus to the growth and development of small businesses.

H.R. 4111 will restructure the Small Business Administration's Small Business Investment Company (SBIC) program. This restructuring will boost investment by the private sector in growth-oriented small businesses, while enhancing the safety and soundness of SBICs. H.R. 4111 also provides a substantial increase in authorized levels of SBA's guaranteed business loan programs. Thousands of small businesses will be able to obtain much-needed credit as a result of the expansion of these programs.

Two-thirds of all jobs in the United States are created by small businesses. This bill ensures that capital, the lifeblood of our economy, is available to help small firms start up and to help tens of thousands of existing firms to expand and grow.

Section 203 of the bill enhances small business contracting goals for a dredging program. In signing the legislation, I note that current law requires the Department of the Army to make every reasonable effort to award the designated contracting business to small business concerns.

Finally, I am pleased to note that section 331 of the bill states that it is the sense of the Congress that "legislation and regulations that enhance the viability of small business concerns, including changes in tax and health care policy, should be given a priority for passage by the Congress." I urge the Congress to act promptly on this section by passing before the end of this legislative session legislation that will truly help small businesses, particularly the capital gains tax cut, the investment tax allowance, and the Administration's proposal to allow small businesses to increase their purchasing power through Health Insurance Networks, making health insurance for their employees more affordable.

GEORGE BUSH

The White House,
September 4, 1992.

Note: H.R. 4111, approved September 4, was assigned Public Law No. 102–366.

Letter to Congressional Leaders Transmitting Proposed Legislation on Idaho Public Lands Wilderness Designation
September 4, 1992

Dear Mr. Speaker: (Dear Mr. President:)

I am pleased to submit for congressional consideration and passage the "Idaho Public Lands Wilderness Act".

The Federal Land Policy and Management Act of 1976 (FLPMA), (43 U.S.C. 1701, *et seq.*), directs the Secretary of the Interior to review the wilderness potential of the public lands.

The review of the areas identified in Idaho began immediately after the enactment of FLPMA and has now been completed. Approximately 1.8 million acres of public lands in 67 areas in Idaho met the minimum wilderness criteria and were designated as wilderness study areas (WSAs). These WSAs were studied and analyzed during the review process and the results documented in 14 environmental impact statements and three instant study area reports.

Based on the studies and reviews of the WSAs, the Secretary of the Interior is recommending that all or part of 27 of the WSAs, totaling 972,239 acres of public lands, be designated as part of the National Wilderness Preservation System.

I concur with the Secretary of the Interior's recommendations and am pleased to recommend designation of the 27 areas (totaling 972,239 acres) identified in the enclosed draft legislation as additions to the National Wilderness Preservation System.

The proposed additions represent the diversity of wilderness values in the State of Idaho. These range from the high desert canyon lands of southwestern Idaho to the lava flows of the Great Rift and Hells Half Acre. These areas span a wide variety of Idaho landforms, ecosystems, and other natural systems and features. Their inclusion in the wilderness system will improve the geographic distribution of wilderness areas in Idaho, and will complement existing areas of congressionally designated wilderness. They will provide new and outstanding opportunities for solitude and unconfined recreation.

The enclosed draft legislation provides that designation as wilderness shall not constitute a reservation of water or water rights for wilderness purposes. This is consistent with the fact that the Congress did not establish a Federal reserved water right for wilderness purposes. The Administration has established the policy that, where it is necessary to obtain water rights for wilderness purposes in a specific wilderness area, water rights would be sought from the State by filing under State water laws. Furthermore, it is the policy of the Administration that the designation of wilderness areas should not interfere with the use of water rights, State water administration, or the use of a State's interstate water allocation.

The draft legislation also provides for access to wilderness areas by Indian people for traditional cultural and religious purposes. Access by the general public may be limited in order to protect the privacy of religious cultural activities taking place in specific wilderness areas. In addition, to the fullest extent practicable, the Department of the Interior will coordinate with the Department of Defense to minimize the impact of any overflights during these religious cultural activities.

I further concur with the Secretary of the Interior that all or part of 57 of the WSAs encompassing 825,217 acres are not suitable for preservation as wilderness.

Also enclosed are a letter and report from the Secretary of the Interior concerning the WSAs discussed above and a section-by-section analysis of the draft legislation. I urge the Congress to act expeditiously and favorably on the proposed legislation so that the natural resources of these WSAs in Idaho may be protected and preserved.

Sincerely,

GEORGE BUSH

Note: Identical letters were sent to Thomas S. Foley, Speaker of the House of Representatives, and Dan Quayle, President of the Senate.

Appointment of Daniel Casse as Special Assistant to the President for Cabinet Affairs
September 4, 1992

The President today announced the appointment of Daniel Casse as Special Assistant to the President for Cabinet Affairs.

Since 1990, Mr. Casse has served as Associate Director and then Deputy Director in the Office of Cabinet Affairs. Prior to arriving at the White House, he served as a special assistant to the director and policy analyst in the Office of National Drug Control Policy and as a researcher in the Secretary's office at the Department of Education. From 1985 to 1987, Mr. Casse was the managing editor of the Public Interest, a public policy quarterly.

Mr. Casse received a bachelor of arts degree from the University of Toronto in 1984 and a master's degree in public administration from the Kennedy School of Government at Harvard University in 1989. He resides in Washington, DC.

Statement by Press Secretary Fitzwater on the August Unemployment Rate
September 4, 1992

The August drop in the unemployment rate, for the second month in a row, is an encouraging sign that the economy is improving. But we cannot be satisfied until every American who wants a job has one.

We continue to urge Congress to pass the President's program of economic incentives to spur economic growth and ensure an even stronger recovery.

Remarks at Octoberfest in Painesville, Ohio
September 5, 1992

Thank you all. What a great turnout. Thank you so very much. Thank you. Thank you very much, Mike. Thank you, Mike DeWine, our next United States Senator. Thank you very, very much for that welcome. Barbara and I are thrilled to be with you, glad to be with you and Fran. It's good to see Bob Bennett, our chairman; national committeewoman Martha Moore over here; and Bob Gardner, who's running for Congress. We want to see him elected. He's sitting over there. Of course, a very special thanks to the Bencics. I'll tell you, what great hosts they are, Steve, Gretel, Martin, Carl, Edith, and Linda. What a wonderful family. When I talk about family values I think of their discipline, their love of country, and their hard work.

I bring greetings today from your Governor and from my very good friend, George Voinovich. What an outstanding Governor you have. He understands this country. You know, Steve told me that this is the first time that the Governor has missed this event since 1966; and the only reason he did it, because he's on a trade mission to Southeast Asia. He's opening up new markets for Ohio goods, and that means creating jobs for Ohio workers. I know he's going to miss all his bratwurst. I'm sure egg rolls taste great, but you can't put syrup on egg rolls. And Voinovich will find that out.

Now, I don't know whether you all got to do what Barbara and I did, but I hope you've all seen Gretel's cake. But you may not know the story behind this enormous cake. I don't want to give away her age, but 50 years ago when she was a little girl, the war in Europe separated her from her mother. The Red Cross came to Gretel's rescue, so today she's returning the favor. Everyone who eats a piece of that cake is contributing food to help the people of south Florida and Louisiana. That is the American spirit, and Gretel, we're very grateful to you.

While we're talking about the tragedy in the south, I want to salute today the contingents of Ohio's finest: the Ohio National Guard 179th Airlift Group, back from their mission of mercy to south Florida, one military person down there helping family after family. It is a wonderful concept, and we're proud of them all. Some of them served in that Desert Storm, too, and they did a first-class job there, believe me. And the country has not forgotten.

So, in summary, it's great to be here in Painesville to help open up this year's Octoberfest. You've got the four basic food groups: pancakes and syrup, bratwurst and beer; and not one stick of broccoli anywhere in sight. This is a first-class——

Well, this celebration has always been a celebration of cultures, but this year, in a very special way, it's a celebration of the spirit. We've witnessed a world of change. Across Europe, across continents, from Panama City to Prague, millions of men and women now celebrate a new birth of freedom.

In Germany—and I think of that because of my friendship with Steve—and in Germany a wall has fallen. We should take great pride in knowing that the German people give us, the United States, great credit for standing up for their unity, for reunification of Germany, and for their freedom. We should be proud of that. For the people here today, people who came to America from the old country, who prayed for this day to come, the change we've witnessed, this change we've worked for, is a miracle come true.

There are those, to quote the poet, who will say that the liberation of humanity, the freedom of man and mind, is nothing but a dream. They are right. It is the American dream. The American dream led to so much of this freedom around the world. Today, our challenge is to bring that spirit home, and Mike DeWine said, home from the towns your parents and grandparents were born in to this new world we call America, and to focus this great Nation on the new mission at hand.

I know the main attraction this morning is pancakes—[*laughter*]—not politics. I salute not only the Republicans that are here, but I know there are many, many Democrats with us, and I'm very proud and pleased about that. But today I want to—and I've got to admit something, with the enthusiasm of this welcome, the temptation is for me to get up here and tear into the Governor of Arkansas, which I've got to do from time to time. But today, and I hope you'll bear with me, I want to just take a few minutes to talk to you about a serious matter, something I hope you'll be thinking about as you go into that voting booth on November 3d, about the way we can change America's health care.

So this isn't a rally speech. I want to talk to you, a little substance, on health care. I want to tell you first a story, a story about the McNally family from Dorset, Ohio. I first learned about them when Tiffany McNally wrote me at the White House 2 years ago. Four members of Tiffany's family have a rare blood disease, and Tiffany, who is adopted, was born with fetal alcohol syndrome. Now, what if Mr. McNally were laid off, or worse still, lost his job? Or what if he found a better job, but the catch was no new health insurer would carry him or his family? He'd have to stay put and let that opportunity pass him by.

Well, that is wrong. That's why we have to change the health care system in America. Health care reform isn't just about studies and cold statistics. It's about real worries and real lives. We have the answers to those worries.

Let's face it, the problem is not the quality of health care. American health care is number one in the entire world. Since 1980, every life expectancy is up; infant mortality is down; death rates from heart disease down; deaths from stroke down. Right now, 200 million Americans have access to quality care system.

But that high quality, high-tech medical care comes at an unacceptable price: An estimated 30 million Americans have no insurance at all, and millions more, like the McNallys, are afraid to change jobs for fear of losing the health insurance that they've got. All told, America's health care now tops $800 billion a year, and the cost is rising 2 to 3 times the rate of inflation. That's why health care reform is a key part of my agenda for economic security for every family in this country.

This year, you watch, health care is going to be a Republican issue. We have a good program. My Democratic opponents are divided between two bad programs, both of which would put Government in charge of health care.

The fact is we can reform the system without pushing our economy into intensive care. We must build on the strengths of the system that's given us the highest quality care in the world, on consumer choice, on innovation and state-of-the-art medicine, while controlling costs and expanding access. We need an efficient health care system built on competition to control costs, not Government control and rationing care. Above all, we need a health care system that gives all Americans real security, security that you can count on, the coverage you need. My plan meets every single one of these objectives.

We can make health care more accessible by making health insurance more affordable. Take a family of two parents and two kids. Let's say the family's income, the total income is $13,000. They're working hard to make ends meet: low enough to put them at the poverty line, high enough to make them ineligible for Medicaid. Right now, that family may fall through the cracks, may not be covered through work, and may not be able to afford any health care coverage at all. Under my plan, that would change. This family would get a $3,750 health care credit, payable to the health care insurer of their choice.

For middle-income individuals and families, all the way up to those making $80,000, my plan provides a health insurance tax credit or deduction that will ease the burden of health insurance costs.

All told, this plan will bring health care coverage to almost 30 million uninsured Americans and new help to nearly 95 million Americans that are struggling to meet health care's runaway costs.

My plan provides security to families like the McNallys and then others that are caught up in what health care experts call "job lock," the fear that because of what they call preexisting medical conditions, changing jobs will cost you and your family your health insurance. We're going to change all of that.

My plan cuts runaway costs by making the system more efficient. And the key is something we call health insurance networks, pooling together individuals and businesses that too often can't afford to offer health insurance to their workers or that worry that one worker's illness or accident could drive everyone else's health insurance right through the roof. Insurance costs obey the law of large numbers: the larger the group being insured, the lower the cost per individual; the broader the risk is spread, the lower the administrative overhead.

We're also going to cut health care costs by wringing out waste and excess in the present system. That's why we have targeted malpractice insurance for reform. You know this, and I know it, and every American knows it: High malpractice premiums mean higher doctors' bills, expensive, unnecessary tests, higher hospital costs, costs passed along not only to the patient but to every American taxpayer. Last year alone, legal costs inflated our doctors' bills by $20 billion. You shouldn't have to pay a lawyer when you go to the doctor.

When health care costs total more than what we spend on our kids' education and our country's national defense combined— education and defense combined, health care costing more—even small changes can save us billions. If we made all the changes I've talked about, my plan would save nearly $400 billion in the next 4 years.

I listen to the American people, and you want to know you've got insurance you can count on. I don't hear you calling for higher taxes to finance a Government takeover of our hospitals. I will never approve such a program.

Yet that is exactly what some of my opponents want, to nationalize our health care system: put Government in control; let Government fix the prices; let Government ration the kind of care that people get and how much, what kind and when they'll get it. Go the Government route, and you know what we'll get: our health care system that combines the efficiency of the House of Representatives post office with the compassion of the KGB over there in Moscow.

You know, we probably have to stop using that comparison. That comparison made a few people hot under the collar. I even got one letter from Russia telling me, "Quit running down the KGB." [*Laughter*]

Nationalize health care, and here's what we're in for: long waiting lines, lists for surgery, shortages of the high-tech equipment responsible for so many of the miracles of modern medicine. One example: Right now—you've got great facilities in Cleveland—but right now the Cleveland Clinic performs 10 coronary bypass surgeries—I see we've got a doctor from the clinic over here. [*Laughter*] Well, that's great. They perform 10 bypass surgeries a day; high tech, high quality, special, excellent surgery without any wait. But if you live across Lake Erie in Canada, the wait for coronary bypass surgery is up to 6 months. And that's not the kind of system that America wants or America needs.

Then there's the cost. According to some studies, nationalized health care would mean a whopping $250 billion to $500 billion a year in new taxes. But you won't hear about higher taxes from the folks that are pushing that scheme. Just ask them about some of the side effects of their plan, and they just say, "Take two aspirin; call me after the election." [*Laughter*]

Well, this is what this election is about: who's got the good ideas, and who's got some lousy ones. We've the right ideas on health care. They have the wrong ones.

My opponent backs a plan that goes by a different name, but in the end it takes you to the same place, nationalized health care. It's called "play or pay." Listen for that one during the fall, "play or pay." Here's what it means: Each employer must "play," meaning shell out for insurance for employ-

ees, or "pay," extract a payroll tax to finance Government health coverage.

"Play or pay" will leave a lot of small businesses, those we are counting on to lead the recovery we need so desperately, with two crummy options: cut workers' wages to pay for mandated health care, or fire some workers and use the savings to cover the rest. According to an independent Urban Institute study, the "pay" part of this plan is no playground. It will require at least a 7-percent payroll tax. Now you small-business people here, you that have your sleeves rolled up running a restaurant or running a neighborhood store of some kind, think about that one.

According to estimates, that kind of tax will cost this country 700,000 jobs. For an employee earning $24,000 a year say, that payroll tax would mean $1,700 chopped right out of his paycheck. Higher prices, lower wages, lost job: Any way you look at it, that is the wrong prescription for America.

So in the end, this "play or pay" is no different from nationalized health care. I'm tempted to call it "pay and pay and pay again." It's an open invitation for employers to stop offering health benefits, throw the problem in the Government's lap, and dump millions of Americans that are working into a public plan like Medicaid.

Right now, the cost of health care eats up 13 percent of all the goods and services that we produce. Do you really want to turn another huge chunk of our economy over to the Government? We can't afford to saddle ourselves with a health care cure that's worse than the disease, especially when we have a much better alternative.

Now you can see why I believe health care is going to be a Republican issue this year. My opponent just isn't up to the mark on health care. A major newspaper that I don't quote too often these days, the New York Times—[*laughter*]—described Bill Clinton's attention to health care issues as, I quote, "occasional." It's no surprise why. After having Governor Clinton for 12 years, one in four folks in Arkansas don't even have health insurance. Bill Clinton has promised he'll do for America what he's done for Arkansas. And my question is: Why would we let him?

I want to start our program that's been sitting up on Capitol Hill for a while moving forward. Move forward on health reform. And Congress comes back from what they call a work period—they've been on vacation for a month and a half—next Tuesday. My opponents are divided. Even they know their proposals won't work. And I say, let Congress start by passing my small-business health care reforms to bring affordable, quality health care to millions of Americans who don't have it now. Make it a Labor Day present to the American worker and to the American family and get off your backsides and do something about it.

If you think I'm a little frustrated with this gridlocked Congress, you are right. We ought to clean House.

On this Labor Day weekend, we should remember what Jefferson called "the sum of good government," whether it respected the right of each one of us. Thomas Jefferson said, and I quote, ". . . a wise and frugal government . . . shall not take from the mouth of labor the bread that it has

earned." In Jefferson's day, doctors made house calls on horseback and life was short. Today, we have miracle medicines that can pluck us from death's door. But all this is of no matter if we can't afford it, not if it is reserved only for the privileged or the prosperous, not if it bankrupts the families of America. We must not take from the mouth of labor the bread that you have earned. We must fix the health care system of America.

Once again, let me say I hope this hasn't been too long and too specific, but this strikes at the core and the well-being of every single family in America. There is no better place to talk about family and family values than it is right here with Steve and Gretel. To all of you, my thanks for this warm Ohio welcome. May God bless the greatest, freest country on the face of the Earth, the United States of America. Thank you all.

Note: The President spoke at 10 a.m. at the Lake County fairgrounds. A tape was not available for verification of the content of these remarks.

Remarks on Arrival in Greenville, South Carolina
September 5, 1992

Thank you all very, very much. What a great welcome back to this wonderful State.

Listen, I am so proud that the First Lady of South Carolina is with us, our old friend Iris Campbell. You've got a great Governor, and you've got a great First Lady. And they represent this State with honor and dignity.

Let me also say, one of the things we've got to do, and I'm glad to see these Inglis signs are, we have got to clean House. We have got to get rid of the gridlocked Congress. So elect this good man standing here to the United States House of Representatives. It is time to clean House and change in Washington. Good idea.

Well, let me just tell you, as I look around all 50 States I see South Carolina out there in the lead for jobs and for bringing new investment into this great State. I was so

proud to stand with Carroll Campbell over there in Germany to get that announcement of a major new plant coming to South Carolina because those Germans have the same respect I do for the workers in the State of South Carolina. They know that by coming here we can produce the best products in the world, and this is going to save this country of ours, move it right into the future. We are going to be able to export more and create more jobs in the United States of America by the free and open trade policies that I support and that Carroll Campbell supports.

I also want to say something about the tragedy to the south, because when Barbara and I were down there in Homestead, Florida, we saw these hats; people that had been helped here in South Carolina during

Hurricane Hugo now reaching out, opening their arms to help others down in Florida. It was a wonderful thing. Your State was helped, and now you are helping the victims of the hurricane down there, Hurricane Andrew. I salute the people of South Carolina and North Carolina who were doing this. It is the best of America: one American reaching out to help another.

Let me just say, we're going to move on now over to the Apple Festival in North Carolina, but I want to say this: I am ready for the fight. We are going to take this battle for a better America to the American people. We are going to win the battle for school choice. It's important that parents can choose where their kids go to school. We are going to win the battle to back up our law enforcement officers and have a little more respect for the victims of crime and a little less for the criminals. We need your help in the Congress for that one. I need Bob up there on that.

We have already helped, thanks to the men and women of South Carolina. I don't think any State did more than South Caroli-na in Desert Storm. I was proud of each and every one of those people that served.

Having set back aggression there, now we're going to extend our exports, take advantage of this more peaceful world and bring more prosperity to the workers in the United States of America.

So thank you all very much for this wonderful turnout. Thanks for your belief, confidence in the United States. You know, one of the biggest differences I have with Governor Clinton: he talks about America being in decline; I talk about America on the rise, competent, able to solve the problems.

So thank you for this warm welcome back. We will clean out the Democrats, and we will clean out the House. We will leave Governor Clinton in Arkansas, letting him—struggling with the worst environmental record in the world.

Thank you all very, very much. Thank you very much for the welcome back.

Note: The President spoke at 12:50 p.m. at the Greenville-Spartanburg Airport. In his remarks, he referred to Republican congressional candidate Bob Inglis.

Exchange With Reporters During a Visit With the Harris Family in Asheville, North Carolina
September 5, 1992

Q. Now that you've got him here, what do you hope to tell the President?

Mr. Roy Harris. Well, we're going to talk about this neighborhood here. I want to make sure that he understands our neighborhood and the neighborhood that he's in right now and how it affects us in policies and decisions that are made. We have a mixed neighborhood here. Therefore, he'll get a chance to see a typical neighborhood.

Q. Are you a registered Republican or Democrat, sir?

The President. These guys, I'll tell you what they want to do——

Mr. Harris. Registered Democrat. [*Laughter*]

The President. A very hospitable one at that, and we are very grateful—[*laughter*]—for their hospitality, I'll tell you. It transcends any of these other things. They invited us, and here we are. They really made us feel at home. We've only been here 5 minutes.

Mrs. Bush. But you ought to tell them a little bit about what the Harrises do for their community.

The President. You tell them.

Mrs. Bush. Well, you do Little League and——

The President. Coaches. She teaches.

Mrs. Bush. Well, she started the Girl Scout troop. They're active in their church. Their children get good marks because their parents care. I mean, just by chance they turned out to be an extraordinary family, and they sort of know what family values are.

The President. Great citizens of their community.

Q. Are you going to try to twist his arm, Mr. President?

Mrs. Bush. You're darn right. [*Laughter*]

The President. I'll leave that to Barbara. [*Laughter*] No, we're not here on that. We're just here because they invited us here, and we're proud to be here and very pleased.

Mr. Harris. It was an invitation for him to come and talk with my two daughters. That was the invitation.

The President. Yes, we had a chance to talk a little on those issues, their education, some of those things. But we'll have a chance to visit.

Q. Well, Mr. Harris, do you think there in the White House that the President really doesn't get a feel for what many neighborhoods are like?

Mr. Harris. The typical example is I went down the street a few minutes ago, and the neighborhood is really happy that this is happening in their neighborhood. They're saying it's not here often that we get a President into our neighborhood, and so everybody is pleased. The church has opened their doors for us; friends across the street, we had to do certain things for them. This is a community. Believe it or not, it's going to be a community effort here, from the food to people loaning us a bread basket, to a number of things that are happening. The community has really participated in this process, and I think they feel very good about it.

The President. That's just wonderful. Well, you're a great spokesman for your community, too.

Thank you all very much.

Q. What do your daughters want to tell the President?

Mrs. Bush. Maybe they want to tell us privately. [*Laughter*]

Mrs. Diantha Harris. Lisa, what did you say you were going to tell Mrs. Bush?

Lisa Harris. Can we play—[*inaudible*].

Mrs. Bush. Sure. [*Laughter*] I'd like that.

Q. Mr. President, what would you like to convey to the Harrises?

The President. Well, we'll have a wide array of things to talk about, the gratitude that we feel in our hearts for their invitation, that's the first thing. When you're welcomed by a family, why, that's what you do, that's what you feel. And I want to know more about their community. Certainly be glad to share with them the views I have on education, family, community itself; try to help others. I mean we were greeted out there by what we call some of the Points of Light, people that are designated; it's so hard, but we have this thousand Points of Light, people helping each other. Well, you do that in your daily lives here. So we can talk about that, plus everything else.

Barbara and I were down in Florida. And a lot of people from South Carolina who had been helped in Hurricane Hugo were there.

Mrs. Bush. North Carolina.

The President. Then we went over to Jeanerette, Louisiana, and there was a whole group from around here, as a matter of fact, in North Carolina. They had just pitched in because people had been over helping on the North Carolina coast.

Mrs. Bush. They had "Remember Hugo" signs.

The President. Remember Hugo. And they were reaching out, helping people halfway across the country. It's just wonderful.

Mr. Harris. There's, I think, 37 churches in the Mud Creek Association that want to do the same thing.

The President. Right from here? Is that right?

Mr. Harris. Want to raise money to help the people in Florida this weekend. It's going to happen in the Mud Creek Association churches tomorrow. So we're all part of it, and I wouldn't be surprised if they end up wanting to bus or truck down there.

The President. Heading down there? A lot of volunteers are pouring in. It's really good, and they're really helping. They're helping reconstruct. I talked to the guy yesterday, Andy Card, and a lot of that debris that was just there has been moved away, cleared out. Military doing a good job, but also the volunteers.

Note: The exchange began at 1:35 p.m. at the Harris residence.

Remarks at the North Carolina Apple Festival in Hendersonville
September 5, 1992

The President. Thank you all very much. Thank you so much. Listen, even the rain can't ruin a great festival like this. This is wonderful, and Barbara and I are thrilled to be here. We have great respect for your Governor, Jim Martin. What a superb job he's done for this State and, indeed, for our country. And may I salute Congressman Taylor, who I understood was going to say a few words; Congressman Cass Ballenger. If we had more like them in the United States Congress, we wouldn't be faced with a grid-locked Congress. So my plea is, keep these guys there, and then help us clean House. Let's get rid of the gridlocked Congress and move this country ahead.

May I thank everybody that arranged all this. In this election you're going to hear a couple of very different versions. My goal is that the United States must remain a military superpower, keeping our defenses up. And I thank all those in North Carolina who served this country in uniform and have done so much to guarantee the peace and guarantee freedom around the world. No State has been more patriotic, none more in the forefront of service.

We've got to remain an economic superpower, and that means we've got to be able to compete. That means we've got to be able to create more jobs in the United States, and that means we must be an export superpower. Let's not turn inward and protect. Let's turn outward, sell American products abroad, and create more jobs at home.

When we go into the voting booth in November, I ask you to consider the experience. I've held a job in the private sector, and I happen to think that's a good experience for President of the United States, private sector job. I also happen to believe that in the fact—they tell you, well, foreign policy doesn't matter; security doesn't matter. I take great pride in the fact that these young people go to bed at night with a lot less fear of nuclear weapons because of the way we've acted over the last 12 years.

I'll tell you what the major issue is in this campaign. The major question in this campaign is this: I believe that the Government is too big and spends too much and taxes too much. The other side wants to tax more and spend more. We cannot let that happen to the United States.

Audience members. Four more years! Four more years! Four more years!

The President. Four more years is what we need to finish this job, 4 more.

Audience members. Four more years! Four more years! Four more years!

The President. You know, let me just mention the tragedy in Florida. We went out this week to try to help people. We took some Federal money that had already been appropriated to use to help farmers whose crops were destroyed. We've led the private sector in helping people in Homestead, Florida, and all across for the hurricane. And Governor Clinton was outraged. He accused me of pandering. Now, that's the same guy that Paul Tsongas called the "Pander Bear." You remember that in the primary. He's now acting like Goldilocks, saying, "Somebody's been sleeping in my bed!"

Here are the facts, pure and simple: We have suggested specific spending cuts and specific tax reductions. And he has told the American people, "I want to increase your taxes by $150 billion and increase spending by $220 billion." We can't have that.

Audience members. Boo-o-o!

The President. Barbara and I are delighted to be here. We know you've been standing out in that rain for a long time. But when Barbara Bush—you know, the other side wants to get us away from talking about family values. You come to a festival like this, and you feel that sense of love and that sense of family. We're going to keep on saying, let's find ways to strengthen the American family, not tear it apart. I might say I am very, very proud of Barbara when she holds an AIDS baby in her arms or teaches some child or adult to read. That is what we mean by strengthening the American family.

My last point is this—you've been standing out there long enough, and I want to eat some apples. The last point is this: The other side says that America is in decline and that we rank somewhere between Germany and Sri Lanka. Well, let me tell Governor Clinton something. I have been around the world many times, and I've worked hard in this country. We are not behind any other country in the world. We are proud. We are patriotic. Don't let them tear down the United States of America. Stand up for us. Don't listen to them.

We can do anything we set our sights to do. So let's have a better system of education. Let's help the people that need it. God bless those from North Carolina who—when people from Florida came to help in Hugo—North Carolina paying it back in spades. I was in Jeanerette, Louisiana, the other day. Here was a group of guys, they'd driven all night to show that North Carolina hospitality and concern for the people of Louisiana. That wasn't the Government. That was the people that were doing it.

Thank you all very, very much for this warm welcome back to this State. I need your support in November. I believe we're going to win. Let us finish the job of helping the United States of America. And yes, let's help those veterans.

God bless you. And thank you very, very much.

Note: The President spoke at 3:10 p.m. at the Henderson County Courthouse.

Message on the Observance of Labor Day
September 5, 1992

On Labor Day, America rightly salutes her working men and women and celebrates their outstanding contributions to our Nation and the world.

From our factories and mines to our construction sites, American labor has led the world in efficiency, productivity, and innovation. American workers, by their matchless ingenuity and resourcefulness, have pioneered advances in aviation, defense, and telecommunications, so it is not surprising that "Made in the U.S.A." remains a universally recognized symbol of quality craftsmanship.

Ever since the first Labor Day parade in New York 110 years ago, this holiday has been one of justifiable celebration and pride, and it remains so today. History shows the extraordinary courage and resilience of the American people, and I know that, by working together, we will overcome the challenges that lie before us—just as we have met every trial in the past.

While our challenges are great, we must remember that our opportunities—and our determination—are greater. The United States will continue to push for free and fair trade, because expanding markets for our goods and services will create jobs. This Administration will also continue to ease the burden on our economy that is caused by excessive Federal regulation and to promote incentives for savings and investment through tax credits and the creation of Enterprise Zones. To help our citizens prepare for the jobs of tomorrow, we are moving forward with America 2000, our National strategy to achieve excellence in our schools.

If there be any solemnity to this Labor Day, let it be only for the passing of summer, because everything else that this day represents—from the spirit of the American worker to the fundamental strength of our free enterprise system—should be a source of pride and hope for all Americans.

GEORGE BUSH

White House Statement on Additional Disaster Relief for Louisiana
September 5, 1992

The President today announced that he has amended his August 26, 1992, declaration of a major disaster in the State of Louisiana to waive State and local cost sharing requirements, where permitted to do so by law, and to allow reimbursement of 100 percent of eligible public assistance costs exceeding $10 per capita.

This additional relief provided by the President is consistent with a request made by Governor Edwin Edwards. It was taken in response to the unprecedented damage and destruction caused by Hurricane Andrew. By waiving customary State and local cost sharing requirements, the President can provide maximum Federal assistance to the people of Louisiana whose lives have been so severely disrupted by this disaster.

This waiver applies to all authorized public assistance. It will provide additional help to the State in its efforts to remove debris from the disaster areas, eliminate immediate threats to public health and safety, and carry out emergency work to save lives. Assistance for temporary housing, crisis counseling, and disaster unemployment will continue to be 100 percent federally funded where allowed under the law.

Remarks Prior to a Redbirds Baseball Game in Louisville, Kentucky
September 6, 1992

Thank you all. What a wonderful holiday welcome. We've got to see a ball game now. Thank you very much. May I just first say what a privilege and thrill it is for Barbara and me to be here. I want to thank Stan for the introduction. I've just been in one of the dugouts talking to the Redbirds, and I also salute the Indianapolis ball club here today. We're going to treat them very kindly. Aren't we, you guys?

But may I also say as an old baseball fan, to be here with Pee Wee Reese, that's a great treat for me, an old fan of his. Also Paul Hornung, I've watched him day-in and day-out, not only in college ball but when he was up there at Green Bay, a superb athlete, a great citizen of Kentucky.

And single out two coaches, Coach Crum and Coach Schnellenberger. Somebody once told me that playing a tie ball game is like kissing your sister. Well, I want to tell you this: The coach did the right thing yesterday. He did it the American way. He took a real shot at it, and we are proud of him and proud of that ball club of his, the Cardinals.

Let me end it by just simply saying I'm here to salute Harvest U.S.A. and Kentucky Harvest. Stan is right, the heartbeat in Louisville and Lexington, Indianapolis, is far louder and far clearer than the heartbeat up in Washington. When one American pitches in to help another, as you're doing now for the victims of this terribly devastating hurricane in south Florida and then again in Louisiana, we salute you. One neighbor helping another, that is the American spirit, the American way. That is what we mean when we talk about Points of Light.

May God bless you all, and may God bless this wonderful American spirit. Thank you so much.

Note: The President spoke at 12:46 p.m. at Cardinal Stadium. In his remarks, he referred to Stan Curtis, founder of Kentucky Harvest; and Denny Crum, head basketball coach, and Howard Schnellenberger, head football coach, University of Louisville.

Remarks to the Polish-American Community in Chicago, Illinois
September 6, 1992

The President. Thank you, Mitch. Thank you all for that great welcome.

Audience members. Four more years! Four more years! Four more years!

The President. Thank you so much for the wonderful introduction. And may I pay my respects to the Governor, Jim Edgar, doing a superb job for the people of this great State. Jim, we're grateful to you. Let me also single out Rich Williamson. We need him in the United States Senate. We've got to change the Congress. We've got to clean the House. We've got to elect Rich Williamson to the Senate. Another old friend, Wally Dudycz, glad to see him and Jack O'Malley and Lou Kasper. The Polish consul general came to greet me, Mr. Jankowski. Ed Moskal, of course, our old, dear friend. And again, I'd like to salute Secretary Ed Derwinski, known so well to everybody here, an outstanding American that has served his country with such distinction.

This past Independence Day, some of you were with us, I traveled to the heartland of Poland to bury a treasure. In the crypt of an ancient cathedral, I stood with President Lech Walesa as the remains of the great patriot Ignacy Paderewski was finally laid to rest in the rich and free Polish soil that conceived and sustained him. And it struck me, this was the fulfillment of Poland's dreams.

Think of what we have seen together in the last few years. We watched a Gdansk electrician, a humble man, stand up for freedom, electrify the world with the charge that all people should be free and be heard. We watched the nation of Poland reform, brimming with a new and different fluid of life, inspired by the passion for freedom. And we watched a Pope named John Paul II, a proud Pole. And as we gather today at this festival, a good time to count our blessings, I can say something no President ever could say before: The cold war is over, and freedom finished first. And Poland is free.

You know, my opponents say——

Audience members. Four more years! Four more years! Four more years!

The President. We've got a lot of work to do for 4 more, I'll tell you.

These critics, the Clinton-Gore ticket, say that I spend too much time on foreign policy. Well, let me tell you this: American schoolchildren used to hide under their desks in drills to prepare for nuclear war. We saw the chance to cut down the threat of nuclear war, and we did it. And does that matter? You bet it matters to the young people that are here right here today. You know, over the past—and everybody in this crowd understands this, Democrat, Republican, liberal, it doesn't matter, you understand this point: Over the past 4 years, more people have breathed the fresh air of freedom than in all of human history. We saw a chance to help, and I did it. And do you say, does that matter? Of course, it does. You bet it does.

Now our challenges are straightforward. This Labor Day weekend we must dedicate ourselves to the challenge: economic security for the working men and working women of America. That is the big challenge, jobs for the American people. You know, in this 21st century America must not only be a military superpower, we've got to be an export superpower, and we've got to be an economic superpower.

Audience members. Four more years! Four more years! Four more years!

The President. My vision is to look forward, to open new markets, to prepare our people to compete, to save and to invest, to strengthen the American family so that we can win.

You know, I've spent half my life in public service, half in the private sector. I built a business, and I met a payroll. And I believe that is a good qualification for being President of the United States, to know what it is to hold a job in the private sector. And Governor Clinton has spent all but a handful of years of his adult life in government. Now he says he respects the small businessman, he loves the private sector. Well, maybe it's a good chance now to give

1489

him a chance to experience what it's like to be in the private sector. Because he isn't going to be President of the United States.

I agree with you, Government has got to help people. But Government is too big, and it taxes too much, and it spends too much of your money. And we've got to get it under control. And so I put a freeze on domestic discretionary spending, plus a plan to control mandatory Federal spending except Social Security. I said at the beginning, don't mess with Social Security. And we are not going to let them touch Social Security. My plan, and it is up before the Congress now, would save nearly $300 billion in over 5 years. And I want to say *Do widzenia* to more than 4,000 wasteful Federal projects, like a national research program, and get into this one, the mating habits of the mink. We do not need to spend your taxpayers' money on that kind of program.

So the gridlocked Congress has balked at my ideas. So now I have a new idea: Give you all a say on it. I want to give you, the taxpayer, the option of taking 10 percent of your income tax and using it for one purpose alone, to reduce the national deficit. Get the mortgage off the back of these young people. Check off 10 percent to get the deficit down. If Congress won't cut spending, let you, the people, do it. And I'll be at your side.

But while we cut Federal spending, we can still set priorities to help people in need to get back on their feet. So this week I took money that had already been appropriated and used it to help farmers whose crops were destroyed. And I said I'd help the private sector rebuild devastated Florida and Louisiana. And let me thank the people of Illinois who reached out to help their fellow man down in the south. You have been magnificent. But anyway, when I did all this to try to help these people, Governor Clinton, of all people, accused me of pandering. This from the man that Paul Tsongas, you remember the little bear, this from the man that Paul Tsongas called the "Pander Bear," the same Paul Tsongas who said on April 7th, the American people are just hearing how cynical and unprincipled Bill Clinton is. That's not from a Republican, that was from a Democrat, Paul Tson-

gas of Massachusetts. And he's right. He is right.

But here are the facts. Governor Clinton proposes at least $220 billion in new spending, just to start. *Newsweek* magazine called the Clinton approach, and I quote, "economic fantasy." And *Newsweek* went on to say that the real cost of the Clinton program is "arguably at least 3 times higher" than he's admitted. And he has mentioned program after program after program that he wants to increase spending for. So while we're eating a little kielbasa, he's offering pie in the sky. Who does he think he's kidding? Not the American people.

You know, I've been one of these guys who is accused of thinking every day is the Fourth of July. Well, I like the way a cartoon summed it up. My opponent thinks that every day is April 15th. You know what happens then. They have this cartoon; it featured a guy at the kitchen table. He said to his wife, "Honey, I figure we can afford all those taxes Clinton and Gore want to raise if I can get two of those jobs they say they'll create." Well, raising taxes doesn't create jobs, it destroys them. You know that. So with the savings that I have proposed, we can cut taxes and get this economy moving again. The difference is tax and spend versus less taxes and less spending.

Now, one other thing. More than 2 percent of our gross domestic product is spent not in the factory, not in the classroom, not in the laboratory but in and around the courtroom. I've never heard of a nation that sued its way to greatness. So I have a plan for the gridlocked Congress to cut down on all these crazy lawsuits that are choking our economy. Too many lawsuits. And as a nation we ought to sue each other less and care for each other just a little bit more. That's my philosophy. That's the way Barbara looks at it.

Another thing, you look around and see these great kids, and you think we've got to do better in education. Three years ago this month, we started a revolution in American education, one called America 2000. Today for the first time, every eligible 4-year-old whose parents choose to participate can get a Head Start on kindergarten. That is progress. That is the way to help the young people in this country. Today for the first time, half our students in college have a Federal loan or grant. Grants and loans are at an all-time high under our administration for these college kids. And we have a new "GI bill" for kids. We want to give every one of you the freedom to pick where your children will learn, any program, any school. I favor school choice. Let the parents decide whether it's public, private, or religious schools.

We've got to do better in education. We've got to do better in law enforcement, backing up the law enforcement people. It's cheaper to send a kid to Yale than to send a kid to jail. Penn State is cheaper than the State pen. But for those who refuse to pitch in and help build up America and instead tear us down, we need to show them what law and order is all about. It's about supporting our police forces and judicial system. God bless the police that stand up against these outrageous criminals.

And it's time we take back the streets of America and support the American family. It is time we let those family values come to the fore. And that means let's reform our welfare system so that families stay together and these fathers that owe the money will stick around and pay what they owe to these mothers that are trying to bring up these kids.

And while we're at it, I've got a plan for health care, and that plan says this: We don't need the Government taking over health care. It doesn't work. We've got the best quality health care. What we need is to pool insurance. What we need are designed—not respect for Government policies but respect for the American family. We've made progress, great progress, and now I ask for your help for a health care reform that will bring insurance to every single family that wants it. That's our proposal. His is to turn it over to the Government.

Now this is the last point. This is the last point, except I want to say a word to this guy over here who feels very strongly about something. He's talking about AIDS. Under my administration the spending for this deadly disease is up from $4.3 billion to a request for $4.9 billion. We care. We are working. And disruptions don't help. What helps is what you feel in your heart. And we will keep on this research until we whip that deadly disease.

So we made a lot of progress. But in others we've got a ways to go. And you ask me why, and I would say three words: the gridlocked Congress. And I know you get tired of people blaming each other, but let me explain something. There are certain numbers that mean something: number 40, Gale Sayers; number 8, Carl Yastrzemski; number 23, a certain basketball player in baggy shorts. Here's one you may not know, number 38. That's how long the same party, the same crowd has been running the United States House of Representatives, 38 years. Ask Millie, our dog, and she'll tell you that's 266 years in a dog life. Change the Congress. Change the Congress. Clean the House. Elect Rich Williamson to the Senate. And while we're at it, elect Elias Zenkich to the House. And while we're at it, let's limit the terms of Congressmen. Let's get some limits out there so things will change.

Let me tell you this. If you detect a little optimism about our country, you're absolutely right. The other side is saying that we're somewhere between Germany and Sri Lanka. They ought to go abroad. Let them go to Poland. Let them look into the eyes of the Polish people who thank America every single day for their freedom. Let Governor Clinton take a look. Let him see what this world is like with freedom and democracy on the march.

We have done it. And we can do it right here at home with your help. God bless our country. Don't let them tear it down. God bless the United States of America. And thank you for this wonderful turnout. Thank you all.

Note: The President spoke at 2:45 p.m. at the Copernicus Center during the Taste of Polonia Festival. In his remarks, he referred to Mitchell P. Kobelinski, president, Copernicus Foundation; Walter Dudycz, Illinois State senator; Jack O'Malley, Cook County State's attorney; Lou Kasper, City of Chicago Republican Party chairman; and

Edward J. Moskal, president, Polish National Alliance. A tape was not available for *verification of the content of these remarks.*

Remarks at the Labor Day Mackinac Bridge Walk in Michigan
September 7, 1992

All right. Who brought the coffee? Now let's go. Governor Engler's here. You know his reputation as a fiscal conservative. When it comes to the taxpayers' money, they say he's so tight that he squeaks when he walks, so we are going to find out about that. [*Laughter*]

We're grateful to see so many people ready for the latest "Big Mac Attack." We're going across this thing. Barbara and I were over in Sault Sainte Marie, and she handed me my sneakers. And she said, "Just do it." Well, that's what we plan to do this fall, I'll tell you.

The only other point I want to make is that this is Labor Day, and to those hard workers across this country, don't let anybody tell you we are a nation in decline. We're a nation on the rise. Our workers are the most productive anyplace in the entire world.

So the big question is, how do we get this country moving so everybody that wants a job has one? And the answer is to spend a little less Government money, tax a little bit less, and stimulate the economy and get it going. And we're going to do that.

Thanks for a great welcome. And I just can't tell you how much we're looking forward to this walk. We'll set a good pace. And I plan to set that pace in November. We need you. Many, many thanks for your support.

Now let's go. We're off. Thank you all.

Note: The President spoke at 7:04 a.m. A tape was not available for verification of the content of these remarks.

Remarks at the Republican Party Labor Day Picnic in Waukesha, Wisconsin
September 7, 1992

Thank you so much. What a marvelous turnout. Waukesha knows how to do it. Thank you all very much. Barbara and I are delighted to be here. May I thank our great United States Senator Bob Kasten and say how lucky we are to have him and Eva in Washington, DC, two of the best. Please get out there and work hard in November. We've got to get more like him in the Senate. Of course, you heard from one of the great Governors in this country, Tommy Thompson, your own. I salute him and Sue Ann. I don't believe I've got a better supporter out there than Tommy Thompson.

May I greet Jim Sensenbrenner. If we had more like him in the Congress you wouldn't have everybody yelling, "Clean House." He's right. Most of them are wrong. We do need to clean House. That brings me to Joe Cook. I'd like to see him elected to the Congress. And then of course, John MacIver, an old friend who has been in these political trenches with me and Tommy and Bob Kasten for a long time; we salute him. Here's a guy who rolls up his sleeves, like so many of you, and just goes to work for what he believes. It's a great part of American politics. I salute him and every other volunteer out there doing the Lord's work. We are going to win because of all of you.

Barbara and I started this morning up at the Mackinac Bridge in Michigan. With us today, incidentally, is Michigan's Governor John Engler over there, another great Republican, John. We had a brisk 50-minute walk across that magnificent Mackinac Bridge. So when we say it's great to be at a picnic, we know what we're talking about. It's nice to be here, no more walks.

Now, this Labor Day we gather at a triumphant moment in history. I can stand before you this morning and can say something no other President could ever say: The cold war is over, and freedom finished first.

But America is not a nation that brags, not a nation that looks behind. We are loyal only to the future. So this Labor Day we must rededicate ourselves to the future of all who punch the time clock, pay the bills, sweat it out at tax time. Our number one priority must be to build economic security for the working men and women of this great country of ours.

Today is the kickoff day for these campaigns. I think the American people feel this one has been going on about 10 months too long, and so do I. But nevertheless, this is the official kickoff day. My opponent will kick off his campaign with a message of fear, telling us that our country is in decline. But I ask you to look beneath the rhetoric and look at the facts.

Governor Clinton will tell you that we're a nation in decline, slipping past Germany, headed south toward Sri Lanka, to use his words. Wrong, absolutely wrong, Governor Clinton. The world's most productive workers are not in Germany. They are not in Japan. They are right here in the United States of America, a lot of them right here today in Wisconsin.

Governor Clinton will tell you that American wages are slipping. And he doesn't mention that since 1985, our workers have earned bigger paychecks and benefits than any other workers in the world. I want to see them even better. Governor Clinton says that people are working harder for less. He won't mention that adjusted personal income is higher than it was 4 years ago. That's because inflation, the thief of the middle class, has been securely locked away.

Now, does this mean all is fine in America? Of course not. But at a time of uncertainty, a time of wrenching global challenge, Governor Clinton wants to scare American workers so that he can slip into office with the failed tax-and-spend policies of the past. Last night, I don't know if any of you heard that Tom Brokaw show, but last night the Governor appeared on the Brokaw show, and the first words out of his mouth were, "I have advocated a tax increase." Well, Governor, that is the wrong prescription for America.

He offers a treasure trove of new Government programs that will cost at least $220 billion more of your money. I say you already give too much to the tax man. He wants to raise taxes by $150 billion just to start; that's just for openers. I want to cut them and get the economy started in high gear.

You heard what Bob Kasten said; he's right. We've been trying to get through this gridlocked Congress some incentives that he and I believe in, locked because of the old thinking of the Democratic leadership that's been in power for 38 years.

So as this campaign gets into full swing, I make one promise. I will talk about real ideas: of making health care available to the poorest of the poor, controlling what you pay when you go to a doctor; about reforming welfare; giving our kids what they deserve, the world's very best schools. My policies will strengthen the most important institution in our Nation, and I am talking about the American family. The liberals are trying to back us away from discussing how to strengthen the family, and we are going to stay with it. America knows that the family is slipping, and we want to help strengthen it by child care and by support for these school choice and whatever it is, welfare reform. So let's keep talking about what America needs: strengthening the American family.

But today, as Governor Thompson said, I want to talk about another roadblock in the way of you and your families' economic security: our crazy, out-of-control legal system. Don't just ask me about what's wrong with our legal system. Check the opinion of that famous enforcer of American justice. I'm not talking about Oliver Wendell Holmes or John Marshall. I mean someone even more famous than that, Hulk Hogan. My grandkids tell me that in his movie last year, Hulk Hogan was confronted with the predictable crop of bad guys, only the bad guys refused to fight. Instead they said, "This is the nineties; we're not going to fight you. We are going to sue you." [*Laughter*]

Well, I believe that one statement sums up a lot of what is wrong in America today. You pick up the newspaper, and the stories roll on out at you. Like the story, true story, about a basketball referee who made a controversial call at the buzzer of a Purdue-Iowa basketball game. Purdue won, and an Iowa souvenir company was suddenly left with a lot of victory souvenirs that weren't in all that much demand. So what did the company do? They sued the referee. Sound crazy? Well, it took 2 years and a lot of money before the case was dismissed by the State supreme court.

Now, understand, law is a noble and honorable profession; but most good lawyers will tell you that the system is out of control. In the past 20 years, the number of civil lawsuits filed in Federal courts has more than doubled. Today the average case takes almost a year to be resolved, and in the past year alone the number of cases were pending for 3 years increased by nearly 15 percent. That means you can file a suit, have time to enroll in a law school, study 3 years, graduate, pass the bar, and then represent yourself on the court the day the decision is handed down. Now, come on.

The NAM, the National Association of Manufacturers, has just finished looking at what this litigation explosion costs our economy. According to a soon-to-be-released study, American consumers and companies will spend up to $200 billion on legal services this year, $200 billion. American businesses now spend more on insurance and legal fees than on training and preparing our workers for the new economy. And that is crazy. As a nation, I believe it's high time that we started suing each other less and caring for each other more. I have proposed a comprehensive plan to reform our civil justice system.

And we must reform our product liability laws. These laws allow people to be compensated for harm caused by a defective product. People ought to receive fair compensation when a product is defective and they get hurt. But like so much of our civil justice system, product liability has careened out of control.

Let me give you just one example. The Will-Burt Corporation of Orville, Ohio, stopped making parts for ladders and scaffolds and aircraft because they couldn't afford the liability insurance. That was bad news for the company's owners, but worse news for the 80 employees, all of whom got pink slips.

Here is the problem. The product liability laws vary from State to State, and the rules have encouraged these crazy lawsuits and outrageous awards. And the cost of insurance keeps going right out through the roof, keeps skyrocketing. Big deal, right? So companies have to pay extra for a few lawyers. But it's not just companies who foot the bill; we all pay higher prices for everything from medicine to stepladders. We never get to see a lot of good products because companies are afraid of excessive lawsuits.

Get this. Almost half of all the money paid out in these kinds of cases goes not to the injured party, but to the lawyers. I don't want to see only lawyers getting rich; I want to see American workers getting rich. And that's the problem. Our product liability system is killing our economic competitiveness, costing Americans secure jobs that you deserve. Our liability costs are many times greater than in Japan and in Europe. Every dollar we spend all around the courtroom is a dollar we won't spending on training, education, research, investment. It could be the difference between no jobs for our kids and good jobs for our kids.

Now, we have to do something about this. Luckily, your great Senator Bob Kasten understands this. He has been fighting to change the system. And he has put forth a plan, which I am for, working with him on, to speed the legal process, settle more cases out of court, and bring some rationality to the product liability system. Once again, a Wisconsin man is in the lead. Our plan is proconsumer, probusiness, prosafety, and projobs. The day my pen signs Senator Kasten's bill is the day we stop undermining the American worker that we salute today on Labor Day.

So why then, if we have all these problems, do we face this crisis? Bob Kasten will tell you in three words, the gridlocked Congress. And that's why I'm here today.

Forty-four years ago next month, another incumbent President came through Waukesha. His name was Harry S Truman. Now, I admit it; Harry and I don't have everything in common. He believed in bigger Government; I don't share that view. But quite frankly, I voted against Truman that year. But still there are some similarities between us.

I've just read that fascinating book, this big, fat book on Truman, a marvelous biography. Harry Truman ran a small business. He knew what it was to meet a payroll, to work for a living in the private sector. And so do I. Harry Truman wanted to join the military and fight for his country. So do I, and I did. Harry Truman ran as an underdog, just as I am. And he liked it, and so do I. Harry Truman admitted when he made a mistake. And God knows I've done the same thing, and I've admitted it.

But most of all, Harry Truman was frustrated by what he called the do-nothing Congress. Listen to Truman's very own words from right here in this very town 44 years ago: "When I say do-nothing, I mean they"—meaning Congress—"have done nothing for the people. They have not listened to the people's demands."

Now, the gridlocked Congress hasn't listened to people either. One example: I favor a balanced budget amendment. So do you. The Congressman from this very district sponsored the balanced budget amendment and then turned around and voted against his own amendment on the House floor. That's what I mean when I say "gridlocked Congress." Clean House.

For years, Americans have complained about this crazy legal system, but once again the gridlocked Congress has refused to act on my reforms, or on Bob Kasten's reforms. Later this week, we finally get a Senate vote on the product liability reform. My message to the gridlocked Congress today is simple: Either fix our legal system,

stop undermining our workers, or we're going to take a broom and do some spring cleaning in November, because we are going to clean House.

Send me some good leaders who will listen to the people, the way this Senator does. Elect Joe Cook to the House of Representatives. Help clean House. That's the message. They talk about change, change the one institution that hasn't budged for 38 years. Change the House.

Well, we're going to clean House, not just so companies spend less time paying lawyers, more time creating jobs, not just so moms and dads can coach Little League without fear of some crazy lawsuit. We're going to clean House so we bring down health care costs, so we improve our schools, we take back our streets from the criminals, and we start backing up our law enforcement officials more and more.

Now before I finish, it's worth mentioning that while I'm in Waukesha this morning, my opponent, guess where he is, he's in Harry Truman's hometown of Independence, Missouri. So let's just have some plain speaking about Bill Clinton, Governor Bill Clinton, and Harry Truman.

Harry Truman never engaged in doublespeak. He told people the truth, not merely what they wanted to hear. Compare that to Governor Clinton's position on reforming our legal system. The head of the lawyers, the head of the trial lawyers in Arkansas, Trial Lawyers Association, said Governor Clinton has, and I quote, "always done what is right for the trial lawyers." I bet Harry Truman would have done what is right for the American people, not for the trial lawyers.

Whether it was the Soviet blockade of Berlin or the invasion of Korea, Harry Truman never flinched from the tough decision. Now, contrast that with Governor Clinton's waffling and wavering about whether he would have followed my lead and stood up to Saddam Hussein and his naked aggression.

Harry Truman prided himself on his own military service, and he frequently visited veterans associations and spoke with great pride about his service to his country.

Last but not least, Harry Truman believed America could not turn our back on the rest of the world, even despite the challenges here at home. Governor Clinton virtually ignores foreign policy and flirts with the dangerous idea of sticking America's head in the protectionist sands.

Harry Truman said, "The buck stops here." On issue after issue, Governor Clinton says, "First, let's blame George Bush," and then, "I'll get back to you later with an answer." I'll tell you, if the buck stops there, then Governor Clinton is offering devalued currency.

Harry Truman was a man of decisiveness, not equivocation. He'd find little in common with Governor Clinton, a man who hedges or ducks on almost every tough issue, a man who seems to feel strongly on both sides of almost every issue that are before this great Nation. I found out something in the Oval Office: You can't have it both ways. You've got to call it as you see it. You have to make the tough decision and then pay the consequences or get the credit. But you can't be on every side of every issue, waffling around, and call that

leadership. That is not leadership.

You know, many people thought Harry Truman would lose in 1948. But he said what was on his mind. He didn't worry about the press. And he never lost faith in the United States of America.

I stand before you with the same passion and that same faith. I will talk about ideas for the next 57 days, ideas that matter, ideas that can deal with the real challenges facing this country, ideas that won't make everyone happy but that will be right for the United States of America.

And like Harry Truman, I believe a new age of America beckons and that we can reap the benefits. With your help, come November we will match our global victory with economic security here at home.

Thank you all for being here. And may God bless the United States of America on this very, very special day. Thank you all.

Note: The President spoke at 10:16 a.m. at the Waukesha County Exposition Grounds. In his remarks, he referred to John MacIver, Wisconsin Bush-Quayle campaign chairman.

Remarks to the Community in Hamtramck, Michigan
September 7, 1992

Thank you, Paul. And thank you, Governor Engler. Thank you very, very much. I love this sign, of all the signs out there: "These are the Poles that count." You are the Poles that count.

Early this morning the Governor and his wife, Michelle, and Barbara and I all joined about 80,000 for a walk across the great bridge up in northern Michigan. He didn't mention it, but I beat the Governor across the bridge. But he says he was just being polite and hanging back with the First Lady.

Today I don't want to talk about politics. I want to talk about something else, something that's near and dear to the hearts of everybody: freedom. May I recognize some of the outstanding leaders who are with us today: Monsignor Milewski; your great

Mayor, Robert Kozaren; my friend the president of the Polish General Council who introduced me, Paul Odrobina; parade chairman Ted Koltowicz; and the grand marshal, Walter Budweil. Thank you all very much.

My fellow Americans, this past Independence Day I traveled to the heartland of Poland to bury a treasure. In the crypt of an ancient cathedral, I stood with President Walesa as the remains of the great patriot and artist Ignacy Paderewski were finally laid to rest in the rich and free Polish soil that conceived and sustained him. And the ripples from that moment, as his remains were consecrated to the earth on that warm summer day in Warsaw, are passing through this crowd here and now. Sons and daughters of Hamtramck, your forebears came to this great country because they too could not countenance a Poland shackled by repression. Rather than cling to native soil bled dry by empty promises, they chose instead to flourish free on foreign soil and to make it their own. Today you are part of the great family that is America.

Fellow Americans, I am proud to be with you in Hamtramck on Labor Day. You are the blood and bone of Copernicus and Chopin and Curie. You are the sweat and sinew that built this city and this industry. And you are the voice and vision of your parents who struggled to be heard and won that struggle, that labor's voice may be heard always, always. You are the inspiration for Americans who watched and prayed and cheered through recent years as the great nation of Poland, racked by the rhythms of war and oppression, rose like a phoenix, a free nation once again.

We watched this new force, not pushing down from a tyrant but up from the people. We prayed for the nation of Poland, reborn, brimming with a new and different fluid of life, inspired by a Pope and by a passion for freedom, for freedom at last. We cheered a Gdansk electrician who electrified the world with the charge that all people should be free and be heard. We stood proud as American labor took to the forefront during the struggle, standing with Solidarity in its darkest hour, firm in the belief that the dream was real.

I stood before you right here in Hamtramck, right here 3 years ago, with this message: Communism has left an ugly scar on Poland. It will heal, but with pain, the pain of insecurity and insolvency. I pledged America's help. Today I return to you to say that this country and our allies have responded forcefully.

First, our concern for Poland's security. On that day here 3 years ago, I called for an end to the cold war. Thank God, the cold war has ended, and thank God, freedom won. America will do what's right to make certain Poland never again braves the chilling tomb of communism.

And second, our concern for Polish solvency. It's been said that communism is not a form of economics, it's the death of economics. So 3 years ago, I called for all to rally 'round with economic efforts to help

pull Poland from an economic grave. I called for giving Poland preferred trade treatment so she can reach out to the world through exports. I called for reducing Poland's debt to ease her burden. I called for investors to help unleash the explosive entrepreneurial energy of the Polish people. I called for loans so the Polish private sector can help her economy blossom. I called for international financial agreements so Poland can build a financial base worthy of a great nation.

In 1989 these and other major initiatives marked a radical new direction for our foreign policy toward Poland and other democracies. In 1992 I've returned to tell you, Democrat or Republican, whoever you're for: All these predictions and pledges have come true, every single one of them.

There are those who tell me that foreign policy doesn't matter, that with our internal challenges America has no business paying attention to the world anymore. I say, tell that to the immigrants of America. Tell that to our children who are free of nuclear nightmare and can dream the sweet dream of peace. I am proud that we helped change the world. Tell that to the American workers who have a new world of consumers eager for the fruit of your labors. On this Labor Day, let me be clear: No one can outproduce, outthink, outcreate the American working man and woman, no one.

So we recognize that the noble experiment taking place in Poland and other nations today is in fact an inspiration and an opportunity for us and the rest of the world. We pledge our support for Poland's security. We pledge our support for Poland's solvency. We pledge to work for a democratic peace, an enduring peace anchored in economic and political freedom. Most of all, we pledge to keep our word. We pledge to keep Poland free.

My friends, we stand today in the twilight of one millennium and the dawn of the next. Never before has humankind beheld such a view. Never before has our Nation been pressured by such deep energies of change and growth reshaping America like the strong hands of a potter on wet clay. But we will survive, and we will thrive. Why? Because the American people are like the great Statue of Liberty that stands in New York Harbor. We're like that great statue, brought over in pieces from the Old World, strapped together with bolts of steel right here on our own American soil, assembled, raised, and anchored on a rock in our own American waters. And we are like that statue because the family that is America came over in pieces as well.

We came as Poles and Hungarians and Chinese and Germans; Japanese, Irish, Swedes, and French; Italians, Russians, Spaniards, Cubans, Koreans, Hondurans, Lithuanians, and Finns; Ukrainians, Latvians, Bulgarians, and Mexicans; Israelis, Albanians, Czechs, Macedonians. And that roster of new Americans goes on and on and never ends. Like that great statue, we came over in pieces. Our cultures were bolted together by hope. Our cross-struts are many. Our strengths are eternal. Our hopes unite us. And our vision is one: a vision of prosperous peace for our children. And the last best hope for that vision is you, the American people.

It's now time to take those same heartfelt urges that made us become the statue and put them to work here at home. This fight for freedom isn't fought on the dark, treacherous borders far from home. This fight for freedom is fought on the economic battlefield by creating new jobs, opening new markets, building new American strengths right here, here and abroad. And this fight is fought with creativity, determination, and investment in the hearts and minds of the American people.

Here in Hamtramck and across this Nation, these are the forces Americans must bring to bear on our future so every American's human potential is stretched to its God-given best. Hamtramck, you can change the world with a gift your mothers and fathers left behind. And today I challenge you to redeem the struggles they endured. Make their labors mean something. Redeem the struggles Solidarity suffered. Redeem the struggles Kosciuszko and Pulaski and, in fact, all the Kowalskis and Janowskis who lived and died and aimed at one simple thing: to be heard, to have a voice, to vote.

Come November 3d, I challenge you to breathe life into the meaning of Labor Day and into the meaning of Solidarity and into the hopes and the dreams of the thousands who have died for the precious right we so often ignore. I challenge you to vote your conscience. I would hope you would vote for me, of course, but only you can know your heart. As you cast that vote, observe how easy it is. And remember how costly, how terribly costly this great gift was to win and to earn and to pass down to us here today.

Ladies and gentlemen, that is the legacy of Hamtramck. That is the legacy of your ancestors' homeland. And that is the legacy of the family of America. Make her proud.

Thank you all. God bless you for this wonderful support. And may God bless a free, an always-free Poland. Thank you very much.

Note: The President spoke at 4:18 p.m. after participating in the Polish Festival parade. In his remarks, he referred to Monsignor Stanley Milewski, chancellor of Orchard Lake St. Mary's, and Paul Odrobina, city councilman and president of the Michigan chapter of the Polish American Congress.

Statement on Signing the Job Training Reform Amendments of 1992
September 7, 1992

Today I am pleased to sign into law H.R. 3033, the "Job Training Reform Amendments of 1992." I believe this legislation, which amends the Job Training Partnership Act (JTPA), will improve an already successful large-scale job training program and make it more responsive to the labor market of the 1990's.

H.R. 3033 will make a major contribution to enhancing the employability of disadvantaged youth and adults. I am particularly pleased that H.R. 3033 incorporates the key features of the Administration's proposal to amend the JTPA.

First, the legislation will maintain the local flexibility and system of performance standards that are the cornerstones of the current JTPA program.

Second, it will target services on youth and adults who are most at risk of failure in the job market, including those who lack basic skills, are high school dropouts, or are dependent on welfare.

Third, H.R. 3033 will enhance program quality by providing more intensive and comprehensive services to participants. These services include an assessment of each participant's skill levels and service needs and the development of individualized service strategies based on the assessment. In addition, participants will receive basic and occupational skills training tied to labor market opportunities that will promote the long-term employability, job placement, and job retention of participants.

Fourth, the legislation will strengthen program accountability by including significant fiscal and administrative improvements.

Fifth, these amendments will provide for a more comprehensive, coordinated human resource system by establishing linkages between Federal programs that will avoid duplication and enhance the delivery of services. For example, Governors will have the authority to establish State Human Resource Investment Councils to oversee the coordination of Federal human resource programs at the State level. Coordination of such programs is a key element in my Job Training 2000 proposal. I am very pleased to have this important step in place as a foundation for Job Training 2000.

In addition, these amendments will establish the innovative Youth Fair Chance program designed to stimulate communitywide action that will provide education and employment opportunities to youth who live in poor, inner city neighborhoods and rural areas. This program will be a vital supplement to our Weed and Seed, Youth Training Corps, Treat and Train, and other urban youth initiatives.

These features of the legislation are essential to improving the already successful track record of the JTPA in providing training and jobs to our most disadvantaged citizens. I wish to express my appreciation for the cooperation that has been exhibited on all sides and has made possible a stronger, more effective Federal job training system.

Finally, I must note that although the Supreme Court has ruled that the Congress and the executive branch may provide benefits to members of Indian tribes, as opposed to Indians defined as a racial group, and I support efforts to offer such benefits, this bill appears to provide some benefits to Alaskan Natives and Hawaiian Natives, as well as other Native Americans in some instances, on the basis of racial categories. I am directing the Secretary of Labor and the Attorney General to consult about whether these provisions can be carried out in a constitutional manner.

GEORGE BUSH

The White House,
September 7, 1992.

Note: H.R. 3033, approved September 7, was assigned Public Law No. 102–367.

Remarks and an Exchange With Reporters on Proposed Disaster Relief Legislation
September 8, 1992

The President. Let me just first express my most sincere condolences at the death of Senator Burdick of North Dakota, a great American, served his country with great distinction. And particularly to our friends from the Senate who are here today, I want to tell you how deeply Barbara and I feel about that loss. I know I speak for everybody here on both sides, the House and the Senate, both sides of the aisle, about the loss of this great Senator.

On to the business at hand. This morning I'm submitting to the Congress emergency supplemental requests to cover the cost of cleaning up the consequences of the devastating hurricane that hit both Florida and Louisiana. There's been a tremendous cooperative effort, many around this table participating to the fullest, private citizens, volunteers, government officials at all levels, to help people who have been so devastated by this storm. And I think it has been a truly bipartisan, put it this way, nonpartisan effort. It's worked very well, I think.

Today we're asking the Congress to join the effort officially on the Hill. We're asking for over $7.6 billion in budgetary resources to pay for everything from temporary shelter to guaranteed loans for new homes. It's a large financial burden, but the personal and human need is even more staggering. And our country must be able to answer the cries for help from those people who have lost so much and yet, I feel, remain so strong. So I'm asking that the Congress move promptly on this legislation with—I'm asking that it not become entangled in other issues. So I would welcome the support of everybody here. We're with you, the Senators and House Members from the affected area. I think we can get this done. Thank you all.

Q. Mr. President, is it your impression the Congress will go along with this request?

The President. Well, one of the things we're going to talk to these leaders about is just exactly that and see what we can do. But I know the Governors of both States, Governor Chiles, Governor Edwin Edwards, are prepared to pitch in. And it is my feeling that the country is together on this one. It's hard——

Q. Does this break the budget?

The President. Some of it unquestionably will be over the budget, not all of it. And I'm going to ask Dick Darman to explain this to the Members here in a minute.

Q. Is this the gridlocked Congress you're asking?

The President. Not on this issue. I don't think there's any gridlock at all, Helen [Helen Thomas, United Press International]. I think the country is together. I think the Members of Congress have been superb. I have spoken out publicly in gratitude for the support of both Governor Chiles and Governor Edwards. So nice try, but not on this issue. We'll go to general quarters on other issues, not this one. We're together on this.

Q. Will anything be accomplished, Mr. President, in this election year session of Congress?

The President. This one's going to get accomplished. We've got to get this done for the people, and I'm confident that it will.

Q. Anything else?

The President. Well, I'll get a little advice on that from some around the table here. Thank you all.

Note: The President spoke at 9:35 a.m. in the Cabinet Room at the White House prior to a meeting with congressional leaders.

White House Statement on Proposed Disaster Relief Legislation
September 8, 1992

Today the President submitted to the Congress emergency supplemental requests to cover the incremental costs arising from the consequences of Hurricane Andrew and Typhoon Omar. The requests are for the Federal Emergency Management Agency (FEMA), the Small Business Administration (SBA), and most of the Cabinet Departments. The requested funds represent a Federal financial response to address the effects of Hurricane Andrew and Typhoon Omar of over $7.6 billion in budgetary resources.

The requests for emergency and related supplemental appropriations for FY 1992 total $2,911.6 million in budget authority and would support additional loan activity of over $3 billion. These funds will be used for a comprehensive range of disaster-related activities including direct assistance to individuals, infrastructure repair, human services, and law enforcement. The additional availability of loans will assist in building and rebuilding homes, facilitate economic recovery through small business loans, and help farmers who have suffered the loss of structures and crops.

In addition to direct emergency and related appropriations, contingent funds of $143 million for FEMA and $75 million in budget authority for SBA (which would support an additional $350 million of new loans) are requested to replenish the depleted contingency funds of these Agencies. Establishment of a disaster-related contingency fund within Funds Appropriated to the President is also requested for $350 million in unanticipated disaster-related needs. These contingent appropriations would become available upon the President's transmittal of subsequent budget requests to the Congress designating each such request as an emergency requirement.

In addition to these emergency funding requirements, $983.9 million in nonemergency funding is requested for the Department of Defense. Of this amount, $205.6 million will be used for replacement of facilities and equipment, cleanup activities, and military personnel support costs stemming from Typhoon Omar in Guam; $297.7 million will be used for similar costs stemming from Hurricane Andrew; and $480.6 million will be used to rebuild the facilities destroyed at Homestead Air Force Base.

The President requested that the legislation in which these funds are provided be kept free of extraneous matters "in order that there may be a minimum of delay in providing necessary funds to the disaster areas."

The President has designated all of the requests, other than the three contingency requests and the request for appropriations to the Department of Defense, as emergency requirements pursuant to the Balanced Budget and Emergency Deficit Control Act of 1985, as amended.

The details of these requests are described in an attachment.

Note: Detailed descriptions of Agencies' specific programs and budget requests were attached to the statement.

Remarks and a Question-and-Answer Session at the B'nai B'rith International Convention
September 8, 1992

The President. Thank you, Senator. Thank you all very much. Please be seated, and thank you. Let me just say what a joy it is to have been introduced by Rudy Boschwitz. The Senate still misses him. He is my friend, and so you can discount some of those kind words. But I'll tell you it was awfully thoughtful of you, Kent and others, to ask Rudy to present me here to this most prestigious order, this group. And thank you for the kind introduction. And Kent, thank you, sir, for what I understand is an extraordinarily successful meeting getting underway. May I salute Ambassador Shoval, with

whom we are working very closely, Israel's Ambassador here in the United States. And of course, the B'nai B'rith leadership who graciously met me when I came here. And to everyone else, it's an honor to be with you today.

Let me express at the outset another personal observation. I was just talking to my good friend George Klein, and others about this, but I want to express my concerns for a good friend of everybody in this room, and that is Max Fisher, who was to be with us today, regrettably is in the hospital. I talked to him, and I'm sure he'll be just fine. That spirit, that Max Fisher spirit and optimism is still just as wonderful as you can possibly imagine and hope for.

Now, we have witnessed, and Rudy talked about this, a world of change. And with change comes new challenges. For America, the end of the cold war means the beginning of a new era, a new era of economic competition that America simply must and will win. In the new world, foreign policy, economic policy, and domestic policy have become one issue. And in order to prevail, the United States must be not only a military superpower but an export superpower and an economic superpower as well.

Yet we know that America is measured by more than the strength of our economy, also by the content of our character and how we serve others. And this willingness to reach out, to help those in need, to recognize across all the divides of color and culture and creed our shared human spirit, this is what B'nai B'rith is all about. For 150 years, the members of this organization have joined a handful of other organizations serving as the Nation's conscience. And part of America's conscience must always be to fight anti-Semitism and other forms of prejudice wherever and whenever they appear. I wish very much, as President, that I could stand before you and today say that anti-Semitism is history. It's not, not when there are hate crimes here at home, brownshirts abroad. That's a sorry commentary on human nature.

Let's all be clear: A world willing to allow Jews to be persecuted is a world certain to allow other tyrannies to emerge. But we're not helpless. And we're doing something about it. In this country, we are aggressively employing the Hate Crimes Act to bring to justice those who traffic in the gutter. Anti-Semitism is an evil idea with an ugly history. And I'll do my utmost, here and now and abroad, so that prejudice is finally, finally, finally banished from the human heart.

In the end, anti-Semitism and prejudice mock and threaten the basic principles upon which the United States is founded. In a letter to the Hebrew congregation of Rhode Island, George Washington wrote, ". . . the government of the United States . . . gives to bigotry no sanction, to persecu-

tion no assistance. . . . While everyone shall sit in safety under his own vine and fig tree, and there shall be none to make him afraid." And here's the difference, the vital difference that sets apart our American creed. For us, freedom of religion is no gift of Government, no privilege to be granted or withheld. It is a fundamental human right.

We can take heart that this American creed is spreading, that people in our time are demanding and getting those rights that they've been denied so long. Changes in our world have come so fast that I say they are nothing short of Biblical, and by that I mean just plain old-fashioned miraculous. Just think about it. Just a few years ago, who would have thought we would no longer live under that horrible threat of nuclear conflagration? Who would have thought the scarring symbol of an era, the divisive Berlin Wall, would be found only in museums or chipped into paperweights? And above all, who would have predicted the Soviet Union would be found only in the pages of history?

And know this: The miracles aren't only confined to Europe. In the Middle East, events have defied all predictions. Today, direct bilateral talks are taking place between Israel and her neighbors. You may recall that we were told we couldn't succeed, we couldn't bring the parties together. But we did. And I want to dwell for a moment on this breakthrough, because I know it matters deeply to everyone in this hall. Let me take you back nearly a year ago to another hall in Madrid. There, gathered around the table, were representatives of Lebanon, Jordan, Syria, Egypt, Palestinians, and Israel. For nearly half a century they had not met all together outside the battlefield. But for the first time they came together not to fight but to talk. I'll never forget as long as I live walking into the meeting room. Then-President Gorbachev was at my side. We were the ones that were to open the meeting; you may remember that. And you could cut the tension with a knife. But when Gorbachev and I spoke afterwards—we chatted about it— we both agreed it had to be one of the most dramatic moments in recent world history.

It was amazing. And we continued to build on those talks.

But then as now, the goal is not just a cease-fire or a truce but peace, real peace: not simply the end of war but genuine reconciliation. A peace both broad and deep; a peace codified by treaties and given life by trade and tourism, by open borders, the fabric of peace knit together even more tightly by the simple human contact of peoples who have known each other far too long as enemies. A comprehensive peace, based on Security Council Resolutions 242 and 338. A peace that at long last will allow the peoples of the Middle East to turn their energies, their resources, their lives to creation rather than destruction, to great works rather than great wars.

Today, as we speak, parties that met first at Madrid are midway through the sixth round of bilateral negotiations. And there has been progress. Delegations are exchanging not only handshakes but, for the first time, written proposals. Public posturing has decreased, and meaningful private dialog has increased. Of course, major hurdles remain. I don't mean to diminish that; they do. And it's going to take time and effort and courage and trust. But there is clearly a way, and increasingly, a will. The evidence is mounting: The many positive steps taken by Israel's new government that improve day-to-day life for Palestinians and signal its seriousness about peace, Egypt's invitation that made it possible for Prime Minister Rabin to make his first trip outside Israel to an Arab country, Syria's relaxation of travel restrictions affecting its Jewish citizens. Further gestures such as an end to the Arab boycott of Israel can only help in bringing about an environment conductive to negotiation and reconciliation. I will continue to oppose that boycott and seek further change.

I am proud of the role that we've played in breaking the long-standing taboo against direct talks between Israel and her neighbors. You see, Israel sought direct talks for 43 years, and it was right to do so. If you do not talk, you can have no hope of making peace. And now there is such a hope.

I'm also proud of what we've done to help end Israel's diplomatic isolation internationally. We finally succeeded, after 16 years of effort, in getting the United Nations General Assembly to repeal what should never have been enacted in the first place. Zionism is not racism, not before, not now, not ever. And as Senator Boschwitz pointed out very generously, thanks in large part to our efforts, China and India and Turkey and many other nations, countries representing more than 2 billion people, now have full diplomatic relations with Israel. Already this has created not only greater contact for Israel worldwide but new economic opportunities.

I know this audience knows of our efforts to open the gates to Jews in the former Soviet Union and also to rescue Ethiopian Jews. You know, 4 years ago when I spoke to you in Baltimore, I noticed a banner hung on the wall that read: Where do Soviet Jews apply for *glasnost*? Some of you all, delegates, may remember that one. As I prepared to come here today, I thought of that banner. I thought of the hopes we had then. And I thought of a pledge that I made, that in every single meeting with Soviet officials I would raise the issue of Soviet Jews. And my friends, I could not forget that banner. I did not forget that pledge. And today, together, we celebrate this miracle: Nearly half a million Jews have come out of the Soviet Union to freedom, to America, to Israel.

Persuading parties to sit down face to face to talk peace, ending Israel's international isolation, assisting in the in-gathering of Jews into Israel: These are the three great aims that have guided Israel from its founding. We didn't just talk about helping Israel in these areas, we delivered. That's a fact of which every American can be proud.

And here's another fact: When the chips were down, when many countries, including Israel, were threatened by the most brutal aggression, America was there. We stopped Saddam Hussein. And that terrible time when the world feared that the cold war would be replaced by a new age of Saddam, that is over, too. I knew when I took the oath of office that every President faces difficult decisions. And I can tell you this: There is no decision more difficult than sending this country's young men and women into combat, sending somebody else's son or daughter to possible death. In the end, it comes down to this: You cannot make that kind of decision unless you are certain you understand what is at stake. I knew what was at stake. And because of the bravery of America's sons and daughters in Desert Storm, America today is safer and Israel today is safer.

Ask yourself this question, where the Middle East would be today, where Israel's security would be today if we had followed the counsel of my critics. Ask yourself where we would be if we had someone in the Oval Office who would have waffled, who would have wavered and wanted to have it both ways. Listen to my opponent's very own words on whether he would have followed my lead and drawn a line in the sand. And here is the exact quotation: "I guess I would have voted with the majority if it was a close vote. But I agree with the arguments the minority made." Where would we be? I'll tell you. We would be facing a nuclear-armed Iraq, dominant in the Middle East, with a chokehold on the world's oil supplies; an Iraq that showed clearly to the rest of the world that aggression against one's neighbors can go unchecked; an Iraq threatening Israel's very existence. Israel's very survival would be at stake. And we'd be talking about whether there was any chance to avoid nuclear Armageddon in the Middle East. Well, Desert Storm swept away that nightmare. And because of America's courage, today we now have the chance to see the dawn of peace in the Middle East.

There is still lots of work to be done. The Middle East, indeed, the world, is still a dangerous place. Terrorists continue to target the innocent. The proliferation of weapons of mass destruction casts a cloud over the region's future. Iraq's Saddam Hussein, however much weaker, defeated, and locked in the prison of his own country, still brutalizes his own people, resists the will of the international community.

The need for Israel to remain strong is beyond question. And it clearly includes having a defensive capability against missile attack. Scud attacks on Israel should have made that clear to everyone in the United States of America. For that reason, I have proposed to Israel that it participate in our development of a global protection system. Let me say to you: You ought to take a good, close look at anyone who claims to be a friend of Israel, at anyone who claims to be serious about Israel's security but opposes development of the defenses like GPALS that may be the most effective way for Israel to defend itself against missile attack. The point is, the need for U.S.-Israel strategic partnership and cooperation remains as strong as ever.

And we're also going to see that partnership at work this week because I am happy to tell you that I am sending to the Congress legislation requesting up to $10 billion in loan guarantees to aid Israel's Government in welcoming its immigrants. [*Applause*] And from that response, I know I can count on the support of everyone in this room to make sure that this proposal becomes law. Yes, we're in tough economic times in this country, but don't let any Member of Congress tell you we can't afford to do this. We can, and we must. Today I ask you: Take that message to Capitol Hill.

I am glad that Prime Minister Rabin and I were able to reach an understanding on loan guarantees when we met up at Kennebunkport last month. He outlined for me the new Israeli government's new priorities, committed to investing in Israel itself, and stood determined to avoid steps that could hamper progress toward peace. I share that commitment. And as a result, we will be able to promote peace and welcome new immigrants at one and the same time. Both are humanitarian undertakings; both deserve our full support. It was important not to choose between them, and I am glad that we are now in a position to promote both of those objectives.

As for the future, I am confident that on most issues, on most occasions, we and Israel will find ourselves in agreement. I, for one, am committed to revitalizing the tradition of full consultations between the United States and Israel on the entire range of issues affecting stability in the Middle East. I know Prime Minister Rabin shares this commitment. And let me emphasize this point: There will be no surprises.

Our support for Israel and its security is

not simply a policy. It is a principle. As I said after Prime Minister Rabin and I met in Maine, this is a relationship based on a shared commitment to democracy and common values, as well as a solid commitment to Israel's security, including its qualitative military edge. This is a special relationship, one specially built to endure.

This relationship is important, especially now, as we enter the new era of uncertainty. Old empires are dying, new nations being born. This is a time when a nation needs to know who it can count on. Israel has a stability of purpose, a strength of spirit that has seen it through dark days. We know Israel will be there for us, just as we will always be there for Israel. Rudy touched on this in the introduction, but no doubt there will be times when we disagree. Even friends disagree. Even Barbara and I disagree from time to time. America will have disagreements with Israel just as we sometimes disagree with Canada and France and Germany and Britain. Those differences are signs of the durability of a strong relationship, of the democratic bonds we share. The point is this: These are disagreements between friends, and I emphasize that word, friends.

There may even be issues where you and I will take opposing sides and things may get hot and words may be exchanged. In the past, I'll never forget this one, some remarks of mine were, I felt, misinterpreted. I have gone on the record expressing my regret for any pain those words caused. Again I want to make it clear, I support, I endorse, and I deeply believe in the God-given right of every American to promote what they believe. It is your right as an individual. It's more than a right. It's your duty as an American citizen.

But let me also say that it is important that we learn how to disagree. The way democracies engage in debate is not without consequence. It is a mark of civility and freedom. I hardly need to tell anyone in this room just what anti-Semitism is. As my friend Abe Foxman, with us today, of the Anti-Defamation League has pointed out, to accuse those who may come to different conclusions on one or another public issue of harboring anti-Semitism is to cheapen the term. That is dangerous. That is deeply

wrong. And when those words, without justice, have been aimed at me, I can tell you, they cut right to the heart.

But let's put all of this aside now and look to the future. I've talked to you here about my optimism for that future. We come together at a blessed time. The cold war is over. And Arab-Israeli peace talks have begun. There is another reason to be optimistic. The American people will soon exercise their unbroken 200-year democratic right to elect a President. And I'm optimistic, too, about the identity of that new President. There I go sounding like Harry Truman. I've got to be careful about that. But seriously, you have made me feel I'm among friends, and I know we've had some differences, but I also hope you'll look at this overall record. But let me leave you with this. However it turns out, commitment to freedom and democracy, to tolerance and opportunity in America and around the world will not change.

You are members of a community that has a long and great tradition of political participation. B'nai B'rith stands for opportunity, for tolerance, for opposition to anti-Semitism and the ugly face of hate in all its forms. You stand, too, for stalwart support for America's close friend and ally, Israel. And now let me say that on all these issues I am proud to stand with you.

In 3 weeks—[*applause*]—and say thank you all. May God bless the State of Israel. And listen, 3 weeks from now—the start of a new year. I wish you a prosperous year; I wish you a year of peace. And may God bless the United States of America. Thank you all very, very much.

The Economy

Q. Mr. President, your words were very clear in your concern about trying to eliminate anti-Semitism and removal of the Arab boycott against Israel. We also applaud your efforts for helping us open the gates for our Soviet and Ethiopian brothers to have the freedom to leave those countries and especially for your supporting the $10 billion loan guarantee.

The President has consented to answer some questions which I will pose to him. Mr. President, the first question: With all the talk about an economy in recession, many Americans believe that the real problem is an economy in decline. What, in your judgment, would it take to reverse this decline?

The President. In the first place, we've had a tough time. It hasn't been only the United States of America. Look around the world. There has been a global recession, certainly a global slowdown. The United States economy has grown anemically for five straight quarters, five straight quarters. But it's so anemic that many areas don't feel it, because to average out a growth like that you have to have some areas doing much worse and some areas doing better.

What it's going to take, it seems to me, to turn the economy around is to get the Government sector of the economy doing less. And that's why I am favoring holding the growth on spending. I will not touch Social Security; I've said that over and over again and have been very faithful to that. But in my view, the Government spends too much and taxes too much. Too much in the public sector, not enough in the private sector.

Now, in my January State of the Union message, I suggested to what I now call the gridlocked Congress that they move on certain incentives to stimulate the economy. Investment tax allowance, for example. A credit for first-time homebuyers to stimulate the housing market. I still believe firmly that a good way to stimulate this economy is a capital gains tax reduction. We are not saving enough, and we're not increasing capital enough. And the way you do that is to cut that capital gains rate. It will increase jobs, increase investment, increase risk-taking. I know I have a big argument with those on the other side of the political aisle, but I believe it would work now just as it worked when it was cut in 1978 as a stimulation.

So the philosophy is cut back on tax-and-spend as an approach, and try to get this Government under control with less regulation, more incentive to save and invest, and certainly do something about the fabric of the Nation. And that is, we're talking here about the need for us to be competitive internationally. We're going to have to do better in the field of education, and our America 2000 program makes a very good

step about that.

I have been concerned about the confidence factor because you've had so much gloom and doom about the economy that people are scared. Yes, things have been slow. But I am not pessimistic in the long run. I simply disagree with my opponent when he talks about this Nation being a nation in decline or ranking somewhere between Germany and Sri Lanka, to use his own words. We don't. Go talk to your friends abroad, and you'll find that we are still, in spite of our difficulty, the envy of the world. Now what we've got to do is get ready and move forward into the future with some optimism. I believe we can do it.

Palestinian State and Middle East Peace

Q. Mr. President, do you still oppose the creation of an independent Palestinian state? And what framework for peace do you see involving and between Arabs and Israelis?

The President. The second part—the answer to the first part is, yes.

Q. And what framework for peace do you see involving and between Arabs and Israelis?

The President. The answer is, yes, I still oppose a Palestinian state. I've been consistent on that for a long, long time. But I think the framework lies in successful step-by-step progress on these negotiations. And once again I don't want to put this in too much of a political context, but I think some in our administration deserve great credit for the diplomacy used in bringing these parties together. And therein is the best framework for the peace.

Let the parties negotiate it out. Let the parties—we're not going to dictate the terms. We shouldn't dictate the terms. Let the parties negotiate it out in face-to-face negotiation. The framework is there. Now our role is to be catalytic, to keep the people at the peace table as best we can, be as helpful as we can in that, and not try to impose some settlement on one party or another. And it takes a while, but we're making some progress, I think.

Separation of Church and State

Q. Jews and others in this country are

very concerned about the separation of church and state. How can you allay fears that the wall of separation is being increasingly eroded?

The President. I don't think the wall is being eroded. Certainly legally it's not, and it shouldn't be eroded. I believe firmly, and I've stated this over and over again, of separation between church and state. Where you get into some complications or some discussion of this is when you get into school choice. I happen to favor it. Some people don't, thinking that it's going to get church and States involved. But what we propose in that area, for example, is to help the families and let them choose.

I was a recipient and I'll bet there's a bunch of other old guys around here that were recipients of the GI bill after World War II. And they didn't say to me, you can take this help from the Government to go to a State school. They said, here, take it and go to whatever school you want, college of your choice. It didn't diminish anything.

And so I think we ought to try the same thing, whether it's public, private, or religious schools. That, in my view, is not merging church and state. What I think of it is a choice for a family that has been demonstrably successful early on.

But the underlying point is, certainly any President of the United States must be always concerned that nothing he or she might do should blur this line of separation between church and state. It is very, very fundamental to our system. And I hope that I can stand up credibly on my record for that principle.

Sale of F–15's to Saudi Arabia

Q. With a final question, we are concerned about news reports that you plan to send to Congress a proposal to sell F–15 jets to Saudi Arabia, especially since Saudi Arabia is in a state of war with Israel and is engaged in an economic boycott of Israel, which also affects the United States, business interests and American jobs. Do you still plan to propose the sale of F–15's to the Saudis?

The President. When you're President, you look at all the issues. You look at everything in the area. One of them, of course, is Israel's qualitative edge. As I said in my remarks, I'm going to keep that in mind. You also look at the domestic economy. You also look at the Persian Gulf and the areas of stress and constraint over there.

No decision has been made. We have made consultations. I do want to make this a little bit, put a little political spin on this, my opponent the other day in St. Louis, big headline, said that he supported the sale. When you are President you have to do a lot of consultation on this. I can tell you no final decision has been made. I don't want to misrepresent it: Consideration is being given to this. But whether there is any difference between the parties for this election on this question, I don't know. But I can guarantee you the qualitative edge that Israel has will not be neglected. And as I say, I will keep fighting for the elimination of the boycott and these other—and for the day when you can sit down and have a peace agreement.

But again, a President has to look at the overall security requirements, and that's exactly what I am doing right now. And I would then have to notify Congress, I'm not sure of the timing on that, if a decision is made to go forward. But again, I will think it all out, make my decision, and call it the way I see it like that umpire does. The buck does stop on that desk in the Oval Office, and you have to make tough calls sometimes.

Q. Mr. President, we are honored to make a special presentation to you today. We have a replica of the famous George Washington letter to which you referred so eloquently in your remarks. The original letter, written in 1790, is one of B'nai B'rith's most prized possessions. It is an historic document because it is the first link in an unbroken chain. Every President from George Washington to you, sir, has championed liberty and justice for all. The worldwide family of B'nai B'rith is proud to present this to you.

The President. Thank you all very, very much. Thank you. A great pleasure.

Note: The President spoke at 11:31 a.m. at the Sheraton Washington Hotel. In his remarks, he referred to Kent Schiner, presi-

dent, B'nai B'rith; George Klein, general chairman, Bush-Quayle '92 Jewish Campaign Committee; and Max M. Fisher, honorary chairman, Bush-Quayle '92 National Finance Committee.

Statement on Virginia Welfare Reform
September 8, 1992

Today, as millions of American schoolchildren return to school, I am pleased that we are approving Virginia's request for welfare waivers. These waivers will allow Virginia to test a program that encourages children of welfare recipients to attend school.

Under Virginia's program, children in grades 6 through 8 in a limited number of schools will be required to attend school, or their families would lose the higher welfare payments and other rewards provided as incentives. To encourage students to stay in school, individual dropout prevention counseling and other needed services will be provided. Families of children who remain truant despite counseling may have their assistance payment further reduced.

Education and job skills are necessary for any person to become a productive member of society. Virginia's program will evaluate whether these incentives improve school attendance and performance.

Message to the Senate Transmitting the Russia-United States Taxation Convention
September 8, 1992

To the Senate of the United States:

I transmit herewith for Senate advice and consent to ratification the Convention between the United States of America and the Russian Federation for the Avoidance of Double Taxation and the Prevention of Fiscal Evasion with Respect to Taxes on Income, signed at Washington on June 17, 1992, together with a related Protocol. I also transmit the report of the Department of State.

The convention replaces, with respect to Russia, the 1973 income tax convention between the United States of America and the Union of Soviet Socialist Republics. It will modernize tax relations between the two countries and will facilitate greater private sector United States investment in Russia.

I recommend that the Senate give early and favorable consideration to the convention and related protocol and give its advice and consent to ratification.

GEORGE BUSH

The White House,
September 8, 1992.

Message to the Senate Transmitting the United Nations Framework Convention on Climate Change
September 8, 1992

To the Senate of the United States:

I transmit herewith, for the advice and consent of the Senate to ratification, the United Nations Framework Convention on Climate Change, adopted May 9, 1992, by the resumed fifth session of the Intergovernmental Negotiating Committee for a Framework Convention on Climate Change ("Convention"), and signed by me on behalf of the United States at the United Nations Conference on Environment and Development (UNCED) in Rio de Janeiro on June 12, 1992. The report of the Department of State is also enclosed for the information of the Senate.

The Convention, negotiated over a period of nearly 2 years, represents a delicate balance of many interests. It embodies a comprehensive approach embracing all greenhouse gases, their sources and sinks, and promotes action to modify net emissions trends of all greenhouse gases not controlled by the 1987 Montreal Protocol on Substances that Deplete the Ozone Layer. It supports an action-oriented approach to net emissions reduction that takes into account specific national circumstances. It provides the basis for assessing the impacts and effectiveness of different national responses in light of existing scientific and economic information and new developments. The Convention encourages cooperative arrangements by providing for joint implementation between and among parties under mutually agreed terms.

The ultimate objective of the Convention is to stabilize greenhouse gas concentrations (not emissions) in the atmosphere at a level that would prevent dangerous human interference with the climate system. In accordance with this objective, the Convention calls on all parties to prepare national inventories of anthropogenic emissions, implement appropriate national and regional programs to mitigate and adapt to climate change, promote technology cooperation (including technology transfer), promote scientific research and monitoring, and promote and cooperate in the full and open exchange of information and in education, training, and public awareness programs. In light of such provisions, this Convention constitutes a major step in protecting the global environment from potential adverse effects of climate change.

The Convention will enter into force 90 days after the 50th instrument of ratification, acceptance, or approval has been deposited. Ratification by the United States is necessary for the effective implementation of the Convention. Early ratification by the United States is likely to encourage similar action by other countries whose participation is also essential. It should be noted that the Convention does not permit reservations.

I recommend that the Senate give early and favorable consideration to this Convention and give its advice and consent to ratification.

GEORGE BUSH

The White House,
September 8, 1992.

Remarks Prior to a Meeting With Republican Congressional Leaders
September 9, 1992

The President. I've invited our leadership, Republican leadership, here this morning to talk about what can get done in this very short session of the Congress. I want the Congress to pass 12 signable appropriations bills. There's 4 weeks available. There's no reason why Congress cannot produce these spending bills individually without resorting to a lot of pork-laden additions to the bills. And I will sign them only if they comply with my budget request.

I also want to see action on some of the things that we've been talking to the American people about over the weekend. We should take a first bold step on legal reform. The civil justice reform legislation designed to change our current inefficient, costly legal system has been pending in Congress for over 7 months without even a hearing. And before adjourning, the Congress should at least seize the immediate opportunity, starting in the Senate this week, and pass the product liability reform bill.

And they can and should take a step, a first step, a needed first step on enacting a health care reform bill by passing portions of my plan, including the small business reform and the medical malpractice reform. These are key ingredients. Time is short. Both can be passed. By acting on these areas, we'll help to provide affordable, quality health care for millions who do not have it now and be a down payment, frankly, to the American people who deserve comprehensive health care reform without higher taxes and without cutting into the quality of United States medicine, which is the best in the entire world. Get the Government further in, and it's going to go down. So we've got to protect the quality as well as making insurance available to all who need it.

And there are other pieces of legislation. I met yesterday with the leaders in the Senate and House. I think we can pass our energy proposal. We need to get a national energy strategy out and approved, and that can be done. There are some others we

might get done. But these that I've outlined here are priority. And I now want to talk to our Members about how we can achieve these ends and hear from them if there's other key objectives to get to that can be accomplished here.

Thank you all very much.

Family Leave Legislation

Q. Mr. President, Democrats are ready to pass a family leave bill. Will you veto it in its present form?

The President. Well, I've got to look at what comes down here, of course, as I always do. But I've expressed my reservations about some of the things that are pending. So let's wait and see what happens. We don't need mandates; we need family leave without loading up small business with a lot more mandates. The concept of family leave I've strongly endorsed. But getting the Government further into it and throwing small businesses over the edge I'm not sure is the way to do it. But let's see what they say.

Q. Do you think the Democrats are playing politics with this issue?

The President. Almost everything, yes. [*Laughter*] No, I do. I believe it. I think the American people believe it. And now I have my chance to take the case to the American people. I've tried to stimulate this economy and been rebuffed. And I think the American people will see that clearly. I don't think they see it yet. But they will when we get through. Of course there's a lot of politics in this.

Note: The President spoke at 8:35 a.m. in the Cabinet Room at the White House.

Remarks to the Community in Norristown, Pennsylvania
September 9, 1992

Thank you so much. Thank you, Dr. Holton. May I congratulate our superintendent for his leadership on America 2000 and on the job he's doing for the whole school system in this area. Good morning to everybody. It's great to be back in Pennsylvania on this first day of school. Any excuse

to get out of class, I know, and here you all are. Thanks for greeting me. May I salute the man you heard from a minute ago, Secretary Alexander, Lamar Alexander. He's come to Washington after great experience in education and in government, and leading us all with this marvelous America 2000 program. We owe him a great vote of thanks, and I'm very pleased to have him with us.

Another old friend is with us today, the Congressman from this district, Larry Coughlin, who is leaving the Congress after marvelous service. But he came in with us. Larry, do you want to stand up there?

May I thank all involved with this visit, particularly Principal Barry Spencer, who has done a great job on all the arrangements and in making these facilities available. Josh Lippy, the president of the student council, I salute him as a student leader. I should add, welcome back to school. I hope you all had a great summer. And out here in the audience are not just students but members of the chamber of commerce, Payson Burt and others that are taking a leadership role. The class of 2000, I salute them, all of you, these participants who got up and read those education goals. I thought they did a first-class job; not a nervous one in the bunch. And I salute all the volunteers, the volunteers that make it happen as we try to reform education. I'll get to the teachers in a minute.

I'm told that many of you were nervous this week, tensions rising about the big event, wondering how you'll handle all the attention. Well, I'm here to put your fears at rest. I know you'll do great against North Penn Friday night.

You know, I want to just give a serious talk this morning. You know, our world has been through a lot of change in the past few years. When my kids were the age of the kids in this room today, they used to practice nuclear disaster drills. The alarms would go off, and they would all crawl under the desks and wait. This happened all across the country, all across many countries. That doesn't happen anymore. As a parent and as a grandparent, I am glad that American kids can grow up in the sunshine of peace. We ought to be grateful for that as a nation.

But now that the cold war is over, the challenge before our Nation is to win the peace, to guarantee that America in the 21st century will be not just a military superpower but also an export superpower, an economic superpower. That's just a fancy way of saying that when you grow up,

you deserve the chance to have a good job and live a better life than your parents and grandparents. You should live the American dream.

That's why I'm here this morning, to talk about how we can build what you need and deserve, the very best schools in the entire world.

Now, I admit, education is not usually found on the front page of the newspaper or at the top of the evening news, but it is the solution for most of what you do see there. As a President and as a grandparent, my loyalty lies with young people, kids like these fifth graders who did such a fantastic job laying out these national education goals this morning. In the year 2000, these fifth graders will graduate from high school. They will have changed so much, we will barely be able to recognize them. I want the schools from which they graduate to have changed so much, that we won't be able to recognize them either.

Four years ago, I said I wanted to lead a revolution in American education. And today, I come before you to report: The revolution is underway.

As President, my job is to set the agenda and mobilize the Nation. I'm proud that the goals the students read this morning are the very first education goals in our Nation's history. They were created by all the Governors, Republicans and Democrats alike, and are being embraced by parents, by teachers, by business and community leaders in town after town, city after city, all across America. Politics is being laid aside. A revolution in education is taking place. If he were here today, I'd shake his hand and salute the Governor of this State, who is holding out his hand to all who want to see America 2000 succeed. He's been a real leader, and we are grateful to him for that, Governor Casey.

I have come to Norristown because you accepted my challenge to reinvent American schools. And again, I salute the principal and the superintendent. Norristown is in the lead, but you're not alone. Today, 1,700 communities in every single State have adopted the vision of what we call America 2000. Seventeen hundred communities have drawn lines in the sand of the future that read, our children must be number one.

The Federal Government should do more than offer congratulations, and we are matching our words with action as we promised.

You've heard about our first goal, making sure every student arrives at school ready to learn. For the first time, every eligible 4-year-old who wants a Head Start on kindergarten can get one. We have asked for record increases in investment for math and science education, to help train teachers. That is consistent with goal number four that was read here, math and science excellence. And I bet you were proud to watch the Olympics and see Jordan and Ewing and Malone slam-dunk the opposition. By the year 2000, I want you, our young people, to be able to slam-dunk the rest of the world in math and science. And we can do it.

Goal number five is to guarantee a skilled, literate work force. My opponent accuses me of cutting education spending. That's just flat wrong. I have proposed record increases in education funding, and during my 4 years, Federal investments in education have increased at a more rapid rate than State and local funding.

But if you think that money alone will reinvent our schools, think again. As a nation, only Switzerland, only Switzerland spends more per student on elementary and secondary education. This doesn't mean we should not make new investments; it means we cannot spend our money on the old way of doing things.

Our schools were basically designed for another age, 100 years ago: a world of Model T cars, in which toasters and flashlights were a big deal; a world in which most clothes were made at home. Imagine, a world without the King of Prussia Mall! [*Laughter*] Hard to believe.

But today, if you apply for a summer job in a car factory, they'll ask you if you can handle mathematics, estimation, and spatial relations, things your mom and dad just didn't have to know. And other things have changed. It's tougher being a parent, tougher being a teacher, and my grandkids tell me it's pretty tough being a kid these days. The world has changed, and so must our

schools.

You don't have to look far for new ideas. Teachers, school board members, parents, business leaders, all are fountains of innovation. They represent the true genius of America, and we must encourage them. Right now, as we gather today, America is responding to this charge. Really, four revolutions are underway.

First, we are in the process of creating hundreds of what we call break-the-mold schools, schools that reject the status quo; for example, a school where students attend all year round. Now, I challenged America to come up with ideas for these schools, and Norristown was one of 700 communities that responded. I applaud you for your energy. I applaud you for your creativity.

Revolution number two has to do with what we teach in our schools. We must demand more of you, so that you can compete in the world economy. Your math teachers are already relying on new, world-class standards, and you are learning more than your older brothers and sisters. By the time today's fifth graders enter high school, we will have new standards in science, history, English, geography, civics, and the arts. And to support these standards, we will have a national examination system, and I call it the American achievement tests, so that parents can know how our kids and our schools are doing.

The third revolution involves a very important person, your teacher. If I can ask a favor, since this is the first day of school, I assume none of you have received any tests back yet. So let's take advantage of the good feeling and say thanks to all the teachers in this room. They are making a difference in your life, and we should applaud them. I'd like to ask them to stand up, all the teachers here. [*Applause*] Thank you all very much.

Let me make this point to the students: When your teachers chose their career, they did it because they love learning and they love helping you to live up to your potential. They certainly didn't do it for self-gain. They did it to help someone else.

Not long ago, as part of my America 2000 effort, I met with some teachers up in Lehigh Valley, and I asked them what was their biggest problem. I thought they might talk about a lack of money or discipline or the drug problem. But they instead talked about all the paperwork and regulations, about getting State government off their back.

I cannot do much about Harrisburg, but this week Congress will consider my legislation to give teachers more flexibility in using Federal funds, as long as they achieve results. Congress wants to give flexibility to just 300 schools. I want to give it to all 110,000 schools. We've got to relieve these teachers of federally mandated paperwork requirements. I trust the teachers, not the Government, to do what's right for our students.

There's one final revolution underway. I think every parent should have the right to choose the school they want for their children.

Not long ago, I was talking with a Milwaukee parent—she and her kid came to the Roosevelt Room right outside of the Oval Office in the White House—her name, Janette Williams. She told me her son Javon went to a crowded school; teachers couldn't pay attention to him. He was so bored, he'd just go home halfway through the day. Then Milwaukee gave some parents the right to choose new schools for their kids. And today, this kid Javon is doing his homework, attending all his classes, even helping clean up around the classroom.

I want to hear more stories like that. My "GI bill" for kids would give thousand-dollar scholarships to children of middle- and low-income families that they can use to spend on any school of their choice. Most parents would choose public schools, but every parent should be able to choose any school, public, private, or religious. Right here in Norristown, almost 6,000 kids, about two-thirds of the school population, would be eligible for this thousand-dollar scholarship. Norristown would receive another $6 million in new Federal funds, not controlled by bureaucrats but parents and teachers. When it comes to choosing schools, I trust parents, not the Government, to do the right thing.

So these are the four revolutions in American education: break-the-mold schools, new standards, getting Government off the teachers' backs, and giving parents real choice. Together these revolutions will change our schools. When these fifth graders come back to visit Miss Ritter and Mrs. Bieler in 8 years from now, they will marvel at how small the desks are and how they have to stoop way over to use the water fountain. But as they look and listen to the school around them, they will say, "Everything else has changed."

Now, as some of you may have heard, there's an election in about 55 days. So before I leave you this morning, I want to take just a moment and contrast my education vision with the opponent's. I want to be fair. When I convened the national education summit—I mentioned it earlier in this speech about—with the Governors present, most of the Governors attended. Governor Clinton's role was constructive. He helped to set these national education goals, and I commend him for that.

However, the facts tell the story about his own record. In 1980, Arkansas ranked 47th in the percentage of adults with high school diplomas, now 48th. Today, they're dead last in the percentage of adults with college degrees.

But that's not the real issue. The real issue is what kind of education President would my opponent be. And in this campaign, Governor Clinton has spent a lot of time courting the education establishment, teachers unions' leaders and the liberal Congress. These people fear change. Look at the education before Congress today. They really don't want to spend more money on education. They want to spend it on the same old system. I wish fixing our schools was that easy; it is not.

A President's job is to set a path and insist that the Nation sticks to it. But Governor Clinton is in with the crowd who say no to break-the-mold schools, no to higher standards, no to less regulation, and no to my "GI bill" for kids. Here's the difference between me and my opponent: He has told the education establishment what they want to hear. And I will continue to tell them what America needs to hear.

You hear a lot of talk about change in this election. But ultimately, change isn't what you say; it is what you do. With your help and the help of millions of other Americans, we have set the forces in motion to literally revolutionize the way we prepare our young people. And I hope you will give me the opportunity to finish that revolution.

To the parents, teachers, community leaders, and students participating in Norristown 2000, I say thank you. You are writing a better chapter in the history of America's next generation.

Thanks for listening. And may God bless each and every one of you, the State of Pennsylvania, and the United States of America. Thank you very much.

Note: The President spoke at noon at Norristown High School. In his remarks, he referred to James N. Holton, superintendent, Norristown Area School District; Barry Spencer, principal, Norristown High School; and Payson Burt, president, Central Montgomery County Chamber of Commerce.

Remarks and a Question-and-Answer Session With Employees of Uniform Tubes in Collegeville, Pennsylvania
September 9, 1992

The President. Listen, it's a pleasure to be here. Thank you all very much. Welcome to the Phil Donahue Show. [*Laughter*] I feel like that, sitting out here. But let me just thank Bruce, all that greeted us, all of you involved in this wonderful company, and all who, particularly, have participated in this education approach. As I look at the country and look at the problems facing us, we're in a transition period. We've been through economic hell in this country. We're poised in my view for a decent and strong recovery, but always at the bottom of this is education for the future.

One of the reasons we are so strongly in support of America 2000 is it trains people for the future. They have this thing: No one is too old to learn. Well, so to demonstrate that, Lamar Alexander, our Secretary of Education who is with me, suggested about a year ago that I learn to run a computer. I'm trying to kill him for that, but nevertheless I use it all the time. I think it does help demonstrate that nobody's too darn old to learn.

Similarly, we're in a mobile economy, and our whole health care reform proposal talks about people being able to move, take their health care with them if they move into another challenging area.

So I just wanted to salute you. I'm pleased to be at this company that's taken the lead in education. It offers everything for the future. We're got to do new ways.

We can't go back to the same old ways that the schools have been run forever. And I'm going to keep pushing for the America 2000 education program, meeting these six educational goals. They're not Democrat or Republican. The Governor of this State has been terribly supportive of this program, and it's one that I don't have to go to Congress for a lot of it. I've got to go to Congress for some of it, but a lot can be done right at the company level or the school level.

So I'm glad to be here for that reason and many others. And I see this guy's T-shirt: "I'll do it tomorrow. I'd rather be fishing." He's right. He's on to something. [*Laughter*] But for 55 days they won't let me do anything like that. No more fishing. I've got to get to work here. And I'm looking forward to the next few days to take this kind of message to the country.

Now, I don't know how we proceed, but fire away on questions. Shoot.

Legislative Agenda

Q. Good morning, Mr. President. What assurances can you give the American people that you'll be more effective working with Congress in your next term?

The President. Good question. I have been criticizing Congress as the gridlocked Congress. People on the other side are talking about change. The one institution that hasn't changed in 38 years is this Congress that can't run a two-bit bank or a two-bit post office. So I've had my battles with them.

We've gotten some things done. We've got a good program on the child care, for example, on the ADA which is bringing the disabled into the mainstream. And it's a very important question. People don't want gridlock. The assurance comes from the fact there are going to be at least 100, maybe as many as 150, new Members of Congress that have to do what I have to do: go out into the neighborhoods, go out into companies like this, take your case to the people, and listen to the people. And I think the kind of changes that people want are the kind that I stand for.

So what I've said I'll do is take these new Members when they get here—heck with the party—bring them into the White House and say, "Let's get these things done: health care reform, Education 2000," whatever the priorities are that come out of this election and education and health care.

I also happen to think—I see these police officers on the line—I'm fighting for a stronger anticrime bill. It's been literally, now, this is not making excuses, it's been bottled up in Congress ever since I've become President. And my case now is, take it to the people. Then if the people support my approach to tougher law enforcement for the neighborhoods, remind the Members of Congress when they come there, and say, "Look, this is what the people want." That's the good thing about a 4-year election cycle. So, sit with the new Members, try to get it done. And I think we can.

Come on, you guys. Here we are. Sir?

Overseas Private Investment Corporation

Q. Being a—[*inaudible*]—to and a proponent of the American worker, what steps has your administration taken to not—[*inaudible*]—the Overseas Private Investment Corporation, OPIC?

The President. We're taking steps to fund it. Because I think when you create more export market, OPIC—and that's exactly what it does—you create more jobs in this country. In this sick and anemic economy, which incidentally, has grown for the last five—hey, just a minute, I haven't finished

yet. [*Laughter*] But no, really, what it does, OPIC secures American—[*inaudible*]—that are selling abroad. And that is what we need. It creates more domestic jobs. So I'm strongly for OPIC. It's done a very good job. More and more American products are being sold because of investments like that.

The Economy

Q. Mr. President, my question is: What personal message would you like to deliver to the former employees of companies like Allied Tank and Anchor Glass, local people who have lost their jobs due to plant closings during your tenure in office?

The President. I'd say we've been caught in a very tough economic time, and we've got to move forward now with incentives to stimulate the economy. If we had had this investment tax allowance, I believe a lot of companies that aren't in business would be in business. I believe it would have stimulated investment.

I happen to believe that the credit for first-time homebuyers that's hung up in this gridlocked Congress would have helped the housing industry. I don't know whether any of these companies sell to that. Some of them are talking about change. We're actually an outmoded process being replaced by something new. There, you've got to do what this company is doing, and what I'm proposing on better education. So it's a combination of all three of these areas.

But let me say this on the economy: It is lousy. We know that. We've been trying to stimulate it. And we're in a global recession. It's not just the United States. Take a look at Canada. Take a look at England and France and Germany. It has been too long.

I do think, with interest rates down, with inflation down, with a "misery index" which reached 21.9 percent under the last time we had a Democrat President and a Democrat House, Congress, down now to around 10 percent, we should be able to recover and recover well. But you've got to do these things we're talking about.

Yes, sir, in the back.

Education

Q. My question, Mr. President, is also referencing to Education Secretary Alexander, and I'm glad he's here. He refers to the many educational entrepreneurships as "sort of defense contractors of the school industry." If there are successes with these programs, what incentives will our communities have to accept them?

The President. I'm not sure—where's Lamar? Do you want to comment on what you've said and then let me try to fill in on the rest of it? Because I'm not sure I've heard him use that expression.

Secretary Alexander. He asks about the—I made a reference to the design teams for the New American Schools Development Corporation that you created. There were 700 applications for that, and 11 were selected. They're going into the business of helping communities create very different schools. The question was, what are the incentives for them?

The incentives for them are the same incentives, Mr. President, that the defense contractors have. What we spend on elementary and secondary education is about exactly the same amount of money in America that we spend on national defense. And defense is going down, and education is going up. So those businesses have the opportunity if they wish to be for-profit—most of them are not, but if they wish to be—of helping school districts in States improve the management of their schools. Now, that would be——

The President. Thank you very much.

What we're talking about here, for those not familiar, is this whole concept of literally revolutionizing the schools. Lots has changed in this country. Employees—work on the floor has changed; a lot of things has changed. Defense has changed. But the schools, elementary and secondary, schools literally have not had fundamental change. So when we talk about the new American schools, we're talking about letting the communities come together, private end of it, teachers and all, and reinvent the schools. Some are going to want year-round schools; some are going to want to have smaller classes, some larger; some different plant and equipment. And we're just challenging the whole system to radically think anew about education.

We spend more on education per capita than any country except Switzerland, and I don't believe a single parent can say that they're happy with the total results. We're grateful to the teachers, but we're not happy with the total results coming out of these schools. And so we've got to do what we're talking about in this whole concept of new American schools. We need some support from Congress. Fortunately, much of it can be done as Pennsylvania 2000 is doing. Again, I cite your Governor, I cite the chamber of commerce, I thank companies like this who are literally saying well, we're going to get the job done. So they go out and invent and innovate, and from that we're going to—other places will learn.

This side's been very quiet over here. Yes, ma'am?

Family Values

Q. Mr. President, in your campaign you talk of the importance of family values, which I agree with. My question is what role, if any, the Government is planning to take in assisting and/or encouraging the country to get back to these values that we've lost sight of?

The President. You know, the opposition wants me to get off talking about family values. We had the mayors of the largest cities in the country, you know, Mayor Bradley of Los Angeles, and some of the smallest, mayors of the League of Cities. They came in; they said, "The largest concern we have for the cities, the problems of the cities, stems from the decline of the American family."

What we're trying to do is change the welfare system, for example, so people have to work if they're going to get a welfare check, or, as in Wisconsin, have to learn; try to get learning and work involved in that. What we're trying to do is give choice in child care or in education so people can choose where their children want to go to school.

But when we talk about family values, it isn't all what the Federal Government can do. A lot of it is things like Barbara tries to do when she holds a little kid and shows compassion or when she works for the volunteer reading program to show that parents ought to read to their kids.

I think we've gotten away from some of

these fundamentals. I think discipline is one. I think respect for the police officers that are out there risking their lives for us every single day is a family value. And so, you know—and that leads to the kind of crime legislation we're supporting.

So it is not demagoguery. It is not suggesting—I was on a thing with Tom Brokaw the other night. Bill Clinton was on there before me. He said, "Are you trying to say you think you and Barbara's family is better than the Clinton family?" I said, "Absolutely not." That's not what we're talking about at all. We're talking about the fabric of our society. We're talking about something that we've taken for granted for years, and that is that it's the family around which everything good happens in the community.

We're not criticizing single mothers. As I told him on that same show, my daughter was one until she got married; she's now married again, very happy. But it isn't trying to be critical of someone else. It's simply trying to identify with what the strength of our country is and then, instead of tearing it down, build it up and find ways to improve it.

So we're going to stay on it. The liberals hate it. They are all over me in these editorials. And I'm going to keep right on it because it is right to try to find ways to help the family, whether it's financial help or whether it's just the moral backing of the President of the United States.

Foreign Policy and Domestic Agenda

Q. I'd like to know what your point of view is, if you're planning to focus more on domestic issues and keep more of our money at home so you support this?

The President. The answer is—you don't want us to give you a long speech on it. I don't know how long ago you were in grade school, but maybe you had to, as everybody else did, my kids did, go under, climb under the desks to worry about some drill against nuclear war. That has dramatically changed. Because we kicked Saddam Hussein, the United States is the sole leader around the world. We are now a military superpower. We've got to stay one. We're an economic superpower, in spite of the lousiness of our economy, and we've got to be an export superpower.

So as I see it now, with freedom and democracy on the march—and I would like to get some credit for that; give plenty of credit to my predecessor, I might add—with Germany reunited, democracy moving in South America, Eastern Europe, these great ethnic areas free, Poland, Lithuania, Latvia, Estonia, that's done. So we can do what I mentioned back here, sell more abroad, but now we've got to use this same energy to change things at home. I believe that we can get the job done because of what I answered this, on the new Congress.

But the answer is not to turn inward. I may have a difference with you on this. I believe the freer trade we've got, the more jobs that means for America. Some are opposing me on the North American free trade agreement, saying it will cost auto jobs. Not so. It will increase the amount of auto jobs we have because we have the most productive workers in the world. Interest rates go into a decision as to whether you put plants abroad or have them here. They are at an all-time low.

So I really don't want to see us turn in. But I do want to see us solve these domestic problems of education, of jobs, of crime and whatever it is. So that's the philosophy that I'm bringing to it and that I'll be talking about out in Detroit tomorrow in a rather long but, I hope, comprehensive speech.

Yes, sir.

Racism, Abortion, and War on Drugs

Q. Good afternoon, Mr. President. I would like to ask you, is there any more that you could do about the moral issues that's messing with our country? I'm talking about racism, as in the Rodney King incident. And I'm talking about abortion, and as you see that that's getting out of hand. And I'm talking about the drug situation, the war.

The President. Very good question. In the first place, racism, anti-Semitism have no place in this country. And I think a President must continue to speak out on it. And I've done that, and I'm going to continue to do it.

Secondly, the answer I gave on the family is very important to the second part of your question.

And thirdly—the third one is on crime? What was the third part you mentioned?

Q. Drugs.

The President. On the drugs. Yes, drugs. We have a strong antidrug strategy. The good news is that use of cocaine has gone down by 60 percent in the last 3 years. The bad news is that it's still pouring in here, these drugs are, mainly from South America, and that the addictive group, the group from about 35 years old, the hard users, have gotten a little worse. It hasn't moved in the right direction. So the answer lies, prevention and treatment. We're spending a lot more money than any administration, and I'm not suggesting that alone can get the job done, and then redoubling our efforts on interdiction. We have some good people that are working with us in Latin America. Gaviria in Colombia has done a good job on it. We're trying to work with Peru and Bolivia on this. But that's a major part of it. And we're using the military much more than we did to try to interdict the flow of narcotics coming into this country.

But once again, here's an area where we really do have to back up those that are out on the streets, our people out on the streets helping, DEA and FBI and local police. And that argues for a strong crime bill. I mean, you've got to put away these hardened criminals. We've got to be tougher on the criminal, and a little more sensitivity for the victims of crime. And that's what our crime bill will do.

So those are the ways that we're trying to approach that problem.

Yes, in the back, sir.

Monetary Policy and Legislative Agenda

Q. I wonder what you have envisioned, once you become elected for the next 4 years, with the building trade industry, and also, back to basics where we start pulling ourself up by the bootstraps and make a good country such as our forefathers have started? And also, the monetary situation, how do you think the dollar will fare, like, strong dollar or whatever?

The President. Let me answer the last part first. One thing a President shouldn't do is say what the level of the dollar is. With the dollar at these levels, most people would agree, we're going to sell a hell of a lot more abroad, and that's good. You can export a lot more. But I don't want my answer to be interpreted as suggesting at what level the dollar should be. That should be set by markets and not by the United States. We can't set our currency like that. It has to respond to international markets.

In terms of the values, I've tried to respond to that one. In terms of the building trades, that gets to the heart of what we're going to be talking about here and trying to do, and that is jobs. I mean, building, I have a proposal in. Again, my opponent will jump on me for saying I'm blaming Congress. On January 20th, we had a State of the Union Message, and in it I suggested an investment tax allowance and that first-time homebuyers credit. It is still sitting there in the United States Congress. And I have to take that case to the people because, in my view, that would have stimulated the building trades and stimulated this kind of employment around the country. I just have to insist on that and try to make the people understand that I haven't just been sitting there. We've been trying to get it done.

Clinton says we're blaming the Congress. Well, as a matter of fact, I am because they're not getting the job done. As I said, I'll work with a new Congress. I've held my hand out to them, but now I've got to define the differences. I want to see a balanced budget amendment. I want to see less taxes and less spending. I've got to contrast that in terms of a vigorous economy with my opponent. And we'll have a debate, and that will all be out there for people to see. I want a balanced budget amendment. I want a line-item veto. If the Congress can't cut spending, give me what 43 Governors have and let me try to cut the excess and save more money for the private sector or for the families that are working. I don't think you're taxed too little. I think we're spending too much.

So I've got to get that philosophy out there and back it up with specifics enough so people will see that we're very serious about this. I believe that will help building trades and everything else. I don't know about city government.

Campaign Strategy

Q. What can we do to help you fulfill your goals?

The President. Vote often. [*Laughter*] No, but seriously, I've never seen a political year like this. I think most people looking at the political process, no matter what party you're on, whether you agree with some of the things I've said here or not, think that this is a weird political year, strange kind of time.

But you see, I am optimistic about this country. I do look around the world, and I see, compared to any other economy or any other country, we're not in decline. We're on the rise. I've got to take that sense of optimism and get enough backing to get done the kinds of programs that I've been advocating and will continue to advocate.

Then the final analysis, and I'll put it this way: I hope, I hope I have earned the trust of the American people in terms of the way I've tried to conduct myself as President. I know there's a big difference. I know there's a lot of differences on issue. But in the final analysis, I'm going to say to the American people: Here's my position on the issue. Here it is on job training; here it is on skills; here it is on education; here it is on accomplishments in foreign policy. Here's the things we haven't done; here's the mistakes I've made. But now I ask for your vote because I think I've been the kind of President in whom you can place your trust. And I'll do that, and I think it will resonate.

Assistance for Displaced Workers

Q. My question to you is, what can you offer the middle- and the older-aged people that have been displaced in the job market?

The President. The program that I talked about in New Jersey the other day of skills training, retraining. We've got a tremendous problem in the defense industry. One of the penalties, you might say, of success is that because we've been successful in reducing the threat to the United States abroad, we've been able to reduce our defense. But as you do that people are thrown out of work. So that argues for the job retraining programs, some of which we have in effect, others of which I have proposed.

So I think that is the major answer, that plus education, to those who are older and still able to be in the workplace.

The other thing is that when we go for our health care program, which is going to keep it in the private sector, provide insurance to those poorest of the poor, that those health benefits will go with the person. In other words, if they leave company X, they don't lose those benefits. I think that, then, gives a certain mobility to the kind of people you're talking about, those that want to move over next door to a new job and still be able to get it.

But the fundamental thing is, get the economy stimulated so young and old will be able to have jobs in the private sector.

Yes, ma'am. Excuse me. Am I out of here? [*Laughter*]

Health Care Reform

Q. I'd like to know what your proposed plan is for, especially for the people who do not qualify for Medicaid and are unable to——

The President. The plan I favor provides, through tax credits and through pooling of insurance and through more managed care, insurance for all.

People come tearing down into our country from Canada and other places because of the quality of U.S. medicine. I do not want to see the quality diminished. People come down to get bypasses in Cleveland because they've got to wait 6 months to get a coronary bypass next door, where they have a nationalized program. I think it would be a big mistake to nationalize it. Our program calls for what I've said, pooling insurance, more use of managed care.

It also calls for something else, and here's one where I have a clear difference from my opponent. It calls for getting rid of some of these frivolous malpractice suits. You cannot coach the Little League without some guy, three and two and doesn't like the call, trying to sue you these days. Neighbor is suing neighbor, and we're suing each other too much. We've got to put some caps on the outrageous limits. Doctors sometimes don't practice delivering babies because they're afraid they're going to be sued, and we've got to get away from that.

That is over $25 billion—different figures—$20 billion to $50 billion a year in terms of your added health costs. I don't know how many have been in the hospital recently, but hospitals are scared. So they say, give the guy three tests instead of one. Make him have test A because we're not sure that we won't be sued if we only give him test B.

So, along with pooling the insurance and making that transportable so people can take it with them wherever they go, we've got to have this concept of malpractice reform which, incidentally, helps pay for the thing without raising people's taxes. So I really think we've got the best idea on health care reform.

Congress is all over me. It was raised by the Senate race here last year. Take a look at the guy. What's happened? They control the Senate. Where's their education bill? Mine's sitting up there languishing. So again, blaming the Congress, well, in this instance, they control both Houses of the Congress. You want health care reform? Where is one? In 3½ years none have come my way.

We've got a good program. And again, one of the good things about this election year is you say to the American people: Here's what I stand for. Let him say what he's for. Here's what I want to get done, regardless of whether you're Democrat or Republican, try to make your voice loud enough so that when we first come in, sit down with those Members of Congress and get this done for the American people. So there we are, and that's the approach I take.

Listen, thank you all very, very much. I appreciate it.

Note: The President spoke at 12:55 p.m. in the model room at Uniform Tubes, Inc. In his remarks, he referred to A. Bruce Mainwaring, chairman of the company, and President César Gaviria of Colombia.

Remarks at a Bush-Quayle Rally in Middletown, New Jersey
September 9, 1992

The President. Thank you all. Thank you, Governor. Listen, thank you for this welcome. What an honor it is to be introduced by Governor Tom Kean, great New Jerseyan, great friend. Thank you, Governor Kean, for heading our campaign. I know that guarantees success.

Now, hello to everybody. A thousand apologies for being, what, 15 minutes late. [*Laughter*] And I'm delighted to be back, back in New Jersey. Allow me to quickly thank my host, Mayor Rosemary Peters; the Vets, Neal Cassidy, Al Thomas, Ben Ferrera, and all the New Jersey veterans in the audience, as well as the Nottingham Little League. What a job they did. And I look forward to seeing Joe Kyrillos in Washington soon where he'll join Congressman Chris Smith.

Audience members. Four more years! Four more years! Four more years!

The President. Four more. And let me acknowledge some New Jersey talent: Bob Franks, Don Francesco, Chuck Haytaian, members of the New Jersey Legislature and members of the Monmouth County Free Holder Board, all good Republicans.

I was not far from here, as the Governor said, almost exactly 4 years ago to the day, and I was campaigning for the Presidency. Our world was very different, largely because of one undeniable fact: A nuclear sword of Damocles hung over our children's head. Well, today I return to this beautiful Garden State to say something no President could ever say before: The cold war is over, and freedom won. Thanks to the sustained effort of brave men and women like the veterans here today, now our kids can go to sleep without nuclear holocaust haunting their dreams. That is real progress for mankind, and I'm proud to have been a part of it.

Audience members. Where was Bill?

Where was Bill? Where was Bill?

The President. We'll let him answer that one. [*Laughter*]

Thanks to folks like veteran Bill Denisson, who's 82 years old and came here tonight just to hear a young guy like me. He deserves credit. Does our children's peace of mind mean anything? You bet it does. We should be proud that together we have made it happen.

Now, America's challenge is straightforward. In the 21st century, America must be a military superpower, an export superpower, and an economic superpower.

And in this election, as the Governor said, you're going to hear two versions of how to do that. Theirs is to look inward and try to protect what we already have. And ours is to look outward, to open new markets, to prepare our people to compete, to strengthen our families, our social fabric, to save and invest, so that we can win.

My agenda starts with a commitment to trade, by opening world markets to the fruits of American labor. My opponent says, turn inward. I say American workers can still outwork, outthink, and outcreate anybody in the entire world. New Jersey, this great State, knows what that's worth better than just about anyone. In this State alone, more than a quarter-million jobs are tied to foreign investment and thousands more to exports.

Understanding the reality of this global economy led me to negotiate the North American free trade agreement. That agreement will create the world's largest free trade zone, a $6 trillion market from the Yukon to the Yucatan, and will create 300,000 American jobs, and that is just in the short run. Governor Clinton used to support it. Now he says, "I'm reviewing it carefully, and when I have a definite opinion, I'll say so."

Well, Walter Lippmann said leadership means guarding, and I quote, "a nation's ideals." Peter Drucker said, quote, "Leadership is action." But you know, nowhere have I seen leadership defined as, "Hey, I'll get back to you later." You can't do that when you're in the Oval Office. You've got to make a decision.

There's a clear choice when it comes to getting the economy going again, too. I spent half my career in the public sector and the other half working for a living in the private sector, running a small business. And I had ulcers to prove it. I think meeting a payroll is a good qualification for being President of the United States. Holding a job in the private sector is a good qualification. What I learned as a businessman is that it's as plain as day that higher taxes do not create jobs. They destroy jobs.

I'll tell you something else I disagree with my opponent about: I believe that Government is already too big and spends too much of your money. That's why I've proposed freezing discretionary spending in a plan to cap the growth of the mandatory spending without touching Social Security. We're not going to mess with Social Security. We're going to control the growth of other spending. And that cap would save almost $300 billion over 5 years, $300 billion. I need your help for that program.

You heard Joe talk about, Joe Kyrillos—so far Congress has balked at making these tough choices. I want to give you, the taxpayer, the option of taking 10 percent of your income tax and using it for one purpose alone: To reduce the budget deficit. Let's get the crushing weight of debt off the backs of these young people here today.

We can take those savings and cut taxes across the board. I've already vetoed one Democratic tax increase, and I'll veto another if I have to. I've got a pen right here in my coat to do just that. No more tax increases.

Now, what about my opponent? What about my opponent?

Audience members. Clean the House! Clean the House! Clean the House!

The President. We've got to clean the House. I'm getting to that, now, just a minute.

Well, my opponent's been in the public sector practically all his professional life. He caught the bug during his work on the McGovern campaign, and he's been at it ever since. In fact, he's either been in public office or trying to get into public office ever since he was 27 years old. Just yesterday, Governor Clinton said, "No government can ever replace the marketplace." Well, now, he sounds like he respects and understands the small business-person. But that's like a guy saying he loves to sail, but he's never been near the water. You've got to understand how it works.

It's reflected in his policies, too. Last week, when Tom Brokaw interviewed both of us and interviewed him, the first words out of the opponent's mouth were, after he said good evening—he did say that. Then he started talking about raising your taxes. We do not need to raise taxes in this country. I found out the hard way. I went along with one Democratic tax increase, and I'm not going to do it again, ever, ever.

He specifically means $150 billion in taxes. That's his proposal. Then he proposes $220 billion in new Government spending, although Newsweek magazine says it might cost 3 times as much as he claims. They called Governor Clinton's plan an "economic fantasy." And they are right.

Of course, he says he only wants to tax the rich. But you know there aren't enough rich folks to pay for his programs. And he endorsed the $100 billion tax increase passed by the congressional Democrats this year. And he's for it. And I'm against it. And who do you think is right?

I ask New Jersey: Does this saxophone song sound familiar, tax and spend? I wish I could bring every American voter to New Jersey to see firsthand what a liberal Governor and a liberal legislature can do to wreck an economy. Thank God we've got some Republicans in there now. When Governor Florio was in cahoots with the Democratic legislature, they acted like every day was April 15th.

I remembered Governor Kean's motto for this State. Well, today, every New Jerseyan knows all too well: A rubber-check legislature and a rubber-stamp executive are not perfect together.

We need tax incentives to get this economy moving. By the way, if you'll give us Joe Kyrillos and a few more like him, I'd be using my pen not to veto tax hikes but to sign tax cuts into law. That's what we need.

The solution to our challenge isn't raising taxes. It's creating more jobs. I know that tourism, for example, is a big part of your great economy. I know it creates thousands of jobs. So, as the Governor said, I came

here in 1988 and promised to clean up, help clean up your beautiful beaches, and I meant it.

First, I promised to end ocean dumping of sewage sludge. Well, the last barge to ever dump sludge in your ocean sailed from New York Harbor last June. No more. When tourists look out over the shore, they won't see sludge barges. They'll see sailboats.

Second, I want to clean up the sewage coming from New York City and points beyond. We've going to compel New York to build those sewage plants so you don't have to put up with their sewage washing up on your shores and ruining your beaches and vacations.

We're finally getting the garbage out of the water. That's what the Government can do when it confronts real problems with real policies based on real ideas, not an old formula from the past.

Now, while my administration's out helping deliver results on the Jersey shore, my opponent is talking a good game. But let me just give you his record on the environment back in his home State.

According to the Institute of Southern Studies, Arkansas ranked dead last for environmental initiatives, and in the amount of toxics they dump in to surface water, per capita, they were 47th. Now, they did better in the amount they pump into the air, they jumped all the way up to 42d worst. They were way up there at 42 in the percentage of rivers and streams that are polluted, too. There's a rumor down there that night fishing is getting more and more popular in Arkansas because it's so easy to spot the fish: They glow at night. They light up. [*Laughter*] Yes, the Governor wants to do for America what he did to Arkansas. Why would you want to let him do that?

You know, my opponent reminds me of a tired guy looking into the medicine cabinet, trying to choose among a bunch of old prescriptions that expired years ago. Old medicine will not cure our ills. Tax-and-spend will not solve our problems. It might kill off the patient. Let's not retreat into the past, with tired, expired remedies. Let's press forward into a new century of global economics where America can compete with the best and win a secure and good life at home.

May I thank the veterans who've provided us this wonderful hospitality. God bless those that served our country here, each and every one of you. May God bless the United States, a nation that is on the rise, not on the decline. Don't listen to the pessimists. May God bless the United States of America. Thank you very much.

Note: The President spoke at 3:04 p.m. at the Veterans of Foreign Wars Hall. In his remarks, he referred to Neal Cassidy, commander, Middletown VFW Post; Al Thomas, chairman, and Ben Ferrera, executive director, New Jersey Veterans for Bush-Quayle; Bob Franks, Republican State Chairman; Donald T. DiFrancesco, president, New Jersey State Senate; and Chuck Haytaian, speaker, New Jersey State Assembly.

Message to the Congress Transmitting the District of Columbia Budget Amendment Request
September 9, 1992

To the Congress of the United States:

In accordance with the District of Columbia Self-Government and Governmental Reorganization Act, I am transmitting the District of Columbia Government's 1993 Budget amendment request.

The District of Columbia Government has submitted a request to increase its FY 1993 capital authority by $60 million and to reprogram $20 million of capital authority from an existing project. The requested increase in authority is needed to fund the District's share of the remaining 13.5 miles of the Washington Metropolitan Area Transit Authority Metrorail system in accordance with the construction schedule adopted in the Fifth Interim Capital Contributions Agreement.

GEORGE BUSH

The White House,
September 9, 1992.

Message to the Congress Transmitting the Ireland-United States Social Security Agreement
September 9, 1992

To the Congress of the United States:

Pursuant to section 233(e)(1) of the Social Security Act, as amended by the Social Security Amendments of 1977 (Public Law 95–216, 42 U.S.C. 433(e)(1)), I transmit herewith the Agreement between the United States of America and Ireland on Social Security, which consists of two separate instruments: a principal agreement and an administrative arrangement. The agreement was signed at Washington on April 14, 1992.

The United States-Ireland agreement contains all provisions mandated by section 233 and other provisions that I deem appropriate to carry out the provisions of section 233, pursuant to section 233(c)(4). It is similar in objective to the social security agreements already in force with Austria, Belgium, Canada, France, Germany, Italy, The Netherlands, Norway, Portugal, Spain, Sweden, Switzerland, and the United Kingdom. Such bilateral agreements provide for limited coordination between the United States and foreign social security systems to eliminate dual social security coverage and taxation, and to help prevent the loss of benefit protection that can occur when workers divide their careers between two countries.

I also transmit for the information of the Congress a report prepared by the Department of Health and Human Services explaining the key points of the agreement, along with a paragraph-by-paragraph explanation of the provisions of the principal agreement and the related administrative arrangement. Annexed to this report is the report required by section 233(e)(1) of the Social Security Act on the effect of the agreement on income and expenditures of the U.S. Social Security program and the number of individuals affected by the agreement. The Department of Health and Human Services has recommended the agreement and related documents to me.

I commend the United States-Ireland Social Security Agreement and related documents.

GEORGE BUSH

The White House,
September 9, 1992.

Message to the Congress Transmitting the China-United States Fishery Agreement
September 9, 1992

To the Congress of the United States:

In accordance with the Magnuson Fishery Conservation and Management Act of 1976 (Public Law 94–265; 16 U.S.C. 1801 *et seq.*), I transmit herewith an Agreement between the Government of the United States of America and the Government of the People's Republic of China Amending and Extending the 1985 Agreement Concerning Fisheries off the Coasts of the United States, as amended, which was effected by exchange of notes at Washington May 12 and July 16, 1992, copies of which are attached. This agreement extends the 1985 agreement for an additional 2-year period, until July 1, 1994, and further amends the agreement to incorporate the latest changes in U.S. laws. The exchange of notes together with the present agreement constitute a governing international fishery agreement within the meaning of section 201(c) of the Act.

Because of the importance of our fisheries relations with the People's Republic of China, I urge that the Congress give favorable consideration to this agreement.

GEORGE BUSH

The White House,
September 9, 1992.

Statement on the Death of Julia Rivera de Vincenti
September 9, 1992

Barbara and I are deeply saddened by the loss of our close personal friend Julia Rivera de Vincenti. She was always an honest and loyal supporter, but much more than that, she was a true friend.

Julia served Puerto Rico with great distinction, and was universally admired. Julia's service did not stop with Puerto Rico. She also served this Nation with great distinction, including her service at the United Nations, where she helped carry forth the message of equity and hope to the entire world.

The Bush family considered Julia a part of our extended family. To her daughter Violeta, Barbara and I send our deepest condolences and prayers.

White House Statement on Fire Danger in the Northwest
September 9, 1992

The President today announced several actions that the administration will take to expedite salvage operations of dead or dying timber in the Northwest and Northern California in order to ease the growing fire danger in that region. Western States, particularly California, are experiencing one of the worst fire seasons in history. This summer alone, there have been over 70,000 wildfires that have destroyed approximately 1.7 million acres of forest and rangeland, burned over 1,200 homes and other buildings, and required the evacuation of over 35,000 people. Fire danger has been particularly acute due to the unusually large volume of timber that is dead or dying because of a 7-year drought that also has exacerbated damage from insects and disease.

The President has directed the Department of Agriculture and the Interior and all other appropriate Federal Agencies to ex-pedite their existing timber salvage sales programs for those areas not falling within spotted owl habitat, where timber harvesting is prohibited by Federal court order. In addition, the Department of Agriculture will issue final regulations updating their policy and procedures for complying with the National Environmental Policy Act (NEPA). The final USDA regulation increases to 1.0 million board feet the amount of dead or dying trees which can be harvested in a single salvage project without having to prepare documentation under NEPA. Pursuant to NEPA and applicable regulations, USDA has determined that timber sales of this magnitude will have no significant environmental effect. In addition to reducing the danger from forest fires, the U.S. Forest Service estimates these actions will increase the timber harvest from these lands by 250 to 450 million board feet for fiscal year 1993.

Remarks and a Question-and-Answer Session With the Economic Club of Detroit in Michigan
September 10, 1992

The President. Thank you all very, very much. Good morning to everyone. Governor Engler, I'm proud to be with you, sir, and thank you for that kind introduction. Greetings to Chick Fisher, your chairman, and Jerry Warren, both of whom have been most hospitable to me. I've been here several times before this most distinguished American forum, and I'm delighted to be back.

This morning I am here for a very serious speech, serious business. I'm releasing today an Agenda for the American Renewal, and I've come here today to introduce it to you and to the Nation.

My agenda diagnoses the economic problems our Nation faces, lays out the principles that should guide us in the years ahead, and explains the integrated approach that I am pursuing to meet the challenge. Over the past weeks I have been discussing certain elements of my economic agenda, and in the weeks ahead I will be expanding on those and other ideas. The document that I'm releasing today shows how the pieces all fit together. But let's begin this morning by stepping back, taking stock of where we are as a great nation in the broader sweep of history.

The American people have just completed the greatest mission in the lifetime of our country: the triumph of democratic capitalism over imperial communism. Today, this year, for the first time since December of 1941, the United States is not engaged in a war, hot or cold. Throughout history, at the close of prolonged and costly wars, victors have confronted the problem of securing a new basis for peace and prosperity. The American people recognize that we stand at such a watershed.

We sense the epic changes at work in the world and in the economy, the uneasiness that stirs the democracies who served as our partners in the long struggle. We feel the uneasiness in our own homes, our own communities, and we see the difficulties of our neighbors and friends who have felt change most directly. We know that while we face an era of great opportunity, we face great risks as well if we fail to make the right choices, if we fail to engage this new world wisely.

But America has always possessed unique powers, and foremost among them is the power of regeneration, to transform uncertainty into opportunity. Only in America do we have the people, the talents, the principles and ideals to fully embrace the world that opens before us.

For America to be safe and strong, we must meet the defining challenge of the 1990's: to win the economic competition, to win the peace. We must be a military superpower, an economic superpower, an export superpower.

My agenda for renewal asks that we look forward, to open new markets, prepare our people to work, strengthen our families, save and invest so that we can win. Our renewal depends on economic growth but growth not for the few at the expense of the many, not for the present at the expense of the future.

In our country we've always prized an entrepreneurial capitalism that grows from the bottom up, not the top down; a prosperity that begins on Main Street and extends to Wall Street, not the other way around.

That's the lesson I learned as a young man, packed up a Studebaker and moved to Texas after another war, at the start of another era. I saw jobs, prosperity, an entire future, built with the hands of ordinary men and women with extraordinary dreams.

Our Nation has never been seduced by the mirage that my opponent offers of a Government that accumulates capital by taxing it and borrowing it from the people and then redistributing it according to some industrial policy. We know that the clumsy hand of Government is no match for the uplifting hand of the marketplace.

My international economic and trade strategy will guarantee our position as an export superpower, extending our global economic reach in tandem with our security presence to stretch beyond our borders so that we can create more jobs within our borders.

At the same time, we need to foster at home the capabilities that will keep us in the lead: radical changes in our education system to prepare our children for a constantly changing workplace; incentives for the entrepreneurs and new technologies to sharpen our competitive edge; job training, health care reform to promote the economic security of our working men and women; and new approaches for reaching out to those who have been left behind, since in the century ahead we will need the talent and the energy of every single American.

Finally, because our greatest strengths flow not from Government but from the personal initiative of free men and women, my agenda aims to check the growth of Government and, in some important ways, to reverse it. Together, the components of this new agenda should renew America according to her most cherished principles.

This renewed America will be empowered toward a grand goal: to nearly double the size of our economy, to $10 trillion, by the early years of the next century.

To place this agenda in a larger context, let me turn briefly to five profound changes now at work in our economy. When Americans gather around the kitchen table at night and talk about how they'll meet a mortgage or pay the doctor's bill, they're feeling these changes in their daily lives. Before the changes have run their course, they will have forever altered the way Americans buy and sell, work, and create.

The first great change in our economy is ironically caused by our very success in ending the cold war. In the short run, deductions in defense spending have meant painful layoffs in many industries, and we are taking steps to ease this transition. But in the medium and long run, deductions in defense spending will free up priceless skills and technologies for peacetime growth.

Second, most of our industries are transforming themselves from old-style hierarchies into flatter organizations, with fewer layers between customer and executive. The new organizations emphasize a skill-based work force, "lean production," and shorter production cycles. From castings to computers, this is a revolution as dramatic as the one made earlier this century, when Henry Ford led the country from craft-based production to mass manufacturing.

While these changes are essential to maintaining our competitive edge, they've come with a cost. Everyone in this room knows that: layoffs, cutbacks among both white- and blue-collar workers. These hard-working people need reassurance, not only about their economic security but about preserving the sense of self-worth that only work can provide.

The third change: While the 1980's brought us the greatest peacetime expansion in our history, the boom also led too many of us to take on too much debt. We have been paying that down, that debt, and lower interest rates have helped us do it. The process is largely over, but consumers and companies remain cautious.

The fourth change involves our financial system. We entered the eighties with a 50-year-old banking system, designed for the days when tellers wore green eyeshades, not for an era when billions, billions of investment dollars can cross borders at the speed of light. In the late seventies, record interest rates and inflation rates rocked this anachronistic system. The less efficient institutions could not survive, obligating the Federal Government to protect the savings of millions of Americans.

Now, this process of paying debt down is nearing its end. Our financial system will become more flexible and efficient. But for now, lenders are cautious and, despite low interest rates, small business still can find it hard to get the credit.

But the most far-reaching of these five changes is the emergence of a global economy. No nation is an island today. One out of every six manufacturing jobs is directly tied to exports. The crops sown from 1 out of every 3 acres of farmland are sold abroad.

Consider some implications of the global economy: When growth slows abroad, as it

has recently, our own growth slows as well. America will only grow in the next century if we can compete globally in every part of the world. So we must seize every opportunity to open new markets, particularly those with the greatest potential for expansion.

Now, in drafting an agenda for America's future, we had to assess our strengths as well as our weaknesses. Conveniently, the other side has discovered many weaknesses and very few strengths. Of course, they might find temporary political gain in portraying America as past her prime, over the hill. But they have no more right to argue, for partisan purposes, that our economy is weaker than it is than I have to understate our problems.

Our strengths are real. Now, here are some facts. The "misery index," the sum of inflation and unemployment, is 10.8 percent, down from 19.6 percent in 1980. Inflation stands at about 3 percent. Interest rates are at a 20-year low. The purchasing power of Americans gives us the highest standard of living in the world. We enjoy the highest homeownership rate of all major industrialized countries. We send 68 percent of our children on to higher education, more than any other country, and well above Germany's 32 percent and Japan's 30 percent. With 5 percent of the world's population, we produce 25 percent of the world's total output and 37 percent of its high-tech products.

Now, I don't mean to suggest that all is well, that we don't need to lead and manage the changes that are transforming our economy. But you can't chart the stars if you think the sky is falling down. Over the past 12 years we have almost doubled the size of our economy. It's as if we'd created two extra economies the size of Germany's from scratch.

How will we meet our goals? Before you hear the specifics of this agenda, let me tell you a little bit about what I believe, because change, if it is to be a force for good, must be guided by principles. The principles that must guide change are the principles that never change.

I believe we are a nation of special individuals, not special interests. Individuals draw their enduring strength from their families, from their neighbors and communities, not from the Government. So I believe we must never ask Government to do what families and neighbors and individuals can better do for themselves and for one another.

I believe, because I've seen it, economic growth comes from the small-business woman who takes a risk on a new product, from the computer hacker working in a garage in a cluttered way; from the merit scholar in south L.A., south central, with a future as big as his dreams.

I believe Government owes it to them and to you to keep tax rates low and make them even lower, to keep money sound, to limit Government spending and regulations, and to open the way for greater competition and freer trade. But I do not believe, as some might, that Government's obligation ends there. As a conservative I believe that Government can help people, offer them hope and opportunity by giving them the means and the confidence to make the decisions that matter in life.

My background has also prepared me for the task of bringing our foreign policies and our domestic policies together to turn our strength as a world power to our advantage as an economic power, to match the security we feel militarily with the economic security that we must build at home. From now on, if America is to lead the world, we need a leader who knows the territory.

My Agenda for American Renewal calls for action on six interconnected fronts. There's no single cause of our present situation. There can be no single cure. The whole of our agenda will be, must be, greater than the sum of its parts.

First: challenging the world. During the cold war, we built a global security structure with military alliances across the Atlantic and the Pacific. In the same way, the post-cold-war era requires strategic economic and trade policy, global in scope and built on our foundation as an economic and export superpower.

We are uniquely positioned to achieve this goal. As the largest fully integrated market in the world, we wield leverage with other countries that want access to our market. As both a Pacific and a European power, we are tied to the largest and most rapidly growing economies across both oceans. As the strongest nation in our hemisphere, we are looked to for leadership by free economies emerging from Chile all the way up to Mexico. The same holds true for the newly born economies of Eastern Europe and the former Soviet Union, where our values, our products, even our language, carry a unique appeal. In Moscow today, the lines at McDonald's are longer than the lines at Lenin's Tomb.

The key to America's growth, expansion, and innovation has always been our openness to trade, investment, ideas, and people. As this openness is at last being reciprocated around the world, we find ourselves again at a special advantage.

The next steps in my strategic trade policy are to secure congressional approval of the North American free trade agreement and to complete the global trade negotiations, the GATT round, creating high-wage American jobs and expanding the pool of customers hungry for the fruits of American labor.

Let me emphasize these agreements are steps, not ends in themselves. So I want to announce today that it is my goal to develop a strategic network of free trade agreements with Latin America; with Poland, Hungary, and Czechoslovakia; and with countries across the Pacific. And then, as these external barriers fall, I believe we can help reduce internal barriers to competition as well in North America, Western Europe, Japan, and elsewhere. Greater competition will encourage entrepreneurial capitalism at the expense of Government power and entrenched interests, spurring unprecedented economic growth.

Traveling around the country I've seen it happen already, particularly in some small businesses, as they strengthen themselves for international competition. A couple of weeks ago, in St. Louis, I visited Public Safety Equipment. They're a company; they make the lightbars that you've seen on police cars. The president of Public Safety told me that a few years ago they recognized they could no longer just sell their products in 50 States, leave it at that. So they took on the world, and now 35 percent of what they make is sold in 48 countries, creating good jobs right here in the United States of America.

Public Safety and the hundreds of thousands of companies like it offer a glimpse into the future I see for all American business. But a business is only as efficient, as resilient, as innovative as the people who keep its books and build its products and devise its strategy. Materials, machines, methods, they'll come and go, but the American worker will remain the key to our economic security.

That brings me, then, to the second part of our agenda: preparing our children. The workplace of the 21st century will be constantly changing. I've heard that from many business people sitting right here at the tables in this hall. We must prepare the American people for a lifetime of learning, to keep a step ahead of that process of change. Now, developed nations need developing minds. The burden will fall on our educational system. As in the past, education should be the ladder that children can climb to better themselves.

Our current school system is not up to the task. Designed for the 19th century, it will collapse under the weight of the 21st. And our educational establishment is caught in the same time warp, where standing still means falling behind.

Money alone is not the answer. The United States already spends more per pupil than any other country but Switzerland. The answer is a radical overhaul of the system itself. If we want to change our country, we simply have got to change our schools.

The catalyst for change, the one reform that drives all others, is school choice, giving children scholarships so that all parents have the freedom to choose which schools will best serve their children. Competition is the principle that must underlie education reform, to break the establishment's monopoly on the system. Competition will not work unless parents are allowed to choose their children's schools, whether it's the public school across town or the parochial school across the street.

Consider just one statistic: In Chicago, 46 percent of public school teachers send their children to private schools. Clearly they know something about monopoly education that my opponent doesn't. Our different approaches to education reform reveal the Grand Canyon that divides me and my opponent. You see the same contrast in child care or health care and a host of other issues. My opponent prefers uniformity to variety and choice, relying on these Government bureaucracies to offer one-size-fits-all service. I don't want to pull everyone down to make everyone equal. I want to give everyone the tools to climb as high as they can dream.

Even as we fix our schools, the question remains: Will there be good jobs for the kids? And that's the third part of my agenda: sharpening businesses' competitive edge. I learned my economics the way most of you did, a lot of late nights sweating over a balance sheet or P&L statement, trying to meet a payroll. I saw that if people are allowed to keep more of what they produce, they will produce more. It's common sense.

When capital is taxed lightly, there's more of it. When it is taxed heavily, it becomes scarce, available only to those who are already wealthy, who need it least of all. That's not the kind of economy that I want.

If capital were more abundant, labor would be more in demand, wages would rise, unemployment lines would shrink. That is the kind of economy that I want. That's why I want enterprise zones in our inner cities and in our rural areas. That's why I want to make this research and development, this R&D tax credit permanent. That's why I want to cut the capital gains tax and index it for inflation.

Those are the fundamentals. I also see three other ways to sharpen the competitive edge of American business:

First, strengthening small business, by cutting taxes, making sure that credit is available, and by lifting the deadweight of Government regulation;

Second, supporting civilian R&D, by bringing the development, production and marketing of technology closer to the consumer;

Third, reforming our legal system. Every year American business and consumers spend up to $200 billion just in direct costs to lawyers, far more than our competitors in Japan and Europe. My "Product Liability Reform and Access to Justice Act" will restore rationality to the system and stop undermining the American worker. This is a fact: We will never lead the world in the 21st century until we learn to sue each other less and care for each other more;

The fourth part of my agenda: promoting economic security for working men and women. Again, common sense shows the way. True security will come only by developing individual capability, not dependency. And that independence, in turn, comes through the private sector, not the Government.

Government's role will be to ease individuals' adjustment to a fast-changing marketplace. The average worker today will change jobs, it's estimated, 10 times over the course of his or her working life. So we need a wider and more flexible range of job training and placement services for both the young and old, the blue- and white-collar worker, and now especially for our workers from the defense industries.

Pensions must be portable, and health care must be affordable. Our health care system today, I think everyone here would agree, provides the best care but at an unacceptable price. More than 30 million Americans have no health insurance. Health care costs are the fastest-rising part of our budget for Government, businesses, and yes, families.

My reforms get to the base of these problems while preserving and building on our system's strengths: our state-of-the-art care, openness to innovation, and consumer choice. Taken together, my reforms cut health care costs by $394 billion over 5 years.

My opponent's plan could eventually place a full 13 percent of our economy under the control of the Federal Government, meaning more bureaucracy, rationed care, inefficient service, and in the end, higher costs.

We must enhance competition and market forces, not restrict them. We must preserve individual choice, not hand decision-making over to centralized bureaucracies. We must reduce the burden on employers and employees, not bury them in a tide of new taxes and Government regulations.

The programs I've outlined and that are detailed in this agenda are based on the principles that will empower all Americans to make their own choices and better their lives. But I believe we need to do more for some of our citizens who have been left behind. And that is the fifth component of this agenda: leaving no one behind. The American dream is nothing more than the belief that all Americans can make a better life for their children. The dream has made us the most dynamic society in the world. It's yet another strength we can draw upon for the challenge ahead. So we must give every American a shot at making good on the dream.

I reject the shopworn logic that sees poverty as a simple lack of income, a kind of economic shortfall that can be replaced with a Government check. A conservative philosophy of empowerment must have at its foundation the creation of character through the ownership of property, through the dignity of work. That means sweeping away the nightmare of crime from our cities, building a core of property owners, creating business incentives, and making individual discipline and self-reliance the goal of all of our programs.

I call the final component of my agenda "rightsizing" Government. You'll recognize that I take the term from the business world, which has a lot to teach those of us in Government. At a time when companies across the country have been restructuring, increasing efficiency, all to prepare for the economic competition of tomorrow, the Federal Government faces an obligation to do the same.

Today the Federal Government spends nearly 24 cents of every dollar, 24 cents of every dollar of the Nation's income. That's the fact: Government is too big and spends too much. The size and structure of Government are relics of a different age, artifacts more suited to the dilemmas of 50 years ago than the problems of today. Every institution in our society has learned that by pushing power down through organizations, by using technology to speed the flow of information, you don't just save money, you improve productivity. It's time for the Government to do the same.

I will streamline Government, consolidating agencies, tightening budgets, and cutting the salaries of highly paid Federal employees. I'll start by cutting the White House budget 33 percent if the Congress cuts its own budget by the same amount. You might say: Why the linkage? Well, with fewer congressional staff badgering us for endless reports and endless visits to Capitol Hill, I know we can cut costs by that amount. I'll cut the salaries of all Federal employees earning more than $75,000 by 5 percent. Taxpayers have tightened their belts. The better-paid Federal workers should do the same.

The agenda I publish today contains specific proposals to cut the fat: a cap on the growth in mandatory spending without touching Social Security; a freeze on domestic spending; a balanced budget amendment; a line-item veto; and a new mechanism, disciplinary mechanism, a check-off box on tax returns to give the taxpayer power to cut the deficit. I will fight to reduce spending and spur growth so we can get this budget in balance.

Unlike my opponent, I do not believe the American people are undertaxed. Quite the opposite: I am committed to cutting taxes across the board. Let me offer an example—this is just an example—as an illustration of what we could do: My cap on the growth of mandatory spending allows for population growth and inflation. It specifically exempts Social Security. But that cap alone, with those caveats, would save about $300 billion over 5 years. If we used just $130 billion in specific spending cuts that I have already proposed—specific spending cuts of $130 billion that I have already proposed—we could cut income tax rates by one percentage point across the board, reduce the small business tax rate from 15 percent to 10 percent, and reduce the tax on capital gains.

That's the direction that I want to go: tax less, spend less, cut the deficit, and redirect our current spending to serve the interests of all Americans. I honestly believe that this is the way, the only way, to control the size of the Federal Government. The facts are painful, but plain: For Congressmen, spend-

ing is power, and they will exercise that power until they have spent every last dime they can squeeze from the working men and women of America. It's as simple as this: Raising taxes won't cut the deficit.

Here, then, is my Agenda for American Renewal. It comes at a time unique in our history, a turning point, a moment when one era is passing away and another is being born. In the agenda published today, you'll find 13 proposals that I intend to achieve in the first year of my second term. I present them as a single program, a unified strategy to make change work for America. Over the last 3 years I've shown how America can change the world, and we've made a respectable start managing the change at home. Our primary task now is to target America.

I intend to fight for this agenda, to fight as hard as I can. With a new Congress—it can have as many as 150 new Members, I am optimistic. If Congress balks, we'll move forward anyway, just as I have done with education, regulatory, and welfare reform. I'll work with our great Governors, like John Engler, with the State and local governments, with the private sector, with anyone who shares the urge to renew our country.

The American people know that the events of recent years have shaken the world. With the close of the cold war we can achieve peace, prosperity, and promise at home. The American people want that. The American people deserve that.

I want America to seize this moment. I want to stimulate entrepreneurial capitalism, not punish it. I want to empower people to make their own choices, not yoke them to new bureaucracies. I want a Government that spends less, regulates less, and taxes less. I will fight without hesitation for a free flow of trade and capital and ideas around the world, because Americans never retreat; we always compete.

My agenda draws together our people and our Government to meet this challenge. We will create a $10-trillion economy, and we will renew America, and we will win the peace.

I know that times have been very, very difficult for many Americans. The world that we knew as children, no matter your age, will never be the same. America will change. That's our destiny. How it will change will soon be decided.

I ask, as you consider the choice that you face, to consider carefully whose agenda for change best fits America's principles, our national experience, and our hopes for lasting peace and prosperity.

Thank you for your attention. And may God bless our great country. Thank you.

Governor Engler. Thank you, Mr. President.

Ladies and gentlemen, we have about a hundred questions for the President. We probably will not get through all of them, but, Mr. President, I will do this from this microphone so that we can expedite this.

The first question deals with the Democratic Congress. Maintenance of the Democratically controlled Congress is highly probable. How do you propose working with them, more effectively with them, over the next 4 years?

The President. Well, I answered that partially in my comments. Not only because of the post office scandal and the bank scandal, there's going to be an enormous change. I've felt that I've had some difficulties with confidence in America, but the Congress has really had problems. The Congress is in a state of change and flux, particularly in the House of Representatives.

So what I've proposed is that when Congress meets—the new one—I will get together with all 100 or 150 Members and say, "Look, you and I have been listening to the same song, the same American people." They want the kind of changes that I've outlined here today, and I believe most Americans really do. And I'll say, "Now let's get together, lay aside partisanship, and let's, in the first 100 days, enact this agenda."

I'm going to have to move fast, but with a new Congress I think we'll have something entirely different than the gridlocked Congress that I've been facing. I really believe that there's going to be that much change. You've already seen it. You've already seen it happening in many of these primaries, and it's still going on.

Governor Engler. This speech was billed as an economic agenda. Why now, in the last 60 days of the campaign? Why not before?

The President. Well, as you may know, I've addressed myself to many of the components of this agenda: health care, several times taking that case to the American people; America 2000, our education program; fighting for our anticrime legislation. So what we've tried to do here today is bring all the elements together that come under this outline I put forward, bring them all together in a comprehensive way.

The most significant thing that I've tried to do is to say, "It's one global economy." We are in this now together, linking international trade to opportunity for the American worker, linking international trade and global peace and security to prosperity for every American job holder. It's that concept, that very broad concept that I think is somewhat different in the presentation today because ingrained in a lot of this are the very same programs, like enterprise zones and these others I've clicked off, that I think are absolutely essential; say nothing of the philosophical difference I have with Governor Clinton: tax and spend versus trying to get the taxing and spending down and get that 24 percent of gross domestic product out of the Government's hand; get it down to 20 percent or get it lower.

So it's trying to put a comprehensive plan out there that encompasses many of the ingredients we've been talking about.

Governor Engler. Last month Governor Clinton was asked about CAFE standards. He said he'd be flexible. What is your position?

The President. Well, I'm not flexible. So we've got a difference. He has proposed, as I understand it, in his plan that the CAFE standards go to 40—I believe it's 40 miles per gallon. There's a wealth of opinion that says that would be devastating to the automobile business. In the name of environment, "Vice President Gore" has been talking about the combustion engine as being the worst threat to society. I've got to be careful with how I quote him, but look it up in his best-selling book. It is scary. It is bad.

Governor Clinton ought to repudiate him or certainly ought to clarify his position. He told some business executives that he was studying the National Academy of Sciences report. I'm told it's a big, fat thing about this, with a square root and all these things through it. So when he gets through reading that, maybe he can take a position on the NAFTA agreement, which he hasn't read either.

But I'm saying that we don't need to go to the extreme. My administration has a good, sound environmental record. But when I went down to Brazil, people of the environmental community, some of them, jumped all over me and said I wasn't leading. Well, let me be very clear, I am not going to go adopt standards, whether it's a CAFE standard of this or whether it's a strange policy regarding an owl, that throw a lot of Americans out of work. And we might as well understand that.

Yet we have a sound environmental record. I'm not apologetic about it at all.

Governor Engler. Why do you hate us trial lawyers so? [*Laughter*]

The President. I might have to hedge if I'd known you were one. [*Laughter*]

Governor Engler. There's an editorial here, "We don't destroy wealth. We just move it around." [*Laughter*]

The President. It's not a question of hating anybody; it's a question that I think the American people understand. When I went to a small town in Idaho, I was expecting to get all kinds of questions on nuclear energy or on wilderness areas. And the community people, the business people, chamber of commerce people, the main subject on their minds were these frivolous lawsuits. When I look at health care, and I see malpractice insurance estimated to cost between $25 to $50 billion a year because of tests that doctors have to give to protect themselves against outrageous suits, I just think we've gone too far and that we ought to control some of these liability—[*applause*]—some of the tort claims, some of these reckless suits.

I have here a distinct—far be it from me to inject to partisan note into this wonderfully nonpartisan audience—[*laughter*]—but I have a real difference with Governor Clinton on this one. The trial lawyers of Arkansas put out a letter saying that he's been with them on everything they've ever asked, and don't worry, just go in for the

Governor so he'll protect against legislation that would try to put some caps on these outrageous suits. We've got a chance right now in the Senate; the Kasten bill is coming up on product liability. And we've got to continue to fight to get through that gridlock up there in the Congress some legislation that would at least lower the burden on the American people, the doctors, whatever it is in terms of too many lawsuits.

Governor Engler. How realistic is it to double the size of our economy by the early years of the next century?

The President. It's realistic when you consider that if you use inflation plus real growth, that is not too heightened a goal. We can do that. You've got to do the math on it, but you're talking about 7 percent, I think. And I believe we can do that. We've had anemic real growth. I'm convinced it is not going to remain anemic in the less than 2 percent area. Coming out of the last recession it got up to 5 percent.

So I think the goal is very much achievable. I might say, I don't want to achieve it by raising inflation, however. I want to get it achieved by real growth. I mean, you can run inflationary policies and grow. So I want to be very careful when I say: one, it's achievable; but two, I want to achieve it with real growth, not with inflationary growth.

Governor Engler. What do you say to the American workers who believe that free trade means jobs lost abroad?

The President. Well, again, I tried to address myself to that one. I think that it means jobs increased in this country. Our trade with Mexico has gone way, way up without this free trade agreement. In my view, it will go up a lot further, and that means American jobs.

We've got experts on the auto industry here, but I am convinced that they are not going to export their factories to Mexico. There are a lot of considerations. One of them is the productivity of the American worker. Another one is interest rates. Another one is capacity, available capacity, in whatever industry we're talking about.

You're going to raise the environmental standards in Mexico. And I think you're going to cut down on the cross-border flow of illegals that I think is burdening a lot of our country, particularly California. I believe in my heart of hearts that what we're going to do is see a massive expansion into that booming market in Mexico. It's already happened in Canada. Our trade with Canada, our largest trading partner, as everyone here knows better than I, has gone way, way up.

I'm convinced the same thing would happen for American agriculture products, not only with Mexico but when we get a finalized agreement with the GATT. Now, that GATT round is on hold until after the French vote on Maastricht. But we're going to keep pushing on it. It has nothing to do with American politics.

I went up there realizing that the unions would take a shot at me on finalizing NAFTA right now when we did, getting an agreement that we can at least get before the Congress. It transcends domestic politics for me. I am so convinced that it will increase markets and increase jobs that I don't have to equivocate. I don't have to hedge. I don't have to read the National Academy of Sciences studies or whoever's doing it. I know enough about it from being briefed by a very able Ambassador Carla Hills to recommend to the American people that we approve NAFTA and approve it just as soon as we possibly can.

Governor Engler. There are a couple more. In black American newspapers across the country, black Republicans are labeled Uncle Toms, opportunists, and lapdogs for white Republicans. Do you have words of encouragement for black Republicans under attack? For black Americans who are Republican, the agenda's the same as for any American. Why can't black Republicans desire the American dream. Is not the same dream for all Americans? Please comment.

The President. He just answered my question. You should be able to have the American dream. And I would ask black voters across this country—a good podium right here to do it—how well have you done under the Democratic Party? Are you going to let people take your vote for granted, promise and forget, promise and forget? Or are you going to try to go with something that's going to give people an enterprise zone so you can bring jobs into the inner

city? Do you favor the old way of doing it in housing, where Government built these big tenements that then go downhill real fast, or do you want a shot at the American dream and owning your own home?

We've got good programs that offer hope and opportunity to black America, to minority Americans wherever they're coming from. And I want to see them enacted. So I would say to black Americans, I know it may be tough in your communities, but you're leaders. You're willing to stand up for principle. And don't blacks care about tough anticrime legislation? Aren't their neighborhoods the ones that are impacted and sometimes the worst because of street crime? Don't we owe them strong anticrime legislation that backs our police officers and doesn't leave them neglected? Don't they have a stake in world peace? Can't a black Republican stand up in his community and say, "I'm delighted that my kid goes to bed at night without the fear of nuclear war that we had before?"

We've got a good agenda. And I'd like to see some more of them stand up and say, "Listen, I am with you. We're with you." And we've got some outstanding black leaders doing just exactly that who are willing to think anew and not be taken for granted.

Governor Engler. When is the debate likely? Are there any restrictions? How much of the press would you like to be directly involved?

There were several questions on this. This is one of them.

The President. I have no problem with the format we used before. I mentioned this on the Tom Brokaw show. I'll debate Governor Clinton. I'm not a professional debater. I'm not an Oxford man—[*laughter*]—and I think he's good at that. I mean, he's got more statistics than there are problems. [*Laughter*]

I know I'm up against a formidable debater, but it's not anything other than, look, I'll be there. I'll let my capable staff figure this out, and whatever they recommend, I'll show up. I think I've done reasonably well in the debates in the past. You ought to try taking on Geraldine Ferraro if you think things were tough. [*Laughter*] We go back a ways on these debates.

So I think there will be debates, and I've already indicated I think the format was very fair, the way we've been doing it in the past. But as I said on Brokaw's, you get some intellectuals out there and the Harvard schools, and they all want you to have 25 debates. And I don't think it's that big a deal, but I'll take my case to the American people any way I can, including debates.

Governor Engler. Well, the last question, Mr. President. Next time in Detroit could we have breakfast, my treat? My name is Patrick Campbell from Edward Township. [*Laughter*] He addresses that to you and Mrs. Bush.

The President. Well, Patrick, it's tough

times. I'll be glad to accept your offer. [*Laughter*]

Governor Engler. Thank you, Mr. President.

The President. Thank you all very, very much. Thank you. A great pleasure to be with you.

Note: The President spoke at 1 p.m. in Cobo Hall. In his remarks, he referred to Charles T. Fisher III, chairman, and Gerald E. Warren, president, Economic Club of Detroit. He also referred to the corporate average fuel economy (CAFE) standards for automobiles.

Remarks at Missouri Southern State College in Joplin, Missouri
September 11, 1992

The President. Thank you so very much.

Audience members. Four more years! Four more years! Four more years!

The President. Thank you all so much. What a welcome. What a great welcome to Southwest Missouri. Thank you all.

First let me salute your—our—great Governor, John Ashcroft. You are lucky to have this man, and what a job he's done for this State. Thank you, John, for that introduction. May I salute another great citizen of Missouri who is working in Washington. If we had more like him, we wouldn't have to clean House. I'm talking about Kit Bond. Send him back. He's doing a superb job there. And of course, another one, your own Mel Hancock with whom I worked on so many issues, delighted he's here. Then our next Governor, the Attorney General now, you know who I'm talking about, Bill Webster, GOP candidate for Governor. May I salute Mayor Johnson, and our host, Dr. Leon.

I spend my days in the Oval Office in Washington. Let me just say it's great to be in the Oval at Missouri Southern State. I think Millie would like it out here in this Oval, I'll tell you.

Four years ago when I spoke on this campus, our country, our cities, our towns were marked by thumbtacks on a war map

inside the Kremlin walls. Today, I stand before you and say something that no President has ever been able to say before: The cold war is over. Freedom finished first.

I think young people understand that reducing the fear of nuclear weapons is something that is very, very important. Peace is precious but precarious. We must know its risks to reap its rewards. For America to be safe and strong, we must win the defining challenge of the 1990's. We must win the economic competition. We must be a military superpower, an export superpower, and an economic superpower. This must be our goal.

Our goal: a $10 trillion economy by the beginning of the next century. The opposition will tell you we can't cut it. I say any way you cut it, America can get the job done. We are not pessimists. We are optimists about this greatest country in the world.

Yesterday I released my Agenda for American Renewal. This is my agenda for action. America's a place where ordinary people can do extraordinary things if only they're set free. Here are my keys to unlock the door.

The first unlocks foreign markets. It's called challenging the world. I want to complete the global trade negotiations and get congressional approval of the North American free trade agreement. Trade with Mexico and Canada already brings $2 billion into this State each year. Our agreement would turn the entire continent into a gigantic free trade zone, a $6 trillion market from Manitoba to Mexico City, and create over 300,000 jobs for American workers.

So do not let the other side try to scare you into thinking we're not up to the job. I believe that when trade is free and fair, American workers can beat the competition fair and square, anywhere. I'm certain of it.

When it comes to exports, I say this continent is not big enough alone for the American worker. I want a free trade agreement with Chile, Poland, and with Hungary. We will have these agreements, and we will lead the world to a new era of commerce. And we will do it by the end of my second term, the end of the next 4 years.

Audience members. Four more years! Four more years! Four more years!

The President. You know, I'd hoped to come here and not talk about my opponent, but I've got to mention this. [*Laughter*] I just have to. He used to support the free trade. First he was for the Mexican free trade agreement. Then he wasn't quite so sure. And now he says, "I'm reviewing it carefully, and when I have a definitive opinion I will say so." Now, are there any history students in the audience? You may recall that Walter Lippmann said leadership means guarding, quote, "a nation's ideals." The Roman historian Tacitus defined leadership as, quote, "reason and judgment." But you know, I studied a little history, and I don't recall ever hearing leadership defined as "Please leave a message, and we'll get back to you later."

It doesn't work that way in the real world. There's no "call-waiting" on the phone in the Oval Office. [*Laughter*] When you're President, when you're Commander in Chief, you have to make decisions, and you have to make decisions whether they're popular or not. And I stand with free trade agreements because they are good for American jobs and American workers.

The second key is preparing our children. Developed economies demand developing minds. Our schools must prepare our kids to compete on a world scale. We must raise standards. We must demand accountability. And we must give parents the right to choose their kids' schools. My "GI bill" for kids would give scholarships to your younger brothers and sisters, your children maybe, so that kids can go to the school that their parents choose. Now, both Clinton and I, Governor Clinton and I, want to change the schools. He wants to change them a little. I want to change them a lot. My opponent says he's for a variety of school choice. His variety: public, public, public. I disagree. Whether it's a public school, a private school, or a religious school, I believe parents, not Government, should choose their children's schools.

The third key must unlock the future: We must sharpen businesses' competitive edge. My opponent wants to do for American business what he's done for Arkansas businesses. But if you ask the entrepreneurs of Arkansas, they'll tell you there's been little hope in Little Rock. Private dollars build more businesses. Public dollars build more bureaucracies. Which do you think will help our economy?

I believe that we must cut the regulations that turn redtape into pink slips. And we've got to put a restraining order out on our legal system. This country is suing itself silly. But the cost to our competitiveness is no laughing matter. Just yesterday, just yesterday on the Senate floor we had a chance to change our product liability system and put an end to these crazy lawsuits that are costing America jobs. But the liberal Democrat leadership heard from their friends, the trial lawyers, and twisted a few arms. When they were finished, they wouldn't even let the issue come up to a vote in spite of the majority wanting to do something about these lawsuits.

Now, ask yourself, which candidate for President will fight against the special interests, the trial lawyers? When it comes to taking on the trial lawyers, my opponent's over in the other corner, sponging their brow. I want to step into the ring for another round and strike a blow against frivolous lawsuits.

The fourth key is promoting economic security. That means job training to ease our workers into the new economy. It means health care reform, proposals that I've introduced to cut almost $400 billion of health care costs over the next 5 years so that you and your neighbors can afford it. And I will bring insurance to the poorest of the poor. Everybody should have a shot at insurance, and that's what our plan does.

Governor Clinton's ideas could end up turning 13 percent of our gross national product over to the Government. I don't like the idea of Uncle Sam, M.D. I don't believe that's the right prescription for America.

And the fifth key, and it's one I know young people are concerned about, is leaving no one behind. My approach to welfare is not how much we hand out but how many we help up. The policies of the past put a roof over people's heads, but they forgot to build the door. We must build that door with housing vouchers, enterprise zones, and workfare reforms. You see, I believe that our policies won't work unless people do, too. Workfare, not welfare.

The final key is what I call "rightsizing" Government. Today the Federal Government spends almost a quarter of every dollar of the Nation's income. Apparently my opponent thinks we're getting off cheap. He's proposed already $150 billion in new taxes and at least $220 billion in brand new spending, and that's batteries and spare parts not included. He's promising a rainbow, but first you've got to hand over the pot of gold.

Recently the people of Missouri voted down a tax increase and sent a message that should echo from coast to coast: Government's not taxing too little; it is spending too much. So send that same Missouri message to Washington when you vote this November.

The agenda that I published yesterday contains specific proposals to cut the fat: caps on the growth in mandatory spending, a freeze on domestic spending, a balanced budget amendment, a line-item veto. Your Governor, your able Governor, Governor Ashcroft, has a line-item veto, and he's used it almost for a quarter of a billion dollars, to keep that in your pockets. Imagine what a President could do with the same power.

I've also proposed a check-off box on tax returns to allow you, the taxpayer, to earmark 10 percent of your income tax to reduce the budget deficit. If Congress won't do it, let's give the taxpayers their own private veto pen.

I am committed in this campaign to providing serious answers to the questions Americans are asking about our future. I've diagnosed the problems and offered serious solutions, not all of which are popular. And I'm asking for a mandate to put my solutions into action and get this country moving.

For now at least, my opponent has chosen a different strategy. Rather than talk about what he wants to do for America, he spends his time belittling my ideas, playing on fears. One example: I want to talk about limiting the growth of spending to get the deficit under control, an idea my opponent says he agrees with. But instead of offering serious ideas of his own, he simply says, "Watch out, senior citizens. Watch out, veterans. Watch out, disabled Americans." It won't work. This administration has strengthened Social Security. We have stood beside the Nation's veterans. We signed legislation that brought the disabled into our economic mainstream. Do not let this Governor try to scare you, America.

Governor Clinton is running a Freddie Krueger candidacy. [*Laughter*] He's more interested in playing on people's fears than in dealing with this country's real problems. I don't want to scare the American people. I want to deal with our real problems. I want to get America moving forward. I am confident that I will win this election because I know America doesn't scare easily. We know the future holds its challenges, but we're not cowards; we're not quitters.

Let me tell you a little story about a fellow born not far from here, in Commerce. Maybe you know him. Mickey Mantle played in the minors right here in Joplin before he went up to the Yankees. His dad was a coal miner, Mutt Mantle, and he worked all his life in the mines so that Mickey wouldn't have to. Then one day Mutt got a long-distance call from his son. The Yankees were sending Mantle back to Joplin. Mickey said, "Dad, I can't play."

Well, Mutt just hung up the phone, jumped in his car, drove through the night to Mickey's hotel. Without a word, he started packing his son's suitcase. Mickey said, "What are you doing?" His dad replied, "You can work the mines with me. You can come back and work in the mines with me. I didn't think I raised a quitter." That night Mutt Mantle drove home all alone.

America is like Mickey Mantle: In face of tough challenges, we never quit. Confronted with the cold war, we didn't flinch, and we won. Confronted with the new economic competition, I say this: America will never retreat. We will always compete, and we will win.

I need your help. The next 53 days are going to be difficult. I've never seen a political year like this in my life. I promise you to continue to advance real issues, and I ask for your support because our ideas are right for America. My opponent says we're a nation in decline. I say America is always on the rise, if we but make the right choices. So for our great country, for America, it's time to step up to the plate and hit it out of the ballpark.

Thank you. God bless each and every one of you, and may God bless the United States of America. Thank you very, very much. Thank you.

Note: The President spoke at 9:30 a.m. on the Oval. In his remarks, he referred to Bernard Johnson, Mayor of Joplin, and Julio S. Leon, president, Missouri Southern State College.

Remarks at the Job Corps Center in Excelsior Springs, Missouri
September 11, 1992

Thank you so much. And may I say to Booker T. Jones, I am just delighted to be here. He's the president, as you know, and CEO of the company that runs this Job Corps Center. Thank you for the introduction, the information, and this warm welcome. And may I also salute one of the Nation's truly great Governors, John Ashcroft. That man has done so much for his country. And two members from the Department of Labor, John Douglas and Wayne Jenkins, are here. And John Thomas is the president of the student body. Thank you, sir, glad you're here.

Just before I got here, I met out at the airport today with a hometown hero, Derrick Thomas. He said something ugly to me about beating the Washington Redskins. But, nevertheless, he runs this Third and Long Foundation, when he's not running down the opposing quarterbacks. On Sundays you know him as number 58, but today he's the number 832, that's the 832d daily Point of Light. And it is a wonderful thing he does. I just wanted to salute him here. Actually, when I got up right next to Derrick I didn't know whether he was a Point of Light or whether he ought to be called a lighthouse. But nevertheless, big guy.

And I know Derrick will agree when I say it's great to see the team spirit here at this Job Corps Center. I read about it, heard about it, and now I get to see it firsthand.

We're in a political season so tough that it makes what goes on in Arrowhead Stadium seem like two-hand touch. So when you're all done with your training, I would like to invite all the carpenters here back to Washington. You see there's a certain House on Capitol Hill that's in need of a little cleaning and a little renovation. You know Bob Vila's show, "This Old House." Well, there's an old House of Representatives right there in Washington that hasn't been cleaned out for 38 years. Let's do something about it.

Let me tell you why I'm here at the Job Corps cutting into your lunch hour. I've just seen firsthand the fruits of your labor, the skills that you will use to succeed in an economy that seems to change, literally, day by day. Today, I want to talk to you about your world and tell you how America as a nation is ready to move forward to a future of peace and prosperity, if we but make the right choices.

As we gather today, I am proud to be the very first President who can say, the cold war is over, and freedom finished first. But with change comes new challenges. The defining challenge of the nineties is to win the peace, to win the competition of this new global economy. In the 21st century, America must be not only a military superpower but an export superpower and an economic superpower. And we start with an honest appraisal of our weaknesses and our strengths. My opponent talks about an America in decline, but just remember, if you want to talk to the most productive workers in the world you don't fly to Japan, you don't have to fly to Germany. You can look right here in the United States of America because the American worker is the most productive worker in the world.

Now, how do we guarantee that our workers will still be the world's most productive and that there will be plenty of high-wage jobs in your future? Yesterday in Detroit, Cobo Hall there, I set out a strategy, what I call my Agenda for American Renewal: six challenges we must meet to move America forward. And I set a goal. Today our national economy is nearing $6 trillion. My agenda will make America the world's first $10 trillion economy by the first years of the 21st century. We can do that.

The Agenda for American Renewal starts with these facts. Right now in our factories one of every six manufacturing jobs is tied to foreign trade. On our farms, produce from 1 in every 3 acres that we harvest will be sold abroad. And in the century ahead and in your lifetimes, the percentage of your paycheck that comes from what America sells abroad is only going to grow. And so, the bottom line in our new world economy is this: exports equal jobs. And I have faith that if we open foreign markets, our workers will satisfy the demand for our products. And so, my agenda starts with a global trade strategy, a network of new free trade agreements from Chile to Hungary, from the Pacific nations to Poland. Give America the opportunity, and I know that we can respond to the needs of any customer anywhere.

But as Booker here knows, developed economies need developing minds. And that's why this Agenda for American Renewal takes aim at the critical challenge: preparing our kids, our children, for the new century ahead. And that literally has to mean a revolution in American education. Competition works in our economy. It's time to bring that same competition to the classroom. I offer a "GI bill" for kids which would give $1,000 scholarships to every parent, so they can choose where their kid should go to school, whether it's public school across town or the private or religious school across the street. You see, I firmly believe that the parents, not the Government, should decide which school is best for the kids.

Now, the third key component of my Agenda for American Renewal: helping America's businesses sharpen their competitive edge. You see, small businesses create two-thirds of all new American jobs, and they're the first to turn change to an advantage in a fast-moving economy. And when you finish this program, a small business is where you'll most likely end up to find a job. We must ease the burden on small business. Small businesses need relief, relief from tight credit, overregulation, taxation, and certainly, litigation. Let me expand on that last point. America has become the land of the lawsuit. Each year we spend, get this one, $200 billion on direct costs to lawyers. I think that is crazy, and I have a plan to put an end to these crazy lawsuits. America won't work until we start suing each other less and caring for one another more. Yesterday the Trial Lawyers Association threw another curve ball to the American people when the majority will in the Senate did the will of the trial lawyers and beat back a chance to do something about liability reform. A sad day in the United States Senate.

Now fourth, my Agenda for American Renewal means promoting economic security for working Americans. That means, it's got to mean health care reform, to make health insurance affordable to all Americans, and make sure you're never locked into the job you want to leave because you're worried that you've got to lose your health care coverage. We're going to make it transferrable. And it also means a pension or a retirement plan that you can take with you throughout your career.

Fifth, the agenda must mean an America that leaves no one behind. That means programs that break the cycle of dependency, that help public housing tenants become homeowners, that help people on welfare find work, that help people without hope take heart. We don't owe every American a living, but we do owe every American an opportunity.

And finally, my agenda won't be complete until we bring change to one of the most change-resistant institutions in America, the Government. I call my idea "right-sizing" Government. But whatever we call it, I know you'll agree, Government is too big, and it spends too much. Here's where I have a major difference with the Governor of Arkansas. He wants to make big Government even bigger. To be precise, he's already on record for at least $220 billion in new spending and $150 billion in new taxes, just for openers. Now, my opponent likes to tell you he'll only raise taxes on the rich. But I'll tell you this, his taxes, he's going to end up taxing all working Americans for the same reason outlaw Willie Sutton robbed banks: because that's where the money is. I don't think people are undertaxed; I think Government spends too much. That's why my agenda includes a new idea to drive down the deficit by giving you, the American taxpayer, if you want to do it, power to earmark a full 10 percent of your Federal dollars for one purpose and one purpose only: to pay down the national debt. If the Congress won't cut that deficit, let the voters do it.

My new plan is comprehensive, filled with specific answers to questions Americans are asking around their dining room tables these days. One of those questions is how will we stay ahead of the changes in the world economy.

According to some studies, just 2 percent of you will work the same job from now until retirement. The average worker can expect to change jobs 10 times during the course of his career. You need real-world security, skills you can put to work now and 10 years from now. But just as you can't

drive a nail without a hammer, you can't build a dream without a job. You're here at Job Corps because you know that it takes more and better skills to earn good jobs, and you decided you were going to do something about that. Well, America has work to do, and we can't let your drive go to waste. Maybe 50 years ago, a strong back might have been enough to get a good job. In our changing economy, it's not enough anymore. What you earned yesterday with sweat you've got to earn tomorrow with skills. That's why last month, I announced new initiatives to focus Federal job training on the kind of real-world skills Americans like you and Americans of all ages need in this new world economy.

To help young people find that first job we have a program called the Youth Training Corps, modeled after Job Corps programs like this one. We want to get these inner-city kids off the mean streets and give them a second chance to build the skills they need to succeed. For older workers who've lost their job or worry that that next pay envelope might bring a pink slip, we've developed a new idea called skill grants. We want to give workers vouchers worth $3,000 to be used towards the training program of their choice. And let me say this: Choice is critical. I don't see job training as an excuse to shoehorn you into whatever program has an open slot or the next box on some bureaucratic checklist. I want to give you the power to go where you want to get training in the kind of career that you choose.

These are some of the ideas I'm talking about to renew America. Many are underway, others just beginning. You see, I am committed in this campaign to providing serious answers to the questions Americans are asking about our future. I have diagnosed the problem; I've offered serious solutions, not all of which are popular—can't do that when you're President. And I'm asking for a mandate to put these solutions into action and get this country moving.

I firmly believe that my opponent, at least for now, has chosen a different strategy. He has chosen a different strategy: Rather than talk about what he wants for America, he spends his time belittling my ideas and playing on fears. One example: I want to talk about limiting the growth of Government spending, which my opponent says he agrees with. But instead of offering any ideas of his own, he simply says, "Watch out, seniors. Watch out, veterans. Watch out, disabled Americans." This fear campaign must not work.

Our administration has strengthened Social Security. I have said time and again I will not mess with Social Security, and we haven't; we've left it sacrosanct. You look at the budgets, and we have stood, not just because I am one, but we have stood beside the Nation's veterans. And we're going to keep on doing that. And he tries to scare the disabled. I signed the most original legislation that brought the disabled into our economic mainstream and gave them a shot at the American dream. And that's what we've been doing, and we ought to deserve some support from the American people for that and not let him scare us. It seems to me Governor Clinton is running a Freddie Krueger candidacy. [*Laughter*] He's more interested in playing on people's fears than in dealing with this country's problems.

You know, I know times are tough and that Americans have real concerns. But I hope America will reject who plays on your fears. You need to hear leaders talking about these ideas, real ideas that are right for our country. You see, we stand on the cusp of a new age in our Nation. We've changed the world—just look back into history—we have literally changed the world. And our children, these children right here, sleep safer because of our actions. They don't worry as kids before them did about the fear of nuclear war. That is significant. That is a major contribution to the world. And now, now we can devote that same energy, that same determination we used to win the cold war to building a safer and more secure America right here at home. With this agenda that I've outlined today, I believe we can renew America and build a better and brighter future.

Thank you all for this wonderfully warm welcome. And may God bless the United States of America. Thank you very, very much. Thank you.

Note: The President spoke at 11:47 a.m. at the Excelsior Springs Job Corps Center. In his remarks, he referred to Wayne Jenkins, Job Corps Project Manager; John I. Douglas, Job Corps Regional Manager; and Derrick Thomas, Kansas City Chiefs football player.

Remarks to McDonnell Aircraft Employees in St. Louis, Missouri
September 11, 1992

Thank you so very much for that warm welcome to McDonnell Douglas. Governor Ashcroft, thank you for your service to the State, for that warm introduction. Let me say it's hard to define a successful bombing mission when you get shot down, but I am confident—[*laughter*]—I am confident that if I had one of these Eagles out there it would have been an entirely different story.

But I'm proud to salute the men and women of McDonnell Douglas, leaders in technology and innovation. I'm delighted to be here with Cass Williams, a union leader of renown, a man I go back with more years than either he or I would like to admit, but a good man and delighted to be

here. No stronger advocate for the workers here.

Kit Bond, of course, I'll say more about in just a minute, but doing a superb job. And yes, I'm counting on him in the Senate.

I have decided to notify Congress to sell up to 72 of your F–15's to the country of Saudi Arabia. I am delighted to make that announcement.

I know that the strength of this corporation extends far beyond the material that you forge into planes. McDonnell Douglas is a pillar of this great community, and you've always given back, and you've been a good neighbor.

I'm also aware that the past few years

have been difficult for this company, for a lot of Americans, as Americans have had to adjust to the reality of a new and more peaceful world. I know that many of you have been anxious about what the future will bring and especially about the status of the Eagle, about the F–15.

I have been sensitive to the impact of this contract on your production line, your jobs. In these times of economic transition, I want to do everything I can to keep Americans at work. But as Commander in Chief, I have a responsibility for the national security of our great country. I had to consider the implications for stability in the Middle East, a tremendously important area for all of us; preserving Israel's qualitative edge; the peacemaking process; the legitimate defense needs of Saudi Arabia; and our ability to work closely with that country, as we did in Operation Desert Storm and as we are now doing in Operation Southern Watch.

I have worked on this issue personally, touching every base, and I am now satisfied that we have adequately addressed each of these concerns and that we can and, indeed, must, for our own interests, go forward with this sale.

Not only has Cass Williams made clear to us the importance of this sale to every working man and woman here, but Kit Bond has never failed. He's never faltered. He's been down to the White House. He's been working his colleagues in the United States Senate. I salute him for what he's doing. We're going to need him now because we're going to take this up, and we are going to get this approved by the United States Congress. We must. Well, put

it this way: I'm going to keep them from disapproving of what I have done properly for the security of this country.

As you know, in addition to the F–15, McDonnell Douglas produces one of the most versatile combat aircraft, the FA–18 strike fighter. We're not only purchasing additional F–18's; we're embarking on a program with the company to develop an improved version of this plane, the F–18 EF. I want to make it clear, I support full funding for the F–18 EF. It is in our interest to do that.

The military technology that you produce is the finest in the world, and it's a tribute to American skill and innovation. It's the same skill and innovation that we must now use to win this global economic competition. For those who have any doubts I would say only, look at the talent that is assembled here today. The American worker can still accomplish great things, more than any other worker anywhere in the world.

So I simply came out to congratulate you on this; to tell you of this determination, this decision I have made, which I am certain is in the interest of world peace, salute you for your work; and thank you for this warm welcome. May God bless each and every one of you. Thank you very, very much.

Note: The President spoke at 3:05 p.m. at the McDonnell Aircraft Company. In his remarks, he referred to Cass Williams, president and directing business representative of the International Association of Machinists, District 836.

Remarks to the Christian Coalition Road to Victory Conference in Virginia Beach, Virginia
September 11, 1992

The President. Thank you, Dr. Pat Robertson. Thank you. Thank you very, very much for that welcome. I'm delighted to be here. Thank you. I am just delighted to be here. Pat, thank you for this rousing welcome and this warm introduction and the

friendship. I tell you, it's a joy to be here with you.

I want to salute the leadership. My respects, of course, to Dede Robertson, who's made us feel so welcome here in this short time, and the family. Some of you missed out on this, but I was embraced by the Robertson family with these wonderful kids and grandkids. So you have a nice way of making us feel at home. Thank you very much.

May I salute my comrade-in-arms in Washington, Senator Warner, who's with us tonight. He's doing an awful lot of work for all the things we believe in. I want to salute the members of the board of this Christian Coalition and also to thank Reverend Sweet. And I understand that Dan Burton was here or is here. And here he is sitting right here—didn't see him when he first walked in—a great Member of the House. You know, if we had more people like Dan, we wouldn't be saying "Clean House!", I'll tell you. May I salute Senators Mark Earley and Ken Stolle.

It is said of some groups that they haven't got a prayer. Well, tonight I'm pleased to be with an audience about whom that will never be said. [*Laughter*] I am delighted to be here in the heart of America's evangelical community. And in recent weeks, you and I have been accused of focusing our energies on what has been called a narrow, irrelevant topic, the American family. Well, I believe it is our critics who are guilty of tunnel vision, because in my mind the family is at the center of America, a source of strength for us as individuals and for America as a nation.

So when I talk about the importance of family, I don't mean to suggest that we should somehow go back to the days of Ozzie and Harriet. Nor do I pass judgment on the kind of family you live in, whether both parents work or just one parent, or whether you're a part of a single-parent family. Families are not measured by "what kind" but by "how close."

I talk about the American family because of something I learn every single day in the Oval Office. When confronting the problems of America, it does no good to attack symptoms. You have to go after the root causes. Ask any mayor, any Governor, any teacher, and yes, any minister, any preacher, and they'll tell you the exact same thing: The one sure way to make America more safe and secure is to make our families more safe and secure.

What are the pressures on the families today? You know them well: schools with low academic standards, young people not learning traditional values that can steady them in an uncertain world. The coarseness of our culture is reflected on some of the most outrageous television shows. The scourge of drugs and violence, these are real issues that Government must address. So I will not be driven away from discussing ways to strengthen the family by those who claim the topic unimportant. Strengthening the family must be a national priority, and it will be as long as I am President of the United States.

If we care about the family, and we all do, then we have to care about the economy, because today one major threat to the American family is a weak economy. And I want to talk about that tonight. Today, family budgets are stretched by rising health care costs. Low-income families are hurt because too often welfare encourages dependency, not personal responsibility. When a mom or dad loses a job, the impact is felt first right at home. So if we care about family, and we all do, we have to figure out a way to make sure that America in the 21st century is more than a military superpower, but we are also an export superpower and an economic superpower.

That's why yesterday in Detroit I laid out my Agenda for American Renewal, a comprehensive plan to create by the early part of the 21st century the world's first $10 trillion economy. With that kind of dynamic growth, we will be able to address all our challenges here at home and take some pressure off our families who are struggling today.

Now, here's where we start. Right now in our factories, one out of every six manufacturing jobs is tied to trade. On our farms, and this may surprise you, on our farms 1 in every 3 acres that we harvest will be sold abroad. America's future lies in building on our strengths to become the world leader in trade.

My opponent spends his energy talking about our weaknesses. He claims, and I quote, that "America is somewhere south of Germany headed for Sri Lanka." He talks about how we're ridiculed around the world. I wish my opponent could see the people of Germany and Eastern Europe whose eyes brighten at the simple word "America." We helped in the reunification of Germany, and they all know it.

I wish my opponent could see what's going on in American factories and businesses despite all our challenges. Don't forget this fact: If you want to talk to the world's most productive workers, you don't buy a ticket to Japan or Germany. You go to Tulsa or Tampa or Tempe. The most productive workers in the world can be found right here in the U.S.A., and we should never let the opposition tell us differently.

I have faith that if we open foreign markets, our workers will satisfy the demand for our products. So my agenda starts with a global trade strategy, to build a network of new free trade agreements not just with Canada and Mexico but with Chile and other Latin American nations, as well as the emerging democracies like Hungary and Poland.

America alone can take advantage of our influence to create unique opportunities for our people. You know, while some say America should turn away from the world economy, I say let's reach out. After all, the American worker will never retreat, and we will always compete. In my view, we will always win. We are the best, and we ought to keep reaching out to help people here at home.

But understand, developed economies need developing minds. That's why this Agenda for American Renewal takes aim at a second critical challenge: preparing our children for the new century ahead. That's going to require, literally require, a revolution in American education.

Dr. Robertson told me that you heard from our distinguished Secretary of Education, Lamar Alexander, today. He's taking this message for America 2000, this change in education, all across our country, and I strongly support him. Competition works in our economy, and I believe it's time to bring some competition to the classroom. I know, as I say, that Lamar was here today, and I'm sure he talked about our "GI bill" for kids. I hope he did. It would give $1,000 scholarships to low- and middle-income parents so that they can choose the school they

want their children to attend.

My opponent says he supports a variety of choice in education. But if you look close, real close, he wants parents to choose between public schools, public schools, and public schools. I want to go further. I support the public schools; I want to go further. Whether it's the public schools across town, though, or the private or religious school right across the street, I believe parents, not the Government, should decide which school is best for their kids.

I was a beneficiary of the GI bill many years ago when I got out. They didn't say to me you can't only go to a State school, or you must go to a religious university or whatever it is. What happened there, these kids coming out of the service were given the GI bill, and they could go to the schools of their choice. It strengthened every single university. The same thing can happen now at the K-through-12 level, and that's what we're talking about here.

Now, the third component of my Agenda for American Renewal: helping America's businesses sharpen their competitive edge. Small businesses create two-thirds of all new American jobs, and they are the first to turn change to advantage in a fast-moving economy. Pat Robertson is a businessman and a darn good one. He'll tell you what holds back business in America today, three things: regulation, taxation, and yes, litigation. And I want to cut them all.

You know, America has become the land of the lawsuit. If you fall off a ladder these days, a trial lawyer will be there to catch you before you hit the ground. [*Laughter*] Each year consumers and companies now spend up to $200 billion on direct payments to lawyers. Japan doesn't do it. Germany doesn't do it.

Just yesterday, and John Warner knows this, just yesterday we had a bill before the United States Senate, the Congress, to reform our product liability laws, to try to finally do something about these outrageous lawsuits. We had more than enough votes, as John will tell you, for passage of the bill. We had well over 50 percent. But the liberal leaders of the Congress heard from their friends the trial lawyers, who twisted a few arms, and when they were finished, we could get 58 votes, not the 60 we needed. We couldn't even get the liability reform up for a vote. The people's will was frustrated by the liberal leaders in the Congress. "Clean House!" is my motto.

I don't think that's right. And while the trial lawyers may not like it, I'm going to keep fighting to reform our legal system. I believe as a nation—I really feel this—that we've got to sue each other less and start caring for one another more.

That brings me to the fourth part of the agenda: providing economic security for all Americans. You know, in the past 4 years, we've done so much to bring peace to the world, but our victory is not complete until we have peace of mind at home. Whether your collar is blue or white, or whether you till the farm or work on the assembly line, Americans today worry about health care. They wonder if they can afford it, and they worry that they might lose it.

Again, we have two alternatives. My opponent offers a plan that would have Government set prices and could eventually lead to having 13 percent of our gross national product under the same people who gave us the House post office. Now, that isn't good enough.

I used to say that the system would give us the efficiency of the House post office and the compassion of the KGB, but I don't say that anymore because I'm getting a lot of Russians mad. They're writing letters saying, quit knocking the KGB. [*Laughter*]

But I have a very different approach, and it's a better approach. You cut the costs by going after the root causes of health care explosion; one of them, medical malpractice. Encourage small businesses to pool their coverage, their insurance coverage, driving down the price. Use the principles of the marketplace to make sure that when it comes to medicine, the intense pain only occurs at the doctor's office, not a month later when you get the bill at home. [*Laughter*]

America can have no spare people if we're to compete in the next century. So the fifth part, then, of our total agenda must mean an America that leaves nobody behind. Welfare as we know it simply has to change. Today's welfare drains taxpayers of hard-earned dollars and recipients of hard-

to-replace dignity. But now, States like Wisconsin are taking the lead, and they're saying, enough is enough. With our help, they're experimenting with programs that reward work and the learning—call it Learnfare—leadership, personal responsibility. We desperately need a welfare system that encourages families to stick together and for those fathers to stick around.

The sixth part of my agenda for America will bring change to one of the most change-resistant institutions in America, the Government. Think about the family budget in 1955. Back then the average family spent 5 percent of its adjusted gross income on Federal taxes. Today the figure is almost 24 percent. Many moms and dads are forced to spend less time with their children so they can feed Uncle Sam's voracious appetite. My opponent has a boundless enthusiasm for Government, and he offers already at least $220 billion in new spending and $150 billion in new taxes. And that's just for openers; that's just to start. And I take a different approach.

Audience members. Boo-o-o!

The President. I believe that the Government is too big, and it spends too much of your money. That's why my agenda includes a new idea to drive down the deficit by giving you, the American taxpayer, the power to earmark a full 10 percent of your Federal tax dollars for one purpose and one purpose only, to get down the national debt.

The same people that don't like the line-item veto and the balanced budget amendment don't like this idea. But they've had their day. Now let's try these new ideas to do something about the deficit that's mortgaging the future of the young people in this country.

So this is the outline, a broad outline of this agenda for America, and it's filled with other ideas. Many are well underway; others are new. But all represent a serious response to the economic challenges of this new age, an answer to the questions being asked around America's dining room tables. I have diagnosed the problem, I think, properly; have offered specific solutions. Not all of them are popular. And I'm asking for a mandate so that we can put my ideas into action immediately and get this economy moving again.

For now, at least, my opponent's chosen a very different strategy. Rather than talk about what he wants to do for America, he spends a lot of his time and his energy belittling my ideas and playing on fears. One example I want to talk about: ways to limit the growth of Federal spending, which every expert will tell you must be done. But instead of offering any spending restraints on his own, Governor Clinton simply goes around saying, "Watch out, senior citizens. Watch out, veterans. Watch out, disabled Americans," the same old scare tactics that they use every 4 years, and it's not going to work.

My administration has strengthened Social Security. I've said I'm not going to mess with it, and I haven't, and we aren't. We stood beside our veterans. And we signed the law, and I'm very proud of this, that brought disabled Americans at long, long last into the economic mainstream. I am not going to let Governor Clinton frighten Americans by telling them these scare stories that crop up by the liberals every 4 years.

And yes, I believe America deserves a serious discussion on the issues, issues like how to renew our Nation by spurring economic growth so that we can help strengthen our families. I'll talk about ideas that deal not just with our immediate challenges

today but will build a safer and a more secure America tomorrow.

So let my opponent do what is safe and politically balanced, and I'm going to keep trying to do what is right for our great country.

Before I leave, let me just say how deeply I support all the work you're doing to restore the spiritual foundation of this Nation. And I say this: The longer that Barbara and I are privileged to live in the White House, the more I understood what Lincoln meant when he said he went to his knees in prayer. I commend you. I join with you in committing to uphold the sanctity of life.

Matthew, chapter 6, verse 21, reminds us, "Where your treasure is, there your heart will be also." And our treasure is with America. With our renewal agenda and your efforts out there in those grassroots, we are joined in a crusade to create an American future that is worthy of its proud past.

Thank you for this exceptionally warm welcome. May God bless this great Nation, the United States of America. Thank you all very, very much. Thank you.

Note: The President spoke at 8:20 p.m. at the Founders Inn and Convention Center. In his remarks, he referred to Pat Robertson, president, Christian Coalition; A. George Sweet, pastor, Atlantic Shores Baptist Church; and Mark L. Earley and Kenneth W. Stolle, Virginia State senators.

Message to the Congress on Trade With China
September 11, 1992

To the Congress of the United States:

Pursuant to the authority vested in me by section 902(b)(2) of the Foreign Relations Authorization Act, Fiscal Years 1990 and 1991 (Public Law 101–246), and section 608(a) of the Departments of Commerce, Justice, and State, the Judiciary, and Related Agencies Appropriations Act, 1992 (Public Law 102–140), I hereby report to the Congress that it is in the national interest of the United States to waive the restric-

tions contained in those acts on the export to the People's Republic of China of U.S.-origin satellites and Munitions List articles insofar as such restrictions pertain to the APSAT, Asiasat 2, Intelsat VIIA, STARSAT, AfriSat, and Dong Fang Hong 3 projects.

Attached is my justification for the aforesaid actions.

GEORGE BUSH

The White House,
September 11, 1992.

Radio Address to the Nation on the Agenda for American Renewal
September 12, 1992

This week I laid out my Agenda for American Renewal, a comprehensive set of answers to the most important question Americans are asking these days: What kind of America will our kids grow up in? My agenda offers the promise of a renewed America, an America with a $10 trillion economy by early in the next century. With that kind of dynamic growth we can address our problems here at home and guarantee that America will remain not just a military superpower but an export superpower and an economic superpower.

Today one out of every six manufacturing jobs is tied to exports. So first, I offer a strategic trade policy, including new free trade agreements with the emerging democracies of Eastern Europe. By increasing trade we increase American jobs. It's as simple as that.

If we want America to compete with other nations, we have to change our schools. Through my America 2000 program we are already reinventing education in almost 2,000 towns and cities. And I want to give scholarships to low- and middle-income students so that parents can choose where their kids go to school, whether public schools, private schools, or religious schools.

Even with new schools, graduates are going to need good jobs. So the third part of my agenda is to sharpen our businesses' competitive edge. That means cutting taxes and regulations on small business. It also means doing away with the crazy lawsuits that strike fear into the hearts of every business man or woman. Get this: American businesses and consumers now spend up to $200 billion each year just on direct costs to lawyers. I don't want to see an America where only lawyers get rich. I want to see an America where workers can get rich.

The fourth part of my agenda is extremely important: to promote economic security for all working people. For example, I have a program to control health care costs, to allow you to take your coverage from job to job, and to make health care available to almost 30 million Americans who simply can't afford it today.

In the 21st century we will need the talents of everyone, regardless of whether you were born in city or suburb. And that's agenda item number five: opportunity for all Americans. It means reforming our welfare system. Already we've given States authority to experiment with programs that don't just give people a check but reward work and personal responsibility.

The final part of my agenda is especially important: "rightsizing" Government. I believe the Federal Government today is too big and spends too much of your money. My opponent wants to raise taxes and raise spending. I put forth almost $300 billion in specific cuts in spending over the next 5 years. I want to use the savings to reduce taxes and get this economy moving, and get the deficit off our children's shoulders.

This is my Agenda for American Renewal. Parts of it are already underway; parts of it are new. I will fight for this agenda with the new Congress and its 150 expected new Members. If Congress balks, I will work with Governors, mayors, teachers, community leaders to keep my agenda moving forward.

My opponent has reached into the medicine cabinet and offered the same tired old prescription: more Government and bigger Government. My agenda for America offers new solutions, solutions that give power to you, not Government. This is the way we will create a $10 trillion economy. This is the way we can match the peace we've achieved around the world with peace of mind here at home.

Thank you for listening.

Note: This address was recorded at 9:50 a.m. on September 10 in the Oval Office at the White House for broadcast after 9 a.m. on September 12.

Remarks on Disaster Assistance for Hawaii Following Hurricane Iniki
September 13, 1992

The President. This weekend, as you know, Hurricane Iniki, one of the most powerful storms in this century, struck the island of Hawaii. Reportedly, some lives have been lost. I talked to the Governor last night, and he told me that the latest estimate was two lives, but nobody is absolutely certain at this point. There have been a lot of injuries, and there's been considerable physical damage. On the island of Kauai, damage is now estimated at approximately $1 billion with 30 percent of the buildings destroyed. Airports and main roads are open now, but 95 percent of the island is without power.

Wallace Stickney, the FEMA Administrator, Pat Saiki, the Administrator of the Small Business Administration—a native Hawaiian—are already out there coordinating the relief operation. They're working closely with Governor John Waihee. And today shipments of water, food, tents, generators, and other relief supplies are being delivered to the island. These efforts involve the cooperation of State officials; FEMA and CINCPAC and the other military people are working closely with the Governor.

In addition to the Governor's request, I've declared most of the island a Federal disaster area, eligible for grants and low-cost loans to cover property losses. We stand ready to provide further assistance for the Governor to speed the relief effort. I had a good talk with him, and he did say that he was satisfied and pleased with the cooperation from the Federal Government, working with State and local officials.

Our hearts go out to the people of Hawaii, and we pledge to stand by them in support at this hour of need.

Thank you all.

Q. Mr. President, are you going——

The President. I have no plans right now.

Note: The President spoke at 8:40 a.m. at Andrews Air Force Base prior to his departure for Irvine, CA. In his remarks, he referred to naval forces under the Commander in Chief, U.S. Pacific Fleet (CINCPAC). Hurricane Iniki struck the island of Kauai on September 11.

Remarks at a Welcome Rally in Anaheim, California
September 13, 1992

The President. Thank you, Mr. President. Thank you very much, President Reagan. May I salute not only President Reagan but Governor Wilson, our master of ceremonies; Bob Dornan, our great Member of Congress, a loyal supporter. I want to thank the Gatlin Brothers, my old friends that are with us today. What a job they do for us. It's great to be in California. And it's especially great to be here with these three Members of the United States Congress, with Senator Seymour. We must reelect Senator Seymour, and we must elect Bruce Herschensohn to the Senate.

Mr. President, last year I was honored to help dedicate your library. When I leave office I look forward to your dedicating mine. Not to be specific, but how are you fixed for 1997?

I love Ronald Reagan for the same reasons you do. First, his sense of humor. No wonder he took Washington by storm. Here was a politician who was funny on purpose. Quite different. [*Laughter*] I'm a Reagan fan for another reason: his eloquence. Ronald Reagan didn't just make the world believe in America again, he made Americans believe in themselves again.

That Great Communicator was indeed the Great Liberator. Abroad, he helped free millions from tyranny. And at home, he helped free millions from a Government that's too big and spends too much of your money. He turned America around. And he turned the days of malaise into "a shining city on a hill," and the American people will never forget it.

Now, I'm not saying these nice things about Ronald Reagan in case he decides to run for President again in 1996. Though I'll confess, if it weren't for a little something called the 22d amendment, he'd be now well into his 12th year of the Presidency. And I'd be going to funerals halfway around the world.

But I say these compliments because the President had that unique ability to peek around the corners of history. Look to Berlin, where a wall has crumbled. Look from Kuwait to Panama, where those once enslaved have been set free. President Reagan predicted communism would land in the dustbins of history, called it the "evil empire." And today imperial communism is not merely E–V–I–L, it is D–E–A–D, dead. So, Mr. President, on behalf of all who love freedom—and look at these signs around here from different countries all over the world—we thank you very much.

Now, as the President said, with the cold war over—and let me say this. Let me interrupt here and just say, I see these POW– MIA banners. We must never, ever forget the POW's and MIA's. And I can assure you we're not going to do that.

With the cold war over, we face a world of transition. Last week in Detroit, I talked about some of those economic changes: the defense industry's adjustment to a more peaceful world; the competitive restructuring of our industry; and most important, the globalization of our economy. No State has felt this transition more than California. And I understand that.

My opponent looks at all that is happening and says we are a nation in decline. He says we are ridiculed and that our economy is sliding below Germany, heading south toward Sri Lanka, Sri Lanka. Come on, Governor, stop picking on small southern states who can't help their leaders take them—can't tell where they take them.

You know, Governor Clinton has it wrong, dead wrong. America is not a nation in decline. We are on the rise. And the lights in the shining city will still shine if we but make the right choices today.

Last week I laid out my plan, my agenda for America's renewal, a comprehensive game plan to create a $10 trillion economy by early in the next century. And my agenda keeps faith with the crusade we called the Reagan revolution. It will decrease what Government must do and increase what individuals may do. It shows what the differences are in the 1992 election: two candidates, two philosophies, two agendas, a Grand Canyon of a divide.

And on the one hand—the left hand, naturally—stands my opponent, a man who started in politics with the McGovern campaign——

Audience members. Boo-o-o!

The President. ——a politician nearly all of his adult life, a man who has known virtually no avocation beyond getting elected.

And on the other hand, you're looking at a man proud to have spent half my life in the private sector working for a living, built a business, met a payroll. And from my own experience, I know that Ronald Reagan had it right: The American people aren't undertaxed; the Government in Washington is overfed. If we had more Congressmen like these sitting here, you wouldn't be yelling, "Clean House!", and I wouldn't be having the problems I'm having with this darned Congress. Send us more like these men.

Take a look at how to get the economy moving again. Just last week, Governor Clinton was interviewed by Tom Brokaw. And his first words were advocating a tax increase. He wants at least, listen, he wants at least $220 billion in new spending, $150 billion in new taxes, just to start.

Audience members. Boo-o-o!

The President. His ideas could lead to a

new training tax and a new payroll tax for his health care scheme. They say that President Reagan thought every day was the Fourth of July. Well, Governor Clinton seems to believe that every day is April 15th. And when it comes to taxes, think of him as Willie Brown with a saxophone. We don't need that in Washington, DC.

I want to take America in an entirely different direction. I have a specific plan to cut the growth of mandatory Government spending by almost $300 billion in the next 5 years. We'll get those taxes down, and we'll get this economy moving again.

Audience members. Viva Bush! Viva Bush! Viva Bush!

The President. What about foreign trade? Ronald Reagan's "peace through strength" made the United States the dominant military presence around the world. And now I want to build on that legacy with a strategic network of trade agreements to keep America an export superpower and an economic superpower. That's why we negotiated the North American free trade agreement, to build the world's largest free-trade zone from Manitoba to Mexico, creating hundreds of thousands of new jobs for the working men and women in America.

And my opponent's position on free trade? Well, first he was for it, and then he changed his mind. And now he says firmly: "When I have a definitive opinion, I will say so." Governor Clinton, here's my opinion: Americans never retreat; we will always compete. And we will always win.

Small business, small business is the backbone of the California economy, begging for relief from taxation, regulation, and litigation. Did you know that each year consumers and companies spend up to $200 billion on direct payment to lawyers? Americans want to know: If an apple a day keeps a doctor away, what works with a lawyer? Well, I have a plan to give business and workers relief by getting rid of these crazy lawsuits. And as a nation, we must sue each other less and care for each other more.

My opponent doesn't think this is a problem. Listen to the president of the Arkansas Trial Lawyers Association, and I quote, "I can never remember an occasion where Governor Clinton failed to do the right thing where we trial lawyers were concerned." While Governor Clinton's in the corner sponging the trial lawyer's brow, I want to get in the ring and strike a blow against all those crazy lawsuits.

And another thing. My opponent says that all this talk of family values is irrelevant. And he's been doing a lot of fearmongering lately, talking about how we want to divide America. You know what I mean when I talk about strengthening the American family. I don't mean to go back to the days of Ozzie and Harriet. Families are measured not by "what kind" but "how close." I speak of strengthening the American family because I believe in dealing not with symptoms but with root causes. You ask Governor Wilson or any Governor, any mayor, any teacher, any preacher: The surest way to strengthen America is to strengthen the American family.

And that's why I want parents, not the Government, to choose their kids' day care. And I want parents, not the Government, to choose your kids' schools. And Pete Wilson is right. We need a welfare system that convinces families to stick together and fathers to stick around.

And about the military. Of America's place in the world, Governor Clinton talks the talk, says he's for a strong military. But he walks the walk of the liberals whose idea of high-tech weaponry is the super-soaker squirt gun. And he wants to slash our budget, our defense budget. He wants to cut it $60 billion beyond what the military experts and our civilian experts tell me is right. These cuts would cost as many as one million jobs in defense, especially in California's hard-hit aerospace industry. He also wants to gut one of Ronald Reagan's greatest legacies, the Strategic Defense Initiative. And he shouldn't do that. We can't let him do that.

Maybe Governor Clinton is simply confused about what exactly SDI does. After all, last week you heard him talk about Patriot missiles, the missiles we used to shoot down Saddam's Scud missiles. Here is what Governor Clinton said of our Scud busters: They go through doors or down chimneys. Whoops! That's not the Patriot. The Patriot shoots down other missiles. Governor Clinton may be a Rhodes scholar, but he is no rocket scientist.

And so here it is.

Audience members. Four more years! Four more years! Four more years!

The President. Here's the sum of it. We have a real clear choice in this election: on to the future with conservatives or back to the drawing board with the liberals; to build on the entrepreneurial policies that Ronald Reagan started or to go back to the liberal agenda that made America look finished.

And I know we have big challenges before us. But following Governor Clinton's prescription for our economy would be like going back to the used car lot, picking up the lemon you sold 12 years before. Only this time it would have higher prices from inflation, skyrocketing interest rates for credit, and a hot air bag thrown in. America, this is not a deal for you.

Like the whole world, America is going through an age of transition. But there's clear sailing ahead if we make the right choices today, if we put our faith in our people, not in Government, if we build to the future, not protect the past.

President Reagan taught us many things. And his first lesson was the enduring power of ideas. In America, the best ideas always triumph. And yes, the polls tell me that we're behind today, but on November 3d, I have no doubt we will finish first. We will win it because our ideas are right for America, and our ideas offer the best hope of matching the peace around the world with the peace of mind here at home. If you believe in these ideas, I ask you to join this crusade to renew America, to make this fair Nation safer, stronger, and more secure.

Thank you, and God bless the United States of America. Thank you all very much. You guys did great. Thank you.

Note: The President spoke at 2:25 p.m. at Yorba Regional Park. In his remarks, he referred to entertainers the Gatlin Brothers and to Willie Brown, Jr., speaker of the California State Assembly. A tape was not available for verification of the content of these remarks.

Remarks to Natural Communities Conservation Planning Organizations in San Diego, California
September 14, 1992

Thank you very much, Bill. Please be seated, and thank you all for that warm welcome at this early hour. I'm delighted to be here. And let me just thank Bill Lowery for the introduction. He's been a joy to work with in the United States Congress. He always keeps in mind his constituents, the people that sent him there. But he always has also had a broad national perspective. I've trusted him, and I've worked with him. And I'm going to sorely miss him inasmuch as he's determined not to stand again for election. But he's a good man, and you've been very, very well served. Let me also acknowledge and thank Doug Wheeler here, the secretary of California resources agency. It's great to be back in California. It's great to be here with him who understands the need to find the balance the right way.

Before I begin, though, let me talk about another situation, the one out in Hawaii. Regrettably, some lives have been lost; the property damage is estimated at a billion dollars. Already relief efforts are well underway. Military aircraft and ships are supplying the island with food and water and generators, tents. And some aircraft are being used to carry tourists who want to leave over to the island of Oahu. We continue to work closely with the Governor to provide whatever assistance possible. And our prayers and good wishes are extended to all who stood in Iniki's path. And I just wanted to say that because following on with Florida and Louisiana, it has been a strange month or so for these natural disasters. And a lot of people have been hurt.

I'm proud that the Federal Government has responded, working closely with the three States involved.

You know, we gather at a very important moment in history. Today I can stand before you and say something that no President has ever been able to say before: The cold war is over, and freedom finished first. With the cold war behind us, the global economy is entering a period of transition. And I know that you, particularly in California, but I know our whole country, and I know you all are feeling the impact, feeling it right here in this wonderfully productive part of California.

The question that voters must ask in this election is this: Who has the ideas, the principles to allow America to rise to our new challenges, to guarantee that in the next century America will remain not just a military superpower but also an export superpower and an economic superpower?

Last week I outlined my Agenda for American Renewal, a comprehensive, integrated set of responses to the challenges that are facing America today. And much of the agenda is underway. Other parts are brandnew. I hope that you and every American will take a look at the ideas and then compare them with my opponent's before you make a decision. I start with the belief that free trade can bring prosperity to California and to the United States. That's why I negotiated the North American free trade agreement, or what we call NAFTA. It will create a $6 trillion market from Manitoba to Mexico and bring thousands of new jobs here to California.

And I want to go further. I want to see a strategic network of trade agreements unique to America and the countries of Eastern Europe; then also in the Pacific Rim. My opponent was once in favor of free trade and NAFTA, and then he changed his mind. Now he says, and here's the quote, "When I have a definitive opinion, I'll say so." Listen, my opinion may not be popular in all places, but I will tell it to you straight: Americans will never retreat, and we will always compete. And we will win.

My opponent really believes we need more Government in Washington. He proposes at least $200 billion in new spending plus $150 billion in new taxes, just to start.

Well, I want to go in the opposite direction. I've put forward specific ideas to control the growth of mandatory Federal spending, that's two-thirds of the budget that heretofore has been uncontrolled, saving over $300 billion over the next 5 years. I want to use the savings to cut the tax rates. I believe very simply that Government is too big and we spend too much of your money. And we've got to turn that around.

Let me give you another difference. Today, American businesses and consumers spend up to $200 billion just on direct services to lawyers. The Japanese don't spend that much, neither do the Germans. And my opponent doesn't think this is a problem. I really believe it's a disgrace. As a nation, we must sue each other less and care for each other more.

So look at every economic issue we face, improving our schools, reforming welfare, controlling health costs, and my opponent and I offer two vastly different approaches. He puts his faith, if you'll analyze his program, in more Government. And I want to put more faith in you, the American people. My opponent's plan includes new taxes, plus steep defense cuts way beyond what the military and civilian experts believe is responsible. And together this program will cost America 2.6 million jobs, with a major impact obviously right here in California, right here in San Diego. My agenda doesn't kill jobs, it protects jobs. It guarantees the national security of this country. And it offers a way to get this economy moving and create in America the world's first $10 trillion economy by early in the next century.

Now, as we create jobs we can re-create dreams for so many Americans and so many Californians. But Americans dream of more than a good job and rising income. As Bill pointed out, we also want clean waters in which to swim, clean air to breathe, and preserves like this in which to enjoy nature. And I have long believed that a strong economy and a clean environment not only can go hand in hand but they must go hand in hand. And here in San Diego, you know so well, a clean environment can be the foundation for a dynamic economy. So I am proud of what my administration has accomplished, proud of the many environmental achievements that Congressman Lowery very, very generously talked about.

And I'm especially proud of the way we've been able to make these advances. We've been able to strike a balance between jobs and the environment by rejecting the stale old ideas of command-and-control regulation and relying instead on new ideas and the power of the marketplace, new technology, new kinds of partnerships.

And that's why I really came up here today. We've come together at this historic ranch house, the site of the first land grant in the State of California, to celebrate a voluntary partnership. And frankly, it's an experiment, an effort to preserve species in their critical habitat while still allowing for economic development. The natural communities conservation planning project tries to bring all parties together voluntarily before regulatory approaches kick in and reduce all flexibility. This will help protect endangered species while still allowing for rational and reasonable economic development. It sounds simple. But very few communities are able to pull it off. I congratulate all of you who are involved in this effort. And I hope other communities across this country will take a look at what you are trying to do here.

Partnership is a principle that can work in environmental policy. And another is in using incentives, not expensive regulations, to stop pollution at its source. Let me just give you one example of what I am talking about: We all know that it can stop money for some businesses and factories to comply with the Clean Air Act. And we also know that, by far, the most polluting cars on the road are these clunkers, like the old Dodge Aunt Edna bought in the early sixties before we had real pollution standards. So we came up with a new idea. We let States allow companies to earn credit for meeting the Clean Air Act standards by buying old cars, taking them off the road, and putting them in the scrap heap. UNOCAL tried doing this right here in southern California. Over 8,000 old cars were turned in. The program cut pollution—now, listen to this— that program cut pollution equal to 150,000 new cars, one million gallons of paint, half the carbon monoxide from refineries and

powerplants in greater Los Angeles, and get this, all the barbecue lighter fluids in the LA basin. [*Laughter*] It had that kind of effect. It's the perfect program. Companies can protect jobs, the air becomes cleaner, and old Aunt Edna finally gets rid of the old Dodge in the garage. And now we're going to apply this program nationwide.

We're also trying to encourage the development of technology. Technology has made possible cleaner cars and cleaner factories, more energy-efficient buildings, less wasteful factories. Technology is not just key to our economic future but to our environmental future as well. One of the lessons that we've learned over the past two decades is that command-and-control regulation freezes this, locks this old technology in place. And you need incentives, you need investment to make new breakthroughs possible.

In this administration, we've launched a broad program of investment in new technologies. They clean the environment. They promote energy efficiency and, in the process, can create an entire new industry to employ you and your children. We started a national technology initiative, linking experts in our Federal labs, where all that great research has been going on, with those in the private sector. And already environmental technology has been the focus of 20 of these ventures, with twice that many small businesses participating. As part of our R&D program, we started a partnership with the major auto companies to develop cars that run on batteries, with no air pollution. And we're working toward lighter materials so that everything from airplanes to automobiles will use less energy and create less pollution. We've increased investment in research and development for new ways to produce and use clean-burning natural gas. And perhaps most important, our national energy strategy gets rid of the roadblocks that will allow these technologies to be adopted in the marketplace. These programs all reject the old command-and-control mentality that drove up the costs and reduced jobs and never achieved the environmental progress that we desired. I am very proud of what we've done.

I'll certainly match my environmental record against my opponent. Under Governor Clinton, Arkansas ranks 50th, worst in the country, for utility of State environmental initiatives, according to an independent analysis by the Institute for Southern Studies. But in his zeal to capture his party's nomination, Governor Clinton has made every promise to every environmental group who sent him a survey. He and his running-mate are advancing a philosophy that goes back to where command-and-control regulation is the only solution, a philosophy that will not only cut jobs but could impede technology, environmental progress, not promote it. And when it comes to the environment, I believe extremism on either side is no virtue. Cooperation, innovation, a faith in technology, these are the virtues that will allow us to protect both jobs and nature.

And let me give you another example of my opponent's inconsistency. It refers to the free trade agreement that I mentioned earlier. I strongly support the free trade agreement. But I am sensitive to concerns about its impact on the environment in Mexico and along the border, not far from here, that goes all the way across Arizona and down into Texas. Governor Clinton claims he's concerned, too. In fact, it's one of the reasons he gives to justify his refusal to take a definite position on the treaty. But at the exact same time he talks about his concern about border pollution, his Democratic friends on Capitol Hill are cutting in half my proposed plan to help protect our border environment. When it comes to environment, Governor Clinton seems to be on one side on one day and on another side the next. And I don't, I honestly do not believe that America needs that equivocation. I believe we've struck the right balance. And with your support, I will fight to keep the right balance.

You remember a few years ago when Time magazine selected its Man of the Year? It selected Planet Earth as the Planet of the Year. And Jay Leno said, "Well, what do you expect? All the judges came from Earth." Well, Time's cover and Jay Leno's joke underscores one fact: The environment is the concern of every Californian, of every American. And we can have a strong environment and a strong economy. Indeed, the way I look at it is we must have both.

I began by talking about the globalization of our economy. I really believe that the question of how America can compete is the defining question not just of this election but of our future. I am very optimistic about our future. If we can create new partnerships like this one, and if we can focus more on preventing a problem than fixing it later, and if we can turn our technological prowess to our environmental advantage, then we face a competitive edge that no other nation can match. But the key is achieving a reasonable balance. And if we do it, we can help. We can renew America. We can make our Nation stronger, safer, and more secure. I am absolutely confident that with your support and with these hundred and some new Members of Congress coming in, that we can get the job done.

Thank you. God bless you. And may God bless the United States of America. Thank you all very much.

Note: The President spoke at 8:20 a.m. at Rancho Penasquitos. In his remarks, he referred to comedian Jay Leno.

Remarks to Vaagen Brothers Lumber Employees in Colville, Washington
September 14, 1992

The President. Thank you all very much. What a wonderful welcome. May I thank your very special Senator, Senator Slade Gorton, for that introduction and much more for all he does for this great State back in Washington, DC. You have an outstanding Senator. And thanks to Duane Vaagen and all of the rest of you for letting us visit here today. I know we've disrupted not only this wonderful facility but a lot of things around town. I'm grateful to the Mayor, Mayor Scott, and the police officials and everybody else who assist in the planning and the success of a visit like this.

I'll tell you, I really enjoyed flying in here in that helicopter. For those of you who haven't been up there, there are a lot of trees around here. So don't listen to some of the critics—[*applause*].

You know, last week out in Detroit, I released an Agenda for American Renewal. I see a sign back there on that. The agenda was based on a fundamental premise: that the challenges America faces, foreign, domestic, and economic, and yes, environmental, are connected; they're linked. The solution to one cannot be divorced from the solution to the other. We need an integrated approach.

We need to bring this integrated approach to the relationship between the economy and the environment. Environmental protection and economic growth must go hand in hand; they can't be divorced from each other. This morning down in southern California, I spoke about ways to bring them together. But frankly, I believe that when it comes to the Endangered Species Act and its application here in the Northwest, the balance has simply been lost.

Like many of you, I love to hunt and hike and fish. I love the outdoors. Like you, I have learned through a lifetime of experience to appreciate and respect the wilderness. I know that you, and you who have chosen to live in this beautiful part of the country, respect and revere these forests as others never can. You resent the implication that earning your livelihood here, with sound management of the forest, makes you less of a conservationist than the city dweller or the suburbanite.

I'm proud of this record, although I don't have the endorsement of some of the extreme environmental groups. But for the past 4 years, we've worked hard to protect our precious environment, and we've accomplished a great deal. Four years ago, I promised Americans a new Clean Air Act. For over a decade, no one could get it done, but we did. My Clean Air Act reduces smog in our cities and gets toxic pollutants out of the air and will cut acid rain in half.

Four years ago, I promised I would protect the environmentally sensitive areas off our coasts from the excesses of offshore drilling. Today, there will be no drilling off the coast of California or Washington and Oregon, not far from here, off the Florida Keys, off the New England coast. We have banned ocean drilling until the year 2000.

Four years ago, I promised to be a good steward of our public lands, and we've added thousands of miles of trails for Americans like you who love the outdoors. We're reopening and upgrading campsites all across America. We've added a million and a half acres to our national parks, wildlife areas, forests, and recreation lands.

The fact is that every American cares about the environment, and most consider themselves environmentalists. That is particularly true here in the Pacific Northwest. Yet Americans today realize that we can protect our lands while also using them for people's benefit. They understand the need for wilderness and recreation areas, as well as the need for paper for our schools and offices and timber for new homes.

Being out here in the great Pacific Northwest, I'm reminded of Teddy Roosevelt, the very first President to focus the attention of the Nation on the condition of our natural resources. Teddy Roosevelt once said this, "Wise forest protection does not mean the withdrawal of forest resources from contributing their full share to the welfare of the people." What President Roosevelt had in mind, and what the American people have always wanted, is balance.

Not far from here is a timber town called Forks. Like Colville, Forks supported a mill, and the mill supported a community. Because of a lack of timber, the mill had to close. Today unemployment in Forks is at 20 percent. The car dealership has closed; the clothing store, gone; the movie theater, shut down. Domestic violence complaints have doubled, just in the past year. Forks is in crisis for a simple reason: The balance that I was talking about, that balance has been lost. I've come here because we must restore the balance.

Listen to Oregon's Senator Mark Hatfield, who was a cosponsor of the original Endangered Species Act back in 1972. This year, he wrote, "There is no question that the act is being applied in a manner far beyond what any of us envisioned when we wrote it 20 years ago." The Endangered Species Act was intended as a shield for species against the effects of major construction projects like highways and dams, not a sword aimed at jobs and families and communities of the entire regions like the Northwest.

But today, when harvesting on Federal timberland is stopped outright by 13 different lawsuits, under 7 different statutes, each inconsistent with the other, the balance has been lost. It's time to fight for jobs, families, and communities. The time has come to talk sensibly. When hundreds of mills have been shut down, thousands of timber workers thrown out of work, and revenues for schools and other local services have been slashed, the balance has been lost. It's time to fight for jobs, families, and communities.

So, as I say, we must talk sense about the Endangered Species Act, about the spotted owl, and about the management of our forests, because it is my firm belief that people and their jobs deserve protection, too.

Audience member. What about AIDS?

Audience members. Four more years! Four more years! Four more years!

The President. Let me digress for one minute. Let me digress. This man has asked a question here. I hadn't planned to discuss this. His question is—if you'll listen, sir, I'll explain to you what about AIDS. AIDS is a serious problem. Under my administration we've appropriated $4.3 billion, ten times as much per victim as for cancer. We've asked for $4.9 billion. We are the leaders in research, and we're going to keep on fighting until we get this thing whipped.

Now, let me go back to the Endangered Species Act. And let me be clear. The basic purpose of the Endangered Species Act is good and noble, to save the rare and threatened species of this country. But today, the act and other laws are being used by people with extreme views, particularly here in Washington and Oregon, to achieve in the courts what no sane official would ever have voted for, the complete lockup of the most productive forests in the entire United States.

The Endangered Species Act, as rigidly interpreted by some courts and as driven by the Congress, has forced an extreme approach and created an unnecessarily tragic situation here in the Northwest. Massive areas of Federal land are being set aside for the owl, virtually ignoring the fact that two-thirds of the Northwest's old-growth forests are already designated as parks, wilderness, or other classifications that prevent harvesting. Each pair of owls—listen, America—gets 3,500 acres to itself, while jobs, families, and communities are being wiped out in the process.

The other side has been talking about a "false choice." They claim that this timber crisis is just politics, and the simple fact is this: The false choice is being driven by extremists who are twisting the Endangered Species Act and its application to the northern spotted owl. So I came up here to set the record straight. Let's do that for the entire country, right here. We have always worked within the parameters of the law to address this problem. But I can tell you this: The law is broken, and it must be fixed.

We have asked the United States Congress for funds to cut enough timber in this region to keep people employed. But these conflicting laws allow challenge after challenge. So this year we sent Congress an alternative plan, a preservation plan that would save 17,000 jobs compared to the recovery plan required by the act. And

Congress has simply failed to act.

My friends, it is time to consider the human factor in the spotted owl equation. My opponent talks about putting people first. Well, we can start right here in the Pacific Northwest.

So, here's what I propose. Here's what I propose:

First, I will not sign an extension of the Endangered Species Act unless it gives greater consideration to jobs and to families and to communities, too. I will not sign it without a specific plan in place to harvest enough timber to keep timber families working in 1993 and beyond. It is time to make people more important than owls.

Second, I will fight to end the injunctions that have put an economic stranglehold on the Northwest, in order to free up the timber that we need today, because the families and the timber communities of the Pacific Northwest need relief now. And I call upon Congress to pass my plan to produce 2.6 billion board feet of timber from Forest Service lands in the Northwest region next year and to pass language that prevents lawsuits from stopping reasonable harvests with reasonable species protection. It is time to put people ahead of process.

Third, my administration will speed the harvesting of dead or dying timber that has been dangerously building up during a 7-year drought. One step is our new rule to allow more timber salvage operations to occur without triggering some of the time-consuming requirements that are blocking progress. This will reduce the risk of fire. It'll provide up to 450 million board feet of timber for the mills in the near term. And it's time, then, to protect jobs with timber that's available now.

Fourth, we will make sure that 100 percent of the raw logs from Washington State-owned public lands are processed here. It's time to put the mills back to work.

Finally, I call upon Congress to pass the spotted owl preservation plan, and that's Senator Gorton's bill which he calls "The Northern Spotted Owl Preservation and Northwest Economic Stabilization Act of 1992." It's time to preserve both owls and jobs. That's what Slade Gorton's act does, and he helps the families in the process.

Now, the Senator mentioned my oppo-

nent, so I will, too. [*Laughter*] My opponent's approach to this problem, to your jobs, is double-speak. When Bill Clinton spoke in Pennsylvania, he said what the Sierra Club wanted to hear. They concluded that Governor Clinton was, quote, "promising the protection of old-growth forests in the Pacific Northwest." And then, when he heard I was coming here, Mr. Clinton cynically held out false hope to timber families by promising, get this, another meeting.

There have already been more than 40 bipartisan meetings of the Northwest congressional delegation on this issue for 3 years. Now, here, you wondered what these are? These are the studies. Look at them. We don't need any more studies of this problem. We need action in the United States Congress. Good heavens, we've produced a pile of studies and proposals this high. The best thing for the timber industry is all the trees it took to print these reports. No more studies. Let's change the law. Let's change the law.

The difference on this is clear. The difference on this is clear. It's as simple as this: My opponent will not fight to change the law to restore balance. And now I know that he's getting famous for being on both sides of every issue. Do you want to know the real views of the other ticket? Senator Gore wrote it in black and white in his book before he knew that he'd be looking for your votes.

In his book, Senator Gore said this, and I quote, "I helped lead the successful fight to prevent the overturning of protections for the spotted owl." And Senator Gore wrote, and I quote, "the jobs will be lost anyway." I challenge Governor Clinton: Do you agree with your running mate? Do you endorse the book that you once called "magnificent"?

It is time we worried not only about endangered species but about endangered jobs, jobs in the timber industry and in agriculture, and in transportation and in recreation as well. All of those are threatened by the Endangered Species Act.

I have come here to tell you that I am a candidate who will respect wildlife, yes, but who will also fight for jobs and families and communities. And I have come here to tell you that I will not stand for a solution that puts at least 32,000 people out of work. I can tell you, that solution will not stand.

I have come here to tell you that we haven't forgotten about the human factor. Because in the end, no matter how you look at it, that's the most important factor of all.

I have come here today to tell you that we can restore the balance, and we must

restore the balance. And with your help, we will restore the balance.

Thank you, and may God bless you. And may God bless the United States of America. Thank you all very much. Thank you.

Note: The President spoke at 1:09 p.m. at Vaagen Brothers Lumber, Inc. In his remarks, he referred to Duane Vaagen, president of the company.

Remarks to Burrill Lumber Employees in Medford, Oregon
September 14, 1992

The President. Mike, thank you, sir. Thank you very—He's getting our props ready for this presentation. [*Laughter*] Now, thank you so much, Mike, for the introduction. Thanks to your wonderful dad and to the entire Burrill family and all of you for letting me visit here today.

Last week in Detroit, I released my Agenda for American Renewal. And the agenda was based on a fundamental premise: that the challenges that America faces, foreign, domestic, economic, and yes, environmental, are connected. The solution to one cannot be divorced from the solution to the other, and we need an integrated approach.

We need to bring this integrated approach to the relationship between the economy and the environment, too. Environmental protection and economic growth must go hand in hand, and they cannot be divorced from each other. This morning, I spoke in California, down in San Diego, about ways to bring them together. But frankly, I believe that when it comes to the Endangered Species Act and its application here in the Northwest, the balance has been lost.

Like many of you, I love to hunt and hike and to fish. Like you, I have learned through a lifetime of experience to appreciate and respect the great outdoors, the wilderness. I know that you, you particularly who have chosen to live in these marvelous parts of the woods, respect and revere these forests as others never can. And you resent

the implication that earning your livelihood here, with sound management of the forest, makes you less of a conservationist than the city dweller or the suburbanite.

For the past 4 years, my administration and I have worked hard to protect the environment, and we've accomplished a great deal. Four years ago, I promised Americans a new Clean Air Act. For over a decade, no one could get it done, but we did. Our Clean Air Act reduces smog in our cities and gets toxic pollutants out of the air and will cut acid rain in half.

Four years ago, I promised that I would protect the environmentally sensitive areas of our coasts from the offshore drilling. And today, there is no drilling off the coast of California, off the coasts of Washington and Oregon, and off the Florida Keys and off the New England coast. We banned that ocean drilling until the year 2000.

Then, 4 years ago, I promised to be a good steward of our public lands. We have added thousands of miles of trails for Americans like you who love the outdoors, and we're reopening and upgrading campsites all across this great country. We've added a million and a half acres to our national parks and wildlife areas and forests and recreation lands.

But the fact is that every American cares about the environment, and most consider themselves environmentalists. That is particularly true here in the Pacific Northwest. Yet Americans today realize that we can protect our lands while also using them for the people's benefit. They understand the need for wilderness and recreation areas, as well as the need for paper for our schools and offices and timber for new homes.

Being out here in the great Pacific, the Northwest, I'm reminded of Teddy Roosevelt, the very first President who focused the attention of the entire Nation on the condition of our natural resources. Teddy Roosevelt once said, "Wise forest protection does not mean the withdrawal of forest resources from contributing their full share to the welfare of the people." What President Roosevelt had in mind, and what the American people have always wanted, is balance.

Not far from here, in the State of Washington, is a timber town called Forks. Forks supported a mill, and the mill supported a community. And because of the lack of timber, the mill had to close. Today unemployment in Forks is at 20 percent. The car dealership is closed; clothing store is gone; movie theater, shut down. Domestic violence complaints have doubled, just in the past year. Now, Forks is in crisis for a simple reason: the balance has been lost. I've come here because we must restore the balance.

Listen to one of the Senators, Senator Mark Hatfield, from here, who was a cosponsor of this original Endangered Species Act back in '72. This year he wrote, "There is no question that the act is being applied in a manner far beyond what any of us envisioned when we wrote it 20 years ago." The Endangered Species Act was intended as a shield for species against the effects of major construction projects like highways and dams, not a sword aimed at jobs, families, and communities of entire regions like the Northwest.

But today, when harvesting on Federal timberland is stopped outright by 13 different lawsuits, under 7 different statutes, each inconsistent with the other, the balance has been lost. And it's time to fight for jobs, for families, and for communities. When hundreds of mills have been shut down, thousands of timber workers thrown out of work, and revenues for schools and other local services have been slashed, the balance has been lost. And it's time to fight for jobs, families, and communities.

So the time has come to talk sense about the Endangered Species Act, about the spotted owl, and about the management of our forests, because it is my firm belief that people and their jobs deserve protection, too.

Let me be clear. The basic purpose of the Endangered Species Act is good and noble: save the rare and threatened species of this country. But today, the act and other laws are being used by people with extreme views, particularly here in this State, here in Oregon, to achieve in the courts what no sane elected official would ever vote for, the complete lockup of the most productive forests in the entire United States.

The entire Endangered Species Act, as rigidly interpreted by some courts and as driven by the Congress, has forced an extreme approach and created an unnecessarily tragic situation here in the Northwest. Massive areas of Federal land are being set aside for the owl, virtually ignoring the fact that two-thirds of the Northwest's old-growth forests are already designated as parks, wilderness, or other classifications that prevent harvesting. Each pair of owls gets 3,500 acres to itself. Meanwhile, jobs and families and communities are being wiped out in the process.

The other side has been talking about a "false choice." And they claim that this timber crisis is just politics. The simple fact is this: The false choice is being driven by extremists who are twisting the Endangered Species Act and its application to the northern spotted owl.

Now let's set the record straight. We've always worked within the parameters of the law to address this problem. But I can tell you this: The law is broken, and it must be fixed. And we have asked the Congress for funds to cut enough timber in this region to keep people employed. But these conflicting laws allow challenge after challenge. We convened the "God squad" to exempt 13 timber sales here in southern Oregon from jeopardy opinions from the Fish and Wildlife Service, and every one of those sales is now enjoined. So this year we sent Congress an alternative plan, a preservation plan, if you will, that would save 17,000 jobs compared to the recovery plan required by the act. And Congress has failed to act on

1559

my plan.

My friends, it is time to consider the human factor in the spotted owl equation. My opponent talks about putting people first. Well, we can start right here in the Pacific Northwest.

So here is what I propose:

First, I will not sign an extension of the Endangered Species Act unless it gives greater consideration to jobs, to families, and to communities. I will not sign it without a specific plan in place to harvest enough timber to keep timber families working in 1993 and beyond. It is time to make people more important than owls.

Second, I will fight to end the injunctions that have put an economic stranglehold on the Northwest, in order to free up the timber that we need today, because the families and the timber communities of the Pacific Northwest need relief, and they need it now. I call upon the United States Congress to pass my plan to produce 2.6 billion board feet of timber from Forest Service lands in the Northwest region next year, and at least 500 million board feet on BLM land. And I ask Congress to tie that plan to language that prevents lawsuits from stopping reasonable harvests with reasonable species protection. It is time to put people ahead of process, and the Congress must understand that.

Third, my administration will speed the harvesting of dead or dying timber that has been dangerously building up during a 7-year drought. One step is our new rule to allow more timber salvage operations to occur without triggering some of the time-consuming requirements that are blocking progress. This will reduce the risk of fire, and it will provide up to 450 million board feet of timber for the mills in the near term. In other words, it's time to protect jobs with timber that's available now and put the mills back to work.

Finally, I call upon the Congress today to pass the spotted owl preservation plan. That's the bill sponsored by Senators Packwood and Hatfield and Slade Gorton, which they call "The Northern Spotted Owl Preservation and Northwest Economic Stabilization Act of 1992." It's a long name, but it's a good bill. And it's time to preserve both owls and jobs, jobs in the timber industry

and in agriculture, transportation, and in recreation as well, where they, too, are threatened by this Endangered Species Act.

Now a word about my opponent. My opponent's approach to this problem—and I'll try to be fair—no, but his approach to this problem, to your jobs, really is—and look at the record—double-speak. When he spoke in Pennsylvania, Governor Clinton spoke in Pennsylvania, he said what the Sierra Club wanted to hear. They concluded that Governor Clinton was, quote, "promising the protection of old-growth forests in the Pacific Northwest." And then, when he heard I was coming here, Mr. Clinton cynically held out false hope to timber families by promising another meeting.

There have already been more than 40 bipartisan meetings of the Northwest congressional delegation on this issue for 3 years. Now, look, here are the studies. We've produced a pile of studies and proposals this high. And the only good reason for the timber industry—the only good news is all the trees it took to print all these darn reports. Look at them. And so I say to Governor Clinton: No more studies.

Help me change the law; that's what needs to happen. The difference on this is clear. I will; I will change it. It's as simple as this: My opponent will not fight to change the law to restore balance.

Now I know that Mr. Clinton, and Governor Doublespeak, I call him—[*laughter*]—but nevertheless is getting famous for being on both sides of these issues. But do you want to know the real views of the other ticket? I hate to bring this word up, but Senator Gore——

Audience members. Boo-o-o!

The President. He wrote it in black and white in his book before he knew that he'd be out there pandering for votes. And in his book, Senator Gore said this, and I quote, "I helped lead"—I want to get it right here—"I helped lead the successful fight to prevent the overturning of protections for the spotted owl." And he wrote, and this is an exact quote, "the jobs will be lost anyway." I challenge Governor Clinton: Do you agree with your running mate? Do you endorse the book that you once called "magnificent"? It is time we worried not only about endangered species but about endangered jobs.

I am here to tell you that I'm the one who will respect the wildlife, yes. I think we all do. We all agree. But I'm also the one who will fight for jobs, for families, and for communities.

I have come here to tell you that I will not stand for a solution that puts at least 32,000 people out of work. It will not stand. I mean it.

I've come here to tell you that we haven't forgotten about the human factor. Because in the end, in the final analysis when all the campaigns are over and all the charge and countercharge takes place, the human factor, that is the most important factor of all.

I've come here today to tell you that we can restore the balance. We must restore the balance. And with your help, we will restore the balance.

May God bless your families, your jobs, your hopes for our great country. And may God bless the United States of America. Thank you all very, very much. Thank you. Thank you all.

Note: The President spoke at 6:30 p.m. at Burrill Lumber Co. In his remarks, he referred to company officers Michael Burrill, president and general manager, and Eugene Burrill, owner. The President also referred to the Endangered Species Act Exemption Committee ("God squad").

Remarks to the National Guard Association in Salt Lake City, Utah
September 15, 1992

Thank you all so much. May I first thank General Ensslin for being my host here today, and all of you for that wonderful reception. And of course, I want to single out Utah's Governor, Norm Bangerter, who's just done a superb job for this—[*applause*]. I see we have some Utah Guard folks here. And while you're clapping, Jim Hanson, a Member of the United States Congress, doing a great job for our country. And may I salute all the leaders of the National Guard.

I understand, with some embarrassment, I understand that some of you may have had to go through room changes to—[*laughter*]—sorry about that. I really feel badly about that. I apologize for any inconvenience. But I really am very, very pleased to be here with you.

I was thinking of giving a political speech, a real stemwinder with catchy sound bites, the usual biting insults. Then I got to thinking: I'm not going to do that; you've already sacrificed enough for your country. [*Laughter*]

Instead, I'd like to talk about a more serious subject: America's national defense and, really, our place in the world. I firmly believe that just because we face stiff chal-

lenges at home, and we do, it doesn't mean that America can pull in its wings and ignore the world outside our borders. Think of the world of change that we've seen the past few years. Today, the Berlin Wall, the Warsaw Pact, the Soviet Union itself, Soviet empire, all are gone, swept away by the most powerful idea known to man, the undeniable desire of every individual to be free. Remember the Communists' claim that history was on their side? Well, today, the "dominoes" all fall in democracy's way.

We must recognize these events for what they were: a vindication of our ideals, but also a victory for the men and women who fought for freedom, because this triumph didn't just happen. Imperial communism didn't just fall. It was pushed, and the National Guard was pushing every inch of the way. From Concord and Lexington Green to the sands of Desert Storm, guardsmen or their forefathers have served with distinction in every major war that America ever fought.

In August of 1990, within days of my decision to draw a line in the sand, more than 4,000 volunteers from National Guard units all across America were activated, airborne and on the way to the Persian Gulf, the first of 767 National Guard units called up during Desert Storm. And when American troops rolled across the Iraqi border, and I'll never forget that day, the National Guard was among the very first to cross.

Here at home, when riots ripped South Central, ripped Los Angeles, the California Guard answered the call, 2,000 in just the first 6 hours. You went into the streets to protect the innocent against the outlaws, to restore the peace.

Late last month, when Hurricane Andrew roared in, again the National Guard answered the call, delivering 215 tons of food, water, and supplies to Miami in the first 24 hours alone, helping bring hot meals and comfort to people who had lost their homes. Guardsmen are working right now to bring comfort to the island of Kauai.

You've all seen the pictures of people hugging the Guardsmen in their fatigues. You know one thing for sure; it wasn't to thank them for their cooking. But nevertheless—[*laughter*]—what the Guard is doing in Homestead and Hawaii and in Lafayette Parish is a godsend. It shows us the true meaning of service, of leadership, of love of country.

This is an important task for which the Guard has and will continue to have the primary responsibility and where we only turn to our Active Forces for backup. Indeed, that happened in the Miami situation, as you know. It's happening now out in Hawaii as well. We need to know that the Guard is there, there for the crises at home, there for the challenges abroad, there when a nation in need looks to you to protect life and liberty.

As all of you know, our cold war victory means a downsizing in our national defenses, Active, Reserve, and Guard alike. But we remain committed to our total force concept: the smallest standing army consistent with our national security and yet large enough to deal with any likely threat. For that total force policy to be effective, a strong Army and Air National Guard are absolutely essential.

Let me be clear: Maintaining strong, capable Reserve and Guard forces will remain essential to our military strategy. You are part of the flexible forces we will need to meet our new military challenges. In fact, we can move certain units or functions from Active Forces to the Reserves to lower costs. At the same time, we recognize the need to be sensitive to the demands placed on individual National Guardsmen, Reservists, and really to their families. As true citizen-soldiers, our Guardsmen must devote time to their families, civilian occupations, or education. If we intrude upon you for every trouble, we may find it hard to keep the very best soldiers that characterize the Guard today.

I know that my opponent will be following me today. So you can expect to hear stories about my administration's cutback of the Guard. Of course, the new National Guard will be smaller, just as our Active Forces are being reduced. Anyone who tells you different is simply not leveling with you. But as long as I am President of the United States, the National Guard will be well-trained and well-equipped. And as Commander in Chief I can assure you, we will never shortchange the National Guard.

Yes, I'm cutting back defense spending with the end of the cold war, through orderly and deliberate downsizing. But don't forget the facts. My opponent proposes to cut nearly $60 billion beyond which my civilian and military experts believe is responsible, $60 billion more than the cuts that I have proposed. Now, let me say this: You cannot cut $60 billion more from defense and not touch the Armed Forces. You simply cannot do it.

We have to be very careful with our defense downsizing. At other times in our history, political leaders rushed to carve apart our military—we remember that—leaving only a hollow shell. Then other Americans paid a big price, paid even with their lives, for those mistakes.

The defense budget is more than a piggy bank for folks who want to get busy beating the swords into pork barrels. The President has got to stand up for an America second to none. And he must be able to say: America is safe, as long as America stays strong.

I learned the value of military strength the hard way, and some of you might identify with this, commanders of the Guard units. I learned it the hard way, by sending our troops into battle. I am proud of our accomplishments, thankful that I've been able to give the order so many Presidents longed to give, for many of our nuclear forces to stand down from alert; proud to be the first President in 50 years to lead an America that's not at war, hot or cold.

But the fact is: For all the great gains we've made for freedom, for all the peace of mind that we've secured for the young people in this country, the world remains a dangerous place. The Soviet bear may be extinct, but there are still plenty of wolves in the world: dictators with missiles, narco-terrorists trying to take over whole countries, ethnic wars, regional flashpoints, madmen we can't allow to get a finger on the nuclear trigger. And you have my word on this: I will never allow a lone wolf to endanger American security. We must remain strong.

No, our work in the world did not end with our victory in the cold war. Our task is to guard against the crises that haven't caught fire, the wars that are waiting to happen, the threats that will come with little or no warning. I make this promise: As long as I am President, our services will remain the best trained, the best equipped, the best led fighting forces in the world. This is the way to guarantee the peace.

Let me add something else that's really close to my heart. Even as we respond to the new challenges, we must never forget those who flew and fought in face of the old. The one hero we must never forget is the hero who has never come home. And I pledge to every American family awaiting word of a loved one: We will continue to demand the fullest possible accounting for every POW and MIA. We will not have normal relations with Hanoi until we are totally satisfied on that account.

I speak of these matters this morning to this very special group because these matters are important. They're important to America. They're important to the whole world.

Like every nation, America today is challenged by a global economic transition. I have outlined my Agenda for American Renewal. It's a comprehensive series of actions that we must take to match our military supremacy by remaining the world's largest export superpower and economic superpower. Yet I hope that in our zeal to concentrate on these problems here at home, we do not forget America's unique role abroad. Other nations still look to us for leadership: military leadership, moral leadership, and economic leadership.

As one who has held this office for 4 years, I hope that when evaluating the two men who want this job, Americans will not ignore the President's role as Commander in Chief.

There's been a lot of controversy swirling around about service to country, about using influence to avoid the military. I've read a great deal of speculation saying that I was going to come out here and use this forum to attack Governor Clinton. I want to tell you, I do feel very strongly about certain aspects of the controversy swirling around Governor Clinton, but I didn't come here to attack him. I came to defend and support the National Guard and those who serve in it.

Four years ago, Dan Quayle was savagely attacked and ridiculed by the national press for going into the National Guard. His critics attacked the Guard as a haven for draft dodgers. Those critics are wrong. Dan Quayle spent 6 years in the Indiana National Guard. He was not sent to Vietnam, but some of his fellow Guardsmen were. And four of them never came back.

No candidate has ever been attacked more unmercifully than Vice President Quayle, but he stood his ground, and he answered every question calmly and with candor. He told the truth. This is service to country, and I am very proud of the Vice President, and I am very proud of the National Guard.

But why do these questions even matter? Why are they part of our national debate? They matter because despite all our problems at home, we can never forget that we ask our Presidents to lead the military, to bear the awful authority of deciding to send your sons and daughters in harm's way.

I remember the night of Desert Storm. Barbara and I had Dr. Billy Graham over for dinner there in the White House. And our family—we still say the blessing at night. So we said our little prayer together, enjoyed some conversation, but my mind, I will confess, was thousands of miles away.

And after dinner—I don't know if you can picture the White House complex—I went down the elevator in the White House and then walked across by the Rose Garden over to the Oval Office, waiting to hear the results of the initial strike. I remember walking along the Rose Garden and thinking. I was wondering if our military estimates were really accurate—General McPeak having briefed me in detail, an amazing briefing of what he was confident the Air Force could do—wondering if it was accurate, if our smart bombs were as smart as Tony McPeak and other experts told me they were. But mostly, I wondered how our young men and women in the sands of Kuwait felt and about their parents back home.

In the months after that fateful night, I received letters from proud parents, and I tried to read as many as I could. But I lingered longest on the occasional note from the parent whose son or daughter had not returned.

This summer, I got a letter from a woman in Illinois. And her son had been lost in a helicopter accident, no body ever discovered. On the day she received word, she received a letter from her son. He said, "Mom and Dad, don't worry about me. I love the Marines, and I love my country." And this July, the mother wrote, "As a Gold Star Mother it is difficult to accept my son's death, but he is alive in my heart. And I could be bitter with the military and God, but my son would never want me to."

I know the commanders here know I feel a little emotional about this. But you get letters like these, and you can almost see the faces, faces of youth and innocence. You feel the weight of the job. Sending a son or daughter into combat, believe me, is the toughest part of the Presidency. Most Presidents never learn that lesson because, thank God, most don't have to ask others to put their lives on the line. But every President might.

Does this mean that if you have never seen the awful horror of battle, that you can never be Commander in Chief? Of course not. Not at all. But it does mean that we must hold our Presidents to the highest standard because they might have to decide if our sons and daughters should knock early on death's door.

I hope that I am reelected President this November. Like my opponent, I believe I'm best qualified. But I wish for something else even more. I hope that whomever is elected to this office, at whatever time in the future, he doesn't have to face the awful decision that I had to face twice. I hope that the next 4 years will pass, indeed, I hope that the next four decades will pass without the blood of young Americans being shed on foreign shores.

Today, we can say this future is possible, but no one can say for sure it will happen. So I commit to you, the proud members and families of the National Guard, that as long as I am fortunate to hold this office, I will fight for a strong defense, for a strong America, for an America that, despite our troubles at home, remains the last beacon of hope and strength around the world.

The Guard has always been a proud part of America's world leadership, and I know you'll continue to help us lead in this new world that we have forged together.

Thank you all, and may God bless the United States of America. Thank you very, very much.

Note: The President spoke at 9:03 a.m. at the Salt Palace Convention Center. In his remarks, he referred to Maj. Gen. Robert F. Ensslin, Jr., Ret., president, National Guard Association, and Gen. Merrill A. McPeak, Chief of Staff, U.S. Air Force.

Remarks to Jeppesen Sanderson Employees in Englewood, Colorado
September 15, 1992

The President. Good morning, Colorado. Thank you all. Thank you very much. Frank, thank you, Frank, for that introduction. Greetings to all: Captain Jeppesen and Paul Sanderson; Horst Bergmann; master of ceremonies, Mark, here; Natalie Meyer, our great Colorado secretary of state; and Gale Norton, Colorado's wonderful attorney general. It's great to be with all of them.

And let me salute our party leaders who are here, Bruce Benson, Ed Jones, Mary Daubman, and the rest of the Colorado Republican team. You're doing a great job. And we are going to win this State.

Audience members. Four more years! Four more years! Four more years!

The President. That's the idea. You got it, you got the message. Now, I'm delighted to see such a great crowd, a fantastic crowd. I'm sure you were told that you'd hear from a guy who loves a good fight, loves to be behind, pull it out at the last minute. Unfortunately, John Elway couldn't be here today. [*Laughter*] But I'm proud to be here. It's the beginning of a new era for America. And I'm proud to be the first President to visit Colorado and say, the cold war is over, and freedom finished first.

But this election is about more than the past; it's about the future. It's about what kind of country we're going to leave for the young kids here today. Here's our challenge: In the next century, America must be not only a military superpower but also an export superpower and an economic superpower. This year you're going to hear two very different versions of how we get there. I want to have us look forward, to prepare our kids to compete, to save and invest, and to strengthen the American family. And if we can do this, when it comes to the new challenges of the nineties, America will finish first again. We have and we will do it again.

A Grand Canyon divides me and my opponent on the issues; two candidates, two very different philosophies. You see it in every issue that we care about: education, health care, economic growth, creating jobs.

My Agenda for American Renewal lays out the answers, shows us the way as clear as a Jeppesen dataplan. And that is very, very clear, if you know anything about this company.

I put my trust in the American people, the same people who made this country the greatest economic power the world has ever seen. I want more competition to keep health care costs down. I want more competition, to give parents the power to choose their kids' schools, to make our schools the very best in the entire world. But for my opponent, it doesn't matter what the problem is, he always sees the same solution: He wants more Government mandates, more Government regulations, and more Government burdens on workers and businesses.

Governor Clinton wants to give Government more power. And I want to give you, the American people, more power. Governor Clinton wants to make the bureaucrat's life easy, to provide one-size-fits-all service in schools and in day care. I want you to be able to choose your schools and choose your day care so that we make your lives easier.

Now, business people here might be a little frightened of this one, but my opponent is for what they call an industrial policy, where Government planners decide how high the American economy will go, and if you try to go any further, they'll tax you down to Earth.

Audience members. Boo-o-o!

The President. And I want to unleash the incredible power of entrepreneurial capitalism so you can climb as high as your dreams will carry you. And that's what this debate is about: the role of Government in America. It's not just the difference between big Government and smaller; it's the difference between a big Government that thinks it knows best and a smaller Government that believes you know better. That's the fundamental difference.

And when it comes to taxes and spending, the difference couldn't be more clear. I hold a firm belief that a Government is too big and it spends too much of your money. And my opponent disagrees. Governor Clinton has already called—and get this now—it's in his plan for $200 billion in new spending. And Newsweek magazine says the real total could be 3 times higher. Right out of the box, he wants to raise taxes by $150 billion.

Audience members. Boo-o-o!

The President. And of course, he says he won't tax you. It's always somebody else: big corporations, foreign investors, the rich. He's even come up with a new twist. He's going to tax jobs, a new training tax and a health care system leading to a new 7-percent payroll tax, all to feed the overfed bureaucrats in Washington, DC.

Audience members. Boo-o-o!

The President. I didn't think you'd be enthusiastic about that. They say I think that every day is the Fourth of July. Well, Governor, I do. I do. I believe America's best days are ahead of us. But Governor Clinton seems to believe that every day is April 15th. And his tired old tax-and-spend philosophy is wrong for this country. We all know that because it's been tried before. And it would be like going back to the used car lot, picking up the lemon that you sold 12 years ago. Only this time it would have higher prices on it from inflation, skyrocketing interest rates for credit, and a hot air bag thrown in. [*Laughter*] America, this is not the deal for you.

Now, I want you to listen closely to him this fall, but you're going to do that, because on issue after issue, he takes one position and then another. He's been spotted in more places than Elvis Presley on these issues. [*Laughter*] Let me give you some specifics. Take the issue, the question of whether to stand up to Saddam Hussein, the defining test of American leadership in the post-cold-war world. Two days after Congress followed my lead—and I had to fight to get them to do that—he said, and I quote, "I guess I would have voted with the majority if it was a close vote. But I agree with the arguments the minority made."

Audience members. Boo-o-o!

The President. Maybe that's why he wants an Oval Office—he spends all his time running around in circles. [*Laughter*] You cannot do that. Being President, the buck

stops there. You can't be on all sides of every question. And when you're in that Oval Office, and when American lives are at stake, you can't take time out to check the latest opinion polls. I had to make the tough decision, and I'm proud of what America did in Desert Storm. And we did the right thing.

How about one of the defining issues of the next 4 years: Whether we're going to continue to open new markets, tap new consumers around the world so we can create more jobs here at home, right here in Colorado, right here at Inverness. I know Americans aren't afraid of competition, because when we compete fairly, we win. And where does Governor Clinton stand? It depends on who he's standing in front of. Sometimes he's for opening markets. But when he talks to the protectionist lobby, he whips out his saxophone and plays a different tune. They asked him about our new plan to open markets in Mexico, and here's what he said: "When I have a definitive opinion, I'll say so." You figure it out. Before he went to the labor unions, he was for the free trade agreement. And when he went there, he had serious reservations. On free trade he backpedals faster than Karl Mecklenburg. [*Laughter*]

And I am going to continue to fight for new markets because, don't kid yourself, the American worker can still outcompete, outthink, and outcreate anyone in the entire world. And there's something else I want to do. I want to get rid of all these crazy lawsuits. They are costing our economy up to $200 billion in a single year. And I think that's crazy. Somebody asked me the other day, "An apple a day keeps the doctor away, what works for lawyers?" [*Laughter*]

Now, my opponent doesn't think this is a problem. You've got Little League people that can't coach who are worried about suits. You've got doctors afraid to deliver babies. You have people out there doing good works, good Samaritan works on the highway, afraid they'll get sued if they stop to help somebody.

Now, here's what the head of the Arkansas Trial Lawyers Association said, and I quote: "I can never remember an occasion where he"—and that's Governor Clinton—"failed to do the right thing where we trial lawyers are concerned." I don't want to do the right thing for the trial lawyers. I want to do right for the American people. And we have got to sue each other less and care for each other more.

So these are some of the things that I'm fighting for. And you'd give me a big hand if you'd give me legislators in Washington who share our vision of America. Give me Bryan Day and Ray Aragon in the U.S. House of Representatives. And do me a special favor. You have a special candidate for the U.S. Senate, the father of the term-limit movement, Terry Considine. And he understands that Government exists to serve the people, not the other way. Give me Terry in the United States Senate, and watch us move this country forward.

You see, I don't think America is a vast collection of interest groups to be appeased, the trial lawyers over here, big labor over there, environmental extremists on the other side, each clamoring for favors from Washington bureaucrats. I believe we are a nation of special individuals, not special interests. And I believe our genius lies in our people, in our families, in our communities, not in the Government.

In this election I'm asking for a mandate to return power to the people, to let Government give you the means and then give you the chance to do it your way. And if

you believe in this mandate, if you believe in these ideas, then I ask you to pull together. For the next 49 days, I ask you to join me and fight for free trade, fight for great schools, fight for giving power to the people.

The polls may show us behind today, but I know we are going to be ahead in November because we have the right ideas. We've done a lot. These young kids don't go to bed at night with the same fear of nuclear weapons and nuclear war that their brothers had or their sisters had. And that is good. That is good. And we have the right ideas to renew America, to make America stronger, safer, and more secure.

Thank you. And may God bless the United States of America. Thank you all very much.

Note: The President spoke at 12:28 p.m. at Jeppesen Sanderson, Inc., in the Inverness Business Park. In his remarks, he referred to company officers Frank Kotulak, project leader, Elrey B. Jeppesen and Paul Sanderson, cofounders, and Horst Bergmann, president and chief executive officer; Mark Bohne, president, Arapahoe County Republican Men's Club, and vice president of public affairs, South Metro Denver Chamber of Commerce; Bruce Benson, Republican State chairman; Ed Jones, State cochair, Bush-Quayle '92; and Mary Daubman, Republican national committeewoman-elect.

Remarks to Sandia National Laboratories Employees in Albuquerque, New Mexico
September 15, 1992

Thank you for that welcome. Thank you so very much. And it's a joy to be introduced by your great Senator, Pete Domenici, steadfast, loyal supporter of the people that sent him to Washington. He knows how he got elected, and he hasn't forgotten. And he does something unique. He votes the way in Washington that he talks in New Mexico, making him quite different than many Members of the United States Senate. And so he's doing a great job for the people

of this State.

I'm also pleased to see two of our Cabinet members here: Secretary Manuel Lujan, a former Congressman from New Mexico, great American; and of course, Jim Watkins, former Chief of Naval Operations, now our Secretary of Energy; both doing a superb job in our Cabinet. And may I salute Steve Schiff and Joe Skeen. If we had more Members of Congress like them everybody wouldn't be yelling at me, "Clean House!"

We've got two good ones right here. And Bruce Twining, the manager of the Department of Energy's Albuquerque office; and let me also especially thank Al and Sig, my two hosts here today. I love that plowshare, I love it. And it's a wonderful thing when you can think what it really signifies. It will have a special place in any library that I'm associated with in the future.

It's great to be back in Albuquerque, this beautiful city, and I understand that you'll host the International Hot Air Balloon Fiesta. I'll leave it to you to decide whether the Presidential candidates should be invited. [*Laughter*]

But I came here today to talk a little bit about the future. And it's really your future. But before I look ahead, a word of thanks for the past, because I can stand before this wonderfully productive and patriotic audience this afternoon and say something no President has ever said before: The cold war is over, and freedom finished first. Where was the cold war won? Well, it was won along the trenches of Korea, on the training fields of our military academies, and inside the pockets of our taxpayers who dug deep and spent $4 trillion over four decades to keep the Soviet bear at bay. But the cold war was won in other places, like right here in Sandia and up on the hill in Los Alamos. And let me quote someone who I'm not in the habit of quoting very often, Leonid Brezhnev. Speaking at the height of the cold war, Brezhnev said, and I quote, "At the present stage, problems of scientific technological progresses are acquiring, quite frankly, decisive importance." Now, I admit that's not exactly the most memorable statement ever made. It's not exactly going to compete with "You got the right one, baby." But Mr. Brezhnev was right: All the courage, all the sacrifice, all the wealth in the world would not have made a difference had we not had scientists on our side.

And so I've come here today on behalf of all Americans, on behalf of all who love freedom, to say thanks to you, thanks to the men and women of Lawrence Livermore, Los Alamos, and Sandia. You were the scientific saviors of the free world. Now you are in the forefront of our effort to help ensure the safe and secure dismantling of former Soviet nuclear warheads. With the historic agreements I've reached with Boris Yeltsin, I know you're awfully busy lately. And yet, although we are now reducing our nuclear forces dramatically, a safe and reliable deterrent remains essential to our national security. Let's not kid ourselves: The Soviet bear may be gone, but there are still plenty of wolves in the woods. And those wolves could turn into full-fledged, fire-breathing dragons if they acquire nuclear capability. And I make this promise: I will never let these threats endanger our kids' security.

In July, I announced a comprehensive strategy to stem the spread of weapons of mass destruction and discourage the use. Today I want to take the next step. With the cold war over, we can do with a smaller nuclear stockpile. And with a smaller stockpile, we need smaller amounts of tritium, an essential ingredient in nuclear weapons. Today I am announcing the immediate deferral of the Department of Energy's billion-dollar program to build a new production reactor for tritium. But the safety of our children is paramount. So I will ask the Congress to redirect $166 million to support the nuclear nonproliferation initiative I announced in July through work done at national laboratories like Sandia. You and your colleagues will develop new technologies to detect and prevent the spread of weapons on land, at sea, and in space. And once again, your scientific brilliance will help make sure that our children sleep soundly and dream the sweet dreams of peace.

Also today I'm asking Congress to reallocate $250 million in funds for the Department of Defense procurement items to provide an increase in research and advance technology programs through DARPA. This research in communications, supercomputers, and manufacturing technology will help protect our national security and strengthen our civilian technology. And by the way, it will employ the talents and skills of more than 3,000 scientists and engineers.

You see, the end of the cold war brings more than new security challenges. It's brought a period of global economic transition. And I know you're feeling the impact right here in New Mexico. But while some will tell you America's in decline, I say the best days are yet to come. The defining challenge of our age is to win the new economic competition, to make sure that in the 21st century America remains not just a military superpower but an export superpower and an economic superpower.

Last week I laid out my Agenda for American Renewal, a comprehensive, integrated strategy to respond to the challenges of this new, more competitive world. My agenda has six parts to start. I want to aggressively pursue free trade agreements with other nations, because American workers never retreat; we always compete. And we will win.

I have a program already well underway to revolutionize our schools. Somebody was asking, what about education? Well, let me say this: You tell me why a nation that can make smart bombs cannot produce the smartest kids in the entire world. I want to sharpen the competitive edge in education. And we can do it.

I want to sharpen the edge of American business, especially small business. And that means relief from taxation, regulation, and yes, litigation.

American men and women deserve economic security. For example, I have a plan to make health care available to every working American and to cut costs through competition. The way I see it, you should only feel the pain in your head when you're at the doctor's office, not 2 months later when you get the bill at home.

America in the 21st century cannot afford to leave anyone behind. And so we need a welfare system that encourages families to stick together and fathers to stick around.

And lastly, but not in the least, we need to change the only institution in our society that has been resistant to change for so many years: the Federal Government, and the United States Congress included. And I have a plan to limit the growth of mandatory Federal spending and save almost $300 billion over the next 5 years. But while we set priorities, Government can still have an important role in responding to the challenges of a new economy.

Look what's going on right here. I got a little bird's-eye view of that in this tour I've just had at the labs right here in Sandia. The same scientific talents that won the cold war are now being put to use in the new economic competition, as we strengthen our high-tech manufacturing base, as we improve our productivity and create the high-paying jobs of the future for you and your kids. I just had a tour of your lab, and I must say I was deeply impressed by what is going on here, especially with your robotics operation. I'm just waiting for one of you to come up with a robot that can give a public speech. I'm sure it will make my life easier and also yours. And I won't ask the national press to touch that one with a 10-foot automated pole.

Listen, inside these labs you're teaching American business how to manufacture, how to take the lead in building new industries of the 21st century. And just as important, you are leading the way to a clean environment. Some say the only way to clean our air and water is with regulation, Government keeping an iron arm on business. And I say there must be a better way. In these walls and at Los Alamos you are devising new technologies in waste reduction and environmentally conscious manufacturing. These technologies will allow us to manufacture products without pollution and achieve the elusive but important balance of good jobs and a clean environment for our children.

So your work is one part of our advanced manufacturing initiative: investing a billion dollars in labs across this Nation to build new industries. And we're fighting to reform the antitrust laws to allow R&D cooperatives to make their research and development tax credit permanent, to expand the small-business innovation research program and regional technology alliances, and to streamline controls on American exports. And every one of these programs is intended to build a sturdy foundation for our 21st century economy. And so if you hear a certain young and energetic Governor saying that we need a strategy to encourage manufacturing, maybe you can bring him here, bring him here to Sandia to show him that the future has already begun. You are doing this right now here in these labs.

You see, here's my belief: If we're going

to reap the fruits of a high-tech harvest tomorrow, we have to plant the seeds today. Our great national labs like Los Alamos and Sandia are working in partnership already with businesses large and small to take ideas from the lab right to the marketplace. And I want to encourage this. That's why my budget for 1993 includes $76 billion for research and development, a record amount. We are investing in basic research: programs like the National Science Foundation, whose budget I've said we must double by 1994; and in health and agricultural research; in projects like the superconducting super collider and the human genome project, through which we can revolutionize our understanding of biology and health care. And we're making a renewed commitment to applied research, spending the process—speeding that up from when the scientist in the laboratory says "Aha!" to when the consumer in the store says, "I want to buy that." We have special programs underway in high-performance computing, space exploration, the advanced materials sciences, and biotechnology. And we are setting priorities, holding the line on money in other areas of Government spending so that we can turn the scientific prowess of America away from creating weapons of mass destruction to creating new industries for mass employment.

Now, Pete Domenici will tell you that not everyone shares our sense of priority, this loyalty to the future. There are many Members of the Congress, mainly on the liberal side, whose idea of robotics is how they mechanically move to satisfy the special interests. And these Members are constantly cutting our investments in tomorrow, to keep dollars pumping into the pork barrel projects today. So let them, let those liberals in Congress keep trying to divert tax dollars away from research and development. I am going to keep fighting for science and fighting for our economic future.

I know this is a time of anxiety in America. Tough questions are being asked around dining room tables. But we have confronted much tougher challenges in our history, and we've won. America is always on the rise because of our incredible capacity for rebirth, regeneration, and renewal. Look what's going on right here at Sandia, the power of science turned in a new and more productive direction. If I were our economic competitors, I'd be trembling in my boots, if I knew what was going on in these great labs.

Almost a 100 years ago, Teddy Roosevelt led America through a period of transition much like this one, another time when the cynics asked, will tomorrow be as good as today? And Teddy Roosevelt said, "We look across the dangers of the great future, and we rejoice as a giant refreshed. But great victories are yet to be won. The greatest deeds yet to be done." You helped bring peace to the world. Look at your work that way. You helped bring peace to the world. And now we turn our energy to a new deed: to build new industries and new jobs and create peace of mind here at home. For you and your colleagues across America, there are new deeds to be done. There are more victories to be won.

So thank you very much for your hard and dedicated work for your country. Thank you for listening. And may God bless the United States of America, the greatest country on the face of the Earth. Thank you very much. Thank you all. Keep up the great work.

Note: The President spoke at 5:07 p.m. at the laboratory. In his remarks, he referred to Albert Narath, president, Sandia National Laboratories, and Siegfried Stephen Hecker, director, Los Alamos Laboratory. Mr. Narath gave the President a plowshare sculpted out of material from a dismantled nuclear weapon.

Statement by Press Secretary Fitzwater on Transmittal of Appropriations Requests to the Congress
September 15, 1992

The President today announced his intention to transmit to the Congress budget amendments for the Department of Defense that would reallocate $250 million of the Department's FY 1993 request to Defense advanced-technology programs. The reallocated funds would be used in the areas of communications, high performance computers, small satellites, sensors to identify environmental contamination, and manufacturing technology. These areas are essential to national security and also have dual-use civilian applications. The funds for these advanced-technology programs would be reallocated from lower priority Defense programs.

Appropriations language was also request-

ed to increase the United States FY 1993 contribution to the Asian Development Bank by $25.5 million. This additional contribution is necessary to maintain United States voting parity with Japan in the Bank. The increased FY 1993 budget authority for the contribution to the Bank would be fully offset by a reduction in the United States contribution to the Asian Development Fund.

The President also transmitted an FY 1992 supplemental appropriations request for the legislative branch. As required by law, appropriations requests for the legislative branch must be transmitted without change.

Remarks and an Exchange With Reporters on Family Leave Legislation
September 16, 1992

The President. One of the things we're going to be talking about here today is family leave. I am very proud of what we have already accomplished for families. We all know the issues on that. We have a child care plan that puts the power in the hands of families and parents, not bureaucrats. We let the family choose their child care and not the Government. We should provide an equally flexible approach to family and medical leave.

I favor family and medical leave, always have. But the real question is how do we achieve that goal? Now the Democrats are sending me a bill. It's been timed for politics. They've been sitting on it for a whole year. It takes one different—approach different from ours.

Unfortunately, they and my opponent believe in a Government-dictated mandate that increases costs and loses jobs. Every Governor that comes in here says, "Please don't create more mandates." But now

they're sending me a mandated program.

Our alternative is to provide a family-oriented solution in the form of a tax credit for small and medium-sized businesses. Our approach both encourages companies to adopt family leave policies and gives them the flexibility to target the specific needs of their employees.

My tax credit approach, and we have it in a bill, has another great big advantage. The Democrat bill covers only businesses with more than 50 employees, leaving out the millions of employees of small firms, those the least likely to get leave. Our solution would provide an incentive to all small and medium-sized companies to provide this important benefit. So, in fact, I think our approach has a broader coverage and includes those most in need.

So I would like to suggest if people are really interested in getting family leave done, and I am, that the Democratic leadership go to work on this. It can be done very, very quickly, and it will not cause a loss of jobs, something that concerns me very much in this small-business arena. We're trying to help small business, not mandate them so that, whether they want to or not, they have to lay people off.

So I would like to see immediate action on this. There's an awful lot of politics at play here. But here's an approach that for those that want family leave can do it; those who are opposed to mandates, as I am and many, many other people are across this country, they can support this very nicely.

So that's where we'd like——

Q. Mr. President, do you know how much it would cost and how would you pay for it?

The President. Well, we're going to be discussing that with the leaders. There are some $60 billion that OMB knows about where we can allocate to this. But that has to all be negotiated out, depending on the size of it and all.

Q. So you are going to veto the bill?

The President. Well, I've sent a veto signal for a long, long time on this. It's just odd that now, after a year up there, it shows up down here 2 weeks before the adjournment of this session. I find that very

peculiar and highly political.

So I'll stay with my past position here. If there's some last minute compromise that can be worked out on existing legislation, fine. I don't see it. Our people, Nick Calio and all, have been struggling very had to try to get something done on family leave that is not a mandate. And therein lies the key.

Q. You didn't offer this bill the last time you vetoed family leave.

The President. Well, we've been trying to work with the Congress to try to get something done. Now here's a clean approach that those who really want family leave should take a look at.

Thank you. Hey, listen, I've got to go to work here. Thank you all very much.

Q. Are you going to be in Lansing on Tuesday?

The President. I don't know where I'm going to be Tuesday. That's a long way away.

Note: The President spoke at 8:15 a.m. in the Cabinet Room at the White House prior to a meeting with Republican congressional leaders. In his remarks, he referred to Nicholas E. Calio, Assistant to the President for Legislative Affairs.

Message to the Congress Transmitting Proposed Family Leave Tax Credit Legislation
September 16, 1992

To the Congress of the United States:

I am pleased to transmit for your immediate consideration and enactment the "Family Leave Tax Credit Act of 1992". This flexible family leave plan will enable 80 percent of the workplaces in the country—the small and mid-sized businesses that often cannot provide family leave—to provide family leave for their employees without costing jobs or stifling economic growth. The proposal will cover 15 million more workers, and 20 times as many workplaces, than the proposals in S. 5.

This legislation will provide a refundable tax credit for up to 20 percent of total com-

pensation, for up to $100 a week—to a maximum of $1,200—for businesses that provide their employees with 12 weeks of family leave. An employee would be eligible to take leave under the following circumstances: the birth of a child, the placement of a child with the employee for adoption or foster care, care for a child, parent, or spouse with a serious health condition, or a serious health condition that prevents the employee from performing his or her job.

This is not federally mandated leave. It instead gives employers positive incentives to adopt responsible family leave policies and gives them the flexibility to target the specific needs of their employees. To qualify for the credit, businesses must adopt nondiscriminatory policies that provide protections for employees' jobs, benefits, and health insurance.

On May 5, 1992, the Administration transmitted the "Health Benefits for Self Employed Individuals Act of 1992" to the Congress. This proposal was also intended to help improve benefits for small businesses, without deterring economic growth, by expanding the deductibility of health insurance from 25 percent of costs to 100 percent of costs. Packaged with the Family Leave Tax Credit, we are providing a strong impetus for small businesses to develop quality benefits programs.

The Department of the Treasury has estimated the cost of the Family Leave Tax Credit at approximately $500 million for FY 1993 and $2.7 billion over 5 years. The combined cost of the Family Leave Tax Credit and the "Health Benefits for the Self Employed" is $740 million in 1993 and $7.7 billion over 5 years. These costs must be offset under the Budget Enforcement Act of 1990. In my 1993 Budget, I identified $68.4 billion of specific mandatory spending reductions. Any of those offsets would be acceptable to the Administration. Additionally, when the self employed tax credit was transmitted to the Congress, over $9.3 billion of these offsets were specifically suggested to pay for the proposal—substantially more than was required. Those same $9.3 billion in offsets are sufficient to pay for the costs of both the self employed deduction and the Family Leave Tax Credit under the Budget Enforcement Act of 1990.

I urge the Congress to take prompt action to generate constructive family leave policies that are consistent with economic growth by quickly passing this legislation.

GEORGE BUSH

The White House,
September 16, 1992.

Message to the Congress Transmitting a Report on United States Government Activities in the United Nations
September 16, 1992

To the Congress of the United States:

I am pleased to transmit herewith a report of the activities of the United States Government in the United Nations and its affiliated agencies during the calendar year 1991, the third year of my Administration. The report is required by the United Na-

tions Participation Act (Public Law 264, 79th Congress; 22 U.S.C. 287b).

GEORGE BUSH

The White House,
September 16, 1992.

Message to the Congress Transmitting the Report on Aeronautics and Space
September 16, 1992

To the Congress of the United States:

It is with great pleasure that I transmit this report on the Nation's achievements in aeronautics and space during 1991, as required under section 206 of the National Aeronautics and Space Act of 1958, as

amended (42 U.S.C. 2476). Not only do aeronautics and space activities involve 14 contributing departments and agencies of the Federal Government, as reflected in this report, but the results of their ongoing research and development affect the Nation as a whole.

Nineteen hundred and ninety-one was a significant year for U.S. aeronautics and space efforts. It included eight space shuttle missions and six successful launches by the Department of Defense. The shuttle missions included the first such mission to focus on astrophysics and the first dedicated to life sciences research. Other shuttle missions included launch of one satellite to study the unexplored polar regions of the Sun and another to collect astronomical data from gamma ray sources. Still another shuttle mission launched a satellite to study global atmospheric change affecting our own planet. In related areas, the Department of Commerce and other Federal agencies have pursued studies of such problems as ozone depletion and the greenhouse effect. Also here on Earth, many satellites launched in 1991 and earlier provid-

ed vital support for the successful prosecution of Operations Desert Shield and Desert Storm to force Iraq to withdraw from Kuwait. And in the aeronautical arena, efforts have ranged from the further development of the National Aero-Space Plane to broad-ranging research and development that will reduce aircraft noise and promote the increased safety of flight.

Thus, 1991 was a successful year for the U.S. aeronautics and space programs. Efforts in both areas have promoted significant advances in the Nation's scientific and technical knowledge that promise to improve the quality of life on Earth by increasing scientific understanding, expanding the economy, improving the environment, and defending freedom.

GEORGE BUSH

The White House,
September 16, 1992.

Letter to Congressional Leaders Reporting on Iraq's Compliance With United Nations Security Council Resolutions
September 16, 1992

Dear Mr. Speaker: (Dear Mr. President:)

Consistent with the Authorization for Use of Military Force Against Iraq Resolution (Public Law 102-1), and as part of my continuing effort to keep the Congress fully informed, I am again reporting on the status of efforts to obtain Iraq's compliance with the resolutions adopted by the U.N. Security Council.

Since the events described in my report of July 16, 1992, Coalition members have decided upon further measures to implement Security Council Resolution 688, which requires Iraq to end the repression of its civilian population immediately, to allow immediate access by international humanitarian organizations to all parts of Iraq, and to make available all facilities for the operation of these organizations. Far from complying with Resolution 688, in recent months Saddam has increased his repression of the civilian population in both the northern and southern parts of the country. In

southern Iraq, according to U.N. Human Rights Commission Rapporteur Max Van der Stoel, Iraqi authorities use jet fighters, helicopter gunships, and scorched earth methods and have drained marshlands, thereby depriving residents of food and leaving them vulnerable to military repression. United Nations workers in southern Iraq, harassed by Iraqi officials, have been unable to learn fully the extent of Iraqi repression.

Members of the Coalition have reviewed means available to assist the United Nations in monitoring Iraqi compliance with Resolution 688. The Iraqi Foreign Minister has informed the United Nations that Iraq would not accept U.N. monitors. The Coalition has decided to begin aerial reconnaissance of southern Iraq to monitor the situation. Moreover, the Coalition has announced that Iraqi aircraft and helicopters will not be permitted to fly south of the 32d parallel. This "no-fly zone" is similar to that established in northern Iraq as part of Operation Provide Comfort and will include expanded monitoring of southern Iraq from the air. As in northern Iraq, United States, British, and French Coalition forces are enforcing the no-fly zone south of the 32d parallel. As a result of the no-fly zone, Iraqi use of aircraft to conduct repression of the civilian population in the region, in particular the bombing of citizens around marsh areas, has stopped.

I have ordered U.S. participation in the enforcement of the no-fly zone and expanded aerial surveillance of southern Iraq under my constitutional authority as Commander in Chief and consistent with the Authorization for Use of Military Force Against Iraq Resolution (Public Law 102–1).

Since the events noted in my last report, the U.N. Special Commission on Iraq (UNSCOM) has continued to investigate Iraq's weapons of mass destruction (WMD) program and to verify the destruction of relevant facilities, equipment, and weapons. The most recent ballistic missile inspection, August 8–18, 1992, found new information on Iraq's ballistic missile program, including confirmation that facilities not previously reported by Iraq were involved in that program. (In July 1992, Iraq had provided what it called a "full, final, and complete" report on its WMD program; as subsequent inspections have revealed, this report is incomplete. U.N. Security Council Resolution 687 required that Iraq provide a full report in April 1991.) The 14th nuclear inspection team, from August 31–September 7, verified the destruction and rendering harmless of facilities and equipment at Ash Sharqat and Tarmiya, two mirror-image facilities for uranium enrichment, and made arrangements for the destruction of remaining facilities. It also began water sampling of Iraqi rivers, to measure any level of radioactivity that might indicate an operative water-cooled reactor nearby. Regular inspections of declared and suspected sites will continue.

These inspection efforts have been subjected to Iraqi interference. Most notoriously, Iraqi authorities refused to admit an UNSCOM team into the Agriculture Ministry for three weeks, even though Resolution 687 requires that Iraq permit "urgent" inspections of any location designated by UNSCOM and Security Council Resolution 707 requires Iraq to allow immediate and unrestricted access to any such area. When the inspection took place, it appeared that information had been removed from the Ministry and files altered. In the weeks before entering the Agriculture Ministry, UNSCOM inspectors suffered petty acts of harassment, demonstrations by large crowds that appeared likely to become violent, vandalism of vehicles, and armed attacks; subsequent inspection teams have also been harassed. For a short time, Iraqi officials voiced opposition to the participation of Coalition members in UNSCOM inspections. They have also said that they will deny UNSCOM access to government ministries.

The Security Council and Coalition members have responded to each Iraqi interference with diplomatic means. We have been prepared to employ stronger measures, however, and our resolve has played a crucial role in obtaining Iraqi compliance. We will remain prepared to use all necessary means, in accordance with U.N. Security Council resolutions, to assist the United Nations in removing the threat posed by Iraq's chemical, biological, and nuclear weapons capability.

UNSCOM continues to face a shortage of funds. We have recently contributed $30 million, bringing our contributions to a total of over $40 million since UNSCOM's inception. We have persuaded other nations to contribute as well and expect at least $30 million in additional contributions to reach UNSCOM in the next several months. More funding will be necessary, however.

Following increasing Iraqi challenges to the work of the Iraq-Kuwait Boundary Demarcation Commission, Iraq informed the Secretary General that it would no longer participate in the Commission's work. Its announcement does not affect the Commission's competence under Security Council Resolution 687. On July 24, the Commission made a further report to the U.N. Secretary General describing its findings on the land boundary between Iraq and Kuwait. On August 26, in Resolution 773, the Security Council welcomed the Commission's decisions and underlined its guarantee of the inviolability of the boundary and its decision to take all necessary measures to that end. The physical demarcation of the land boundary is expected to be completed by the end of the year. In addition, in October the Commission plans to renew its consideration of the offshore boundary.

Since my last report, the U.N. Compensation Commission has continued to prepare for the processing of claims from individuals, corporations, other entities, governments, and international organizations that suffered direct loss or damage as a result of Iraq's unlawful invasion and occupation of Kuwait. The next session of the Governing Council of the Commission is scheduled in Geneva September 21–25, 1992, with a further meeting in December.

At an informal meeting on August 7, the Governing Council discussed the continuing serious financial difficulties confronting the Commission. These difficulties persist, despite a $2 million dollar loan from the Kuwaiti Government, received in June, and an additional $1 million dollars from the United States, which was noted in my last report. The Commission must now develop computer software and services needed to process claims, at an estimated one-time cost of $2.8 to $6.6 million and an annual cost of about $1.2 million. Unless funding is found immediately, the Commission's financial difficulties threaten to delay or halt the entire compensation process.

Meanwhile, the Commission has released to governments the forms for claims by governments and international organizations (Form F). On July 6, the Department of State distributed the forms for claims by corporations and other entities (Form E) to over 500 potential U.S. claimants. The Department also continues to collect and review over 1,500 claims received from individuals and has scheduled its next filing of such claims with the Commission in September.

In accordance with paragraph 20 of Resolution 687, the Sanctions Committee has received notices that approximately 3.1 million tons of foodstuffs have been shipped to Iraq thus far in 1992. The Sanctions Committee also continues to consider and, when appropriate, approve requests to send to Iraq materials and supplies for essential civilian needs. Iraq, in contrast, has for months maintained a full embargo against its northern provinces. Iraq has also refused to utilize the opportunity under Resolutions 706 and 712 to sell $1.6 billion in oil, most of the proceeds from which could be used by Iraq to purchase foodstuffs, medicines, materials, and supplies for essential civilian needs of its population. The Iraqi authorities bear full responsibility for any suffering in Iraq that results from their refusal to implement Resolutions 706 and 712.

Through the International Committee of the Red Cross (ICRC), the United States, Kuwait, and our allies continue to press the Government of Iraq to comply with its obligations under Security Council resolutions to return some 800 detained Kuwaiti and third-country nationals. Likewise, the United States and its allies continue to press the Government of Iraq to return to Kuwait all property and equipment removed from Kuwait by Iraq. Iraq continues to withhold necessary cooperation on these issues and to resist unqualified ICRC access to detention facilities in Iraq.

I remain grateful for the support of the Congress for these efforts and look forward to continued cooperation toward achieving our mutual objectives.

Sincerely,

GEORGE BUSH

Note: Identical letters were sent to Thomas S. Foley, Speaker of the House of Representatives, and Dan Quayle, President of the Senate.

Statement on the Death of Millicent Fenwick
September 16, 1992

I was saddened to learn of the death of former Representative Millicent Fenwick of New Jersey. Mrs. Fenwick represented the highest ideals of public service: integrity, devotion to principle, and commitment to the public interest. I knew and admired her.

Mrs. Fenwick dedicated herself to New Jersey and to the United States. Mrs. Fenwick's service as town council member, State assemblywoman, consumer affairs director, and U.S. Representative are a testimony to her devotion to her State and her country. She will be missed but also long remembered as a conscientious and effective public servant.

White House Statement on Additional Disaster Relief For Hawaii
September 16, 1992

The President today announced that he will amend his September 12, 1992, declaration of a major disaster in the State of Hawaii where permitted to do so by law. He will waive State and local cost sharing requirements and allow reimbursement of 100 percent of eligible public assistance costs exceeding $10 per capita.

The additional relief to be provided by the President is consistent with a request made by Governor John Waihee. It will be granted in response to the extraordinary damage and destruction caused by Hurricane Iniki. By waiving customary State and local cost sharing requirements, the President will provide maximum Federal assistance to the people of Hawaii whose lives have been so severely disrupted by this disaster.

This waiver will apply to all authorized public assistance under the law. It will provide additional help to the State in its efforts to remove debris from the disaster areas, eliminate immediate threats to public health and safety, and carry out emergency work to save lives. Assistance for temporary housing, crisis counseling, and disaster unemployment will continue to be 100 percent federally funded where allowed under the law.

Statement by Press Secretary Fitzwater on the President's Meeting With Lebanese-American Leaders
September 16, 1992

President Bush met today with a group of prominent Lebanese-Americans and His Eminence, John Cardinal O'Connor, to review the situation in Lebanon in light of the recent elections. The President reaffirmed the longstanding commitment of the United States to the unity, sovereignty, independence, and territorial integrity of Lebanon, the dissolution of all armed militias, and the withdrawal of all non-Lebanese forces. Consistent with these goals, the United States remains committed to the full and rapid implementation of both the spirit and the letter of the Taif agreement.

The President also expressed his support for steps that strengthen the Lebanese Armed Forces in its efforts to expand its national authority. The President also reiterated his belief that the ongoing negotiations between Lebanon and Israel offer the best means to bring about a secure border for the peoples of both countries. Finally, the President noted that he looks forward to the day when Americans can again travel in safety to Lebanon, a day which can only come when the militias are disarmed and no longer free to threaten either Lebanese or Americans.

Statement by Press Secretary Fitzwater on Russia's Withdrawal of Troops From Cuba
September 16, 1992

We welcome the decision by Russia to withdraw the former Soviet infantry brigade from Cuba. President Bush sought this result in discussions with President Gorbachev and, more recently, with President Yeltsin. This is further proof of the international isolation of the Castro regime from the community of nations. We remain committed to freedom and democracy being fully realized by all Cuban people and look forward to the day when Cuba joins the democracies of the Western Hemisphere.

Remarks to the Community in Enid, Oklahoma
September 17, 1992

Thank you. Please be seated. Good morning, everyone, and thank—[*applause*]—hey, let me tell you something. There's something about Enid. You really make a guy feel at home.

May I thank Don Nickles. I'll have more to say about him in just a minute. And while I'm on the subject of thanks, let me compliment Mark McCord on his introduction of Senator Nickles and getting this whole event together, all the civic clubs. And I want to thank all the leaders here on the dais joining me this morning and bring attention to several guests here. In particular, I want two to join me in the United States Congress this fall: Bob Anthony right here, you see him behind us, and Ernest Istook, running in the Fifth District; and Charles Ford for the State senate. And may I salute Mr. Grey and Mr. Divelbliss and Mr. Key and Mary Rumph, our leaders; Neva Hill; and thank you very much for your leadership, all of you back there and all of you out here, on your efforts on behalf of the Republican Party here in Oklahoma.

Let me just say a word about your Senator. I work with him closely. He has taken the lead in changing this alternative minimum tax that will help stimulate the domestic drilling business. We don't need to depend on foreign oil so much. He understands the importance of a strong defense, and I thought of that when he and I flew in on Air Force One to Vance. We must keep our country strong. Yes, we've made progress, but we've got to stay strong. He understands American agriculture and the need to sell abroad. Oklahoma sets the pace in agricultural exports. And Don Nickles is with you every inch of the way.

Now, I've come here today to the Bright Star of the Great Plains to discuss perhaps the most serious issue that Americans face this fall. This is a wonderful turnout, and politics is in the air. But today I approach this opportunity you've given me not as a rally but as a chance to discuss for the whole Nation our economic future and of the very real choices that my opponent and I offer for shaping that future. It's a serious talk, not a rally speech, and I hope you'll bear with me.

Enid is the perfect place for this discussion, for in many ways your community is a metaphor for America. Here in your history we can find the forces that have made us the world's greatest economic power.

Yesterday, as Don was reminding you,

you marked the 99th anniversary of the Land Race, a peculiarly American experiment. The Government set up the competition in 1893 but then got out of the way, stood back, to let free people work, work their miracles. And 99 years later, we see the results all around us: hard-working ranchers, some of the world's best oilmen. Enid has become a thriving center of commerce, a hub of transportation, a producer of goods sold in every corner of the Earth. A Government planner might conjure up this miracle, but only a free people could have produced it. The lesson it teaches should guide us as we look to the challenges ahead.

We stand today at the edge of a new era. At the close of a long and costly war, democracy now is sweeping the globe. The fear of nuclear holocaust that gripped us for 45 years is receding. Our kids no longer go to bed at night worried about nuclear war. That is dramatic change. These are world-shaping changes, and I am proud of the role that my administration has taken in bringing them about.

Now we have an opportunity to refocus our attention to the problems at home. Americans recognize the world is in transition. We feel it in our homes and in our neighborhoods.

In Detroit last week at the Detroit Economic Club, I presented my Agenda for American Renewal, a look at what's wrong in America and what's right. I offered a comprehensive, integrated approach to win the new global economic competition, to create the world's first $10 trillion economy by early in the next century. My agenda includes 13 actions that I will pursue in the first year of my second term, and I will fight for every one of them.

I want to be specific about what I have to offer America because I want a mandate to change things and to govern. I built a mandate in the Persian Gulf, and look what we got done. I want to do the same thing here at home, because just as America has achieved a lasting political and military security, we can and will forge an economic security, right here in Oklahoma, right here in all the rest of the States in the United States of America.

Yes, change is underway because change is the nature of America. Oklahomans know that. Yet change must be a tool for us, not against us. So we must never grasp change blindly, without considering seriously where these changes will lead us or what they will mean in our daily lives.

That's why this afternoon—or this, yes, almost afternoon—I want to lay out the differences between my agenda and my opponent's plan. These distinctions are fundamental. They shape our approach to every major issue in this election from education to health care to the renewal of the American economy.

The first difference is the most profound, for it goes to the heart of the matter: What makes our economy grow? Or more precisely, who makes an economy grow? My answer is individual working men and women make it grow. My opponent puts his faith in different people, the Government planners. He believes that Washington, the Government, will produce economic growth through, quote, and here's his word, "investing," unquote, your money more wisely than you can. To understand where these differences come from, you have to look at the differences in who we are and what we believe.

I came out west, like a number of you. Let's see, in 1948 Barbara and I moved over across the way to Midland and Odessa to work in the oil field supply business and then to become an independent producer and a drilling contractor. I spent half my adult life in business, and I have the ulcers to prove it. [*Laughter*] With a lot of help, a lot of help from the tool pushers and the roughnecks and the drilling superintendents and everybody else, and then some strong Oklahoma partners, I built a company from the ground up, created jobs, and paid my taxes.

By contrast, my opponent chose to run for office at an exceptionally early age. He wanted to determine how the people's taxes should be spent, how to shape people's lives through more government programs.

I never forgot, nor will I, my days in the Texas oil fields: some successes; yes, some dry holes; some twist-offs; some flawless completions. I never forgot the economic philosophy that I learned there in the field, to unleash the aspirations of the ordinary person with the extraordinary dream. Aspirations lead to enterprise. Enterprise creates jobs and wealth and the opportunity that knows no difference among color, creed, or social class.

You look at the differences. My opponent and his advisers propose something quite different. Their writings refer to European models and industrial policy, and that's an academic term for letting the Government pick economic winners and losers. Their ideal is not the entrepreneur but the Government planner, the lawyer, or the policy professor who flatters himself that he understands the American economy better than the workers and the entrepreneurs who have their sleeves up and really make it work.

My opponent and his advisers can trace their intellectual roots to the social engineering ideas popular at the turn of the century. Those old social—some of you historians remember this—those old social engineers advocated large-scale Government ownership to give the State the leading role in society and economy. Today, European governments are still selling off the inefficient industrial monstrosities that were born from those ideas, and Mexico and Argentina to our south are soaring because they're also ridding themselves of government-owned enterprises.

Over the years those early social engineers became interventionist liberals who wanted to create a welfare state. They sought to level the differences, to tax success, to redistribute wealth. They ended up paralyzing the private sector. That's one reason that some European countries today are stuck with unemployment rates around, if not higher than 10 percent. It's why ordinary Europeans are rebelling against anything that even smacks of the elite central government.

Now, my opponent is drawn to these views. He and a number of his advisers studied them at Oxford in the 1960's. But they are shrewd enough to know that the welfare state doesn't sell in America. So my opponent labels his latest technique for Government management "investment." Those are his words. No matter what you call it, it's still big-time Government spending directed by Washington planners who want to reorder social and economic priorities. We cannot have that.

I ask you to look at the plans. My opponent's approach exploits the market but fundamentally distrusts it. Where the market can be rough-edged, they prefer academic tidiness. Where the market is often unpredictable, they prefer the false certitude of social engineering, fashioned by a new economic elite of the so-called best and brightest. The best and the brightest are right out here in middle America where you know what's going on. From Santa Monica to Cambridge, my opponents are cranking up their models, ready to test them on you.

So at a decisive moment in history comes your choice about who should lead the American economy, the Government planner or the entrepreneur, the risktaker. I stand with the private sector and with the risktaker. From Mexico to Eastern Europe, from Russia to South China, command-and-control economies have been dismissed as failures. The individual is being set free, private enterprise unleashed, bureaucracies shut down. At the exact moment that the rest of the world is going our way, why should we ever want to go their way? What are we supposed to say to a world suddenly copying our ideas about free enterprise? Just kidding? [*Laughter*]

This is the most fundamental disagreement between us: whether the driving engine of growth is Government interventionism or entrepreneurial capitalism. But from this one disagreement flow many, many others with important practical consequences for our economy, our Nation, and yes, for your family.

Take our second disagreement over the issue of taxes. He wants to raise taxes. I want to cut taxes. You see, I believe our tax system is fundamentally the product of a wartime economy. The cost of fighting two World Wars and a cold war vastly expanded the number of people who had to pay taxes and raised marginal tax rates.

High tax rates created pressure for exceptions, tax loopholes. The discovery and enlarging of loopholes has, in turn, created a vast industry of accountants and lawyers and tax specialists, all paid by special interests seeking favored treatment.

During the 1980's—and I think you all will remember this—we slashed the tax on labor, increasing incentives for work and creating 21 million jobs. Now we need to lower the tax on capital, encouraging more investment that will create more jobs. My opponent calls for raising marginal rates again. His approach will cut the demand for labor, unless you happen to be a lawyer or an accountant or a lobbyist.

There's a motive to his madness. My opponent needs the money to pay for his social engineering, and he says it will come from the rich. He neglects to mention that two-thirds of the, quote, "rich" he's targeting are family farmers and small-business owners. His theory is that you may not live the lifestyle of the rich and famous, but you can be taxed like you do.

This leads me to our third major difference: Government spending. Again, the contrast couldn't be more plain. He wants to raise Government spending. I want to cut it.

The Federal Government today—now listen to this one—spends almost a quarter of every dollar of our national income. When you add State and local spending, your local taxes, your State taxes, the figure is about 35 cents out of every dollar going to some level of government.

My opponent thinks Government should be bigger. He's already called for $220 billion in new spending, on top of today's $1.5 trillion, so Government can lead our economy with new, quote, "investments." Newsweek suggests that the actual cost could be 3 times that.

My proposal to reduce the growth of spending has three parts: a cap on the growth of mandatory spending, excluding Social Security; a freeze on domestic spending; and the elimination of 246 programs and more than 4,000 projects that we don't need and that we cannot afford.

I want this discipline, and so does Don Nickles, I might add. I want this discipline backed up with a balanced budget amendment and a line-item veto. I want to give you the right to take up to 10 percent of your tax payment and dedicate it solely to cut spending and the deficit.

My opponent says he would like to cut a Government program, too, one program in the entire Federal budget, the honeybee subsidy, worth $11 million. Incidentally, on that subject, that worldwide important subject of the honeybee, Senator Gore has voted two times to save the honeybee subsidy.

My opponent ducks the subject of serious spending cuts. He's proposed only about $7 billion in cuts in mandatory spending over 5 years. That amounts to about 2 percent of what we've proposed to cut the growth of mandatory spending, excluding Social Security. What I proposed cut it by $300 billion. The trends are clear. He wants to increase Government's share of the national wealth, and I want to decrease it.

Now, the fourth defining difference: opening foreign markets for American goods. Again, there's two contrasting approaches. Oklahoma is one of the Nation's leading grain exporters; 65,000 Oklahoma jobs are supported by trade. That number will grow if we open more foreign markets. That's why I've negotiated the North American free trade agreement, or they call it NAFTA, and why I want a network of free trade agreements with other countries.

I want lower priced goods for American consumers. I know that, given the chance, the American worker can outthink, outcompete, outcreate any worker in the entire world. That's true of the Oklahoma farmer, and that's true of the Oklahoma manufacturer.

Now there was a time when my opponent said he favored open trade. Other times, usually after meeting with the big union leaders, the bosses up there in Washington, he has no opinion at all. In fact, the labor bosses.have let him off the hook, saying they won't press him on this issue until after the election. Now, asked about the free trade pact with Mexico, he now says and here's an exact quote, "When I have a definitive opinion, I'll say so." You cannot be on all sides of every issue if you want to be President of the United States of America.

That indecision could have disastrous consequences. Make no mistake: An indecisive President will produce a protectionist trade policy. Over the past 20 years, Congress has become much more protectionist. Changes in the way Congress operates have significantly increased the power of individual Members. The established special interests have targeted each one with a great deal of success. These local interest groups will conspire with their clients in Congress to keep out competition altogether. Only the President can speak for the national interest.

The marriage of convenience between the special interests and powerful Congressmen poses particular dangers to free trade. Entrepreneurs are very good at taking advantage of foreign markets. They are not good at taking these lobbyists out to lunch. So if you feel that Oklahoma is right in exporting as much of its wheat as it does, then you must have a President who is firmly committed to opening markets, at home and abroad.

You know, frankly, I believe that when Americans shop we should give the first look to products marked "Made in the U.S.A." Our quality revolution has made American products the best in the world, but they will only remain the best if American business opens itself to competition. Competition gave American business its competitive edge, and competition will keep it sharp.

Then there's a fifth difference between my opponent and me: our attitudes toward Government regulation, mandates, and monopolies. I want to minimize Federal intrusion in the workings of the marketplace. My opponent sees regulation as he sees taxes and spending, as a chance to reorder society according to the planner's blueprint.

Of course, I believe firmly in Government's obligation to protect the health and safety and rights of its citizens, of course. I fought for both the Clean Air Act and the Americans With Disabilities Act. Both will require new regulations, but we're proceeding to implement them in the most efficient and least burdensome way possible.

Last year, Americans expended 5.3 billion hours just to keep up with Federal regulations. That's like watching every pro-football game on television back-to-back for the next 12,268,000 years. [*Laughter*] That's not including playoffs.

That's why I have ordered a top-to-bottom review of Government regulations to assess each new rule's impact on economic growth. In this agenda I am outlining, I have called for adding "sunset" provisions to all new regulation.

Look at health care, a case study of our different attitudes toward Government regulation. I believe everybody should have health care. My health care reform will bring health care to those without it by giving them the means to choose the kind of care they want. It will harness the forces of competition to control costs. In keeping the Government out, it keeps the quality of our health care up. Our health care is the finest in the world, and I want to keep it that way.

My opponent, by contrast, says that Government will simply issue an edict: Costs shall not rise. He will order businesses to provide health care or pay for it, though he never quite says how. It sounds simple, sounds even seductive.

But that's not the way the world works. My opponent's new dictates and taxes won't cure the health care problem; they will just make the economy sicker. From Warsaw to Prague to Moscow, Government price controls have led to one thing: rationing of service. In health care, that will mean longer lines, inefficient service, and lower quality.

Our difference in approach to Government's role shows up across the board.

In child care, I fought to empower parents to choose from a public agency, a relative, or a church. Give the parents the choice. My opponent wanted a Government-knows-best policy.

In education, I am fighting to give parents scholarships to choose the best schools for their kids: public, private, or religious. My opponent bows to the special interests who say parents should only choose Government schools.

Now, lastly, my opponent and I disagree on an issue crucial, absolutely crucial, to small businesses and also to small communities. I believe that our legal system is out of control, heading for an accident. The litigation explosion has discouraged risktaking and innovation, the life's blood of entrepreneurial capitalism. Today Americans spend up to $200 billion in direct costs to lawyers, far more than our competitors in Asia and Europe.

Again, when it comes to legal reform, the difference is clear: I'm for it, and my opponent and the trial lawyers want to kill it. In fact, one trial lawyer from Arkansas solicited funds for my opponent by writing, "I can never remember an occasion when he failed to do the right thing where we trial lawyers were concerned."

A truly competitive America cannot afford a President who worries about doing the right thing for the trial lawyers. You see, I believe we need to sue each other less and care for each other more. These, then, are the six core differences between my agenda and my opponent's plan. There are others, but all relate to America's central challenge: the challenge of securing peace and prosperity in a totally new era.

We may talk about the same issues, but the similarity ends there. My opponent and I both hope to take America off in very different directions.

He would unite the Presidency and the Congress to achieve one end above all others: more Government; a Government that taxes more and spends more and regulates more, encourages more lawsuits and shuts off more products from the markets that Americans create.

Those aren't new ideas. They're bad ideas, and they've been tried before.

Buying my opponent's prescription for the economy would be like going out to the used car lot down the road and buying the lemon that you got rid of 12 years ago. Only this time, there would be higher taxes, higher interest rates, and higher inflation. This is not a good deal for America.

Now, on July 20th, 1988, my opponent nominated Michael Dukakis for President. It was a rather lengthy speech; makes this one look like the Gettysburg Address. [*Laughter*] He praised Michael Dukakis then as a master of innovation, the architect of the Massachusetts Miracle. [*Laughter*] Six months later the miracle was a curse, and Massachusetts teetered toward bankruptcy.

I think America can do without that kind of innovation. There are some kind of changes America simply cannot afford.

I look to a different kind of future. We can build on our strengths. With inflation kept safely behind bars, our entrepreneurs can turn to the challenges they love to face, transforming their dreams into wealth, their risktaking into jobs for all Americans.

The result won't be the mirage of innovation conjured up by Government planners. It will be a wave of genuine innovation and prosperity, created by free men and women, exploiting opportunities unprecedented in our history.

If you get the feeling I'm optimistic about the future of the country, you are right. We're the United States of America. So this is the choice we face. This is the choice we face in November. So I ask when you make that choice, please consider carefully which candidate's agenda best fits your beliefs, our national heritage, and our hope for a lasting peace.

Thank you so much for listening. And may God bless the United States of America. Thank you. Thank you very much.

Note: The President spoke at 10:15 a.m. in the Enid Convention Hall. In his remarks, he referred to Mark McCord, president, Greater Enid Chamber of Commerce; Norman L. Grey, Mayor of Enid; Charles Divelbliss, Garfield County Republican chairman; Clinton Key, Republican State chairman and chairman, Oklahoma Victory '92; and Mary Rumph, Oklahoma Republican national committeewoman.

Remarks to the Community in Jonesboro, Georgia
September 17, 1992

The President. What a fantastic welcome. Thank you very, very much. Thank you all very much for that warm welcome. I am delighted to be here, and I'm especially glad to be with the residents of Avery of Walnut Creek and thank them for this impromptu block party. You really know how to make a guy feel at home here.

May I salute Jerry Kopp, not only our chairman but a man whose vision is bringing this place alive, thank him for his leadership, thank him for his hospitality. We've got a great host here today.

I also want to salute and thank the members of the Atlanta Home Builders who are with us here today. The president-elect is here, Charles Bussey. Also we're expecting Congressman Newt Gingrich, whose plane was about to land, and I salute him as one of our leaders in the Congress.

But let me just mention two candidates with us today. We've got to get Mac Collins elected to the House of Representatives. We need new blood. We need people that think as you and I do on trying to solve the problems of this country. As for the Senate, I would like to see us get some new Senate leaders up there, and Paul Coverdell is the man.

You know, he's already served our administration with great distinction. He has the courage and he has the commitment to work with me to get the budget deficit down. Because of that commitment, in this State, where for a while Ross Perot captured the imagination of many people because of his commitment to get the deficit down, Paul has now been endorsed by the Perot leadership in this State. I think that's a tribute to his integrity and his commitment to getting the debt off the backs of these young people.

When you're done here, I'd like you to all pack up and go to Washington, because there's a certain House on the Hill that's in need of a little renovation. You know Bob Vila's old show, "This Old House"? Well, back in Washington there's an old House on Capitol Hill that hasn't been cleaned out for 38 years. We've got to clean House. We need these two people elected there.

Audience members. Clean the House! Clean the House! Clean the House!

The President. "Clean the House!" is right.

Well, I'm pleased to be here with you today because you're building here at 1270 Larkwood Drive, and it isn't just a house. The way I look at it, it's a part of the American dream for the family who will call it a home.

And now that the cold war is over, the defining challenges of the nineties are to win the peace and to win the competition in the new global economy. Let me give it to you straight. In the 21st century America must be not only a military superpower, but an economic superpower and an export superpower.

In this election you're going to hear varying versions of how to do this. My opponent wants to look inward, to pretend that we can protect what we already have. Yours and mine is to look forward, open up new markets, prepare our people to compete, strengthen the American family, and save and invest so that when it comes to the global competition, America will win, just as we did in the cold war.

What we need is this: an agenda for the American renewal, a strategy that reaches out to the world in a way that makes a difference right here in this county and in your neighborhoods and in your lives. We've got to build on the fundamentals of lower tax rates, limits on Government spending, less redtape, less regulation, and more trade and more competition to generate the growth that this country needs, which means opportunity.

I think that in the nineties, Government can add to this growth by building opportunity and hope for individuals, empowering families and communities. And my agenda for renewal is a blueprint for long-term growth. But near-term, right now, we all know that we've got to jump-start this economy, to put America back to work.

Let me tell every would-be homebuyer and everybody familiar with the homebuilding industries: Back in January, 8 months ago, you might remember this, I challenged the Congress to pass a new incentive, a $5,000 tax credit for these first-time homebuyers. I proposed that credit for two reasons: First, because I knew that coming out of troubled times, housing is traditionally the sector that pulls this economy forward. I also wanted to help the young families, the ones that are struggling to save for that first home, because the American dream, after all, really starts right here with a home of your own.

This year alone, my plan would have meant more than 120,000 new housing starts and 220,000 new jobs in the economy, including jobs for carpenters and plumbers and plasterers. For the average first-time homebuyer right in this county, that tax credit would have been the equivalent of 8 months worth of mortgage payments, right here at 1270 Larkwood. It's like getting your down payment back and more.

And my plan, you know what's happened to it, it is still sitting, stalled by the do-nothing liberal leadership that puts politics ahead of helping people. The opposition feels the only chance they can have to win is if everything is bad. They refuse to act, and it's time to put people ahead of political gain in this country.

You know, rule number one in the housing business is build from the ground up. Well, given what you've seen in Congress this year, I think this is one time you ought to raise the roof. Go after these people. Clean them out. They've been there 38 years. Give us some new leadership in both the Senate and the House.

You know, the housing business is no different than a lot of other small businesses. I see small business as the engine to pull this economy forward, generating jobs and opportunity. My opponent sees small business as the goose that laid the golden egg. Here's what he wants: $150 billion in new taxes to a payroll tax for health care to a training tax. Governor Clinton wants to squeeze small business to bankroll big Government, and we cannot let him do that. So I say keep your hands off the housing industry. America's small businesses need relief, relief from taxation and overregulation and, yes, relief from these frivolous lawsuits. We're suing each other too much and caring for each other too little.

Last month, I was in Michigan, western Michigan, talking to a group of small-business leaders. And I talked to a guy who runs an asphalt paving company. He said, "Mr. President, when a regulation doesn't make sense, it's the worker who pays with his job."

Excessive regulation is a huge hidden cost in housing. The single most expensive item in a home these days isn't sheetrock; it's not the drywall; it isn't all the lumber, even the land underneath. The single most expensive item in a new home is that piece of paper you stick inside the front window, the building permit. All the regulations that it represents can add up to 20 to 35 percent of the cost of these houses. That's why I put a freeze on new Federal regulations to give businesses like this a chance to make it, a chance to improve, a chance to get ahead.

For those in the housing business and those potential consumers, let me say this: Today I'm announcing an important regulatory reform that will make housing more affordable, a reform that does not require action by the Congress, thank heavens. It will substantially reduce the insurance premium on FHA-insured 15-year mortgages, with benefits to both the homebuyers and the homebuilders.

Now, this action is no substitute for the legislation I want, the one I proposed back in January. But I will continue to do everything I can on my own to get the economy moving, even if Congress sits on its hands.

Now, there are some good signs for the housing industry. I think most people here in Georgia know it. The housing affordability index is almost double what it was 10 years ago. Interest rates today are lower than at any time since 1973. The last time a family could get a mortgage this low, milk was 98 cents a gallon and the Braves' Hank Aaron was still chasing Babe Ruth's record. That was some time ago.

So let me tell you what the lower interest means to you and to the American family. Lower interest rates mean real money, real savings for every American who buys a home, every family that refinances a mortgage. It means money in your pocket, as much as $2,000 a year or more that instead of paying to the bank you can put in the bank. Nationwide, over the past 2 years alone, that is like a $26 billion tax cut for America's homeowners.

Now, that is good news. But we've got to do even better. Some studies show that three-quarters of all renters are ready to become buyers if they could muster up the down payment. If Congress had passed my plan when I asked them to, if Congress had acted to help that first-time homebuyer, you'd see almost 400,000 more "Sold" signs on front lawns all across America. Workers in the homebuilding industry wouldn't be worried about pink slips; they'd be too busy working overtime.

So today let me make a suggestion to you: Come November, send me a Congress that shares our view to get this country moving, to get the economy moving.

Audience members. Clean the House! Clean the House! Clean the House!

The President. And if you say, give me one good reason you'll get Congress to act, I'll give you about 150. That's the number of new faces that we'll probably see next year in the Congress.

I'll be candid: I want every last one of them to be a Republican, of course. But whatever party they come from, even if they were first elected before some of you were born, they'll come back with a new appreciation of what you want, a complete set of instructions from the American people that say it's time for Congress to change. I am convinced with a new Congress, a Congress made up of so many new people, we can get the job done. I'll sit down with them all the day after the election, say, "You've listened to the American people. I've listened to the American people. Now let's get things going forward in this country and put aside all these politics."

Don't forget what happened the last time Democrats controlled both ends of Pennsylvania in Washington, DC. The "misery index," the malaise days, the "misery index" was over 20 percent, and mortgage rates were so high, sky high, there was a lockout for millions of Americans who wanted to buy their own home. We've seen what happens when the party of tax-and-spend operates without any checks and balances, and we cannot do that to the American people again.

I've set out in my program 13 specific challenges, initiatives, actions, challenging the new Congress to take in the first 100 days of my second term. And November 3d, I'm looking for a mandate to move forward, to move forward on this Agenda for American Renewal, an agenda that builds a stronger, more secure America that we want for ourselves and certainly for these kids here.

We've got to remember this one fundamental fact: America is the envy of the world. Governor Clinton and Senator Gore would have you believe that we're a nation, here's what they said, somewhere south of Germany but just ahead of Sri Lanka. They are wrong. We are the most respected nation in the entire world. We're that, not because our Government is great but because our people are great and because the American people are builders and dreamers and dreamers who build.

I am delighted to be here. Let me tell you this. I'm sorry that Barbara is not here. She's meeting me in downtown Atlanta in a few minutes. But I am absolutely convinced that we're going to have change this year. We're going to have a new Senator from the State of Georgia, Paul Coverdell. Clearly, we've got to elect Mac to the House. He's a good man, and he knows what change is all about.

I don't care what the liberals think about it; I am not going to stop talking about strengthening the American family, the values that we have tried to emulate in the White House. So let them knock us. Let them tear us down. I will continue to find ways to help every family in America strengthen the values that we hold so dear.

Thank you. Now elect these good men. Vote for me. And may God bless each and every one of you. Thank you.

Note: The President spoke at 3:39 p.m. at a homesite in the Avery of Walnut Creek development. In his remarks, he referred to

Jerry Kopp, president, Koppar Corp. (developer of Avery of Walnut Creek), and chairman, Republican Party of Clayton County.

White House Fact Sheet: Regulatory Reform to Reduce Costs of Homeownership
September 17, 1992

As part of his continuing effort to reform and streamline Government regulations, the President today announced that the Department of Housing and Urban Development (HUD) will release today an important reform designed to reduce the cost of homeownership and thereby to spur residential construction.

The President acknowledged that this reform, which does not require congressional action, will have a more limited impact than the $5,000 tax credit for first-time homebuyers that he has proposed to Congress. But the President declared, "I will continue to do everything I can on my own to get the economy moving, even if Congress sits on its hands."

The administrative change released today will reduce mortgage insurance premiums on 15-year FHA-insured mortgages. HUD estimates that for those who choose a 15-year mortgage, this change will reduce the up-front FHA insurance premium by an average of $650 (based on an average loan of $65,000). It will also reduce the annual insurance premium by $165 to $325—for a total savings of approximately $2,500 to $6,000 over the life of the loan. This change is made possible by HUD's determination that 15-year mortgages pose a significantly smaller risk to the FHA insurance fund than longer term mortgages.

Remarks at Olympic Flag Jam '92 in Atlanta, Georgia
September 17, 1992

Thank you all very much. Bill Hybl, thank you for that introduction; and to Lieutenant Governor Pierre Howard and Ambassador Andy Young and Robert Holder, IOC member Anita DeFrantz; entertainers, special entertainers, Dick Clark and Whitney Houston, Gladys Knight; and of course, Billy Payne, a Bulldog on the field, a bulldog for these Olympics. Sir, I salute you for what you've done for Atlanta and all America.

You know, it's been said that if the South begins anywhere, it begins in Atlanta. Let me speak for millions of Americans: If the 1996 Olympics begin anywhere, they begin in Atlanta tonight. Look at this wonderful new dome—what a metaphor for this region's can-do spirit—and this setting, thousands of Georgians, all members of the family called America. Look at this Olympic flag, a symbol of the kind of world we want where differences are solved peacefully, not violently. What a great night to be back in the heart of the South.

A little while ago Whitney Houston sang about a "precious moment in time." And already you should be proud of some precious memories, for once again, the South has made the impossible possible. Skeptics said that no American city could impress the Olympic committee so soon after Los Angeles, but you did. Their trust means Atlanta will host the 100th anniversary of the Olympic games. Skeptics said you'd never win the games on your first attempt, no city ever had, but you did. In 1996 you'll host a record number of countries, the largest peacetime event of the 20th century.

The games are coming just as Americans are coming together. The capital of Georgia is about to become the sports capital of the entire world. As it does, let's remember past Olympics, for this event is like a tapestry, seamless, indivisible. And for me, tonight is like Yogi Berra says, "*Déjà vu* all over again."

Last month I got to meet the 1992 summer Olympic team at the White House. And the team competed hard, as America always has, competed to win and did, as America always does. Think of it, in Barcelona we won 108 medals, the most ever since 1904 in a nonboycotted Olympics.

The games showed how the Olympics have changed the world, changed the world for the better, athletically as well as economically. They occurred without boycotts, without terrorism, without politics, and that is as it should be.

Carl Sandburg once wrote, "The Republic is a dream. Nothing happens unless first a dream." With us tonight are the people who this year made dreams a reality. They showed how the Olympics are not just poetry in motion but history in action; athletes, heroes who made us proud to be Americans and made America proud.

Ladies and gentlemen, I give you, and I am proud to present, the United States Olympic athletes.

Note: The President spoke at 8:07 p.m. in the Georgia Dome. In his remarks, he referred to William J. Hybl, president, U.S. Olympic Committee; and Robert Holder and Billy Payne, cochairman and chairman, Atlanta Committee for Olympic Games.

Letter to Congressional Leaders on Cable Television Legislation
September 17, 1992

Dear Mr. Speaker: (Dear Senator:)
(Dear Congressman:)

I am writing to express my strong opposition to the Conference Report to accompany S. 12 (Cable Television Consumer Protection and Competition Act of 1992), which the House and Senate will consider in the next several days.

This legislation will hurt Americans by imposing a wide array of costly, burdensome, and unnecessary requirements on the cable industry and the government agencies that regulate it. The heavy-handed provisions of the bill will drive up cable industry costs, resulting in higher consumer rates, not rate reductions as promised by the supporters of the bill.

The bill will also restrain continued innovation in the industry, cost the economy jobs, reduce consumer programming choices, and retard the deployment of growth-oriented investments critical to the future of our Nation's communications infrastructure.

My vision for the future of the communications industry is based on the principles of greater competition, entrepreneurship, and less economic regulation. This legislation fails each of these tests and is illustrative of the Congressional mandates and excessive regulations that drag our economy down.

Congress would best serve consumer welfare by promoting vigorous competition, not massive re-regulation.

For these reasons I will veto S. 12 if it is presented to me, and I urge its rejection when the House and Senate consider the Conference Report.

Sincerely,

GEORGE BUSH

Note: Identical letters were sent to Thomas S. Foley, Speaker of the House of Representatives; Robert H. Michel, House Republican leader; George J. Mitchell, Senate majority leader; and Robert Dole, Senate Republican leader.

White House Statement on Additional Disaster Relief for Guam
September 17, 1992

The President today announced that he has amended his August 28, 1992, declaration of a major disaster in the Territory of Guam to waive Territory and local cost sharing requirements, where permitted to do so by law, to allow reimbursement of 95 percent of eligible public assistance costs exceeding $10 per capita, and to waive the cost sharing requirement for the individual and family grant program as allowed under the provisions of the Insular Act.

This additional relief provided by the President was in response to a request made by Gov. Joseph Ada. It was taken in response to the unprecedented damage and destruction caused by Typhoon Omar. By waiving customary Territory and local cost sharing requirements, the President can provide maximum Federal assistance to the people of Guam whose lives have been so severely disrupted by this disaster.

Nomination of United States Ambassadors to Bosnia-Hercegovina, Croatia, and Slovenia
September 17, 1992

The President today announced his intention to nominate Victor Jackovich, Mara M. Letica, and E. Allan Wendt as Ambassadors to Bosnia-Hercegovina, Croatia, and Slovenia, respectively. The naming of Ambassadors will complete the establishment of full diplomatic relations with these nations. Their mandate is to foster a viable political, economic, and trading partnership between the United States and these countries, including the development of democratic and market-oriented reforms. The dispatch of our Ambassadors will allow the U.S. to work more closely with Bosnia, Croatia, and Slovenia to bring about a settlement of the conflicts in the region. In addition, their mission is to encourage the ongoing peace negotiations, including facilitating the delivery of humanitarian assistance to those suffering in the region.

Victor Jackovich, of Iowa, a career member of the Senior Foreign Service, class of Counselor, to be Ambassador of the United States of America to the Republic of Bosnia and Hercegovina. Currently Mr. Jackovich is the executive assistant to the Counselor at the United States Information Agency. Prior to this, he was in the Bulgarian Language Training School at the Department of State, 1990–91; Cultural Affairs Of-

ficer in Moscow in the former Soviet Union, 1988–90; Information Officer in Nairobi, Kenya, 1983–86; Cultural Affairs Officer in Bucharest, Romania, 1980–83; and Branch Public Affairs Officer in Kiev in the former Soviet Union, 1979–80. Mr. Jackovich also served as the Chief of the Yugoslav Service at the Voice of America, 1976–78.

Mr. Jackovich graduated from Indiana University (B.A., 1970; M.A., 1971). He was born on April 24, 1948, in Des Moines, IA. Mr. Jackovich is married, has one child, and resides in Arlington, VA.

Mara M. Letica, of Michigan, to be Ambassador of the United States of America to Croatia. Currently Ms. Letica is an attorney and general counsel of the Letica Corp. in Rochester, MI. She is a founder of the Croatian American Association, where she has served as secretary-treasurer from 1990 to 1992. The association was founded to provide information about the independence movement in Croatia and to support U.S. recognition of Croatia.

Ms. Letica has also served as an attorney with Bullivant, House, Bailey, Pendergrass and Hoffman, P.C., in Portland, OR, 1982–85; and in the office of prosecuting attorney criminal division in Seattle, WA, 1980. Through the Letica Corp., Ms. Letica has organized humanitarian assistance programs to Croatia and Bosnia-Hercegovina.

Ms. Letica graduated from the University of Michigan (B.A., 1976) and the University of Puget Sound (J.D., 1981). She was born January 11, 1955, in Kaiserslautern, Germany. Ms. Letica is married, has two children, and resides in Bloomfield Hills, MI.

E. Allan Wendt, of California, a career member of the Senior Foreign Service, class of Minister-Counselor, to be Ambassador of the United States of America to the Republic of Slovenia.

Since 1987, Ambassador Wendt has served as Senior Representative for Strategic Technology Policy at the State Depart-

ment. Prior to this, he served as Deputy Assistant Secretary of State for International Energy and Resources Policy, 1981–86; Counselor for Economic and Commercial Affairs at the American Embassy, Cairo, Egypt, 1979–81; Director of the Office of International Commodities at the State Department, 1975–79; and State Department fellow at the Council on Foreign Relations, 1974–75. He was given the Department of State's Award for Heroism in 1968.

Ambassador Wendt graduated from Yale University (B.A., 1957) and Harvard University (M.P.A., 1967). He was born November 8, 1935, in Chicago, IL. Ambassador Wendt currently resides in Orange County, CA.

Remarks to AT&T Employees in Basking Ridge, New Jersey
September 18, 1992

Please be seated, and thank you very much, Dr. Mary Stewart. Thanks for the welcome. Thank you very much, and good afternoon. What a wonderful introduction by such a wonderfully experienced person. Dr. Stewart, thank you very, very much. And good afternoon to everyone.

I want to first recognize she who came up with me on the airplane today, Secretary Lynn Martin. She is doing a great job for this country as Secretary of Labor. I'll have more to say about her own labors in the context of this speech. But I want to thank her for being with us. She is a former Member of Congress. She is now leading this enormous Department and doing a first-class job.

As to Tom Kean, your former Governor, my longtime friend, I couldn't be more pleased. He is heading up our campaign effort here, and I can't think of any better formula for success in this State because of his own record, the respect with which he's held. It is just a wonderful thing. Barbara and I are just delighted to have him at our side in this fight.

Another one is Congressman Dean Gallo, who has been a leader for me and who's helping this State and this community a great deal in the House of Representatives.

If we had more like him, we wouldn't hear everybody yelling at me, "Clean House!" everyplace I went. So that was nice.

Of course, I'm grateful to the chairman, Bob Allen, and to everyone at AT&T. I think it's a good thing that you provide a forum for political people to bring their views to a community. A lot of companies duck it; they dodge it. Then they end up writing me letters griping about how things are. This one is out front. Bob Allen has always been willing to take a position. He stands for something, and so do the people that work with him. So I want to express my thanks to not only those that are in this room but those that might be plugged into some fancy high-tech AT&T communications system around here. But the company does good work and certainly is a great corporate citizen of this wonderful community.

I want to thank the speaker who's here, Chuck Haytaian. He is leading the New Jersey Legislature. All States are caught up in enormous battles. And I'm very, very proud of him.

With me today also are two women that came up with us from Washington, both of them standing there. Connie Horner is an Assistant to the President in terms of personnel. She gave up an enormous job as number two in the largest Department in the Federal Government. She's over now working with us in the White House in charge of all of our personnel. You all know the size of the Federal Government. So believe me, that's a major assignment, and I'm delighted she came.

Next to her, some of you may know our household word, our household symbol now, Marlin Fitzwater. Well, Marlin's able deputy is Judy Smith, standing over next to Connie. You may have seen her on television fencing with or supporting the press, depending what kind of mood she's in— [*laughter*]—as we go around this country. But I just am so pleased that they're here with us today.

You know, I remember standing in the Rose Garden just last year and awarding a prize, Environment and Conservation Challenge Award, to AT&T for your world-class work in reducing air pollutants. It's great to be here and see firsthand the folks who made it happen. That was a national honor well deserved by you and those who work with you.

But there's something also sad, and Tom touched on it, about being in this neck of New Jersey today, and I'd like to just take a minute or two to explain why.

You lost one of your most remarkable citizens on Wednesday when Congressman Millicent Fenwick died at the age of 82. She was an incredible person. And many portrayed her as the "pipe-smoking grandmother," but she preferred "hard-working grandmother." She said it had the same number of syllables—typical of Millicent. [*Laughter*] And she spent her whole life climbing obstacles and helping others to do the same.

Yes, she was born to a life of privilege. But in the early thirties, her marriage split up, and she moved to New York alone, deep in debt, with a couple of kids. She wanted to get a job selling stockings at a department store, but they turned her away. She hadn't earned a high school diploma. She stuck with it, finally rising to be an editor of Vogue magazine.

Her kids grown up, Millicent came home to New Jersey and started to get involved in town politics. She was the first woman member of the Bernardsville Borough Council. She ran then for the State assembly and won and served as State consumer affairs director.

Then at 64, when most people are settling down, Millicent was just starting to make this fantastic reputation in Congress. I was honored to know her very, very well indeed. She helped run my campaign here in this State in 1980. She was deeply principled in politics for all the right reasons, to fulfill a deep and burning desire to achieve justice for all people.

Her commitment to the underdogs of the world was matched only by her wit. Once a State legislator said to her, "I've always thought of women as kissable, cuddly, and smelling good." Millicent replied, "That's the way I feel about men, too. I only hope for your sake that you haven't been disappointed as often as I have." [*Laughter*] Well, who but Millicent? Enough said.

Well, Millicent Fenwick lived during interesting times. She saw a world transformed outside our borders, and she helped lead that transformation. You remember her assignment after she left the Congress was to go off into a marvelous agency helping people in the food area. But while these remarkable changes took place overseas, here in America a quieter and even more profound revolution has been unfolding, and Millicent was a part of that, too.

I'm talking about a move toward human justice at its most basic level, the movement toward equality of the sexes, a movement that cuts across social and ideological boundaries and touches all our lives. Of course, before we all get carried away with the congratulations, we have to admit—and Lynn and I were talking about this coming up here on the plane—that we have a ways to go. I did not come here today just as one more man, but I'm here as a President whose policies affect your lives.

Last week I unveiled, and Dr. Stewart very generously talked about this, my Agenda for American Renewal, answers to the questions that Americans are asking around their kitchen tables. The agenda is a comprehensive strategy to guarantee that by the early part of the 21st century, America will enjoy the world's first $10 trillion economy. I have several priorities; most are well underway. I want to open new markets and new customers for the products you produce. I want to create new schools for a new age. I want to sharpen businesses' competitive edge, with relief from taxation, regulation, and certainly from litigation. I want to reach out to all Americans, and I want to dramatically reduce the size and the scope of the Federal Government.

That's my agenda. But today, I'm here to talk about a special priority on my agenda, providing economic security for American working men and women. The first order of business, as I said, is to admit that there is still unfinished business. Women work as hard as men and still earn less, and that's not acceptable. Most working women do more than equal work on the job and at home, and that's not acceptable, either.

Many women are trying to do it all alone. Look, divorce happens, and I know it from my own family, my own daughter. I've seen what single mothers are up against, the kind of pressures, trying to do 36 hours of work in a 24-hour day.

As a nation, we must confront these challenges head-on. Not talk, not slogans, not political rhetoric, we need Government policies that help men and women meet their responsibilities at home. And that means child care. It means family leave policies. It means child support enforcement. It means cheaper health care.

Both candidates in this election are talking about these issues. But we offer entirely different solutions. The other side puts their faith in Government, Government mandates. On issue after issue, their solution comes down to giving more power to Government. I put my faith in you. I want to give you the power to help yourself. The other side's ideas sound very enticing. But you have to ask, "Will they work for me? Will they make a difference in my life?"

In thinking about this, I refer you to a story about William II, the Emperor of Germany. He saw himself as a man's man, which I guess means he was the kind of Kaiser who, when he got lost, would refuse to ask anybody directions. [*Laughter*] Well, the Kaiser got in his head that he could design a better battleship. So he drew up plans and sent them to the naval architect for him to study. And the architect said the

Kaiser's battleship would be absolutely the finest one on Earth. It would be as fast as a speedboat. Its range and its power would overwhelm the enemy. Everybody on board would feel like they were lounging in their living room. There was only one teeny, tiny problem: If the boat were built and actually placed in the water, it would sink.

Well, I'm afraid a lot of policies that have been coming out of Capitol Hill the past few years do that. All are designed to use Government to achieve great things on your behalf. But look closely, and I suggest that they just might not float in water.

Let me give you a few examples. You decide for yourself.

This week, Congress sent me what's called family leave legislation. The bill has the noble goal of allowing a mom or dad to leave a job in order to take care of a new baby, maybe care for a sick parent. The bill would require companies to keep the job open for 3 months until the employee could come back to work.

Now, I believe family leave is necessary, and our families need it. A lot of companies are providing it. This one right here does; AT&T is one. You should be proud of your farsighted leadership on this. But the bill Congress sent me this week would force every company with more than 50 employees to provide family leave. If companies don't foot the bill, they break the law. Now, that's one approach, and I offer another one. I want to give all businesses incentives in the form of credits, tax credits to offer family leave.

It's an election year, so congressional leaders have sent me their mandatory approach. They've been sitting on it all year long, I might add. Now, with 2 weeks to go in this session of the Congress, or 3, sent it to me and dared me not to sign it. I want to explain why I can't support their approach.

First of all, our economy is sluggish. Here in New Jersey and all across the country it's sluggish. Think of the ad agencies, the printing companies, other suppliers in your neighborhoods and people that you work with every day. They're still cutting budgets and payrolls, and I don't want to load on more Federal mandates that will force them to lay off people.

You might say, "You're protecting the rich." But, you know, entrepreneurs aren't all rich. In fact, more and more people are taking their pensions and starting their own small businesses. By the year 2000, women will run the majority of these businesses.

Here's another point to consider: You and I know the best benefit packages often come from the largest employers. They're the ones that can provide the benefits. Small companies are usually where parents have to make the tough choice between work and family. But the other side's approach exempts the smallest employers. My approach offers incentives to those companies, and it will cover the 40 percent of American workers who won't be covered by the other side's plan.

One more thing: Think of the impact mandated family leave has on hiring decisions. I know it's not supposed to happen, but how many employers will think, why not hire a man instead of a woman? He won't leave to have a child. He won't leave to care for his family. This is illegal, and we must enforce the law. But mandated family leave could encourage this subtle kind of discrimination.

I don't think you'll hear these kinds of details discussed in the media. But I'm going to take a stand because to me, it's not worth putting politics ahead of progress.

Let me talk just about another job-related issue, something that's called the glass ceiling. Today, companies are promoting some women in greater numbers, but not fast enough. So a lot of talented women are going into the businesses for themselves.

This isn't just a corporate problem; we're seeing the same thing happen in Government. And I'm proud of our record in promoting women. But I'm especially proud that we've put talented women in important economic positions: running the Department of Labor, running the Department of Commerce or the Small Business Administration, or handling all of our trade negotiations. The women I work with tell me they don't want any special opportunity; they just want the right to succeed or fail, to be measured by the same standard as men.

We want to see the Lynn Martins of corporate America succeed, too. That's why this Secretary of Labor, Lynn Martin, has made shattering the glass ceiling a top priority. She's making sure that companies who receive your tax dollars through Federal contracts make career opportunities available to women.

Let's talk child care for a moment. You see a difference in philosophies here. Congress wanted a Government-run child care program, a mandated program emanating from some subcommittee and then working its way through the Congress. I heard from parents who wanted the right to choose the best child care for their children. It might be a public school. It might be a church or a synagogue, an aunt's house. And the point is, you want to make the choice, not be told where to go by some county clerk. Congress wanted to give the money directly to county agencies and limit the family's alternatives. I fought for giving vouchers directly to parents, so you can choose the best care, regardless of who provides it. Our way was better, and on this one we won.

Now we're having a similar debate, major national debate, over health care. Costs are rising more than 10 percent a year. It's putting pressure on families. It's the fastest growing item in this enormous Federal budget. Once again, the other side wants the Government alone to solve the problem, either by directly taking over our health care system or by indirectly getting involved in setting prices and mandating benefits. Now, that idea sounds appealing to some, but it will end up meaning longer lines and less flexibility for you and for your families.

I offer an entirely different approach, sitting up there now in the United States Congress awaiting action. I want to give companies incentives to provide coverage and use competition to drive down costs. I want to get at the root cause of raising prices, including skyrocketing malpractice insurance. I want to let small businesses pool their coverage, insurance coverage, so they can get the same price breaks as larger companies do. My plan will lower costs through competition, extend coverage to the poorest of the poor—insurance coverage—extend coverage to 30 million Americans who cannot afford it today and build on the strengths of our system, which already provides the highest quality care in the world.

You see people coming from all over the world to come to America for health care. Why? Because we have the highest quality care. If you take it out of the private sector and you put it in the public sector, you can guarantee that it will no longer be that beacon for quality. I believe my approach is right. I believe it's right for the citizens of this country, and I believe it's right when it comes to a philosophy of government.

Now, here's something that really bothers me. Five million women today in America are entitled to child support from ex-husbands. Now, you know how many of those women get all they are entitled to? About half. About half. I think it's outrageous that a father in Pennsylvania can be shopping for a new Corvette, while his ex-wife in New Jersey is struggling to shop for food. And I think it's time that the long arm of the law taps every deadbeat dad on the shoulder and says, pay up, or else.

There's a lot more in this agenda. We've made it so you can take a pension from job to job. Our health care proposal, the health care goes from job to job. We've provided incentives for student aid. Today one out of two students at a college or university gets a Federal loan or grant. And the purpose is the same: to protect working men and women, to make it easier to raise a family.

But listing the exact details of every program isn't as important as the philosophy behind them, a philosophy that says: Ultimately, the only way to make people more secure is to give you more power, give you, the individual, more power over the decisions that affect your jobs and family budgets.

If we're going to use the power of Government to move us forward, we need to use the power of Government to help, not hinder; not to add new barriers to opportunity but to remove old ones. I started by talking about the economic challenge before America, and I'd like to close the same way because ultimately that's what this election is about: Who has the ideas that can help America win the global economic competition? When you stop to consider all the challenges we face in this Nation, let's not ignore some of the advantages.

Here in America, we send more of our students to higher education, more than any other nation, twice as many as Germany and more than twice as many as Japan. More than half of these American students are women. Basically, we have twice as many educated people as our competitors. It's because America is the only nation that really tries to base opportunity on character and talent alone.

The changes of the past few decades have improved the lives of all Americans. But more than that, they've improved our society. They've made us stronger as we face the stiff challenges ahead. The policies that I've outlined today are designed to build on our strengths, to help us take advantage of the talents of every American, to strengthen all our families so that we can make America safer and more secure.

I have seven granddaughters. Maybe I better rephrase that: Barbara and I have seven granddaughters. [*Laughter*] I don't want to be killed when I get down to Maryland. [*Laughter*] The oldest is 15 years old. And the world that she enters today will be much different than the world that Barbara and I entered many years ago. If my granddaughter wants to go out to Texas and start an oil company, she can do it. If she wants to write the "Vogue Book of Etiquette," she can do that, too. If she chooses another line of work, if she chose to stay home and raise her kids, well, I'll give her love and support. She won't have to answer to anyone about the choices she's made. If she wants to try and run for President, she can do that, too. And I hope she does.

I'm very glad that my grandchildren face these opportunities, but they will only be able to take advantage of them if America remains the most dynamic place on this great Earth. I think the path to economic security lies with less Government, less regulation, more freedom and respect for families and individuals.

So what I offer in this election is simple: a new path to a renewed America, based on some tried and true values. That's how we're going to build a safer, more secure America for all of us and certainly for our kids, your kids, and my grandkids.

Thank you for listening. And may God bless the United States of America. Thank you all very much.

Note: The President spoke at 2:54 p.m. at

the AT&T corporate headquarters. In his remarks, he referred to Mary L. Stewart, president, Stewart Management Group, and Chuck Haytaian, speaker of the New Jersey State Assembly.

Letter to Congressional Leaders on the North American Free Trade Agreement
September 18, 1992

Dear Mr. Speaker: (Dear Mr. President:)

In accordance with section 1103(a)(1) of the Omnibus Trade and Competitiveness Act of 1988 ("Act"), I am pleased to notify the House of Representatives and the Senate of my intent to enter into a North American Free Trade Agreement (NAFTA) with the Governments of Mexico and Canada.

This historic agreement represents a comprehensive charter to liberalize trade and investment flows on this continent. NAFTA will link us to our first- and third-largest trading partners, Canada and Mexico, respectively, to create one of the world's largest and richest markets, with over 360 million consumers and over $6.4 trillion in annual output. It will enhance the ability of North American producers to compete in world markets, spur economic growth on the continent, expand employment, and raise living standards.

We are at the dawn of a new era. The threat of global nuclear warfare is gone. The prolonged Cold War struggle against totalitarianism, fought over half a century through immense sacrifices by countless American men and women, has ended in freedom's victory.

Just as America prevailed in the Cold War, we must continue to lead the world in the global economy of the next century. Exports are vital to the health of the U.S. economy, accounting for 70 percent of our economic growth since 1988, and supporting the jobs of more than 7.5 million Americans. We must continue to expand our exports by strengthening our lead in technological innovation, by giving American firms and workers the tools to compete and win in international competition, and by negotiating effective agreements to open foreign markets to U.S. goods and services.

The NAFTA eliminates tariffs and other barriers to the flow of goods and services between the United States, Mexico, and Canada. It lifts barriers to investment, strengthens the protection of intellectual property, and improves upon trade rules that govern our bilateral trade relations to ensure that U.S. firms can reap the full rewards of the market opportunities NAFTA creates.

Fifteen months ago, the Congress endorsed the extension of the fast track procedures to allow the NAFTA negotiations to proceed. The fast track has been a shining example of bipartisan cooperation to enhance our Nation's future.

I am deeply mindful of the commitment I made during the fast track debate to achieve a balance in the NAFTA that will not only expand our economic growth but also facilitate adjustment for U.S. workers and protect the environment.

While NAFTA will create new, high-wage export-oriented jobs through expanded trade, we have a responsibility to ensure that all U.S. workers, including those affected by NAFTA, have the skills to compete in global markets. Accordingly, last month I proposed a comprehensive new Federal job training program for all dislocated U.S. workers, including the relatively small number who face adjustments because of NAFTA. It will be funded at $2 billion annually—nearly triple the current budget for all of our existing worker training and assistance services.

I remain equally committed to ensuring that NAFTA improves environmental protection. The NAFTA contains unprecedented provisions to benefit the environment. In addition, we are moving forward with a comprehensive environmental agenda with the Government of Mexico—an agenda that NAFTA made possible.

The trade of a nation reflects its aims and aspirations. The choice before us is stark—to retreat into protectionism or move forward to new horizons of challenge and opportunity in an expanding global economy. Our Nation won the Cold War because of its faith in the abiding power of free people, free markets, and free trade in goods and ideas. We must continue to lead and to trade, confident of our ideals and principles and the ability of American firms and workers to prevail in free and fair competition.

I look forward to working closely with the Congress to develop appropriate legislation to approve and implement this historic agreement.

Sincerely,

GEORGE BUSH

Note: Identical letters were sent to Thomas S. Foley, Speaker of the House of Representatives, and Dan Quayle, President of the Senate.

Notice of Intention To Enter Into a North American Free Trade Agreement With Canada and Mexico
September 18, 1992

On September 18, 1992, under section 1103(a)(1)(A) of the Omnibus Trade and Competitiveness Act of 1988, I notified the House of Representatives and the Senate of my intention to enter into a North American Free Trade Agreement with the Government of Canada and the Government of Mexico.

Pursuant to section 1103(a)(1)(A) of that Act, this notice shall be published in the *Federal Register.*

GEORGE BUSH

The White House,
September 18, 1992.

[*Filed with the Office of the Federal Register, 2:26 p.m., September 18, 1992*]

Remarks to the G–7 Finance Ministers and Bank Governors
September 20, 1992

Please be seated, and welcome to the White House. May I thank you all for coming. Secretary Brady and Chairman Greenspan were most interested in having this little get-together, and so am I and everybody at the White House. May I salute Minister Solchaga and Mr. Camdessus and just say welcome to the White House.

First, I know it's a difficult time, extremely difficult, and I salute the spirit of this meeting, the meetings that you've been having. Given the important events in Europe this week, in particular the turmoil in the financial markets and the vote in France on the European Community's Maastricht Treaty, I believe it is important for me to share with you my views. Together, we must establish an international economic system that meets the demands of the post-cold-war era. While the topics may be complex, they affect the day-to-day life of all of our citizens, the interest rates they pay on mortgages, inflation that can eat away at pensions, trade, and then growth that creates jobs.

First and foremost, I want to assure you of the United States commitment to be strongly engaged in a positive, steady fashion to help build global prosperity. I am working to strengthen America to compete with you, not retreat from you.

Next, I want to affirm our country's support for a European integration that opens markets and, in the process, enhances Europe's capability to be our partner in the great challenges we face in this new era. The exact form of integration is, of course, for our partners to determine, and we will stand with them as they do so.

Over recent years, we've been largely successful in returning to a regime of price stability. This stability will enable our entrepreneurs, our businesses, our workers to concentrate on building new technologies, real productive assets, savings, and jobs. We must combine this price stability with more vigorous economic growth. And therefore, we must examine ways to strengthen our international economic and monetary systems further, not only in Europe, which is experiencing exchange rate instability at the moment, but in the global economy.

In this context, I believe it is important in the months ahead for the G–7 nations, the U.S., our European partners, Canada, and Japan, to enhance the efforts we made in the past to review our economic policies and strengthen our economic coordination process. The aim of the coordination process in this new era should be to promote a healthy and progressive world economy and a stable monetary system. I believe the political leadership of our nations will need to play an increasingly active role in this work by reviewing our different economic perspectives and reinforcing possible agreements.

In seeking to strengthen the coordination process over the longer term, the United States will advocate to our economic partners that we explore the development of an independent reference point for our multilateral surveillance process.

We believe it could be useful in strengthening the coordination process to more intensely utilize an economic indicator that compares the relationship among our currencies and a basket of commodities, including gold. This commodity price indicator should be used in conjunction with other measures of economic performance such as growth, exchange rates, external imbalances as we work to coordinate our economic policies.

Finally, the United States also pledges its full commitment to policies that will strengthen the fundamentals for sustainable long-term growth. That includes a successful Uruguay round to expand world trade for all market economies, old and new. No politics of this country, let me just assure you, will interfere with our efforts for the United States side to conclude a successful—the successful conclusion of the GATT round. It also includes limits on the growth of our mandatory spending programs here in this country so that we can reduce our deficits. It includes an effort to dismantle internal rigidities that obstruct the creative process of building new businesses, helping people develop new skills, and shifting capital to investments where it will contribute to greater growth.

Over the past few years we have succeeded beyond our greatest expectations in offering hundreds of millions of free people the opportunity to build a secure economic future. But the very scope of the change has left all our publics uncertain, anxious about the future. It is our duty to build a global economic, financial, and trading structure for this new era, one that will help people translate hope into peace and prosperity for generations to come.

I know that together we can create an exciting future if we proceed cooperatively and confidently. I just wanted to get everybody together to tell you that I pledge the United States to the fulfillment of that task. We will work with you. Once again, congratulations on the way you're approaching the situation that faces us all now, the situation of cooperation and determination that I think really is capturing the imagination of people all around the world. The United States will stay with you. We will stay in here as partners, doing our level-best to be a part of the solution.

So thank you very much for coming. It is a Sunday afternoon, and what we wanted to do is simply to—Barbara and I—to invite you all through a rather informal receiving line down here, and then welcome you to a little hospitality at the White House.

Thank you very much for coming.

Note: The President spoke at 6 p.m. in the *East Room at the White House. In his remarks, he referred to Carlos Solchaga, Spain's Minister of Economy, Finance and Commerce, and Michel Camdessus, managing director, International Monetary Fund.*

Address to the United Nations General Assembly in New York City
September 21, 1992

Thank you, Mr. President, to you, sir, and Mr. Secretary-General and distinguished guests. Forty-seven years ago, I was a young man of 21, and like thousands of others of my generation, I'd gone off to war to help keep freedom alive. But 47 years ago this month, the war was finally over, and I was looking forward to peace and the chance to begin my life in earnest. Nineteen forty-five, it marked a moment of promise, not just for me but for all of mankind. A great struggle against dictatorship had been fought and won. Across the globe we all looked forward to a future free of war, a world where we might raise our children in peace and freedom. And this institution, the United Nations, born amidst the ashes of war, embodied those hopes and dreams like no other.

But the hopes and dreams of 1945 remained unfulfilled. Communist imperialism divided the world in two; our hopes for peace and our dreams of freedom were frozen in the grip of cold war. And instead of finding a common ground, we found ourselves at ground zero. Instead of living on Churchill's "broad, sunlit uplands," millions found that there was, as Arthur Koestler so chillingly wrote, "darkness at noon." And instead of uniting the nations, this body became a forum for distrust and division among nations. And in a cruel irony, the United Nations, created to free the world of conflict, became itself conflict's captive.

I, too, lived through those disputes. I sat where you sit, proudly so, served in this Assembly. I saw in my time the consequences of the cold war's hot words on the higher missions of the United Nations. And now 47 years later, we stand at the end of another war, the cold war, and our hopes and dreams have awakened again.

Driven by its own internal contradictions and banished by the people's undying thirst for freedom, imperial communism has collapsed in its birthplace. Today, Russia has awakened, democratic, independent, and free. The Baltic States are free, and so too are Ukraine and Armenia and Belarus and Kazakhstan and the other independent states, joining the nations of Central and Eastern Europe in freedom.

The fear of nuclear Armageddon between the superpowers has vanished. We are proud to have done our part to ensure that our schoolchildren do not have to practice hiding under their desks for fear of nuclear attack as the generation before them.

I am proud also to salute the courageous leaders with nuclear responsibilities: President Yeltsin, Kravchuk, Nazarbayev, Shushkevich, who join me in ending the superpower standoff that risked nuclear nightmare. This is the first General Assembly to seat you as truly independent and free nations. And to you and the leaders of the other independent states, I say: Welcome home; we are now truly United Nations.

With the cold war's end, I believe we have a unique opportunity to go beyond artificial divisions of a first, second, and third world to forge instead a genuine global community of free and sovereign nations; a community built on respect for principle of peaceful settlements of disputes, fundamental human rights, and the twin pillars of freedom, democracy and free markets.

Already the United Nations, especially the Security Council, has done much to fulfill its original mission and to build this global community. U.N. leadership has been critical in resolving conflicts and brokering peace the entire world over. But securing democracy and securing the peace in the century ahead will be no simple task. Imperial communism may have been vanquished, but that does not end the challenges of our age, challenges that must be overcome if we are finally to end the divisions between East and West, North and South that fuel strife and strain and conflict and war.

As we support the historic growth of democracy around the world, I believe the community of nations and the United Nations face three critical, interrelated challenges as we enter the 21st century:

First, we face the political challenge of keeping today's peace and preventing tomorrow's wars. As we see daily in Bosnia and Somalia and Cambodia, everywhere conflict claims innocent lives. The need for enhanced peacekeeping capabilities has never been greater, the conflicts we must deal with more intractable, the costs of conflict higher.

Second, we face the strategic challenge of the proliferation of weapons of mass destruction, truly the fastest growing security challenge to international peace and order.

And third, we face the common economic challenge of promoting prosperity for all, of strengthening an open, growth-oriented free market international economic order while safeguarding the environment.

Meeting these challenges will require us to strengthen our collective engagement. It will require us to transform our collective institutions. And above all, it will require that each of us look seriously at our own governments and how we conduct our international affairs. We too must change our institutions and our practices if we are to make a new world of the promise of today, if we're to secure a 21st century peace.

With you today, I would like to discuss these three challenges: peacekeeping, proliferation, and prosperity. And I'd like to use this opportunity to begin to sketch how I believe the international community can work together to meet these three challenges and how the United States is chang-

ing its institutions and policies to catalyze this effort.

Let me begin with peacekeeping. The United Nations has a long and distinguished history of peacekeeping and humanitarian relief. From Cyprus and Lebanon to Cambodia and Croatia, the blue beret has become a symbol of hope amid all that hostility, and the U.N. has long played a central role in preventing conflicts from turning into wars. Strengthened peacekeeping capabilities can help buttress these diplomatic efforts.

But as much as the United Nations has done, it can do much more. Peacekeepers are stretched to the limit while demands for their services increase by the day. The need for monitoring and preventive peacekeeping, putting people on the ground before the fighting starts, may become especially critical in volatile regions. This is especially the case because of the rapid and turbulent change that continues to shake Eastern Europe and Eurasia.

Across the lands that once were imprisoned behind an Iron Curtain, peoples are reasserting their historical identities that were frozen in communism's catacomb. Where this is taking place in a democratic manner with tolerance and civility and respect for fundamental human rights and freedoms, this new democratic nationalism is all to the good. But unfortunately, we need only look to the bloody battles raging in places such as the former Yugoslavia to see the dangers of ethnic violence. This is the greatest threat to the democratic peace we hope to build with Eastern Europe, with Russia and Eurasia, even more so than economic deprivation.

We fully support the efforts of NATO and CSCE and WEU, the C.I.S. and other competent regional organizations to develop peacekeeping capabilities. We are convinced that enhanced U.N. capabilities, however, are a necessary complement to these regional efforts, not just in Europe and Eurasia but across the globe.

I welcome the Secretary-General's call for a new agenda to strengthen the United Nations' ability to prevent, contain, and resolve conflict across the globe. And today, I call upon all members to join me in taking bold steps to advance that agenda. I, therefore, will be discussing with my colleagues the merits of a special meeting of the U.N. Security Council to discuss the Secretary-General's proposals and to develop concrete responses in five key areas:

One, robust peacekeeping requires men and equipment that only member states can provide. Nations should develop and train military units for possible peacekeeping operations and humanitarian relief. And these forces must be available on short notice at the request of the Security Council and with the approval, of course, of the governments providing them.

Two, if multinational units are to work together, they must train together. Many nations, for example, Fiji, Norway, Canada, and Finland, have a long history of peacekeeping. And we can all tap into that experience as we train for expanded operations. Effective multinational action will also require coordinated command-and-control and interoperability of both equipment and communications. Multinational planning, training, field exercises will be needed. These efforts should link up with regional organizations.

Three, we also need to provide adequate logistical support for peacekeeping and humanitarian operations. Member states should designate stockpiles of resources necessary to meet humanitarian emergencies including famines, floods, civil disturbances. This will save valuable time in a crisis.

Four, we will need to develop planning, crisis management, and intelligence capabilities for peacekeeping and humanitarian operations.

And five, we must ensure adequate, equitable financing for U.N. and associated peacekeeping efforts.

As I said, we must change our national institutions if we are to change our international relations. So let me assure you: The United States is ready to do its part to strengthen world peace by strengthening international peacekeeping.

For decades, the American military has served as a stabilizing presence around the globe. I want to draw on our extensive experience in winning wars and keeping the peace to support U.N. peacekeeping. I have directed the United States Secretary of Defense to place a new emphasis on peacekeeping. Because of peacekeeping's growing importance as a mission for the United States military, we will emphasize training of combat, engineering, and logistical units for the full range of peacekeeping and humanitarian activities.

We will work with the United Nations to best employ our considerable lift, logistics, communications, and intelligence capabilities to support peacekeeping operations. We will offer our capabilities for joint simulations and peacekeeping exercises to strengthen our ability to undertake joint peacekeeping operations. There is room for all countries, large and small, and I hope all will play a part.

Member states, as always, must retain the final decision on the use of their troops, of course. But we must develop our ability to coordinate peacekeeping efforts so that we can mobilize quickly when a threat to peace arises or when people in need look to the world for help.

I have further directed the establishment of a permanent peacekeeping curriculum in U.S. military schools. Training plainly is key. The United States is prepared to make available our bases and facilities for multinational training and field exercises. One such base nearby with facilities is Fort Dix. America used these bases to win the cold war, and today, with that war over, they can help build a lasting peace.

The United States is willing to provide our military expertise to the United Nations to help the U.N. strengthen its planning and operations for peacekeeping. We will also broaden American support for monitoring, verification, reconnaissance, and other requirements of U.N. peacekeeping or humanitarian assistance operations.

And finally, the United States will review how we fund peacekeeping and explore new ways to ensure adequate American financial support for U.N. peacekeeping and U.N. humanitarian activities. I do believe that we must think differently about how we ensure and pay for our security in this new era.

While the end of the cold war may have ended, the superpower nuclear arms competition, regional competition, weapons of mass destruction continue. Over 20 countries have or are developing nuclear, chemical, or biological weapons and the means to deliver them. At a time when the United States and its former adversaries are engaged in deep historic cuts in our nuclear arsenals, our children and grandchildren will never forgive us if we allow new and unstable nuclear standoffs to develop around the world.

We believe the Security Council should become a key forum for nonproliferation enforcement. The Security Council should make clear its intention to stem proliferation and sanction proliferators. Reaffirming assurances made at the time the Nuclear Non-Proliferation Treaty was negotiated, I proposed that the Security Council reassure the non-nuclear states that it will seek immediate action to provide assistance in accordance with the charter to any non-nuclear weapons state party to the NPT that is a victim of an act of aggression or an object of threat of aggression involving nuclear weapons.

I also call for the indefinite renewal of the Nuclear Non-Proliferation Treaty when it is reviewed in 1995. I believe we must explore ways that we can strengthen linkages between these suppliers' clubs, the Nuclear Suppliers Group, Australia Group, and the Missile Technology Control Regime, and specialized U.N. agencies. Here, I would like to note UNSCOM's productive efforts to dismantle the Iraqi weapons of mass destruction program and the International Atomic Energy Agency's continuing good work.

But as the U.N. organizations adapt to stop proliferation, so, too, must every member state change its structures to advance our nonproliferation goals. In that spirit, I want to announce my intention today to work with the United States Congress to redirect the United States Arms Control and Disarmament Agency, known to some of you as ACDA, to refocus its talents on providing technical support for nonproliferation, weapons monitoring and destruction, and global defense conversion. Under the direction of the Secretary of State, ACDA should be used not only in completing the traditional arms control agenda, but, just as importantly, in providing technical assistance on our new security agenda.

Even as we work to prevent proliferation of weapons of mass destruction, we must be realistic and guard ourselves against proliferation that has already taken place. Therefore, we're working toward a cooperative system for defense against limited ballistic missile attacks. And we fully intend to have other nations participate in this global protection system.

While expanded peacekeeping capabilities and improved nonproliferation efforts will be critical for building an enduring peace, shared economic growth is the long-term foundation for a brighter future well into the next century. That's why I stated yesterday, during a moment of international uncertainty, that the United States would be strongly engaged with its global partners in building a global economic, financial, and trading structure for this new era. At the same time I urge that our global responsibilities lead us to examine ways to strengthen the G–7 coordination process. I affirmed America's support for European integration that opens markets and enhances Europe's capability to be our partner in the great challenges that we face in this new era.

While the exact form of integration is, of course, for Europeans to determine, we will stand by them. Economic growth is not a zero-sum process. All of us will benefit from the expanded trade and investment that comes from a vibrant, growing world economy.

To ensure that the benefits of this growth are sustained and shared by all, fair and open competition should be the fuel for the global economic engine. That's why the United States wants to complete the Uruguay round of the GATT negotiations as soon as possible and to create a network of free trade agreements beginning with the North American free trade agreement. At the same time we need to recognize that we have a shared responsibility to foster and support the free market reforms necessary to build growing economies and vibrant democracies in the developing world and in the new democratic states. This should be done by promoting the private sector to build these new economies, not by fostering dependency with traditional government-to-government foreign aid.

Since World War II, foreign assistance often served as a weapon in the cold war. Obviously, we will still use critical foreign assistance funds to meet legitimate security needs. As our humanitarian operations in Somalia and northern Iraq, Bosnia, and the former Soviet Union will testify, we will continue our robust humanitarian assistance efforts to help those suffering from man-made and natural disasters.

But foreign aid as we've known it needs to be transformed. The notion of the hand-out to less developed countries needs to give way to cooperation in mutually productive economic relationships. We know that the more a nation relies on the private sector and free markets, the higher its rate of growth; the more open to trade, the higher its rate of growth; and the better a country's investment climate, the higher its rate of growth.

To move from aid, what I would call aid dependency, to economic partnership, we propose to alter fundamentally the focus of U.S. assistance programs to building strong, independent economies that can become contributors to a healthy, growing global economy. Now, that means that our new emphasis should be on building economic partnerships among our private sectors that will promote prosperity at home and abroad also.

Working with our Congress, I will propose a top-to-bottom overhaul of our institutions that plan and administer foreign assistance, drastically reducing the bureaucracy that has built up around Government-based programs; streamlining our delivery systems; and strengthening support for private sector development and economic reform. The Agency for International Development, AID, another institution born during the cold war, needs to be fundamentally and radically overhauled. Promoting economic security, opportunity, and competitiveness will become a primary mission of the State Department.

Our assistance efforts should not be charity. On the contrary, they should promote mutual prosperity. Therefore, using existing foreign affairs resources, I will propose creating a $1 billion growth fund. The fund will provide grants and credits to support U.S. businesses in providing expertise, goods, and services desperately needed in countries undertaking economic restructuring.

I will also support significantly increasing the programs of the Export-Import Bank to ensure that U.S. products and technology promote investment in worldwide economic growth. The United States will work with its global partners, especially the G-7 nations, to enhance global growth at this key point in world history as we end one era and begin another. None of us can afford insular policies. Each of us must contribute through greater coordinated action to build a stronger world economy.

Ladies and gentlemen, I realize that what I've outlined today is an ambitious agenda. But we live in remarkable times, times when empires collapse, ideologies dissolve, and walls crumble, times when change can come so fast that we sometimes forget how far and how fast we've progressed in achieving our hopes for a global community of democratic nations.

In the face of today's changes, with the loss of so much that was familiar and predictable, there is now a great temptation for people everywhere to turn inward and to build walls around themselves: walls against trade, walls against people, walls against ideas and investment, walls against anything at all that appears new and different. As the Berlin Wall fell, these walls, too, must fall. They must fall because we cannot separate our fate from that of others. Our peace is so interconnected, our security so intertwined, our prosperity so interdependent that to turn inward and retreat from the world is to invite disaster and defeat.

At the threshold of a new century we can truly say a more peaceful, more secure, more prospering future beckons to us. And for the sake of our children and our grandchildren, and for the sake of those who perished during the cold war, and for the sake of every man, woman, and child who kept freedom's flame alive even during the darkest noon, let us pledge ourselves to make that future real. And let us pledge ourselves to fulfill the promise of a truly United Nations.

Thank you, and may God bless you all. Thank you very much.

Note: The President spoke at 11:02 a.m. in the General Assembly Hall at the United Nations.

Message to the Senate Transmitting the Organization of American States-United States Headquarters Agreement
September 21, 1992

To the Senate of the United States:

With a view to receiving the advice and consent of the Senate to approval, I transmit herewith the Headquarters Agreement Between the Government of the United States of America and the Organization of American States ("the Agreement"), signed at Washington on May 14, 1992. I transmit also, for the information of the Senate, the Report of the Department of State with respect to this Agreement.

The Agreement will place the status of the Organization of American States ("OAS") in the United States on a clear legal basis and will underscore our commitment to the Organization. The Agreement in large measure elaborates and codifies the existing arrangements governing the presence of the headquarters of the OAS in the United States. However, it departs from existing arrangements in several respects. It extends diplomatic agent-level privileges and immunities to a small number of high level OAS officials. It exempts non-U.S. national OAS officials from state and local as well as federal income tax on their OAS earnings and benefits. It affords the OAS immunity from judicial process but in exchange for such immunity obligates the OAS to resolve certain (mainly commercial) disputes through a mutually agreed mechanism or, failing agreement, to submit such disputes to binding arbitration.

Although the Agreement provides that the U.S. will not exclude or expel OAS officials or experts for acts performed in their official capacity, Article XVII specifically states that "nothing in this Agreement shall be construed as in any way limiting the right of the United States to safeguard its own security, or its right completely to control the entrance of aliens into any territory of the United States."

Other provisions address the form and substance of the Official Travel Document; the procurement of communications facilities by the OAS; the disposition of the headquarters property in the event the OAS should cease to maintain headquarters in Washington; the provision of public services to the headquarters; and the privileges and immunities accorded OAS officials and experts.

No implementing legislation is required for the United States to perform its obligations under the Agreement. As a treaty, the Agreement will override federal, state, and local law with respect to privileges, immunities and exemptions to the extent such laws are inconsistent with its provisions. The provisions of the Agreement are not inconsistent with U.S. immigration laws, which will provide the basis for meeting the commitments established by the Agreement for the admission of aliens.

I recommend that the Senate give early and favorable consideration to the Agreement and give its advice and consent to approval.

GEORGE BUSH

The White House,
September 21, 1992.

Nomination of Robert Gregory Joseph To Be an Assistant Director of the United States Arms Control and Disarmament Agency
September 21, 1992

The President today announced his intention to nominate Robert Gregory Joseph, of Virginia, to be an Assistant Director of the U.S. Arms Control and Disarmament Agency (Bureau of Verification and Intelligence). He would succeed Manfred Eimer.

Since 1990, Dr. Joseph has served as U.S. Commissioner to the U.S. Standing Consultative Commission at the Department of State. From 1987 to 1990, he served as Principal Deputy Assistant Secretary of Defense and Deputy Assistant Secretary for Nuclear Forces and Arms Control at the Department of Defense. He has also served as Director of Theater Nuclear Forces at the Department of Defense, 1985–87, and as the United States Representative to the Nuclear Planning Group at NATO Headquarters in Brussels, Belgium, 1982–85.

Dr. Joseph graduated from St. Louis University (B.A., 1972); the University of Chicago (M.A., 1973); and Columbia University (M.Ph.L., 1976; Ph.D., 1978). He was born September 29, 1949, in Williston, ND. Dr. Joseph is married, has two children, and resides in Alexandria, VA.

Designation of Charles R. Hilty as Chief Financial Officer of the Department of Agriculture
September 21, 1992

The President today designated Charles R. Hilty, of Ohio, Assistant Secretary of Agriculture for Administration, as Chief Financial Officer of the Department of Agriculture. He will serve in these positions concurrently. This is a new position.

Currently Mr. Hilty serves as Assistant Secretary of Agriculture for Administration. Prior to this he served as Associate Deputy Secretary of Agriculture, 1991. Mr. Hilty has also served as minority staff director for the House Committee on Agriculture in the U.S. House of Representatives, 1984–91, and as administrative assistant in the office of Congressman Edward Madigan, 1978–84.

Mr. Hilty graduated from Bowling Green State University (B.S., 1960). He served in the Ohio National Guard, 1960–66. He was born November 6, 1934, in Bluffton, OH. Mr. Hilty is married and currently resides in Washington, DC.

Nomination of Marshall Fletcher McCallie To Be United States Ambassador to Namibia
September 21, 1992

The President today announced his intention to nominate Marshall Fletcher McCallie, of Tennessee, a career member of the Senior Foreign Service, class of Counselor, to be Ambassador of the United States of America to the Republic of Namibia. He would succeed Genta Hawkins Holmes.

Since 1990, Mr. McCallie has served as Deputy Chief of Mission at the U.S. Embassy in Pretoria, South Africa. Prior to this, Mr. McCallie served in several positions with the U.S. Department of State, including Deputy Chief of Mission at the U.S. Embassy in Lusaka, Zambia, 1988–90; Director of the Junior Officer Division with the Bureau of Personnel, 1986–88; Nigeria desk officer with the Bureau of African Affairs, 1984–86; political counselor at the U.S. Embassy in Monrovia, Liberia, 1982–84; and economic officer at the U.S. Embassy in Abu Dhabi, 1979–82.

Mr. McCallie graduated from Vanderbilt University (B.A., 1967) and the Fletcher School at Tufts University (M.A., and M.A.L.D., 1974). He served in the U.S. Air Force, 1967–71. He was born June 21, 1945, in Chattanooga, TN. Mr. McCallie is married, has two children, and resides in Washington, DC.

Nomination of Mark Johnson To Be United States Ambassador to Senegal
September 21, 1992

The President today announced his intention to nominate Mark Johnson, of Montana, a career member of the Senior Foreign Service, class of Minister-Counselor, to be Ambassador of the United States of America to the Republic of Senegal. He would succeed Katherine Shirley.

Since 1991, Mr. Johnson has served as executive assistant to the Under Secretary of State for Management at the U.S. Department of State. He has served in several positions with the Department of State, including Deputy Chief of Mission at the American Embassy in Kuwait City, Kuwait, 1991; Deputy Chief of Mission at the American Embassy in Cairo, Egypt, 1989–90; Deputy Assistant Secretary of State for Legislative Affairs, 1986–89; economic counselor at the American Embassy in Nairobi, Kenya, 1983–86; and a legislative management officer in the Office of Legislative Affairs, 1981–83.

Mr. Johnson graduated from Georgetown University (B.S., 1968) and George Washington University (M.A., 1970). He was born January 12, 1946, in Twin Falls, ID. Mr. Johnson currently resides in Great Falls, MT.

Remarks to the Community in Springfield, Missouri
September 22, 1992

Thank you all very, very much. Thank you very much. And let me just say to Governor Ashcroft how appreciative I am for that rousing introduction. And let me tell you, it's a joy to be back. I keep showing up in this marvelous part of the country.

I understand that I owe a vote of gratitude to Ben Parnell, a leading, most respected Democrat who gave an outstanding talk here; to Hal Gibbs, a former leader in the Perot organization who is now suited up and working hard for us. And I'm grateful to him, grateful to both of them. To an old friend, Johnny Morris, the only thing I feel deprived of is I can't go by that marvelous outlet here and enhance your economy— [*laughter*]—because I love fishing and I love the outdoors. And I respect Johnny Morris as one of our leading environmentalists in the entire United States. He's sensible, and he speaks for the sportsmen all across this country.

And of course, seeing modestly sitting in the front row over here my old, dear friend whom Barbara and I respect and love, who's been with us at Camp David, with whom I campaigned 4 years ago, Moe Bandy. I'll tell you, it's a joy to have him here. And I also want to pay my respects to the Congressman. I haven't seen Mel Hancock; maybe he's not with us. But he's a great Representative for this area. And of course, I was privileged to ride in with Don Gann, who is the neighboring State rep, a man that serves with John Ashcroft with such distinction in the capital.

So let me on with the business at hand. John has set the course and set the agenda for today's comments. These trips today will take me to six different States.

Two weeks ago in Detroit, I presented to the American people my Agenda for American Renewal. It is a clear-eyed look at what's wrong with our country and also what's right about our country. I offered a comprehensive, integrated approach to win the new global economic competition so that by early in the next century, the world's first $10 trillion economy will be found right here in the United States of America.

Last week, I discussed in detail how my vision of our future differs from that of the opponent. The differences simply could not be deeper. The stakes, as John points out, the Governor points out, could not be higher. Basically, it comes down to this: My opponent believes that Government planners can manage the economy better than the workers and small-business men and women who actually make it grow. I respect Government, but I don't put my faith in it. I put my faith in the tax-paying, hard-working men and women of America.

The first shot out of the box Governor Clinton says that he wants to raise taxes that will kill jobs. I want to see them cut to help Americans create jobs. Governor Clinton wants to increase—he's already said this—increase Federal spending by at least $220 billion. I want to cut it by that and more. I want the differences to be clear and sharp. And then the American people, then you will make a choice.

You know, the American people are interviewing two men for the same job. Now, you know me. My record is on the table, over the years. You know its shortcomings; I admit I've made mistakes. And I hope you know my record's strengths. And in my agenda I've told you what I intend to do to build on that record. I have spoken from my heart about the great optimism that I feel for this Nation, how I know we can rise above our challenges today and achieve an even better tomorrow.

My opponent has taken a very different path. He hasn't hesitated a minute to try to tear down everything we've accomplished for 12 years, to find everything he can about what's wrong with America. While I've been talking about ideas, he and his people have admitted publicly that their focus is on the negative, on what's wrong. For month after month, Governor Clinton has persisted in attacks on me; persistent, unrelenting, and many very personal in nature. Frankly, he has distorted my record, and his campaign cochairman even called me a racist. And this week the Governor unveiled, for the first time in this Presidential race, negative campaigning, negative television advertising, first one of this campaign.

So far, right up to today in Springfield, I have resisted the urge to focus on Governor Clinton's record. Frankly, I have felt that Americans want a positive debate. But I must tell you, I am very tired of the distortions, tired of the half-truths. The stakes are too high to let America be deceived by a negative campaign. So today, for really the first time, I have chosen to lay it on the line, talk about my opponent's record, talk facts, talk about the record in Arkansas, the Governor's record. And that means explaining the Grand Canyon that separates his rhetoric from the reality of his record. You need to know this because our country's future is literally on the line. You need to know whether you can trust Bill Clinton to take America where it needs to go in the next 4 years. Because once you buy what he's selling, there's no refund.

I hear candidate Clinton is up in Michigan today talking about debates. Well, I propose a debate for him today: candidate Clinton versus Governor Clinton. You see, we've all heard what candidate Clinton says he can do for America. But that's very different from what Governor Clinton has done to Arkansas, to the good people of Arkansas. And I want to stress this: My argument is not with the people of Arkansas, it is not. They are good, decent, hard-working people. Frankly, they deserve treatment better than they've received from Governor Clinton. So here we go.

Let me begin with an issue of concern to

every American, every fairminded American: civil rights. Governor Clinton says, and I quote, "Everybody knows I have the best civil rights record." His words. His modesty overwhelms me. [*Laughter*] But how does his record stand? Some of you may know that in 1968, when I was a Congressman from Texas, I supported the Fair Housing Act. It wasn't popular with some of my constituents. Times have changed, of course, and nowadays 41 States have laws banning housing discrimination, 41. But Arkansas is not one of them, even though my opponent has been Governor for 12 years. Forty-six States have human relations agencies that safeguard citizens against discrimination, but not Arkansas under his leadership. Forty-eight States have basic civil rights laws that ban discrimination and guarantee equal opportunity, but not Arkansas. That's right: Arkansas is only one of two States in America without a civil rights statute.

Candidate Clinton likes to talk about my 1990 veto of the Democratic Congress' quota bill. I did veto that bill, and I'll veto any other quota bill that the liberals cook up. I am for civil rights. And I am against quotas. That is not a contradiction. So last year, after tough negotiations with Congress and beating back two attempts to ram down my throat and the people's throat a quota bill, I did proudly sign a major civil rights bill without resorting to quotas. In addition, I fought for the Americans with Disabilities Act, the most sweeping civil rights legislation in 30 years, that brings those with disabilities into the mainstream and gives them as shot at the American dream. And I'm proud of it.

What about Governor Clinton? Even though his party enjoys overwhelming control of the Arkansas Legislature, Governor Clinton has still not brought a civil rights bill to the people of Arkansas. So when you hear the candidate Clinton's rhetoric all across this country about civil rights, Governor Clinton's record just does not stand up.

Now, consider another issue: economic fairness. You know, candidate Clinton is playing the old game that liberals love to play, class warfare: divide Americans, rich from poor, one group from another. And he's good at it. Candidate Clinton is very good at that, using the same tired, twisted, partisan statistics to explain how the poor can only get richer if the rich get poorer. According to candidate Clinton, the last 10 years have been a nightmare. Well, I've got news for him. It is not true. The Urban Institute back in Washington is not usually sympathetic to me, but listen to what they had to say about the 1980's: "When one follows individuals rather than statistical groups defined by income, one finds that, on average, the rich got a little richer and the poor got much richer." Now, that's the truth. Our policies of cutting taxes have spurred growth for all Americans.

Yes, we've got tough times now. But it's fair to look at the whole record. And candidate Clinton doesn't think this is a fair result. He doesn't think it's fair. It's maybe because Governor Clinton doesn't have much experience with tax fairness in his own State. Governor Clinton has more than doubled—if you want a horror story, listen to this—he has more than doubled Arkansas State spending since 1983. And he has paid for it by raising the taxes that hurt poor and working families the most. My opponent has raised and extended his sales tax repeatedly, and he has opposed removing that tax from groceries. Governor taxes—"Governor Taxes"—sorry. [*Laughter*] Freudian slip. Governor Clinton raised taxes on beer and started taxing mobile homes, too. And he more than doubled Arkansas' gas tax to 18½ cents per gallon. Governor Clinton even taxed food stamps until the Federal Government forced him to stop. And as if working families in Arkansas did not have enough problems, he's even tried to tax child care.

When it comes to taxes, Governor Clinton can't seem to get enough. Last year, he signed the largest tax increase in Arkansas history. I signed a tax increase once, and I've regretted it ever since. I admit it when I make a mistake. And therein lies the difference. Let me quote from an article in the Arkansas Gazette on all of this. "In the Clinton era," it says, "the State tax system has become more and more regressive. It has become, step by step, a pretty bad system, stacked against the ordinary taxpayer and consumer, stacked for the rich and special interest." End of quotation. Now, that's been his tax policy in Arkansas. Look at what it did to that State's economy—a wonderful State, but look what it did to the economy. The per capita income, for example—that's the bottom line for working men and women, how much income on average each of them have—well, at the end of the 1980's, Arkansas ranked 48th in the Nation, per capita income, only about 73 percent of the national average. And that was even lower than the 75 percent in 1980. The poor people have been going backwards under this man. And what about all those good manufacturing jobs that candidate Clinton talks about? Well, average hourly earnings for Arkansas manufacturing workers ranked 47th in 1980. By 1989, they had dropped to 50th.

Now candidate Clinton says he wants to do to the American economy what Governor Clinton's done to Arkansas: Arkansas taxes, Arkansas income, Arkansas jobs. And I don't think he's kidding. I wish he were. Candidate Clinton wants the biggest tax increase in history. He hasn't even got there yet, and he's proposing the largest tax increase in history. And that's not even counting his payroll taxes for training and also those that would be required under his health care plan. And that's not fair. That simply is not fair for every working man and woman in America.

Another issue, one near and dear to the hearts of every American, rural and urban, and that's crime. Candidate Clinton likes to talk tough. You'll hear him criticize me about Federal aid to State and local law enforcement. But in fact, since 1989, we've proposed a 59-percent increase in Federal spending to fight crime. You'll also hear candidate Clinton make some pretty impressive claims about crime control in Arkansas. Wrong. Wrong again. Not. [*Laughter*] Candidate Clinton, meet Governor Clinton. During the 1980's, the Nation's overall crime rate during the eighties actually declined. But not in Arkansas. In fact, Governor Clinton's State had the biggest increase in overall crime rate in the entire Nation, nearly 28 percent. Again, this is not fair to the good people of Arkansas.

What about violent crimes? Arkansas' violent crime rate went up more than 58 percent, one of the worst records in the entire

Nation. Why? Well, I've got a few hunches. Arkansas ranks near rockbottom in every important per capita law enforcement expenditure: for prisons, 46th; for judicial and legal systems, 50th. And when it comes to spending for police officers, Arkansas ranks 49th. And in Arkansas, when the prison door slams shut on a convicted criminal, he knows it won't be long before it opens up again. As incredible as it sounds, as incredible as it sounds, most inmates in Arkansas serve less than one-fifth of their sentence behind bars. That's the worst record in the entire Nation. The people of Arkansas deserve to walk their streets without fearing that some crazy convict is going to ruin their lives, some guy let out of jail far too early.

Now, contrast the situation in Arkansas with what we've been doing on the Federal level. Most Federal inmates serve at least 85 percent of their full sentence. And I think it's pretty simple: If you take liberties with the law, you're going to lose your own liberties for a long, long time. When you look at Governor Clinton's record on law enforcement, it's not surprising that last week, the Fraternal Order of Police in Little Rock gave me their endorsement for President of the United States of America. And that is the verdict of the police officers in Governor Clinton's own backyard. They agree with me. You do not coddle criminals; you stand up for the law-abiding citizens in this country.

I'm really enjoying getting this record out here. Now let's look at another contrast. It's been 11 long months of his hammering me. And we're just starting today right here Springfield because I want the American people to know the truth. I want them to know the facts. I want them to know the truth.

Let's look at another contrast between candidate Clinton's rhetoric and Governor Clinton's record: with children. In his new book, candidate Clinton says that America has failed to provide its children with either the best education or adequate protection from violence. That's what the candidate says. Now how about the Governor? Look at the facts. During the 1980's, Arkansas fell from 47th to 48th place in the percentage of adults with a high school diploma. Arkansas' rankings on its primary college entrance examination, known as ACT, have declined overall. Twenty-eight States use the ACT as their primary college entrance test. The New York Times recently reported that in 1979, Arkansas ranked 20 out of those 28. The State's latest available ranking is down to 25th out of the 28.

And we know that more than three-quarters of Arkansas high school graduates require remedial instruction when they get to college. It's not fair to them. Think about it, 75 percent of Arkansas college students spend their first year of college relearning what they missed out on in high school. Now these are bright, dynamic young people. And they deserve better than a failed education system. And when it comes to the percentage of adults with a college degree, Governor Clinton's Arkansas still ranks 50th.

Now, when it comes to protecting children from violence, you should know this: My opponent's record is, in one word, appalling. The facts are not pretty. But America should listen to the facts. During the 1980's, the death rate of American children 14-and-under improved dramatically across the country. But in Arkansas, it got worse. The State ranked 49th in 1989. In the late 1980's, Arkansas' rate of violent deaths for teenagers soared at 3 times the national average. And over the decade, child abuse reports shot up 130 percent. Now, behind that statistic are tales of heartbreaking tragedy. The young people over in Arkansas deserve to have their hearts healed.

Now, it's hard to believe that Governor Clinton was unaware of what was going on. Throughout the 1980's, study after study contained detailed findings and recommendations; a cry for help, if you will. And he even commissioned some of these studies himself. In 1990, his own department of human services reported that "frequent and widespread" official failures had placed the children of Arkansas in, again a quote, "imminent peril." Still Governor Clinton did nothing. And finally, a group of child welfare advocates took the Governor to court. They filed a Federal class action naming him as lead defendant. And on June 8th, less than 4 months ago, my opponent finally

settled. And now candidate Clinton promises to crack down on violence against children.

Now to what Johnny Morris is famous for and that Governor Ashcroft can take great pride in, the environment. I love to hike. I love to camp out. I love to go fishing. I like to go hunting. And you've heard me talk about the importance of protecting the environment many times. But to me real eloquence is action, and I have acted. There's our historic Clean Air Act, cutting acid rain in half, we did that. We banished offshore oil rigs from sensitive beaches on both coasts and added a billion dollars worth of new forests and parks for our children to enjoy. In the past 3 years, our Environmental Protection Agency has assessed more than half of all the civil penalties and criminal fines in the history of EPA, more than $200 million. To those who spoil our lakes and air we are saying: Mess with our children's health and you will pay.

Those are facts. And that is the record, a record I am very proud of on the environment; a sound, progressive record. But candidate Clinton calls America's environmental record since 1989 a disaster. And he promises, quote, "real environmental policy" that will, again quote, "challenge Americans and demand responsibility at every level." My advice: Let's take candidate Clinton at his word. Demand that candidates run on their records. I'm prepared to do that. We've got a good record to take to the American people, the people of Missouri. I'll stand by my record. Now, let's see if he can stand on his. And again, I'm going to be very, very factual.

Earlier this year, my opponent was asked to name a single Arkansas law that exceeds Federal environmental standards. He couldn't do that, not one. The Governor has accepted generous campaign contributions, free plane rides from Arkansas' powerful chicken industry. And the industry is the ultimate source of, and I'll put this as delicately as I possibly can, fecal coliform bacteria, which pollutes hundreds of miles of Arkansas rivers. Governor Clinton did create an animal waste task force to deal with the issue. But the task force subcommittee was headed by a chicken executive. And they decided that controls on what they call "chicken litter," unquote—[*laughter*]—should be purely voluntary. It's hard to keep this clean, but I'm telling you the record is bad over there. But I guess with Governor Clinton, some things do run thicker than water. [*Laughter*]

Last year, the Institute for Southern Studies released an extraordinarily detailed, State-by-State study of environmental quality and progress. And let me quote the Institute's research director: "In the areas of policy—laws passed, not task forces or commissions set up to study a problem—Arkansas was 50th, the worst in the Nation." Arkansas residents want clean air and clean water. They're sportsmen just like you all are, just like I am. They love the outdoors just like you do and just like I do. And they should not be last in the entire Nation.

And finally, let's talk about health care. As you might expect, my opponent and I have two vastly different approaches to the problem. I want to use competition to expand coverage, preserve quality, drive down the costs. And candidate Clinton's plan could eventually bring our health care system under the control of the Federal Government. Until last month, candidate Clinton pretended that his plan wouldn't cost a dime. But then someone at USA Today got him to admit what I've been saying all along: His plan would require a new payroll tax. And I say small business does not need any more taxes. Let's do it my way. A new payroll tax will kill jobs, especially in the small businesses that we're looking to to create the new jobs we need in this country. It'll cut wages.

But since we're talking about our records today, consider this, too. Candidate Clinton says, "Health care should be a right, not a privilege." And yet, under Governor Clinton, Arkansas has one of the Nation's worst health insurance crises. More than 42 percent of Arkansas workers, the second highest percentage in the entire Nation, don't even have employer-paid health insurance. And the New York Times says a full 25 percent of all State residents have no health insurance at all. Candidate Clinton now says America, quote, "can't afford 4 more years" without a solution to our health care problem. And I totally agree with that. But Gov-

ernor Clinton took a long time to come around. Early last year, in his fifth term as Governor, he finally signed a bill to provide bare-bones coverage to people who have gone uninsured for more than a year.

And so there you have it. Nothing personal, just the facts. And next time you hear candidate Clinton promise to be a progressive change agent for the entire United States, think of civil rights and taxes in the State he's left behind. Think of crime and child abuse and education in that great State of Arkansas. Think of the environment that he's neglected, the health care problems he's ignored. Think about all this the next time candidate Clinton says he will do for America what he's done for Arkansas.

It is true we're having a big debate about America's future. But first you have to learn who's really on the other side. And you have to know: Is it the words of candidate Clinton or the actions of Governor Clinton? We've seen over the last 9 months that candidate Clinton appears willing to say anything to anyone. But the record of Governor Clinton proves that it doesn't matter what the candidate will say to anyone, because he won't deliver. So either way, whether it's candidate Clinton or Governor Clinton, I believe that Bill Clinton is wrong to be President of the United States of America.

You know, I feel better now, because when I started this morning, I explained how for months Governor Clinton has distorted my record. And I sat there through primary after primary, one assault by another—not all by Governor Clinton, I might add, joined by a handful of other guys that have fallen by the wayside—and I'd made a decision. I was President; I was trying to do something to help this country. And I chose not to fight back until now, because I believe Americans want action from their President. And I believe they want positive ideas, want real solutions to our challenges.

But I simply cannot let Governor Clinton's distortions go unanswered. His own record must be exposed because look at what is at stake. This man has the gall to go around America and promise the moon, when on issue after issue, the sky has fallen in in his own backyard. I say Arkansas deserves better. And I mean that. I say America deserves better. And I say America deserves more than learning what's wrong; we need to know what works to build a safer and more secure future for these kids over here. And this is what I offer in this campaign: experience, character, and ideas that are right for America.

My agenda contains 13 specific actions that I'm going to fight to accomplish in the first year of my second term, with all those new Congressmen that are coming in as a result of the confusion and disarray in the House. And I'm going to get them done. I'm going to get these things done with your help, because America has what it takes to win the economic competition, to win the peace. So let's get on with the job.

And thank you for this exceptionally warm welcome, this Missouri welcome. And may God bless the greatest country on the face of the Earth, the United States of America. Thank you all.

Note: The President spoke at 8:53 a.m. in the University Plaza Convention Center. In his remarks, he referred to John Morris, chairman, Bush-Quayle Outdoors Coalition; entertainer Moe Bandy; and Don Gann, Missouri State legislator.

Remarks on Arrival in Tulsa, Oklahoma
September 22, 1992

Thank you all very much. What a fantastic rally. Thank you so very much, and good morning, Oklahoma. I'm delighted to be back. May I first salute J.C., the man that introduced me, my friend. You should be very proud to have a man of his character and experience in office here in the great State of Oklahoma. J.C., thank you very, very much.

Before I share just a few remarks with you on our campaign, as I look at national priorities, one of them simply must be the reelection of your great Senator, Don Nickles. We need him in Washington. And you know, everyplace I go you hear people saying, "Clean House! Clean House!" We've got a good man in Jim Inhofe. Reelect him, and then send Jerry Hill to the United States Congress. We've got to change it.

I am just delighted to be here. May I pay a special tribute to these great bands: the Hornets, the Warriors, the Indians, and the Eagles. It's great to be back in one of the great States for high school football. All four of these schools won their football games last weekend. Good news.

May I also just say a word to those who work for the great company that puts together that fabulous fighting machine, the F-15, the people at McDonnell Douglas.

Thanks for hosting us here, and good luck with the new sale abroad. And I want to say hello also to those who work for the great Rockwell Industries, two giants of American industry, employing men and women who are the best workers in the entire world.

You know, for the past few weeks I've been traveling the length and the breadth of this fantastic country of ours, stumping for the economic ideas that I believe in: an Agenda for American Renewal. I want to create new markets for American products and new jobs for American workers. You see, we never retreat; we always compete. And we will always win. We are the United States of America.

And yes, we've had some tough times in this country, but don't believe the pessimists on the other side who can only win by tearing down America. We're coming out of our difficulties, and we are leading the world, and we'll continue to do so as long as I'm your President.

Big difference in this election. He wants to spend more and tax more. I want to see the Federal Government spend less, and I want to see us taxed less, so private sector can get the job done. I'm standing in Tulsa, Oklahoma, one of the great oil capitals of the world. I want to see a change in our tax system that benefits the independent oil people so we can get those rigs running again. Change the alternative minimum tax, and watch what Tulsa and the rest of Oklahoma can do.

Frankly, we are trying hard to give small business relief from taxation, from regulation, and yes, from litigation. We are suing each other too much, and we should care for each other more. I want to change all the lawsuits up there.

Another big objective, and we're on the right track, is we want to change the American schools. I want to give these young people the finest education in the entire world. I want to give the parents the right to choose the schools, whether it's public, private, or religious.

We've got a good health care program for America, and I want to use competition to cut the cost of health care, make it available to you and your neighbors. And the way I see it, you should only feel the pain when you're in the doctor's office, not a month later when you get the bill in the mail. And so, do not go for the Clinton plan that says get the Government further involved; go for our plan that says provide insurance to all, and keep the quality of health care we now have.

You know, for about 11 months, Governor Clinton has been attacking me and my record, and I've sat back trying to get things done for this country. Month after month he's persisted in these unrelenting attacks, many of them quite personal in nature, distorting my record; and his campaign cochairman even called me a racist. And this week Governor Clinton unveiled the first negative television advertising of the campaign. He fired the first negative campaign shot, and I am not going to take it anymore. I'm going to take his record to the American people as well as my own.

And so let's see how the American people—how they feel after they understand the facts about his record. In Springfield, Missouri, a few minutes ago I talked about the overall record. And today I'm coming by some of the other States that are near Arkansas to move beyond the record and find out what he has actually done in Arkansas, or put it this way, done to the good people of the State of Arkansas. First,

my argument is not with the people of that great State. They are good; they are decent; they are hard-working. And they deserve better treatment than they've received from their Governor.

The other side is eager to debate. We'll probably have a debate. But for openers, let them debate each other. Let one side, as candidate Clinton, a promising young man who seems to be willing to promise anything to get elected; and on the other is Governor Clinton, whose record in Arkansas is a series of broken promises.

Now let me look at just one issue today because I think of the people of Oklahoma as fair. Let's take a look at the civil rights record. Candidate Clinton says, and I quote, "Everybody knows that I have the best civil rights record." Well, that is a very modest statement by the Governor saying he has the best civil rights record. But let's see if his rhetoric is matched by his record.

Some of you may know in 1968 when I was a Member of Congress from Texas that I voted for a fair housing act. It was not a popular vote with my constituents. But times have changed now, and nowadays 41 States have laws banning housing discrimination—41 States, including the great State of Oklahoma. Arkansas is not one of them, and that man's been Governor for 10 or 12 years. He's talked a lot and done nothing.

Forty-eight States, the young people here might be interested, have basic civil rights law, 48 that ban discrimination and guarantee equal opportunity, and Oklahoma is proud to be one of them. But not Arkansas. Arkansas is one of only two States without a civil rights statute. What has the Governor been doing, other than talking about fairplay?

Governor Clinton goes around criticizing my 1990 veto of the Democrat Congress' quota bill. Well yes, I did veto that bill, and I'll veto any other quota bill that the liberals cook up in Washington, DC. I am for civil rights, and we've got a good record on that. And I am against quotas. And that is not a contradiction. I'm proud last year to have signed a very good equal opportunity bill, and it had no quotas in it. Now, even though his party enjoys overwhelming control of the Arkansas Legislature, he still hasn't brought a civil rights bill to the people of Arkansas. So when you hear candidate Clinton, his rhetoric about civil rights, remember Governor Clinton's record in Arkansas.

You know, Bill Clinton talks a very good game. He's got more statistics than there are problems out there, but his actions betray his words. In Arkansas, individual income has slipped; crime is up relative to the Nation; children's test scores get weaker; while streams of air get more polluted. If you go swimming in that Arkansas River, keep your mouth closed and hold your nose. They are doing a terrible job on pollution.

So again, candidate Clinton talks one way, and Governor Clinton has a very, very different record. Governor Clinton proves that it doesn't matter what the candidate says. He simply will not deliver. So whether it's candidate Clinton or Governor Clinton, the message is the same: Bill Clinton is the wrong man to accept your trust to be President of the United States of America. I will let you all make up your mind about service to country when it comes to war and peace. I will take my record with pride to the American people. We have stood tall, and freedom has prevailed.

Not far from here, you know, is the birthplace of Will Rogers, the man who said he wasn't a humorist, he just watched the Government and reported what happened.

Well, I don't know what he'd say about Governor Clinton. Maybe he would say that here's a guy with the gall to promise the Moon to America while the sky is falling down in his own backyard. But I really believe we can do better, and I say America deserves better.

And yes, we have challenges, and yes, we have problems. But this agenda of mine will confront our challenges. There's going to be over 100 new Members of Congress, maybe 150. And the day I am reelected and they are elected, I'll sit down with them and say, "Now let's improve our schools; let's fight for America's security; let's do something about these lawsuits that are plaguing America; let's do something about health care; let's get on with the business of governing this Nation and solving our problems."

And so what I will be offering the voters, and I ask for your support, is experience, ideas that are right for America. And I hope that my character will pass muster with you, the American people.

Thank you very much, and may God bless this great State. And thank you for this fantastic welcome to Oklahoma. Thank you very much.

Note: The President spoke at 11:12 a.m. at the Tulsa International Airport. In his remarks, he referred to Johnnie Cherblanc, master of ceremonies for the event.

Remarks on Arrival in Longview, Texas
September 22, 1992

The President. Thank you very, very much. Thank you so much. It's an honor and privilege to be introduced by Florence Shapiro, not only the Mayor of Plano but going to be a member of the Texas Senate. We need her. She's typical of our great women leaders in our State of Texas. Thank you, Florence. I want to thank our State chairman, Jim Oberwetter, who is here somewhere; Rob Mosbacher, the Texas Victory '92 chairman; Barbara Patton, the Bush-Quayle cochairman; and our master of

ceremonies, Jim Offutt. Let me say it's great to be back in east Texas, great, where the people understand the values that make this country strong.

You know, Longview brings back many memories. Back when I started a business out in west Texas and then down on the Gulf Coast, where I met a payroll, learned the basic truth about things like the role of Government and the power of the individual, I stood here at this very airport, I believe it was 22 years ago, and saw a former

President come into this airport. And I am proud to be back here as President of the United States, asking for your support for 4 more years.

Here in Texas, I learned something, and I learned that prosperity doesn't come just from the hallowed halls of Government. It comes from the hard work, the imagination, and the industry of men and women like you here today. I'm grateful to you for coming out to this rally. I'm glad to see all the bands and participants here, glad to see the Kilgore Rangerettes. I wish they'd go up to Washington for a few days. They could go over and take a look at the Congress and put those high-kicking boots to good use, help us to "clean House." You talk about kicking it, they're the ones to do it.

Now, you know, for the past few weeks I've been traveling the length and breadth of our country, and what a great country it is, stumping for the ideas that I believe in, the Agenda for American Renewal. I want to open new markets for our American products and new jobs for American workers. Americans never retreat; we always compete. And we always win. Let's open these foreign markets.

I have a fundamental difference with the Governor next door. I believe Government is too big and spends too much of your taxpayers' money. I want to do something about it. He wants to raise taxes and increase spending. I want to cut taxes and cut spending.

Good news today for the Nation, good news today on housing starts: They are up, the largest increase in 18 months. Inflation is down. Interest rates are down. Productivity is up. And the economy is poised for a recovery. We must not let Governor Clinton get in and tax it back into oblivion. I want to see incentives. I want to see incentives, and one of them ought to apply to the domestic oil business. We want to change the alternative minimum tax so we can get on with the business of developing more domestic resources and less dependency on foreign oil.

You know, it's small-business people, small-business women, small-business men that saved this economy when the going has been tough. They need relief from taxation,

regulation, and yes, from litigation. As a nation, we spend up to $200 billion a year on lawsuits. As a nation, we ought to sue each other less and care for each other more.

I see a lot of young people here today and welcome. Let me say this about education: I want to give the young what they truly deserve, the finest schools in the entire world. I want to give every parent and every family the right to choose their children's schools, whether they're public, private, or religious.

You know, I believe the Governor next door, Governor Clinton, has made up his mind: The only way he can win is to tell everybody how horrible things are about this country. He has persisted on attacking me day-in and day-out, many of the attacks personal. He has distorted and, I would say, told the untruths about my record. This week, he unveiled—started in, the first one to do it—the first negative campaign ad. He's the one that says, watch out for the Republicans. Watch on the television, the first negative campaign ads in the Presidential race of 1992 belong to that sorry ticket of Clinton and Gore. It's a sad thing.

I have taken it for 11 months, listening to these guys. And I'll tell you today: I'm starting to dish it out and tell the truth about his record. So, this morning for openers, I went to the State of Missouri, and I laid out the Clinton record, just the facts, telling the truth. I'm stopping by these States, our State and others, that are neighbors to the State of Arkansas so that we can get past this campaign rhetoric of his and look at what he's done for the people of Arkansas or, should I say, done to the good people of that great State. Look, they are good, decent people next door. They are good, hard-working people, and they deserve better treatment than they've received from their Governor.

You know, the other side keeps talking, you hear him talking about debate, they want to change the rules from the debate rules that have been in effect for the last four Presidential campaigns. Now he wants to change them. But now they ought to have a debate. On the one hand, you ought to have candidate Clinton; he'd be over here. On the other side, promising everything, Governor Clinton. They ought to debate each other on the issues.

Each stop here along the way in this six-State swing, I'm talking about various issues. And let me talk today just about affordable health care, something that I am desperately interested in providing to every man, woman, and child in this country. As you might expect, my opponent and I have two vastly different ideas how to go about this. I want to use the competition to expand coverage, making insurance available to the poorest of the poor, to everybody else, everybody, preserve quality, and allow you to spend less of your paycheck on health insurance.

He has a different approach. He expresses so much enthusiasm for Government, he would have Government get involved in setting health care prices and perhaps eventually get involved in running our health care system. We do not need the Government to run it. We need to protect quality and provide insurance to all. You'd think he'd learn from the way the Democrats ran the House post office. They can't run that; they can't run a bank. Why in heaven's name do they think they can run the health insurance programs?

You know, this guy, he's too much. Up until a few weeks ago Governor Clinton pretended that his plan wouldn't cost a dime. But then someone at USA Today—you know the paper that got him to admit what I've been saying all along: his plan would require a new payroll tax on the back of, you've got it, small business. Now, I don't know about you, but I think small-business men and women pay enough in taxes already. We cannot let him do this to the American economy.

You know, he says that health care should be a right, not a privilege. Yes, I think everybody should have health care. But yet, look at his record as Governor, not the candidate but Governor Clinton. Arkansas has one of the Nation's worst health insurance crises. More than 42 percent of Arkansas workers, decent, hard-working people, 42 percent, the second highest percentage in the entire Nation don't have employer-paid health insurance at all and a full 25 percent have no health insurance at all. He talks

one way around the Nation; he delivers misery at home. We do not need that for the Nation.

You know, early last year in his fifth term as Governor, Governor Clinton finally signed a bill to provide bare-bones coverage to people who have gone uninsured for more than a year. Last fall, even his minimal plan had still not been implemented. Even today, not a single insurance company has ever set up a single policy for anyone under Governor Clinton's model program.

So, on this issue, on health care—and I could be talking about the environment, whatever—on this one, look at the Grand Canyon between the words of candidate Clinton, running around the country criticizing me, and the actions of Governor Clinton, which is a sorry record by any Texas standard.

I love fishing and hunting. I know everybody in east Texas does, too. I flew over some beautiful bass lakes, and I got thinking about Governor Clinton's record on the environment. Some of you may have tried to fish or swim in the Arkansas River. You may have heard that night fishing is catching on over there. The rivers are so polluted that the fish glow in the dark. He has a lousy record on the environment, and we across the line in Texas have a good record on the environment.

You know, on issue after issue he talks a great game, but his actions betray his words. While he makes promises, the workers, the decent, hard-working men and women of Arkansas, their standard of living weakens and their crime rate rises up faster than the rest of the Nation. Their children's test scores slip, and Governor Clinton cannot muster the courage to even put in a basic civil rights law like we have right here in Texas. Forty-eight States have them, but not Arkansas. That is not fair. There's not fairplay in Arkansas.

So in other words, what I'm asking the American people today on this six-State swing is to take a look at the record that he's laid down, and then compare that against the rhetoric that he's trying to take all across the country, and be careful, because it's slippery when wet. [*Applause*] You're right.

We've got a lot of challenges, and we have a lot of problems, but we've got a great future. I see that airplane sitting over there, and I don't want to start telling you war stories, but that's the kind of torpedo bomber I flew in World War II. I was shot down in that airplane in World War II, and I am proud that I served my Nation in combat. I am proud that since I have been President we have reduced the threat of nuclear war so young men and women go to bed at night without that awesome fear of nuclear war.

We have changed the world, and now I'm asking for your help to bring honor and decency right back here at home and change things to make things better for the people of Texas and the other 49 States. We can do it. We've got a sound record. We are on the right track. Now I need the help of the American people to guarantee 4 more years to finish the job.

Audience members. Four more years! Four more years! Four more years!

The President. I am very proud to be back home. We are going to carry Texas, and we are going to win this election because we are right on the issues and because I have been telling the truth all along. Thank you very, very much.

May God bless you all. Thank you so very, very much for this wonderful rally. What a fantastic turnout. I love the signs, man. Thank you.

Note: The President spoke at 1:17 p.m. at Longview County Airport.

Remarks on Arrival in Shreveport, Louisiana
September 22, 1992

The President. Thank you so very much for this great welcome back to Louisiana. First-class, first-class all the way. Thank you very much. May I thank Sheriff Larry Deens for that wonderful introduction and thank him and the other law enforcement officers who are here to back me up. We back up the law enforcement officers of this country, and we ought to continue to back up the law enforcement officers of this country that are giving their lives for us every single day.

I'm also proud to be here with Jim McCrery. We need him in the United States Congress. Please reelect him, and send him back. He's doing a first-class job, not just for Louisiana but for the values and the programs we hold so dear. May I thank Mayor Hazel Beard of Shreveport, delighted to be with her, and former Governor Treen, one of the great Governors of this State, an old friend of Barbara's and mine, glad to see Dave; Mayor Dement, Mayor George Dement.

It's great to be here in Shreveport. Let me say to those law-and-order, sound, sensible, conservative Democrats who are with us at this rally and standing with me here, I am grateful to each and every one of you for your loyal support. I will not let you down.

You know, for the last few weeks I've been traveling the length and breadth of America, stumping for the economic ideas that I believe in. We call it the Agenda for American Renewal. We must renew America, and with these economic ideas and your support, we can do just exactly that.

Here are some of the fundamentals. We want to open up new markets for American products and in the process create new jobs for American workers, and that means the North American free trade agreement with Mexico. Louisiana sells a lot there now. With this trade agreement we're going to sell a lot more, and that means more jobs for the people of Louisiana.

One big difference I have with our neighboring Governor: I believe that Government is too big and spends too much of your money. And he thinks, and he has already advocated big tax increases and big spending increases. Frankly, I want to see us cut those taxes and provide incentives, especially for those of you in the oil industry. We've got to get that domestic oil industry moving again.

This morning there was some good news. It may not have gotten onto the evening news around here yet, but let's keep our fingers crossed: Housing starts made the largest increase in the last 18 months, strong improvement in housing. Inflation is down. Interest rates are low. Our economy is poised for a takeoff if we make the right choices in November.

The answer, the way to do that is to get the President and get the Members of Congress that will give small businesses relief from taxation, from regulation, and yes, from litigation. We are suing each other too much and caring for each other too little. You know, we spend up to $200 billion, $200 billion a year on lawyers and lawsuits. People are afraid to coach Little League, doctors afraid to deliver babies because they're going to get sued by some crazy lawsuit. We've got to put an end to it, and we've got to stand up against the lobbies that are keeping that from happening.

When you see the young people that are here or any of the crowds across this country, I want to give our kids what they deserve, the best, the very best education in the entire world. I want every parent to have the freedom to choose the school of their choice, whether it's public, private, or religious schools.

So these are just a part of what we call the agenda——

Audience members. Four more years! Four more years! Four more years!

The President. I'm for that.

Audience members. Four more years! Four more years! Four more years!

The President. These are just a part of what we call the Agenda for American Renewal. While I've been outlining these positive ideas, my opponent has chosen to focus his energies on the past. Month after month, 11 straight months, Governor Clinton has persisted in his attacks on me, unrelenting attacks, many of them very personal in nature. He's distorted the record. And this week he launched the first one in the Presidential year, the first negative campaign commercials, the first ones.

So far I've kind of resisted the urge to focus heavily on his record. But I've got to tell you: I'm tired about the exaggerations; I am tired about the lies, and I am ready to fight back and tell the truth about his record in Arkansas.

So this morning up in Springfield, Missouri, I laid out the Clinton record. I'm stopping by some States that are neighbors of Arkansas, including my State of Texas and your State of Louisiana, so that we can move beyond the rhetoric and see what he's really done for the good people of Arkansas or, put it this way, what he's done to the good people of Arkansas. And they are good people. Look, my argument isn't with them at all. They're good, hard-working, decent people. They deserve better treatment than they've received from Governor Clinton.

The other side says they're eager to debate. I've debated every time we've had elections, and we'll probably have debates. We're not going to do it on his terms alone, but we'll have debates. But until then, until then I've got an idea for debate: candidate Clinton, standing here, debating Governor Clinton and his record, standing over here. And here's what we'll get.

Here in Louisiana I'd like to talk a moment about the struggle of importance to every parent, every teacher, every student, and that's the hard-fought battle to take back our streets from the druggies and the crackheads and the thugs that are criminals in this country.

Sheriff Larry Deens is right. The good sheriff knows what he's talking about. Candidate Clinton likes to talk tough on crime. You'll hear him criticize me about support for local law enforcement. Well, those criticisms are off the mark. We have increased Federal spending, that's your tax money, on Federal law enforcement activities by 43 percent over the last 4 years, and we've done it for one reason: The brave men and women in law enforcement, police officers, sheriffs, whatever they may be, don't need our rhetoric. They need equipment, and they need manpower, and they need the support of every law abiding citizen.

Well, candidate Clinton doesn't acknowledge this record. But you will hear candidate Clinton make some pretty impressive claims about crime control in Arkansas. When it comes to crime, I just wish that candidate Clinton out around the country, the Doberman pinscher, would meet Governor Clinton, the chihuahua. [*Laughter*]

Let me tell you what I mean. Here are the facts, and I challenge that reaction squad of his to tell me what's wrong. Pure and simple facts: During the 1980, the Nation's overall crime rate actually went down, but not in Arkansas. In fact, Governor Clinton's State had the biggest increase in the overall crime rate in the entire Nation, nearly 28 percent. Now, explain that to the good people of Arkansas.

What about violent crime? Arkansas violent crime rate went up more than 58 percent, one of the worst records in the entire Nation and a heck of a lot worse than where we're standing right here in Louisiana. You've done a much better job here.

I don't believe Governor Clinton is committed to the issue. Once again, here are the facts; these are facts. Arkansas ranks near the bottom in every important per capita law enforcement expenditure: for prisons, 46th; for judicial and legal systems, 50th; and when it comes to per capita spending for police officers, Arkansas ranks 49th. That is not good enough for the United States of America.

Here's another one, and these good law enforcement officers know what I'm talking about. In Arkansas when the prison doors slam shut on a convicted criminal, he knows it won't be long before the door opens up again. As incredible as it may seem, most inmates in Arkansas serve less than one-fifth, one-fifth of their sentences behind bars. That does not happen in Louisiana. That does not happen in Louisiana. It does not happen in Texas, and it doesn't happen in Mississippi. When it comes to keeping criminals behind bars, Governor Clinton has the worst record in the entire Nation. Do not let him do that to the United States of America.

You know, if you play Monopoly in Little Rock, the card would read like this, "Do not pass go. Go directly to jail." And then you'd turn it over and it says, "Don't worry. You'll be back in a minute. You'll be back out in a minute."

Look, contrast that with what we've been doing on the Federal record. I'm very proud to talk about my record in law enforcement. Most Federal inmates serve at least 85 percent of their full sentences. Sure it costs money, but it takes a real commitment.

But my philosophy is simple. If someone takes liberty with the law, we ought to put them behind bars, and we ought to make them stay there and stare at the ceiling for a good, long time, because, you see, I think we ought to have less sympathy for the criminal and a lot more sympathy for the victims of crime. When you look at his record on law enforcement, it's not surprising that last week the Fraternal Order of Police in Little Rock endorsed me for the President of the United States of America. That's how the police in his own backyard feel about it. So when you hear candidate Clinton's rhetoric about being tough on crime, just remember Governor Clinton's record. Two entirely different things. Slippery when wet.

You know, in the White House I've found something out. You can't be on all sides of each question. You can't say on the one hand I'm for this and on the other hand for that. When it comes to making a call on something as tough as Desert Storm, you've got to say, "Here's what we're going to do." You have to lead. You have to be unafraid. You cannot do what this Governor does, take one side of the issue one day and another side the other. You can't be all things to all people.

Audience members. Bush means business! Bush means business! Bush means business!

The President. You know, I kind of enjoy this after 11 months of hearing them bash my brains out up there. It's wonderful to be able to stand up and say the truth about this record. He talks a good game, but his actions betray his words. And he travels the Nation making all kinds of promises. You've got a special group, call him. He'll be for whatever you're for. [*Laughter*] And while he travels the Nation, Arkansas' workers' income slumps; their children's test scores slide in comparison to other States; their rivers grow more polluted. The fish light up at night over there. [*Laughter*] Their crime rises faster than every other State, and that is a fact. That is not political rhetoric. That is a fact. He is promising America the Moon, while the sky is falling down in his own wonderful State, and it is a great State. And the people have been had by this treatment.

Whether it's candidate Clinton or Governor Clinton, the message is the same: He is not the leader for America. I say we can do better, and I say America deserves better. And yes, we've got problems, and yes, we have big challenges. But our agenda confronts these challenges. We've had a global recession. We've got one kind of complex world economy. And I believe with my record in war and peace and beating down the communist aggression and winning in Desert Storm and bringing democracy around the world, that I am the person to renew America with these ideas.

I have one last—no, I'm not going to talk about the draft today. Let the American people make up their mind on that. All I'll say about the draft is I am proud that I put on the uniform and fought for my country.

Let me say this: You know, Barbara and I got home at 11:30 this morning to the White House from—we were up in New York and now took off early this morning. People say, "Well, don't you get a little tired?" Yes, you get tired, but you get refurbished. You sense the strength of America when you come to States like this and see turnouts like this.

Clinton says this, he says, "We're in decline. We are somewhere between", I think the quote was "somewhere between Germany and Sri Lanka." I don't know if he's ever been out of Little Rock until this campaign, but let me tell you something. We are not somewhere between Germany and Sri Lanka. We are the most respected nation on the face of the Earth, and we want to use what we've done to make life better for people here at home.

Thank you all for this great, great turnout. And may God bless the United States of America. Thank you.

Note: The President spoke at 2:55 p.m. at Shreveport Regional Airport. In his remarks, he referred to George Dement, Mayor of Bossier City, LA.

Remarks on Arrival in Greenville, Mississippi
September 22, 1992

The President. Thank you all. Thank you, Kirk. Thank you, Governor Fordice.

Let me just start off by telling the people of Mississippi something you already know. You've got a great Governor, a great new Governor fighting for the people here, and a wonderful wife, Pat. May I salute our State chairman, Evelyn McPhail, a great political leader; I see her family's here; and national committeewoman, Suzanne Rogers; and my old friend whose hometown we're in, longtime political warrior, Clarke Reed. I'm proud to be standing next to him.

You know, you keep hearing the cry up there in Washington, "Clean House!" all around the country because of the mess the Congress has made of things. But you've got two people that we don't want to clean; we want to keep them there forever. I'm talk-ing about Trent Lott, and I'm talking about Thad Cochran, two great United States Senators.

I want to take some catfish back with me; so I'd like to ask somebody to bring it to me. [*Laughter*] I love these signs: Arkansas for Bush. We're not giving up on one single State around here.

You know, for the past few weeks I've been traveling the length and breadth of our wonderful country, campaigning for the economic ideas that I believe in, my Agenda for American Renewal. I want to open up new markets for American products, create new jobs for American workers, because American workers never retreat; we always compete. And we always win. We must open up the markets.

All you hear out of the Clinton camp is

gloom and doom. Let me tell you, the figures released this morning show that housing starts, a key indicator, are the largest increase in 18 months. Inflation is down. Interest rates are low. Our economy is poised for a takeoff if we make the right choice in November. Elect me as President. Do not put this recovery at risk.

Audience members. Four more years! Four more years! Four more years!

The President. You know, the backbone of Mississippi is small business, small-business men, small-business women. I believe that small business will be the sturdy horse pulling the wagon of a recovering economy. So I want to give small business relief from taxation, from regulation, and yes, from litigation.

You know, this is a ghastly figure, but do you know that Americans spend up to $200 billion in one year on lawyers and lawsuits? I think that is outrageous. As a nation we ought to sue each other less and care for each other more. Help me put a lid on these outrageous lawsuits.

I am so glad to see so many kids here today. I want to give our kids what they truly deserve, the finest schools in the entire world. And I want every parent all across this country to have the freedom to choose their schools for their kids, whether it's public, private, or religious.

There's so much more to our Agenda for American Renewal: fighting crime, fighting drugs, many other things. But while I've been out talking positively for the future, my opponent has chosen to fix his energies on the past. Month after month, I believe it's about 11 months now, Governor Clinton has persisted in these one-sided attacks on me, distorting my record, telling untruths about what I've been trying to do for this country. Do you remember all the things about negative, "be careful of the Bush campaign" negative? This week Governor Clinton launched the first nationwide negative television advertisements. So far up to now I've resisted going after him. But I tell you, I'm tired of these exaggerations, and today I started to fight back. Today I started to fight back, and we're going to talk about his record, his record next door. It is not fair to the people of Arkansas.

Audience members. Hit him again,

harder, harder! Hit him again, harder, harder! Hit him again, harder, harder!

The President. I will; just a minute here. [*Laughter*]

You know, today we've been to all six States surrounding Arkansas, and I want to see that we can move beyond Governor Clinton's rhetoric and see what he's really done for the people next door, for the people of Arkansas or, put it this way, what he's done to the good people in the State of Arkansas.

I support the people over there. I've been there many, many times. They are good, hard-working, decent people. They deserve better treatment than they have had from that Governor of theirs for 10 years.

You know, you hear a lot about debates. Governor Clinton is talking up there in Michigan, waving his arms around, talking about my being afraid to stand up with him. Who is he to call me afraid, for heaven sakes?

The other side says they're eager to debate. Well, I've got an idea. On the one side you can have candidate Clinton, standing over here. And then over here you can have Governor Clinton, and let them debate: the rhetoric versus the record. Let him talk about a series of broken promises. Let's just look at one issue, and that's the need to give the middle class, you who pay the bills and do the work, a big, fat chunk of the American pie.

Candidate Clinton, standing here, is playing the same old game that the liberals always play, class warfare. You've heard it over and over again. Candidate Clinton is good at it, using the same tired, twisted, partisan statistics to explain how the poor only get richer if the rich get poorer.

Let me tell you this: According to candidate Clinton, the one over here, the last 10 years have been a nightmare. Well, if you look at the facts, it simply is not true. Inflation is down. Interest rates are down, and the American worker is still the most productive in the entire world.

You know, back in Washington they have this thing called the Urban Institute, not usually one of my most ardent admirers. But listen to what they have to say about the 1980's, and I quote, "The rich got a little richer, and the poor got much richer." That is the truth. Our conservative policies of cutting taxes have meant more money in the pockets of all Americans. Candidate Clinton doesn't think it is fair, but maybe it is because Governor Clinton doesn't have much experience with tax fairness right across the border in Arkansas.

He talks about my record. Let me talk about his, factually. He's more than doubled Arkansas's spending since '83. He's paid for it by raising taxes that hurt working families the most. He's raised and extended his sales tax repeatedly. He's more than doubled Arkansas's gas tax. He's even taxed food stamps until the Federal Government forced him to stop. He started taxing mobile homes, and then he raised taxes on beer, and then he tried to tax child care. I guess it doesn't matter whether the burp is from the beer or the baby bottle, he's going to slap a tax on it. I don't think we need that. I don't think we need that for the United States of America.

Listen to what the Arkansas paper—I'm going right to his homefront for this one—said about his tax policies. "If Congress followed the example Bill Clinton has set as Governor, it would pass a tax program that would hit the middle class the hardest." Well, I don't want to favor the rich at the expense of the middle class. I want to cut taxes for all working Americans so that everyone can get rich because that's what America is all about.

Candidate Clinton wants to do for the American economy what Governor Clinton has done to Arkansas. I've got one question: Why in the world should we let him do that to us? As a candidate now he's come out of the box, and he has already proposed the largest tax increase in American history. That's not even counting the payroll taxes that he wants to slap on for training and health care.

Now, you tell me, is that fair to the middle class? The answer is no. He's been talking the talk of economic fairness, sounding like Robin Hood: Rob from the rich and give some crumbs to the poor. But Governor Clinton has been more like Captain Hook, scaring the wits out of the middle class. And I believe in something entirely different. I believe that Government is too big and spends too much of your money. I want to change that.

That's why I want that line-item veto and the balanced budget amendment and that tax cut-off to let people check their box on their income taxes. If the Congress can't do it, let the American people do it. Let me follow through to get these taxes down and get this deficit down.

Audience members. Clean the House! Clean the House! Clean the House!

The President. There's a good idea. They say "Clean the House!" I'll tell you, there's going to be 150 new Members of Congress or something like that. The day I am re-elected, I'll sit down with them, and I'll say "Look, the American people said they don't want to spend more. They don't want to tax more. They want to get Government under control. They want to do something about crime. Now, you new Members of Congress help me get all this done in the first 100 days. Give the people a break."

You know, I feel the same way on this tax situation as Kirk Fordice does. He went to the mat with that State legislature to ease the tax burden on the working men and women. Governor Fordice might not have won that first round, but he's going to come back again and again. He knows the same as I know that you can spend your money better than any Government planner can. Low taxes are the way to get the economy moving again.

So whether the issue is fairness, the environment, health care, civil rights, fighting crime, improving our schools, candidate Clinton promises America the moon, while Governor Clinton watches the sky fall in over in Arkansas. He has a lousy record, and I don't want him to do to the United States that which he has done to the great State of Arkansas.

You know, I'm proud to be back in Mississippi, and I think of this one, as Kirk referred to it, as one of the most patriotic of States. I will say this—no, I am not going to bring up the draft issue. But let me just simply say I am proud that I wore the uniform of the United States of America, and I am proud that I served.

We have a great country. We are the

leader of the entire world. Soviet communism is dead. Peace is on the move all around the world. And Governor Clinton says we're a nation in decline. He ought to get outside of Little Rock and travel and find out that we are the most respected nation on the face of the Earth. I want to keep it that way by keeping us strong, keeping us determined, keeping us economically viable at home.

You have a great, proud State, and I'm proud to be back in it. May God bless the people of Mississippi and the people of the United States of America. Thank you very, very much.

Note: The President spoke at 5:19 p.m. at Greenville Municipal Airport. In his remarks, he referred to Clarke Reed, State chairman, Bush-Quayle '92.

Remarks to the Community in Memphis, Tennessee
September 22, 1992

The President. Thank you. Thank you very much. What a wonderful welcome.

Audience members. Four more years! Four more years! Four more years!

The President. Thank you all very much. May I salute at first Congressman Sundquist. You're lucky; you've got a great Member of the United States Congress. Barbara Bush, off on some other part of the campaign trail, sends her love to Martha Sundquist, the great wife of Don. May I say how pleased I am to have been introduced by one of the truly great members of the Cabinet, a man who served this country with such distinction, a national leader for education, Governor Lamar Alexander. What a class act.

May I thank and salute Dr. House, the superintendent of the schools here in Memphis; Dr. Langsdon, the Shelby County GOP and B-Q, the Bush-Quayle chairman in '92. And may I single out Dr. Walters— [*applause*]—I didn't know kids clapped that much for a principal, but you're right. She is outstanding. And also Jakene Ashford, who greeted me earlier, the student body president. You've got a class-act president of this school, too.

You know, I left the White House at 6:40 this morning. We started out on the campaign trail in Springfield, Missouri. This is the sixth State we've visited in just a little over 12 hours. But you know, I can't think of a better place to finish this day than Memphis, Tennessee, home of the blues, home of the wet and dry ribs, the Old South, and the new pyramid. And of course, the home of Elvis himself. Rest assured, I'm talking about Elvis Presley, not Elvis Clinton.

You know, for the past few weeks I've been all across America stumping for the economic ideas I believe in. We call it the Agenda for American Renewal. I want to open new markets for American products, create jobs for American workers because— don't listen to the other side—Americans never retreat. We always compete, and we always win. That is the American spirit.

If you listen to that Clinton-Gore ticket, you think everything is wrong. This morning new figures came out. Housing starts are up, the largest increase in a year and a half. Inflation is under control. Interest rates remain low. And I believe the stage is set, after a long, begrudging anemic growth, set for an economic recovery if we make the right choices in November. I need 4 more years to finish the job.

Audience members. Four more years! Four more years! Four more years!

The President. That's what we want.

You know, the choice before the American people is really clear. Governor Clinton has already started with his program. He wants more Government and higher taxes. That is bad for America.

Audience members. Boo-o-o!

The President. I believe in something completely different, and so does Don. I believe that Government is too big and spends too much of your money, and I want to cut taxes and provide incentives to get this economy moving again. You know, small business will be the horse pulling the wagon on our recovering economy. And so I want to give small businesses relief from taxation and regulation and litigation.

You know parents don't coach Little League for fear; doctors don't deliver babies for fear. Today Americans spend up to $200 billion a year on lawyers and lawsuits. And I think it's crazy. As a nation we've got to sue each other less and care for each other more.

I have one wish above all others, though, and as I look out at the young faces in this audience, I think of the potential of our great country and of the challenge of our schools. Your great Governor, Lamar, puts our challenge in education this way: When the fifth graders graduate from high school, they will have changed so much we will barely recognize them. But for our young people to succeed, our schools will have to change so much that we barely recognize them either.

That's why I am so excited about America 2000 movement, the program to literally revolutionize education in this country. I am excited about our new American schools, about our higher standard for students, about freeing teachers from Government bureaucracy, and about giving every parent the choice to choose the best school for their child to learn in.

So one of the reasons I came here to this wonderful institution is to say thanks to Memphis, because you are the big part, a major part of America 2000. You are a leader in a revolution that is changing America from the schoolyard right on up. And so to the parents and the teachers and the business leaders and the community activists, I say thanks for caring about the kids, thanks for being loyal to Memphis' future.

Of course, there's another reason I came here today. As one or two of you may have heard, there's an election coming up in November. I have been traveling all across America making my case for our renewal agenda. While I've been outlining my positive ideas for the future, Bill Clinton has chosen to focus his energy on the past. And literally, you go back now, a lot of you are

students about government and politics, month after month, for the last 11 months, Governor Clinton has persisted in attacking me, distorting my record. This week he unveiled the campaign's first negative commercial. He's been saying, "Oh, wait until the Republicans go negative." It is the Clinton-Gore ticket that has aired the first national negative ads.

Audience members. Boo-o-o!

The President. Now I have a confession to make. I haven't talked much about his record because I think the American people would rather hear a positive discussion about what we'll do to renew America. But I will also admit that I'm a little tired of having my own record distorted, and I think it's time we don't just listen to what he says, but take a look at what Governor Clinton does.

That is what I've been doing today. That's exactly what I've been doing today, from Missouri to Oklahoma to Texas to Louisiana to Mississippi, and now in the great State of Tennessee, pointing out the facts, no exaggeration about Governor Clinton's record on economic fairness, on civil rights or lack thereof, on the environment, on health care. Over and over you see the same pattern emerging: Governor Clinton promises the Moon to America while the sky is falling in on Arkansas.

Regrettably for the young people in that State, the wonderful young kids across the way in Arkansas, education is no different. In his new book, candidate Clinton says America has failed to provide its children with either the best education or adequate protection from violence. And I disagree. I am proud of what we've done to promote America 2000. And I am especially proud of the leadership of that great son of Tennessee, Lamar Alexander.

And yes, sure, Governor Clinton, candidate Clinton, is critical of our record. But what has Governor Clinton done? Here are the facts. Let me give it to you. You're not going to like it, on behalf of your friends in Arkansas, but here's the record. Here are the facts, pure and simple. During the 1980's, Arkansas fell from 47th to 48th place in percentage of adults with a high school diploma. Arkansas' rankings on its primary college entrance exam, the ACT, have declined. Twenty-eight States use the ACT as their primary college entrance test. The New York Times reported that in 1979, Arkansas ranked 20th out of those 28. In its latest ranking, it's down to 25th out of 28. While we're going up in the Nation, he's going down in the State of Arkansas.

Audience members: Boo-o-o!

The President. It is not fair to the young people there. It is not fair to the young families across the way. We know that more than three-quarters of Arkansas high school graduates require remedial instruction when they get to college. Think about that. Three out of four Arkansas college students spend their first year of college relearning what they missed in high school. That is not fair to the families of Arkansas. When it comes to the percentage of adults with a college degree, Governor Clinton's Arkansas still ranks 50th, 50th in the entire Nation.

Now, these are facts, pure and simple. And you can see there's a Grand Canyon by what candidate Clinton says about improving education and what Governor Clinton has actually done.

If you believe as I do, if you believe education is important, I ask you to look beyond the rhetoric. Look at the record. I have fought for higher standards. I have fought for less regulation. I have fought to reinvent our schools. I have fought for parental choice. These ideas are not popular in all places. But if you care about education, I think you must look at the two candidates and ask yourself a simple question: When it comes to reforming our schools, which candidate will tell America what it wants to hear and which will tell America what it needs to hear?

Enough talk of politics for the day. It's been a long, long day. It's been a wonderful day. And as you can imagine, campaigns can be grueling. Once in a while I'll get home, you know, after midnight, after being attacked in the press and the craziest mood I've every seen out there. And Barbara will ask me this simple question, "You know, we've got a good life; we've got a wonderful family. Why do you put up with it?" And I'll tell you why I put up with it, why I want 4 more years: I want it for the

children, for the bright-faced kids I see on their parents' shoulders at rallies all across the Nation, for the young people right here tonight.

Don Sundquist tells me that there are six young people from Russia with us this evening. They're part of an exchange program. Think about it. Think about how 10 years ago such a program might never be possible. Think about how 5 years ago these very kids sat halfway around the world knowing nothing of our world but fearing, as our own families, our own kids did, that the world they knew might be destroyed in a moment with the mere press of a finger on a button. Well, that terrible, awful nightmare has receded from our children's minds. And today these Russian kids can join with Memphis kids, and they can read stories together and play basketball and laugh at the same jokes and share the same sweet memories and think of all that has happened to make this possible.

In another time, in another age, Thomas Paine wrote these simple words, "We have the power to begin the world again." Well, we have begun our world again. Our new world is a world of hope. It's a world of promise, a world of peace, a world of unprecedented opportunity. I want our children to realize the magic of this new world, to believe in miracles, just as we can look at our Russian friends here tonight and say, "Miracles have finally come true."

If we can renew the world, and I take great pride in the fact that our administration has literally changed the world, made peace a reality and not a dream, made democracy on the march, made tranquility around the world something real and something we can touch and feel. If we can change the world, then I have no doubt that we can renew America, and we can strengthen our economy. We can reinvent our schools.

There is much work to be done, and I believe I am the leader to do it. That is why I am running for reelection, and that is why I ask for your support. And don't ever let the Governor from across the way convince you that we are a nation in decline. We are the most respected, freest, greatest nation on the face of the Earth, and I want to lead you for 4 more years.

Thank you, and may God bless the United States of America. Thank you very, very much.

Note: The President spoke at 7:45 p.m. at Craigmont High School.

Message to the Senate Returning Without Approval the Family and Medical Leave Act of 1992
September 22, 1992

To the Senate of the United States:

I am returning herewith without my approval S. 5, the "Family and Medical Leave Act of 1992." This bill would mandate that public and private employers with 50 or more employees provide their employees with leave under certain circumstances.

I want to strongly reiterate that I have always supported employer policies to give time off for a child's birth or adoption or for family illness and believe it is important that employers offer these benefits. I object, however, to the Federal Government mandating leave policies for America's employers and work force. S. 5 would do just that.

America faces its stiffest economic competition in history. If our Nation is to succeed in an increasingly complex and competitive global marketplace, we must have the flexibility in our workplaces to meet this challenge. We must ensure that Federal policies do not stifle the creation of new jobs or result in the elimination of existing jobs. The Administration is committed to policies that create and preserve jobs throughout the economy—serving the most fundamental need of working families.

My Administration is also strongly committed to policies that foster a complementary relationship between work and family and encourage the development of a strong employer-employee partnership. If these policies are to meet the diverse needs of our Nation, they must be carefully, flexibly, and sensitively crafted at the workplace by employers and employees, and not in Washington, D.C., through Government mandates imposed by legislation such as S. 5.

Therefore, I have transmitted to the Congress legislation to establish an alternative flexible family leave plan that will encourage small and medium-sized businesses to provide family leave for their employees.

My flexible family leave plan is based on a refundable tax credit for businesses that establish nondiscriminatory family leave policies for all their employees. A refundable tax credit of 20 percent of compensation (for a credit of up to $100 a week—to a maximum total credit of $1,200) would be available for all businesses with fewer than 500 employees, for a period of family leave up to 12 weeks in length. Family leave would include the birth or adoption of a child or the care of a seriously ill child, parent, or spouse. It also would cover a serious health condition that prevents the employee from performing his or her job. This approach will cover almost all workplaces—smaller companies that S. 5 does not cover that are less likely to provide leave to their employees. My plan covers about 15 million more workers than would be eligible under S. 5 and 20 times the number of workplaces. Those not affected by my plan work for large businesses, which generally have established family leave policies.

I want to emphasize again that my bill will help where the concern is most acute—with small and medium-sized businesses and the workers in those businesses. S. 5 misses these key workplaces by excluding businesses with fewer than 50 employees. We know that these hard-pressed small companies usually offer fewer benefits than large firms, that they generate most of our new jobs—in fact, they provide the majority of people with their first job—and that they are more likely to employ women and reentrants to the labor force. Under my proposal, many more of the millions of men and women employed by smaller businesses would be able to take advantage of family leave.

The tax credit approach to the family leave issue will provide the flexibility workers and employers need to enable them to establish the optimal package of benefits that meets their particular needs. This way the parties can decide which package of benefits is best suited to them. In addition, because a tax credit is not a mandate, it does not put struggling firms at an economic disadvantage in the global marketplace. It maintains the competitiveness of American business while providing the benefits American workers need. It provides positive incentives, not mandates with veiled costs that impede growth.

Both the House and Senate passed family leave legislation almost 1 year ago, but they have kept it in the filing cabinet until now. That is nearly an entire year with no action or any willingness to depart from a federally mandated approach, only an interest in politicizing the issue.

I have proposed a truly flexible family leave program. I am willing to work with the Congress to get it passed and signed into law immediately.

There appears to be a pattern here. Three years ago, my Administration had a fundamental disagreement with these same congressional committees on child care policy. It took the Democratic-controlled Congress more than a year to get the point—I would not buy a Government-controlled and mandated child care program. When they got serious, we rapidly hammered out flexible child care legislation patterned after my proposal, that allowed *individuals* to choose their benefits.

The same holds true for family leave. If the Congress is serious about encouraging family leave, I ask those Members of Congress who have joined me in the past in opposing Government mandates to work with me again. The Congress should pass a family leave bill quickly that provides positive incentives for family leave and is responsive to the needs of workers and employers.

GEORGE BUSH

The White House,
September 22, 1992.

Remarks to the Bush-Quayle Independent Business Coalition in Greensboro, North Carolina
September 23, 1992

Let me just, at the outset, thank Miller Hicks and Pat Harrison for serving as the cochairmen on our Independent Business Coalition. And also to Jack Laughery who— I'm not sure the statistics anymore qualify him as what we say is a small-business man or small-business person because of the success he's had. But he does know what it means to start a business from scratch and to fight the excesses of regulation and taxes. And of course, I'm just delighted to see everyone else here, small-business men and women who are supporting me. And Pat, thanks for the very kind words.

In a few minutes I'm going to outline in some considerable detail some new initiatives, coupled with the ones we've already made, that I think will spur small-business

investment in this country. And I think it is fitting to stand here with people who represent the very backbone of the American economy, people who know what it's like to meet a payroll, build an inventory, sell a product, and most of all, create jobs.

I can tell you this, that of all the experiences in my life, starting a business and working for a living and meeting a payroll and fighting with the regulators trained me for this job better than any other facet of my career. Half of my adult life in the private sector, the other half, adult life, half of it also in the public sector. And I think that's a good qualification for President, to have met a payroll. You all have done that. And in just a few minutes, as I say, I'm going to spell out an agenda that will encourage entrepreneurial capitalism—entrepreneur, a big name for risk-taking, starting something—a coherent agenda for sharpening our competitive edge as a nation so that we can win.

As I'll say inside—and I don't want to give you both barrels in here—but Germany and Japan tax capital at one percent and zero. And we've got it way up there. They say this is a tax break for the rich—my eye. It stimulates investment and business creation, and it is very, very important. So it's much more than that one item in the Tax Code, too, and I'll talk more about that later.

It's about helping small businesses hire new workers and increase productivity, which is vital if we're going to compete. And I'm confident we can compete. It's about freeing up the businesses from redtape and the excesses of regulation. And it's about helping people provide for their workers, but doing it—I'm talking about health care, training—but doing it in a way that just doesn't break the back of the small business that's struggling anyway and make them lay off workers in order to accommodate some Federal mandate from Washington, DC. That's about helping more people in the sum realize the American dream.

So what I'm doing is asking people to compare our agenda versus Governor Clinton's agenda. He relies heavily—and this is not a charge I can't back up—on Federal mandates, dictating from Washington how leave should be handled or how health care should be handled, and we don't need that. Our proposals are not that; they are structuring the tax system so as we can encourage the creation and success of more small businesses. He relies an awful lot on what I think would result in terrible redtape, and we don't. And most importantly, his plans tax jobs. And I think ours create jobs.

We've been through a tough time in this country. As you can see from recent events in the world, actually, the American economy is doing better than most of the global economy. So they can lower all the blame they want on me, but what I'm trying to do is guarantee that the recovery, which is coming and, frankly, working in some places, will not be set back by more Government control and Government answers. That's a big difference. And that's what will come out on these debates.

So, thank you again for this warm endorsement. Thank you for what you're doing to create jobs and, through that, helping men and women in this country as well as demonstrating what true capitalism really means, true risk-taking really means. I'm proud to be here, back in this State. Now, we're going to go in and spell out in some detail a plan that I hope captures the imaginations of small-business men and women all across this country. We're with you, and now I want to demonstrate it as cohesively and as forcefully as I possibly can.

Thank you all for being with us.

Note: The President spoke at 9:25 a.m. in the Biltmore Room of the Joseph S. Koury Convention Center. In his remarks, he referred to Jack Laughery, chairman and chief executive officer, Hardee's Food Systems.

Remarks to the Triad Business Community in Greensboro, North Carolina
September 23, 1992

Thank you, Tom. Thank you very, very much, and what a wonderful welcome back to this State. Thank you all. Please be seated. It's an honor to be introduced by a successful, honored small-business man, Tom Coble. Thank you, sir, for those kind words. I also want to salute the woman who's done so much to advance the interests of American small businesses, our Administrator of the Small Business Administration, Pat Saiki, former Member of Congress and now head of our SBA in Washington. And also to, of course, to salute the inimitable, marvelous Governor of this State, Jim Martin. What a job he's done for the country and for North Carolina. And salute, too, congressional candidates Barbara Gore Washington of the 12th District and Richard Burr of the 5th District. I'm glad to be with them.

And with us are our two national leaders of our Independent Business Coalition, Pat Harrison and Miller Hicks, both here with us today. Here's Miller over here, and where's Pat? Whoops, she didn't make the head table—sitting out here. [*Laughter*] She should have; she's an outstanding business success. Pat, stand up. And Miller, you've got to stand up and let them see you. These people are pulling together this national small-business coalition, Independent Business Coalition, we call it.

Well, I've come here to Greensboro to talk about small business and really to drive home for the Nation the fact that businesses, like the ones that come together in the Triad business community, generate the hope and pride and the jobs that hold America together.

Take Joe Koury, a well-respected member of the Triad and the father of four beautiful girls. Now, Joseph wasn't always the one-man conglomerate that we see today. He started small, began building his empire in the early years after World War II, buying up the old Army barracks here in Greensboro and turning them into housing, sometimes for the same GI's who'd trained there before going off to war, now come home to start a family. And that ingenuity, that spirit of enterprise, that drive and dream tells us the meaning of opportunity, the meaning in America. And it's all over this great—I don't want to start singling people out, but my friend Jack Laughery is another one right here from this State who exemplifies the American dream, starting, taking risk, building. And it's a wonderful thing, and it's a wonderful epitome of the spirit of this State, in my view.

Now today, America's economy is working its way through a period of profound change. And incidentally, it's not just America, it's international change. You saw the recent ups and downs in the international currency market. Other countries even now look to our economy as the envy of the world. And you see it here in North Carolina, these changes, just the way you do all across the country. Many of our larger companies have retrenched and, indeed, they've restructured, and I know that these changes have been difficult for many working Americans. But America's small businesses have shown a staying power, creating new products by the thousands, new jobs literally by the millions.

Let me give you one statistic that will drive home just what I mean. In the 1980's, the numbers of workers employed by the Fortune 500 companies actually went down. But in that same decade, small businesses boomed, adding 16 million new jobs.

The simple fact is small businesses are often the first to adapt to a changing world, the first to turn change to advantage, the force at the leading edge of economic recovery. And that's why it is absolutely critical that we do all we can to strengthen small businesses, remove obstacles that stand in their way, and create incentives that unleash America's entrepreneurial genius. Helping small business reach for its dreams is the key to my Agenda for American Renewal.

I've set a goal to make America the first, the world's first $10 trillion economy in the early years of the 21st century. And when we get to that goal, not if but when—and it is very achievable, look at the numbers—it won't be the chairmen of the Fortune 500 we have to thank. It will be the men and women who run the small businesses that power America, the men and women, for example, of the Triad business community.

Right now, small businesses employ over half of our Nation's work force. Small businesses create two-thirds of the new jobs in America. Small businesses are hothouses for innovation and risk-taking, new ideas, the very engine of entrepreneurial capitalism that pulls the economy forward.

I know because I've been there myself. I did, as Mr. Coble said, run a small business, started it from the ground up, with a lot of help, obviously, from coworkers and partners. I know what it's like to sweat out a deal and shop for credit, stay up late worrying how you're going to meet the next payroll. I've even got the ulcers, or had them back then, to prove it. That is a fact. So let me tell you, I happen to think that meeting a payroll is not a bad qualification for being President of the United States of America.

I might peripherally make the point that the contrast with my opponent couldn't be clearer. He's spent almost his entire life in government. When he wasn't in government, he practiced law and taught law school. He even worked in the Congress for his part-time job. Not exactly the credentials we're looking for these days. So it shouldn't surprise you that when it comes to the economy, my opponent thinks Government should lead. All I ask you to do is compare the plans directed by the bureaucratic planners who couldn't run a business anywhere but into the ground.

Now I believe Government can play a role in helping small business, no question. But it is a role of support, not the lead; not to put the new bureaucracy of Government planners in the business of picking winners and losers but to help America do what it does best: to make way for the American entrepreneur, the little guy with the big idea. So I've put together a program to strengthen small business, a program that will work because it understands how small businesses work. This is one important part of my comprehensive Agenda for American Renewal.

I'm releasing the full program today in a report I call "Encouraging Entrepreneurial Capitalism." Now, here is the report, and I hope we can make some, at least, available to people here today. But we can get them to you. That's a fancy name for small-business savvy America is known for. Some of the ideas are ones that we've been pushing for, for years; some are new. All of them are solid, sensible ways to strengthen small business. Now let me detail, and some of this is quite detailed, what my program does.

First, it will help small businesses get started. You see, many new businesses literally begin at home when entrepreneurs convert their own "nest egg" into capital. Germany does not tax capital gains at America's punitive rates; neither does Japan. One of them, I believe, is zero percent; and the other, I believe is Japan, is one percent. If we want to compete and win, it's time to reward the risk-takers who turn their dreams into tomorrow's jobs. It is time to cut the tax on capital gains. The liberals continue to insist that that's a break for the rich. It isn't. It is clearly an incentive to start new companies and employ more people.

And because you've got to crawl before you can walk, we're also helping small businesses with an aggressive micro-loan program from a few hundred dollars up to $25,000 at the critical early stages when new ventures are—I think we would all agree at that stage, new businesses are most vulnerable. That's how we'll help entrepreneurs get their ideas off the ground, get their businesses up and running.

But today I want to take our efforts one step further. I am proposing a 5-year, $20 billion small-business initiative to lift tax and regulatory burdens off the back of small business and to cut the costs of capital.

We start by knocking down the corporate tax rate on small businesses from 15 to 10 percent. And this new initiative will smooth the way for small-business startups by increasing the small-business deduction limit from $10,000 to $25,000. It will allow entrepreneurs to deduct $2,500 of those startup costs that most of you remember in the very first year.

My initiative includes steps to simplify tax laws for small businesses, changes that will result in almost $5 billion a year in tax relief and should allow most small businesses to file a one- or two-page tax return. And finally, it eliminates capital gains on newly issued small-business stock. That will serve as an incentive to create new businesses.

Part three of this small business program is to help existing small businesses find credit. The best idea in the world cannot work without capital. Entrepreneurs simply can't do it alone. They need credit to set up shop and to expand. Right now, you and I know that the credit crunch has hit small businesses hard. That's why we've been working with bankers and regulators across the country to free up the flow of credit to companies like yours. Our regulatory reform, for example, by the SEC, has made it easier for small businesses to raise capital through stock, through these offerings of stock, and to help growing firms to get from Main Street to Wall Street.

I've had the Small Business Administration, I have Pat Saiki here working overtime to help the credit-starved businesses. This year alone, we have increased by more than 50 percent the loan guarantees offered by her Agency, the SBA, more than $6 billion for men and women with good ideas who want to turn those dreams into jobs.

Small business is one of the most effective ways to bring minority Americans into the economic mainstream. That's why later today, Pat Saiki will release our plan to streamline the SBA's minority small-business program to bring economic opportunity to entrepreneurs all across America.

And tomorrow Pat's going to go on to south Florida to kick off what we call the green-line program, a program that we test-marketed up in New England, to provide a revolving line of credit to help small businesses bridge the gap between production and payment. This green-line initiative, incidentally, should be especially helpful to small firms that are seeking to get back to business as usual after Hurricane Andrew.

Now fourth, we have got to help small businesses hire new workers and increase productivity. Small businesses, like every employer in America, will benefit from education reforms like America 2000, our program; from our expanded job training initiatives; from enterprise zones; from legal reform that ends those sky's-the-limit lawsuits that can drive a small business into bankruptcy. We've got to do something about these crazy lawsuits. Even all of that, though, is not enough.

That's why I support aggressive new export promotion programs to help small businesses crack new markets abroad and create new jobs here at home. You see, in the 21st century, America must be not just a military superpower but an economic superpower and an export superpower. For a long time, it was felt that small businesses were too little to sell abroad and compete abroad. That's changed. We want to facilitate more sales from small business into this vast export market that lies ahead. Right now, a fraction of America's companies, 15 percent, account for 85 percent of America's exports. We've got to open these new markets for America's small businesses; we've got to tap their explosive potential to make new customers not just down the street but around the world.

Small business is already helping us pioneer new worlds, leading the way, for example, in the biotechnology revolution. That's one reason that I strongly support a 100-percent increase in Federal research and development funds to help small businesses generate the technologies of tomorrow.

And fifth, we've got to free small businesses from the tangle of redtape and regulation. Vice President Quayle has filled me in on a meeting that he had not long ago with Richard Allen, who runs a furniture manufacturing company over in High Point. Federal reporting rules have gotten so bad that he's had to hire new staff just to read regulations. Now frankly, that's one kind of job creation we could do without. Filling out Federal forms should not be a full-time job. That's why, in January of this year, I ordered a freeze on Federal regulations. You work long and hard for your success, and you should spend your time doing business, not doing paperwork.

And finally, we've got to help small businesses provide for their workers, to help the 15 million Americans who are self-employed. So I want to raise the deduction for health insurance from 25 to 100 percent. I want to reform health insurance, give small companies the same advantage that bigger companies have when they shop for health care coverage by encouraging small companies to pool together to buy insurance.

We want to create tax incentives to help small businesses offer their employees family leave, not do what the liberal Congress wants me to do, slap another mandate on small businesses' back. I'm not going to do that. I believe in family leave, and I believe our approach to facilitating family leave through tax credits is a far better way than putting new mandates on a guy who is struggling to make ends meet and would have to lay off people to meet the costs of that program. We want to expand small businesses' ability to offer the portable pensions people will need in a dynamic economy.

Taken together, that's a strong package, a comprehensive package to give real-world help right now to the small businesses that make this economy grow. You'll notice a lot of it, through tax relief, is removing the burden of Government from the back of small business.

Now, I think it's fair to say, and ask dispassionately: What about my opponent? What is his plan for small business? The difference could not be sharper. You see, I see small business as the backbone of the American economy. Mr. Clinton, Governor Clinton, sees small business as the goose that lays the golden eggs.

Bill Clinton's got big plans for bigger government and to pay for it, he's got the tax plan for almost every day of the week: Start with $150 billion in new taxes. That's not my saying he's doing it; this is what he actually has proposed. Then add a payroll tax for training, he's already proposed that, 1½ percent across the board for small businesses, every business. And then add a health care plan that will lead to a 7-percent payroll tax to finance the inevitable Government takeover of health care.

And I tell you, it's taxing just to talk about this whole program ahead. Somebody said, that taxes my memory. And Clinton says, that's a good idea, let's try it. [*Laughter*] Yesterday, nobody believes this, but I did make a subconscious slip. I spoke up when I was going on about the different plans, and I called him "Governor Taxes." And I quickly corrected it.

But now, "Governor Taxes" says yes, he wants to raise taxes, and rolls out his standard soak-the-rich rhetoric. You listen to him. But what he won't tell you is this: Two out of every three people hit by Governor Clinton's tax hike would be small-business owners or family farmers. And these folks are not millionaires, they are Mom and Pop, Incorporated. We cannot let him slap a tax on small business.

Take a look at what Governor Clinton's tax plan would mean for small businesses right here in this State. If you're like the typical small business, you operate with a profit margin of about 2 percent. Some clearly do better; some are struggling to make it 2 percent. Your market is too com-

petitive for you to pass on costs by raising prices. That can happen in large companies that dominate the market. You can't do it as a small-business man. You already feel that you've already cut your costs, your operating costs, to the very bone.

And so when Bill Clinton's new taxes kick in, you have a choice, a tough choice. His payroll taxes alone amount to 4 to 5 percent of your operating expenses. That's your profit margin and then some. So here's your choice: You can board up the windows, or you can get out the pink slips. You can continue to operate, but to do so you're going to have to lay off some of your rather small work force.

Now, I want to invite Governor Clinton and his advisers to follow along for a little business math. Just over half of all small businesses with between 10 and 20 employees have annual sales of $500,000 to $1 million. That's a 2-percent profit margin and in the best case gives that business, say, a $20,000 profit. Now, Governor Clinton's new taxes would cost that company between $46,000 and $56,000. So after you've handed over your profit to the Government, the only way to pay the rest of the tax is putting someone out of work, cutting down on your overall payroll account. And in the case of my example, that's 2 or 3 employees, 2 or 3 people out of less than a 20-person company who lose their jobs.

Now, just think about that. Those two or three people aren't just numbers; they're not some names on a payroll sheet. They're real people. They're friends and neighbors, men and women with families to feed and mortgages to pay.

Now, if that two or three still doesn't sound like much, keep this one in mind. In North Carolina alone, 25 percent of the workers, of all workers, 638,000 people, work in companies the same size as the one in my example, companies that will be crippled by Bill Clinton's new taxes. Across this State, North Carolina has thousands of businesses with less than 10 employees: grocery stores, more than 3,000; more than 2,500 small furniture stores; 4 out of every 5 companies in the building trades; bookstores, beauty shops, laundries, video stores, and TV repair shops, and the list goes on and on and on. And for them, Bill Clinton's tax plan means one thing, misery on Main Street.

You see, I don't think these central planners understand this. America is a Nation of small businesses, and to those small businesses, they'll take a big hit under Governor Clinton's tax plan. And my opponent could not do more damage to America's risk-takers, entrepreneurs, if he'd declared war on small businesses. Well, if you're like me, you've got to say: Small business should not be big Government's piggy bank.

All I ask is that you people here and the people across the country take a look for a moment at my approach and then contrast that with Governor Clinton's. You see, I want to strengthen small businesses across America by lowering taxes, increasing R&D. Bill Clinton wants to tax small businesses and small-business owners so he can give big Government a raise.

I want to cut redtape, eliminate excessive regulation, and reform the ruinous legal system that's crippling this economy and killing small businesses. We really must get these suits under control. We are suing each other too much and caring for each other too little in this country. Now, Bill Clinton wants to saddle these—or his plan would saddle these new small businesses with new mandates; the old ones too, the existing ones—new or old small businesses, all with new mandates. And he's told the trial lawyers of America he wouldn't take away even one little loophole.

How about health care? Job training? Family leave? I want to reform our health care system, extend coverage to all Americans, and use the markets to drive costs down while keeping the quality, the great quality of American health care, up. And as I said before, Bill Clinton's plan will mean a payroll tax and more Government control.

I want to give displaced workers a voucher to get the training they want. And Bill Clinton wants to put a payroll tax on employers. I want to use tax credits to encourage businesses to provide workers family leave. Well, my opponent? You see the pattern: more Government rules, more Government redtape.

You know, they sent this family leave bill down to me the other day. They sent it down just for fine timing in terms of politics. And I vetoed it, and I sent it right back. I am for family leave, but I am not for putting further mandates on small business. Let's do it through tax relief, not through running people out of business.

Bill Clinton's got a "punt, pass, and kick" plan: Punt the problem over to business. Pass the costs along. And kick the American worker right where he carries his wallet.

Now, you've got a choice in this election. A choice between two different philosophies, two different directions to take this great country. Bill Clinton puts his faith in the so-called best and brightest, in his old Oxford cronies who believes that Government knows best, just like the social welfare crowd that pulled Britain down before Maggie Thatcher and John Major pumped some life back in.

Well, I put my faith in the American people, and I want to see you keep control of the decisions that really matter in life. And when Bill Clinton says Government knows best, I say you know better. Let me sum it up this way: His plan is wrong for America. And mine is right.

Here's what Bill Clinton and the "Government first" crowd just really don't get. They don't get it. They don't understand: Government can print money, but it simply cannot create wealth. The great ideas that make this economy grow don't begin in the marbled halls of some Federal building back in Washington, DC. More great ideas, more of our gross domestic product, our GDP, begins at a basement workbench, at a computer on someone's kitchen table, with the savings you set aside to start a business of your own.

And America, don't let them teach the American people, particularly the young, that America is a nation in decline. We are simply not. We are the most respected leader in the world, militarily and economically. And in spite of the economic difficulties we've had and are enduring, America, believe me, is the envy of the world, not because its Government is great but because its people are great. Because the American people are builders and dreamers who build.

We need a Government that understands

that fundamental fact. And my program, my Agenda for American Renewal, will make the next American century a new American century, a time of peace and prosperity for all.

Thank you once again for this warm North Carolina welcome, and may God bless the United States of America. Thank

you very much.

Note: The President spoke at 9:50 a.m. at the Joseph S. Koury Convention Center. In his remarks, he referred to Tom Coble, president, Coble Dairy, and Greensboro Small Businessman of the Year.

Remarks at Pennsylvania State University in State College, Pennsylvania
September 23, 1992

The President. Thank you very, very much. What a wonderful rally. What a great day at Penn State. Thank you, Coach Paterno——

Audience members. Four more years! Four more years! Four more years!

The President. Thank you, Joe; thank you, Coach. It is a great—thank you very, very much. Thank you. Thank you very much, Coach Paterno. It's one thing to have to play after one of your pep talks, but it's a little tougher to have to give a speech after one of your pep talks. Thank you for that great introduction. Last time I gave a speech on a college campus, one student came up to me afterwards and said, "That was the best imitation of Dana Carvey I've ever seen." [*Laughter*] I never knew I had such talent.

But let me just say a word about the coach. And I'm talking to the choir here, but a lot of people won't take a position; a lot of people out in life want to protect themselves and not stand up for what they believe in. So in a tough political year when a man with the standing of Coach Joe Paterno stands at my side as a friend and speaks for me, I am very, very grateful to him not just for the support but for his courage.

Just to get this rally open, I want to do to Governor Clinton this year what Penn State did to Cincinnati last year. I'm glad I'm not running against Joe Paterno and also glad I'm not running against that world-renowned baton twirler, John Mitchell. Where is the man? There he is, right back

there. You can't see him, but I can; real talent. Now before I get started, let me simply acknowledge some up here with me on the dais, two great Members of Congress, Bud Shuster and Bill Clinger. If we had more people like these two in the Congress, the American people wouldn't have those brooms out, yelling "Clean House!" But as a matter of fact, we ought to clean House.

May I salute Sue Paterno and Tricia Giannini—and thanks, Tricia, the president of the college Republicans; she did a great job on this rally—and so many others working on behalf of the party in Pennsylvania; and Anne Anstine, our chairman; Joyce Haas, Mary Dunkel.

I didn't come here today, you'd be happy to know, to give a big rally or a grand speech. I came here to talk a bit about where we've been and where we are and what I want to do to get us where we've got to be. You know, as I was walking through the old "Main" I saw a plaque on the wall. Not too shiny, but then again, it didn't need to be. It was dedicated to 374 Americans who died in World War II, all from Penn State. I was there, and I survived to see a lot of history between then and now, the heated battles and a long cold war, won by people with the right stuff and the people with the right ideas. We stood fast. We stayed strong, and I am the first President that can say we won the cold war. It is over. And people say, "Are you better off?" Well, I think it's a good thing that every kid on this campus goes to bed at night without the same fear of nuclear war that the generations precedent had.

But the challenges we face today are different, and so are the demands. The challenge of the nineties is to win the economic competition, to win the peace.

Yesterday I went to six States. For months now my opponent is taking me on and taking this country down. So I figured it was time to introduce candidate Clinton to Governor Clinton, because the rhetoric and the reality are like night and day. You know what we discovered? Whether it's candidate Clinton or Governor Clinton, it doesn't matter. Governor Clinton is wrong for the United States of America if you want to move this country forward.

Some in the press will be saying, "Well, talking about the Governor's policy record is like going after an unarmed man." Well, I say, he should have armed himself. He should have packed more than promises. My opponent and I may argue towards some of the same ends, but we start from radically different premises, premises built on different experience and different philosophies. I will point out the differences in our visions, because I believe it explains the differences in our views.

Two weeks—hey, listen, maybe we can get this guy to shut up. I'll answer your question. He's raising—no, seriously, he's raising a legitimate question. He's asking about AIDS. It's a terrible curse. We have spent $4.3 billion on that. I have asked now for $4.9 billion. No researcher in this country is going to rest until we find the cure for AIDS. And so we care about it.

Two weeks ago in Detroit, I presented my views and my Agenda for American Renewal. I didn't just hammer away at what's wrong with America. I gave fair due to what's right. I offered a comprehensive, integrated approach to win the new global economic competition, to create the world's first $10 trillion economy by the dawn of the century. My opponent will say we can't do it. I say: When America sets its sights on a goal, we always succeed. We are the United States of America.

Audience members. U.S.A.! U.S.A.! U.S.A.!

The President. This agenda that I have out there, this detailed agenda contains 13 actions, specific actions that I will pursue in the first year of my second term, and I will fight for them harder than the Nittany Lions, fourth quarter, fourth down, goal to go, and that's tough. That's tough. So I'm asking the people for nothing more, nothing less, than a mandate to move this country forward. I will work with the hundred and some newly elected Members of Congress who will listen to the people to move this country forward.

And yes, I want a debate. I want a debate over issues and an argument over ideas. I will stand on my record, and I won't let that Arkansas Governor run away from his record, either. You know, I think the American people have a right to know what they're buying into. Because remember, if you buy what candidate Clinton is selling, there's no refund. There's no rebate. Actually, it's more like a permanent payment plan. I don't think we need that for the United States of America.

On one issue, and I think it's the fundamental issue in this campaign, my opponent and I have just agreed to disagree. It's a question of how our economy grows and how our country works. It's kind of like "Jeopardy"; it all comes down to how you ask the question. My opponent asks what makes the economy grow. And his answer, and look at his program, is Government planners and projects and programs. I ask who makes this country go. And my answer is you, the individual working men and women, building and buying in the freedom of a market.

My opponent believes that the Government will, quote, and here are his words, "invest," unquote, your money smarter than you can. I don't see it that way. I say the smart money is on the smart people, like standing right out here in this beautiful day in Pennsylvania.

You know, it's crazy. Some of you all are studying history, and it's a crazy thing. At the very moment when Russia and Eastern Europe and the whole world is turning our way, why would we want to go back their way? All of a sudden, all around the world, people are turning to free markets and to free trade and to freedom. Now that the world is finally catching on, what are we supposed to say, "just kidding," and start their way? No.

The world is sending us a message we should already know: Government planning, social engineering, centralized economies do not work. We know what works: Freedom works.

Audience members. Four more years! Four more years! Four more years!

The President. Thank you all very much. That's what we're after, 4 more. Look, in this discussion I'm not just talking about political freedom. I'm talking about the freedom to save, to invest, to work, and for you and your families to keep more of what you earn.

A major difference between the candidates is taxes. My opponent has already said he wants to raise taxes, and I want to lower taxes. During the eighties we lightened the tax load on labor, creating 21 million jobs. I know there are some economics majors out here, but you don't have to crunch numbers to figure it out: The less you tax of something, the more you get of it. If we cut taxes on investment, we'll get more investment. More investment means more jobs for the working men and women in the United States of America.

Now, listen to this because this is factual. My opponent disagrees. In Arkansas he's taxing everything he can get his hands on: groceries, beer, gas——

Audience members. Boo-o-o!

The President. I knew you wouldn't like that one—mobile homes, cable TV, used cars, airplanes, coal. He was even taxing food stamps until the Federal Government forced him to stop.

Audience members. Boo-o-o!

The President. That's the truth. I guess that's why yesterday my subconscious spoke up, and by accident, and it was an accident, down there in the South, I actually called him "Governor Taxes." And I'm sorry, I apologize.

Audience members. Bush! Bush! Bush!

The President. We disagree on taxes. And guess what: We disagree on Government spending. He wants to raise Government spending, and I want to cut it.

The Federal Government today spends almost one quarter out of every dollar of our national income. He apparently thinks that's cheap. On top of the $1.5 trillion we already spend today, he's proposed $220 billion in brand-spanking-new spending. Newsweek thinks his true total could be 3 times as high as that. Frankly, I can't think of why anyone would want the Government to grow one inch bigger. Maybe my opponent thinks there's just that much more of it to love.

The fourth difference: Opening foreign markets to American goods is a big, key difference. Exports support over 400,000 jobs right here in the State of Pennsylvania. I want lower priced goods for American consumers and new customers for American goods. I believe in free trade because I believe that when trade is free and fair, America beats the competition fair and square, anytime.

You know, there was a time when Governor Clinton said he favored open trade. Other times, usually after meetings with big union guys, he wasn't so sure. Well, what will it be? Well, when he's asked for his opinion on the free trade agreement with Mexico and Canada he said, quote, "when I have a definitive opinion, I'll say so." Well, I've got news for the Governor: There's no call-waiting in the Oval Office. You can't have it both ways. You've got to make up your mind. I am for creating more jobs in the United States by increasing our exports.

Finally, when it comes to legal reform, and this is a tough one, the Governor and I parted company before we even met. I believe that our legal system is out of control and headed for a crash. And it's running roughshod over all the small businesses, scaring the wits out of anyone who wants to take the risk and try out something new. Today, Americans spend up to $200 billion in one year in direct costs to lawyers. Now, that's got to stop. Americans need to stop suing each other so much and caring for each other more.

You talk about special interests. One trial lawyer from Arkansas solicited funds for my opponent by writing, and here's his quote, "I can never remember an occasion when he failed to do the right thing where we trial lawyers were concerned." Well, how touching. We do not need someone to do the right thing for the special interests. We need a President who will do things right for all the American people. We need to put a lid on these lawsuits, put limits on these crazy lawsuits.

Now, this fall I'm going to continue to talk about what's right, even if it's not in fashion. The Governor wishes I wouldn't talk about foreign policy. It makes him very uncomfortable, and I won't ask him why. But I will ask him what the heck he's talking about when he describes a President's, quote, here's what he called it, a President's "powerless moments when countries are invaded, friends are threatened, Americans are held hostage, and our Nation's interests are on the line." That's the end of the quote.

Well, let me say, Governor Clinton: If America is powerless when our Nation's interests are on the line, who else do you suppose is going to take care of us? My America is not powerless. My America takes care of its interests. When we have to fight, we're willing to do it if the cause is just.

Someone once said that, "You learn more about character on the 2-yard line than anywhere else in life." I don't know whether Joe agrees with that. But I've been there. America has been there. But there's one

thing about America: We never back down. We never give up. We never retreat. We always compete. And we always win. That is the United States of America.

Audience members. U.S.A.! U.S.A.! U.S.A.!

The President. And I have faith in our great country. Clinton talks about our country being somewhere below Germany, but north of Sri Lanka. He ought to open his eyes and look around. We are the most respected country in the entire world. Now, we enhanced the peace, and now let's take that power and use it to help every working man and woman in this country.

May God bless you all. Joe, again, my thanks. And thanks to all of you for this fantastic rally. Thank you so very much. Thank you.

Note: The President spoke at 1:20 p.m. on the Old Main Lawn. In his remarks, he referred to Joe Paterno, head coach, Pennsylvania State University Nittany Lions football team, and his wife, Sue; Anne Anstine, chairman, Pennsylvania State Republican committee; Joyce Haas, central Pennsylvania coordinator, Bush-Quayle '92; and Mary Dunkel, Centre County coordinator, Bush-Quayle '92.

Statement on Signing the Dire Emergency Supplemental Appropriations Act, 1992
September 23, 1992

Today I am signing into law H.R. 5620, an Act that provides supplemental appropriations for disaster assistance to meet urgent needs resulting from Hurricane Andrew, Hurricane Iniki, and Typhoon Omar. This will make urgently needed assistance available immediately.

H.R. 5620 provides $10.6 billion in emergency funding for disaster programs of the Federal Emergency Management Agency (FEMA), the Small Business Administration (SBA), and a number of other departments and agencies. These departments and agencies are continuing to provide assistance to victims of the natural disasters. The FEMA funds will be used to provide individuals

and families with temporary housing assistance and to provide loans and grants for the repair and replacement of property. The SBA funds will be used to provide low-interest loans to individuals and businesses located in areas affected by the disasters.

In accordance with the applicable provisions of the Balanced Budget and Emergency Deficit Control Act of 1985, as amended, I am designating the funding identified in the Attachment, "Emergency Supplemental Appropriations for Recent Disasters," as emergency requirements.

In addition to disaster-related emergency funding, H.R. 5620 provides nonemergency FY 1992 supplemental appropriations of

$3.5 billion for costs related to Operation Desert Shield/Desert Storm, and $2.1 billion for other purposes, including a cost-of-living adjustment for veterans compensation and pension payments. This Act also provides $500 million in FY 1993 appropriations, subject to the enactment of authorizing legislation, for urban aid to distressed cities.

GEORGE BUSH

The White House,
September 23, 1992.

Note: H.R. 5620, approved September 23, was assigned Public Law No. 102–368.

Message on the Observance of Rosh Hashanah, 1992
September 23, 1992

I am pleased to offer greetings to American Jews and to Jewish men, women, and children in Israel and around the world as you observe the High Holy Days.

Beginning with the new year 5753 on Rosh Hashanah, Jews everywhere engage in 10 days of solemn self-reflection and prayer in preparation for Yom Kippur. As you conclude this period of repentance with the Day of Atonement—a day dedicated to forgiveness and renewal—you will affirm your belief in the mercy and justice of our Creator, while at the same time setting inspiring examples of charity and brotherhood.

In their emphasis on reconciliation and renewal, these observances have special significance not only for Jews but also for peoples around the globe who have benefitted from the rich cultural and religious traditions of Judaism. Here in the United States, centuries-old Judaic law and tradition helped to shape the fundamental moral vision on which our Nation was founded. With these High Holy days, that legacy continues to shape our society, as all of us can take inspiration from your acts of repentance, tolerance, and forgiveness.

This year, the High Holy Days are also marked by a special sense of hope, as the people of the Diaspora welcome improved prospects for peace among Israel and her Arab neighbors. For the first time, the peoples of the Middle East are engaged in direct negotiations that are aimed at achieving a comprehensive, just, and lasting peace. On this occasion, Americans of every race and creed join with you in praying for greater understanding and cooperation among all nations.

Barbara joins me in wishing you L'Shanah Tova—may you be inscribed in the Book of Life for a good year.

GEORGE BUSH

Note: This message was released by the Office of the Press Secretary on September 25.

Presidential Determination No. 92–47—Memorandum on Action in Support of Peacekeeping Operations in Nagorno-Karabakh
September 24, 1992

Memorandum for the Secretary of State, the Secretary of Defense

Subject: Drawdown of Commodities and Services from the Inventory and Resources of the Department of Defense to Assist Peacekeeping Operations in Nagorno-Karabakh

Pursuant to the authority vested in me by section 552(c)(2) of the Foreign Assistance Act of 1961, as amended, 22 U.S.C. 2348a(c)(2) (the "Act"), I hereby determine that:

(1) as a result of an unforeseen emergency, the provision of assistance under Chapter 6 of Part II of the Act in amounts in excess of funds otherwise available for such assistance is important to the national interests of the United States; and

(2) such unforeseen emergency requires the immediate provision of assistance under Chapter 6 of Part II of the Act.

I therefore direct the drawdown of commodities and services from the inventory and resources of the Department of Defense of an aggregate value not to exceed $2 million in support of peacekeeping operations in Nagorno-Karabakh.

The Secretary of State is authorized and directed to report this determination to the Congress and to arrange for its publication in the *Federal Register*.

GEORGE BUSH

[*Filed with the Office of the Federal Register, 3:32 p.m., November 2, 1992*]

Note: This memorandum was released by the Office of the Press Secretary on September 25.

Remarks to Motorola Employees in Schaumburg, Illinois
September 25, 1992

Thank you for that Motorola welcome. Thank you for that warm welcome to Motorola. I can't for the life of me understand why you give me such a pleasant welcome. You've been standing out here a long, long time. But I'm sure glad to be here. It's a great pleasure, of course, to have been introduced by Ronnie Haggert and then to be here with Governor Jim Edgar, one of the truly great Governors in the United States, and also be here with a longtime friend, your Congressman, my former colleague, my former colleague Phil Crane, two strong supporters of this high-tech economy of tomorrow. I'm delighted to be here with the men and women of Motorola, winners of the first Baldrige Award.

I hope you know how important that is. I hope you know just how important that is not just to Motorola but to the entire coun-

try because, under the leadership then of Bob Galvin and certainly George Fisher, this company set an example for others. And now that coveted award that you won for the very first time is sought after by thousands of companies across this country. They're setting an example of quality. We have the best workers, and we have the best quality when we set our mind to it.

So I thank George Fisher, and I thank Bob Galvin, an old friend standing here. I thank Gayle Landuyt, who gave us a tour. Marvelous, it was an absolutely fantastic tour. I don't know where she is. Oh, there she is right there. Let's hear it for Gayle. Come on, you guys, you chauvinists, get clapping. [*Applause*] She's embarrassed, and I'm happy.

But no, seriously, I came to pay tribute to your skills, your creativity, your hard work because if you use this as a microcosm of our country, they're writing the future for our whole country, the future for the United States of America. What you're doing is the perfect put-down for the professional pessimists, the doomsayers, some of whom say we cannot compete in a changing world. You've taken the challenges of this new world, and you've done what America has always done, reinvented them as opportunities for yourselves, for your families, and for every single American.

You know, a few weeks ago in Detroit, I presented my Agenda for American Renewal. It is an integrated strategy for keeping America competitive in the new century. After our visit here this morning, I'm heading over to the University of Chicago, where I will expand on one part of this agenda, how to sharpen America's competitive business edge. You see, I believe that we will succeed in the new world not by making Government bigger but by making private business better. That's what Motorola's been doing. The genius, and it's true genius, the genius that will take our country forward is not found in the committee rooms and the bureaucratic beehives in Washington. It's found right here in companies like this. Of course, I'm not denying that Government has a role, but it's a role of supporting the private sector, not leading it.

Now the professional pessimists don't want you to hear this, but that's what we've been doing for 4 years, laying a groundwork to help American business compete in this new global economy. That's why we've been working diligently to open markets for American goods, making America the greatest export superpower that the world has ever seen.

We've had tough economic times in this country, tough economic times in the European countries with whom we trade; our economy doing better than theirs. But it is exports, it is companies that export that have saved the day in these difficult times. Again, I salute your leadership in all of that.

I hope you don't mind if I point out a difference with my opponent. My opponent isn't sure exactly how he feels about free markets, open markets. And sometimes he says he's for them; other times, especially when he's talking to the special interests, he hedges his bets. But when American jobs are at stake, a President cannot hem and haw, can't waffle, can't waver in his commitments, say, "On the one hand I'm for this; on the other I'm for that." You've got to work night and day to open those markets for American workers.

You look at the radio equipment you're building right here, the trunked radio equipment. Before 1989, American manufacturers of this equipment were effectively cut out of the Japanese market, couldn't sell there. Well, we went to work. We got an agreement, opened up that market, and now your systems cover 85 Japanese cities. I salute your management, and I take pleasure that we were at your side in this effort.

That success has been repeated over and over again. And Governor Clinton won't tell you and neither will the media, so let me tell you. Over the last 4 years our exports to Japan have grown 12 times faster than our imports from Japan. That is good, and you are a fundamental part of this. Those are new customers for the products you build. New customers abroad mean new jobs right here in the U.S.A. Somebody ought to tell my opponent Americans do not retreat; we compete. And we're going to win.

You may not have yet read in today's paper the timely news about our mutual success for semiconductor sales in Japan. Our Government and the Japanese Government announced a significant increase in foreign semiconductor sales in the second quarter to Japan, a step-up to 16 percent of their market share. Now, this is importantly attributable to effective negotiations by administration officials over many preceding months. And it's your achievement even more because your company had led the industry effort to gain access to that important market and had designed and produced the quality devices and the circuits that the Japanese want. You are leading by this kind of innovation, this kind of research, this kind of competition.

Our products are clearly the best in the world. Give them the chance, and Americans can outwork, outthink, outcreate anybody, anytime, anywhere. And you're demonstrating that.

Now, we have to keep that edge. We must keep that edge, especially in the kind of new technologies that you're specializing in here. My opponent says he wants to do the same, but the answer is very different from mine. He and his advisers talk about industrial policies, economic plans designed by a Government elite. The planners dictate the terms, pick and choose their favorite technologies, pick and choose corporate winners. If you're lucky, they let the private sector have a piece of the action. All of it is paid for with new tax dollars from the middle class. I think that is absolutely wrong, and you have demonstrated that it's wrong.

They say Government knows best. I say private industry knows better. So we really need to move the power away from the Government bureaucrats and closer to the consumer and the producer, closer to the people who build the products and the people who want to buy them.

That's why we've made it a top priority to move ideas out of the Government research lab—and they're very, very good; I believe that you people that have worked with them will say they're good people there, good scientific talent—to move new ideas out of the Government research labs and into the marketplace.

You see, it's happening right here at Motorola. Motorola has already signed a number of what we call CRADA's, the cooperative research and development agreements, with these Government research labs. I'm told several more of them are in the works. And we're taking the best science from these Government labs and letting you, the efficient workers and leaders, put it to work for the American consumers.

We've got 1,400 similar agreements up and running with businesses across the country, and that's double the number from

a year ago. Each one is based on a simple philosophy: When it comes to keeping American business competitive, Government can facilitate; it should never dictate.

Now, this may be news to the Governor from Arkansas. This may be news to him, but it won't be news to you. We know what made America the envy of the world, and we know how to keep it that way. We need to open markets, not close them. We need smaller Government, not bigger Government. We need more free enterprise, not less of it. That's what this choice really boils down to in the fall, a choice between the architects of the future and the patrons of the past.

I am very confident about this country. You know, the Governor talks about, "We're a nation in decline, somewhere south of Germany and north of Sri Lanka." He ain't been there, man. [*Laughter*] There is great respect for the United States all around the world. It's not just because we've won the cold war. It's because they see products like the ones coming out of this building here as the best in the entire world.

So we're going to stay in there, and we are going to build this future together. So don't let the pessimists talk you down. You're showing the rest of this country that America is a rising nation now, just as we always have been.

Thank you all for this wonderful day. May God bless each and every one of you. Thank you very, very much.

Note: The President spoke at 12:53 p.m. at the Motorola plant. In his remarks, he referred to Motorola officers Veronica Haggert, corporate vice president, Washington office; George Fisher, chairman of the board; Robert W. Galvin, former chairman of the board; and Gayle A. Landuyt, director of manufacturing.

Remarks at the National Technology Initiative Conference in Chicago, Illinois
September 25, 1992

Thank you all very much. Thank you. It's a pleasure and honor to be back on this campus. Thank you, Barbara Franklin, our able Secretary of Commerce. Let me say how pleased I am to also have with me two of the other top officials in our Government: the Secretary of Energy, Jim Watkins, who has served his country in several roles with great distinction, and of course, one that's I'm sure well-known to many of the scientists here, Dr. Allan Bromley, who is the Science Adviser to the President, has just worked in so many ways to further the aims of science in this country.

I want to thank Dr. Laumann for his hospitality, the provost, and say that I am glad to be back on the campus. I'm at risk here because I'll leave out others who have served their country, but I just had the pleasure of shaking hands once again with the former Attorney General, your own Ed Levi, who has served not only in Government at the highest levels but also has done such a remarkable job in academia. George Shultz I single out as a former professor here and a former great Secretary of State. And of course, his Deputy there, a business leader now coming to this faculty, Ken Dam, who I believe will be at the law school, but another outstanding American. So you can see that Chicago is still getting a good combination of public service and then outstanding academic credentials. And I feel honored to be here. I want to thank the Governor, who is doing a great job for this State, for being at my side, and also salute Susan Solomon, who was named Scientist of the Year by R&D Magazine.

So here we go. I would remind you that Illinois' most famous son and the first Illinois Republican, Abraham Lincoln, once said that the struggle of today is not altogether for today; it's for a vast future also. And that's why I've come to this great university for this lecture, to the city in the heart of the most confident nation on Earth, to talk to you today. In less than 6 weeks—there's going to be a little politics

in this, too—[*laughter*]—no, but in less than 6 weeks you face a fundamental choice about the future of our great country, about the kind of America we'll seek to build, about the direction that we're going to take.

A few weeks ago out in Detroit, I laid out the direction in which I hope to go. I called it the plan for American renewal. My strategy is integrated, tying economic policy and foreign policy and domestic policy all together because they, in fact, are related.

I put it simply: Our defining challenge in the nineties is to win the economic competition, to win the peace. So my agenda outlines the steps that we can take today to make America more competitive both now and in the future. And one key step is to invest in technology.

Today I want to talk to you about my program for investing in civilian research and development. I want to talk about how we can speed the process through which American businesses and entrepreneurs can turn the fruits of that R&D into successful products and American jobs.

I included investment in civilian R&D in my Agenda for American Renewal for a very specific reason. In the information age, when capital and ideas can move around the world literally in seconds, investments in R&D and in the technologies of tomorrow can improve our productivity. That is the key, the fundamental key to increasing economic growth. And growth means an improved standard of living for the American people.

In the old days, economists would tell you that capital and labor were the two ingredients that you needed to make the economy produce. Today, it's universally accepted that a third ingredient is needed, knowledge. We need the best ideas in the world, and America has always had them. For decades, American scientists have produced the most scientific literature, the most new patents, the most Nobel prizes. We are investing in basic research to keep that lead.

But to win today's economic competition we must have processes that can speed the route from the laboratory to the marketplace. We need investments in applied R&D. We need capital to turn the abstract idea into concrete results. We need a work force with the brainpower and the skills to take these technologies and turn them into the best quality products anywhere on Earth.

If we succeed in creating these building blocks, we will succeed in creating jobs. Just look at Jim Edgar's State, your State, Illinois; 588,000 jobs in this State are tied to high technology. That's over 11 percent of Illinois' work force. My agenda states that we must sharpen the competitive edge of the American business. But it rests on the core belief, a simple core belief, that the source of our success has always been the immense power of entrepreneurial capitalism. And that is a key difference from the vision of—the differences between me and Governor Clinton in this election.

You see, my opponent has also been talking about investing in civilian R&D during this election. But my opponent's rhetoric stops, falls short in four key respects. And I'd just like to ask you to compare.

First, he puts his faith in the ability of the Government to pick the right investments, industrial policy we call it, to control the resources, to determine which particular product and process will be favored by the bureaucrats in Washington. I want to empower the businessman or the businesswoman. I want them to develop a range of products, picked not by industrial planning, not by the planner but by the power of the marketplace.

Second, while Governor Clinton may be claiming he's going to make the right play, Congress is intercepting the ball and running it in just exactly the opposite direction. In each of the past 4 years, my R&D budget has been cut by Bill Clinton's allies in the other party on the Hill, the pork-happy partisans I call them in my more congenial times, up there in Congress. [*Laughter*]

In fact, right now—look, this year, the Democratic leaders in the Congress, with whom the Clinton campaign is consulting each and every day, have slashed my proposed increase for the National Science Foundation, headed by your own Walter Massey. They've zeroed out my proposed initiative in magnetically levitated high-speed rail. They've reduced our investment in computers and advanced materials and manufacturing R&D. While the Governor talks high-tech, his allies in Congress walk away from it.

Governor Clinton's own plan, for all the talk about research, would gut the foundation of American science and technology enterprise by cutting university reimbursements for R&D by $3 billion, almost one-third. Under his plan the ability of great universities like the University of Chicago to conduct world-class research, in my view, that would be compromised.

Third, the promises of the candidate don't match the record of Governor Clinton. The most recent report card on technology indicators, and that was published by the Corporation for Enterprise Development, rated Arkansas near the bottom among States in virtually every category. For technology resources, Arkansas got an "F."

Now, he's not even lining up the fundamentals for a high-tech world. At the end of the 1980's, Arkansas ranked 48th in the percentage of adults with high school diplomas. Three-quarters of Arkansas' high school graduates needed remedial education when they get to college. So it's odd for him to talk about high-tech when the residents of his State have to worry about getting out of high school.

Finally and most importantly, he proposes to finance his many promises with a massive tax increase that will smother the very growth on which our success depends. I had a Freudian slip the other day—and it was; nobody believes it when I say this—Clinton was "Governor Taxes." But he has proposed the largest, really, the largest tax increase in American history, $150 billion. And that's just for openers. To pay for his other promises, he'll have to tax small businesses, the main source of jobs in our economy and the heroes of high technology. So let's be clear: These high-tax policies will kill high-tech's businesses. Even the Governor is beginning to see that these tax policies are catching up.

Yesterday he talked about the health care plan. It was the third different plan in 3 months, his third different plan. First he said the plan would not require any new taxes. Then, in his second version, he admitted there would be a buy-in tax for employers. Now he's walking away from that, too. Yesterday, in the third version, he moved toward my plan, even using some of the same terms.

The rhetoric certainly sounds better. It uses words like "competition" and "preserving quality." But when you strip away the double-speak, it is the same old thing. In his plan in any version, employers have to provide the insurance that his national health board says is right, or they pay what Governor Clinton calls a mandatory premium. What he calls a mandatory premium you and I call a tax. It is plain and simple. Worse yet, we all become part of a national health care spending limit set by a Government-appointed board. We all know what that means: long lines and price controls that will only kill competition, will only lead to rationed health care.

So the Governor really is in more places than Elvis on this one. One thing—and I say this having been there—one thing about the Oval Office, you have to take positions. Whether it's on war and peace or whether it's on bills you veto or whatever it is, you can't conceal them, and you don't get to change you mind every time the heat gets turned up.

The direction that I propose at its heart is future-oriented and outward-looking. I do not believe that Americans should fear competition, because I believe when it comes to new ideas, America can compete. And America can win. So I've worked to open markets, to get our work force ready to compete, and both as a Government and as a society, to invest in the future. In short, I believe we should compete, not pull back, not retreat. I believe we can do it without a massive expansion of the Federal Government that reaches into the pocket of every American taxpayer.

Let me talk about the elements of this competition. First, open markets. My opponent said America is in decline. He used the analogy somewhere below Germany but just above Sri Lanka. Well, that is not the way others look at this country, certainly not the way I look at this country. But the fact is that we are winning new markets for American goods and services right now, even though the world economy has been very difficult.

Just look at our export performance over these past 4 years. We've increased exports by 40 percent. We have gained worldwide market share in manufacturing output. Our exports to Japan have grown 12 times faster than our imports. The average American simply does not understand that. And high-tech exports have led the way. Since 1987, our trade surplus in advanced technology products has grown by more than 80 percent. So I have a message for the pessimists: We can compete, and we can win.

For us to continue to win new markets for America, we need a more open world trading regime. So we've worked to complete this famous North American free trade agreement, referred to as NAFTA, which will create almost 200,000 jobs right here in the United States. We've worked for a successful conclusion of the Uruguay round. Now that one's been hung up, as you know, in the Maastricht agreements, the vote, particularly the vote in France, the very recent vote in France on the Maastricht agreements. We're going to keep pushing for that, however. We've completed individual agreements with Japan, Korea, Mexico, and countries around the world to open markets for technology and protect American intellectual property so that the incentive to generate new ideas and create new products remains.

Now, again, my opponent has waffled on NAFTA. He would risk our ability to expand trade by supporting antitrade legislation on Capitol Hill. The tax on foreign investment, believe me, the tax on foreign investment in the United States will not only lock out high-wage, high-skill jobs here, it will invite retaliation that will undercut the growth in exports which is absolutely key to the growth in our economy.

Let's talk about education and preparing our children to meet the challenges of the 21st century. Governor Clinton has said that we've reduced investment in education. And candidly, again, he is wrong. Education this year got the biggest increase in my budget. It is up 41 percent over 1989. We've placed a particular emphasis on math and science education, boosting it by more than two-thirds since 1989 so that this year's budget's going to be able to use Federal assets to help train over 770,000 teachers in these math and science skills that are absolutely essential for teaching our kids.

Let's talk about investing in the future. We've been working to promote the technologies that will make us more competitive in the future, but it's time to set the record straight on this. The Governor said we've reduced investment in civilian R&D. That is simply not true. Here is the record: My budget this year would increase civilian R&D by 44 percent over 1989 levels. Civilian basic research is up 36 percent, and applied civilian R&D is up 49 percent. So when the Governor talks about investing in civilian R&D, the fact is we are already doing it. If I weren't doing it, Allan Bromley, sitting over my shoulder, would kill me, absolutely kill me, because he's brought to the fore the need to keep us on the cutting edge when it comes to science and technology.

Now, let me explain what we're doing. Two years ago we pulled every Federal Agency together to launch a new program to develop the supercomputers of tomorrow, computers 1,000 times more powerful than today's. Our vision is to see industry develop a supercomputer the size of a desktop PC and to do it within 4 years. We also proposed a nationwide communications network, an information backbone that will transmit 1,000 times more information than we can today in one second. This year, we proposed over $800 million, that's a 23-percent increase, for this high-performance computing and communications initiative.

Last year we launched another cross-cutting technology plan, an investment of over $1.8 billion in the materials of tomorrow. Now, these new kinds of materials will help us make products that are stronger, lighter, and faster, everything from cars to airplanes to military equipment. And we've launched a $4 billion program in biotechnology research and proposed to knock down the regulatory barriers that might prevent tech-

nologies in this area from helping us to cure disease, grow more crops, or clean up the environment.

We're using technology to tackle a really unfortunate legacy of the war, the cold war, the environmental problems left from making weapons that defended freedom around the globe. Winning the peace means managing dangerous materials more effectively. Today we're using the scientific expertise of our marvelous Federal labs, whose scientists first devised these bombs, to find new technologies for stopping weapons proliferation and for protecting our children from environmental threats.

I take great pride, great joy as a grandparent that the young people in this country go to bed at night without the same fear of nuclear war that their older brothers or their fathers and mothers did. That is a major advancement, and yet we still have problems in the nuclear age. We cannot turn our back on them. And Jim Watkins, our able Secretary, is contending with these problems daily.

But look, I'm here today because a successful strategy for winning the economic competition requires more than just the investment in R&D, whether it's basic or applied. In a fast-paced world of shorter product cycles and faster communications, the key to victory is moving ideas and technologies from the laboratory bench to the commercial marketplace faster than ever before.

That's what this National Technology Initiative, or NTI, is all about. This is the 11th NTI meeting that we've had, each in a different part of the country, each designed to help speed the transfer of technology from our Federal labs and universities to the private and commercial sector. We're working to make it easier to deal with the Federal Government as a partner. If you attend the workshops and visit the technology fair, you'll get a window on today's opportunities and an early start on tomorrow's successes.

One year ago, I directed the Secretaries of Commerce, now Barbara Franklin, Secretary of Energy Jim Watkins to increase the number of cooperative research and development agreements signed between our Federal facilities and the private partners.

These CRADA's, as they are called, help speed the transfer of the most promising technologies from the Government to the private sector so they can be developed into commercial products and services.

In the one year since that directive was issued, we've doubled the numbers of these agreements. There are now more than 1,400 operating and in place, computers, ceramics, environmental cleanup. We are achieving an unprecedented level of success in taking the best ideas from our labs and turning them into American products. In these days, it's fundamental: American jobs.

Today we are signing several new breakthrough agreements. One involves two Federal labs and three private industry partners working to determine the right mix for burning pelletized trash along with coal to generate electricity. The results will be cleaner air, less trash in our landfills, and more jobs in Illinois. Second, we'll bring the Oak Ridge National Lab together with IBM to extend America's leadership in high-performance computing. The third one involves a partnership between General Motors and the National Institute of Standards and Technology, NIST, to develop new software to solve problems in automated manufacturing equipment.

These agreements provide rules of the road, protection of patents and intellectual property and other understandings so that technology transfer is not just a concept, but a job-producing reality.

Our program reflects a fundamental belief about the path to successful technology development. Our efforts to transfer technology from the labs to invest in the most promising technologies of tomorrow have recognized the fact that the private sector must be the one to commercialize these technologies.

To help in that task, to spread information about best practices and new processes, my administration has also established seven regional manufacturing tech centers around the country. These centers will introduce new equipment and improve manufacturing processes for small and medium-sized firms. You know, since 1989, more than 6,000 companies have used the services provided by these centers. And we plan to start up four more of them next year.

Now, again in the politics, my opponent proposes to create hundreds of centers. He doesn't say how long it will take to build them, but I can tell you this: We don't need a massive bureaucracy. We want to share best practices, not necessarily every practice that a Government planner wants to push.

I think the fundamental point is this: Rather than waiting for the bureaucrats and planners to decide what's best, I believe that we should foster the kind of partnerships that will allow the private sector to help identify and commercialize the most promising technologies, those in which we are pursuing leadership today.

In next year's budget, we will launch a new initiative to increase our investment in R&D into new technologies to advance the manufacturing process. You know, today's factories face a different set of challenges from those of a generation ago. In the face of fast-changing requirements, more flexibility is needed. We want to advance the development of systems in software, robotics, artificial intelligence, to make this flexibility possible for all kinds of companies. The Government will help with technological leaps so that American firms can leap ahead in the marketplace.

One of the most quintessentially American figures of our time, a scientist, a research and development scientist, John Wayne, you remember him, once said that, "Tomorrow is the most important thing in life."

When the shouting is finished and all this campaign winds down to its end, it will come down to a very personal and serious decision for every American: What kind of tomorrow do you want? Do you want a tomorrow in which we look forward and take on the competition or one where we turn inward to protectionism and pull back? Do you want a tomorrow in which we invest in the technologies that can make us more competitive or in which we allow the patrons of the past to spend our future away? Do you want a tomorrow in which work and innovation are rewarded or in which we turn back down the path of higher taxes and more regulation?

When Americans step into that booth this year, they will face a fundamental choice about the kind of future that they want. I have come today out here to Chicago to offer my ideas for a future full of promise. I am optimistic about the future of this country. Let there be no mistake about it: Regardless of what we have been through, I am absolutely convinced that the young people that many of you in this room teach have an exceptionally bright future ahead, a future in which America works, America competes. And America wins.

So I thank you for being a part of this future in your own way—put the politics aside for a moment. I've been told by Allan Bromley and others of the fantastic R&D capability, scientific know-how right here in this room today. And I ask you to visualize the same kind of future I've outlined to you.

Many, many thanks for your attention. And may God bless our great country. Thank you very, very much.

Note: The President spoke at 2:26 p.m. in Mandel Hall at the University of Chicago. In his remarks, he referred to Kenneth W. Dam, Max Pam professor in American and foreign law, University of Chicago.

Remarks to Working Families for Bush-Quayle in Chicago
September 25, 1992

Let me put it this way, I'm glad to be running against Governor Clinton instead of Randy here. [*Laughter*] He is tough. I mean that was a wonderful introduction and wonderful comments. And thank you very, very much. Thank all of you here and out there for being here.

Let me, of course, salute the Governor, Jim Edgar. You've got a first-class Governor in this State. And I'm very proud to have his support. May I greet Sam Panyotovich, the State representative. And to all of you, thank you for being with us.

When I first heard I was heading for the Windy City, I was afraid I was going up to Capitol Hill, as Randy was talking about them. Instead, here I am, glad to be back in this city of big shoulders and very, very proud to have the endorsement of these hard-working men and women.

Two men ask for your support this year and ask America to decide where we're going. Two different philosophies, two very different agendas, two candidates shaped by where each of us has been. My opponent started in politics with George McGovern. He spent almost his whole career on a government payroll. Kind of like a contestant on "Jeopardy": Alex Trebek would say, "The answer to everything," and Bill Clinton would answer, "What's 'More Govern-

ment'?"

My background's very different. I started a business. As Randy said, I met a payroll of working men and women. I learned that higher taxes and spending do not create jobs, they destroy jobs. And every day in the economy, every day, is high noon. I spent half of my adult life in public service and the other half in private sector. And I think that's a good mix, a good combination.

Sending Uncle Sam into the world to fight, burdened by higher taxes, is like sending Norm Schwarzkopf into Kuwait to fight with one hand tied behind his back. I didn't do the latter, and I do not want to see this country burdened further by taxes.

That's why my comprehensive approach to win the new global economy is built on lower taxes, lower spending, and less regulation. It's not a tax break for the rich, it's a jobs break for America. This Agenda for American Renewal that Randy very generously mentioned can create the world's first $10 trillion economy by the dawn of the next century, not by turning inward but by reaching out to free markets and free trade and freedom itself, the freedom to save, to invest, to work, to keep more of what you earn.

This won't surprise you, but Governor

Clinton disagrees. Maybe that's why last week in a Freudian slip—didn't do it on purpose—I referred to him as "Governor Taxes." I was in Texas, I think, at the time. But nevertheless, he does want to raise taxes. He's already come out and said he wants to raise them $150 billion, boost Government spending by $220 billion. And that slogan of his is "Putting people first." Well, based on what he'd do to the U.S. taxpayer, it should be "Putting it to the people first."

Now, most of you have families. Think about the family budget in 1955. Back then, the average family spent 5 percent of its adjusted gross income on Federal taxes. Today the figure is up to about 24 percent. We don't need a President who makes things worse. Yes, we've had tough economic times. Every country of our major trading partners in Europe have tough economic times. It's not simply the United States. The question is, who's best to get us out of these difficult times. You can't tax grocery and beer and gas and cable TV as my opponent has done in Arkansas. We do need lower taxes. We need spending to get lower priced goods for American consumers. And we need customers for American goods.

So look around you here. We've got six unions represented, I believe, union members from locals like UAW 551, the Operating Engineers, Carpenters Local 60, auto workers, pilots, the building trade, steel workers and tradesmen. And every day that you go to work, compete; do not retreat. And you work like the dickens. You strive to excel. You know that whether it's Munster, Indiana, or Rosemont, Illinois, it doesn't matter. When trade is free and fair, America beats the competition fair and square, anywhere.

I wish I could tell you that he agrees on this point. Very hard to tell. On the North American free trade agreement, which I'm absolutely convinced is going to increase jobs, he says, "When I have a definitive opinion, I'll say so." You can't waffle when you're President of the United States. You've got to make the tough calls. Sometimes you make people happy, sometimes not so happy. But you can't have both sides of every single issue. Somebody mentioned the fuel standards, the CAFE standards. Let me just tell you his position here, if I can

figure it out. In April he wanted to hike them from the current level, 27 miles per gallon, to, this is a quote, "40 to 45 miles per gallon." Later it became a goal of 40 or 45 miles a gallon.

On issue after issue he is on one side and then the other, showing up in more places than Elvis Presley. And this 45 miles per gallon would kill off the auto industry. He went over and met with some auto industry leaders here, and he said, well, I'm studying. They've got a National Academy of Science study about this thick, and he's sitting there reading it every night in the campaign trail? Come on. There's plenty of information out about that. He's not studying that, I don't believe.

But you've got to take a position in this job, that's what I'm saying. I'll take a stand for policies that favor the working family. I want real reform, reform of that welfare system for example, to help the families stay together and make the fathers stick around some. And I'm the one who will keep the inflation low so that money buys more at the supermarket and every senior, every member of a union who has saved all his life is not going to have those savings wiped out by inflation anymore.

We got the interest rates down, so the working families can buy that first home. I'm for keeping the fuel standards at 27.5, not risking the future of the auto workers in this country by trying to make some environmentally extreme statement to keep the Sierra Club happy and at the same time throwing auto workers out of work. The worst environment of all is to be cold, broke, and unemployed. And so we've got to remember that.

Above all, I'm the one who will keep faith with the people who trust me, just as I have faith and trust in you. And the campaign is about trust. Some out there don't like the concept that I talk about, strengthening the American family. But we try to exemplify strength in family. I want to see discipline. I want to see families reading to their kids. I want to see the neighborhoods safe. I want to back up the local law enforcement officers, to whom we are beholden for many, many things. I put all of these under the heading of strengthening the

American family. So let the liberal elite criticize it. Let them distort my position. But we are going to keep fighting for the American family, to keep it strong.

I heard Governor Edgar mention something about international affairs. You wouldn't think world peace had anything to do with anything, given the way the Clinton campaign doesn't even want to discuss it. It's Ted back here, Ted Myeka, is that right? Well, okay, he comes here, he fights before he's even a citizen for our country. I said, "Where do you come from? What's your ethnic background?" "Poland." Look, I take great pride in the fact that it was under my Presidency that Poland is free and they are democratic. And there's a lot of these countries that are free and democratic because, with the backing of good men and women like these with me here today, we stayed strong. We didn't listen to the nuclear-freeze crowd or those that were demonstrating against the United States of America. We stood strong. And the result is democracy and freedom in Poland and Czechoslovakia, the Balkans, and all across the way.

So it's a wonderful thing. And there's another thing. You see this little guy here. I take great pride in the fact that that kid does not go to bed the same as some of you did a few years ago, worrying about nuclear war. I think that's an important change. So when we talk about change, let's get credit for some of the changes that make the world a little more peaceful. You think about these freedoms out there, and I don't have to lecture to a patriotic group like this, but I didn't work to help bring freedom to Eastern Europe to now lose it out here, right in this country.

We're going to fix these classrooms.

We're going to make it better. We're going to give parents the choice of whatever schools they want to send their kids to, public, private, or religious, and help them do just that. And so we're going to keep fighting: Child care where the parents get the choice, and not rule out, as some of these liberals would have you believe—if a church has a child care center there, why, of course the parents ought to have a choice to send the kid to that as well as have some Government-dictated, bureaucratically controlled child care center. So we're trying to strengthen the family, we're trying to strengthen the community, and we're darn sure trying to strengthen the American economy.

Last word: It is very easy to get on a bandwagon when somebody thinks the other guy's going to win, the front-runner. I'm going to win this election, and it's not going to be because I'm so smart. But it's because hard-working men and women who value their families and treasure their neighborhoods are going to stand with me when the going is tough, just like these guys have done, these women and men who are working for a living, and put principle ahead of dictation from some group.

So I'm very honored. This is one of the nicest events that I could possibly have been invited to attend, because it comes from principle. It comes from people that are willing to stand up based on fundamental principle.

Thank you very, very much for being here. Thank you very much.

Note: The President spoke at 5:45 p.m. at the Hilton Hotel. In his remarks, he referred to Randy Peters, recording secretary, United Auto Workers Local 551.

Letter to Congressional Leaders Reporting on the Cyprus Conflict
September 25, 1992

Dear Mr. Speaker: (*Dear Mr. Chairman:*)

In accordance with Public Law 95–384 (22 U.S.C. 2373(c)), I am submitting to you this bimonthly report on progress toward a negotiated settlement of the Cyprus question. This report covers the months of May and June 1992.

Representatives of the U.N. Secretary

General returned to the Eastern Mediterranean area and met separately with President Vassiliou and Mr. Denktash in Cyprus from May 8 through 12. Consultations followed in Ankara and in Athens with the Prime Ministers and other officials of the Greek and Turkish Governments. The Secretary General's representatives returned to New York to prepare their report to the Secretary General on the status of the negotiating effort.

Based on that report, the Secretary General sent letters on June 1 to the leaders of both Cypriot communities, inviting them to talks in New York starting on June 18. In his letter, the Secretary General suggested separate talks with each leader (so-called "proximity talks") covering the eight topics of the U.N. "set of ideas," starting, in accordance with Security Council Resolution 750, with outstanding issues, in particular the issues of territorial adjustment and displaced persons. The Secretary General proposed further that, if the leaders of the two communities were within agreement range on all eight topics, the proximity talks could be followed by joint meetings. Both leaders accepted the Secretary General's invitation.

Also on June 1, the Secretary General invited the Governments of Greece and Turkey to designate senior officials to be in New York for the duration of the talks. Both Governments responded positively, and each had a senior representative in New York for the meetings.

The Secretary General's representatives returned again to the area to prepare for the June 18 meetings. U.S. Special Cyprus Coordinator Nelson Ledsky went to the area at the same time to back up the efforts of the U.N. negotiators. The U.N. negotiators and Ambassador Ledsky met separately in Nicosia with President Vassiliou and Mr. Denktash between June 7 and June 12. Ambassador Ledsky also traveled to Athens where he met with officials of the Greek Government.

I discussed the Cyprus question with Prime Minister Demirel of Turkey and with President Vassiliou of Cyprus at the Rio "Earth Summit" (U.N. Conference on Environment and Development) on June 11 and 12, 1992, emphasizing the importance we attach to a peaceful, fair, and permanent solution to the Cyprus question.

In the days immediately before the opening of the New York talks, the U.S. Special Cyprus Coordinator met in New York with the leaders of the two Cypriot communities, with the senior representatives sent to New York by the Governments of Greece and Turkey, and with teams of experts sent by the Governments of the United Kingdom, France, and Russia. These contacts continued throughout the June meetings.

The talks in New York began, as scheduled, on June 18 and continued through June 23. During this first phase, the U.N. Secretary General met on five occasions separately with each community leader. As planned, the talks initially focused on the issue of territorial adjustment, and both sides were shown a map prepared by the U.N. Secretariat. (The map was designated a "non-map" by mutual agreement.) During the proximity negotiations the U.N. negotiators daily briefed representatives of the five permanent members of the Security Council.

On June 23, the proximity talks were recessed, by mutual agreement, due to the need of the U.N. Secretary General to be away from U.N. Headquarters in New York. Before the recess the Secretary General hosted an amicable joint meeting with the two community leaders. The Secretary General and the two leaders agreed to resume the talks in New York on July 15. The resumed talks will be the subject of my next report.

Talks aimed at arriving at a fair and permanent negotiated resolution of the Cyprus issue were successfully started during the period covered by this report. We will continue to follow and to assist however possible the U.N. Secretary General's effort to arrive at an overall framework agreement, which will benefit all Cypriots.

Sincerely,

GEORGE BUSH

Note: Identical letters were sent to Thomas S. Foley, Speaker of the House of Representatives, and Claiborne Pell, Chairman of the Senate Committee on Foreign Relations.

Message to the Congress Reporting on the National Emergency With Respect to Export Control Regulations
September 25, 1992

To the Congress of the United States:

1. On September 30, 1990, in Executive Order No. 12730, I declared a national emergency under the International Emergency Economic Powers Act (IEEPA) (50 U.S.C. 1701, *et seq.*) to deal with the threat to the national security and foreign policy of the United States caused by the lapse of the Export Administration Act of 1979, as amended (50 U.S.C. App. 2401, *et seq.*), and the system of controls maintained under that Act. In that order, I continued in effect, to the extent permitted by law, the provisions of the Export Administration Act of 1979, as amended, the Export Administration Regulations (15 C.F.R. 768, *et seq.* (1991)), and the delegations of authority set forth in Executive Order No. 12002 of July 7, 1977, Executive Order No. 12214 of May 2, 1980, and Executive Order No. 12131 of May 4, 1979, as amended by Executive Order No. 12551 of February 21, 1986.

2. I issued Executive Order No. 12730 pursuant to the authority vested in me as President by the Constitution and laws of the United States, including IEEPA, the National Emergencies Act (NEA) (50 U.S.C. 1601, *et seq.*), and section 301 of title 3 of the United States Code. At that time, I also submitted a report to the Congress pursuant to section 204(b) of IEEPA (50 U.S.C. 1703(b)). Section 204 of IEEPA requires follow-up reports, with respect to actions or changes, to be submitted every 6 months. Additionally, section 401(c) of the NEA requires that the President, within 90 days after the end of each 6-month period following a declaration of a national emergency, report to the Congress on the total expenditures directly attributable to that declaration. This report, covering the 6-month period from April 1, 1992, to September 30, 1992, is submitted in compliance with these requirements.

3. Since the issuance of Executive Order No. 12730, the Department of Commerce has continued to administer and enforce the system of export controls, including antiboycott provisions, contained in the Export Administration Regulations. In administering these controls, the Department has acted under a policy of conforming actions under Executive Order No. 12730 to those required under the Export Administration Act, insofar as appropriate.

4. Since my last report to the Congress, there have been several significant developments in the area of export controls:

—As the nations of Central Europe and the former Soviet Union continue their progress towards democracy and market economies, United States Government experts have been working with officials of Albania, Bulgaria, the Czech and Slovak Federal Republic, Hungary, Poland, Romania, the Baltic States, and many republics of the former Soviet Union to implement and strengthen their export control systems, including pre-license inspections and post-shipment verifications. These developments will facilitate enhanced trade in high technology items and other commodities in the region, while helping to prevent unauthorized shipments or uses of such items. At the same time, we have been engaged in activities with the Central and Eastern European countries to assist in the prevention of proliferation of weapons of mass destruction and corresponding technology.

A significant result of these activities was the removal of Hungary from the list of proscribed destinations to the list of free world destinations on May 1, 1992, thereby liberalizing export controls with respect to Hungary and easing the burden on exporters dealing with Hungary. This action should facilitate a significant increase in exports and reexports to Hungary. (57 F.R. 19805, May 8, 1992.)

—Working diligently with our Coordinating Committee (COCOM) partners to streamline multilateral national security controls, we are pleased to report the following important developments:

—Elimination of nearly all individual license requirements for exports to

COCOM and cooperating countries, enabling exporters to ship items without prior agency approval. (57 F.R. 18819, May 1, 1992.)

—Elimination of most U.S. reexport authorizations for U.S.-origin goods going from COCOM and cooperating countries to most third countries, except when destined to a country or region of proliferation concern. (57 F.R. 18817, May 1, 1992.)

—Liberalized licensing requirements on exports to Hong Kong and New Zealand, following their designation as COCOM cooperating destinations. (57 F.R. 19334, May 5, 1992.)

—At the June 1992 High-Level Meeting in Paris, in response to a proposal from former Secretary of State James Baker, our COCOM allies agreed to establish a new "COCOM Cooperation Forum" (CCF) to include the 17 members of COCOM, the newly independent states of the former Soviet Union (NIS), and most recently other Central and Eastern European nations. The CCF hopes to engage these nations in further establishing controls for sensitive goods and technologies, and to provide an impetus for wider access by those countries to controlled items. The first High-Level Meeting of the CCF is scheduled for late November of this year.

—Also at the June High-Level Meeting, the COCOM partners agreed to significantly liberalize export controls on telecommunications exports to the NIS, which should facilitate rapid and reliable telecommunications between the NIS and the West, as well as modern, cost-effective domestic telecommunications systems.

—The Department of Commerce also recently revised the regulations governing the Distribution License procedure, thereby allowing expanded use of this special license and eliminating many current prior-approval requirements. The Distribution License, which permits multiple exports of controlled items to approved consignees in eligible countries without prior review of individual transactions, is used by approximately 125 of the largest exporters to export computers and other items to many countries. (57 F.R. 18815, May 1, 1992.)

—In my last report, I noted that the Department of Commerce issued a conforming regulation to bring the Commerce Control List (CCL) into line with special country- and commodity-based controls. In this action, the transfer from the State Department to the Commerce Department of licensing jurisdiction over certain civil aircraft inertial navigation equipment was implemented. (57 F.R. 4553, February 6, 1992.) This transfer of items formerly included in the State Department's U.S. Munitions List (USML) to the CCL is ongoing. The majority of overlaps between the USML and the CCL were eliminated in the April 25, 1992, amendment to the USML. (57 F.R. 15227.) In the future, certain commercial telecommunications satellites, imaging technologies, and navigational technologies will be removed from the USML and added to the CCL.

—We are continuing our efforts to address the threat to the national security and foreign policy interests of the United States posed by the spread of weapons of mass destruction and missile delivery systems. As such, we have been working with our major trading partners to strengthen export controls over goods, technology, and other forms of assistance that can contribute to the spread of nuclear, chemical, and biological weapons and missile systems.

—At the June 1992 meeting of the 22-nation Australia Group (AG), a consortium of nations that seeks to prevent the proliferation of chemical and biological weapons (CBW), the delegates agreed to establish a refined common control list for exports of dual-use biological equipment and to increase from 50 to 54 the number of precursor chemicals subject to control. The Commerce Department is in the process of publishing rules reflecting the changes to conform the U.S. list to the AG list.

—The United States has also been a key participant in the ongoing Chemical Weapons Convention (CWC) negotiations in Geneva, Switzerland. On September 3 the Conference on Disarmament, which is the drafting body for the CWC, forwarded to the United Nations General Assembly, a draft CWC, which includes a prohibition on the design, development, production, or use of chemical weapons, as well as destruction of chemical weapons production facilities and stockpiles. The United States strongly supports these provisions.

—In April, the 27-nation Nuclear Suppliers Group (NSG), in which the United States participates, formally established a multilateral regime to control nuclear-related dual-use items similar to the nuclear-referral list currently administered by the Department of Commerce. The Department is working to publish a rule to conform the U.S. list with the NSG list.

—At the June-July plenary session in Oslo, the Missile Technology Control Regime (MTCR) members welcomed Greece, Ireland, Portugal, and Switzerland to their ranks, bringing the total membership to 22 nations. The MTCR members also agreed to amend the Guidelines and Equipment and Technology Annex to ensure adequate control of delivery systems for *all* types of weapons of mass destruction—including chemical and biological weapons, as well as nuclear weapons. The MTCR partners expect to have the revised Guidelines in effect by the end of October 1992.

—The Commerce Department has also participated in implementation of missile technology sanctions imposed by the Department of State under Title XVII of the National Defense Authorization Act for FY 1991 (Public Law 101–510). Sanctions, which include denial of export licenses, have been imposed on the following foreign entities: ARMSCOR (South Africa), Changgwang Credit Corporation (North Korea), China Great Wall Industry Corporation (PRC), China Precision Machinery Import-Export Corporation (PRC), Glavkosmos (Russia), Indian Space Research Organization (ISRO–India), Lyongaksan Machineries and Equipment Export Corporation (North Korea), Ministry of Defense (Syria), Ministry of Defense and Armed Forces

Logistics (Iran), Space and Upper Atmosphere Research Commission (SUPARCO–Pakistan), and Syrian Scientific Research Center a/k/a Centre d'Etudes et Recherches Scientifique (Syria). The sanctions imposed in June 1991 on the two Chinese entities were recently waived.

—In the area of supercomputers we have established a supercomputer safeguard regime with Japan, and we are negotiating with our European trading partners to expand this regime. Under the provisions published in May, exports of supercomputers to Canada do not require a license, exports to Japan may be made under General License GCT, and both Distribution Licenses and individual validated licenses are available for exports to many Western European destinations with only minimum safeguards. Supercomputer exports involve sensitive national security and foreign policy interests, such as cryptology, strategic defense, and submarine warfare; the multilateral safeguard regime is therefore intended to establish uniform and effective international policies and procedures to protect supercomputers from unauthorized end-uses and end-users, without unnecessarily burdening U.S. exporters. (57 F.R. 20963, May 18, 1992.)

—At the beginning of the year, I announced the lifting of the U.S. embargo against Cambodia in response to the United Nations-directed comprehensive political settlement of the decades-long Cambodian conflict. In April the Commerce Department issued a rule removing Cambodia from the list of embargoed countries and revising licensing policies and procedures affecting Cambodia and Laos to allow these countries to receive general license treatment for exports and reexports of many items. (57 F.R. 11576, April 6, 1992.)

—More recently, the Department issued a rule permitting commercial exports of humanitarian goods—including food, building materials, and health and educational items to Vietnam, under a new general license. This liberalization in export control policy is consistent with the step-by-step process for normalizing relations with Vietnam, and should further reduce paperwork and expand trade to benefit America's exporters. (57 F.R. 31658, July 17, 1992.)

—Finally, our enforcement efforts are proceeding apace as we continue to enforce export controls vigorously. The export control provisions of the Export Administration Regulations are enforced jointly by the Commerce Department's Office of Export Enforcement and the U.S. Customs Service. Both of these agencies investigate allegations and, where appropriate, refer them for criminal prosecution by the Justice Department. Additionally, the Commerce Department has continued its practice of imposing significant administrative sanctions for violations, including civil penalties and denial of export privileges.

—Commerce's Office of Export Enforcement (OEE) has continued its vital preventive programs such as pre-license checks and post-shipment verifications, export license review, and on-site verification visits by teams of enforcement officers in many countries. The OEE has also continued its outreach to the business community to assist exporters with their compliance programs and to solicit their help in OEE's enforcement effort. The OEE has initiated its well-received Business Executive Enforcement Team (BEET) to enhance interaction between the regulators and the regulated.

—The OEE has also initiated a new program—the Strategic and Non-proliferation Enforcement Program (SNEP)—which targets critical enforcement resources on exports to countries of concern in the Middle East and elsewhere.

—In one of many successful enforcement efforts, following his plea of guilty to several counts of an indictment charging him with violating U.S. export control laws, Don Danesh, an Iranian national doing business in the United States, was sentenced to serve 12 months in jail and placed on supervised probation for an additional 36 months. Danesh's associate, Ray Amiri, also an Iranian national doing business in the United States, is expected to be sentenced in the near future following his guilty plea. In developments related to the criminal case, on May 29, 1992, the Acting Assistant Secretary for Export Enforcement renewed an order temporarily denying the export privileges of Amiri, his company, and Danesh. (57 F.R. 24242, June 8, 1992.)

—In the last 6 months, the Department has continued to enforce the antiboycott law vigorously. The Office of Antiboycott Compliance (OAC) is fully staffed with 30 full-time employees, and OAC has doubled the level of civil penalties it seeks to impose within the statutory $10,000 per violation maximum. The total dollar amount of civil penalties imposed so far in fiscal year 1992 approaches $2 million, the second largest amount in the history of the program.

—During this 6-month reporting period, significant civil penalties were assessed against several companies in antiboycott compliance cases. Among them, by Order of May 19, 1992, L.A. Gear, Inc., was assessed a civil penalty of $404,000 to settle allegations that the company complied with boycott requests from a customer in Kuwait and that it failed to report its receipt of boycott requests. On August 12, 1992, the Bank of Baroda, one of India's largest banks, was assessed a civil penalty of $502,000 to settle allegations that it implemented letters of credit containing prohibited boycott conditions and that it failed to report its receipt of boycott requests. After reviewing data related to the financial condition of the bank, the Department agreed to suspend payment of $227,000 of the $502,000 civil penalty.

5. The expenses incurred by the Federal Government in the 6-month period from April 1, 1992, to September 30, 1992, that are directly attributable to the exercise of authorities conferred by the declaration of a national emergency with respect to export controls were largely centered in the Department of Commerce, Bureau of Export

Administration. Expenditures by the Department of Commerce are anticipated to be $19,186 million, most of which represents program operating costs, wage and salary costs for Federal personnel, and overhead expenses.

6. The unrestricted access of foreign parties to U.S. goods, technology, and technical data, and the existence of certain boycott practices of foreign nations, in light of the expiration of the Export Administration Act of 1979, continue to constitute an unusual

and extraordinary threat to the national security, foreign policy, and economy of the United States. I shall continue to exercise the powers at my disposal to retain the export control system, including the antiboycott provisions, and will continue to report periodically to the Congress.

GEORGE BUSH

The White House,
September 25, 1992.

Notice on Continuation of Emergency Regarding Export Control Regulations
September 25, 1992

On September 30, 1990, consistent with the authority provided me under the International Emergency Economic Powers Act (50 U.S.C. 1701, *et seq.*), I issued Executive Order No. 12730. In that order, I declared a national emergency with respect to the unusual and extraordinary threat to the national security, foreign policy, and economy of the United States in light of the expiration of the Export Administration Act of 1979, as amended (50 U.S.C. App. 2401, *et seq.*). Because the Export Administration Act has not been renewed by the Congress, the national emergency declared on September 30, 1990, and extended on September 26, 1991, must continue in effect beyond September 30, 1992. Therefore, in accordance with section 202(d) of the Na-

tional Emergencies Act (50 U.S.C. 1622(d)), I am continuing the national emergency in order to deal with the threat posed by the unrestricted access of foreign parties to United States goods, technology, and technical data and by the existence of certain boycott practices of foreign nations.

This notice shall be published in the *Federal Register* and transmitted to the Congress.

GEORGE BUSH

The White House,
September 25, 1992.

[*Filed with the Office of the Federal Register, 12:16 p.m., September 25, 1992*]

Message to the Congress on Continuation of the National Emergency With Respect to Export Control Regulations
September 25, 1992

To the Congress of the United States:

On September 30, 1990, in light of the expiration of the Export Administration Act of 1979, as amended (50 U.S.C. App. 2401, *et seq.*), I issued Executive Order No. 12730, declaring a national emergency and continuing the system of export regulation, in-

cluding antiboycott provisions, under the International Emergency Economic Powers Act (50 U.S.C. 1701, *et seq.*). Under section 202(d) of the National Emergencies Act (50 U.S.C. 1622(d)), the national emergency terminates on each anniversary of its declaration unless I publish in the *Federal Register* and transmit to the Congress notice of its continuation.

I am hereby advising the Congress that I have extended the national emergency declared in Executive Order No. 12730. Attached is a copy of the notice of extension.

GEORGE BUSH

The White House,
September 25, 1992.

Message to the Senate Returning Without Approval the Family Planning Amendments Act of 1992
September 25, 1992

To the Senate of the United States:

I am returning herewith without my approval S. 323, the "Family Planning Amendments Act of 1992." This legislation would extend and amend the Federal family planning program under title X of the Public Health Service Act.

If the scope of S. 323 were limited to family planning, I would approve it. My Administration has an excellent record in support of family planning. About this there can be no question. Our approach to reauthorizing title X was embodied in a bill transmitted to the Congress on February 25, 1991. We need a family planning program to deliver preventive, pre-pregnancy services.

Unfortunately, S. 323 is unacceptable because it would override current regulations that are designed to maintain the title X program's integrity as a pre-pregnancy family planning program. The bill would require projects supported by title X family planning funds to counsel pregnant women on, and refer them for, abortions. Such a requirement is totally alien to the purpose of the title X program. Title X is a quality health care program that provides pre-pregnancy family planning information and services and refers pregnant women to health care providers who can ensure continuity of care.

Under current regulations, upheld by the United States Supreme Court, pregnant women who seek services from clinics funded by title X would be referred to qualified providers for prenatal care and other social services, including counseling. Moreover, nothing in these regulations prevents a woman from receiving complete medical information about her condition from a physician. The Supreme Court specifically found that the regulations regarding the title X program in no way violated free speech rights.

In a memorandum to Department of Health and Human Services Secretary Louis Sullivan on November 5, 1991, I reiterated my commitment to preserving the confidentiality of the doctor/patient relationship. In that memorandum, I also repeated my commitment to ensuring that the operation of the title X family planning program is compatible with free speech and the highest standards of medical care. My memorandum makes clear that there is no "gag rule" to interfere with the doctor/patient relationship. There can be no doubt that my Administration is committed to the protection of free speech.

I have repeatedly informed the Congress that I would disapprove any legislation that would transform this program into a vehicle for the promotion of abortion. Unfortunately, the Congress has seen fit to entangle this family planning program in the politics of abortion.

I believe that the title X family planning program should be reauthorized. I now urge the Congress to adopt a bill that promotes true family planning rather than requiring Federal tax dollars to be used in a manner that promotes abortion as a method of birth control.

GEORGE BUSH

The White House,
September 25, 1992.

Message to the Congress Transmitting Proposed Legislation on Federal Pay Reduction
September 25, 1992

To the Congress of the United States:

I am pleased to transmit today for your immediate consideration and enactment the "Federal Pay Reduction Act of 1992." This legislation is part of my Agenda for American Renewal. The proposal is an important step toward "rightsizing" our Government—making it more fiscally responsible and reducing its size and structure. Also transmitted is a section-by-section analysis.

There are many in America who are out of work or uncertain of their prospects. The Federal deficit constrains the capacity to rejuvenate the economy. It is therefore appropriate that those who lead the Government make a personal contribution—toward reducing the deficit and as a symbol of our understanding of the concerns of so many Americans. Accordingly, this proposal would reduce the salary of the President, the Vice President, and the Speaker of the

House of Representatives by a full 10 percent. For other leaders in our Government—Members of Congress, senior officials paid more than $75,000 in all three branches of the Government, and high-ranking military officers—the pay reductions would be 5 percent. An otherwise scheduled pay increase in January 1993 for these officials would not take place.

Under our Constitution, the President's salary can only be changed at the beginning of a new term of office. Pay reductions for all others affected will take place with the first pay period beginning on or after January 20, 1993. It is therefore essential that this legislation be enacted immediately, before the adjournment of the current Congress.

GEORGE BUSH

The White House,
September 25, 1992.

Appointment of John G. Keller, Jr., as Deputy Assistant to the President for Special Activities
September 25, 1992

The President today announced the appointment of John G. Keller, Jr., as Deputy Assistant to the President for Special Initiatives.

Since 1991, Mr. Keller has served as Under Secretary of Commerce for Travel and Tourism at the Department of Commerce. Prior to this, Mr. Keller served as Deputy Assistant to the President and Director of Presidential Advance, 1989–91. From 1987 to 1989, he worked in the Office of the Vice President as Deputy Assistant to the Vice President and Director of Advance and as Deputy Director of Advance, 1986–87 and 1984–85, respectively. He was also a confidential assistant to the

Director at the U.S. Fish and Wildlife Service from 1985 to 1986. Mr. Keller has acted as a lead advance representative, 1982–84, and as a volunteer advance representative, 1981–82. In addition, he was the scheduling and advance coordinator for George Bush's Presidential campaign in 1979–80. His work experience has allowed him to travel over one million miles and has taken him to more than 70 foreign countries and every State in the Nation.

Mr. Keller graduated from Iowa State University (B.A., 1982). He was born August 10, 1958, in Washington, DC. Mr. Keller is married and resides in Sterling, VA.

Nomination of Eric J. Boswell To Be Director of the Office of Foreign Missions at the Department of State
September 25, 1992

The President today announced his intention to nominate Eric J. Boswell, of California, a career member of the Senior Foreign Service, class of Minister-Counselor, to be Director of the Office of Foreign Missions, Department of State, with the rank of Ambassador. He would succeed David C. Fields.

Since 1990, Mr. Boswell has served as Executive Director of the Bureau of Near East and South Asian Affairs at the U.S. Department of State. He has also served with the Department of State as administrative minister-counselor at the American Embassy in Ottawa, Canada, 1987–90; administrative counselor at the American Embassy in Amman, Jordan, 1985–87; Deputy Executive Director of the Bureau of European and Canadian Affairs, 1983–85; personnel officer for Near East assignments with the Bureau of Personnel, 1980–83; and consular officer at the American consulate general in Quebec, Canada, 1977–80.

Mr. Boswell graduated from Stanford University (B.A., 1970). He served in the U.S. Army, 1968–69. He was born May 31, 1945, in Naples, Italy. Mr. Boswell currently resides in Washington, DC.

Nomination of William Lucas To Be Director of Community Relations Service at the Department of Justice
September 25, 1992

The President today announced his intention to nominate William Lucas, of Michigan, to be Director of Community Relations Service at the U.S. Department of Justice, for a term of 4 years. He would succeed Grace Flores-Hughes.

Since 1989, Mr. Lucas has served as Director of the Office of Liaison Services at the Department of Justice. From 1988 to 1989, Mr. Lucas served as an attorney with the firm of Evans and Luptak in Detroit, MI. In 1987, he was a Harvard fellow at the John F. Kennedy School of Government. He has also served as Commissioner of the Commission on the Bicentennial of the United States Constitution, 1986–89; county executive for Wayne County, MI, 1983–86; and sheriff of Wayne County, MI, 1970–83.

Mr. Lucas graduated from Manhattan College (B.S., 1948) and Fordham Law School (LL.B., 1962). He was born January 15, 1928, in New York City. Mr. Lucas is married, has five children, and resides in Arlington, VA.

Remarks on Beginning a Whistlestop Tour in Columbus, Ohio
September 26, 1992

What a great day in Ohio. Barbara and I are delighted to be here. May I salute our longstanding friends, George and Janet Voinovich, and say you are very lucky in this State to have this man as your Governor. Also I want to single out another one, and that's Chalmers Wylie. He and I went to Congress on the same day, and he served Columbus with great distinction. If we had more like him they wouldn't be yelling all the time, "Clean House!" to get rid of all those Democrats that have been there in control for 38 years, for 38 years.

I want to see John Kasich reelected. I want to thank your great Mayor, Greg Lashutka. My gosh, you've got a good one here in Columbus, Ohio. Also, if you really want to help change this country, elect Mike DeWine to the United States Senate.

May I thank and give a special salute to the Marching Tigers. Others can blow the saxophone, but I'll stand with the Purple Pride of Pinkerton. You try to say that. [*Laughter*] It's great to be back in Ohio. It's a great, beautiful day, football weather. I should say "Buckeye weather" here.

You know, over the next couple of days we're taking our crusade to Ohio and to Michigan, eight towns and cities, over 233 miles. We're going to talk about what it takes to match peace around the world with peace of mind here at home. For 4 months another candidate for President has been tearing down the United States of America, running the country down. Maybe he's inhaled too many of those bus fumes. I think he did inhale them. Well, let's get that bus off the side of the road, because on this train trip we're going to blow the whistle on Governor Clinton. I am tired of his lousy record in Arkansas.

Here's what we're going to do. We're going to talk about what's right about America and what we're doing to change it, what we need to do to change Congress, change the direction of the country. Then we're also going to talk about what's going on down in Arkansas and who is doing that to the good people of that State. He has a lousy record in Arkansas, and we don't need that for the United States of America.

So for the next 2 days it's "All aboard, America." The Spirit of America is on its way, and it's all aboard for a better future where Government serves the people, not the other way around. It's all aboard for the freedom to save and invest and, yes, to keep more of what you earn. It's all aboard for an agenda which can renew and literally change America, just as America, and I am proud to have been a significant part of this, has reduced the threat of nuclear war for these young people here today.

And so what do we want for America? We want smart schools and safe streets. We want to lower taxes and less regulation. We want to strengthen families that are working, hoping, and building and dreaming. That's very different than what the Governor of Arkansas is proposing.

You know, my granddad knew how America was blessed, and he lived here in Columbus. His company, Buckeye Steel, made couplings for the railroads. My father was born here in Columbus, Ohio. He was raised as a child, lived over on East Broad Street for a while. He knew how this city loved the American spirit, how you lived it from one generation to the next. And today, Barbara and I are very proud to begin this voyage in a city which has blessed our family, a city that we love.

For you see, this train trip is much more than about my reelection. It's about creating an America where every day has that spirit of the Fourth of July, the kind of America these young people here today deserve. That is the real spirit of America, always been and always will be.

Now we're off to Marysville and Arlington and Bowling Green and then on into Michigan, the heart of America, the real America. With this spirit we see here today, we are going to win this election.

Thank you all very, very much. May God bless each and every one of you. Thank you very, very much, indeed. All aboard!

Note: The President spoke at 9:45 a.m. on the observation deck of the Spirit of America train at the Old Mound Freight Yard station.

Remarks to the Community in Marysville, Ohio
September 26, 1992

The President. Thank you very, very much. What a great Ohio day. Thank you very, very much. Thank you all for this wonderful welcome to Marysville. May I salute your great Governor, George Voinovich, who's with us on this train, and thank him for what he's doing for creating jobs in Ohio and jobs across this country through his trip—bringing up these exports. We need to hear more like it. We need more Governors like George Voinovich.

Also I want to introduce to all of you—maybe he's been introduced—another old friend who has served this State well, and now I want to see him in the United States Senate, Mike DeWine, Lieutenant Governor. Congressman Kasich is here, and my old friend Congressman Chalmers Wylie. And of course, your Congressman, Paul Gillmor, is here and his wife, Karen, who will make a great State senator. And may I make a special plea to send David Hobson to the United States Congress. We need to give Paul Gillmor some help in Washington. We need to clean House. And may I salute the Monarchs and the——

Audience members. Clean the House! Clean the House! Clean the House!

The President. You're right, man. May I salute the Monarchs, the Wildcats, and the Panthers.

You know, somebody told me that some of you around here always wear a button, normally wear a button that says, "Reelect Barbara Bush's husband." Well, I like that because, you see, I think we have the best First Lady in the entire world.

You know, some of you yelling "Clean House!", I couldn't help but notice the sign down the street on McCullough's Hardware. It says, "All I want for Christmas is a new Congress." Not a bad idea. Let's get this country moving forward.

May I salute the veterans that are here from Richmond and Marysville and elsewhere, men and women that served their country with great distinction. I salute the veterans. I salute those who put on a uniform and served their country.

You know, we take this train through Marysville this morning to discuss what kind of an America we want. I want an America that is a military superpower—we've got to stay strong—an economic superpower and an export superpower; an America where every person who wants the dignity of work can find it, because you just can't build a home without a hammer, you can't build a dream without a job.

I have laid out my Agenda for American Renewal, a comprehensive, integrated series of steps to create here in America, by early in the next century, the world's very first $10 trillion economy. I believe that the only way to achieve prosperity is by opening foreign markets to American goods and services. You see, I have faith in the American worker and in the American farmer, who can still outwork, outproduce any other worker in the entire world.

You know, George Voinovich, as you all know, recently visited Japan. He talked with the chairman of Honda, and the chairman told him flat out that the workers here in Marysville were not as good as Japanese workers; he told them they were better than Japanese workers.

On free trade, and I'm talking about jobs with Honda here in Marysville, on free trade, my opponent hasn't even made up his mind yet. But he does want to slap a tough tax on foreign plants in the United States, including the Honda plant right here in Marysville.

Audience members. Boo-o-o!

The President. Now, you slap a tax on Honda, and they'll take the jobs and go somewhere else. I want more jobs for American workers, not by raising taxes but by getting taxes down.

You've got great workers here in Marysville, like American workers everywhere. You never retreat; you always compete. And you always win. That is the American spirit. We pulled this wonderful train, the Spirit of America, into Marysville today to talk about how we'll win the economic competition.

Now, Governor Clinton, if you'll excuse the expression, Governor Clinton says that our economy is, and I quote—listen to the way he talks about America—"sliding past Germany, heading south toward Sri Lanka." Those are his words. He ought to stop knocking the greatest country on the face of the Earth. He ought to understand that we are the most admired and respected country on the face of the Earth. Let's not knock the United States of America.

You know, we all know that we've had some tough times here. But we're in a global economy. Take a look at the economies of Europe, where they suffer with the high taxes and the big government that Clinton favors. We have lower unemployment, stronger growth. That doesn't sound like Sri Lanka to me. We are the United States. Interest rates are below the 20-year lows. Inflation is under control. Our economy is ready to move. And Governor, that doesn't sound like Sri Lanka to me.

So we must not take a risk about this economy. Our economy could slide into a disaster if we go back to the misery days of Jimmy Carter, if we make the wrong choice. That's why today we are going to blow this whistle on Bill Clinton, take his record to the people of Ohio. Here's what worries me: He's promising to do for the national economy what he's done for Arkansas. Now, when you look at the record, you realize that's not a promise; it is a threat.

You know, I know that Marysville hosted the hot air balloon festival last month. Well, when you think of politicians, every day is a hot air balloon festival. So let me stick to the facts today on Governor Clinton's record, his rhetoric.

Arkansas was, indeed, one of the poorest States when Bill Clinton became Governor, and 12 years later, it is still on the bottom. The problem is not with the good people of that State, not at all. The problem is with the leader, who criticizes me at every turn but has failed to move his own State up the ladder. That is the fact, and we don't want him doing that for the United States of America.

You want to know the record? All right, here it is. Governor Clinton raised and extended the sales tax over and over again. He taxed groceries. He taxed mobile homes. He doubled the tax on gasoline. And yes, he raised the tax on beer. Bad.

Audience members. Boo-o-o!

The President. I'm tempted to say that listening to this will kind of tax your patience, but why give him another idea.

Now, Governor Clinton is no friend of the middle class. Don't take my word for it, though. Listen to his hometown newspaper, the Arkansas Gazette: "In the Clinton era"—this is exactly what it says—"In the Clinton era the Arkansas tax system has become stacked against the ordinary taxpayer and consumer; stacked for the rich and the special interest."

I do not want a tax system that just benefits the rich. I want a tax system that helps all working people get rich. That is the American way.

Audience members. Four more years! Four more years! Four more years!

The President. You know, what a great rally. My heavens.

Now, Governor Clinton says he's seen the light. In this campaign, he's come right out—in the beginning; this is before he gets through—and he said he wants $150 billion in new taxes. But don't worry, he says, all the money will come from the rich, all those people who drive Jaguars and eat that quiche and drink that champagne, all those who inherit their money.

And we've heard that song before. Jimmy Carter sang it. Walter Mondale sang it. Michael Dukakis sang it. They're going after the rich, but the middle class always gets up singing the blues. Big Government gets the gold, and you get the shaft. We do not need to raise taxes in this country.

Now, listen to this. Governor Clinton says he'll raise it, he'll raise the $150 billion by taxing the top 2 percent of Americans, all those people who make over $200,000. But whoops, that's not the top 2 percent. The Treasury Department says the top 2 percent of Americans begins with individuals with incomes taxable of $64,800. But there's not enough money at that level. So to get the full $150 billion, Bill Clinton would have to tax individuals at $36,600 a year. I do not think these people are spending their time on the Riviera. They are the hard-working men and women and families in the United States. We must not let him raise their taxes.

But it gets worse. I hate to ruin this beautiful day. It gets worse. Governor Clinton has made a lot of promises in this campaign. He's already called for Government spending increases of at least $220 billion. Newsweek magazine says the real cost is arguably at least 3 times that high.

Now the liberal Congress is salivating, waiting to pass all these new programs. But where will he get the money? Where will Governor Clinton get the money? Listen to the folks who know Bill Clinton best. The Pine Bluff Commercial, a newspaper in Arkansas, I quote: "If Congress followed the example that Bill Clinton has set as Governor of Arkansas, it would pass a tax program that would hit the middle class the hardest."

That is the big secret of this campaign. To capture all the revenue that he wants to raise, to pay for all these promises, Bill Clinton will have to go after the middle class. I am not going to let him do that, and neither are you.

Audience members. Hit him again, hit him again, harder, harder! Hit him again, hit him again, harder, harder!

The President. I'm getting to that.

Just think about what the Clinton plan could mean right here in Marysville, Ohio. Listen to this. Let's say you're a 40-year-old fireman with about 29,000 bucks in taxable income. Governor Clinton would have you give the Government another $1,000 a year. That money could help you pay for your kids' education, and you should keep it in your hands. Or let's say you are a licensed nurse, making about $28,000 in taxable income. Governor Clinton could have you to fork over another $890 a year. That money could be used to fix the car or help pay your mortgage. And you ought to be allowed to keep it, not send it to Washington, DC.

This is a fundamental issue in this election. Governor Clinton trusts Government planners to make better decisions than you can. I believe that you can invest your money, make your own decisions better than any Government planner or any mandating Congressman in Washington, DC.

Governor Clinton says he wants to gather the so-called best and the brightest, all the economists and lawyers and lobbyists who studied with him over there in Oxford during the war, and bring them to Washington to figure out how to fix all your problems. I want to give more power to you, freedom to you, because in my mind, America's best and brightest are standing right here in Marysville, Ohio, and other towns like it across this great country.

So to sum it up, Bill Clinton's taxes are wrong for America. Bill Clinton's Arkansas record is wrong for America. And any way you cut it, Bill Clinton is wrong to be President of the United States of America.

As Barbara said, her mother was born here and grew up here in Marysville. And I know the town's slogan is the place where "the grass is always greener." But it might as well make it the slogan for our great country. And sure, we have problems. And sure, we face our challenges. But you ask a European or ask an Asian, as George Voinovich said, America is still number one in the entire world.

Look around, look around this community at the new jobs, at the Americans competing in a new world economy, and you see our capacity for renewal. Government did not build this great Nation, and Government alone will not renew our great Nation. People built it, people who believe in family, people who believe in hard work, people just like you standing out here on this magnificent Ohio day.

So he offers you more Government, and I offer more power to the American family, more power to the American people. And I stand before you as a leader who has served his country in war and in peace; a leader with the experience, hopefully the character, the ideas to keep the great train of America rolling along to a more safe and a secure future.

These are exciting times. America is not in decline. We are a strong, respected, rising nation. I ask for your trust for another 4 years to lead this great Nation.

May God bless you all. And may God bless the United States of America. Thank you very, very much. Thank you all.

Remarks at the Centennial Family Picnic in Arlington, Ohio
September 26, 1992

The President. Thank you very, very much. What a wonderful welcome to Arlington. Thank you so much. I just wish each and every one of you could have been on this train ride from Columbus here. It has been magnificent, a wonderful turnout of the true American spirit, a welcome by Ohio that has warmed our hearts. Then to come here for this icing on the cake, this fantastic rally. We are very, very glad to be with you on your 100th anniversary.

In case you didn't see him when we walked in, I want to be sure you salute and honor a great, a truly great Governor, George Voinovich. What a job he's doing for this State. Your Congressman, Mike Oxley, and I go back a long, long time. You've got one of the best. If we had more like him, everybody wouldn't be yelling, "Clean House!" We need to clean House, but we need more like Mike Oxley to get the job done for America.

I believe Mike DeWine is with us. I haven't seen him on this stop. He's been along with us. But let me say, whether he's here or not, we must clean House, and that means we need a new Senator. Please elect this great Lieutenant Governor to the United States Senate.

Mayor Suter, may I thank you and all the citizens here for this warm welcome. I'll tell you, as we were leaning out of the train coming around the bend here, you could just sense the feeling of this marvelous community gathering. And we are very, very grateful to you.

I understand that your local deputy, Kreg Sheets, is here, or he was here a minute ago, he's the guy all dressed up because he's getting married in less than an hour; there he is, right here. We wish him well. Kreg, we want to wish you and Kris Martin all the very, very best in a great life of happiness ahead.

Now, today's been a wonderful day for Barbara and me: the sendoff from my dad's birthplace in Columbus, Ohio; then a stop in Marysville, which is where Barbara's mother was born; and then the trip here through this gentle, beautiful, highly productive Ohio farmland. People greeting us on both sides of the Spirit of America, great sounds and sights, it has been a wonderfully moving day where you can't help but count your blessings and say America is the greatest, freest country on the face of the Earth.

We saw all kinds of farmers lined up along the railroad tracks. We saw a dairy farmer holding up a sign. It said he'd be "pulling for me." Well, that ought to ruin your lunch, but that's what I saw. [*Laughter*]

We knew the best still lay ahead of us: this town, this lunch, Rosemary Orwick's pasta noodles. I'm not quite sure what's more difficult, working with Congress or getting Rosemary to divulge her secret recipe I'm about to sample here.

There's a lot at stake in this election. We have won great victories around the world. The kids here in this beautiful cross section of America can go to bed at night without the same fear of nuclear war that the older generation had. That is a wonderful accomplishment for the United States of America, and we ought to take great pride in it.

Now, it's time, with all these dramatic changes around the world that we've helped bring about—decline and fall of the Soviet empire; Middle Eastern enemies talking to each other; democracy on the move south of our border; the great countries of Eastern Europe free, free at last— it's now time to roll up our sleeves and renew America, just as our ancestors did. We want an America of the best schools in the world. We want safe neighborhoods and safe streets. And that's what I'm fighting for against this Congress in Washington, DC.

We want lower taxes and less regulation. An America working and hoping and building, where every day is like the Fourth of July for our families and for these young people here today.

I'm not going to ruin this magnificent picnic with a long political speech, but let me just say that the question before you in this election is very simple. My opponent believes that America should pay more taxes because Government planners, senior little chairmen up there in the Congress, bureaucrats can spend your money more wisely than you can. And I don't believe that for one single minute.

You know, all of this talk about class warfare and a talk of moderation and going after the rich, he's got a big tax increase aimed right at the heart of middle America. I don't think we need that. I believe you should keep more of your hard-earned dollars because you can invest them more wisely.

In my second term, and believe me there will be one, I will continue to be doing for this Nation which your great Governor is doing for Ohio, opening up new markets for our products and creating new jobs for our workers. We can outhustle the workers in any other country if we open those foreign markets to American expertise. That's what I'm trying to do.

So we will be working to hold the line on Government spending and taxes and regulation, to cut the health care costs down with my health care program that provides everybody in this country that needs it insurance. We keep the quality of health care, but we then provide insurance to people, and we do not get the Government further involved like some of the socialist systems around the world. We've got the best; we want to make it better and make it available to all.

The liberals in Washington don't like it, but let me tell you something: I am going to keep trying to find ways to strengthen the American family. The family is our strength, and the family needs to be supported, not divided. And how do you do that? You do it by giving parents more choice in child care or in schools. You do it by reforming welfare so that the young girl is in school and tries to save a little money,

save over $1,000, her mother doesn't get thrown off of welfare. Reform the system to keep families together, rather than trying to drive them apart.

Strengthen the family by making our neighborhoods safer. I strongly back our local law enforcement people, our firefighters, our policemen, our county sheriff's people. I back them all the way because they are fighting for the American family by cutting down crime in our neighborhoods all across America.

So when I talk about strengthening the family, it's this and so many things else. And I might say something about our First Lady. When she holds in her arms a baby stricken by AIDS or cancer, she's sending the signal that we ought to love each other more. And when she sits there in the White House and reads to a group of kids, she's setting an example for parents and families all across this country, because reading to kids is important. So don't let the liberals scare us away from strengthening the American family. We are right, and you are right. And this part of America knows exactly what I'm talking about.

In its great 100 years, Arlington has seen its children march off to war, its young men and women; seen its old cry, in the old seen the cry of the tears of depression. And you've marveled at the arrival of new technology and treasured this sturdy foundation of the traditional values that we're talking about here. Through every change, America has emerged stronger, and it is the same today.

Our challenges look difficult, and we've got big challenges. If you look around the world, you'll see the whole world is facing economic challenges. Whether it's in Europe or wherever else it is, there's enormous economic change taking place. In spite of what my opponent says, the United States, although we've got to do much better, is the envy of the entire world, whether it's our economy, our military strength, our system of freedom.

So I am not one who wants to get to be President again by complaining about the United States or tearing it down or saying, as Governor Clinton does, that we are somewhere less than Germany and a little better than Sri Lanka. We are the United States of America, the envy of the entire world because we have stood for freedom. And we can do anything we set our sights on.

My faith is in the American people. My faith is with the people, to give the people the power that comes from less Government, less taxes, less regulation, and more confidence in the neighborhoods and in the communities and in the young people we're surrounded with here today.

So I come here as an optimist about America, and I want to finish the job that I have started. I believe this: It's not that I need to be President, but it is that I want to finish the job and strengthen the institutions, and particularly the family that we've talked about. We've made a big start. We are the envy of the world. And I am proud

that these kids go to bed at night without the same fear of nuclear war that their predecessors did, much, much prouder than I could be of anything else.

But now, I ask for your support; 4 more years to strengthen America, bring us back, bring economic opportunity to all. And may God bless our great country. And thank you all very, very much.

And Mayor, will you come up?

Audience members. Four more years! Four more years! Four more years!

The President. This is a little symbol that's flown over the Capitol. This is for Arlington on its 100th birthday. Many, many thanks and congratulations.

Note: The President spoke at 2:21 p.m. at Arlington Park. In his remarks, he referred to Dean Suter, Mayor of Arlington.

Remarks to the Community in Findlay, Ohio
September 26, 1992

Hey, listen, it's great to be back in Findlay. We want to come down and shake a few hands, but thanks for this welcome. We've had a great trip across, all the way from Columbus through Marysville, Arlington. Here we are in Findlay, and on we go. But I'll tell you something: This is a great part of the United States. Do not let Bill Clinton tell you that this is a nation in decline. We are the best in the entire world. We can solve every problem we've got.

Here's a guy that's got a good idea. He's saying, "Clean House!" Let's clean House in the Capitol, and let's get this country going forward again. Clean the House. That's exactly right. Those guys have been in control of the House for 38 years, and it's time to clean House, get rid of them and get a good team in like your Representatives right here from Findlay. We need more.

It's been a wonderful day. By the way, don't vote for a man that's going to raise

your taxes and raise spending all at the same time. Do not put Governor Clinton in that White House.

One last word, and then we'll come down, Barbara and I, down to say hello down there. But one last word. I see these young people here today, and I take great pride in the fact that they go to bed at night with a lot less fear of nuclear weapons. Bill Clinton says foreign affairs don't mean anything. I say world peace means an awful lot.

Now let's get this country moving by less taxes and less spending, less regulation, more emphasis on strengthening the American family and less emphasis on spending and taxing, like Clinton and Gore want.

Thank you all very, very much.

Note: The President spoke at 3:30 p.m. on the observation deck of the Spirit of America train.

Remarks to the Community in Bowling Green, Ohio
September 26, 1992

The President. What a great welcome back to Bowling Green. Thank you all. Thank you very, very much. Thank you, Representative Gardner. Barbara and I just want to say it's great to be back in Bowling Green. It's good to see your great Congressman, Congressman Gillmor, doing a great job for the United States. If we had more like him we would not have to clean House. But we've got to clean 'em out—not him. Send us more like him. Give us more Congressmen like this one.

May I salute State Senator Montgomery; thank Representative Gardner; thank Bowling Green's Mayor Hoffman and my good friend and former Congressman Del Latta. You've had great public servants up here.

You know, we weren't tuned in. So who won the football game? Just kidding. Well done.

Well, listen, we're in the midst of a great train ride, 233 miles across Ohio and into Michigan. Now, I don't want to suggest we're picking up support, but Barbara and I were looking out the window a couple miles ago, and we saw a bunch of cows doing the wave. Things are coming along.

We saw all kinds of animals on this trip, and in this crowd somewhere we caught sight of the chicken, a chicken. Don't worry. What's one chicken, compared to thousands of Falcons? There he is, the chicken. I'm not sure if that chicken is from Oxford, England——

Audience members. Boo-o-o!

The President. ——or if he's the one that dumps that fecal coliform bacteria into the Arkansas River.

No, the election is about your future: What kind of America you want to live in. I want an America where every graduate of this great school can find a good, decent job.

I have laid out my Agenda for American Renewal, a comprehensive, integrated plan, so America can win the economic competition. I want to open up new foreign markets for our products, because the American worker never retreats; we always compete.

And we always win.

I want to see us reform a legal system that is careening out of control, faster than a lawyer can chase an ambulance. As a nation, we must sue each other less and care for each other more. Enough of these reckless lawsuits.

I am proud, you wouldn't get it from listening to the Clinton-Gore ticket cry, but I am proud that under my administration half the college students in America now receive some form of Federal grant or tuition assistance. We have increased the aid for students.

Here's another difference I have with the Governor of Arkansas: I want to strengthen our elementary and secondary schools by giving every parent the right to choose their children's school, public, private, or religious.

But while I'm talking about the positive things, Governor Clinton insists on cutting America down. While I'm focusing on the future, he is engaged in a deliberate campaign of distortion. I've had it up to here. So let's talk about his record. If he wants to talk about the past, if the Governor wants to talk about the past, let's do it. We pulled this train in here this afternoon to blow the whistle on Governor Clinton and his record in Arkansas.

Audience members. Four more years! Four more years! Four more years!

The President. You know, let me tell you, the people of Arkansas, and I used to live right next door to them, the people of Arkansas are good and decent. And frankly, they deserve much better leadership than they're getting. Here's the scary part: Governor Clinton says he wants to do for the national economy what he's done for Arkansas. If you look at his record, you'll see that's not a promise. That's a threat. We can't have it.

Okay, he wants to talk specifics. Listen to these: Governor Clinton has raised and extended the sales tax, over and over. He taxed groceries. He taxed mobile homes. He doubled the tax on gasoline. And he even raised the tax on beer. How do you like that?

Audience members. Boo-o-o!

The President. Now he says he's seen the light. In this campaign, he proposes $150 billion in new taxes, plus at least $220 billion in new spending. But don't worry; don't worry. He says it will all come from the rich, the top 2 percent, people who make over $200,000.

But here's the truth. To get the money that he needs for this tax plan and spend plan, the $150 billion he's raised in new taxes, he would have to raise taxes on every individual with over $36,600 a year in taxable income.

Audience members. Boo-o-o!

The President. That is a fact. These aren't people that hang out on the Riviera. These aren't the people on the "Lifestyles of the Rich and Famous." These are good people who work hard all day, and frankly, you deserve a break, not more taxes.

But you know, it's worse than this. I don't want to ruin your day, but let me just finish this record. It is worse than this. He has promised a new program every time he makes a speech. But he hasn't said how he'll pay for them. He'll need hundreds of billions of dollars more, beyond the tax increases he's already proposed. You might say, where is he going to get the money?

Well, listen to a newspaper from Governor Clinton's own home State, the Pine Bluff Commercial. They said, and I quote, "If Congress followed the example Bill Clinton set as Governor of Arkansas, it would pass a program that hit the middle class the hardest."

That is a quote from the people that know best. So if the past is any guide, Bill Clinton will go to where the money is. He'll take it right out of your pocketbook, right from the middle, hard-working class in this country. He's not going to stop at just taxing the rich. He's going to raise taxes on the middle, and I'm not going to let him do it.

Just think about what the Clinton plan would mean right here in Bowling Green. Let's say you are working in a campus administration. You get maybe, what, $38,000 a year in taxable income. Governor Clinton could have give you another $1,700 to the tax man. I say you should use that money, keep it to pay your bills, not to pay off some special interest.

Here's how he responds: He says, forget it, "I'm a different kind of Democrat." Yes, I've heard that one. Listen to his first political boss, George McGovern. McGovern says, and here's what I quote, "The Democratic ticket is much more liberal underneath, and they will show it after they are elected." Let's see that they are not elected to this high office.

Audience members. Four more years! Four more years! Four more years!

The President. He says he's a different kind of Democrat. You tell me what's so different about socking it to the middle class. We do not need that kind of difference.

You know, I know Governor Clinton is concerned with his lack of foreign policy experience, and frankly, I take great pride in the fact that these young people here go to bed at night without quite the same fear of nuclear weapons and nuclear war that our predecessors have.

So Governor Clinton doesn't think foreign policy is important. But anyway, he's trying to catch up. You may have seen this in the news. He was in Hollywood, seeking foreign policy advice from the rock group U2. Now, understand, I have nothing against U2. You may not know this, but they tried to call me at the White House every night during their concert. But the next time we face a foreign policy crisis, I will work with John Major and Boris Yeltsin. And Bill Clinton can consult Boy George. I'll stay with the experts.

But, you know, this U2 is not a description of Governor Clinton's foreign policy. It's a description of his economic plan. You, too, can pay higher taxes. You, too, can watch inflation waste—write out your paycheck. You, too, can see the U.S. get used to 10 percent unemployment, where it was when we last had a Democratic President and a Democratic Congress.

I say forget this economic policy. You, too, deserve better, and we have the program to move this country ahead. I offer America a responsible program but a smaller Government, a Government that sees that not every problem can be solved back there along the Potomac but understands that the real strength of America is right here in places like Bowling Green.

Our world is filled with so much opportunity, unlike we've ever known before. We've stood fast for freedom, and now the world is embracing our ideas. And in this election I'm the one that stands for freedom and democracy, freedom through strength, freedom from big Government, freedom from the arrogance of the bureaucrat, freedom from the long arm of the tax man. I stand for these things because they are the way we can build a safer and more secure America so that you can fulfill your dreams.

Governor Clinton goes around saying we are a nation in decline, somewhere south of Germany and better than Sri Lanka. Let me tell you something: We are the most respected nation in the entire world, and don't ever let him forget it.

I am very proud to have served this Nation in war and in peace. I ask your support for 4 more years to lead this great country to a new prosperity and a new greatness.

Thank you for this fantastic Bowling Green welcome. And may God bless the United States of America. May God bless our great country. Thank you very, very much. Thank you so much. Thank you guys. "Millie, not Willie."

Note: The President spoke at 5:02 p.m. at the Reed and Frazee Streets railroad tracks. In his remarks, he referred to Randy Gardner, State representative; Betty Montgomery, State senator; and Wesley Hoffman, Mayor of Bowling Green.

Remarks to the Community in Plymouth, Michigan
September 26, 1992

The President. All right. Great train trip. Thank you all very much. Thank you, Governor. What a great Governor the State of Michigan has. I'm so proud of John Engler. You know, Barbara and I are on a 233-mile train ride through the great heartland of America. We just came across the line into Michigan and let me tell you, Barbara and I think it is fantastic to be here in Plymouth and see this marvelous turnout. Thank you all very, very much. May I salute Michelle Engler, as well as the Governor; Mayor Robert Jones; your great State chairman, Dave Doyle. May I ask you a big favor. It's a favor for the whole country that you help me clean House in Washington and send Bob Geake to the United States Congress. We need him.

Audience members. Clean the House! Clean the House! Clean the House!

The President. Clean the House. Clean it out. Give the American people a break; clean that institution out. Thirty-eight years it's been controlled by those same liberal Democrats. Clean House! Send this man to Washington.

You know, this is the last stop for tonight. For today, on this fantastic journey, filled with incredible sights and sounds, we've seen entire towns turned out beside the tracks to say hello to this train, this Spirit of America. We've seen the faces of young people, fresh faces, young faces; some waving flags, some with these great signs like we see here, all proud to be a part of America. And the election is about these young people's future, what kind of nation we want them to grow up in.

I want an America where everyone can find a good job, because you can't build a home without a hammer, and you can't build a dream without a job. And if they do what I've been saying in terms of incentives, we would be creating jobs today. We need to do it. Another thing is we need to open foreign markets for our products so we can create good jobs in America, because the American worker never retreats; we always compete. And we always win.

Help me get people in the Congress who will help reform a legal system that is careening out of control, faster than a lawyer can chase an ambulance. [*Laughter*] As a nation, we've got too many of these crazy lawsuits. Doctors can't practice, people can't coach Little League for fear of these suits. As a nation we've got to sue each other less and care for each other more.

And we have a plan to literally reinvent American education, to give these young people the very best schools in the entire world. I want to give every parent the right to choose their children's schools, public, private, or religious.

I believe we need to reform our Government and make it serve you, not the other way around. Governor Clinton says he is the candidate of change, but he opposes the most important change this year: limiting the terms of the Members of the Congress. Let's limit those terms and get on with this.

These are just some of the ideas I'm fighting for: health care reform, a sound environmental record, great energy strategy. But while I'm out there trying to find ways to rebuild America, build it up, Bill Clinton is spending his energy tearing down America. The only way he can win is if he convinces the American people that we're in decline. And we are not. We are the United States of America, the most respected nation on the face of the Earth. So don't listen to that gloom and doom. While I'm focusing on the future of these kids, he's out there distorting our record. I am proud of the record, and I will stand by it. But if candidate Clinton wants to talk about the past, that's okay. We pulled the train here this evening to blow the whistle on Governor Bill Clinton. Just like that sign says.

And here's the record for you; just take a comparison. As Governor of Arkansas, Bill Clinton raised and extended the sales tax. He taxed groceries. He taxed mobile homes. He doubled the tax on gasoline. And he even raised the tax on beer. How do you like that one? And he says—here's the really scary part—he says he wants to do for America what he's done for Arkansas. I don't know whether that's a promise or a threat. It's terrible, though. We can't have that. There's another sign, "We will not let Clinton do to the United States what he did to Arkansas." Lady, you are right.

Hey, look, he has already proposed, just for openers, $150 billion in new taxes plus at least $220 billion in new spending. But don't worry, he says, don't you worry, it will all come from the rich guys, top 2 percent, people who make over $200,000. But here's the truth. To get the money he needs for his plan, the $150 billion that he's promised in new taxes, Governor Clinton would have to raise taxes on every individual with over $36,600 a year in taxable income. And we cannot let him do that. If you listen to Clinton and Gore, he thinks these people are the ones who hang out on the Riviera. They're not the "Lifestyles of the Rich and Famous." These are good people who work hard all day, and they deserve a break, and you deserve a break. Do not get this Arkansas taxer in there.

But it's even worse—I'm sorry to bring you gloomy news—it's even worse than this. Bill Clinton has promised a new program every time he makes a speech. But he hasn't said how he's going to pay for them. To pay for all these promises, he'll need hundreds of billions of dollars more beyond the tax increases he's already proposed. And you might say, where is he going to get the money?

And listen to the newspaper from Governor Clinton's own State, the Pine Bluff Commercial. They said, and here's an exact quote, "If Congress followed the example of Bill Clinton, the one he set as Governor of Arkansas, it would pass a program that hit the middle class the hardest." We cannot let that happen to the young families in this country. Bill Clinton says he wants to hit the rich, but the middle class will take it on the chin. And I'm not going to let him do it. The middle class will get the shaft, and we're not going to have that happen.

And besides that, I think his ideas are all wrong for America. I want to put more power with the family and the American people and local governments. And he wants to put more with those codgy old subcommittee chairmen in Washington. Let's give the power back to the people here.

And so, here's the difference on philosophy. You know what he wants to do on tax-and-spend. And I say Government is too big, and it spends too much of your money. And let's get something done about that in the new Congress that's coming up. To give you more power—that's what it's about. To choose your own schools. I believe parents should be able to choose the schools, private, public, or religious. I believe parents ought to be able to choose day care centers, not have some mandated program out of Washington, DC. And I believe you ought to have more power to keep your hard-earned tax dollars.

You know, Governor Clinton is already talking about pulling together the best and the brightest—all the lobbyists, economists, lawyers, all those guys, liberal guys that were hanging out with him in Oxford when some of you were over there fighting—and have them solve all of America's problems.

I've got a very different vision: a responsible Government but a smaller Government, a Government that sees not every problem can be solved along the Potomac but understands that the real strength of America is right here in places like Plymouth, Michigan.

We saw great sights today coming in here, rolling hills and golden cornfields, vivid proof of why our great Nation is the most bountiful and special place on the face of the Earth. And while America is a land of extraordinary physical beauty, America is even more a land of extraordinary people. Because Americans had the courage to stand for freedom, our children today do not know the fear of nuclear weapons. And I am proud to have been a part of that. Governor Clinton says that the United States is somewhere below Germany and just above Sri Lanka. And I say to him he ought to open his eyes. Because of what you did—and many of you here today—in Desert Storm, we are the most respected nation on the face of the Earth. And don't let him tear down America. Don't let him tear it down. Because we had the courage to stand for freedom, the world today now holds unprecedented opportunity. We've got to be ready for it. And in this election, I am proud of my record as Commander in Chief of the Armed Forces. I'm going to take the case to the American people that

you can't be on both sides of every issue when you make a tough decision. You've got to do what is right for the United States.

So the bottom line is freedom. And I bring my case to you, and I say, look, we have just begun to fight. We've accomplished a great deal. The world is a much more peaceful place. Our new education program is rolling. We've got a health care program to bring insurance to every family in this country without getting the Government to run our medicine. And we've got all these programs that work if you can get us some help in the Congress.

Here's what's going to happen. Already we've got over a hundred, a hundred new Members of Congress will be there. And I'll sit down with them and say, look, the American people are tired of gridlock. Whether you're Democrat or Republican, here's my hand. Let's take this country forward once again. We can do it. We are a nation on the rise, not a nation in decline.

And the last point I would make is this. The last point I would make is this: I hope I have earned your trust to be President of the United States. And I know very well we've got the best First Lady in the entire world, who has earned your trust to be the First Lady. And Barbara and I want to do everything we can to help strengthen the American family: back up our law enforcement officers, give parents choice, help these kids learn to read, strengthen the greatest institution we've got, which is the American family. Give me 4 more years to get the job done.

Thank you very, very much. Thank you so much for this fantastic rally. This is great. Thank you so much.

Audience members. Four more years! Four more years! Four more years!

The President. Thanks a lot. The skies are clearing.

Note: The President spoke at 8:30 p.m. at the Plymouth train station. In his remarks, he referred to Dave Doyle, chairman of the Michigan Republican State committee.

Letter Accepting the Resignation of Edward J. Derwinski as Secretary of Veterans Affairs
September 26, 1992

Dear Ed:

It is with great regret and with sincere appreciation for your dedicated service to our country that I accept your resignation as Secretary of Veterans Affairs. However, I'm delighted that you are willing to now devote your great energies to speeding our message of renewal across America as Deputy Co-Chairman of our Campaign.

When I appointed you as Secretary of Veterans Affairs in 1989, I knew that you were the right person to represent the more than 25 million men and women who have served in our Nation's Armed Forces, as well as some 53 million of their dependents and survivors. As one who began his career as an enlisted member of the United States Army, you have a long and distinguished record of compassion and support for those who have so ably defended our Nation. You can be proud of your role in strengthening a Department of nearly 250,000 employees, the second largest civilian work force in the United States Government, and I am grateful to you for helping to lead the Administration's efforts to protect veterans benefits while promoting more effective management of existing veterans programs.

While Operation Desert Storm constituted a resounding victory for freedom and the rule of law, it also brought new challenges to the Department of Veterans Affairs. However, you proved your determination to meet them, and I salute you for that. At a time when our Nation proudly celebrates the expansion of democracy around the globe and the potential for increased international cooperation in this post-Cold War era, you have rightly reminded all Americans of our tremendous debt to our veterans.

From your service in the Army to your many achievements in the United States House of Representatives, the Department of State, and now, the Department of Veterans Affairs, your contributions to our Nation have been substantial; your loyalty and concern for others, inspiring. I am grateful for your friendship and support, and Barbara joins me in sending best wishes to you and Bonnie for the future.

Sincerely,

GEORGE BUSH

Dear Mr. President:

It is an honor for me to accept your request to serve as your campaign's Deputy Chairman for Ethnic Coalitions. I hereby tender my resignation as Secretary of Veterans Affairs so that I may devote my full energies to this vital role and uphold your determination to keep VA free of any political label.

As I leave the position you appointed me to 3½ years ago as the first Secretary of the new cabinet-level Department of Veterans Affairs, I do so with deep appreciation for your support in bringing effective and compassionate health-care and benefits services to the Nation's veterans. Your personal concern for their well-being has been consistently demonstrated with record levels of resources committed to VA programs.

I welcome the opportunity that I will now have to bring your solid record of achievement in furthering the ideals of democracy and liberty abroad to this important bloc of American voters.

Thank you for your confidence in my ability to be of service to you in the homestretch of the re-election campaign.

Respectfully,

EDWARD J. DERWINSKI

Note: These letters were made available by the Office of the Press Secretary but were not issued as White House press releases.

Statement by Press Secretary Fitzwater on Military Cooperation With Israel
September 26, 1992

In accordance with the United States on-going commitment to the preservation and maintenance of Israel's qualitative military edge, President Bush and Israeli Prime Minister Rabin have reached agreement on certain measures that will be initiated by the United States in the very near future. These measures include the supply of Apache and Blackhawk helicopters and the pre-positioning of advanced defense equipment in Israel. They will be implemented pursuant to previously enacted legislation which authorized the transfer to Israel and pre-positioning in Israel of defense articles drawn from U.S. stocks. It was further agreed that there will be closer ties between the two countries' armed forces, cooperation on technology upgrades, and the start of discussions on Israel's participation in the Global Protection System.

These initiatives represent a significant effort in reaffirming the United States long-standing commitment to a strategic partnership with Israel and will effectively maintain Israel's qualitative edge. The United States and Israel intend to continue consultations for the purpose of determining additional measures necessary to maintain Israel's qualitative military edge.

Remarks to the Community in Wixom, Michigan
September 27, 1992

The President. Thank you, Wixom. Thank you, Governor Engler. What a great Sunday welcome. Thank you very, very much. May I thank Governor John Engler, your great Governor, and his wife, Michelle, on the train with us here today. May I single out your Mayor, Wayne Glessner, and thank him. Barbara Dobb, you've got a great State representative here, Barbara Dobb, and may I ask you to send Joe Knollenberg to Congress so we can clean the House. For 38 years, 38 years one party has controlled the House. And everyplace I go people are saying, "Clean House!" Give us Joe Knollenberg; let's start the job right here in Wixom.

Well, it's great to wake up in this great State of Michigan. You know, this isn't just any campaign stop; it's Oakland County. When we carry Oakland County, we are going to carry the great State of Michigan. When we carry Michigan, we're going to earn 4 more years to renew this country. We've changed the world. Now we must renew America.

You know, the stakes are very high because this election is about your future and the kind of America you want to live in. A few weeks ago in Detroit, I laid out my Agenda for American Renewal, a series of steps to guarantee that in the next century America will be the economic superpower. We will lead by renewing our schools, by freeing small business from taxation, regulation, and, yes, these reckless lawsuits and by holding the line on Government spending and by getting your taxes down, not up.

You know, Governor Clinton pretends foreign policy means nothing. But I am proud of my leadership in foreign policy, proud of America's leading role in ridding—[*applause*]—proud of ridding the fear of nuclear war from these young people here today. We have done it; we have changed America.

I hope that my character and I know my experience qualify me to meet the challenges of the nineties. Because in this new economy, the path to prosperity and jobs lies in opening markets and getting ready to compete. Today, American products have a newfound respect all around the world. We have the best workers in the entire world right here in Michigan. Just ask the men and women who make the great Lincoln cars, and they'll tell you our workers never retreat, we always compete. And we always win.

I want to do what's right for America. My opponent will tell America so many different things because he wants to do what's right to win an election. Let me give you just one example of what I mean.

I believe that you can balance the needs of the economy and the environment. Indeed, we have to. Here in Wixom, you've achieved this delicate balance, and you should be commended, you're leading the way. I have worked at the national level to protect the environment. We're cutting acid rain in half. I am proud we've added a million and a half acres of parks and forests so that our kids and grandkids will have space to play and enjoy nature.

Now, Government Clinton's environmental policies in Arkansas can be described in only one word: abysmal. According to the Green Index, Arkansas ranked dead last in the Nation in policies to protect the environment, dead last. That is not good enough for America. You know, I don't want to suggest that the Arkansas rivers are polluted. But you know, Governor Clinton sometimes thinks he can walk on water. Living around the Arkansas water, Arkansas River, he can walk on water. Hey listen, that's the only place the fish light up at night. It's the only place the fish teach their young ones how to jog instead of swim. You talk about pollution; we don't need that for the rest of the United States.

But look, in his zeal to capture his party's nomination he's jumped over to the other extreme. If there's anybody that's interested in the auto industry here, listen to this. He has proposed raising car fuel standards to 40 to 45 miles per gallon by the turn of the century. Now, there is a couple of big problems with that idea. For one, the scientists say it's not possible; you'd have to make cars out of papier mache. For another, these standards would toss 40,000 auto workers out on the unemployment line right here in Michigan. And you and I cannot let that happen to the workers in Michigan. The big labor bosses think they can convince him after the election, Lane

Kirkland mentioned that himself, where we're going to let him off the hook until after the election. We cannot go to 45-miles-per-gallon CAFE standards and still have a strong auto industry.

You know, we're cleaning up the air. We're promoting clean burning American fuels. We're not doing it by killing jobs but by creating jobs. I have a good, sound environmental record, but I will not go to the Clinton-Gore extremes and needlessly throw Americans out of work.

This guy's environmental programs are terrible, but there's one thing worse. And I'm talking about his tax-and-spend policy. Governor Clinton wants to do for the national economy what he's done for Arkansas. If you look at his record you'll see that that's not a promise, it is a threat. As Governor of Arkansas, Bill Clinton raised and extended the sales tax over and over. He taxed groceries. He taxed mobile homes. He doubled the tax on gasoline. And he even raised the tax on beer. That is the fact, and we don't need that for America.

Now, Governor Clinton says he's seen the light. He's promised $150 billion in new taxes plus at least $220 billion in new spending. But don't worry, he says, it will all come from the rich, that's the top 2 percent, people who make over $200,000, he says. Well, here's the truth. To get to $150 billion, even with his other plans, Governor Clinton would have to raise the tax rates on every individual with over $36,600 a year in taxable income. That is a fact, and we cannot let him do that to the United States. People making $36,000, those aren't people hanging out on the Riviera. That's not the "Lifestyle of the Rich and Famous." These are good people who work hard all day, and they deserve a break.

Every time the guy opens his mouth he promises a new program. But he hasn't said how he'll pay for them. He'll need hundreds of billions of dollars more beyond the tax increases he's already proposed. Where's he going to get the money? Right out of your pockets.

Audience members. Boo-o-o!

The President. Now, let me read you a quote from a paper right in his own backyard. This isn't Detroit, this is Pine Bluff,

Arkansas, the Pine Bluff Commercial. They said, and I quote, "If Congress followed the example Bill Clinton set as Governor of Arkansas, it would pass a program that hit the middle class the hardest." And that is a quote from the people who know Bill Clinton best. So if the past is any guide, Governor Clinton will go to where the money is, and he'll take it from the middle class. Let's not let him do that to the hard-working people of America.

For 11 months he's been mistalking about my record, misdirecting it, misstating it. I've just started in the last couple of days because the American people need to know this. Think about what the Clinton tax plan will do right here in Wixom. Let's say you've got a good job at the Lincoln plant. Say you get 38,000 bucks a year in taxable income. Governor Clinton would have you give another $1,700 to the tax man. And I say you could better use that money for your kids' education or paying a mortgage on a house.

In Detroit I unveiled our plan. There's a fundamental issue in this election. We both have presented our plans for America. He wants to pay for it by raising taxes. I want to pay for mine by reigning in Government spending. I want you to help me reign in the big spenders, let you keep a little more of what you earn.

I propose that every taxpayer have a chance to make a little check on his tax return to cut Government debt and force the Congress to cut spending. If we do that, the Congress will have to listen to the people. It's a good idea, and the Democrats hate it. If the Congress won't cut the spending, let the people do it. The people have more power if we make our representatives more accountable. And so I say this: It is time to limit the terms of the Members of Congress. Give Government back to the people, term limits.

Here is the bottom line. The Clinton taxes are wrong for the middle class. The big Government philosophy is wrong for the White House and for your house. Any way you cut it, Bill Clinton is wrong to be President of the United States of America.

I offer a responsible Government; a changed Congress; a smaller Government; a Government that serves people, not the other way around; a Government that understands the real strength of America is right here, right here. It's not all in DC; it's right here in Wixom, Michigan. That's where the power is. Give the power back to the people.

The entire world has been in a global recession. You hear Bill Clinton talk about it, it's everything's my fault. Fine, I'll take my share of the blame. But look around Europe. Look at Canada. The entire world has had tough economic time. And the very nations that have adopted the strategy Governor Clinton proposes, the nations of Europe, are enduring higher unemployment and worse hardship than we are. I believe the world economy is poised to get moving again, and America would lead the way. We must have a United States that will take the lead but not if we take the risk of adopting the failed strategies that are being rejected in Europe, not if we take the risk by going back to the failed policies of big Government, and not if we take the risk of socking it to the middle class with higher taxes.

Let me just say a word. Governor Clinton would have us believe that world affairs and national security mean nothing. I am proud that I led this country to stand up against aggression in Desert Storm. I'm proud of the men and women here.

Governor Clinton can only get elected by tearing down America. He talks about America being less than Germany and a little more than Sri Lanka. Open your eyes, Governor Clinton. We are the most respected nation on the face of the Earth.

As we stood for freedom abroad, we stand for freedom at home, freedom from big Government, freedom from the arrogance of the bureaucrat, freedom from the bosses who tell everybody what to do, freedom from the long arm of the tax man.

Today, I know the people of Wixom are marking this visit by signing the names on a wall, a wall that will be preserved for history. And I am flattered by this action. But I ask you to come build something much, much larger: to renew our Nation, to make it a better place for the young people here today, to strengthen the American family in every way we possibly can, to make it a safer and more secure America for us and for all those who will come after.

We are blessed with the greatest, freest, most wonderful country on the face of the Earth. Help me move it forward; give me 4 more years, and let's change America for the best.

Thank you, and may God bless you all.

Thank you very much.

Audience members. Four more years! Four more years! Four more years!

Note: The President spoke at 11:35 a.m. on the observation deck of the Spirit of America train. In his remarks, he referred to Lane Kirkland, president, AFL–CIO.

Remarks to the Community in Milford, Michigan
September 27, 1992

Listen, thank you all very, very much. Barbara and I are thrilled to be here, delighted to be with your great Governor, John Engler, and Michelle. And let me just tell you what a great day it is to be in Michigan. Even the Clinton people are nice around this State. It's wonderful. [*Laughter*]

We've made a great dramatic change for world peace. To listen to Governor Clinton talk about it, foreign affairs and national security is nothing. I am proud to have served my country in wartime, and I'm proud to have served it in peace. And I am proud that because of our leadership, we have far less fear of nuclear weapons today. And now we need your help to renew America. We cannot let a tax-and-spend Governor come in and change things in that direction. Let's change them by holding the line on taxes, cutting back on this spending, and giving power to the people of Michigan. That's what we've got to do.

Thank you for a great day. We don't want this train to run late, but we do want to say hello and say thank you very much for this warm welcome.

Don't listen to Governor Clinton when he tries to tear down this country and say we're somewhere below Germany and above Sri Lanka. Never forget we are the United States of America, the greatest country on the face of the Earth. We can overcome every problem we've got, but don't do it by putting in the Arkansas Governor who wants to raise your taxes and raise spending. Give me 4 more years. Leave Barbara as the best First Lady in the entire world. And let's win this election. Let us win this election.

Thank you very, very much. All aboard! All aboard! All aboard!

Note: The President spoke at 12:25 p.m. on the observation deck of the Spirit of America train.

Remarks to the Community in Holly, Michigan
September 27, 1992

What a great day. My heavens, beautiful. Thank you, thank you very, very much. What a beautiful day in Holly. My heavens. Thank you, President Regan. Has a nice ring to it. [*Laughter*] May I salute Governor Engler and Michelle Engler, who have been on this train for us. You've got a great Governor here, a great Governor in this State.

You know, everyplace I go I see people yelling, "Clean House! Clean House!" Elect Dick Chrysler now, and help us clean House.

Mayor Regan, I'm told that your full title is the president of the village of Holly. Well, I'm also told you're a Democrat, but you stopped wearing a Clinton button about a week ago, I'm told. I don't know if it's just to be polite, but thank you very much. Keep the Clinton button in the drawer, and come on over to our side. I salute you as the president of this township. And thank you all, every single citizen, for this wonderful, warm welcome. You can't help but feel great about America when you see something like this.

I'm told that this is the last day of your Renaissance Festival. I might ask to borrow some of the knight's armor; it would sure come in handy with Governor Clinton's daily attacks.

Barbara and I are in the middle of a great tour of this heartland of America, 233 miles from Ohio up through Michigan, building up for November 3d. I have spelled out a comprehensive agenda for America's renewal, a comprehensive, integrated, detailed plan so that in the 21st century America will reign as the economic superpower in the entire world.

Governor Clinton and Senator Gore seem to think that foreign affairs is not important, leadership for world peace is not important. Well, let me say this: I am proud of our record in standing up against aggression halfway around the world. I am proud that we put an end to the cold war. I am proud that Poland and the Baltic States are free, and I'm proud of America's role in ridding our children's dreams of the nightmare of nuclear war. That is big progress, dramatic progress. Thank God these kids don't worry about it. We should get credit for having fought hard against, standing true against that Soviet empire, now working with the new and democratic countries around the world. Yes, national security is important. And don't let Governor Clinton and Senator Gore cut into the muscle of our defense. We've got to stay strong.

I believe, having been in business and meeting a payroll, that my experience qualifies me to handle this new economy. Because today, the path to prosperity and jobs lies in opening foreign markets for our products. Because the American worker never retreats, he competes. And we will win.

I also want to see us, and here's one where Governor Clinton completely op-poses me, I want to see us reform a legal system that is out of control. Doctors are scared to deliver babies because of lawsuits; some dads are afraid to coach Little League because of crazy lawsuits; people are scared to help a victim in a highway accident along the road because of lawsuits. We've got to put an end to these crazy lawsuits, and I need your help to do it. We've got to sue each other less and care for each other more in this great country of ours.

I've got a very different approach from Governor Clinton when it comes to education and child care. I want to give every parent the right to choose their children's schools, whether it's public, private, or religious. Put the power with the families. I want to fundamentally reform our Government, make it work for you and not the other way around. Governor Clinton says, "Well, I'm for change," but he opposes the single most important change offered this year and that's limiting the terms of the Members of Congress. The time has come to limit those terms.

While I'm trying to find out ways, because I am optimistic about this country, to build up the United States, Governor Clinton insists on cutting America down. Well, I am focusing on the future, and he's engaged in a deliberate campaign of distortion. I think it's a sorry thing when the only way you can win an election is to tell everybody how bad things are. Look, we are the United States of America. We are the best in the entire world. Now let's make things better for the workers here at home.

You know, I'm a little tired of the distortion, so we pulled this train in here this afternoon to blow the whistle on Bill. You know, let's really take a look, after about 11 months of knocking me down, let's take a look at what's happening, if you've got a minute, on Arkansas itself. The first place, I lived next door to them. The people of Arkansas are decent and wonderful and warm people. They deserve a lot better than they've got, I'll tell you. Governor Clinton wants to do for the national economy what he's done for Arkansas. But if you look at his record you'll see that's not a promise, that's a threat. And we don't need it.

Let me tell you why I feel that way. Governor Clinton raised and extended the sales tax over and over. He taxed groceries. He taxed mobile homes. He doubled the tax on gasoline. And he even raised the tax on beer. Enough is enough. We do not need that kind of taxation at the Federal level.

Now, Governor Clinton says he's seen the light. In this campaign, he's proposing $150 billion in new taxes, that's not counting taxes that he put on small business for health care, plus at least $220 billion new spending. But don't worry, don't worry about that. He says it's all going to come from the rich guys, the top 2 percent. But the problem is, and here's the real truth on it: To get the money he needs for his plan, the $150 billion he's promised in new taxes, Governor Clinton would have to raise tax rates on every individual with incomes over $36,600 a year. That is $36,600. These are not people on the "Lifestyles of the Rich and Famous." These are good people who work hard every day, and you deserve a break. Do not let him get in there and do that to the American people.

Depending who he's speaking to, every time he turns around he's got a new way to spend your money. But he hasn't said how he's going to pay for all these new programs. He'd literally need hundreds of billions of dollars more. And don't kid yourself. While Governor Clinton is pulling promises out of the sky with one hand, he's pulling the dollars out of your wallet with the other.

Listen to this newspaper, don't take my word for it, listen to this newspaper from his own front yard in Pine Bluff, Arkansas, the Pine Bluff Commercial. Here's what it said: "If Congress followed the example that Bill Clinton set as Governor of Arkansas, it would pass a program that hit the middle class the hardest." And I am not going to let him win. I am not going to let him do that to the United States of America.

We figured this out coming up here. Let me give you an example. Say you've got a good job earning 38,000 bucks a year in taxable income. Governor Clinton would have you give another $1,700 to the tax man. And I say you ought to be able to use that to pay for your kids' education, to meet the mortgage on the house, to put into the savings, not send it back to the IRS.

Now, when I point out what Governor Clinton really stands for, he says, "Hey, forget my record. Forget the facts." But he says, "I'm a different kind of Democrat." But what's different about him? George McGovern, he worked for him. Jimmy Carter, he voted for him. Michael Dukakis, he nominated him. And he didn't forget about Walter Mondale, he borrowed the tax increase from him. He's not different in the way we want difference and change in this country.

Now just think about his teaming up with those Democrats on Capitol Hill. It gives me ulcers just thinking about it. We would have a rubber-check Congress and a rubber-stamp President. And remember the last time this country had that. The "misery index," unemployment and inflation, was at 20 percent. And now we've beat it back to 10. We don't need to go back to the "misery index" days of Democratic control of both ends of Pennsylvania Avenue.

I need this change in Congress. The only defense I've had to help the taxpayer is vetoing 33 bills in the United States Congress, standing up for fiscal discipline. I'll tell you what though: You give me that line-item veto; Congress can't do it, then watch us get the job done.

I just ask you to think how Governor Clinton and the Congress together will treat the middle-income taxpayers: the same way as the Michigan offense treated the Houston Cougars yesterday. Michigan pounced on the Cougars; Clinton's going to pounce on your wallet. Watch it. Guard it.

I say forget his plans to spend more and tax more. You deserve to keep your hard-earned dollars, and you can invest them better than any Government bureaucrat. When it comes to the Presidency, we simply cannot afford to take a risk. The Government is ready, the economy is ready. We're moving now with inflation down and interest down. We're moving towards a better recovery. But we must not set it back by more spending and more taxes.

I've proposed and will insist on, with these new Members of Congress, a responsible Government but a smaller Government; a Government that serves the people, and not the other way around; a Government that understands that the real strength of America is right here in places like Holly, Michigan. It is not back in Washington, DC.

As Barbara and I take this train across the middle of this beautiful heartland of America, we see some wonderful sights, the smiling faces of kids out there. But we hear the voices of concern. And keep in mind that the entire world has been in a global recession. It's not just the United States that's had difficulties. Not one single one of those economies in Europe would be unhappy to trade with us. They all envy us, every single one. But now we're ready to move. And the very nations that have adopted the strategy that Governor Clinton proposes, those nations of Europe are enduring higher unemployment and hardship than we are.

I believe this economy is ready now. America will lead the way. But not if we take the risk of adopting the failed strategies that are being rejected in Europe and that have failed the socialist country in Eastern Europe. Not if we take the risk of socking the middle-class taxpayer again. Not again. And I say to America, we will not risk our future by adopting the failed policies of the past.

You know, our world is filled with opportunity. You wouldn't get it from the press; you darn sure won't get it out of Clinton and Gore. But we are great and we are strong, and we have a marvelous opportunity now with a better education system, a better child care system. I'm fighting for health care reform. I'm fighting to back up these police officers here who are trying to help us bring peace and tranquility to our neighborhoods, frustrated at every turn by the liberal Democrats. We are going to get

a new crowd in Congress, and we are going to move this country forward.

You know, Governor Clinton talks about—this guy kills me. When you come across this country in a train—he talks about this country being something less than Germany and a little more than Sri Lanka. He ought to open his eyes. We are the most respected country on the face of the Earth, and I'm glad I've had a part in helping restore that respect for America.

So here's the difference: I stand for freedom, freedom from big Government, freedom from the arrogance of the bureaucrat, freedom from the long arm of the tax man. And I stand for these things because they are the way we can build a safer and more secure America, and so that you can fulfill your dreams.

There's a lot of debate out there these days. But let me say this: I am proud that I served this military and our country in wartime. I am proud I served my Nation. I am proud that I brought change, peaceful change for democracy and freedom around the world. I am fighting hard to get this economy on the move, and I need your help. And don't let the other side tear down the greatest country on the fact of the Earth.

Thank you all. And may God bless you on this beautiful day. And I happen to think we've got the best First Lady in the entire world, too. Thank you all. What a wonderful welcome. Turn it around. Show them. Thank you very much. What a great day. What a welcome. Thank you all. Hi, kids.

Note: The President spoke at 1:15 p.m. on the observation deck of the Spirit of America train. In his remarks, he referred to Ardath Regan, president of Holly.

Remarks on Concluding a Whistlestop Tour in Grand Blanc, Michigan
September 27, 1992

The President. Thank you very, very much. Thank you. Four more, that's it, 4 more of them. Thank you very, very much,

Governor Engler. You have a great Governor in the State of Michigan. Thank you, John Engler. May I salute Mrs. Engler and thank Mayor Crane. Thank you all for this fantastic hospitality. And may I salute Dick Chrysler and Megan O'Neill, both of whom are running for the United States Congress. It's great to have two great people running for the Congress. Let us clean House, change the Congress. Get rid of that tired old leadership, and get some new blood in there. Clean House!

And may I salute the three great bands who are here: the Grand Blanc High School Cats, Montrose High School, and Davison High School. You make us all feel welcome. Barbara and I want to thank all of you for this unbelievable reception there. You know, this is the end of a 233-mile tour across America's heartland, building momentum for this election. And you give a guy a feeling of confidence. I am absolutely convinced we are going to beat that Governor of Arkansas and win this election.

You know, for 233 miles, we've been hanging off the back of this marvelous train, waving to people. We've seen some incredible sights: kids and pets and rolling farmlands and factories, thousands and thousands of enthusiastic Americans. We've also seen some great signs out there. One of them said, "Blow the whistle on Bill." That's exactly what we're here to do. Then we must have—saw one guy who obviously was a student of the Arkansas environmental record of Governor Clinton. His sign said, "Arkansas fish for Bush." The fish are tired down there of all that pollution. It's the only place they light up at night. [*Laughter*] You talk about the environment—take a look at that Arkansas River, and I'll have more to say about that in a minute.

We've even seen some chickens along the way. Here's one back here. But I can't figure out if that chicken is talking about the draft. I can't figure that out. Or maybe he's talking about that Arkansas River again, where they're dumping that—I've got to be careful here—that fecal, some kind of bacteria, into the river. Too much from the chicken. [*Laughter*]

You know, this election is like every election, a referendum of what kind of America we want for the young people that are here today. And we have laid out a renewal plan. We call it the Agenda for American Renew-

al. It is a comprehensive and integrated plan so that in the 21st century America will reign as the economic superpower of the entire world. We still have the best economy in the whole world. Now let's make it better.

Tomorrow in Dallas some supporters of Ross Perot will gather to hear what both campaigns have to offer. And we're going to send a team just to make a case for the agenda that I offer for America. Mine is the only agenda that includes cutting the growth of mandatory Government spending, cutting the size of Government, and reducing the Federal deficit because that is the way to give the kids here today a better America tomorrow. I'm afraid that Governor Clinton offers more of the old big taxes, big Government; no serious plan to control the deficit. And when you compare our ideas, it is a very clear choice. He wants to do what is right to win an election, and I want to do what is right to win the global economic competition.

Well, you might say, how are we going to do it? Down the street a little bit is a small business called Impact Auto Collision. The owner of that business lost his job with GM so he decided to start his own business, and today it's going strong. This is the story of human renewal, a story of American renewal. It is happening all across America. No people are more resilient than the American people. No people can rise better to any challenge if Government pursues the right policies. Send me a Congress that will help, and we will pursue the right policies for the next 4 years.

You see, I believe that small business is going to create the real opportunity and the new jobs in this economy. Bill Clinton looks at small business as the goose that laid the golden egg. And he wants to tax you. I see small business as the sturdy house, that sturdy horse that's going to pull the American economy into the next century. And I want to give you relief from taxes and build a strong residence, a strong house, a strong economy for everybody.

You know, our legal system today is another thing. He refuses to change it. He's in the pocket of the trial lawyers. And our legal system today is careening out of control. Doctors are afraid to deliver babies. Some guys are afraid to coach Little League because they get sued. Some are afraid to stop at a highway accident for fear somebody will sue them later on. And the victims in the car crash sometimes, therefore, lose out because of outrageous lawsuits. And as a nation, we've got to stop that. We've got to sue each other less and care for each other more. Help me put a cap on these outrageous lawsuits. As a nation, we've got to sue each other less.

But Bill Clinton wants to go another way. He wants to increase Government regulation, not cut it. Listen, here's what he wants to do on automobiles. You all know something about automobiles. He wants to go to 40 or 45 miles per gallon on these CAFE standards. And there's a couple of problems with this idea. Scientists say we can't do it. It could throw 40,000 Michigan auto workers out of work. Help me defeat Governor Clinton and those crazy environmental standards. We've got a good record on the environment, far better than this chicken has in Arkansas. And I want you to know that we've got a good one, but we don't have to come down on the side of throwing auto workers out of their jobs. I am not going to do that.

I want to see us fundamentally reform our Government. Governor Clinton says he's for change, but he opposes the single most important change offered this year. You see, he is against it, and I am for it. I want to limit the term for Members of the United States Congress. I want to see some change in there. A President's terms are limited; why shouldn't Congress be limited?

While I'm trying to find ways to build America up, the only way Governor Clinton can win is to tell everybody how bad everything is. And for 11 months he's been doing just that, tearing down America. He says we are somewhere less than Germany but a little higher than Sri Lanka. And to him I say: Open your eyes, Governor Clinton. We are the most respected nation on the face of the Earth. And one of the reasons is when we were faced with a tyrant halfway around the world, and the President had to make a tough choice, I didn't do what he did, be on one side of the issue one day, another the other. I said, we are going to

have to fight for what is right. We did it. The young men and women of Desert Storm restored the pride to the United States. And I am proud of that role. And I am proud of this record. And I'll stand for it. To listen to Governor Clinton and Gore talk, you'd think foreign affairs and national security means nothing. I am very proud that every young person here today goes to bed without that same fear of nuclear war that their predecessors had. That is progress, and we should be grateful for it.

Now, we're talking about blowing the whistle on Bill. But you see, the people of Arkansas are good and decent folks, and they deserve another leader down there who will give them a better deal. But let me tell you what happened. Governor Clinton says he wants to do for the national economy what he's done for Arkansas. But if you look at his record you'll see that's not a promise, that's a threat. He's extended and raised the sales tax over and over again. He taxed groceries. He taxed mobile homes. He doubled the tax on gasoline. And he even raised the tax on beer. I don't think we need that now for the United States at our level.

Governor Clinton says he's seen the light. In this campaign, he's proposing already $150 billion in new taxes plus at least $220 billion in new spending. But don't worry, he says, we can take it all from the rich guys, people with over $200,000. But here's the problem. Here's the truth. To get the money he needs for this plan, the $150 billion he's promised in new taxes, Governor Clinton would have to raise tax rates on every individual with over $36,600 a year in taxable income. That is $36,600. These are not the people on the "Lifestyles of the Rich and Famous." These are not people that are driving Jaguars. These are people who are hard at work every single day. And we cannot let him do that to the working men and women of this country.

But it's even worse, if you can take a little more bad news here. Governor Clinton has promised a new program every time he makes a speech. He's got more answers than there are problems, but he hasn't said how he'll pay for them. We'll need hundreds of billions of dollars more, beyond the tax increases that he's already proposed. So don't kid yourself. When Governor Clinton is pulling promises out of the sky with one hand, he's pulling dollars out of your wallet with the other. We cannot let that happen to the American people.

Hey, listen, you don't have to take my word for it. Listen to the Pine Bluff Commercial, a paper right in his home State, right in his home area. And they said this: "If Congress followed the example that Bill Clinton set as Governor of Arkansas, it would pass a program that hit the middle class the hardest." And I am not going to let him do that to the American people. You know Grand Blanc. Let me tell you what it would do to somebody right here. Let's say you've got a good job. Let's say you're earning 38,000 bucks a year in taxable income. Governor Clinton would have you give another $1,700 to the tax man. And I say that you ought to be free to use that money to pay for your kids' education or to pay the mortgage on your house and not send it to Washington, DC.

Governor Clinton says, "Forget my record."

Audience members. Four more years! Four more years! Four more years!

The President. Governor Clinton says— you know, here's what gets me—he says, "I'm a different kind of Democrat." He says. But what's different about him? George McGovern, he worked for George. Jimmy Carter, he voted for him, brought us the highest "misery index" in modern time. Michael Dukakis, he nominated him. And he didn't forget Walter Mondale, he borrowed his tax increase from him. Different? What's so different about that?

I'll tell you one real worry I've got. Just think about him teaming up with those spending Democrats on Capitol Hill. I've had to pass 33 vetoes to protect the taxpayer against those maniacs. So imagine what it would be if they controlled both ends of Pennsylvania Avenue. We'd have a rubber-check Congress. That's what they are. And we'd have a rubber-stamp President. And you watch out for your wallet if that ever happens.

So I say forget his plans to spend more and tax more. You deserve to keep your hard-earned dollars, and you can invest them better than any Government bureaucrat. And when it comes to the Presidency, we simply must not take a risk. This is serious business. The decisions you face in the Oval Office are not easy decisions. You can't be on one side of the issue one day and then on the other the other day. You can't keep everybody happy. You've got to be honest. You've got to call them as the umpire does, call them as you see them, take the heat when it comes with it. And you can't waffle around, whether it's on your record in the military or whether it's on your service as the Governor, or wherever it is. You've got to call them straight. And I am asking for your trust for another 4 years.

I honestly believe that that big Government philosophy is wrong for America at this time. And any way you cut it, I believe Governor Clinton, with this philosophy of tax and spend, is the wrong man to be President of the United States. I hope I have earned your trust for 4 more years in this high office. You know, I'll take my share——

Audience members. Four more years! Four more years! Four more years!

The President. When you make a mistake in life, you ought to admit it. You ought to stand up and admit it. And I've taken my share of the heat, and I'm perfectly prepared to do that. But I want to point out that it isn't just the United States that had difficulties. The entire world has been in a bit of a global recession. And there isn't one country in Europe that wouldn't trade their economy for the economy of the United States of America, our problems notwithstanding.

And the nations that have gone downhill are the ones that have endorsed the Clinton plan of more taxes, more socialist ideas, more Government. We don't need that. The nations of Europe now that are recovering are on the road for democracy and freedom, and that's what we want to keep here, and that's what we want to help extend around the world. So we must not adopt for the great United States the failed strategies that are being rejected in Europe. We're not going to take a risk by socking it to the middle class right here in this country.

You know, I think our world is filled with great opportunity, unlike any that we have known before, if we in America can rise to the challenge. We have stood fast for freedom. And now the world is embracing our ideas. And in this election, I stand for freedom, freedom from big Government, freedom from the arrogance of the bureaucrat, and freedom from the long arm of the tax man. That's the kind of freedom we need more of in the United States of America.

At the end of this trip—I came here to ask for your support. We've got a lot of reasons. I happen to think we've got the best First Lady in the entire world. And I think when she reaches out her hands to the kids in teaching them to read, she's setting an example for family. And when she holds an AIDS baby in her arms, she's showing the kind of compassion that all Americans feel. And I want to find ways through choice in schools and choice in education to strengthen the American family. The heartbeat of America is our family, and we ought to strengthen it, not tear it down by lousy welfare programs and things that don't work.

We have a great country, and we can make it even greater. So thank you for this fantastic turnout today. It is good for the soul. It makes me more convinced than ever that I will have 4 more years to finish the job.

Audience members. Four more years! Four more years! Four more years!

The President. Let this chicken back here tell you what's wrong about America. I'll tell you what's great about it. We are the freest, fairest country on the face of the Earth. Now let's make it even better.

Thank you, and may God bless each and every one of you.

Note: The President spoke at 3:30 p.m. on the observation deck of the Spirit of America train. In his remarks, he referred to Greg Crane, Mayor of Grand Blanc, and an audience member dressed in a chicken costume.

Statement on Signing the Civil Liberties Act Amendments of 1992
September 27, 1992

Today I am pleased to sign into law H.R. 4551, the "Civil Liberties Act Amendments of 1992." This legislation fulfills the commitment that this country made in 1988 to individuals of Japanese ancestry who were interned or relocated during World War II, and to their families.

In the Civil Liberties Act of 1988, the United States apologized for the wrongful internment and relocation of innocent, loyal individuals and promised monetary compensation to each such person (or his or her heirs). The funds provided by this bill will ensure that all of these individuals are compensated as promised. These payments are compelled by justice, and I am pound to sign this bill into law.

H.R. 4551 also makes important technical amendments to the 1988 Act, which will help to ensure fair treatment of claimants and smooth administration of this program.

No monetary payments can ever fully compensate loyal Japanese Americans for one of the darkest incidents in American constitutional history. We must do everything possible to ensure that such a grave wrong is never repeated.

GEORGE BUSH

The White House,
September 27, 1992.

Note: H.R. 4551, approved September 27, was assigned Public Law No. 102–371.

Remarks to the Community in St. Louis, Missouri
September 28, 1992

Thank you very much for that kind introduction, Chief Harmon. Let me say that I've heard a good deal about the work of this chief and of this police force. And I salute every man and woman who's out there in the St. Louis police force laying their lives on the line for us every single day of their life. We ought to be grateful to those who wear the uniform, and I'm certainly grateful to this group.

And may I salute our great Governor, John Ashcroft, and fantastic Senator, Senator Jack Danforth. It's delightful to be in Fox Park, St. Louis, a friendly city. Actually, my mother grew up here. My brother lives here, cousin lives here. And I love that heartbeat of St. Louis. So thank you for this welcome.

A word to those in this parish. I want to apologize to everyone who was counting on the usual Sunday bingo game last night. I hear that the Secret Service spoiled your fun when they had to check out the building. I'm sorry you missed the game. It was smart, though, to stay away. Believe me, you don't want to be jumping up suddenly and yelling "Bingo!" around these Secret Service guys.

This has all the earmarks of a political gathering, but I really want to talk to you today about what I consider a foremost, a first and most basic function of Government: to protect every American citizen from violence, at home and on the streets. Now, there's nothing new about that. Security is one big reason Government was created in the very first place. But what is new are the terrible forms that violence has taken recently, beyond anything our Founding Fathers could have imagined.

A whole generation has grown up with the threat of nuclear terror hanging like a sword over its head. And it's been horrible. Our kids had nightmares. It seemed like it would never end. Well, it did end. And today I can stand up here and say something that no other President could ever say before: the cold war is over. Freedom finished first.

Now, we must win the peace right here at home, in the streets of Fox Park. In too many places, our grandparents and grandchildren lock themselves behind the bars on their windows, afraid to come out from a jail called home. This simply must end.

We've made progress against violent crime. We've slowed it dramatically the past 12 years. And we're beginning to turn the tide on the drugs that so often fuel it. But we got soft on crime way back in the sixties, and we paid for it. Then by the time we cracked down again in the eighties, violent crime had gone up 400 percent in 20 years. Since we cracked down, it's gone up just 27 percent in a little over 10 years, and the overall crime index is actually down.

So we've stemmed the tide, in a sense, prevented millions of crimes. But of course, that is simply not enough. It's never enough. The face of crime is changing fast, and we need our laws to react just as quickly, so that we can beat it.

Let me give you a timely example. Carjacking: a brandnew word for a brandnew crime. Someone figured out it's easy to steal a car when it's already running, with the keys in the ignition. Of course, the owner's behind the wheel. So the criminal uses a gun. I want to tell you a story that literally sickens me, as I'm sure it will you, but describes what we're up against.

Just a few weeks ago, in a nice neighborhood near Baltimore, a woman was sitting in her car at a stop sign. In broad daylight, two men forced her out of her car and drove off. But she was tangled in the seatbelt, trying desperately to save her baby. The mother was dragged for almost 2 miles. The thieves tried to knock her off by banging into a fence, and tragically, she died. And you know what they did with her little baby? They tossed her out of the car like a piece of trash. Miraculously, that baby survived.

And you know what? America is going to survive, too. We cannot put up with this kind of animal behavior. These people have no place in a decent society. And as far as this President's concerned, they can go to jail, and they can stay in jail, and they can rot in jail for crimes like that. For that to happen, we need tough laws that don't bend over backwards protecting the criminal while saying to the victim, "Tough luck, buddy."

Let's look for a minute at the Arkansas record and see where Governor Clinton stands. The average inmate in Arkansas served less than one-fifth of his sentence last year. Most Federal inmates serve at least 85 percent of their full sentence. Violent crimes in that State, in Arkansas, went up almost 60 percent in the eighties, over twice the national average. Arkansas had the Nation's biggest increase in overall crime and the third-biggest in violent crime.

This kind of record is not right for Arkansas, and it is not right for America. If you don't believe me, just ask the Fraternal Order of Police in Little Rock, Arkansas. They know Governor Clinton's record best, and they're endorsing me for President of the United States. The police know better than anyone that we're all vulnerable: men, women, children; white, black, brown; young, old; rich and poor. To a bullet or a blade we all look just the same.

Americans deserve a Government that goes after the problem, that prevents and punishes crime and helps the victims, lifts up the victims of crime. That's why I want to see America make a move at the Federal level to step forward and support State and local police around the country in real, concrete ways. We need to help them fight.

That's why 1,201 days ago, on June 5, 1989 [June 15, 1989] [1]—the same day Mikhail Gorbachev first hinted that the Berlin Wall might someday fall—I sent a comprehensive crime bill to Capitol Hill. I offered the hand of partnership to Congress and asked it to help me fight crime on a national level.

Listen to this: Since I first sent that bill to the Hill in 1989, here in the United States, we've had almost 60,000 murders, 260,000 rapes, 1,600,000 robberies, and 2,600,000 assaults. By the way, 506 of those violent

[1] *White House correction*

crimes took place right here in Fox Park. Think about that. Across America that's enough assault victims to fill the city of St. Louis more than six times over, victims brutalized while that bill languished on Capitol Hill.

Now, I know the numbers are staggering. I know that Americans sit down in front of their TV's at night, watch the news, and say: Why doesn't somebody do something about this incredible mess? People are dying in the streets, for heaven's sake. Well, 1,201 days later, Congress still has not acted on my crime bill. I think if they had a glacier on Capitol Hill, they'd name it Speedy. You ought to try and get something done there.

But frustrating as this crime bill has been, it's still my job as President to get results. There are good people on both sides of the issue, working in good faith for a compromise. And I will not rest until this matter is settled.

This very week, we are now finally close to an agreement on a bill the Congress could send me, and I'll sign. The compromise bill could include, for example, a workable death penalty for horrible murders, committed by terrorists, assassins, and drug lords. It should target the shocking violence we see on television: the drive-by shootings and gang turf wars. This deadly behavior deserves deadly punishment. It should include provisions recommended by former Supreme Court Justice Powell to short-circuit an endless process of appeals that make a mockery of justice. There are other items prompting strong feelings on all sides, but we're making a good faith effort to reach a compromise.

So I want you to know what's on my crime agenda. I'm not asking for anything but common sense and reasonable justice, especially for women, children, and the elderly victims of crime. I think I can get some of these items this year. Then, I'll come back to get more of them next year.

Let me click off about eight key points here. First, apprehend and severely punish these carjackers, like the ones I just described. I want to make carjacking a Federal offense with harsh penalties. And I want thugs who take cars at gunpoint to stay in a cell so long that when they get out they're too old to drive.

Second, I keep talking about strengthening the family, well, here's one for you: Call the deadbeat dads onto the carpet. Right now, a single mother here in Missouri can be struggling to keep the kids fed and clothed on her small salary, while their father's up in Chicago somewhere, picking out a new Chevy truck with terrycloth pom-poms and a gunrack. Now, he could be way behind in child support, but no one can touch him because he's across the State lines. Well, I think that's a disgrace, and it's about time the long arm of the law reaches out over that State line, taps that deadbeat dad on the shoulder, and says loud and clear: time to pay up; cough up the cash or go to jail.

The third, strengthen the laws dealing with sexual and domestic violence. For starters, we need to protect the victim. It is bad enough a rape victim is attacked in the first place. Then she takes the stand, and then she gets worked over and attacked by the rapist's lawyers. I say that makes two too many attacks.

And I want repeat sex and domestic violence offenders behind bars until trial. Today, even a repeat offender can get arrested, be out on bond hours later, stalking his next victim or beating his wife and kids for turning him in. I want him detained until trial, and I want the prosecution to be able to use past convictions against him. Any of you law enforcement officers knows this, but right now, certain details can't even be mentioned in court, so-called little details like the fact that everyone and their dog within a country mile knows the guy acts this way regularly. And that's wrong. Let him pay for what he's done.

Fourth, crack down on gang violence. I want gangs to be treated like the criminal enterprises they are. That way, we can go after the leaders, and we can deal harshly with them, and we can untie the hands of good cops so they can clean up decent neighborhoods. I also want to toughen the penalties for using juveniles in crimes. Some of the gangs right now can send underage kids out to do their dirty work because they're minors and they'll get off if they're caught. I think the older gang mem-

bers should be punished harshly for treating these little kids like bullet fodder.

Fifth, protection for the elderly. It is absurd that the folks who have contributed to this society all through their lives have to live in terror when they're old and frail just because some young punks see them as an easy target. They're as low as the thugs who pick on children. I want to beef up the laws that put these thugs behind bars.

Sixth, the habeas corpus reform. Habeas corpus is supposed to protect the innocent, but it's turned into a ridiculous perversion of the law. Can you believe that a lot of these petitions drag on for more than a decade? Criminal lawyers use it to postpone justice. A guilty verdict can mean seemingly endless appeals that choke our courts and delay justice. It's about time we put a stop to this travesty. Let them have one habeas corpus petition and be done with it. And that's what I'm trying to do in that crime bill right now.

The seventh, a Federal death penalty. I think certain acts of violence deserve the ultimate penalty. I'm talking about assassinations, murder for hire, terrorism, and other depraved acts. Add to that the new urban violence we see with gangs, drive-by shootings, random violence, gang massacres. These people are merchants of death, who trade in death. The death penalty is warranted in these cases. And I wish Congress would move and do something about it.

And eighth—and this one's short—firearms. I want much tougher penalties for criminal use of firearms, period. Tighten up the law, and take the risk away from these law enforcement officers.

Now, I'm not saying that tougher laws are going to fix absolutely everything. I'm a firm believer in justice, but I think punishment is only part of the solution. The other part has a more human face. Tomorrow's criminals are still just kids today. And while I believe in resources for law enforcement and in reform for law enforcement, I also believe that at some point early in life, a youngster at a critical juncture can be steered to a life of right or a life of terrible wrong. It all depends on the kind of soil you plant these kids in and how you nourish them. I just had a wonderful briefing upstairs by the chief and some of our community leaders, including the pastor of this church, and what impressed me is what the community is doing to help these kids before they get caught up in this wave of criminality.

All of this is why I believe that our "Weed and Seed" program, the Federal program, is so very crucial. "Weed and Seed," that means going into a rough neighborhood, eradicating the "weeds" of violent crime that can choke a young life and then replacing them with "seeds" of social opportunity and reform. That's what Operation Crackdown in St. Louis is all about: the Federal Government, working with local law enforcement, reclaiming crack houses and giving them back to the community. And that's what your—the chief talked about your COPS program, here in Fox Park, is all about, too, on a local level. Real people making real changes in your own neighborhood.

You know, just the other day, only a few blocks from here, police officers raided a crack house on Ohio Avenue. And as those officers came out of the house with those drug dealers handcuffed, the neighbors—maybe some of you all were there—came out to their porches and gave those police a standing ovation and a cheer. That's what this country is hungry for. Americans want to take crime out of their neighborhoods and put the neighbors back. And we've got to weed the poison growth from the soil,

and in its place, plant the seeds of hope.

I know there's a craving. I know you just want to be able to walk down to Worth's Market or down to Fox Park here for a stroll or over to Bartlett's Grocery Store for a newspaper or Mary's Restaurant for a cup of coffee, even if she is a Democrat— [*laughter*]—and you want to do it knowing you're safe in your own neighborhood that you've helped build and kept alive.

I think John Mirgaux said it best. He lives in this neighborhood and knows about that old crack house over on Ohio. He said he and his wife, Eleanor, had been thinking about selling their house and just moving out, moving away from the drugs and all the ugly crime. But you know, he's lived in Fox Hill his whole life. It's his neighborhood. And after the raid, he and Eleanor did some thinking. And he put it this way. He said, "You know, I've been waiting for this to happen. Now we're going to make a stand."

Please join us. Join John and Eleanor and Ohio Avenue and Fox Park and St. Louis and Missouri and this whole United States and make a stand against crime today, because the people deserve it.

Thank you all so very much for listening. May God bless Fox Park, Missouri. And God bless the United States of America. Thank you all very, very much.

Note: The President spoke at 10:21 a.m. in the parish hall at St. Francis de Sales Roman Catholic Church.

Remarks at the East Dallas Renaissance Neighborhood Project in Dallas, Texas
September 28, 1992

The President. Thank you so much. I love what Michael Fells said about his house. That's the way we all ought to feel about our homes. And I was very proud of that.

Thanks to all of you for this great Dallas welcome. May I salute your wonderful Mayor, an old friend of mine and Barbara's, Steve Bartlett, doing an outstanding job for this wonderful area, this wonderful city.

Also I want to salute Judge Lee Jackson and your Congressman, a Congressman, not this district but right next door, Sam Johnson, doing a fine job for Dallas. May I salute our sheriff, Sheriff Bowles, and our new police chief from Dallas, been here a while, doing a great job with the law enforcement community, Chief Bill Rathburn over here.

While I'm in the neighborhood, I want to

recognize Meadows Foundation for their work restoring homes, restoring hope in this community. I saw a little bit of that when Steven here and Dirk and Cheryl, Cheryl Harley, showed me around this house that they are fixing to restore. So I'm just delighted to be here. Also pleased to welcome a cross-town guest from west Dallas, Mr. Artrous Hill, who for 41 years ran the barber-shop on Puget Street. When the drug epidemic came to west Dallas, Mr. Hill's landlords were the local crack dealers until U.S. marshals and the Dallas police put them out of business.

Audience member. Chicken George, why don't you debate?

The President. [*Laughter*] Listen to this guy. There are going to be debates.

May I say a word about the chicken question? May I say a word about—you're talking about the draft record chicken or are you talking about the chicken in the Arkansas River? Which one are you talking about? Which one? Get out of here. Maybe it's the draft. Is that what's bothering you?

All right now. As I was saying before being so rudely interrupted, I was telling about Mr. Hill who owns his own barber shop. His west Dallas neighborhood is on the way back, on the way back just the way all of you here in east Dallas are on the move forward.

You know, I came here to talk about the progress we're making in our quest to make America more safe and secure. But first let me just say a word about the dominant issue in this campaign, and that's the economy.

The American voter this year is confronted with two choices, two candidates with two very different economic strategies. If Governor Clinton is elected, by next year we will have hundreds of billions of new Government spending, higher taxes on the middle class, and no restraints on Federal spending, and even more pressure on the Federal deficit.

So Governor Clinton claims he knows a way to reduce the budget deficit by increasing taxes on the middle class and giving Congress more of your money to spend. I believe the way to reduce the deficit is by making tough choices and cutting Government spending.

That's why we put forward a plan, a serious program to control the growth of spending with almost $300 billion in savings over 5 years. I've gone on the record, targeted 246 programs, 4,000 wasteful projects that I want to eliminate altogether. I want to use these savings to reduce the deficit, to reduce the tax burden on the working men and women, and still do what's right by our neighborhoods.

You know, this is a tough time for the world economy. But the brighter days are right here around the corner, and America can and will lead the way forward if we make the right choices this November.

Whether it's the building of a strong economy or strengthening our families or keeping our streets safe, I put my trust in the people. That's why I am delighted to be here today to salute all of you for helping take this community back, helping make east Dallas a safe place to live, to raise kids, to stake a claim on the American dream.

The neighbors we've seen and the neighbors I've heard from—I don't care about the politics—they are doing what is right. They are here to help build a neighborhood and protect their homes. Now, this community is one community that is breaking out of the cycle of violence in America.

You know, in the past year, overall crime in the city of Dallas is down 13.7 percent. Violent crime, murder, rape, robbery, assault, has dropped 14.1 percent. That is good news. It represents thousands of hours of hard work for the Dallas police, for the sheriff's department, for the crime watch groups like Mill Creek and others all across Dallas. You deserve to be congratulated— right there.

But it does not make the crimes that take place every day any less real. The building behind us here brought the reality of crime close to home, literally, right next door. You know the Mohawk as a crime haven, a crime den, a crack den, not as home but as a house of horror. Some weekend nights, I'm told, as many as a hundred cars line Swiss Avenue, bringing customers in search of heroin and crack and marijuana. Addicts used to roam this neighborhood, offering to do odd jobs for $10, the price of a crack high.

One day a crackhead fired a gun at Michael Fells as he was sitting on his front porch. And in 2 months' time last spring police made more than 200 arrests at that one address alone. But all that has changed. The morning of June 5, the day U.S. marshals and Dallas police swept in and seized this building, that day many of you came out to cheer, to celebrate the day that the law came back to this street. Today the Mohawk doesn't just have a history, it has a future.

But, you know, the change taking place here is just the beginning. Each one of you is going to have to do your part in taking back the streets and then keeping this community crime free. I'm here today to tell you as President, we can help. The key to a new approach, one that combines a no-nonsense approach to crime with social programs that promise real help. Too often in the past we've pursued our social programs and our law enforcement efforts on totally separate tracks. As a result, many of our urban revitalization efforts are cut short by crime.

You know, what I'm talking about is this: We build public housing only to see these buildings taken over as crack houses. We build model schools only to see them become war zones where fear follows teachers and students right into the classroom. Then we build playgrounds for children only to see them become battlegrounds for drug pushers. When a neighborhood is overridden by crime, businesses are driven away, taking jobs and opportunities with them.

We're tackling each one of these issues, each one of these problems, with a new approach that we call "Weed and Seed." "Weed and Seed" is not so much a new spending program as a whole new method of operating. Let me tell you how it works. As the first step, Federal, State, and local enforcement officers concentrate their efforts on neighborhoods like this one. Working with you, the community, they "weed" out the gangs, the criminals and the crackheads and the drug dealers. As the streets are reclaimed from the criminals, community policing is put in place to help hold every inch of the ground that we've taken. Police commanders attend community meetings; officers patrol neighborhoods on foot; and residents feel safe knowing who is on the beat in their area.

Finally, the broad array of Federal, State, and local government and private sector community revitalization programs are brought to bear on the community, to "seed" in long-term stability, growth, and opportunity. Drug prevention programs, Head Start, job training, health care programs, community development grants, all are applied together in one place and at one time in a true working partnership with the community.

"Weed and Seed" is already up and running in Fort Worth and in 19 other cities across the country. This year I asked the Congress for $500 million to fund "Weed and Seed" programs in 50 or more communities. I know east Dallas would like to be one of them. Congress has appropriated the money, but they have not authorized it. I wouldn't bother you with these fine congressional distinctions, but I have to because unless Congress acts, Dallas or any American city for that matter won't get one single dollar of what it needs.

You need help, and you need it now. If you work the late shift at some convenience store, you shouldn't have to worry about whether you're going to be safe walking home. If you're sitting on your porch, you shouldn't have to be on the lookout for a car full of hoods with a gun. If you need to run out for milk and bread late at night, you shouldn't have to worry about who you'll run into at the corner of Swiss and Moreland. This is your home and your community and the place your children play. You deserve to be safe here.

It pains me to say that every day we're being forced to learn a new vocabulary for crime. Back in Washington we've had a wave of what they now call carjackings, where a criminal steals a car, not when it's parked but when you're sitting in a parking lot or waiting at a red light. Just this month, carjackers stole the car of a woman taking her small daughter to her first day of preschool. They dragged the woman to her death and tossed her little baby out of the window. Something is wrong in our cities, something is wrong in our society when crimes like that are commonplace. We will not and cannot stand by and see innocent people terrorized, innocent people paralyzed by fear. We've got to be tougher on the criminals. Carjackers or crack dealers, whatever the crime may be, we've got to draw the line. I ask you to get Congress to give me the support we need to draw the line against them.

But this we know: Tough talk won't do it. My opponent in this Presidential race talks a tough game, but I would like you just for a minute to take a look at the Arkansas record and see where Governor Clinton stands. The average inmate in Arkansas served less than one-fifth of his sentence last year. Most Federal inmates serve 85 percent of their sentence. Violent crimes in Arkansas went up almost 60 percent in the eighties, over twice the national average. Arkansas had the Nation's biggest increase in overall crime and the third biggest in violent crime. This kind of record is not right for Arkansas, and it is not right for America.

Just ask the Fraternal Order of Police in Little Rock, Arkansas. They know Governor Clinton's record best, and they're endorsing me for President. I'm very proud of that endorsement.

As President, I pushed Congress to put tough talk aside and take action. I sent my comprehensive crime package to Congress more than 3 years ago, June 15th, 1989, to be exact. What's happened since then? The fall of the Berlin Wall, the end of Soviet communism, the invasion and the liberation of Kuwait, and Congress has sat on my crime package for 1,201 days, 1,201 days. In those 1,201 days here in Dallas alone, 1,441 people have been murdered. In those 1,201 days, 3,997 have been raped. All told, in those 1,201 days, 79,903 have been victims of violent crime.

Each one of those days, another innocent person becomes a statistic. We do not have another day to waste. We need this comprehensive crime package. We need more prisons, more police, more swift and certain punishment. We need a Federal death penalty for cop killers and drug kingpins. Tough new provisions against sex crimes and domestic violence, we need that also. We need to make carjacking a Federal offense, apply Federal racketeering laws to help us go after gangs. We need to strike a blow for responsibility by using Federal law to enforce child support payments from all those deadbeat fathers.

We must get reforms. I believe in backing up our police officers, and we need reforms to put a stop to the endless appeals that make a mockery of justice for the victims of crime. We need reforms that slam shut the revolving door of justice that far too often lets these criminals go free.

What you're doing here puts you on the side of the angels. But you cannot do it alone. You can't do it if the system mocks the victims and if criminals own the streets and law-abiding citizens are prisoners in their own homes.

Let's get our cities and our citizens and our cops the help that they need, the help they must have to drive crime and drugs off our streets and out of our lives, here in east Dallas and all across the United States of America. Let's make some changes in Congress and clean House. Absolutely!

Thank you for this wonderful, warm welcome of east Dallas. It's a privilege to spend this time in your community. May God bless the United States of America. Thank you very much.

Note: The President spoke at 2:45 p.m. at Swiss Avenue. In his remarks, he referred to Michael Fells, resident and member of the Mill Creek Homeowners Association; Lee Jackson, Dallas County judge; and Steven Hugh, Dirk Newton, and Cheryl Harley, co-owners, 4514 Swiss Avenue apartment complex renovation project.

Message to the House of Representatives Returning Without Approval the United States-China Act of 1992
September 28, 1992

To the House of Representatives:

I am returning herewith without my approval H.R. 5318, the "United States-China Act of 1992," which places additional conditions on renewal of China's most-favored-nation (MFN) trade status.

I share completely the goals of this legislation: to see greater Chinese adherence to international standards of human rights, free and fair trade practices, and international nonproliferation norms. However, adding broad conditions to China's MFN renewal would not lead to faster progress in advancing our goals. To those who advocate this approach, let me set the record straight.

Our policy of comprehensive engagement lets the Chinese know in no uncertain terms that "business as usual" is not possible until they take steps to resolve our differences. Through multiple, focussed measures, we are eliciting the results we seek.

This year China joined global efforts to control the spread of nuclear weapons and ballistic missiles by declaring adherence to the Missile Technology Control Regime's (MTCR) guidelines and parameters and signing the Nuclear Proliferation Treaty (NPT). Chinese behavior remains MTCR-consistent, and we have begun a dialogue with the Chinese on their responsibilities under the NPT. We continue to monitor vigilantly China's weapons export practices. We have used the sanction authorities available successfully and remain prepared to do so again if necessary.

We have made progress on the resolution of outstanding trade issues with our agreements to protect Intellectual Property Rights and to ban prison labor exports. I will not allow, however, market access to remain a one-sided benefit in China's favor while our bilateral trade deficit grows. If China fails to reduce trade barriers, we are prepared to take trade action under the statutory guidelines of section 301 of the Trade Act of 1974.

The limited steps China has taken on human rights are inadequate. But our human rights dialogue gives us an avenue to express our views directly to China's leaders. Significant improvement in China's human rights situation, including freedom for all those imprisoned solely for the peaceful expression of their beliefs, remains our objective. It is easy to be discouraged by the pace of progress in this area. But it would be a serious mistake to let our frustration lead us to gamble with policies that would undermine our goals.

Withdrawing MFN or conditioning it, such that it will be withdrawn at a later date, will not promote these goals. H.R. 5318 imposes unworkable constraints on our bilateral trade. Among the casualties of this bill would be the dynamic, market-oriented regions of southern China and Hong Kong, as well as those Chinese who support reform and rely on outside contact for support.

The impact of this bill would extend beyond the state enterprise system, harming independent industrial and agricultural entities that have sprung up in China since the advent of economic reform and its opening to the outside. These family-owned and operated entities are interlinked in the manufacturing process with large, state-controlled factories and marketing agencies. They would not be shielded from the effects of this bill.

Americans too would be affected. This year our exports to China will climb to about $8 billion. China's retaliation for the loss of MFN would cost us this growing market and thousands of American jobs. We would cede our market share to our foreign competitors who impose no restrictions on their trade with China, at a time when China is taking market-opening measures that our trade negotiators fought to obtain.

Our policy seeks to address issues of vital concern to us and looks to the future of our relations with a country that is home to almost one-quarter of the human race. MFN is a means to bring our influence to bear on China. Comprehensive engagement is the process we use to transform this influence into positive change. The relationship between these two key elements of our China policy is a powerful one, and the absence of one element diminishes the potency of the other. We continue to advance broad U.S. objectives without imposing economic hardship on Americans because both elements of our policy are in place.

Engagement through our democratic, economic, and educational institutions instead of confrontation offers the best hope for reform in China. MFN is the foundation we need to engage the Chinese. H.R. 5318 places conditions on MFN renewal for China that will jeopardize this policy and includes a requirement that infringes upon the President's exclusive authority to undertake diplomatic negotiations on behalf of the United States.

In order to protect the economic and foreign policy interests of the United States, I am returning H.R. 5318 to the House of Representatives without my approval.

GEORGE BUSH

The White House,
September 28, 1992.

Statement by Press Secretary Fitzwater on the Circuit Court Decision on the Marbled Murrelet
September 28, 1992

The administration is disappointed that the Ninth Circuit Court of Appeals has refused to stay an order by the Seattle Federal District Court requiring the Fish and Wildlife Service to immediately decide whether to list the marbled murrelet as a threatened species under the Endangered Species Act. The district court also issued a temporary restraining order preventing timber sales in selected areas of the Pacific Northwest's national forests. The court order will require a listing decision for the marbled murrelet to be made prematurely, before additional biological information necessary to make an appropriate decision is obtained.

These rulings will result in additional hardships for timber families and communities in the Pacific Northwest already suffering high rates of unemployment as a result of court injunctions to protect the spotted owl. The premature listing of the marbled murrelet is further evidence that several statutes relating to forest management and species protection are in need of reform by Congress.

This recent development provides another clear message to Congress that it must enact appropriate timber management legislation, such as proposed by the administration, to address the timber supply crisis in the Pacific Northwest as quickly as possible. The administration will continue to work for a balanced solution to this problem, one which will provide sufficient timber to keep Northwest mills operating and workers employed while providing protection for endangered species.

Remarks on Arrival in Blountville, Tennessee
September 29, 1992

The President. You know, Naomi says this is the first time that she's introduced a President. But look at it this way, this is the first time I've ever been introduced by such a wonderful person, Naomi Judd. And I'm just pleased to have her with us on Air Force One.

You know, lest you didn't know it, we

have a great Secretary of Education, as Secretary, Lamar Alexander, a former Governor of this State. I'm very proud to be with him. And of course, my old friend Howard Baker is still beloved not only in Tennessee but all across this country as a great leader. And may I salute another old friend. If we had more like these three that I'm about to introduce, everybody would not be yelling at me, "Clean House!" because you've got three greats in Jimmy Quillen, in Don Sundquist, and Jimmy Duncan right here with us today. Send us more like these three, and let's get this country moving again.

Audience members. Clean the House! Clean the House! Clean the House!

The President. That's it, we've got to clean it.

And about these three characters over here, Barbara Bush and I are their friends, and we are very proud of that. They don't know how to throw horseshoes. We had them at Camp David, and they came in second, third, and fourth. [*Laughter*] But in life they're coming in first because of their talent and because of Larry's fighting back. And I'll tell you, we are very proud to have the Gatlin Brothers at our side. And of course, may I salute Sarah Sellers, our national committeewoman, and our great chairman in this State, Tom Hopper. They tell me we are going to win Tennessee, and they are absolutely right. I also want to salute the Volunteer High School Marching Band. Thank you all for being with us.

This campaign, like every campaign for the Presidency, is about a simple question: What kind of America do we want for the young people here today? I want an America that remains a military superpower, but is the greatest economic superpower on the face of the Earth. We're going to make it even better.

You know, I have spelled out a specific agenda for America's renewal, a specific comprehensive plan, an integrated agenda to create in America the world's first $10 trillion economy. I am proud of America's leadership role in ending the cold war, proud of the sons and daughters who wowed the world in the sands of Saudi Arabia. The Democrats want us to forget it, but we are not. I will continue to thank the

sons and daughters of Tennessee who served with honor in Desert Storm. We're not going to let Bill Clinton forget that this was a proud moment in the history of the United States.

Audience members. Where was Bill? Where was Bill? Where was Bill?

The President. I don't know where he was. I'll tell you where he was on the war. You want me to answer the question? On Desert Storm he was on both sides. He was for the people that opposed it, but he was for those that supported me. That's a great thing, but you can't do that as President of the United States of America. You've got to make the tough call.

But now what we've got to do is work with these great Members of Congress, using our experience to lead the way to new markets for American products because that is how we're going to create more good jobs for people all across the United States of America. You see, small business will create two-thirds of the new jobs in the new economy. Governor Clinton, well, he promises small business higher taxes and more redtape. I promise small business relief from taxation, regulation, and litigation.

You know, we spend almost $200 billion a year on direct costs to lawyers. Japan doesn't pay that and neither do the European countries. My opponent doesn't think this is a problem. He's in cahoots with the trial lawyers, and they spend so much time in court that their favorite song is "A Boy Named Sue." [*Laughter*] But here is my view. We've got to take the pressure off doctors who are scared to practice or Little League coaches who are afraid to coach. We've got to sue each other less in this country and care for each other more.

I am proud of my record. All the Governor of Arkansas does is go around tearing me down, tearing our country down, saying we're less than Germany and a little more than Sri Lanka. He ought to open his eyes. We are the most respected country on the face of the Earth.

But if you'll bear with me for just a minute, if he wants to talk about the past, fine. But let's take a look at what's going on in Arkansas. The people there are decent.

They are hard-working. They are sound, grassroots people. But there's a lot they don't know about their Governor's record and a lot you don't know about it. The more you find out about it the more you know that Governor Clinton is wrong for President of the United States. He is wrong for America.

Look at the issue of crime. We simply have got to take back our streets from the crackheads and the criminals. Candidate Clinton, oh, he talks a tough game. But in Arkansas, the average criminal served just one-fifth of his sentence, and then he's let back out on the streets. Compare that to the Federal prisons for which I am responsible. The average inmate there serves 85 percent of his sentence. When it comes to crime, I am not much for letting these prisoners out of jail early. If you steal a car or you beat up some elderly woman, you ought to go to jail. And I say this: You should not be let out until you're eligible for a birthday salute from Willard Scott.

Hey, don't take it from me, though. Listen to those in Arkansas. Ask the police over there in Little Rock. The cops who know Bill Clinton best have endorsed me as the best candidate for President of the United States.

The same thing on every issue. I think of Howard Baker and the others standing here as leaders in fairplay on civil rights matters. Governor Clinton says he's for civil rights, but Arkansas doesn't even have a basic civil rights law.

He says he's for the clean environment, but the Institute of Southern Studies ranked Arkansas 50th in environmental politics. It's the only place where fish teach the young fish to jog instead of swim. That's how polluted the rivers are over there. I love fishing. I'm a bass fisherman. The fish in Arkansas light up at night because of what the chickens are doing to the river.

Governor Clinton says he's for high-tech. But under Clinton, Arkansas has been falling behind in high school. Three out of every four Arkansas graduates spend their first year in college relearning what they were supposed to learn in high school. That is not fair to those young people over across the way.

Let's take a look at the economy. All we

hear from him is how bad things are. I know we've been through some tough economic times. But we are affected, of course, by the global economic situation. Our competitors in Europe would trade places with us in a minute. Yet Governor Clinton offers America that European social welfare state politics: more Government, more special interest spending, and more taxes on the middle class. That is wrong for America.

If you can take another horror story this early in the morning, let me tell you this: He has raised and extended the sales tax, including a tax on baby formula, vegetables, and other groceries. He raised the gas tax. He raised the mobile home tax. And for those of you ESPN watchers, he even taxed cable TV and slapped a tax on beer. How do you like that?

Audience members. Boo-o-o!

The President. Now he says he's seen the light. In this campaign he's proposing at least $150 billion, direct proposal, in new taxes, plus at least $220 billion in new spending. "Don't worry," he says, "I'll get it all from the rich, people making over $200,000 a year, the top 2 percent." But here's the problem, and here is the truth. To get the money that he needs for his plan, the $150 billion that he's already promised in new taxes, he would have to get his money not from those with over $200,000, but from every individual with taxable income over $36,600, and that is not good for America. These people aren't out there on the "Lifestyles of the Rich and Famous." They work hard, and they deserve a break. That's just the start of his tax campaign against the middle class. He will need hundreds of billions of dollars more to pay for all these programs he's promised.

There's an old saying: When you hunt ducks you go where the ducks are. Well, he's hunting for ways to pay for all his promises, and he's going back to tax the middle class because that's where the bucks are.

Listen to the news. Don't take my word for it. You listen to the newspaper from his own backyard, the Pine Bluff Commercial. Here's what they say, "If Congress followed the example that Bill Clinton set as Governor of Arkansas, it would pass a program that hit the middle class the hardest." I say the middle class has been hit hard enough already. The Pine Bluff paper is not bluffing.

Let me give you one example. Let me just—this is an example. Say you're a third-grade teacher with about 22,000 bucks a year in taxable income. Governor Clinton could have you fork over another $430 a year to the tax man. I say that you ought to be able to use that money to pay for your kids' education, pay the mortgage on the house, not send it up to the IRS in Washington, DC.

And Governor Clinton will say, oh, I'm on the side of the middle class. But he says then, well, I'm going to have it both ways. Consider his principled stand on both sides of the Gulf War—I mentioned that—when he said, and here's an exact quote, an exact quote, "I guess I would have voted with the majority if it was a close vote, but I agree with the arguments the minority made." Now, how would that be for a Commander in Chief when you've got to stand up against aggression halfway around the world?

Audience members. Boo-o-o!

The President. One day Governor Clinton says, "Well, I'll never run for President." The next year he announces he's running for President. One day he says he's for the North American free trade agreement. Then he says, "Well, I haven't made up my mind yet." One day he's for raising fuel efficiency standards on cars. And the next day he says, "Well, I'm flexible on that one." One day he says the middle class deserves a tax break. And the next day he's plotting new ways to hit the middle class to pay for all his programs.

If he ever became President of the United States, and he won't, we'd have to replace the American eagle with a chameleon. That is not the way it works in the Oval Office. You cannot come down on both sides of every issue. You have to take your lumps, and you have to take a stand. I don't think that we can take a risk on Governor Bill Clinton to be President of the United States of America.

You know, I've made mistakes as President. Different than him, I've admitted when I'm wrong. But I believe I've been a good leader, willing to make the tough calls. I'm a leader whose ideas are right for America.

I stand before you today asking for your support so that we can go to work with a new Congress to fix the problems that stand in the way of this country; so that we can reform our health care system and reinvent, as Lamar is so eloquently stating, reinvent our American schools; so we can retrain our workers from one generation and create jobs for the next; so that we can cut Government spending and cut taxes and get this economy moving again; and also, so that we can limit terms for the Members of the United States Congress and give Government back to the people. Now, this is our agenda.

If you want one who has a statistic for every problem, go ahead and cast your vote for the other guy. But if you're looking for a leader of experience, a leader of ideas, a leader who shares your values, a leader who understands that America's real strength is not in Government but in places like this marvelous town right here today in your great State of Tennessee, then I know I can count on your support on November 3d.

Governor Clinton says that we are a nation in decline, somewhere less than Germany and a little better than Sri Lanka. I say we are the greatest, freest country on the face of the Earth. Now let's make life better for everybody at home by using that same courage and leadership we have to change the world.

Thank you, and may God bless the people of Tennessee and the United States of America. Thank you all very, very much. What a wonderful rally.

Note: The President spoke at 10:17 a.m. at Tri-City Regional Airport. In his remarks, he referred to former Senator Howard Baker; entertainers Naomi Judd and the Gatlin Brothers; and Sarah Sellers, member, Tennessee State Republican executive committee.

Remarks on Arrival in Knoxville, Tennessee
September 29, 1992

The President. Thank you. What a great Tennessee welcome.

Audience members. Four more years! Four more years! Four more years!

The President. This is fantastic. Thank you, Knoxville. Thank you very, very much. Thank you, Knoxville, Tennessee. This is fantastic.

Let me thank Naomi Judd for being with us. I'm the guy who's honored. What a wonderful entertainer and a great personality and a wonderfully strong character we have standing here today in Naomi Judd. And may I salute your former, some of you all's former president of the great university here, our marvelous Secretary of Education, Lamar Alexander; and another Tennessean known nationally as a true leader, a true, honest, decent, strong leader in a Congress that was crying out for it and still is, I'm talking about Howard Baker.

You know, you hear a lot of calls—everyplace I go, people have brooms and they're yelling, "Clean House! Clean House! Change the Congress!" If we had more Congressmen like Jimmy Duncan and more like Don Sundquist and Jimmy Quillen with us here today, we wouldn't have to clean House. But since we do, help us clean House and get this country moving again.

May I salute another old friend, longtime friend for Barbara and me, Victor Ashe, the Mayor of this city. And also I understand our county executive, Dwight Kessel, is here. And that brings me also to another special friend who's taking it out on the trail for me, Ricky Skaggs. I'm just delighted to be with him; and standing over here, another good one, another great one, T.G. Sheppard. Thank you very much for being with us.

Now, first let me start with a word about the polls and the talking heads. [*Laughter*] Every one of them said that Tennessee would lose to Georgia, and every one of them said that Tennessee would lose to Florida. So much for the polls, and so much for the talking heads. Enough of it. We're going to win this election.

This campaign, like every campaign, is about a simple question: What kind of America do you want for the young people that are here today? I'll tell you what kind of an America I want and am working for, an America that is not just a military superpower but the greatest economic superpower in the entire world. That means more jobs for the American people.

I have laid out a comprehensive Agenda for American Renewal, a specific, integrated agenda to create in America the world's first $10 trillion economy. We can get that happening by moving to change the Congress and moving forward with my program.

The Democrats don't like my even talking about it, but I am very proud of our record in ending and winning the cold war, proud of the way the sons and daughters of Tennessee performed in the sands of Saudi Arabia. It was a proud moment, not a moment to be forgotten.

The Clinton ticket feels that I ought not to talk about foreign policy. I want to use my experience to lead the way to new markets for America products because that is how we are going to create good American jobs, the same leadership that changed the world. Now let's make America better and renewed.

But look, we all know that if we're going to compete abroad and do what I am talking about with markets, we've got to make changes at home. It's small business that creates two-thirds of the new jobs in the new economy, and Governor Clinton promises small business higher taxes and more redtape.

Audience members. Boo-o-o!

The President. And I promise relief from regulation and taxation and, yes, relief from these crazy lawsuits that are killing us in this country.

If we're going to compete in this new world, in this new economy, we must reform our schools. I am very proud of our great Secretary of Education, Lamar Alexander. I am proud of our national America

2000 program; proud that we're raising standards; proud that we're freeing up the teachers, and God bless them all, freeing them up from regulation and redtape; and proud that we are designing totally new schools for a new century. And I thank our Secretary. I thank these communities in Tennessee that are working to rebuild American education.

Lamar and I want to go further. The parents of today's Volunteers had the power to choose the best college for their kids. I want that same choice for elementary and high school. My "GI bill" for kids will give parents and fundamental resources they need and the right to choose the best schools for their kids, whether they're public, private, or religious.

Now, these are some of my ideas and what we're fighting for and what this election is about. I'm proud of our record, and I'll stand by it in November. But if candidate Clinton wants to talk about the past, then I say I'm ready. Let's take a look at what's been going on in Arkansas. Sorry to ruin your day, but we've got to look at the record.

There's a lot you don't know about this man, and the more you find out, the more you know is that he's wrong for America. We cannot take a risk with this great country of ours. Take a look at the issue of education. As long as I'm standing here with some greats on education, let me put it this way: Governor Clinton was part of the national summit which set our education goals. I've given him credit for participating in that, and so has Lamar Alexander.

But in Arkansas, his rhetoric does not match his record. He talks about a high-tech economy that Arkansas is 48th in the percent of students who have high school diplomas. Three out of every four Arkansas high school graduates spend his first year in college relearning what they were supposed to learn in high school. I think America must do a lot better than that.

I think of Tennessee as a fairplay State when it comes to race. It's the same thing on every issue with him. Governor Clinton says he's for civil rights, but Arkansas doesn't even have a basic civil rights law. He says he's for a clean environment, but the Institute of Southern Studies ranks Ar-

kansas 50th, 50th in environmental policies. It's the only place where mother fish teach baby fish to jog instead of to swim—[*laughter*]—it's so polluted in that river over there. Governor Clinton says he's been tough on crime. But in the eighties, Arkansas' crime increases far outstripped the Nation. The Little Rock police say it all, because they have endorsed me for President of the United States of America.

Now let's take a look at the economy. I know America has had some tough times. I know families are concerned, worried about the next job. Those out of work are worried about how they're going to get back to work. But understand, we are being affected by a global economic slowdown. It isn't just the United States. Look at Europe. Look at Canada. Look at other countries around the world. Our competitors in Europe would trade places with us in a minute. And yes, Governor Clinton offers America the European social welfare state policies——

Audience members. Boo-o-o!

The President. ——more Government, more special interest spending, more regulation, and more taxes on the middle class. We cannot let him do that to the taxpayers in this country.

This is not simply campaign rhetoric. As Governor, he raised and extended the sales tax, including a tax on baby formula, vegetables, and other groceries. He raised the gas tax. He taxed mobile homes. For those of you ESPN watchers, he even taxed cable TV. Then he put a tax on beer just for an add-on.

Audience members. Boo-o-o!

The President. I knew the college crowd wouldn't like that too much. [*Laughter*]

Governor Clinton now says, well, he's seen the light. In this campaign he's proposing at least, and look at the record, $150 billion in new taxes, plus at least a $220 billion in new Federal spending. "But don't worry," he says, "I'll get it all from the rich, from the top 2 percent."

But the problem is, here's the truth, to get the money that he needs for this plan, everybody that's analyzed it says this, the $150 billion that he's promised in new taxes, Governor Clinton would have to get his money from every taxpayer and every individual with taxable income over $36,000. And these are not people that you see out there on the "Lifestyles of the Rich and Famous." They deserve a break, not a tax increase.

The problem is, this is just for openers. He'll need hundreds of billions of dollars more to pay for every one of these programs that he's proposed. There's an old saying: When you go hunting for ducks, hunt where the ducks are. Well, he's hunting for ways to pay for all of his promises, and he's going to go right smack to the middle class because that's where the bucks are. So watch your wallets. Watch your pocketbooks. He's coming right after you. Don't let him say anything different.

On this one you don't have to take my word for it. Go right to his neighborhood. Go to Pine Bluff and listen to the Pine Bluff Commercial. Here's what it says: "If Congress followed the example that Bill Clinton set as Governor of Arkansas, it would pass a program that hit the middle class the hardest." He's going to treat the middle class the way Johnny Majors' team treated Cincinnati last Saturday, exactly. The Volunteers pounced on the Bearcats, and he's going to pounce on your wallet. Look at the record. We cannot let this happen to America.

I'll give you a factual example. Let's say you're a nurse just starting out with about $22,000 a year in taxable income. Governor Clinton would have you fork over another 430 bucks a year to the tax man. I say that you ought to be able to use that to help your kids' education or pay the mortgage on the house and not send it to the IRS in Washington, DC.

But he says, "Hey, forget about this. Forget my record. Forget the facts. Don't talk about Arkansas and my record there. I am a different kind of Democrat." But what is different about him? George McGovern, Bill Clinton ran Texas for him in 1972. He learned his liberalism from George McGovern, and in that campaign he was out there front for George McGovern. Then Jimmy Carter, Bill Clinton wore the same moderate costume; but at least Carter meant it, even though he brought us the highest "misery index" in modern times. Then Mi-

chael Dukakis, Clinton nominated him in an endless nomination speech, I might say. [*Laughter*] Then he praised the Massachusetts Miracle right before it went south and the economy collapsed. America does not need this kind of different Democrat. There are some wonderful Democrats out there, but we don't need this kind, this McGovern, Carter, Dukakis Democrat.

Now, Governor Clinton wants you to trust the America's economy is going to improve if you turn full control of your paycheck over to the crew that already runs the United States Congress. He wants tax-and-spend Government plannings, those kind of planners to have total control over the executive branch, too.

They tried this 12 years ago, and we ended up with double-digit inflation. We had interest rates sometimes as high as 18 percent, and we had a "misery index" over 21 percent, unemployment and inflation added together. It took years to wring inflation and high interest rates out of the American economy. I want to strengthen our economy and protect your paycheck from the ravages of inflation. We cannot go the tax-and-spend route anymore. It all boils down to this. At this time in our history we simply cannot take the risk of Governor Clinton in the White House.

You know, I've been in the Oval Office, and I've faced some tough decisions. It's not easy. You cannot be on all sides of every question when you're a President of the United States. I stand before you today admitting mistakes, but saying I called them as I saw them. I hope I brought the character and integrity to this high office that you can respect and appreciate.

So I came here to ask for your support so that we can get to work with the new Members of Congress, Democrat and Republican alike, to fix the problems that stand in the way of this country; so that we can reform our health care system and we can literally reinvent our schools; and so that we can retrain the workers from one generation and create jobs for the next; so that we can cut Government spending and taxes and get this economy moving again; and that we can pass an amendment to limit the terms of Members of the United

States Congress and give the Government back to the people.

Now, if you want a guy that has a statistic for every problem, your man is the Governor of Arkansas. He's got more statistics than there are problems: 38 percent of this, 28 percent of that. But he's got to face up to the fact that as President you can't have it all ways; you've got to make the tough calls.

If you're looking for a leader of experience, a leader of ideas, a leader who shares your values, and a leader who understands that America's real strength is not in Government but in places like Alcoa, a leader you can trust, then I know that I can count on your support. I need it to be President of the United States for 4 more years.

Let me say this: I am very proud of the sons and daughters of Tennessee that have worn the uniform of the United States of America. You are a great and proud Volunteer State. Governor Clinton wants us to forget that we have changed the world. I am not going to let him forget that the young men and women that fought in Desert Storm helped us change the world and make it much more peaceful for every young person here today.

I ask for your trust. I ask for your trust, and I will not betray it. I ask for your vote, and I hope I have earned it.

He can talk about the United States being lower than Germany and someplace above Sri Lanka. I'll end this way: We are the most decent, fairest, strongest country on the face of the Earth. Let's not tear it down. Let's build it up. We are Americans.

May God bless you all, and thank you very, very much. Thank you so much.

Note: The President spoke at 12:11 p.m. at McGhee-Tyson Airport. In his remarks, he referred to entertainers Ricky Skaggs and T.G. Sheppard.

Remarks on Arrival in Chattanooga, Tennessee
September 29, 1992

The President. Thank you very much.

Audience members. Four more years! Four more years! Four more years!

The President. Four more. Four more. That's what we need. What a great Tennessee welcome. Thank you all. Thank you so much.

Audience members. We love you, George.

The President. Thank you. Thanks for that Chattanooga welcome. Let me thank two special guests with us today: of course, an old friend of mine and Barbara's, Ricky Skaggs, one of the great entertainers, great American; and also, I'm the one that's honored to be introduced by Naomi Judd, also a great American talent. I love country music, because country music loves America. Today we get to hear it all across Tennessee.

May I also welcome those others here standing with me: Senator Howard Baker, one of the great leaders of this country. All across the country we hear words of "Clean House! Clean House!" People are tired of the Democrats that have controlled Congress for 38 years. And if we had more like Don Sundquist here and Jimmy Duncan, we wouldn't be yelling that. But we need more. Where's Zach? Here's a way to help clean—get Zach up there.

May I pay my special respects to the Forrester Sisters. The Forrester Sisters are here. I'm told that they have a popular song called "I Choose You Again." Well, I take that personally.

Audience members. Four more years! Four more years! Four more years!

The President. I've got to get this going here. This campaign, like every campaign, is about a very simple question: What kind of America do we want for the young people here today? I'll tell you the kind of America that I want, an America that is not just a military superpower but the greatest economic superpower in the world and an export superpower.

I have laid out a detailed agenda for America's renewal, a specific, comprehensive, integrated agenda to create in America the world's very first $10 trillion economy. We can do it if you give us the support in Congress and reelect me for 4 years.

The other side acts like foreign affairs and national security means absolutely nothing, but I am very proud of our leadership in winning the cold war and proud of the way the sons and daughters of Tennessee stood fast and proud in the sands of Saudi Arabia, standing up against aggression.

Now I want to use that leadership and that experience in international affairs to lead the new market for American products, because that is how we will create more good jobs for the greatest workers on the face of the Earth, the American worker. And if we're going to compete in the global economy, and I'm confident we will, we've got to reduce that budget deficit and remove the burden from the backs of these kids that are here with us today.

Governor Clinton has gone through the entire Federal budget——

Audience members. Boo-o-o!

The President. ——and he has spelled out exactly one Federal program he would cut out, and that is the $11 million Federal honeybee subsidy. Believe me, no one will be stung by that courageous decision on the part of the Governor of Arkansas.

I have put specific programs forward to eliminate 4,000 projects, 246 programs, and to control the growth of the spending that's out of control, the mandatory spending programs, saving almost $300 billion over the next 5 years. But I want to go further. I want that line-item veto to discipline the Congress. I want a balanced budget amendment to the Constitution to discipline that spendthrift Congress. I want to give you, the taxpayer, the right to make a check on your income tax return, earmarking up to 10 percent of your tax return to go to reduce the Federal deficit. If the Congress doesn't have the guts to take a whack at the budget deficit, let the taxpayers have the ax and give it a try.

You know, I'm proud—this guy's fired up over here. I am proud of my record, and I'll stand by it in November. But if Governor Clinton, candidate Clinton, wants to talk about the past, let's look at what's been going on over in the great State of Arkansas, and they're wonderful people there. But let's look at the record. There's a lot you don't know about my opponent, and the more you find out, the more you know that he is wrong for America.

Look at health care reform. Take a look at health care reform. We need it desperately. But he says, no more pressing problem faces America. And yet after five terms in office, 40 percent of Arkansas residents don't have health insurance with their jobs, one of the highest rates in the entire Nation. We can do better than that.

It's the same on every issue. Tennessee's a fairplay State. Governor Clinton says he's for civil rights. But Arkansas doesn't even have a basic civil rights law. He says he's for clean environment, but the Institute for Southern Studies ranked Arkansas fifth in environmental policies.

And I'm told that there's a new aquarium in town, and maybe they'll have a live fish from the polluted White River in Arkansas. No, really, that would be a rare species exhibit. [*Laughter*] I love to fish. Sometimes I fish at night. In the river over there, you can fish at night because the fish light up at night from the pollution in that river.

You talk about a polluted river, you talk about cheap chicken—I've got to be careful—chicken fecal coliform bacteria. That's what dumps into the river. It's the only place where the mother fish don't teach their fish to swim. They teach them to jog, it is so polluted in that Arkansas river. A lousy record. We don't need that for the United States.

You know, Bill Clinton says—here's another issue, one of real concern, because when I see the police officers here, members from the sheriff's department, I think of our bill hung up in the Congress to back these law enforcement officers, to support them because they're supporting our families. But Bill Clinton says he's tough on crime? Listen to this: Arkansas prisoners get let out of jail after serving one-fifth of their sentence.

Audience members. Boo-o-o!

The President. And his hometown police force endorse me for President of the

United States of America.

Audience members. Four more years! Four more years! Four more years!

The President. You guys are too much.

Audience members. Four more years! Four more years! Four more years!

The President. I will continue to battle in the Congress, with the help of these Congressmen, to get a crime bill that gives a little more sensitivity and support for the victims of crime and a little less for the criminals themselves.

I know that many families are worried, and I know we've had some really tough economic times. But understand, we are being affected not just by what's at home but by a global economic slowdown. Our competitors in Europe would trade places with us in a minute. Yet Governor Clinton offers America the European social welfare state policy: more Government, more regulation, more special interest spending, and spending more taxes, tax bills, putting more taxes on the middle class. We simply cannot let that happen to our great country.

He's been going after me for 11 months, but how about this one? Governor Clinton raised and extended the sales tax, including a tax on baby formula, vegetables, and other groceries. He raised the gas tax. He raised the tax on mobile homes. And for those of you ESPN watchers, he even taxed cable TV. And then for good measure, he put a tax on beer. Try that one on.

Audience members. Boo-o-o!

The President. But now, here's good tidings of great joy. Governor Clinton says he's seen the light. In this campaign he is proposing at least $150 billion in new taxes, plus at least—that's not the worst of the news—a $220 billion new spending bill. Don't worry, he's going to take it all out of the very rich, those that make—the top 2 percent.

But here is the problem, and here is the truth. To get the money he needs for this plan of his, the $150 billion he's promised in new taxes, he would have to get his money from every individual with a tax income over $36,000. That is not the "Lifestyles of the Rich and Famous." That is going after your pocketbook.

Audience members. Boo-o-o!

The President. We're going after him.

Don't you worry about it. Just the start of his tax campaign—wait a minute, you haven't heard the worst of it. I'm sorry, that's just the start of his tax campaign against the middle class. He will need hundreds of billions of dollars more to pay for all the spending programs he's promised. He's going after the nurses, the teachers, the hardware store owners. I say you can spend your money better yourself on your home or educating your kids.

Ask him about it, and he'll take both sides. He'll say, on the one hand, I'm for you, and on the other, I'm for you over here. And when you're President of the United States you've got to make the tough decisions. You can't waffle. You can't go around like a chameleon all the time. You've got to say what you're for and vote that way.

I'll give you an example. I think of the sons and daughters of Tennessee that served in Desert Storm as among the most patriotic people in the entire world. Consider Governor Clinton's principled stand on both sides of the Gulf war when he said, and here is an exact quotation—remember now, this man wants to be Commander in Chief—and here is the exact quotation, "I guess I would have voted with the majority if it was a close vote, but I agree with the arguments the minority made." What kind of leadership position is that?

Audience members. Boo-o-o!

The President. He's like that on a lot of issues. He turns up in more places than Elvis Presley. You know, I saw a tape on this the other day, looking right into the camera saying, "I will not run for President. I will finish my 4 years if you people of Arkansas elect me." The very next year he says, "I'm running for President." One day he says he's for the North American free trade agreement, and then he says, "Well, I've got to study it. I haven't made up my mind yet." One day he says the middle class deserves a tax break, and the next day he's plotting new ways to hit the middle class for all his programs. One day he's for an automobile fuel efficiency standard, CAFE standard, of 45 miles per gallon. And that would throw a lot of Tennessee auto workers out of their jobs. The next day he says,

"Well, I'm studying it." When you're President of the United States, privileged to sit in that Oval Office, you've got to make a decision. You cannot sit there being all things to all people.

We do not expect the man to win, but don't expect him to level with the American people. If he ever got to be President, we'd have to take off the American eagle as our symbol and put on a chameleon. We don't need that for the head of the United States of America.

So it boils down to this—I'm having fun because for 11 months I've wanted to go after this guy and his record, and now we're doing it. It is great.

It simply boils down to this: We cannot take a risk on Governor Clinton to become President Clinton. You know, I've been in that Oval Office, and I've faced some tough decisions, made some mistakes, hopefully called a lot of them right. But believe me, I've tried hard to be a good and principled leader, willing to make the tough calls. I am a leader whose ideas are right for the United States of America.

So I came here to this great part of Tennessee today, asking for your support so I can go to work with a new Congress to fix the problems that stand in our way. We've got to reform our health care system, reinvent our public schools.

And let me salute Lamar Alexander, our great Secretary of Education. What a job he has done. For Lamar and for me it's not enough to change things. We want to reinvent them and back up our teachers and the people, the local people that know what's best for Tennessee education.

We're going to reinvent the schools, and then we want to retain the workers from one generation and create jobs for the next. So that we can cut Government spending, cut these taxes to get this economy moving again, and pass term limits for Members of Congress and give the Government back to the people.

Let me tell you something. I am very proud that I served our country in the uniform of the United States of America. That helped me make a tough decision when Saddam Hussein moved out and tried to take over another country. Again, I salute every person in the United States that was willing to stand up and fight against aggression and for the United States of America and for freedom.

As the result of what happened, you have ancient enemies talking to each other in the Middle East. You have democracy on the move, and Russia—who would have thought that possible. You have far less fear of nuclear war today than when I became President of the United States.

Now what we've got to do, and what I can do with your help, is to take that same principled leadership and lift up and renew America. I ask for your support for 4 more years as President of the United States.

May God bless our great country. May God bless the United States of America. Thank you very much.

Note: The President spoke at 2:15 p.m. at Lovell Field. In his remarks, he referred to Zach Wamp, Republican candidate for House of Representatives in Tennessee's Third Congressional District.

Remarks at Austin Peay State University in Clarksville, Tennessee
September 29, 1992

The President. Thank you, Naomi. And may I welcome just a few people: first, our Secretary of Education, a great Tennessean, Lamar Alexander, what a job he's doing for education; and Senator Howard Baker, great American leader. Congressman Sundquist, your great Congressman, is here with us today, and Congressman Duncan. And may I salute the president, President Oscar Page, and thank him for this hospitality; and Coach Ray Gregory. Coach Gregory, congratulations on being named Tennessee football coach of the year, a great honor. May I also salute my introducer, Naomi, I'm very, very proud that she's been with us today; and thank Ricky, Ricky Skaggs, who you heard from, who's a wonderful entertainer and a good friend to Barbara and me. And my special appreciation to a great friend and a great entertainer, the legendary, one and only Crystal Gayle. Crystal, thank you so much. And Crystal's sister Peggy Sue is here. Four years ago we went on a bus trip across Illinois, and we won the State. So this is a good omen. We are going to win Tennessee.

Before I make a few campaign remarks I have a few things to say about a topic that's been on a lot of minds recently. And I hope you'll bear with me because I want to talk to you and to the rest of the Nation from this wonderful campus about Presidential debates.

Two weeks ago, I proposed to Governor Clinton that we debate. I proposed that we do so on the same terms and conditions that have been used in prior Presidential debates, and that the Vice Presidential candidates do so as well. Governor Clinton has failed to respond to this proposal. But, in fact, it is reported that he is afraid for his campaign to sit down with our campaign to negotiate arrangements for the debate.

I have debated in all of my prior campaigns for President. I continue to think that it's important that debates be held. You see, I believe strongly that it is not up to any self-appointed body to determine the basis on which debates will be held but rather up to the candidates themselves. This basic principle was expressly recognized by both national political parties when the resolution establishing the Commission on Debates was first adopted.

Because of the importance of this election, the strength of my convictions about what is right for this country, and my belief that a Clinton Presidency would be wrong for America, I think it is important that voters have an opportunity to see and hear from the candidates themselves in publicly televised debates. I also believe that the candidates should not be afraid to accept and respond to questions from the press during the course of Presidential debates.

Americans will go the polls 5 weeks from today. I regret that Governor Clinton has not accepted the traditional approach to Presidential debates, the approach that's been in effect for many, many years. But nevertheless, in order to move this process forward, I hereby challenge my opponent to a debate on every Sunday evening between October 11th and November 1st.

This would mean that there would be four televised Presidential debates, more than ever held in any Presidential election. And if Ross Perot decides to enter the race, I'd be pleased to see him included in these debates.

Now, furthermore, to allow these arrangements to move forward quickly, I would be willing to see two of the debates proceed under the format which has been used in all these previous Presidential elections and two proceed under this single moderator format. In addition, I think that during the 5-week period, there should be at least two Vice Presidential debates with one based on each format.

I feel quite confident that Governor Clinton will accept this proposal, since his campaign chairman has indicated in the past that Governor Clinton would debate, and now I quote, "with moderators, without moderators, in a studio, out of a studio, three questioners, one questioner." So I have no doubt that there will be organizations willing to sponsor these debates. If Governor Clinton is serious about debating, he will accept this challenge, and he will instruct his campaign officials to meet promptly with my campaign officials to work out the details directly between the parties. Let's get it on!

What are we going to be talking about in these debates? What are we going to be talking about in them? Well, this campaign, like every campaign, is about a simple question: What kind of America do we want for the graduates of this great school, for all the young people here today? My opponent will tell you that America is in decline. I would remind him of what anyone will tell you on the streets of Europe or Asia: America is still the most respected, the most admired, the most dynamic nation in the entire world. I'm tired of hearing Clinton drag down the United States of America.

I'm proud. I am proud of our leadership, proud that we led the way in reducing nuclear weapons so that our kids can sleep free from the nightmares of nuclear war. It's a fitting place to say this, right near Fort Campbell, and I am proud of how we stood up to Saddam Hussein, kicking him—[*applause*]—proud of the Screaming Eagles from Fort Campbell's 101st Airborne. In the sands of Saudi Arabia, they showed that no other nation can match the courage of the men and women of America.

Now our challenge is to put our talents to work to win the new global economic competition, to create a high-tech, high-growth economy with good jobs for you and all your classmates. I have laid out my agenda, detailed Agenda for American Renewal, a specific, comprehensive, integrated agenda to create in America the world's very first $10 trillion economy. I want to use this international experience, international leadership to open up new markets for American products, because that is how we will create good jobs for American workers.

Small business will create two-thirds of the new jobs in the new economy. Governor Clinton promises small business higher taxes and more redtape. I promise relief from taxation, regulation, and litigation. Get the regulations off of the back of the small-business people in this country.

With Lamar Alexander's leadership and assistance, we're proud that today half the students in 4-year colleges across Tennessee receive Federal grants or loans. No one told you what college you had to go to. You had the freedom to choose your school. Now we are fighting to reinvent America's elementary and high schools by giving every parent the right to choose their children's schools, public, private, or religious.

We have a good plan to give Government vouchers to soldiers and others caught in the transition of the economy so that they may learn new skills and find the dignity of work.

Here's something else I want: to limit the terms of Members of the United States Congress. Governor Clinton says he's the candidate of change, but he opposes this, the most profound change offered this year. Presidents serve limited terms. The same rule ought to apply to the other end of Pennsylvania Avenue. So let's approve term limits and give Congress back to the American people.

I might add this, that if we had more Congressmen like Don Sundquist up there, everybody wouldn't be yelling at me, "Clean House!" But while we're at it, let's have that little chant, "Clean House!" We've got to get rid of that old 38-year-old governance that has controlled Congress for 38 years. Let's change it. You want to make real change in America? Help me change the Congress and move this country forward.

These are just some of my ideas and some of what I'm fighting for. I'm proud of my record, and I'll stand by it in November. But if candidate Clinton wants to talk about the past, I say okay, let's look at what's going on in Arkansas.

The people there—and I know them; I've been there many, many times, lived next door—they are decent and hard-working people. But the more you know about their Governor, the more you know that he's wrong for America. Governor Clinton says he's for civil rights. But Arkansas doesn't even have a basic civil rights law. He says he's for high-tech, but under Bill Clinton, Arkansas has been falling behind in high school. Three out of every four Arkansas graduates spend their first year in college relearning what they were supposed to learn in high school. That is not fair to the people of Arkansas.

Bill Clinton says he wants to get tough on crime. But his crime rate rises faster than the Nation's. I support the law enforcement officers all across the country, and I am very proud that the police in Little Rock, Arkansas, endorse me for President of the United States of America. America deserves better than that sorry Arkansas record of Governor Clinton.

Look at the economy, the major issue in this campaign. I know America's endured some tough economic times. Families are hurting. But understand, we are being affected, and all students know this, by a global economic slowdown. Our competitors in Europe would trade places with us in a minute. And yet Governor Clinton offers America the European social welfare state policies: more Government, more special interest spending, and more taxes on the middle class. That is not good for America.

Audience members. Boo-o-o!

The President. As Governor—I know I hate to ruin a beautiful afternoon like this, but listen to this one—as Governor, Bill Clinton raised and extended the sales tax, including a tax on baby formula, vegetables, and other groceries. He raised the gas tax. He taxed mobile homes and cable TV. And, oh yeah, he slapped a tax on beer.

Audience members. Boo-o-o!

The President. Yes. I had a feeling that would not be very popular here. Now the Governor says he's seen the light. In this campaign he's proposing at least $150 billion in new taxes, plus at least $220 billion in new spending. But don't worry, he says, "I'll get it all from the rich," people who make it over $200,000, the top 2 percent.

But here's the truth and problem: To get the money he needs for his plan, the $150 billion he's promised in new taxes, Governor Clinton would have to get his money from every individual with taxable income over $36,600. That's just the start of his tax campaign against the middle class. Governor Clinton will need hundreds of billions of dollars more to pay for all the programs that he's promised.

The newspaper in his own backyard, the Pine Bluff Commercial, says that "If Congress follows Bill Clinton's example, it would pass a tax program that would hit the middle class the hardest." These are not people, Governor Clinton, on "Lifestyles of the Rich and Famous." These are your parents, your parents, my friends. These are the people that work hard and pay the bills and sweat it out at tax time. They deserve a break, not a new tax.

Let me give you one example. Let's say after you graduate, you get your first job with about, say, $22,000 a year in taxable income. Governor Clinton could have you fork over another 430 bucks a year to the tax man. I say you ought to be able to use that money to pay the rent or spend a week at the lake on vacation, not have to send it back to the IRS in Washington, DC.

So, at this time in the great history of the United States, I don't think we can take the risk on a tax-and-spend candidate with no experience. You see, I've been in the Oval Office, and I have faced some very tough decisions, and of course, I've made mistakes. When I make a mistake, I admit it. But I believe I've been a good leader, willing to make the tough calls, and I'm a leader whose ideas are right for America.

I stand before you today, asking for your support so that we can get to work with a new Congress to fix the problems that stand in the way of this country; so that we can reform our health care system; that we can literally reinvent our schools; so that we can retrain workers from one generation and create jobs for the next; so that we can cut Government spending and taxes and get this economy moving again.

This is the agenda that I have to offer. If you are looking for a leader of experience, a leader of ideas, a leader who shares your values, and a leader who understands that America's real strength is not in Government but in places like Clarksville, then I know I can count on your support on November 3d.

I have only one regret today, and that is that the greatest First Lady this country— well, I'd better be careful, but our great First Lady is not with me. I'm very proud of Barbara Bush. I see a sign over here that's talking about the family. I think that my wife has done an awful lot, when she holds an AIDS baby in her arms or when she sits and reads with kids in the lobby there at the Diplomatic Entrance to the White House, to show what we mean as a family when we say, let's strengthen the American family. Read to the kids. Teach them discipline. Help them.

I've been privileged to be your President. We did it through some very, very tough times. One of the things that shaped my life is that I served my country in uniform, and I'm very, very proud of that. I salute those here from Fort Campbell and elsewhere who are also serving their great country.

Don't listen, don't listen to the other side that is tearing down this country. We are the greatest, strongest, fairest, freest country on the face of the Earth. Let's keep it that way.

May God bless you all. May God bless the United States of America. Thank you very,

very much. What a great rally. Thank you all.

Note: The President spoke at 4:04 p.m. in Dunn Center.

Remarks to the Community in Nashville, Tennessee
September 29, 1992

The President. Thank you very much for that warm welcome. Thank you, thank you, thank you. Hey, listen, how do you ever adequately—please be seated, and let me just say what a joy it is to be here today. I don't know how I possibly can begin to thank these fantastic entertainers that are standing up with me right now, I'll tell you, Baillie and the Boys, the Oak Ridge Boys, and Paul Overstreet, and Mark Chestnut; of course, Lee Greenwood and Chet Atkins and, oh, there's so many. Naomi, thank you for being with us all day long, and, Crystal, thank you for appearing with me. It really makes a tremendous difference. It really brings the crowds alive. And I'm grateful to each and every one of you. And, Goober, your jokes were all right, too. [*Laughter*] And thank you.

May I salute Roy Acuff. My heavens, what an inspiration he's been to all of us in this country. And as President, you get to do many wonderful and happy things, and one of the things I've enjoyed the most was when I had the honor of presenting to Roy the most prestigious award we have for the arts, the National Medal of the Arts, up at the White House. He deserved it, and he's a fine, fine, fine legend in his own time.

You know, I don't know whether Naomi or Crystal are still speaking to me, or Ricky Skaggs, who was with us on this trip. But as far as I'm concerned, this is a wonderful day, traveling all across the width and breadth of this great State. I can't think of a better place to finish this swing than right here at the Mecca of country music.

You know, last week on one of the networks there was a story asking why country music had become such a big part of national politics. I won't speak for any other politicians, but I love country music. Leave politics aside, I love it because country music loves America. I don't start listen-ing—listen to this crowd—just at election time. I listen to it every night of my life, and I love it. I can flip on 98.7 on the dial at Washington, DC, and all the cares of all these talking heads and media freaks and everybody else go flying out. It is wonderful.

May I salute Howard Baker who's with us here today. Congressmen Sundquist and Duncan; and of course, our great Secretary of Education, Lamar Alexander.

It's a funny thing, who was it, Naomi talked about family. I get a funny feeling that some on the opposition camp want to have us stop talking about the fundamental importance of strengthening the American family. But I'm not going to stop talking about it because we must find ways to stand for the values of family and faith. Sometimes those values like family and faith become unpopular, a little out of sync in some places. But never, never here and never in country music. It's always there. Country music reminds us that for all our faults, America still is the very best, the finest country on the face of the Earth.

We've had a lot of difficulties, but I don't like it one single bit when I find somebody trying to be President and the only way he can get there is by tearing down and talking down the United States of America. I want to talk it up. I believe in our country. I am very proud.

To listen to Clinton and Gore, they don't think foreign affairs or national security is important. I am proud of how we helped win the cold war so that our children can sleep without that nightmare of nuclear war and nuclear weapons and dream the sweet dreams of peace.

I am proud that when Saddam Hussein stuck his forces across into Kuwait that we were the country, we were the ones, the sons and daughters of Tennessee, that said,

"No way. You're through. You're out." Right there we showed that courage is a fundamental part of the American character. We are not going to forget what those men and women did, no matter how the other side tries to move the debate away. We're going to stay with the pride that we feel in this country.

I'm not going to get into the one subject that's racing all around the politics, but let me just put it this way: I am very proud that I served my country in the uniform of the United States of America. I hope it has made me a better Commander in Chief. And I hope it has made me a sensitive one, because the toughest decision that a President has to make is to commit somebody else's son or daughter into combat. I think that experience has been extraordinarily useful.

But now what we've got to do is to take the leadership that helped shape the entire world, that brought an end to the cold war, that brought democracy to countries all across the world who have lived behind communist tyranny, and say, now take the leadership that did that and change things dramatically here at home. That's what the debate is about, and that's what the election is about.

We can feel the impact in our neighborhoods now as we take this message of hope and economic opportunity all across the United States of America. You see, what I must do now in the last 5 or 6 weeks, whatever we have left—should be able to tell you right down to the hour; it's been that kind of a year, but—[*laughter*]—we've got two entirely different views as to how to respond to the challenge. Beneath all his rhetoric and all of his talk of partnership and new ways, Governor Clinton basically offers America more of the old way, more Government, more spending, more redtape, more middle class taxes.

Audience members. Boo-o-o!

The President. You know, I had the honor, coming in here, to call a real legend on the phone, Minnie Pearl, beloved daughter of Nashville. Leaving the politics aside, Barbara and I just love her, and we wanted to just wish her good health. Ronald Reagan used to describe the liberal spending programs as being something like Minnie

Pearl's hat: "They look great, but they have all these big price tags dangling from them." [*Laughter*] And so that's the way I look at the Clinton program.

I don't think we can afford that kind of a program of tax and spend. And yes, I believe that Government can do good things. But fundamentally, I believe that the key to renewing America won't be found in some Washington bureaucracy, but right here, right here in the heartland of America, in places like Nashville, Tennessee.

So in this campaign we're talking about turning the power, giving the power to the American people. I want to break down the barriers, bureaucratic barriers, to world trade, so that we can create more jobs for the American workers. I want to get rid of all of these crazy lawsuits that keep mothers and fathers from coaching Little League, these lawsuits that keep doctors from practicing medicine. As a nation, frankly, we've got to sue each other less and care for each other more.

With the great leadership and help of Lamar Alexander, I want to give parents, not the Government, the right to choose their kids' school, whether public, private, or religious.

But most of all, we've got to get the Government under control by cutting Government spending and cutting taxes, because I believe that you can spend your money better than any Government subcommittee or Government bureaucrat. So we've got some big differences. I believe Governor Clinton, just to put it mildly—I'm an objective observer here—I believe Governor Clinton's ideas are wrong for America. That is the bottom line, and I've got to take that case to the American people.

A couple of hours ago, over at Austin Peay University, I challenged Governor Clinton to a debate, the last four Sundays of this campaign, four nationally televised debates. I said that I'd be flexible about the format, but I believe that the American people deserve to hear our ideas because only they can make the right choice in November. I hope that the Governor will respond and accept. We've been hearing a lot about him. I've seen all those chickens out there at these various events. [*Laughter*] I didn't know whether they were talking about the draft or the pollution in the Arkansas River.

Look, I know, I don't pretend to be the world's greatest debater. I didn't go to Oxford. I know, I know I'm not very good on statistics. This guy's got more statistics than there are problems. [*Laughter*] But what I do have is a fundamental commitment to values and hopefully some character to go with it.

Something else I have is faith in the American people, faith in all the beauticians and bartenders and Boy Scouts and great singers. I believe that America will win the economic competition if Government just gives these people the tools and then gets the heck out of the way and lets America get the job done.

I'll tell you what really gets me about this. I don't want to get wound up here, these guys have lots to do—but it burns me up right in the bottom of my gut to hear Governor Clinton talking about this country being a nation in decline. He says we're south of Germany and a little north of Sri Lanka. Well, he ought to open his eyes and look around the world. We are the most respected, the fairest, the most decent country on the face of the Earth. Thank God I don't have to get reelected by going around tearing down the United States of America.

I wish Barbara Bush were here. Not only does she keep me in line, but I think she's been the greatest First Lady we've had. I'll tell you something; I'll tell you why we're going to win this election: We really care. We have been honored—I say we, the both of us—to live in this wonderful White House, the symbol to countries all around the world of freedom and democracy. We've tried very, very hard to keep the public trust, to honor the office that we've been privileged to hold.

Now I'm going to ask the American people: Let us finish this job. Let us have this economy recover. Let's offer hope and opportunity to all Americans. Give me 4 more years to finish the job.

Thank you, and may God bless our great country. I can't do it as well as Lee Greenwood, but God bless the United States. God bless the U.S.A. Thank you very much.

Note: The President spoke at 7:20 p.m. at the Roy Acuff Theater. In his remarks, he referred to entertainers Baillie and the Boys, the Oak Ridge Boys, Paul Overstreet, Mark Chestnut, Lee Greenwood, Chet Atkins, Naomi Judd, Crystal Gayle, George "Goober" Lindsey, Roy Acuff, and Ricky Skaggs.

Message to the Congress Reporting on the State of Small Business
September 29, 1992

To the Congress of the United States:

It is my pleasure to submit my third annual report on the state of small business. America's small business owners are individuals with countless new ideas, employers and workers who produce a vast array of goods and services, taxpayers who pay many of the bills, and economic pioneers who help decide the future direction of our economy. In their endless variety, small firms help create a flexible, diverse, and lively marketplace.

For generations, entrepreneurial business owners have been in the forefront of the dynamic economic changes that continually revitalize our democracy. In the early days of our Republic, small business innovators led the way in developing more productive farming technologies. Greater agricultural productivity eventually freed other entrepreneurs to develop and commercialize new manufacturing processes. These processes and manufactured products set a new standard for America—and for the world. But America's small business innovators did not stop there. They started another revolution by anticipating and responding quickly to the demands that grew out of the new, higher standard of living—demands for services and sophisticated new information technologies.

Small businesses have made important contributions to the economy, not only by introducing new products and processes and creating jobs, but also by making the economy more adaptive and flexible—by retaining workers longer during recessions and hiring workers earlier as expansions begin.

There is no doubt that 1991 was not an easy year for the American economy or for small business. The recession that began in the third quarter of 1990 carried over into 1991. Business formation rates were down, and business closings were up. The flow of financing slowed as banks and businesses grew more cautious about business expansions.

Yet in this recession, as in other economic downturns, small businesses continued to function as a source of jobs, creating many of the new jobs in the economy. Rather than lay off workers, many small firms tightened their belts in other areas. And they continued to innovate, introduce new products, and contribute to their communities.

Our economy has begun to grow again. Still, small firms face difficult challenges in the months and years ahead. The truth is that health care costs are too high and the unmet need for health coverage is great in small businesses. And of all employers, small businesses are least able to afford the expensive mandates that have been advocated by some. The proposal I presented to the Congress would not resort to mandates, but would build on the strengths of our private health care system to make health insurance affordable for America's workers and their families.

Adjustments occurring in our financial institutions have made it difficult for many worthy small businesses to find the capital they need to start up or expand. Therefore, my Administration is taking steps to encourage investment in business ventures in a number of ways. I have proposed that the Congress cut the capital gains tax so that investors will have an incentive to buy into new ventures. Another proposal I have made is to create an investment tax allow-

ance that would assist in starting new firms.

And we can encourage some new investment by adapting programs that are already underway. For example, the Small Business Administration is working with banks to implement innovative loan programs that are channeling funds to smaller firms in some of the most economically depressed areas.

Another obstacle that can stand in the way of small firm growth is too much regulation. My Administration this year instituted a moratorium on new Federal regulations to give Federal agencies a chance to review and revise their rules. And we are looking at ways to improve our regulatory process over the long term so that regulations will accomplish their original purpose without unduly hindering economic growth.

We also need to encourage innovation—such as that exhibited by thousands of small high technology firms—by making the research and experimentation tax credit permanent. My Administration is committed to exploring the promise of new technologies.

This report documents the increasing, healthy diversity of our small business community, as minority- and women-owned businesses enter the marketplace in record numbers. I want to keep encouraging that diversity through our Federal procurement programs.

I also want to see more of the Nation's economically depressed communities reap the benefits of business growth. To that end, I have asked the Congress to pass my enterprise zone legislation, which will provide incentives to businesses that start up in specially designated areas, particularly in inner cities.

Looking to the future, it is clear that we need to improve our educational system so that America's workers, particularly in small firms, will be in a better position to compete in a more and more sophisticated global marketplace. My America 2000 education strategy is designed to give parents, teachers, and communities more freedom and flexibility in designing education programs to meet their needs—and to make America the world's leader in education.

Many of these proposals for economic recovery and growth are being enacted now; others will require action by the Congress. I am committed to working with the Members of Congress to develop and enact a broad economic plan we can all live with. These combined actions will help small business to move ahead to create the economic revolutions that will lead us into the 21st century.

GEORGE BUSH

The White House,
September 29, 1992.

Message to the Congress Transmitting the Report of the National Institute of Building Sciences
September 29, 1992

To the Congress of the United States:

In accordance with the requirements of section 809 of the Housing and Community Development Act of 1974, as amended (12 U.S.C. 1701j–2(j)), I transmit herewith the 15th annual report of the National Institute of Building Sciences for fiscal year 1991.

GEORGE BUSH

The White House,
September 29, 1992.

Remarks at the National Salute to the President and His Black Appointees
September 30, 1992

The President. Thank you very much. Josh, thank you, Josh Smith.

Audience members. Four more years! Four more years! Four more years!

The President. Thank you, Josh Smith, and all of you. Thank you very much, Josh, and thank all of you. My heavens, 27 different States, I'm told, represented here by all of you. Josh, I can't begin to thank you, not only for your friendship and loyal support but your service to the Government, to the people, I would put it that way, and also for your outstanding commitment to small business and your own accomplishments in that field.

I also want to acknowledge Josh's wife, Jackie Jones-Smith, who is the Chairman of the Consumer Product Safety Commission; my old friend Milton Bins here, chairman of the Council of 100. Kay James from the Office of National Drug Control Policy gave up an awful lot to move over there to fight this drug scourge, and I'm very proud of her.

Reverend Thad Garrett, we all know Thad. He ought to be praying more and talking less out there on the campaign—[*laughter*]—I need that, I'll tell you. But somebody once gave me a little rug, and it said, "What would we do without friends?" I am grateful that Thad and so many others out here are true and loyal friends. When the going is tough, they're hanging in there.

I want to salute Fred Brown, the chairman of the National Council of Black Republicans. I was very grateful to Reverend Larry Haygood for that invocation, for his leadership in education, for his commitment and faith. Thank you, sir, for coming and for doing that.

Of course, I can't say too much about Lou Sullivan. I love it when we talk about genuine health care reform for this country. He summarized it in his remarks there, giving me the credit. But he's out there on the cutting edge. When a paper like the New York Times, which has not been overly friendly to me this year—[*laughter*]—points out that we've got a sound, or the best of the health care reform programs out there, why, I'm very grateful to Lou. He's tireless in taking the message across the country, and he's leading this, the largest Government bureau, with such distinction and honor. I tell you, we're lucky to have him in the Government.

Ginger is not clapping too hard. Maybe she wants him back; I don't know. But nevertheless. [*Laughter*]

May I salute Gary Franks, distinguished Member of Congress. I don't see him, but I know he's here. Where's Gary? Well, he's not here. All right, he's late. [*Laughter*] He's to be here; Andy Ireland, a Member of the United States Congress, with us here today, too.

I want to single out a warrior. Some of you know her just by seeing her on television. Some of you know her for seeing her at my side as I climb on the helicopter or Air Force One or go to take on some political debate. And I'm talking about Marlin's able deputy, Judy Smith, who is standing right over here. Judy, I don't want this to come out wrong, but you talk about tough women. [*Laughter*] I mean, she is strong, and in a wonderful way. She takes it and can dish it out just as well. It is tough out there in that press arena. But boy, she's doing a superb job for me and I think for the country because she gets out our position on fundamental issues that are important to the Nation.

Let me just talk for a few minutes. I'm off to Wisconsin in a few minutes and then to New Jersey. So I want to just talk a little bit about the concerns that we share about the future of this great country, about the choice that we have in shaping that future. I will spare you a stemwinding political oration, but I will just point out that we've got a great task before us, and the differences are clear. With the end of the cold war that Reverend Haygood very generously referred to, now we've got to turn our attention to winning the new global economic competition.

The other side is telling us everything that's wrong about the economy, and I'll accept my share of the blame. But we're caught up in something worldwide. And any fair-minded observer knows that it's not just the United States that's had difficult economic times. It's England. It's France.

It's Canada. It's Germany now. A lot of countries in this, and we have the strongest economy of all of them. It's my objective to make it even stronger. I call that winning the peace, for only then will we keep the promise of opportunity that is the birthright of every American. I am proud of the fact that our kids go to bed at night without that same fear of nuclear weapons that their predecessors had. This is, I think, a significant accomplishment, and I salute everyone in our administration that worked to help end that nuclear nightmare.

But now we've got to do the same thing, apply that same leadership, and lift this country up. You know, the Governor, Governor Clinton, and I offer very different choices. They're really based on very different philosophies, different experience. He's spent most of his life in government. He believes that government, kind of a Washington elite, should take the lead in shaping the economy. He uses the word "investing": investing your money, that's taxpayers' money, more wisely than you can as entrepreneurs and individuals.

Well, that's not the way I see it at all. Like so many of you, I've spent exactly 50 percent of my adult life in business and 50 percent in government. Not with the sparkling success that some in this room have had as business people, but nevertheless, I understand it. I built a business from the ground up. I met a payroll, created jobs, and worked for a living. I happen to think that that is a good qualification for being President of the United States, because I believe it's a prospering small business or large business environment that's going to do more to help people. Put it this way, a job in the private sector is going to do more to help people than Government programs can.

I learned in that private sector what many of you not only have learned but have mastered: what makes an economy grow. It is not central planning, quote, "investing," unquote, the taxpayers' money. It is not the people who take your taxes and spend them. It is you who make the economy grow, ordinary men and women with the extraordinary dreams who have the grit to make those dreams real. And I'm very grateful to what Josh does in taking this message of small business out around this country.

That understanding is really at the heart of what Larry Haygood again referred to as the Agenda for American Renewal. I talk about the global economy and then what we're going to do now to be the lead. We are the only remaining military superpower. We have the strongest economy; I want to help make it stronger. I want to see us become an export superpower as well. To do this, we've got to unleash the energy, the brainpower of our workers and our entrepreneurs, and again, particularly in small business because this is the area that employs the most and takes the risks and creates the new opportunities.

I want to encourage investment so that wages rise and those unemployment lines shrink. That's why I'm helping small business in particular and, hopefully, all business in general. We unveiled a good small business program the other day down in North Carolina. I'll just touch on a couple of points: Reducing the corporate tax rate for small business 15 percent to 10 percent; increasing the amount of equipment that small business can expense, and thus that would create more jobs and new opportunities; simplifying the tax filing. Most small-business people know that the onerous reporting for tax purposes takes too many work hours, too many people hours, and we're trying to change that. Then, of course, I still feel that to stimulate risktaking, the reduction in the capital gains is very, very important, bringing people into the enterprise zones in the minority areas; a reduction in capital gains, a break on that will help attract jobs to the areas that need it the very most.

So to the business people here, we are trying to streamline so you won't have to be second-guessed back here in Washington by some bureaucratic establishment. And that's why we've put an end to the Federal regulations that turn redtape into pink slips. We just put out a moratorium on them. We're going to go forward with safety and health; obviously we have to do that. But we've got a moratorium, a blanket on new regulations, recognizing that there is too much control and regulation on the back of the

small entrepreneur and the small-business person.

We really do want to do what Lou was talking about, and that is to make health insurance available to everyone. We want to make health care more accessible and more affordable for everyone. That's why we're all—have our shoulders to the wheel, fighting for health care reform without burdening small businesses with expensive new mandates and more payroll taxes.

Our program is good. It keeps the quality of American health care where it belongs, number one in the entire world, and still says to those who cannot get insurance, we're going to make it available to you through pooling, and also we're going to reduce the costs. We're doing something about these crazy malpractice suits and also doing something about lifting the regulatory burden and streamlining the operating processes of our health care system.

So we've got a good program there, and I hope that it'll get the kind of support in the very next Congress that we need to have it enacted into law.

I want to reward the risktakers who bring capital and jobs to our inner cities; I touched on that. But it's very interesting to me that when we went to Los Angeles in the wake of the South Central problems, all the civic leaders there were saying we must have enterprise zones. It's an idea whose time has come. We ought to try it at the Federal level. So we're fighting hard to bring the enterprise zones into reality.

On issue after issue, you see the very sharp differences between my opponent and me, because he really does want a Government. He's already proposed more taxes, more spending, more regulations. He's already proposed programs that would result in the latter, in the last item, and tax plans and spending plans that would tax at the outset $150 billion more in taxes and $220 billion more in spending. It's going to kill off a lot of small business.

So we want to free up, instead, the genius of American enterprise and initiative. This is going to be one of the clearest distinctions as people begin to really make up their minds on this election.

Let me be clear: I am not anti-Government. Government must never shirk its responsibilities. The fine men and women honored here today who I've been proud to have at my side for the past 3 years are a testament to the good work that Government can do. We believe it's Government's role to create opportunity, though, and not stifle it, and to clear the path for individual accomplishment, not to block it; to facilitate, not to dictate. Together, we believe that there is no room in our country, and I want to repeat this here, for discrimination of any kind whatsoever. As long as I am President, I am going to do absolutely everything I can in my power to drive bigotry and anti-Semitism and racism from our great land.

You know, I hope you know that I have strong feelings about this. Lou and Josh and I were talking. I'm not sure the American people know how strongly I feel about this. That's one of the reasons I hope we get these debates on. We've proposed four debates with the Governor. Let him step up now and debate. We've accepted his formula for two of them, and so, we'll have an opportunity there without any filters, without any Monday morning quarterbacks telling you what you thought you heard, to take the case directly to the American people.

I've tried in my public life—like supporting fair housing when I was a Member of Congress from Texas and fighting for I think decent civil rights legislation, whether it's the ADA bill or an antidiscriminatory civil rights bill. I think we got, and others here have mentioned this very generously, an excellent record of appointing officials on the content of their character and their competence to positions of high authority in the Government. I am proud of what both Josh and Lou talked about, to have appointed a higher percentage of blacks and women in the history of the Presidency to important positions.

Some are here with us today: Gwen King at the Social Security Commission, who is now going on to new pursuits. I mentioned Kay James, who served with such distinction in several capacities. Some are nonpolitical. I think it's a wonderful thing that Colin Powell is the Chairman of the Joint Chiefs. I don't know anything about his pol-

itics, and I couldn't care less. I know something about his character, though. I know something about his ability, though. I know something of how it is when he's making tough, tough decisions regarding the life of somebody else's son and daughter, and that's all I need to know in selecting the best Chairman of the Joint Chiefs.

Connie Newman, we all know her, how she served with great distinction in this administration; and a most beloved figure, Joyce Berry. I mentioned Lou, of course. I mentioned Josh for the Commission. But we've got others, Carla Hills, Antonia Novello, Lynn Martin, Bernadine Healy, all women in high-level positions. I'm proud of Wayne Budd over at Justice. You talk abut a tough assignment, there's a decent man and a man of honor, fulfilling an extraordinarily tough assignment over at the Department of Justice. My old friend Art Fletcher is head of the Commission.

Let me tell you something: I am not going to let the political diatribes going on out there and attacks coming out of some radical groups diminish the pride I take in having appointed Clarence Thomas to the Supreme Court. So let others try to smear a decent man. I'm standing with him. He's going to be a great Justice. You watch. You just wait. He's just beginning. He's going to be outstanding.

So we're here to salute all of you—I came over to do that—and to thank you, those in Government, for serving and serving with integrity. I'll tell you something: Our administration has been a clean administration. You look back over your shoulders. We haven't had scandals because we have honorable men and women who sacrifice to serve their country. I'm proud of each and every one of you. And in terms of those others who are out in the private sector employing people, creating opportunity, living the American dream, I salute you as well. We want to facilitate what you're doing, not get Government in the way and make it tougher.

So this is the message we'll be taking to the American people, and I believe we're going to get this job done. It has not been a very pleasant political year for Barbara Bush and me; I'll have to confess that.

Indeed, I've been around the political track for a long time, and I've never seen quite the anger and the ugliness in the political process, the willingness to twist and distort and make things ugly. But it's worth it; you know it. It is worth it because we have accomplished a lot for this country. We've accomplished a lot on the world scene as well. Now I want to finish the job, finish the job by bringing opportunity and hope to all Americans, and I am very grateful to each and every one of you.

Thank you, and now off to the political wars. May God bless the United States of America. Thank you.

Note: The President spoke at 9:23 a.m. at the J.W. Marriott Hotel.

Remarks to the Law Enforcement Community in Oshkosh, Wisconsin
September 30, 1992

Thank you all on this beautiful day in Oshkosh. I am delighted to be here. I want to thank the Mayor and ask that he not send the bill—[*laughter*]—but thank him for the presentation. And I am very, very grateful to the men and women in law enforcement who are standing here, Officer DeBraska and Paul Bucher particularly, were up here speaking. It's also an honor to be introduced by one of the Nation's great, Governor Tommy Thompson. You're lucky out here, and I hope you know it.

But I am very honored and pleased to receive the endorsement of Wisconsin's law enforcement community: the State troopers, the Sheriffs Department Association, the Military Police Association, the Milwaukee Police Association.

You know, keeping our neighborhoods safe and secure is one of the fundamental responsibilities of government. It takes a tough, no-nonsense approach, one that puts our sympathy with the victims of crime, not with the criminals. After all, hard time is what criminals should get, not the innocent kids and older Americans who have to live in fear of violence. In this election, two candidates are talking tough on crime, but just one candidate is taking action. All I ask, and will be asking the American people in these debates if the other guy ever shows up—[*laughter*]—is look at the record.

Look at the record. Arkansas ranks near the bottom in every important per capita law enforcement expenditure: for prisons, 46th in the Nation; for judicial and legal systems, 50th; and when it comes to spending for police officers, Arkansas ranks 49th. Since 1989, we've proposed a 59-percent increase in Federal spending to fight crime.

Here's another snapshot on the Arkansas situation: Last year under Governor Clinton, Arkansas' criminals on average served just one-fifth of their sentence before they were back out on the street. They did crime, and then they serve one-fifth of the time. That is not right. And let me contrast that with the Federal inmates, the ones who fall under the Federal jurisdiction, my jurisdiction: Arkansas one-fifth of the time, and the Federal prisons an average 85 percent of their full sentence. A big difference in favor of the police officers, in favor of the victims of crime.

Crime is one more issue, one more area where the Governor of Arkansas cannot kind of slickly talk his way past his record. If you want to know who's really tough on crime, look around you here today. Look at the people that are out on the front line, putting their lives at risk for you and me every single day. That's who we ought to support, not worrying about how kind we want to be to these criminals.

And speaking of those who are on the front line, I was delighted—take a look at the Fraternal Order of Police in Little Rock, Arkansas. They've lived with Governor Clinton for 12 years, and they know his record best. And they endorsed me for President of the United States.

To you who put your lives on the line

every day, let me just say you have my thanks. But much more than that, you have our strong support. You are on the side of the law, and I am on your side. I wish you had a little more clout with the United States Congress. For 1,091 days, I believe the figure is, they are sitting on a strong anticrime bill that I sent up there 3½ years ago. And they've done absolutely nothing with it. That is not fair to the men and women who wear the uniform, who are out there supporting us. Whether it's in the courts or on the streets, we need to back them up with strong Federal anticrime legislation.

You know, with your strong support, I know that we can take back the streets and we can turn back the threat of drugs and crime and make our communities safer and more secure.

So thank you all very, very much, women and men of law enforcement, for your vote of confidence. May God bless the men and women who serve us. Thank you very, very much. Thank you.

Note: The President spoke at 11:20 a.m. at Wittman Regional Airport. In his remarks, he referred to Robert Jungwirth, Mayor of Oshkosh.

Remarks to the Community in Fond du Lac, Wisconsin
September 30, 1992

The President. Thank you, Governor Thompson. Thank all of you for that warm Fond du Lac welcome. And it's great, great to be here in your city, great to be back in the State of Wisconsin. Let me just say how pleased I am to be here with your Lieutenant Governor, Scott McCallum, who's doing a great job for the State; Anita Anderegg, the county executive here, a real leader; Cate Zeuske, the State treasurer. And let me also thank my longtime friend John MacIver, our Bush-Quayle Wisconsin chairman, for all his efforts. Unless you don't know it, you've got one of the greatest Governors in Tommy Thompson in the entire United States of America. He is an outstanding national leader. He's doing great things for this State. And he's working most cooperatively with Washington. I am very, very proud that he is my close, dear friend. And Barbara feels exactly the same way about him. I see some Tom Petri signs. We've got to reelect him to the United States Congress. He's a good man, a good Congressman. Reelect him.

Now, I understand that I'm visiting here the day before the Democratic candidates come to town.

Audience members. Boo-o-o!

The President. I can't resist saying, I don't think this is the last time that I'll be ahead of the Democratic ticket. We are going to win this election in November.

Audience members. Four more years! Four more years! Four more years!

The President. There's been a lot of discussion in the past week about Presidential debates. I think debates are important. I think the American people deserve to see the two candidates side by side. So yesterday, down in Tennessee, I challenged my opponent to a series of four television debates, the last four Sundays before the election. I said I'd be very flexible about the format, but I was eager to have the American people compare my ideas with Governor Clinton's. We have offered to meet with Governor Clinton's campaign anywhere, anytime. And so far at least, Governor Clinton has responded to my challenge the same way he responds to issues like free trade, fuel efficiency standards, and middle class taxes: He waffles. I can't find him. He's lost. He's missing in action. He refuses on this issue to take a position one way or the other, just like on all these other issues.

So this morning I renew my challenge to Governor Clinton: Let's have our people sit down, work this out. Let's have four debates with the formats that I like and the format that you like. And I'm no Oxford debater. I didn't spend a lot of time over in

Oxford, England, in the debating society. But I say let American people decide. Let's get up there and get it on, side by side.

Now, when we sit down to debate, and I hope the Governor will take a stand to agree to them, we should discuss the most important question: What kind of America do we want for the young people here today? Because of your sacrifice, because of your commitment, we have helped reduce the fear of nuclear annihilation. Today, our kids can dream the sweet dreams of peace without fear of nuclear war. And I am proud that that happened when I have been President of the United States. You listen to Governor Clinton, you might think national security of this country and foreign affairs are not important. They are. We've changed the world.

Now we face a new challenge. We must win the new global economic competition because that is the only way we'll create good jobs for our kids and our grandkids. And I've laid out my call for an Agenda for American Renewal, a comprehensive, integrated agenda to create in America by the 21st century the world's very first $10 trillion economy. And we can do it. We are Americans.

I know that many Americans are anxious about our economy today, concerned about our future. But we need to understand that we are experiencing the impact of a global economic slowdown. It isn't just the United States. It's being felt here at home, but it's also felt in Asia and Europe. Those countries would switch with us in a minute regarding economies.

My opponent spends a lot of time cutting down America, tearing it down, telling everybody how bad he thinks things are. I would remind him of a few facts, like the fact that when you go looking for the world's most productive workers and farmers, you don't look to Japan, you don't look to Germany; you look right here in the United States of America.

We need to build on our strengths. And so my agenda starts with a commitment to free and fair trade. And I want to use my experience in international affairs to open new markets for our products and services, because the American worker never retreats; we always compete. And we always win.

The people of Fond du Lac know this, but small business is the backbone of what we call the new American entrepreneurial capitalism. Small business will create two-thirds of the new jobs in this new economy. Governor Clinton promises small business relief from taxation, regulation, and yes, litigation. But if we're going to stay with him, we better see what the record is. He has a lousy record on regulation. And he certainly has a lousy record on litigation.

Now, if we're really going to renew America, attention must be paid to our children. It is tough to be a kid in America today. The face of poverty is too often a fresh face. The ignorant mind is too often—a young mind is too often something you can lose. And the spirit of hope and opportunity has too often been taken away from the young. We know what works to help our kids. We know, for example, that if you give a low-income kid a head start on kindergarten, they end up doing much better in school. And I am proud that today, for the very first time, every eligible kid who wants a head start can get one. That happened on my watch, and I'm very proud of it.

I am proud of our education revolution. Already 1,700 schools, including many right here in Wisconsin, have signed on to the national crusade to raise standards, to free the teachers—God bless those teachers—to free them from redtape, and to literally reinvent American schools. I want to go farther and give every parent the right to choose the best schools for their kids, public, private, or religious.

But if we really want to help those kids, we have to change the American system of child support. And the statistics there are not pretty: 1989, fathers were absent from 10 million families. Only a little more of half of absent parents are ordered to pay child support. Those required to pay, only half do, on time and in full. And only one in five absent parents pay for kids' health care. Each year, $5 billion in court-ordered child support, $5 billion, fails to reach families and kids who desperately need it.

These working parents, mostly mothers, are trying to keep their families going, trying to work, keep the kids on track, pay the bills. They need that check every month, and they deserve it. And I believe that since I took office we've made a very good start. We are now able to identify 50 percent more fathers of the kids of single moms, and we increased by more than 40 percent the cases of child support collections. With the aggressive leadership of Governors like your great Tommy Thompson, States collect over $2 billion more in child support. And that's a whole lot of good kids who are now getting some lunch money, money that they deserve.

That's something you and Wisconsin can take pride in. But the job's not finished. Today I want to build on your success with a new initiative called Project KIDS. Project KIDS will require all States to recognize and enforce other States' child support orders. And that will make it much easier to cross borders and catch those deadbeat parents in other States. We will require organizations who receive support from the Legal Services Corporation to devote 10 percent of their Federal funds to helping mothers who need legal help track down a deadbeat dad. And we will say to deadbeat parents: If you owe child support and you haven't paid, then you're going to pay a price. You'll get no passport, no professional licenses, no housing or student loans, or any other help from the Federal Government until you do right by your children. So the bottom is, if you haven't done what's right for your kids, don't expect any help from Uncle Sam from this day forward.

Now, by taking these steps, we think we can help reduce the stress on so many families. We can help single parents. And most importantly, we can lend a big hand to kids.

Now, while we're on the subject, maybe it's worth taking just a few minutes to consider Governor Clinton's record with children. I hate to do this to you on this beautiful sunny day here in Wisconsin. But in this area as in so many others, Governor Clinton talks a good game, but his record leaves something to be desired. Welfare is a kids' issue, because the more we can get people off welfare and into work, the more we strengthen the family. Here in Wisconsin, you are the leading State. Tommy Thompson is making real progress, promoting per-

sonal responsibility. Governor Clinton talks a good game, but when you look behind the rhetoric, there's nothing there. He's got a TV ad that talks about cutting the welfare rolls in Arkansas. What he neglects to mention is that while some people were leaving welfare, even more were going onto welfare. Since Bill Clinton was elected Governor, Arkansas' welfare rolls have increased by 19 percent, 13 percent faster than the rest of the Nation.

Now, he says he wants to do for America what he's done for Arkansas.

Audience members. Boo-o-o!

The President. I don't know whether that's a promise or a threat. America deserves better than that.

Look at the facts. Look at the facts about Arkansas. In the late 1980's, Arkansas' rate of violent deaths for teenagers soared at 3 times the national average. Over the decade, child abuse reports shot up 130 percent. And behind each one of those cases is a story of heartbreak. Arkansas' kids deserve to have their hearts healed.

Arkansas faced a special crisis of abuse in the State's foster homes. For years Governor Clinton ignored the problem until he was sued by welfare advocates in his own State. And only this summer, in the middle of his campaign, did he settle a lawsuit and take any steps to improve these homes. Now he's running around our great country, claimed to be an advocate for children. I urge all Americans, young and old, to take a look not just at his rhetoric but a hard look at Governor Clinton's record. I believe America can do better, and I believe we must do better by the young people in this country.

The economy is the major issue, let's look at it, a major issue in this campaign. When Bill Clinton became Governor 12 years ago, Arkansas, yes, was one of the poorest States in America. Today, Arkansas is still stuck at the bottom. And Bill Clinton's policies are responsible. As Governor, he raised and extended the sales tax, including a tax on baby formula, vegetables, and other groceries. He raised the gas tax. He taxed mobile homes and cable TV. And just for good measure he threw in a tax on beer. Now, how do you like that one?

Audience members. Boo-o-o!

The President. I didn't think you guys would like it. Now Governor Clinton says he's seen the light. In this campaign he's proposing at least $150 billion in new spending. But don't worry, he says, "I'm going to get it all from the rich," the people who make over $200,000, the top 2 percent. Well, but here's the truth, and here's the problem. To get the money he needs for his plan, the $150 billion that he's promised in new taxes, Governor Clinton would have to get his money from every individual with taxable income over $36,000. Now, these are not people on the "Lifestyles of the Rich and Famous." You deserve a break, not a further tax increase.

Audience members. Four more years! Four more years! Four more years!

The President. Look, you see, that's just the start of the tax campaign though, campaign against the middle class. He has literally made hundreds of promises in this campaign. He hasn't said how he'll pay for any one of his new programs. But his own hometown newspaper, the Pine Bluff Commercial, says, "If Congress followed the example that Bill Clinton set as Governor of Arkansas, it would pass a program that hit the middle class the hardest." We do not need that for the United States of America.

Now, the good Governor says he's going after all the millionaires, but he'll end up hitting all the nurses and teachers and cab drivers and construction workers. I say you pay enough to the tax man already. We do not need to add taxes to the working families in this country.

So it boils down to this: We cannot take a risk of a candidate with no experience, no track record, whose ideas and agenda are wrong for America. That is the basic thing: Governor Clinton is wrong for America.

Let me tell you something. In the Oval Office you face tough decisions. You cannot be on all sides of every question. You've got to call them as you see them. And I've made mistakes. Like any American, I'll admit it when I make a mistake. But I believe I've been a good, strong leader, willing to make the tough calls. I'm a leader whose ideas are right for America.

I stand before you today asking for your support so that we can change America, just as we have changed the entire world. I want a second term in office so we can continue to renew our schools, reform welfare, give our children a better shot at the American dream, and so we can continue to make lives better for American children by matching the peace around the world and by giving our kids peace of mind right here at home.

Let me say something, in conclusion, about service to country. I am very proud that I served my country in the uniform of the United States of America. I think that has helped me be a good Commander in Chief when we had to stand up against aggression halfway around the world. And that standing up against aggression has changed the world. Don't listen to the Governor who says we're less than Germany and slightly ahead of Sri Lanka. We are the most respected nation on the face of the Earth, admired by every country, the friends we have and those that used to be our foes.

So now, help me take that kind of leadership and help me change America to make life better for every single family in our great country. We are going to win Wisconsin, and we are going to win the Presidency because our ideas are right for America, this generation and generations to come.

May God bless the United States of America, the greatest country on the face of the Earth. Thank you very, very much.

Note: The President spoke at 12:45 p.m. in Veterans Memorial Park.

Remarks to the Law Enforcement Community in Newark, New Jersey
September 30, 1992

The President. Thank you all so very much. I mean, this is a tremendous event. I just can't tell you how much I appreciate the support of these men and women standing here. It transcends me personally. I think the fact is that this country must strongly support our law enforcement people. And I am grateful for this endorsement.

Let me just say that all of these organizations are important, the endorsement of the members of the New Jersey law enforcement community: the New Jersey Fraternal Order of Police; the Newark Policemen's Benevolent Association; New Jersey State Fraternal Association representatives that are here; representatives of the New Jersey Sheriffs Association and groups from Newark to Nutley, Glen Ridge, East Orange, Bloomfield, Belleville, Verona, Port Authority, Essex County; police, jails and prosecutors office; Union County and Montclair to the Morris County sheriff's office. And that's a fine endorsement, I'll tell you. I treasure them all and the support of these individuals.

I think we would all agree that keeping America's neighborhoods safe and secure is one of the most fundamental responsibilities of government. It takes a tough, no-nonsense approach, one that puts our sympathy with the victims of crime, not with the criminals. After all, hard time is what criminals should get, not the innocent kids and older Americans who have to live in fear of violence. In this election, the candidates both are talking tough on crime, but just one is taking action. All I'm going to ask the American people to do between now and November is to look at the record.

Arkansas ranks near the bottom in every important per capita law enforcement expenditures: for prisons, 46th; judicial and legal systems, 50th; and when it comes to spending for police officers, Arkansas ranks 49th. Since 1989, my administration has proposed a 59-percent increase in Federal spending to fight crime.

Here is another snapshot of the situation in Arkansas: Last year under Governor Clinton, Arkansas' criminals on average served just one-fifth of their sentence before they were back on the street. They did the crime, and they serve one-fifth of the time. That is not right. That's not protection for every family in this country. The Federal situation, the area under my control: Inmates who fall under my jurisdiction serve an average of 85 percent of their full sentence. And I'm not too happy of that; I would like to see it 100 in most of those cases.

But anyway, crime is one more issue where the Governor of Arkansas can't talk his way past his record. If you want to know who's really tough on crime, take a look at the people that are out there risking their lives for you and me every single day of their lives. Take a look at the people on the front lines. Take the Fraternal Order of Police down in Little Rock, for example. They lived with Bill Clinton for 12 years, and they know his record best. And they have endorsed George Bush for President of the United States.

Let me remind some of these officers of something some of them know and then might be new to some others. For 4 years I've kept a badge, a police badge, and I brought it along with me. I keep this in the desk in the Oval Office. I'm sure you've seen pictures of the President's desk on the television. This is number 14072 of the New York police force, city of New York. And I was given this by Police Lieutenant Matt Byrne. He gave it to me. It's the badge that his son Eddie wore the day he was gunned down by a gang of crackheads. And as Matt asked, I have kept that badge as a reminder of all the brave police officers who put their lives, put your lives, on the line for us every single day.

And yes, I'm grateful for this endorsement, these many endorsements, but it transcends that. You have my thanks for your service to your country. You have my support. You're on the side of the law, and I am on your side. With your strong support, I am absolutely convinced that we can make dramatic progress, more progress turning back the threat of drugs and crime, making our communities more safe and more secure. We talk of strengthening family. One way to strengthen family is give the families neighborhoods that are free of these criminals. That's what these people with me here today do every single day of their lives. And I am very, very grateful, grateful for this vote of confidence.

May God bless the men who wear the badge and the women who wear the badge and serve our great country. Thank you very much. Thank you all.

Audience members. Four more years! Four more years! Four more years!

Note: The President spoke at 5:42 p.m. at Newark International Airport.

Remarks to Construction Workers in Newark
September 30, 1992

The President. Thank you all.

Audience members. Four more years! Four more years! Four more years!

The President. Thank you guys. What a great welcome. This Richie—I'm glad to have been running against Clinton instead of this guy, I'll tell you. Richie Tissiere, thanks a lot. And may I salute also, as Rich did, appropriately in my view, our great Governor Tom Kean. We miss him, and hope—[*applause*]

I'm glad to be here with my new favorite number, 472. Thank you all very much. You know, as Tom said, Richie's a passionate advocate of the rights of working men and women and creating jobs. His reputation extends far beyond the borders of New Jersey. It's an honor to accept his invitation to join you here today. I've just invited him to come and be my guest at the Oval Office, and we're going to talk over some of the problems you guys face.

Now I know the work you do every day is rewarding, but it can also be back breaking in many cases here, even dangerous. I know that last Friday along the turnpike you were reminded of just how dangerous your work can sometimes be. And so before I go into a few remarks on the political situation, let me just say that Barbara and I were talking about this and that our hearts go out to the friends and families of the three who were involved in Friday's tragic accident. True working heroes, and our prayers are with all of you who call them friends.

Look, this afternoon I came to speak candidly at what's at stake in our election next month. And boy, did you give me a good, warm welcome walking into this place. I'll tell you, it's good for the soul. And it's been a good day.

I just came here after being endorsed by most of the law enforcement people in the State. I'm proud to have their endorsement because, I think we would all agree, we'd better stand with the law enforcement community against the criminal element and strengthen our neighborhoods. And they supported me, and I'm glad to have their support.

Right this minute, Governor Kean tells me that my opponent is over at his university. He got out of there fast. And so I figured that I'd take my case to the working people in New Jersey. I want to say as long as Governor Clinton is this nearby, I hope he accepts my challenge for four head-on-head debates. Let's get it on. Let's get it on, stand up there with him.

I've got plenty of questions to ask of him, and they relate to a lot of things that this crowd here cares about. So, I hope that they agree and sit down and get this format settled. I agreed to do two of the debates his way and ask only that they be done, two, the way that's been done under the last four Presidents and last four challengers. It seems to me that's fair enough. But he's been talking awful brave, sending these chickens around. Let's see him show up for the debates now.

For generations you know, and Rich touched on this, our Nation sacrificed, shed the tears of war so that freedom could triumph around the globe. As a young man, yes, I was proud to wear a military uniform and serve my country. That experience shaped my character. And I hope it has made me a better Commander in Chief of the Armed Forces of this country. For those that served in the country, let me put it this way: I do not loathe the military. When Governor Clinton wrote and said loathe the military, I said that's a shame. These people served their country with distinction and honor. We ought to salute them, not loathe them. Rich was telling me that many in this room served and sacrificed for an idea, a simple idea. It's called freedom. And today because of your efforts, backed by the taxpayers I might say, I can stand before you and say something no other President ever said: The cold war is over, and freedom finished first. We can all be proud of that as Americans.

Listen to the media and these talking heads and you listen to the opponents, you'd think that world peace doesn't mean anything. But does it matter at home? Of course, it does. Rich, you've got two grandkids, Richard and Rachel. Today because of America's sacrifice, these two kids and all our kids and grandkids won't have their days ruined by the thoughts of nuclear war. And does that matter? You bet it does. Look at these kids here.

I am very proud we got rid of those enormously destabilizing missiles when I sat down there in the marvelous White House with Boris Yeltsin. You think it wouldn't matter at all if you listened to the debate on the other side. It is very important to the future of these kids.

But look, this election isn't about the victories of the past. It's about what we're going to do in the future and our hopes for the future. It's about how we can win a new economic competition. Rich touched on it. We're in a global situation now. Not one of those European economies would hesitate a minute to trade for the United States in spite of the fact that we've got enormous economic difficulties. So I've put forward an Agenda for the American Renewal. It's a comprehensive series of steps that we've got to take to realize the global opportunity before us. My opponent likes to run down our country, say we're less than Germany, a little more than Sri Lanka. And I say we are still the greatest country on the face of the Earth.

Everybody in the world knows that, even if he doesn't, if you're looking for the most productive workers in the world, you turn to the United States of America. And so the question is this, even in these tough times how do we build on our strength? How do we keep America number one? How do we sell more abroad? My opponent has a great tendency to try to be all things to all people. Then they go before a business group and say one thing, labor group and then say another. And I am simply not going to do that.

Let me say straight out that the first part of my agenda is to promote free and fair trade, to open markets to American goods so that we can create more jobs right here in New Jersey. This is a trading State. One out of six jobs already depend on sales abroad. New Jersians know that. The American worker never retreats; we compete. And we win. So I'm going to keep on working to open these markets for our products.

Governor Clinton talks about a program of transportation investment. I'd like to point out we have one. It's a darned good one. I am proud that we have a 6-year $150 billion commitment to rebuild these roads and highways. And as we start the jackhammers and get the steamrollers moving, we will create over half a million new jobs, many right here in New Jersey. You deserve the work, and this bill will get the job done. We need new roads and bridges and highways, and we're going to keep on fighting for them.

And when it comes to the economy, my opponent and I have very different views. Beneath all his rhetoric about change, lies a very old policy: bigger Government in Washington, bigger bureaucracies, and more taxes on the working men and women of this country. I am going to stand up and fight him every inch of the way to get the taxes down, not raise them.

You know, for 11 months this guy's been

out telling falsehoods about my record, 11 months. I've just started defining the real record and talking about what he's done to the people of Arkansas. And when he became Governor 12 years ago, yes, Arkansas was one of the poorest States. But today they are stuck on the bottom. And Bill Clinton's policies are the reasons why. And we cannot let him do that to America.

He raised and extended the sales tax. He included a tax on baby formula. He included a tax on vegetables and other groceries. He raised the gas tax. And he taxed mobile homes and cable TV. You'd better iron it down, you'd better nail it down, or he'll tax it, whatever it is. We cannot have that for the United States. Coming out of the box, he's already proposed $150 billion new taxes, the biggest tax increase in American history. "And don't worry," he says, "I'll get it all from the rich." He says, "That's the top 2 percent."

But the problem is to get the money he needs from that new plan, the $150 billion that he's promised in new taxes, he'd have to get his money from every individual with a taxable income over $36,000 just to start. Then he's made literally more promises. And to pay for them, if he's going to do it the same way he says he's going to do taxing people, he has to tax families over about $22,000. And that is not the "Lifestyles of the Rich and Famous," that's you, your families, and everybody that's working for a living in this country. We cannot let it happen.

Hey listen, don't take my word for it. You don't have to take my word for it. Here's the Pine Bluff Commercial that's in his own State. Here's what he says: "If Congress followed the example that Bill Clinton set as Governor of Arkansas, it would pass a program that hit the middle class the hardest." And I don't think the Pine Bluff paper is bluffing. Let's say you work on the turnpike earning about $22,000 a year in taxable income. You already send $3,300 to the tax man. And he would have you fork over another $430 a year to send into the taxes so that Washington can figure it out. We do not need that for the United States of America.

And so we've got some big differences, and that's one of the reasons I look forward

to the debate. You don't need a crystal ball to think what he'd do to the national economy. We've got problems enough already, and they're big ones. And as I say, they're global. But if you want to know what it would be like under him, just look at New Jersey under Jim Florio for openers.

Audience members. Boo-o-o!

The President. Bring back Tom Kean. That's the way I feel about it. No, really. You had a big-spending Governor and a legislator to go along with him, Jim Florio. And look what happened: almost $3 billion in new taxes driving away half a million jobs, I'm told, in manufacturing and services. And here's the worst part: A State that had led the Nation, led the Nation under your friend Tom, became a laggard under Jim Florio. And I don't want to see that happen to the United States of America under Governor Clinton.

Florio did the same. This is an interesting point. Florio pushed through the massive increase in the sales tax, taxes that fell predominately on you and your families, the working people, and the elderly. Those are exactly the same people that Governor Clinton is aimed at in Arkansas. And I know he was recently in New Jersey, embracing Governor Florio. I would suggest that while Bill Clinton has his arm around Florio, he's really after the wallet in your pocket. So let's have him keep his hand off your hard-earned money. They deserve each other.

I believe we can invest, build our roads, and invest in America. But we can, and indeed we must, do it without raising taxes on the working family of this country. All we've got to do is set priorities. Here's Bill Clinton on the spending: He looked through the entire Federal budget. He found one program to cut, the $11 billion subsidy for honeybee growers. Believe me, no one's going to get stung by that courageous cut.

There is much more that can be taken out of it. I have spelled out 4,000 Government programs specifically that I'd eliminate, along with 246 programs. I've put forth a Government plan to control the growth of Government spending without touching Social Security and cutting almost $300 billion over the next 5 years. We've got to get the Government shaped to serve the people, not having the people serve the Government.

So, that's the only way we can cut taxes and still make our investment and create jobs for the working men and women. That's the major difference we've got in the campaign. And then buying my opponent's policies would be like going back to a used car lot, picking up the lemon you dropped off about 12 years ago, only this time there would be higher interest, higher taxes, and higher inflation thrown in. We simply cannot let this happen to the families and the working men and women of this country.

You know, Rich referred to this, we have changed the world in the past 4 years. And we've got to use that same talent to change America. Look, I'm the first to admit everybody's human. When I make a mistake, I admit it. And I've made mistakes. But I believed then that I, putting that aside, that I've been a good President. We've tried; Barbara and I have tried very hard——

Audience members. Four more years! Four more years! Four more years!

The President. We have tried very hard to uphold——

Audience members. Four more years! Four more years! Four more years!

The President. Come on, you guys. I've tried very hard to be a good leader. Barbara and I have tried very hard to uphold the principles that make this country strong. People talk about family values, and a lot of the press don't like it and the liberals don't like it. But I know what's important. It is important we find ways to strengthen and honor the American family, not rip it asunder by welfare programs that don't work.

We've got to strengthen the American family and that's what we're trying to do. When she reads to children or we go out and do things with families, we're trying to say let's strengthen the institution that has held this country together for years and years and years: respect for families, respect for law enforcement, discipline in schools, choice so that parents can choose the schools they want, private, religious, or public. All of those things strengthen the American family.

I am very grateful to you for this wonderful turnout and this enthusiastic response. And let me say this: Let somebody else tear American down. I am proud to have worn the uniform of the United States. I had to make some very tough decisions as President, particularly when you have to send somebody else's son or daughter off to a war. That is a tough decision to make. But we did it, and in the process we redeemed America as the strongest, fairest, most decent nation on the face of the Earth. And now I want to use that same leadership to lift up the families in this country and to give every working man and woman a better shot at the American dream.

I need your help. And thank you. And may God bless the United States of America.

Audience members. Four more years! Four more years! Four more years!

Note: The President spoke at 6:34 p.m. at the Heavy and General Construction Laborers Local 472 union headquarters. In his remarks, he referred to Richie Tissiere, president and business manager of Local 472.

Message to the House of Representatives Returning Without Approval the District of Columbia Appropriations Bill
September 30, 1992

To the House of Representatives:

I am returning herewith without my approval H.R. 5517, a bill providing appropriations for fiscal year 1993 for the District

of Columbia.

Although I do not object to the funding provided by the bill, its language concerning the use of funds for abortion is unacceptable. I have stated my intention to veto any bill that does not contain language that prohibits the use of all congressionally appropriated funds to pay for abortions except when the life of the mother would be endangered if the fetus were carried to term. The limitation I propose is identical to the one included in the District of Columbia Appropriations Acts for FY 1989, FY 1990, FY 1991, and FY 1992.

H.R. 5517 would place such a limitation on the use of Federal funds to pay for abortion. However, the bill would permit congressionally appropriated local funds to be used for abortions on demand. As a matter of law, the use of local funds in the District of Columbia must be approved by the Congress and the President through enactment of an appropriations act. Under these circumstances, the failure of H.R. 5517 to prohibit the use of all funds appropriated by the bill to pay for abortions, except in the limited circumstances mentioned above, is unacceptable.

From the outset of my Administration, I have repeatedly stated my deep personal concern about the tragedy in America of abortion on demand. As a Nation, we must protect the unborn. H.R. 5517 does not provide such protection. I am therefore returning H.R. 5517 without my approval.

GEORGE BUSH

The White House,
September 30, 1992.

Statement on Signing the Tourism Policy and Export Promotion Act of 1992
September 30, 1992

Today I am signing into law S. 680, the "Tourism Policy and Export Promotion Act of 1992." The Act authorizes appropriations for the United States Travel and Tourism Administration. This Federal agency promotes the United States as an international travel destination. It assists small and medium-sized U.S. travel and tourism companies in entering and competing in the international market.

The travel and tourism industry is America's third largest retail industry. It employs over six million workers, making it America's third largest employer. In 1991, travel and tourism generated $344 billion in receipts, accounting for a trade surplus of $16.8 billion. Both receipts and the surplus are expected to grow even larger in 1992. The health of this industry is important to our economic recovery.

In signing this legislation, I must note my concerns with one provision. S. 680 would establish the Rural Tourism Development Foundation as a charitable and nonprofit corporation to assist in the development and promotion of rural tourism. Although most of the provisions in the Act demonstrate an intent to establish the Foundation as a private entity, there are certain provisions that undermine this conclusion. Entities that are neither clearly governmental nor clearly private should not be created because they blur the distinction between public and private entities in a way that may diminish the political accountability of Government.

On balance, I believe the Congress intended to create the Foundation as a private entity. However, in order to remove any doubt as to the nature of the Foundation, I instruct the Attorney General and the Secretary of Commerce to prepare legislation for submission to the next Congress to amend this Act to ensure that the Foundation is considered solely a private entity.

GEORGE BUSH

The White House,
September 30, 1992.

Note: S. 680, approved September 30, was assigned Public Law No. 102–372.

Message to the Congress Transmitting Proposed Legislation on Violent Crime
September 30, 1992

To the Congress of the United States:

I am pleased to transmit for your immediate consideration and enactment the "Violent Crime Control Act of 1992." Also transmitted is a section-by-section analysis.

In a speech I delivered recently at the DeSales Catholic Church in Fox Park, Missouri, I outlined my crime agenda for the remainder of this Congress and for next year. I discussed several issues of particular concern to the families of this country such as carjacking, sexual and domestic assault, and gang violence. The enclosed legislative proposal addresses these critical problems.

As you know, I first proposed a comprehensive crime bill to the Congress on June 15, 1989. I again submitted a bill to the 102nd Congress on March 11, 1991. That bill, which has yet to be enacted, includes provisions for restoring and expanding the Federal death penalty, ending the abuse of habeas corpus, reforming the exclusionary rule, and establishing additional crimes and penalties involving the criminal use of firearms. The failure of the Congress to pass these pro-law enforcement proposals is particularly frustrating in light of the broad bipartisan support they enjoy.

I know that there is currently an effort being made to forge a genuine compromise that would include effective death penalty provisions and a version of habeas corpus reform that would be acceptable to me. It is my hope that the Congress will present me with such a compromise, one that is truly meaningful for Federal, State, and local law enforcement. This apparent willingness to work realistically on crime legislation provides the basis for me to call on this Congress to act quickly in its final days to pass the additional crime-fighting measures I am today proposing.

The bill I am transmitting today addresses several of the most significant current threats to public safety. It includes:

1. *New tools for fighting sexual violence* such as increased penalties, new rules of evidence and conduct for trial lawyers, expanded restitution for victims, and grants to State and local law enforcement.

2. *Anti-carjacking provisions* in the form of a new Federal crime, expanded use of law enforcement grants to the States, and a study of devices to prevent carjacking.

3. *Provisions for combatting domestic violence* such as a new Federal offense covering spouse abuse, violations of protective orders, and stalking, and a comprehensive grant program to fight domestic violence and enforce child support obligations.

4. *Anti-gang amendments,* including a new RICO-type offense for street gang activities, a new offense for involving a minor in the commission of a violent crime, and broadened adult prosecution of violent juveniles.

5. *New laws for child support enforcement* that will give the Federal Government the ability to punish criminally "deadbeat dads" who leave a State in order to avoid child support or who are significantly late in the payment of child support obligations. The legislation will also assist the States in the enforcement of child support orders.

6. *Increased penalties for crimes against the elderly* that will punish and deter criminals from assaulting or defrauding senior citizens.

7. *New crimes and penalties for the criminal use of firearms* such as a mandatory 10-year sentence for using a semiautomatic firearm in the course of a violent or drug trafficking crime, and a mandatory 5-year sentence for possession of a gun by a dangerous felon.

As the 102nd Congress draws to a close, the Congress has an opportunity to pass legislation that will have a major impact on many of the most serious crime problems facing Americans. The public wants decisive action from government to combat the menacing presence of violent criminals. Let us address this unfinished agenda now.

GEORGE BUSH

The White House,
September 30, 1992.

Message to the Congress Reporting on the National Emergency With Respect to Haiti
September 30, 1992

To the Congress of the United States:

1. On October 4, 1991, in Executive Order No. 12775, I declared a national emergency to deal with the threat to the national security, foreign policy, and economy of the United States caused by events that had occurred in Haiti to disrupt the legitimate exercise of power by the democratically elected government of that country (56 FR 50641). In that order, I ordered the immediate blocking of all property and interests in property of the Government of Haiti (including the Banque de la Republique d'Haiti) then or thereafter located in the United States or within the possession or control of a U.S. person, including its overseas branches. I also prohibited any direct or indirect payments or transfers to the *de facto* regime in Haiti of funds or other financial or investment assets or credits by any U.S. person or any entity organized under the laws of Haiti and owned or controlled by a U.S. person.

Subsequently, on October 28, 1991, I issued Executive Order No. 12779 adding trade sanctions against Haiti to the sanctions imposed on October 4, 1991 (56 FR 55975). Under this order, I prohibited exportation from the United States of goods, technology, and services, and importation into the United States of Haitian-origin goods and services, after November 5, 1991, with certain limited exceptions. The order exempts trade in publications and other informational materials from the import, export, and payment prohibitions, and permits the exportation to Haiti of donations to relieve human suffering as well as commercial sales of five food commodities: rice, beans, sugar, wheat flour, and cooking oil. In order to permit the return to the United States of goods being prepared for U.S. customers by Haiti's substantial "assembly

sector," the order also permitted, through December 5, 1991, the importation into the United States of goods assembled or processed in Haiti that contained parts or materials previously exported to Haiti from the United States. On February 5, 1992, it was announced that this exception could be applied for on a case-by-case basis by U.S. persons wishing to resume a pre-embargo import/export relationship with the assembly sector in Haiti.

2. The declaration of the national emergency on October 4, 1991, was made pursuant to the authority vested in me as President by the Constitution and laws of the United States, including the International Emergency Economic Powers Act (50 U.S.C. 1701 *et seq.*), the National Emergencies Act (50 U.S.C. 1601 *et seq.*), and section 301 of title 3 of the United States Code. I reported the emergency declaration to the Congress on October 4, 1991, pursuant to section 204(b) of the International Emergency Economic Powers Act (50 U.S.C. 1703(b)). The additional sanctions set forth in my order of October 28, 1991, were imposed pursuant to the authority vested in me by the Constitution and laws of the United States, including the statutes cited above, and implemented in the United States Resolution MRE/RES. 2/91, adopted by the Ad Hoc Meeting of Ministers of Foreign Affairs of the Organization of American States ("OAS") on October 8, 1991, which called on Member States to impose a trade embargo on Haiti and to freeze Government of Haiti assets. The present report is submitted pursuant to 50 U.S.C. 1641(c) and 1703(c), and discusses Administration actions and expenses directly related to the national emergency with respect to Haiti declared in Executive Order No. 12775, as

implemented pursuant to that order and Executive Order No. 12779.

3. On March 31, 1992, the Office of Foreign Assets Control of the Department of the Treasury ("FAC"), after consultation with the Department of State and other Federal agencies, issued the Haitian Transactions Regulations ("HTR"), 31 C.F.R. Part 580 (57 FR 10820, March 31, 1992), to implement the prohibitions set forth in Executive Orders No. 12775 and No. 12779. Since my last report, there have been two amendments to the HTR.

On June 5, 1992, new section 580.211 was added (57 FR 23954, June 5, 1992) prohibiting vessels calling in Haiti on or after that date from entering the United States without authorization by FAC. This amendment is explained more fully in section 6 of this report. In addition, effective August 27, 1992, new section 580.516 (57 FR 39603, September 1, 1992) authorizes the exportation to Haiti of certain additional food items (corn and corn flour, milk (including powdered milk), and edible tallow), as well as the issuance of specific licenses permitting, on a case-by-case basis, exports of propane for noncommercial use. Copies of these amendments are attached to this report.

4. The ouster of Jean-Bertrand Aristide, the democratically elected President of Haiti, in an illegal coup by elements of the Haitian military on September 30, 1991, was immediately repudiated and vigorously condemned by the OAS. The convening on September 30, 1991, of an emergency meeting of the OAS Permanent Council to address this crisis reflected an important first use of a mechanism approved at the 1991 OAS General Assembly in Santiago, Chile, requiring the OAS to respond to a sudden or irregular interruption of the functioning of a democratic government anywhere in the Western Hemisphere. As an OAS Member State, the United States has participated actively in OAS diplomatic efforts to restore democracy in Haiti and has supported fully the OAS resolutions adopted in response to the crisis, including Resolution MRE/RES. 2/91 and MRE/RES. 3/92.

5. In the first year of the Haitian sanctions program, FAC has made extensive use of its authority to specifically license transactions with respect to Haiti in an effort to mitigate the effects of the sanctions on the legitimate Government of Haiti and on the livelihood of Haitian workers employed by Haiti's export assembly sector having established relationships with U.S. firms, and to ensure the availability of necessary medicines and medical supplies and the undisrupted flow of humanitarian donations to Haiti's poor. For example, specific licenses have been issued (1) permitting expenditures from blocked assets for the operations of the legitimate Government of Haiti, (2) permitting U.S. firms with pre-embargo relationships with product assembly operations in Haiti to resume those relationships in order to continue employment for their workers or, if they choose to withdraw from Haiti, to return to the United States assembly equipment, machinery, and parts and materials previously exported to Haiti, (3) permitting U.S. companies operating in Haiti to establish, under specified circumstances, interest-bearing blocked reserve accounts in commercial or investment banking institutions in the United States for deposit of amounts owed the *de facto* regime, (4) permitting the continued material support of U.S. and international religious, charitable, public health, and other humanitarian organizations and projects operating in Haiti, and (5) authorizing commercial sales of agricultural inputs such as fertilizer and foodcrop seeds.

6. The widespread supply of embargoed goods, particularly petroleum products, to Haiti by foreign-flag vessels led to the adoption on May 17, 1992, by the Ad Hoc Meeting of Ministers of Foreign Affairs of the OAS of Resolution MRE/RES. 3/92 urging, among other things, a port ban on vessels engaged in trade with Haiti in violation of the OAS embargo. There was broad consensus among OAS member representatives, as well as European permanent observer missions, on the importance of preventing oil shipments to Haiti. Vessels from some non-OAS Caribbean ports and European countries have been involved in trade, particularly oil supplies, that undermines the embargo.

In response to Resolution MRE/RES. 3/92, section 580.211 was added to the HTR on June 5, 1992, prohibiting vessels calling in Haiti on or after that date from entering the United States without FAC authorization. Vessels seeking such authorization must demonstrate that all calls in Haiti on or after June 5 were (1) for transactions exempted or excepted from the applicable prohibitions of the HTR, (2) specifically licensed by FAC, or authorized by an OAS Member State pursuant to Resolution MRE/RES. 3/92, or (3) made under a contract of voyage that was fully completed prior to the vessel's proposed entry into a U.S. port.

Strict enforcement of the new regulation has benefitted from the close coordination between FAC, the U.S. Embassy at Port-au-Prince, the U.S. Customs Service, the U.S. Navy, and the U.S. Coast Guard in monitoring vessel traffic to and from Haiti.

7. Since the issuance of Executive Order No. 12779, FAC has worked closely with the U.S. Customs Service to ensure both that prohibited imports and exports (including those in which the Government of Haiti has an interest) are identified and interdicted and that permitted imports and exports move to their intended destinations without undue delay. Violations and suspected violations of the embargo are being investigated, and appropriate enforcement actions have been initiated.

Since my last report, penalties totalling more than $30,000 have been collected for U.S. banks for violations involving unlicensed transfers from blocked Government of Haiti accounts or the failure to block payments to the *de facto* regime. Additional penalties totaling nearly $175,000 have

been proposed for other violations of the HTR, including penalties against the masters of vessels violating the new regulation, effective June 5, 1992, applicable to vessels calling in Haiti on or after that date.

8. The expenses incurred by the Federal Government in the 6-month period from April 4, 1992, through October 3, 1992, that are directly attributable to the authorities conferred by the declaration of a national emergency with respect to Haiti are estimated at $2.3 million, most of which represent wage and salary costs for Federal personnel. Personnel costs were largely centered in the Department of the Treasury (particularly in FAC, the U.S. Customs Service, and the Office of the General Counsel), the Department of State, the U.S. Coast Guard, and the Department of Commerce.

9. The assault on Haiti's democracy represented by the military's forced exile of President Aristide continues to pose an unusual and extraordinary threat to the national security, foreign policy, and economy of the United States. The United States remains committed to a multilateral resolution of this crisis through its actions implementing the resolutions of the OAS with respect to Haiti. I shall continue to exercise the powers at my disposal to apply economic sanctions against Haiti as long as these measures are appropriate, and will continue to report periodically to the Congress on significant developments pursuant to 50 U.S.C. 1703(c).

GEORGE BUSH

The White House,
September 30, 1992.

Notice on Continuation of Haitian Emergency
September 30, 1992

On October 4, 1991, by Executive Order No. 12775, I declared a national emergency to deal with the unusual and extraordinary threat to the national security and foreign policy of the United States constituted by the grave events that had occurred in the Republic of Haiti to disrupt the legitimate

exercise of power by the democratically elected government of that country. On October 28, 1991, by Executive Order No. 12779, I took additional measures by prohibiting, with certain exceptions, trade between the United States and Haiti. Because the assault on Haiti's democracy represented by the military's forced exile of President Aristide continues to pose an unusual and extraordinary threat to the national security, foreign policy, and economy of the United States, I am continuing the national emergency with respect to Haiti in accordance with section 202(d) of the National Emergencies Act (50 U.S.C. 1622(d)).

This notice shall be published in the *Federal Register* and transmitted to the Congress.

GEORGE BUSH

The White House,
September 30, 1992.

[*Filed with the Office of the Federal Register, 11:41 a.m., September 30, 1992*]

Message to the Congress on Continuation of the National Emergency With Respect to Haiti
September 30, 1992

To the Congress of The United States:

Section 202(d) of the National Emergencies Act (50 U.S.C. 1622(d)) provides for the automatic termination of a national emergency unless, prior to the anniversary date of its declaration, the President publishes in the *Federal Register* and transmits to the Congress a notice stating that the emergency is to continue in effect beyond the anniversary date. In accordance with this provision, I have sent the enclosed notice, stating that the Haitian emergency is to continue in effect beyond October 4, 1992, to the *Federal Register* for publication.

The crisis between the United States and Haiti that led to the declaration on October 4, 1991, of a national emergency has not been resolved. The assault on Haiti's democracy represented by the military's forced exile of President Aristide continues to pose an unusual and extraordinary threat to the national security, foreign policy, and economy of the United States. The United States remains committed to a multilateral resolution of this crisis through its actions implementing the resolutions of the Organization of American States with respect to Haiti. For these reasons, I have determined that it is necessary to maintain in force the broad authorities necessary to apply economic pressure to the *de facto* regime in Haiti.

GEORGE BUSH

The White House,
September 30, 1992.

Message to the Senate Transmitting the Barbados-United States Taxation Protocol
September 30, 1992

To the Senate of the United States:

I transmit herewith for Senate advice and consent to ratification the Protocol Amending the Convention Between the United States of America and Barbados for the Avoidance of Double Taxation and the Prevention of Fiscal Evasion with Respect to Taxes on Income signed on December 31, 1984, which protocol was signed at Washington on December 18, 1991. I also transmit for the information of the Senate the Report of the Department of State.

In addition, I transmit herewith, for the information of the Senate, Understandings Regarding the Scope of the Limitation on Benefits Article in the U.S.—Barbados Protocol. Although not submitted for the advice and consent of the Senate to ratification, this document is relevant to the consideration of the protocol by the Senate.

The protocol amends the 1984 income tax convention with Barbados, which has been in force since February 28, 1986, to modify certain provisions of the convention. I recommend that the Senate give early and favorable consideration to the protocol and give its advice and consent to ratification.

GEORGE BUSH

The White House,
September 30, 1992.

Letter to Congressional Leaders Transmitting a Report on a Schedule for Resumption of Nuclear Testing Talks
September 30, 1992

Dear Mr. Speaker: (Dear Mr. President:)

Enclosed, pursuant to section 3140 of the National Defense Authorization Act for Fiscal Years 1992 and 1993 (Public Law 102–190; 105 Stat. 1581), is a Report on a Schedule for Resumption of Nuclear Testing Talks. The report is in both classified and unclassified versions.

Sincerely,

GEORGE BUSH

Note: Identical letters were sent to Thomas S. Foley, Speaker of the House of Representatives, and Dan Quayle, President of the Senate.

Presidential Determination No. 92–48—Memorandum on Counternarcotics Assistance for Colombia
September 30, 1992

Memorandum for the Secretary of State, the Secretary of Defense

Subject: Presidential Determination to Drawdown DOD Stocks for Counternarcotics Assistance for Colombia

Pursuant to the authority vested in me by Section 506(a)(2) of the Foreign Assistance Act of 1961, as amended, 22 U.S.C. 2318(a)(2) (the "Act"), I hereby determine that it is in the national interest of the United States to drawdown defense articles from the stocks of the Department of Defense, defense services of the Department of Defense, and military education and training for the purpose of providing coun-

ternarcotics assistance to Colombia.

Therefore, I hereby direct the drawdown of up to $7 million of such defense articles from the stocks of the Department of Defense, defense services of the Department of Defense, and military education and training for the purposes and under the authorities of Chapter 8 of Part I of the Act.

The Acting Secretary of State is authorized and directed to report this determination to the Congress, and to arrange for its publication in the *Federal Register*.

GEORGE BUSH

[*Filed with the Office of the Federal Register, 4:10 p.m., October 8, 1992*]

Presidential Determination No. 92–49—Memorandum on Disaster Assistance for Pakistan
September 30, 1992

Memorandum for the Secretary of State, the Secretary of Defense

Subject: Presidential Determination to Drawdown DOD Stocks for Disaster Assistance for Pakistan

Pursuant to the authority vested in me by Section 506(a)(2) of the Foreign Assistance Act of 1961, as amended, 22 U.S.C. 2318 (a)(2) (the "Act"), I hereby determine that it is in the national interest of the United States to drawdown defense articles from the stocks of the Department of Defense, defense services of the Department of Defense, and military education and training, for the purpose of providing disaster assistance in Pakistan.

Therefore, I hereby authorize the furnishing of up to $5 million of such defense articles from the stocks of the Department of Defense, defense services of the Department of Defense, and military education and training, for the purposes and under the authorities of Chapter 9 of Part I of the Act.

The Acting Secretary of State is authorized and directed to report this determination to the Congress and to arrange for its publication in the *Federal Register.*

GEORGE BUSH

[*Filed with the Office of the Federal Register, 4:11 p.m., October 8, 1992*]

Statement by Press Secretary Fitzwater on the National Education Goals Panel Report
September 30, 1992

This year's report of the National Education Goals Panel shows we have made strides in increasing the high school completion rate of our youth and in eradicating drug use in schools. These positive results are the most compelling evidence of the effectiveness of the reform policies we have pursued over the past 3 years.

The President called the Nation's Governors together in 1990 for an education summit in Charlottesville, Virginia, where the participants set a strategic vision to improve American education by concentrating their efforts on reaching six national education goals. The National Education Goals Panel is charting the progress toward achieving these goals.

The President today recognizes those who have embraced the goals and who are working to establish rigorous national standards for what American children should know and be able to achieve. Continued support for this initiative and for the President's efforts to establish a voluntary system of achievement tests tied to world class standards will ensure that all citizens are able to live, work, and compete in an international marketplace.

Appointment of Andrew M. Carpendale as Deputy Assistant to the President for Policy Planning, Development, and Speechwriting
September 30, 1992

The President today announced the appointment of Andrew M. Carpendale as Deputy Assistant to the President for Policy Planning, Development, and Speechwriting.

Since June 1992, Mr. Carpendale has served as Deputy Director (Designate) on the State Department's Policy Planning Staff. He oversaw planning staff work on Western and Eastern Europe, Russia, and Eurasia, as well as political-military issues and arms control. From May 1990 to May 1992, he was Director of Speechwriting and Senior Adviser for Russian and Eurasian Affairs, Policy Planning Staff, Department of State. His duties included overseeing speechwriting for the Secretary of State as well as advising the Director of Policy Planning on issues related to Russian and Eurasian affairs. From January 1989 to April 1990, he was Special Assistant to the Director of Policy Planning.

As an undergraduate, Mr. Carpendale studied at the University of California, Santa Barbara, and the London School of Economics, receiving his bachelor's degree in June 1984 from the University of California in political science and economics. He received his master's degree from the University of California, Berkeley, in December 1986. He currently resides in the District of Columbia.

Excerpt of a White House Fact Sheet on the Child Support Enforcement Initiative—Project KIDS
September 30, 1992

The President announced today a new comprehensive child support enforcement strategy to ensure that absent parents pay child support, no matter where they live. The President's initiative, Project KIDS (Keep Irresponsible Dads Supportive), will:

Require wage withholding for absent parents. Universal employer income withholding would be required, and payroll withholding would follow absent parents from job to job. The tax withholding forms would be updated to include information on child support responsibilities.

Overdue child support will become tax liabilities. Delinquent absent parents would face stiff penalties, and delinquent payments would be treated as tax liabilities collectible by State tax authorities and the Internal Revenue Service. Payments collected would be paid to custodial parents.

Recognize all child support orders in all States. Require all States to recognize and enforce child support orders established in other States. Place jurisdiction for child support disputes in one State.

Interstate nonpayment of child support as a Federal crime. Parents who fail to meet major interstate child support obligations, or who leave the State to evade those obligations, could face imprisonment.

Cover health services in child support orders. Absent parents would be required to cover children under their employer's health plan when coverage is available at reasonable cost.

Restrict access to Federal benefits for nonpaying parents. Any parent who is delinquent in child support payments would need a payment or deferral plan before qualifying for any new Federal benefits. Existing benefits will be garnished in the amount of the award and sent directly to the custodial parent.

Keep up with absent parents. Custodial parents will get better access to existing records to track down absent parents, and new information will be kept to track down "deadbeat dads" when they change jobs.

No payment/no passport. Deadbeat parents could not qualify for a passport, and existing passports could be withdrawn.

No payment/no professional license. Deadbeat parents could not have State or Federal professional licenses issued or renewed.

No payment/no Federal loans or loan guarantees. If deadbeat parents have not met obligations or do not have a plan to do so, they could not qualify for FHA home loans, guaranteed student loans, or any other Federal loan guarantee.

Report all delinquent parents to credit bureaus. Deadbeat parents will risk losing access to private credit.

Better legal services for custodial parents. Any legal services organization receiving funds from the Legal Services Corporation (LSC) must use at least 10 percent of its LSC funding to help eligible custodial parents obtain child support.

Make the Federal Government a model employer. Require up-to-date employer records and immediate payroll withholding.

Statement on Signing the Older Americans Act Amendments of 1992
September 30, 1992

Today I am signing into law H.R. 2967, the "Older Americans Act Amendments of 1992." The bill extends and amends important programs under the Older Americans Act of 1965 (OAA) and the Native American Programs Act of 1974 (NAPA), including provisions for a White House Conference on Aging.

H.R. 2967 strengthens provisions of the OAA and supports expanded opportunities and services for our Nation's 42 million older Americans.

The OAA has enabled millions of older Americans to live with independence and dignity in their own homes and communities. Programs sponsored under the OAA have had many positive results. They have provided older persons with a range of supportive in-home and community services; led to the development of gerontological curricula at our Nation's universities and colleges; and tested innovative ways of better meeting the needs of older persons. The OAA also provides opportunities for part-time employment for low-income persons aged 55 or older.

H.R. 2967 promises to further these goals. It provides for the increased participation of minority elders in OAA programs and sets up intergenerational services at meal sites in public schools that will benefit both older Americans and at-risk children. It also offers supportive services to the thousands of family caregivers who make it possible for the frail elderly to remain in their own homes and communities.

This bill supports the goal of the OAA to end the tragedy of elder abuse. It establishes a new Elder Rights Title of the OAA to consolidate long-term care ombudsman services, legal assistance, and outreach and counseling for elderly who are institutionalized or at risk of losing their independence.

H.R. 2967 also extends the programs under NAPA. These programs have had an important role for nearly two decades in promoting the social and economic self-sufficiency of Native Americans through grants to the governing bodies of Indian tribes and other Native American groups.

The bill, however, does contain provisions that raise constitutional concerns regarding the separation of powers. One provision would establish a policy committee for the White House Conference on Aging that is not clearly legislative or executive. I must therefore interpret the policy committee's role as entirely advisory. H.R. 2967 also requires the Secretary of Health and Human Services to submit recommendations and final guidelines to improve nutrition services to the Speaker of the House and the President pro tempore of the Senate. As the head of the executive branch, I will interpret this provision so as to maintain my constitutional authority to supervise my subordinates as I deem appropriate.

H.R. 2967 expands legislation to aid older Americans and their families. It is one way of demonstrating our commitment and thanks to those older people who have done so much to make America the great Nation that it is today.

GEORGE BUSH

The White House,
September 30, 1992.

Note: H.R. 2967, approved September 30, was assigned Public Law No. 102–375. This statement was released by the Office of the Press Secretary on October 1.

Remarks at the Ethanol Waiver Announcement Ceremony
October 1, 1992

Thank you all very much, and welcome to the Rose Garden. Please be seated. Let me just thank Senator Dole and Congressman Michel, two of our leaders of the Congress, for being here; Governor Edgar, the Governor of Illinois, with me; Tim Trotter from the Corn Growers, from the National Corn Growers; and Bill Reilly over here. Bill, come up here now. We need you up here to show a little hands across the border here. [*Laughter*] Ann Veneman is here from the Ag Department, the Deputy Secretary; Linda Stuntz, the Deputy Secretary of Energy, is with us, Linda; and other Members of Congress. Welcome, all. Governor Thompson wanted to be here, Tommy Thompson, but could not make it this afternoon.

I've asked you all to come here today because we have a very positive announcement, one that will help America's farmers, one that will help clean our air, and one that will promote our energy security by increasing the use of domestically produced renewable fuels.

I'm announcing today that the administration has decided to effectively grant a one-pound volatility waiver for ethanol, and to do so in a way that is fully consistent with the Clean Air Act and protective of the environment. This one-pound waiver will apply to all reformulated gasoline blended with ethanol sold in northern U.S. cities in up to 30 percent of the market of these cities. As you know, the Clean Air Act requires that the smoggiest of these cities

reduce smog-forming emissions by 15 percent in the summer months. And to make sure that this reduction is achieved, we will require that the volatility of gasoline sold in these cities be reduced to 7.8 pounds per square inch.

Gasoline with this volatility level is being sold in southern cities under current regulations right now. So we have confidence that it can be achieved at little cost to the consumer. In fact, our estimate is that the effect on the price of gasoline would be only about three-tenths of a penny.

Our program also permits ethanol use to expand even further. The Governors of States in the northern tier will have the right to allow a waiver on a higher percentage of the market, and if they order further compensating emission reductions. The waiver we are announcing today will apply to all the cities in the north that are required to adopt reformulated gasoline by 1995 and to all northern cities in States that choose to opt into this program.

When southern States choose to opt into the reformulated gas program, they will be able to choose between the regular reformulated gasoline program and one in which ethanol is granted a one-pound waiver for up to 20 percent of the market, with offsetting volatility reductions that would require that gasoline with 7.0 RVP be sold.

Again, we expect gasoline of this kind to be sold in California in 1996, so we know it is possible to proceed in this way. In addition, if ethanol blenders can secure voluntary agreements to get this lower volatility gasoline, they can receive a corresponding waiver under the regular reformulated gasoline program in the South.

Today's waiver is just one part of our program to promote ethanol. We're also going to work for the enactment of an additional tax incentive for ETBE. We're going to expedite the development of the complex model that measures all types of emissions so that the full smog-reducing benefits of ethanol can be measured. For the coming winter, we're going to make sure that all 39 cities that need help in reducing carbon monoxide participated in the oxygenated fuel program.

The bottom line is this: Clean-building ethanol can help reduce pollution. It is domestically produced. It is renewable. This waiver will allow ethanol to participate in both the summer and winter programs required under the Clean Air Act. It will do so in a way that protects all of the environment, all of the environmental benefits that we worked so hard for when that law was enacted.

I know that this question of how to allow ethanol to play a role in our reformulated gasoline program has been extraordinarily complex and a very difficult one. But I am pleased that this creative solution allows us to proceed in a way that is good for farmers, good for rural America, good for the environment in our cities, and good for American consumers and motorists.

So I congratulate all those who have worked hard to achieve this result. Thank you all very much for coming. Thank you very much. That concludes our little ceremony.

Well, I'm very pleased. I was just asking Bill if he feels very comfortable with it, and he does. And God knows, he's got good environmental credentials, the best.

Well, thank you all very much for coming down. Concludes a happy event. Thank you.

Note: The President spoke at 2:35 p.m. in the Rose Garden at the White House. In his remarks, he referred to William K. Reilly, Environmental Protection Agency Administrator.

Statement on Senate Ratification of the Strategic Arms Reduction Treaty
October 1, 1992

I am pleased that the Senate today gave its consent to the ratification of the Strategic Arms Reduction Treaty, START. The START negotiations began 10 years ago. These long years of negotiations culminated in an historic agreement, first with the Soviet Union and then with Russia, Ukraine, Byelarus, and Kazakhstan; true strategic arms reductions, not just limitations or controls.

START reduces United States and former Soviet strategic weapons by about 40 percent and makes even deeper cuts in the weapons of greatest concern, fast-flying ballistic missiles.

It also helps to ensure that the demise of the Soviet Union does not stimulate nuclear proliferation. In START, Ukraine, Byelarus,

and Kazakhstan have all agreed to join the Nuclear Non-Proliferation Treaty as non-nuclear-weapon states and to guarantee the elimination of strategic nuclear forces from their territory.

Finally, this historic agreement has paved the way for further path-breaking steps and far-reaching reductions. In large part because of START's verification provisions, I was able in my September 1991 and January 1992 initiatives to make major *unilateral* nuclear reductions and successfully challenge Presidents Gorbachev and Yeltsin to do the same. Of even greater significance, the START framework permitted President Yeltsin and me to reach agreement at our summit meeting last June, after just 5 months of negotiation, on extraordinary further reductions in strategic nuclear weapons. All the agreements reached over the past year, beginning with START, will reduce our strategic nuclear forces by about 75 percent from their 1990 level. As such, START and follow-on understandings have done much to reverse the hands on the nuclear doomsday clock.

With the Senate's action this morning, the United States will be prepared to ratify the START Treaty once the other four parties have acted. I would note with satisfaction that the Government of Kazakhstan has already approved START, and I urge the remaining parties, Russia, Byelarus, and Ukraine, to approve this historic treaty promptly, so its mandated reductions can begin without delay.

Message to the Congress Reporting Budget Deferrals
October 1, 1992

To the Congress of the United States:

In accordance with the Congressional Budget and Impoundment Control Act of 1974, I herewith report seven deferrals of budget authority, totaling $930.9 million.

These deferrals affect International Security Assistance programs as well as programs of the Agency for International Development and the Departments of Agriculture, Defense, Health and Human Services, and State. The details of these deferrals are contained in the attached report.

GEORGE BUSH

The White House,
October 1, 1992.

Note: The report detailing the deferrals was published in the Federal Register on October 9.

Statement on Signing the Continuing Appropriations Bill
October 1, 1992

I am today signing this legislation to provide for the continuing operation of the Government for the brief period between now and October 5, 1992, during which legislation is enacted providing for annual appropriations. I note that in some cases this bill incorporates by reference appropriations levels determined by action by one or both houses of Congress as of October 1, 1992. Because laws can be enacted only by the action of both houses and the President, see U.S. Const., Art. I, sec. 7; *INS v. Chadha*, 462 U.S. 919 (1983), I sign this bill on the understanding that no action taken on that date subsequent to my approval at 8:10 a.m. o'clock E.D.T. is incorporated. For the same reason, section 106(b) can be effective only if interpreted to mean enactment of the referenced appropriations bills into law.

GEORGE BUSH

The White House,
October 1, 1992.

Note: H.J. Res. 553, approved October 1, was assigned Public Law No. 102–376.

Statement by Press Secretary Fitzwater on Assistance to Refugees of Nagorno-Karabakh
October 1, 1992

The United States is contributing more than $2,150,000 to the American Red Cross (ARC) to provide emergency food and shelter for Armenian refugees who have fled the conflict in Nagorno-Karabakh and are currently in Armenia.

The ARC will use these funds to provide food assistance to 15,000 families. This assistance will be in the form of monthly food parcels meant to supplement nutritional shortfalls experienced by the refugee population. The funds will also be used to provide emergency shelter in the form of winterized tents. These tents will provide emergency shelter for up to 5,970 persons.

This assistance is in addition to U.S. Government contributions to the International Committee of the Red Cross (ICRC) of more than $2,840,000 in support of its humanitarian aid to war victims, refugees, and other vulnerable groups in Armenia and Nagorno-Karabakh. These contributions together provide a total of $5 million for humanitarian assistance to Armenian refugees and victims of conflict since January 1992.

In addition to these contributions, the President has authorized $2 million in U.S. Government support for a CSCE Observer Force to promote a peaceful settlement to the Nagorno-Karabakh conflict. The President has also offered Armenia $15 million under the Food for Progress program.

They are an expression of the administration's support for the Armenian Government led by President Levon Ter-Petrosyan and of our commitment to help achieve a lasting peace in the area.

Remarks on Signing the Energy and Water Development Appropriations Act, 1993
October 2, 1992

Let me just say this is a good morning here. And thank you all for coming, some from a long way. I first want to welcome those who are here from the Superconducting Super Collider Laboratory, those here, and also say welcome to those that are watching this back in Texas. My greetings to the Members of Congress who fought hard for this legislation.

We're here today to take another step into the future, an American future that really offers unprecedented opportunities in our country's history. The task before us is to grasp those opportunities and to make them available for every American.

The great question today is not whether America will compete in the new century. You and I know that we will. The question is how we compete, how we remain the world's leader, not only militarily and politically but economically as well. In large measure, the answer lies in pushing back the frontiers of human knowledge so that daring and ideas and dreams of this decade become the everyday life of the next. We have part of that answer before us this morning, a cornerstone of our agenda to keep America at the forefront of science.

The appropriations bill that I'm about to sign provides support for all fields of science and technology. It ensures that one of the greatest adventures in human knowledge will continue. The superconducting super collider is to basic research what the All-Star game is to baseball. Already it has brought together the finest scientific minds in the world, academic scientists, industrial technologists, laboratory researchers, a collection of talent and brainpower not seen since the great research projects of World War II; and all of this scientific talent, backed by the greatest workers in the world at all levels.

In the short term, the superconducting super collider will mean jobs, at least 7,000 first-tier jobs across the country, and already 23,000 contracts have been awarded to businesses and to universities. I'm especially pleased by the participation of those small businesses from 40 States who will help build the SSC.

In the longer term, the tangible benefits of the SSC will be felt by every single American. Time and again, history has shown that advances in abstract knowledge have the most practical of consequences. The work done with the SSC will bear fruit in new industries, new jobs, new breakthroughs in medicine and chemicals, transportation, and electronics. The list stretches into fields of knowledge we can only imagine today.

Ten days from now, we will mark the 500th anniversary of a dramatic landfall, the moment when Christopher Columbus set foot in a new world. And his spirit of fearless exploration survives. Today, Americans set sail not for new continents but for new ideas, not for new passageways but for new ways of knowing. Our frontier is the human imagination; our vessel, the super collider.

I believe that the bill I'm about to sign shows us that we've reached a consensus about the super collider and more really about the future.

I thank all of you here today who share our commitment, who worked so hard to ward off the shortsighted attempts to kill off the super collider. With your help and faith, we will ensure that America remains for all its people the country of tomorrow.

Thank you all very much for coming. And now I have the honor to sign this bill. I congratulate once again every single Member of Congress who worked with these leaders of Congress here with us today to bring this about.

Note: The President spoke at 8:04 a.m. in the Roosevelt Room at the White House. H.R. 5373, approved October 2, was assigned Public Law No. 102–377.

Statement on Signing the Energy and Water Development Appropriations Act, 1993
October 2, 1992

Today I have signed into law H.R. 5373, the "Energy and Water Development Appropriations Act, 1993." The Act provides funding for the Department of Energy. The Act also provides funds for the water resources development activities of the Corps of Engineers and the Department of the Interior's Bureau of Reclamation, as well as funds for various related independent agencies such as the Appalachian Regional Commission, the Nuclear Regulatory Commission, and the Tennessee Valley Authority.

I am pleased that the Congress has provided funding for the Superconducting super collider (SSC). This action will help us to maintain U.S. leadership in the field of high-energy physics. SSC-related research has spawned, and will continue to spawn, advances in many fields of technology, including accelerators, cryogenics, superconductivity, and computing. The program serves as a national resource for inspiring students to pursue careers in math and science. SSC-related work will support 7,000 first tier jobs in the United States. In addition, 23,000 contracts have been awarded to businesses and universities around the country.

I must, however, note a number of objectionable provisions in the Act. Specifically, Section 507 of H.R. 5373, which concerns nuclear testing, is highly objectionable. It may prevent the United States from conducting underground nuclear tests that are necessary to maintain a safe and reliable nuclear deterrent. This provision unwisely restricts the number and purpose of U.S. nuclear tests and will make future U.S. nuclear testing dependent on actions by another country, rather than on our own national security requirements. Despite the dramatic reductions in nuclear arsenals, the United States continues to rely on nuclear deterrence as an essential element of our national security. We must ensure that our forces are as safe and reliable as possible. To do so, we must continue to conduct a minimal number of underground nuclear tests, regardless of the actions of other countries. Therefore, I will work for new legislation to permit the conduct of a modest number of necessary underground nuclear tests.

In July 1992, I adopted a new nuclear testing policy to reflect the changes in the international security environment and in the size and nature of our nuclear deterrent. That policy imposed strict new limits on the purpose, number, and yield of U.S. nuclear tests, consistent with our national security and safety requirements and with our international obligations. It remains the soundest approach to U.S. nuclear testing.

Sections 304 and 505 of the Act also raise constitutional concerns. Section 304 would establish certain racial, ethnic, and gender criteria for businesses and other organizations seeking Federal funding for the development, construction, and operation of the Superconducting super collider. A congressional grant of Federal money or benefits based solely on the recipient's race, ethnicity, or gender is presumptively unconstitu-

tional under the equal protection standards of the Constitution.

Accordingly, I will construe this provision consistently with the demands of the Constitution and, in particular, monies appropriated by this Act cannot be awarded solely on the basis of race, ethnicity, or gender.

Section 505 of the Act provides that none of the funds appropriated by this or any other legislation may be used to conduct studies concerning "the possibility of changing from the currently required 'at cost' to a 'market rate' or any other noncost-based method for the pricing of hydroelectric power" by Federal power authorities.

Article II, section 3, of the Constitution grants the President authority to recommend to the Congress any legislative measures considered "necessary and expedient." Accordingly, in keeping with the well-settled obligation to construe statutory provisions to avoid constitutional questions, I will interpret section 505 so as not to infringe on the Executive's authority to conduct studies that might assist in the evaluation and preparation of such measures.

GEORGE BUSH

The White House,
October 2, 1992.

Note: H.R. 5373, approved October 2, was assigned Public Law No. 102–377.

Statement on National Energy Strategy Legislation
October 2, 1992

I strongly urge the 102d Congress to pass the national energy strategy before it adjourns. For the last 18 months, my administration has worked diligently with the Congress to produce the most comprehensive national energy strategy in 20 years. This bipartisan legislation was crafted not in a time of crisis but in a time when our long-term energy needs could be addressed with balance and reason.

The conference report to the national energy strategy will soon come before the

Congress. This bill is good news for Americans. The legislation will increase conservation efforts, promote domestic renewable resources and alternative fuels, increase competition in the electric utility industry and reduce consumer costs, and remove regulatory barriers to increased use of clean-burning natural gas. The bill also provides much-needed alternative minimum tax (AMT) relief for independent oil and gas producers, thus removing a substantial disincentive to domestic oil and gas production.

Congress has demonstrated overwhelming support for the national energy strategy. The Senate passed this legislation on July 30 by a vote of 93–3, and the House passed it on May 27 by a vote of 381–37. This legislation should not fall victim to the end-of-year rush to adjourn. The Congress should not adjourn without passing this legislation.

Statement on Humanitarian Assistance to Bosnia
October 2, 1992

All Americans, and people of compassion everywhere, remain deeply troubled by the cruel war in Bosnia and the broader turmoil in what was Yugoslavia. We took several important initiatives in August, and today I am announcing further steps to help ease this conflict.

The United States has been working intensively with other concerned nations to contain the conflict, alleviate the human misery it is causing, and exact a heavy price for aggression. This international effort has produced some results. The recent London conference set up an international mechanism for addressing all aspects of the Yugoslav problem and put in motion an active negotiation. The tenuous truce in Croatia is holding. International observers are on their way to neighboring countries and other parts of the former Yugoslavia to prevent the violence from spreading. The United Nations trade embargo has idled roughly half the industry of Serbia, whose leader bears heavy responsibility for the aggression in Bosnia. Our demand that the Red Cross be given access to detention camps has begun to yield results, and the release of detainees has now begun. The U.N. resolution we obtained to authorize "all necessary measures" to get relief supplies into Bosnia has led to the creation of a new U.N. force to be deployed for that purpose.

We will continue to honor our pledge to get humanitarian relief to the people of Sarajevo and elsewhere in Bosnia. To this end, I have directed the Secretary of Defense to resume American participation in the Sarajevo airlift tomorrow morning. I wish I could say that there is no risk of attack against these flights, but I cannot, although we are taking precautions. We can be proud of the Americans who, along with courageous personnel from other countries, will go in harm's way to save innocent lives.

Still, the savage violence persists in Bosnia. Despite agreements reached at the London conference, Bosnian cities remain under siege, the movement of humanitarian relief convoys is still hazardous, and innocent civilians continue to be slaughtered. At London, the parties agreed to a ban on all military flights over Bosnia. Yet the bombing of defenseless population centers has actually increased. This flagrant disregard for human life and for a clear agreement requires a response from the international community, and we will take steps to see that the ban is respected.

Now, a new enemy is about to enter the battlefield: winter. Some weeks ago, I asked for an assessment of the effects that the combination of war and winter could inflict on the suffering people of Bosnia. The answer was profoundly disturbing: thousands of innocent people, some uprooted, others trapped, could perish from cold, hunger, and disease. Anticipating this danger, the United States has been working with other nations and with the United Nations to mount a major expansion of the international relief effort and to support the tireless negotiations of U.N. and EC envoys, Cyrus Vance and David Owen, to get the fighting stopped.

I want the American people to know what the United States intends to do to help prevent this dreadful forecast from becoming a tragic reality. I have decided to take a number of further steps:

First, having authorized a resumption of U.S. relief flights into Sarejevo, I am prepared to increase the U.S. share of the airlift.

Second, we will make available air and sea lift to speed the deployment of the new U.N. force needed immediately in Bosnia to protect relief convoys. The United States will also provide a hospital and other critical support for this force.

Third, the United States will furnish $12 million in urgently needed cash to the U.N. High Commissioner for Refugees for the purpose of accelerating preparations for the winter. This is in addition to the $85 million in financial and material support we have already committed.

Fourth, we will offer to the United Nations and the Red Cross help in transporting and caring for those who are being freed from detention camps. We have already provided $6 million for this purpose.

Fifth, in cooperation with our friends and allies, we will seek a new U.N. Security Council resolution, with a provision for enforcement, banning all flights in Bosnian airspace except those authorized by the United Nations. If asked by the United Nations, the United States will participate in enforcement measures.

Sixth, we are taking steps in concert with other nations to increase the impact of sanctions on Serbia. I call on the Serbian authorities to cooperate fully with the United Nations and to comply with its resolutions.

Seventh, we have been working with the United Nations, European Community, and our other allies to introduce an international presence into Kosovo. The United States and the international community will continue to monitor the situation closely.

There is no easy solution to the Bosnian conflict, let alone the larger Balkan crisis. So we will persist in our strategy of containing and reducing the violence, making the aggressors pay, and relieving the suffering of victims, all the while lending our full support to the quest for a settlement. History shows that what this troubled region needs is not more violence but peaceful change, and I am confident that the steps I am announcing today will help the innocent victims, strengthen the hand of the negotiators and reinforce the pressures for peace.

Statement on the Glass Ceiling Commission
October 2, 1992

I am pleased to recognize the inaugural meeting of the Glass Ceiling Commission, which will focus on examining and eliminating discriminatory barriers to the advancement of women and minorities to senior positions in the workplace.

The Commission's work will complement the ongoing effort that I have made a priority in my administration: to assure women and minorities an opportunity to serve in upper echelons in Government, to be measured by the same standard as men. I have made record numbers of appointments of women and minorities to senior-level positions. I am proud that I appointed a talented team of women to the most senior economic positions, and I would like to see the business world follow my lead.

I am certain that under Secretary of Labor Lynn Martin's leadership, the Commission will aggressively pursue its 4-year agenda. The work of this Commission will help equip the Nation to make the most of every member of the 21st century work force.

Presidential Determination No. 93–1—Memorandum on Refugee Admissions
October 2, 1992

Memorandum for the United States Coordinator for Refugee Affairs

Subject: Determination of FY 1993 Refugee Admissions Numbers and Authorization of In-Country Refugee Status Pursuant to Sections 207 and 101(a)(42), Respectively, of the Immigration and Nationality Act

In accordance with section 207 of the Immigration and Nationality Act ("the Act") (8 U.S.C. 1157), and after appropriate consultation with the Congress, I hereby make the following determinations and authorize the following actions:

a. The admission of up to 132,000 refugees to the United States during FY 1993 is justified by humanitarian concerns or is otherwise in the national interest; provided, however, that this number shall be understood as including persons admitted to the United States during FY 1993 with Federal refugee resettlement assistance under the Amerasian immigrant admissions program, as provided in paragraph (b) below.

Ten thousand of these admissions numbers shall be set aside for private sector admissions initiatives, and may be used for any region. The admission of refugees using these numbers shall be contingent upon the availability of private sector funding sufficient to cover the reasonable costs of such admissions.

b. The 122,000 funded admissions shall be allocated among refugees of special humanitarian concern to the United States as described in the documentation presented to the Congress during the consultations that preceded this determination and in accordance with the following regional allocations; provided, however, that the number allocated to the East Asia region shall include persons admitted to the United States during FY 1993 with Federal refugee resettlement assistance under section 584 of the Foreign Operations, Export Financing, and Related Programs Appropriations Act of 1988, as contained in section 101(e) of Public Law 100–202 (Amerasian immigrants

and their family members); provided further that the number allocated to the former Soviet Union shall include persons admitted who were nationals of the former Soviet Union, or in the case of persons having no nationality, who were habitual residents of the former Soviet Union, prior to September 2, 1991:

> Africa—7,000
> East Asia—52,000
> Former Soviet Union—50,000
> Eastern Europe—1,500
> Near East/South Asia—7,000
> Latin America/Caribbean—3,500
> Unallocated (funded)—1,000

Utilization of the 122,000 federally funded admissions numbers shall be limited by such public and private funds as shall be available for refugee and Amerasian immigrant admissions in FY 1993. You are hereby authorized and directed to so advise the judiciary committees of the Congress.

The 1,000 unallocated federally funded numbers shall be allocated as needed. Unused admissions numbers allocated to a particular region within the 122,000 federally funded ceiling may be transferred to one or more other regions if there is an overriding need for greater numbers for the region or regions to which the numbers are being transferred. You are hereby authorized and directed to consult with the judiciary committees of the Congress prior to any such reallocation.

The 10,000 privately funded admissions not designated for any country or region may be used for refugees of special humanitarian concern to the United States in any region of the world at any time during the fiscal year. You are hereby authorized and directed to notify the judiciary committees of the Congress in advance of the intended use of these numbers.

c. An additional 10,000 refugee admissions numbers shall be made available during FY 1993 for the adjustment to permanent resident status under section 209(b) of the Act (8 U.S.C. 1159(b)) of aliens who have been granted asylum in the United States under section 208 of the Act (8 U.S.C. 1158), as this is justified by humanitarian concerns or is otherwise in the national interest.

In accordance with section 101(a)(42) of the Act (8 U.S.C. 1101(a)(42)) and after appropriate consultation with the Congress, I also specify that, for FY 1993, the following persons may, if otherwise qualified, be considered refugees for the purpose of admission to the United States within their countries of nationality or habitual residence:

a. Persons in Vietnam.

b. Persons in Cuba, El Salvador, Guatemala, and Haiti.

c. Persons in the former Soviet Union.

You are authorized and directed to report this Determination to the Congress immediately and to publish it in the *Federal Register.*

GEORGE BUSH

cc: *The Secretary of State, The Attorney General, The Secretary of Health and Human Services*

[*Filed with the Office of the Federal Register, 2:33 p.m., October 13, 1992*]

Nomination of Sean Charles O'Keefe To Be Secretary of the Navy
October 2, 1992

The President today announced his intention to nominate Sean Charles O'Keefe, of Virginia, to be Secretary of the Navy. He would succeed H. Lawrence Garrett III.

Currently Mr. O'Keefe serves as the Acting Secretary of the Navy. Prior to this, he served as Comptroller and Chief Financial Officer of the Department of Defense, 1989–92. He has also served as minority counsel for the Senate Appropriations Committee, Defense Subcommittee, 1987–89; minority staff director for the Senate Ap-

propriations Committee, Defense Subcommittee, 1986–87; majority professional staff member, Senate Appropriations Committee, Defense Subcommittee, 1981–85; and budget analyst with Naval Sea Systems at the Department of Defense, 1980–81.

Mr. O'Keefe graduated from Loyola University (B.A., 1977) and Syracuse University (M.P.A., 1978). He was born January 27, 1956. Mr. O'Keefe is married, has three children, and resides in Arlington, VA.

Statement by Press Secretary Fitzwater on the President's Telephone Conversation With Turkish Leaders on the Missile Accident
October 2, 1992

The President spoke today with President Turgut Özal and Prime Minister Suleyman Demirel of Turkey to express the intense sorrow and regret of the United States for the unfortunate and tragic accident involving ships of our two navies during the multination NATO exercises in the Mediterranean. The President expressed profound sympathy for the families of the victims and

assured the Turkish leaders that a full and complete investigation of this tragic accident would be undertaken.

Note: On October 2, the U.S.S. "Saratoga" accidentally fired two missiles, hitting a Turkish destroyer and killing five of its crew.

Remarks to the Community in Clearwater, Florida
October 3, 1992

Thank you all very, very much. Please be seated. At long last he's made his intentions clear. I'm delighted that Sidney will not be a candidate for President of the United States. [*Laughter*] It's a confusing enough year with the way it is. But thank you, sir, to you and your family for this introduction. Sidney and I go back a while, and he's been a loyal and strong friend and supporter. He's certainly been a marvelous citizen of this community and of our great State of Florida. So thank you very much.

Allow me quickly to single out a couple of others: Sandra, thank you, and best of luck to you; we have Bill Grant with us, another friend, and I want to see some real changes in the Congress, and he's running for the Senate; and Jeanie Austin, the vice chairman of the Republican National Committee, sitting over here, a Floridian; and Marian Keith, longtime GOP volunteer and a resident of On Top of the World, right back there. And a special welcome to Gerald McRaney. He's a great campaigner, a man of principle, and I'm very proud to have him at my side. Mac will be traveling with us all across Florida today, and we love having him along. Except every time I get going on a little too long, he makes me drop in the aisle of Air Force One and do 50 pushups. [*Laughter*]

But in honor of the "Major's" presence, I'd like to start this morning with an announcement related to the area, regarding MacDill Air Force Base. As you know, Mac-Dill played a big role in bringing an end to the cold war and certainly in Desert Storm. Now I'm pleased to announce that the Air Force and the National Oceanic and Atmospheric Administration, NOAA, will work together to make MacDill a major center for NOAA's fleet of research aircraft. This is a good decision. It represents a big victory for Senator Connie Mack and Congressman Bill Young, who are both back in Washington today. And also to give credit, I want to single out Al Austin, the chairman of the MacDill Response Group, a Floridian who played a big role in finding a use for Mac-

Dill that will serve the national interest and also provide a major boost to the area's economy. So it's good news, and I'm glad to be able to announce it here in Florida today.

Now about this little matter of an election a month from today. This campaign, like every campaign, is about a simple question: What kind of America do we want for our kids and for our grandkids? My opponent says that America is over the hill. At the Democratic Convention, he said he saw the U.S. sliding down the list of nations, somewhere past Germany and heading for Sri Lanka.

Well, maybe he ought to open his eyes. Maybe he ought to look at the respect with which we're held all around the world. Maybe the Governor needs to walk the streets of Europe and talk to the people of Asia, and they'd remind him of a few facts: Americans are still the most educated people in the world. In spite of our difficulties, the American economy is still the most dynamic in the world, American workers still the most productive. Any way you measure it, America is still on top of the world. That's the way it is.

So how do we stay number one? That's the question. I've laid out an Agenda for American Renewal, a comprehensive, integrated agenda to create in America the world's very first $10 trillion economy. My agenda for renewal demands that we open new markets for American products because that is the way we are going to create the new jobs for American workers. My agenda prepares our young people to excel in science and math and English because that's the way they will outperform the Japanese and the Germans. My agenda helps strengthen the American family because we must never forget: Family is still the foundation of our Nation.

I might just say, I'm a little prejudiced, but I think we have one of the great First Ladies of all time. I wish Barbara were here, because she feels as I do on strengthening family. When she sits there in the

Diplomatic Entrance of the White House and reads to those kids, it's sending a signal to parents to help your children. When she holds an AIDS baby in her arms, it sends the compassion that we all ought to feel, one for another. She feels as strongly as I do that we've got to find ways to strengthen the fabric of society by strengthening the American family.

This agenda for America's renewal promotes savings and investment, because in America the future is our children's birthright. So here's what I'm fighting for: To reinvent, literally reinvent American education and give every American the fundamental right to choose the best school for their children. Fighting to reform our crazy legal system, because as a nation we must sue each other less and care for each other more. These suits are out of hand.

Then to use market and competition to cut the cost of health care and make it available to all your neighbors. And it seems to me if you see a doctor once, you shouldn't have to go back a month later when you get the bill to be treated for aftershock. [*Laughter*] So we have a good new health reform program, and I think it's time to bring some sanity to our health care system.

I want to bring real change to Washington by limiting the terms of the Members of Congress and give the power back to real people. The President's terms are limited; why not limit the terms of some of those old geezers up there that have been for about 50 years?

Finally, I'm fighting for economic security for every man and woman in America. And I know that Social Security and Medicare are important to all of you, to all of us. And I'm sure some of you have heard my opponent's ads on the subject. Understand, Governor Clinton's a very ambitious politician. That's fine. But in his first try on the national scene he's using the oldest trick in the world, trying to scare America's seniors.

Here are the facts: I have proposed a comprehensive program to reform our health care system, to improve health care for all Americans. The only proposal I've made to—will affect Medicare benefits is to give people with highest incomes a smaller Government subsidy. But I believe we can

get big savings by cutting the fat out of an inefficient system, by going after things like the $25 billion in potential savings in malpractice insurance. But we can reform health care without cutting your health benefits. I have protected them as President, and I'm going to continue to protect them.

Bill Clinton's got a different idea. He wants the Government to get involved in setting prices, setting health care prices. But the experts said it could force people to wait in lines for treatment they want and need. Governor Clinton's plan would require $218 billion in cuts in Medicaid and Medicare over the next 5 years. So at the same time he's scaring you, he will not tell the seniors across this State and across the country where he's going to get the over $200 billion in savings that he wants. I think you deserve an answer to this.

These are the facts. They are pure and simple facts. It's the same with Social Security. In 1983, most people will probably remember this, in 1983, we took steps to make sure Social Security would stay financially sound, and we have kept it that way. No matter what Governor Clinton says, as long as I am President, Social Security will remain safe and sound. As I said in the State of the Union Message, and I repeat it here, I will not mess with Social Security, and I will not let Congress mess with Social Security. I will not let anyone take a knife to your Medicare benefits.

Now, ultimately none of us will be secure without a strong economy. And that's a fundamental issue of the campaign. And the differences in approach couldn't be more dramatic. I know America's endured some very tough economic times. But understand, we are being affected, and most people know this, by a global economic slowdown. Our competitors in Europe would trade places with us in a minute. Yet Governor Clinton offers America the European social welfare state policies: more Government, more special interest spending, more taxes on the middle class.

As Governor, Bill Clinton raised and extended the sales tax, including a tax on vegetables and other groceries. He raised the gas tax. He taxed mobile homes. He even taxed cable TV, taxes that hit the middle class and seniors the hardest. Now in this campaign, he says he's changed his ways. He's proposing at least $150 billion in new taxes plus at least $220 billion in new spending. But don't worry, he says, I'll get it all from the rich, the people who make over $200,000, that top 2 percent.

Well, yesterday in the Washington Post, his economic spokesman was quoted admitting to a reporter that the top 2 percent is not people over $200,000. He said that was just shorthand. Well, he's right. It's shorthand. Governor Clinton's plan is shorthand for socking it to the nurses and the teachers and the cab drivers and the middle class people who always get the shaft. I am not going to let it happen. We're going to take this case to the American people.

To get the money, to get the money that he needs for this plan, the $150 billion that he's promised in new taxes, he would have to get his money from every individual with taxable income over $36,600. That is a fact. These aren't the folks you see on "Lifestyles of the Rich and Famous." They work hard, and they deserve a break.

But that's just a start, because hardly a day goes by when candidate Clinton isn't signing on some plea for some new Government spending program. Before he's done, Bill Clinton is going to need hundreds of billions of dollars more to pay for all the programs he's promised. You've got every right to say, well, who will pay? The same people who always pay, the people who work hard and sweat it out at tax time. Bill Clinton wants you to sweat harder for the tax man, and I say his ideas deserve a cold shower.

Just some examples: Let's say your daughter's a third grade teacher with about $22,000 a year in taxable income. She already pays about $1,300 in taxes. Governor Clinton could have her fork over another $430 a year to the tax man; that is, if he's going to pay for all the social programs and pay for the additional spending that he's already proposed. I say that that woman ought to be able to use that money to pay for the grandkids' education or pay the mortgage on her house, not to send it back to the IRS.

Bill Clinton can protest all he wants, but

his numbers do not add up. I'm not going to let him take the difference out of your income.

Now, whenever I say this, Governor Clinton says it's outrageous. He'd never consider taxing the middle class. He's, quote, here's what he says about himself, "a different kind of Democrat." Well, there's nothing different about $150 billion in new taxes right out of the chute. There's nothing different about at least $220 billion in new Government spending, spending he's already proposed. There's nothing different in Bill Clinton's record in Arkansas where he's treated the middle class like a piggy bank to pay for all his programs.

Remember Mike Dukakis, the tank driver? [*Laughter*] Well, Bill Clinton nominated him for President 4 years ago. This year, according to an article in the New York Times, 39 of Governor Clinton's economic proposals are virtually identical to the ideas Governor Dukakis was pushing: higher taxes, more spending, a bigger deficit. I say simply: These things are wrong for America. We've got fundamental differences here. I'm getting warmed up on you, because I think we're going to have three debates; so I'm practicing here today.

Governor Clinton wants you to believe that the American economy will improve if you turn full control of your paycheck over to the crew that already runs the Congress. He wants the tax-and-spend Government planners to have total control over the executive branch, too. Last time they tried this, we ended up with double-digit inflation and rising interest rates and a "misery index," inflation and unemployment, over 20 percent.

Think about what inflation does to people on fixed incomes. Bill Clinton and his friends in Congress would let the lion of inflation out of its cage. I say, let's lock it away; keep it from your bank account; keep your savings sacrosanct, not to be wiped out by inflation.

So my case to the American people is this: At this time in our history, we simply cannot take the risk on a President with no national experience and a miserable Arkansas record to run on.

Since I've been in the Oval Office I've

faced some very difficult decisions. That's what you pay me to do. And yes, I've made some mistakes. When I make a mistake, I'll admit it. But I believe I've been a good leader. I've tried to make the tough calls. I've tried to make the tough calls, willing to tell people not what they want to hear but what they need to hear. And I stand before you today asking for your support so that we can get to work with a new Congress to fix the problems that stand in the way of this country, and so that we reform our health care system, that we literally reinvent our schools, so that we can retrain workers from one generation and create jobs for the next, and so that we can cut Government spending and cut taxes to get this economy moving again, and so that we can limit terms of Members of the Congress

and give Government back to the people.

If you're looking for a leader of experience and ideas, a leader who shares your values, a leader who knows that America's heartbeat can be found not in Washington but in places like Clearwater and Largo and St. Pete and Tampa, then I hope I can count on your support on November 3d.

Thank you all very, very much. And may God bless the United States of America. Thank you all. Thank you.

Note: The President spoke at 9:25 a.m. at the On Top of the World community. In his remarks, he referred to Sidney Colen, chairman of the community's board; Sandra Mortham, Florida State representative; actor Gerald McRaney; and Al Austin, chairman, Hillsborough County Victory '92.

Remarks to the Community in Fort Lauderdale, Florida
October 3, 1992

The President. Thank you, Colonel Bud Day, and thank all of you for being here. Let me also single out two Floridians: Jeanie Austin, who is the cochairman of the Republican National Committee, a great daughter of Florida with us today; and also the man I want to see elected to the United States Senate, Bill Grant, a good Congressman, a good man. And may I salute Guy Sanchez and Commander Donald Feak; and also a couple of friends of mine that came up on the plane, Andy Mill and Chris Evert, two of Fort Lauderdale's favorites over here. May I thank Gerald McRaney, a man of principle, who's campaigning. I'm glad to have "Major Dad" on my side, I'll tell you.

I'm sure some of you young ones are wondering what this is. This thing is a TBF Avenger. And I remember the first time I saw one of these. I could hardly wait to try it out. And then my flight instructor told me a curious aerodynamic fact. When the thing was loaded, it could fall faster than it can fly. I proved that a couple of times out in the Pacific flying one of these things. I took my flight training right here at Fort Lauderdale. It was quite a few years ago.

I am very pleased to be here to talk about the——

Audience members. Where was Bill? Where was Bill? Where was Bill?

The President. I am very pleased to be here to talk about the choice for this November. This campaign, like every campaign, is about a simple question: What kind of America do you want for the young people that are here today?

My opponent likes to tear America down. He says that we are, in his words, "south of Germany, heading toward Sri Lanka." Well, maybe he ought to talk to a few folks in Germany or Asia, and they'll remind him of a few facts: Our people are the best educated. Our economy is still the most dynamic, and our workers the most productive. America is the greatest economic superpower the world has seen. I intend to keep it that way and make it better. I don't like Governor Clinton tearing down the United States of America.

Audience members. We want Bush! We want Bush! We want Bush!

The President. I have laid out a comprehensive Agenda for American Renewal. It's a comprehensive, integrated agenda to create, right here in the United States, the world's very first $10 trillion economy. You go with my plan, and we can do just that.

Here's what we've got to do. We've got to look forward, to open new markets for our products because that's the way we're going to create new jobs and better wages for our workers. My agenda charts a way to prepare our young people to excel in math and English and science because that's the way our kids will beat the socks off the Germans and the Japanese in economic competition. This agenda provides ways to strengthen the American family because families are the foundation of our Nation. I'm going to keep on talking about strengthening the family. And as the colonel said, Governor Clinton wants to gut our military forces. He wants to cut $60 billion beyond what my military experts say is responsible.

Audience members. Boo-o-o!

The President. My agenda cuts defense, but only so far, because the only way America can stay safe is for America to stay strong. The reason we whipped Saddam Hussein is we stayed strong.

So here's what I'm fighting for, is to reinvent American education and give every parent the right to choose the best school for their kids, public, private, or religious; to reform our crazy legal system. We've got too many crazy lawsuits, and it is time that we sue each other less and care for each other more in this country.

With the help of that new Congress, I'm determined to cut the size of Government, because Government is too big and spends too much of your money. I want to limit, limit the terms—

Audience member. Clean the House!

The President. That's a good idea. The man says, "Clean House!" Wait a minute, I'll tell you how to do it.

Audience members. Clean the House! Clean the House! Clean the House!

The President. We need to do that, I'll tell you. We need to do that, and one thing we need to do is limit the terms for the Members of Congress and give Congress back to the people. The President's terms are limited; limit the Congress.

These are just some of the things I'm

fighting for. But while I'm talking about the future, Governor Clinton only wants to talk about the past.

Audience members. Four more years! Four more years! Four more years!

The President. Clinton only wants to talk about the past. I say, if you want to talk about the past, take a look at Arkansas. These are good people, good, honorable, patriotic Americans, and they've had a bad leader. The more you know about him, the more you'll understand: Bill Clinton is wrong for America.

You know, he says he's for civil rights, but Arkansas doesn't even have a basic civil rights law. He says he's for a clean environment, but the Institute of Southern Studies ranked Arkansas the 50th in environmental policies, right down to the bottom.

Audience members. Boo-o-o!

The President. Governor Clinton would want us to believe he can walk on water. And maybe he can, over there in Arkansas in those rivers, they're so polluted. The Governor says he's tough on crime, but under him, Arkansas's crime rate has gone right through the roof, has risen 2 times faster than the Nation's. You don't have to take my word for it. Ask the police officers who know Bill Clinton the best, the people in Little Rock. The police officers in Little Rock have endorsed me for President of the United States.

Let me talk for just a minute about the economy. We've been through some tough economic times. But understand, we're being affected by a global economic slowdown. Our competitors in Europe would trade places with the United States in a minute. And yet, Governor Clinton offers for America this kind of European social welfare state with bigger Government and higher taxes. And we don't need it.

Audience members. Boo-o-o!

The President. Don't listen to what he's saying today. He is wanting to slap more taxes on the middle class.

Audience members. Boo-o-o!

The President. Let me give you the facts. He is proposing at least $150 billion in new taxes and at least $220 billion in new spending. "Don't worry," he says, "I'll take it all from the rich. I'll take it all from those who are the top 2 percent."

But the problem is this: To get all the money he needs for that plan he's come up with, the $150 billion that he's promised in new taxes, Governor Clinton would have to get his money from every individual with taxable income over $36,600. And to pay for his other promises, he'll have to sock it to the cab drivers, the teachers, the nurses, and the day-to-day citizens. And we can't let him do that.

Audience members. Boo-o-o!

The President. He wants the middle class to sweat more and send it to the IRS. I say his ideas deserve a cold shower. Do not give him a chance.

You know, we had some television ads on, exposing the truth about who's going to pay for all Governor Clinton's promises, and then he gets mad. Even today he's got a new ad on television trying to fog the issue. He's scared that you're going to find out the truth before November 3d.

His economic plan does not add up. Someone is going to have to foot the bill, and Governor Clinton says it won't be the middle class. But you cannot raise $150 billion in taxes and pay for at least $220 billion in new spending without touching the middle class. Middle class taxpayers believe that Governor Clinton won't touch their paychecks like they believe that Hurricane Andrew was a gentle spring shower. We cannot let him touch the middle class on taxes.

Now, you see he's got a habit of never trying to take a position on a tough issue. I've finally figured out why he compares himself to Elvis. The minute he has to take a stand on something, he starts wiggling. One day he looks right in with those blue eyes into the camera and says he's not going to run for President of the United States; the next thing you know, he announces his campaign. One day he says he's for a good trade agreement that we want, the North American free trade agreement, and then he says, "I haven't made up my mind yet." One day he says the middle class deserves a tax break; the next day he's piling up spending programs that the middle class have to pay for.

Just 2 days ago in Wisconsin, he read a speech on foreign policy. It sort of sounded like a college term paper. Governor Clinton said, and I quote—this has to do with the war in Iraq—he said, "I supported the President when it became necessary to evict Saddam Hussein from Kuwait." He said that the other day. But last year, here's what he said, "I guess I would have voted with the majority if it was a close vote, but I agree with the arguments that the minority made."

Audience members. Boo-o-o!

The President. This is crazy. You cannot act like that as a Commander in Chief. This guy couldn't remember in detail that he didn't inhale 20 years ago, and he can't remember what came out of his mouth 20 minutes ago. I think we've discovered a new disease: Clintonesia. [*Laughter*] The symptoms: weak knees, sweaty palms, and an incredible desire to say anything on all sides of every issue, depending on who you are trying to please.

So let me just comment about the young people here. You cannot keep everybody happy. You've got to call them as you see them. You've got to make tough decisions. We better not replace the American eagle with a chameleon in the White House. We still have some very tough problems both at home and abroad. I don't think that we ought to put our bet on a leader with no experience and a sorry record in his home State.

You know, this place is special for me. I mention it because this is where I took that final flight training before I went overseas, at the old Naval Air Station here. I was just a kid. I was 19 at the time. Maybe that's why I've never forgotten the lessons that military service teaches. It shaped my character, and I hope that that service to country has made me a better Commander in Chief, because I respect our military and the veterans. I respect the military. I do not loathe them, as Governor Clinton said in that famous letter. I respect them. I support the veterans, and we have a special trust with the veterans. We must protect them, and we will always stand beside the brave men and women who stood up for their country. And by the way, I do believe that serving in uniform is a good criterion for being Commander in Chief of the Armed

Forces.

No, the question between our Agenda for American Renewal and the Clinton plan is like night and day. But the fundamental points are two: One, I don't believe we're a country south of Germany and just above Sri Lanka. I believe we are the best, fairest, most decent country on the face of the Earth, and I will never tear down America.

The last point relates to trust. I believe when people go into that voting booth, they're going to ask themselves the question: Who do I trust to the privilege, the honor, the duty of serving the United States of America as President? I hope I have earned your trust. Barbara and I have worked very, very hard, and I ask for your support for 4 more years.

Thank you, and God bless you all. Thank you.

Note: The President spoke at 2:25 p.m. at Hollywood International Airport. In his remarks, he referred to Col. George (Bud) Day, Congressional Medal of Honor recipient; Guy Sanchez, representative of VFW Post 11297; Donald P. Feak, commander of VFW Post 1966; downhill skier Andy Mill; and tennis champion Chris Evert.

Remarks to the Community in Orlando, Florida
October 3, 1992

The President. Thank you very much. All right, you guys, thank you. Thank you very much.

Audience members. Four more years! Four more years! Four more years!

The President. What a fantastic rally. And let me say, I've got great respect for Pat Williams. Wasn't he great up there, I'll tell you, giving us that warm introduction. As for Gerald McRaney, "Major Dad," he's been a great campaigner, and I'm proud to have him at our side. I want to salute Congressman Bill McCollum. I'm not sure he made it. But he's a good man, and he obviously—if we had more like him, they wouldn't be yelling "Clean House!" all the time. But we've got the answer to cleaning House in John Mica and Bill Tolley with us here today. We've got Bill Grant running for the Senate. More like that and we are going to get a real advantage here in the Congress and change America. Help me clean House. Thank you, everybody, for this great welcome. It's wonderful to be back in this City of Light, this City Beautiful.

Before I begin, let me just make a serious comment on what happened in Tampa this morning. We were followed out of town by a tornado which devastated some residential areas, tragically killed four people. On behalf of Barbara and me, our hearts and prayers go out to the family and the victims and all others whose homes were in that tornado's path. We've seen, and I saw it again today in Homestead, that Floridians are strong and good people. You've had your fair share of natural disasters, and I want to just express my concern and say, Florida's fighting back. Never make a mistake about that.

I might say, on a brighter note, I am very pleased that we have reached agreement with the Clinton campaign to hold three Presidential debates beginning next Sunday. I look forward to going head-on-head with Governor Clinton and Ross Perot. I'm especially pleased that Americans will be able to compare our ideas side by side without any media filter and get the facts and the truth to the American people. I didn't go to Oxford, so I'm not the world's greatest debater. But I know how to tell the truth, and that may make a difference.

Audience members. Four more years! Four more years! Four more years!

The President. Let me say this. This election and what we'll be putting in perspective in the debates out there is asking the rhetorical question: What kind of an America do you want for the young people here today? My opponent rips our country down and says that we're a nation in decline, somewhere between Germany and Sri

Lanka. He ought to open his eyes. We are the most respected nation on the face of the Earth.

Now let's use that leadership that changed the world and brought democracy and peace to all the countries moving around the world, and bring that same progress and prosperity to every working man and woman in this country. That's why I want 4 more years.

You might say, how do we stay number one economically, and we are when you look around the world. We do it this way: Here's the agenda for America's renewal. It is a comprehensive, factual plan, integrated plan to create the world's first $10 trillion economy in the next few years. We can do it because we are the United States of America.

One way you do it is to turn away from protection and open up new markets abroad for American products. We must become an export superpower. We can do it if we don't listen to the siren's call of protection emanating from the other camp.

This agenda prepares our young people to excel in science and math and English, because this is the way we're going to outcompete the Germans and outcompete the Japanese. This agenda helps strengthen the American family because family is still the foundation of our Nation. I worry when it's weak, and I want to see us help strengthen it. We've got to literally reinvent American education and give every parent a fundamental right to choose the public schools, private schools, or religious schools. Parental choice will make all the schools better.

One thing that Governor Clinton doesn't want to touch, and I want to see done and done quickly, is to reform our crazy legal system so that we sue each other less and care for each other more.

He has already advocated spending, and he hasn't even started yet, already advocated $220 billion in more spending. I want to get the spending down and the taxes down. Here's the way we'll do it: Give me that balanced budget amendment; give me that check-off; and give me that line-item veto; and let me do what the Congress can't do.

And another thing, give us these three good men for the United States Congress. Then let's say, let's limit the terms for the Members of Congress. A President's terms are limited. Limit the Congress' and give it back to the people.

Now these are just some of my ideas. I hate to ruin this program, but I think we ought to take a little look at Arkansas because this man's trying to get elected by doing one thing: Tear down the country, say we're down, and criticize the President. If that's fair game, let's take a look at Arkansas.

Now first, the people of Arkansas are good and decent. We live right next door to them in Texas. They are good and decent people, but there's a lot they don't know about their Governor and a lot you don't know. And the more you think about it and the more you find out, the more you know he is wrong for America.

Audience member. Tell him!

The President. I am.

He says he's for civil rights. He says he's for civil rights. Arkansas doesn't even have a basic civil rights law. I have passed a sound bill, sound civil rights bill, a sound ADA bill, the best creative piece of civil rights legislation in the last two decades. He hasn't even done one single thing for fairplay in the State of Arkansas.

He says he's for a clean environment, but the Institute for Southern Studies ranked Arkansas 50th in environmental policy, 50th.

Audience members. Boo-o-o!

The President. The Governor sounds like he can walk on water. Well, you can do it over there in that Arkansas River. [*Laughter*] No, really. There's so much fecal coliform bacteria in the river that the fish teach their kids to jog rather than swim. [*Laughter*]

Governor Clinton says he's tough on crime, but crime in Arkansas has increased twice as fast as the rest of the Nation. And the cops who know him best, the Fraternal Order of Police in Little Rock, Arkansas, have endorsed me for President of the United States.

This guy says he wants to do for the country what he's done for Arkansas, and I say, why in the world would we let him?

Audience members. Boo-o-o!

The President. That is a real threat. We

can't let him do that. Now, look at the economy, a major issue in the campaign. And look, I know we've had tough times. Families are worried; people are out of work. But I'll tell you something: We need to understand that it's bigger than America. We're feeling a global economic slowdown. Everybody knows that. It's worse overseas. Not one single country over there wouldn't trade in a minute for our economy.

So, yet, Governor Clinton offers to America that same kind of tired European social welfare approach to life that has failed them. We don't need that in this country. He has already proposed $150 billion in new taxes, $220 billion in new spending. Don't worry, don't worry, he says, he'll take it all out of the top 2 percent, everybody making over $200,000. But the truth is, to get the money for his plan, that $150 billion, Governor Clinton would have to get his money from every American with taxable income over $36,600. It's not just the top, and these people are not Shaquille O'Neal. They're not rolling in millions. These are your neighbors.

So I've got an idea, though. We ought to do what Shaquille would do and stuff the Governor's tax increase right into the front row. But on top of this—I hate to ruin this marvelous rally—but on top of this, Governor Clinton will literally need hundreds of billions of dollars more to pay for all the programs he's promised. You say, who's going to pay? The same people who always pay: those who work hard, pay their bills, sweat it out at tax time. He wants you to sweat harder for the tax man, and I say his ideas deserve a cold shower. We cannot do that for this country.

You're a third grade teacher making 22,000 bucks a year in taxable income; he could slap you with another 430 bucks a year in taxes. I say you ought to be able to use that money to pay for your kids' education, take a shot at the mortgage. You don't need to send it up to the IRS in Washington, DC. And therein lies the biggest single difference on this election: tax and spend versus holding down taxes, holding down spending, and return the power to the people of the United States.

I've got another. You know, for 11 months this guy and bunch of these other Democrats have been around tearing me up, and I'm having a good time now getting this thing in focus. I enjoy it. This guy is on every side of every issue. You talk about "slippery when wet"—[*laughter*]—listen to this: One day, Bill Clinton tells Arkansas he'll never run for President—I've seen the tape of it—and 8 months later, he's out there running for President, announcing his campaign. One day he says, I'm for the North American free trade agreement; then he backs away. Now today the Washington Post reports that tomorrow the Governor is poised to switch again and support the trade agreement. Watching him go back and forth on the issues is mind-boggling. It's like watching a Chinese ping-pong match. [*Laughter*]

One day he says the middle class deserves a tax break, and the next day he's plotting new ways to give the middle tax the greatest honor of paying for all his programs. If he ever became President, and he won't, we'd have to replace the eagle with a chameleon.

Now, I'll give you another example. I'll give you another example. Look at the question of whether to follow my lead and stand up against Saddam. Just 2 weeks ago in Washington Bill Clinton read a speech on foreign policy—it sounded like a college term paper—and he said, and I quote, he said this, "I supported the President when it became necessary to evict Saddam Hussein from Kuwait," end quote. But 2 years ago, when I was trying to mobilize the whole country behind it, fighting not only the demonstrators out there in front of the White House that Saddam misunderstood and a lot in the media and plenty in the United States Congress, here is what Governor Clinton said: "I guess I would have voted with the majority if it was a close vote, but I agree with the arguments the minority made." Now, tell me what kind of leadership that would be for a Commander in Chief of the United States Armed Forces.

Audience members. Boo-o-o!

The President. No, we've got too much on one side and then another side. I've found one thing about the Oval Office: You can't make everybody happy. You're bound to make mistakes, but you've got to do like the umpire. You've got to call them as you see them and stay with it and tell the truth as you go along.

I'll tell you why I'm going to win the election. In the first place, we've got a better plan, an Agenda for American Renewal. Secondly, the young people in America go to bed at night without that same fear of nuclear war the generations ahead of them had. Thirdly, when people go into that voting booth, they're going to ask themselves this question: Who do I trust to be empowered with the dignity, prestige, and the enormous power of President of the United States? And I have worked hard to uphold that trust. Yes, I've made mistakes. But I have not betrayed the public trust. I have been a strong leader. And now I ask for your support for 4 more years to finish the job and get this job done.

Thank you all, and God bless you. God bless you all. Thank you very much.

Note: The President spoke at 6:05 p.m. at the Church Street Market. In his remarks, he referred to Patrick Williams, general manager, Orlando Magic basketball team.

Message to the Senate Returning Without Approval the Cable Television Consumer Protection and Competition Act of 1992
October 3, 1992

To the Senate of the United States:

I am returning herewith without my approval S. 12, the "Cable Television Consumer Protection and Competition Act of 1992." This bill illustrates good intentions gone wrong, fallen prey to special interests.

Contrary to the claims made by its proponents, this legislation will not reduce the price Americans pay for cable television service. Rather, the simple truth is that under this legislation cable television rates will go up, not down. Competition will not increase, it will stagnate. In addition, this legislation will cost American jobs and discourage investment in telecommunications, one of our fastest growing industries.

S. 12 is clearly long on promises. Unfortunately, it is just as clearly short on relief to the American families who are quite rightly concerned about significant increases in their cable rates and poor cable service. Although the proponents of S. 12 describe the bill as procompetitive, it simply is not. Indeed, the only truly competitive provision, one that would have expanded the ability of telephone companies to compete with cable companies in rural areas, was dropped from the bill at the last minute.

S. 12 tries to address legitimate consumer concerns, but it does so by requiring cable companies to bear the costs of meeting major new federally imposed regulatory requirements and by adopting costly special interest provisions. For example, the bill requires cable companies for the first time to pay broadcasting companies, who have free access to the airwaves, to carry the broadcasters' programs. The undeniable result: higher rates for cable viewers.

Beyond increasing consumer costs, the bill takes certain key business decisions away from cable operators and puts them in the hands of the Federal Government. One provision, which is unconstitutional, requires cable companies to carry certain television stations regardless of whether the viewing public wants to see these stations. Another special interest provision would put the Federal Government in the position of dictating to cable companies to whom and at what price they could sell their programs. These types of federally mandated outcomes will discourage continued investment in new programs to the detriment of cable subscribers who have come to expect a wide variety of programming and new services.

I believe that the American people deserve cable television legislation that, unlike S. 12, will deliver what it promises: fair rates, good programming, and sound service.

GEORGE BUSH

The White House,
October 3, 1992.

Note: S. 12, which passed over the President's veto on October 5, was assigned Public Law No. 102–385.

Remarks to the Community in Dover, Delaware
October 5, 1992

The President. Thank you very, very much. Thank you, Governor Castle. Hey, listen, you've got an outstanding Governor, one of the greatest in the United States, and he's going to make an outstanding Member of the United States Congress, too.

Before I get started here may I single out all these marvelous bands, the—[*applause*]—just a minute, you guys—Caesar Rodney High School Band and their show choir, the Dover High School Band and their select chorus, and the Smyrna High School Band and the great soloist, Marva Thomas.

I am delighted to be here. And Mike, not only have you done a great job, but I am grateful to you for that kind introduction. Good afternoon, everyone. What a spectacular Delaware day. And what a fantastic turnout. We are going to carry the State of Delaware.

May I salute Lieutenant Governor Dale Wolf, another outstanding leader. Your Mayor, with whom I just met, Aaron Knopf; Basil Battaglia, our great State chairman; and the cast of fine candidates that have joined us here today. Donna Lee Williams over here, the candidate for insurance commissioner. Philip Cloutier, the candidate over here for Lieutenant Governor. And we've got to keep the governorship in Republican hands. Gary Scott is our outstanding candidate; vote for him for Governor. And I just talked to another friend of mine, a man with whom I served in Congress. He and I went there on the very same day back in the late sixties. I'm talking about your outstanding Senator, Bill Roth. I talked to him. He's doing a great job for this State, and he's a good friend.

But I came over to Dover this afternoon to talk a little bit about the choice that we face this November. This campaign, like every one, is about a simple question: What kind of America do we want for the young people here today? I have laid out my Agenda for American Renewal, a specific, comprehensive, integrated agenda so we can create in America the world's very first $10 trillion economy by the end of this decade. My agenda for renewal asks that we look forward to open new markets for American products so we create new jobs for American workers. The answer is to expand our exports. We want to prepare our young people to work so they have the tools to compete and win, and to strengthen the American family because family is still the foundation of our great Nation. And we've got to save and invest because America must always put tomorrow ahead of today. Those are the four things we must do.

So here's what I am fighting for: I want to literally reinvent American education and give every American the fundamental right to choose the best schools for their children, public, private, or religious. And I salute Governor Castle for the leadership role that he is taking with our America 2000 program. It is new, it is revolutionary, and it puts the power in the hands of the teachers and the parents where it belongs. Mike, thank you very much for your leadership.

Another one: I want to reform our crazy legal system because as a nation we must sue each other less and care for each other more. It has gone too far when these crazy lawsuits keep people from coaching Little League, doctors from delivering babies, or whatever it is. We must put a cap on these outrageous lawsuits, and we've got to stand up against the special interests in Congress who are keeping us from doing just exactly that. Clean House!

I want to use competition to cut the cost of health care and make it affordable and accessible for you and your families. And our program provides insurance to the poorest of the poor and still keeps the quality of American medical care up there as number one in the world.

And finally, I'm fighting for economic security for every man, woman, and child in America. If we are truly to renew America, we must pay special attention to those who have been left behind. Today is National Child Health Day, a good time to remind ourself that America's greatest resource is her people. As we move into the new century, we cannot afford to lose a single American to indifference and to neglect. Good intentions and noble rhetoric are not enough. Our actions must match our words. When it comes to children's health, the actions of my administration has spoken loud and clear. And so, let's take a quick look at the record. Since I took office, we have increased spending on children's programs by 66 percent to over $100 billion a year. From infant mortality to childhood immunizations to making sure that our neediest kids get nutritious foods they need, we've done more than talk about children's health. And we haven't stopped there, believe me. We've increased Head Start funding by 127 percent, $600 million this year alone, so that every eligible 4-year-old will be able to start school ready to learn. We did it. And now let's take that case to the American people.

We've also pushed through a 96-percent increase in the earned income tax credit, putting another $5.5 billion in the hands of those hard-working, low-income, working parents. And our program encourages them to stay off welfare and stay on the job and gives them a leg up in providing stability and security for their families. We've got to support the families through this kind of program. Now these are good, solid programs, programs that work for families, not against them. But nobody should be fooled that we can spend our way out of problems. The bottom line for all our programs should be strengthening the family. And we must encourage families to stick together and

those deadbeat fathers to stick around and do what they're obliged to do under the law.

Look at our child care reform. I pushed through my comprehensive child care program 2 years ago with Bill Roth's help and the help of others. The liberals in Congress wanted to create a brave new child care bureaucracy. I said let's try something different, and we did. We let parents, not the Government, choose the child care they want for their kids, whether it's in a church basement or a public school or in a neighbor's house. It gives parents the means and lets the parents make the choice. And that's what we need for this country. Just last week, I proposed a new tough child support policy. We're telling these deadbeat fathers: You can run, but you can't hide. And you will support the family you're responsible for—no if's, no and's, no but's. You're going to pay up.

Now, I hate to ruin this beautiful day, but that's our record, and I'm proud of what it is. But what about Governor Clinton?

Audience members. Boo-o-o!

The President. I hate to do this to you. I hate to do this to you, but let me tell you something. For about 11 months, he and those other Democrats have been ill-defining what we're trying to do, and now let me tell you what he has done. I know that he always talks a good game, but behind his word is a very different reality, the reality of his record as Governor of Arkansas.

Now, when it comes to protecting the children of Arkansas, the facts about his record are not pretty. But America must look at those facts because Governor Clinton isn't leveling with the American people. And during the 1980's, the death rate for American children, 14 and under, improved dramatically across the country, but in Arkansas it got worse. The State ranked 43d in 1987, and 2 years later it fell to 49 out of 50. And that is not what we want for the entire United States of America.

In the late 1980's, on Governor Clinton's watch, Arkansas' rate of violent death for teenagers soared at 3 times the national average. And over the decade, child abuse reports shot up 130 percent. Now, it's hard to believe Governor Clinton was unaware of what was going on. Throughout the 1980's, study after study offered detailed findings and recommendations—a cry for help, if you will—and Bill Clinton even commissioned some of these studies himself. And in 1990 his own department of human services reported, and here is the quote, "Frequent and widespread official failures had placed the children of Arkansas in imminent peril." And still Governor Clinton did nothing. At last, a group of child welfare advocates had to take him to court, and they filed a class action suit naming him as the lead defendant. And finally 4 months ago, Governor Clinton settled. Bill Clinton's child health record in Arkansas is absolutely appalling. He ought to stop attacking me and try to help the good people of Arkansas before he becomes President of the United States.

There's no other word for it, appalling. Look at how his State matches up with other States: 45th in the well-being of children, 45th in low-weight babies, 47th in the percentage of children in poverty. And despite that record, the Governor travels the country calling himself an advocate for children. Well, maybe the children of Arkansas would be better off if he spent less time talking about them and more time trying to help them. They deserve better. The children of America deserve better. We've got a good record to take to the American people on child care and child support. And on issue after issue you see this same huge gap between Clinton's rhetoric and Governor Clinton's record.

Bill Clinton says he's for civil rights. And I am proud that we passed two historic civil rights bills since I've been President of the United States, the ADA bill and the Civil Rights bill. But Arkansas is one of two States that doesn't have even a basic civil rights law. He says he's for high-tech, but under Bill Clinton, Arkansas's been falling behind in high school. Three out of every four Arkansas graduates spend their first year in college relearning what they were supposed to learn in high school. You don't want that for Delaware, and I don't want that for the United States.

I'm just getting warmed up. [*Laughter*] Listen, take a look at our North American free trade agreement with Mexico and Canada, NAFTA. I launched NAFTA, this free trade agreement, because it will create high-wage jobs for Americans right here in Delaware, right here in the United States. And I fought for it every step of the way because it is the right thing to do. That's what Presidential leadership is all about.

Once upon a time, Bill Clinton said— here's one of the great problems, he's on all sides of every issue—once upon a time, he said he was for NAFTA, this free trade agreement. Then the labor bosses told him that they were against it. So he said he wasn't sure if he was for it or against it. And now he's looked at the polls, he's seen that the American people want NAFTA, so just yesterday he said he's for it. And then again, maybe he's not. You see, he's saddled his support for this bill with all kinds of reservations and qualifications. He says we need special provisions to help workers, and he's right. That's why I've already proposed $10 billion in job retraining programs to do just exactly that. And he says we need to complete NAFTA with environmental agreements, and he's right. That's why I have already negotiated with the Mexicans separate agreements, environmental agreements with the Mexican Government. And when I've asked Bill Clinton's Democratic friends in Congress to fund my proposals to clean up our border with Mexico, they said no.

But Governor Clinton won't let those facts get in the way. It doesn't matter what's right or what's wrong, he just tells people what he thinks they want to hear. You cannot do that when you are President of the United States. You have to make the tough calls. You can't be everything to everyone. And you cannot come down on both sides of the issue and call it leadership.

Look at the economy, the major issue in this campaign. I know America has had some tough economic times, but understand, we're being affected by a global economic slowdown. Our competitors in Europe, every single one of them, would trade places with us in a minute. And yet, Governor Clinton offers America the same European social welfare state policies: more Government, more special interests, more special interest spending, and more taxes on the middle class.

As Governor, Bill Clinton raised and extended the sales tax, including a tax on vegetables and other groceries. He raised the gas tax. He taxed mobile homes. And he even taxed cable TV. And he's now out telling us we need to raise taxes on the American people by $150 billion. We are not going to do that. In this campaign, he's going to get out there and do something else that we don't like. He says he's going to raise these taxes again, as I said, $150 billion worth, but only on the rich. Well, don't bet on it. To get the money he needs for this plan of his, just the $150 billion that he has promised in new taxes, Governor Clinton would have to get his money from every individual with taxable income over $36,600. And that's just for starters. Listen to the newspaper from his own backyard, the Pine Bluff Commercial. Here's what they say: "If Congress followed the example that Bill Clinton has set as Governor of Arkansas, it would pass a tax program that would hit the middle class the hardest."

And there you have it: higher taxes on the middle class, more spending, a bigger deficit. And America deserves something better as we come out of these slow economic times and move this country ahead. At this time in our history, we simply cannot afford that kind of change. The man goes all around the country saying change, change, change. And with his kind of change, all you're going to have left in your pocket is a little change. We cannot let him do that to the American taxpayer.

So the bottom line is, Bill Clinton is wrong for America. Let him straighten out Arkansas before he tries to be President of the United States.

You know, I see a lot of young people here, and let me say this: I've been in the Oval Office now for 3½ years, close to 4. And in that office you face tough decisions, and you make mistakes. And when you make mistakes, you ought to say, look, I fouled this one up, or I made a mistake. That's the human way; in my view that's the American way. But I've also made some very tough calls. And I believe I've been a principled, strong leader. We have changed the world. We have literally changed the world the past 4 years. And I, too, want to

salute those men and women in the armed services right here from Dover who did the right thing in Desert Storm. We've changed the world. And now let's use that same energy and that same enthusiasm and that same vision to change the United States of America, to make life better for every single citizen in this country.

And the last point I'd make is this: I believe we need a smaller Government in Washington and bigger opportunities, bigger opportunities in places like Dover and New Castle. I see an America where health care is more affordable; where we've reinvented education, creating these new schools for a new century. I see an America where we spend less time suing and more time caring and where we take back our streets from the crackheads and the criminals through tough anticrime legislation. I see an America where we limit the terms for Members of Congress. The President's term is limited. Let's limit the terms for Congressmen and give it back to the American people.

Audience members. We want Bush! We want Bush! We want Bush!

The President. For 38 years, one party has controlled the House. And no wonder these people here feel we ought to clean House. Let's clean it out. Get Mike Castle in there. You've got a great Governor. You've got an honest, decent Governor. Put him in there, and watch the change begin.

So, if you're looking for a leader with some experience and someone who shares your values and who understands that America's real strength is not in Government but in places like Dover and Camden and New Castle, then I know I can count on your support for 4 more years on November 3d.

Audience members. Four more years! Four more years! Four more years!

The President. In this very historic setting one can't help but look over one's shoulders at history. One can't help but recognize how magnificent our system is. And you know, in these tough political times—and this has been about as ugly a political year as I've ever seen—the media has been rolling down the tracks in their own inimitable way, and it's not been very pleasant. The campaigning and stuff is not very much fun. But Barbara and I have tried to uphold the trust that was placed in us by the American people. Yes, I think we have the best First Lady in a long, long time. And I know it's tough going, although rallies like this make it just great.

But when people go into that booth, I think that in addition to all these issues, I think they're going to say: Who has made the tough decisions? But much more impor-tant, they're going to say: Who do I trust? Who has the character to lead this country for 4 years? And on that basis, I ask for your support as President of the United States so I can finish the job.

Thank you all, and may God bless you. Thank you very, very much.

Note: The President spoke at 3:12 p.m. on the Green in front of the old statehouse.

Statement on Signing the Civil War Battlefield Commemorative Coin Act of 1992
October 5, 1992

I am signing into law H.R. 5126, the "Civil War Battlefield Commemorative Coin Act of 1992." H.R. 5126 authorizes the Secretary of the Treasury to mint coins in commemoration of the 100th anniversary of the beginning of the protection of Civil War battlefields. The proceeds will go to the nonprofit Civil War Battlefield Founda-tion to be used for the preservation of his-torically significant Civil War battlefields.

This legislation provides a nonfederal funding mechanism to enhance the protec-tion of Civil War battlefields. The minting of these coins will cost the taxpayers noth-ing. The monies raised will make a major contribution to the preservation of our Civil War heritage. The greatest beneficiaries of this bill will be the future generations of Americans who will be able to relive more of the history of the Civil War era.

Today, many of America's battlefields face unprecedented development pressures, and there is renewed interest in protecting them. My Administration has embarked on an ambitious campaign to identify and pro-tect important battlefields through the American Battlefield Protection Program. This program is a national public/private partnership overseen by the Secretary of the Interior. The Civil War Battlefield Foundation is a privately established entity dedicated to raising funds for this endeavor. This legislation is timely in that it coincides with, and supports, this important program.

Innovative public/private partnerships such as the kind supported by this legisla-tion are a necessity if we are going to pre-serve our heritage to the fullest possible extent. Therefore, it is with great pleasure that I approve H.R. 5126.

GEORGE BUSH

The White House,
October 5, 1992.

Note: H.R. 5126, approved October 5, was assigned Public Law No. 102–379.

Statement on Signing the Department of the Interior and Related Agencies Appropriations Act, 1993
October 5, 1992

I have signed into law H.R. 5503, the "Department of the Interior and Related Agencies Appropriations Act, 1993." H.R. 5503 provides funds for various programs of the Departments of the Interior and Energy, the Forest Service (Department of Agriculture), and the Indian Health Service (Department of Health and Human Services). Funding for other agencies such as the Smithsonian Institution and the United States Holocaust Memorial Council is also included.

This Act provides funding for important Federal recreation and conservation activities, including the expansion of national parks, forests, and wildlife refuges. Many nationally significant natural and cultural resources will be protected by the appropriations provided in this Act.

I do have concerns with certain provisions of the Act. The Congress has included funding for a number of unnecessary, low-priority construction projects and ineffective programs. These funds would be more effectively utilized for my America the Beautiful initiative for national parks, forests, wildlife refuges, and other public lands.

I strongly object to the reduction in the Act for the new natural gas research and development program. The National Energy Strategy (NES) concluded that the use of domestically abundant natural gas resources could increase energy security and improve the environment. This reduction will impede the development of ultra-high efficiency gas turbines and other gas technologies that are needed to achieve NES goals.

A number of provisions in the Act condition the authority of executive branch officials to use funds otherwise appropriated by this Act, or to take other specified actions, on the approval of various committees of the House of Representatives and the Senate. These provisions constitute legislative vetoes similar to those declared unconstitutional by the Supreme Court in *INS* v. *Chadha.* Accordingly, I will treat them as having no legal force or effect in this or any other legislation in which they appear.

GEORGE BUSH

The White House,
October 5, 1992.

Note: H.R. 5503, approved October 5, was assigned Public Law No. 102–381.

Letter to Congressional Leaders Reporting on Panamanian Government Assets Held by the United States
October 5, 1992

Dear Mr. Speaker: (Dear Mr. President:)

1. I hereby report to the Congress on developments since the last Presidential report on April 7, 1992, concerning the continued blocking of Panamanian government assets. This report is submitted pursuant to section 207(d) of the International Emergency Economic Powers Act, 50 U.S.C. 1706(d).

2. On April 5, 1990, I issued Executive Order No. 12710, terminating the national emergency declared on April 8, 1988, with respect to Panama. While this order terminated the sanctions imposed pursuant to that declaration, the blocking of Panamanian government assets in the United States was continued in order to permit completion of the orderly unblocking and transfer of funds that I directed on December 20, 1989, and to foster the resolution of claims of U.S. creditors involving Panama, pursuant to 50 U.S.C. 1706(a). The termination of the national emergency did not affect the continuation of compliance audits and enforcement actions with respect to activities taking place during the sanctions period, pursuant to 50 U.S.C. 1622(a).

3. Of the approximately $6.2 million remaining blocked at this time (which includes approximately $100,000 in interest credited to the accounts since my last report), some $5.6 million is held in escrow by the Federal Reserve Bank of New York at the request of the Government of Panama. Additionally, approximately $600,000 is held in commercial bank ac-

counts for which the Government of Panama has not requested unblocking. A small residual in blocked reserve accounts established under section 565.509 of the Panamanian Transactions Regulations, 31 CFR 565.509, remains on the books of U.S. firms pending the final reconciliation of accounting records involving claims and counterclaims between the firms and the Government of Panama.

4. I will continue to report periodically to the Congress on the exercise of authorities to prohibit transactions involving property in which the Government of Panama has an interest, pursuant to 50 U.S.C. 1706(d).

Sincerely,

GEORGE BUSH

Note: Identical letters were sent to Thomas S. Foley, Speaker of the House of Representatives, and Dan Quayle, President of the Senate.

Presidential Determination No. 93–2—Memorandum on Assistance to Kenya and Somalia
October 5, 1992

Memorandum for the Secretary of State

Subject: Determination Pursuant to Section 2(c)(1) of the Migration and Refugee Assistance Act of 1962, as Amended— Kenya and Somalia

Pursuant to section 2(c)(1) of the Migration and Refugee Assistance Act of 1962, as amended, 22 U.S.C. 2601(c)(1), I hereby determine that it is important to the national interest that $1,500,000 be made available from the United States Emergency Refugee and Migration Assistance Fund to meet the urgent and unexpected needs of Somali refugees, conflict victims, and displaced persons in Kenya and Somalia.

You are hereby directed to inform the appropriate committees of the Congress of this determination and the obligation of funds under this authority and to publish this memorandum in the *Federal Register*.

GEORGE BUSH

[*Filed with the Office of the Federal Register, 3:58 p.m., October 15, 1992*]

Statement by Press Secretary Fitzwater on the Veto of the Cable Television Consumer Protection and Competition Act of 1992
October 5, 1992

We stood for lower cable bills for the consumer through increased competition. This is an important principle. We genuinely believe that our approach would be a better way to increase the variety of services available to the consumer at lower prices. We now call on the House of Representatives to support the American consumer and sustain the President's veto.

Note: S. 12, which passed over the President's veto on October 5, was assigned Public Law No. 102–385.

Statement by Press Secretary Fitzwater on the End of the Civil War in Mozambique
October 5, 1992

We welcome the agreement signed October 4 in Rome ending the civil war in Mozambique and establishing the basis for democratic multiparty elections by October 1993. We congratulate the Government of Mozambique, RENAMO, and the Italian mediators on this important breakthrough.

Now that a cease-fire has been agreed to, we expect that all parties will redouble their efforts to overcome the severe humanitarian crisis in Mozambique brought about by the war and drought. Tens of thousands of Mozambicans in remote areas of the country are reported to be facing famine. While limited deliveries have been made to some areas, a much wider effort is required to avert a large-scale human catastrophe. We call on the United Nations, international relief agencies, and all Mozambicans to work together to address this crisis promptly. The U.S., which contributed over $150 million in food and other humanitarian assistance to Mozambique in FY 1992, is prepared to participate generously in this effort.

Nomination of Gerald R. Riso To Be Chief Financial Officer of the Department of Housing and Urban Development
October 5, 1992

The President today announced his intention to nominate Gerald R. Riso, of Virginia, to be Chief Financial Officer of the Department of Housing and Urban Development. This is a new position.

Since 1991, Mr. Riso has served as Deputy Assistant Secretary for Student Financial Assistance at the Department of Education. He has also served as a senior partner with Riso and Dempsey, 1989–91; Associate Director for Management at the Office of Management and Budget and Chief Financial Officer of the United States, 1987–89; Assistant Secretary for Policy, Budget and Administration at the Department of the Interior, 1985–87; vice president at Korn/Ferry International, 1984–85; and Deputy Commissioner of the Immigration and Naturalization Service at the Department of Justice, 1982–84.

Mr. Riso graduated from Lafayette College (B.A., 1953) and Wharton Graduate School (M.G.A., 1957). He served in the United States Army, 1953–55. He was born January 30, 1930, in New York, NY. Mr. Riso is married, has six children, and resides in Washington, DC.

Appointment of Chester Paul Beach, Jr., as Associate Counsel to the President
October 5, 1992

The President today announced the appointment of Chester Paul Beach, Jr., as Associate Counsel to the President.

Since February 1992, Mr. Beach has served as Principal Deputy General Counsel of the Department of Defense. Prior to this, he was Principal Deputy General Counsel of the Department of the Navy and conducted the Navy's administrative inquiry regarding the A–12 aircraft program. As Special Assistant to the Under Secretary and Secretary of the Navy from 1987 to 1989, Mr. Beach headed the Navy's Procurement Task Force supervising the Navy's response to the "Ill Wind" procurement fraud investigation, and the Navy Management Review Task Force that implemented the 1989 Defense Management Report. Mr. Beach served on active duty as a captain in the U.S. Army from 1981 to 1987 in Germany and Washington, DC.

Mr. Beach is a graduate of Vanderbilt University in Nashville, TN, receiving a Bachelor of Arts degree *magna cum laude* in 1976, and the University of Chicago Law School, Chicago, IL, receiving a J.D. degree in 1980. He was born in Memphis, TN, and currently resides with his wife, Kathy, in Alexandria, VA.

Nomination of Jeni Brown Norris To Be an Assistant Secretary of Housing and Urban Development
October 5, 1992

The President today announced his intention to nominate Jeni Brown Norris, of Virginia, to be an Assistant Secretary of Housing and Urban Development for Public Affairs. She would succeed Mary Shannon Brunette.

Since 1989, Ms. Norris has served as vice president for public affairs and publications at the Export-Import Bank of the United States. She has also served as a consultant to Secretary Jack Kemp at the Department of Housing and Urban Development, 1989; executive assistant to the Deputy Under Secretary for International Labor Affairs at the Department of Labor, 1988–89; and Director of Public Affairs and Deputy Director of Audience Relations at the Voice of America, 1983–88.

Ms. Norris attended the University of Mainz, West Germany. She was born October 24, 1949, in Gustavsburg, West Germany. Ms. Norris resides in Hume, VA.

Statement on Signing Legislation Waiving Federal Immunity Relating to Solid and Hazardous Waste
October 6, 1992

I am signing into law H.R. 2194, which waives Federal sovereign immunity for violation of Federal, State, and local laws and regulations related to solid and hazardous waste.

Four years ago I promised the American people that I would make the Federal Government live up to the same environmental standards that apply to private citizens. By signing this bill, we take another step toward fulfillment of that promise.

My Administration has made a concerted effort to ensure that Federal facilities have the resources to meet the requirements of our Nation's environmental laws. Since 1989, we have tripled funding for the cleanup of wastes at Federal facilities and for bringing them into compliance with applicable environmental laws. Our FY 1993 budget proposed $9.5 billion for environmental cleanup and compliance at Federal facilities. The $5.5 billion request for Department of Energy environmental restoration and waste management activities represented an increase of $1.1 billion. This was approximately 26 percent above enacted FY 1992 levels. I am pleased that the Congress has agreed to fund these requests.

The objective of the bill is to bring all

Federal facilities into compliance with applicable Federal and State hazardous waste laws, to waive Federal sovereign immunity under those laws, and to allow the imposition of fines and penalties. During the development of H.R. 2194, my Administration supported this objective, but insisted that the legislation recognize unique situations presented by activities of the Department of Defense and the Department of Energy. I commend the Congress for the effort made to address these situations.

This Administration will strive to comply fully with the legislation. I want to emphasize, however, that several provisions of H.R. 2194 will require special effort and the cooperation of regulators and other interested parties to ensure that national compliance goals are met. My Administration views this legislation as a unique opportunity for a positive and constructive relationship between the various parties to ensure that enforcement actions and the assessment of fines and penalties will be exercised within a fair framework.

I look forward to a cooperative effort under this legislation to accomplish our national compliance goals and promote the implementation of efficient, cost-effective waste management programs.

In signing this bill, I wish to clarify the question of the source of payment of fines and penalties. H.R. 2194 is silent on this matter. House Report 102–111 suggests that Federal agency appropriations would be the source when the agency concedes liability or agrees to pay after an administrative hearing. However, the Judgment Fund would be the source if the agency disputed the matter and sent it to the Attorney General for defense. The Judgment Fund provides for the payment of judgments, awards, and settlements that are not otherwise provided.

This approach would put incentives in the wrong place and muddy the lines of responsibility within the Federal Government. It would take away the coercive effect penalties might have on the agencies and turn the waiver of sovereign immunity into a revenue sharing program. Accordingly, fines or penalties imposed as a result of this legislation will be paid from agency appropriations, unless otherwise required by law.

Finally, section 102(a)(3) of the bill amends the Solid Waste Disposal Act to subject the Federal Government to "all civil and administrative penalties and fines" imposed with respect to solid waste or hazardous waste, including penalties and fines "imposed for isolated, intermittent, or continuing violations." The conference report on H.R. 2194 indicates that under the latter provision, the Federal Government may be penalized "notwithstanding the holding of the Supreme Court in *Gwaltney of Smithfield, Ltd. v. Chesapeake Bay Foundation, Inc.*, 484 U.S. 49 (1987)." The Supreme Court's decision in *Gwaltney* rested in part on constitutional principles of standing and mootness. *See* 484 U.S. at 65–67; *id.* at 70–71 (Scalia, J., concurring in part and concurring in the judgment). I must note that no statute, and certainly no conference report, can overcome these principles.

GEORGE BUSH

The White House,
October 6, 1992.

Note: H.R. 2194, approved October 6, was assigned Public Law No. 102–386.

Statement on Signing Legislation Waiving Printing Requirements for Subsequent Appropriations Bills
October 6, 1992

I have signed into law H.J. Res. 560, which waives the printing requirements of sections 106 and 107 of title 1 of the United States Code with respect to subsequently presented appropriations bills during the 102nd Congress. I do so to avoid any confusion as to my ability to act on any form of appropriations legislation presented to me after certification by the Committee on House Administration of the House of Representatives that the form is a true enrollment. In signing the joint resolution, I express no view on whether it is necessary to waive the provisions of title 1 before I exercise my prerogatives under Article I, Section 7 of the Constitution.

GEORGE BUSH

The White House,
October 6, 1992.

Note: H.J. Res. 560, approved October 6, was assigned Public Law No. 102–387.

Statement on Signing the Department of Transportation and Related Agencies Appropriations Act, 1993
October 6, 1992

I have signed into law H.R. 5518, the "Department of Transportation and Related Agencies Appropriations Act, 1993." This Act includes funding necessary to maintain and improve our transportation system and to support transportation safety.

I am very disappointed that the Congress cut Federal-aid highway funding $1.3 billion below what I requested. This reduced highways funding will result in 65,000 fewer highway jobs being supported in the coming year. The reduced funding level also could lead to deterioration of the Nation's highway infrastructure. This would slow economic growth and job creation by increasing the transportation costs of goods in interstate commerce. The Congress could have funded Federal-aid highways at the requested level by not funding low priority programs and earmarked projects. Furthermore, the flexibility I proposed for the States to allocate funds according to their own priorities is not provided.

The bill contains an unnecessary and costly auto labeling requirement that may conflict with our international obligations on origin and labeling. In implementing this new requirement, the Department of Transportation will make every effort to provide accurate and meaningful information to consumers while minimizing costs.

The bill purports to require the Secretary of State to inform the Government of Panama within three months of the "dissatisfaction of the Government of the United States concerning inadequate compliance by Panama with the enforcement provisions of Annex V of the International Convention for the Prevention of Pollution from Ships." While I am concerned that this convention be properly enforced, decisions of whether and when to communicate with foreign governments are the sole province of the President. I will, therefore, treat this provision only as an indication of congressional concern in this area.

I am disappointed at the undue intrusion into the management of the Department of Transportation contained in this bill. This intrusion includes earmarking funds for projects that should be awarded based on established, objective criteria.

Nevertheless, the amount of funding provided by H.R. 5518 is consistent with my budget request, and thus allows progress toward a freeze in domestic discretionary budget authority. Because the bill provides funding for the continuance of important transportation programs within this level, I have signed it.

GEORGE BUSH

The White House,
October 6, 1992.

Note: H.R. 5518, approved October 6, was assigned Public Law No. 102–388.

Statement on Signing the Departments of Veterans Affairs and Housing and Urban Development, and Independent Agencies Appropriations Act, 1993
October 6, 1992

I have signed into law H.R. 5679, the "Departments of Veterans Affairs and Housing and Urban Development, and Independent Agencies Appropriations Act, 1993."

The Act provides important funding for the space program, environmental protection, and programs for our Nation's veterans.

The Act provides the funds necessary to maintain a balanced civil space program. Space Station Freedom, an essential step in meeting our future space objectives, is funded at a level that will keep the project on schedule during fiscal year 1993.

H.R. 5679 also meets important needs of our Nation's veterans. The Act provides $14.6 billion for VA Medical Care, an increase of $1 billion over the FY 1992 enacted level. With this increase, funding for VA Medical Care will have grown by 28 percent since FY 1990.

The Act provides funding for a range of environmental protection programs. I am pleased that the Act funds my request for EPA construction grants targeted to high-priority, coastal secondary treatment facilities, such as Boston Harbor, New York, Los Angeles, and San Diego. Expedited construction of these facilities can help clean the water on America's coasts.

Regrettably, the Act provides significantly less funding than I requested for EPA to carry out environmental commitments in support of the North American Free Trade Agreement. Despite my urging the Congress to fund fully these vital environmental initiatives, the Act cuts $47 million from the request to control border area sewage flows that pose a public health threat to citizens in San Diego and Calexico, California, and Nogales, Arizona. These cuts will severely constrain the Administration's efforts to clean up the U.S.-Mexico border and to support our proposed program of U.S.-Mexico environmental cooperation.

I also regret that, for the fourth year in a row, the Congress has chosen to reduce my request to clean up hazardous waste sites. This year's $176 million reduction in EPA's Superfund program brings the total reduction over 4 years to $643 million. These reductions unnecessarily delay the cleanup of these sites.

I am particularly troubled that the Congress has cut over $1 billion in civilian research and development programs within NASA, EPA, and NSF. These cuts will have a significant impact on a broad range of important research and education efforts, including my request for crosscutting initiatives in materials science, biotechnology, global change research, high performance computing and communications, and math and science education. These investments are important in maintaining our Nation's economic competitiveness, and they are critical in the training of our next generation of scientists and engineers. These investments also contribute to sustaining our commitment to environmental stewardship.

Although the Act provides funds for priority activities requested by the Administration, several housing provisions are flawed. I am greatly concerned over the inadequate funding levels for the Administration's important housing initiatives that emphasize tenant choice and homeownership opportunities. The Congress has provided only $361 million out of a requested $1 billion for the HOPE program, a program that would enable low-income people to take control of their lives through homeownership.

I am also disappointed that the Congress has reversed some previously enacted reforms critical to the financial health of the Federal Housing Administration (FHA) mortgage fund. Eliminating the 57-percent limit on the amount of closing costs a borrower can finance with an FHA mortgage will cause an increase in homeowner defaults, weakening the FHA fund and hurting homebuyers. The Congress has also increased the maximum single-family mortgage above $125 thousand—an amount that was agreed upon by the Congress and the Administration in the National Affordable Housing Act. This increase moves FHA away from its traditional role as a financial resource for middle- and lower-income buyers.

On the other hand, I am pleased that the Congress agreed to the Administration's request that it remove a prohibition on the issuance by HUD of a rule that would prevent the provision of housing subsidies to vacant public housing units.

The Act directs the Environmental Protection Agency, the National Aeronautics and Space Administration, and the Resolution Trust Corporation each to award 8 percent of funding for Federal contracts to businesses owned or controlled by minorities or women. A congressional grant of Federal money or benefits based solely on the recipient's race or gender is presumptively unconstitutional under the equal protection standards of the Constitution. Ac-

cordingly, I will construe these provisions consistently with the demands of the Constitution, and, in particular, I direct the heads of the relevant agencies not to award monies appropriated by this Act solely on the basis of race or gender.

Although I am disappointed that this bill contains damaging cuts in HOPE tenant ownership, civilian research and development, U.S.-Mexico border cleanup, and Superfund, I recognize that the bill does fund important veterans programs, space initiatives, and environmental programs at acceptable levels. In addition, the total level of spending in the bill maintains progress toward the achievement of my proposal to freeze domestic discretionary spending. For these reasons, I am signing the bill.

GEORGE BUSH

The White House,
October 6, 1992.

Note: H.R. 5679, approved October 6, was assigned Public Law No. 102–389.

Statement on Signing Legislation on Commemorative Olympic Coins, Reform of the United States Mint, and For Other Purposes
October 6, 1992

I am approving H.R. 3654, a bill "To provide for the minting of commemorative coins to support the 1996 Atlanta Centennial Olympic Games and the programs of the United States Olympic Committee, to reauthorize and reform the United States Mint, and for other purposes."

I am proud that the United States Mint, the Atlanta Committee for the Olympic Games, and the United States Olympic Committee have worked together to develop a unique coin program that offers the potential of $100 million in profits to be evenly divided between the two Olympic committees. By working together to maximize the sale of these coins we will assist our Olympic athletes. This program will also have a positive economic impact and help create jobs for the people of Georgia.

This is a wonderful opportunity to sup-

port those goals that are important to every citizen in this country—the successful hosting of the 1996 Centennial Olympic Games of Atlanta, Georgia, and the continued participation of our athletes in the Olympic Games.

In approving this legislation, I must, however, note that certain provisions concerning the newly established Numismatic Public Enterprise Fund might be construed to infringe on my constitutional authority to determine what legislative proposals to submit to the Congress and to supervise and guide executive branch officials. I will construe these provisions so as not to interfere with the President's constitutional duties.

GEORGE BUSH

The White House,
October 6, 1992.

Note: H.R. 3654, approved October 6, was assigned Public Law No. 102–390.

Statement on Signing the Foreign Operations, Export Financing, and Related Programs Appropriations Act, 1993
October 6, 1992

I am signing into law H.R. 5368, the "Foreign Operations, Export Financing, and Related Programs Appropriations Act, 1993." The Act provides funding for bilateral and multilateral foreign assistance, international security assistance, and for programs in the Department of State, the Agency for International Development, the Peace Corps, the Export-Import Bank, and several smaller agencies.

I am pleased that the Act provides authority and funding for several high priority programs including: loan guarantees for Israel; an increase in the U.S. quota for the International Monetary Fund; bilateral assistance to the former republics of the Soviet Union; appropriations for the Enterprise for the Americas Initiative; and appropriations for international security programs including Turkey, Greece, and Portugal.

Several provisions of the Act purport to require, or to forbid, certain international negotiations by the United States or the adoption by the United States of certain positions in international institutions or negotiations. Under our constitutional system, however, the President alone is responsible for such negotiations, and the Congress may not decide which negotiations the President will undertake or what position the United States will adopt. Similarly, provisions directing the placement of United States diplomatic personnel abroad intrude upon the President's authority for the conduct of international relations. Nor may the Congress condition the availability of funds on the President's surrendering his discretion in these areas. I will, therefore, treat all such provisions as purely precatory.

I retain the same concerns about section 565, prohibiting certain dealings with foreign governments and other persons, that I have expressed in signing previous appropriations acts.

Finally, I note that the various reporting requirements of this Act would have to be construed in light of the President's authority to protect against the disclosure of state secrets and national security information.

GEORGE BUSH

The White House,
October 6, 1992.

Note: H.R. 5368, approved October 6, was assigned Public Law No. 102–391.

Statement on Signing the Legislative Branch Appropriations Act, 1993
October 6, 1992

I have signed into law H.R. 5427, the "Legislative Branch Appropriations Act, 1993." While I regret that the Congress has rejected my proposal for a 33 percent reduction in congressional staffs, I need not repeat here the compelling reasons for such a reduction. However, I am compelled to comment upon two troublesome features of this bill.

First, I object to section 315, which establishes a "Task Force on Senate Coverage" for the purpose of "studying" whether various statutes that now apply to the private sector and/or the executive branch should also apply to the United States Senate.

This is not the sort of complex, difficult question that requires deliberation by a blue-ribbon panel. The Congress need not look beyond James Madison's warning in *Federalist Paper No. 57* that "[i]f [the American] spirit shall ever be so far debased as to tolerate a law not obligatory on the Legislature as well as on the people, the people will be prepared to tolerate anything but liberty." Rather than "study" the issue, the Congress should quickly eliminate this unseemly practice by passing the Accountability in Government Act that I proposed in April.

I would also note the limitations placed on the Task Force's authority to take even the small step of examining this issue. Although the bill mentions several statutes by name, it ignores the Civil Rights Act of 1964, the Rehabilitation Act, and other civil rights laws. The current "coverage" of the Congress by these laws is a sham, since it denies congressional employees the same rights to trial before a judge or jury enjoyed by other Americans. The bill also excludes consideration of whether the Congress should be covered by the Independent

Counsel provision of the Ethics in Government Act, if that statute is reauthorized. And even as to the small number of laws remaining for consideration by the Task Force, the Task Force's mandate reaches only the Senate, not the House.

Second, provisions establishing the Commission on the Bicentennial of the United States Capitol present constitutional concerns. Even though the voting members of the Commission will all be Members of Congress, section 324(a) of the bill, if broadly construed, could be interpreted to allow the exercise of significant governmental authority by the Commission. So construed, this provision would be unconstitutional under the Appointments Clause of Article II, section 2, and the Incompatibility Clause of Article I, section 6. To avoid this constitutional infirmity, I will interpret section 324(a) of the bill as authorizing the Commission to perform only ceremonial and advisory functions within the legislative branch.

GEORGE BUSH

The White House,
October 6, 1992.

Note: H.R. 5427, approved October 6, was assigned Public Law No. 102–392.

Statement on Signing the Treasury, Postal Service, and General Government Appropriations Act, 1993
October 6, 1992

I have signed into law H.R. 5488, the Treasury, Postal Service, and General Government Appropriations Act, 1993.

This Act provides funding for several Administration priorities, including programs that address the crisis of drugs in our country. These include drug interdiction activities in the United States Customs Service and drug rehabilitation and treatment programs financed through the Office of National Drug Control Policy.

I am pleased that the Congress has provided the funding I requested for my efforts to control unnecessary and burden-

some Federal regulations through the regulatory review process headed by the Council on Competitiveness. Reviewing Federal regulations is an essential part of the President's constitutional responsibility to take care that the laws be faithfully executed. Regulatory review ensures that regulations issued by the executive branch protect the health and safety of the American people while taking into consideration the economic interests of American consumers.

In implementing this regulatory review process, the Council on Competitiveness, the Office of Management and Budget, and the agencies take great care to ensure that the public participation provisions, as well as all other elements of the Administrative Procedure Act, are carried out in all respects. My advisers, including the Council members, the Office of Management and Budget, and the agencies, also ensure that agency rule-making decisions are supported by the public record maintained by the relevant agency pursuant to the Administrative Procedure Act.

I note that the Conference Report suggests certain operating procedures for the Council on Competitiveness. This report language is not legally binding, and the procedures it suggests would inappropriately interfere with my duty to oversee the executive branch. As previously stated, current procedures ensure that the regulatory process includes public participation and that decisions are based on the public record.

It is also essential that the President, the Cabinet, and other advisers be provided frank, candid advice about issues that may be raised in the regulatory process. The procedures proposed in the Conference Report would interfere with my ability to obtain such advice by requiring internal discussions among my Cabinet and my advisers to be reduced to writing and put on the public record. Such restrictions on the President's Cabinet or advisers, if imposed by the Congress, would be unprecedented and unconstitutional. I am, therefore, directing the Council on Competitiveness to

continue to implement the regulatory review process in a manner that is consistent with current law and with my constitutional responsibilities.

I also note that, certain provisions in the bill—those concerning regulatory review by the Office of Management and Budget (OMB) and the management of the Postal Service—could be interpreted to interfere with my authority under the Constitution to supervise the decision-making process within and management of the executive branch. In order to avoid this constitutional difficulty, and without recognizing the Congress's authority to impose these restrictions, I will interpret them to permit such supervision through other means.

A number of provisions in the Act condition the President's authority, and the authority of affected executive branch officials, to use funds otherwise appropriated by this Act on the approval of various congressional committees. These provisions constitute legislative vetoes similar to those declared unconstitutional by the Supreme Court in *INS v. Chadha.* Accordingly, I will treat them as having no legal force or effect in this or any other legislation in which they appear.

GEORGE BUSH

The White House,
October 6, 1992.

Note: H.R. 5488, approved October 6, was assigned Public Law No. 102–393.

Statement on Signing the Departments of Commerce, Justice, and State, the Judiciary, and Related Agencies Appropriations Act, 1993
October 6, 1992

I have signed into law H.R. 5678, the "Departments of Commerce, Justice, and State, the Judiciary, and Related Agencies Appropriations Act, 1993."

During the past few years, I have continually sought increased resources for Federal law enforcement. While we have achieved substantial progress in this area, the Congress has been unwilling to support fully my

efforts to combat violent crime and drugs, placing public safety at greater risk. Once again, I am disappointed that this Act cuts more than $500 million from my request to support the fight against crime and drugs. Obviously, this will hamper the Justice Department's efforts to combat violent crime. Additional funding could have been provided to fight crime if the Congress had agreed to terminate or reduce other unwarranted programs as proposed in my FY 1993 budget request.

The results of the congressionally imposed cuts will be manyfold. First, the Federal Bureau of Investigation will not be able to hire additional agents. Second, the Drug Enforcement Administration will be unable to complete major planned drug investigations. Third, my plan for the systematic expansion of prison operations will be curtailed. Fourth, the Immigration and Naturalization Service will be forced to operate at a level below FY 1992, meaning less enforcement on our Nation's borders. Finally, Federal prosecutors will be unable to handle their mounting case loads, thereby delaying putting criminals behind bars.

In addition, I note that section 611(b)(1) of the Act incorporates by reference a provision that grants certain authority only to those Members of the Board of Directors of the Legal Services Corporation who have been confirmed by the Senate. Under Article II of the Constitution, the President has the power "to fill up all Vacancies that may happen during the Recess of the Senate." Under the Constitution, such recess appointees enjoy the same powers assigned to Senate-confirmed officers. Provisions purporting to grant authority only to individuals confirmed by the Senate interfere with the President's recess appointment power, and are unconstitutional.

I would also note my strong objections to the inclusion of an amendment to the criminal post-employment statute in an appropriations bill, without benefit of any public discussion of the merits, without any appreciation of the recently enacted comprehensive amendments to the post-employment statute, and without regard for the implications of targeting for coverage just one position.

Nevertheless, the overall amount of funding provided by H.R. 5678 is consistent with my budget request, and thus allows progress toward a freeze in domestic discretionary budget authority to be maintained. Because the bill provides funding for the continuance of many important programs within this level, I have signed it.

GEORGE BUSH

The White House,
October 6, 1992.

Note: H.R. 5678, approved October 6, was assigned Public Law No. 102–395.

Statement on Signing the Department of Defense Appropriations Act, 1993
October 6, 1992

I have signed into law H.R. 5504, the "Department of Defense Appropriations Act, 1993." The Act provides funding for Department of Defense programs.

I note that in specifying appropriations ceilings on specific programs for "Defense Reinvestment for Economic Growth," the Congress provided flexibility to allocate the total amount of such appropriations. This will allow the President to ensure that such appropriations are used only for defense-related functions, consistent with the Budget Enforcement Act and the appropriate role of the Department of Defense.

I am concerned that the Act requires American taxpayers to indemnify States and localities, with respect to certain claims that may arise in connection with real property transferred to them by the Department of Defense. This provision discourages the Department of Defense from transferring to States and localities real property no longer needed by the Department, an unfortunate outcome of H.R. 5504 by that should be corrected in future legislation.

Section 9009 of H.R. 5504 and the last proviso in section 105 of the Classified Annex incorporated in H.R. 5504 by reference, which purport to limit the authority to protect certain national security information through the establishment of special access programs, shall be construed consistent with the constitutional authority of the President to protect national security information.

GEORGE BUSH

The White House,
October 6, 1992.

Note: H.R. 5504, approved October 6, was assigned Public Law No. 102–396.

Statement on Signing the Hawaiian Homes Commission Act Amendments
October 6, 1992

I am signing into law S.J. Res. 23, consenting to certain amendments to the Hawaiian Homes Commission Act, notwithstanding reservations I have concerning the Act itself. This joint resolution gives the United States consent to a number of amendments to the Hawaiian Homes Commission Act that were adopted by the State of Hawaii. This consent is necessary because section 4 of the "Act to provide for the admission of the State of Hawaii into the Union," Public Law 86–3, 73 Stat. 4 (1959), requires that amendments to the Hawaiian Homes Commission Act be approved by the National Government. I am signing this bill because it gives effect to the desires of the government of the State of Hawaii. But I wish to note my concern over the process by which the National Government must give its consent to matters that are solely within the competence of the State of Hawaii. Such a procedure is at tension with federalism principles that lie at the heart of our system of government. There is no question that the administration of the public lands in question here can be competently handled by the State government.

I also wish to express another concern. Because the Act employs an express racial classification in providing that certain public lands may be leased only to persons having a certain percentage of blood "of the races inhabiting the Hawaiian Islands prior to 1778," the continued application of the Act raises serious equal protection questions. Moreover, the Congress has not conducted the type of examination of the reasons for and the need to use this classification that the Supreme Court has stated is necessary to legitimate such classifications as an exercise of the Congress' Fourteenth Amendment enforcement powers.

Thus, while I am signing this resolution because it substantially defers to the State's judgment, I urge that the Congress amend the "Act to provide for the admission of the State of Hawaii into the Union," Public Law 86–3, so that in the future the State of Hawaii may amend the Hawaiian Homes Commission Act without the consent of the United States, and note that the racial classifications contained in the Act have not been given the type of careful consideration by the Federal Government that would shield them from ordinary equal protection scrutiny.

GEORGE BUSH

The White House,
October 6, 1992.

Note: S.J. Res. 23, approved October 6, was assigned Public Law No. 102–398.

Nomination of Douglas Alan Brook To Be Director of the Office of Personnel Management
October 6, 1992

The President today announced his intention to nominate Douglas Alan Brook, of Virginia, to be Director of the Office of Personnel Management for a term of 4 years. He would succeed Constance Berry Newman.

Currently, Mr. Brook serves as Acting Director of the Office of Personnel Management. He has also served as Assistant Secretary of the Army for Financial Manage-

ment, 1990–92; president of Brook Associates, Inc., 1982–90; and vice president of Libbey-Owens-Ford Co., 1979–82.

Mr. Brook graduated from the University of Michigan (B.A., 1965; M.A., 1967). He served in the U.S. Navy on active duty, 1968–70, and in the Naval Reserve, from 1971 to the present. He was born January 15, 1944, in Chicago, IL. Mr. Brook is married and resides in Vienna, VA.

Appointment of Clifford T. Alderman as Special Assistant to the President for Intergovernmental Affairs
October 6, 1992

The President today announced the appointment of Clifford T. Alderman as Special Assistant to the President for Intergovernmental Affairs.

Since November 1990, Mr. Alderman has served as Deputy to the Special Assistant to the President for Intergovernmental Affairs. Prior to this, he served as Deputy Director of External Affairs in the Office of the Secretary at the U.S. Department of the Interior, 1989–90. From 1987 to 1988, Mr. Alderman served as the executive director of the

Connecticut Bush-Quayle campaign. From 1985 to 1987, Mr. Alderman served on the field staff of the Fund for America's Future. From 1983 to 1985, Mr. Alderman worked in the political analysis office of the Republican National Committee.

Mr. Alderman graduated from American University with a Bachelor of Science degree in 1983. Mr. Alderman was born on April 8, 1961, in Bristol, CT. He currently resides in Alexandria, VA.

Remarks at the Initialing Ceremony for the North American Free Trade Agreement in San Antonio, Texas
October 7, 1992

May I start off by saluting President Salinas and Prime Minister Mulroney, Secretary Serra, Minister Wilson: Welcome to the city of San Antonio. I thank the other foreign dignitaries, Governors, mayors, and Members of our Congress and my Cabinet, so many from the business community from all three countries that are here.

We've just been talking about this, and

this meeting marks a turning point in the history of our three countries. Today the United States, Mexico, and Canada embark together on an extraordinary enterprise. We are creating the largest, richest, and most productive market in the entire world, a $6 trillion market of 360 million people that stretches 5,000 miles from Alaska and the Yukon to the Yucatan Peninsula.

NAFTA, the North American free trade agreement, is an achievement of three strong and proud nations. This accord expresses our confidence in economic freedom and personal freedom, in our peoples' energy and enterprise.

The United States, Mexico, and Canada have already seen the powerful and beneficial impact of freer trade and more open markets. Over the past 5 years, as President Salinas reduced trade barriers under his bold reform program and as Prime Minister Mulroney and I implemented the United States-Canadian Free Trade Agreement, trade between our three countries has soared. In 1992 alone, that trade will reach an estimated $223 billion, up $58 billion just since 1987.

If anyone doubts the importance of trade for creating jobs, they should come to this great State, come to the Lone Star State. In 1991, Texas exports totaled $47 billion, just from this State. And of that amount, over $15 billion went to Mexico, almost 2½ times as much as 5 years ago. This export boom goes well beyond one State, well beyond Texas. Virtually every State has increased exports to Mexico in the past 5 years.

NAFTA means more exports, and more exports means more American jobs. Between 1987 and 1991, the increase in our exports to Mexico alone created over 300,000 new American jobs. These are high-wage jobs. In the case of merchandise exports, those jobs pay a worker a full 17 percent more than the average wage.

Free trade is the way of the future. I've set a goal for America to become, by the early years of the next century, the world's first $10 trillion economy, and NAFTA is an important element in reaching that goal. With NAFTA, as more open markets stimulate growth, create new products at competitive prices for consumers, we'll create new jobs at good wages in all three countries.

NAFTA will do these things and remain consistent with our other international obligations, our GATT trade obligations. Let me be clear that I remain committed to the successful conclusion of the Uruguay round of trade negotiations this year.

But NAFTA's importance is not limited to trade. We've taken particular care that our workers will benefit and the environment will be protected. As a result of NAFTA, the U.S. and Mexico are working more closely than we ever have to strengthen cooperation on such important labor issues as occupational health and safety standards, child labor, and labor-management relations.

Then, on the environment, an issue of critical concern for all three leaders here today, we have agreed on practical, effective steps to address urgent issues such as border pollution, as well as longer term problems, such as preventing countries from lowering environmental standards to attract foreign investment. I salute the two gentlemen standing next to me, Prime Minister Mulroney and President Salinas, for their commitment and their leadership to this environment that we all share. As proof of that commitment, the United States and Mexican Governments have already developed a comprehensive, integrated plan to clean up air and water pollution and other hazardous waste along the Rio Grande River.

I know for some NAFTA will be controversial precisely because it opens the way to change. Some of NAFTA's critics will fight the future, throw obstacles in the way of this agreement, to mask a policy of protectionism. But history shows us that any nation that raises walls and turns inward is destined only for decline. We cannot make that choice for ourselves or for our children. We must set our course for the future, for free trade.

Mr. President and Mr. Prime Minister: This accord underscores the principle that democratic, market-oriented nations are natural partners in free trade. We owe it to our fellow citizens to bring this agreement into effect as soon as possible, and I pledge my support to that end.

Thank you very much.

Note: The President spoke at 3:06 p.m. at the Plaza San Antonio Hotel. In his remarks, he referred to Jaime Serra Puche, Mexico's Secretary of Commerce and Industrial Development, and Michael Wilson, Canada's Minister of International Trade.

Presidential Determination No. 93–3—Memorandum on Trade With Afghanistan
October 7, 1992

Memorandum for the Secretary of State

Subject: Assistance to and Trade with Afghanistan

By virtue of the authority vested in me by section 620D(b) of the Foreign Assistance Act of 1961, as amended (22 U.S.C. 2374(b)), I hereby determine that furnishing assistance to Afghanistan with funds authorized to be appropriated under that Act is in the national interest of the United States because of substantially changed circumstances in Afghanistan.

By virtue of the authority vested in me by section 2(b)(2)(C) of the Export-Import Bank Act of 1945, as amended (12 U.S.C. 635(b)(2)(C)), I hereby determine that Afghanistan has ceased to be a Marxist-Leninist country within the definition of such term in subparagraph (B)(i) of section 2(b)(2) of that Act (12 U.S.C. 635(b)(2)(B)(i)).

In accordance with section 118(c)(1) of Public Law 99–190 (99 Stat. 1319), I hereby provide notice of my intention to restore nondiscriminatory trade treatment to the products of Afghanistan no sooner than 30 days following receipt by the Congress of this memorandum.

Attached to this determination is a Statement of Justification for these actions, setting forth, among other things, a description of U.S. national interests in resuming assistance and normal trade ties with Afghanistan.

You are authorized and directed to report these actions to the Congress and to publish this memorandum in the *Federal Register*.

GEORGE BUSH

[*Filed with the Office of the Federal Register, 4 p.m., October 15, 1992*]

Note: The attached justification was published in the Federal Register on October 19.

Statement by Press Secretary Fitzwater on Free Elections in Kuwait
October 7, 1992

The President is pleased to note that this week Kuwait held free parliamentary elections. The United States has been a strong supporter of this process since the Amir's decision to hold elections was announced during the Iraqi occupation. We have also been encouraged by the statement by the Crown Prince that the Kuwaiti Government will soon propose legislation to amend the constitution to broaden the electorate and specifically to give women the right to vote in future elections. The Amir and the Kuwaiti people are to be congratulated on this latest stage in Kuwait's progress toward full recovery and reconstruction.

These elections reaffirm Kuwait's hard-won independence and the freedoms enjoyed by the Kuwaiti people, in sharp contrast to the agony the Iraqi people still endure from Saddam. The gulf between Kuwait's determination to begin a democratic process and Saddam's brutalities against the Iraqi people is a vivid reminder of why the coalition had no choice but to use force to liberate Kuwait. The United States remains committed both to supporting Kuwait in its physical and political reconstruction and to support the efforts of the Iraqi opposition toward building a democratic future for the people of Iraq.

Remarks at the Port of New Orleans, Louisiana
October 8, 1992

The President. Thank you, Governor Treen. Good morning, everybody, and thank you, thank you for that warm welcome. May I salute David Treen, who did a great job as Governor of this State; my friend Congressman Bob Livingston. If we had more Members of Congress like him, they wouldn't be yelling at me "Clean House!" all the time. We've got a good one here. May I salute our Secretary of State, Fox McKeithen; and Peggy Wilson, right here with me; Ron Brinson, the president and CEO of the Port of New Orleans; and of course, our old friend, a great Louisianian serving at my side in the White House, Henson Moore.

You know, it's a very special pleasure for me—I'm going to take my coat off. It's hot out here, man. It's a very special pleasure to be here. Let me tell you one of the reasons why. Thirty-five years ago I came back to this city—I came here many, many times— came back here to the Bienville Street Wharf down the way a bit to christen a new offshore oil rig. I was a small-business man with an office right here near here in downtown New Orleans and the offices also over at Cameron and Morgan City and Lafayette. I grew to know this State and to love Louisiana and the people, the food, the music, the fondness for the old, and the passion for the new. I am glad to be back here today because it brings back a lot of memories, and you make me feel right at home. Thanks for this warm welcome.

I mentioned offshore drilling. I am for the offshore drilling industry. Ask the super-environmentalists, the Clinton-Gore ticket, exactly where they stand and then try to get them to keep their word. They waffle on every single issue.

This morning I want to say, or this afternoon, just a few words about the economic challenge facing this great country of ours, about the powerful force of trade, a force that will shape the lives, the livelihood of these children here today. And let me just say I salute the Taylor's kids, and Pat Taylor, who helps get them educated.

In this campaign, I have laid out an Agenda for American Renewal. It is a comprehensive series of steps to win the new global economic competition, to create here in America by early in the next century the world's very first $10 trillion economy.

My agenda spells it out in detail what we must do to achieve that goal, the priorities I'm fighting for. I want to literally, to begin with, we have got to literally reinvent American education and give every parent the right to choose their kids' schools, public, private, or religious. Governor Clinton said it won't work, and I say I do remember that it worked pretty well for the GI bill, and it can work for all the parents today. So let's fight for that.

I want to reform our legal system. Frankly, we must limit these crazy lawsuits. As a nation we must sue each other less and care for each other more. I don't care, the liberals don't like this one, but I want to see us strengthen the American family because family is still the foundation of our Nation.

I want our Nation to save and invest more. And we can do this only by reducing the size of the Federal Government, because today's Government is too big, and it spends too much of your money.

I want to limit the terms of Members of Congress and take Congress away from the special interests and give it back to you, the American people.

These are steps that we must take to realize the global opportunity before us, to place more of our neighborhoods on the path to prosperity. But we can begin by grasping a unique opportunity to break down century-old barriers to the free flow of goods and ideas, by fighting to open new markets. Because you know as well as I do, given the right chance, the American worker can outthink, outcompete, outwork any other worker in the entire world.

I was over in San Antonio yesterday to mark a turning point in the history of North America. Yesterday will be remembered in history, for along with President Carlos Salinas of Mexico and Prime Minister Brian

Mulroney of Canada, we watched the signing of a truly historic agreement, the North American free trade agreement or NAFTA. And over the next 15 years, NAFTA will create the largest free trade area in the world, an economic trading area with over 360 million customers and over $6 trillion in annual output.

Trade between the United States and Mexico and Canada has already increased by over 70 percent in the past 5 years. This agreement strengthens our partnership, and most of all, it creates good jobs for American workers. And that has got to be the goal. Everybody in the Port of New Orleans knows what I'm talking about. This agreement allows the United States to build on our lead as the export superpower.

America already sells more products abroad than any other nation in history. Over the past 3 years, despite a sluggish world economy, U.S. exports have increased more than 30 percent and more than $20 billion of these goods passed right through the Port of New Orleans. And you know what this means for the city.

Audience members. Four more years! Four more years! Four more years!

The President. You know what this means for the city, don't you? As the Saints' fans might say, "Cha-ching!" You know, today, Louisiana is the Nation's eighth largest export State with over $16 billion in export sales. Almost 70,000 jobs come from manufactured exports. You send chemicals to Australia and cotton to China and paper to France. You see, where's that—there it is, this yellow tractor right here, it's headed for Chile. But no matter what we're putting in these ships, we're going to mow down the international competition. We can't do it if we're protectionists. We do it by things like NAFTA, this forward-looking agreement.

You know, Louisiana leads the way, all right, but the rest of America isn't far behind. Already, one in six American manufacturing jobs is supported by trade. For those who worry that our children will not enjoy high wages, consider this fact: On average, trade-related jobs pay 17 percent more than the average U.S. wage. So, if we want the sons and daughters of steelworkers to earn a good living and get their share of the American dream, we have to promote trade, and we have to do it right now.

You see, the world has changed dramatically over the past few years.

Audience members. Four more years! Four more years! Four more years!

The President. Where once leaders gathered to find ways to evade conflict, now we must meet to find new ways to promote opportunity. And where once our progress was measured only by a crisis averted, in the new world it will be measured by new jobs created. And I learned the lessons of trade not from a textbook over in Oxford, England, not from a briefing paper, but from the only teacher that counts, real-world business experience.

Even back in the days back there in the late fifties and sixties when I was coming here to New Orleans to work with these oil rigs, I learned that the more my company could sell abroad, in Japan in our case or South America or the Middle East, the more jobs we could create for Louisiana roughnecks and drillers and tool-pushers. My company drilled wells off this coast. The skill of our workers made us the very best in the entire world. And as we drilled abroad, we created good jobs for U.S. workers. It was true then, and it is true today. So don't listen to that measure of protection.

Over the years, I sensed that the world was becoming more like us and saw people in China and Europe demand more of our cars, our computers, even our colas. That is why I am so excited by the new era that lies before us, lies ahead for these kids. You know, I know times have been tough here in America, but we must keep in mind, this is a global economic downturn. The nations of Europe suffer higher unemployment, higher interest rates, higher inflation. But we can and we will lead the way to a new era of prosperity, if we have the courage to do what is right today.

I believe that America is uniquely suited to lead this new world, just as we led the old one. Despite all the pessimism, all the tearing down of the United States of America, don't forget a few facts. We have the world's largest market. We sell more high-tech products than any other nation. Our workers are more productive than the Germans, more productive than the Japanese, more productive than any other men and women in the entire world. And so don't let that Clinton-Gore ticket tell you how bad everything is.

You know, in the cold war, we used our military might to force alliances, to push them together all across the Atlantic and the Pacific. Today, we can use our economic strength to forge new trade alliances, push them together. NAFTA is only the first. I see other trade agreements with nations in Europe and Latin America and Asia. As we tear down barriers, we create good, high-paying jobs for American workers, and that is what this Nation desperately needs.

You know, there used to be a great distinction, but that old distinction between foreign policy and economic policy has simply vanished. To build a strong economy at home, we must be strong and aggressive abroad. That's why I believe that the American people have a clear choice this November between an experienced leader with a clear global vision and a Governor with no international experience, who can't seem to make a decision on any issue at all, any day of the week.

Audience members. We want Bush! We want Bush! We want Bush!

The President. There's a great article up there in USA Today. Get a look at it, this morning's USA Today. It chronicles Governor Clinton's changing positions on ten issues, from taxes to term limits to the Gulf war. I challenge you to read this article and tell me where Bill Clinton stands on any of these important issues. He says all things to all people. In the White House, I've found out something. You have to take a stand. You can't keep everybody happy. You've got to call them as you see them and do what is right and not waffle.

I see these signs out here about NAFTA, this free trade agreement. Well, take that for an example. When he started his campaign, Bill Clinton sounded like a staunch defender of free trade. Then, he sought the endorsement of some powerful labor people, particularly the labor leaders in Washington. Before long, he announced he was undecided. Finally, last week, Governor Clinton looked at the polls one more time and came out for NAFTA.

But then, he waffled. He said, "I'm for it—but." He said he didn't want the agreement to encourage strikebreakers from coming into the country. The agreement already prevents that. The agreement takes care of that. It isn't going to happen. He said he didn't want the agreement to allow contaminated food to come into the country. That's already been taken care of in this agreement. He said he didn't want the agreement to allow other countries to flood our market with imports, but part of the agreement is devoted to providing safeguards against that. He said he has reservations about the environmental impact of the agreement, and yet the National Wildlife Federation, our nation's largest environmental organization, has already endorsed the agreement.

So here is the bottom line. In the White House, you cannot have it both ways on tough issues. The phone in the Oval Office doesn't have a call-waiting button. When you're President of the United States, "maybe" cannot be your middle name.

This is especially important when you're fighting for free and fair trade. And today, the U.S. Congress is a riot of conflicting interests. As I said, I wish we had many more like Bob Livingston. Many Members are loyal to the future and understand that free trade is the way to create jobs. But others are only loyal to whomever gives them the biggest campaign check, and they back down to every group seeking a new tariff or a trade wall. As President, only I can stand up against irrational impulses of protectionism. And as President, only I can speak for the national interests and fight for the jobs of the future.

There was nothing inevitable about this trade agreement. It is the product of thousands of hours of grueling negotiation, hundreds of detours avoided, thousands of diversions ignored. Only the unwavering resolve of three governments, the steadfast commitment of visionary leaders like Brian Mulroney of Canada and President Carlos Salinas of Mexico brought this dream to life.

We must guarantee that America will remain the world's export superpower. Governor Clinton waffles and hedges his bet, and I'm going to bet on our future. I'm going to fight for good jobs to go right in this port and ship our goods abroad, every one of them made by American workers in the United States.

Audience members. We want Bush! We want Bush! We want Bush!

The President. I care about America leading this new economy, right here. I just didn't read about free trade in a textbook somewhere; I feel it. I've learned it all my life.

And here at this port, you know that the future lies in reaching out, in tearing down barriers, in selling American products in every corner of the globe. Now let's get the job done, together.

I am proud of what we have accomplished the past 4 years to make freedom victorious, to make our children safer. You know, Governor Clinton doesn't seem to care, but I think it's a big deal that our kids, our children, go to bed every night safer from the scourge of nuclear weapons. I am proud that my administration had a lot to do with that. And we did it by standing up against aggression. The sons and daughters of Louisiana that served in Desert Storm deserve our thanks and deserve our support. And so do those that served in Vietnam.

Now we must build on our accomplishment and meet the challenge of a global economy. America cannot be timid, we cannot be uncertain. That is not our nature. We must be aggressive. We must lead. We must keep our eyes fixed on the future, for that is where our opportunity lies.

This is the kind of leadership I've given America. As we've changed the world the past 4 years, this is the kind of leadership that I offer for the next 4 years, as we create jobs and renew this country we love so dearly. Do not let them tear down the United States of America. We are the best and freest and fairest country on the face of the Earth. Our future looks bright. Now let's get to work and create jobs here in America for all.

Thank you. Thank you. And may God Bless our great country. Thank you very much. Thank you all.

Note: The President spoke at 2:08 p.m. at the Nashville Avenue Wharf. In his remarks, he referred to Peggy Wilson, New Orleans council member; W. Henson Moore, Assistant to the President for Intergovernmental Affairs; and Patrick F. Taylor, who developed the Taylor plan for financing higher education for low- and moderate-income students.

Remarks to the Law Enforcement Community in New Orleans
October 8, 1992

Well, thank you, Ron, Pete, and I am very pleased to receive this endorsement. I am very pleased. Louisiana has got a great law enforcement community, and this is a wonderful occasion for me. The Police Association of New Orleans and the other representatives of law enforcement community here with us today, I just thank you all from the bottom of a very grateful heart.

Let me just say a word to the family and friends of Officer Norvin Powell, who dedicated a lifetime of service to the small town of Winfield, Louisiana. Two weeks ago, officer Powell responded to a routine break-in. Then after a struggle with the burglar,

Powell lay dead, and the burglar escaped. He didn't get far. After an 18-hour manhunt, he was arrested. Tragically, Officer Powell's handcuffs were still attached to one wrist. Powell took a stand. He made a difference in his community. On behalf of a grateful nation, while I'm here, I simply want to pay tribute here to this outstanding officer and others like him all across this country.

You know, keeping neighborhoods safe and secure has got to be one of the fundamental responsibilities of government. It takes a tough, no-nonsense approach, one that puts our sympathy with the victims of crime, not the criminals. Ron set out the principles that I feel are absolutely essential for a President as related to law enforcement. After all, hard time is what criminals should get, not the innocent kids and older Americans who have to live in the fear of violence.

In this election, two candidates are talking tough on crime, but just one candidate is taking action. Now, you can look at the record. Last year under Governor Clinton, Arkansas criminals on average served just one-fifth of their sentence before they were back out on the street. They did the crime, and they served one-fifth of the time.

So I think you'll see the contrast when I tell you that the Federal inmates, inmates who fall under my jurisdiction, serve an average of 85 percent of their full sentence. Crime is one more issue where the Governor of Arkansas can't talk his way past his record. If you want to know who's really tough on crime, look to the people out there on the front lines.

Take the Fraternal Order of Police over in Little Rock. They lived with Governor Clinton for 12 years. They know that Arkansas ranks rock bottom for every important per capita crime dollar it spends: prisons, 46th; judicial and legal systems, 50th. And when it comes to spending for police officers, Arkansas ranks 49th. They know Bill Clinton's record best, and they are endorsing George Bush for President of the United States.

So let me say to the law enforcement officers and the associations that are represented here today: For 4 years I've kept a badge, an officer's badge 14072, in my desk in the Oval Office. A retired New York police lieutenant, Matt Byrne, gave me that badge some time ago. It's his son's badge, Eddie Byrne, who wore the badge the day he was gunned down by a gang of crackheads. As Matt asked, I have really kept that badge right there in that center drawer of the Oval Office desk, kept it there as a reminder of all of the brave officers who put your lives on the line for us every single day.

As President, you have my thanks. But much more than that, you have my support. You're on the side of the law, and I am on your side. With your support, I know that we can turn back the threat of drugs and crime. I know that we can make our communities much safer and much stronger.

I thank you very much, each and every one of you, for this vote of confidence. And may God bless the men and women who wear the badge. Thank you all.

Note: The President spoke at 3:25 p.m. at Belle Chasse Naval Air Station. In his remarks, he referred to Ronald J. Canatella, president, Police Association of New Orleans, and Peter Dale, Louisiana State coordinator for law enforcement, Bush-Quayle '92.

Remarks at a Victory '92 Dinner in Houston, Texas
October 8, 1992

The President. Thank you all very much. Thank you.

Audience members. Four more years! Four more years! Four more years!

The President. Thank you, President Reagan. Thank you, my friend, and thank you for all that you taught me in those 8 years when I was privileged to serve at your side.

Let me also give my thanks to Barbara, working so hard up in New York tonight, but all across this country; to President Gerald Ford, for whom I have unlimited respect; for my running mate and my partner, Vice President Dan Quayle, out there in St. Louis, and Marilyn; and to Bob Dole and Bob Michel. I couldn't ask for two finer, more principled leaders in the two Houses of Congress, and I just wish we had control of both Houses to move this country forward even faster.

I was touched by what my friend Arnold

Schwarzenegger said. He is a friend, and I value that friendship. And to all of you and the good friends watching in over 100 cities and in 30 States, you have touched my heart this evening.

Let me also add my special thanks to Ted Welch, who ran this whole effort, to Bob Mosbacher, to Rob Mosbacher, next to me here, to all our finance chairs, and of course, a great party chairman, Rich Bond, the chairman of the Republican National Committee.

This evening is for our entire ticket, from top to bottom, the proud Republican team. As you can imagine, I'm not in the habit much lately of quoting polls. [*Laughter*] But Rob reminded me of something; I couldn't help but notice that new poll that came out just last night. It wasn't CNN or ABC or Gallup or the Wall Street Journal; it was that little kids' magazine, Weekly Reader. They polled over 600,000 kids across America: 39 percent wanted Bill Clinton for President and 56 percent wanted George Bush.

Before you think that the pressure of the past few months has gone to my head and that I'm seeking solace in fourth graders— [*laughter*]—let me point out something. Weekly Reader is not a bad thermometer of what happens in elections. That particular poll hasn't been wrong since 1956. But this is admittedly a weird year, the strangest year I can ever remember in politics, and I don't want to leave anything to chance. So when the Democrats leave Washington next week, or in the next few days, I'm asking Bob Dole, Bob Michel, and all the other Republicans to sneak up to Capitol Hill and pass the 28th amendment, lowering the voting age to 5-year-olds. Let Governor Clinton take his saxophone and go after the MTV vote—[*laughter*]—we'll tear him apart on "Sesame Street."

But seriously, forget the polls. Forget the pundits. We are going to win this election. And we're going to lead this Nation for 4 more years. And let me tell you three reasons why I remain so confident.

The first is our record. We've heard a lot of talk this year about what's wrong with America. But let's not lose sight of the grand victory that we have helped win for all humanity.

As I study for the debate this Sunday, my thoughts went back to another debate 12 years ago. I believe it was in Cleveland with President Reagan, between Jimmy Carter and then-challenger Ronald Reagan. In his closing statement, President Carter, speaking from the heart, talked about how he'd had a conversation with his daughter, Amy, in which she said that the control of nuclear weapons was the greatest problem facing mankind. Some laughed. I didn't, and nor did President Reagan.

Well, President Carter and many well-meaning people advocated at that point a nuclear freeze. Remember the freeze movement? But President Reagan and I fought for a policy of peace through strength. And 12 years later, over a billion people in every corner of the globe have taken their first breath of freedom. Tonight, as millions of American kids pull back the covers and shut off their talking Barbie dolls, they think not of nuclear weapons, but of the sweet and satisfying dreams of peace. Does that matter? You bet it does.

The second reason we'll win is because our ideas make sense to middle class Americans.

Governor Clinton likes to quote statistic after statistic, all kind of tearing down America, pointing out how bad everything is. But our problems are never put in the context of a global slowdown. Only now, only in the past few days, have people really started to compare our solutions.

Governor Clinton likes to say that he's, quote, "a different kind of Democrat," unquote. Well, to me there's nothing different about $150 billion in new taxes, more than Michael Dukakis and Walter Mondale combined. There's nothing different about making pie-in-the-sky promises with one hand while pulling dollars out of working people's wallets with the other. In June, Governor Clinton proposed $220 billion in new Government spending. And he called it "investment." And he used that same tone that doctors use when they say, this shot won't hurt you one bit. [*Laughter*]

I thought that would satisfy Governor Clinton's appetite, but it turned out to be just an hors d'oeuvre. We did a little calculating. Since that day in June, Governor

Clinton has promised at least another $200 billion, quote, "in investments." Those are just the ones we've been able to put a price tag on, a billion dollars in new promises every single day. And so Governor Clinton has earned a new nickname, Billion Dollar Bill. [*Laughter*] But who is going to pay Bill's bills? The same people who always pay, the middle class. They're going to do it.

A couple of weeks ago, the National Association of Business Economists compared Governor Clinton's billion-dollar-a-day spending plan with my progrowth policies of smaller Government and lower taxes. And the vast majority said that under our plan, under my plan, inflation would be lower, interest rates would be lower, and the budget deficit would be smaller.

Governor Clinton said this week that his side is, quote, "on the right side of history." But I fear his inexperience is showing. From Managua to Moscow, history is moving away from taxes and regulation and central control. History is casting aside the Government planner, who spends the wealth of nations, and lifting up the men and women who create it. No, Governor Clinton, history is on our side, and that's why we will make history in 25 days.

I believe the third reason—I really believe this one—one reason we will win, in a word, is trust. We've spent most of the time in this campaign talking about economic and domestic policy, as well as we should, because those are the most important problems facing us today. We should remember, however, that when we elect a President of the United States, we're electing someone who at any time may have to deal with the awesome decision of sending someone else's young son or daughter, America's men and women, into battle.

I had to make that decision in 1989, and then again in Desert Storm. The President we entrust with these decisions must have character, honesty, and integrity. Last night on the Larry King show, I was asked about some issues in my opponent's background. Let me repeat the point I made, because I feel so strongly about it: My opponent has written that he once mobilized demonstrations in London against the Vietnam war. I simply for the life of me cannot understand how someone can go to London, another country, and mobilize demonstrations against the United States of America when our kids are dying halfway around the world.

The issue here isn't patriotism. You can demonstrate all you want here at home. Barbara and I look out, as Ron and Nancy did, out of the White House, and there's somebody out there every single day, properly protesting or raising objections, exercising their rights. That's part of America. But I can't understand someone mobilizing demonstrations in a foreign county when poor kids, drafted out of the ghettos, are dying in a faraway land. You can call me old-fashioned, but that just does not make sense to me.

I think the American people respect experience and character and proven ability to make a tough decision. I hope that means that they will vote for me on November 3d.

It has been said that a friend is someone who knows everything there is to know about you and likes you anyway. [*Laughter*] And, tonight, I would add that the definition of a friend is someone who stands by your side while you're behind, so that you can pull ahead. Barbara and I are blessed with thousands of friends, and you have touched our hearts tonight. As we say a hearty thanks to all of you, I remind you that our struggle is to more than win an election; our struggle is to renew America so that we can match the peace we have achieved in the world with that peace of mind here at home.

Tonight, you have given me the strength and the passion and the inner confidence to take our ideas to the American people for 25 more days. You're sending me into St. Louis for that debate with a full head of steam.

Thank you for your support. And God bless the United States of America. Thank you all very, very much.

Note: The President spoke at 9:08 p.m. in the J.W. Marriott Hotel. In his remarks, he referred to Arnold Schwarzenegger, Chairman, President's Council on Physical Fitness and Sports; Robert Mosbacher, Sr., gen-

eral chairman for finance, Republican National Committee; and Robert Mosbacher,

Jr., chairman, Texas Victory '92.

Remarks to the National Fraternal Order of Police in Cincinnati, Ohio
October 9, 1992

Hey, listen, Dewey, let me just tell you at the outset how grateful I am not just for that kind introduction but for this fantastic endorsement. I'll say more about it in a minute. I appreciate this warm welcome, and I do mean warm. [*Laughter*] I'm delighted to be back in the Cincinnati area, and I am very pleased to salute not only Dewey Stokes but Ralph Orms, the FOP secretary; Ken Gorman, the chairman of the board of trustees; Gil Gallegos and George Austin and all the members of the executive board. I especially want to recognize the officers from Dayton who came here today in remembrance of your fallen comrade, Officer Bill Whalen.

I'm delighted and honored to accept this most prestigious endorsement here today as the preferred Presidential candidate of the National Fraternal Order of Police, and I thank you for your support. As most people across this country know, you're one of the strongest voices of the law enforcement community in the entire country, and I'm grateful you're speaking on my behalf. This country is going to see a real comeback on election day when we come storming back to victory. I really believe it's going to happen.

I will continue to say what I am for, and I will continue, because a lot of the people around are not helping us do this, to define Governor Clinton for what he is and for what his record is. I am confident when people go into the voting booth they are going to say, this President has the character and the trust to lead this country for another 4 years. We are going to turn it around because of people like you who want to do what's right for America, aren't afraid to take a position, to stand up. I believe beyond a shadow of a doubt that this Bill Clinton—I really honestly believe this—

is wrong for America at this time.

Now, look at his record. Look at the record. He is a typical tax-and-spend, big Government, tax-and-spend, coddle-the-criminal man. We don't need that. Don't take my word for it. Ask the folks who know the record best. Ask your brothers and sisters in Little Rock, Fraternal Order of Police in Arkansas, Governor Clinton's hometown. They're endorsing not their Governor, but you guessed it, they are endorsing George Bush for President of the United States of America. They're doing this not out of personal spite, but they're doing this because of the record. Arkansas ranks near rockbottom for every important per capita crime dollar it spends: for prisons, 46th; for judicial and legal systems, 50th; and when it comes to spending for police officers, Arkansas ranks 49th.

No wonder crime went up faster in Arkansas during the 1980's than in any other State. If you don't give your police the tools they need, you can't expect them to do the job.

Dewey Stokes very generously spelled out some of our record, and I would like to compare my record to Governor Clinton's. Since 1989, I've proposed a 59 percent increase in Federal spending to fight crime. As for charges that my administration short-shrifted State and local law enforcement, a charge that this Governor recklessly keeps putting forward, the fact is that spending under the Eddie Byrne Memorial Grant Program for State and local law enforcement is more than 3 times what it was when I became President of the United States.

Here's something that the victims of crime might be interested in; there's more to it. Last year, under Governor Clinton, the average Arkansas criminal served less than one-fifth of his sentence. Then he's back out on the streets. Apparently, down in Arkansas you do the crime but not the time.

Most Federal inmates under my jurisdiction serve at least 85 percent of their full sentences. I have had very little support from the national media in putting these facts into perspective, but we've got time. With this endorsement and your help, we are going to get the facts into the record. The record, I might say, gets a little unnerving when you consider the damage that a soft-on-crime President could do to law enforcement nationwide.

After all, maybe the single most vital legacy a President can leave behind is his record of judicial appointments. Everybody in this room—maybe you know it better than others across the country, but everybody here knows the judicial appointments are terribly important to strong law enforcement. I ask that you compare the Carter record to the Reagan-Bush era, and you can see how the Democratic appointments are still hurting us.

The record clearly shows that Carter left us with judges far more sympathetic to the suspect's rights than judges appointed by Ronald Reagan. According to one independent study that NBC News reported just the other night, Carter appointees are almost 5 times more likely to champion the suspect's rights over the rights of a victim.

Well, my record on this is clear. In 1988, I told the American people that, like my predecessor, I would appoint judges who interpret and apply the law and do not try to rewrite the law from the Federal Bench. I pledged my appointments would give more consideration to victims' rights than to criminals' rights, and that is exactly what I have done. The results are clear. The Supreme Court has handed down a series of sensible decisions allowing victims to be heard and justice to be served.

Now, would Governor Clinton's appointments be similar? Well, all the names of possible Supreme Court appointees coming from his camp are rabidly opposed to the death penalty. The name Clinton himself has mentioned as recently as Saturday night, with my wife sitting there, was Governor Cuomo of New York. So much for

capital punishment and so much for the thugs who kill cops. We do not need that kind of appointment to the Supreme Court of the United States.

It is plain wrong and deeply unfair to ask law enforcement officers, who are out there on the streets putting their lives on the line for us, to do their job and then see their good work undone by judges who turn those criminals right back out on the sidewalk. I am on the side of the victim. And let there be no mistake about that. I say it is high time that we turn around this judicial trend to be soft on criminals and hard on the people in blue.

The bottom line on November 3d is this: When it comes to crime, if you liked Carter I, you will love Carter II. [*Laughter*] America simply cannot afford that. We need a President to help you take criminals off the streets and keep them off the streets. I believe I am that person, and that's what I stand for as President of the United States.

I support the brave men and women who wear the blue because you know better than anyone that we are all vulnerable: men, women, and children; white, brown, and black; young and old; rich and poor. To a bullet, to a blade we all look just the same.

You alone stand in the breach. We don't thank you enough. To tell you the truth, I don't believe we can thank you enough. The best we can do is to give you our support, and we can fight for justice when one of your comrades falls in the line of duty.

That's why my crime bill calls for a Federal death penalty for cop killers. It will go into law if Congress gets around to voting on it, and I believe they will. There's going to be a lot of new Members of Congress this time, the one institution that hasn't changed for 38 years. We need to clean House. While it won't bring back the six brave police officers who were killed across the Nation just in the past few weeks, at least it will take the animals off the street who commit the ultimate horror by gunning down the heroes in blue.

I want to tell you why you folks are so often on my mind. I mentioned Eddie Byrne. I know Dewey; he probably knows Eddie Byrne's father. For 4 years I've kept this badge in my desk there in the Oval Office. You've probably seen that desk on the television, where all the visitors come in. I keep this badge, 14072, in my desk in the Oval Office. A retired New York officer, Lieutenant Matt Byrne, gave it to me. This is the badge that his son, Eddie, wore the day he was gunned down by a crackhead. Matt, the dad, asked me to keep that badge as a reminder of all you brave officers who put your lives on the line every single day. I've kept it, and I always will. As President, you have my lasting thanks, but much more than that, you have my support. You can count on that.

With your strong support, I know that America can indeed do what so many here today are working on every single waking minute, and that is turn back the threat of drugs and crime, the fear of our young and old, and make our communities safe and strong and secure once again.

You know, I talk and Barbara talks and the Quayles talk about family values. There are a lot of people trying to distort what that means. To me, it means a lot of things. It means support for the children. It means families staying together. It means deadbeat dads supporting the mother. It means a lot of things, including choice in schools and choice in child care. Many things come to-gether. But one thing it means is support for law enforcement, because families must be entitled to safe places to raise their children.

You, more than any other Americans, are out there guaranteeing that part of this battle. We are not going to stop talking about family values because the liberals don't like it. We're going to keep on talking about it.

Now that same crowd is on me in another item. I said that I didn't think it was right to be demonstrating against your country in a foreign land when soldiers are being held captive and soldiers are dying in Vietnam. I feel strongly about that. You let the liberal elite do their number today, trying to call me Joe McCarthy. I'm standing with American principle. It is wrong to demonstrate against your country when your country is at war, and I'm not going to back away from it one single bit.

Thank you all for this fantastic support. And may God bless the greatest, freest country on the face of the Earth, the United States of America.

Note: The President spoke at 4:30 p.m. at the Holiday Inn Eastgate. In his remarks, he referred to Dewey Stokes, president, National Fraternal Order of Police.

Remarks on Arrival in Columbus, Ohio
October 9, 1992

The President. Thank you all.

Audience members. Four more years! Four more years! Four more years!

The President. Thank you very, very much. You've got a great Governor in George Voinovich, and his wife, Janet, is with us here today. Let me say, while we're at it, everyplace I go they're holding up these signs saying "Clean House!" I want to see us helping the Senate, too, by sending Mike DeWine to the United States Senate. I salute my former classmate in Congress, Chalmers Wylie, who's stepping aside. We want to see Debbie Price win that congressional seat. Help us clean House.

It's great to be back here in Ohio. Maybe some of you kids don't know this, but I love coming back here. My granddad ran a business here, Buckeye Steel. My father was born and raised in Columbus, Ohio. A couple of weeks ago we started that wonderful train trip right here in Columbus. This city and this State have been good to us. I believe I've kept the faith, and we believe in the same things: hard work, community, respect for law, duty, honor, and country. That is our code, and we all believe in that.

Now, I've got a big debate coming up Sunday night, and I'm going to talk about these things. I don't pretend I'm the world's greatest debater. You may not always agree, but you know where I stand. I think a President must trust the people, and the people must trust their President. You can compare this to the Governor of Arkansas. The man likes to take both sides on every issue, and he's the reason we're having three debates. One is for Governor Clinton to state his position, and the other two are for him to change his mind. I've never seen anything like it. You can't do that in the Oval Office. You can't waffle. You can't be everything to everybody.

This election is about the kind of America that we want for the young people here, and it's about remaining the world's number one economic power. We can do that with my agenda for America's renewal. It is a comprehensive, integrated plan to create a $10 trillion economy after the turn of the century, and I believe we can do it.

The agenda believes in preparing our young people to excel in science and math and English. And we've got to literally reinvent American education and give every parent a fundamental right to choose their kids' schools, whether public, private, or religious. That will make all the schools better. Parents who favor school choice can start by choosing a President who agrees with them on choice.

Another thing we've got to do is reform our legal system. We've got to control these crazy lawsuits. We've got to sue each other less and care for each other more.

So this agenda is what I'm fighting for, reducing the deficit, reducing taxes by cutting Federal spending. I am seeking a mandate for a balanced budget amendment, for the line-item veto, and for term limits on the United States Congress. I want every taxpayer here to be able to check a box on your tax form targeting up to 10 percent of your income to reduce the deficit. If Congress won't do it, let the taxpayer have a shot at it.

Now I've told you what I'm for, and now let me tell you what you're up against this election year. It's the difference between talk and action, a history of empty promises. The Governor of Arkansas says he's for civil rights. That State doesn't even have a basic civil rights law. Arkansas is one of two States that don't have a civil rights law. He says he's for a clean environment, but the Institute of Southern Studies ranked Arkansas 50th, 50th in terms of environment, dead last in environmental policy. It's the only place the fish light up at night because of pollution down there.

He says he's tough on crime, but crime in Arkansas has increased twice as fast as the rest of the Nation. The cops who know him best, the Fraternal Order of Police in Little Rock, Arkansas, turned their back on him and endorsed me for President of the United States. Earlier today with the Ohioan at my side, Dewey Stokes, right here in Ohio, I proudly accepted the endorsement of the National Fraternal Order of Police, a great, big push for the Bush campaign.

But I think the big difference is on taxes.

Audience members. Four more years! Four more years! Four more years!

The President. Governor Clinton wants to raise your taxes. He's already proposed $150 billion in new taxes and $220 billion in new spending. He announced this using the same words doctors use, "This shot won't hurt you one single bit." Don't believe it.

You know, we added up some of the provinces since that day in June. He's promised at least another $200 billion in investments, he calls it, without saying how he's going to pay for them. Those are just the first few that we've been able to put a price tag on, one billion dollars in new promises every single day. He's earned the nickname Billion Dollar Bill, and we don't need that now as President of the United States.

You know, he says, "Don't worry, we're going to take it out of the rich guys, the top $200,000." But the truth is—you look at the program—to get the money for his plan, to get the $150 billion, he'd have to hit Americans with taxable income of over $36,000. Then to pay for all the rest of his spending, you've got to take it down to about $24,000 a year. Those aren't rich people. Those are the hard-working men and women in this country, and we can't let him slap a tax on them.

Now, think of this Sunday night as you listen to the debate. Judge us not as politicians but as leaders and as human beings, and ask who best reflects your values, and vote for who you trust to lead America at home and abroad.

Barbara and I have tried to uphold the trust of the American people every day we have been in that White House. I hope we have earned your support. Ohio is important. I ask you to work hard. Give me your vote. We have changed the world, and now let's lift everyone up in America and change America.

Thank you, and God bless you all. Thank you very much. Thanks for coming.

Note: The President spoke at 6:03 p.m. at Port Columbus International Airport.

Statement on Signing the Rocky Mountain Arsenal National Wildlife Refuge Act of 1992
October 9, 1992

I am pleased to sign into law H.R. 1435, the "Rocky Mountain Arsenal National Wildlife Refuge Act of 1992." This Act provides for the future establishment of a national wildlife refuge at the Rocky Mountain Arsenal immediately outside of Denver, Colorado. The refuge will be a unique addition to the National Wildlife Refuge System, for both the natural resources it supports and the fish and wildlife-related public uses it provides for Denver residents and all Americans.

The 26 square miles of land at the Arsenal have provided valuable wildlife habitat for many species since the Arsenal was established in 1942. Despite some of the land being contaminated by military and industrial use, the Arsenal continues to host wildlife populations rarely found in such proximity to a major urban area.

A significant population of endangered bald eagles, averaging nearly 100 birds, winters there, along with an extraordinarily high number of hawks. Extensive prairie dog towns cover over 5,000 acres at the Arsenal, and deer, coyotes, burrowing owls, migratory waterfowl, and other species are readily observable.

An essential objective of this Administration is to develop increased opportunities for urban populations to learn about wildlife and the environment. Approximately 50,000 visitors have toured the Arsenal in the past 2 years to view its wildlife and learn about the ongoing contaminant clean-up. Once the refuge is established, the site will educate and enthrall thousands more.

We have done an outstanding job to date of implementing the remediation process at the Arsenal while preserving its wildlife. This legislation, the result of close and bipartisan cooperation between the Administration and members of the Colorado congressional delegation, builds on that effort.

The Act ensures that the ongoing Superfund cleanup process will fully protect humans and the environment and will not be altered by the ultimate designation of the area as a wildlife refuge. Once the Environmental Protection Agency certifies that the remediation process is complete, the Arsenal will officially become the Rocky Mountain Arsenal National Wildlife Refuge.

The Act also acknowledges the need to coordinate management of the refuge with the operation of the nearby Denver International Airport, which will open next year.

The very idea of converting the Rocky Mountain Arsenal into a national wildlife refuge would have been inconceivable a few years ago. Our success in doing so demonstrates that, when we focus on opportunities rather than problems, we can match the resilience of nature with human ingenuity. In signing H.R. 1435, I applaud this approach to resolving the Nation's environmental problems and urge its application to other challenges that confront us.

GEORGE BUSH

The White House,
October 9, 1992.

Note: H.R. 1435, approved October 9, was assigned Public Law No. 102–402.

Letter to Congressional Leaders Transmitting the Report of the White House Conference on Indian Education
October 9, 1992

Dear Mr. Speaker: (Dear Mr. President:)
    Section 5502 of Public Law 100–297, as amended by section 306 of Public Law 102–27, requires that I submit to the Congress the final report of the White House Conference on Indian Education and recommendations with respect to the report.
    Enclosed are a "Response to the Recommendations of the Report of the White House Conference on Indian Education,"

the final report of the Conference, and an executive summary.
    Sincerely,

GEORGE BUSH

Note: Identical letters were sent to Thomas S. Foley, Speaker of the House of Representatives, and Dan Quayle, President of the Senate.

Statement by Press Secretary Fitzwater on the Death of Willy Brandt
October 9, 1992

The President was deeply saddened to learn of the passing of a great German statesman and patriot, Willy Brandt.
    Willy Brandt was a towering figure of the postwar era, a man of vision and courage. History will crown him as a stalwart champion of freedom and democracy, who, as Governing Mayor of Berlin during the city's darkest days, fearlessly faced down a Soviet menace that threatened the lives and ideals of his beloved city and people. History will also record his as a powerful voice for reconciliation between East and West. First as Foreign Minister and then as Chancellor, he actively pursued a relaxation of tension in Europe that made the world a safer place for us all. The collapse of communism and

the onward march of democracy in Eastern Europe and the former Soviet Union soundly vindicate his bold vision of two decades ago.
    Americans will remember Willy Brandt not only as a champion of freedom and democracy but also as a steadfast friend of the United States. His strong support of the transatlantic community reflected his belief that close German-American cooperation was crucial to the preservation of peace and promotion of freedom and democracy.
    Together with our German friends and all those who fought in the causes to which Willy Brandt dedicated his life, the American people mourn his loss.

Designation of Arlene Holen As Chairman of the Federal Mine Safety and Health Review Commission
October 9, 1992

The President designated Arlene Holen, of the District of Columbia, as Chairman of the Federal Mine Safety and Health Review Commission. She would succeed Ford Barney Ford.

Since 1990, Ms. Holen has served as a commissioner of the Federal Mine Safety and Health Review Commission. Prior to this, Ms. Holen has served as a member of the Coal Commission, 1990; as an Associate Director for Human Resources, Veterans and Labor, for the Office of Management and Budget at the White House, 1988–90; and as a senior economist with the Council of Economic Advisers at the White House, 1985–88.

Ms. Holen graduated from Smith College (B.A., 1960) and Columbia University (M.A., 1963). She was born July 5, 1938, in New York, NY. Ms. Holen is married, has two children, and currently resides in Washington, DC.

Remarks on Arrival in St. Louis, Missouri
October 11, 1992

The President. Hey, listen, thank you for this great welcome, a marvelous sendoff for the big debate, and the countdown to the election. I'm absolutely convinced we're going to win this election. I believe we're going to win the election because we are right on the issues. Our record is good, and we're not going to let this guy distort it anymore.

You know, the only way they can win is if they try to convince the American people that America is in decline. That's what they're telling us. We are number one; we're going to make life better for everybody. But don't let them tell you things are bad. It is so sick.

Thank you all very much. Keep your TV's on. Thanks a lot.

Audience members. Four more years! Four more years! Four more years!

Note: The President spoke at 1:25 p.m. at Lambert-St. Louis International Airport. A tape was not available for verification of the content of these remarks.

Presidential Debate in St. Louis
October 11, 1992

Jim Lehrer. Good evening, and welcome to the first of three debates among the major candidates for President of the United States, sponsored by the Commission on Presidential Debates. The candidates are independent candidate Ross Perot; Governor Bill Clinton, the Democratic nominee; and President George Bush, the Republican nominee.

I am Jim Lehrer of "The MacNeil/Lehrer NewsHour" on PBS, and I will be the moderator for this 90-minute event, which is taking place before an audience here in the Athletic Complex on the campus of Washington University in St. Louis, Missouri.

Three journalists will be asking questions tonight. They are John Mashek of the Boston Globe; Ann Compton of ABC News; and Sander Vanocur, a freelance journalist. We will follow a format agreed to by representatives of the Clinton and Bush campaigns. That agreement contains no restrictions on the content or subject matter of the questions.

Each candidate will have up to 2 minutes for a closing statement. The order of those as well as the questioning was determined by a drawing. The first question goes to Mr. Perot. He will have 2 minutes to answer, to be followed by rebuttals of one minute each from Governor Clinton and then President Bush.

Distinction Among Candidates

Gentlemen, good evening. The first topic tonight is what separates each of you from the other. Mr. Perot, what do you believe tonight is the single most important separating issue of this campaign?

Mr. Perot. I think the principal issue that separates me is that 5½ million people came together on their own and put me on the ballot. I was not put on the ballot by either of the two parties. I was not put on the ballot by any PAC money, by any foreign lobbyist money, by any special interest money. This is a movement that came from the people.

This is the way the framers of the Constitution intended our Government to be, a Government that comes from the people. Over time we have developed a Government that comes at the people, that comes from the top down, where the people are more or less treated as objects to be programmed during the campaign, with commercials and media events and fear messages and personal attacks and things of that nature.

The thing that separates my candidacy and makes it unique is that this came from millions of people in 50 States all over this country who wanted a candidate that worked and belonged to nobody but them. I go into this race as their servant, and I belong to them. So this comes from the people.

Mr. Lehrer. Governor Clinton, one-minute response.

Governor Clinton. The most important distinction in this campaign is that I represent real hope for change: a departure from trickle-down economics, a departure from tax-and-spend economics, to invest and

grow. But before I can do that I must challenge the American people to change, and they must decide.

Tonight I say to the President: Mr. Bush, for 12 years you've had it your way. You've had your chance, and it didn't work. It's time to change. I want to bring that change to the American people, but we must all decide first we have the courage to change for hope and a better tomorrow.

Mr. Lehrer. President Bush, one-minute response, sir.

President Bush. Well, I think one thing that distinguishes is experience. I think we've dramatically changed the world. I'll talk about that a little bit later, but the changes are mind-boggling for world peace. Kids go to bed at night without the same fear of nuclear war. And change for change's sake isn't enough. We saw that message in the late seventies when we heard a lot about change. And what happened? That "misery index" went right through the roof.

But my economic program, I think, is the kind of change we want. And the way we're going to get it done is we're going to have a brandnew Congress. A lot of them are thrown out because of all the scandals. I'll sit down with them, Democrats and Republicans alike, and work for my Agenda for American Renewal which represents real change.

But I'd say, if you had to separate out, I think it's experience at this level.

Experience

Mr. Lehrer. Governor Clinton, how do you respond to the President—you have 2 minutes—on the question of experience? He says that is what distinguishes him from the other two of you.

Governor Clinton. I believe experience counts, but it's not everything. Values, judgment, and the record that I have amassed in my State also should count for something. I've worked hard to create good jobs and to educate people. My State now ranks first in the country in job growth this year, fourth in income growth, fourth in the reduction of poverty, third in overall economic performance, according to a major news magazine. That's because we believe in investing in education and in jobs.

We have to change in this country. You know, my wife, Hillary, gave me a book about a year ago in which the author defined insanity as just doing the same old thing over and over again and expecting a different result. We have got to have the courage to change. Experience is important, yes. I've gotten a lot of good experience in dealing with ordinary people over the last year and a month. I've touched more people's lives and seen more heartbreak and hope, more pain and more promise than anybody else who's run for President this year. And I think the American people deserve better than they're getting. We have gone from first to 13th in the world in wages in the last 12 years since Mr. Bush and Mr. Reagan have been in. Personal income has dropped while people have worked harder in the last 4 years. There have been twice as many bankruptcies as new jobs created.

We need a new approach. The same old experience is not relevant. We're living in a new world after the cold war. And what works in this new world is not trickle-down, not Government for the benefit of the privileged few, not tax-and-spend but a commitment to invest in American jobs and American education. Controlling American health care costs and bringing the American people together, that is what works. And you can have the right kind of experience and the wrong kind of experience. Mine is rooted in the real lives of real people. And it will bring real results if we have the courage to change.

Mr. Lehrer. President Bush, one minute to respond.

President Bush. I just thought of another, another big difference here between me—I don't believe Mr. Perot feels this way, but I know Governor Clinton did, because I want to accurately quote him. He thinks, I think he said, that the country is coming apart at the seams. Now, I know that the only way he can win is to make everybody believe the economy is worse than it is. But this country's not coming apart at the seams, for heaven sakes. We're the United States of America. In spite of the economic problems, we are the most respected economy around the world. Many would trade for it.

We've been caught up in a global slowdown. We can do much, much better. But we ought not to try to convince the American people that America is a country that's coming apart at the seams.

I would hate to be running for President and think that the only way I could win would be to convince everybody how horrible things are. Yes, there are big problems. And yes, people are hurting. But I believe that this Agenda for American Renewal I have is the answer to do it. And I believe we can get it done now, whereas we didn't in the past, because you're going to have a whole brandnew bunch of people in the Congress that are going to have to listen to the same American people I'm listening to.

Mr. Lehrer. Mr. Perot, a minute response, sir.

Mr. Perot. Well, they've got a point. I don't have any experience in running up a $4 trillion debt. [*Laughter*] I don't have any experience in gridlocked Government where nobody takes responsibility for anything and everybody blames everybody else. I don't have any experience in creating the worst public school system in the industrialized world, the most violent, crime-ridden society in the industrialized world.

But I do have a lot of experience in getting things done. So if we're at a point in history where we want to stop talking about it and do it, I've got a lot of experience in figuring out how to solve problems, making the solutions work, and then moving on to the next one. I've got a lot of experience in not taking 10 years to solve a 10-minute problem. So if it's time for action, I think I have experience that counts. If it's more time for gridlock and talk and finger-pointing, I'm the wrong man.

Character Issues

Mr. Lehrer. President Bush, the question goes to you. You have 2 minutes. And the question is this: Are there important issues of character separating you from these other two men?

President Bush. I think the American people should be the judge of that. I think character is a very important question. I said something the other day where I was accused of being like Joe McCarthy because I questioned—put it this way—I think it's wrong to demonstrate against your own country or organize demonstrations against your own country in foreign soil. I just think it's wrong. Maybe, they say, well, it was a youthful indiscretion. I was 19 or 20, flying off an aircraft carrier, and that shaped me to be Commander in Chief of the Armed Forces. And I'm sorry, but demonstrating—it's not a question of patriotism. It's a question of character and judgment.

They get on me, Bill's gotten on me about "Read my lips." When I make a mistake, I'll admit it. But he has not admitted the mistake. And I just find it impossible to understand how an American can demonstrate against his own country in a foreign land, organizing demonstrations against it, when young men are held prisoner in Hanoi or kids out of the ghetto were drafted.

Some say, well, you're a little old-fashioned. Maybe I am, but I just don't think that's right. Now, whether it's character or judgment, whatever it is, I have a big difference here on this issue. And so we'll just have to see how it plays out. But I couldn't do that. And I don't think most Americans could do that.

And they all say, well, it was a long time ago. Well, let's admit it then, say, "I made a terrible mistake." How could you be Commander in Chief of the Armed Forces and have some kid say, when you have to make a tough decision, as I did in Panama or in Kuwait, and then have some kid jump up and say, "Well, I'm not going to go. The Commander in Chief was organizing demonstrations halfway around the world during another era"?

So there are differences. But that's about the main area where I think we have a difference. I don't know about—we'll talk about that a little with Ross here in a bit.

Mr. Lehrer. Mr. Perot, you have one minute.

Mr. Perot. I think the American people will make their own decisions on character. And at a time when we have work to do and we need action, I think they need to clearly understand the backgrounds of each person. I think the press can play a huge role in making sure that the backgrounds

are clearly presented in an objective way. Then make a decision.

Certainly anyone in the White House should have the character to be there. But I think it's very important to measure when and where things occurred. Did they occur when you were a young person in your formative years, or did they occur while you were a senior official in the Federal Government? When you're a senior official in the Federal Government, spending billions of dollars in taxpayers' money, and you're a mature individual and you make a mistake, then that was on our ticket. If you make it as a young man, time passes.

So I would say just look at all three of us, decide who you think will do the job, pick that person in November, because, believe me, as I've said before, the party's over, and it's time for the cleanup crew. And we do have to have change. And people who never take responsibility for anything when it happens on their watch, and people who are in charge——

Mr. Lehrer. Your time is up.

Mr. Perot. ——the time is up. [*Laughter*]

Mr. Lehrer. Time is up.

Mr. Perot. More later.

Mr. Lehrer. Governor Clinton, you have one minute.

Governor Clinton. Ross gave a good answer, but I've got to respond directly to Mr. Bush. You have questioned my patriotism. You even brought some rightwing Congressmen into the White House to plot how to attack me for going to Russia in 1969–1970, when over 50,000 other Americans did.

Now, I honor your service in World War II. I honor Mr. Perot's service in uniform and the service of every man and woman who ever served, including Admiral Crowe, who was your Chairman of the Joint Chiefs and who's supporting me. But when Joe McCarthy went around this country attacking people's patriotism, he was wrong. He was wrong. And a Senator from Connecticut stood up to him, named Prescott Bush. Your father was right to stand up to Joe McCarthy. You were wrong to attack my patriotism. I was opposed to the war, but I love my country. And we need a President who will bring this country together, not divide it. We've had enough division. I want to lead a unified country.

Mr. Lehrer. All right. We move now to the subject of taxes and spending. The question goes to Governor Clinton for a two-minute answer. It will be asked by Ann Compton.

Taxes

Ann Compton. Governor Clinton, can you lock in a level here tonight on where middle-income families can be guaranteed a tax cut or, at the very least, at what income level they can be guaranteed no tax increase?

Governor Clinton. The tax increase I have proposed triggers in at family incomes of $200,000 and above. Those are the people who, in the 1980's, had their incomes go up while their taxes went down. Middle-class people, defined as people with incomes of $52,000 and down, had their incomes go down while their taxes went up in the Reagan-Bush years because of six increases in the payroll taxes. So that is where my income limit would trigger.

Ms. Compton. So there will be no tax increases below $200,000?

Governor Clinton. My plan, notwithstanding my opponent's ad, my plan triggers in at gross incomes, family incomes of $200,000 and above. And then we want to give modest middle-class tax relief to restore some fairness, especially to middle-class people with families with incomes of under $60,000.

In addition to that, the money that I raise from upper income people and from asking foreign corporations just to pay the same income on their income earned in America that American corporations do will be used to give incentives back to upper income people. I want to give people permanent incentives on investment tax credit like President Kennedy and the Congress inaugurated in the early sixties to get industry moving again; a research and development tax credit; a low-income housing tax credit; a long-term capital gains proposal for new business and business expansions.

We've got to have no more trickle-down. We don't need across-the-board tax cuts for the wealthy for nothing; we need to say, here's your tax incentive if you create American jobs the old-fashioned way.

I'd like to create more millionaires than were created under Mr. Bush and Mr. Reagan, but I don't want to have 4 years where we have no growth in the private sector. And that's what's happened in the last 4 years. We're down 35,000 jobs in the private sector. We need to invest and grow, and that's what I want to do.

Mr. Lehrer. President Bush, one minute, sir.

President Bush. I have to correct one thing. I didn't question the man's patriotism; I questioned his judgment and his character. What he did in Moscow, that's fine. Let him explain it. He did. I accept that. What I don't accept is demonstrating and organizing demonstrations in a foreign country when your country's at war. I'm sorry, I cannot accept that.

This one on taxes spells out the biggest difference between us. I do not believe we need to go back to the Mondale proposals or the Dukakis proposals of tax-and-spend. Governor Clinton says $200,000, but he also says he wants to raise $150 billion. Taxing people over $200,000 will not get you $150 billion. And then when you add in his other spending proposals, regrettably, you end up socking it to the working man.

That old adage that they use, "We're going to soak the rich, we're going to soak the rich," it always ends up being the poor cab driver or the working man that ends up paying the bill. And so I just have a different approach. I believe the way to get the deficit down is to control the growth of mandatory spending programs and not raise taxes on the American people. We've got a big difference there.

Mr. Lehrer. Mr. Perot, one minute.

Mr. Perot. We've got to have a growing, expanding job base to give us a growing, expanding tax base. Right now, we have a flat-to-deteriorating job base, and where it appears to be growing is minimum-wage jobs. So we've got to really rebuild our job base. That's going to take money for infrastructure and investment to do that. Our foreign competitors are doing it; we're not.

We cannot pay off the $4 trillion debt, balance the budget, and have the industries of the future and the high-paying jobs in this country without having the revenue. We're going to go through a period of shared sacrifice. There's one challenge: It's got to be fair.

We've created a mess and don't have much to show for it, and we have got to fix it. And that's about all I can say in a minute.

Mr. Lehrer. Okay. Next question goes to President Bush for a 2-minute answer, and it will be asked by Sandy Vanocur.

U.S. Troops in Europe

Sander Vanocur. Mr. President, this past week your Secretary of the Army, Michael Stone, said he had no plans to abide by a congressional mandate to cut U.S. forces in Europe from 150,000 to 100,000 by the end of September 1996. Now, why, almost 50 years after the end of World War II and with the total collapse of the Soviet Union, should American taxpayers be taxed, support armies in Europe, when the Europeans have plenty of money to do it for themselves?

President Bush. Well, Sander, that's a good question. And the answer is: For 40-some years, we kept the peace. If you look at the cost of not keeping the peace in Europe, it would be exorbitant. We have reduced the number of troops that are deployed and going to be deployed. I have cut defense spending. And the reason we could do that is because of our fantastic success in winning the cold war. We never would have got there if we'd gone for the nuclear-freeze crowd; never would have got there if we'd listened to those that wanted to cut defense spending. I think it is important that the United States stay in Europe and continue to guarantee the peace. We simply cannot pull back.

Now, when anybody has a spending program they want to spend money on at home, they say, well, let's cut money out of the Defense Department. I will accept and have accepted the recommendations of two proven leaders, General Colin Powell and Dick, Secretary Dick Cheney. They feel that the levels we're operating at and the reductions that I have proposed are proper. And so I simply do not think we should go back to the isolation days and start blaming foreigners.

We are the sole remaining superpower. And we should be that. We have a certain disproportionate responsibility. But I would ask the American people to understand that if we make imprudent cuts, if we go too far, we risk the peace. And I don't want to do that. I've seen what it is like to see the burdens of a war, and I don't want to see us make reckless cuts.

Because of our programs, we have been able to significantly cut defense spending. But let's not cut into the muscle. And let's not cut down our insurance policy, which is participation of American forces in NATO, the greatest peacekeeping organization ever made. Today, you've got problems in Europe still bubbling along, even though Europe's going democracy's route. But we are there. And I think this insurance policy is necessary. I think it goes with world leadership. And I think the levels we've come up with are just about right.

Mr. Lehrer. Mr. Perot, one minute, sir.

Mr. Perot. If I'm poor and you're rich and I can get you to defend me, that's good. But when the tables get turned, I ought to do my share. Right now we spend about $300 billion a year on defense. The Japanese spend around $30 billion in Asia. The Germans spend around $30 billion in Europe.

For example, Germany will spend a trillion dollars building infrastructure over the next 10 years. It's kind of easy to do if you only have to pick up a $30 billion tab to defend your country. The European Community is in a position to pay a lot more than they have in the past. I agree with the President, when they couldn't, we should have; now that they can, they should.

We sort of seem to have a desire to try to stay over there and control it. They don't want us to control it, very candidly. So it I think is very important for us to let them assume more and more of the burden and for us to bring that money back here and rebuild our infrastructure. Because we can only be a superpower if we are an economic superpower, and we can only be an economic superpower if we have a growing, expanding job base.

Mr. Lehrer. Governor Clinton, one minute, sir.

Governor Clinton. I agree with the general statement Mr. Bush made. I disagree that we need 150,000 troops to fulfill our role in Europe. We certainly must maintain an engagement there. There are certainly dangers there. There are certainly other trouble spots in the world which are closer to Europe than to the United States. But two former Defense Secretaries recently issued reports saying that 100,000 or slightly fewer troops would be enough, including President Reagan's former Defense Secretary, Mr. Carlucci. Many of the military experts whom I consulted on this agreed.

We're going to have to spend more money in the future on military technology and on greater mobility, greater airlift, greater sealift, the B–22 airplane. We're going to have to do some things that are quite costly, and I simply don't believe we can afford, nor do we need to keep 150,000 troops in Europe, given how much the Red Army, now under the control of Russia, has been cut; the arms control agreement concluded between Mr. Bush and Mr. Yeltsin, something I have applauded. I don't think we need 150,000 troops.

Let me make one other point. Mr. Bush talked about taxes. He didn't tell you that he vetoed a middle-class tax cut because it would be paid for by raising taxes on the wealthy and vetoed an investment tax credit paid for by raising taxes on the wealthy.

Taxes

Mr. Lehrer. All right. We go now to Mr. Perot for a 2-minute question, and it will be asked by John Mashek.

John Mashek. Mr. Perot, you talked about fairness just a minute ago, on sharing the pain. As part of your plan to reduce the ballooning Federal deficit, you've suggested that we raise gasoline taxes 50 cents a gallon over 5 years. Why punish the middle-class consumer to such a degree?

Mr. Perot. It's 10 cents a year, cumulative. It finally gets to 50 cents at the end of the fifth year. I think "punish" is the wrong word. Again, you see, I didn't create this problem; we're trying to solve it.

Now, if you study our international competitors, some of our international competitors collect up to $3.50 a gallon in taxes. And they use that money to build infra-

structure and create jobs. We collect 35 cents, and we don't have it to spend. I know it's not popular. And I understand the nature of your question. But the people who will be helped the most by it are the working people who will get the jobs created because of this tax. Why do we have to do it? Because we have so mismanaged our country over the years, and it is now time to pay the fiddler. And if we don't, we will be spending our children's money. We have spent $4 trillion worth. An incredible number of young people are active in supporting my effort because they're deeply concerned that we have taken the American dream from them.

I think it's fitting that we're on the campus of a university tonight. These young people, when they get out of this wonderful university, will have difficulty finding a job. We've got to clean this mess up, leave this country in good shape, and pass on the American dream to them. We're got to collect the taxes to do it. If there's a fairer way, I'm all ears. Ah-h-h. [*Laughter*]

But see, let me make it very clear. People don't have the stomach to fix these problems, I think it's a good time to face it in November. If they do, then they will have heard the harsh reality of what we have to do. I'm not playing Lawrence Welk music tonight.

Mr. Lehrer. Governor Clinton, you have a minute, sir.

Governor Clinton. I think Mr. Perot has confronted this deficit issue, but I think it's important to point out that we really have two deficits in America, not one. We have a budget deficit in the Federal Government, but we also have an investment, a jobs, an income deficit.

People are working harder for less money than they were making 10 years ago: two-thirds of our people, a $1,600 drop in average income in just the last 2 years. The problem I have with the Perot prescription is that almost all economists who have looked at it say that if you cut the deficit this much this quick, it will increase unemployment, it will slow down the economy. That's why I think we shouldn't do it that quickly. We have a disciplined reduction in the deficit of 50 percent over the next 4 years. But first, get incentives to invest in this economy, put the American people back to work. We've got to invest in growth. Nine Nobel Prize-winning economists and 500 others, including numerous Republican and Democratic business executives, have endorsed this approach because it offers the best hope to put America back to work and get our incomes rising instead of falling.

Mr. Lehrer. President Bush, one minute, sir.

President Bush. The question was on fairness. I just disagree with Mr. Perot. I don't believe it is fair to slap a 50-cent-a-gallon tax over whatever many years on the people that have to drive for a living, people that go long distances. I don't think we need to do it.

You see, I have a fundamental difference. I agree with what he's talking about in trying to get the spending down and to discipline, although I think we ought to totally exempt Social Security. But he's talking tough medicine, and I think that's good. I disagree with the tax-and-spend philosophy. You see, I don't think we need to tax more and spend more and then say that's going to make the problem better. And I'm afraid that's what I think I'm hearing from Governor Clinton.

I believe what you need to do is some of what Ross is talking about: control the growth of mandatory spending and get taxes down. He's mentioned some ways to do it, and I agree with those. I've been talking about getting a capital gains cut forever. And his friends in Congress have been telling me that's a tax break for the rich. It would stimulate investment. I'm for an investment tax allowance. I am for a tax break for first-time homebuyers. And with this new Congress coming in, gridlock will be gone and I'll sit down with them and say, let's get this done. But I do not want to go the tax-and-spend route.

Mr. Lehrer. All right. Let's move on now to the subject of jobs. The first question goes to President Bush for 2 minutes, and John will ask that question. John?

The Defense Industry

Mr. Mashek. Mr. President, last month you came to St. Louis to announce a very lucrative contract for McDonnell Douglas to build F–15's for Saudi Arabia. In today's Post-Dispatch, a retired saleswoman, a 75-year-old woman named Marjorie Roberts, asked if she could ask a question of the candidates, said she wanted to register her concern about the lack of a plan to convert our defense-oriented industries into other purposes. How would you answer her?

President Bush. Well, I assume she was supportive of the decision on McDonnell Douglas. I assume she was supporting me on the decision to sell those airplanes. I think it's a good decision. I took a little heat for it, but I think it was the correct decision to do. And we've worked it out, and indeed, we're moving forward all around the world in a much more peaceful way. So that one we came away with which—in creating jobs for the American people.

I would simply say to her, look, take a look at what the President has proposed on job retraining. When you cut back on defense spending, some people are going to be thrown out of work. If you throw another 50,000 kids on the street because of cutting recklessly in troop levels, you're going to put a lot more out of work. I would say to them, look at the job retraining programs that we're proposing. Therein is the best answer to her.

And another one is, stimulate investment and savings. I mean, we've got big economic problems, but we are not coming apart at the seams. We're ready for a recovery with interest rates down and inflation down, the cruelest tax of all; caught up in a global slowdown right now, but that will change if you go with the programs I've talked about and if you help with job retraining and education.

I am a firm believer that our America 2000 education problem is the answer. A little longer run; it's going to take a while to educate, but it is a good program. So her best hope for short term is job retraining if she was thrown out of work at a defense plant. But tell her it's not all that gloomy. We're the United States. We've faced tough problems before. Look at the "misery index" when the Democrats had both the White House and the Congress. It was just right through the roof.

Now, we can do better. And the way to do better is not to tax and spend but to retrain, get that control of the mandatory spending programs. I am much more optimistic about this country than some.

Mr. Lehrer. Mr. Perot, you have one minute, sir.

Mr. Perot. Your defense industries are going to have to convert to civilian industries, many of them are. And the sooner they start, the sooner they'll finish. And there will be a significant transition.

And it's very important that we not continue to let our industrial base deteriorate. We had someone who I'm sure regrets said it in the President's staff, said he didn't care whether we make potato chips or computer chips. Well, anybody that thinks about it cares a great deal. Number one, you make more making computer chips than you do potato chips. Number two, 19 out of 20 computer chips that we have in this country now come from Japan. We've given away whole industries.

So as we phase these industries over, there's a lot of intellectual talent in these industries. A lot of these people in industries can be converted to the industries of tomorrow. And that's where the high-paying jobs are. We need to have a very carefully thought through phaseover.

See, we practice 19th century capitalism. The rest of the world practices 21st century capitalism. I can't handle that in a minute, but I hope we can get back into it later. The rest of the world, the countries and the businesses would be working together to make this transition in an intelligent way.

Mr. Lehrer. Governor Clinton, you have one minute, sir.

Governor Clinton. We must have a transition plan, a plan to convert from a defense to a domestic economy. No other nation would have cut defense as much as we already have without that. There are 200,000 people unemployed in California alone because we have cut defense without planning to retrain them and to reinvest in the technologies of the future here at home. That is what I want to do.

This administration may say they have a plan, but the truth is they have not even released all the money, the paltry sum of money that Congress appropriated. I want

to take every dollar by which we reduced defense and reinvest it in technologies for the 21st century: in new transportation, in communication, and environmental cleanup technologies. Let's put the American people to work. And let's build the kind of high-tech, high-wage, high-growth economy that the American people deserve.

Mr. Lehrer. All right. The next question goes to Mr. Perot for a 2 minute answer. It will be asked by Ann.

Ann?

Jobs Program

Ms. Compton. Mr. Perot, you talked a minute ago about rebuilding the job base. But is it true what Governor Clinton just said, that that means that unemployment will increase, that it will slow the economy? And how would you specifically use the powers of the Presidency to get more people back into good jobs immediately?

Mr. Perot. Step one: The American people send me up there, the day after election, I'll get with the—we won't even wait until inauguration—I'll ask the President to help me, and I'll ask his staff to help me. And we will start putting together teams to put together—to take all the plans that exist and do something with them.

Please understand, there are great plans lying all over Washington nobody ever executes. It's like having a blueprint for a house you never built. You don't have anywhere to sleep. Now, our challenge is to take these things, do something with them.

Step one: You want to put America back to work, clean up the small business problem. Have one task force at work on that. The second: You've got your big companies that are in trouble, including the defense industries, have another one on that. Have a third task force on new industries of the future to make sure we nail those for our country, and they don't wind up in Europe and Asia. Convert from 19th to 21st century capitalism. You see, we have an adversarial relationship between Government and business. Our international competitors that are cleaning our plate have an intelligent relationship between Government and business and a supportive relationship.

Then, have another task force on crime,

because next to jobs, our people are concerned about their safety. Health care, schools, one on the debt and deficit. And finally, in that 90-day period before the inauguration, put together the framework for the town hall and give the American people a Christmas present, show them by Christmas the first cut at these plans. By the time Congress comes into session to go to work, have those plans ready to go in front of Congress. Then get off to a flying start in '93 to execute these plans.

Now, there are people in this room and people on this stage who have been in meetings when I would sit there and say, is this one we're going to talk about or do something about? Well, obviously, my orientation is let's go do it.

Now, put together your plans by Christmas. Be ready to go when Congress goes. Nail these things—small business, you've got to have capital; you've got to have credit; and many of them need mentors or coaches. And we can create more jobs there in a hurry than any other place.

Mr. Lehrer. Governor Clinton, one minute.

Governor Clinton. This country desperately needs a jobs program. And my first priority would be to pass a jobs program, to introduce it on the first day I was inaugurated. I would meet with the leaders of the Congress, with all the newly elected Members of the Congress, and as many others with whom I could meet between the time of the election and the inauguration. And we would present a jobs program.

Then we would present a plan to control health care costs and phase in health care coverage for all Americans. Until we control health care costs, we're not going to control the deficit. It is the number one culprit. But first we must have an aggressive jobs program.

I live in a State where manufacturing job growth has far outpaced the Nation in the last few years; where we have created more private sector jobs since Mr. Bush has been President than have been created in the entire rest of the country, where Mr. Bush's Labor Secretary said the job growth has been enormous. We've done it in Arkansas. Give me a chance to create these kinds of jobs in America. We can do it. I know we

can.

Mr. Lehrer. President Bush, one minute.

President Bush. Well, we've got a plan announced for what we can do for small business. I've already put forward things that will get this country working fast, some of which have been echoed here tonight: investment tax allowance, capital gains reduction, more on research and development, a tax credit for first-time homebuyers.

What I'm going to do is say to Jim Baker when this campaign is over, "All right, let's sit down now. You do in domestic affairs what you've done in foreign affairs. Be the kind of economic coordinator of all the domestic side of the house, and that includes all the economic side, all the training side, and bring this program together." We're going to have a new Congress. And we're going to say to them, "You've listened to the voters the way we have. Nobody wants gridlock anymore. And so let's get the program through."

And I believe it will work, because, as Ross said, we've got the plans. The plans are all over Washington. And I have put ours together in something called the Agenda for American Renewal. And it makes sense. It's sensible. It creates jobs. It gets to the base of the kind of jobs we need. And so I'll just be asking for support to get that put into effect.

Mr. Lehrer. The next question goes to Governor Clinton for 2 minutes. It will be asked by Sandy.

Federal Reserve Board Chairman

Mr. Vanocur. Governor Clinton, when a President running for the first time gets into the office and wants to do something about the economy, he finds in Washington there's a person who has much more power over the economy than he does: the Chairman of the Federal Reserve Board, accountable to no one. That being the case, would you go along with proposals made by Treasury Secretary James Brady and Congressman Lee Hamilton to make the Federal Reserve Board Chairman somehow more accountable to elected officials?

Governor Clinton. Well, let me say that I think that we might ought to review the terms and the way it works. But frankly, I don't think that's the problem today. We have low interest rates today. At least we have low interest rates that the Fed can control. Our long-term interest rates are still pretty high because of our deficit and because of our economic performance.

And there was a terrible reaction internationally to Mr. Bush saying he was going to give us 4 more years of trickle-down economics and other across-the-board tax cuts and most of it going to the wealthy with no real guarantee of investment. But I think the important thing is to use the powers the President does have on the assumption that given the condition of this economy, we're going to keep interest rates down if we have the discipline to increase investment and reduce the debt at the same time. That is my commitment.

I think the American people are hungry for action. I think Congress is hungry for someone who will work with them, instead of manipulate them; someone who will not veto a bill that has an investment credit, middle class tax relief, research and development tax credits, as Mr. Bush has done. Give me a chance to do that.

I don't have to worry, I don't think, in the near term, about the Federal Reserve. Their policies so far, it seems to me, are pretty sound.

Mr. Lehrer. President Bush, you have one minute.

President Bush. I don't think the Fed ought to be put under the Executive Branch. There is separation there. I think that's fine. Alan Greenspan is respected. I've had some arguments with him about the speed in which we might have lowered rates.

But Governor Clinton, he talks about the reaction to the markets. There was a momentary fear that he might win, and the markets went "rrrfft"—down like that—[*laughter*]—so I don't—we can judge on—the stock market has been strong. It's been very strong since I've been President. And they recognize we've got great difficulties. But they're also much more optimistic than the pessimists we have up here tonight.

In terms of vetoing tax bills, you're darn right. I am going to protect the American taxpayer against the spend-and-tax Con-

gress. And I'm going to keep on vetoing them because I don't think we are taxed too little. I think the Government's spending too much. So Governor Clinton can label it tax for the rich or anything he wants. I'm going to protect the working man by continuing to veto and to threaten veto until we get this new Congress, when then we're going to move forward on our plan. I've got to protect them.

Mr. Lehrer. Mr. Perot, one minute.

Mr. Perot. Keep the Federal Reserve independent, but let's live in a world of reality. We live in a global economy, not a national economy. These interest rates we have now don't make any sense. We have a $4 trillion debt, and only in America would you finance 70 percent of it 5 years or less. So 70 percent of our debt is 5 years or less, it's very interest-sensitive.

We have a 4-percent gap between what we pay for treasuries and what Germany pays for 1- to 5-year treasuries. That gap is going to close because the Arabs, the Japanese, and folks in this country are going to start buying German treasuries because they can get more money.

Every time our interest rates go up 1 percent, that adds $28 billion to the deficit or to the debt, whichever place you want to put it. We are sitting on a ticking bomb, folks, because we have totally mismanaged our country. And we had better get it back under control.

Just think, in your own business, if you had all of your long-term problems financed short term, you'd go broke in a hurry.

Mr. Lehrer. We're going to move to foreign affairs. The first question goes to Mr. Perot for a 2-minute answer, and Sandy will ask it.

Foreign Affairs

Mr. Vanocur. Mr. Perot, in the post-cold-war environment, what should be the overriding U.S. national interest? And what can the United States do, and what can it afford to do to defend that national interest?

Mr. Perot. Again, if you're not rich, you're not a superpower, so we have two that I'd put as number one. I have a "1" and "1a." One is, we've got to have the money to be able to pay for defense. And we've got to manufacture here. Believe it or not, folks, you can't ship it all overseas. You've got to make it here. And you can't convert from potato chips to airplanes in an emergency. You see, Willow Run could be converted from cars to airplanes in World War II because it was here. We've got to make things here. You just can't ship them overseas anymore. I hope we talk more about that.

Second thing, on priorities, we've got to help Russia succeed in its revolution and all of its republics. When we think of Russia, remember we're thinking of many countries now. We've got to help them. That's pennies on the dollar compared to renewing the cold war.

Third, we've got all kinds of agreements on paper and some that are being executed on getting rid of nuclear warheads. Russia and its republics are out of control or, at best, in weak control right now. It's a very unstable situation. You've got every rich Middle Eastern country over there trying to buy nuclear weapons, as you well know. And that will lead to another five-star migraine headache down the road. We really need to nail down the intercontinental ballistic missiles, the ones that can hit us from Russia. We've focused on the tactical; we've made real progress there. We've got some agreements on the nuclear, but we don't have those things put away yet. The sooner, the better.

So in terms of priorities, we've got to be financially strong. Number two, we've got to take care of this missile situation and try to get the nuclear war behind us and give that a very high priority. And number three, we need to help and support Russia and the republics in every possible way to become democratic, capitalistic societies and not just sit back and let those countries continue in turmoil, because they could go back worse than things used to be. And believe me, there are a lot of old boys in the KGB and the military that like it better the way it used to be. Thank you.

Mr. Lehrer. Governor Clinton, one minute.

Governor Clinton. In order to keep America the strongest nation in the world, we need some continuity and some change. There are three fundamental challenges. First of all, the world is still a dangerous

and uncertain place. We need a new military and a new national security policy equal to the challenges of the post-cold-war era; a smaller permanent military force, but one that is more mobile, well-trained, with high-technology equipment. We need to continue the negotiations to reduce nuclear arsenals in the Soviet Union, the former Soviet Union, and the United States. We need to stop this proliferation of weapons of mass destruction.

Second, we have to face that in this world economic security is a whole lot of national security. Our dollar is at an all-time low against some foreign currencies. We're weak in the world. We must rebuild America's strength at home.

Finally, we ought to be promoting the democratic impulses around the world. Democracies are our partners. They don't go to war with each other. They're reliable friends in the future. National security, economic strength, democracy.

Mr. Lehrer. President Bush, one minute.

President Bush. We still are the envy of the world in terms of our military; there's no question about that. We're the envy of the world in terms of our economy, in spite of the difficulties we're having; there's no question about that. Our exports are dramatically up.

I might say to Mr. Perot, I can understand why you might have missed it because there's so much fascination by trivia, but I worked out a deal with Boris Yeltsin to eliminate, get rid of entirely, the most destabilizing weapons of all, the SS–18, the big intercontinental ballistic missile. I mean, that's been done. And thank God it has, because the parents of these young people around here go to bed at night without the same fear of nuclear war. We've made dramatic progress.

So we've got a good military—the question that says get a new military, get the best in the world—we've got it, and they're keeping the peace. They're respected around the world, and we are more respected because of the way we have conducted ourselves.

We didn't listen to the nuclear freeze crowd. We said, peace through strength. It worked, and the cold war is over. America understands that. But we're turned so inward we don't understand the global picture. We are helping democracy. Ross, the FREEDOM Support Act is something that I got through the Congress, and it's a very good thing because it does exactly what you say, and I think you agree with that, to help Russian democracy. We're going to keep on doing that.

Mr. Lehrer. All right, Next question is for Governor Clinton, and John will ask it.

China-U.S. Relations

Mr. Mashek. Governor Clinton, you've accused the President of coddling tyrants, including those in Beijing. As President, how would you exert U.S. power to influence affairs in China?

Governor Clinton. I think our relationships with China are important, and I don't think we want to isolate China. But I think it is a mistake for us to do what this administration did when all those kids went out there carrying the Statue of Liberty in Tiananmen Square, and Mr. Bush sent two people in secret to toast the Chinese leaders and basically tell them not to worry about it. They rewarded him by opening negotiations with Iran to transfer nuclear technology. That was their response to that sort of action.

Now that voices in the Congress and throughout the country have insisted that we do something about China, look what has happened. China has finally agreed to stop sending us products made with prison labor not because we coddled them but because the administration was pushed into doing something about it. Recently the Chinese have announced that they're going to lower some barriers to our products, which they ought to do since they have a $15 billion trade surplus with the United States under Mr. Bush, the second biggest surplus of all, second to Japan.

So I would be firm. I would say, if you want to continue most-favored-nation status for your government-owned industries as well as your private ones, observe human rights in the future. Open your society. Recognize the legitimacy of those kids that were carrying the Statue of Liberty. If we can stand up for our economic interests, we ought to be able to pursue the democratic interests of the people in China. And over the long run they'll be more reliable partners.

Mr. Lehrer. President Bush, you have one minute.

President Bush. Well, the administration was the first major country to stand up against the abuse in Tiananmen Square. We are the ones that worked out the prison labor deal. We are the ones that have lowered the barrier to products, the Carla Hills negotiation. I am the one that said, let's keep the MFN because you see China moving toward a free market economy. To do what the Congress and Governor Clinton are suggesting, you would isolate and ruin Hong Kong. They are making some progress, not enough for us. We were the first ones to put sanctions on. We still have them on some things.

But Governor Clinton's philosophy is isolate them. He says don't do it, but the policies he's expounding of putting conditions on MFN and kind of humiliating them is not the way you make the kind of progress we are getting. I have stood up with these people, and I understand what you have to do to be strong in this situation. It's moving, not as fast as we'd like. But you isolate China and turn them inward, and then we've made a tremendous mistake. I'm not going to do it. I've had to fight a lot of people that were saying "human rights." We are the ones that put the sanctions on and stood for it. And he can insult General Scowcroft if he wants to. He didn't go over to coddle. He went over to say——

Mr. Lehrer. Mr. President, you're over——

President Bush. ——you must make the very changes they're making now.

Mr. Lehrer. One minute, Mr. Perot.

Mr. Perot. China's a huge country, broken into many provinces. It has some very elderly leaders that will not be around too much longer. Capitalism is growing and thriving across big portions of China. Asia will be our largest trading partner in the future. It will be a growing and a closer relationship. We have a delicate tightwire walk that we must go through at the present time to make sure that we do not cozy up to tyrants, to make sure that they don't get the impression that they can suppress their people. But time is our friend there because their leaders will change in not too many years, worst case. And their country is making great progress.

One last point on the missiles. I don't want the American people to be confused. We have written agreements, and we have some missiles that have been destroyed, but we have a huge number of intercontinental ballistic missiles that are still in place in Russia. The fact that you have an agreement is one thing. Until they're destroyed, some crazy person can either sell them or use them.

Mr. Lehrer. All right. The next question goes to President Bush for a 2-minute answer, and Ann will ask it.

Bosnia and Somalia

Ms. Compton. Mr. President, how can you watch the killing in Bosnia and the ethnic cleansing, or the starvation and anarchy in Somalia, and not want to use America's might, if not America's military, to try to end that kind of suffering?

President Bush. Ann, both of them are very complicated situations. I vowed something, because I learned something from Vietnam: I am not going to commit U.S. forces until I know what the mission is, until the military tell me that it can be completed, until I know how they can come out.

We are helping. American airplanes are helping today on humanitarian relief for Sarajevo. It is America that's in the lead in helping with humanitarian relief for Somalia. But when you go to put somebody else's son or daughter into war, I think you've got to be a little bit careful, and you have to be sure that there's a military plan that can do this.

You have ancient ethnic rivalries that have cropped up as Yugoslavia is dissolved or getting dissolved. It isn't going to be solved by sending in the 82d Airborne, and I'm not going to do that as Commander in Chief. I am going to stand by and use the moral persuasion of the United States to get satisfaction in terms of prison camps, and we're making some progress there, and in terms of getting humanitarian relief in there.

Right now, as you know, the United States took the lead in a no-fly operation up there, no-fly order up in the United Nations. We're working through the international organizations. That's one thing I learned by forging that tremendous and greatly, highly successful coalition against Saddam Hussein, the dictator: Work internationally to do it. I'm very concerned about it. I'm concerned about ethnic cleansing. I'm concerned about attacks on Muslims, for example, over there. But I must stop short of using American force until I know how those young men and women are going to get out of there as well as get in, know what the mission is and define it. I think I'm on the right track.

Ms. Compton. Are you designing a mission that would——

Mr. Lehrer. Ann, sorry, sorry. Time is up. We have to go to Mr. Perot for a one-minute response.

Mr. Perot. If we learned anything in Vietnam, it's you first commit this Nation before you commit the troops to the battlefield. We cannot send our people all over the world to solve every problem that comes up.

This is basically a problem that is a primary concern to the European Community. Certainly we care about the people. We care about the children. We care about the tragedy. But it is inappropriate for us, just because there's a problem somewhere around the world, to take the sons and daughters of working people—and make no mistake about it, our all-volunteer armed force is not made up of the sons and daughters of the beautiful people. It's the working folks that send their sons and daughters to war, with a few exceptions. Very unlike World War II when FDR's sons flew missions; everybody went. It's a different world now. It's very important that we not just, without thinking it through, just rush to every problem in the world and have our people torn to pieces.

Mr. Lehrer. Governor Clinton, one minute.

Governor Clinton. I agree that we cannot commit ground forces to become involved in the quagmire of Bosnia or in the tribal wars of Somalia. But I think that it's important to recognize that there are things that can be done short of that and that we do have interests there. There are, after all, two million refugees now because of the problems in what was Yugoslavia, the largest number since World War II, and there may be hundreds of thousands of people who will starve or freeze to death in this winter.

The United States should try to work with its allies and stop it. I urged the President to support this air cover, and he did, and I applaud that. I applaud the no-fly zone, and I know that he's going back to the United Nations to try to get authority to enforce it. I think we should stiffen the embargo on the Belgrade government. I think we have to consider whether or not we should lift the arms embargo now on the Bosnians, since they are in no way in a fair fight with a heavily armed opponent bent on ethnic cleansing. We can't get involved in the quagmire, but we must do what we can.

Mr. Lehrer. All right. Moving on now to divisions in our country. The first question goes to Governor Clinton for two minutes, and Ann will ask it.

Family Values

Ms. Compton. Governor Clinton, can you tell us what your definition of the word "family" is?

Governor Clinton. A family involves at least one parent, whether natural or adoptive or foster, and children. A good family is a place where love and discipline and good values are transmuted from the elders to the children, a place where people turn for refuge and where they know they're the most important people in the world.

America has a lot of families that are in trouble today. There's been a lot of talk about family values in this campaign. I know a lot about that. I was born to a widowed mother who gave me family values, and grandparents. I've seen the family values of my people in Arkansas. I've seen the family values of all these people in America who are out there killing themselves, working harder for less in a country that's had the worst economic years in 50 years and the first decline in industrial production ever.

I think the President owes it to family values to show that he values America's families. Whether they're people on welfare, you're trying to move from welfare to work; the working poor, whom I think deserve a tax break to lift them above poverty if they've got a child in the house and working 40 hours a week; working families, who deserve a fair tax system and the opportunity for constant retraining. They deserve a strong economy. I think they deserve a family and medical leave act. Seventy-two other nations have been able to do it. Mr. Bush vetoed it twice because he says we can't do something 72 other countries do, even though there was a small business exemption.

So with all the talk about family values, I know about family values. I wouldn't be here without them. The best expression of my family values is that tonight's my 17th wedding anniversary, and I'd like to close my question by just wishing my wife a happy anniversary and thanking my daughter for being here.

Mr. Lehrer. President Bush, one minute.

President Bush. Well, I would say that one meeting that made a profound impression on me was when the mayors of the big cities, including the Mayor of Los Angeles, a Democrat, came to see me, and they unanimously said the decline in urban America stems from the decline in the American family. So I do think we need to strengthen family. When Barbara holds an AIDS baby, she's showing a certain compassion for family. When she reads to children, the same thing.

I believe that discipline and respect for the law, all of these things, should be taught to children, not in our schools but families have to do that. I'm appalled at the high, outrageous numbers of divorces. It's happened in families; it's happened in ours. But it's gotten too much, and I just think that we ought to do everything we can to respect the American family. It can be a single-parent family. Those mothers need help. One way to do it is to get these deadbeat fathers to pay their obligations to these mothers. That will help strengthen the American family. And there's a whole bunch of other things that I can't click off in this short period of time.

Mr. Lehrer. Mr. Perot, you have one minute.

Mr. Perot. If I had to solve all the problems that face this country and I could be granted one wish as we started down the trail to rebuild the job base, the schools, and so on and so forth, I would say a strong family unit in every home, where every child is loved, nurtured, and encouraged. A little child, before they're 18 months, learns to think well of himself or herself, or poorly. They develop a positive or negative self-image. At a very early age, they learn how to learn. If we have children who are not surrounded with love and affection— see, I look at my grandchildren and wonder if they'll ever learn to walk because they're always in someone's arms. I think, my gosh, wouldn't it be wonderful if every child had that love and support, but they don't.

We will not be a great country unless we have a strong family unit in every home. And I think you can use the White House as a bully pulpit to stress the importance of these little children, particularly in their young and formative years, to mold these little precious pieces of clay so that they, too, can live rich, full lives when they're grown.

Mr. Lehrer. New question, 2-minute answer, goes to President Bush. Sandy will ask it.

Legalization of Drugs

Mr. Vanocur. Mr. President, there's been a lot of talk about Harry Truman in this campaign, so much so that I think tomorrow I'll wake up and see him named as the next commissioner of baseball. [*Laughter*]

President Bush. We could use one.

Mr. Vanocur. The thing that Mr. Truman didn't have to deal with is drugs. Americans are increasingly alarmed about drug-related crimes in cities and suburbs, and your administration is not the first to have grappled with this. Are you at all of a mind that maybe it ought to go to another level, if not to what's advocated by William F. Buckley, Jr., and Milton Friedman, legalization, somewhere between there and where we are now?

President Bush. No. I don't think that's the right answer. I don't believe legalizing narcotics is the answer. I just don't believe that's the answer. I do believe that there's some fairly good news out there. The use of cocaine, for example, by teenagers is dramatically down. But we've got to keep fighting on this war against drugs.

We're doing a little better in interdiction. Many of the countries that used to say, "Well, this is a United States problem. If you'd get the demand down, then we wouldn't have the problem," are working cooperatively with the DEA and other law—the military. We're using the military more now in terms of interdiction. Our funding for recovery is up, recovering the addicts.

Where we're not making the progress, Sander, is in—we're making it in teenagers. And thank God, because I thought what Ross said was most appropriate about these families and these children. But where we're not making it is with the confirmed addicts. I'll tell you one place that's working well, and that is the private sector, Jim Burke and this task force that he has. You may know about it. Tell the American people, but this man said, "I'll get you a million dollars a day in pro bono advertising," something that's very hard for the Government to do. He went out and he did it, and people are beginning to educate through this program, teaching these kids you shouldn't use drugs.

So we're still in the fight. But I must tell you, I think legalization of narcotics or something of that nature, in the face of the medical evidence, would be totally counterproductive. And I oppose it, and I'm going to stand up and continue to oppose it.

Mr. Lehrer. Mr. Perot, one minute.

Mr. Perot. Any time you think you want to legalize drugs, go to a neonatal unit, if you can get in. They are between 100 and 200 percent capacity up and down the East Coast, and the reason is crack babies being born. Baby's in the hospital 42 days; typical cost to you and me is $125,000. Again and again and again, the mother disappears in 3 days, and the child becomes a ward of the State because he's permanently and genetically damaged. Just look at those little children, and if anybody can even think about legalizing drugs, they've lost me.

Now, let's look at priorities. We went on

the Libyan raid, you remember that one, because we were worried to death that Qadhafi might be building up chemical weapons. We've got chemical warfare being conducted against our children on the streets in this country all day, every day, and we don't have the will to stamp it out.

Again, if I get up there, if you send me, we're going to have some blunt talks about this. We're really going to get out in the trenches and say, "Is this one you want to talk about or fix?" Because talk won't do it, folks. There are guys that couldn't get a job third shift in a Dairy Queen, driving BMW's and Mercedes, selling drugs. These old boys are not going to quit easy.

Mr. Lehrer. Governor Clinton, one minute.

Governor Clinton. Like Mr. Perot, I have held crack babies in my arms. But I know more about this, I think, than anybody else up here because I have a brother who's a recovering drug addict. I'm very proud of him. But I can tell you this: If drugs were legal, I don't think he'd be alive today. I am adamantly opposed to legalizing drugs. He is alive today because of the criminal justice system.

That's a mistake. What should we do? First, we ought to prevent more of this on the street. Thirty years ago there were three policemen for every crime. Now there are three crimes for every policeman. We need 100,000 more police on the street. I have a plan for that. Secondly, we ought to have treatment on demand. Thirdly, we ought to have boot camps for first-time nonviolent offenders so they can get discipline and treatment and education and get reconnected to the community, before they are severed and sent to prison where they can learn how to be first-class criminals.

There is a crime bill that, lamentably, was blocked from passage once again, mostly by Republicans in the United States Senate, which would have addressed some of these problems. That crime bill is going to be one of my highest priorities next January if I become President.

Mr. Lehrer. Next question is to you, Mr. Perot. You have 2 minutes to answer it, and John will ask it.

Racial Harmony

Mr. Mashek. Mr. Perot, racial division continues to tear apart our great cities, the last episode being this spring in Los Angeles. Why is this still happening in America? And what would you do to end it?

Mr. Perot. This is a relevant question here tonight. First thing I'd do is during political campaigns, I would urge everybody to stop trying to split this country into fragments and appeal to the differences between us, and then wonder why the melting pot's all broken to pieces after November the 3d.

We are all in this together. We ought to love one another, because united teams win and divided teams lose. If we can't love one another, we ought to get along with one another. If you can't get there, just recognize we're all stuck with one another, because nobody's going anywhere. Right? [*Laughter*]

Now, that ought to get everybody back up to let's get along together and make it work. Our diversity is a strength. We've turned it into a weakness.

Now, again, the White House is a bully pulpit. I think whoever's in the White House should just make it absolutely unconscionable and inexcusable. And if anybody's in the middle of a speech at, you know, one of these conventions, I would expect the candidate to go out and lift him off the stage if he starts preaching hate, because we don't have time for it.

Our differences are our strengths. We have got to pull together. In athletics, we know it. You see, divided teams lose; united teams win. We have got to unite and pull together. And there's nothing we can't do. But if we sit around blowing all this energy out the window on racial strife and hatred, we are stuck with a sure loser, because we have been a melting pot. We're becoming more and more of a melting pot. Let's make it a strength, not a weakness.

Mr. Lehrer. Governor Clinton, one minute.

Governor Clinton. I grew up in the segregated south, thankfully raised by a grandfather with almost no formal education but with a heart of gold who taught me early that all people were equal in the eyes of God. I saw the winds of hatred divide people and keep the people of my State poorer than they would have been, spiritually and economically. I've done everything I could in my public life to overcome racial divisions. We don't have a person to waste in this country.

We are being murdered economically because we have too many dropouts. We have too many low-birth weight babies. We have too many drug addicts as kids. We have too much violence. We are too divided by race, by income, by region. I have devoted a major portion of this campaign to going across this country and looking for opportunities to go to white groups and African-American groups and Latino groups, Asian-American groups and say the same thing: If the American people cannot be brought together, we can't turn this country around. If we can come together, nothing, nothing can stop us.

Mr. Lehrer. Mr. President, one minute.

President Bush. Well, I think Governor Clinton is committed. I do think it's fair to note—he can rebut it—that Arkansas is one of the few States that doesn't have any civil rights legislation.

I've tried to use the White House as a bully pulpit, speaking out against discrimination. We passed two very forward-looking civil rights bills. It's not going to be all done by legislation, but I do think that you need to make an appeal every time you can to eliminate racial divisions and discrimination. And I'll keep on doing that and pointing to some legislative accomplishment to back it up.

I have to take 10 seconds here at the end—the red light isn't on yet—to say to Ross Perot, please don't say to the DEA agents on the street that we don't have the will to fight drugs. Please, I have watched these people. The same for our local law enforcement people; we're backing them in every way we possibly can. But maybe you meant that some in the country don't have the will to fight it. But those that are out there on the front line—as you know; you've been a strong backer of law enforcement; really, I just want to clear that up— have the will to fight it. And frankly, some of them are giving their lives.

Mr. Lehrer. Time, Mr. President. All right, let's go now to another subject, the subject of health. The first question for 2 minutes is to President Bush, and John will ask it.

AIDS

Mr. Mashek. Mr. President, yesterday tens of thousands of people paraded past the White House to demonstrate their concern about the disease AIDS. A celebrated member of your Commission, Magic Johnson, quit, saying that there was too much inaction. Where is this widespread feeling coming from that your administration is not doing enough about AIDS?

President Bush. Coming from the political process. We have increased funding for AIDS. We've doubled it, on research and on every other aspect of it. My request for this year was $4.9 billion for AIDS, 10 times as much for AIDS victim as per cancer victim. I think that we're showing the proper compassion and concern. So I can't tell you where it's coming from, but I am very much concerned about AIDS, and I believe that we've got the best researchers in the world out there at NIH working the problem. We're funding them. I wish there was more money, but we're funding them far more than any time in the past. We're going to keep on doing that.

I don't know, I was a little disappointed in Magic, because he came to me and I said, "Now, if you see something we're not doing, get ahold of me, call me, let me know." He went to one meeting, and then we heard that he was stepping down. So he's been replaced by Mary Fisher, who electrified the Republican Convention by talking about the compassion and the concern that we feel. It was a beautiful moment. And I think she'll do a first-class job on that Commission.

So I think the appeal is, yes, we care. The other thing is, part of AIDS, it's one of the few diseases where behavior matters. And I once called on somebody, "Well, change your behavior. If the behavior you're using is prone to cause AIDS, change the behavior." The next thing I know, one of these ACT-UP groups is out saying, "Bush ought to change his behavior." You can't talk about it rationally. The extremes are hurting the AIDS cause. To go into a Catholic mass in a beautiful cathedral in New York under the cause of helping in AIDS and start throwing condoms around in the mass, I'm sorry, I think it sets back the cause. We cannot move to the extreme.

We've got to care. We've got to continue everything we can at the Federal and the local level. Barbara, I think, is doing a superb job in destroying the myth about AIDS. All of us are in this fight together. All of us care. Do not go to the extreme.

Mr. Lehrer. One minute, Mr. Perot.

Mr. Perot. First, I think Mary Fisher was a great choice. We're lucky to have her heading the Commission. Secondly, I think one thing, that if I were sent to do the job, I would sit down with FDA, look exactly where we are. Then I would really focus on let's get these things out. If you're going to die, you don't have to go through this 10-year cycle that FDA goes through on new drugs. Believe me, people with AIDS are more than willing to take that risk. We could be moving out to the human population a whole lot faster than we are on some of these new drugs. So I think we can expedite the problem there.

Let me go back a minute to racial divisiveness. All-time low in our country was the Judge Thomas-Anita Hill hearings, and those Senators ought to be hanging their heads in shame for what they did there.

Second thing, there are not many times in your life when you get to talk to a whole country, but let me just say this to all of America: If you hate people, I don't want your vote. That's how strongly I feel about it.

Mr. Lehrer. Governor Clinton, one minute.

Governor Clinton. Over 150,000 Americans have died of AIDS. Well over a million and a quarter Americans are HIV-positive. We need to put one person in charge of the battle against AIDS to cut across all the agencies that deal with it. We need to accelerate the drug approval process. We need to fully fund the act named for that wonderful boy, Ryan White, to make sure we're doing everything we can on research and treatment. The President should lead a national effort to change behavior to keep our children alive in the schools, responsible behavior to keep people alive. This is a matter of life and death.

I've worked in my State to reduce teen pregnancy and illness among children. And I know it's tough. The reason Magic Johnson resigned from the AIDS Commission is because the statement you heard tonight from Mr. Bush is the longest and best statement he's made about it in public. I'm proud of what we did at the Democratic Convention, putting two HIV-positive people on the platform, and I'm proud of the leadership that I'm going to bring to this country in dealing with the AIDS crisis.

Mr. Lehrer. New question for Mr. Perot. You have 2 minutes to answer, and Ann will ask it.

Entitlement Programs

Ms. Compton. Mr. Perot, even if you've got what people say are the guts to take on changes in the most popular and the most sacred of the entitlements, Medicare, people say you haven't a prayer of actually getting anything passed in Washington. Since the President isn't a Lone Ranger, how in the world can you make some of those unpopular changes?

Mr. Perot. Two ways. Number one, if I get there, it will be a very unusual and historical event because—*[laughter]*—because the people, not the special interests, put me there. I will have a unique mandate. I have said again and again, and this really upsets the establishment in Washington, that we're going to inform in detail on the issues through an electronic town hall so that they really know what's going on. They will want to do what's good for our country.

Now, all these fellows with thousand-dollar suits and alligator shoes running up and down the Halls of Congress that make policy now, the lobbyists, the PAC guys, the foreign lobbyists, what have you, they'll be over there in the Smithsonian—*[laughter]*—because we're going to get rid of them. The Congress will be listening to the people. And the American people are willing to have fair, shared sacrifice. They're not as stupid as Washington thinks they are. The American people are bright, intelligent, caring, loving people who want a great country for their children and grandchildren. They will make those sacrifices. So I welcome that challenge. And just watch, because if the American people send me there, we'll get it done.

Now, everybody will faint in Washington. They've never seen anything happen in that town. [*Laughter*] This is a town where the White House says, "Congress did it." Congress says, "The White House did it." And I'm sitting there and saying, "Well, who else could be around?" And then when they get off by themselves, they said, "Nobody did it." [*Laughter*] And yet, the cash register is empty. And it used to have our money, the taxpayers' money, in it, and we didn't get the results. We'll get it done.

Mr. Lehrer. Governor, one minute.

Governor Clinton. Ross, that's a great speech, but it's not quite that simple. [*Laughter*] I mean, look at the facts. Both parties in Washington, the President and the Congress, have cut Medicare. The average senior citizen is spending a higher percentage of income on health care today than they were in 1965 before Medicare came in. The President's got another proposal to require them to pay $400 a year more for the next 5 years.

But if you don't have the guts to control cost by changing the insurance system and taking on the bureaucracies and the regulation of health care in the private and public sector, you can't fix this problem. Costs will continue to spiral. Just remember this, folks: A lot of folks on Medicare are out there every day making the choice between food and medicine. Not poor enough for Medicare, Medicaid; not wealthy enough to buy their medicine. I've met them, people like Mary Annie and Edward Davis of Nashua, New Hampshire, all over this country. They cannot even buy medicine. So let's be careful. When we talk about cutting health care costs, let's start with the insurance companies and the people that are making a killing instead of making our people healthy.

Mr. Lehrer. One minute, President Bush.

President Bush. Well, first place I'd like to clear up something, because every 4 years the Democrats go around and say, "Hey, Republicans are going to cut Social Security and Medicare." They've started it again. I am the President that stood up and said, "Don't mess with Social Security." And

I'm not going to, and we haven't. We are not going to go after the Social Security recipient. I have one difference with Mr. Perot on that because I don't think we need to touch Social Security.

What we do need to do, though, is control the growth of these mandatory programs. And Ross properly says, "Okay, there's some pain in that." But Governor Clinton refuses to touch that, simply refuses. So what we've got to do is control it, the growth. Let it grow for inflation; let it grow for the amount of new people added, population. And then hold the line. I believe that is the way you get the deficit down, not by the tax-and-spend program that we hear every 4 years, whether it's Mondale, Dukakis, whoever else it is. I just don't believe we ought to do that. So hold the line on Social Security, and put a cap on the growth of the mandatory program.

Mr. Lehrer. New question. It is for Governor Clinton, 2-minute answer. Sandy will ask it.

Health Care Costs

Mr. Vanocur. Governor Clinton, Ann Compton has brought up Medicare. I remember in 1965 when Wilbur Mills of Arkansas, the chairman of Ways and Means, was pushing it through the Congress. The charge against it was it's socialized medicine. One, you never——

Governor Clinton. Mr. Bush made that charge.

Mr. Vanocur. Well, he served with him 2 years later in 1967 where I first met him. The second point, though, is that it is now skyrocketing out of control. People want it; we say it's going bonkers. Is not the Oregon plan, applied to Medicaid rationing, the proper way to go, even though the Federal Government last August ruled that violated the Americans with Disabilities Act of 1990?

Governor Clinton. I thought the Oregon plan should at least have been allowed to be tried because at least the people in Oregon were trying to do something.

Let me go back to the main point, Sandy. Mr. Bush is trying to run against Lyndon Johnson and Jimmy Carter and everybody in the world but me in this race. I have proposed a managed competition plan for health care. I will say again: You cannot control health care costs simply by cutting Medicare. Look what's happened. The Federal Government has cut Medicare and Medicaid in the last few years. States have cut Medicaid; we've done it in Arkansas under budget pressures. But what happens? More and more people get on the rolls as poverty increases. If you don't control the health care costs of the entire system, you cannot get control of it.

Look at our program. We've set up a national ceiling on health care costs tied to inflation and population growth set by health care providers, not by the Government. We provide for managed competition, not Government models, in every State, and we control private and public health care costs.

Now, just a few days ago, a bipartisan commission of Republicans and Democrats, more Republicans than Democrats, said my plan will save the average family $1,200 a year more than the Bush plan will by the year 2000; $2.2 trillion in the next 12 years; $400 billion a year by the end of this decade. I've got a plan to control health care costs. But you can't just do it by cutting Medicare. You have to take on the insurance companies, the bureaucracies, and you have to have cost controls, yes. But keep in mind, we are spending 30 percent more on health care than any country in the world, any other country. Yet, we have 35 million people uninsured. We have no preventive and primary care. The Oregon plan is a good start if the Federal Government is going to continue to abandon its responsibilities.

I say if Germany can cover everybody and keep costs under inflation, if Hawaii can cover 98 percent of their people at lower health care costs than the rest of us, if Rochester, New York, can do it with two-thirds of the cost of the rest of us, America can do it, too. I'm tried of being told we can't. I say we can. We can do better, and we must.

Mr. Lehrer. President Bush, one minute.

President Bush. Well, I don't have time in 30 seconds or one minute to talk about our health care reform plan. The Oregon plan made some good sense, but it's easy to dis-

miss the concerns of the disabled. As President, I have to be sure that those waivers which we're approving all over the place are covered under the law. Maybe we can work it out. But the Americans for Disabilities Act, speaking about sound and sensible civil rights legislation, was the foremost piece of legislation passed in modern times. So we do have something more than a technical problem.

Governor Clinton clicked off the things: You've got to take on insurance companies and bureaucracies. He failed to take on somebody else, the malpractice suit people, those that bring these lawsuits against— these frivolous trial lawyers' lawsuits that are running costs of medical care up by $25 billion to $50 billion. He refuses to put anything—controls on these crazy lawsuits.

If you want to help somebody, don't run the costs up by making doctors have to have five or six tests where one would do for fear of being sued, or have somebody along the highway not stop to pick up a guy and help him because he's afraid a trial lawyer will come along and sue him. We're suing each other too much and caring for each other too little.

Mr. Lehrer. Mr. Perot, one minute.

Mr. Perot. We've got the most expensive health care system in the world. It ranks behind 15 other nations when we come to life expectancy and 22 other nations when we come to infant mortality. So we don't have the best. Pretty simple, folks, if you're paying more and you don't have the best, if all else fails go copy the people who have the best who spend less, right? But we can do better than that. Again, we've got plans lying all over the place in Washington. Nobody ever implements them.

Now I'm back to square one: If you want to stop talking about it and do it, then I'll be glad to go up there and we'll get it done. But if you just want to keep the music going, just stay traditional this next time around, and 4 years from now you'll have everybody blaming everybody else for a bad health care system. Talk is cheap. Words are plentiful. Deeds are precious. Let's get on with it.

Mr. Lehrer. And that's exactly what we're going to do. That was, in fact, the final question and answer. We're now going to move to closing statements. Each candidate will have up to 2 minutes. The order, remember, was determined by a drawing. And Mr. Perot, you were first.

Closing Statements

Mr. Perot. Well, it's been a privilege to be able to talk to the American people tonight. I make no bones about it: I love this country. I love the principle it's founded on. I love the people here. I don't like to see the country's principles violated. I don't like to see the people in a deteriorating economy and a deteriorating country because our Government has lost touch with the people. The people in Washington are good people; we just have a bad system. We've got to change the system. It's time to do it because we have run up so much debt that time is no longer our friend. We've got to put our house in order.

When you go to bed tonight, look at your children. Think of their dreams. Think of your dreams as a child. And ask yourself, "Isn't it time to stop talking about it? Isn't it time to stop creating images? Isn't it time to do it?" Aren't you sick of being treated like an unprogrammed robot? Every 4 years they send you all kinds of messages to tell you how to vote and then go back to business as usual. They told you at the tax and budget summit that if you agreed to a tax increase, we could balance the budget. They didn't tell you that that same year they increased spending $1.83 for every dollar we increased taxes. That's Washington in a nutshell right there.

In the final analysis, I'm doing this for your children, when you look at them tonight. There's another group that I feel very close to, and these are the men and women who fought on the battlefield, the children, the families of the ones who died, the people who left parts of their bodies over there. I'd never ask you to do anything for me, but I owe you this, and I'm doing it for you. I can't tell you what it means to me at these rallies when I see you and you come up, and the look in your eyes. I know how you feel, and you know how I feel. And then I think of the older people who are retired. They grew up in the Depression. They fought and won World War II.

We owe you a debt we can never repay you. And the greatest repayment I can ever give is to recreate the American dream for your children and grandchildren. I'll give it everything I have if you want me to do it.

Mr. Lehrer. Governor Clinton, your closing statement.

Governor Clinton. I'd like to thank the people of St. Louis and Washington University, the Presidential Debate Commission, and all those who made this night possible. And I'd like to thank those of you who are watching. Most of all, I'd like to thank all of you who have touched me in some way over this last year, all the thousands of you whom I've seen. I'd like to thank the computer executives and the electronics executives in Silicon Valley, two-thirds of whom are Republicans, who said they wanted to sign on to a change to create a new America. I'd like to thank the hundreds of executives who came to Chicago, a third of them Republicans, who said they wanted a change. I'd like to thank the people who started with Mr. Perot who have come on to help our campaign. I'd like to thank all the folks around America that no one ever knows about: the woman who was holding the AIDS baby she adopted in Cedar Rapids, Iowa, who asked me to do something more for adoption; the woman who stopped along the road in Wisconsin and wept because her husband had lost his job after 27 years; all the people who are having a tough time; and the people who are winning, but who know how desperately we need to change.

This debate tonight has made crystal clear a challenge that is as old as America: the choice between hope and fear, change or more of the same; the courage to move into a new tomorrow or to listen to the crowd who says, "Things could be worse."

Mr. Bush has said some very compelling things tonight that don't quite square with the record. He was President for 3 years before he proposed a health care plan that still hasn't been sent to Congress in total; 3 years before an economic plan; and he still didn't say tonight that that tax bill he vetoed raised taxes only on the rich and gave the rest of you a break, but he vetoed it anyway.

I offer a new direction: Invest in American jobs, American education, control health care costs, bring this country together again. I want the future of this country to be as bright and brilliant as its past, and it can be if we have the courage to change.

Mr. Lehrer. President Bush, your closing statement.

President Bush. Well, let me tell you a little what it's like to be President. In the Oval Office, you can't predict what kind of crisis is going to come up. You have to make tough calls. You can't be on one hand this way and one hand another. You can't take different positions on these difficult issues.

Then you need a philosophical—I'd call it a philosophical underpinning; mine for foreign affairs is democracy and freedom. Look at the dramatic changes around the world. The cold war is over. The Soviet Union is no more, and we're working with a democratic country. Poland, Hungary, Czechoslovakia, the Baltics are free. Take a look at the Middle East. We had to stand up against a tyrant. The United States came together as we haven't in many, many years. We kicked this man out of Kuwait. In the process, as a result of that will and that decision and that toughness, we now have ancient enemies talking peace in the Middle East. Nobody would have dreamed it possible.

I think the biggest dividend of making these tough calls is the fact that we are less afraid of nuclear war. Every parent out there has much less worry that their kids are going to be faced with nuclear holocaust. All this is good.

On the domestic side, what we must do is have change that empowers people, not change for the sake of change, tax and spend. We don't need to do that anymore. What we need to do is empower people. We need to invest and save. We need to do better in education. We need to do better in job retraining. We need to expand our exports, and they're going very, very well indeed. We need to strengthen the American family.

I hope as President that I've earned your trust. I've admitted it when I make a mistake, but then I go on and help try to solve the problems. I hope I've earned your trust, because a lot of being President is about trust and character. And I ask for your support for 4 more years to finish this job.

Thank you very, very much.

Mr. Lehrer. Don't go away yet. I just want to thank the three panelists and thank the three candidates for participating, President Bush, Governor Clinton, and Mr. Perot. They will appear again together on October the 15th and again on October 19th. Next Tuesday there will be a debate among the three candidates for Vice President.

And for now, from Washington University in St. Louis, Missouri, I'm Jim Lehrer. Thank you, and good night.

Note: The debate began at 6:03 p.m. in the Field House at Washington University.

Remarks to the Community in St. Louis
October 11, 1992

Thank you all. Thanks for that great rally. And thanks for the welcome back to Missouri. Thank you very, very much. Fantastic. Hey listen, I think you guys were—I am glad to be out of that tag-team match over there. I think with my dear friends the Gatlin Brothers here and Lee, my other dear friend Lee Greenwood, you had the best of all worlds being over here, not over there.

You know, these debate things, the tension mounts. But there's one good thing about them: You can look right into that camera and take your message, unfiltered, right out there to the American people. You can get around, and I think our message is a message of hope. The other side would have you believe—and the only way they can win is if they try to convince the American people that we are a nation in decline. And we are not. We are the United States. We are a rising nation, the most respected in the entire world.

Yes, we have problems. And on our Agenda for American Renewal we've got the answer to fix them. But it would be a sorry thing to think the only way you can do it is to tear down our country. And I'm glad I had an opportunity tonight to stand up for America and stand up for what is right.

We need to win this State, and I need your help. But we also need something else. We need to reelect Senator Kit Bond. He's doing an outstanding job there in the Senate. He's here with us tonight, and a great United States Senator. If we had more like him, we wouldn't have people going around yelling "Clean House!" We need to clean House and Senate; but keep Senator Bond there and send more like him, and watch us move this country forward. Clean

the House, that's right.

You heard me tonight on there getting my 2 minutes in every once in a while, I'll tell you. But all I want to say to you is thank you for this. Do not let them get you discouraged about the United States. I believe I am going to win this election because I believe I have the trust of the American people. The election is about world peace. The election is about who has brought change. Governor Clinton talks about change, change, change; that's all you'll have left in your pocket if you put him in there. We don't need any more tax-and-spend. Stay with our program, and watch us move this country forward.

Thank you all. And on a night like this, Lee says it better, but "God Bless the U.S.A." Thank you all very, very much.

Note: The President spoke at 8:30 p.m. at St. Louis Community College at Forest Park. In his remarks, he referred to entertainers the Gatlin Brothers and Lee Greenwood.

Remarks on Signing the Benjamin National Franklin Memorial Commemorative Medal and Fire Service Bill of Rights Act in Springfield, Pennsylvania
October 12, 1992

Curt, thank you so very much. And I just can't tell you what this event means to me. I want to offer a special salute to Curt Weldon. He has got to be, when you look at the whole Nation, the firefighter's, the emergency responder's best friend. He is unbelievable in his steadfast support for everything we believe in. Curt is very generous in his assessment of my role, but it is his work, his labor, his efforts that make this historic bill here—gives us this bill to sign today. I want to salute Chief Gallagher; Gene Bidoli, the president of the Firemen's Association of Delaware County. I want to salute the 20 national presidents that are here today representing a million and a half emergency responders all across our great country.

It's an honor to be here. And I guess like every kid in America, I grew up wondering

whether I could ever be a fireman. Barbara saw me drilling a hole in the Lincoln Bedroom the other day, trying to put a fire pole down, curving it around to go down into the Oval Office. But I am here today to sign the Benjamin Franklin National Memorial Commemorative Medal and Fire Service Bill of Rights Act. It authorizes the minting of a medal commemorating Benjamin Franklin's contribution to the advancement of science and the American fire service.

The activities funded through the sale of the medal we're going to authorize today will help to carry out your important bill of rights. The proceeds will help promote education and training programs, a greater public awareness and support of the many hazards of firefighting and emergency response. And they will help assure that should the ultimate tragedy occur, your loved ones will be taken care of.

The list of benefits from this medal goes on and on, and so does the courage of the American firefighters. And I know that it can be touch and go in some situations, some of the calls that you respond to, the danger that every firefighter faces when entering a burning building or responding to an accident. For your bravery and for your unfailing dedication, I say this from the bottom of my heart: Thank you on behalf of all Americans.

Also included in this act is the Fire Service Bill of Rights. It is a tribute to all of you. It acknowledges the important contributions that firefighters make to their communities. But most of all, the Fire Service Bill of Rights is long-awaited and much-deserved recognition for all you do for your country.

As some of you may know, Teddy Roosevelt is among my favorite Presidents in history, and let me share with you what his

father said to him on his 16th birthday. He said, "We are not placed here to live exclusively for ourselves." And you serve, you serve. You serve not only for yourselves alone, obviously, but for the family called America.

And on behalf of that family, thank you. May God bless each and every one of you. All of you are heroes in my book. And may God bless the State of Pennsylvania and this wonderful country that we are fortunate enough to live in, the United States of America.

And now you will see me sign enthusiastically and make official this very important act. Thank you all very much.

Note: The President spoke at 11:35 a.m. at Springfield Township Fire Co. No. 44. In his remarks, he referred to U.S. Representative Curt Weldon. H.R. 2448, approved October 12, was assigned Public Law No. 102–406. A tape was not available for verification of the content of these remarks.

Remarks to the Community in Springfield
October 12, 1992

The President. Thank you very, very much. Give them the sign. [*Laughter*] Thank you very, very much. Let me say it's great to be back here in Springfield, great to be back in this all-important part of Pennsylvania, and great to be accompanied by one of the true national leaders who is your Congressman, Curt Weldon. He's doing an outstanding job.

I hope some of you tuned into last night's political talk-a-thon. I don't pretend to be an Oxford debater, but I think I did OK. What we're going to do is continue to tell the truth about this country, and let the voters decide 3 weeks from whenever it is—tomorrow. Three weeks away. We need your support.

You know, listening to our opponents, you might think they want you to believe that America is a nation in decline. And of course, we've got our challenges, but we should never forget that our people are still

the best educated; our economy, in spite of the problems, the most dynamic; our workers are still the most productive, more productive than any other workers in the entire world. And I am proud of what we have done to strengthen America's leadership all around the world.

Four years ago we said we'd bring America's disabled into the mainstream, and we delivered. I said we would do what no President has done in 10 years, and that is start to clean our air and get rid of acid rain, and we delivered. I said we would strengthen the family by letting parents, not the Government, choose our kids' child care, and we delivered again.

I am very proud that on my watch more than a billion people, almost one-fifth of the entire population of the world, have enjoyed the first breath of freedom. I'm proud that we stood up to the bully of Baghdad and led the world to saying no to aggression.

I am especially proud that the children here today, the young people, will grow up in a world that is safer because we reduced the fear of nuclear war. But as you people know, the Soviet bear may be gone, but there are still some wolves in the woods. It may be tempting to believe that we can turn the American Commander in Chief into the Maytag repairman. But there are still dangers in the world, and you've got to ask who do you trust to keep your families secure.

Governor Clinton has absolutely no experience in international matters, and I am the President who has led the world and made these kids safer. I ask for your support on that basis.

You see, the new world brings new challenges and new opportunities. We're part of a global economy, and this is no time to hand the wheel to a novice. When it comes to steering America through the new global economic challenges, America needs a driver who knows the highway. Do not take a risk on America's future.

I have laid out my Agenda for American Renewal, the steps that we must take to win the economic competition, to build a prosperous, secure nation for all the kids here today. And step number one is to tear down the barriers to free and fair trade so that we can create good jobs for American workers.

Yes, we've been caught up in a global economic slowdown. We have to understand that the nations of Europe would switch for our economy in a fast minute. We have lower inflation and lower interest rates. We're the world's leading exporter. And when you shop in the world, chances are that the goods in the stores say not "Made in Japan," not "Made in Germany" but "Made in the U.S.A."

Audience members. U.S.A.! U.S.A.! U.S.A.!

The President. And by opening up foreign markets, we will provide good jobs for our kids and our grandkids. You know, already the average export-related job pays 17 percent more than a traditional job. So if we want our sons and daughters of steelworkers to have good jobs, we must fight for free and fair trade. I am proud of our administration that last week signed the North

American free trade agreement, forging a $6 trillion market from Manitoba to Mexico. NAFTA will create 175,000 new American jobs.

In my second term, we will fight for new agreements with the nations of Europe and Asia and Latin America. And just as we once used our military alliances to win the cold war, we can use these economic alliances to win the new business war. We are number one. Let's make ourselves even stronger.

But let's be serious about one point: If we're going to win that competition in the new economy, we've got to do it, and we've got to do it by changing our schools. You know, we already spend more per pupil than any of our major industrial competitors and yet our kids rank near the bottom in math and science. We need to embrace new ideas. And again, I'm proud of what we've done already. Never in history has America had national education goals. But today we do. Now let's build on that goal to give every kid here a better education. Never before in America have almost 2,000 communities committed to literally reinventing our schools. And today they are. But we can't stop here. So in my second term I want to give every parent in America the right to choose their kids' school, public, private, or religious.

But you know, reforming education will not be enough if our graduates can't find jobs. So we have to strengthen American business. The past 4 years have not been easy. American companies are restructuring. But almost every American industry—steel, computers, biotech—is stronger than just a few years ago. Small business is the backbone of this economy, creating two out of every three jobs. Small business will lead the economic recovery if we can provide the kind of tax relief I'm fighting for, relief from taxation, regulation, and litigation.

America spends up to $200 billion every year on direct cost to lawyers. Japan doesn't spend this, and neither does Germany. I want to take on these trial lawyers and reform our lawsuit-happy legal system. People don't even dare coach Little League because they'll get sued. You see a guy lying along the highway, and you don't dare stop because you think somebody will sue you for trying to help. Or if you're a doctor, you don't dare deliver babies because you're afraid some crazy patient will sue you with a malpractice suit. Well look, we sue each other too much, and we care for each other too little. Let's start doing it the other way: care for each other more and sue each other less.

Step four is this: We've got to cut the cost of health care. With our current health care system, you get sick twice, first when you go to the doctor and then a month later when you get the bill. I want to reform this malpractice insurance. I want to use competition to drive the cost down. I want to make insurance available to absolutely everybody: the poorest of the poor right up through the overworked, overtaxed middle class. My plan does that, and we still keep the quality of American health care. Let's not go to socialized medicine; let's go to competitive medicine. A good doctor ought not to be a luxury, not something reserved for the privileged few: not here, not in Pennsylvania, not in America, not anymore. Pass my health care reform. Give me new Members of Congress. Clean out the House. Give us more like Curt. Give us people that will pass this kind of legislation.

Priority number five is to reach out to every American because in the next century we need the talent of every person from the city to the suburbs to the furthest rural town. And to do this we must take back our streets from the crackheads and the criminals. We must back our law enforcement people. Today I've just come from a marvelous meeting of 20 leaders of national firefighting people. And we've got to make them safe by better law enforcement. We must protect those who are helping us.

I'm proud that under my administration about 85 percent of the people served their full sentences on Federal crimes. We have appointed Federal judges who have a little less respect for the criminal and a lot more for the victims of crime. And that's the kind of judges we need.

But we want to do even better with tough new laws for new crimes like carjacking and special laws for crimes against women and the elderly. And so I put forward a specific plan to eliminate over 4,000

Government projects, almost 250 programs that waste your hard-earned tax dollars. And I want to control the growth of mandatory Federal spending without touching Social Security. Leave Social Security safe.

As Curt knows, the Congress can't do anything about the deficit, so give me a chance. Give me a balanced budget amendment, a line-item veto, a check-off on our tax return. A check-off on the tax return to take the deficit off our children's shoulders. We've got to get the job done, and the current Congress won't do it. The good news is because of the fraud in the banks and the post offices, we're going to have a lot of new Congressmen. And I'll sit down and say, let's change America. Let's get the deficit off the back of these kids.

Governor Clinton simply cannot stand up to the congressional bosses. He refuses to endorse term limits. I say let's limit the terms of Members of Congress and give the Government back to the people.

So this is some of our agenda for America's renewal. It's a comprehensive, it's an innovative, a new approach, a new plan, and it offers the promises of a very different America than the plan Governor Clinton proposes.

Now, look at each of the items I've mentioned and you'll see the difference. I hate to ruin this beautiful sunny day in Springfield, but I've got to tell you a little bit factually about Governor Clinton's record.

On the question of the North American free trade agreement, he was first for it and then against it. Now he's for it again. You can't do that. They don't serve waffles in the Oval Office on these tough issues. You have to take a position. You can't keep everybody happy, but you've got to take a position. You can't be on all sides of every issue.

In education Governor Clinton talks a good game, but he's flunked the test in Arkansas. He can't reform American schools because he doesn't want to attend the very powerful union leaders. I want to support the teachers, not the teachers' union. He wants to listen to the union and not to the teachers.

You see the same thing when it comes to small business. Governor Clinton and the trial lawyers act like Boris and Natasha in those old Bullwinkle cartoons, you remember? They play goo-goo eyes with each other. He wants small business to pay a stiff new payroll tax for health care, and that would drive away jobs in small business. And we don't need to destroy jobs; we need to create jobs.

And on crime, I have been endorsed, because we have a strong record of backing the law enforcement officers, by the National Fraternal Order of Police. And get this, the police in Little Rock, the ones who know Governor Clinton best, have endorsed me for President of the United States.

Here's the biggest difference of all. Here is the biggest difference of all. Where I want to make Government smaller, Governor Clinton has already proposed—worse than Mondale, worse than Dukakis—$150 billion in new taxes. And that ain't all of it, man. He's also proposed over $200 billion in new spending, and he hasn't got there yet. We cannot have that. You've got to ask who's going to pay for it. He says sock it to the rich. There aren't that many people that are rich. What he's going to do is stick it right to the cab driver, the teacher, the nurse, the firefighter, the construction workers. I say we need to help the middle class, not sock it to them with more taxes.

So we've got two fundamentally different philosophies of Government. He puts his faith in more Government, in special interests, in higher taxes to pay for all his promises. And I offer smaller Government, lower taxes, and more power to the people so that we can renew America.

The Democrats don't like it when I talk about it, but we've got to find ways to strengthen the American family, not tear it apart at the shreds by crazy social legislation. When Barbara Bush reads to those children in the Diplomatic Entrance to the White House, she's saying, "Love your kid. Read to the children. Strengthen the American family." And that's what we must do. [*Applause*] And I agree with you. I think we've got the best First Lady in a long, long time.

You know, as I told them last night, in the Oval Office, the buck does stop there. You've got to make tough decisions. You can't keep everybody happy. When you make a mistake you pick up and go on and try to continue to help the American people. When you do something wrong, do like a family person does, say, "Look, I made a mistake and now I want to go forward." I believe I have been a good, strong leader in tough times for the United States of America.

Audience members. Four more years! Four more years! Four more years!

The President. I believe I have the ideas, the experience, and the character to lead again so that together we can make our Nation more safe and more secure. Let us not take a risk on America's future. I ask for your trust so that I can finish this job. I am proud of the United States. I do not tear it down. I want to lift it up and make life better for every single American.

And may God bless you all. May God bless you. And thank you for this fantastic show of support. I am very, very grateful to you. Thank you all.

Note: The President spoke at 11:57 a.m. at the Springfield Township Municipal Amphitheater.

Remarks to Farm and Business Groups in Grand Rapids, Michigan
October 12, 1992

Thank you very much. Well, thank you all. And let me just thank everybody, thank Jim and Tom, Noelle and Brian. Pay respects to our Governor, who is rapidly crossing out the fact that his wife, Michelle, is not with us today, which is our loss. She's doing a first class job as first lady of this State, and I'm very proud to have these endorsements from the leading farm and business groups in Michigan.

You know, the global economy—and we're in a global economy—is in transition. And still, compared to the other countries of the world, the American economy is in relatively good shape. Industrial manufacturing—up, versus Japan. In the Bush years, farm income and family income averaged highest under any President. And inflation is way down, as we've heard. Low interest rates mean good news for farmers, homebuyers, small-business men and women.

The real question then in this election is: Where do we go from here? And Governor Clinton offers a billion dollars a day in new promises, at least $150 billion which he's already proposed in new taxes to be paid by, of course, small businesses, farmers, and middle class. He says soak the rich, but the whole country knows better.

I want to make Government smaller, make opportunity larger. And I propose controlling the growth of mandatory spending, eliminating wasteful Government spending, while still making the necessary investments in job training, education, and in high-wage industries of the future.

Last month, the National Association of Business Economists compared our two directions, Governor Clinton's and mine. And the vast majority said that under the Bush agenda, inflation would be lower, interest rates would be lower, and the budget deficit smaller. Michigan voters ought to look at our plans in detail and ask which will make their jobs, their families more secure. The Michigan farm and business community has done that, and I am very proud to accept their support in our crusade to renew America for the next 4 years.

Thank you all very, very much.

Note: The President spoke at 3:55 p.m. at Kent County International Airport. In his remarks, he referred to Gov. John Engler of Michigan; James Barrett, president, Michigan Chamber of Commerce; Tom Guthrie, vice chairman, Michigan Farm Bureau AgriPac; Noelle Clark, chairwoman, Michigan chapter, National Federation of Independent Businesses; and Brian Wellman, chairman, Michigan Homebuilders Association.

Remarks to the Community in Holland, Michigan
October 12, 1992

The President. Thank you, Governor. What a fantastic rally. Thank you all. Wall-to-wall people at Hope. This is beautiful. Thank you so very much. And may I thank your great Governor, John Engler, and salute your Lieutenant Governor, Connie Binsfeld, who's with us. And Peter Hoekstra, who we've got to have as a Member of the Congress. If we had more people in Congress like Peter, they wouldn't be yelling at me, "Clean House!" We've got to clean House, and one way to do it: Get Peter in there and others like him. Good, solid, Michigan people.

Out there in the audience is someone you ought to be very proud of, the man I had the pleasure of meeting awhile back, Professor Harvey Blankespoor, and his wife, Marlene. Great leader, great educational leader. And of course, it's a great pleasure

to be here at Hope College, and great to be back in Michigan.

Now, may I begin by congratulating the Flying Dutchmen on your big victory Saturday. You know, I also couldn't help but notice that one of Michigan's great companies, the Herman Miller Corporation, made the furniture for last night's Presidential debate. They did a great job. Things got so hot in there that I commend whoever made the decision to nail the podiums to the floor. [*Laughter*] But, you know, Governor Clinton has a tendency to take two positions on every issue. So maybe Herman Miller should make a fourth podium, one for Clinton when he's for something and one for Clinton when he's against it.

You listen to him, and also to some degree to Ross Perot, and you get the feeling that America is a nation in decline. And yes, we've got our challenges. But we should never forget that our people are still the best educated; our economy, in spite of a world slowdown, the best, the most dynamic; and our workers the most productive, more productive than any other workers in the entire world. And that is the fact. I am proud of what we've accomplished the past 4 years: to strengthen America's leadership. We are respected around the entire world. And we are number one.

Let's talk about the record. Four years ago, I said we would bring the disabled into America's economic mainstream. And we delivered with the Americans for Disability Act, the best piece of civil rights legislation in decades.

I said I would do what no President has done for 10 years, 20 years and start to clean our air of acid rain. And we delivered. I said we would strengthen the family by letting parents, not the Government, choose our kids' child care. And we delivered on that, too. I'm also proud that on our watch more than a billion people, almost one-fifth of the population of the entire world, have enjoyed their first breath of freedom. Democracy and freedom are on the move.

And while Governor Clinton waffled, I stood up to a Baghdad bully, and we led the world in saying no to aggression. And I'm especially proud that the children here today will grow up in a world that is safer because we reduced the awful threat, the nightmare of nuclear weapons. That is a major accomplishment. But you know, while the Soviet bear may be gone, there are still wolves in the woods. It may be tempting to believe that we can turn the American Commander in Chief into the Maytag repairman, but there are still real dangers in the world. You must ask, who do you trust to keep your families secure?

This is about big things. It's about the Presidency. And Governor Clinton has absolutely no international experience. I am the President who has led the world and made our children safer.

Audience members. Four more years! Four more years! Four more years!

The President. You see this new world, the new world today brings new challenges and also new opportunities. We are part of a global economy, and this is no time to hand the wheel to a novice to take a risk with the United States. When it comes to steering America through the new global economic challenges, America needs a driver who knows the highway. And I am that man.

I have laid out this agenda for America's renewal, the steps that we must take to win the new economic competition, to build a prosperous, secure nation for all the kids here today. Step number one is to tear down barriers to free and fair trade so that we can create good jobs for American workers. Today, we're in a global downturn. But while there is anxiety here at home, we have to understand that the nations of Europe would switch places with us in a minute. We have lower inflation. We have lower interest rates. And we are the world's leading exporter. When you shop in the world, chances are that the goods in the store may say not "Made in Japan," not "Made in Germany" but "Made in the U.S.A."

And so we're going to pry open new foreign markets. In so doing, we will provide good jobs for our kids and our grandkids. Already the average export-related job pays 17 percent more than a traditional job. So if we want the sons and daughters of auto workers to have good jobs, we must fight for free and fair trade. I'm proud of our record, and I'm proud that last week we signed the historic North American free trade agreement, forging a $6 trillion market from Manitoba to Mexico. And that will create 175,000 additional American jobs.

In the second term, we're going to fight for new agreements with the nations of Europe and Asia and Latin America. Just as we once used our military alliances to win the old cold war, we can use our economic alliances to win the new business war. Because give the American worker the chance and they will outthink, outcompete, outproduce any other worker on the face of the Earth.

Let's not kid ourselves. We're not going to compete in this new economy if we don't do better by education, if we don't change our schools. We already spend more per pupil than any of our major industrial competitors, and yet our kids in K through 12 rank near the bottom in math and science. We need to embrace new ideas.

And again, I am proud of what we have done already. Never in the history has America had national educational goals. Today we do. That happened under my being President of the United States. Never before in America have almost 2,000 communities committed to literally reinventing their schools. Today they are.

But we can't stop here. So in my second term, I want to give every parent in America the right to choose their kids' schools, public, private, or religious.

Audience members. Four more years! Four more years! Four more years!

The President. Reforming education, though, reforming education won't be enough if our graduates can't find jobs. So we have to strengthen American business. The past 4 years have not been easy as American companies restructure. But almost every American industry—steel, computers, cars, biotechnology—is stronger now than just 4 years ago. Small business is the backbone of our new economy, creating two out of every three new jobs. And small business will lead the new economic recovery if we can provide the kind of relief that I am fighting for, relief from taxation, regulation, and litigation.

You know I'm not anti-lawyer, but let me tell you something. We spend up to $200 billion every year on direct costs to lawyers. Japan doesn't spend this; Germany doesn't. And I want to take on those ambulance chasers and reform our lawsuit-happy legal system. You see, when doctors are afraid to practice, when people are afraid to help somebody along the highway, when coaches are afraid to coach Little League, my message is this: As a nation, we must sue each other less and care for each other more.

Step number four of my agenda is to create economic security for every working man and woman in this country. And that means cutting the cost of health care. With our current health care system, you get sick twice, first when you go to the doctor, then a month later when you get the bill.

I want to reform malpractice insurance. I want to use competition to drive costs down and make affordable insurance available to everyone in the United States, including the poorest of the poor. And my health care plan does exactly that without taxing small business. A good doctor should not be a luxury, not something reserved for the privileged few: not here, not in Michigan, not in America, not anymore.

Priority number five is to reach out to every American, because in the next century we need the talent of every person from the city to the suburbs to the furthest rural town. And to do this, we must take back our streets from the crackheads and the criminals. We're fighting for strong anti-crime legislation. And I'm proud that under my administration most Federal inmates serve at least 85 percent of their full sentence, while in Arkansas they serve 20 percent.

Audience members. Boo-o-o!

The President. We have appointed judges, and I will continue to do that, who have no respect for the criminals and a lot more concern for the victims of crime. But we must do better. We just passed a bill with tough laws against new crimes like carjacking. And now we need special laws for crimes against women and crimes against the elderly. Everybody should be secure in his or her own home. The way I see it, if you steal a car or if you mug an elderly woman, you ought to go to jail, and you shouldn't be let out until you're eligible for a birthday salute from Willard Scott.

The final part of my agenda is simply this: I believe that Government is too big and spends too much of your money. So I have put forward a specific plan to eliminate 4,000 Government projects, almost 240 programs that waste your hard-earned tax dollars. I want to control, as I said last night, to get this deplorable deficit down. We have got to control the growth of mandatory Federal spending without touching Social Security. We've got to do it. It means a little pain, but we cannot saddle the generations represented here today with more and more Federal debt.

And here's something that would help. I'm fighting for a balanced budget amendment to the Constitution. I am fighting for a line-item veto. And I want to give every taxpayer the power to designate up to 10 percent of your income tax to be used for one purpose only: to take the deficit off our children's shoulders. Congress won't make the tough choices, so it's time for some tough medicine. Governor Clinton won't stand up to the congressional bosses and endorse term limits. So I say let's limit the terms of Members of Congress and give Government back to the people.

And this, then, is my agenda for America's renewal. It offers the promise of a very different America than the plan Governor Clinton proposes. I hate to ruin this beautiful day, but just look for a minute at each of the items I've mentioned today, and you'll see the difference.

On the question of the North American free trade agreement, Governor Clinton was first for it and then against it. Now he's for it again. They do not serve waffles in the Oval Office. On tough issues, you have to take a stand. You can't be everything to everybody.

In education, Governor Clinton talks a good game, but he's flunked his test in Arkansas. And Governor Clinton can't reform American schools because he doesn't want to offend the powerful unions. I want to offend the unions and lift up the teachers, not the other way around. And so the Governor—one side and then the other—he tells the education establishment what they want to hear. I want to tell them what they need to hear.

You see the same thing when it comes to helping small business. Governor Clinton and the trial lawyers act like Boris and Natasha—remember the old Bullwinkle cartoons—goo-goo eyes with each other. [*Laughter*] And Governor Clinton doesn't want to touch the legal system. And he wants small business to pay a stiff new payroll tax for health care, which would drive away your jobs. And we do not need to destroy jobs by socking a tax to small business. We need to create jobs.

And on crime, which I mentioned—I told you what I'm for—but on crime, here's all you need to know about him. The prestigious National Fraternal Order of Police, the nationwide organization, have endorsed me for President. And the police in Little Rock, the ones who know Governor Clinton best,

Little Rock, have endorsed me for President of the United States.

But here is the biggest difference and most important. Where I want to make Government smaller, Governor Clinton has already proposed, look at his plan, $150 billion in new taxes——

Audience members. Boo-o-o!

The President. ——and he has promised well over $220 billion in new spending. We cannot have that.

Audience members. Boo-o-o!

The President. You've got to ask, who's going to pay for all those bills, all the promises? And the answer is: not the rich guys. It's the cab drivers, the barbers, the beauticians, the construction workers. And I say it is time to help the middle class.

And so we've got two very different, very different views of America. Governor Clinton puts his faith in more Government, in special interests, in higher taxes to pay for all these promises. And I offer smaller Government, lower taxes, and more power to the people so that we can renew America.

Today, as you know, is this glorious Columbus Day, and I'd like to point out that when Columbus set sail on his voyage, Spain's motto was three words: *ne plus ultra*. All you Latin students out there know that this meant "no more beyond." And after Columbus returned from his discovery, Queen Isabella dropped the first word from her country's motto. And now it reads *plus ultra*, "more beyond."

And today we can say the same thing of the United States of America. We have triumphed around the world, but there is "more beyond," more to reach for, more to reach for right here at home: better schools; safer streets; stronger families; a dynamic, growing economy where you can live your dreams. This is the future that I offer America. And that is why I ask for your support to finish the job.

Audience members. We want Bush! We want Bush! We want Bush!

The President. Thank you for this fantastic rally. And may God bless the United States of America. Thank you very much.

Note: The President spoke at 5:10 p.m. at Hope College.

Statement on Signing the Instrument of Ratification for the United Nations Framework Convention on Climate Change
October 13, 1992

Today I have signed the instrument of ratification for the United Nations Framework Convention on Climate Change, which I submitted to the U.S. Senate for advice and consent on September 8, 1992. The Senate consented to ratification on October 7, 1992. With this action, the United States becomes the first industrialized nation (and the fourth overall) to ratify this historic treaty.

I signed this convention on June 12, 1992, in Rio de Janeiro at the United Nations Conference on Environment and Development (UNCED). The convention was also signed by 153 other nations and the European Community. Today I am calling on them to join us in ratifying the convention as soon as possible and making a prompt start in its implementation.

The Climate Convention is the first step in crucial long-term international efforts to address climate change. The international community moved with unprecedented speed in negotiating this convention and thereby beginning the response to climate change.

As proposed by the United States, the convention is comprehensive in scope and action-oriented. All parties must inventory all sources and sinks of greenhouse gases and establish national climate change programs. Industrialized countries must go further, outlining in detail the programs and measures they will undertake to limit greenhouse emissions and adapt to climate change and quantifying expected results. Parties will meet on a regular basis to review and update those plans in the light of evolving scientific and economic information.

Since UNCED, the United States has begun to refine its national action plan, based on the U.S. climate change strategy first announced in February 1991 and updated in April 1992. The United States was one of the first nations to lay out its action plan, which will reduce projected levels of net greenhouse gas emissions in the year 2000 by as much as 11 percent.

Through such measures as the newly enacted national energy legislation, the Clean Air Act Amendments of 1990, the Intermodal Surface Transportation Efficiency Act of 1992, and other programs and policies of this administration, I am confident the United States will continue to lead the world in taking economically sensible actions to reduce the threat of climate change.

The United States is also assisting developing nations with their treaty obligations. Specifically, we are committed to providing $25 million to help such nations fund "country studies" that will inventory each country's sources and sinks of greenhouse gases and identify options for mitigating and adapting to climate change. The United States hosted an international workshop from September 14 to 16 at the Department of Energy's Lawrence Berkeley Laboratory in California to plan these country studies.

We look forward to the December session of the Intergovernmental Negotiating Committee, December 7–10 in Geneva, to discuss with other parties how best to move forward in promoting the objectives of the treaty.

Statement by Press Secretary Fitzwater on Namibia's Accession to the Nuclear Non-Proliferation Treaty
October 13, 1992

The United States welcomes and commends the Government of Namibia's accession on October 7, 1992, to the Nuclear Non-Proliferation Treaty (NPT). The administration has been encouraging President Nujoma to make this important decision. Namibia's accession to the NPT represents a positive response to the international community's heightened concern about the global spread of weapons of mass destruction.

The United States firmly believes this action by Namibia represents another important step toward strengthening international security as well as peace and cooperation in southern Africa.

Letter to Congressional Leaders on the Partial Suspension of the Davis-Bacon Act
October 14, 1992

Dear Mr. Speaker: (Dear Mr. President:)

I hereby report that I have exercised my statutory authority under section 6 of the Davis-Bacon Act, 40 U.S.C. 276a–5, to suspend the provisions of sections 276a to 276a–5 of the Davis-Bacon Act in the event of a national emergency. I have found that the conditions caused by Hurricanes Andrew and Iniki constitute a "national emergency" within the meaning of section 6. I have, therefore, suspended the provisions of the Davis-Bacon Act in designated areas in the States of Florida, Louisiana, and Hawaii.

This action is more fully set out in the enclosed proclamation that I have issued today.

Sincerely,

GEORGE BUSH

Note: Identical letters were sent to Thomas S. Foley, Speaker of the House of Representatives, and Dan Quayle, President of the Senate. The proclamation is listed in Appendix E at the end of this volume.

Statement by Press Secretary Fitzwater on Russian Action To Resolve Questions Concerning the Korean Airlines Flight 007 Incident
October 14, 1992

Russian President Boris Yeltsin met today in Moscow with U.S. Ambassador Robert Strauss and family members of Americans killed in the Soviet shootdown of Korean Airlines flight 007 in September 1983. President Yeltsin offered his condolences to the American people, the American families of the victims, and the other countries involved. He also transferred to the United States important documents and information concerning the shootdown from Soviet archives, including information pertaining to the aircraft's black box.

The President is deeply grateful to President Yeltsin for this courageous effort to resolve the many questions which still linger from one of the cold war's greatest tragedies. President Yeltsin's actions demonstrate once again the benefits from the new U.S.-Russian relationship which is grounded in cooperation, respect, and a commitment to forge together a new era of peace.

Today's meeting followed years of discussion of the KAL tragedy between the United States and the Soviet and Russian Governments. The President and other senior American officials have raised this issue repeatedly during the last 2 years in an effort to discover the truth concerning the deaths of 63 American citizens who were aboard the flight.

The delegation of American family members will continue discussions with the Russian Government in Moscow this week on the important issues that remain to be resolved, including disposition of the remains and personal effects of the victims which may have been uncovered during the Soviet search effort, the families' desire to hold a memorial service near the crash site, and *ex gratia* payments to each American family. The administration supports the family members in their efforts to reach a final resolution of all issues concerning this tragedy.

Statement by Press Secretary Fitzwater on the 1992 Winners of the Malcolm Baldrige National Quality Awards
October 14, 1992

The President today congratulates the five winners of the 1992 Malcolm Baldrige Quality Award for excellence in quality management.

The winners in the manufacturing category are AT&T Network Systems Group/ Transmission Business Unit of Morristown, NJ, and Texas Instruments Inc. Defense Systems and Electronics Group of Dallas, TX. The winners in the service category are AT&T Universal Card Services of Jackson-

ville, FL, and the Ritz-Carlton Hotel Co. of Atlanta, GA. In the small business category, the winner is the Granite Rock Co. of Watsonville, CA.

The Baldrige Award is given annually, in memory of the late Commerce Secretary Malcolm Baldrige, to acknowledge exemplary efforts of U.S. companies in instilling in their workplaces a commitment to quality products and services.

Statement on Signing the Advisory Council on California Indian Policy Act of 1992
October 14, 1992

I am signing into law H.R. 2144, the "Advisory Council on California Indian Policy Act of 1992." The Council is to review the status of, and Federal policy towards, California Indian tribes.

In 1978 the Department of the Interior established the Federal Acknowledgment Process to ensure that all petitions for recognition as a federally recognized tribe would be evaluated in an objective and uniform manner. The process, developed with the support of the Indian tribes and the

Congress, provides each petitioning group the opportunity for an unbiased, detailed review of its petition.

I support the Federal Acknowledgment Process for the review of all petitions for tribal recognition. It is a stated policy objective of the Administration to restore terminated tribal entities, as appropriate. I do not, however, support establishment of separate recognition procedures or policies exclusive to one State. I note that the members of the Council created under this Act are effectively selected by various California Indian tribes. Thus they are not appointed in conformity with the Appointments Clause of the Constitution, Article II, section 2, clause 2. I sign this bill on the understanding that the Council will serve only in an advisory capacity. In particular, I note that the tribal and descendency lists created by the Council may not, without further congressional action, serve as the basis for determining eligibility for Federal funds or benefits.

Finally, I am also troubled that, although the advice of the Council may influence important decisions, members and staff have been specifically exempted from any restrictions involving financial conflicts of interest. There does not appear to be any justification for this exemption. In order to protect the integrity of the Council, I direct the Secretary of the Interior, in consultation with the Director of the Office of Government Ethics, to ensure that, as a condition of appointment, members and staff of the Council agree to abide by appropriate standards of conduct set forth in 5 C.F.R. 2635.

GEORGE BUSH

The White House,
October 14, 1992.

Note: H.R. 2144, approved October 14, was assigned Public Law No. 102–416. This statement was released by the Office of the Press Secretary on October 15.

Presidential Debate in Richmond, Virginia
October 15, 1992

Carole Simpson. Good evening, and welcome to the second of three Presidential debates between the major candidates for President of the United States. The candidates are the Republican nominee, President George Bush; the independent, Ross Perot; and Governor Bill Clinton, the Democratic nominee.

My name is Carole Simpson, and I will be the moderator for tonight's 90-minute debate which is coming to you from the campus of the University of Richmond in Richmond, Virginia.

Now, tonight's program is unlike any other Presidential debate in history. We're making history now, and it's pretty exciting. An independent polling firm has selected an audience of 209 uncommitted voters from this area. The candidates will be asked questions by these voters on a topic of their choosing, anything they want to ask about. My job as moderator is to, you know, take care of the questioning, ask questions myself if I think there needs to be continuity and balance, and sometimes I might ask the candidates to respond to what another candidate may have said.

Now, the format has been agreed to by representatives of both the Republican and Democratic campaigns, and there is no subject matter that is restricted. Anything goes. We can ask anything. After the debate the candidates will have an opportunity to make a closing statement.

So, President Bush, I think you said it earlier, let's get it on.

President Bush. Let's go.

Ms. Simpson. And I think the first question is over here.

Foreign Trade and Domestic Jobs

Q. I'd like to direct my question to Mr. Perot. What will you do as President to open foreign markets to fair competition from American business and to stop unfair competition here at home from foreign countries so that we can bring jobs back to the United States?

Mr. Perot. That's right at the top of my agenda. We've shipped millions of jobs overseas, and we have a strange situation because we have a process in Washington where after you've served for a while, you cash in, become a foreign lobbyist, make

$30,000 a month, then take a leave, work on Presidential campaigns, make sure you got good contacts, and then go back out.

Now, if you just want to get down to brass tacks, first thing you ought to do is get all these folks that have got these one-way trade agreements that we've negotiated over the years and say, "Fellas, we'll take the same deal we gave you." They'll gridlock right at that point, because, for example, we've got international competitors who simply could not unload their cars off the ships if they had to comply, you see, if it was a two-way street, just couldn't do it.

We have got to stop sending jobs overseas. To those of you in the audience who are business people, pretty simple: If you're paying $12, $13, $14 an hour for factory workers, and you can move your factory south of the border, pay $1 an hour for labor, hire young—let's assume you've been in business for a long time; you've got a mature work force—pay $1 an hour for your labor, have no health care—that's the most expensive single element in making a car—have no environmental controls, no pollution controls, and no retirement, and you don't care about anything but making money, there will be a giant sucking sound going south. So if the people send me to Washington, the first thing I'll do is study that 2,000-page agreement and make sure it's a two-way street.

I have one last part here. I decided I was dumb and didn't understand it, so I called the "Who's Who" of the folks that have been around it. And I said, "Why won't everybody go south?" They say, "It would be disruptive." I said, "For how long?" I finally got them up for 12 to 15 years. And I said, "Well, how does it stop being disruptive?" And that is, when their jobs come up from $1 an hour to $6 an hour, and ours go down to $6 an hour, then it's leveled again. But in the meantime, you've wrecked the country with these kinds of deals. We've got to cut it out.

Ms. Simpson. Thank you, Mr. Perot. I see that the President has stood up, so he must have something to say about this.

President Bush. Well, Carole, the thing that saved us in this global economic slowdown has been our exports, and what I'm trying to do is increase our exports. If,

indeed, all the jobs were going to move south because of lower wages, there are lower wages now, and they haven't done that. So I have just negotiated with the President of Mexico the North American free trade agreement, and the Prime Minister of Canada, I might add. I want to have more of these free trade agreements because export jobs are increasing far faster than any jobs that may have moved overseas. That's a scare tactic, because it's not that many. But any one that's here, we want to have more jobs here, and the way to do that is to increase our exports.

Some believe in protection. I don't. I believe in free and fair trade. That's the thing that saved us. And so I will keep on, as President, trying to get a successful conclusion to the GATT round, the big Uruguay round of trade which will really open up markets for our agriculture, particularly. I want to continue to work after we get this NAFTA agreement ratified this coming year. I want to get one with Eastern Europe. I want to get one with Chile. Free and fair trade is the answer, not protection.

As I say, we've had tough economic times, and it's exports that have saved us, exports that have built——

Ms. Simpson. Governor Clinton.

Governor Clinton. I'd like to answer the question, because I've actually been a Governor for 12 years, so I've known a lot of people who have lost their jobs because of jobs moving overseas, and I know a lot of people whose plants have been strengthened by increasing exports.

The trick is to expand our export base and to expand trade on terms that are fair to us. It is true that our exports to Mexico, for example, have gone up, and our trade deficit's gone down. It's also true that just today a record-high trade deficit was announced with Japan.

So what is the answer? Let me just mention three things very quickly. Number one, make sure that other countries are as open to our markets as our markets are to them. If they're not, have measures on the books that don't take forever and a day to implement.

Number two, change the Tax Code. There are more deductions in the Tax Code

Photographic
Portfolio

Overleaf: At the Republican National Convention in Houston, TX, August 20. **Left:** Visiting the Job Corps Center in Excelsior Springs, MO, September 11. **Below:** Addressing Burrill Lumber Co. employees in Medford, OR, September 14. **Right:** Greeting White House staff at the Old Executive Office Building en route to the Richmond, VA, Presidential debate, October 15.

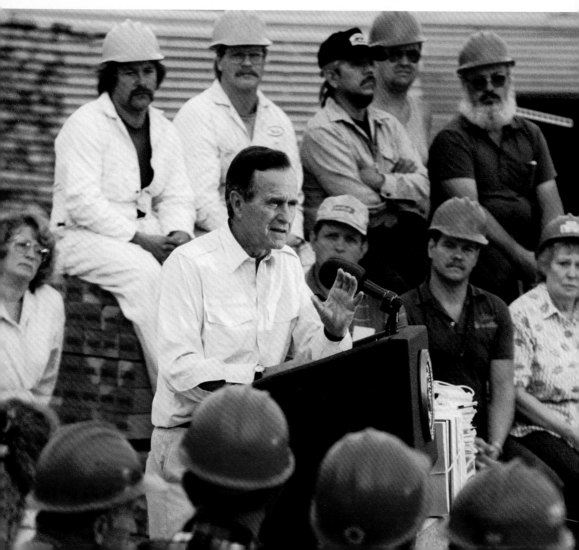

Greeting supporters during campaign whistlestop tours. **Right:** Plymouth, MI, September 26. **Below:** Gainesville, GA, October 20.

Above: Greeting cadets at the United States Military Academy [a]
West Point, NY, January 5. *Left:* Surveying damage caused by Hurricane Andrew in Lafayette, LA, August 26. *Above right:* Wit[h]
Secretary of Commerce and Industrial Development Jaime Serra Puche and President Carlo[s]
Salinas of Mexico, U.S. Trade Representative Carla A. Hills, an[d]
Minister of International Trade Michael Wilson and Prime Minister Brian Mulroney of Canada at the initialing ceremon[y]
for the North American Free Trade Agreement in San Antonio[,]
TX, October 7. *Below right:* Touring the Bonka Orphanage Center in Somalia, January 1. *Overleaf:* At Camp David, MD, September 11.

for shutting plants down and moving overseas than there are for modernizing plants and equipment here. Our competitors don't do that. Emphasize and subsidize modernizing plants and equipment here, not moving plants overseas.

Number three, stop the Federal Government's program that now gives low interest loans and job training funds to companies that will actually shut down and move to other countries, but we won't do the same thing for plants that stay here. So more trade, but on fair terms, and favor investment in America.

Ms. Simpson. Thank you. I think we have a question over here.

Federal Deficit

Q. This is for Governor Clinton. In the real world, that is, outside of Washington, DC, compensation and achievement are based on goals defined and achieved. My question is about the deficit. Would you define in specific dollar goals how much you would reduce the deficit in each of the 4 years of a Clinton administration and then enter into a legally binding contract with the American people that if you did not achieve those goals that you would not seek a second term? Answer yes or no, and then comment on your answer, please.

Governor Clinton. No, and here's why; I'll tell you exactly why, because the deficit now has been building up for 12 years. I'll tell you exactly what I think can be done. I think we can bring it down by 50 percent in 4 years and grow the economy.

Now, I could get rid of it in 4 years in theory on the books now, but to do it you'd have to raise taxes too much and cut benefits too much to people who need them, and it would even make the economy worse.

Mr. Perot will tell you, for example, that the expert he hired to analyze his plan says that it will bring the deficit down in 5 years, but it will make unemployment bad for 4 more years. So my view is, sir, you have to increase investment, grow the economy, and reduce the deficit by controlling health care costs, prudent reductions in defense, cuts in domestic programs, and asking the wealthiest Americans and foreign corporations to pay their fair share of taxes,

and investing in growing this economy.

I ask everybody to look at my economic ideas. Nine Nobel Prize winners and over 500 economists and hundreds of business people, including a lot of Republicans, said this is the way you've got to go. If you don't grow the economy, you can't get it done. But I can't foresee all the things that will happen, and I don't think a President should be judged solely on the deficit.

Let me also say we're having an election today. You'll have a shot at me in 4 years, and you can vote me right out if you think I've done a lousy job. I would welcome you to do that.

Ms. Simpson. Mr. President?

President Bush. Well, I've got to—I'm a little confused here because I don't see how you can grow the deficit down by raising people's taxes. You see, I don't think the American people are taxed too little. I think they're taxed too much. I went for one tax increase, and when I make a mistake, I admit it, say that wasn't the right thing to do. Governor Clinton's program wants to tax more and spend more: $150 billion in new taxes, spend another $220 billion. I don't believe that's the way to do it.

Here's some things that will help. Give us a balanced budget amendment. He always talks about Arkansas having a balanced budget, and they do. But he has a balanced budget amendment; have to do it. I'd like the Government to have that. I think it would discipline not only the Congress, which needs it, but also the executive branch.

I'd like to have what 43 Governors have, the line-item veto. So if the Congress can't cut, we've got a reckless spending Congress, let the President have a shot at it by wiping out things that are pork barrel or something of that nature.

I've proposed another one. Some sophisticates think it may be a little gimmicky. I think it's good. It's a check-off. It says to you as a taxpayer—say, you're going to pay a tax of $1,000 or something; you can check 10 percent of that if you want to in one box, and that 10 percent, $100, or if you're paying $10,000, whatever it is, $1,000, check it off, and make the Government, make it lower the deficit by that amount. If the Congress won't do it, if they can't get together and negotiate how to do that, then you'd have a sequester across the board. You'd exempt Social Security. I don't want to tax or touch Social Security. I'm the President that said, "Hey, don't mess with Social Security." And we haven't.

So I believe we need to control the growth of mandatory spending, back to this gentleman's question, that's the main growing thing in the budget. The program that the President—two-thirds of the budget, I, as President, never get to look at, never get to touch. We've got to control that growth to inflation and population increase, but not raise taxes on the American people now. I just don't believe that would stimulate any kind of growth at all.

Ms. Simpson. How about you, Mr. Perot?

Mr. Perot. Well, we're $4 trillion in debt, and we're going into debt an additional $1 billion, a little more than $1 billion, every working day of the year. Now, the thing I love about it—I'm just a businessman. I was down in Texas, taking care of business, tending to my family. This situation got so bad that I decided I had better get into it. The American people asked me to get into it. But I just find it fascinating that while we sit here tonight, we will go into debt an additional $50 million in an hour and a half.

Now, it's not the Republicans' fault, of course, and it's not the Democrats' fault. What I'm looking for is who did it? Now, they're the two folks involved; so maybe if you put them together, they did it. Now, the facts are we have to fix it.

I'm here tonight for these young people up here in the balcony from this college. When I was a young man, when I got out of the Navy, I had multiple job offers. Young people with high grades can't get a job. The 18- to 24-year-old high school graduates 10 years ago were making more than they are now. In other words, we were down to—18 percent of them were making—the 18- to 24-year-olds were making less than $12,000. Now that's up to 40 percent. And what's happening in the meantime? The dollar's gone through the floor.

Now, whose fault is that? Not the Democrats; not the Republicans. Somewhere out there there's an extraterrestrial that's doing this to us, I guess. [*Laughter*] And every-

body says they take responsibility. Somebody, somewhere has to take responsibility for this. Put it to you bluntly, the American people: If you want me to be your President, we're going to face our problems. We'll deal with the problems. We'll solve our problems. We'll pay down our debt. We'll pass on the American dream to our children. I will not leave our children a situation that they have today.

When I was a boy, it took two generations to double the standard of living. Today it will take 12 generations. Our children will not see the American dream because of this debt that somebody, somewhere dropped on us.

Ms. Simpson. You're all wonderful speakers, and I know you have lots more to add. But I have talked to this audience, and they have lots of questions on other topics. Can we move to another topic, please?

We have one up here, I think.

Presidential Campaign

Q. Yes, I'd like to address all the candidates with this question. The amount of time the candidates have spent in this campaign trashing their opponents' character and their programs is depressingly large. Why can't your discussions and proposals reflect the genuine complexity and the difficulty of the issues to try to build a consensus around the best aspects of all proposals?

Ms. Simpson. Who wants to take that one? Mr. Perot, you have an answer for everything, don't you? Go right ahead, sir. [*Laughter*]

Mr. Perot. No, I don't have an answer for everything. As you all know, I've been buying 30-minute segments to talk about issues. Tomorrow night on NBC from 10:30 to 11, eastern, we're going to talk about how you pay the debt down. So we're going to come right down to that one, see. We'll be on again Saturday night 8 to 9 o'clock on ABC. [*Laughter*]

Ms. Simpson. Okay, okay.

Mr. Perot. So the point is, finally, I couldn't agree with you more, couldn't agree with you more. And I have said again and again and again, let's get off mud wrestling. Let's get off personalities, and let's talk about jobs, health care, crime, the things that concern the American people. I'm spending my money, not PAC money, not foreign money, my money to take this message to the people.

Ms. Simpson. Thank you, Mr. Perot. So that seems directed. He would say it's you gentlemen that have been doing that. Mr. Clinton, Governor Clinton, how do you— President Bush, how would you like to respond?

President Bush. Well, first place, I believe that character is a part of being President. I think you have to look at it. I think that has to be a part of candidate for President or being President. In terms of programs, I've submitted, what, four different budgets to the United States Congress in great detail. They're so heavy they'd give you a broken back. Everything in there says what I am for. Now, I've come out with a new agenda for America's renewal, a plan that I believe really will help stimulate the growth of this economy.

My record on world affairs is pretty well-known because I've been President for 4 years. So I feel I've been talking issues. Nobody likes "who shot John," but I think the first negative campaign run in this election was by Governor Clinton. And I'm not going to sit there and be a punching bag. I'm going to stand up and say, "Hey, listen, here's my side of it." But character is an important part of the equation.

The other night, Governor Clinton raised—I don't know if you saw the debate the other night, suffered through that. [*Laughter*] Well, he raised a question of my father. It was a good line, well-rehearsed and well-delivered. But he raised a question of my father and said, "Well, your father, Prescott Bush, was against McCarthy. You should be ashamed of yourself—McCarthyism."

I remember something my dad told me. I was 18 years old, going to Penn Station to go into the Navy. He said, "Write your mother," which I faithfully did. He said, "Serve your country." My father was an honor, duty, and country man. And he said, "Tell the truth." And I've tried to do that in public life, all through it. That has said something about character.

My argument with Governor Clinton— you can call it mud wrestling, but I think

it's fair to put it in focus—is I am deeply troubled by someone who demonstrates and organizes demonstration in a foreign land when his country's at war. Probably a lot of kids here disagree with me, but that's what I feel. That's what I feel passionately about. I'm thinking of Ross Perot's running mate sitting in the jail; how would he feel about it? But maybe that's generational. I don't know.

But the big argument I have with the Governor on this is this taking different positions on different issues, trying to be one thing to one person here that's opposing the NAFTA agreement and then for it; what we call waffling. And I do think that you can't turn the White House into the waffle house. You've got to say what you're for. And you have got to——

Ms. Simpson. Mr. President, I am getting time cues, and with all due respect, I'm sorry.

President Bush. Excuse me, I don't want to—no, go ahead, Carole.

Ms. Simpson. Governor Clinton.

President Bush. I get wound up because I feel strongly.

Ms. Simpson. Yes, you do. [*Laughter*]

Governor Clinton. Let me say first of all to you that I believe so strongly in the question you asked that I suggested this format tonight. I started doing these formats a year ago in New Hampshire, and I found that we had huge crowds because all I did was let people ask questions, and I tried to give very specific answers. I also had a program starting last year.

I've been disturbed by the tone and the tenor of this campaign. Thank goodness the networks have a fact check so I don't have to just go blue in the face anymore. Mr. Bush said once again tonight I was going to have a $150 billion tax increase. When Mr. Quayle said that, all the networks said: that's not true; he's got over $100 billion in tax cuts and incentives.

So I'm not going to take up your time tonight, but let me just say this. We'll have a debate in 4 days, and we can talk about this character thing again, but the Washington Post ran a long editorial today saying they couldn't believe Mr. Bush was making character an issue, and they said he was the greatest political chameleon, for changing his positions, of all time.

Now, I don't want to get into that——

President Bush. Please don't say anything by the Washington Post.

Governor Clinton. Wait a minute. Let's don't—you don't have to believe that. Here's my point. I'm not interested in his character. I want to change the character of the Presidency. And I'm interested in what we can trust him to do and what you can trust me to do and what you can trust Mr. Perot to do for the next 4 years. So I think you're right, and I hope the rest of the night belongs to you.

Ms. Simpson. May I—I talked to this audience before you gentlemen came, and I asked them about how they felt about the tenor of the campaign. Would you like to let them know what you thought about that, when I said, "Are you pleased with how the campaign's been going?"

Audience members. No!

Ms. Simpson. Who wants to say why you don't like the way the campaign is going? We have a gentleman back here?

Focusing on Issues

Q. If I may, and forgive the notes here, but I'm shy on camera. The focus of my work as a domestic mediator is meeting the needs of the children that I work with by way of their parents, and not the wants of their parents. I ask the three of you, how can we as, symbolically, the children of the future President, expect the two of you, the three of you, to meet our needs, the needs in housing and in crime and you name it, as opposed to the wants of your political spin doctors and your political parties?

Ms. Simpson. So your question is——

Q. Can we focus on the issues and not the personalities and the mud? I think there is a need—if we could take a poll here with the folks from Gallup, perhaps—I think there is a real need here to focus at this point on the needs.

Ms. Simpson. How do you respond? How do you gentlemen respond to——

Governor Clinton. I agree with him.

Ms. Simpson. President Bush?

President Bush. Let's do it. Let's talk about programs for children.

Q. Could we cross our hearts, and it sounds silly here, but could we make a commitment? You know, we're not under oath at this point, but could you make a commitment to the citizens of the United States to meet our needs, and we have many, and not yours again? You know, I repeat that; that's a real need I think that we all have.

President Bush. I think it depends on how you define it. I mean, I think, in general, let's talk about these issues, let's talk about the programs. But in the Presidency, a lot goes into it. Caring goes into it; that's not particularly specific. Strength goes into it; that's not specific. Standing up against aggression; that's not specific in terms of a program. This is what a President has to do.

So, in principle, though, I'll take your point. I think we ought to discuss child care or whatever else it is.

Ms. Simpson. And you two?

Governor Clinton. Ross had his hand up.

Mr. Perot. No hedges, no ifs, ands, and buts, I'll take the pledge, because I know the American people want to talk about issues and not tabloid journalism. So I'll take the pledge, and we'll stay on the issues.

Now, just for the record, I don't have any spin doctors. I don't have any speechwriters. Probably shows. [*Laughter*] I make those charts you see on television even. [*Laughter*] But you don't have to wonder if it's me talking. Hey, what you see is what you get. If you don't like it, you've got two other choices, right?

Governor Clinton. Wait a minute. I want to say just one thing now, Ross, in fairness. The ideas I express are mine. I've worked on these things for 12 years, and I'm the only person up here who hasn't been part of Washington in any way for the last 20 years. So I don't want the implication to be that somehow everything we say is just cooked up and put in our head by somebody else. I worked 12 years very hard as a Governor on the real problems of real people. I'm just as sick as you are by having to wake up and figure out how to defend myself every day. I never thought I'd ever be involved in anything like this.

Mr. Perot. May I finish?

Ms. Simpson. Yes, you may finish.

Mr. Perot. Very briefly?

Ms. Simpson. Yes, very briefly.

Mr. Perot. I don't have any foreign money in my campaign. I don't have any foreign lobbyists on leave in my campaign. I don't have any PAC money in my campaign. I've got 5½ million hard-working people who have put me on the ballot, and I belong to them.

Ms. Simpson. Okay.

Mr. Perot. And they are interested in what you're interested in. I'll take the pledge. I've already taken the pledge on cutting the deficit in half. I never got to say that. There's a great young group, Lead or Leave, college students, young people who don't want us to spend their money. I took the pledge we'd cut it out.

Ms. Simpson. Thank you. We have a question here.

Domestic Infrastructure

Q. Yes. I would like to get a response from all three gentlemen. And the question is, what are your plans to improve the physical infrastructure of this Nation, which includes the water system, the sewer system, our transportation systems, et cetera? Thank you.

Ms. Simpson. The cities. Who is going to fix the cities, and how?

President Bush. I'd be glad to take a shot at it.

Ms. Simpson. Please.

President Bush. I'm not sure that—and I can understand if you haven't seen this because there's been a lot of hue and cry. We passed this year the most farthest looking transportation bill in the history of this country since Eisenhower started the interstate highways, $150 billion for improving the infrastructure. That happened when I was President. So I am very proud of the way that came about, and I think it's a very, very good beginning.

Like Mr. Perot, I am concerned about the deficits. And $150 billion is a lot of money, but it's awful hard to say we're going to go out and spend more money when we're trying to get the deficit down. But I would cite that as a major accomplishment.

We hear all the negatives. When you're President, you expect this. Everybody's running against the incumbent. They can do better; everyone knows that. But here's something that we can take great pride in because it really does get to what you're talking about. Our home initiative, our homeownership initiative, HOPE, that passed the Congress is a good start for having people own their own homes instead of living in these deadly tenements.

Our enterprise zones that we hear a lot of lip service about in Congress would bring jobs into the inner city. There's a good program. I need the help of everybody across this country to get it passed in substantial way by the Congress.

When we went out to South Central in Los Angeles—some of you may remember the riots there. I went out there. I went to a boys club, and every one of them, the boys club leaders, the ministers, all of them were saying, pass enterprise zones. We go back to Washington, and very difficult to get it through the Congress.

But there's going to be a new Congress. No one likes gridlock. There's going to be a new Congress because the old one, I don't want to get this man mad at me, but there was a post office scandal and a bank scandal. You're going to have a lot of new Members of Congress. And then you can sit down and say, "Help me do what we should for the cities. Help me pass these programs."

Ms. Simpson. Mr. President, aren't you threatening to veto the bill, the urban aid bill, that included enterprise zones?

President Bush. Sure, but the problem is you get so many things included in a great big bill that you have to look at the overall good. That's the problem with our system. If you had a line-item veto, you could knock out the pork. You could knock out the tax increases, and you could do what the people want, and that is create enterprise zones.

Ms. Simpson. Governor Clinton, you're chomping at the bit.

Governor Clinton. That bill pays for these urban enterprise zones by asking the wealthiest Americans to pay a little more, and that's why he wants to veto it, just like he vetoed an earlier bill this year. This is not mud slinging. This is fact slinging.

President Bush. There you go.

Governor Clinton. A bill earlier this year—this is fact—that would have given investment tax credits and other incentives to reinvest in our cities and our country. But it asked the wealthiest Americans to pay a little more. Mr. Perot wants to do the same thing. I agree with him. I mean, we agree with that.

Let me tell you specifically what my plan does: My plan would dedicate $20 billion a year in each of the next 4 years for investments in new transportation, communications, environmental cleanup, and new technologies for the 21st century. We would target it especially in areas that have been either depressed or which have lost a lot of defense-related jobs.

There are 200,000 people in California, for example, who have lost their defense-related jobs. They ought to be engaged in making high-speed rail. They ought to be engaged in breaking ground in other technologies, doing waste recycling, clean water technology, and things of that kind. We can create millions of jobs in these new technologies, more than we're going to lose in defense if we target it. But we're investing a much smaller percentage of our income in the things you just asked about than all of our major competitors. Our wealth growth is going down as a result of it. It's making the country poorer, which is why I answered the gentleman the way I did before.

We have to both bring down the deficit and get our economy going through these kinds of investments in order to get the kind of wealth and jobs and incomes we need in America.

Ms. Simpson. Mr. Perot, what about your plans for the cities? You want to tackle the economy and the deficit first.

Mr. Perot. First, you've got to have money to pay for these things. So you've got to create jobs, and there are all kinds of ways to create jobs in the inner city. Now, I am not a politician, but I think I could go to Washington in a week and get everybody holding hands and get this bill signed, because I talked to the Democratic leaders, and they want it. I talked to the Republican leaders, and they want it. But since they are bred from childhood to fight with one another rather than get results, I would be glad to drop out and spend a little time and see if we couldn't build some bridges.

Now, results is what counts. The President can't order Congress around. Congress can't order the President around. That's not bad for a guy that's never been there, right? But you have to work together. Now, I have talked to the chairmen of the committees that want this; they're Democrats. The President wants it. But we can't get it because we sit here in gridlock because it's a campaign year. We didn't fund a lot of other things this year, like the savings and loan mess. That's another story that we're going to pay a big price for right after the election.

The facts are, though, the facts are the American people are hurting. These people are hurting in the inner cities. We're shipping the low-paying, quote, "low-paying" jobs overseas. What are low-paying jobs? Textiles, shoes, things like that that we say are yesterday's industries. They're tomorrow's industries in the inner city.

Let me say in my case, if I'm out of work, I'll cut grass tomorrow to take care of my family. I'll be happy to make shoes. I'll be happy to make clothing. I'll make sausage. You just give me a job. Put those jobs in the inner cities, instead of doing diplomatic deals and shipping them to China, where prison labor does the work.

Washington Gridlock

Ms. Simpson. Mr. Perot, everybody thought you won the first debate because you were plain-speaking, and you make it sound, oh, so simple. "We'll just do it." What makes you think that you're going to be able to get the Democrats and Republicans together any better than these guys?

Mr. Perot. If you asked me if I could fly a fighter plane or be an astronaut, I can't. I've spent my life creating jobs. It's something I know how to do, and very simply in the inner city, they're starved. You see, small businesses is the way to jump-start the inner city.

Ms. Simpson. Are you answering my question? [*Laughter*]

Mr. Perot. You want jobs in the inner city? Do you want jobs in the inner city? Is that your question?

Ms. Simpson. No, I want you to tell me how you're going to be able to get the Republicans and Democrats in Congress——

Mr. Perot. Oh, I'm sorry.

Ms. Simpson. ——to work together better than these two gentlemen.

Mr. Perot. I've listened to both sides. If they would talk to one another instead of throwing rocks, I think we could get a lot done. And among other things, I would say, okay, over here in this Senate committee, to the chairman who is anxious to get this bill passed, to the President who's anxious, I'd say, "Rather than just yelling at one another, why don't we find out where we're apart; try to get together. Get the bill passed, and give the people the benefits, and not play party politics right now."

I think the press would follow that so closely that probably they would get it done. That's the way I would do it. I doubt if they'll give me the chance, but I will drop everything and go work on it.

Ms. Simpson. Okay. I have a question here.

Gun Control and Crime

Q. My question was originally for Governor Clinton, but I think I would welcome a response from all three candidates. As you are aware, crime is rampant in our cities. In the Richmond area, and I'm sure it's happened elsewhere, 12-year-olds are carrying guns to school. And I'm sure when our Founding Fathers wrote the Constitution, they did not mean for the right to bear arms to apply to 12-year-olds. So I'm asking, where do you stand on gun control, and what do you plan to do about it?

Ms. Simpson. Governor Clinton?

Governor Clinton. I support the right to keep and bear arms. I live in a State where over half the adults have hunting or fishing licenses or both. But I believe we have to have some way of checking handguns before they're sold, to check the criminal history, the mental health history, and the age of people who are buying them. Therefore, I support the Brady bill, which would impose a national waiting period, unless and until a State did what only Virginia has done now, which is to automate its records. Once you automate your records, then you don't have to have a waiting period, but at least you can check.

I also think we should have, frankly, restrictions on assault weapons, whose only purpose is to kill. We need to give the police a fighting chance in our urban areas where the gangs are building up.

The third thing I would say doesn't bear directly on gun control, but it's very important. We need more police on the street. There is a crime bill which would put more police on the street, which was killed for this session by a filibuster in the Senate, mostly by Republican Senators. I think it's a shame it didn't pass. I think it should be made the law, but it had the Brady bill in it, the waiting period.

I also believe that we should offer college scholarships to people who will agree to work them off as police officers. I think as we reduce our military forces, we should let people earn military retirement by coming out and working as police officers.

Thirty years ago there were three police officers on the street for every crime. Today, there are three crimes for every police officer. In the communities which have had real success putting police officers near schools where kids carry weapons, to get the weapons out of the schools, or on the same blocks, you've seen crime go down. In Houston there's been a 15-percent drop in the crime rate in the last year because of the work the Mayor did there in increasing the police force. So I know it can work. I've seen it happen.

Ms. Simpson. Thank you.

President Bush?

President Bush. I think you put your finger on a major problem. I talk about strengthening the American family. It's very hard to strengthen the family if people are scared to walk down to the corner store and send their kid down to get a loaf of bread. It's very hard. I have been fighting for very strong anticrime legislation: habeas corpus reform, so you don't have these endless appeals; so when somebody gets sentenced, hey, this is for real. I've been fighting for changes in the exclusionary rule, so if an honest cop stops somebody and makes a technical mistake, the criminal doesn't go away. I'll probably get into a fight in this room with some, but I happen to think that we need stronger death penalties for those that kill police officers.

Virginia's in lead in this, as Governor

Clinton properly said, on this identification system for firearms. I am not for national registration of firearms. Some of the States that have the toughest antigun laws have the highest levels of crime. I am for the right—as the Governor says, I'm a sportsman, and I don't think you ought to eliminate all kinds of weapons.

But I was not for the bill that he was talking about because it was not tough enough on the criminal. I'm very pleased that the Fraternal Order of Police in Little Rock, Arkansas, endorsed me, because I think they see I'm trying to strengthen the anticrime legislation. We've got more money going out for local police than any previous administration.

So we've got to get it under control. And as one last point I'd make: drugs. We have got to win our national strategy against drugs, the fight against drugs. We're making some progress, doing a little better on interdiction. We're not doing as well amongst the people that get to be habitual drug users. The good news is, and I think it's true in Richmond, teenage use is down of cocaine substantially, 60 percent in the last couple of years. So we're making progress. But until we get that one done, we're not going to solve the neighborhood crime problem.

Ms. Simpson. Mr. Perot, there are young black males in America dying at unprecedented——

Mr. Perot. I would just make a comment on this.

Ms. Simpson. Yes, I'm getting——

Mr. Perot. Oh, you're going to elaborate. Okay, excuse me.

Ms. Simpson. ——to the fact that homicide is the leading cause of death among young black males, 15 to 24 years old. What are you going to do to get the guns off the street?

Mr. Perot. On any program, and this includes crime, you'll find we have all kinds of great plans lying around that never get enacted into law and implemented. I don't care what it is, competitiveness, health care, crime, you name it. The Brady bill, I agree that it's a timid step in the right direction, but it won't fix it. So why pass a law that won't fix it?

Now, what it really boils down to is can

you live—we have become so preoccupied with the rights of the criminal that we have forgotten the rights of the innocent. In our country, we have evolved to a point where we've put millions of innocent people in jail, because you go to the poor neighborhoods and they've put bars on their windows and bars on their doors and put themselves in jail to protect the things that they acquired legitimately. Now, that's where we are.

We have got to become more concerned about people who play by the rules and get the balance we require. This is going to take, first, building a consensus in grassroots America. Right from the bottom up, the American people have got to say they want it. And at that point, we can pick from a variety of plans and develop new plans. And the way you get things done is bury yourselves in the room with one another, put together the best program, take it to the American people, use the electronic town hall, the kind of thing you're doing here tonight, build a consensus, and then do it and then go on to the next one. But don't just sit here slow dancing for 4 years doing nothing.

Ms. Simpson. Thank you. Thank you, Mr. Perot.

We have a question up here.

Term Limits

Q. Please state your position on term limits. And if you are in favor of them, how will you get them enacted?

President Bush. Any order? I'll be glad to respond. I strongly support term limits for Members of the United States Congress. I believe it would return the Government closer to the people, the way that Ross Perot is talking about. The President's terms are limited to two, a total of 8 years. What's wrong with limiting the terms of Members of Congress to 12? Congress has gotten kind of institutionalized. For 38 years, one party has controlled the House of Representatives. And the result? A sorry little post office that can't do anything right and a bank that has more overdrafts than all of Chase Bank and Citibank put together.

We've got to do something about it. I

think you get a certain arrogance, bureaucratic arrogance if people stay there too long. So I favor, strongly favor term limits. And how to get them passed? Send us some people that will pass the idea, and I think you will. I think the American people want it now. Everyplace I go, I talk about it, and I think they want it done.

Actually, you'd have to have some amendments to the Constitution because of the way the Constitution reads.

Ms. Simpson. Thank you.

Governor Clinton?

Governor Clinton. I know they're popular, but I'm against them. I'll tell you why. I believe, number one, it would pose a real problem for a lot of smaller States in the Congress who would have enough trouble now making sure their interests are heard. Number two, I think it would increase the influence of unelected staff members in the Congress who have too much influence already. I want to cut the size of the congressional staffs, but I think you're going to have too much influence there with people who were never elected who have lots of expertise.

Number three, if the people really have a mind to change, they can. You're going to have 120 to 150 new Members of Congress. Now, let me tell you what I favor instead. I favor strict controls on how much you can spend running for Congress, strict limits on political action committees, requirements that people running for Congress appear in open public debates like we're doing now. If you did that, you could take away the incumbent's advantage, because challengers like me would have a chance to run against incumbents like him for the House races and Senate races, and then the voters could make up their own mind without being subject to an unfair fight. So that's how I feel about it, and I think if we had the right kind of campaign reform, we'd get the changes you want.

Ms. Simpson. Mr. Perot, would you like to address term limitations?

Mr. Perot. Yes. Let me do it first on a personal level. If the American people send me up to do this job, I intend to be there one term. I do not intend to spend one minute of one day thinking about reelection. It is a matter of principle. My situation

is unique, and I understand it. I will take absolutely no compensation. I go as their servant.

Now, I have set as strong an example as I can. And at that point, when we sit down over at Capitol Hill—tomorrow night I'm going to be talking about Government reform. It is a long subject; you wouldn't let me finish tonight. If you want to hear it, you can get it tomorrow night. [*Laughter*] But the point is, you'll hear it tomorrow night. But we have got to reform Government.

If you put term limits in and don't reform Government, you won't get the benefit you thought. It takes both. So we need to do the reforms and the term limits. And after we reform it, it won't be a lifetime career opportunity. Good people will go serve and then go back to their homes, and not become foreign lobbyists and cash in at 30,000 bucks a month, and then take time off to run some President's campaign.

They're all nice people. They're just in a bad system. I don't think there are any villains, but boy, is the system rotten.

Ms. Simpson. Thank you very much.

We have a question over here.

Health Care Reform

Q. I'd like to ask Governor Clinton, do you attribute the rising costs of health care to the medical profession itself, or do you think the problem lies elsewhere? And what specific proposals do you have to tackle this problem?

Governor Clinton. I've had more people talk to me about their health care problems, I guess, than anything else. All across America, people who have lost their jobs, lost their businesses, had to give up their jobs because of sick children—so let me try to answer you in this way.

Let's start with the premise. We spend 30 percent more of our income than any nation on Earth on health care. And yet, we insure fewer people. We have 35 million people without any insurance at all, and I see them all the time. One hundred thousand Americans a month have lost their health insurance just in the last 4 years.

So if you analyze where we're out of line with other countries you come up with the following conclusions: Number one, we spend at least $60 billion a year on insurance, administrative costs, bureaucracy, and Government regulation that wouldn't be spent in any other nation. So we have to have, in my judgment, a drastic simplification of the basic health insurance policies of this country, be very comprehensive for everybody. Employers would cover their employees. Government would cover the unemployed.

Number two, I think you have to take on specifically the insurance companies and require them to make some significant change in the way they rate people in the big community pools. I think you have to tell the pharmaceutical companies they can't keep raising drug prices at 3 times the rate of inflation. I think you have to take on medical fraud. I think you have to help doctors stop practicing defensive medicine. I've recommended that our doctors be given a set of national practice guidelines and that if they follow those guidelines, that raises the presumption that they didn't do anything wrong. I think you have to have a system of primary preventive clinics in our inner cities and our rural areas so people can have access to health care.

But the key is to control the costs and maintain the quality. To do that, you need a system of managed competition where all of us are covered in big groups, and we can choose our doctors and our hospitals from a wide range, but there is an incentive to control costs. And I think there has to be—I think Mr. Perot and I agree on this—there has to be a national commission of health care providers and health care consumers that set ceilings to keep health costs in line with inflation plus population growth.

Now, let me say, some people say we can't do this, but Hawaii does it. They cover 98 percent of their people, and their insurance premiums are much cheaper than the rest of America. So does Rochester, New York. They now have a plan to cover everybody, and their premiums are two-thirds the rest of the country. This is very important. It's a big human problem and a devastating economic problem for America. I'm going to send a plan to do this within the first 100 days of my Presidency. It's terribly important.

Ms. Simpson. Thank you. Sorry to cut you short, but, President Bush, health care reform.

President Bush. I just have to say something. I don't want to stampede—Ross was very articulate. Across the country, I don't want anybody to stampede to cut the President's salary off altogether. Barbara is sitting over here, and I—[*laughter*]—but what I have proposed, 10 percent cut, downsize the Government, and we can get that done.

She asked the question, I think, is whether the health care profession was to blame. No. One thing to blame is these malpractice lawsuits. They are breaking the system. It costs $20 to $25 billion a year, and I want to see those outrageous claims capped. Doctors don't dare to deliver babies sometimes because they're afraid that somebody's going to sue them. People don't dare, medical practitioners, to help somebody along the highway that are hurt because they're afraid that some lawyer's going to come along and get a big lawsuit.

So you can't blame the practitioners or the health—and my program is this: Keep the Government as far out of it as possible, make insurance available to the poorest of the poor through vouchers, next range in the income bracket through tax credits, and get on about the business of pooling insurance. A great, big company can buy—Ross has got a good size company, been very successful. He can buy insurance cheaper than mom-and-pop stores on the corner. But if those mom-and-pop stores all get together and pool, they, too, can bring the cost of insurance down.

So I want to keep the quality of health care. That means keep Government out of it. I don't like this idea of these boards. It all sounds to me like you're going to have some Government setting price. I want competition, and I want to pool the insurance and take care of it that way.

Here's the other point. I think medical care should go with the person. If you leave a business, I think your insurance should go with you to some other business. You shouldn't be worrying if you get a new job as to whether that's going to—and part of our plan is to make it what they call portable, big word, but that means if you're working for the Jones Company and you go to the Smith Company, your insurance goes with you. I think it's a good program. I'm really excited about getting it done, too.

Ms. Simpson. Mr. Perot?

Mr. Perot. We have the most expensive health care system in the world. Twelve percent of our gross national product goes to health care. Our industrial competitors, who are beating us in competition, spend less and have better health care. Japan spends a little over 6 percent of its gross national product; Germany spends 8 percent.

It's fascinating. You bought a front-row box seat, and you're not happy with your health care. You're saying tonight we've got bad health care but very expensive health care. Folks, here's why. Go home and look in the mirror. You own this country, but you have no voice in it the way it's organized now. If you want to have a high-risk experience comparable to bungee jumping—[*laughter*]—go into Congress sometime when they're working on this kind of legislation, when the lobbyists are running up and down the halls. Wear your safety-toe shoes when you go. [*Laughter*] And as a private citizen, believe me, you are looked on as a major nuisance. The facts are, you now have a Government that comes at you. You're supposed to have a Government that comes from you.

Now, there are all kinds of good ideas, brilliant ideas, terrific ideas on health care. None of them ever get implemented because—let me give you an example. A Senator runs every 6 years. He's got to raise 20,000 bucks a week to have enough money to run. Who's he going to listen to, us or the folks running up and down the aisle with money, the lobbyists, the PAC money? He listens to them. Who do they represent? Health care industry. Not us.

Now, you've got to have a Government that comes from you again. You've got to reassert your ownership in this country, and you've got to completely reform our Government. And at that point, they'll just be like apples falling out of a tree. The programs will be good because the elected officials will be listening, too. I said the other night I was all ears and I would listen to any good idea. I think we ought to do plas-

tic surgery on a lot of these guys so that they're all ears, too, and listen to you. Then you get what you want, and shouldn't you? You paid for it. Why shouldn't you get what you want as opposed to what some lobbyist cuts a deal, writes the little piece in the law, and it goes through. That's the way the game's played now. Until you change it, you're going to be unhappy.

Ms. Simpson. Thank you.

Governor Clinton, you wanted one brief point.

Governor Clinton. One brief point. We have elections so people can make decisions about this. The point I want to make to you is, a bipartisan commission reviewed my plan and the Bush plan and concluded—there were as many Republicans as Democratic health care experts on it—they concluded that my plan would cover everybody, and his would leave 27 million behind by the year 2000, and that my plan in the next 12 years would save $2.2 trillion in public and private money to reinvest in this economy. The average family would save $1,200 a year under the plan that I offered, without any erosion in the quality of health care. So I ask you to look at that.

You have to vote for somebody with a plan. That's what you have elections for. If people say, "Well, he got elected to do this," and then the Congress says, "Okay, I'm going to do it." That's what the election was about.

Ms. Simpson. Brief, Governor Clinton. Thank you.

We have a question right here.

Personal Impact of the Economy

Q. Yes, how has the national debt personally affected each of your lives? And if it hasn't, how can you honestly find a cure for the economic problems of the common people if you have no experience in what's ailing them?

Mr. Perot. May I answer it?

Ms. Simpson. Well, Mr. Perot, yes, of course.

Mr. Perot. Who do you want to start with?

Q. My question is for each of you, so——

Mr. Perot. Yes, it caused me to disrupt my private life and my business to get involved in this activity. That's how much I care about it. Believe me, if you knew my family and if you knew the private life I have, you would agree in a minute that that's a whole lot more fun than getting involved in politics.

I have lived the American dream. I came from a very modest background. Nobody's been luckier than I've been, all the way across the spectrum, and the greatest riches of all are my wife and children. It's true of any family. But I want all the children, I want these young people up here to be able to start with nothing but an idea like I did and build a business. But they've got to have a strong basic economy. And if you're in debt, it's like having a ball and chain around you.

I just figure as lucky as I've been, I owe it to them, and I owe it to the future generations. And on a very personal basis, I owe it to my children and grandchildren.

Ms. Simpson. Thank you, Mr. Perot. Mr. President.

President Bush. Well, I think the national debt affects everybody. Obviously, it has a lot to do with interest rates——

Ms. Simpson. She's saying you personally.

Q. You, on a personal basis, how has it affected you?

Ms. Simpson. Has it affected you personally?

President Bush. Well, I'm sure it has. I love my grandchildren. I want to think that——

Q. How?

President Bush. I want to think that they're going to be able to afford an education. I think that that's an important part of being a parent. If the question—maybe I get it wrong. Are you suggesting that if somebody has means that the national debt doesn't affect them?

Q. What I'm saying——

President Bush. I'm not sure I get it. Help me with the question, and I'll try to answer it.

Q. Well, I've had friends that have been laid off in jobs——

President Bush. Yes.

Q. I know people who cannot afford to pay the mortgage on their homes, their car payment. I have personal problems with the national debt. But how has it affected you? And if you have no experience in it,

how can you help us if you don't know what we're feeling?

Ms. Simpson. I think she means more the recession, the economic problems today the country faces rather than——

President Bush. Well, listen, you ought to be in the White House for a day and hear what I hear and see what I see and read the mail I read and touch the people that I touch from time to time.

I was in the Lomax AME Church. It's a black church just outside of Washington, DC, and I read in the bulletin about teenage pregnancies, about the difficulty that families are having to make ends meet. I talked to parents. I mean, you've got to care. Everybody cares if people aren't doing well. But I don't think it's fair to say you haven't had cancer, therefore you don't know what it's like. I don't think it's fair to say, whatever it is, if you haven't been hit by it personally. But everybody's affected by the debt, because of the tremendous interest that goes into paying on that debt, everything's more expensive. Everything comes out of your pocket and my pocket. So it's that. But I think in terms of the recession, of course, you feel it when you're President of the United States. That's why I'm trying to do something about it by stimulating the export, investing more, better education system.

Thank you. I'm glad you clarified it.

Governor Clinton. Tell me how it's affected you again? You know people who have lost their jobs and lost their homes?

Q. Yes.

Governor Clinton. Well, I've been Governor of a small State for 12 years. I'll tell you how it's affected me. Every year, Congress and the President sign laws that make us do more things; it gives us less money to do it with. I see people in my State, middle class people, their taxes have gone up from Washington and their services have gone down, while the wealthy have gotten tax cuts.

I have seen what's happened in this last 4 years when, in my State, when people lose their jobs there's a good chance I'll know them by their names. When a factory closes, I know the people who ran it. When the businesses go bankrupt, I know them.

And I've been out here for 13 months, meeting in meetings just like this ever since October with people like you all over America, people that have lost their jobs, lost their livelihood, lost their health insurance.

What I want you to understand is, the national debt is not the only cause of that. It is because America has not invested in its people. It is because we have not grown. It is because we've had 12 years of trickle-down economics. We've gone from 1st to 12th in the world in wages. We've had 4 years where we've produced no private sector jobs. Most people are working harder for less money than they were making 10 years ago. It is because we are in the grip of a failed economic theory. And this decision you're about to make better be about what kind of economic theory you want, not just people saying, "I want to go fix it," but what are we going to do.

What I think we have to do is invest in American jobs, in American education, control American health care costs, and bring the American people together again.

Ms. Simpson. Thank you, Governor Clinton. We are a little more than halfway through this program, and I'm glad that we're getting the diversity of questions that we are.

And I don't want to forget these folks on the wings over here, so let's go over here. Do you have a question?

Entitlement Programs

Q. Yes, I do. My name is Ben Smith. I work in the financial field, counseling retirees. And I'm personally concerned about three major areas. One is the Social Security Administration or trust fund is projected to be insolvent by the year 2036. We've funded the trust fund with IOU's in the form of Treasury bonds. The pension guaranty fund which backs up our private retirement plans for retirees is projected to be bankrupt by the year 2026, not to mention the cutbacks by private companies. And Medicare is projected to be bankrupt maybe as soon as 1997.

I would like from each of you a specific response as to what you intend to do for retirees relative to these issues, not generalities but specifics, because I think they're

very disturbing issues.

Ms. Simpson. President Bush, may we start with you?

President Bush. Well, the Social Security—you're an expert and I could, I'm sure, learn from you the details of the pension guaranty fund and the Social Security fund. The Social Security system was fixed, about 5 years, and I think it's projected out to be sound beyond that. So at least we have time to work with it.

But on all of these things, a sound economy is the only way to get it going. Growth in the economy is going to add to the overall prosperity and wealth. I can't give you a specific answer on pension guaranty fund. All I know is that we have firm Government credit to guarantee the pensions, and that is very important.

But the full faith in credit of the United States, in spite of our difficulties, is still pretty good. It's still the most respected credit. So I would simply say, as these dates get close you're going to have to reorganize and refix as we did with the Social Security fund. I think that's the only answer. But the more immediate answer is to do what this lady was suggesting we do, and that is to get this deficit down and get on without adding to the woes, and then restructure.

One thing I've called for that has been stymied, and I'll keep on working for it, is a whole financial reform legislation. It is absolutely essential in terms of bringing our banking system and credit system into the new age instead of having it living back in the dark ages, and it's a big fight. I don't want to give my friend Ross another shot at me here, but I am fighting with the Congress to get this through.

You can't just go up and say, "I'm going to fix it." You've got some pretty strong-willed guys up there that argue with you. But that's what the election's about; I agree with the Governor. That's what the election is about. Sound fiscal policy is the best answer, I think, to all the three problems you mentioned.

Ms. Simpson. Thank you.

Mr. Perot?

Mr. Perot. Just on a broad issue here. When you're trying to solve a problem, you get the best plans. You have a raging debate about those plans. Then out of that debate, with leadership, comes consensus. And if the plans are huge and complex, like health care, I would urge you to implement pilot programs. Like the older carpenter says, measure twice, cut once. Let's make sure this thing's as good as we all think it is at the end of the meeting.

Then, finally, our Government passes laws and freezes the plan in concrete. Anybody that's ever built a successful business will tell you, you optimize, optimize, optimize after you put something into effect. The reason Medicare and Medicaid are a mess is we froze them. Everybody knows how to fix them. There are people all over the Federal Government if they could just touch it with a screwdriver could fix it.

Now, back over here. See, we've got a $4 trillion debt, and only in America would you have $2.8 trillion of it, or 70 percent of it, financed 5 years or less. Now, that's another thing for you to think about when you go home tonight. You don't finance long-term debt with short-term money. Why did our Government do it? To get the interest rates down. A one-percent increase in interest rates in that $2.8 trillion is $28 billion a year.

Now, when you look at what Germany pays for money and what we don't pay for money, you realize there's quite a spread, right? You realize this is a temporary thing and there's going to be another sucking sound that runs our deficit through the roof.

You know, and everybody's ducking it so I'm going to say it, that we are not letting that surplus stay in the bank. We are not investing that surplus like a pension fund. We are spending that surplus to make the deficit look smaller to you than it really is. Now, that puts you in jail in corporate America if you kept books that way, but in Government it's just kind of the way things are. That's because it comes at you, not from you.

Now then, that money needs to be—they don't even pay interest on it, they just write a note for the interest.

Ms. Simpson. Mr. Perot, can you wrap it up?

Mr. Perot. Sure. But the point, see, do you want to fix the problem or sound-bite it? I understand the importance of time, but see, here's how we get to this mess we're in. This is just 1 of 1,000.

Ms. Simpson. But we've got to be fair.

Mr. Perot. Now then, to nail it, there's one way out, a growing, expanding job base, a growing, expanding job base to generate the funds and the tax revenues to pay off the mess and rebuild America. We've got to double hit. If we're $4 trillion down, we should have everything perfect, but we don't. We've got to pay it off and build money to renew it, spend money to renew it, and that's going to take a growing, expanding job base. That is priority one in this country. Put everybody that's breathing to work. I'd love to be out of workers and have to import them, like some of our international competitors.

Ms. Simpson. Mr. Perot, I'm sorry, I'm going to——

Mr. Perot. Sorry.

Ms. Simpson. And I don't want to sound-bite you, but we are trying to be fair to everyone.

Mr. Perot. No, absolutely. I apologize.

Ms. Simpson. All right, Governor Clinton.

Governor Clinton. I think I remember the question. [*Laughter*] Let me say first of all, I want to answer your specific question, but first of all, we all agree that there should be a growing economy. What you have to decide is who's got the best economic plan. We all have ideas out there, and Mr. Bush has a record. I don't want you to read my lips, and I sure don't want you to read his. [*Laughter*] I do hope you will read our plans.

Now, specifically——

President Bush. [*Inaudible*]—first rule?

Governor Clinton. ——one, on Medicare, it is not true that everyone knows how to fix it; there are different ideas. The Bush plan, the Perot plan, the Clinton—we have different ideas. I am convinced, having studied health care for a year, hard, and talking to hundreds and hundreds of people all across America, that you cannot control the costs of Medicare until you control the cost of private health care and public health care with managed competition, ceiling on cost, and radical reorganization of the insurance markets. You've got to do that. We've got to get those costs down.

Number two, with regard to Social Security, that program, a lot of you may not know this: It produces a $70 billion surplus a year. Social Security is in surplus $70 billion. Six increases in the payroll tax—that means people with incomes of $51,000 a year or less pay a disproportionately high share of the Federal tax burden, which is why I want some middle class tax relief.

What do we have to do? By the time the century turns, we have got to have our deficit under control, we have to work out of so that surplus is building up, so when the baby boomers like me retire, we're okay.

Number three, on the pension funds, I don't know as much about it, but I will say this: What I will do is to bring in the pension experts of the country, take a look at it, and strengthen the pension requirements further, because it's not just enough to have the guarantee. We had a guarantee on the S&L's, right? We had a guarantee, and what happened? You picked up a $500 billion bill because of the dumb way the Federal Government deregulated it. So I think we are going to have to change and strengthen the pension requirements on private retirement plans.

Ms. Simpson. Thank you. I think we have a question here on international affairs, hopefully.

Foreign Affairs

Q. We've come to a position where we're in the new world order. And I'd like to know what the candidates feel our position is in this new world order and what our responsibilities are as a superpower.

Ms. Simpson. Mr. President?

President Bush. We have come to that position. Since I became President, 43, 44 countries have gone democratic. No longer totalitarian, no longer living under dictatorship or communist rule. This is exciting. This new world order to me means freedom and democracy.

I think we will have a continuing responsibility, as the only remaining superpower, to stay involved. If we pull back in some isolation and say we don't have to do our share, or more than our share, anymore, I believe you're going to just ask for conflagration that we'll get involved in in the future. NATO, for example, has kept the peace for many, many years. I want to see us keep fully staffed in NATO so we'll continue to guarantee the peace in Europe.

But the exciting thing is the fear of nuclear war is down. You hear all the bad stuff that's happened on my watch. I hope people will recognize that this is something pretty good for mankind. I hope they'll think it's good that democracy and freedom is on the move. And we're going to stay engaged, as long as I am President, working to improve things.

You know, it's so easy now to say, hey, cut out foreign aid, we've got a problem at home. I think the United States has to still have the Statue of Liberty as a symbol of caring for others. We're right this very minute, we're sending supplies in to help these little starving kids in Somalia. It's the United States that's taken the lead in humanitarian aid into Bosnia. We're doing this all around the world.

And yes, we've got problems at home. I think I've got a good plan to help fix those problems at home. But because of our leadership, because we didn't listen to the freeze, the nuclear freeze group—do you remember: "Freeze it," back in about in the late seventies. "Freeze, don't touch it. We're going to lock it in now, or else we'll have war." President Reagan said, "No. Peace through strength." It worked. The Soviet Union is no more. Now we're working to help them become totally democratic through the FREEDOM Support Act that I led on. A great Democratic Ambassador, Bob Strauss over there, Jim Baker, all of us got this thing passed, through cooperation, Ross. It worked with cooperation. And you're for that, I'm sure, helping Russia become democratic.

So the new world order to me means freedom and democracy, keep engaged, do not pull back into isolation. We are the United States, and we have a responsibility to lead and to guarantee the security. If it hadn't been for us, Saddam Hussein would be sitting on top of three-fifths of the oil supply of the world, and he'd have nuclear weapons. Only the United States could do this.

Excuse me, Carole.

Ms. Simpson. Thank you.

Mr. Perot.

Mr. Perot. Well, it's cost-effective to help Russia succeed in its revolution. It's pennies on the dollar compared to going back to the cold war. Russia's still very unstable. They could go back to square one and worse. All the nuclear weapons are not dismantled. I'm particularly concerned about the intercontinental weapons, the ones that can hit us. We've got agreements, but they're still there. With all this instability and breaking into Republics and all the Middle Eastern countries going over there and shopping for weapons, we've got our work cut out for us. So we need to stay right on top of that and constructively help them move toward democracy and capitalism.

We have to have money to do that. We have to have our people at work. See, for 45 years, we were preoccupied with the Red Army. I suggest now that our number one preoccupation is red ink in our country. And we've got to put our people back to work so that we can afford to do these things we want to do in Russia.

We cannot be the policeman for the world any longer. We spend $300 billion a year defending the world. Germany and Japan spend around $30 billion apiece. It's neat. If I can get you to defend me and I can spend all my money building industry, that's a home run for me. Coming out of World War II, it made sense. Now the other superpowers need to do their part.

I'll close on this point: You can't be a superpower unless you're an economic superpower. If we're not an economic superpower, we are a used-to-be, and we will no longer be a force for good throughout the world. If nothing else gets you excited about rebuilding our industrial base, maybe that will, because job one is to put our people back to work.

Ms. Simpson. Governor Clinton, the President mentioned Saddam Hussein. Your vice president and you have had some words about the President and Saddam Hussein. Would you care to comment?

Governor Clinton. I'd rather answer her question first, and then I'll be glad to, because the question you ask is important. The end of the cold war brings an incredible opportunity for change, the winds of

freedom blowing around the world, Russia demilitarizing. It also requires us to maintain some continuity, some bipartisan American commitment to certain principles.

I would just say there are three things that I would like to say. Number one, we do have to maintain the world's strongest defense. We may differ about what the elements of that are. I think the defense needs to be with fewer people and permanent armed services, but with greater mobility on the land, in the air, and on the sea, with a real dedication to continuing development of high-technology weaponry and well-trained people. I think we're going to have to work to stop the proliferation of weapons of mass destruction. We've got to keep going until all those nuclear weapons in Russia are gone and the other Republics.

Number two, if you don't rebuild the economic strength of this country at home, we won't be a superpower. We can't have any more instances like what happened when Mr. Bush went to Japan and the Japanese Prime Minister said he felt sympathy for our country. We have to be the strongest economic power in the world. That's what got me into this race, so we could rebuild the American economy.

Number three, we need to be a force for freedom and democracy. We need to use our unique position to support freedom, whether it's in Haiti or in China or in any other place, wherever the seeds of freedom are sprouting. We can't impose it, but we need to nourish it. That's the kind of thing that I would do as President, follow those three commitments into the future.

Ms. Simpson. Okay, we have a question up there.

Education

Q. We've talked a lot tonight about creating jobs. But we have an awful lot of high school graduates who don't know how to read a ruler, who cannot fill out an application for a job. How can we create high-paying jobs with the education system we have? And what would you do to change it?

Ms. Simpson. Who would like to begin? The education President?

President Bush. I'd be delighted to, because you can't do it the old way. You can't do it with the school bureaucracy controlling everything. And that's why we have a new program that I hope people have heard about. It's being worked now in 1,700 communities—I bypassed Congress on this one, Ross—1,700 communities across the country. It's called America 2000. It literally says to the communities: Reinvent the schools, not just the bricks and mortar but the curriculum and everything else. Think anew. We have a concept called the New American School Corporation, where we're doing exactly that.

So I believe that we've got to get the power in the hands of the teachers, not the teachers union—what's happening up there? [*Laughter*] So our America 2000 program also says this: It says let's give parents the choice of a public, private, or religious school. And it works. It works in Milwaukee. A Democratic woman up there taking the lead in this, the Mayor up there on the program, and the schools that are not chosen are improved. Competition does that.

So we've got to innovate through school choice. We've got to innovate through this America 2000 program. But she is absolutely right. The programs that we've been trying where you control everything and mandate it from Washington don't work.

The Governors—and I believe Governor Clinton was in on this, but I don't want to invoke him here—but they come to me, and they say, please get the Congress to stop passing so many mandates telling us how to control things. We know better how to do it in California or Texas or wherever it is. So this is what our program is all about. I believe—you're right onto something—that if we don't change the education, we're not going to be able to compete.

Federal funding for education is up substantially. Pell Grants are up. But it isn't going to get the job done if we don't change K through 12.

Ms. Simpson. Governor Clinton?

Governor Clinton. First of all, let me say that I've spent more of my time in life on this in the last 12 years than any other issue. Seventy percent of my State's money goes to public schools. I was really honored when Time magazine said that our schools have shown more improvement than any

other State in the country except one other. They named two States showing real strides forward in the eighties. So I care a lot about this, and I've spent countless hours in schools.

But let me start with what you've said. I agree with some of what Mr. Bush said, but it's nowhere near enough. We live in a world where what you earn depends on what you can learn, where the average 18-year-old will change jobs eight times in a lifetime, and where none of us can promise any of you that what you now do for a living is absolutely safe from now on. Nobody running can promise that. There's too much change in the world.

So what should we do? Let me reel some things off real quick, because you said you wanted specifics. Number one, under my program we would provide matching funds to States to teach everybody with a job to read in the next 5 years and give everybody with a job a chance to get a high school diploma, in big places, on the job.

Number two, we would provide 2-year apprenticeship programs to high school graduates who don't go to college, in community colleges or on the job.

Number three, we'd open the doors to college education to high school graduates without regard to income. They could borrow the money and pay it back as a percentage of their income over the couple of years of service to our Nation here home.

Number four, we would fully fund the Head Start program to get little kids off to a good start.

Five, I would have an aggressive program of school reform. More choices in the—I favor public schools or these new charter schools. We can talk about that if you want. I don't think we should spend tax money on private schools, but I favor public school choice. I favor radical decentralization in giving more power to better trained principals and teachers with parent councils to control their schools. Those things would revolutionize American education and take us to the top economically.

Ms. Simpson. Thank you, Governor Clinton. What the question is—what is it going to cost?

Q. What is it going to cost?

Ms. Simpson. What is it going to cost?

Governor Clinton. In 6 years—I budget all this in my budget. In 6 years, the college program would cost $8 billion over and above what—the present student loan program costs 4. You pay $3 billion for busted loans, because we don't have an automatic recovery system, and a billion dollars in bank fees. So the net cost will be $8 billion 6 years from now, in a trillion-plus budget: not very much.

The other stuff, all the other stuff I mentioned costs much less than that. The Head Start program, full funding, would cost about $5 billion more. It's all covered in my budget from the plans that I've laid out, from raising taxes on families with incomes above $200,000, and asking foreign corporations to pay the same tax that American corporations do on the same income; from $140 billion in budget cuts, including what I think are very prudent cuts in the defense budget. It's all covered in the plan.

Ms. Simpson. Mr. Perot, you on education, please.

Mr. Perot. Yes. I've got scars to show from being around education reform. The first words you need to say in every city and State and just draw a line in the sand—public schools exist for the benefit of the children—you're going to see a lot of people fall over it, because any time you're spending $199 billion a year, somebody's getting it, and the children get lost in the process. So that's step one.

Keep in mind in 1960 when our schools were the envy of the world, we were spending $16 billion on them. Now we spend more than any other nation in the world, $199 billion a year, and rank at the bottom of the industrialized world in terms of educational achievement. One more time, you've bought a front-row box seat and got a third-rate performance. This is a Government that's not serving you.

By and large, it should be local. The more local, the better. Interesting phenomenon, small towns have good schools, big cities have terrible schools. The best people in a small town will serve on the school board. You get into big cities, it's political patronage, stepping stones. You get the job, give your relatives the janitor's job at $57,000 a year, more than the teachers make. And with luck, they clean the cafeteria once a week. [*Laughter*]

Now, you're paying for that. Those schools belong to you, and we put up with that. As long as you put up with that, that's what you're going to get. These folks are just dividing up 199 billion bucks, and the children get lost.

If I could wish for one thing for great public schools, it would be a strong family unit in every home. Nothing will ever replace that. You say, "Well, gee, what are you going to do about that?" Well, the White House is a bully pulpit, and I think we ought to be pounding on the table every day. There's nothing—the most efficient unit of Government we'll ever know is a strong, loving family unit.

Next thing. You need small schools, not big schools. A little school, everybody's somebody. Individualism is very important. These big factories, everybody told me they were cost-effective. I did a study on it. They're cost-ineffective. Five thousand students: why is a high school that big? One reason. Sooner or later, you get 11 more boys that can run like the devil, that weigh 250 pounds, and they might win district. Now, that has nothing to do with learning.

Secondly, across Texas, typically half the school day was nonacademic pursuits. In one place, it was 35 percent. In Texas, you could have unlimited absences to go to livestock shows. Found a boy—excuse me, but this gives the flavor—a boy in Houston kept a chicken in the bathtub in downtown Houston. Missed 65 days going to livestock shows. Finally had to come back to school, the chicken lost his feathers. That's the only way we got him back. [*Laughter*] Now, that's your tax money being wasted.

Now, neighborhood schools. It is terrible to bus tiny little children across town. It is particularly terrible to take poor, tiny little children and wait until the first grade and bus them across town to Mars where the children know their numbers, know their letters, have had every advantage; the end of the first day, that little child wants out.

I close on this: You've got to have world-class teachers, world-class books. If you ever got close to how textbooks were selected, you wouldn't want to go back the second day. I don't have time to tell you the stories. [*Laughter*]

Ms. Simpson. No, you don't. [*Laughter*]

Mr. Perot. Finally. If we don't fix this, you're right, we can't have the industries of tomorrow unless we have the best educated work force. And here, for the disadvantaged children, you've got to have early childhood development, the cheapest money you'll ever spend. The first contact should be with the mother when she's pregnant. That little child needs to be loved and hugged and nurtured and made to feel special, like you children were. They learn to think well or poorly of themselves in the first 18 months.

Ms. Simpson. Thank you, Mr. Perot.

Mr. Perot. Within the first few years, they either learn how to learn or don't learn how to learn. If they don't, they wind up in prison, and it costs more to keep them in prison than it does to send them to Harvard. I rest my case.

Ms. Simpson. Thank you. President Bush, you wanted to add something.

President Bush. I just had a word of clarification because of something Governor Clinton said. My school choice program, "GI bill" for kids, does not take public money and give it to private schools. It does what the GI bill itself did when I came out of World War II. It takes public money and gives it to families or individuals to choose the school they want. Where it's been done, those schools, like in Rochester, those schools that weren't chosen find that they then compete and do better. So I think it's worth a shot.

We've got a pilot program. It ought to be tried: school choice, public, private, or religious, not to the schools, but to—46 percent of the teachers in Chicago, public school-teachers, send their kids to private school. Now, I think we ought to try to help families and see if it will do what I think, make all schools better.

Governor Clinton. I just want to mention if I could——

Ms. Simpson. Very briefly.

Governor Clinton. Very briefly. Involving the parents in the preschool education of their kids, even if they're poor and uneducated, can make a huge difference. We have a big program in my State that teaches mothers or fathers to teach their kids to

get ready for school. It's the most successful thing we've ever done.

Just a fact clarification real quickly. We do not spend a higher percentage of our income on public education than every other country. There are nine countries that spend more than we do on public education. We spend more on education because we spend so much more on colleges. But if you look at public education alone, and you take into account that we have more racial diversity and more poverty, it makes a big difference. There are great public schools where there are public school choice, accountability, and brilliant principals. I'll just mention one, the Beasley Academic Center in Chicago. I commend it to anybody. It's as good as any private school in the country.

Ms. Simpson. We have very little time left, and it occurs to me that we have talked all this time and there has not been one question about some of the racial tensions and ethnic tensions in America. Is there anyone in this audience that would like to pose a question to the candidates on this? Yes?

Women or Minority Presidential Candidates

Q. What I'd like to know, and this is to any of the three of you, is aside from the recent accomplishments of your party, aside from those accomplishments in racial representation and without citing any of your current appointments or successful elections, when do you estimate your party will both nominate and elect an Afro-American and female ticket to the Presidency of the United States?

Ms. Simpson. Governor Clinton, why don't you answer that first.

Governor Clinton. Well, I don't have any idea, but I hope it will happen sometime in my lifetime.

Q. I do, too.

Governor Clinton. I believe that this country is electing more and more African-Americans and Latinos and Asian-Americans who are representing districts that are themselves not necessarily of a majority of their race The American people are beginning to vote across racial lines, and I hope it will happen more and more.

More and more women are being elected. Look at all these women Senate candidates we have here. You know, according to my mother and my wife and my daughter, this world would be a lot better place if women were running it most of the time.

I do think there are special experiences and judgments and backgrounds and understandings that women bring to this process, by the way. This lady said here, how have you been affected by the economy? I mean, women know what it's like to be paid an unequal amount for equal work; they know what's it like not to have flexible working hours; they know what it's like not to have family leave or child care. So I think it would be a good thing for America if it happened, and I think it will happen in my lifetime.

Ms. Simpson. Okay. I'm sorry we have just a little bit of time left. Let's try to get responses from each of them.

President Bush or Mr. Perot?

President Bush. I think if Barbara Bush were running this year she'd be elected. [*Laughter*] But it's too late.

You don't want us to mention appointees but when you see the quality of people in our administration, see how Colin Powell performed—I say administration, he's in the military.

Q. I said when's your guess?

President Bush. You weren't impressed with the fact that he performed——

Q. Excuse me, I'm extremely impressed with that.

President Bush. Yes, but wouldn't that suggest to the American people then here's a quality person, if he decided that he could automatically——

Q. Sure. I just wanted to know——

President Bush. ——get the nomination of either party? Huh?

Q. I'm totally impressed with that. I just wanted to know is when is your guess of when.

President Bush. Oh, I see. You mean time?

Q. Yeah.

President Bush. I don't know. Starting after 4 years. [*Laughter*] No, I think you'll see——

Ms. Simpson. Mr. Perot?

President Bush. I think you'll see more

minority candidates and women candidates coming forward.

Ms. Simpson. Thank you.

President Bush. This is supposed to be the year of the women in the Senate. Let's see how they do. I hope a lot of them lose.

Ms. Simpson. Mr. Perot, I don't want to cut you up any more, but we only have a minute left.

Mr. Perot. I have a fearless forecast. Unless he just won't do it, Colin Powell will be on somebody's ticket 4 years from now. Right? Right? You wanted—that's it. Four years.

Ms. Simpson. How about a woman?

Mr. Perot. Now, if he won't be, General Waller would be a—you say, why do you keep picking military people? These are people that I just happened to know and have a high regard for. I'm sure there are hundreds of others.

President Bush. How about Dr. Lou Sullivan?

Mr. Perot. Absolutely.

President Bush. Yeah, good man.

Mr. Perot. Absolutely.

Ms. Simpson. What about a woman?

Mr. Perot. Oh, oh.

President Bush. My candidate's right back there.

Mr. Perot. I can think of many.

Ms. Simpson. Many?

Mr. Perot. Absolutely.

Ms. Simpson. When?

Mr. Perot. How about Sandra Day O'Connor as an example? Dr. Bernadine Healy.

Ms. Simpson. Good.

Mr. Perot. National Institutes of Health. All right, I'll yield the floor. Name some more.

President Bush. Good Republicans. [*Laughter*]

Ms. Simpson. Thank you. I want to apologize to our audience because there were 209 people here, and there were 209 questions. We only got to a fraction of them, and I'm sorry to those of you that didn't get to ask your questions, but we must move to the conclusion of the program.

It is time now for the 2-minute closing statements. By prior agreement, President Bush will go first.

Closing Statements

President Bush. May I ask for an exception because I think we owe Carole Simpson a—anybody who can stand in between these three characters here and get the job done—we owe her a round of applause. [*Applause*] Just don't take it out of my time.

Ms. Simpson. That's right.

President Bush. I feel strongly about it, but I don't want it to come out of my time.

Ms. Simpson. That's right. [*Laughter*]

President Bush. No, but let me just say to the American people: In 2½ weeks, we're going to choose who should sit in this Oval Office, who to lead the economic recovery, who to be the leader of the free world, who to get the deficit down. Three ways to do that: one is to raise taxes; one is to reduce spending, controlling that mandatory spending; another one is to invest and save and to stimulate growth.

I do not want to raise taxes. I differ with the two here on that. I'm just not going to do that. I do believe that we need to control mandatory spending. I think we need to invest and save more. I believe that we need to educate better and retrain better. I believe that we need to export more, so I'll keep working for export agreements where we can sell more abroad. And I believe that we must strengthen the family. We've got to strengthen the family.

Now, let me pose this question to America: If in the next 5 minutes a television announcer came on and said, there is a major international crisis, there is a major threat to the world, or in this country a major threat, my question is, if you were appointed to name one of the three of us, who would you choose? Who has the perseverance, the character, the integrity, the maturity to get the job done? I hope I'm that person.

Thank you very, very much.

Ms. Simpson. Thank you, Mr. President. And now a closing statement from Mr. Perot.

Mr. Perot. If the American people want to do it and not talk about it, then I'm one person they ought to consider. If they just want to keep slow dancing and talk about it and not do it, I'm not your man. I am results oriented. I am action oriented. I've built my businesses getting things done in 3 months that my competitors took 18 months to do.

Everybody says, you can't do that with Congress. Sure you can do that with Congress. Congress, they're all good people. They're all patriots. But you've got to link arms and work with them. Sure, you'll have arguments. Sure, you'll have fights. We have them all day, every day. But we get the job done.

Now, I have to come back in my close to one thing, because I am passionate about education. I was talking about early childhood education for disadvantaged little children. Let me tell you one specific pilot program where children who don't have a chance go to this program when they're 3. Now, we're going back to when the mother is pregnant, and they'll start right after they're born, starting when they're 3 and going to this school until they're 9, and then going into the public school in the fourth grade—90 percent are on the honor roll. Now, that will change America. Those children will all go to college. They will live the American dream.

I beg the American people, anytime they think about reforming education, to take this piece of society that doesn't have a chance, and take these little pieces of clay that can be shaped and molded and give them the same love and nurture and affection and support you give your children. Teach them that they're unique and that they're precious and there's only one person in the world like them, and you will see this Nation bloom. We will have so many people who are qualified for the top job that it will be terrific.

Now, finally, if you can't pay the bills, you're dead in the water. We have got to put our Nation back to work. Now, if you don't want to really do that, I'm not your man. I'd go crazy sitting up there slow dancing that one. In other words, unless we're going to do it, then pick somebody who likes to talk about it.

Now, just remember, when you think about me, I didn't create this mess. I've been paying taxes just like you. And Lord knows, I've paid my share, over $1 billion in taxes. And for a guy that started out with everything he owned in the trunk of his car, that ain't bad.

Ms. Simpson. I'm sorry, Mr. Perot. Once again——

Mr. Perot. But it's in your hands. I wish you well. I'll see you tomorrow night on NBC, 10:30 p.m., 11 p.m., eastern. [*Laughter*]

Ms. Simpson. And finally, last but not least, Governor Clinton.

Governor Clinton. Thank you, Carole, and thank you, ladies and gentleman. Since I suggested this format, I hope it's been good for all of you. I've really tried to be faithful to your request that we answer the questions specifically and pointedly. I thought I owed that to you. And I respect you for being here, and for the impact you've had on making this a more positive experience.

These problems are not easy. They're not going to be solved overnight. But I want you to think about just two or three things. First of all, the people of my State have let me be their Governor for 12 years because I made commitments to two things, more jobs and better schools.

Our schools are now better. Our children get off to a better start, from preschool programs and smaller classes in the early grades. We have one of the most aggressive adult education programs in the country. We talked about that.

This year, my State ranks first in the country in job growth, fourth in manufacturing job growth, fourth in income growth, fourth in the decline of poverty. I'm proud of that. It happened because I could work with people, Republicans and Democrats. That's why we've had 24 retired generals and admirals, hundreds of business people,

many of them Republican, support this campaign.

You have to decide whether you want to change or not. We do not need 4 more years of an economic theory that doesn't work. We've had 12 years of trickle-down economics. It's time to put the American people first, to invest and grow this economy. I'm the only person here who's ever balanced a government budget, and I've presented 12 of them and cut spending repeatedly. But you cannot just get there by balancing the budget. We've got to grow the economy by putting people first, real people like you.

I got into this race because I did not want my child to grow up to be part of the first generation of Americans to do worse than their parents. We're better than that. We can do better than that. I want to make America as great as it can be, and I ask for your help in doing it.

Thank you very much.

Ms. Simpson. Thank you, Governor Clinton.

Ladies and gentlemen, this concludes the debate, sponsored by the Bipartisan Commission on Presidential Debates. I'd like to thank our audience of 209 uncommitted voters who may leave this evening maybe being committed. And hopefully, they'll go to the polls like everyone else on November 3d and vote.

We invite you to join us on the third and final Presidential debate next Monday, October 19th, from the campus of Michigan State University in East Lansing, Michigan.

I'm Carole Simpson. Good night.

Note: The debate began at 9 p.m. in Robins Center at the University of Richmond.

Remarks to the Community in Edison, New Jersey
October 16, 1992

The President. Thank you very, very much. And I am delighted to be back here in New Jersey. Great to be in Middlesex County, and great to fly over in that helicopter with Governor Tom Kean. I wish he

were still Governor of this State. While we're talking about good—whoops—got a Democratic bee here. [*Laughter*] Let me just say at the beginning that New Jersey needs Bob Franks and Al Palermo in Washington. We've got to clean House. Get Bob Franks and Al Palermo down there.

You know, this week on your TV screens you saw a spectacle of intense competition, breathtaking battle of wits and courage, a spine-tingling fight to the finish. I am talking about the Pirates-Braves game, of course. [*Laughter*] You know, I sort of identify with the Atlanta Braves, because politics is like baseball: It ain't over until the last batter swings. And we are going to win this election.

We're going to surprise the pundits— what's this bee here?—surprise the pundits, annoy the media, and hit a home run on November 3d. The reason is clear: Our ideas are better for America. My opponents, sorry opponents, pathetic, try to tell you that America is in decline, and we are not in decline. Not so. Our people are still the best educated, and our economy is still the most dynamic. Our companies and our workers are still more productive than any other in the entire world.

You know——

Audience members. Bush! Bush! Bush! Four more years! Four more years! Four more years!

The President. You know, if we'd have listened to this nuclear——

Audience members. Four more years! Four more years! Four more years!

The President. You know, we've led the United States through a very difficult global transition, and I am very proud that the world is safer for our kids. And does that matter? You bet it does. The fear of nuclear war is less.

We've kept our economy afloat when many of those European economies are drowning, and the Europeans would trade with us in one minute. We've kept inflation down. We've kept interest rates down. We have made our industries stronger and more competitive. And I am proud of our leadership.

For all his rhetoric about change, Bill Clinton offers a very old path: more Government, more regulation, and more taxes; more Government, more regulation, and more taxes.

Audience members. Boo-o-o!

The President. We must not let Clinton do this to our country.

Audience members. We want Bush! We want Bush! We want Bush!

The President. All right. Listen to this program. Let me tell you about Governor Clinton's program. In June, Governor Clinton promised $150 billion in new taxes, plus $220 billion in new spending. I thought that would satisfy his appetite, but that's just an hors d'oeuvre, because ever since then Bill Clinton has made new promises, $1 billion in new Government spending every single day.

Audience members. Boo-o-o!

The President. Who is going to pay Bill's bill? Of course, Governor Clinton says he's only going to tax the rich. But everybody out there with $22,000 in income better be ready, because he's going to sock it to the working people in this country.

Audience members. Boo-o-o!

The President. He'll go after the cab drivers and the teachers and the nurses and the middle class.

Let me say this: Higher taxes do not create new jobs. They destroy that. You've seen it when their man, Governor Florio, was elected. Governor Florio has too much taxes. So does Governor Clinton. That Florio-Clinton combination, they kicked half a million jobs out of New Jersey. When Governor Kean was here, we were building jobs.

But I have a very different agenda, a plan to control the growth of mandatory spending and get the taxes down so we can create good jobs, create them. We're going to win the new economic competition. Our Agenda for American Renewal includes the steps that we must take to create good jobs today and build a stronger America, and some of these ideas are being tried. But working with a new Congress, we're going to put this entire agenda into effect and get America moving, get rid of these Democrats from Congress and get them moving.

Audience members. We want Bush! We want Bush! We want Bush!

The President. One way to do it is to tear down barriers to free and fair trade so that we can create good jobs for American workers. In the past 3 years, our exports to Japan have increased 12 times faster than our imports from Japan. Whether you shop in

Tokyo or Trenton, chances are that the goods don't say "Made in Japan" or "Made in Germany," they say "Made in the United States of America."

Today in New Jersey one out of every six jobs is tied into foreign trade. And the average export-related job pays 17 percent more than the traditional job. So if we want the sons and daughters of steel workers to have good jobs, we've got to fight for free and fair trade. Do it the New Jersey way, more exports.

We've already got a great new trade agreement—one that Governor Clinton has waffled on. He waffles on everything. He's on one side and then the other. We've got a good trade agreement, and I'm going to fight for more trade agreements. Just as we once used our military alliances to win the cold war, we will use our economic alliances to win the new business war.

[*At this point, audience members interrupted the President's remarks.*]

I wish these draft dodgers would shut up so I can finish my speech. It's pathetic.

Audience members. Where was George? Where was George? Where was George?

Audience members. We want Bush! We want Bush! We want Bush!

The President. You see—these guys. Where was Bill?

Audience members. We want Clinton! We want Clinton! We want Clinton!

The President. No. You see, I'm glad we've led in foreign policy, because now we'll use those alliances that have made the world more peaceful to bring more prosperity to the workers right here in America.

I also want to do for the country what Governor Kean has tried to do when he was Governor here, change our schools. Make our education system better for all. I am proud of what we have done already. We have educational standards nationally for the first time in the history of this country. We want to let the parents choose the schools, public, private, or religious. Every parent should be able to choose his children's schools.

You know, I believe that small business is the backbone of our economy creating two out of every three new jobs. Bill Clinton wants to slap a tax on small business. I say if we really want to help small business, let's give them relief from taxation, regulation, and litigation.

Now, let me mention just another subject the New Jerseyans know about, and that is auto insurance. At the root of many of our problems is a legal system that is out of control. I want to do something about these crazy lawsuits. Governor Clinton and the trial lawyers do not want to do anything about it.

You know, 15 percent of American companies report that they have laid off workers because of high premiums from liability insurance. Experts estimate that over $20 billion of our health care costs come from doctors and nurses doing unnecessary tests because they're afraid that a lawyer is going to sue them, and auto insurance costs continue to rise, as New Jerseyans know better than almost anyone. One big cause is our lawsuit-happy legal system. Thousands of people enter frivolous lawsuits for pain and suffering. But the lion's share of the benefits goes not to people who are injured but to the trial lawyers. I say we must reform our malpractice laws and our product liability laws.

When Congress comes back, I'm going to introduce a new proposal to allow all Americans to opt out of the so-called pain and suffering standard. You know, this reform allows States to go even further than New Jersey's landmark insurance reforms.

Audience members. Bill's a fake! Bill's a fake! Bill's a fake!

The President. Thank you very much.

But anyway, this proposal will save American drivers 20 to 30 billion dollars in insurance premiums every year.

So these are part of our Agenda for American Renewal. But the election is a lot more about other things, the best economic plan. It's about another virtue, and it's called trust. It's called trust. Who do you trust to be President of the United States?

You know, I've got to tell you, I enjoyed last night's debate, and I'm grateful to have a chance to have Americans compare my views with my opponents'. But it's difficult to debate Clinton because he comes down on every side of every issue. You can't do that as President of the United States.

You've got to make a decision. You can't be popular to every group. And yes, he ought to tell the truth.

Audience members. We want Bush! We want Bush! We want Bush!

The President. Thank you. Look, a lot of being President is about respect for that office and about telling the truth and serving your country. You are all familiar with Governor Clinton's various stories on what he did to evade the draft. He still has not leveled with the American people. He still hasn't told the truth.

Last night you heard Governor Clinton state that he was absolutely against allowing parents to use tax dollars to send their kids to private or religious schools. But he used to be for the idea.

What about limiting the terms of Members of Congress? I am strongly for it. He said he was interested, and now he's against it. Let's limit the terms of Members of Congress.

Just this morning in the Los Angeles Times, there's an article suggesting that Governor Clinton is already preparing yet another economic program, with billions of dollars more in new spending. But his advisers won't spell it out until after the election.

Now, you might say, why is this important? Because there's a clear pattern to Governor Clinton's past, a pattern of deception. Character does matter. A pattern of deception is not right for the Oval Office. You cannot be leader of the world, you cannot be leader of this country if you have a pattern of deception.

You know, last night Governor Clinton said he was not interested in my character. He said, I quote, "I want to change the character of the Presidency." Well, let me tell you something. You cannot separate the character of the President from the character of the Presidency. They go together. You cannot be one kind of man and another

kind of President. It is that simple.

You know, I've been there. I've had to make some tough decisions in that Oval Office. I hope this doesn't happen, but the next President who may have to send our young men, women in harm's way. And the next President will have to stand up to the special interests and that big-spending Congress. In the White House you cannot make everybody happy, and you have to level with the American people. He is not capable of doing that.

So my problem is this pattern of deception. We cannot have this pattern of deception brought into the Oval Office. I believe you cannot lead the American people by misleading the American people.

Now, you know, we've had Presidents from the South and from the North; Presidents who were rich, Presidents who were poor. But rich or poor, southern or northern, you must have integrity. And that's what it takes to lead this great land.

I think the American people are beginning, as they focus in on the final part of this election, they're saying: Who do you trust? Who do you believe? Who do you trust to be in the Oval Office?

You know, last night in that debate I asked the American people to imagine what would happen if a crisis occurred that could affect you and your family. Who would you prefer to lead in a crisis? And so this is the question that I'm going to ask all of you to ask when you go into that voting booth. I hope because of my character, my judgment, my ideas, that I have earned your trust to lead America again.

Thank you all, and may God bless you. Thank you for a wonderful rally. Thanks a lot. Thank you so much.

Note: The President spoke at 4:23 p.m. at Middlesex County Community College.

Statement on Signing the Dayton Aviation Heritage Preservation Act of 1992
October 16, 1992

I am signing into law H.R. 2321, the "Dayton Aviation Heritage Preservation Act of 1992," which establishes the Dayton Aviation National Historic Park in Ohio as an addition to the National Park System. The park will preserve certain historic sites in the Dayton, Ohio, area that are associated with the Wright brothers and the early development of aviation. The Act will recognize the national significance of these sites and the achievements of the Wright brothers, two of our most distinguished Americans.

The Act also establishes the Dayton Aviation Heritage Commission to assist Federal, State, and local authorities in preserving and managing historic resources related to aviation in the Dayton area. The commission is composed of 13 members, most of whom are appointed by the Secretary of the Interior from recommendations of various State and local officials. The majority of members are effectively selected by various nonfederal officials and thus are not ap-pointed in conformity with the Appointments Clause of the Constitution, Article II, section 2, clause 2. Therefore, I sign this bill on the understanding that the commission will serve only in an advisory capacity and will not exercise Government power.

It should also be noted that the FY 1993 Interior Appropriations Act (Public Law 102–381) reduces the funds available for National Park Service management by approximately $42 million from my budget request. I question the wisdom of establishing new units of the National Park System that fail to meet the criteria established by the National Park Service when the Congress is not providing the existing system with adequate funding.

GEORGE BUSH

The White House,
October 16, 1992.

Note: H.R. 2321, approved October 16, was assigned Public Law No. 102–419.

White House Fact Sheet: Consumer Choice in Auto Insurance
October 16, 1992

President Bush announced a proposal today that would allow consumers to save 20 to 30 percent on their auto insurance premiums, for a potential nationwide savings of $20 to $30 billion annually. These savings would be achieved by giving consumers the opportunity to waive their right to sue for pain and suffering damages (thereby also insulating themselves against lawsuits for such damages) and to elect insurance coverage payable by their own insurer regardless of fault.

The Problem

The current auto insurance system is a source of consumer outrage. Insurance premiums, now more than $1,000 per car in many areas, grew at almost 3 times the rate of inflation in the 1980's, forcing many lower income Americans to drive uninsured.

A root cause for escalating rates is the pain and suffering component of tort awards. Nationwide, coverage for pain and suffering awards constitute 15 percent of insurance costs, while litigation costs (which are driven largely by the prospect of pain and suffering awards) account for another 10 percent.

There are other wasteful costs as well under the current system, such as incentives to inflate medical costs. In particular, a recent study by the Insurance Research Council showed that people involved in auto accidents obtain more expensive medical treatment if they file a claim against the other driver than if they collect from their own insurer, regardless of fault.

If there were fewer lawsuits for pain and suffering, overall auto insurance rates could drop sharply. Under current law, however, consumers cannot purchase auto insurance that omits coverage for pain and suffering.

The Solution

The President stated that on the first day of the next session of Congress, he will submit legislation proposing a Federal statute to permit purchasers of automobile insurance to opt out of pain and suffering claims.

Under the President's proposal:
- Consumers would be allowed to waive their right to sue for noneconomic (i.e., pain and suffering) damages. In return, they would be insulated from noneconomic damage claims by other motorists.
- Those electing to waive the right to sue for noneconomic damages would purchase personal insurance protection coverage, under which they would collect economic damages without regard to fault from their own insurer instead of suing other motorists. This would largely eliminate litigation costs and avoid the lengthy payment delays (usually 18 months or more) that are common under the current system.
- Those motorists not waiving this right would retain their coverage under the tort liability system. They would purchase coverage from their own insurer to cover all damages (for both economic and noneconomic losses) negligently caused by drivers who elect the personal insurance protection plan.
- All motorists would retain the right to sue for pain and suffering caused by intoxicated or criminally negligent drivers.
- All motorists would also be able to sue for all economic damages based on fault in excess of their own insurance coverage.

The Benefits of the President's Proposal

Although the proposal would benefit all motorists, the greatest cost benefits would go to consumers in high-premium areas, and especially to poor inner-city residents, many of whom now drive illegally without insurance. This proposal presents a sharp contrast to the nonmarket approaches preferred by the Democrats, such as mandatory rollbacks, surcharges on insurers, and rigid rate regulation, which try to force businesses to engage in losing ventures. This proposal also reinforces the President's call for legal reform and makes clear that consumer empowerment and choice is the key to better insurance.

Statement on Signing the Community Environmental Response Facilitation Act
October 19, 1992

I am signing into law H.R. 4016, the "Community Environmental Response Facilitation Act," which requires Federal agencies that intend to terminate operations on real property to identify those portions of the property that are not contaminated by hazardous waste or petroleum products.

The Act would, among other things, require agencies to obtain the concurrence of the appropriate State official in order to complete identification of certain property as uncontaminated. If this requirement were understood to allow the State official to prevent a Federal agency from disposing of property, then the Act would, in effect, be granting Federal Executive power to a person who has not been appointed in conformity with the Appointments Clause of the Constitution, Article II, section 2, clause 2.

In order to avoid this constitutional difficulty, I instruct all agencies affected by this Act to construe a State official's failure to concur as a statement of that official's views, but not as a bar to transfer of the property. Because the Act nowhere states the consequences of a failure to concur, a Federal agency may terminate operations on a property and dispose of it, in accordance with applicable Federal laws, regardless of whether a State official fails to concur in the identification of it as uncontaminated.

GEORGE BUSH

The White House,
October 19, 1992.

Note: H.R. 4016, approved October 19, was assigned Public Law No. 102–426.

Letter to Congressional Leaders Reporting on the Cyprus Conflict
October 19, 1992

Dear Mr. Speaker: (Dear Mr. Chairman:)

In accordance with Public Law 95–384 (22 U.S.C. 2373(c)), I am submitting to you this bimonthly report on progress toward a negotiated settlement of the Cyprus question. This report covers the months of July and August 1992.

The New York negotiations resumed, as scheduled, on July 15 on the same basis as they had recessed with the Secretary General having separate meetings with the leaders of the two Cypriot communities ("proximity talks").

On the first day of this new negotiating session, the U.N. Secretary General gave his "set of ideas" for a Cyprus settlement, including a U.N. suggested map of territorial adjustments, to the two Cypriot delegations. Both sides accepted the documents and signalled their readiness to use them as the basis for negotiations. Mr. Denktash, however, objected to the U.N. map, and after lengthy discussion with the U.N. negotiators over several weeks, indicated his intention to accept a Turkish Cypriot federated state that constituted "29 plus percent" of a future Cyprus federated republic, a formulation he had accepted in the mid-1980s. Mr. Denktash made several specific proposals, none of which came close in quality or quantity to the territorial adjustments suggested in the U.N. map. The Secretary General's account of the negotiations on this issue is detailed in paragraphs 17 through 29 of his August 21 report to the Security Council on his mission of good offices in Cyprus, which is attached to this letter.

The question of displaced persons was also discussed in detail during the July-August negotiations. The Turkish Cypriot side accepted the principles of the right to return and the right to property, provided that "practical difficulties" on the Turkish Cypriot side would be taken into account. Mr. Denktash wanted particularly to exempt certain categories of Turkish Cypriots from the obligation to vacate their current homes and to provide a review mechanism for cases in which there were conflicting claims. The Greek Cypriot side agreed, the Secretary General reported, that, in this as in all other respects, the "set of ideas" provided the basis for reaching an overall framework agreement. Paragraphs 27 through 32 of the Secretary General's August 21 report cover the negotiations on displaced persons.

The U.N. negotiators reviewed the other six headings of the "set of ideas," including constitutional arrangements, with the two Cypriot community leaders on the last days of the proximity talks.

In all, the U.N. Secretary General and his representatives had more than three dozen separate meetings with the two leaders between July 15 and August 11. During this period and during the direct talks that followed, the U.S. Cyprus Coordinator, Ambassador Nelson Ledsky, and the U.S. Ambassador to Cyprus, Robert Lamb, were in New York to coordinate with the U.N. negotiators, with the representatives of the two

Cypriot communities, Greece, Turkey, and with representatives of the other permanent members of the U.N. Security Council. These consultations continued during the July-August negotiations, and representatives of the United States and the other four permanent members of the Security Council were briefed almost daily by the negotiators on the progress of the talks. There were also numerous informal contacts with the two Cypriot delegations as well as the numerous consultations with the representatives of the five permanent Security Council members indicated above.

On August 11, the Secretary General announced that the two sides had made enough progress to warrant moving to direct discussions. The two Cypriot leaders agreed that these face-to-face discussions would focus first on displaced persons, then on constitutional arrangements, then territory, and then to the other issues in the "set of ideas."

In the 3 days that followed, the Secretary General conducted four meetings between the two Cypriot leaders. On August 14, the Secretary General suggested and the two leaders agreed to another pause in the talks. The parties agreed that the talks would resume on a face-to-face basis on October 26 at the U.N. headquarters in New York.

On August 21, the Secretary General issued the attached report to the Security Council. The Secretary General's report covers his efforts to resolve the Cyprus problem during the period from April 10, 1992, through August 21, 1992. The report has annexed to it the entire U.N. "Set of ideas on an overall framework agreement on Cyprus" (previously referred to in my letters to the Congress as the "set of ideas") including the map that contains the Secretary General's suggestions for territorial adjustments.

On August 26, 1992, the U.N. Security Council passed Resolution 774 of August 26, 1992 (attached), which, among other points, endorsed the Secretary General's report and the "set of ideas," including the suggested territorial adjustments reflected in the map contained in the annex to the report, as the basis for reaching an overall framework agreement. Resolution 774 called on the parties to manifest the necessary political will and to address in a positive manner the observations of the Secretary General for resolving the issues covered in his report.

The Resolution expressed the Security Council's expectation that an overall framework agreement will be concluded in 1992 with 1993 as the transitional year envisioned in the "set of ideas." It reaffirmed the Council's position that the Secretary General should convene, following the satisfactory conclusion of the face-to-face talks, a high-level international meeting to conclude an overall framework agreement, in which the two Cypriot communities and Greece and Turkey would participate.

In Resolution 774, the Security Council also reaffirmed its position that the present status quo is unacceptable and called on the Secretary General to recommend alternate courses of action to resolve the Cyprus problem should an agreement not emerge from the talks that will reconvene in October.

I fully endorse the sentiments expressed in Security Council Resolution 774 and call on the parties to continue their work toward an agreement, which will benefit all the people of Cyprus.

During the course of the July-August New York negotiating session, I announced the appointment of Mr. John Maresca as the new U.S. Special Cyprus Coordinator. Mr. Maresca will replace Ambassador Ledsky, who has retired from the U.S. Foreign Service after a long and distinguished career. I would like to applaud and commend to your attention the outstanding achievement of Ambassador Ledsky in moving forward the U.N. Cyprus negotiations.

Sincerely,

GEORGE BUSH

Note: Identical letters were sent to Thomas S. Foley, Speaker of the House of Representatives, and Claiborne Pell, Chairman of the Senate Committee on Foreign Relations.

Statement by Press Secretary Fitzwater on Implementation of the Clean Air Act
October 19, 1992

Today the Environmental Protection Agency is announcing that 41 more cities are attaining health standards for ground-level ozone (smog) and 13 more cities are attaining health standards for carbon monoxide. With over 35 million Americans breathing more easily than in 1988, this is a great American success story.

These improvements are due to a combination of cooler weather since 1988 and the actions this administration has taken in the last 4 years, including reducing the volatility of gasoline and passage of the Clean Air Act. The Bush administration is committed to continuing to clean our air through the full implementation of the Clean Air Act.

Remarks on Arrival in Lansing, Michigan
October 19, 1992

Thank you, Marti. Listen, this is a big moment. And Marti, thank you for those glowing words. I am pleased to receive the endorsement not only of two key members of the Perot campaign, Marti Plender and Jim Jenkins, but so many other Perot people.

All along in this campaign we've shared a common concern to take immediate action to get our economy moving again. And now we share something else: We agree that my plan is the best plan to jump-start the economy and to create jobs.

We agree, as Ross Perot's national coordinator, Orson Swindle, said this weekend, that a vote for Bill Clinton is a vote for disaster. Bill Clinton will not be able to control this spendthrift Congress. We've got the agenda, and we've got the ideas that will turn this economy around and get the deficit under control. And we can do it without giving Government more of your money to spend. Hold the line on taxes!

You know, some in the media will tell you the election's almost over, but the American people have a very different opinion. And this endorsement, coming at this critical moment, shows we are moving in the right direction, gathering strength, and we are winning the battle of ideas that will take us to victory on November 3d.

Thank you all very much. Thank you for coming out here today.

Note: The President spoke at 2:32 p.m. at the Capital City Airport. In his remarks, he referred to Marti Plender and Jim Jenkins, former key organizers for Ross Perot in the Grand Rapids and Detroit areas.

Presidential Debate in East Lansing, Michigan
October 19, 1992

Jim Lehrer. Good evening. Welcome to this third and final debate among the three major candidates for President of the United States: Governor Bill Clinton, the Democratic nominee; President George Bush, the Republican nominee; and independent candidate Ross Perot.

I am Jim Lehrer, of "The MacNeil/Lehrer NewsHour" on PBS. I will be the moderator for this debate, which is being sponsored by the Commission on Presidential Debates. It will be 90 minutes long. It is happening before an audience on the campus of Michigan State University in East Lansing.

The format was conceived by and agreed to by representatives of the Bush and Clinton campaigns. And it is somewhat different than those used in the earlier debates. I will ask questions for the first half under rules that permit followups. A panel of three other journalists will ask questions in the second half under rules that do not. As always, each candidate will have 2 minutes, up to 2 minutes, to make a closing statement. The order of those as well as that for the formal questioning were all determined by a drawing.

Gentlemen, again, welcome. And again, good evening.

Credibility

It seems, from what some of those voters said at your Richmond debate and from polling and other data, that each of you, fairly or not, faces serious voter concerns about the underlying credibility and believability of what each of you says you would do as President in the next 4 years.

Governor Clinton, in accordance with the draw, those concerns about you are first. You are promising to create jobs, reduce the deficit, reform the health care system, rebuild the infrastructure, guarantee college education for everyone who is qualified, among many other things, all with financial pain only for the very rich. Some people are having trouble, apparently, believing that is possible. Should they have that concern?

Governor Clinton. No. There are many people who believe that the only way we can get this country turned around is to tax the middle class more and punish them more. But the truth is that middle class Americans are basically the only group of Americans who have been taxed more in the 1980's and during the last 12 years even though their incomes have gone down. The wealthiest Americans have been taxed much less even though their incomes have gone up.

Middle class people will have their fair share of changing to do and many challenges to face, including the challenge of becoming constantly reeducated. But my plan is a departure from trickle-down economics, just cutting taxes on the wealthiest Americans and getting out of the way. It's also a departure from tax-and-spend economics because you can't tax and divide an economy that isn't growing.

I propose an American version of what works in other countries. I think we can do it better: invest and grow. I believe we can increase investment and reduce the deficit at the same time if we not only ask the wealthiest Americans and foreign corporations to pay their fair share, we also provide over $100 billion in tax relief in terms of incentives for new plants, new small businesses, new technologies, new housing, and for middle class families, and we have $140 billion of spending cuts.

Invest and grow: raise some more money; spend the money on tax incentives to have growth in the private sector; take the money from the defense cuts and reinvest it in new transportation and communications and environmental cleanup systems. This will work.

On this, as on so many other issues, I have a fundamental difference from the present administration. I don't believe trickle-down economics will work. Unemployment is up. Most people are working harder for less money than they were making 10 years ago. I think we can do better if we have the courage to change.

Mr. Lehrer. Mr. President, a response.

President Bush. Do I have one minute? Just the ground rules here.

Mr. Lehrer. Well, you have roughly one minute. We can loosen that up a little bit. But go ahead.

President Bush. He doesn't like trickle-down Government, but hey, I think he's talking about the Reagan-Bush years where we created 15 million jobs. The rich are paying a bigger percent of the total tax burden. What I don't like is trickle-down Government. I think Governor Clinton keeps talking about trickle-down, trickle-down, and he's still talking about spending more and taxing more.

Government, he says, invest Government, grow Government. Government doesn't create jobs. If they do, they're make-work jobs. It's the private sector that creates jobs.

And yes, we've got too many taxes on the American people, and we're spending too much. That's why I want to get the deficit down by controlling the growth of mandatory spending.

It won't be painless. I think Mr. Perot put his finger on something there. It won't be painless, but we've got to get the job done. But not by raising taxes.

Mr. and Mrs. America, when you hear him say we're going to tax only the rich, watch your wallet, because his figures don't add up, and he's going to sock it right to the middle class taxpayer and lower if he's going to pay for all the spending programs he's proposed. So we have a big difference on this trickle-down theory. I do not want any more trickle-down Government. It's gotten too big. I want to do something about that.

Mr. Lehrer. Mr. Perot, what do you think of the Governor's approach, what he just laid out?

Mr. Perot. Well, the basic problem with it is it doesn't balance the budget. If you forecast it out, you still will have a significant deficit under each of their plans, as I understand them. Our challenge is to stop the financial bleeding. If you take a patient into a hospital that's bleeding arterially, step one is to stop the bleeding. And we are bleeding arterially.

There's only one way out of this, and that is to stop the deterioration of our job base, to have a growing, expanding job base to give us the tax base. See, balancing the budget is not nearly as difficult as paying off the $4 trillion debt and leaving our children the American dream intact. We have spent their money. We have got to pay it back. This is going to take fair-shared sacrifice.

My plan balances the budget within 6 years. We didn't do it faster than that because we didn't want to disrupt the economy. We gave it off to a slow start and a fast finish to give the economy time to recover. But we faced it, and we did it. And we believe it's fair-shared sacrifice.

The one thing I have done is lay it squarely on the table in front of the American people. You've had a number of occasions to see in detail what the plan is and at least you'll understand it. I think that's fun-

damental in our country that you know what you're getting into.

Mr. Lehrer. Governor, the word "pain," one of the other leadership things that's put on you is that you don't speak of pain, that you speak of all things—nobody's going to really have to suffer under your plan. You've heard what Mr. Perot has said. He said to do the things you want to do, you can't do it by just taking the money from the rich. That's what the President says as well. How do you respond to that? The numbers don't add up.

Governor Clinton. I disagree with both of them. Let me just follow up here. I disagree with Mr. Perot that the answer is to put a 50-cent gas tax on the middle class and raise more taxes on the middle class and the working poor than on the wealthy. His own analysis says that unemployment will be slightly higher in 1995 under his plan than it is today. As far as what Mr. Bush says, he is the person who raised taxes on the middle class after saying he wouldn't. Just this year Mr. Bush vetoed a tax increase on the wealthy that gave middle class tax relief. He vetoed middle class tax relief this year.

Furthermore, under this administration, spending has increased more than it has in the last 20 years, and he asked Congress to spend more money than it actually spent. Now, it's hard to outspend Congress, but he tried to for the last 3 years.

So my view is the middle class is the—they've been suffering, Jim. Now, should people pay more for Medicare if they can? Yes. Should they pay more for Social Security if they get more out of it than they've paid in and they're upper income people? Yes. But look what's happened to the middle class. Middle class Americans are working harder for less money than they were making 10 years ago, and they're paying higher taxes. The tax burden on them has not gone down; it has gone up.

I don't think the answer is to slow the economy down more, drive unemployment up more, and undermine the health of the private sector. The answer is to invest and grow this economy. That's what works in other countries, and that's what will work here.

Mr. Lehrer. As a practical matter, Mr. President, do you agree with the Governor when he says that the middle class—the taxes on the middle class—do your numbers agree that the taxes on the middle class have gone up during the last——

President Bush. I think everybody is paying too much taxes. He refers to one tax increase. Let me remind you it was a Democratic tax increase. I didn't want to do it, and I went along with it. I said I made a mistake. If I make a mistake, I admit it. That's quite different than some. But I think that's the American way.

I think everyone is paying too much. But I think this idea that you can go out and—then he hits me for vetoing a tax bill. Yes, I did, and the American taxpayer ought to be glad they have a President to stand up to a spending Congress. We remember what it was like when we had a spending President and a spending Congress and interest rates—who remembers that—they were 21.5 percent under Jimmy Carter, and inflation was 15. We don't want to go back to that. So yes, everybody's taxed too much, and I want to get the taxes down, but not by signing a tax bill that's going to raise taxes on people.

Mr. Lehrer. Mr. President, when you said just then that you admit your mistakes, and you looked at Governor Clinton and said—what mistake is it that you want him to admit to?

President Bush. Well, the record in Arkansas. I mean, look at it. And that's what we're asking America to have? Now, look, he says Arkansas's a poor State. They are. But in almost every category, they're lagging. I'll give you an example.

He talks about all the jobs he's created in 1 or 2 years. Over the last 10 years since he's been Governor, they're 30 percent behind. They're 30 percent of the national average. On pay for teachers, on all these categories, Arkansas is right near the very bottom.

You haven't heard me mention this before, but we're getting close now, and I think it's about time I start putting things in perspective. I'm going to do that. It's not dirty campaigning, because he's been talking about my record for half a year here, 11 months here, and so we've got to do that.

I've got to get it in perspective.

What's his mistake? Admit it, that Arkansas is doing very, very badly against any standard: environment, support for police officers, whatever it is.

Mr. Lehrer. Governor, is that true?

Governor Clinton. Mr. Bush's Bureau of Labor Statistics says that Arkansas ranks first in the country in the growth of new jobs this year, first——

President Bush. This year.

Governor Clinton. ——fourth in manufacturing jobs; fourth in the reduction of poverty; fourth in income increase. Over the last 10 years we've created manufacturing jobs much more rapidly than the national average. Over the last 5 years our income has grown more rapidly than the national average. We are second in tax burden, the second lowest tax burden in the country. We have the lowest per capita State and local spending in the country.

We are low-spending, low tax burden. We've dramatically increased investment and our jobs are growing. I wish America had that kind of record, and I think most people looking at us tonight would like it if we had more jobs and a lower spending burden on the Government.

Mr. Lehrer. Mr. Perot, if you were sitting at home now and just heard this exchange about Arkansas, who would you believe?

Mr. Perot. I grew up five blocks from Arkansas. [*Laughter*] Let's put it in perspective. It's a beautiful State. It's a fairly rural State. It has a population less than Chicago or Los Angeles, about the size of Dallas and Fort Worth combined. So I think probably we're making a mistake night after night after night to cast the Nation's future on a unit that small.

Mr. Lehrer. Why is that a mistake?

Mr. Perot. It's irrelevant. [*Laughter*]

Mr. Lehrer. What he did as Governor of Arkansas——

Mr. Perot. No, no, no. But you can't—I could say that I ran a small grocery store on the corner, therefore, I extrapolate that into the fact that I could run Wal-Mart. That's not true. I carefully picked an Arkansas company, you notice there, Governor.

Mr. Lehrer. Governor?

Governor Clinton. Mr. Perot, with all respect, I think it is highly relevant, and I think that a $4 billion budget in State and Federal funds is not all that small. I think the fact that I took a State that was one of the poorest States in the country and had been for 153 years and tried my best to modernize its economy and to make the kind of changes that have generated support from people like the presidents of Apple Computer and Hewlett-Packard and some of the biggest companies in this country, 24 retired generals and admirals, and hundreds of business executives are highly relevant.

And you know, I'm frankly amazed that since you grew up five blocks from there you would think that what goes on in that State is irrelevant. I think it's been pretty impressive.

Mr. Perot. It's not——

Governor Clinton. And the people who have jobs and educations and opportunities that didn't have them 10 years ago don't think it's irrelevant at all. They think it's highly relevant and wish the rest of the country——

President Bush. I don't have a dog in this fight, but I'd like to get in on it.

Governor Clinton. You think it's relevant.

President Bush. Governor Clinton has to operate under a balanced budget amendment. He has to do it. That is the law. I'd like to see a balanced budget amendment for America, to protect the American taxpayers. Then that would discipline not only the executive branch but the spending Congress, the Congress that's been in control of one party, his party, for 38 years. We almost had it done. And that institution, the House of Representatives—everyone's yelling "Clean House!" One of the reasons is we almost had it done, and the Speaker, very able, decent fellow, I might add, but he twisted the arms of some of the sponsors of that legislation and had them change their vote.

What's relevant here is that tool, that discipline that he has to live by in Arkansas. And I'd like it for the American people. I want the line-item veto. I want a check-off so if the Congress can't do it, let people check off their income tax, 10 percent of it, to compel the Government to cut spending. If they can't do it, if the Congress can't do

it, let them then have to do it across the board. That's what we call a sequester. That's the discipline we need. And I'm working for that to protect the American taxpayer against the big spenders.

Leadership

Mr. Lehrer. Mr. President, let's move to some of the leadership concerns that have been voiced about you. They relate to something you said in your closing statement in Richmond the other night about the President being the manager of crises, and that relates to an earlier criticism that you began to focus on the economy, on health care, on racial divisions in this country only after they became crises. Is that a fair criticism?

President Bush. Jim, I don't think that's a fair shot. I hear it. I hear it echoed by political opponents, but I don't think it's fair. I think we've been fighting from day one to do something about the inner cities. I'm for enterprise zones. I have had it in every single proposal I've sent to the Congress. Now we hear a lot of talk, "Oh, well, we all want enterprise zones." Yet the House and the Senate can't send it down without loading it up with a lot of these Christmas tree ornaments they put on the legislation.

I don't think in racial harmony that I'm a laggard on that. I've been speaking out since day one. We've gotten the Americans for Disabilities Act, which I think is one of the foremost pieces of civil rights legislation. And yes, it took me to veto two civil rights quota bills, because I don't believe in quotas, and I don't think the American people believe in quotas. I beat back the Congress on that, and then we passed a decent civil rights bill that offers guarantees against discrimination in employment, and that is good. I've spoken out over and over again against anti-Semitism and racism, and I think my record as a Member of Congress speaks for itself on that.

What was the other part of it?

Mr. Lehrer. Well, it's just that—you've spoken to it, I mean, but the idea—not so much in specifics——

President Bush. Yes.

Mr. Lehrer. ——but that it has to be a crisis before it gets your attention.

President Bush. I don't think that's true at all. I don't think that's true. But, you know, let others fire away on it.

Mr. Lehrer. Do you think that's true, Mr. Perot?

Mr. Perot. I'd like to just talk about issues, and so——

Mr. Lehrer. You don't think this is an issue?

Mr. Perot. Well, no. But the point is that's a subjective thing. The subjective thing is when does President Bush react. It would be very difficult for me to answer that in any short period of time.

Mr. Lehrer. Well, then, I'll phrase it differently then. He said the other night in his closing words in Richmond that one of the key things that he believes the American people should decide among the three of you, is who they want in charge if this country gets to a crisis. Now, that's what he said. And the rap on the President is that it's only crisis time that he focuses on some of these things. So my question to you—we're going to talk about you in a minute.

Mr. Perot. I thought you'd forgotten I was here. [*Laughter*]

Mr. Lehrer. No, no, no. No, no. But my question to you is—so, if you have nothing to say about it, fine. I'll go to Governor Clinton. But——

Mr. Perot. I will let the American people decide that. I would rather not critique the two candidates.

Mr. Lehrer. All right.

Governor, what do you think?

Governor Clinton. The only thing I would say about that is I think that on the economy, Mr. Bush said for a long time there was no recession and then said it would be better to do nothing than to have a compromise effort with the Congress. He really didn't have a new economic program until over 1,300 days into his Presidency and not all of his health care initiative has been presented to the Congress even now.

I think it's important to elect a President who is committed to getting this economy going again and who realizes we have to abandon trickle-down economics and put the American people first again and who will send programs to the Congress in the first 100 days to deal with the critical issues that America's crying out for leadership on:

jobs, incomes, the health care crisis, the need to control the economy. Those things deserve to be dealt with from day one. I will deal with them from day one. They will be my first priority, not my election year concerns.

Mr. Lehrer. Mr. President.

President Bush. Well, I think you're overlooking that we have had major accomplishments in the first term. But if you're talking about protecting the taxpayer against his friends in the United States Congress, go back to what it was like when you had a Democratic President and a Democratic Congress. You don't have to go back to Herbert Hoover. Go back to Jimmy Carter. Interest rates were 21 percent. Inflation was 15 percent. The "misery index," unemployment, inflation added together, it was invented by the Democrats, went right through the roof. We've cut it in half, and all you hear about is how bad things are.

You know, you remember the question, "Are you better off?" Well, is a homebuyer better off who can refinance the home because interest rates are down? Is a senior citizen better off because inflation is not wiping out their family savings? I think they are. Is the guy out of work better off? Of course he's not. But he's not going to be better off if we grow the Government, if we invest, as Governor Clinton says, invest in more Government.

You've got to free up the private sector. You've got to let small business have more incentives. For 3 months—three quarters I've been fighting, three quarters, been fighting to get the Congress to pass some incentives for small business, capital gains, investment tax allowance, credit for first-time homebuyers, and it's blocked by the Congress. Then if a little of it comes my way, they load it up with Christmas trees and tax increases. And I have to stand up in favor of the taxpayer.

Staying the Course

Mr. Lehrer. We have to talk about Ross Perot now, or he'll get me, I'm sure.

Mr. Perot, on this issue that I have raised at the very beginning and we've been talking about, which is leadership as President of the United States, the concerns—my reading of it, at least—my concerns about you, as expressed by folks in the polls and other places, it goes like this: You've got a problem with General Motors. You took over $750 million, and you left. You had a problem in the spring and summer about some personal hits that you took as a potential candidate for President of the United States, and you walked out. Does that say anything relevant to how you would function as President of the United States?

Mr. Perot. I think the General Motors thing is very relevant. I did everything I could to get General Motors to face its problems in the mid-eighties while it was still financially strong. They just wouldn't do it. Everybody now knows the terrible price they're paying by waiting until it's obvious to the brain dead that they have problems. [*Laughter*]

Now, hundreds, thousands of good, decent people, whole cities up here in this State are adversely impacted because they would not move in a timely way. Our Government is at that point now. The thing that I am in this race for is to tap the American people on the shoulder and to say to every single one of you: Fix it while we're still relatively strong. If you have a heart problem, you don't wait until the heart attack to address it.

So the General Motors experience is relevant. At the point when I could not get them to address those problems, I had created so much stress in the board, who wanted just to keep the Lawrence Welk music going, that they asked to buy my remaining shares. I sold them my remaining shares. They went their way; I went my way, because it was obvious we had a complete disagreement about what should be done with the company.

But let's take my life in perspective. Again and again on complex, difficult tasks, I have stayed the course. When I was asked by our Government to do the POW project, within a year the Vietnamese had sent people into Canada to make arrangements to have me and my family killed. And I had five small children. And my family and I decided we would stay the course, and we lived with that problem for 3 years.

Then I got into the Texans' war on drugs program, and the big-time drug dealers got

all upset. Then when I had two people imprisoned in Iran, I could have left them there. I could have rationalized it. We went over, we got them out, and we brought them back home. And since then, for years, I have lived with the burden of the Middle East, where it's eye-for-an-eye and tooth-for-a-tooth country, in terms of their unhappiness with the fact that I was successful in that effort.

Again and again and again, in the middle of the night, 2 or 3 o'clock in the morning, my Government has called me to take extraordinary steps for Americans in distress. And again and again and again, I have responded. And I didn't wilt, and I didn't quit.

Now, what happened in July we've covered again and again and again. But I think in terms of the American people's concern about my commitment—and I'm here tonight, folks. I've never quit supporting you as you put me on the ballot in the other 26 States. When you asked me to come back in, I came back in. And talk about not quitting, I'm spending my money on this campaign. The two parties are spending your money, taxpayer money. I've put my wallet on the table for you and your children. Over $60 million at least will go into this campaign to leave the American dream to you and your children, to get this country straightened out, because if anybody owes it to you, I do. I've lived the American dream. I'd like for your children to be able to live it, too.

Mr. Lehrer. Governor, do you have a response to the staying the course question about Mr. Perot?

Governor Clinton. I don't have any criticism of Mr. Perot. I think what I'd like to talk about a minute is, since you asked him the question, was the General Motors issue. I don't think there's any question that the automobile executives made some errors in the 1980's, but I also think we should look at how much productivity has increased lately, how much labor has done to increase productivity, and how much management has done. We're still losing a lot of auto jobs, in my judgment, because we don't have a national economic strategy that would build the industrial base of this country.

Just today, I met with the presidents and the vice presidents of the Willow Run union near here. They both said they were Vietnam veterans supporting me because I had an economic program that put them back to work. We need an investment incentive to modernize plant and equipment. We've got to control the health care costs for those people. Otherwise we can't keep the manufacturing jobs here. We need a tough trade policy that is fair, that insists on open markets in return for open markets. We ought to have a strategy that will build the economic and industrial base.

So I think Mr. Perot was right in questioning the management practices. But they didn't have much of a partner in Government here as compared with the policies the Germans and the Japanese followed. I believe we can do better. That's one of the things I want to change. I know that we can grow manufacturing jobs. We did it in my State, and we can do it nationally.

CAFE Standards

Mr. Lehrer. Mr. President, do you have a response?

President Bush. To this?

Mr. Lehrer. Yes.

President Bush. Well, I wondered when Governor Clinton was talking to the autoworkers whether he talked about his and Senator Gore's favoring CAFE standards, those are fuel efficiency standards, of 40 miles per gallon. That would break the auto industry and throw a lot of people out of work.

As regarding Mr. Perot, I take back something I said about him. I once said in a frivolous moment when he got out of the race, if you can't stand the heat, buy an air conditioning company. I take it back because I think he said he made a mistake. The thing I find is if I make a mistake, I admit it. I've never heard Governor Clinton make a mistake.

But one mistake he's made is fuel efficiency standards at 40 to 45 miles per gallon will throw many autoworkers out of work, and you can't have it both ways. There's a pattern here of appealing to the autoworkers and then trying to appeal to the spotted owl crowd or the extremes in the environmental movement. You can't do it as President. You can't have a pattern of one side of the issue one day and another the next.

So my argument is not with Ross Perot; it is more with Governor Clinton.

Mr. Lehrer. Governor, what about that charge that you want it both ways on this issue?

Governor Clinton. Let's just talk about the CAFE standards.

Mr. Lehrer. All right.

Governor Clinton. That's the fuel efficiency standards. They're now 27.5 miles per gallon per automobile fleet. I never said, and I defy you to find where I said—I gave an extensive environment speech in April. I said that we ought to have a goal of raising the fuel efficiency standards to 40 miles a gallon. I think that should be a goal. I never said we should write it into law if there is evidence that that goal cannot be achieved. The National Science Foundation did a study which said it would be difficult for us to reach fuel efficiency standards in excess of 37 miles per gallon by the year 2000.

I think we should try to raise the fuel efficiency. And let me say this: I think we ought to have incentives to do it. I think we ought to push to do it. That doesn't mean we have to write it into the law.

Look, I am a job creator, not a job destroyer. It is the Bush administration that has had no new jobs in the private sector in the last 4 years. In my State we're leading the country in private sector job growth. But it is good for America to improve fuel efficiency.

We also ought to convert more vehicles to compressed natural gas. That's another way to improve the environment.

NAFTA

Mr. Lehrer. Mr. Perot, based on your experience at General Motors, where do you come down on this? This has been thrown about, back and forth during this campaign from the very beginning about jobs and CAFE standards.

Mr. Perot. Well, everybody's nibbling around the edges. Let's go to the center of the bull's eye to the core problem. Believe me, everybody on the factory floor all over this country knows it. You implement that NAFTA, the Mexican trade agreement, where they pay people $1 an hour, have no health care, no retirement, no pollution controls, et cetera, et cetera, et cetera, and you're going to hear a giant sucking sound of jobs being pulled out of this country right at a time when we need the tax base to pay the debt and pay down the interest on the debt and get our house back in order. We have got to proceed very carefully on that.

See, there's a lot I don't understand. I do understand business. I do understand creating jobs. I do understand how to make things work. And I've got a long history of doing that. Now, if you want to go to the core problem that faces everybody in manufacturing in this country, it's that agreement that's about to be put into practice.

But here, very simply, everybody says it will create jobs. Yes, it will create bubble jobs. Now, watch this. Listen very carefully to this: One-time surge while we build factories and ship machine tools and equipment down there. Then year after year for decades they will have jobs. And I finally thought I didn't understand it. I called all the experts, and they said, "Oh, it will be disruptive for 12 to 15 years." We haven't got 12 days, folks. We cannot lose those jobs. They were saying Mexican jobs will eventually come to $7.50 an hour and ours will eventually go down to $7.50 an hour. It makes you feel real good to hear that, right?

Let's think it through, here. Let's be careful. I'm for free trade philosophically, but I have studied these trade agreements until the world has gone flat, and we don't have good trade agreements across the world. I hope we'll have a chance to get into that tonight, because I can get right to the center of the bull's eye and tell you why we're losing whole industries in this country. Excuse me.

Mr. Lehrer. Just for the record, though, Mr. Perot, I take it then for your answer you do not have a position on whether or not enforcing the CAFE standards will cost jobs in the auto industry.

Mr. Perot. Oh, no. It will cost jobs. But that's not—let me say this: I'd rather, if you gave me two bad choices——

Mr. Lehrer. Okay.

Mr. Perot. I'd rather have some jobs left here than just see everything head south, see?

Mr. Lehrer. So that means no—[*laughter*]—in other words, you agree with President Bush, is that right?

Mr. Perot. No, I'm saying our principal need now is to stabilize the tax base, which is the job base, and create a growing, dynamic base. Now, please, folks, if you don't hear anything else I say, remember millions of people at work are our tax base. One quick point: If you confiscate the Forbes 400 wealth, take it all, you cannot balance the budget this year. Kind of gets your head straight about where the taxes year-in and year-out have got to come from. Millions and millions of people at work.

Mr. Lehrer. I wanted—yes, sir.

President Bush. Well, I'm caught in the middle of NAFTA. Ross says, with great conviction, he opposes the North American free trade agreement. I am for the North American free trade agreement. My problem with Governor Clinton, once again, is that one time he's going to make up his mind, he will see some merit in it. But then he sees a lot of things wrong with it. And then the other day, he says he's for it; however, then we've got to pass other legislation. When you're President of the United States, you cannot have this pattern of saying, "Well, I'm for it, but I'm on the other side of it." And it's true on this, and it's true on CAFE.

Look, if Ross were right and we get a free trade agreement with Mexico, why wouldn't they have gone down there now? You have a differential in wages right now. I just have an honest philosophical difference. I think free trade is going to expand our job opportunity. I think it is exports that have saved us when we're in a global slowdown, a connected, global slowdown, a recession in some countries. It's free trade, fair trade that needs to be our hallmark, and we need more free trade agreements, not fewer.

Mr. Lehrer. Governor, a quick answer on trade, and I want to go on to something else.

Governor Clinton. I'd like to respond to that. You know, Mr. Bush was very grateful when I was among the Democrats who said he ought to have the authority to negotiate an agreement with Mexico. Neither I nor anybody else, as far as I know, agreed to give him our proxy to say that whatever he did was fine for the workers of this country and for the interests of this country.

I am the one who is in the middle on this. Mr. Perot says it's a bad deal. Mr. Bush says it's a hunky-dory deal. I say, on balance, it does more good than harm if we could get some protection for the environment so that the Mexicans have to follow their own environmental standards, their own labor law standards, and if we have a genuine commitment to reeducate and retrain the American workers who lose their jobs and reinvest in this economy.

I have a realistic approach to trade. I want more trade. I know there are some good things in that agreement, but it can sure be made better.

Let me just point out, just today in the Los Angeles Times, Clyde Prestowitz, who was one of President Reagan's leading trade advisers, and a lifelong conservative Republican, endorsed my candidacy because he knows that I'll have a free and fair trade policy, a hard-headed realistic policy, and not get caught up in rubber-stamping everything the Bush administration did. If I wanted to do that, why would I run for President, Jim? Anybody else can run the middle class down and run the economy in a ditch. I want to change it.

President Bush. I think he made my case. On the one hand, it's a good deal, but on the other hand, I'd make it better. You can't do that as President. You can't do it on the war, where he says, "Well, I was with the minority, but I guess I would have voted with the majority."

This is my point tonight: We're talking about 2 weeks from now you've got to decide who is going to be President. And there is this pattern that has plagued him in the primaries and now about trying to have it both ways on all these issues. You can't do that. If you make a mistake, say you made a mistake and go on about your business, trying to serve the American people.

Right now we heard it. Ross is against it. I am for it. He says, "On the one hand, I'm for it, and on the other hand, I may be against it."

Mr. Lehrer. Governor——

Governor Clinton. That's what's wrong with Mr. Bush. His whole deal is, you've got to be for it or against it, and you can't make it better. I believe we can be better. I think the American people are sick and tired of either-or solutions, people being pushed in the corner, polarized to extremes. I think they want somebody with common sense, who can do what's best for the American people. I'd be happy to discuss these other issues, but I can't believe he is accusing me of getting on both sides.

He said trickle-down economics was voodoo economics. Now, he's its biggest practitioner. Let me just say——

President Bush. I've always said trickle-down Government is bad.

Governor Clinton. I could run this string out a long time, but remember this, Jim: Those 209 Americans last Thursday night in Richmond told us they wanted us to stop talking about each other and start talking about Americans and their problems and their promises. I think we ought to get back to that. I'll be glad to answer any question you have, but this election ought to be about the American people.

Mr. Lehrer. Mr. Perot?

Mr. Perot. Is there an equal time rule here tonight?

President Bush. Yes.

Mr. Perot. Or do you just keep lunging in at will? I thought we were going to have equal time, but maybe I just have to interrupt the other two. Is that the way it works this——

Mr. Lehrer. No. Mr. Perot, you're doing fine. Go ahead. Whatever you want to say, say it.

Foreign Lobbyists

Mr. Perot. Now that we've talked all around the problem about free trade, let's go again to the center of the bull's eye.

Mr. Lehrer. Wait a minute. I was going to ask—I thought you wanted to respond to what we were talking about.

Mr. Perot. I do. I do. I just want to make—these foreign lobbyists, this whole thing. Our country has sold out to foreign lobbyists. We don't have free trade. Both parties have foreign lobbyists on leave in key roles in their campaigns. If there's anything more unwise than that, I don't know what it is. Every debate, I bring this up, and nobody ever addresses it.

I would like for them to look you in the eye and tell you why they have people representing foreign countries working on their campaigns. And you know, you've seen the list; I've seen the list. We won't go into the names. But no wonder they—if I had those people around me all day every day telling me it was fair and free, I might believe it. But if I look at the facts as a businessman, it's so tilted. The first thing you ought to do is just say, "Guys, if you like these deals so well, we'll give you the deal you gave us." Now, Japanese couldn't unload the cars in this country if they had the same restrictions we had, and on and on and on and on and on.

I suggest to you that the core problem—one country spent $400 million lobbying in 1988—our country. And it goes on and on. And you look at a Who's Who in these campaigns around the two candidates. They're foreign lobbyists taking leaves. What do you think they're going to do when the campaign's over? Go back to work at 30,000 bucks a month representing some other country. I don't believe that's in the American people's interest.

I don't have a one of them, and I haven't taken a penny of foreign money, and I never will.

Mr. Lehrer. Mr. President, how do you respond to that? Mr. Perot has made that charge several times, the fact that you have people working in your campaign who are paid foreign lobbyists.

President Bush. Most people that are lobbying are lobbying the Congress. I don't think there's anything wrong with an honest person who happens to represent an interest of another country for making his case. That's the American way. What you're assuming is that that makes the recipient of the lobbying corrupt or the lobbyists themselves corrupt. I don't agree with that.

But if I found somebody that had a conflict of interest that would try to illegally do something as a foreign registered lobby, the laws cover this. I don't know why—I've never understood quite why Mr. Perot was

so upset about it, because one of the guys he used to have working for him, I believe, had foreign accounts. Could be wrong, but I think so.

Mr. Perot. Soon as I found it out, he went out the door, too.

President Bush. Well, I think you've got to look at the integrity and the honor of the people that are being lobbied and those that are lobbyists. The laws protect the American taxpayer in this regard. If the laws are violated so much—but to suggest if somebody represents a foreign country on anything, that makes him corrupt or against the taxpayer, I don't agree with it.

Mr. Perot. One quick relevant specific. We're getting ready to dismantle the airlines industry in our country, and none of you know it. I doubt, in all candor, if the President knows it. But this deal that we're doing with BAC and USAir and KLM and Northwest—now, guess who is on the President's campaign big time? A guy from Northwest. This deal is terribly destructive to the U.S. airline industry. One of the largest industries in the world is the travel and tourist business. We won't be making airplanes in this country 10 years from now if we let deals like this go through.

If the press has any interest tonight, I'll detail it to you. I won't take 10 minutes tonight; all these things take a few minutes. But that's happening as we sit here today. We hammerlock the American companies, American Airlines, Delta, the last few great we have, because we're trying to do this deal with these two European companies. Never forget, they've got Airbus over there, and it's a government-owned, privately owned consortium across Europe. They're dying to get the commercial airline business. Japan is trying to get the commercial airline business. I don't think there are any villains inside Government on this issue, but there sure are a lot of people who don't understand business. And maybe you need somebody up there who understands when you're getting your pocket picked.

Mr. Lehrer. Governor, I'm sorry, but that concludes my time with——

Governor Clinton. Boy, I had a great response to that.

Mr. Lehrer. All right. Go ahead, quickly.

Just very briefly.

Governor Clinton. I think Ross is right and that we do need some more restrictions on lobbyists. We ought to make them disclose the people they've given money to when they're testifying before congressional committees. We ought to close the lawyers' loophole; they ought to have to disclose when they're really lobbying. We ought to have a much longer period of time, about 5 years, between the time when people can leave executive branch offices and then go out and start lobbying for foreign interest. I agree with that.

We've wrecked the airline industry already because there's all these leveraged buyouts and all these terrible things that have happened to the airline industry. We're going to have a hard time rebuilding it. But the real thing we've got to have is a competitive economic strategy. Look what's happening to McDonnell Douglas. Even Boeing is losing market share because we let the Europeans spend 25 to 40 billion dollars on Airbus without an appropriate competitive response.

What I want America to do is to trade more, but to compete and win by investing in competitive ways. And we're in real trouble on that.

Mr. Lehrer. I'm going to be in real trouble if I don't bring out—it's about time——

President Bush. I promise it's less than 10 seconds.

Mr. Lehrer. Okay.

President Bush. I heard Governor Clinton congratulate us on one thing. First time he said something pleasant about this administration. Productivity in this country is up. It is way up. Productivity is up, and that's a good thing. There are many other good ones, but I was glad he acknowledged that.

Mr. Perot. I've volunteered—now, look, I'm just kind of a, you know, cur dog here. I was put on the ballot by the people, not special interest, so I have to stand up for myself. Now, Jim, let me net it out. On the second debate, I offered, since both sides want the enterprise zones but can't get together, I said I'll take a few days off and go to Washington and hold hands with you, and we'll get it done. I'll take a few days off, hold hands with you, and get this airline thing straightened out, because that's im-

portant to this country.

That's kind of pathetic I have to do it, and nobody's called me yet to come up, I might mention—[*laughter*]—but if they do, if they do, it's easy to fix. If you all want the enterprise zones, why don't we pass the dang thing and do it? Right?

Mr. Lehrer. All right. Now we're going to bring in three other journalists to ask questions. They are Susan Rook of CNN, Gene Gibbons of Reuters, and Helen Thomas of United Press International.

You thought you'd never get in here, didn't you?

President Bush. Uh-oh.

Mr. Lehrer. Okay, we are going to continue on the subject of leadership, and the first question goes to Governor Clinton for a 2-minute answer. It will be asked by Helen Thomas. Helen?

The Draft Issue

Helen Thomas. Governor Clinton, your credibility has come into question because of your different responses on the Vietnam draft. If you had to do it over again, would you put on the Nation's uniform? And, if elected, could you, in good conscience, send someone to war?

Governor Clinton. If I had to do it over again, I might answer the questions a little better. You know, I had been in public life a long time and no one had ever questioned my role, and so I was asked a lot of questions about the things that happened a long time ago. I don't think I answered them as well as I could have.

Going back 23 years, I don't know, Helen. I was opposed to the war. I couldn't help that. I felt very strongly about it, and I didn't want to go at the time. It's easy to say in retrospect I would have done something differently.

President Lincoln opposed the war, and there were people who said maybe he shouldn't be President. But I think he made us a pretty good President in wartime. We've got a lot of other Presidents who didn't wear their country's uniform and had to order our young soldiers into battle, including President Wilson and President Roosevelt. So the answer is, I could do that. I wouldn't relish doing it, but I wouldn't shrink from it.

I think that the President has to be prepared to use the power of the Nation when our vital interests are threatened, when our treaty commitments are at stake, when we know that something has to be done that is in the national interest. And that is a part of being President. Could I do it? Yes, I could.

Mr. Lehrer. A reminder now, we're back on the St. Louis rules, which means that the Governor had his answer, and then each of you will have one minute to respond.

Mr. President.

President Bush. Well, I've expressed my heartfelt difference with Governor Clinton on organizing demonstrations while in a foreign land against your country when young ghetto kids have been drafted and are dying.

My argument with him on—the question was about the draft is that there is this same pattern. In New Hampshire, Senator Kerry said you ought to level, you ought to tell the truth about it. And April 17th, he said he'd bring out all the records on the draft. They have not been forthcoming. He got a deferment, or he didn't. He got a notice, or he didn't. I think it's this pattern that troubles me more than the draft. A lot of decent, honorable people felt as he did on the draft. But it is this pattern.

And again, you might be able to make amendments all the time, Governor, but as President, you can't be on all these different sides, and you can't have this pattern of saying, well, I did this, or I didn't. Then the facts come out, and you change it. That's my big difference with him on the draft. It wasn't failing to serve.

Mr. Lehrer. Your minute is up, sir.

Mr. Perot, one minute.

Mr. Perot. I've spent my whole adult life very close to the military; feel very strongly about the people who go into battle for our country; appreciate their idealism, their sacrifices; appreciate the sacrifices their families make. That's been displayed again and again in a very tangible way.

I look on this as history. I don't look on it, personally, as relevant. I consider it really a waste of time tonight when you consider the issues that face our country right now.

Mr. Lehrer. All right. The next question goes to President Bush, and Gene Gibbons will ask it.

1990 Budget Agreement

Gene Gibbons. Mr. President, you keep saying that you made a mistake in agreeing to a tax increase to get the 1990 budget deal with Congress. But if you hadn't gotten that deal you would have either had to get repeal of the Gramm-Rudman deficit control act or cut defense spending drastically at a time when the country was building up for the Gulf war and decimate domestic discretionary spending, including such things as air traffic control. If you had it to do all over again, sir, which of those alternatives would you choose?

President Bush. I wouldn't have taken any of the alternatives. I believe I made a mistake. I did it for the very reasons you say. There was one good thing that came out of that budget agreement, and that is we put a cap on discretionary spending. One-third of the President's budget is at the President's discretion, or really, the Congress', since they appropriate every dime and tell the President how to spend every dime. We've put a cap on the growth of all that spending, and that's good. And that's helped. But I was wrong because I thought the tax compromise, going along with one Democratic tax increase, would help the economy. I see no evidence that it has done it.

So what would I have done, what should I have done? I should have held out for a better deal that would have protected the taxpayer and not ended up doing what we had to do or what I thought at the time would help.

So I made a mistake. You know, the difference, I think, is that I knew at the time I was going to take a lot of political flak. I knew we'd have somebody out there yelling, "Read my lips." And I did it because I thought it was right. And I made a mistake. That's quite different than taking a position where you know it's best for you. That wasn't best for me, and I knew it in the very beginning. I thought it would be better for the country than it was. So there we are.

Mr. Lehrer. Mr. Perot, one minute.

Mr. Perot. The 101 in leadership is be

accountable for what you do. Let's go back to the tax and budget summit briefly. Nobody ever told the American people that we increased spending $1.83 for every dollar of taxes raised. That's absolutely unconscionable. Both parties carry a huge blame for that on their shoulders. This was not a way to pay on the deficit. This was a trick on the American people. That's not leadership.

Let's go back in terms of accepting responsibilities for your actions. To create Saddam Hussein over a 10-year period, using billions of dollars of U.S. taxpayer money, step up to the plate and say it was a mistake. To create Noriega using taxpayer money, step up to the plate and say it was a mistake. If you can't get your act together to pick him up one day when a Panamanian major has kidnaped him, a special forces team is 400 yards away and it's a stroll across the park to get him, and if you can't get your act together, at least pick up the Panamanian major who they then killed, step up to the plate and admit it was a mistake. That's leadership, folks.

Now, leaders will always make mistakes. And I'm not aiming at any one person here. I'm aiming at our Government. Nobody takes responsibility for anything. We've got to change that.

Mr. Lehrer. I'll take responsibility for saying your time is up.

Mr. Perot. I'm watching the light.

Mr. Lehrer. All right.

Governor Clinton, one minute, sir.

Governor Clinton. The mistake that was made was making the "read my lips" promise in the first place just to get elected, knowing what the size of the deficit was, knowing there was no plan to control health care costs, and knowing that we did not have a strategy to get real economic growth back into this economy. The choices were not good then.

I think at the time the mistake that was made was signing off on the deal late on Saturday night in the middle of the night. That's just what the President did when he vetoed the family leave act. I think what he should have done is gone before the American people on the front end and said, "Listen, I made a commitment, and it was wrong. I made a mistake because I couldn't

have foreseen these circumstances. And this is the best deal we can work out at the time."

He said it was in the public interest at the time, and most everybody who was involved in it, I guess, thought it was. The real mistake was the "read my lips" promise in the first place. You just can't promise something like that just to get elected if you know there's a good chance that circumstances may overtake you.

Mr. Lehrer. All right, Mr. Perot, the question is for you. You have a 2-minute answer, and it will be asked by Susan Rook.

Leadership

Susan Rook. Mr. Perot, you've talked about going to Washington to do what the people who run this country want you to do. But it is the President's duty to lead and often lead alone. How can you lead if you are forever seeking consensus before you act?

Mr. Perot. Let's talk about two different subjects. In order to lead, you first have to use the White House as a bully pulpit and lead. Then you have to develop consensus, or you can't get anything done. That's where we are now. We can't get anything done. How do you get anything done when you've got all of these political action committees, all of these thousands of registered lobbyists, 40,000 registered lobbyists, 23,000 special interest groups, and the list goes on and on and on, and the average citizen out here just working hard every day. You've got to go to the people. I just love the fact that everybody, particularly in the media, goes bonkers over the town hall. I guess it's because you will lose your right to tell them what to think. [*Laughter*] The point is, they'll get to decide what to think.

President Bush. Hey, you've got something there.

Mr. Perot. I love the fact that people will listen to a guy with a bad accent and a poor presentation manner talking about flip charts for 30 minutes, because they want the details. See, all the folks up there at the top said, people, "The attention span of the American people is no more than 5 minutes. They won't watch it." They're thirsty for it.

You want to have a new program in this country? If you get grassroots America excited about it and if they tap Congress on the shoulder and say, "Do it, Charlie," it will happen. That's a whole lot different from these fellows running up and down the halls whispering in their ears now and promising campaign funds for the next election if they do it.

Now, I think that's going back to where we started. That's having a Government from the people. I think that's the essence of leadership, rather than cutting deals in dark rooms in Washington.

Mr. Lehrer. Governor Clinton, one minute.

Governor Clinton. Well, I believe in the town hall meetings. They started with my campaign in New Hampshire. I think Ross Perot has done a good job in having them. And I, as you know, pushed for the debate to include 209 American citizens who were part of it in Richmond a few days ago. I've done a lot of them, and I'll continue to do them as President.

But I'd also like to point out that I haven't been part of what we're criticizing in Washington tonight. Of the three of us, I have balanced a government budget 12 times. I have offered and passed campaign finance reform; offered, pushed for, and passed in public referendum lobbyist restrictions; done the kinds of things you have to do to get legislators together, not only to establish consensus but to challenge them to change. In 12 years as Governor, I guess I've taken on every interest group there was in my State at one time or another to fight for change. It can be done. That's why I've tried to be so specific in this campaign: to have a mandate, if elected, so that Congress will know what the American people have voted for.

Mr. Lehrer. President Bush, one minute.

President Bush. I would like the record to show the panelists that Ross Perot took the first shot at the press. My favorite bumper sticker, though, is "Annoy the Media. Reelect President Bush." [*Laughter*] I just had to work that in. Sorry, Helen. I'm going to pay for this later on.

Look, you have to build a consensus, but in some things—Ross mentioned Saddam Hussein. Yes, we tried, and yes, we failed to bring him into the family of nations. He had the fourth largest army. But then when he moved against Kuwait I said, this will not stand. And it's hard to build a consensus. We went to the U.N. We made historic resolutions up there. The whole world was united. Our Congress was dragging its feet. Governor Clinton said, "Well, I might have been with the minority, let sanctions work. But I guess I would have voted with the majority."

A President can't do that. Sometimes he has to act. In this case, I'm glad we did, because if we'd have let sanctions work and had tried to build a consensus on that, Saddam Hussein today would be in Saudi Arabia controlling the world's oil supply, and he would be there maybe with a nuclear weapon. We busted the fourth largest army, and we did it through leadership.

Mr. Lehrer. All right, we're going to go on to another subject now, and the subject is priorities. And the first question goes to you, President Bush, and Susan will ask it.

Women Advisers

Ms. Rook. President Bush, gentlemen, I acknowledge that all of you have women and ethnic minorities working for you and working with you. But when we look at the circle of the key people closest to you, your inner circle of advisers, we see white men only. Why, and when will that change?

President Bush. You don't see Margaret Tutwiler sitting in there with me today?

Ms. Rook. The key people, President Bush.

President Bush. What?

Ms. Rook. The key people, the people beyond the glass ceiling.

President Bush. I happen to think she's a key person. I think our Cabinet members are key people. I think the woman that works with me, Rose Zamaria, is about as tough as a boot out there and makes some discipline and protects the taxpayer. Look at our Cabinet. You talk about somebody strong, look at Carla Hills. Look at Lynn Martin, who's fighting against this glass ceiling and doing a first-class job on it. Look at our Surgeon General, Dr. Novello. You can look all around and you'll see first-class, strong women.

Jim Baker's a man. Yes, I plead guilty to that. [*Laughter*] But look who's around with him there. I mean, this is a little defensive on your part, Susan, to be honest with you. We've got a very good record appointing women to high positions and positions of trust. And I'm not defensive at all about it.

What we've got to do is keep working, as the Labor Department is doing a first-class job on, to break down discrimination, to break down the glass ceiling. I am not apologetic at all about our record with women. You think about women in Government. I think about women in business. Why not try to help them with my small business program to build some incentives into the system?

I think we're making progress here. You've got a lot of women running for office. As I said the other night, I hope a lot of them lose, because they're liberal Democrats, and we don't need more of them in the Senate or more of them in the House. But nevertheless, they're out there. And we've got some very good Republican women running. So we're making dramatic progress.

Mr. Lehrer. Mr. Perot, one minute.

Mr. Perot. Well, I've come from the computer business, and everybody knows women are more talented than the men. So we have a long history of having a lot of talented women. One of our first officers was a woman, a chief financial officer. She was a director. And it was so far back, it was considered so odd. And even though we were a tiny little company at the time, it made all the national magazines.

But in terms of being influenced by women and being a minority, there they are right out there, my wife and my four beautiful daughters. And I just have one son. So he and I are surrounded by women telling us what to do all the time. [*Laughter*]

Iraq

For the rest of my minute, I want to make a very brief comment here in terms of Saddam Hussein. We told him that we wouldn't get involved with this border dispute, and we've never revealed those papers that were given to Ambassador Glaspie on July 25. I suggest, in the sense of taking responsibility for your actions, we lay those papers on the table. They're not the secrets to the nuclear bomb.

Secondly, we got upset when he took the whole thing, but to the ordinary American out there who doesn't know where the oilfields are in Kuwait, they're near the border. We told him he could take the northern part of Kuwait, and when he took the whole thing, we went nuts. And if we didn't tell him that, why won't we even let the Senate Foreign Relations Committee and the Senate Intelligence Committee see the written instructions for Ambassador Glaspie?

President Bush. I'd like to reply on that. That gets to the national honor. We did not say to Saddam Hussein, Ross, "You can take the northern part of Kuwait." That is absolutely absurd. Glaspie has testified——

Mr. Perot. Where are the papers?

President Bush. ——and Glaspie's papers have been presented to the United States Senate. So please——

Mr. Perot. If you have time, go through NEXIS and LEXIS, pull all the old news articles. Look at what Ambassador Glaspie said all through the fall and what have you, and then look at what she and Kelly and all the others in State said at the end when they were trying to clean it up. And talk to any head of any of those key committees in the Senate. They will not let them see the written instructions given to Ambassador Glaspie. And I suggest that in a free society owned by the people, the American people ought to know what we told Ambassador Glaspie to tell Saddam Hussein. Because we spent a lot of money and risked lives and lost lives in that effort, and did not accomplish most of our objectives. We got Kuwait back to the Amir; but he still got his nuclear, his chemical, his bacteriological, and he's still over there, right? I'd like to see those written instructions. Sorry.

Mr. Lehrer. Mr. President, when you— just make sure that everybody knows what's going on here. When you responded directly to Mr. Perot then——

President Bush. Yes.

Mr. Lehrer. ——you violated the rule, your rules. Now, I'm willing——

President Bush. I apologize. When I make

a mistake, I say—[*laughter*].

Mr. Lehrer. No, no, no. I just want to make sure that everybody understands. If you all want to change the rules, we can do it.

President Bush. No, I don't. I apologize for it. But that one got right to the national honor.

Mr. Lehrer. All right. Okay.

President Bush. And I'm sorry.

Mr. Lehrer. Okay. But Governor Clinton, you have a minute.

Women Advisers

Governor Clinton. Susan, I don't agree that there are no women and minorities in important positions in my campaign. There are many. But I think even more relevant is my record at home. For most of my time as Governor, a woman was my chief of staff, an African American was my chief cabinet officer, an African American was my chief economic development officer.

It was interesting, there was a story either today or yesterday in the Washington Post about my economic programs. My chief budget officer and my chief economic officer were both African Americans, even though the Post didn't mention that, which I think is a sign of progress. The National Women's Political Caucus gave me an award, one of their good guy awards, for my involvement of women in high levels of government. I've appointed more minorities to positions of high levels in government than all the Governors in the history of my State combined before me.

So that's what I'll do as President. I don't think we've got a person to waste. I think I owe the American people a White House staff, a Cabinet, and appointments that look like America, but that meet high standards of excellence, and that's what I'll do.

Mr. Lehrer. All right. The next question goes to you, Mr. Perot, for 2 minutes. It's a 2-minute question, and Helen will ask it. Helen?

Investigations

Ms. Thomas. Mr. Perot, what proof do you have that Saddam Hussein was told that he could have—do you have any actual proof, or are you asking for the papers? And also, I really came in with another question.

What is this penchant you have to investigate everyone? Are those accusations correct, investigating your staff, investigating the leaders of the grassroots movement, investigating associates of your family?

Mr. Perot. No, they're not correct. And if you look at my life for the first—until I got involved in this effort, I was one person. And then after the Republican dirty tricks group got through with me, I'm another person, which I consider an absolutely sick operation. And all of you in the press know exactly what I'm talking about. They investigated every single one of my children. They investigated my wife. They interviewed all my children's friends from childhood on. They went to extraordinary, sick lengths. And I just found it amusing that they would take two or three cases where I was involved in lawsuits and would engage an investigator, the lawyers would engage an investigator, which is common. And the only difference between me and any other businessman that has the range of businesses I have is I haven't had that many lawsuits.

So that's just another one of those little fruit-loopy things they make up to try to, instead of facing issues, to try to redefine a person that's running against them. This goes on night and day. I will do everything I can, if I get up there, to make dirty tricks a thing of the past. One of the two groups has raised it to an art form. It's a sick art form.

Iraq

Now, let's go back to Saddam Hussein. We gave Ambassador Glaspie written instructions. That's a fact. We've never let the Congress and these Foreign Relations—Senate Intelligence Committee see them. That's a fact.

Ambassador Glaspie did a lot of talking, right after July the 25th, and that's a fact, and it saw the newspapers. You pull all of it at once and read it, and I did, and it's pretty clear what she and Kelly and the other key guys around that thing thought they were doing.

Then, at the end of the war when they had to go testify about it, their stories are a total disconnect from what they said in

August, September, and October. So I say, this is very simple: Saddam Hussein released a tape, as you know, claiming it was a transcript of their meeting, where she said, "We will not become involved in your border dispute," and in effect, "You can take the northern part of the country."

We later said, "No, that's not true." I said, well, this is simple. What were her written instructions? We guard those like the secrets to the atomic bomb, literally. Now, I say: Whose country is this? This is ours. Who will get hurt if we lay those papers on the table? The worst thing is, again, it's a mistake. Nobody did any of this with evil intent. I just object to the fact that we cover up and hide things, whether it's Iran-*contra*, Iraqgate, or you name it. It's a steady stream.

Mr. Lehrer. Governor Clinton, you have one minute.

Governor Clinton. Let's take Mr. Bush for the moment at his word. I mean, he's right, we don't have any evidence, at least, that our Government did tell Saddam Hussein he could have that part of Kuwait. And let's give him the credit he deserves for organizing Operation Desert Storm and Desert Shield. It was a remarkable event.

But let's look at where, I think, the real mistake was made. In 1988, when the war between Iraq and Iran ended, we knew Saddam Hussein was a tyrant. We had dealt with him because he was against Iran. The enemy of my enemy maybe is my friend.

All right, the war is over. We know he's dropping mustard gas on his own people. We know he's threatened to incinerate half of Israel. Several Government Departments, several, had information that he was converting our aid to military purposes and trying to develop weapons of mass destruction. But in late '89, the President signed a secret policy saying we were going to continue to try to improve relations with him, and we sent him some sort of communication on the eve of his invasion of Kuwait that we still wanted better relations.

So I think what was wrong—I give credit where credit is due, but the responsibility was in coddling Saddam Hussein when there was no reason to do it and when people at high levels in our Government knew he was trying to do things that were outrageous.

Mr. Lehrer. Mr. President, you have a moment—a minute, I'm sorry.

President Bush. It's awful easy when you're dealing with 90/90 hindsight. We did try to bring Saddam Hussein into the family of nations. He did have the fourth largest army. All our Arab allies out there thought we ought to do just exactly that. When he crossed the line, I stood up and looked into the camera and I said, "This aggression will not stand." We formed a historic coalition, and we brought him down. We destroyed the fourth largest army, and the battlefield was searched, and there wasn't one single iota of evidence that any U.S. weapons were on that battlefield. The nuclear capability has been searched by the United Nations, and there hasn't been one single scintilla of evidence that there's any U.S. technology involved in it.

What you're seeing on all this Iraqgate is a bunch of people who were wrong on the war trying to cover their necks here and try to do a little revisionism. I cannot let that stand, because it isn't true. Yes, we had grain credits for Iraq, and there isn't any evidence that those grain credits were diverted into weaponry, none, none whatsoever. And so I just have to say it's fine. You can't say there, Governor Clinton, and say, "Well, I think I have supported the minority"—let sanctions work or wish that it would go away—"but I would have voted with the majority." Come on, that's not leadership.

Mr. Lehrer. The next question goes to Governor Clinton, and Gene Gibbons will ask it. Gene?

Banking Situation

Mr. Gibbons. Governor, an important aspect of leadership is, of course, anticipating problems. During the 1988 campaign, there was little or no mention of the savings and loan crisis that has cost the American people billions and billions of dollars. Now there are rumblings that a commercial bank crisis is on the horizon. Is there such a problem, sir? If so, how bad is it, and what will it cost to clean it up?

Governor Clinton. Gene, there is a problem in the sense that there are some problem banks. And on December 19th, new regulations will go into effect which will, in effect, give the Government the responsibility to close some banks that are not technically insolvent but that are plainly in trouble.

On the other hand, I don't think that we have any reason to believe that the dimensions of this crisis are anywhere near as great as the savings and loan crisis. The mistake that both parties made in Washington with the S&L business was deregulating them without proper capital requirements, proper oversight and regulation, proper training of the executives. Many people predicted what happened, and it was a disaster.

The banking system in this country is fundamentally sound, with some weak banks. I think that our goal ought to be, first of all, not to politicize it, not to frighten people; secondly, to say that we have to enforce the law in two ways. We don't want to overreact as the Federal regulators have, in my judgment, on good banks so that they've created credit crunches that have made our recession worse in the last couple of years, but we do want to act prudently with the banks that are in trouble.

We also want to say that, insofar as is humanly possible, the banking industry itself should pay for the cost of any bank failures, the taxpayers should not, and that will be my policy. I believe we have a good, balanced approach. We can get the good banks loaning money again in the credit crunch, have proper regulation on the ones that are in trouble, and not overreact. It is a serious problem, but I don't see it as the kind of terrible, terrible problem that the S&L problem was.

Mr. Lehrer. President Bush, one minute.

President Bush. Well, I don't believe it would be appropriate for a President to suggest that the banking system is not sound; it is sound. There are some problem banks out there. But what we need is financial reform. We need some real financial reform, banking reform legislation. I have proposed that, and when I am reelected I believe one of the first things ought to be to press a new Congress, not beholden to the old ways, to pass financial reform legislation that modernizes the banking system,

doesn't put a lot of inhibitions on it, and protects the depositors through keeping the FDIC sound. I just was watching some of the proceedings of the American Bankers Association, and I think the general feeling is most of the banks are sound. Certainly there's no comparison here between what happened to the S&L's and where the banks stand right now, in my view.

Mr. Lehrer. Mr. Perot, one minute.

Mr. Perot. Well, nobody's gotten into the real issue yet on the savings and loan. Again, nobody's got a business background, I guess. The whole problem came up in 1984. The President of the United States was told officially it was a $20 billion problem.

These crooks—now, Willie Sutton would have gone to own a savings and loan rather than rob banks. He robbed banks because that's where the money is; owning a savings and loan is where the money was.

Now, in 1984 they were told. I believe the Vice President was in charge of deregulation. Nobody touched that tar baby until the day after election in 1988, because they were flooding both parties with crooked PAC money. And it was, in many cases, stolen PAC money. Now, you and I never got a ride on a lot of these yachts and fancy things it bought, but you and I are paying for it. And they buried it until right after the election.

Now, if you believe the Washington Post and you believe this extensive study that's been done, and I'm reading it, right after election day this year they're going to hit us with 100 banks. It'll be a $100 billion problem. Now, if that's true, just tell me now. I'm grown up. I can deal with it. I'll pay my share. But just tell me now. Don't bury it until after the election twice. I say that to both political parties. The people deserve that, since we have to pick up the tab. You've got the PAC money. We'll pay the tab. Just tell us.

Mr. Lehrer. All right, Mr. Perot. The next question, we're going into a new round here on a category just called "differences." And the question goes to you, Mr. Perot, and Gene will ask it. Gene?

Government Reform

Mr. Gibbons. Mr. Perot, aside from the deficit, what Government policy or policies do you really want to do something about? What really sticks in your craw about conditions in this country, beside the deficit, that you would want to fix as President?

Mr. Perot. The debt and the deficit. Well, if you watched my television show the other night, you saw it. If you watch it Thursday, Friday, Saturday this week, you'll get more. So, a shameless plug there, Mr. President. But in a nutshell, we've got to reform our Government or we won't get anything done. We have a Government that doesn't work. All these specific examples I'm giving tonight, if you had a business like that, they'd be leading you away and boarding up the doors. We have a Government that doesn't work. It's supposed to come from the people. It comes at the people. The people need to take their Government back.

You've got to reform Congress. They've got to be servants to the people again. You've got to reform the White House. We've got to turn this thing around. It's a long list of specific items, and I've covered it again and again in print and on television. But very specifically, the key thing is to turn the Government back to the people and take it away from the special interests and have people go to Washington to serve.

Who can give themselves a 23-percent pay raise anywhere in the world except Congress? Who would have 1,200 airplanes worth $2 billion a year just to fly around in? I don't have a free reserved parking place at National Airport. Why should my servants? I don't have an indoor gymnasium and an indoor tennis court, an indoor every other thing they can think of. I don't have a place where I can go make free TV to send to my constituents to try to brainwash them to elect me the next time. And I'm paying for all that for those guys.

I'm going to be running an ad pretty soon that shows—they promised us they were going to hold the line on spending, a tax and budget summit—and I'm going to show how much they've increased this little stuff they do for themselves. It is Silly Putty, folks, and the American people have had

enough of it.

Step one, if I get up there, we're going to clean that up. You say, how can I get Congress to do that? I'll have millions of people shoulder-to-shoulder with me, and we will see it done warp speed, because it's wrong. We've turned the country upside down.

Mr. Lehrer. Governor Clinton, you have one minute. Governor.

Governor Clinton. I would just point out on the point Mr. Perot made, I agree that we need to cut spending in Congress. I've called for a 25-percent reduction in congressional staffs and expenditures. But the White House staff increased its expenditures by considerably more than Congress has in the last 4 years under the Bush administration, and Congress has actually spent $1 billion less than President Bush asked them to spend. Now, when you outspend Congress, you're really swinging.

That, however, is not my only passion. The real problem in this country is that most people are working hard and falling further behind. My passion is to pass a jobs program to get incomes up with an investment incentive program to grow jobs in the private sector, to waste less public money and invest more, to control health care costs and provide for affordable health care for all Americans, and to make sure we've got the best trained work force in the world. That is my passion.

We've got to get this country growing again and this economy strong again, or we can't bring down the deficit. Economic growth is the key to the future of this country.

Mr. Lehrer. President Bush, one minute.

President Bush. On Government reform?

Mr. Lehrer. Sir?

President Bush. Government reform?

Mr. Lehrer. Yes. Well, to respond to the subject that Mr. Perot mentioned.

President Bush. How about this for a Government reform policy? Reduce the White House staff by a third after or at the same time the Congress does the same thing for their staff; term limits for Members of the United States Congress. Give the Government back to the people. Let's do it that way. The President has term limits. Let's limit some of these guys sitting out here tonight. Term limits, and then how about a balanced budget amendment to the Constitution? Forty-three States, more than that, States have it, I believe. Let's try that.

You want to do something about all this extra spending that concerns Mr. Perot and me? Okay, how about a line-item veto? Forty-three Governors have that. Give it to the President. If the Congress isn't big enough to do it, let the President have a shot at this excess spending. A line-item veto, that means you can take a line and cut out some of the pork out of a meaningful bill. Governor Clinton keeps hitting me on vetoing legislation. Well, that's the only protection the taxpayer has against some of these reckless pork programs up there. I'd rather be able to just line it right out of there and get on about passing some good stuff, but leave out the garbage. Line-item veto, there's a good reform program for you.

Mr. Lehrer. The next question goes to Governor Clinton. You have two minutes, Governor, and Susan will ask it.

Taxes

Ms. Rook. Governor Clinton, you said that you will raise taxes on the rich, people with incomes of $200,000 a year or higher. A lot of people are saying that you will have to go lower than that, much lower. Will you make a pledge tonight below which—an income level that you will not go below? I am looking for numbers, sir, not just a concept.

Governor Clinton. You can read my plan. My plan says that we want to raise marginal incomes on family incomes above $200,000 from 31 to 36 percent; that we want to ask foreign corporations simply to pay the same percentage of taxes on their income that American corporations pay in America; that we want to use that money to provide over $100 billion in tax cuts for investment in new plant and equipment, for small business, for new technologies, and for middle class tax relief.

Now, I can tell you this: I will not raise taxes on the middle class to pay for these programs. If the money does not come in there to pay for these programs, we will cut other Government spending, or we will slow down the phase-in to the programs. I

am not going to raise taxes on the middle class to pay for these programs.

Now, furthermore, I am not going to tell you "Read my lips" on anything because I cannot foresee what emergencies might develop in this country. And the President said never, never, never would he raise taxes, in New Jersey. Within a day, Marlin Fitzwater, his spokesman, said, now, that's not a promise. So I think even he has learned that you can't say "Read my lips" because you can't know what emergencies might come up.

But I can tell you this: I'm not going to raise taxes on middle class Americans to pay for the programs I've recommended. Read my plan. And you know how you can trust me about that? Because you know, in the first debate, Mr. Bush made some news. He had just said Jim Baker was going to be Secretary of State, but in the first debate he said no, now he's going to be responsible for domestic economic policy. Well, I'll tell you, I'll make some news in the third debate: The person responsible for domestic economic policy in my administration will be Bill Clinton. I'm going to make those decisions, and I won't raise taxes in the middle class to pay for my program.

Mr. Lehrer. President Bush, you have one minute.

President Bush. That's what worries me, that he's going to be responsible. He would do for the United States what he has done for Arkansas. He would do for the United States what he's done to Arkansas. We do not want to be the lowest of the low. We are not a nation in decline. We are a rising nation. My problem is, I heard what he said. He said, "I want to take it from the rich, raise $150 billion from the rich." To get it, to get $150 billion in new taxes, you've got to go down to the guy that's making $36,600. And if you want to pay for the rest of his plan, all the other spending programs, you're going to sock it to the working man.

So when you hear "tax the rich," Mr. and Mrs. America, watch your wallet. Lock your wallet, because he's coming right after you just like Jimmy Carter did, and just like you're going to get—you're going to end up with interest rates at 21 percent, and you're going to have inflation going through the roof. Yes, we're having tough times. But we do not need to go back to the failed policies of the past when you had a Democratic President and a spendthrift Democratic Congress.

Mr. Lehrer. Mr. Perot.

Governor Clinton. You permitted Mr. Bush to break the rules, he said to defend the honor of the country. What about the honor of my State? We rank first in the country in job growth. We've got the lowest spending, State and local, in the country and the second lowest tax burden. The difference between Arkansas and the United States is that we're going in the right direction, and this country's going in the wrong direction. And I have to defend the honor of my State.

Mr. Lehrer. We've got a wash, according to my calculations. We have a wash. And we'll go to Mr. Perot for one minute. In other words, the violation of the rule; that's what I meant.

Mr. Perot. I'm the only one that's untarnished at this point.

Mr. Lehrer. That's right, you're clean. [*Laughter*]

Mr. Perot. I'm sure I'll do it before it's over.

The key thing here, see, we all come up with images. Images don't fix anything. You know, I'm starting to understand it. You stay around this long enough, you think about—if you talk about it in Washington, you think you did it. If you've been on television about it, you think you did it. [*Laughter*] What we need is people to stop talking and start doing.

Now, our real problem here is they both have plans that will not work. The Wall Street Journal said your numbers don't add up. And you can take it out on charts; you look at all the studies that different groups have done; you go out 4, 5, 6 years: We're still drifting along with a huge deficit.

So let's come back to harsh reality. Everybody said, "Gee, Perot, you're tough." I say, well, this is not as tough as World War II; and it's not as tough as the Revolution. It's fair-shared sacrifice to do the right thing for our country and for our children. And it will be fun if we all work together to do it.

Mr. Lehrer. This is the last question, and it goes to President Bush for a 2-minute answer. And it will be asked by Helen.

Presidential Campaign

Ms. Thomas. Mr. President, why have you dropped so dramatically in the leadership polls, from the high eighties to the forties? And you have said you will do anything you have to do to get reelected. What can you do in 2 weeks to win reelection?

President Bush. Well, I think the answer to why the drop, I think, has been the economy in the doldrums. Why I'll win is I think I have the best plan of the three of us up here to do something about it. Mine does not grow the Government. It does not have Government invest. It says we need to do better in terms of stimulating private business. We've got a big philosophical difference here tonight between one who thinks the Government can do all these things through tax and spend, and one who thinks it ought to go the other way.

So I believe the answer is, I'm going to win it because I'm getting into focus my agenda for America's renewal, and also I think that Governor Clinton's had pretty much of a free ride on looking specifically at the Arkansas record. He keeps criticizing us, criticizing me; I'm the incumbent. Fine. But he's an incumbent. And we've got to look at all the facts. They're almost at the bottom on every single category. We can't do that to the American people.

Then, Helen, I really believe where people are going to ask this question about trust—because I do think there's a pattern by Governor Clinton of saying one thing to please one group and then trying to please another group. I think that pattern is a dangerous thing to suggest would work for the Oval Office. It doesn't work that way when you're President. Truman is right: The buck stops there. You have to make decisions, even when it's against your own interest. I've done that. It's against my political interests to say go ahead and go along with the tax increase. But I did what I thought was right at the time. So I think people are going to be looking for trust and experience.

Then, I mentioned it the other night, I think if there's a crisis, people are going to say, "Well, George Bush has taken us through some tough crises, and we trust him to do that." So I'll make the appeal on a wide array of issues.

Also I've got a philosophical difference—I've got to watch the clock here—I don't think we're a declining nation. The whole world has had economic problems. We're doing better than a lot of the countries in the world. And we're going to lead the way out of this economic recession across this world and economic slowdown here at home.

Mr. Lehrer. Mr. Perot, you have one minute.

President Bush. That's why I think I'll win.

Mr. Lehrer. Mr. Perot, you have—sorry. Excuse me, sir. Mr. Perot, you have one minute.

Mr. Perot. I'm the last one, right?

Mr. Lehrer. No. Governor Clinton has a minute after you. Then we have the closing statements.

Mr. Perot. One minute after you?

Mr. Lehrer. Right.

Mr. Perot. I'm totally focused on the fact that we may have bank failures, and nobody answered it. I'm totally focused on that fact that we are still evading the issue of the Glaspie papers. I'm totally focused on the fact that we still could have enterprise zones, according to both parties, but we don't. So I'm still focused on gridlock, I guess.

I'm also focused on the fact that isn't it a paradox that we have the highest productivity in our work force in the industrialized world and at the same time have the largest trade deficit, and at the same time rank behind nine other nations in what we pay our most productive people in the world. We're losing whole industries overseas. Now, can't somebody agree with me that the Government is breaking business' legs with these trade agreements? They're breaking business' legs in a number of different ways. We have an adversarial relationship that's destroying jobs and sending them overseas, while we have the finest workers in the world. Keep in mind the factory worker has nothing to do with anything except putting it together on the factory floor. It's our obligation to make sure that we give him the finest products in the

world to put together, and we don't break his legs in the process.

Mr. Lehrer. Governor Clinton, one minute.

Governor Clinton. I really can't believe Mr. Bush is still trying to make trust an issue after "read my lips" and "15 billion new jobs" and embracing what he called "voodoo economics" and embracing an export enhancing program for farmers he threatened to veto and going all around the country giving out money and programs that he once opposed. But the main thing is he still didn't get it, from what he said the other night to that fine woman on our program, the 209 people in Richmond. They don't want us talking about each other. They want us to talk about the problems of this country.

I don't think he'll be reelected because trickle-down economics is a failure, and he's offering more of it. And what he's saying about my program is just not true. Look at the Republicans that have endorsed me, high-tech executives in northern California. Look at the 24 generals and admirals, retired, who have endorsed me, including the deputy commander of Desert Storm. Look at Sarah Brady, Jim Brady's wife, President Reagan's Press Secretary, who endorsed me because he knuckled under to the NRA and wouldn't fight for the Brady bill. We've got a broad-based coalition that goes beyond party, because I am going to change this country and make it better with the help of the American people.

Mr. Lehrer. All right. That was the final question and answer, and we now go to the closing statements. Each candidate will have up to 2 minutes. The order was determined by a drawing. Governor Clinton, you are first. Governor.

Closing Statements

Governor Clinton. First I'd like to thank the Commission and my opponents for participating in these debates and making them possible. I think the real winners of the debates were the American people. I was especially moved in Richmond a few days ago when 209 of our fellow citizens got to ask us questions. They went a long way toward reclaiming this election for the

American people and taking their country back.

I want to say, since this is the last time I'll be on a platform with my opponents, that even though I disagree with Mr. Perot on how fast we can reduce the deficit and how much we can increase taxes on the middle class, I really respect what he's done in this campaign to bring the issue of deficit reduction to our attention. I'd like to say to Mr. Bush, even though I've got profound differences with him, I do honor his service to our country. I appreciate his efforts, and I wish him well. I just believe it's time to change.

I offer a new approach. It's not trickle-down economics; it's been tried for 12 years, and it's failed. More people are working harder for less, 100,000 people a month losing their health insurance, unemployment going up, our economy slowing down. We can do better. And it's not tax-and-spend economics. It's invest and grow, put our people first, control health care costs and provide basic health care to all Americans, have an education system second to none, and revitalize the private economy. That is my commitment to you. It is a kind of change that can open up a whole new world of opportunities to America as we enter the last decade of this century and move toward the 21st century. I want a country where people who work hard and play by the rules are rewarded, not punished. I want a country where people are coming together across the lines of race and region and income. I know we can do better.

It won't take miracles, and it won't happen overnight. But we can do much, much better if we have the courage to change. Thank you very much.

Mr. Lehrer. President Bush, your closing statement, sir.

President Bush. Three weeks from now—two weeks from tomorrow, America goes to the polls. You're going to have to decide who you want to lead this country to economic recovery. On jobs, that's the number one priority, and I believe my program for stimulating investment, encouraging small business, brandnew approach to education, strengthening the American family, and yes, creating more exports is the way to go.

I don't believe in trickle-down Government. I don't believe in larger taxes and larger Government spending.

On foreign affairs, some think it's irrelevant. I believe it's not. We're living in an interconnected world. The whole world is having economic difficulties. The U.S. is doing better than a lot. But we've got to do even better. If a crisis comes up, I ask: Who has the judgment and the experience and, yes, the character to make the right decision?

Lastly, the other night on character, Governor Clinton said it's not the character of the President but "the character of the Presidency." I couldn't disagree more. Horace Greeley said, "The only thing that endures is character." And I think it was Justice Black who talked about "Great nations, like great men, must keep their word." And so the question is: Who will safeguard this Nation? Who will safeguard our people and our children?

I need your support. I ask for your vote. And may God bless the United States of America.

Mr. Lehrer. Mr. Perot, your closing statement, sir.

Mr. Perot. To the millions of fine, decent people who did the unthinkable and took their country back in their own hands and put me on the ballot, let me pledge to you that tonight is just the beginning. These next 2 weeks we will be going full steam ahead to make sure that you get a voice and that you get your country back.

This Thursday night on ABC from 8:30 to 9, Friday night on NBC from 8 to 8:30, and Saturday night on CBS from 8 to 8:30, we'll be down in the trenches, under the hood, working on fixing the old car to get it back on the road. [*Laughter*]

Now, the question is: Can we win? Absolutely we can win, because it's your country. The question really is: Who do you want in to the White House? It's that simple. Now, you've got to stop letting these people tell you who to vote for. You've got to stop letting these folks in the press tell you you're throwing your vote away. You've got to start using your own head.

Then the question is: Can we govern? I

love that one. The "we" is you and me. You bet your hat we can govern, because we will be in there together, and we will figure out what to do. You won't tolerate gridlock. You won't tolerate endless meandering and wandering around. You won't tolerate nonperformance. And believe me, anybody who knows me understands I have a very low tolerance for nonperformance also. Together we can get anything done.

The President mentioned that you need the right person in a crisis. Well, folks, we've got one. And that crisis is a financial crisis. Pretty simply, who's the best qualified person up here on the stage to create jobs? Make your decision and vote on November the 3d. I suggest you might consider somebody who's created jobs.

Second, who's the best person to manage money? I suggest you pick a person who's successfully managed money. Who's the best person to get results and not talk? Look at the record; make your decision.

Finally, who would you give your pension fund and your savings account to to manage? And the last one, who would you ask to be the trustee of your estate and take care of your children if something happened to you?

Finally, to you students up there, God bless you. I'm doing this for you. I want you to have the American dream. And to the American people, to the American people, I'm doing this because I love you. That's it. Thank you very much.

Mr. Lehrer. Thank you, Mr. Perot. Thank you, Mr. President. Thank you, Governor Clinton, for being with us tonight and the previous debates. Thank you to the panel.

The only thing that is left to be said is, from Michigan State University in East Lansing, I'm Jim Lehrer. Thank you, and good night.

Note: The debate began at 7 p.m. in Wharton Center for the Performing Arts at Michigan State University. During the debate, the following persons were referred to: Rose M. Zamaria, Deputy Assistant to the President and Director of White House Operations; April C. Glaspie, former U.S. Ambassador to Iraq; and John H. Kelly, former Assistant Secretary of State for Near Eastern and South Asian Affairs.

Remarks at a Post-Debate Rally in Lansing, Michigan
October 19, 1992

The President. Thank you very much.

Audience members. Four more years! Four more years! Four more years!

The President. What a fantastic rally. Thank you all very, very much. Thank you for this great Lansing welcome.

May I first thank Mel McDaniel; and of course, another old friend, Fred Travalena; and Wynonna Judd, a great friend of the Bush family. We're delighted that she is here. Many thanks.

Anybody watch the debate? I believe we won, but I believe we won because our ideas are right for America, and Governor Clinton is wrong for America. And I think the American people know that the Presidency is a position of trust. I believe character is important.

Let me say how pleased I am and pleased at our campaign. This State is headed by one of the truly great Governors, John Engler, with us today. I am very very lucky. I watched how he did it. The polls had him down, and he fought back, and he won for Michigan. We're going to do exactly the same thing. We're going to do it.

Our Lieutenant Governor is here somewhere, Connie Binsfeld; the chairman of our party, Dave Doyle, right here in Michigan; and our national committee people, Chuck Yobb and Betsy Devost. We've got a first-class political team, and that's why we're going to win.

One point I made tonight, and I feel strongly in my heart about it, being President, is that the next President is going to have to stand up against the special interests in that big-spending Congress. And I believe I'm the one to do that. You cannot be all things to all people, try to keep every single group—you've got to call them as you see them, as the umpires do in the World Series. I have done it, and I believe that's why the American people will put their trust in me.

And yes, you had to stand for principle. You heard the revisionists out there tonight trying to make something of it. But I looked into the camera and told the American people that Saddam Hussein's aggression will not stand, and it didn't stand.

I really believe that tonight——

Audience members. We want Bush! We want Bush! We want Bush!

The President. I believe that right here, right here at this rally, the first post-debate event, we are starting to move. We are going to close this thing up, and we're going to win it on November 3d.

I'm going to stay out on the road. A while back I said I'll do what it takes to win, and I mean I'm going to outhustle this guy, outwork him. I'll take my message to the American people. Let him talk about making Government bigger. I want to get that deficit down by getting rid of some of this taxation and getting rid of some of this Government spending.

I loved it when I told the American taxpayer—tomorrow, listen, you'll hear the last—just a few hours ago, you hear them talk about tax the rich. You cab drivers, you beauticians, you schoolteachers, watch your purse. They're going to come right after you. We cannot let that happen to the American people.

With all respect, with all respect, I had a lot of fun when I reminded some of the media about that bumper sticker, "Annoy the Media." "Annoy the Media. Reelect

George Bush." I probably shouldn't have done it. You know, they always have the last word. But, gosh, that was fun. [*Laughter*]

Well, I have never lost confidence. I have always been convinced, because of our record and because of my belief in America as a rising nation, that we would win this election. And tonight I'm never more certain of it.

That Clinton-Gore ticket would make the Carter years look like a bonanza. We cannot go back to the tax-and-spend years: interest rates up at 21 percent and inflation up through the roof, every senior citizen getting wiped out, the "misery index" going through Gore's ozone hole up there someplace. We're not going to go back. We're going to go forward, because we are America. And my confidence is with the American worker, not with the big Government. Besides that, we've got the best First Lady in the world, and we'd better keep her there.

So thank you. All I ask now is that you take this enthusiasm, do what the Governor tells you: Get to the polls. Get our message of hope and opportunity and power to the people, out to the voters of Michigan. We will win this State, and we will win the national election.

Thank you. And may God bless the United States of America. Thank you very much.

Note: The President spoke at 9:35 p.m. at the Lansing Civic Center. In his remarks, he referred to entertainers Mel McDaniel, Fred Travalena, and Wynonna Judd. A tape was not available for verification of the content of these remarks.

Question-and-Answer Session in Atlanta, Georgia
October 20, 1992

Mr. Nigut. We want to welcome everyone to our town hall meeting, "Ask George Bush." Mr. President, we're delighted that you could be with us in Georgia this evening. We have, as you know, an audi-

ence of 33 people who say they are still undecided voters. Just before you came into the studio I asked them to tell me, after last night's debate, how many were still undecided. Most of them raised their hand, said they're still trying to make up their mind. So this is your opportunity to address their questions.

The President. That sounds like a reasonable deal. They all look relatively sane and— [*laughter*].

The Economy

Mr. Nigut. Let me start, to get the ball rolling, and then turn immediately to questions from the audience—ask you a quick question. Coming out of the debates last night, there are some people who say that the campaign schedules today say a lot about how these last 2 weeks of the campaign is playing out. Your opponent Governor Clinton is off campaigning in States that at this stage of the campaign typically would no longer be vulnerable to a Democratic candidate, but they feel they are. You've come south where many people feel you should have been able to build your base a long time ago.

The last poll that we conducted with the Atlanta Journal Constitution suggests that this is a very tight race here, but that your job approval rating has been high in Georgia. Thirty-three percent of the core Republicans said they're not particularly pleased with your job. Have you in some way let them down? And if you have, how do you get them back in these final 2 weeks?

The President. I think the major problem has been the economy. And we're going to get them back because I think people are going to decide when they go into that voting booth on trust, on proven leadership. I think character is important. And then I think people are going to, in the final analysis, compare economic approaches. I just don't happen to think we need to tax people more and spend more. So I've got to get that in focus.

But look, it's not just the United States, the whole world has been through a tough economic time. This will come as a surprise, perhaps, but we're an interconnected world, and we're leading most of the European economies, the great European economies. Our growth rate is twice what Japan's is. Yet I hear everybody comparing, talking about how great Japan is, and we ought to do better. Of course, we ought to do better.

But we're going to lead the way out of what's been an economic slowdown.

I think the economy has been the major problem for the working men and women in this country, for the unemployed. I believe that our proposals, the agenda for America's renewal, is what's going to change it and make it better.

Mr. Nigut. Well, I promised that I would ask very few questions and give the audience most opportunities. A number of people wanted to ask questions based on last night's debate. These people all watched the debate last night, so I wanted to first turn to a few people who said they had specific followups to last night.

Would you please stand up? You started to talk before about a couple of questions that were lingering after the debate last night.

Iraq

Q. Well, I think that Mr. President has made it an issue of the character and judgment of one of his challengers, and Mr. Perot last night challenged him and was very adamant about maybe his character or judgment. I would like him to respond to the allegations of quote, unquote, Iraqgate or the Glaspie papers. He said that you were dealing with Saddam Hussein, helped build him up and gave him the opportunity to move into Kuwait.

The President. I heard what he said. He also strongly opposed the war, and he said that we had not leveled with the American people on the Glaspie—that was Ambassador Glaspie. Let me tell you something. Every single paper, including Secretary of State's notes, which is unprecedented, was taken up to the United States Congress and looked at in detail. And after the event, Secretary Baker went and explained that to Mr. Perot, who said he hadn't known that.

So I hope that one is cleared up, because you had congressional hearing after congressional hearing. My position on Iraq was we did try to make Saddam Hussein into somebody a little more sane. You know, when the war in Iran and Iraq ended, Saddam Hussein had the fourth largest army. Our Arab friends were saying, "Try to bring him along. We don't need a radical in our midst. Try to help him." We had letters, incidentally, from many of the people now critical on trying to sell American grain to Iraq, including the two Senators from Arkansas: "Please sell grain to Iraq on credit."

Mr. Nigut. Is this an issue that still concerns you?

The President. Can I just finish?

Mr. Nigut. Yes, I'm sorry.

The President. Because what happened is he then refused to come along and do what we encouraged him to do. And we knocked his socks off, thanks to the sons and daughters of Georgia who did what most Americans do: When called, they served, and they served with great distinction. It was a proud moment, and people are now trying to revise it and make it something it's not.

Mr. Nigut. Are you satisfied? You still have some lingering question?

The Character Issue

Q. Well, no. In the second debate I think that the audience participants tried to keep the character and judgment issue out of the room.

The President. Well, may I respond? Do you think character is not important?

Q. No, I do think it's important, Mr. President.

The President. But they did try to keep it out of the room, and it belongs on the front page. A President must have character. You know, the way I described it last night, Clinton said it's not the character of the President but "of the Presidency." That is absolutely ridiculous. I am judged on my character every single day. Every President must be judged on that. And so must he be judged on his character, and so must Mr. Perot. Character is vital. It is essential, because you have to have the trust of the whole world when you're President, or lack thereof.

So I'm not going to let some guy stand up and say what I can talk about or what I can't. I happen to think that every schoolchild ought to think their President has a certain degree of character. Maybe Mr. Clinton's got it; maybe Mr. Perot's got it. But certainly it belongs as a matter for discussion.

Mr. Nigut. Let's move on to another question. We talked to some people in here earlier and most of them said their decision now is between you and Governor Clinton. But a few said they still like Ross Perot, and you were one of them. What did you want to ask the President today?

Domestic Airline Industry

Q. Mr. President, my question is twofold. It involves the airline industry. I would like to know why it appears that we are being so cooperative with foreign airlines and we've abandoned the weaker carriers of the United States. One, specifically in the past involving the demise of Eastern Airlines, why did you defy the recommendation of the National Mediation Board to form a Presidential emergency board to address this transportation crisis? And secondly, specifically in the present, why are you promoting policies which appear to give foreign airlines nearly total freedom to invest and operate within the United States with little or nothing in exchange for the United States airlines?

The President. Tell me about the mediation board. Remind me of what that was, would you?

Q. It had to do with investigating Lorenzo's actions involving the bankruptcy of Eastern Airlines.

The President. I'll tell you what my philosophy is on these matters. As much as possible, it is to let these disputes be handled by private sector. I don't believe the Government ought to get in at all times. The one that Mr. Perot was hitting out about last night was an attempt for the British Airways to purchase USAir. You've got a major dispute raging. The USAir employees everyplace you go are holding up picket signs, not picket signs but saying, "Hey, protect my job. Let the merger go through." And then you've got the other airlines like Delta, outstanding airline headquartered right here, American Airlines saying, "Wait a minute. It's not fair to let British come in here under USAir and then not let us have access to the British market."

Mr. Nigut. Of course, Eastern Airlines' bankruptcy and the decision not to allow mediators to come in was of enormous concern here in the Atlanta area because we have some 5,000 Eastern employees who lost their jobs.

The President. Sure it is. But my point—I was getting to the point. The point is, all USAir employees are saying, "Let British take over," and all Delta Airline people are saying, "Don't do it." This one has to be resolved by Government because of the routing and all of that. It's being negotiated now, and I'm not hiding behind this. But it would be most inappropriate for the President to take a position on it while the Department of Transportation is handling it. It will come to me. Everything does. And then you have to say, "I'm for this," or against it.

But on the other one, I just don't believe that the Government ought to intervene in all of these things.

Mr. Nigut. All right, thank you, sir.

The President. That's a big difference we've got on some of this philosophy.

Mr. Nigut. Thank you, sir.

The economy everyone identifies as a crucial issue. Does someone in the group want to ask an economic question of the President right now? Who has something they want to——

Improper Display of Canadian Flag

The President. I want a baseball question, if I could.

Mr. Nigut. We do have, actually——

The President. Only because I've got a serious thing I want to say.

Mr. Nigut. Go ahead. We're calling on you because the President mentions baseball. You've got your Braves T-shirt on. You get special treatment here today.

The President. You don't have to ask baseball, but I just want to use this program, Bill, if I can to say something about the flag situation. Maybe I could do it before; then you'd be unfettered by my trying to define what you should ask about.

But here's the thing on the Canadian flag inadvertently flown upside down. If that had happened in Canada and we'd have seen the United States flag flown upside down, every American would have been very, very upset. This was a mistake. Certainly, nobody would ever do anything like that on purpose.

So what I wanted to use your program for is to say how badly I feel about it, how badly all the American people feel about it, how much we value our friendship with Canada. They are our strongest trading partner in the whole world, and we would do nothing to hurt the national pride of Canada. So, on behalf of all Americans, I simply wanted to apologize to the people of Canada and suggest we try to keep this now, from now on, out of the marvelous baseball rivalry between Atlanta and Toronto. And that's all I want to say.

Mr. Nigut. How are you going to feel tonight? We are likely to see—they're planning on flying a lot of American flags upside down tonight in Toronto. How are you going to feel if you see that?

The President. Well, I won't like it, because when you see the American flag flown upside down, as a person that served in the Armed Forces and fought for my country, I would find that inappropriate. I guess I'd have to say I understand the passions of the Canadians, but I would simply ask them to have the same respect for the American flag that all Americans have for their flag, and recognize, as I said last night, if you make a mistake, whatever it is, hey, say, "I made a mistake," and get on about the Nation's business.

But I use this because the Prime Minister of Canada is a wonderful man. He's a friend to the United States, and he gets pounded in Canada for his friendship. Don't mistake it; he's pro-Canadian. I suspect he's rooting hard for Toronto. But I just wanted him to know how strongly Americans feel. End this discussion now, please.

Social Security

Q. I'm a lunchroom lady, and this is something—I'm really very privileged. How many times do we get that opportunity, you know, us little folks down here? But I am concerned about Social Security. I'm about, well, a little less than 20 years away from it, but I'm concerned about if I'm going to have it when I get up there. And I have a 2-week-old granddaughter that, in 62 years—I know that's a long time, but she's going to be there, too, someday. I want to know that we have that available to us when we're ready for it.

The President. First place, I think you'll remember that I'm the President that said in the State of the Union Message, don't mess with Social Security, don't touch it. Last night, perhaps inadvertently, Governor Clinton said something about those that take out more than they put in ought to do something about it. He may have misspoken, so I want to be fair about that. That's messing with Social Security. Ross Perot has proposed some kind of tax on Social Security. We ought not to mess with it.

It was fixed in a bipartisan agreement under the Reagan administration, I think in '83 or '84, in there. It is solvent well into the—way after the turn of the century, up until about 2030 or something like that. If it needs further adjustments then, it should be fixed then. You'll still be alive, but I don't think I'll be around wrestling with the problem in the year 2030. And we ought not to fool around with it.

In my budget plan, this Agenda for American Renewal, I say we've got to control the growth of these mandatory programs, but set Social Security aside. It's not a welfare program. It originally was to be a supplement to people's incomes. It's sacrosanct.

So I think you can tell your daughter that the system is sound, and if it's not sound when she gets up there, my age, it will be made sound. But the big thing for now is, don't fool around with it, leave it separate as we try to control the growth of other spending programs.

Mr. Nigut. All right, Mr. President. We have a question over here, please.

Urban Initiatives

Q. I would like to know—as you already know, the black people of this Nation and the black African-American people feel that we have been made a mockery of and that our issues are not being faced. We have not been addressed, and we have not had the proper opportunities that we should have in this country. We would, at this time, like to know specifically what you plan to do in order to get our vote this time around. After 12 years of being in office, what do you plan to do this time around to prove to us that you are capable of being our leader

in this next 4 years?

The President. That's a good question. I'm delighted that you're undecided, because so many are traditionally taken for granted by one party. They'll vote the straight lever on the other side and be had by local officials and by the United States Congress.

We've got a good urban program. I don't know if you're talking about urban America. But if you're talking about urban America, the best thing for minority Americans is to bring the jobs into urban America. And we've got this program called enterprise zones. Now we're getting a lot of lip service from the Democrats, but they've been unwilling to pass it. They control the Senate, and they control the House, and they've controlled them both for 38 years.

Enterprise zones says, look, give a tax break to businesses, make it worth their while to come into the urban centers and create jobs. I think our anticrime program benefits minority families more than others because some of those areas are the ones that are most afflicted by bad crime statistics. I think that homeownership is a far better concept than these big public tenements where the residents don't have the pride. I think tenant management, which we have pioneered, is a much better answer to urban hopelessness than having some Government official trying to run the places where people live.

So all of these things, in my view, would raise the quality of life for people. It's not just for minorities, but I think it would disproportionately help the minorities. We've really got a good urban program.

Mr. Nigut. I apologize, sir. We have to pause for a break, and we'll be back with you in just a moment.

[*At this point, the television station took a commercial break.*]

Mr. Nigut. We're back with our town hall forum with George Bush, President of the United States. We want to get right back to questions. Go ahead.

Mortgage Loan Discrimination

Q. My question is about homeownership. My wife and I hope to become homeowners in the near future and therefore favor the tax credit to the first-time homebuyer. My question is, how can we as minorities be assured of this tax credit if we can't get equal lending from our banking community?

The President. First place, the first-time homebuyer should be thrilled about my proposal. The way it works is you give a $5,000 credit to the family that's never owned a home before, for the first time. It is hung up, regrettably, in the Democratic Congress. They will not pass it. And it is the best possible thing that you could do.

Obviously, the credit that you need to buy on the home has to come from your own full faith in credit, your own standing. But this is a major break for homeowners, and besides that, it would stimulate the economy. Along with building homes goes a lot of other industries that outfit the houses and refrigerators and furniture. And so it really is essential. I'm not sure I fully answered your question, but your credit—this won't help your borrowing. It will help it that you have $5,000 less you'll have to come up with. But it's really stimulative for the housing industry.

Is that it? Did I get to it fully?

Mr. Nigut. I'm sorry. I'm going to walk right in front of the camera to get you here on that.

Q. Well, you touched on it. I'm talking about a couple of weeks ago our local paper ran an article where blacks and other minorities are being discriminated against on the lending, from the lending community. I think it's 18 percent or so, being denied. And the credit standing wasn't one of the biggest issues for denial.

The President. Well, the credit standing should be the only issue for denial. I mean, if you have discrimination against anybody in housing or in loaning, that is against the law, and it must not continue.

Mr. Nigut. What are you suggesting we do? Any ideas—how we enforce——

The President. Well, I'd go right to the local officials here and get something done about it. You're looking at a man who, as a Congressman from Texas, voted for open housing. My view was if you've got kids dying—coming out of the ghettos—in Vietnam—they ought not to come back and find that they couldn't live where they

wanted to live. So I'm a fair housing person.

You're talking about something that is already against the law, where people discriminate against, lenders, because of their race is what I think you're saying. That is purely against existing Federal law. You ought to go get it enforced by the local law enforcement people and, if they're violating a Federal law, by the Federal law enforcement.

Tax Credit for First-Time Homebuyers

Mr. Nigut. A quick followup on what you've made a big issue out of it in the campaign, and that's your break, your tax credit, for first-time homebuyers. How much does it cost, and how do we pay for it?

The President. It costs very little because it stimulates the whole industry, and when you get industry stimulated you have much more jobs. Frankly, I think it would be income-productive, because housing is going to lead the way out of this slowdown, in some areas, recession. So there is some good news——

Mr. Nigut. But you acknowledge that initially we take a pretty big chunk of income tax——

The President. Not that big. I can't give you the exact figure, but it's not enormous, and it will be far more offset by growth. Housing sales, incidentally, were up yesterday. I don't know; I didn't hear that on the top of the news last night. It may have been in there somewhere, but it's very difficult to get any good news out. That's good news for America.

Mr. Nigut. Let me turn to another question.

The Economy

Q. Four years ago, I voted for you, and I was a freshman in college. And now it's 4 years later, and I just graduated. I've worked really hard in school, and I was looking forward to entering the job market. But I'm very undecided about the whole economic issue, and I'm already discouraged before I've even started. What is your economic plan to have someone offer me who's just entering the job market?

The President. You're caught up in what

has been a global recession. It's not just the United States. I'll take my share of the blame for the United States. I'm not going to take all of it because I think there's a lot of fault as to how things can be better. But this agenda for Americans' renewal that puts emphasis on investment is job-creating. I mentioned the homebuyers tax credit. I might talk about an investment tax allowance; it would stimulate job creation. You know I'm for the capital gains reduction. And the opposition—except I think Mr. Perot may be for it—but the opposition says this is a tax break for the rich. It is not. It is to stimulate entrepreneurship, the creation of new businesses.

So I would suggest that the best answer to the economic recovery which is needed are these incentives that I've proposed as recently as January of this year, all hung up by a Congress that has to win by having things bad. I wouldn't be sitting here probably if the economy was growing at 3.5 or 4 percent, and it's not. But I think these incentives that I proposed are the way to make the economy grow.

Herein I have a big difference with Governor Clinton. He says, "grow the economy," get the Government to use what he calls investment. Government investment does not create the kind of job that you're looking for. It creates bureaucracy.

Mr. Nigut. Have you made a decision at least tentatively about which of the three Presidential candidates you believe has the kind of programs that will make sure you'll find good work down the road?

Q. Well, like I said before, I voted for the President 4 years ago. So to begin with, I was leaning toward him, but now I've gone back and forth just because of the different economic plans. I'm just not sure.

The President. Let me throw in another selling point. [*Laughter*] Four years ago you were a college freshman. Did you ever worry about nuclear war back then? Did you? You worry less about it now. But most kids that vintage, 4 years ago, would share the same fear of nuclear war that their parents had. We've changed all that.

All I ask is to be judged on the whole record, and I really think that's dramatic. Forty-three more countries are free and democratic, since I've become President,

around the world. You've got ancient enemies talking to themselves. That may not affect the job market, but it does affect the climate in which we're going to grow and create opportunity.

Again, I get back to—last night I had this big argument with him about exports. Exports are going to save the job market. They're the only thing that saved it in this slow growth or in a recession.

Health Care

Mr. Nigut. Mr. President, we have a voter here who is very concerned about health care and who has said frankly that he has been a supporter of yours in the past but needs to hear more from you about the whole issue of health care before he makes up his mind.

Q. I think the American people understand your ability as a leader and to lead us in international affairs. I think we understand that that's really second to none, and we appreciate the job that you've done in the last 4 years. We also believe, I think, that if you understand us and our domestic problems as well as you understand the international affairs, that you will do as good a job here as you've done internationally. The question is, have you lost touch with America? Have you lost touch with us?

My case in point is health care. When you have a monopoly such as the health care system, and I do mean monopoly because you have pills that cost, for 20 pills they cost $500. That's monopoly because without that this person is not going to survive. What do you do about the inequities in the health care system? You want a cap——

Mr. Nigut. [*Inaudible*]—I understand your concern, and you're asking a terrific question. But if we could give the President a chance to respond.

Q. Basically, it's the inequities in the health care system that are there. I can't afford health care in 5 years with the way it's going up. As a middle class person it will be out of sight. I've had a doctor say we can't do an operation for a loved one because I didn't have enough insurance. What's going to happen to the rest of us if middle class America is being squeezed?

The President. That's a very good question. Let me tell you, you know why some of the doctors say that, or why the doctors say you've got to have five tests instead of one? Because they're afraid of being sued. They're afraid of these malicious lawsuits. Part of my health reform plan is to put a cap on these malicious lawsuits.

The trial lawyers have a very powerful lobby. And you go look up where the contributions come from. People talk about lobbies and power groups; the trial lawyers are solidly behind Governor Clinton. He refuses to do anything about malpractice. And you're right, $25 billion to $50 billion in additional costs come from malpractice.

Now, that's part of the answer. But that's why the doctors are telling you this. Some of them give up practicing medicine. Some people give up coaching Little League because they're afraid of being sued. Some people see a wreck along the highway, and they want to stop and help their fellow man, and they say, "I'm not going to do it because I read about a lawsuit that wiped out a guy like me. I moved his head, and the next thing, he dies, and I'm sued for trying to be a good Samaritan."

Mr. Nigut. Are you convinced that eliminating frivolous lawsuits, or allegedly frivolous lawsuits, are the first big step, or is the problem much larger than that?

Q. I don't think that's the issue. I don't think the people——

The President. I thought you asked about the doctors.

Q. No, I agree that that should be taken care of, but I don't believe the person at the lower income that needs just basic health care is being addressed by attacking the lawsuit issue. They're just worried that——

The President. Well, let me finish then. I got cut off.

Mr. Nigut. Let's let him respond.

The President. I think we have the best health care reform plan. What it does, it provides vouchers to the poorest of the poor. There are a lot of people, 40, 38 million people that have no insurance. It provides insurance to the poorest of the poor. For the middle income, it provides tax credits and breaks, so it's the equivalent of a sustenance there to help you buy insurance. It keeps the Government out of it.

My big argument with Government and Clinton, he wants another Government board to set prices. Anytime you have Government intervention in the market, prices go up. So I believe our health care plan—and I hate guys that say, have you read my speech or looked at my program, and then make you read 30 pages—take a look at it because it does address itself to these ever-increasing costs.

Mr. Nigut. Mr. President, thank you. We've got to take another quick break, and we'll be back after this.

[*At this point, the television station took a commercial break.*]

Mr. Nigut. We're back with more questions for the President. We talked a little about health care before the break and we have a followup question.

Q. I think all of your proposals for access to health care are great, but we need money now for preventative care. Our funding for AZT ran out this year, and we need money to get into the neighborhoods and teach prenatal care so that we don't have the expensive burdens on the other end. I want to ask how you can help us with that.

The President. Well, I would only refer you to the fact that money from the Federal Government for health care has increased dramatically. The problem you have is you don't have unlimited resources. Take AIDS funding on research, for example. We've doubled, in the last 4 years, the Federal participation in research and treatment and all of this. We're up to $4.9 billion, 10 times as much for AIDS victims as per cancer victim, what the Federal Government can do. We're operating at these enormous deficits. And so, I'd like to sit here and say, the Federal Government can solve this problem, or the Federal Government can solve the problems of urban America by spending more. I don't believe we can do it.

I think the best thing the Federal Government can do is to continue to be as compassionate as possible on funding for health care. It's way up, believe me; just look at the numbers. But it's got to be done as much as possible by participation of others also. We cannot do it and then say, "Well, I'm going to get the deficit down." You can't be taxed much more.

So the President is faced with the problem: How do you help these hospitals for the indigent, and yet, how do you protect the taxpayer's wallet. I've concluded that we've got about the right balance for what we can do right now.

Mr. Nigut. What do we spend at a Grady hospital on a baby who is born prematurely because of a lack of prenatal care?

Q. As much as $100,000 in a year.

Mr. Nigut. So the question, of course, is, are you robbing Peter to pay Paul on this?

The President. I don't get the question.

Mr. Nigut. In the sense that, without prenatal care and spending for prenatal care, you end up getting bigger bills down the road?

The President. Spending for prenatal care—my point is—it's up by the Federal Government. My point is, I don't believe anybody can say the Federal Government alone can solve the problems of prenatal care. We've got a great Secretary of HHS. He comes right from Atlanta, Lou Sullivan, one of the outstanding medical people. He was head of Morehouse College here. I think he's reached about as good a sensitive balance in terms of support for programs like this as he can do, if he is restricted on the funds.

We're operating at such big deficits. I don't like to sound hopeless, but I say we have increased support for all of these things. Somebody's got to be responsible to the taxpayer or to the young woman who is trying to get a job, and they all interact. So I hope we can help more.

Mr. Nigut. All right. We'll try to get a few more questions.

Family Values

Q. I'm a divorced father, and I support four children. During your campaign, you've allowed the Vice President and others to make family values a political issue. I just wondered why you did that. And if you could go back, since you're running a distant second now in the polls, if you could go back, would you change that as being an issue?

The President. Oh, no. No. I think family values is critical. Now, if you're talking about am I trying to define that a one-parent family is no good and two-parent families are perfect, that's not the case. I'm talking about when Mayor Bradley of Los Angeles came to see me, along with other mayors, he said the major concern of urban decay is the decline of family values. He was talking about discipline. He was talking about respect. He was talking about helping people to learn. He was talking about respect for law enforcement. He was talking about strengthening the family through choice, or I'm talking about it, in child care or schools.

So please, I wouldn't go back because I believe family is important. When Barbara reads to these children, she's trying to say, "Hey, parents ought to read to kids." When you talk about discipline, Federal Government can't do that. But respect for the law is a family value, respect for your parents.

So I'm glad you gave me a chance to clear it up because nobody is saying single parents are wrong. My respect for you, supporting four kids is great. My respect for the father that runs away from the mother and leaves her to do it without any support has—I think that's disgraceful. So we're trying to pass laws to reform the welfare system, and I'm glad you gave me a chance to clear it up.

Mr. Nigut. Very quickly—I want to get other people in, but you're shaking your head.

Black Americans

Q. I still don't believe that the issue that I presented to you was answered. I mean, I——

The President. What is your question again, ma'am?

Q. ——but I still think you should let us know what can you do to make us believe that you are qualified to be a black Afro-American people President?

The President. Well, I thought I just told you that the best thing to do is to bring jobs and hope to the inner city, to do things different, and to get some people in the Congress that agree with me instead of trying to perpetuate the hopelessness that's brought to bear on some of these neighborhoods.

I think welfare reform is important. I believe making people learn and work when they're on welfare is important. Now, you may disagree with me. But I think dependency on welfare is terrible. Give people a better break in education. Give them a better break in health care. But then let everybody else pitch in and be part of the American dream. I think we're doing tremendous amounts in terms of helping people, and I want to make it so people can help themselves more.

Now, I've told you housing programs and all of this. But maybe we just disagree. But I'd say to black Americans, don't be taken for granted all the time. Don't vote that straight lever and go right down the way your predecessors did, and then wake up in despair. Try something different.

Mr. Nigut. I'm sorry, another question if we can.

School Choice

Q. My statement and question is about education. Seeing that some middle class taxpayers are actually saving the government State and Federal money by making great sacrifices, like my husband and I to send our daughter to private school, could it be possible for some of us that we work so hard to give our children a good education, get a tax break, such as a rebate in school taxes?

Mr. Nigut. I think you've just been served up a home run pitch here, Mr. President. [*Laughter.*]

The President. Well, I have.

Forty-six percent of the public school-teachers in Chicago send their kids to private school. I have a big difference with Governor Clinton on this one. I believe, and our "GI bill" for kids suggests, if it worked for the GI bill for people coming after World War II—the Government said, here's the money, to the family, to the soldiers, and you go to the school of your choice, private, public, or religious. And the State schools got better if they weren't chosen. Public schools, exactly the same thing: Give the parents a voucher, if they go to public school or private school, or religious school. And that then starts, as it has in Milwaukee, competition. And the schools not chosen, the public schools are getting better. There's a black woman up there named Polly Williams, a big, strong Democrat, and she thinks that her kid was maligned by the public school system. She was given, under their program, choice. She sent that kid to a private school, and now he's a high attainer. The school that wasn't chosen is doing much better because they have to compete. So we've got the program for you.

Q. As far as my question goes, I don't think I quite get—what I was asking is, we, as middle class taxpayers trying to make a sacrifice to send our daughter to private school. It's a misconception that people seem to think that everybody that sends their children to private school is well off or rich, and we are not. My question was, is it possible that in the future you will have a program that will look at us, at middle class Americans trying to work hard——

The President. Our program gives you a break. Our program gives you a break so you can get assistance in sending your—to the school of your choice. School choice, religious, private, public, that's what I favor, and you're just exactly the guy that would benefit from our program. Help me get it through the Congress.

Mr. Nigut. Well, we have so many people, Mr. President, who would like to still ask you questions. Their hands are in the air, but unfortunately, we've come to the end of our time. So what I want to do is finish by saying, thank you very much. We are truly delighted you could be with us tonight.

The President. It's like the last inning. I love baseball. Played it; love it. Remember the last inning of the Braves game when everybody went to the exits, and the Braves knocked it out of the park. Now they're in the World Series. Great pride. That's exactly what's going to happen in this election. So stay tuned.

Mr. Nigut. Last 2 weeks, we'll watch you carefully. Thank you, sir, very much. And thanks to our audience for all their wonderful questions.

Note: The question-and-answer session was

taped at 10:02 a.m. at the WSB–TV studios for evening broadcast. WSB–TV newsman Bill Nigut served as moderator for the session.

Remarks on Beginning a Whistlestop Tour in Norcross, Georgia
October 20, 1992

The President. What a great Georgia day. Thank you for that great welcome. It is great to be in the land of the free and the home of the Braves. Thank you all very much.

You know, everywhere I go I see signs that say "Clean House!" We need more Members of Congress like Newt Gingrich. And I'm delighted to have been introduced by him. So send us more like Newt and also, while we're at it, let's clean Senate and elect Paul Coverdell to the United States Senate.

I am very proud to have at my side today the Governor of South Carolina, Carroll Campbell, one of the outstanding Governors in the entire United States. I'm glad he's here, and of course, my friend and supporter in the Senate, Strom Thurmond. I'll tell you, he does a great job for this country. May I thank Brooks Coleman, our master of ceremonies. And may I salute the world's best First Lady, Barbara Bush. I'm proud she's out here today.

Audience members: Barbara! Barbara! Barbara!

The President. And I like all these signs around here. I referred to that one the other night, last night in the debate. I love it. And we're going to show them on November 3d exactly how it works.

You know, baseball is like politics. So forget about all these polls. Forget people telling you how you think. On election day, on election day we're going to show America that it ain't over until Cabrera swings, and that is exactly the way it's going to be.

Anybody out here see the debate last night?

Audience members. Yes.

The President. The thing I like about it is we had a chance to lay out the differences, the choice for the American people: a vast difference between experience, a vast difference on philosophy, and a vast difference

on character and confidence in the United States. I hope I stand for all four, and I challenge my opponent on all four.

You know, there was one scary moment in that debate last night, and that's when Governor Clinton said that he would do for America what he's done for Arkansas. You talk about a real threat.

Audience members. Boo-o-o!

The President. Here he is, running with Mr. Ozone, Senator Gore, and Arkansas is 50th in the environmental initiatives; 49th in high school dropouts; 45th in overall well-being of children; 75 percent of the kids that graduate from high school have to get remedial reading, remedial education when they go to college; and their income and their jobs and their wages lag the Nation. We cannot let him do for the United States what he's already done to Arkansas.

I've got to admit, I agreed with the feisty little guy from Dallas on one thing, when he said the grocery store is no preparation for Wal-Mart. I thought that was a pretty good line. Let me put it in baseball terms: The Little League ain't any preparation for the Atlanta Braves, either.

You know, we had a chance to talk about the economy. And yes, we've been going through some tough times, but what we don't need is a dose of lousy medicine. He wants to raise taxes by $150 billion and increase spending by $220 billion.

Audience members. Boo-o-o!

The President. And we cannot let him do that to the United States.

Audience members. Boo-o-o!

The President. And you know who's going to pay it. He says, "I'm going to sock the rich." That won't get him any money at all. What he's going to do is sock it to the cab driver and the nurse and the beautician and the housewife. I will protect against all these tax increases that Clinton wants to load on you, the taxpayer.

You know, I've got a difference in philosophy. I think that we're taxing too much and spending too much. He wants to tax more and spend more. Do not let this happen to the United States of America.

I believe in a State like Georgia one of the things that's going to save us and lead the recovery is more exports, more free and fair trade. I will continue to fight to expand our exports, because we have the best workers, the best products anywhere in the world. Let them have competition in foreign markets, and we will create more American jobs.

Another big difference—I can't even remember whether I mentioned it last night; I think I did—is the difference I have with him on legal reform. I want to reform our legal system and stop these crazy lawsuits. We've gone too far. Doctors are afraid to practice medicine; Little League guys are afraid to coach; somebody along the highway sees a victim, and they're afraid to stop because if they move the body a little bit to bring comfort, somebody's going to sue them for doing the wrong thing. We sue each other too much and care for each other too little in this country. And we've got to change that.

You saw the differences last night on education. I want to give parents the right to choose their schools, public, private, or religious. Give the middle class a break. Give the middle class a little relief.

Health care: He wants to put a Government board in there. I want to reform health care and make insurance available to all, the poorest of the poor, give the middle class a break on it. Keep the Government out of the health care business, and let's compete and make our health care the best and most affordable in the entire world.

Very candidly, we've got a big difference on crime. I was delighted the other day when the FOP, the Fraternal Police Officers came up to Washington from Little Rock, Arkansas, and that police group endorsed me for President of the United States. They did it because I agree with Strom Thurmond, who is fighting for tough anticrime legislation. We need to support the police officers more and have a little less sympathy for the criminals themselves.

I am for reforming Government. I am with Newt Gingrich and Strom Thurmond because I want a balanced budget amendment to the Constitution. I want a line-item veto. I want to give you, the people, a taxpayer check-off so we must compel the Congress to get this Federal deficit down. And I want to give the Congress back to the people by having term limits up there, too—there are term limits on the President—term limits for the Members of Congress.

Lastly, I made a distinction last night. Governor Clinton said in Richmond, it's not the character of the President that counts, it's "the character of the Presidency." I repeat today, especially to the young people, these two are inseparable. These two are inseparable. You cannot flip-flop on the issues every single time. One day you said you told the full truth on your sorry draft record, and the next day it comes out you haven't.

On Desert Storm, that was a proud moment for the sons and daughters of Georgia. Governor Clinton said, "Well, I probably was with the minority," or "I supported the minority, but I probably would have voted with the majority." You cannot waffle. You cannot turn the White House into the waffle house.

It is his pattern. It is his pattern of trying to be all things to all people. You simply cannot have a pattern of deception. You cannot separate the character of the Presidency from the character of the President. I have tried to be a faithful custodian of the trust you have placed in me. Barbara and I have tried to protect and revere the White House, where we are privileged to live, and I will do that for 4 more years.

Audience members. Four more years! Four more years! Four more years!

The President. You cannot literally flip-flop on all these issues and lead. You cannot lead by misleading. You can't say one day, "Well, I think Toronto is great, but I'm for the Braves." You've got to take a position. I am for the Braves, courageously.

My last point is simply this: The opposition would have you believe that the United States is a nation in decline. Governor Clinton said, well, we're something less than, paraphrasing, we're something less than Germany, but a little better than Sri Lanka. Let me tell him something. We are the best, the fairest, the most decent, and the strongest country on the face of the Earth.

And yes, our economy needs fixing, but we're caught up in something global. We're in an interdependent world. Our economy, in spite of its ailment, is doing better than Germany and Japan and England and France. With our leadership and our agenda for America's renewal, we are going to lead our way to economic recovery around the entire world, meaning jobs for the American worker.

Thank you for this fantastic turnout, and don't let him say we are second class. We are the United States, the freest, fairest, greatest nation on the face of the Earth. And I need your support, and I ask for your vote. Thank you all, and God bless you.

Note: The President spoke at 12:15 p.m. beside the Spirit of America train.

Remarks to the Community in Gainesville, Georgia
October 20, 1992

The President. Thank you, Dow Williams. And thank you, Gainesville. What a fantastic rally. I am grateful to you, and it makes me think we are going to win this election.

Let me just say how pleased I am to be accompanied on this trip by two of America's greats: Governor Campbell, the Governor of South Carolina, and Senator Strom Thurmond, the great United States Senator. And you know, everyplace I go I see signs that say, "Clean House!" Let me say let's also clean Senate and send Paul Coverdell to the United States Senate.

May I thank Dow Williams, who's our master of ceremonies, and everybody responsible for this fantastic rally. And let me say this: One left me in Norcross. I expect I will see her in the White House Thursday night, but I am very proud of our First Lady, Barbara Bush, who sends you her very best.

It is great to be in the land of the free and the home of the Braves. You know—you got it. This is what we're going to do to Governor Clinton, Clinton-Gore. You know, baseball's exactly like politics. So you forget about all these crazy polls. Don't let these newscasters tell you what's happening or how to vote. On election day we're going to show America it ain't over 'til Cabrera swings, and that's exactly the way it's going to be.

Anybody see that debate last night? Well, it seems to me we had a chance to lay out the difference before the American people. I was talking about a difference in experience, a difference in philosophy, and, yes, a difference in character. And I think all three of those things matter.

The scariest moment of that debate was when Governor Clinton said he wanted to do for the United States what he's done to Arkansas. That scares me. We cannot have that. I hate to ruin a beautiful rally on a sunny day in Gainesville, but let me tell you something: Arkansas is the 50th out of 50 States in environmental initiatives; 49th in high school diplomas; 45th in well-being of children; and incomes and jobs and wages lag the entire Nation. We do not need that for the greatest country on the face of the Earth.

Audience members. Four more years! Four more years! Four more years!

The President. I thought——

Audience members. Four more years! Four more years! Four more years!

The President. Four more!

You know, I agreed with one thing that Ross Perot said. He said, the grocery store is no preparation for Wal-Mart, and I think he's right. This is the big leagues. You can't have it both ways on every issue. You've got to say what you think, admit your mistakes, and lead and not waffle. I am that kind of a leader, and the other man is the waffler.

I had a chance to point out last night—he didn't like it a bit—that Governor Clinton has already said he wants to raise your taxes by $150 billion. He wants to spend——

Audience members. Boo-o-o!

The President. I'm sorry. He wants to spend $220 billion. He says he'll take it all from the rich. All you cab drivers, all you nurses, all you boys club workers, all you watch out, because he's coming right after your wallet, coming right after it. We are not going to let him tax the American people anymore.

He wants trickle-down Government. We do not need bigger Government in Washington, DC. We need to control that growth in spending, give the over-taxed taxpayer a little relief, and get this deficit down. That is my program.

Georgia is a great export State. We create a lot of export jobs here. I think exports are going to lead our way to a new prosperity for the entire world. Let's not go back to protection. Let's open up those foreign markets to Georgia's goods. Our American workers can outproduce any workers, any part of the world. We are the best.

Everybody here knows this, but it is small business that creates the new jobs. Two-thirds of the new jobs come from small businesses. And the small businesses need relief from taxation, regulation, litigation. Clinton would sock the taxpayer with more. I say no, lighten up on small business, and let them create jobs.

Last night, I can't remember whether we talked about it in the debate, but one big difference I have with this man is he doesn't care about these lawsuits. My view is we are suing each other too much and caring for each other too little. We ought to do something about these crazy lawsuits. We spend over $200 billion a year on lawyers, and that's too much. We've got some darn good ones, and I hope they're here. But we've got to put a cap on these crazy lawsuits.

Last night, we showed a big difference on education. We've got a lot of kids here. I think it's time to give the parents the choice and the help to send their kids to the schools they want, public, private, or religious. I think it's time we have a new health care system that makes insurance available to the poorest of the poor, gives the middle class a tax break, but does not turn it over to the Federal Government. The Federal Government can't run the post office too well, and we ought to do better in health care.

On crime, I've got a fundamental difference with the Governor, because I believe we ought to be a little more sympathetic to the victims of crime and a little less sympathetic to the criminals themselves. In Arkansas, prisoners spend 20 percent of their term in jail. In the Federal system it is 85. We do not need to be more lenient; we need to back up the families and the law enforcement officers and bring law and order back to our communities.

You know, one of the best visits I've had as President of the United States is when a group of young men from the Fraternal Order of Police came to see me, and they were from Little Rock, Arkansas, endorsing me for President of the United States.

Last night, we talked about reforming Government. I do believe we need to get this deficit down, and here's three ways to do it: Give me what many of the Governors have. Give me a balanced budget amendment, and make this Congress save money. Give me a line-item veto. Forty-three Governors have it. Let the President draw a line through those wasteful programs. Congress can't do it. Give me the chance.

I want a check-off on the tax returns so if a person says, "I'm concerned about the deficit," they can check off 10 percent of their tax they send to the Government, and then the Congress and the President must reduce the deficit by that much. Discipline the Federal Government.

One other idea where I have a big difference with the status quo and with Governor Clinton and Mr. Gore is I believe that we ought to have term limits on the Members of the United States Congress.

I do believe character counts. We're talking about the Presidency. We are talking about who is privileged and honored to serve in that hallowed White House. Character counts, and I don't believe you can flip-flop on every issue.

Governor Clinton is on one side of the war. He was saying, "Well, I agree with the minority, but I guess I would have voted for the majority." When you're President, you've got to make a tough decision. We did it, and Georgia's sons and daughters behaved with honor, and we kicked Saddam Hussein all the way out of Kuwait. And we restored the honor of the United States.

Audience members. Four more years! Four more years! Four more years!

The President. My objection——

Audience members. Four more years! Four more years! Four more years!

The President. Four more!

My concern about Governor Clinton is there is a pattern of deception. It flip-flops. It's on the right-to-work laws. It's on free trade. It was on the war itself. It was on term limits. You cannot be all things to all people. You can't say one day, "Well, I'm for the Blue Jays, but maybe I'll be for the Atlanta Braves." I'm for the Braves, and that's the way it is.

Listen, you guys——

[*At this point, the audience chanted the Braves cheer.*]

The President. Wasn't that great? You know, I'll make one serious comment here that transcends politics. But I know all Georgians, everyone in the United States was upset when we saw the Canada flag inadvertently, by mistake—everyone's human—make an error, and their flag was flown upside down. This morning I apologized to the people of Canada. They understand. They are our friends and our allies. They have respect for our flag, and we have respect for theirs. They are great people, and I hope they come in second in the World Series.

In conclusion, let me say this: In the Richmond debate—maybe some of you had to suffer through that one—Governor Clinton said it's not the character of the President, it's "the character of the Presidency." And I said, no, you can't separate the two. When I see these kids out here, I am more determined than ever not only to serve with honor, not only to show compassion and concern for the people of this country but to enact the programs that are going to help the young people and lead them to a new prosperity and a new hope.

We have literally changed the world. These kids go to bed at night without the same fear of nuclear war that their mothers and their dads and their older brothers and their sisters had. That is dramatic change. And because of our leadership we are, indeed, the most respected nation in the world. Now help me take that same leadership and lift up the American people, because our best days are ahead. We are the United States.

May God bless the United States of America. Thank you all very, very much. What a great rally. Thank you.

Audience members. Four more years! Four more years! Four more years!

The President. Thank you so much. Thank you all. Great rally. Thank you, Gainesville. Thank you, Georgia. Thank you, the United States of America. We are going to win this election. Thank you so much. All aboard!

Note: The President spoke at 2:25 p.m. on the observation deck of the Spirit of America train.

Remarks to the Community in Cornelia, Georgia
October 20, 1992

The President. Thank you all very much. Thank you. Four more! Thank you all very, very much. Thank you for this great Cornelia, Georgia, welcome. It's a beautiful day in Georgia, and it's a bright day for the United States. We are going to win this election.

You know, all across the country I see signs, "Clean House!" I'd like to see a new Congressman in Washington, Dan Becker. But while we're talking about it, while we're talking about it, let's do something great. Let's clean Senate and send Paul Coverdell to the United States Senate.

I was so pleased to be accompanied on

this trip by one of the truly great American public figures, Senator Strom Thurmond of South Carolina. What a great American he is. And also proud to have at my side in this campaign, as in the last, one of the great young, upcoming Governors of the country, Governor Carroll Campbell of South Carolina.

And may I thank Russ Spangler for arranging all of this, being our master of ceremonies. And let me say this: I am sorry that she's not with us—she was in Norcross and is now off in another State—but I think in Barbara Bush we have the best First Lady in a long, long time. She sends her love. She sends her love. And let me put it this way: It's great to be in the land of the free and the home of the Braves. Chop 'em.

Forget all these polls. Forget them. We are going to win on election day. We're going to show America it ain't over 'til Cabrera swings. And by the way, I'll make a confession. I don't like—I don't watch them anymore—I don't like these Sunday morning inside-the-beltway talk shows emanating from Washington. I'm going to sic Rick Flair on some of those talking heads. I'm glad he's here with us today, great American sports figure and a wonderful guy.

Now, I've got to ask you a question: Did anyone see the debate last night? Well, it seems to me we had a good, clean shot to go right into the living rooms across Georgia and across the United States and to lay out a choice for the American people, a vast difference in experience, a vast difference in the philosophy, and a vast difference in character among those who want to be President. A scary moment in the debate came when Governor Clinton said, "I want to do for America what I've done to Arkansas." We can't let that happen.

Audience members. Boo-o-o!

The President. Hey, listen, we've got a lovely day out here. But let me just click off a few statistics. I don't want to sound like Governor Clinton, but I've got a few statistics of my own. Fiftieth, here's Arkansas for you, 50th in environment initiatives; 49th in schools, students with high school diplomas; 45th in the overall well-being of children; income, jobs, wages lag the entire Nation. We must not let him do to us what he has done to Arkansas.

My feisty little friend from Texas, Ross Perot, had one thing right. He said the grocery store is no preparation for Wal-Mart. Well, I think the man's on to something.

But you know, on the economy, we've had a tough time. We're caught up in a global slowdown, in some areas, a global recession. Governor Clinton talks about the United States being less than Germany and more than Sri Lanka. He ought to open his eyes. We are still, in spite of our problems, the envy of the world. What I want to do is help America jobs recover. The way not to do that is do what Clinton wants. He wants to raise your taxes by $150 billion and spend $220 billion more just for openers out of Washington, DC, and we cannot let him do that to the American people.

He says, "Oh, let's let the rich guys pay it." There aren't enough of them. There are not enough Ross Perots out there. The middle class is going to have to pay. So do not elect somebody that starts out of the box saying, "I want to raise your taxes, and I want to increase spending."

It is my belief that Government taxes too much and spends too much. Help me right-size the Congress, right-size the Federal executive branch, and right-size the Government. With the new Members of Congress coming there, we are going to be able to sit down with them and change things and protect the taxpayer and the young people of this country.

I want to create more jobs. Exports have saved us. We have the most productive workers in the entire world, and I want to see us create more jobs in this country that will sell more competitively abroad. We can do it, and I believe we will.

We've got to reform our health care system. I think it's a crying shame that doctors don't dare deliver babies because they're afraid of a lawsuit. Or some of you guys won't coach Little League because you're worried some nutty parent's going to sue you, or some lawyer will get ahold of them. Or you pass an automobile accident on the street, and you're afraid to stop and help somebody because you're afraid a lawyer will come along, get the family of the victim to sue you. We can't do that. We've got to sue each other less and care for each other more. I need your help to make that change in this country.

The hope of the country is the young people here. The hope of the country are the Raiders. And we ought to give them the best possible education. That's why I favor school choice for parents, public, private, or religious schools. Help the parents strengthen the American family. The liberals don't like it when I talk about family values, but let me tell you something: When you come here to the State of Georgia, I think the Nation understands what I mean. We need to strengthen the American family through choice, teaching discipline, respect for the law enforcement officers. Help me strengthen the American family. And one way you do that is by getting better, tougher anticrime legislation.

Let me tell you this: In Arkansas, people go to jail, and they spend 20 percent of their term in jail. Under the Federal law, it's 85 percent. Let's pass some laws that have a little more concern for the police officers and the victims of crime and a little less for the criminals.

You know, one of the great meetings—I have been privileged to be your President and have a lot of fascinating meetings in that marvelous Oval Office—one of the very best was when I met with eight men from Little Rock, Arkansas, the other day. Grassroots, they could be the neighbors of everybody here in Cornelia. They came and said, "We are for you." And they were the Fraternal Order of Police of Little Rock, Arkansas. That says something about who's going to support the law enforcement.

Now, give me your help in this next term in reforming the Government. Give me a balanced budget amendment. Make us live within our means. Give me a check-off that says every taxpayer can check up to 10 percent of his tax returns to go to lowering the deficit, and make the Congress adjust. If they won't, cut it across the board. Give the people the power. And give me those line-item vetoes so I can cut out the pork and protect you, the taxpayer. While we're at it, I'd like to see term limits for the United States Congress. They've been around there too long. The Presidency's term is limited. Let's give the Congress back to the people by limiting those terms.

You know, I had a chance last night in the debate to point it out, but Governor Clinton in the Richmond debate said it's not the character of the President, it is "the character of the Presidency." Let me tell you something. They are inseparable. They are locked. Barbara and I have tried to be good stewards and custodian of the American dream and of that precious White House. And we have exemplified, I hope, enough courage and enough statesmanship to merit the trust of the American people.

But character is important, and you cannot in that Oval Office be all things to all people. You go forward, and if you make a mistake, you say, "Hey, listen, I was wrong about that one." But you keep on going, serving the people. Governor Clinton tries to be on every side of every issue, and you cannot have that as President of the United States.

I am very proud of the courage and backing I got from Georgia when I had the toughest decision of my life to make, and that is whether you send somebody else's son or daughter to fight for this country. I fought for my country, and that helped. But I'll say to you as President, it is not an easy decision. And Georgia backed me. The people here did.

But Governor Clinton said, "Well, I agreed with the minority"—meaning let sanctions work and all of that; let's not commit ourselves—"but on the other hand, I would have voted with the majority." You cannot waffle as President of the United States of America. If he were a baseball fan he'd say, "Well, I'm for the Blue Jays. But then, on the other hand, I may be for the Braves." I'm for the Braves, taking a firm commitment here. Give it to 'em. [*Applause*] You're right.

Let me say this: It's like Harry—remember Harry Truman? They'd say, "Give 'em hell, Harry." And he said, "Look, I just tell the truth, and they think it's hell." I just tell the truth, and he thinks it's hell.

You know, I believe we're going to win this election. I'm absolutely confident in my heart of hearts. Don't believe these crazy polls. Don't believe these nutty pollsters. Don't let these guys tell you what you think. You have a debate, you see what you think. And then 2 seconds later some crackpot comes on and tells you what you think. We don't need that in the United States. They don't like it, but that's the truth.

Audience members. Four more years! Four more years! Four more years!

The President. Four more! That's what we need to get this job done.

Audience members. Four more years! Four more years! Four more years!

The President. Let me tell you something. You know, these days have been some difficult times. I've been blessed. You saw one of my sons here and my twin granddaughters here. And like a lot of people in this audience, I've been blessed by strong family, a wonderful wife to back you up when the going is tough. I want to serve 4 more years because I really want to help people.

I think we've got the best answer in health care. I think we've got the best answer in education. And there's another reason: I don't believe for one single minute that this Nation is a nation in decline. I've served; I understand the world. We're caught in something international

here, and it is the United States of America that is going to lead the way to better lives for our people here, but also for a better world. And I want to continue this job.

I am grateful that these high school kids here go to bed at night without the same fear of nuclear war that their older brothers and their sisters had. And that happened under my Presidency.

So don't let people try to get into the White House by telling everything that is wrong with this great country. We are the greatest, the fairest, the best nation on the face of the Earth. And may God bless our country.

And thank you for this tremendous support. Thank you so much. I'll never forget it. A beautiful day in Georgia. Thank you. This gets me fired up for the next one. I can't tell you what this has done for my spirits. Thank you very, very much. God bless you all. Thank you.

Note: The President spoke at 4:15 p.m. on the observation deck of the Spirit of America train. In his remarks, he referred to professional wrestler Rick Flair.

Remarks to the Community in Spartanburg, South Carolina
October 20, 1992

The President. Wall to wall people. Thank you all. This has been a wonderful day, taking this train through Georgia and South Carolina. This is the icing on the cake. I am delighted to be with your great Senator and my great friend, Strom Thurmond. When you talk about a national leader, you've got a great Governor in Carroll Campbell, respected all across this country. I salute him, and I salute Iris. And I'm delighted to have Rick Flair on our side. I want to thank Barry Wynn and all of you who helped make this rally such a fantastic success.

You know, everyplace I go, I see signs that say, "Clean House!" Well, I've got an idea: Send Bob Inglis to the United States Congress. Get a good man up there. And while we're at it, let's clean Senate, and send Tommy Hartnett, my old friend, to

the United States Senate. We need a change. That institution's control hasn't changed in 38 years, the Congress. It is time to clean House and send us these two good new people.

Well, I'm told that the world's entire supply of Pepto Bismol is made at the Procter and Gamble camp right down the road in Greensville. After the past couple of months of campaigning, I'm sure sales must be soaring. But look at it this way: Two weeks from tonight, all this will be over, and I will be reelected President of the United States.

Let me give you a little advice. They've been so wrong before. Don't listen to these pundits telling you how to think, and don't listen to these nutty pollsters. Remember, things are decided in the last couple of weeks of this campaign. And now people are going to decide: Who do I trust to be the leader of the free world and the United States?

I wonder if any of you saw the debate last night. Well, I think——

Audience members. George Bush! George Bush! George Bush!

The President. ——I think the country saw a vast difference there, a difference in principle, a difference in philosophy, a difference in experience, a vast difference in character. I ask for your support on the basis of all of those.

You know, for 11 months, Governor Clinton and the rest of those liberals have been running around criticizing not only our country but me and my record. I think before people go to the polls, they need to know a couple of statistics about his record. Arkansas is the 50th out of 50 States in environment initiatives.

Audience members. Boo-o-o!

The President. I'm sorry. They are the 49th in students with high school diploma. They are 45th in the overall well-being of children; and in incomes, in jobs, and in wages, they lag the entire Nation. We do not need that for the United States of America.

You know, let me tell you what he said last night in case you didn't hear it. He said, "I want to do for the United States what I've done for Arkansas." We can't let that happen. No way.

Ross Perot was right on one thing. He said the grocery store is no preparation for Wal-Mart. I thought that was a good line. But here's the dangerous part: Governor Clinton wants to raise your taxes by $150 billion and increase spending by $220 billion. We're not going to let him do that.

I don't know how many people standing around here make over $200,000, but I'll guarantee you one thing: His figures don't add up. And to get that $150 billion, he's going to have to go after your wallet. So when he says "tax the rich," you taxpayers, you hard workers, you people that believe in the American dream, watch out. It will turn into a nightmare.

I've got a different philosophy. I believe the Federal Government is too big, and it spends too much. He wants to see it spend more and tax more.

We've been caught up in something global. The global economy has slowed down. Though it hurts when anyone is out of work, I think it's fair to note that the American economy, in spite of our problems, is still a lot better than all the European economies or Japan or Canada. We are the United States, and I want to make it better, not worse.

I want to expand our exports so our textile products and our other products made in this great State can find free and fair markets all around the world. We are leading in exports; let's keep it up.

Audience members. U.S.A.! U.S.A.! U.S.A.!

The President. Let me remind you that it is small business that creates most of the jobs, and it is small business that doesn't need to pay any more taxes. It needs relief from regulation and taxation and litigation. Let's get the job done. We've got too many crazy lawsuits, and Governor Clinton is owned by the pocket of the trial lawyers. We ought to sue each other less and care for each other more in this country.

Governor Clinton wants to slap a tax on foreign investors. Well, let me ask right here in South Carolina. You do that, and you don't get a BMW plant. I would welcome BMW to South Carolina because they know our workers are the best anyplace in the world. I congratulate your Governor for taking a lead role in bringing that great business to this State. I want to promote that kind of investment in the United States of America. That means jobs for the American people, and we're going to keep on working for that.

Another area we've got a big difference is education. I told you about Arkansas' sorry record. But I'll tell you a big difference. You see, I believe parents ought to have the right to choose and the help—for money, to choose private, public, or religious schools for their kids. I think we need more support for the teachers and the local communities and a little less for the bureaucrats.

On health care, my plan provides insurance for the poorest of the poor, tax breaks for the middle class. But it does not turn the health care of this country over to the Government. We don't need that. We need market forces.

On crime, I believe we ought to be a little tougher on the criminal and have a little more concern for the victims of crime. Nobody in this country has fought harder for good, strong anticrime legislation than your own and my friend Senator Strom Thurmond.

You know, the other day in the Oval Office, I had a visit from about eight guys from Arkansas. They came up to pledge their support, and they represented the Fraternal Order of Police of Little Rock, Arkansas. They are supporting me for President of the United States. So is the National Fraternal Order of Police because they know that I back up the law enforcement officers. They are fighting for us every day of their lives, and we ought to support them.

You heard another difference last night— talking about reducing and reforming Government. I'll tell you how to get this deficit down: Give us a balanced budget amendment to this Constitution. Give us a check-off so that people that care about the deficit can say, "Hey, I'm going to check in this box, 10 percent of my taxes must go to reduce the deficit." If Congress can't do the job, make them do the job. I strongly support a line-item veto. Forty-three Governors have it. Give it to the President. Let us try to make it work. I like the idea of getting the power out of the Congressmen and back to the people. I favor term limits for the Congress.

Lastly, Governor Campbell touched on it, but let me say I've got a big difference with Governor Clinton. He says it's not the character of the President but "the character of the Presidency." I say they're one and the same thing. They're locked in. You cannot sit in that Oval Office and waffle. Do not turn the White House into the waffle house. You've got to stand up. You've got to stand up and make a tough decision. When I had to make that tough decision on Desert Storm, Governor Clinton was saying this, here's what he said: "I'm for the minority, but I guess I would have voted for the majority." What kind of Commander in Chief would that make?

Audience members. Boo-o-o!

The President. I worry about the pattern

of deception, on one side of an issue one day and then the opposite side the other. You cannot do that as President of the United States.

Let me tell you another one, and this concludes it. Governor Clinton and Senator Gore, the Ozone Man, is going around the world—[*laughter*]—you listen to some—hey, this guy is strange. They've got Gore muzzled back now. You have no timber workers, only a bunch of owls, if you listen to him. You'd have no farmers, only a great big wet hole out there somewhere, if you listen to him.

But here's the point: They differ. They differ. They want bigger Government. He talks about growing Government. I want to grow the private sector. I want to grow jobs in the private sector.

But the big difference is, to get elected they've got to convince the American people that the United States is a nation in decline, and we are not. We are number one in the economy, in security, in standing up for freedom and democracy.

Audience members. We're number one! We're number one! We're number one!

The President. I believe in the American people. And I have had the honor—and my family shared it with me, one son here tonight and my daughter-in-law, twin granddaughters. And certainly, I happen to think we've got the best First Lady that we could possibly ever have, Barbara Bush. We have been privileged as a family to live in that White House, and I've been privileged to serve as President. But I now want to do this: We've literally changed the world. And Carroll was very generous in his assessment. But when I look around here and see these young people, we've got lots to do. We've got all kinds of opportunity. And I want to take that same leadership and, with a brandnew Congress, lift up the lives of the young people here tonight.

We are not a nation in decline. We are a nation on the move. With our education and our job retraining and our caring for people, we are going to make America better. We're going to create jobs worldwide, and I will see that we continue to be the most respected leadership country in the entire world.

Thank you all, and may God bless the United States of America. Thank you very much.

Audience members. Four more years! Four more years! Four more years!

The President. Thank you very much.

God bless you all.

Note: The President spoke at 8:20 p.m. beside the Spirit of America train. In his remarks, he referred to Barry Wynn, master of ceremonies.

Remarks to the Community in Gastonia, North Carolina
October 21, 1992

The President. What a fantastic welcome. Thank you, thank you very much. Thank you so much. Thank you very, very much. Thank you, Alex. Let me just say this about Alex McMillan and Cass Ballenger: If we had more men of distinction, people of their character, people wouldn't be saying, "Clean House!" Keep both these guys in the Congress, and send us a lot more like them.

May I say what a pleasure it is to be here with both the Mayors of Renlo and Gastonia. I'm delighted to be welcomed by both of them. In fact, for good luck we've even thrown in the Mayor of Charlotte, North Carolina, over here, Mayor Vinroot. I'm delighted to see him. And, of course, I'm honored once again to be standing next to one of the truly great Governors in the United States, Jim Martin. You've been very, very lucky.

You've been very, very lucky for these last few years, and now I hope you'll keep this record going by sending Jim Gardner back to be Governor of this State. And also, when they yell, "Clean House!" they're starting to yell, "Clean Senate!" And well they should because we need Lauch Faircloth in the United States Senate.

I heard the introduction he got, but let me just put a P.S. on it: I am very honored to have with us one of the country's senior statesmen and most respected leaders in the whole country, Strom Thurmond. What a wonderful man he is.

I don't know if you watched the ball games, but I hope you see my Braves jacket because the Braves are going to win the World Series. Now, you've got the chop going. You got it.

Did any of you all watch that debate on

Monday night? You said that, not me. Now, wait a minute. [*Laughter*] Well, I think we had a chance to lay out the choice before Americans, the vast difference on philosophy, on issues, and yes, the vast difference on character. Character matters.

We also had a chance to put into focus this man's record. This sign says it pretty well: 50th in environmental initiatives. I would add, 50th in percentage of adults with college degrees; 50th in per capita spending on criminal justice; 49th in per capita spending on police protection; 48th on percentage of adults with high school diplomas; 48th in spending on corrections; 46th, teachers' salaries; 45th in the overall well-being of children. And he said, "I want to do for the country what I've done for Arkansas."

Audience members. Boo-o-o!

The President. We cannot put him in the White House. He's like a struggling Little League manager wanting to go to the Atlanta Braves. We're not going to have it happen.

I think the biggest difference between us really relates to what he calls change. He wants $150 billion in new taxes. He wants $220 billion new spending. And he wants trickle-down Government, big Government trickling down to the people, and we aren't going to let him get that.

Yesterday he backed off a little bit, once again flip-flopping, one side of an issue one day, one on another. Now he says, well, he didn't mean it, when they pointed out to him he would have to tax the middle class. And he said, "Well, maybe I'll slow down reducing the deficit."

We can get this deficit down by controlling spending and without raising taxes. That is my position.

He talks about change, change, change. The last time we got that kind of change we had interest rates at 21 percent; we had inflation at 15 percent; we wiped out every family budget. We do not need a liberal Democrat in the White House with this spendthrift Congress we've got. He talks about change. He talks about change. That's all you'll have left in your pocket if his program goes in, believe me.

So how do we help people? Here's the way we do it. We open up new markets for the products made right here in North Carolina. We have the best workers. Now expand our markets so those products can be sold in this interrelated world economy.

How do we do it? We put some incentive in there for small business. Big guys can take care of themselves. Give some incentives to small business to remove the regulation, help with the taxes.

We've got to do something about these crazy lawsuits. Governor Clinton is in the pocket of the trial lawyers. Let me tell you something: Up to $200 billion is spent on lawyers. We ought to sue each other less as a country and care for each other more.

We've got a good health care program. It's backed by these two Members of the Congress, a good program. Governor Clinton wants to get the Government setting the prices. I want to provide insurance to every American, help the middle class with tax credit, help the poorest of the poor with vouchers, get insurance provided for all, but keep America's quality of health care up while making it accessible to all. We've got to do that.

Education: We've got a good record; 1,700 communities across this country, some North Carolina communities in the lead, literally revolutionizing education. It is not good enough to have education refuse to change. We are going to do it. We are going to give parents a choice of schools, religious, public, or private. We've increased Pell grants for kids going to college by far more than any other administration. We're going to fight for choice, and we are going to make these schools better. But we're not going to do it by trickle-down Government, having Governor Clinton tell us how to run our schools all across this country.

You know, all along the line I see these police officers at these crossings, and it makes me count my blessings for those men and women who are out there defending our neighborhoods against the criminals. We need more strong anticrime legislation in this country. We need to back up our police officers more and have a little less concern about the criminals themselves. Nobody in this country is fighting harder for strong anticrime legislation than your neighbor and my friend Strom Thurmond. We owe him a vote of thanks for what he's doing.

The other day—one of the best visits I've ever had in the White House—we had a group of, I think it was six or eight men. They came to see me, and they said, "We support you for President." They were the leaders of the Fraternal Order of Police from Little Rock, Arkansas, and they joined the National Fraternal Order of Police, saying, "We've got to get strong legislation. We support President Bush for reelection."

I don't think we need more of the status quo. I told you what it was like when Jimmy Carter left and when those liberal Democrats controlled both the White House and the Congress. Remember now, those interest rates were 21 percent. Inflation was wiping out every senior citizen; it was at 15 percent. And remember, it led us into a deep recession where unemployment got far higher than this today.

So what have we got to do? We've got to reform the Government. Send me new Members of Congress, and we will. Give me that line-item veto to cut down on the spending. Give the taxpayers a check-off on their tax returns. And if you care as much about the deficit as I do, check off 10 percent of your income tax and make the Congress and the White House cut that deficit by cutting spending.

I want a balanced budget amendment to the Constitution. The Governors have it. Give it to the President, and let's get this country on the move. I want to give the Congress back to the people and get some term limits. The President's term is limited. Let's limit the Members of Congress.

My big difference with Governor Clinton, though, is——

Audience members. Clean House! Clean House! Clean House!

The President. Clean House! You've got it.

The big difference I've got with Governor Clinton relates to being on all sides of all issues. You know, as President you cannot do that. When I had to make a tough decision, a rather lonely decision, to commit the sons and daughters of North Carolina to battle, where was Governor Clinton? He said, well, I'm with the minority—I'm paraphrasing—I am with the minority—they wanted sanctions to work; they wanted to let Saddam Hussein have it the way he was, and hoped we'd back him out—I'm with the minority, but I guess I would have voted with the majority. What kind of leadership is that? That is not leadership. That is pathetic.

We made a tough call, and we kicked Saddam Hussein out. We busted the fourth largest army, and we resurrected the image of the United States all around the world.

No, we do not need a pattern of deception. It isn't one single issue. It's not simply whether—I'm still offended by the fact that anybody, when your country is at war, would go to a foreign country and organize demonstrations against the United States. I'm against that.

But it is not just that. It is this flip-flop and pattern of deception on one issue after another, whispering to one union what they want to hear and then going out and saying something different. Fuel efficiency standards, spotted owls, term limits, trade agreements, you name it: He is on both sides of the issue, and a President cannot do that. You simply cannot lead by misleading. I ask the American people to look at this Arkansas record and then listen to his rhetoric, and let's tell the truth to the people.

When that telephone rings in the Oval Office or at the White House late at night, and you have to make a decision, you cannot be all things to all people. If you make a mistake, you do what you people do. You stand up and say, "I blew it. I was wrong. Let's go on about the Nation's business." But do not try to be something

you're not. Do not try to tell them one thing and then do something else.

You notice the Sun just came out. Well, let me tell you something: That's what's going to happen on election day. Don't believe these crazy pollsters. Don't believe these nutty pollsters. You know my favorite bumper sticker: "Annoy the Media. Reelect President Bush." They don't like it. They don't like it a bit. They don't like it, but I love the American people, and this train trip is fantastic. You get outside of that beltway; you take your case to genuine Americans. My case is the right case for this country, because I want to make life better for every kid here.

Let me tell you something. They say, what is your—what accomplishments you like—take the best out of? What do you like the most? I'm proud that we put choice in child care. I'm proud that we passed an ADA bill that says to the disabled, you have a shot at the American dream. I'm proud of what we did in clean air, try to help this environment so they'll have a better chance when they get older. But I'll tell you one thing that pleases me the most: We have lowered the threat of nuclear war so every kid here will have a safer future. That is good.

Now I ask your support, and I ask your help to get this economy moving again so we can make life better for every single young person here. With your help and with your support, I will be reelected President and will serve the people for 4 more years.

Thank you. And may God bless the United States of America. May God look after us. We are the world's leader. Let's keep it that way. Thank you very much. Thank you guys very much. Thank you. All aboard. All aboard. Thanks a lot. What a great rally. Thank you, kids. Chop 'em up. You got it.

Note: The President spoke at 10:25 a.m. beside the Spirit of America train. In his remarks, he referred to Joe Lawing, Mayor of Renlo; James B. Garland, Mayor of Gastonia; and Richard Vinroot, Mayor of Charlotte.

Remarks to the Community in Kannapolis, North Carolina
October 21, 1992

The President. Lynn, thank you, and thank all of Kannapolis and all of North Carolina for this wonderful welcome. I'm delighted to be with you on this beautiful North Carolina day.

Again, my thanks to Lynn Safrit, and thank you for the introduction. Thank all of you for the welcome. Let me say at the beginning here, I am so proud to have the leadership and the support of your great Governor, Jim Martin. What a job he's done for this State. And I salute the three Members of the United States Congress that are with me, standing here, Cass Ballenger and Alex McMillan, and Strom Thurmond, the indefatigable Strom Thurmond from next door here. If we had more Senators like Strom and Jesse Helms, we'd be in great shape in that Senate. That's why I'm for Lauch Faircloth for the Senate. I hope you'll send him up there and clean Senate as well as cleaning House.

Audience member. Clean the House!

The President. The man says, "Clean the House," and he's right. Well, let's start by sending Coy Privette up to the Congress. I served in the Congress years ago with Jim Gardner. I want to see him elected to the governorship to continue the work Jim Martin has done.

Also may I salute another American great. I think you've heard from him; I hope you have. You know him, you respect him as I do, and I'm talking about Darryl Waltrip here. What a great American, great fellow. We're so proud of his record and what he stands for.

It's great to be here today. I've got to ask this question: Did any of you all see that debate 2 nights ago or 3 nights ago, whatever it was? Well, let me tell you something. I hope what you saw was a vast difference in philosophy, approach to this great country of ours, and I hope you saw a difference in character, because that's what's going to decide this election.

You know, Governor Clinton talked about his record in Arkansas, and I don't want to ruin a beautiful gathering like this, but let

me just——

Audience member. Please don't. [*Laughter*]

The President. I've got to do it. I've got to put it in perspective. Listen to this now, facts: Arkansas rates 50th in the quality of environmental initiative; 50th in the percentage of adults with college degrees; 50th in per capita spending on criminal justice; 49th in per capita spending on police protection; 48th in percentage of adults with a high school diploma; 48th in spending on corrections; 46th on teachers' salaries; 45th on the overall well-being of children. And Governor Clinton said the other night, "I want to do for the country what I've done for Arkansas." We cannot let him do that. You cannot do that.

It's like sending some Little League guy to coach the Braves. The Braves are going to win. You've got the chop going. Governor Clinton's like the guy that says, well, I might be for Toronto, but on the other hand, I'm for the Braves. You've got to make a commitment. I am for the Braves. Let's be clear on that one.

You know, all we hear about from that Clinton-Gore outfit is change, change, change, and that's all you'll have left in your pocket if they go in and start raising your taxes and increasing spending. He got a little mad at me when I pointed out what he said he wanted. He said he wants $150 billion in new taxes, $220 billion in new spending, and I call that trickle-down Government, big Government trickling its way down to the people. Let's make it the other way, have the people telling the Government what to do.

I remember the last time we had the kind of change he wants to bring to Washington. I hate to bring this one up, but how many remember the "misery index" that was invented not by us but by the liberal Democrats, unemployment and inflation added together? It was 21 percent. Now it's 10. How many remember what interest rates were back then when the Democrats controlled the White House and the Congress? Twenty-one percent. We cannot have that kind of change for the American people.

No, that's change all right. And, as I say, we can't have change for the sake of change. We've got to keep this country moving. I've got a proposal, it's called the agenda for America's renewal, that will cut this spending down. I'll tell you how I'm going to do it. I'm going to get this new Congress, working with these Congressmen here who are good and solid, to give me a line-item veto to cut out some of the pork out of the budget.

We're going to insist to do what the people want: Give the Federal Government a balanced budget amendment and take the burden off the backs of these young people. You want to get the deficit down? Give the taxpayer a check-off. Let the taxpayer say, "Okay, I'm checking this box on my income tax. Ten percent of my tax must go for reducing the deficit by reducing spending." If they can't do it, make it mandatory. Make it obligatory.

A couple of other ideas. I don't believe that the answer is to pull inward. I believe we ought to open markets abroad for agriculture, for our textile products, for whatever it is. We've got the most productive workers in the world. Now let's hammer out new markets, so North Carolina will continue to do what it's doing, growing and prospering.

Another thing is small business. We've got some big ones right around the corner here, but small business is what drives this country. We need less regulation. We need tax breaks, investment tax allowance. We need a capital gains incentive so small business can prosper. We do not need more Clinton-Gore big Government.

I think every American worries about health care. I believe our proposal to provide insurance to the poorest of the poor, to provide tax credit to the overworked and overtaxed middle class is the way to go, because it provides the quality of our health care, keeps that, and yet makes insurance available to all. And when you leave one job, the insurance goes with you. That's a very important part of it. Keep the quality of the health care, but do not let the Government get in and tell us how to run health care.

On education, I am proud of our record. We have 1,700 communities across the land, North Carolina in the lead in many of its communities, literally reinventing our education. Let me be clear on the big difference with Governor Clinton. I believe that the parents should be able to choose. Just as parents choose day care now because of us, let them choose the school of their choice, public, private, or religion, and help them get that. Help them do it. Let's try it. That will make the public schools better. It worked in the GI bill after the war. State schools prospered. It will work for public schools to prosper if we try something different. School choice: Let the family stay together and have a say in all of this.

You know, coming along this trip on the train, I was talking to the Governor and these Congressmen about it. It makes me give thanks and count my blessings for those who serve in law enforcement, and I've tried to back them. Strom Thurmond here, your neighbor, has been a leader for tougher laws to go after these criminals, and we've been blocked by a soft-thinking United States Congress.

But when I see those police officers and sheriffs' people and whatever it is, I count my blessings for what they do in our neighborhood. The other day, we had a visit from six or eight people, came to see me. They were from Arkansas, and they came to give me their endorsement. The Fraternal Order of Police in Little Rock, Arkansas, are backing me for President of the United States. So let's support them. Let's support our law enforcement community.

You know, the last point I want to make relates to character. I don't quite understand it when Governor Clinton said in Richmond, Virginia—he put it this way, it's "the character of the Presidency," not the character of the President. I don't believe that. I believe it's both. I believe that the President influences the Presidency. I have tried to keep the public trust, and I believe Barbara has kept the public trust. I don't think you can be on all sides of every issue and keep the public trust.

Some of these guys were talking about Desert Storm. It was a proud moment in our history, and no State did more than North Carolina when their sons and daughters went there, none. And let me remind you where Governor Clinton is when I had to say a prayer up at that little chapel in Camp David a couple of days before we had to commit your sons and your daughters to war. Governor Clinton was saying this as soon as that tough vote was taken a couple of weeks before that moment. He said, well, I was with—this is a paraphrase—I could support the minority view, but I guess I would have voted for the majority.

If we'd have listened to that view, Saddam Hussein would be in Saudi Arabia today, controlling three-fifths of the world oil, and he'd have a nuclear weapon. Because we made a tough decision that didn't play both sides of the aisle, the fourth largest army in the world was defeated by your sons and your daughters. It's a proud moment, and don't let them try to convert it into something bad.

On every issue, whether it's the right to work, one day he's on one side of it; another day when he's talking to the labor bosses he's on the other side of it. On term limits, I'm for it. One day he says he's for it, and the next day he's against it. On the free trade, whatever it is, he's on one side and then another.

There's a pattern here of deception. And you cannot have a President who's going to try to be all things. You've got to make the tough decision. When you're right, get a little credit if you can, but when you're wrong, admit your mistakes and go on trying to lead this great country.

Audience member. Let's keep him in Arkansas——

The President. Well, let's do that, and let's also not turn the White House into the waffle house. We can't have that. We had breakfast at the Waffle House today, a little symbolism. Very good breakfast, I might add, but there was a message in that. I don't think the American people want a President who's going to try to be all things to all people.

You know, let me put it this way. Sometimes as President you're faced with pretty tough decisions. Sometimes the phone rings at night and you've got to make a call, or in the day you've got groups coming to compete for your interest and your activities and whatever it is, your vote. But it's a wonderful thing, the Presidency of this country. I want to be elected not to keep a job, but I want to continue to try to help the young people.

Today the young people go to bed at night without the same fear of nuclear war that they had 4 years ago, and we helped accomplish that for the whole world. Today democracy is on the move to the south and across the world. And yes, we're caught up in an international economic slowdown, in some places, a recession. But our economy—you'd never get it from this media—our economy is doing better than Canada and Germany and England and Japan and France.

Now, my goal is to make it even better still. We've got to help the people of this country. It's the United States that's going to lead our way to economic recovery at home and to global economic recovery so we can sell more products from this State all around the world.

So the job is not yet finished. And yes, we have changed the world. And yes, I'm proud that interest rates are far less than they were when we came in and inflation under control so every senior citizen is not threatened by being wiped out by this cruelest tax of all. But we've got much to do.

So I came here today to say we are not a nation in decline. Do not listen to the pessimists, these liberal Democrats posing as a friend of America. We are the number one nation in the world. Now help me make it even better.

Audience members. Four more years! Four more years! Four more years!

The President. The American dream is still alive. And let me say in conclusion, the longer I am in this White House the more I understand what it means to say we are one Nation under God. Don't you ever forget it.

So with faith and with your support, we are going to show the pundits are wrong. We are going to do what Truman did and show these pollsters don't know what they're talking about. The American people will give us this victory.

Thank you, and be sure to go to the polls. May God bless the United States of America. Thank you very, very much. Thank you all. Thank you, kids.

Note: The President spoke at 12:45 p.m. beside the Spirit of America train. In his *remarks, he referred to Lynn Safrit, president, Kannapolis Chamber of Commerce, and Darryl Waltrip, former NASCAR champion.*

Remarks to the Community in Thomasville, North Carolina
October 21, 1992

The President. What a great North Carolina day. Thank you, Governor Jim Martin. I'll tell you something, the people of North Carolina are lucky to have such a quality man of character leading this State as Jim Martin. Now we've got to keep that character and quality going by electing Jim Gardner to be the next Governor of North Carolina.

I'm delighted to see a man here who supports me and supports our country so much. Congressman Howard Coble. If we had more like him they wouldn't be yelling "Clean House!" at me. We need more like him. While we're at it, we need to help our distinguished guest today, Senator Strom Thurmond, one of America's truly greats over here. We need to help him by cleaning Senate, and that means send our friend Lauch Faircloth to the United States Senate. Lauch Faircloth is one of the great—he'd be a great Senator. He'll go up there and change things, and the status quo is what's wrong. We need him in the Senate. Send him up there. He's doing just great.

Then we've got another sportsman here. I think of North Carolina as a sporting State, one that loves athletics. Charlotte's coming on strong. We've got Darryl Waltrip right here, one of America's greats. So we've got them all, and now we're ready to go.

Let me thank everybody responsible for this wonderful rally—the great bands from Thomasville, East Davidson, and Ledford High Schools. It's great to be here with last year's State champions, the Thomasville High School Bulldogs.

Can I tell you something as a satisfied customer? You've got to make the best furniture in the entire world. Not only is it made right here, but also there's a certain generosity of spirit by the companies and the workers involved, because I'm told that you were sending furniture to the victims of Hurricane Andrew. That is the American spirit, and I'm very grateful to you.

Now on to the business at hand. Did anybody watch that debate the other night? Let me tell you, I thought we did all right. I thought we did okay. But let me tell you this. What I think you saw was a vast difference in experience, certainly a vast difference in philosophy, and a vast difference in character, and character matters for President of the United States.

Governor Clinton made a horrible comment. He said he wants to do for the United States what he's done for Arkansas. That would be terrible.

Audience members. Boo-o-o!

The President. Let me click off some gloomy statistics, and then we'll get on to something a little more positive. Arkansas—he's got this Ozone Man on the ticket with him, you know, Gore. Arkansas ranks the 50th in quality of environmental standards. It ranks 50th in per capita spending on criminal justice. It ranks 49th in per capita spending on police protection. It ranks 48th in percentage of adults with high school diplomas. It is 48th on spending on corrections, 46th on teachers' salaries, and 45th in the overall well-being of children. You cannot take a failing Little League coach and put him on to coach the Atlanta Braves, manage the Braves.

He calls this change. He says he's the candidate of change. Well, let's take a close look at what he offers. How about this one for openers, and he hasn't got there: $150 billion in new taxes and $220 in new spending. That is trickle-down Government, and we don't need it in Washington, DC. He says he'd sock it to the rich. Watch out, middle America. Watch out, struggling nurse or family person. He's going to stick it right in your wallet, and you don't need that anymore. Let's get the taxes down and the spending down.

The last time we got that kind of change, you don't have to go back to Herbert Hoover. Go back to when you had a liberal Democrat in the White House and you had a Democrat spendthrift Congress that Lauch Faircloth wants to change. Go back and take a look. That was in the days of Jimmy Carter. Now, do you remember what interest rates——

Audience members. Boo-o-o!

The President. Sorry, gang, but it's true. Do you remember what the interest rates were? Twenty-one and a half percent. Twenty-one percent. Inflation was robbing every senior citizen in this country—15 percent. We cannot go back to that failed policy. You keep going with that kind of change, and change is all you'll have left in your pocket. We've got to do better.

My philosophy is this: Cut the spending and cut the taxes and put more money, put more money into the pockets of the American working man. One way to do that is create more markets abroad. It's exports that have saved us in this global slowdown. We've got to increase exports, create more markets for the goods that are produced right here in North Carolina, and we can do it. But we can't do it by turning inward.

It's small business that creates the jobs in this country, and we ought never to forget it. They create two-thirds of the new jobs. That means we need relief for taxation from small business. We need relief from regulation; and certainly, we need relief from litigation. We are suing each other too much in this country and caring for each other too little. Legal reform is what we need. It's a sorry thing when malpractice insurance is running health care costs up for every American. When a guy sees somebody lying by the highway and doesn't dare stop to help him because they're afraid some trial lawyer will come along and sue him, when a person doesn't coach Little

League because he's scared of getting a lawsuit by some nutty lawyer, it is time to put a lid on this. Sue each other less, care for each other more.

One big difference I've got is with him on health care. He wants to put a Government board in to kind of ration out the health care of this country. I want to make insurance available to the poorest of the poor. I want to give a tax credit to middle America so they can get a little relief, and make insurance available to everybody, but keep the quality up. We've got the best doctors in the world. Keep the quality up by keeping Government under control.

A big difference on education. You see, he wants to put the control more in Washington. And I say this: We want to put control in the hands of the families. We did it in child care, and now I want to do it in school choice. Help parents send their kids to all schools, public schools, private schools, and religious schools. And he won't do that. I am proud that under my administration more money is going to kids to help them go to college than anytime in the history of this country.

You know, as I ride along the rails and I see these crossings, I see law enforcement people out helping us at every crossing. Let me just say this: Strom Thurmond, one of the great leaders for strong anticrime legislation, is fighting in the Senate to make our laws tougher so that we back up our law enforcement officials and have more consideration for the victims of crime and less for the criminals. That's what we've got to do.

And what is Arkansas' policy? Arkansas' prisoners spend 20 percent of their sentences in jail. That's not good enough.

Audience members. Boo-o-o!

The President. If a guy busts a law, and certainly, if they kill a law enforcement officer, they ought to stay there until they get on Willard Scott's program on that 100th birthday.

You heard the difference the other day between how we get the Government spending down. I'll give you three ideas. You give us Lauch Faircloth, and we're going to help Strom get that job done: one, a balanced budget amendment; two, a taxpayers' check-off that says if you're concerned about the deficit, check your tax return, and 10 percent of it has to go to lowering the deficit. If Congress can't make the priorities, make them cut right straight across the board until we get the job done. The last one is, I want that line-item veto. Forty-three Governors have it. Forty-three Governors have it. Let's stop that pork barrel spending, do what's right for the American people, but not do what's right for the reelection of every Member of the United States Congress. Frankly, I like the idea of turning the Congress back to the people by putting on term limits. The President is limited; why not the Congress?

You know, the other night I guess one of the big differences came—this was in the Richmond debate—when Governor Clinton said it's not the character of the President. He says it's "the character of the Presidency." And to that I say, they're inseparable. You cannot separate it out, and character matters.

The liberals don't like it when I talk about family values, but America knows what I mean. We've got to strengthen the family. They don't like it when I say, yes, we're one Nation under God. And we are, and we'd better never forget it.

But my argument with the Governor of Arkansas is you can't please everybody. I found that out in this job. You've got to call them as you see them. If you make a mistake, you admit it. You don't try to cover it up and say one thing to one group and another thing to another group, and therein is a question of character. On everything from the right-to-work laws, to term limits, to free trade, to the Persian Gulf, he's tried to be on one side and then another. And you cannot do that as President, and that is a matter of character.

There's a pattern of deception here, and America better look at it. There is a pattern of deception. I love what Governor Martin said about the patriotism of this State, serving your country. And yes, North Carolina responded perhaps more than any other State in Desert Storm.

But where was Governor Clinton? Where was Governor—never mind. Don't let this guy say that. You're going to get me in trouble with the media, and who would want to do that?

But let me remind you of where this man that wants to be Commander in Chief of the Armed Forces—this one didn't happen 23 years ago, this one happened about a year and a half ago. And what he said was—at the time, I had to make a very tough decision, leading the country and the Congress to make a tough decision—he said this. He said, "Well, I agreed with the minority, but I guess if it were a close vote, I guess if it were a close vote I would have voted with the majority." If we had listened to him, Governor Martin is right, Saddam Hussein would be in downtown Saudi Arabia and controlling the world oil supply and have a nuclear bomb. We didn't listen to that kind of waffle. We went ahead and made a tough decision. Character counts. Character matters. You cannot be all things to all people. And yes, it matters.

Let me say this. First place, I wish Barbara Bush were here because I think we've got a great First Lady. But, you know, she and I have talked about this, and as you know, we are blessed in our family. We're blessed with a bunch of grandkids, blessed with five wonderful children. And so, life has treated us pretty good. But when people are hurting in this country you feel it. You feel it right in your heart. And so I want to win this election not because I need this job, but I want to continue to serve the American people and lift up the hopes of these kids. We have literally changed the world.

Audience members. Four more years! Four more years! Four more years!

The President. We have literally changed the world. The kids in these bands over here go to bed at night without that same fear of nuclear war that gripped their parents, and that is substantial change for world peace.

Now what we've got to do is take that same leadership with a new and changed Congress, and there will be one, and lift up America. We are not, as Clinton says, a nation in decline. We are the greatest, fairest, freest nation on the face of the Earth. And now let's make it better. Now let's make it better. Help me. But the change I'm talking about: Remember, send Lauch Faircloth to the United States Senate. We must change the Senate. Reelect Howard Coble. Let's move America forward.

And thank you, and may God bless this greatest country on the face of the Earth. Thank you all very much.

Note: The President spoke at 3:12 p.m. on the observation deck of the Spirit of America train.

Remarks to the Community in Burlington, North Carolina
October 21, 1992

The President. Thank you. What a magnificent crowd. And let me tell the people of North Carolina something they already know: You have one great Governor in Jim Martin.

Let me say a word about the man that's also walking down here, Jesse Helms. He's served this country with great distinction and honor in the United States Senate. I am proud that he and Dot are Barbara's and my friends. You are lucky to have him up there. And if we had more like him they wouldn't be yelling, "Clean House!" Send Lauch Faircloth to the Senate to join Jesse, and let's get the job done.

And of course, I'm proud to be in the district of another old friend, a guy I've campaigned with and for whom I have great respect, and I'm talking about Howard Coble, who's right here with us. He's working the other side of the State right this minute, but it is important that we elect the Lieutenant Governor to be Governor of this State, Jim Gardner. I know him well, served with him in the Congress.

Now, I've got to ask this rhetorical question: Did anyone have the opportunity to see that debate a couple of nights ago? Well, I'll tell you something. What I think we saw and what I think the Nation saw was a vast difference in experience, in philosophy and, yes, a difference in character. I hate to ruin this beautiful rally here today, but I must share with you a little bit about Governor Clinton's record in Arkansas—a sorry record.

Audience members. Boo-o-o!

The President. Now, please be fair as I click off these wonderful statistics. Arkansas and the people there are good. I lived next door to them. They're good, strong, wonderful people, and they're entitled to better

than this. They are 50th in the quality of environmental initiatives; they are 50th in the percentage of adults with college degrees; they are 50th in per capita spending on criminal justice; they are 49th—they have worked to ooze their way up one—in per capita spending on police protection; they are 48th in percentage of adults with a high school diploma; they are 48th in spending on corrections; they are 46th on teachers' salaries; they are 45th in the overall well-being of children. And the other night Governor Clinton said to this country, "I want to do for you, the rest of the country, what I've done for Arkansas." We cannot let him do that.

He's on all sides of all issues. He's like the guy that says, "Oh, I'm for the Toronto Blue Jays, but I might as well be for the Braves." I'm for the Braves. You've got to make the tough decisions.

But Governor Clinton calls this, what he's running on, a change. He's the candidate of change. But you've got to look close at what he's offering: $150 billion in new taxes and $220 billion in new spending. I call that trickle-down Government. We don't need that. And he says he'll take it all from the rich. But everybody out there making about $25,000 hold on to your wallet, watch your pocketbooks, he's coming after you. Watch your wallets, Mr. and Mrs. America.

And Jesse and I were talking about this, talking about change. The last time we had a liberal Democrat in the White House and a big-spending Congress, Jesse was there, and he remembers it well. And Jimmy Carter left—interest rates were at 21.5 percent. We don't need that kind of change. Inflation got up at about 15 percent, and every senior citizen that worked all their lives to save their money saw it going up in smoke with the cruelest tax of all. We don't need that kind of change, either. Keep talking about that kind of change, and change is all you're going to have left in your pocket if this guy ever got in there. And we don't need that.

My plan—and it's backed strongly by these two great Senators here today, Strom Thurmond and Jesse Helms—is to cut the spending and cut the taxes and put more money in your pocket. And in the process, that will create more jobs. I'll tell you how we're going to get that spending under control in just a minute. But in the longer term issues, we've got to open new markets for our products.

North Carolina workers can outproduce, outhustle any other workers in the world. We need access to foreign markets and more export jobs. That's what I'm trying to do. And we need to get the burden of regulation and taxation off the back of the small businesses. I don't know much about Newlon Hardware, but I'll bet there's not a guy working over there that thinks he's paying too little in taxes. Let's give them a little relief: a little regulatory relief, a little relief by investment tax allowances, a little relief for the first-time homebuyer. Give them a break so they can buy a home. Give them a capital gains so you can start new businesses. And let's see this country move.

I've got a big difference with Governor Clinton on another thing. I worry about the doctors. Some of them can't practice medicine for fear of being sued all the time. I worry about Little League coaches that don't want to coach because they're afraid some crazy lawyer is going to come along and bring a lawsuit on them. I worry about the American spirit, when people pass by people that are hurt on the road for fear if they pick them up and help them, somebody will sue them. We are suing each other too much and caring for each other too little. And we've got to stop these crazy lawsuits. And Governor Clinton owes his election, his past elections to the trial lawyers. He refuses to move for tort reform and putting a cap on these lawsuits. Send me some new Members of Congress, and let's get that job done.

In health care, we've got a good program. But I want to keep the quality of the medicine up. I want to provide insurance to the poorest of the poor through vouchers. I want to give the middle class tax relief for—so they can buy this insurance. I want to see us pool insurance, get the costs down, provide it to all. But I don't want to see the Government run insurance. They can't even run a post office or a silly bank up in Congress, and we don't want to have the Government doing it.

In education, we've got to do better. And we've got a good program, America 2000. It says to the communities like Burlington, you design it. You teachers, you PTA people, avoid the bureaucracy in that big union that controls the teachers far too much. Give the teachers a shot themselves, and we will revolutionize education in this country. One way to do it is to give the parents more choice. Give them a little assistance to choose between private, public, and religious schools, and give the parents a chance. We did it in child care; let's do it in education.

In crime, I hate to bring this one up, Arkansas has got a sorry record on that, a sorry record. You get a guy into jail in Arkansas, 20 percent of his sentence is all they serve, and that's not good enough. We've got here today Strom Thurmond, who is fighting in the Congress against all the liberals to make tough anticrime legislation. My view is make it tougher, have a little more concern for those police officers out there, and a little less for the criminal.

I said I'd mention the approach to how we want to get that deficit down. You've got to control the growth of mandatory spending. But here's three ideas that haven't been tried. You want to try some change, try this. Give us a balanced budget amendment to the Constitution, and make us balance the budget. How about this one: Give a check-off to the taxpayer. Those that are concerned about the deficit, check it off. Ten percent of your funds will then have to go in, but it will have to go for lowering the Federal deficit. The Congress is going to have to make offsets on the spending. And the third one is this: 43 Governors have it. They can take a pen and line it right through the budget, knocking out the pork. Give the President the line-item veto. Congress has failed. Give me a shot at it.

We hear all this talk from Clinton and Gore about change. I love this sign: "Bill, you're just blowing smoke." And the American people are not going to believe this. Blowing it out. I don't know about inhaling. That's not my line. That's somebody else's over here.

But let me say, let me end this way. I don't know if you heard in the debate we had in Richmond, Governor Clinton said it's not the character of the President, he said, it's "the character of the Presidency." I don't believe that. I believe they're interlocked. I don't believe you can have a person in that White House unless he stands for principles in character. And I don't believe blowing smoke is the answer. I don't believe you can flip-flop on every issue, whether it's the right-to-work laws—whisper to the unions you're against it, then in the South say you're for it. Term limits—in one place he's for it, one place he's against it. Free trade—one place he's for it, the next time he has to tell the unions, oh, no, I've got problems. CAFE standards are going to drive the autoworkers out of their jobs—one place he's for it, another he is against it. You cannot be the waffle house if you want to be in the White House.

Let me remind you about the position on the war. You've got a lot of revisionists up there in Washington trying to make something bad out of something noble. But let me tell you something: When I had to make that tough decision and commit the sons and daughters of North Carolina to go in there and defeat the fourth largest army in the world, we did it. We did it. And I didn't waffle. I led. And where was Governor Clinton? About the time of that tough decision, he said, "Well, I'm with the minority, but I guess I would have voted with the majority." You cannot waffle when it comes to the national security of the United States of America. You cannot lead by misleading.

Sometimes that phone rings in the White House, and you can't say maybe. You've got to say, here's what I believe. And you might make mistakes. Then you do what you teach your kids to do. You say, if you're

wrong, say it and go on about representing the American people. Hold your head up, and do the best you can, but not waffle and be on every side of every issue.

The biggest difference I have, I believe, with Governor Clinton and the Ozone Man with him, Senator Gore—where is he up there? You put those environmental—I'm an environmental man, but I'm not going to throw every worker out of work because of some snail darter or some smelt or some owl.

But the biggest difference I have is they go around trying to win by saying that America is in decline. They say that we're less than Germany—this is their words, or Clinton's words—less than Germany, but a little above Sri Lanka. They ought to open their eyes. We are the most respected nation on the face of the Earth.

I see these young people here today, and frankly, I take great pride in the fact that we have literally changed the world. Soviet communism is gone; ancient enemies are talking peace in the Middle East. Saddam Hussein is back in his box, and we have lowered the threat of nuclear war from the face of the Earth.

And now let's bring that leadership together. Give Jesse some support in the Senate with Lauch Faircloth. Give Howard Coble some support with new Members of Congress. When they yell "Clean House!", they mean send us some new ones up there to help him. Do that, and then let's try to make life better.

We're in an international slowdown in this economy. The United States is doing better than most of our trading partners. And with my program for America's future we are going to lift this country up, make life better for every single worker, and restore total hope to these young people here today.

May God bless the United States. And many, many thanks for this fantastic rally. Thank you all very much. Duty, honor, and country—you're right.

Note: The President spoke at 5:42 p.m. on the observation deck of the Spirit of America train.

Remarks at the State Fair in Raleigh, North Carolina
October 21, 1992

The President. Thank you very, very much. And let me say at the outset, let me say at the beginning how proud I am to be standing here with your great Senator, Jesse Helms, and to be introduced by him. With us all day today is Strom Thurmond from South Carolina, another great leader, a man that is fighting for strong anticrime legislation in that Senate. Every place I go people talk about cleaning House, changing the Congress. Well, let's clean Senate and send Lauch Faircloth to the United States Senate.

I've known your Governor, I've known Jim Martin for a long time. And I'm not saying this just because I'm here, but I think he has been one of the truly great Governors in the entire United States. And I served in the Congress with the man who must succeed him, when he was there, Jim Gardner. Please elect him to be Governor of this State. Speaking of cleaning House, let's get Vicky Goudie up there to try her part, and Don Davis, too. Then, of course, the real celebrity of the night, king over here, Richard Petty. You know, in the President you get a lot of thrills. One of mine was standing next to Richard at this last Daytona 500 and hearing that crowd who worship him, embrace him with their cheers. It was a wonderful day in American sports, and I am proud to have Richard as my friend. Besides that, I was in this fair headquarters and I heard what he had to say—14 laps behind and moving and ended up 4 ahead. I like that.

Well, it's great to be at the fair, and you've got a lot of things going: cotton candy, cotton candy, cotton candy. [*Laughter*] I know you all are doing a lot at the fair, but did anyone see that debate Monday night? It's a marvelous thing, those—I don't particularly like them, but there's one good thing about those debates. You can get your message out unfiltered. It was a good thing because the American people saw a choice, a difference in philosophy, a difference in experience, and a difference in character.

What I didn't get to do is to spell out in enough detail the Arkansas record. I'm sorry to ruin it, but I've got to tell you a little bit about it, because for 11 months the liberal Democrats, and Bill Clinton in the fore, have been misrepresenting my record. So I think the American people are entitled to know some facts about his record in Arkansas. Here we go.

You won't be cheering when I get through these numbers: 50th in the quality of environmental initiatives; 50th in the percentage of adults with a college degree——

Audience members. Boo-o-o!

The President. Sorry about that—50th in spending on criminal justice; 50th in spending on police protection; 49th in percentage of adults with a high school diploma; 48th in spending on corrections; 46th on teachers' salaries——

Audience members. Boo-o-o!

The President.——45th in the overall well-being of children. Now, Governor Clinton said in the debate, "I want to do for America what I've done for Arkansas." We cannot let him do that. We're not going to let him do that.

Audience members. We want Bush! We want Bush! We want Bush!

The President. You know, it's like taking the manager of the team that finished last in the Little League and saying, you go up and manage the Atlanta Braves. It doesn't work that way when you want to be President of the United States.

Governor Clinton calls this change. Let me tell you something; he calls himself a candidate of change. Let's look close at what he offers: to openers, $150 billion in new taxes, bigger than Mondale and Dukakis together—we can't have that—and $220 billion in new spending when I last heard from him. Now he's changing the plan a little bit.

Audience members. Waffle, waffle, waffle!

The President. Hey, listen, I'm getting to the waffle house part. I'm just getting warmed up here, you guys.

What he's talking about is saying to the working man in this country, give us more of the money. Let the Federal Government figure it out, and we'll let it trickle down to you. We do not need trickle-down Government. We need to cut taxes and cut spending and get the people a break.

You hear Clinton talking about Herbert Hoover. He doesn't have to go back any further than Jimmy Carter. Let me remind you of this. Jesse alluded to this. You remember the "misery index"? They invented it. The libs invented it, inflation and unemployment added together. It got up to 21 percent under Jimmy Carter, and it's 10 with us. We cut it in half. Everybody buying a home, or everybody trying to buy one, I ask you to remember what it was like when the Democrats controlled the White House and, as Jesse said, the other end of Pennsylvania Avenue, the Congress. Interest rates were 21.5 percent. And we don't need to go back to that for the good of America.

This is change, all right. Change, that's what you're going to have left in your pocket if you put this guy in the White House.

Let me tell you what else we've got to do. We've got to increase the markets for North Carolina products all around the world. We've got the best workers in the world in America. Now let's sell more abroad.

We've got to get the tax burden off of small business. I mean build some incentives into it, investment tax allowance, capital gains, whatever it takes; less regulation, less taxation, because they provide two-thirds of the jobs for America. Relief for small business.

Hey, fella, quiet.

Then we've got to change the legal reform. We're suing each other too much in this country and not caring for each other enough. We've got to put some lid on the lawsuits in this country. Clinton is in the pocket of the trial lawyers, and we can't let that happen.

On health care, I don't want to get the Government involved. I want to provide insurance for the poorest of the poor, and I want to do it through vouchers and tax credits and keep the quality but provide insurance for all Americans.

On education, we are providing more grants to kids to go to college than at any time in the history of this country. Now I want to bring it down to the elementary, K through 12, and what I want to do is this: Give the parents the choice between private, public, and religious schools. Give them a break. That's going to help the public schools as well as the others.

On crime, we've got to be a little tougher on the criminals and have a little more sympathy for the victims of crime. I might say I was very proud to have been endorsed by the Fraternal Order of Police from Little Rock, Arkansas.

You know, they talk a lot over there on the other side about getting the deficit down. But here's three ideas for you. Let's pass a balanced budget amendment and make the Congress get it down. Here's another idea: Give the taxpayer a check-off on his income, 10 percent to go to reduce spending. Make them reduce that spending. Then give them a line-item veto. Let the President cut right through that waste. Three good ideas.

My biggest problem with Governor Clinton is that he's on one side of the issue one day and on the other, the other day. We cannot let the White House turn into the waffle house. We can't do that. He'll take one position on right to work in the right-to-work State, and in the other States he says he's against it. On term limits, which I am in favor of, he is for it in one State and against it in another.

On the Persian Gulf war, where the sons and daughters of North Carolina served with such distinction, here's what Governor Clinton said. Think of this in terms of the Commander in Chief of the Armed Forces. He said, "Well, I agree with the minority, but I guess I would have voted with the majority." What kind of leadership is that?

Audience members. Boo-o-o!

The President. You cannot lead the American people by misleading them. Nobody is perfect. If you make a mistake, admit it. That's the American way. Then go on about leading the country. But do not try to be all things to all people.

Let me tell you this: I'm very sorry Barbara is not here because I think we've got the best First Lady we can possibly have. But she and I have tried very hard to uphold the public trust. The White House is your house. The Presidency is your Presidency. We have tried to keep that place decent and honorable so all the American people can look up to the White House.

Let me just add that sometimes that telephone rings there at night, and you have to make a decision. You can't wait. You can't procrastinate. You can't take a poll or have a town meeting or have a referendum. You've got to make a decision. That's what being President is all about.

I am very proud to have served my country in war. I put on a uniform and fought for the United States, and I am honored and proud to be President of the United States. I want to succeed in this campaign, not that I need the job, but I want to lift up these kids here today. We are in a global recession, a global slowdown. The United States economy is doing better than most of the European countries, Japan, Germany, Canada, you name it. But with my program, the one I have proposed, and with 150 new Members of Congress, we are going to lift this country up. We are going to help these kids here tonight. We are going to lead the way out of this into economic recovery.

Thank you very much. And may God bless the United States of America. And may God bless the wonderful people of the State of North Carolina. Thank you very much.

Note: The President spoke at 9 p.m. at the State Fair Grounds.

Memorandum of Disapproval for the Jena Band of Choctaws of Louisiana Restoration Act
October 21, 1992

I am withholding my approval of S. 3095, entitled the "Jena Band of Choctaws of Louisiana Restoration Act."

S. 3095 would establish the Jena Band of Choctaw Indians in Louisiana as a distinct, federally recognized Indian tribe.

It is important that all groups seeking Federal recognition as an Indian tribe should go through the established Federal acknowledgment process. The process was established with the encouragement and support of the Indian tribes and the Congress to deal uniformly and consistently with requests for acknowledgment. The acknowledgment process is objective, applies fair criteria, and provides each petitioning group the opportunity for an unbiased, detailed evaluation of its documented petition.

S. 3095 would circumvent the standard Federal acknowledgment process, establish a precedent that would weaken the Department of the Interior's acknowledgment process, and encourage other groups to seek statutory recognition outside this well-established process. Further, it would be inequi- table to other groups seeking Federal acknowledgment. Finally, it is inconsistent with the standard practice of "restoring" Federal recognition to only those tribes that have been previously recognized and legislatively terminated.

S. 3095, in using the term "restore," automatically assumes the Band was formerly recognized as the Band claims. This claim is based on the fact that, for a few years in the 1930's, the United States funded a school for Indians at Jena, Louisiana, and, in 1938, considered relocating Jena families to Mississippi, but did not do so. The limited provision of funds for education and the consideration to relocate Jena families were actions based on the identification of members of the group as Indians, not on identification of the group as a tribe. There is a distinction between identifying individuals as Indians versus Federal recognition of a tribe, which establishes a perpetual government-to-government relationship.

Enactment of S. 3095 would circumvent and weaken the Federal acknowledgment process and be unfair to other groups similarly situated. For these reasons, I am withholding my approval of S. 3095.

The White House,
October 21, 1992.

GEORGE BUSH

Remarks at a Rally in Vineland, New Jersey
October 22, 1992

The President. Thank you, Frank. First of all, let me just thank Vineland. I have never seen such a wonderful rally. And it's great for the morale. As Frank says, it's a great day for Vineland. I'll say it's a great day for George Bush. And this will go all across the country.

You know, everyplace I go, I see signs, because people are sick and tired of the Congress, the way it's been for the last 38 years, controlled by the liberal Democrats. Everyplace I go, I see signs saying, "Clean House!" One way to clean it is to send Frank LoBiondo down to the United States Congress.

I want to thank State Senator Bill Gormley, who came to meet us. I want to thank Governor Kean, my great leader here and a great Governor. If you had him, people would be a lot more happy in New Jersey. And of course, Mayor Joe Romano, who's standing here with me, give him great credit for all this, and Lou de Marco and so many others. I am so very pleased to be here.

In 12 days, we get right down to the log. We get right down to the vote. In 12 days, the American people are going to have to decide: Who has the character, who do you trust to be President? And I ask for your vote on that basis.

We are caught up in a global recession. The United States economy is doing better than most of the economies, but we're not doing well enough. The last thing we need is to put another liberal Democrat in there who wants to raise taxes and raise spending. We have a plan, the agenda for America's renewal, to get us out of this economic rut. And I see the "Deep-six the Luxury Tax." We don't need a luxury tax. We need less tax.

You know, I hate to ruin this beautiful rally, but we've got to put things in perspective, because Governor Clinton keeps talking about—in the debate, he said something scary. He said, "I want to do for America what I've done for Arkansas." No way. No way.

Audience members. Boo-o-o!

The President. In his 10 years in Arkansas, jobs, wage, income growth have lagged the Nation, every single category. He talks about reforming health care; after 10 years with Bill Clinton, almost half of Arkansas' workers don't have employer-paid health insurance. They are 49th in the entire Nation. Don't let him do that to the United States.

Arkansas ranks 50th in the Nation in the percentage of adults with high school diplomas, 50th. Three out of four Arkansas students after they graduate from high school, go to college, and then they need remedial education, relearning what they're supposed to learn in high school. They are good people down there. They deserve better leadership.

The nonpartisan Corporation for Enterprise Development gave Arkansas failing grades for economic development, an "F" for employment, an "F" for high technology, an "F" for economic development. We cannot let him do that to the rest of the country.

Now he's campaigning across the country saying he's the candidate for change. Yes, he wants to raise taxes by $150 billion. He wants to raise spending by $220 billion. You listen to that kind of change, and that's all you'll have left in your pocket, change. We don't need it.

The guy's all over the field. Yesterday he was out there in the West someplace saying it would be hypothetical to discuss what programs he would cut to pay for all these promises. Well, someone's going to have to pay the bill, and it won't be a hypothetical taxpayer. You cannot get all the money he wants to spend from the rich and from the middle class. He's going right after your wallet, man. If you hold a job on Main Street here, he's going after you. So button it up, and vote for me.

Audience members. Bush! Bush! Bush!

The President. You saw it. I'm not just making this up. You saw it when Governor Florio came in here, working with that legislature.

Audience members. Boo-o-o!

The President. You saw what happened. Don't do it to the country. Do not do it to the country.

Governor Clinton is talking about, well, we really need change. He wants to put the White House in the same hands of the big spenders in Congress. The last time we had this, do you remember what the "misery index" was? They invented it—20 percent; it's now 10. Do you remember what the interest rates were? Twenty-one and a half percent, with Carter in the White House and the libs controlling the Congress. We cannot go back. We have got to go forward by getting Government spending down and our taxes down.

I think New Jersey, because I think of you all as a great export State, you're broad-minded. You look around and send a lot of New Jersey products all around the world. We must open more markets abroad so the productive workers in New Jersey can sell your products all around the world. Do not turn in, turn out. We are the leaders in the world.

You know, there are 72,000 jobs in New Jersey tied to exports, 225,000 jobs to foreign investment of one kind or another. And Bill Clinton waffles on free trade, tax foreign investment, threatening 4.5 million U.S. jobs by socking it to them. You've got to open markets. You've got to encourage investments. And I want to open these new markets and encourage our workers. We can outcompete anyone, anywhere in the world. I have confidence in America.

You look around this town, and you'll see that it is small business that employs people,

not the big ones. They do their part, but it's the small ones that create new jobs and new opportunity. So what I propose for small business is to give them relief from excessive taxation, relief from regulation, and relief from these crazy lawsuits that get inflicted on the people.

You know, it's a sad thing in this country when doctors are afraid to deliver babies in case some of these crazy lawsuits are going to come in and sue them; or somebody doesn't want to coach Little League, afraid they're going to get sued; or when somebody's riding along the highway and sees an accident, they don't want to stop and help the person that's hurt because they're afraid some crazy trial lawyer's going to come along and sue. We've got to sue each other less and care for each other more.

I am very proud of Governor Tom Kean's record, when he was Governor, on education. He was forward-looking. Now he's part of the leadership on a program called America 2000. It puts the power in the hands of the teachers and the local communities. It bypasses the powerful union that thinks it's speaking for the teachers. It puts the power in the hands of the people.

We are literally going to revolutionize education. And one way we're going to do it is this: We're going to do it like the GI bill worked. I have a "GI bill" for kids. And we're going to say to parents: The power should be in your hands. We are going to help you financially to choose the school of your choice, public, private, or religious.

We've got a good program on health care. Give me a couple of more Congressmen like Frank here, and we'll get that job done. What it says is, don't throw the baby out with the bathwater. Keep insurance going for everybody. Help the poorest of the poor; tax breaks for the middle class; create insurance pools; and leave the Government out of the insurance business. Get the private citizens involved so everyone has insurance for health care.

I've got a real big difference, I've got a tremendous difference with Governor Clinton on law enforcement. I see these police officers out here, and I think we ought to support them more, and a little less concern for the criminals. The other day—one of the great visits I've had as President when people come to the Oval Office—this one was about six or eight guys came up to see me. They were all members of the Fraternal Order of Police. They endorsed me, and they were from Little Rock, Arkansas. Eighty-five percent of the criminals that are sentenced under Federal law fulfill their full term, and in Arkansas, 20 percent do. The rest of them get going out of there, and they shouldn't do that. We've got to be tougher on the criminal. Don't listen to the liberals who want to tell it the other way around.

Governor Clinton talks about taxing more and spending more. Let me tell you what I want to do. Here's a four-point program for you: Give me a balanced budget amendment, and make us get that deficit down. Give the taxpayers that are concerned about the deficit a 10 percent—check on a box—10 percent of your income. If you want to apply that to the deficit, then that law will compel the Congress to cut spending by that amount. We can get the deficit down by letting the people do the job Congress has been unwilling to do. And one of the others is to give us a line-item veto. Let the President cut through this pork. The fourth point, and I like this one, is, you know, Presidents serve limited terms. One way to give the Congress back to the people is to have term limits for this Congress.

But I think the reason I'll win this election is going to boil down in the last 2 weeks, as all elections do, to character and to trust. You know, Justice Hugo Black—I mentioned this—did any of you see that debate out there in—all right. I mentioned this: I believe that great nations, like great men, should keep their word. And my argument with Governor Clinton is he tries to be all things to all people. In the Oval Office you cannot do that. But you have to make the tough decision. If you make a mistake, you say, "Listen, I made a mistake. Let's go forward." But you cannot lie, and you can't be all things to all people.

Over and over again, Governor Clinton is trying to be all things to all people. On free trade, first he was for it; then he hadn't made up his mind; now he's for it, maybe. On the Persian Gulf, here's what he said, he said, "I agree with the arguments of the minority but then again, I guess I would have voted for the majority." If we'd have listened to that kind of waffle, Saddam Hussein would control the world's oil and have a nuclear bomb. We kicked him out.

These decisions are not easy, but we cannot let him make the White House into the waffle house. I went down there and had a little breakfast there at the Waffle House in North Carolina to get the point across. You cannot be all things to all people.

He said in the debate you've got to separate the character of the—he says it this way, he says it's not the character of the President, it is "the character of the Presidency." That is not true. They're interlocked. Countries look to us to see whether the President will keep his word and make the tough decisions. On the basis of character and trust, I ask for your support as President of the United States.

Audience members. Four more years! Four more years! Four more years!

The President. You know, if I'd have stood here in Vineland 4 years ago and said that Soviet communism would be dead, and said that Eastern Europe would be democratic, and said that ancient enemies were talking peace around the world, and said to these kids 4 years ago, we are going to reduce if not all but eliminate the threat of nuclear war, you would have said not only is he smoking, but he's inhaling. All that has happened. All that has happened.

The Soviet bear may be gone, and yes, we've changed the world dramatically and made it better, but there are still some threats out there. So I want to keep this country strong. And now I want to use that leadership that has literally changed the world: lift up the American worker, guarantee these kids that they are going to have a better future. It can't be done by waffling. It's got to be done through leadership.

I'm very sorry that Barbara Bush isn't here because I think we've got a great First Lady, and I want to see her stay there. But she and I have tried very hard to keep the public trust, to take the trust you placed in us and live with dignity and honor in that White House. And now some say to me,

"Well, why do you want to be President?" It's not a question of wanting to be President. It's a question of finishing the job for the young people here today.

I am going to win this election. Don't listen to these nutty pollsters trying to tell you how to think. I wonder how many people out here have ever been called by a pollster. Well, not very many show a hand, one guy. We got about 10,000, 15,000 people here. I don't know who they talk to,

but they're inhaling, and we're going to win this election.

Thank you. Thank you, and may God bless the United States of America.

Note: The President spoke at 12:16 p.m. at Seventh Street and Landis Avenue. In his remarks, he referred to Louis de Marco, longtime New Jersey Republican Party member.

Remarks on Arrival in Trenton, New Jersey
October 22, 1992

The President. Thank you very, very much. Thank you, guys.

Audience members. Four more years! Four more years! Four more years!

The President. Thank you, New Jersey. Thank you, Chris. You know, everyplace I go, you see these signs that say, "Clean House!" If we had more Congressmen like Chris Smith, we wouldn't be saying, "Clean House!" And I want to salute not only Chris but Governor Tom Kean. What a great job he did for this wonderful State. I want to thank the Mayor, Rosemary Pramuck, and everybody else who's done a superb job on this rally.

May I say that I am proud to share this stage with Joe Cicippio back here, a true American hero. Great courage, you talk about courage and stick with—my heavens, that man has shown us all an awful lot. And we learn from that kind of courage in this country. I want to thank him for his perseverance. And I am proud that our policy of not negotiating has freed all the American hostages.

Well, I can hardly believe it, but 12 days from today, the fate of this country and, indeed, of the free world is in your hands. And I ask for your support for 4 more years to lead this Nation.

It's going to spell out——

Audience members. Four more years! Four more years! Four more years!

The President. The question that Americans will answer and that the whole world will be watching for the answer to is:

Whose idea do you trust to lead America out of this global recession, to create new jobs, and to keep trust and character in the White House?

For 11 months, Governor Clinton and the other liberal Democrats have been running around distorting our record. So I want to just spend a little time, not ruin this beautiful day in New Jersey but a little time to remind America of Governor Clinton's own record in Arkansas. Here we go: They are— I think of this State and all we've done to work with the New Jersey officials to help clean up the beaches—in Arkansas, his record is the 50th in quality of environmental initiative; 50th in percentage of adults with college degrees; 50th in per capita spending on criminal justice; 49th—they're moving up—in per capita spending on police protection; of their students that graduate from high school, 75 percent of those that go on to college need remedial education; 48th in the percentage of adults with high school diplomas; 48th in spending on corrections; 46th in teachers' salaries; 45th in the overall well-being of children. And the other night in that debate, he says, "I want to do for America what I've done for Arkansas." No way.

Audience members. Boo-o-o!

The President. No way. It makes you think of the guy that's failed; he's 0 and 10 in the Little League, and he wants to manage the Braves. You can't do that.

He calls this change. He calls himself the

candidate of change. Now, let's look a close look at what he offers. Chris mentioned it, $150 billion, this is for openers, $150 billion in new taxes; $220 billion in new spending. That is called trickle-down Government. It goes right from the top into your pocket. And we don't need that anymore. He says he's going to take it from the rich. I think everybody's heard that one before. He's not going to take it from the rich. If you drive a cab, teach school, trying to make ends meet in the household, watch your wallet, gang; he's coming after you. And we're not going to let it happen on November 3d.

He says he can work with Congress. I remember the last time we elected a southern Governor to go up there and work with this spendthrift Congress. Thank God we've got guys like Chris. Let me remind you of what it was like, though, because that's what he wants to do; program sounds identical. When Jimmy Carter left office, same kind of situation: inflation wiping out every senior citizen, every family, every saver with 15 percent; and interest rates, remember, 21.5 percent. We do not need that kind of change. Family budgets were wiped out, hopelessness and despair, the world standing, not even believe in the credibility of the President of the United States. And that was changed. And if you listen to that kind of change, change is all you'll have left in your pocket. We don't need that.

You heard my program the other night. We're going to get that Government spending down and get the tax rates under control and let the private sector provide the growth. Let small business move out and employ more people in this State.

I'm not the kind of guy that likes to attack the media. I like to needle them once in a while, though. You remember the bumper sticker—who's got one of those bumper stickers? I'd like to show it to you. It's my favorite, there it is, my favorite bumper sticker, "Annoy the Media. Reelect President Bush." It's great. It's fantastic. I sure hope they've got a good sense of humor back there. [*Laughter*]

But really, let me tell you this—we'll see how they play it tonight on the news. In early October, this was just announced today, the number of Americans filing new claims for jobless benefits fell to a 2-year

low. Now, this is a good sign. We've still got big problems, but that's a good sign. We've had 3 months in a row with unemployment going down. But I don't hear too much noise about it out of here.

I'm not saying we don't have problems. We've got plenty of them. But we're not going to improve them by raising taxes and raising Government spending, I'll guarantee you that.

Here's what I want to do. I want to see us expand our markets abroad. You know, we've been in a global recession. The United States, you can't tell this from Clinton and Gore, the Ozone Man, but I'm telling you, the United States is leading all these world economies. It's not just my failure, if you listen to the Democrats. We're caught up in something global. And the way we'll get out of it is to increase our exports. New Jersey sells an awful lot of product abroad, sells a lot. Open these markets is what I say. Get those New Jersey products going into worldwide markets, and you watch us lead out of this recession.

I'd like to pin down Governor Clinton on this one because he's got all kinds of mandates he wants to stick on small business. But one of them was his health care plan that would sock it to the small business. And instead of that, I believe that small business employs two-thirds of the people in this country. And they need relief from taxation and regulation and litigation.

And I said yes, litigation. We need legal reform. We spend up to $200 billion a year on lawyers. I don't have anything against lawyers. I do have something against these crazy malpractice lawsuits, these lawsuits that keep a neighbor from helping a neighbor, afraid of getting sued, that keep a Little League coach afraid of coaching because some crackpot dad is going to sue him with a big trial lawyer at his side. We got to sue each other less and care for each other more.

And yes, we need to do something about health care. But what we don't need: to get the Government to try to run it. Congress couldn't even run a two-bit bank and screwed up a two-bit post office. Now they want to run the health care.

My plan provides insurance to the poorest of the poor; says to the middle class, we're going to give you tax breaks; says that your health insurance will be portable if— leave one job, it goes with you; pools insurance so the rates come down; goes after malpractice; and it does not turn to the Government for rationing. Anytime Government rations, the price goes up. Let's get it down by pooling insurance.

Tom Kean was and is one of the great education leaders in this country. He and I both know that our America 2000 program to literally revolutionize education is the way to go. What we are doing is trying to give parents a choice, say to a parent: You should be able to choose, and we'll help you, whether your kid goes to public school, private school, or a religious school.

Governor Clinton always knocks my background, but did you know that he drove in from Hope into someplace else, a bigger place in Arkansas, to go to a parochial school? Forty-six percent of the schoolteachers in the public schools in Chicago send their kids to private school. If you give parents a choice, not only will the schools that are chosen improve, but it will show as it has in Milwaukee that those that are left behind will pick themselves up and compete and be better for those kids that are left there.

I think of the police officers and the sheriff's department and those that are helping enforce the law here as dedicated Americans, and we owe them a vote of thanks for trying to keep our neighborhood free of these crackheads and backing up the law. And you don't get that way by coddling the bad elements.

The other day, I told them at this last rally, it was a very moving meeting for me. Just before I left the White House, I think it was eight guys that came up to see me. And they were your basic grassroots family people, hard-working men, and they came to endorse me for President. And they were the Fraternal Order of Police from Little Rock, Arkansas.

The last point, we got to reform the Government. We've got to get it right-sized. And I'll tell you what I'd do. I've got a program for getting the deficit down. Let me tell you what it is: Give the Nation the balanced budget amendment to make the

Congress get it down.

Give the taxpayer a check-off on his tax return. And if you feel as strongly about the deficit as your neighbor or as I do, check 10 percent of your taxes, send it in, and that 10 percent then will have to be offset by a reduction in Government spending. Congress can't do it, let the people do it.

Forty-three Governors have this one— give the President the line-item veto to cross out all this stuff.

And I like the idea of giving the Congress back to the people, putting term limits on for the new Members of Congress.

I'll tell you something, I think the defining moment in the debate was when Governor Clinton in Richmond said it's not the character of the President, he said, it's "the character of the Presidency." And I say to everybody here, the two are interlocked. You cannot separate them. You cannot separate those two things.

I'm not asking for sympathy; I'm just telling you sometimes those decisions are tough. Sometimes you've got to make a decision that doesn't keep anybody happy. Sometimes you have to make a decision that might send somebody else's son or someone else's daughter into harm's way, as I had to do in Desert Storm. And you cannot waffle. You've got to look the American people in the eye and say, this is what we're going to do. And if you make a mistake, admit it, and then go on about the people's business.

But in time after time, Governor Clinton waffles, trying to make one person happy and then the group opposing him happy. And you can't do it, whether it's free trade or if it's right to work or whatever it is. Here's what he said on the war; here's what he said in Desert Storm—how's this, try this one on for a Commander in Chief. He said, "Well, I agreed with the minority." You remember the minority were telling me you can't do this, you can't do that, you've got to let sanctions work. "I agree with the minority, but I guess I would have voted with the majority." Leadership? That is a waffle house, and we can't have it for the American people.

Now, every President, every decision the President makes in one way or another affects the lives of others. And let me tell you something about character and trust: I've messed up a time or two, but Barbara and I have worked hard to uphold the public trust by living there in that White House. We've tried to conduct ourselves with decency and honor because I do believe in duty, honor, and country.

And now we're getting down to a choice: Who do you trust to be the leader of the free world and the President of the United States?

Audience members. Four more years! Four more years! Four more years!

The President. Governor Clinton——

Audience members. Bush! Bush! Bush!

The President. Governor Clinton wants to win by saying we are a nation in decline. Somewhere, he puts it this way, somewhere

less than Germany and a little more than Sri Lanka. Let me tell you something, we have problems. We have big, tough economic problems, and people are hurting. But we are the United States, the most respected nation on the face of the Earth. And I will not apologize for this country.

I am proud that I served my country in uniform. I am proud to be serving as President. And I came here to say this: I need your support because I want to finish the job.

And may God bless America. May God bless our great country. Thank you all very much.

Note: The President spoke at 2:07 p.m. at Trenton-Robbinsville Airport. In his remarks, he referred to Joseph Cicippio, former American hostage held in Lebanon.

Remarks at a Rally in Ridgewood, New Jersey
October 22, 1992

The President. Thank you. It's great to be here. Thank you. What a beautiful day in New Jersey. And let me tell you something: This marvelous crowd convinces me that I will be reelected for 4 more years in 12 days from now.

I want to thank Bob Grant. I want to thank Bob Grant. He always brings people he's for some good luck. And I want to thank your Congressman, Marge Roukema. You've got a great Congressman in Washington, DC. Everywhere I go, people yell, "Clean House!" If we had more like Marge, you wouldn't be doing that. But we need a new Congress to work with her to change America.

Audience members. Four more years! Four more years! Four more years!

The President. This guy's fired up, up here.

Let me also say that I still wish that Governor Tom Kean were Governor of the State of New Jersey, I'll tell you. May I thank Mayor Pat Mancuso. And may I say a belated congratulations to the Ridgewood Maroons, the State champions, football

champions.

And so, I come into this State feeling good. Something's happening out across this country. Something is happening. We're moving up on this guy. And remember, the vote is not over until November, when people vote on November 3d. And we are going to win the election because we are right for the American people.

Here's what's going to decide it; here's what's going to decide it: When people go into that booth, they're going to have to ask themselves, who do you trust to lead America out of a global recession? Who do you trust to create new jobs? Who has the experience and the ideas to lead the United States of America?

For a long time, for a long time, Governor Clinton and a handful of others running for President, for about a year, have been misrepresenting our record. And so today, I want to run the risk of ruining what is a lovely recession—a lovely reception— [*laughter*]—wait'll you hear this, you'll know what I'm talking about. I've got to give you just a little bit on the Arkansas record. We've got to get in perspective. Watch out, here it is.

The 50th, Arkansas is the 50th in the quality of environmental initiatives; they are the 50th in the percentage of adults with a college degree; they are 50th in the per capita spending on criminal justice; they are 49th in per capita spending on police protection. When a kid gets out of high school, 75 percent of them in college need remedial learning. They are 48th in adults with a high school diploma; 48th on support for corrections; 46th on teachers' salaries; 45th on the overall well-being of children. And the other night Governor Clinton says, "I want to do for America what I've done for Arkansas." No way.

Audience members. Boo-o-o!

The President. No way. No way. No way. It's like taking a guy in the Little League, taking a manager of the Little League team that finished last, and say he ought to be managing the Braves. There's a big difference between failing in Arkansas and leading the United States of America.

I'll give you a little idea of what he has already said he wants: $150 billion in new taxes, $220 billion in new spending. He talks about trickle-down; that is trickle-down Government. Government's not yet to create a job that means anything; small business does that. Let's help small business, not big Government.

Audience members. Four more years! Four more years! Four more years!

The President. It's easy when the times are tough. And yes, we've got a tough economy. We happen to have one of the best in the world. It's not as good as I want it, but we're in a global slowdown, a global recession. And we've got to change things. But what we don't need to do is go back, what it was like when the Democrats controlled the White House and the Congress, which they've controlled for 38 years.

I want to remind you of what it was like. Interest rates, some here are too young to remember, 21.5 percent. We don't want that for the United States. Inflation was 15 percent. The "misery index" was going through the ozone hole that Gore talks about all the time. And we cannot go back to the failed policies of the past.

Audience members. Four more years!

Four more years! Four more years!

The President. Our idea is to get the Government under control and get Government spending and the taxation bill down. I saw a horrible sign here. It says "Clinton equals Florio." No, we cannot do that to the United States. There it is. The guy's got it right there.

In early October, the number of Americans filing new claims for jobless benefits—to a 2-year low. We just got this announcement today. It's a good sign. And I can't wait to turn on the evening TV tonight and hear good news for America; I'm sure they'll report it. So far I haven't heard too much about that. We've had unemployment down for the last 3 months. I haven't heard too much about that. And my favorite bumper sticker, Tom, you got it? Here's my favorite bumper sticker of all, "Annoy the Media. Reelect Bush." What is it about these guys?

Let me tell you what we've got to do, and New Jersey knows this, we've got to open up markets abroad. New Jersey can outproduce, outhustle—our workers can outproduce, outhustle any, anywhere in the world. But we've got to open up these markets. We've got to outcompete the rest of the world. We don't turn inward, we turn outward and sell New Jersey products in markets all around the world, and that's what I stand for.

A lot of you people here today are small-business people. And that means they employ two-thirds of the people in this country, two-thirds. And they're not taxed too little. They're not regulated too little. They're taxed too much and regulated too much, and they're sued too much. Let's change all three.

I'm not, hey look, I'm not against lawyers. What I'm against is malpractice lawsuits that keep doctors from practicing. I'm against lawsuits so if a person goes by and sees a person lying on the side of the road in a car accident and then they're afraid to pick them up and help them because somebody is going to sue them; or a Little League coach who's afraid to coach because some nutty trial lawyer is going to come in and sue the opposition. I'm sorry, we are suing each other too much in this country and caring for each other too little. And we've got to change it.

And Governor Clinton owes his election to the trial lawyers in the past. And we've got to stand up against those people and put some caps on these ridiculous lawsuits that are costing health care alone $25 to $50 billion. Do something about it. Change it. That's the kind of change we need.

We've got a good health care program that's going to get insurance available to the poorest of the poor; tax credit to the over-worked middle class; get the insurance portable so it goes with you from job to job; change malpractice. But do not let the Government run the health care program. And don't let the Congress do it. Congress can't run a two-bit bank or a two-bit post office. Don't let them do anything except change; change them out. Give Marge some company up there that's sensible like she is.

We've got a good education program—reform education, America 2000. Tom has been in the lead of it, taking our case for new American schools all across the country, saying to the parents, you ought to be able to choose. You ought to choose whether you want your kid to go to a public, private, or religious school. It worked for the GI bill; it will work for public education, too.

Everyplace I go we are so well supported by the law enforcement community. And very candidly, we have been fighting hard to get decent, strong support for our law enforcement community in the Congress. And it's been frustrating. But my idea is we ought to have more support for the police and less support for the criminals. We need people in Congress that will stand up and support us.

The other day, I think it was eight people came up to see me. And they were the salt of the Earth, strong family people, dedicated to the values of this country. They are supporting me for President. And they are the Fraternal Order of Police from Little Rock, Arkansas.

And speaking of support from labor, I'm glad to see the guys from 472 here. Heads are on right, strong workers, the best, the best.

Now here's—let me, let me—I get wound up, too wound up here, but I want to tell you another approach. I'm concerned about the deficit. Marge is concerned about the deficit. Parents are concerned about the deficit because they don't want their kids having their future mortgaged anymore. So I'll give you four ideas: One of them, give me a balanced budget amendment to the Constitution and make us, make the Congress and the Executive do something about it.

I like the idea also of giving the taxpayer a check-off on his income tax at the end of the year. And he or she can check a box, pay the tax. Ten percent of it would then go, and have to go to reducing the Federal deficit. And that would force the Congress to offset with spending cuts. We need to give the people the power to get this down.

I think we ought to give the power of the Congress back to the people. The President's terms are limited. I favor term limits for the Congress.

And lastly, they send me bill after bill, and it's got 3 good things in it and 25 bad things. Or it will have 20 good things and 4 bad things. And I want that, you've got it, I want that line-item veto that 43 Governors have.

Audience members. Four more years! Four more years! Four more years!

The President. I'll tell you why I really believe I'm going to win this election. I'll tell you why: I don't believe that the country is going to turn to a man who said in his debate it isn't the character of the President, it is "the character of the Presidency." They are interlocked. You cannot separate the leadership of the President from the character of the Presidency.

And you cannot be all things to all people. You've got to say, here's what I believe. And if you make a mistake, you do what you all do: you say, I was wrong about that; now I'm going to get on about the Nation's business. You can't be on all sides of all questions, whether it's term limits, where he is one day, someplace else the next. CAFE standards, one day he wants 45 miles per gallon—drive every auto worker out of business—the next day, oh, he's going to study it a little more. A furry owl out on the West Coast, oh, he's all for the owl, but then he sees the timber workers, "Oh well,

I'll study that one a little more."

You can't do that as President of the United States. I had to make a tough decision. Some of you may have agreed with it; some of you didn't. But when Saddam Hussein took over Kuwait, I determined that we were going to kick him out of Kuwait, and we did.

And where was Bill? He said, here's exactly what he said, he said, "I agreed with the minority, but I guess I would have voted with the majority." What kind of leadership is that? Flip-flop, flip-flop, everything to all people. You can't do it. Look the American people in the eye and say, this is what I'm for. I'll call them as I see them. I'll be right, I'll be wrong, but I'm going to tell you the truth. I'm not going to be all things to all people. You can't do it.

And so I think character is important. And I think trust is important. And Barbara and I have tried very hard as a family to uphold the public trust. The honor of living in this, the most fantastic "people's house" in the entire world. We have changed the world. These kids go to bed at night without the same fear of nuclear war that their mothers and dads had. And that is significant challenge and significant change.

And now what we've got to do is take that same leadership, and working with the new Congress—and there will be one, there will be over 100 new Members of the United States Congress—say, I want to sit down with you the minute this election is over and do the people's business. Get on with the business of lifting up every family in this country and telling them, not like Clinton does, that we're a Nation in decline, but we are the best, the fairest, most decent country in the entire world. And now let's make life better for every single American.

Thank you all. Thank you very, very much, and may God bless the United States of America. May God bless our great country. Thank you.

Note: The President spoke at 3:35 p.m. at Veterans Memorial Park. In his remarks, he referred to Bob Grant, WABC radio talk show host.

Question-and-Answer Session in Secaucus, New Jersey
October 22, 1992

Rolland Smith. We're very excited about tonight's exclusive event. This is not a debate. It's not a news conference. It is a chance for the President to interact with our studio audience. Our audience tonight is made up of a cross-section of the State's residents, people from all walks of life, and I've got a handful of questions that the viewers have phoned in.

But now please join me in welcoming the President of the United States, George Bush.

The President. Thank you very, very much. Thanks a lot.

Mr. Smith. Obviously, a warm welcome for you, Mr. Bush.

The President. Well, it was very nice.

Mr. Smith. Are you ready for questions?

The President. Sure. Fire away.

Health Insurance

Q. I'm a health care worker from Bloomfield, New Jersey. My question to you is, if elected President again, what would you do to keep down the spiraling cost of health care insurance, and at the end of 4 years will everyone have health care, health insurance?

The President. Rolland, you're on a subject that I think is of paramount importance to everyone. Our health care plan works like this: It provides vouchers to the poorest of the poor to get—give an insurance to the kind of overworked next layer in the tax structure. It gives tax credits up to 3,750 bucks for the family. It pools insurance. I don't believe that we need to go the Government route. I believe that the way to get these costs down is through competition, providing insurance for all.

One of the ways you get costs down, to get to the second part of your question, is to do something about malpractice insurance. I've got a big difference with Governor Clinton on this one. It costs $25 to $50 billion, these crazy lawsuits, and what happens—if you're in the field, I'm sure you know this probably a heck of a lot better than I do—but what happens is, doctors, to protect themselves against these crazy lawsuits, do more testing than is required. Hospitals, to protect themselves, sometimes say, well, instead of giving one test, give three.

So we've got to do something about malpractice insurance. We have got to continue to make the field more competitive. I say pooling will bring down the costs, and then we've got to really get started and try to be sure that everyone is insured. I believe that will bring the costs down. We're also in an electronic age, and this automatic billing and this putting everything together in this managed care, all of those will contribute to getting the cost down. The first thing I think is to get the insurance available for all. There's a lot of people that are not covered now, and we're going to do that.

I think I can get it done, too, because the Congress has got—hey, they've had different ideas, but here's what's going to happen. You're going to have a whole bunch of new Congressmen because of the scandals in the Congress, and I believe then people will say, let's get the people's business on. And I've taken this case to the people, and I think this plan will be the one they try. So I'm a little more optimistic than I was a couple of months ago.

Thank you. Good question.

Incentives for Small Business

Q. Your opponent Ross Perot has promised to help allocate funds for startup businesses to create jobs. What would you do in your administration, help raise startup capital for inventors like me to create jobs right now? And why should I vote for you again, which I would like to do, but we're currently being strangled by the economy?

The President. Well, let me put the economy in perspective first, if I can. We're in what's called a global slowdown, or a global recession. I'll take my share of the blame. But when you look at Germany and Canada

and France and the European countries, it's hard to believe, we're doing better than they are. It's the U.S. that's going to lead the way out.

The answer to your question—I don't think Perot said he's going to give small businesses money. Our small-business program says give tax incentives, an investment tax allowance. I want to get that through the Congress. I want to do a capital gains. People say a capital gains cut is a tax for the rich; the enemy, the opposition says that. It's not. It's going to stimulate investment in new businesses. A person's going to take a risk if they know they can keep a little more of what they earn.

So it's that. You talk about small business getting stimulated, my credit for first-time homebuyers says to a homebuyer who never owned a home: You're going to get $5,000 credit. It stimulates a lot of businesses that supply the housing industry. So I think those three things—cutting down on the paperwork, regulation strangling a lot of small businesses, is the way to get it done.

Q. Yes. But right now, the SBA loans are for businesses that are in business. And for startups, the capital is not available. You cannot——

The President. I don't want to mislead you. I don't think the Government will put money in risktaking. I don't think the Government—see, I think—and I don't think Ross Perot will do that. He may. He's got enough money. He can do anything he wants to do. But I don't think—[*laughter*].

Q. I wish he'd lend some to me right now.

The President. No, I know. But, I mean, I don't think anybody will say that the Government, the taxpayers—you've got a good idea, maybe, but I don't think everybody here should be asked to see if it works or not.

Q. True.

The President. I do think what you do is when you get it started, you ought to be able to get loans at a better rate if you're a small business. You ought to be able to do better on the insurance. And SBA is doing better now, and I think that's the approach I'd take.

Mr. Smith. Did that answer your question?

Q. Thank you very much.

The President. Good luck to you on that.

Family Values

Q. Mr. President, the issue of family values has been raised during this campaign. Unfortunately, your opponent and the media has focused on what is a family rather than on what are values. If reelected, how will you get the focus back on values and get the country on track related to this issue?

The President. Well, you're onto something. We talk about family values. And the more liberal side of the political equation say, who are you to tell us what size family there ought to be, or something of that nature. I was on another network here. I've got to be a little careful. But the question was, "Do you and Barbara think your family is better than the Clintons or the Gores?" I said, "You're missing the point."

I put it like this: The mayors, including Tom Bradley, a Democrat from Los Angeles, came to see me, the mayors from the National League of Cities, little towns, big towns, Republicans, Democrats. They said the biggest single concern of urban decay is the decline in the American family. So let me tell you—and it doesn't mean you have to have a two-parent family. But what it does mean is kids ought to be taught discipline; kids ought to be taught respect for the law; kids ought to have parents read to them. Government can't do this. Parents ought to have choice in child care. We've already got that in the law. I think choice in education is good. I think it strengthens family for a mother and a father or a mother alone or whoever it is raising a kid to be able to choose a choice and get help from the Federal Government for public school, private school, or religious school.

When Barbara reads to kids, I think it's saying, you ought to read to your children. So it's a broad array of things that I at least have in my heart when we talk about family values. We are not going to be scared away from it. You can't legislate it. It's not something where you can pass a family value act and say, okay, everybody adhere to these standards. It's something

we know is wrong. When you have 13-year-old pregnancies going up and up and up, don't tell me family values is not important. It is. So that's what I'm talking about.

How you do it, how you strengthen it, a lot of it is through the private sector. He won't tell you this, but I will. We have a program called Points of Light, and it salutes those in communities all across the country that help others. This station does something for family values. They're, I think, the 12th Point of Light out of 1,000, the 12th one named. Everyone here, I'm told, participates in education, helping adopt a school or whatever it is. If a parent's not there, these people are there to help out and say, get the kid so everyone knows his name and everybody can lift him up, dust him off on the playground, and put him back in the game. Family values, sometimes it's a parent. A lot of times, because of the way families break up and we've got so darn many divorces and stuff, it's got to be community. This station is doing it. I think they strengthen families.

Anyway, that's the end of speech. If I go too long—I get wound up, Rolland, so you say, look, to me, because we don't want to deprive them. You just—and I'll try to make the answers short.

School Choice

Q. Mr. President, I'm concerned about the voucher system. The Milwaukee school system, I understand, was the first school system in America to institute such a system where they have publicly subsidized private school choice programs. Their attrition rate has been remarkably high, 46 percent. It doesn't seem to be working. And I'm concerned about the program, number one. And secondly, is this a violation of principle of separation of church and state?

The President. No, it's not a violation. The GI bill was not a violation. I'm old enough to have gotten out of the war, and they gave me the GI bill. You know, it didn't say you have to go to a religious school, public school, or private school. It worked. Those schools that weren't chosen picked themselves up and did better.

Milwaukee is working. If it weren't why would the Mayor, a Democrat, why would

Polly Williams, a black former member—I think she was a Democrat in the State legislature, whose own child has benefited from this choice, come down to the White House, as they did a few months ago, and say you ought to try it nationally? I don't know about the numbers. All I know is they believe it is really working there.

It's not violation of church and state because the money goes to the family, the voucher goes to the family. And it's not just Milwaukee, but it is working.

Do we have time to tell this example? She mentioned Polly Williams, a black mother whose child was in a bad public school, one that wasn't achieving anything. They said, "Your kid is dysfunctional, or he can't keep up." She said, "He's not dysfunctional. He's a good kid." And she arranged through this program to get the kid into a private school; chose a different school, and the kid is really achieving now. And the school that he left, she tells me, is trying to do better now.

So I don't think it's a—I know it's not a violation of church and state, and we ought to try something different. We've used the same educational system for years. We're spending more money now, my administration is, than any other administration on education, and I'm not happy with the results. So try something different. That's my—— [applause].

The Economy

Q. I'm a self-employed sports photographer. A few days ago you were quoted in the local newspaper as saying when the history of the recession is written, the recession will have ended five quarters ago, four quarters ago?

The President. Five.

Q. What we've been reading also in the papers is that the majority of people in the country are still having trouble finding work. Thousands of people are still being laid off. The gross national product is either flat or down. Exports were down last month. I don't understand. Could you please explain how you justify that statement?

The President. Good question. The definition of a recession that I was using, and it's the technical definition, is two straight quarters of negative growth. Do you agree with that?

Q. That's one definition of it, yes.

The President. Well, what's another one? Another definition is, if you're out of work it's a depression, not a recession. So that is the technical definition. We have had five straight quarters of economic growth. And that's what I was referring to. I'm not trying to say people aren't hurting. We've had 3 straight months of national unemployment going down. Today, we had the lowest unemployment claims announced in the last couple of years. So there are some encouraging signs.

Interest rates are down. If you're a saver, you're not getting wiped out by inflation. If you're borrowing money, had a home mortgage, you can refinance it and save a pretty good chunk of change. The last time the Democrats had the White House and the Congress, interest rates were 21.5 percent.

Q. They were also that high under Mr. Reagan's term as well.

The President. Well, if they were, it was for a month or two, because they've been down now. And the point is they're way down, because the "misery index" that was invented by the Democrats of inflation and unemployment was 21, and now it's 10.

All I'm saying is, not everything is good. But I'm telling you—you asked me how I arrived at that——

Q. You said the recession would have been over 5 months ago. I think a lot of people in this country would disagree with you. And the definition of terms——

The President. May I finish and let me answer that for you? I sent up to the Congress—this guy asked the right question on small business—a bill to put in an investment tax allowance, stimulate business. I put in one on a capital gains tax. I put in one that said this first-time homebuyer should get a credit. All three of those would stimulate the economy, and none of them have come down to the White House. That's what I was referring to. You may not agree with it, but that's what I was referring to. And I'm convinced it would have—past pluperfect, or whatever it is—stimulated the economy. I'm absolutely convinced of it.

Balanced Budget Amendment

Q. Mr. President, you are a supporter of the balanced budget amendment to the United States Constitution. Can you please tell us why you have never presented to Congress a balanced budget?

The President. I've presented four of them. I can't do it in one—you mean in one year?

Q. Balanced budget, yes.

The President. You can't do it in a year.

Q. Any year. One balanced budget. Well, then, why the proposal of a balanced budget when it's almost impossible to achieve?

The President. Let me clear it up for you. The balanced budget amendment would have to be phased in. There's no way you can balance it in one year. Everybody concedes that. But I have submitted 4 straight years to the Congress. It's printed—I'd get a hernia lifting it. Really, it's out there, and it brings it down each time to zero after 4 or 5 years, 5 years.

The balance budget amendment would discipline not only the Congress but the executive branch. The States live under it. Governor Clinton talks about he's balanced the budget in Arkansas. He has to. That is the law. We got it very close in the last Congress. We got down—I think the votes separated were about six votes out of a mainly Democratic-controlled Congress. And six or seven of the people that had cosponsored it got the leaderships to twist their arms out of their sockets, and they voted against the thing they cosponsored.

It's not magic, but it will discipline the Government. So will a line-item veto. So will the check-off I've proposed. The check-off says to a taxpayer, look, if you care about the deficit, check 10 percent of your taxes that have to go to reduce the deficit. Can't be offset by spending increases.

So I really think these——

Q. Will that affect entitlements, though? Won't that affect some of the entitlements, the 10 percent checking-off?

The President. No. Well, it will affect getting the budget deficit down, and that depends on how the Congress and the President do. Here's what we're going to have to do to get it down. There isn't any easy for-

mula. There's no free lunch out there anymore. You're going to have to control the growth of the mandatory spending programs. You don't have to cut them, but they can't grow as fast. And that I really believe is the answer. Set Social Security aside. Don't touch it, and control the growth of the mandatory programs. Two-thirds of the budget, the President never gets to sign it, never gets to touch it. It's automatic because, as you say, it's an entitlement.

Gridlock

Q. Mr. President, you criticized the gridlocked Congress, and you just did again——

The President. Yes.

Q. ——that gentleman's question. Yet, President Reagan didn't seem to have that much trouble getting major legislation such as tax reform accomplished. Why haven't you been able to do the same thing?

The President. I think we have on some things, child care. One of the great things is the Americans for Disabilities Act. It says to the handicapped or the disabled, we're going to get you into the mainstream, a major bipartisan agreement. A lot of Presidents tried to get the revised Clean Air Act. I happen to believe strongly in clean air. We passed that with this Congress. We passed the highway bill, $150 billion infrastructure bill. So we've gotten a lot of things done. But on this one, I've got a big difference with—maybe with—I know I do with him, but he isn't in the Congress. Thank heavens. We've got enough guys like him. [*Laughter*]

No, but we've got a big difference. I mean, I honestly believe that the Democrats that control the Congress, not all but those that control it, have a very different philosophy of priorities. And I think that's why we haven't been able to get these financial incentives through.

But here's why the gridlock will end: Congress has got it so fouled up with the post office and a bank—they can't run a two-bit bank. One party has controlled it for 38 years. Just by accident they should have changed control, and it hasn't happened. Now you're going to have over 100 new Members of Congress, some Democrats, some Republican. But they're going to have to listen to the voters, as I do. I think you're going to see the ability to move, certainly in the first year. The best time for the new President to do something, particularly one that doesn't have to run again, doesn't have to worry about any politics, is in that first 120 days. I think that's how you break the gridlock.

The Arkansas Record

Q. Good evening, Mr. President. To get away from the economy, I would just like to know, are the American people ever going to know the truth about Governor Clinton's record in Arkansas before election?

The President. Well, I'm trying to get it out. You know, I tried to point it out in the last debate. I didn't do it in the first couple of debates, and I think I made a tactical mistake because he has been talking about my record. And I think, very candidly—I don't want to sound harsh or critical in the lovely ambience like this. However, I think he's been very unfair about it. And I think I'll take my share of the responsibility. Unlike him, if I make a mistake, I'll admit it.

But Arkansas is near the bottom on every single category. He says they've done better in jobs. He takes one period, one month. And for 10 years as Governor, they have achieved 30 percent of what the rest of the Nation did. On education, 75 percent of the kids that graduate from high school there have to have remedial education when they get to college. I mean—the environment, 50th. He said the other day, "I want to do for the United States what I've done for Arkansas." And I'm thinking, my God, please don't do that. We've got enough problems.

So the record will be out there. And some say, well, that's negative campaigning. And I'll say, where have you been for the last 11 years with this guy and six others like him knocking my brains out? So I think we need to take that case out there.

Administration Accomplishments

Q. Mr. President, what would you consider to be your single most important accomplishment as President?

The President. Domestic or foreign?

Q. Domestic.

The President. Domestic. I mentioned some of them. I believe in the environment, the Clean Air Act. I think I take the most personal joy in the Americans for Disabilities Act. Worldwide, the fact that these kids go to bed without the same fear of nuclear war.

Innovation in Education

Mr. Smith. Mr. President, a teacher from the Kentler School in Westwood, New Jersey, had her kids write some questions for you, and this one is, "What do you think about expanding the school year?"

The President. I think it ought to be decided by local school districts. I think we've got to innovate in this country. My America 2000 program bypasses the mandates from Congress and says to communities, you decide. You want a shorter school year, fine. You want a longer school year, fine. You want a different kind of school building, but let's innovate. Let's try new things. That's why I answered as I did on school choice.

War on Drugs

Q. I'm a mother of three children, and I'd like to know in the next 4 years how are you going to continue to fight drugs?

The President. Well, we've got to win it, and we haven't won yet. We've made progress. Teenage use of cocaine is down 60 percent. The addictive drug use, regrettably, is going the wrong way. Back the law enforcement people; do better in interdiction, although we've made some great strides working with Colombia, Peru, and all of these countries. And then back up the law enforcement people with tougher, not weaker but tougher, anticrime legislation that puts these real dealers away for a long, long time, no appeals, not getting them out early. He's trying to get me to do this quicker, but that's a quick and dirty answer. And education, education and rehabilitation.

Republican Party Platform

Q. Good evening, Mr. President. I voted for you, sir, in 1988 because I thought you were a moderate. I'm voting for Governor Clinton in '92 because he's the moderate. And the thing is, your convention—Pat Buchanan, Pat Robertson, extreme right-wing jargon—I mean, it didn't seem to fit with George Bush and the George Bush we knew in 1988. Can you talk about it?

The President. I'd be glad to talk about it. Our party has room for plenty of diversity in it. The Democrats' convention wouldn't even let somebody speak if they differed on that very sensitive question of abortion. The Governor of Pennsylvania wasn't even allowed to have any air time. And so I'll be glad to talk about it. Our convention was accused by the Governor of New York, the illustrious Mario Cuomo, right in the front page of the New York Post, of being like the Nazis. His cochairman called me a racist, and you can condone this, as a professor? I'm sorry. I don't think that's right.

We have diversity. I don't agree with everything in the platform, and I don't agree with every spokesman at our convention. So we've got a large——

Q. So you don't necessarily stand behind the platform of the Republican Party?

The President. Not necessarily every part of it. I differ with——

Q. What do you disagree with?

The President. Well, I've already told you my position on abortion. I hope you know what it is. I'm against this wanton abortion. But I don't—favor rape, incest, and the life of the mother as exceptions to it. So I'm not going to necessarily be bound. I'm the President. I'll say what I'm for and what I'm against. I've got to argue with you, I've got to argue on this liberal perception that this is some kind of a racist, reactionary situation there. It isn't. You talk about family values, and the libs say, oh, we shouldn't do that. We should do it. This is vital to the American people, and we ought to endorse it.

The Character Issue

Q. Mr. President, I'm a comrade in arms from World War II. Unlike you, I'm a doughboy, not a flyboy. I'm very much bothered by Clinton's record on the draft. I have with me his letter that was published in the New York Times February 13, '92, Mr. President, in which he states, "I stayed up all night writing a letter to the chairman of my draft board stating: after all, would he please draft me as soon as possible."

That's what he said. His very next paragraph, he said, "I never mailed the letter." Now, my question to you, Mr. President, did he ever submit himself into the draft before he was saved by the draft lottery number?

The President. I'll be honest with you—I'm not ducking your question—I don't know the answer. What I do know is on April 17th he said, "I will get all my records out." It hasn't happened.

My argument with Governor Clinton, I have a different view of service to country, and I have a different view of organizing demonstrations in England when you've got ghetto kids dying in Vietnam. But I was told by some that that's a little old-fashioned. My argument is broader. It is this pattern of saying one thing and then the truth coming out on the other side of it.

Some say character is not an issue. He said it's "the character of the Presidency," not the character of the President. And I could not disagree with him more. I believe they're interlocked. So I think he ought to tell the truth.

Iraq

Q. Mr. President, I'm self-employed. I'd like to switch for a moment to some overseas events. Today's Bergen Record, there was an article—I have it here—that states that three Federal agencies are investigating U.S.-made equipment that was recently found at a nuclear development site in Iraq by U.N. inspectors. In Monday's debate you said that no U.S. technology was used in Iraq's nuclear weapons development program. How do you account for this discrepancy?

The President. I believe this is dual-use equipment. I believe this is dual use that was cleared. If it's not, somebody screwed up, or somebody took equipment that shouldn't have been shipped over there, or not. We never, ever tried to support Saddam Hussein in building his nuclear capability. It is the United States that guarantees he doesn't have one.

So if there was some high-level, you know, just really special level technology that got there, it got there without the knowledge of the United States. But what I saw today—I don't know about the Bergen Record—was dual-use tech—have you got what kind of equipment it was?

Q. It said that it was an electronic welding machine that we shipped to Iraq in 1988 under Commerce Department license.

The President. Okay, well, if it was licensed, that's dual use. I have no problem with that.

Q. For general military purposes, it says.

The President. Okay. If it was dual use, it can have a civilian use and others. Some equipment did this. Some computers were in that category. But if it was designed strictly to build up a nuclear capability, it shouldn't be there, and I hope none was there. That's what I was talking about, and I hope it didn't get there.

Q. Isn't it a bit naive, though, to think that if a country like Iraq with a madman like Saddam Hussein at the helm would not try to use some of this equipment for nuclear development?

The President. No, I don't think it was naive if the equipment itself is not going to enhance his nuclear capability. I don't think so.

But look, we were trying to bring him into the family of nations. They just finished a war. He had the fourth biggest army in the world. Our friends over in that part of the country who became our allies thought we were too tough on him, thought we were going to drive him into a more totalitarian position. And we had a good program. It included sending grain over there. And it didn't work. The guy then went in and took Kuwait, and we knocked his brains out.

And you've got a lot of Democrats who didn't want to move at all down there trying to make something to cover their own necks and trying to make it look like they were right all along. If I had listened to them, Saddam Hussein would be in downtown Riyadh in Saudi Arabia, and he'd have had a nuclear weapon. So we tried; didn't work. Admit it, go on and do your business. In this case, put him back in his box and destroy the fourth largest army.

[*At this point, the television station took a commercial break.*]

Foreign Loans

Mr. Smith. We're back with America again. Our studio audience is made up of a cross-section of New Jersey residents, and let's get to some of our questions. This one was called in, Mr. President, on our 800 number: How much of our national debt is attributed to loans to other countries?

The President. Oh, I can't tell you the figure. Not anything substantial in terms of the total debt. But gosh, I don't think I could even estimate it for you. Do you consider a grain credit a loan? And you know, you get things where we guarantee loans, but they are not technically loans. I'd say I'd just have to get her name and address and——

Mr. Smith. She was probably wondering if it was a large percentage.

The President. No, it's not a large percentage. It's a substantial amount of bucks, but in terms of the total debt, it is not. But let me say: Have you got her address, because I think she's entitled to a decent answer.

Mr. Smith. I have just the name and other—I'm sure she'll call in.

The Environment

Q. Mr. President, if I were a Clinton supporter because of his stand on environmental issues, what would you say to convince me that you're at least as concerned, if not more so, than Governor Clinton? And also, how does Millie feel about reintroduction of the wolves into our national parks?

The President. All right. On the Clinton record, one of the reasons I have to do a better job in describing Arkansas is they are 50th in the Nation. He said the other night in the debate, "I want to do for America what I've done for Arkansas." That wouldn't be very good. We've got a good record on the wilderness. We've got a good record on EPA enforcement. We passed the Clean Air Act that no other President has been able to do. We've got a good record on planting a billion trees a year in forestry.

So I am not on the extreme of the environment. I believe that you can get compatibility between jobs and in the environment. But I would ask only that you compare these things and more that I've named with what his record actually is. I don't think that's negative campaigning. I think that's comparative.

I don't think Millie's got a position on the wolves, but—[*laughter*]—I'm a little wary about that because I think again I'd come down on the side of the people out there that are making their living. I wouldn't want to do something that's going to wipe out their cattle herds.

Q. Do you feel that you're the environmental President?

The President. I think I've done well, yes. Don't think we get much credit for it, but I've clicked off some of the reasons I think we should. I came to New Jersey, and I said, "We're going to give you Federal help to clean up the beaches, and we're going to stop ocean dumping." In that area I think we're doing all right. That was easy.

Cable Television Consumer Protection and Competition Act

Q. Mr. President, you recently vetoed cable television legislation that would have controlled the sometimes exorbitant fees these companies could charge. Did the veto have anything to do with the fact that your son Neil networks for the owner of one of the largest cable television systems in the country?

The President. No, it didn't. I never talked to him about it. I just hope that you're right and that your cable rates go down. My view is that the—and I lost, I lost to the Congress on this. It was a battle of the networks versus the cables, and the networks won. Now I hope your cable rates go down, as they told you they were going to, because I'm out of this. I tried to keep them down by not putting in more regulations. That's why I felt that way. But please be sure and write me when your cable rates go down. I'm waiting. They're not going to do it. I don't believe they'll do it.

They had a big battle, cable versus the networks. I said, "Look, we don't need more regulation." We got beat, and I hope that the other side is right, because they represented that the rates are going to come down. We'll see.

College Loans

Q. My question is regarding education.

I've read that you're in favor of cutting Federal aid to families who earn $20,000 and over. As a student, this would affect me severely. Is it true?

The President. No. Twenty thousand dollars over, cutting Federal aid for what?

Q. For student assistance.

The President. Well, what we've done is increase Pell grant money. I don't believe that the richest of the rich—and I don't think it's $20,000—should get the same benefits for scholarships for college—are you talking about college aid? Yes—that everybody else gets. I just think it ought to have some means tests in there.

American Protesters in Foreign Countries

Q. My question is a followup to the idea of the distinction between demonstrating here or demonstrating in a foreign land, which I find difficult to understand. But divorcing it for a minute and following your logic, wouldn't it also be wrong, show lack of character or bad judgment if the person running for President were from your generation and, instead of protesting Vietnam, he had protested U.S. treatment of Japanese Americans by quarantining them outside one of our embassies in a foreign land while we were at war with Japan during World War II?

The President. You mean to go to—would it have been wrong to be protesting in Japan during World War II?

Q. No, Japan—in one of our embassies. Let's say, Mexico, Canada, whatever it happened to be, outside and organizing demonstrations, protesting American policy, while we are at war with a foreign country?

The President. Well, gosh. Back then, I don't think anybody would have done that. It was quite different. It's hard for people to understand it. I make a distinction. We get protests out there, Barbara and I do. We have dinner in a little dining room upstairs in the White House, and you look out, and there's always some group out there. Sometimes they're a bunch of weirdos, and sometimes they're very genuine, people that want to protest something, and I understand that. It's a distinction that I think has a difference, but it's legally—I'm not a lawyer, so I can't prove it.

I just think it is morally indefensible—and maybe it is generational, because I did fight for the country, and I was in combat. I just think it's morally indefensible to go to a foreign country, particularly with the record that we heard a little bit about here tonight, and organize demonstrations against your own country in a foreign land. Come to the White House and do it. It's not legal—it's not a legal difference. It's not a legal difference. It's just—tell you what I think—obviously have a little trouble getting you to agree with me.

North American Free Trade Agreement

Q. Mr. President, with your recently signed trade pact, do you really believe that it's going to create more jobs for us——
The President. Absolutely, yes.
Q. ——companies will go down to Mexico, and they'll get cheap labor. How many people do you really believe will relocate from here to go down there and work?
The President. I don't think many will, because if they were—let me ask you this question: If the labor union bosses in Washington are right, and we're going to ship a lot of jobs abroad, why is Haiti not the manufacturing capital of the world today? They've got the lowest wages. Why is American business not pouring into Haiti?

This is going to create—the gentleman's talking about the North American free trade agreement, and that is going to create jobs. It is exports that have saved us in this economy, export jobs in America. And so I disagree with those.

If it's going to lose jobs, you may have one or two, but then retrain. Have the best retraining program in the world, and reach out and create jobs.

Q. It would be nice to retrain if the companies were still here. But if they're going there, they're going to get the cheap labor there. They're not going to——
The President. Well, why haven't they already gone?
Q. Because they did not have the trade pact now. Now they do, they can go down there and get the cheaper labor.
The President. Well, no, they can go right now. They can locate in these countries. See, the trade pact doesn't just give license to move a business down there. You can go right now. Take your factory, move to Haiti, and you couldn't get a darn thing done.

Q. How would they bring it back if there wasn't a trade agreement to send products back into the United States, because we weren't going to take all their products. Now that we have this trade pact, we can——
The President. I see what you—I think you're making a good case for protection, and I think protection is just 180 degrees wrong. What I think we need to do is expand markets. We're in a global economy. It's no longer just the U.S. We can't live behind these borders. We're caught up in a global slowdown, recession in some countries, growth going down. And so I believe that the way to get out of it is—no, the way to get out of it is to continue to sell more abroad. New Jersey is an export State. You've got a great port. You're moving product out of here. So we just have a difference in philosophy.

Mr. Smith. It's also a question State, and we have a lot of them for you. [*Laughter*]
The President. All right, sorry.

Wilderness Conservation

Q. I'm an outdoorsman, as I know you are. I enjoy my fishing. What are you going to do to protect our national forests and parks from people who want to chop the trees down, the lumber companies, and destroy most of them and kill off the animals?
The President. I don't think you can do that. I think we've got to have good, strong conservation policies. I think we do. We've done something about the old growth forests. We've stopped this slashing approach that you're talking about, although I think that's been going on—better balance on that is being found. And I am an outdoorsman. I am a sportsman. And I think we can take great pride in the stewardship of the parks under me. More wilderness has been created. I don't want to have so much that you deny people access. But we have created more, not less, wilderness areas than any previous administration. But you raise a tough question because you do have to find a balance. We're going to keep striving to do that.

Child Support Enforcement

Mr. Smith. Mr. President, this came in on one of our 800 numbers. It says it's from John from New York. He says, "I'm 13 years old. My father hasn't paid child support for a year. What will you do to make sure that deadbeat dads pay?"

The President. Try to pass laws to crack down on them. And we have to do that. It is simply unfair, and we submitted legislation again that I think makes sense. They don't get the passport. They don't get a lot of things that the Federal Government can control if they don't pay up. And I believe that the kid is right. We've got to put legislation through to back up these families and get these deadbeat dads to do what they're supposed to do.

Entitlement Programs for the Disabled

Q. Mr. President, my major concern is the cut in Social Security benefits for the disabled, health care benefits for the disabled, job opportunities for the disabled, and a change in the Social Security law to allow disabled people to work without having their benefits penalized.

Mr. Smith. What's your question?

The President. How do I feel about those?

Q. Yes.

The President. Americans for Disabilities Act really is helpful to the disabled. The other, second part of it: Do not fool around with Social Security benefits. Don't touch them. I pledged to the Congress in the State of the Union, do not mess with Social Security, and we haven't. So I think we've got to leave that sacrosanct from this lady's very appropriate question, "How are you going to get the deficit down without cutting benefits." You control the growth of the others to population and to inflation, but don't touch Social Security.

Education

Q. Mr. President, what educational reforms will be used in your next 4 years in the White House?

The President. What what?

Q. Educational reforms.

The President. Educational reforms: America 2000 is our main educational reform. It addresses K through 12. Parental choice I've touched about. Programs to get

the communities involved. We have a thing called the New American School Corporation. And I might say, unlike Governor Clinton, I oppose the English-only legislation that bounces around in these various States because I think it would result in discrimination. And perhaps I'm a little sensitive because I have two grandchildren who are half Mexican, and it makes you a little more simpatico. I think the answer is to go with this America 2000 program that's really going to put the emphasis back at the local community level.

Unions don't like it. The teachers union doesn't like it, but they've never been for me anyway so I'm not going to worry about that. [*Laughter*] And I want to support the teachers, the teachers, not the NEA. Bilingual, we've got a—I'm sorry I missed it—we've got a strong bilingual program. Money for bilingual is up under the Education Department.

Bosnia

Q. Mr. President, do you have any plans for United States involvement in the struggle in Bosnia?

The President. Well, we're involved. We're trying to help in a relief sense. I don't have any plans to put troops in there. When you commit someone else's son or daughter to war, it's a pretty burdensome thing. And I won't do that until the military, Colin Powell, Cheney, come to me and say, "Here's what we need to do. Here's what our mission is. And here's how those kids are going to get out." Vietnam, we didn't do it that way. We made a big mistake. Saudi Arabia, we did do it the way I say, and something good happened.

But I think the answer is to continue to push on emergency relief. I also think that what we're doing—we took the lead in the U.N. on something called the no-fly zone, passing a resolution, which is now international law, that says the Serbian planes will not fly. And so far they've watched it.

The big question comes: What if they do? Then the President has to make another decision. Do you permit it, or do you do something about it? We can do something about it. The question is—we'll cross that bridge when we come to it. But I'm not considering sending American kids into this very complicated ethnic, historically ethnic battle over there. It is so sad, too.

Foreign Policy

Q. Mr. President, first of all, I want to tell you that my patient this morning was Father John Connally, and he took a census among the—[*inaudible*]—students in Ramsey, New Jersey. He found that you were an overwhelming favorite, 2 to 1.

The question is the following: Mr. President, the American people owe you a major debt of gratitude for your helping bring the cold war to an end. However, in spite of this, bloodshed in Yugoslavia. Russian troops are still in European nations, and there are still missiles aimed at the U.S. There is continental unrest in the Mideast.

Mr. Smith. Your question, please.

Q. Do you feel that Governor Clinton would be equipped to handle these problems? What, if anything, do you know about his background in foreign affairs?

The President. Well, that's what we call a slow ball in the trade. You can see the seams going across the plate. [*Laughter*] He has no experience in it. But you put your finger on a problem. There's still danger in the world, and that's why I do not want to cut the defense spending more. We've already cut it by billions of dollars, reduced the troop level by billions. But there are wolves in the woods. And the doctor put his finger on some of them. And we've got to stay persuasively strong to enhance the road, the democratic road for these countries, to be sure those nuclear weapons come out.

One thing I take great pride in is the fact that I worked out a deal with Yeltsin to eliminate these SS–18 missiles, the most destabilizing intercontinental ballistic missiles. We've got that in writing. But we've got to stay persuasively strong to be sure that the deal is finalized and that the troops go out of these Eastern European and these Baltic countries and that peace prevails.

Mr. Smith. Mr. President, thank you. You've had almost an hour to answer the questions from people of New Jersey. Is there anything you'd like to say to our viewing audience tonight?

The President. Well, I don't want to take advantage of them and make the normal political pitch. But let me just say this: That I am not pessimistic about America. I've got a big difference—when Governor Clinton says we're somewhere less than Germany and more than Sri Lanka, I don't agree with that. We're going through an awful difficult time. But it's the United States that's going to lead the world out of recession.

And I will be appealing in the last 10 days here on the basis of trust. You know, I admit to making mistakes, but I also have kept the trust, and so has Barbara Bush. We've been good custodians of the people's house. I think character is vitally important, and I'm going to appeal on that basis. We've got the program. Here's our agenda. I think we can get that in with new Members of Congress.

But the Presidency is more than that, and I want to finish what we've started. I want to lift up these kids and give them hope. Here's a college graduate; it's not right that she's out there now wondering how she's going to get her first job. Her family has struggled to educate her. And I think this agenda is the way to get it done and still get this fiscal discipline back in the mix. So that will be my appeal as we go right down to the wire in the last 10 days.

Mr. Smith. Will you be glad when it's over?

The President. Oh, golly, I sure will. It's been the craziest year. With all respect, and present company excluded, I've never seen the media in such—the one I get the biggest kick out of—I hold up a bumper sticker that says, "Annoy the Media. Reelect Bush." People know what it means.

Audience members. Four more years! Four more years! Four more years!

Mr. Smith. Thank you, Mr. President.

Note: The question-and-answer session began at 7 p.m. at the WWOR-TV studios. WWOR-TV anchorman Rolland Smith served as moderator for the session.

Remarks on Developments in the POW/MIA Situation
October 23, 1992

The President. May I start by thanking General Vessey and Senator McCain. And also, demonstrating the bipartisan nature of this effort, I want to thank Senator Kerry for being here and Senator Smith, both extraordinarily active in trying to get to the bottom of this matter we want to discuss for a minute here.

Let me welcome also representatives from a group representing a group of brave Americans, the families of those still missing in Indo-China. I've visited with some of you all, but I want to welcome you to the Rose Garden. I've read your letters and listened to your stories. It is a powerful mixture of pride and fear: proud of your warrior's service, but fearful that you will never know his fate.

Early in our administration, we told Hanoi that we would pursue a policy that left behind the bitterness of war but not the men who fought it. Our approach was called the "Road Map." It was designed to gain the fullest possible accounting of MIA's. It's been a tough road to follow. You see, for all of us the POW/MIA issue is a question of honor, of oath-sworn commitment kept. It's a Nation's test of its own worth, measured in the life of one lone individual.

To help gain the fullest possible accounting, I asked General Vessey, a former Chairman of the Joint Chiefs of Staff, to continue to serve as my personal representative to Hanoi. He has had, as we all know, many years of distinguished service. But of all his many missions, he might tell you that this is the toughest task he has ever faced.

He's worked countless hours; he's traveled endless miles, but he's been persistent and steadfast. And under his leadership, policy began to work. Hanoi has yielded the remains of 269 American servicemen.

We secured the right to go anywhere in Vietnam to investigate reports of live Americans. We began excavating battlegrounds of Indo-China, searching for the remains of our servicemen. In these searches we never found anyone alive, but we vowed to follow every lead. And then last summer, we got our first glimpse of Vietnam's vast set of wartime archives. With proof of the archives' existence in hand, once again I asked General Vessey to undertake a mission to Hanoi, and called on a man I greatly admire, Senator John McCain, himself a former POW, to accompany the General.

The Vietnamese have tremendous respect for Senator McCain, a respect that transcends country and culture. And because of this, as General Vessey just told me, Senator McCain was absolutely critical to this mission. General Vessey and Senator McCain have just now reported to me and to others here on their mission, and I'm pleased to announce this morning that our policy has achieved a significant, a real breakthrough.

Hanoi has agreed to provide us with all, and I repeat, all, information they have collected on American POW's and MIA's. This includes photographs, artifacts, detailed records on Americans who fell into Vietnam's hands.

Hanoi's records will at last enable us to determine the fate of many of our men. And we still await the return of their remains, but already my representatives have begun to provide answers to families who have waited and prayed for decades. It pains me beyond words to say we may never know what happened to each and every American, but we will spare no effort to learn the truth.

Early in my term as President, we initiated worldwide investigations to determine the fate of our missing men, not only in Vietnam but in all the battles of the cold war. Along the way we've had significant help from Senator Kerry and Senator Smith who head this select POW/MIA committee. And I think we all stress this point: This is a bipartisan effort. It must transcend partisan politics in every way.

From Russia, we've had cooperation with President Yeltsin, pledging full cooperation. We've begun to learn the fate of Americans missing since Stalin's regime. And North

Korea's returned the first American remains in over 40 years.

Today, finally, I am convinced that we can begin writing the last chapter of the Vietnam war. I want to stress that it is only a beginning, but it is a significant beginning. It was a bitter conflict, but Hanoi knows today that we seek only answers without the threat of retribution for the past.

As we cooperate in bringing that painful era to a close, Vietnam and the United States can begin to look towards the future. And to begin that process, we have extended a very modest disaster assistance to flood the ravaged areas of Vietnam—to those that have been hurt the most by the flood. I've also directed my administration to work with Hanoi in developing ways to help identify Vietnam's MIA's and increase humanitarian assistance to the disabled Vietnamese veterans of the war.

Now we will begin reviewing what further steps we can take with Hanoi. We appreciate what's been done, and now we are redetermined to go forward to see what more we can do.

Today is a day of significance for all Americans. It is so because today again we honor those who chose to serve and who gave themselves in the supreme measure of devotion to their country. We're honoring them by at long last approaching a point where we can fully keep faith with their loved ones and bring them peace. So I am proud to be standing here with four who are making a significant contribution to America's search for the full truth.

Thank you all for coming. And General Vessey, my special thanks to you, sir, for once again serving your Nation with such distinction.

General Vessey. Thank you, sir.

The President. Thank you all very much.

Note: The President spoke at 8 a.m. in the Rose Garden at the White House.

Remarks at a Laurel County Rally in London, Kentucky
October 23, 1992

The President. Thank you, Senator. Thank you, Mitch McConnell. And I am so proud to be introduced by your Senator, who is doing a superb job for this State in Washington. If we had more like him they wouldn't be yelling, "Clean House!" or clean out the Senate. He is a star, and you're lucky to have him up there. Mitch, thank you.

But I'll tell you what you can do: You can improve things for this State and for the Nation, getting people that think as we do on these issues, and send David Williams to the Senate, elect him. He can do it.

As far as my former chairman and great friend Hal Rogers goes, I know he's surrounded in this wonderful part of Kentucky by friends. But every once in a while you strike up a strong personal friendship built on respect and, yes, love. And we Bushes feel very strongly, Barbara and I feel very strongly about Hal Rogers. You must reelect him to the United States Congress.

I want to thank Superintendent Joe McKnight and Roger Marcum, the principal, for permitting us to have this beautiful rally on this beautiful Kentucky day. Pay my respects to Melda Barton, our national committeewoman, Melda Barton Collins; and State rep Tom Johnson; and the chairman of our campaign, Tom Handy; and our celebrity guest, the family man from "Family Feud," Ray Combs.

I still remember my great visit here 4 years ago to the town named Bush, Kentucky. And I saw the fire department and the Bush Elementary School, and I met George Bush, the postmaster. This part of Kentucky—you have a wonderful way of making somebody feel at home. Someone mentioned to me the results of the South Laurel High School student referendum, and I understand it went pretty well. And let me just say to all of those from South

Laurel High and North Laurel High, you're as smart as you look.

I also know that just 10 miles down the road is where Colonel Sanders started his first restaurant. He said something that Governor Clinton ought to learn from; he said, "The bucket stops here." [*Laughter*] And Governor Clinton better understand, if he wants to be President of the United States, you can't take one side of an issue one day and one another. You've got to tell the truth.

I think the Colonel would have approved of our offering for America, our own original recipe: ideas, experience, and yes, character. I don't want to ruin this beautiful rally here, but I think it is appropriate inasmuch as Governor Clinton and the rest of the liberals have been trying to misdefine my record, let me tell you about the Arkansas record. They are 50th in the quality of environmental initiatives; they are 50th in the percentage of adults with college degrees; they are 50th in per capita spending on criminal justice; 49th—they're going up, getting better—in per capita spending on police protection; 48th in percentage of adults with a high school diploma; 48th in spending on corrections; 46th on teachers' salaries; 45th in the overall well-being of children. And the other night, in a debate, Governor Clinton said, "Now I want to do for America what I've done for Arkansas." We cannot let him do that.

Audience members. Boo-o-o!

The President. The people of Arkansas, and you know it, are good people, and they deserve better. And the people of the United States better not gamble on this lousy record. He's like the guy on the Little League that finished last, then wanting to go up and manage the Braves as they come back.

Governor Clinton talks about change, change, change, change; he used the word something like 53 times in a debate. But let's look at what he offers. Change—tax and spend is what he's really talking about. Arkansas for the eighties lagged the Nation in growth. And in 1991, Clinton says, "We did better; we led the Nation." Well, the only way to get Arkansas' economy moving was for Governor Clinton to get out of the State. He was out of there in '91, running

for President, the only time they did better than the national average.

And if you want to get the economy in this country moving—and I do, and we've got the ways to do it—is to send him back to Little Rock and keep him there.

I don't believe there's a person out here that works for a living thinking he's paying too little in taxes. And yet, Governor Clinton has already proposed $150 billion in new taxes and $220 billion in new spending. You talk about trickle down, that is trickle-down Government. Give the Government your wallet, man, and step back and let Washington solve the problem. We cannot do that to the taxpayer.

But again, my problem is this pattern of being on one side, that he has, and then on another. He says he's going to get it from the rich. There are not enough rich people around to get all that dough he's talking about. So what happens? He comes after you. If you drive a cab, work in a coal mine, whatever it is, watch out. Watch your wallet; he's coming right after you. And I'm not going to let him do that to the American people.

Yesterday, or the day before, he admitted that he may not be able to pay for his programs without taking it from the middle class. And so what does he do? Gives the programs up and says, well, I'm not going to do that. One day he's for one thing; one day for the next.

The last time we tried this kind of change, I would ask you to remember what happened. When the Democrats controlled the White House—and this same crowd controls the Senate and the House that has controlled it for 38—58 years—38 years, whatever it is—interest rates, do you remember what they were? They got to 21.5 percent, and inflation was 15 percent. And we do not need that kind of change for the United States of America.

With us, interest rates are down, and homeowners can refinance their mortgages. Inflation is down, and senior citizens are not getting wiped out by that, the cruelest tax of all. We will get it down further by controlling the growth of Federal spending and giving you a break on your taxes, particularly small business.

Change, change, change, this Clinton is bad enough, but when you throw Gore in— you heard what Senator McConnell said— you know who's going to get gored, the people that are working for a living in Kentucky, if you go for this carbon tax. I call him Mr. Ozone; he's way up there. We've got to be down where the people are, trying to solve these problems. You try their formula for change and that's all you're going to have left in your pocket, believe me.

Now, I want to get these taxes down, spending under control, and there's a good way to do that. Let me give you a little formula. Mitch believes it. Hal Rogers believes it. We fought for it. And we've got a few more good people, good men and women from Kentucky joining us there. Here's the way we'll do it. One, we will have a balanced budget amendment that makes the President and the Congress get this budget in balance in 5 years. Second, we'll get them to give us a check-off. If Congress can't handle it, let the people do it. You can check off 10 percent of your taxes to go, must go, no way around it—to reducing the Federal deficit. And I want that for the taxpayers. And the third idea is to give me what 43 Governors have, and if the Congress can't do it, give me that line-item veto. And let's cut out the pork and the waste from the Federal budget.

In this country it's small business that produces the jobs. And that's why we favored investment tax allowance or a capital gains reduction or a tax credit for the first-time homebuyer so we can stimulate jobs and investment and support small business, not do as Governor Clinton want to do, manage the economy. He calls it investing. The Government cannot invest. It is the people that invest, and he ought to understand that.

And health care, he wants a Government board again to settle everything. I want to provide insurance to the poorest of the poor. I want to pool the insurance. I want to give vouchers to the poor, tax credit to the more affluent. And then we're going to get these insurance costs down by something else; we are going to go after those crazy malpractice suits that are driving the cost of medicine right through the roof. We

are suing each other too much, and we care for each other too little. And we've got to change it. We need more people in the Congress like Hal and Mitch to get that job done.

You know, everybody in every State is concerned about crime. Arkansas' prisoners for example, spend 20 percent of their term in prison. They get off with serving one-fifth of the sentence. Under the Federal program, it is 85 percent. You see, I have a different theory. I believe we ought to have more support for these police officers out here and a little less worry about the criminals.

We had a great meeting, these police guys that are out there on the line for us. It's the same in Kentucky as other States. But the other day I had a visit from six or eight of them in the Oval Office. And that's a majestic office. You meet the world leaders, and you see all the people from all across this country. But this one was very special. Eight people, I believe it was, and they came up to say, we are for you for President. They were the Fraternal Order of Police from Little Rock, Arkansas. And I was very proud to have their support.

So we must back them up. We must win this war against crime and drugs with our "Weed and Seed" program, backing the law enforcement officers and getting tough anticrime legislation.

But I think the biggest difference as we get down to the polls, and the reason I'm convinced I will win this election, is this: I honestly believe that character counts. I believe that people look to the President of the United States not just in this country but all around the world. And I think his character has a lot to do with how they view our country.

The other night Governor Clinton said in the debate it's not the character of the President, he said, it is "the character of the Presidency." Wrong. They're interlocked. You've got to treat this office with respect and give it the dignity and the honor it deserves. And you don't get that there by saying one thing one day and changing your position. You look into the eyes of the American people and you say, this is what we're going to do. And if you make a mistake, a President does what you have to do. You say, hey, I was wrong about that, and I'm going to continue to do the American people's business. But you cannot be all things to all people.

Let me give you some examples. Governor Clinton says on free trade one day, "Well, I'm for it." And then he goes to the big unions up in Washington, and he says, "Well, I've got some serious reservations." On right-to-work laws, doesn't matter if you're for them or against them, but you can't be on both sides of it. He says, "Well, I'm for them," in Arkansas. He goes to the unions that are up in New Hampshire, and he says, "I'm against them."

On the Persian Gulf, a very tough decision that I had to make to commit somebody else's son, somebody else's daughter to combat. I had to make a decision and had to lead, and I couldn't equivocate. And here's what Governor Clinton said. He said, "I guess I agreed with the minority," that's those who wanted to give sanctions a chance, "I agree with the minority, but I guess I would have voted with the majority." What kind of Commander in Chief can waffle and change his position like that?

I have big differences with him, and I know some here might disagree with them. I still feel in my heart-of-hearts that when your country is in a war, you don't go to another country and lead demonstrations against your country. And when you say to the American people, "I'm going to tell you the full truth on the draft on April 17th," and then they're silent, hoping the issue goes away, I don't think that's right either. A lot of people opposed the war. Some of them said, "Well, I'm not going to even stick around." But they didn't change their story. They weren't one thing one day and then trying to preserve their political viability the next. You cannot waffle. You cannot equivocate when you're President of the United States of America.

You know, some days in the Oval Office—it could be at night in the White House or over in the Oval Office in the day—the telephone rings, and the decisions aren't always easy ones. They're decisions where principle has to be invoked, and where you have to say what you think you really believe in your heart-of-hearts is right. And that's why I believe you cannot separate the character of the President from the character of the Presidency. They are one and the same thing. They are locked in.

I will be asking the American people to consider that important point. We've got the economic program, an agenda for America's renewal. We've got a foreign policy record that gives great credit to the United States and those who have stood strong. Isn't it a wonderful thing that the young people behind me today go to bed at night without the same fear of nuclear war that many of you had? International communism is dead. And Germany's reunited. And ancient enemies are talking to each other in the Middle East. And democracy is on the move south of our border. Now we must take that same leadership and with this new Congress—and there's going to be 100, at least 100 new ones coming up there—with that new Congress we are going to lift this country up. We are going to make life better for every single kid that is here today.

Don't you believe it when Clinton-Gore go around this country saying we are a nation in decline, everything is bad. That is not so. Yes, some people are hurting. Our program will help them. But we are the United States of America. We don't need a man whose only hope to get into office is by criticizing and tearing down. I want to build and lift up.

And I ask for your support. I ask for your vote. And may God bless the United States of America. Thank you all very much.

Note: The President spoke at 12:07 p.m. at the South Laurel High School.

Statement on Signing the Wild Bird Conservation Act of 1992
October 23, 1992

I am signing into law H.R. 5013, the "Wild Bird Conservation Act of 1992." I take great pleasure in signing this Act because it promotes the conservation of wild exotic birds and provides for other measures related to fish and wildlife conservation. It also demonstrates our global leadership in the protection and conservation of wildlife.

Over the past 4 years, my Administration has played a strong role in the development of a world conservation strategy. The United States is a long-standing member of the Convention on International Trade in Endangered Species of Wild Fauna and Flora (CITES). This Act provides an important mechanism for the United States to implement the decisions and resolutions agreed to under CITES. Other nations, including those within the European Community, have also acted to regulate imports of exotic wild birds whose populations may be detrimentally affected by trade.

Furthermore, this Act authorizes the Secretary of the Interior to support the management efforts of other nations in the conservation of their wild birds. Funds to assist these countries will be made available through the Exotic Bird Conservation Fund established by this Act.

Our action here exemplifies our commitment to wildlife conservation around the world. By strengthening our wildlife import policies and by encouraging the wildlife management programs of other countries, this Act will help to prevent any further decimation of wild bird populations.

I commend the bipartisan leadership of the House Merchant Marine and Fisheries Committee as well as a broad range of groups, including conservation organizations, importers, scientists, breeders, humane organizations, and the pet industry, for working with the Administration on this legislation.

George Bush

The White House,
October 23, 1992.

Note: H.R. 5013, approved October 23, was assigned Public Law No. 102–440.

Statement on Signing Legislation Establishing Asian/Pacific American Heritage Month
October 23, 1992

Today I am signing into law H.R. 5572, which designates May of each year as "Asian/Pacific American Heritage Month." In May 1990, I was proud to extend Asian Pacific American Heritage Week to a full month celebration. Therefore, I am pleased to have the Congress join me in recognizing the important contributions of Asian Pacific Americans and the impact of their distinct and dynamic cultures on our great Nation.

As President I have witnessed poignant and difficult times for Asian Pacific Americans, but I know the tremendous value of Asian Pacific Americans to this country. Much as others who have come to our shores, Asian Pacific Americans came here seeking freedom and yearning for the American Dream. And like other immigrants, Asian Pacific Americans are finding it—in the arts, in business, in science, in public service—across the spectrum of achievement. I am pleased to pay tribute to the significant contributions of Asian Pacific Americans.

George Bush

The White House,
October 23, 1992.

Note: H.R. 5572, approved October 23, was assigned Public Law No. 102–450.

Remarks on Signing the Cuban Democracy Act of 1992 in Miami, Florida
October 23, 1992

The President. Thank you very, very much. And may I thank Armando for that warm introduction and all of you for this reception. I am very, very pleased to be here. It's great to be among so many friends. This is a very special day, and we've got one standing up here who deserves very special credit, our great Senator Connie Mack. And also a great friend, Congressman Ileana Ros-Lehtinen, joined in the Congress now by Lincoln, Lincoln Diaz-Balart. And may I salute the veterans of the 2506 Brigade who are here, heroes of America and heroes in your homeland. Tomas Garcia Fuste and Armando Perez Roura, Ariel Ramos. Of course, let me recognize another old friend, Carlos Salman, and Al Cardenas and Jorge Mas. Where's Jorge? Hey, Jorge is the only guy that can take on that "60 Minutes" crowd and come out ahead. You know, that was very good. [*Laughter*] He did. He did just great, and he's one of the key forces, of course, as so many in this room, but he was one of the very key forces behind this Cuban Democracy Act. And let me offer a very special recognition to the representatives of La Unidad, champions of a free Cuba.

Now, we share a history, a commitment to struggle. We've worked years toward this single goal, common dream, because everyone here wants a free and democratic Cuba. Today I am delighted to take the next step toward that dream with the Cuban Democracy Act of 1992. Our policies and principles rest on a single belief: For freedom to rise in Cuba, Fidel Castro must fall.

Audience members. Viva Bush! Viva Bush! Viva Bush!

The President. In today's democratic world, Communist governments no longer hold sway. Cuba's special relationship with the former Soviet Union has all but ended.

And we've worked to ensure that no other government helps this, the cruelest of regimes. And the result: Literally, you look around the world and you see that Castro has literally become an outcast among dictators. He's not a leader; he's what you call a warden. His beaches are not borders but his confines of freedom. And the tide is running out. For years, this Cuban community has energized Miami. Someday freedom-loving people will change that island for the better, just like America has changed the entire world. And none of us should rest and relax until we stop those who mock the rights that we treasure, rights of speech and religion and assembly and economic freedom.

One hundred years ago, the Abraham Lincoln of Cuba, the great patriot José Marti, said simply, "To beautify life is to give it an aim." To beautify life is to give it an aim. And I agree with that. Our aim is human liberty.

Audience members. Viva Bush! Viva Bush! Viva Bush!

The President. People are choosing liberty all over the world by their votes. The Cuban people deserve no less. That's why this Cuban Democracy Act strengthens our embargo. It will speed the inevitable demise of the Cuban Castro dictatorship. The legislation that I sign today reflects our determination, mine and yours, that the Cuban Government will not benefit from U.S. trade or aid until the Cuban people are free. And it reflects another belief: I'm not going to let others prop up Castro with aid or some sweetheart trade deal.

All of this is not designed to hurt the Cuban people. I am saddened by their suffering and loss of freedom. Many of you in this room have families there, and I'm saddened by families that are split apart and sons and daughters lost at sea. Let's make it clear: Cuba suffers because Castro refuses to change. Our policy and this bill allow for humanitarian donations of food and medicine to nongovernment organizations in Cuba, help that will get to the Cuban people. And it allows for improved communications between the United States and Cuba, so that all of you can maintain contact with family members.

Our policy is the only way to put it, plain and simple: Democracy, Mr. Castro, not sometime, not someday, but now. Put it this way: We simply will not provide life support to a dictatorship which is dying. There will never be normal relations with Cuba as long as Castro sustains this illegitimate regime, as long as he intimidates and does violence to a brave and courageous people.

I have challenged him before, and now I challenge him again. Mr. Castro, let a United Nations human rights representative come to your island nation.

Audience members. Viva Bush! Viva Bush! Viva Bush!

The President. Mr. Castro, put your leadership to the test of the ballot box, and let your people decide. Call off your secret police, and let the Cuban people choose their leaders and their future. Let your people live in freedom. That is the message to Cuba today.

You know, when Cuba is free, a million free Cuban Americans will be united with their long-suffering Cuban brothers. Nowhere has the pain and anguish of family separation been more eloquently stated than in a letter that Barbara received from Major Orestes Lorenzo, who is with us here today. Where is the major? Right here. As all of you know, he heroically escaped from Cuba when he flew his Mig to south Florida a year and a half ago, asked for political asylum. But he could not free his family. Despite humanitarian pleas from the world over, Castro keeps Vicky, Major Lorenzo's wife, and their two little sons, Alexander and Reyniel, hostage there in Cuba. I want to say to the major here today and to all of you that I will keep working until all Cuban families are united again in freedom.

You know, Castro likes to say that any person who wants to leave Cuba may go. Well, all it takes, he says, is an American visa. Well, over a year ago we issued a visa

for the major's family, and still they're barred from leaving that country. The answer is today to Mr. Castro: Do what's decent. Do what's right. You say everybody can leave; let the Lorenzo family go.

One cannot help but be emotional, looking around this room and seeing the commitment here. I get it in a very special way, obviously, through my son Jeb, who's a friend to many here, and through my dear friend Armando Codina who introduced me, who sensitizes me to this struggle that everyone in this room has been involved in.

We've been in this, and I say "we" proudly, we've been in this for a long time, and we are not going to back away from this commitment. We're not going to listen to these editorials that tell me how to run the foreign policy of this country and to change this policy.

Audience members. Four more years! Four more years! Four more years!

The President. We are not going to waffle on our commitment, and we're not going to quit until—we've got a little enthusiasm over here—until that is achieved. You must remember that this administration—and I am the President who pressed the Soviets and the Russians to cut back their support and pull out their troops and send an unmistakable signal to Cuba of its complete isolation. And we're the ones, you and I together, who urged our friends in Latin America to let Castro know that he's out of things, he's a has-been. It is my firm belief, I really believe this, that during my second term as President, you will be reunited with your loved ones.

Audience members. Viva Bush! Viva Bush! Viva Bush!

The President. And I know, I am certain in my heart that I will be the first American President to set foot on the soil of a free and independent Cuba.

Thank you. Thank you all, and God bless you. Now I will sign the Defense Authorization Act, giving the force of law to the Cuban Democracy Act of 1992.

Note: The President spoke at 5:48 p.m. at the Omni Hotel. In his remarks, he referred to Armando Codina, chairman, Codina-Bush Group; Tomas Garcia Fuste, WQBA radio talk show host; Armando Perez Roura, WAQI radio talk show host; Ariel Ramos, newspaper reporter, Diario Las Americas; Carlos Salman, real estate broker; Al Cardenas, attorney; and Jorge Mas, chairman, Cuban American National Foundation. The President also referred to the 2506 Brigade, *the military unit which participated in the Bay of Pigs invasion. H.R. 5006, the National Defense Authorization Act for Fiscal Year 1993, approved October 23, which incorporated the Cuban Democracy Act of 1992, was assigned Public Law No. 102–484.*

Statement on Signing the National Defense Authorization Act for Fiscal Year 1993
October 23, 1992

Today I am signing into law H.R. 5006, the "National Defense Authorization Act for Fiscal Year 1993." H.R. 5006 authorizes appropriations that provide for a national defense adequate to meet foreseeable threats to the national security. It generally supports the Administration's major defense priorities, including key elements of the Strategic Defense Initiative and the B–2 program. I am also pleased that the bill includes the Cuban Democracy Act, which will help establish a free and democratic Cuba.

I have signed this Act notwithstanding the reservations that I have regarding certain of its provisions. I am particularly concerned about provisions that purport to derogate the President's authority under the Constitution to conduct U.S. foreign policy, including negotiations with other countries. A number of provisions purport to establish foreign policy by providing that it shall be "the policy of the United States" or "the goal of the United States" to undertake specific diplomatic initiatives. Consistent with my responsibility under the Constitution for the conduct of diplomatic negotiations, and with established practice, I will construe these provisions to be precatory rather than mandatory. Other provisions purport to require reports to the Congress concerning diplomatic negotiations. I sign this bill with the understanding that these provisions do not detract from my constitutional authority to protect sensitive national security information.

In addition, H.R. 5006 would assign new domestic, civil functions of government to the Department of Defense and the Armed Forces. These roles include community medical care; local school funding; training of civilian children; establishing new government data bases on U.S. defense businesses; establishing plans for U.S. industries; assisting and funding Federal, State, local, and private nonprofit industrial support efforts; and providing broad adjustment grants to communities. For the most part, the objectives of these provisions are laudable. The functions prescribed are not, however, appropriate roles for the military. Accordingly, I direct the Secretary of Defense to implement these provisions in a manner that will do the least damage possible to the traditional role of the military. Where particular provisions of H.R. 5006 cannot be implemented consistent with the traditional role of the military, I direct the Secretary of Defense to draft and propose to the Congress remedial legislation.

I am also concerned that two provisions of H.R. 5006 might be construed to impinge on the President's authority as Commander in Chief and as head of the executive branch. Section 1303 purports to prohibit the use of appropriations to support a level of U.S. troops in Europe greater than 100,000 after October 1, 1995, and section 1302 purports to require a 40 percent cut in U.S. forces overseas after September 30, 1996, absent a war or national emergency. American forces abroad are a stabilizing influence in a volatile world and provide a ready means to protect American interests. Ill-considered cuts to America's forward presence diminish America's ability to help keep the peace in the future in various regions of the world. I shall construe these provisions consistent with my authority to deploy military personnel as necessary to fulfill my constitutional responsibilities.

I note with disappointment that included within this bill is a provision that will lessen the impact of the honoraria restriction on a very select group of individuals rather than the career work force as a whole. I have strongly supported a Governmentwide amendment, and I believe that passage of this limited exemption sends a message that Federal employees need not be accorded the respect and fair treatment they deserve. As a result, the credibility of all of the standards to which we ask employees to adhere is undermined.

I also note that section 330, under which the Secretary of Defense may "settle or defend" certain claims, should not be understood to detract from the Attorney General's plenary litigating authority. Accordingly, to the extent provided in current law, the Secretary of Defense will "settle or defend" claims in litigation through attorneys provided by the Department of Justice.

Section 4217 provides overbroad authority to the Government to collect data on technology and the industrial base from American businesses. Collecting such data through subpoena, administrative search warrants, and other investigative techniques authorized by this section will not contribute to America's economic strength and could intrude unacceptably into the lives of those who own and work in the Nation's businesses. Accordingly, I do not anticipate that the authority provided by section 4217 will be exercised.

As for title XVI, which prohibits exports of certain goods or technologies listed on the Department of Commerce Control List, I will interpret this provision as applying solely to items listed as requiring a validated license for export to Iran or Iraq. I find no indication of intent to override the congressionally endorsed regulatory provisions regarding exports from abroad of foreign-made products that incorporate certain minimal U.S.-origin content. As to the contract sanctity provision, I consider the reference date to be the date of enactment of this law. The Secretary of Commerce shall promptly issue such interpretive guidance and implementing regulations as may be required.

Finally, the bill contains a number of provisions for the disposition of Federal real property interests that would circumvent the provisions of, or regulations related to, the Federal Property and Administrative Services Act of 1949. Effective and efficient management of such real property matters generally is best accomplished in accordance with the Property Act.

GEORGE BUSH

The White House,
October 23, 1992.

Note: H.R. 5006, approved October 23, was assigned Public Law No. 102–484.

Question-and-Answer Session in Miami
October 23, 1992

Tom Wills. The President of the United States, George Bush, faces Florida voters in 11 days. Tonight he is here in Miami to answer their questions.

Ann Bishop. Good evening. With Tom Wills, I'm Ann Bishop. Tonight from across the State, President Bush will be answering the concerns on the issues on the minds of Floridians. We're going to get right to it, and our first question is from Jacksonville.

Consultation on the Economy

Q. Good evening, Mr. President. During the first debate you acknowledged that while the present economy is nowhere nearly as bad as your opponents would like for the American people to believe, there is room for improvement. My question is, if you're reelected President, would you be willing to offer an invitation to Ross Perot or to Bill Clinton to discuss their economic plans?

The President. That's easy. I think the answer is yes. But if I'm elected, it will be to put in my economic plan, and I think I will be because I think we've got the best plan. But I meet with opposition leaders all the time as President of the United States, and certainly I'd be willing to discuss it with them.

Tax Increase

Q. Good evening, Mr. President. Excluding your tax increase decision, if you could rewrite the history of the last 4 years, what one decision would you change?

The President. I gave you the main one. My view is if you make a mistake, you admit it. It's a little unusual in politics, but I think it's the thing you do. I made a mistake going along with that major Democratic tax increase. I say a mistake. It had some good things in it, put the caps on the discretionary spending programs, but it raised taxes. It was my belief that that was something we ought to do that would help the economy. I don't think it did at all.

I can't think of anything that fits into that league as something that I would view as a mistake of that proportion. I'm sure I make plenty of them, but give me some time and I might get back to you with it. I'm not sure this is a good time to be pointing out all your weaknesses, either. [*Laughter*]

Cuba

Mr. Wills. Just before President Bush came to be here with us tonight he was in downtown Miami, and he signed into law the Cuban Democracy Act. Now, Mr. President, as you know, the Democrats have accused you of trying to make some political hay on this issue. Our first question, sir, tonight here in Miami, is concerning Cuban-American relations.

Q. Good evening, Mr. President. Welcome to south Florida. My question is: Within the next 4 years, Cuba will join the nations that have democracies. What will you do and what will your administration do to help the people of Cuba?

The President. Well, I hope you're right.

And I think you're right, because I don't think Castro can continue to swim against the worldwide tide. The tide in this hemisphere is against him, but so is the worldwide tide. Everybody wants democracy, freedom, market economies. Of course, Castro's got none of that. I think the answer is then to move forward with investment support for him.

You see, it's going to be private. The thing that's going to make Cuba move forward fast is you have so many Cuban-Americans who have done well and want to invest and create businesses. It's not going to be a drain on the American taxpayer. It is going to be investment that solidifies their democracy.

I don't think we're going to need special programs. We've got programs in the Caribbean for those countries, Caribbean Basin Initiative. We've got a debt forgiveness program that has helped move Argentina and Brazil and other countries towards democracy. Many countries, 43 more countries have become democratic since I've been President, 43. Cuba will be the next one, I hope.

But it's not going to require a lot of Government aid. Everybody hates foreign aid. It's not going to require that. It's going to require investment. These are industrious people. We've seen what they can do here in this country. With freedom down there, they can do the same thing.

The Economy

Q. Good evening, President Bush. In 1980, my home mortgage was 18.5 percent. We had a cold war, hostage problems, and global inflation, but my family and I had good jobs, savings with high interest, and excellent health insurance. Today I have inadequate health insurance, no savings. My children and their children are without jobs. My oldest daughter is losing her home with a 7.5-percent mortgage. My home in a mobile park is facing liquidation. There is a global recession and homelessness. Granted, with the cold war over my family could sleep better at night, but now my own party's opening speaker at our convention tells us we're facing a religious and cultural war. Can you tell me why I am any better off today than I was 4 years ago?

The President. Well, you're better off in the sense of interest rates, clearly. We've got to go back to the days when the Democrats controlled both the White House and the Congress, which they've controlled for 38 years. Interest rates were 21 percent. Clearly, it's better to have them at where they are now. You can refinance homes. Inflation is lower. That's the cruelest tax of all if you were a saver. I'm not sure you were a saver.

I don't, I'm not sure I understand what you mean about a cultural war. I had the mayors from the leading cities come to see me. They were the board of directors of the National League of Cities. You know what they told me? They told me the major cause for urban decay was the decline in the American family. These were not right-wing nuts or leftwing nuts. Mayor Tom Bradley of Los Angeles was one of them; smalltown mayors that were Republicans from North Carolina; Plano, Texas, mayor. And this discussion of family is not something that I'm going to be driven away from. We've got to find ways to strengthen it. That's talking about driving drugs out of the community.

In some ways you're worse off, if you've got all those problems for your kids. But in many ways, you're better off, and I would cite some of the statistics that I've given you. I just hope that with this new job training program we've got, a program to get the burden of Government off of people like you, that we can do better.

But you're right, it's a global recession. I don't know how many people know this: Our economy is growing twice as fast as Japan's. People don't believe that. Germany had a negative growth. We have grown, albeit anemically, for five straight quarters. So when you're going through a tough economic time, you're bound to have hardships. I'm sorry you've got those, but I believe that job retraining, education, and stimulation of this economy for small business is the answer. I really do. Very good question.

POW–MIA's

Q. Good evening, President Bush. My name is Jill Hobbs. My father is Navy Com-mander Donald Richard Hobbs, and he has been missing in Vietnam since 1968. As you can imagine, this has been a very painful, heartbreaking, frustrating situation for my family for the last 24 years. Now with all the new information that's coming out of Vietnam, I would like to know what you plan to do to ensure that all of the live prisoners are returned, that all remains are repatriated, and that complete and truthful accounting of all our POW's and MIA's is given. I want to know what hope I have that I'll find out the truth about my father's fate.

The President. You have a lot more hope today than you did yesterday because this announcement that I made in the Rose Garden with General Vessey is a very significant breakthrough. Here's General Vessey, who is the former head of the Army, marvelous man, head of the Joint Chiefs, too. He went over there and came back with a lot of pictures, a lot of information that they had denied even existed before.

We think that today the announcement I made in the Rose Garden is a significant breakthrough, and I hope it leads to evidence that will be comforting to your family. But we just have to keep pressing on, and we're going to keep pressing on, trying to follow every single lead.

You're talking to somebody whose comrades died in combat. My roommate, this is ancient history, but my roommate was missing on the very first flight that I was in combat in the Pacific. So I hope it sensitizes me a little. I can't say I really know what you're going through.

But I think you ought to take some heart from this breakthrough today because I really believe that Vietnam now is going to—we're going to follow up to be sure they do this, but that they've turned over a new leaf. They're saying, no more obfuscation; we're going to put people in the archives. They've come out with 5,000 pictures. John McCain is a former prisoner, now a Senator; he came back with—they gave him, handed him pictures that he didn't know existed of his being pulled out of the water.

So I hope it leads to clues, and certainly we will follow up any leads on anybody that might be alive. But we've got to get the remains back, too. It's a breakthrough, and I just hope it proves to be something that is comforting to your family.

Child Care

Q. Good evening, Mr. President. My question, sir, is, what does your administration plan on doing to help the middle class as far as child care? It's beginning to look as though the poor and the rich are the only ones that can afford to have children. If reelected, what does your administration plan to do to help the middle class?

The President. One of our accomplishments was passing a child care bill, adequately financed, that gives parents the choice. When I came into office there was a prohibition against all but mandated—almost all but mandated child care centers. In other words, the Congress would say, here's the kind of child care you have to have. I think it strengthens the family to do what we've done, get legislation through a not altogether friendly Congress at times, and get it through to give the parents the choice for child care.

It is funded, and I hope that it's of benefit to you. There are limits in terms of how much a person is making. I don't remember the exact cutoff price, and maybe you're a little beyond that. But I believe that we've taken a major step forward in child care, and I hope it will benefit your family. There are no new bills planned for it.

Mr. Wills. Mr. President, we have tried to bring together here in our four cities voters, citizens from all walks of life. And this next question comes to you, sir, from a man who is 17 years old.

Education

Q. Good evening, Mr. President. Mr. President, I am planning to go to college within the next year. But my family may not be able to afford my higher education. It is a problem that many students and their families face in this community. As President of the United States, what will you specifically do if you are reelected to provide my generation with the educational opportunities that we need to succeed in life?

The President. First place, we've already doubled the funding for what they call Pell grants; that's for university. And I hope you've applied for that. Maybe—I don't know, again, what your circumstances are. But we've doubled the funding on the Pell grants, which is the major way of going forward for college students. And again, as I say, I hope that really helps.

Our main education program relates to getting kids ready for college. Frankly, we haven't done a good enough job for that. And many can't simply get into the college. So our program is called America 2000. It revolutionizes, literally revolutionizes education. It bypasses the old educational bureaucracy. It puts choice in the hands of parents for public, private, or religious schools.

Now, some say to me, "Hey, that's going to weaken the public schools." It hasn't worked that way with a woman named Polly Williams, a black woman up in Milwaukee. The mayor, a Democrat, in Milwaukee strongly supports it. And we believe that if you get the quality of elementary and K through 12 education, that more people will be able to qualify for existing scholarships.

Then I think the answer to your question is keep trying to do as much as we can in the scholarship field and the student loan field for kids like you that probably need some support to go through the college of your choice.

Health Care

Q. My 5-year-old had this question. One of the perks afforded you as President is what basically amounts to universal health care. Since you don't believe in universal health care for the American people, why is it that you utilize this benefit when you can clearly afford to pay your own medical bills? And why isn't this same program good enough for the American people?

The President. Well, you've got a bright 5-year-old with very good English, "utilizing my benefits." [*Laughter*] That kid's not going to have any trouble getting a scholarship.

I'll tell you, I'm Commander in Chief of the Armed Forces, and the Armed Forces provide this. This has traditionally been provided to the President. I have no apologies for it. But the kid is wrong in one thing. I hate to say that about your kid; she's very bright if she's that interested. My plan provides insurance for all. For the poorest of the poor you get a voucher. For the next group, like this guy's family back here, you're going to get assistance. You're going to get tax credit.

What I don't want to do is go to a plan that nationalizes—in some areas they call it socialized medicine—but say nationalizes medicine where you lower the quality of health care. The answer is to provide insurance to all, do more in terms of preventative medicine. Under Dr. Lou Sullivan, our HHS Secretary, we've moved out very well on that.

We've got to do more to get the costs of all this down. One of the things where I differ with Governor Clinton is, I think we've got to do something about these malpractice suits and these awful lawsuits that are raising the costs to the tune of $25 to $50 billion.

But put it this way: If your 5-year-old thinks the only way that you're going to get universal health care coverage is to have mandated Government coverage, I disagree with her. I think it's better to use this whole brandnew system of pooling insurance to provide insurance to the poorest of the poor and right on up. So we just have a philosophical difference. No difference about wanting to get it done, though.

Abortion

Q. Good evening, Mr. President. Your firm stand against legalized abortion has been clearly stated in the past and during this campaign. I'd like to ask you this: If the Supreme Court reverses the *Roe* v. *Wade* decision during your next term in office, do you think that States that outlaw abortion should make it a capital crime——

The President. No.

Q. ——that is, equating abortion with murder? And if so, do you think that women that receive the abortions and the doctors that perform them should be subject to the death penalty and/or life imprisonment?

The President. No, no. The answer is no to all of the above. But I do oppose abortion.

You know, I think it's wrong to have 28 million abortions over the last few years. I don't believe you ought to have abortion for a—put it this way: If a 13-year-old kid can't even get her ears pierced without parental approval, don't you think we ought to have some restraints? Don't you think that that kid ought to have to get permission from the parents? I believe in adoption. I believe in life. I know my position isn't particularly popular with some, but this is something I feel in my heart; take your case to the American people.

But no, on the criminal penalties you're talking about.

Deficit Reduction

Q. Mr. President, good evening. How is your proposal on allowing people to designate income tax proceeds toward debt reduction and spending cuts supposed to work? And do you believe a citizen would be willing to spend his or her own money toward debt reduction?

The President. Debt reduction—I'll get to his—there's three things we need: We need a balanced budget amendment to the Constitution. A lot of the States have it. We need a line-item veto that says to the President, if Congress can't cut it, you can cut out the pork by drawing a line through whatever line you want in the veto, in the bill. Then they can override you if they want to.

On this proposal he's talking about, it's a new one that I have made. And what it says to the taxpayer is, when you go fill out your tax form, if you care as much about deficit reduction as other things, you can then kick off 10 percent, a little box on the tax return. That will all be added up. Say it comes to $40 billion, all the people that fill out the tax return, added to $40 billion. Then you have to use that money to reduce the debt.

And that's going to mean, then, that Congress is going to have to, working with the administration, reduce spending by that much. And that gets to be difficult. But it forces it; it forces the equation. And if they can't do it in negotiation, then you do what they call a sequester. The sequester goes right across the board, not touching Social Security, but right across the board to get the spending down.

It's rather simple. And some of the liberal economists ridicule it. But I believe those three things together can make a significant difference on getting this deficit off the back of young people like you. When your kids come along, if we don't we're going to be in real problems for the future.

That isn't easy. I mean, I can't stand here and tell this audience or the audience in Orlando or Jacksonville or Tampa that it's going to be easy. I want to control the growth of the mandatory spending program, not cut them, control the growth to inflation and to allow for population. But that means they're not going to be able to grow as fast. They can grow, not be cut, but not grow as fast.

Those things together I think are the way we're going to get this deficit down. And that check-off ought to be tried. If it doesn't work, change the law.

Hurricane Andrew Recovery Efforts

Mr. Wills. Sir, as you know, the people here in south Florida for the past many weeks now have been trying to recover from the devastating effects of Hurricane Andrew. The next person you're going to hear from really tonight is in the category of a special guest.

Q. Mr. President, Alex Muxo, city manager of the city of Homestead.

Mr. Wills. And I should add, Mr. President, that Alex is a nonpartisan officeholder, neither Democrat nor Republican.

The President. I'll tell you what I think about him in a minute. [*Laughter*]

Mr. Wills. He wants to tell you what he thinks about you.

The President. I know he does.

Q. Mr. President, first of all, on behalf of all the south Dade community, we really thank you from the bottom of our heart for your support in this last few months. As a matter of fact, tomorrow will be the 2-month anniversary of Hurricane Andrew, which we all know the devastation caused in our community.

Although your leadership was unwavering, you know the outcome of what happened with the Congress with Homestead

Air Force Base. One of the biggest concerns that we have now is if the medical facility and the PX isn't built immediately, this community, south Dade, Dade County, Monroe, and West Palm Beach and Broward, have the chance of losing as much as 80,000 retirees because those facilities aren't there. What can you do to move that along so we can keep these people in our community?

The President. Well, let me answer Alex's question. But let me tell you about this guy because—and this is not a slow ball—he's an independent. He's strong out there. He does what he thinks is right. Here's a man who, when his own home was devastated, was out looking after people in the community, and that said an awful lot to me. I think it said a lot to the people of Florida and the people across the country. And I think it stimulated a lot of support not just from us, from the Federal Government, but it served as an inspiration to what I call the Points of Light, the people here where they got this program Rebuild. You see a guy like this—do it.

I hope we can push it. I hope we can get it moving. What Alex is talking about is, I made a decision that we were going to rebuild Homestead. I got hit by Congressmen and Senators from different parts of the country because in a shrinking defense budget they saw a chance to get this money to build the installations in their area or keep the bases in their area or transfer the facilities, you know, the intelligence facilities, antidrug facilities, somewhere else.

We got beat on it. We got some money, got a little, not near as much as we wanted. On this one, I think we just have to push on it and get it done. I don't think it's to be controversial. I mean, I think it's something we can get through. Our bureaucracy is what I think the problem is.

But we'll keep pushing. I mean, it's been an inspiration to the whole country. I will say this to the audience: Government can do a lot. When the Government's spending over its head, it can't do as much as it would like. But the private sector response on this is absolutely amazing. You go out there and you see people from North Carolina who were helped by you all when their

Hurricane Hugo came along, and now they've responded. I went to Louisiana. There was a bunch of people from North Carolina and South Carolina over there, so that American spirit of helping one another is still there. I think you all demonstrated it as vividly as anything out of this hurricane situation.

Correctional Facilities

Q. With your present tax policies, what will you do to assist major cities and counties with their overcrowded prison populations on a State and local level?

The President. We have put more money into State and local police than ever. Spending is up for Federal. But we can't do the whole police corrections facilities bit. That can't be done by the Federal Government. We have expanded the Federal prisons. The Federal prisoners—you know this, given your life to corrections—have spent 85 percent of their time in jail. A lot of the States have a much less rigorous program.

We have an assistance program to corrections institutions, but I just hate to stand here and try to promise you that we can increase it. What we have done is increase the funding considerably for Federal prisons, and we've increased it for local law enforcement support, but not as much in the prison field.

Now the answer, I guess, is to continue to try to help as much as we can and then press forward with programs that are going to reduce the incidence of crime.

I come back to a program we call "Weed and Seed," where you weed out the criminals. I don't know whether you've had any—working with it at all. But it's a good new approach, gets across partisan lines. It says weed out the criminals and then seed the communities with hope. Then that gets to our whole urban agenda, so people have jobs in these cities through enterprise zones and tenant management, homeownership, as opposed to the hopelessness and despair that results in the crimes that you, fortunately, are helping on.

Women's Health Care

Q. Women's health could be a prime area of research for the National Institutes of Health, especially in the areas of breast, ovarian, and cervical cancer. However, Dr. Healy, the Director of the NIH, has stated that focus on women's health was not necessary. How would you in your next term ensure that the NIH increased research and funding in women's health?

The President. Well, again, I don't want to be under false colors. Every question, almost, says how much more money can you spend from the Federal Government, every one. And I can understand it. There is a new program for breast cancer, and it's pretty well financed out of HHS. I'll have to look at the NIH funding. I don't remember Ms. Healy saying that, Dr. Healy. She's a very able head of NIH.

And I'm not trying to put you down at all, because, look, that is a tremendously important cause. The next question I'll get will probably be on AIDS. We're spending up from $4.2 billion to $4.9 billion. And people say, "Well, you got to do more." I'm standing here telling these guys how we're going to get the deficit down. You can't do it painlessly. You can't do it by slapping more taxes on an overtaxed population. So we're dealing with somewhat of a restricted budget in doing all these things.

But let me check on NIH. I'm not just putting you off, but I don't believe that NIH is opposed to any women's health care efforts. And our early prevention programs that Dr. Sullivan is sponsoring can help get the problem—you're a nurse, so you know much more about it than I do—but can help before you have to be putting the serious treatment to people.

Ross Perot

Q. My regards to you, President Bush. My question to you is, why is there such an integrity vacuum in today's government? The silent majority, like myself, can find more answers and solutions to the problems in America today in a book written by Ross Perot, "United We Stand," than by any of the present elected officials. And why haven't you initiated a special group of highly trained individuals to address these problems one by one until each Department has been corrected?

The President. That's a good question. But you see, I differ with Mr. Perot. I don't want to touch Social Security. He has in his program doing something about reducing Social Security for some. I don't think we ought to do that. I think we ought to set Social Security aside. It's not just another guaranteed program. It is a rather sacrosanct program with a trust fund. And so I have a difference with him on that.

I don't think we need a 50-cent—in your hand there in that plan is a 50-cent-a-gallon gasoline tax. Now, a lot of people have to ride to work, and where you have big distances, that is overwhelming. Or if you're a cab driver, the poor guy's trying to make ends meet, or a truck driver, he doesn't need to pay 50 cents more per gallon.

So I don't want to spend a lot of time looking at things that I'm opposed to. Now, in terms of what Perot is suggesting in terms of really having to do something on the spending side, I think he's on to something there, but not in these specifics that I've given you. And so I'm not going to spend the taxpayers' money with having a whole new group of people coming in to study something that I'm certainly not—going to oppose, or that people will oppose if they elect me. I mean, I don't think a Social Security increase or a gasoline tax is the answer at this time.

So that's why I would—but don't let me try to put you down by saying there's no good ideas in there; there are. I think we've got enough study groups. What we need to do is get something done.

I've got one difference with him. You just can't open the hood, say fix it. I mean, you've got to work with the Congress. And I don't mean to put the blame—I'll accept blame. But when you're working with Congress, it ain't that easy, believe me. Look at Alex's problem. Here we had a problem that would have helped the community just to keep something that was there, rebuild it. You've got all these contrasting interests. I go up as President, say restore Homestead, and you can't dictate to them. They're tough. You've got to hit them over the head like that mule with a two-by-four.

But the good news, there's good news, they screwed up that two-bit bank up there and that post office so bad that there are going to be 100 new Members of Congress. And maybe we can get things moving much

quicker the next term.

AIDS

Q. Good evening, Mr. President. I bring a question that comes from clients and other professionals in my agency. They'd like to know why over the last 4 years when the Names Project has been in Washington three times, you have not visited the Names Project, which now contains more than 26,000 panels for those who have died of AIDS?

The President. Well, that's a good question. I have felt a little bit unloved by the AIDS community. We have spent, as I say, far more money on research, far more, I think, money on compassionate programs. We've got the NIH with their great researchers out there geared up. What happens to me when I go out—and I shouldn't judge the whole community by the excesses, but they've got an outfit called ACT–UP. And they come to my home and throw condoms around and behave in a very bad fashion. They break up your political appearances.

I don't think that helps the cause any. And I don't want to be a lightning rod in a compassionate project like this quilt project by going out there. I can take it. Good God, I've seen worse characters than those. But they don't help the cause any. For me to go as a lightning rod out onto those grounds to be yelled at and screamed at and as a symbol, I don't think it helps the AIDS problem.

The AIDS problem requires compassion, requires understanding. Both Barbara and I have been to clinics and held AIDS babies and tried to demonstrate the concern we feel. But to be a lightning rod for the excesses, I don't think that is good for the President of the United States. And that's my very frank feeling on it.

Maybe we differ. Maybe you can make a case for ACT–UP. I can't. When they come to a guy's home, little home village, and stand there with outrageous behavior, I'm afraid I just have to say I don't agree with that. I don't agree with them going into a Catholic cathedral, when people are on their knees worshiping, and start throwing condoms around. I don't want to be the symbol for that kind of behavior. I want to help that. I want to help with research. I want to see compassion. But I don't want to be the catalyst for excess. That's why I didn't do it.

Communism

Q. As a major foreign policy accomplishment, you have consistently maintained in this campaign that you deserve credit for the dissolution of communism. How can you prove that communism is virtually dead when more than one billion Chinese and, importantly, more than 10 million Cubans in our backyard are still committed to undemocratic governments?

The President. Well, I don't say communism is totally dead. I say imperial communism is, if not dead, stretched out on the slab there about to be buried, because you don't have the Soviet Union anymore. For years we had a cold war going on between the Soviet Union. That ended. That ended when I was President. And I think our policies had a lot to do with it.

Do you remember, do you remember about 12 years ago people were saying, "Nuclear freeze, the only way you're going to solve nuclear terror for the kids is to freeze, stop right where we are." If we'd have done that, there would have been no driving force to get the Soviet Union moving towards democracy and to get rid of their nuclear weapons. I stood out there in the East Room of the White House and made a deal with Yeltsin to get rid of every single SS–18. Those are the big, destabilizing, multiwarheaded nuclear missiles. That is a major accomplishment for all the kids.

But you're right. I gave a big speech here today on Cuba. The guy's trying to keep his snorkel out of the water. Castro, he's not reaching out trying to corrupt the Dominican Republic and these other people.

And China, we've got big differences with them. What's happening in China, though, is their economic side of the house is moving toward market forces. And that's going to lead them to political change. That's why I don't want to cut off relations with China.

I'm glad you asked it because if I left the impression that I think there's no more communism anywhere, I should clear that up. There is, but it's not what I call imperial communism that's trying to take over its neighbors. Thanks for giving me the opportunity. I didn't realize I'd been that unclear on it.

Space Programs

Q. I'm an aerospace worker. In obtaining funding for space station, it's been tough going through the Democrat-controlled Congress. My question is, specifically, how committed will your new administration be towards funding our space station and our future space programs at Kennedy Space Center?

The President. Rick, I'm committed, and my word is on the line on that. It's in every budget we've sent forward. We're going to continue to fight for it. One of the places I might be able to do better on is to convince people that the research that goes into the space station and the space station itself will benefit not just those interested in space but all mankind. Now, you guys know this. The fallout in medicine and other fields from our space effort already has been appreciable. Agriculture has benefited.

So I am committed. I will keep fighting for it. We have a big fight with Congress because when money is tight, as it is, you've got to set priorities. But research and development is going to lead this country to a brandnew level of prosperity for young people. And you guys are on the cutting edge. So we're going to fight again in the next Congress for it.

Ms. Bishop. Mr. President, Diane Tass is with us, and she has a question not only important to the country but terribly important to this community.

Airline Industry

Q. I wanted to know, Mr. President, how do you plan to support some of these airlines that are being edged out by the big three or four, and especially for just the average traveler who, once we get down to three or four airlines, we're not going to be able to travel on vacations? Also I want to know how you feel about the USAir-British Airways alliance.

The President. Good questions. First I've got to start off with, we may have a philosophical difference. I don't believe it's the Government's role to say how many airlines there are going to be, which ones are going to survive, which ones not. The market has to do that for the most part, unless you want to go to state-owned airlines. And I don't want to do that.

So we're just going to have to be as competitive as possible. The problem with my argument is, a little bit, is that there are some Government controls on airlines because the routes are set. But I still don't want to see Government saying who's going to get in, who can't get in, who's got to get out.

On the USAir deal, it's a tough one right now. It boils down to this, that British Air wants to take over USAir. USAir workers are picketing me out here in the field when I land, wherever I land, wherever there's any USAir. Standing next to them in the field are the American Airline pickets, all decent, wonderful Americans, all concerned about their jobs. American Airlines are saying, "Don't let British come in and take over USAir unless we get access to the European markets."

Now, here's what will seem like a hedge to you. This matter is now under adjudication with the Secretary of Transportation. And to prejudge what his decision is, I would be—I wouldn't be run out of office, but I'd have a lot of explaining to do in the legal community. And I'm not going to do it. But it is being heard. The interests are very difficult because you've got people whose jobs are going to be threatened one way or the other. It will come to me. I'm not ducking it; it will come to me. But I have to wait until we hear from the Department before I tell you what I think is going to happen on the British Air-USAir proposed merger.

On balance, on general statement, please discount airlines, I think we need more access to foreign markets in everything, whether it's agriculture or whether it's textiles or whatever it is. Exports have saved us in an extraordinarily difficult global recession, and exports are going to lift us up and lead us out of it. But they aren't if we don't hammer away and get more access to foreign markets.

Thank you.

Retraining Military Personnel

Q. Good evening, Mr. President.

The President. Hi.

Q. Good evening, Mr. President. I'm Sergeant Oliver, stationed at MacDill Air Force Base. What type of program or help will you offer those military members who are now being forced out of the military?

The President. Just signed a bill today, the Defense Authorization Act, which also included this Cuban Democracy Act, I might add, signed it in Miami. And that has a significant numbers of millions, up in the hundreds of millions, for retraining and relocation.

The sergeant puts his finger on something. Because we were successful, Desert Storm, around the world, we are cutting back on defense. I've cut back on it significantly. My opponent Governor Clinton and Ross Perot want to cut it $50 billion more. I'm not going to do that. I'm going to wait until I get a recommendation by Colin Powell and Dick Cheney, in whom I have total trust and whom the Nation trusts, because I think, even though there are problems in this world, I mean, a lot of the problems have been solved, there still are wolves out there. And we'd better be strong.

But back to your question. The new defense authorization bill authorizes significant funds for exactly what you're talking about. But let's not let them cut into the muscle of our defense.

Taxes

Q. It is my understanding that capital gains tax reduction is actually supported by Bill Clinton. Is he not letting the public know this because a reduction of capital gains would actually help the middle class as much, if not more, than it would help the so-called wealthy? And isn't it true that the only time we should be happy about taxes is when ours are going down and not when anybody else's are going up?

The President. Well, you're my kind of guy. That's what I think. [*Laughter*] But for years the Democrats have been beating up on me saying capital gains is a tax break for the rich. Let me tell you something. For months I've been asking the Congress to pass an investment tax allowance, a tax credit for the first-time homebuyer, and a cut in capital gains, not to help some rich guy but to create new small businesses. Small businesses employ two-thirds of the people. Jobs in the private sector would have been enhanced. I'm going to keep on fighting for breaks for small business, and one of them is capital gains.

I cannot get that point across. And if Governor Clinton is for it, he's whispering in one place and then—the first bad thing I've said about the guy tonight. But look, you can't be on all sides of every issue. And if he's for it, stand up and get his Members of Congress, who allegedly are—who are opposed to it, to say, "I will support this man. I will get it through." I have big differences with him, and this may be one of them. But if he's for it, he's whispering it to the business guys but not saying anything to the rest of the people about it.

Young Voters

Q. Mr. Bush, Bill Clinton and Al Gore have reached out to young voters with their recent appearances on MTV. Why have you and Vice President Quayle rejected such opportunities to reach out to 18- to 24-year-old voters?

The President. Hey, we're trying to reach out to them with programs. I'm not too much of a mod MTV man. But I don't think what program you appear on—I can't play the saxophone, but I know a good deal about issues. And so you can't be everywhere. I think our programs have strong appeal for young people, whether it's education reform or whether it's on the health care so their families have a much better break on that, whether it's on college scholarships where our record is superb in terms of these Pell grants.

But look, there's something funny going on in American politics. I've been doing this kind of program since 1978 in forums that were called "Ask George Bush." And I like it. I feel comfortable.

Some of the programs to get out there and kind of outdo Oprah or Phil Donahue, that's not my style. Maybe MTV would be a good one, and I'll think about it. But you can't do them all, and you shouldn't be judged by whether you go on one single network or one single program. That's my answer.

National Debt

Q. Good evening, President Bush. How do you envision American life and standard of living in 5 to 10 years if the national debt isn't controlled?

The President. Not good. But I think we can control it. You've got to start by controlling the growth of mandatory spending and not do it by raising people's taxes. And I think that will stimulate economic growth.

We're limping along. We've had five straight quarters of economic growth. The definition of recession is two straight quarters of negative growth. We haven't had negative growth for five quarters. That's over a year and a—maybe six now, because the end of September, I think we'll find we grew. So we've had very anemic growth, caught up in an economic global recession in some countries, slowdown in others. We're going to come out of that. The way we're going to come out of it, I believe, is by controlling the growth of our spending, by stimulating through the kinds of tax proposals I told him about, and getting this country growing. After the last recession, we grew at 5.4 percent. Now we're growing at 1.7 or 1.8 percent, maybe up into 2 now. And it's too anemic.

So you've got to have economic programs that are going to stimulate growth. And when that happens, then the standard of living, the standard of living goes up. Personal income is up in this country. Agricultural income has reached a high under our administration. Please don't wait to hear about that on the top of the CBS evening news or NBC or ABC—I've got to be careful here—because you don't get much good economic news out there. The unemployment claims went down yesterday, the biggest since, I think, 2 years, and I didn't even hear about it on the news.

I'm not saying everything's perfect. A lot of people are hurting. But don't despair about the future standard of living if we get in there and bring a lot of new Members of Congress and say, now let's do what the people want done. I don't think they want their taxes raised. I do think they want to stimulate the economy.

Family Leave Bill

Q. Mr. President, time and time again you have used your veto power to go against the wishes of the American public. You did this by vetoing the family leave bill, something that I feel our country really needed. At a time when your campaign has pushed for family values, how could you veto the bill? And please don't tell me that it was so it wouldn't hurt small businesses. From what I understand——

The President. That's a good answer to it.

Q. ——those with less than 50 employees would have been exempt. Is that true?

The President. They would have been exempt, but we have a better idea. In the first place, I keep telling everybody here, and I'll tell them up there, the thing that's going to lead us out of this into recovery is small business. They do not need any more mandates from Washington.

My approach was a tax credit approach. And that includes—what are those eyes going up? You don't agree with it. [*Laughter*] I saw you rolling your eyes. But my approach says why not the lower than 50? Why not the mom-and-pop store? Why not others? And my program would have covered them all. You want to go with having the Government dictate all this, and to say that that veto makes me less on family? I'm sorry. I reject it. It's a philosophical difference. And let's get a little more support out of these who think the Government can do it all for some ways to strengthen the American family, as those mayors urged us to do.

I'm for family leave. I am not for needlessly burdening small businesses. So I am telling you what you don't want to hear. Sorry about that.

Enterprise Zones

Q. I'd like to ask you, considering the financial constraints facing cities yet the increasing need, would you support a plan to offer low or interest-free loans to local or State governments for infrastructure improvements?

The President. I'd rather do it through enterprise zones. I'd rather do it through tax breaks to bring jobs into the inner cities. That's my priority. And it's a program—

when L.A. blew up, L.A., South Central, the Mayor, the Governor, and Peter Ueberroth all came back. I arranged for a meeting in the Cabinet Room with the Speaker and Gephardt, the leader of the Democrats in the House, and the Senate leaders. All three of those people from California said the way to help the cities is through enterprise zones, urban enterprise zones. So that's my preferred approach, rather than the one you suggest. I really think it will work. I believe it will work.

Aid to Russia and the Federal Budget

Q. My question is as follows: Do you believe that the United States must invest a significant amount of money in the Russian economy in order to help Mr. Yeltsin's newfound democracy, prevent a resurgence of the hardliners, and perhaps initiating a new cold war? And part two of the question is, how do you think this would influence in balancing the budget?

The President. The answer to your question is yes, I believe it. We have already passed on a bipartisan basis a thing called the FREEDOM Support Act. It's like an insurance policy. It says we spent trillions of dollars in the cold war, and now Boris Yeltsin, the guy that stood on the tank and brought democracy forward in Russia, needs support. The Russian people need it. And we've already done it. I don't think we need more of that regard.

But you raise a good point. Anything we do of that nature makes balancing the budget more difficult, any spending. All these programs we're being asked about tonight makes getting the deficit down hard. So what you have to do is put together a budget, as I do every year. Four straight years I've had budgets that get in balance, putting to the Congress over 5 years. You can't do it in one. Included in the last one is funding for the FREEDOM Support Act.

But the man's on to something. I mean, I happen to think that this is an insurance policy with Russia. I don't want to see them go back to totalitarianism. Let's hope that this approach keeps them from doing that. But it costs money. And we've got to recognize it every time. Whether it's a program here or a program there, the taxpayer is bearing the burden.

Haiti

Q. Mr. President, your own immigration officials interviewed Haitian refugees and found 40 percent were not economic migrants but had credible fears of political persecution in Haiti. We correctly give asylum to Cuban refugees. Why since May have you ordered the Coast Guard to repatriate all of the Haitian boat people to a dictatorship we don't even recognize and which the State Department says executes and tortures its own people and which actually fingerprints the arrivals in Port-au-Prince and photographs them? And lastly, if you're really serious about restoring Haiti's ousted democratically elected government, why do you let oil and other essential supplies reach Haiti's dictators from Europe?

The President. Let me answer the last part first. We're not trying to starve the people of Haiti, and we're not trying to freeze them or cook them or do anything of that nature.

On the first part of your question, this information that 40 percent are considered political refugees, I'd like to see the documentation of that because our program says the law will apply. Political refugees have access to asylum.

What I don't want to do is to see these merchants of death, these guys that rent these leaky boats or build them, then sell passage to poor people, who offer them the hope of coming to America, and then have a rescue operation—some of them not rescued—at sea. We had a program to screen these people in Haiti. I must have different information than you, but I've got pretty good information as President of the United States that these people are not being persecuted when they go to file their claims for asylum. So we've got a factual difference there.

Q. In the Embassy, a case has come to our attention—it's not the first one—of a man who applied in June at the Embassy; 3 months later they invited him for an interview, but he'd been dead 9 days. Earlier a man's toenails had been ripped out. There are 11,000 people that your own asylum officers in Guantanamo, for 6 months before June, said had credible fears of per-

secution in Haiti, and they'd been allowed to come here and ask for asylum. But now you send everybody back.

The President. That's exactly my point. If they find cases like that, they're allowed to apply.

Q. But now you're sending them back with no asylum interviews whatsoever, right to the docks to get fingerprinted by the Haitian military.

The President. But I am told that when they go back there, there is not this persecution. You've raised it; let me take a look at it.

Aristide going back, we support that. I've got to be a little careful as President on what I say about him and how it works and what he's doing here. Our policy has been to support the OAS, the Organization of American States, to get this man back, not because of a great love for any individual but because of a commitment to democracy. I don't like to see democracy aborted by a coup. It isn't working too well because you don't have the public support that he once had. But we're going to stay with that for a while. But shutting down the oil is not that easy either. You ask the naval people about that.

Mr. Wills. Mr. President, I hate to stop this discussion——

The President. Kind of interesting debate, though.

Mr. Wills. ——but I've got to move on to Tampa-St. Petersburg for our next question, sir.

The Character Issue

Q. Good evening, Mr. President. I wanted to find out from you what is the goals of your administration for the next 5 years? And also, I am a person who served in the military, and my father served before me, and I want to find out your thoughts on the integrity of the person who will serve in the White House?

The President. The goals are restore economic prosperity to this country. That is the single overriding goal. As Commander in Chief of the Armed Forces, as custodian of the national security, I've got to guarantee against threats to the United States or threats to the free world, really, and I take that responsibility very, very seriously.

In terms of the next person to serve there, I have had differences with Governor Clinton. And some say to me, "You're old-fashioned. I find it difficult to understand how the Commander in Chief reacts," taking the position that he did, that it's okay to organize demonstrations against your country when your country is at war in a foreign land. People say, "What's the difference in a foreign land?" I don't know. I make a distinction. If you want to protest, come to the White House and do it. That's the American way. Everybody else does. Why don't you come along and do that? But I have big differences.

But my differences with Governor Clinton in terms of the custodianship of the—or the being Commander in Chief is the problem that he has with kind of coming down on one position. On the war he said, "I agree with the minority, but I guess I would have voted for the majority." You can't do that in the Oval Office. You have to make a decision. And sometimes it's painful, and you'll make a mistake and you say, "Look, I fouled that up. I made a mistake."

But on the war, we did the right thing, and I thought his position was waffling around out there. So I can't pass judgment on how anybody else would behave. But I've tried to uphold the honor. Honor, duty and country: I believe in that. I believe in service to country. And I think I'm a better Commander in Chief because I fought for my country. I don't think it's a mandatory requirement, but I just think it's made me more sensitive when you have to commit somebody else's son or someone's daughter to combat, having been there.

Mr. Wills. Mr. President, we've run out of time. Thank you so much for being here with us tonight.

That was our last question. We know there are so many others. We'd like to get them all in, but we have used up all of our time. We hope that the Florida News Network, through their town meetings, has helped you make an informed choice on November 3d.

Ms. Bishop. I'm sure last month you saw Governor Clinton on our town meeting, and the Florida News Network has issued an invitation to Ross Perot. We are waiting for his response. We thank all of you for joining us on television. Thank you here in our studio and our other studios around the State.

And of course, thank you, Mr. President, for being with us.

The President. Thank you all very, very much.

Note: The question-and-answer session began at 8 p.m. at the WPLG–TV studios. News anchors Ann Bishop, WPLG–TV, and Tom Wills, WJXT–TV, Jacksonville, FL, served as moderators for the session. In his remarks, the President referred to Gen. John W. Vessey, USA, ret., Special Emissary to Hanoi for POW–MIA Affairs.

Statement on Signing the Depository Institutions Disaster Relief Act of 1992
October 23, 1992

Today I am signing into law H.R. 6050, the "Depository Institutions Disaster Relief Act of 1992." The Act provides the banking regulatory agencies with limited discretion to waive or modify certain regulatory requirements. These requirements needlessly restrict the flow of banking and credit services to areas devastated by Hurricanes Andrew and Iniki and the Los Angeles riots.

This legislation will provide welcome relief to federally insured depository institutions and their customers in these shattered neighborhoods and help expedite recovery efforts.

Following a meeting with bankers in south Florida in early September, my Administration first proposed legislation to assure the full participation of banks, thrifts, and credit unions in the process of recovery from disasters or major emergencies. This Act stems from the Administration's original proposal and will be very helpful to the residents of south Florida, south-central Louisiana, Kauai, and Los Angeles.

This is the first banking legislation in a decade that does nothing but reduce regulatory burdens. I urge the next Congress to build upon this measure by the passage of my Credit Availability and Regulatory Relief Act (CARRA), which would reduce the excessive regulatory burden on the banking industry generally and permit banks to provide the credit needed for sustained economic growth.

GEORGE BUSH

The White House,
October 23, 1992.

Note: H.R. 6050, approved October 23, was assigned Public Law No. 102–485.

Letter to Congressional Leaders Transmitting a Report on Trade With Canada
October 23, 1992

Dear Mr. Chairman:

Pursuant to section 103 of the United States-Canada Free-Trade Agreement Implementation Act of 1988 (Public Law 100–449), I am pleased to submit the attached report and related documents pertaining to an action to amend Annex 301.2, which pertains to rules of origin.

Sincerely,

GEORGE BUSH

Note: Identical letters were sent to Dan Rostenkowski, chairman, House Committee on Ways and Means, and Lloyd Bentsen, chairman, Senate Committee on Finance.

Remarks to the Community in Montgomery, Alabama
October 24, 1992

The President. Thank you very much. Wow! Thank you very much. And I am so very pleased to be back in this great State on this beautiful Saturday day. Let me just say I want to pay my respects to your Governor. I want to thank Mayor Emory Folmar, my long-time, longstanding friend. I'll give you a little advice. If you want to win a State and if you want to win it with conviction and honor, get Emory Folmar at your side. I am proud he is at mine. And also, I want to salute my bass fishing friend, Ray Scott, who has made this great Alabama pastime a national pastime. I have threatened to him that when this election is over, with a much more relaxed attitude, I'm coming back to Pintlala, Alabama, and catch some bass.

And of course, I would be remiss if I didn't single out Bill Dickinson, who has served this area with such distinction in the Congress. If we had more like him, they wouldn't be holding up these signs everywhere I go saying, "Clean House!" We must clean House. We'll get this guy up there, get Terry Smith up there, and we'll clean the House out, I'll tell you. Now, also while we're at it, let's clean Senate and elect Rick Sellers to the United States Senate. And I want to say, here's the guy. Now vote for this man. Come on, Rick. Another man, Don Sledge, running in another area for Congress, good luck to you. Terry Everett is running for the Dickinson seat, and we've got to get him elected there. So thank you all. And I'm told that we had a——

Audience member. [*Inaudible*]—man, Kervin Jones.

The President. Hey, what district? For the 7th District. Hey, listen, we get these guys elected and we won't see those signs saying, "Clean House!" We will have done our part. Besides, he's big enough to whip 'em all up there, so—[*laughter*]—that's good. We need that man there, I'll tell you.

Now, may I thank the Jefferson Davis and Lee High School participants around here. Great job. And finally, Bart Starr. You know, I look over my shoulder and see a great son of Alabama, the legendary quarterback Bart Starr. You know, many years ago in the frozen tundra of Wisconsin, Bart Starr led those Packers to a stunning playoff victory against the Dallas Cowboys. And let me tell you something, he is here today because that accentuates the fact that we are going to achieve another stunning upset victory and represent these people in the United States for 4 more years. Thank you, Bart.

Now, I hate to ruin this beautiful Saturday, but I do think we must get in perspective, before the American people go to the polls, the Arkansas record. The people in Arkansas—everyone in Alabama knows it because we have friends, we in Texas, you in Alabama have friends in Arkansas—they are good and decent and honorable people. But let me tell you what the record has been with Bill Clinton. They are the 50th in the quality of environmental initiatives; 50th in percentage of adults with college degrees. They are 50th in per capita spending on criminal justice. They are 49th in per capita spending on police protection; 48th in percentage of adults with a high school diploma; 48th in spending on corrections; 46th on teachers' salaries; 45th in the overall well-being of children. And the other night, Governor Clinton said in that debate in Michigan, he said, "I want to do for America what I've done for Arkansas." No way. We cannot let him do that. It's like sending the guy who finishes last in managing the Little League in Montgomery, telling him to manage the Braves. We don't need that kind of change.

This guy talks about change. That's all your going to have left in your pocket if we listen to his program. And here it is—all right, you taxpayers, get ready—this is before he's even gotten started: $150 billion in new taxes, bigger than McGovern and Dukakis put together; $220 billion in new spending. And I call that trickle-down Government. Give it to the Government, and you never see it again. He says he'll get it from the rich. But the rest of you guys out there that have to work for a living, you nurses or you teachers or you cab drivers or you truck drivers, watch your wallet. There aren't enough rich people to pay for this guy's promises and all Al Gore's extreme environmental positions. There are not enough so he's coming after you. Watch your wallet, America. This guy is coming after you. But I'm not going to let him do it.

Audience members. Four more years! Four more years! Four more years!

The President. All right, it's fine to stand up and point out all the things that are wrong. And yes, we've got problems, and yes, people are hurting, and yes, some people at work want to know where they're going to get the jobs, how they're going to keep them. But let me tell you something. The last time we tried his kind of change, when you had a liberal Democrat in the White House and that same old crowd controlling the Congress, who remembers? He changed inflation, all right; he changed it up to 15 percent. He destroyed the family budgets. And the interest rates—some of you homeowners remember what they were—they were 21 percent. We do not need that kind of change for America.

My view is to cut that spending, get the Government spending down and the taxes down, and then stimulate investment in small business, not in Government but in small business. They create two-thirds of the jobs, two-thirds. Give them a tax break, and get America back to work.

The doom-and-gloom crowd is a little too much. You know, my favorite bumper sticker—I don't know whether we've got any of them around here—there's a marvelous—yes, it's here, right over there. That's over there: "Annoy the Media." They wouldn't know good news if it hit them in the face. Have you gotten this from your television yet? Have you heard this on the television at night, that unemployment claims have gone down to the lowest in 2 years? Have you heard that inflation is down, that interest rates are down, that total employment is 93 percent, inflation 2.5 to 3 percent, home mortgages are 8 percent? Now, ask yourself this: Can Bill Clinton do better than this, or will he make things worse? I think he'll make things worse.

Here's what we're going to do. We're going to increase our exports. We're going to create more jobs right here in Montgomery, Alabama, and all across this country that are concerned with exports. Exports have saved us in what is essentially a global recession or a global slowdown. Our economy—don't listen to Governor Clinton, you'll never hear this; nobody will report it on the news—is doing better than Japan, doing better than Germany, doing better than Europe, doing better than Canada. It's not good enough; it's not good enough. We're going to create export jobs by barging into those foreign markets. And that means prosperity for people in Alabama. Not protection, exports.

And I'll tell you another one where I've got a big difference with the Governor from Arkansas. That is on legal reform. I think it's a shame when people don't dare coach Little League because some crazy trial lawyer is going to come along and try to sue them; or when somebody sees an automobile accident and they don't dare stop along the highway because if they move a person, trying to help them, and then it doesn't work out, somebody's going to sue him for caring; and when a doctor is afraid to practice and deliver babies because of a crazy suit. We've got to sue each other less and care for each other more.

I heard Mayor Folmar talking about health care. And yes, he is right, we need health care for all. Our program provides health care insurance to the poorest of the poor. Then it gives tax breaks to the income bracket above that that are trying to make ends meet. It gets pooling of insurance, works with managed care, does something about malpractice insurance. But it does something else: It provides the best quality of health care. We have the best. And I don't want to drive these doctors out of medicine by putting the Government further into medicine.

There's another area where I have a big difference with Governor Clinton, and that is on crime. Arkansas prisoners spend 20 percent of their sentences in jail; the Federal, the one I'm responsible for, 85 percent. I believe we need tougher laws that back up these dedicated people on the highways, these police officers in the neighborhoods, the sheriff's people. We need to back law enforcement. And in doing that, we will be strengthening the neighborhoods for every single family in this country.

One of the great meetings we had was in the Oval Office, I think it was last week. I think it was eight people came to see me. They were up there and said, we are supporting you. And they were from Arkansas. They were from the Fraternal Order of Police in Little Rock, who endorsed me for President of the United States. Good, decent, hard-working people.

We talk about reforming the Congress. Let's challenge Governor Clinton to say where he stands on these items: I want a balanced budget amendment to make the Congress get this deficit down. I want a check-off, to have a check-off on the income tax form. You can check up to 10 percent. And then you put it up there and add them all together across the country, and that is the force of law to make Congress reduce spending by that amount. And I believe it will work.

And another one is—time has come for it, 43 Governors have it. I get legislation by this crazy Congress coming down there every day; two good things in it, eight bad. Give the President what the Governors have. Get the deficit down by giving me that line-item veto, cross it out.

I'll tell you, I'll tell you there's another thing. I'll tell you what's going to really decide this election at the last minute. It's going to be a question of character and trust. And I believe, I hope I have earned the trust of the American people. What you do—you represent the American people's interest in that Oval Office, and you have to make tough decisions. And sometimes you make a mistake. You're human like everybody else, and you say, I make it. You look people in the eye and say, we're going to go forward together. But you cannot be on every side of every issue. It is a question of character, if you try to whisper one thing here and do something else there.

Governor Clinton tries to have it both ways. And yes, it's a fair issue. Flip-flopping on right to work: He's from a right-to-work State, says he's for it there; whispers up to the big labor unions, "I'm against it." Term limits: one place he's for it, one place he's against it. Free trade: one time he's for it, then he's against it. In the debate you heard him say, "Well, I'm for it, but I'll have to"—you can't say "but"; you've got to make a decision.

The biggest difference I had with him was on the war. I had to make a tough decision. And Alabama responded with pride, great strength. The sons and daughters did something noble: They busted up the fourth largest army and kicked this aggressor out of Kuwait. And now we're having a lot of revision coming out. It was a noble moment, and where was Governor Clinton? He said this: Well, I was with the majority—I'm paraphrasing—I was with the majority—and this I'm not paraphrasing—but I guess I would have—with the minority, but I guess I would have voted with the majority. You cannot waffle. You cannot make the White House into the waffle house.

And so I do believe that character and trust matters. I've got a big difference with him, and I know people here might or might not agree with me. I was a product of World War II, and I fought for my country, and I think that's made me a good Commander in Chief. I don't think everybody had to do that to be Commander in Chief. I don't believe that's the way to do it. I still think it is wrong, when your brothers are held prisoners in a Hanoi prison camp or kids are drafted out of the ghetto of Birmingham and Montgomery or New York City to serve their Nation, to be over in another country organizing demonstrations against your Nation. I just think it's wrong. I think it's wrong. But what I think is—do we have the word "wronger"? But what I think is worse, what I think is worse is if you don't level, if you don't tell the truth. One day, he says he got a draft notice; the next day, he didn't. One day, he

said, well, he wanted to go into the ROTC; the next day, he didn't. You've got to level. If you make a mistake, look the American people in the eye and say, I was wrong about that. And the American people forgive, but they are entitled to have something other than waffling and a pattern of deception as President of the United States.

Audience members. Four more years! Four more years! Four more years!

The President: Thank you for this great rally. I have—excuse me for drinking all this water up here, but I had 2 miles running out by your magnificent Shakespeare Festival building out there. It was superb.

But let me tell you this. I'm very sorry she's not here, but very candidly, I think we've got a great First Lady in Barbara Bush. We have tried very hard to exemplify what's right and decent about America, exemplify the trust and faith we have in the American family. Liberals don't like it, but it's right. We've got to strengthen the family: read to the kids; teach them right from wrong; support the law enforcement people and the teachers; teach discipline; give choice in child care or choice in education. We believe in these things. And when Barbara reads to those kids, she's saying every parent should read to their kids, take the time to lift them up and to make them better. And that's what we're talking about, and we've tried to do it.

Life has been good to the Bush family. There's no question about that. We're very, very lucky with our grandkids and a wonderful four sons and a great daughter. And so I have no complaints on the personal side at all. People say, well, why do you want to do this? It's ugly out there. You're getting clobbered by the national media over and over again. Can't be any fun. The answer is, something transcends your own personal well-being. And what transcends it for me is we have literally changed the world. These kids here go to bed at night without the same fear of nuclear war that their parents had. And that is a major change. And now what I want to do through the programs I've touched on today is make life better and more challenging by creating more opportunity in employment or education for every young person here today.

That is why I want to be your President. I ask for your support and your trust. And may God bless the United States of America. Thank you very much. Thank you all. A great rally and a beautiful day.

Note: The President spoke at 10:40 a.m. at the Atlanta Crossing Shopping Center.

Remarks on Signing the Energy Policy Act of 1992 in Maurice, Louisiana
October 24, 1992

The President. Please be seated. And I want to thank Jack, Jack Wilson, for making all this possible. He ain't making any money while we're standing here, with that rig waiting for a little more action. But it's very, very nice of him to do this. And I'm grateful to him, to the superintendent, the tool pushers, all the guys here and those from Arco, a company for whom Jack is drilling this rig. And Chip Rimer and Leon Smith, particularly, I want to thank. Also I want to single out Secretary Jim Watkins, our Secretary of Energy, my mate in the Cabinet. He is doing a superb job. And we invited several Members of the United States Congress who have been interested in this, and I don't know that they're here. But I want to thank the Louisiana delegation who worked hard, and all of you have fought hard to strengthen America's energy future. And it's an honor to have you here today and to be with you.

Two years ago our administration proposed a national energy strategy. It was a blueprint to promote economic growth and make the country more secure. And our strategy was based on the simple premise that the greatest single energy resource America possesses is the wisdom and enterprise of its citizens. The last 2 years have seen much hard work, many hundreds of hours of hard study and negotiation. And we know, and I know especially because I used to be in this business, how rough it's been on those who have been working the oilfields and the drilling business and, yes, in the production business as well. But now our efforts have borne fruit, and this afternoon, right here, and it's fitting it happens in the shadow of a drilling rig, we're going to sign the Energy Policy Act of 1992.

We're in a political year, but I think it's only fitting to say that this bill is a tribute to many, the work of many people. And it's not a Republican accomplishment or a Democratic accomplishment; it's an accomplishment for all America. And the Senate, to be very fair about it—I wish the guy would see the light on the rest of the things, but Bennett Johnston deserves great credit because he's been working closely with Jim Watkins on this. So give credit where credit is due. And I'll talk to him about something else later on, you know what I mean? [*Laughter*] But I salute him. And I salute Senator Malcolm Wallop, the Senator from Wyoming, who also was very active in all of this. And in the House, the Democratic chairman over there, John Dingell, deserves credit and Phil Sharp and then Republican Carlos Moorhead. So I mean it when I say it's a team effort. Jim can bring that out and talk to you about that. He'll certainly confirm it because he's working with all of them, as well as with his colleagues in the Cabinet.

Another—but this one that I mentioned earlier deserves very special praise—and a man of vision and integrity, and that's Jim Watkins. I'll tell you, he has stayed in this thing from day one, fought against a lot of political odds, changed and worked and given and taken, but we've ended up with good, sound national energy. So once again, I want to thank Jim Watkins for what he's done. For 3 years he's been fighting this battle, working to strengthen America's energy industry through more than 90 administrative actions so that we may compete in this new world economy. And he's already made great progress, but the bill, in our view, will accelerate progress. And it's a crowning achievement.

The Energy Policy Act will increase domestic energy production, and in the process we all—you know this better than most Americans—that means there will be less reliance on foreign oil, foreign energy. And it will promote conservation and efficiency. And it will create American jobs. The IPA—what was that figure?

Secretary Watkins. Forty-five thousand jobs just next year.

The President. All right, Jim is telling me there's a new estimate by IPAA, which is the Independent Petroleum Association, that will create 45,000 American jobs next year, 7,000 wells. And we're doing this not by resorting to the failed methods of Government control but by unleashing the genius of the private sector; guys like Jack, tool pushers and roughnecks like these guys standing right here.

And the act, now, it's got other facets to it that get across the broad energy spectrum. The act increases competition in the way that electricity is generated and sold. And that will cut prices, reducing the strain on family budgets across the country. By the year 2010, and most of you look young enough to think you'll be around by then, our reforms will save the average household $150 a year in annual electricity bills. The act also improves licensing procedures for new nuclear power plants, safe use of nuclear power, guaranteeing that this safe and clean resource will help meet our needs for the next century. It also encourages the development and use of clean-burning alternative fuels so that the robust production of energy will go hand in hand with a clean environment.

The act provides much needed tax relief for you, our Nation's independents, independent oil and gas producers. By far the most important change that we make as it affects the independents is to reform the alternative minimum tax to better reflect the risk, the risk that it takes to explore for oil. And that will create good jobs, as Jim

has pointed out to me just now once again, good jobs all across the oil States. The reform will allow producers to keep more of your hard-earned money to reinvest in the production of some domestic fossil fuels. And the facts are simple: We must work to produce more of our energy here at home and import less from abroad. And our national security demands it. Future generations deserve it. And now we can make sure that it will be done.

I spent much of my life, and Barbara at my side, in the oil business, starting out in west Texas in the supply business and then in the land drilling business, in the offshore drilling business, as well as the production business, doing some wild-catting and producing some oil. And I saw firsthand how the Government can sometimes help. But I also saw firsthand, particularly when I was in the offshore business, how the Government can hinder things with too darn much regulation. And so what we're trying to do is cut through the regulation. And I believe that I do understand the men and women who are out there trying to meet America's energy needs. I believe that this act opens a new era in which Government acts not as a master but as a partner and the servant.

Once again, to the families in south Louisiana and other places who have been hurting, we understand that. And I do think that this act, with the repeal particularly of the alternative minimum tax, offers a much, much brighter future. And I'm proud to be back in this wonderful part of the world.

Thank you all very, very much. Now you're going to see how it works when you sign some of this legislation.

Note: The President spoke at 5:05 p.m. at Jack-Wade Drilling, Inc. In his remarks, he referred to Jack Wilson, president and owner, and Leon Smith, tool pusher, Jack-Wade Drilling, Inc.; Charles J. Rimer, drilling engineer, Arco Oil and Gas Co.; and Senator J. Bennett Johnston. H.R. 776, approved October 24, was assigned Public Law No. 102–486.

Statement on Signing the Energy Policy Act of 1992
October 24, 1992

Today I am signing into law H.R. 776, the "Energy Policy Act of 1992." My action today will place America upon a clear path toward a more prosperous, energy efficient, environmentally sensitive, and economically secure future.

Soon after I took office I directed the Secretary of Energy, Admiral James Watkins, to prepare a comprehensive and balanced National Energy Strategy (NES) in recognition of the vital importance of energy to our economy and to our daily lives and the need for changes to Government policies and programs to take full advantage of the tremendous resources our Nation possesses.

Under Admiral Watkins' leadership, the NES was issued in February 1991 to provide a blueprint for our energy future while ensuring that our environmental and economic goals would also be met. Proposed legislation to implement some of its core features was sent to the Congress on March 4, 1991, and with the support of leading members of the congressional energy committees, sound energy legislation was finally enacted by overwhelming margins in both Houses.

There is much that is good for America in this new law. It contains a landmark provision furthering competition in the way electricity is generated and sold, thus lowering prices while ensuring adequate supplies. It also contains licensing reforms that will help to preserve the option of using more nuclear power—which now supplies one-fifth of our electric power—in the future. Our near total dependence upon petroleum to fuel cars and trucks will begin to decline because of provisions to encourage the development and use of clean burning alternative fuels. Research and development on a host of exciting new energy technologies—including advanced clean coal, natural gas, renewables, and conservation—will be greatly increased. America's independent oil and natural gas producers will be allowed to keep more of their hard-earned money for reinvesting in the production of domestic fossil fuels, so we will produce more here and import less from abroad. Finally, this bill will upgrade postsecondary math and science education for low-income college students so that they will have a better opportunity to contribute to their country and thereby enrich their lives as well as ours.

These are some of the highlights of this legislation. The chief highlight, however, is this: In all of these great and worthy endeavors, Government will serve as the partner of private enterprise, not as its master. This approach will allow our Nation to reap the benefits of the greatest single energy resource we possess—the entrepreneurial spirit of free men and women.

This new energy policy now takes its rightful place alongside our initiatives in clean air, trade, and other areas that together form a solid basis for my Agenda for American Renewal. This agenda will enable us to approximately double the size of our economy over the next decade and achieve the world's first $10 trillion economy.

I must note, however, that there are several provisions that the Congress has added to the NES that raise constitutional issues.

Various provisions of the Act must be interpreted consistent with the Appointments Clause of the Constitution, which requires that authority under Federal law be exercised only by officers of the United States, and not by private organizations and State officials.

For example, numerous provisions added by title I of the Act, including various provisions in sections 101, 121, and 123, purport to require the Secretaries of Housing and Urban Development, Agriculture, and Energy to amend Federal standards or testing procedures to "conform to" or "be consistent with" standards or procedures to be established in the future by private organizations. Consistent with the Appointments Clause, the Secretaries should, when exercising their responsibilities under these provisions, reserve for themselves the final decision whether or to what extent to adopt these standards or procedures. In particular, the title I provisions must be interpreted as authorizing, but not requiring, the Secretaries to change Federal standards or procedures in response to changes promulgated by the private organizations specified in title I.

Similarly, provisions of the Public Utility Holding Company Act of 1935 (as added by sections 711 and 715 of this Act) purport to condition exemptions for wholesale generators and foreign utility companies on the consent of every State commission having jurisdiction over the relevant utility company, and section 2407(c)(1) of the Act purports to condition the Federal Energy Regulatory Commission's granting of certain licensing exemptions on the licensee's compliance with terms and conditions set down by Alaska's fish and wildlife agency. In administering these provisions, the Federal Energy Regulatory Commission should reserve for itself the final decision regarding the exemptions, while requiring that notice be given to the relevant State authorities and taking their views into account. In particular, the Commission need not regard non-concurrence by any such State authority as sufficient to require denial of an exemption.

Certain portions of section 901, relating to the Uranium Enrichment Corporation, must also be interpreted to avoid constitutional problems. In particular, the provisions adding section 1312 (b) and (c) to the Atomic Energy Act of 1954 (AEA), and which subject the Corporation to Federal environmental laws and to the Occupational Safety and Health Act, must be construed not to authorize litigation in court between the Corporation and other Federal agencies as long as the Corporation is wholly owned by the government. Similarly, new section 1315 of the AEA, which authorizes a Transition Manager to exercise the powers of the Corporation until a quorum of the Board of Directors has been "appointed and confirmed," must be interpreted so as not to interfere with my authority under Article II, section 2 of the Constitution to make recess appointments to the Board. And new section 1306(c) of the AEA, which requires that certain materials be made available to the Comptroller General at his request,

must be construed as limited by other applicable law, including Executive privilege. (The same applies to section 2605(1)(3), which authorizes the Indian Energy Resource Commission to obtain certain information from Federal agencies.)

Other provisions of this legislation must likewise be construed to avoid constitutional difficulties.

Sections 1211(a) and 1332(a) of the Act purport to direct the Secretary of Energy to enter into agreements with the Administrator of the Agency for International Development and other agency heads. If these officers are unable to reach such agreements, they must send their competing versions of proposed agreements to the President, who shall within 90 days determine which version shall be in effect. I will interpret these provisions consistent with my inherent constitutional authority as head of the executive branch to supervise my subordinates in the exercise of their duties, including my authority to settle disputes that occur between those officials through means other than those specified in the statute.

Sections 1332(g)(3) and 1608(g)(3) of this Act direct the Secretary of Energy to "consult with government officials" and other persons in certain foreign countries regarding technology transfer programs. Sections 3020(c) and (d) of the Act purport to direct the course of objectives of negotiations concerning the establishment of a Consultative Commission of Western Hemisphere Energy and Environment and to require that the Commission include representatives of legislative bodies, presumably including the Congress. Under the Constitution, it is the President, not the Congress, who articulates the foreign policy goals of the Nation, who decides whether and when to negotiate agreements with foreign nations or otherwise consult with them, and who represents the United States in international bodies. I will, therefore, construe these provisions merely to express the sense of the Congress with respect to the matters to which they refer.

Section 3021(a) of the Act directs agencies to expend 10 percent of the amounts obligated for certain contracts under the

Act with organizations that may be defined on the basis of race, ethnicity, or gender. A grant of Federal money or benefits based solely on the recipient's race, ethnicity, or gender is presumptively unconstitutional under the equal protection standards of the Constitution. Consistent with these standards, I will construe these provisions so as not to allow the expenditure of monies solely on the basis of race, ethnicity, or gender.

Finally, several provisions of the Act purport to require officers of the executive branch to submit reports to the Congress containing recommendations for legislative action, and to submit certain other reports "to the President and the Congress." I will construe these provisions in light of my constitutional duty and authority to recommend to the Congress such legislative measures as I judge necessary and expedient, and to supervise and guide my subordinates, including the review of their proposed communications to the Congress.

GEORGE BUSH

The White House,
October 24, 1992.

Note: H.R. 776, approved October 24, was assigned Public Law No. 102–486.

Remarks and a Question-and-Answer Session in Lafayette, Louisiana
October 24, 1992

The President. Kind of the Phil Donahue of southern Louisiana. [*Laughter*] But let me just say to all the people in this great State, a State in which I used to work, and in an area, this one, an area in which I used to work, that we have just come from signing a very important piece of national legislation. I signed the national energy strategy bill. And those who work in the oilfields and do either drilling or production or the service work should know that the IPAA has just suggested that the legislation we signed will result in 45,000 more jobs in the oil patch next year and many more rigs running.

That brings us to a major difference that I have with the Clinton-Gore ticket on this question of energy. Senator Gore was quoted in California—and I don't have, I didn't write down the exact quote, but it is going to be played verbatim with his voice tomorrow—that he thought the ban on off-shore drilling that exists in California should be extended to all the coastal waters of the United States.

Audience members. Boo-o-o!

The President. And I don't agree with that. And that's an exact quote. It will be played with his voice. Obviously, he is now doing what Governor Clinton is doing, and that's waffling; say, "Well, I didn't mean it like that." But you can't do that. You cannot go to Santa Barbara, California, and say one thing and then come to southern Louisiana or the coast of Texas and say another. Not if you want to be President of the United States.

You caught me on an up day. I am absolutely—I am going to get to some questions, but I've got to finish this one pitch. We've had a long, long, long trail here and one of the worst years I've ever seen in terms of politics. My favorite bumper sticker is "Annoy the Media. Reelect Bush." And people know what I mean. People know fairplay when they see it.

But the great thing about this kind of event is you can take the questions, you can take your case directly to the people, in this instance, the people of Louisiana. So I'll be glad to take—I don't know how we're going to proceed here, but I'll be glad to follow my leader.

Campaign Issues

Dud Lastrapes. I personally think some good things are going to be in store for you in this great country of ours November 3d. How do you feel about the election on Tuesday?

The President. Better than I do about this mike. [*Laughter*] No, I do feel that, I have said all along, I believe we're going to win. I believe we're going to win because we have the best program.

We are caught up in a global slowdown, a global recession. To listen to Clinton and Gore, they would say it's all my fault. Unlike them, when I make a mistake, I say so. But we are caught up in something global, and what we're trying to do is lead the way out of this by increasing our exports, by holding the line on Government spending and taxes, and by providing incentives to small business. That will get this economy going. And that is why I believe I will win.

Also there's another thing, and it's called character and trust. And in the debate Governor Clinton said, in Richmond, Virginia, he said it's not the character of the President but "the character of the Presidency." Wrong. They are interacted. They're locked. And you better be—if you're going to be there in the Oval Office and a situation comes up like Desert Storm, you can't have it both ways. He said, I favored the minority position—that's a paraphrase, and this is the exact quote—"but I guess I would have voted with the majority." You cannot do that if you want to lead. You can't be all things to all people.

So, I believe character and trust are making a difference. And I think Barbara and I—we've tried very hard to uphold the trust that any President gets who is privileged to serve in the Oval Office. And I think in the final analysis, when people go into the voting booth, that is what's going to make me reelected for 4 more years.

Go ahead, get them going. You've got the question? There's one right behind you. He's next. This guy's next. Go ahead.

Q. I just want to say that we're rooting for you. And I want to ask you how you like AHS so far.

The President. Like what?

Q. How you like Acadiana High so far?

The President. All right. I like it so far, a very compatible group and very friendly people. And I would repeat I used to have offices down here, our company, little companies down in Morgan City and Cameron and Ulma and indeed for Lafayette for a while. And so I feel comfortable and at home here.

All right. Yes, sir.

Government Gridlock

Q. Clinton and them can't touch you on foreign policy, so they're trying to play this game that somehow or the other they have something better for us in the economic area. And what I don't understand is that for years you've been sending plans on education, on the economy, and so forth to Congress, but it doesn't seem to get out to the people. And I would like to get some comments on that.

The President. Well, let me comment. And it's a very important point. We were able to get some key things done in the early days before the Democrats, and I'd say liberal Democrats, who control both Houses of Congress made a determination, and that determination was about a year and a half ago, that nothing good was going to happen on my watch. Early on, I held out my hand to them. In the first State of the Union, I said, let's put aside the bickering, and let's get something done.

We did. We got a child care act that gives parents the choice of where to put their kids and what kind of child care. We've got an ADA, an Americans with Disabilities bill, the best piece of civil rights legislation in a long time. And it says to somebody disabled, we're going to help you get into the mainstream, not be on some program but work your way into the mainstream with the kind of assistance we can give. And we had several other accomplishments. We got a good highway bill last year, $150 billion to start building the infrastructure. We got homeownership going.

But in the last few, couple of years, the last year or so, they've made a determination. The only way they can win is if they convince the American people how bad everything is and that I'm not doing anything about it. And so I have had to veto legislation that's come my way, to protect the taxpayer.

We've got a good energy program, fortunately, we did get through, and to give credit, it was bipartisan to get that passed. We've got a good energy program. But we're hung up on things that would help the city. I believe in enterprise zones to bring jobs into the cities, give tax credits. I believe in much more in the way of home-ownership. I believe our "Weed and Seed" program to ferret out the criminals and then help people in the neighborhoods stay, fight against drugs is a very important program. And we're not getting the support from the Congress, and there's a gridlock.

But here's why it will change. Because the Congress, controlled by one phase of the Democratic Party for 38 years, 38 years they've controlled the House of Representatives. Those guys can't run a two-bit post office or a lousy little bank. And now, though, because of that, you're going to see at least 100 new Members. And I'm going to say, look, the country is tired of gridlock. Here's my agenda for America's renewal. Here are our priorities. Now let's work together, Democrat, Republican, whoever, form new coalitions. And in that first 120 days, let's get something done for the people, the people that are hurting in this country.

Taxes

Q. Mr. President, I'm a senior here at Acadiana. I was wondering, we've been hearing all this talk about the middle class. What parts of Governor Clinton's economic policy should the middle class America be worried about?

The President. I'd be worried about tax increases. He says, "I want to raise taxes $150 billion, and I want to spend $200 billion." And he says, don't worry about it, though, this will come out of the rich. There aren't enough rich guys around. There aren't enough to, out of the top 2 percent, raise the revenues he wants.

I believe—and I was told this, I don't watch these deadly talk shows any Sunday anymore. I can't stand them. All they do is make me angry. But I heard that one of them, that his spokesman kind of admitted that they were going to have to sock it to people that made over—I don't know what it was—$40,000 or $50,000. I'm telling you it's going to hit $25,000 if you do all the things he talked about on top of the $220 billion that he's got.

Health care is a good example. We've got

a good program through tax credits and through vouchers to bring insurance to the poorest of the poor. It keeps the quality of medicine up. It goes against these crazy malpractice lawsuits that are costing medical care $25 billion to $50 billion. And it does not sock a tax on the middle class.

But the Clinton program was at one point—I don't know whether it's changed recently—but was at one point aimed directly at about a 7 percent tax on the middle class, the small-business people that would end up hitting the middle class. Small-business people are not big, rich guys with over $200,000.

So we've got big differences in those and many other areas.

Small Business

Q. Mr. President, I just want to say it's an honor to be in this room with you. Concerning small business, my family owns a small construction company. We do a lot of Federal highway work. And I want to know, when you're reelected, how you can help us to cut back on insurance, because insurance is eating all small businesses alive.

The President. Andy, I wish I had an easy answer for you on that one. I'm thinking here as to how that can be done. The only way it's going to be done is through more competition. Maybe that will come with more growth. But in terms of saying to you there's a Government program to do it, I must tell you, I don't think there is.

Q. Is there any way small businesses can be grouped together?

The President. Well, that's the program we're using in health care, and yes, that might be a very good approach for business. But I believe it ought to be done through the auspices of business without the Government in it. But it can be done, because when you pool like we're talking about for health care, a small grocery store in a— somebody, a mom-and-pop shop across the street, that they all get together, and we facilitate, that prices will go down and the insurance coverage will be more extensive.

So the principle is good. I'm just not sure that I can say that the Government ought to do it. But it's a very valid principle.

1990 Budget Agreement

Q. Mr. President, in 1988, when you were running, you said, "No new taxes." And then you sought to compromise with the Democrats. In hindsight I think we all see that we can't compromise with serpents. Are you willing to stand fast when you are reelected and say, "Override my veto"?

The President. I've done that many times. And he's right. I made what I admitted was a mistake. At the time I thought it was the right thing to do, because we—one good thing about that 1990 bill, we got a cap, a firm cap on the discretionary domestic spending.

For the kids here, two-thirds of the budget is mandatory spending; the President never gets a shot at it. It's called entitlements. One-third of it is the rest of the Government spending. It's very extensive, but it's not as much as the two-thirds.

There we did, out of that bill, we got a cap on it so that they cannot spend more than provided under the budget, which is something that's quite different. But to go with a tax increase, I think, was a mistake. And since then I have vetoed bill after bill, and I'm going to keep on vetoing, but with a new Congress I believe we can do much better.

Campaign Advertising

Q. Mr. President, first of all, I'd like to thank you from the bottom of my heart for my family and my two daughters for what you did with Reagan's great years and what you've done for the last 4 years, first of all.

The President. Thank you, Butch.

Q. I have a two-part question. I don't presume to know what your national campaign does or knows or how they try to run their business. But it seems like on the national and local news here in this area that the Clinton-Gore commercials are running three and four to one of your commercials. So I don't know if you have people who are supposed to monitor that and take care of it—and wait, the second part is, in the last debate, Slick Willie—pardon the term—when he summarized the debate, said that his differences with Perot were, number one, how long it would take to bring down the deficit; and number two, how much to tax the middle class. How could—why has

that not been made into an ad and run it, run it, run it, run it?

The President. We need this guy up there telling our—*[applause]*. Butch, I don't know, Butch, the answer to the numbers of ads that are running. I'll tell you this, though: Louisiana is priority. I must and I believe I will carry this State. But I can't give you the formulation on it.

But on the major ads we are running we are spelling out as clearly as we can the differences that get to this gentleman's question about socking it to the middle class. And I did have a chance in the debates to spell that out. We're going to keep on hitting it because the fundamental philosophical difference is tax and spend versus constraint on spending and taxes. So we're going to keep hitting that theme.

And I don't know the numbers of ads that are being used, but we're not neglecting this key State. It's a battleground, and we've got to win it.

The Media

Q. I'm about to graduate from college in journalism. And you started out by saying "Annoy the Media. Vote for Bush," and that sort of thing. What exactly is your problem in detail with the media, and what advice could you have for me as I start out in that field?

The President. My advice to you in the field is be objective if you want to be a journalist, if you want to be a journalist. If you want to be a columnist or an editorialist, then, of course, that's a different ball game. But I think be objective. I have never seen media having these programs at night analyzing each other, saying, are we being fair? They know very well they wouldn't be having these programs if there was some question about that.

Look, they got the last word. I'm going to pay for telling you this, because they've been all over me like ugly on a whatever it is out here. But nevertheless—*[laughter]*—but I've gotten tired of it. And everybody knows it's been unfair. But the great thing about winding up a campaign is, you get out and take your case to the people.

But seriously, there's a new wave of journalism where the journalists themselves slant the stories. And this isn't a charge, this is a fact. And you say how to do it? I would like to see more objectivity in the news columns and let them slug me in the cartoons and the editorials and the columns and these nuts that come on there on these talking heads.

I'll tell you one other thing. I'll tell you another thing while I'm at it: The minute these debates are over you have a commentator saying who won it. Why can't—let the American people decide who won?

Ross Perot

Q. Mr. President, after you are reelected would you consider using Ross Perot as one of your advisers?

The President. Well, it depends what he would be advising on. I mean, I've got some differences with him because, for example, I don't believe that we need a 50-cent-a-gallon gasoline tax. I just don't think that is—[*applause*]. But on other things, he's a successful man. He's been a big success. He's been very—be fair about it—he's been very helpful on the prisoner of war thing at various times. And so, you know, the door would be open to a lot of people. I'll reach out as best I can across a wide spectrum, because God knows I don't have a lock on all the answers.

But there are some differences. I don't believe we need to tax Social Security benefits. I've been the President that said Social Security is sacrosanct; leave it alone; don't mess with it. And I have a difference.

So on your question generally, look, I could take all the advice and all, especially from very successful people. So the answer is affirmative.

The Economy

Q. Mr. President, with a little more than one week until election, will your campaign focus on the continuing signs of improvement in the economy?

The President. Well, we will do it, and we need some help, because for 3 straight months, unemployment has gone down. And all I hear is: Bad news for President Bush; job market shrinks. For five straight quarters—I'm talking quarters, a year-and-a-half, maybe six, because those figures will be out, I believe this week—we have had

growth in this economy, albeit anemic growth. It's been very slow. But there hasn't been any negative growth.

Germany was down this past month, a negative growth. Japan, we're growing twice as fast as they are. Our economy, with interest rates down and inflation down, is far better than most of the European economies. But to listen to Clinton-Gore and their friends jump on me, they say it's all my fault. I'll take the blame. I make a mistake, I admit it.

Ninety-three percent of the people are working. Now, they're afraid. They're scared they might not have that job tomorrow. So I'd like—all I ask is a fair presentation and then an objective look at who has the best answers to stimulate the economy, particularly small business, and lift these people out of this fear that I understand they have. And I believe it can be done.

One last point: Governor Clinton can only win if he convinces everybody that things are really bad, worse than they are. He says that the American economy is something—I don't have the exact quote, but I'll paraphrase with accuracy—less than Germany but something more than Sri Lanka and that we are the mockery of the world. That is not right. We are the most respected nation in the world, and we are going to lead the world into recovery, if we don't go the tax-and-spend route.

Hurricane Andrew Recovery Efforts

Q. I'd like to welcome you to Lafayette. And before I ask a question, I'd like to thank you for your concern and personal help during our recent hurricane. That was quite an experience for our State.

The President. Let me interrupt just simply to say one, thank you. And I think the Federal Government did respond. But in fairness, a lot of the local officials, some Democrat, some Republican, responded masterfully. And something else happened, something else happened in that hurricane. And I saw this community; the community responded. And sometimes it's what we call the Points of Light, one citizen helping another. So I think the congratulations should very well go to the people of the community. Excuse the interruption.

Confidence in United States

Q. That leads into my question. Each evening when I get home, I watch the 6 p.m. news or the 5:30 p.m. news, and I see stories about what's wrong with our country. And yet in that same news hour, I look at the coverage of what's going on in the rest of the world and how many countries are in turmoil, and their economies are in trouble. You mentioned the Points of Light. How can we send a message out to the Americans that we live in the best country in the world? We may have our problems from time to time, but things are good here.

The President. Well, I think people have a fundamental confidence in the United States. And our Points of Light program, where we recognize a thousand—it could be, it's just a sample of all the good that's being done for others—I think helps in that regard. Voluntarism helps. But I don't know the answer to how to project it out across the world.

I do know this, that most countries still look to us with envy in terms of the economy and with gratitude because we do respond, like in the suffering in Bosnia and Sarajevo and the suffering in Somalia. It's the United States, it's us, it's you, your money that responds.

So we'll continue to do that in a—showing the concern we feel whether it's for the hurricane victims. But in terms of the overall status, I think people just have to have a quiet confidence that the United States is not in decline and that with the programs we're talking about and with a new Congress we can really lift up the kids and give them a little more hope.

You know—you didn't ask for this, but let me just say, they ask me a lot and they ask Barbara a lot, what is it that you—maybe you're a failure, or what did you do wrong or sometimes what did you do right? One of the things that gives me the greatest sense of pride and joy, literally joy in my heart, is that the young people go to bed at night, because of a lot of the way my predecessor worked and the way we've worked, without that same fear of nuclear war. And I think that's a major accomplishment, and I think it's significant.

And yet, if you listen to these critics out there that are on my case all the time, the accomplishments in world peace and the demise of international communism, they say, don't talk about that, nobody cares. I think there's a feeling in America, well, we've done something noble, we've done something good. And it's the taxpayers and the citizens who stayed with the policy of peace through strength that finally can say, we've made the world a little better for others. And there's something there. It doesn't help the guy that's out of work, but it's good for our soul to know that there is some decency around.

All right, now, where? We're coming to this side? Yes, ma'am.

Education and Health Care

Q. Hi, Mr. President, I'm so happy you came to Lafayette to give a personal visit to us. But my concern is how do you plan to help middle class Americans with funding their child's education, their college education? And what about the soaring health costs for middle class Americans? I'm really concerned about that.

The President. Everyone is, in both areas. Education: we have doubled, almost doubled Pell grants. Education: I happen to believe for K through 12 that before you get to K, Head Start is important. We have increased dramatically the funding for the Head Start program, which is a really good program.

On education generally, we've got to revolutionize education. We simply can't go with putting a Band-Aid here and a Band-Aid there. And we have a program, I hope you've heard of it, called America 2000. And what it does is to literally—it bypasses the educational establishment. It says to the community, we're going to help you, Federal help, to literally reinvent the schools. Some are going to want longer hours, some shorter. Some are going to want different size classrooms. Some are going to want to try a different curriculum. Some are going to want—okay, you kids hold your nose—to have year-round schools. Some are going to want to try it one way or another. And we've got to do that in this country. We have to innovate and make that elementary part of education better.

What was the second part? You said education and health care?

Health care: Our health care proposal provides insurance through vouchers to the poorest of the poor and to the middle class you asked about, tax credits. And it does what this gentleman was asking about in small business, but in health care it pools the insurance, which will get the cost down. It goes after malpractice. And I believe that that is the answer.

And the reason I like this one better than "pay or play" or the Canada system is we do have the best quality of health care, and we've got to keep that quality by keeping the Government's role to what I've said it is. I think both would bring relief to families that are really worried about health care costs.

Energy Policy

Mr. Lastrapes. One last question.

The President. My gosh, it goes fast when you're having fun.

Q. Thanks for coming, Mr. President. I'm a small independent producer and operator in this State, and I would like to focus a little bit more on the energy policy, which I also endorse. Thank you for being here on that.

I produce and operate here in this State. I live in this State. I work in this State, I work other people in this State and I spend my money in this State. My point is, one, we need to come home. And secondly, about that energy policy, how is it going to affect me here in this State? And secondly, what is it going to do? I know it's going to do a lot internationally and create jobs here and focus our economy here, but where is that going to come back on us, coming home on that?

The President. You mean the energy strategy, or what?

Q. What's the timetable on that?

The President. Well, the estimate by the IPAA, you know who they are, and they estimate 45,000 jobs. Our Secretary of Energy is here, got much more detail. But the reason they do that is we changed the alternative minimum tax. And that alternative minimum tax, as you know, just took the incentive right out of doing any drilling.

It just slammed the oil industry in the effort to try to level out all taxes. It was a tremendous mistake back several years ago. So that is the biggest thing that's going to help the domestic drilling and producing business. That one won't help internationally. I mean, it will make us less dependent on foreign oil because we'll stimulate drilling and production in this country.

One thing it did not have in it that I favor is the opening up of ANWR. I think that can be done, but it doesn't help us, a small independent or an independent. But it does help the national security because it will have more energy coming from inside the United States.

And the super-environmentalists, the ones way out on the extreme, use the same argument against that that they used against the pipeline. They kept talking about those—what was that animal? The caribou? They said if you put the Alaska pipeline in, you're going to have—the caribou is going to be extinct. The caribou are having one hell of a time up in Alaska with that pipeline. There are more of them around than you can shake a stick at. It's the best thing that ever happened to those caribou.

And the same arguments are now being used on ANWR. And I have a good record on the environment, but it is not an extreme. I believe you need to find the balance between good strong environmental protection for the future of these kids and for growth and families.

I've got a big argument out there with Gore and Clinton on the spotted owl. I mean, I'm all for the spotted owl, a feathery, fine-looking little bird, but I'm also worried about those 30,000 families that might be thrown out of work.

Well listen, I see that the ripcord has been pulled and thousands of hands—I'm sorry, I really do have to run. We're going back to Washington, my last night tonight in Washington before the election. Then we'll be campaigning and ending up in Houston, Texas, on Monday night.

But thank you all for this wonderful welcome. And please go to the polls. Do not neglect it. The guy that stays home is not doing his part by citizenship. And I am absolutely confident that if you go to the polls and you work the phone banks and you do the sometimes tough but always effective things in politics, that you have seen the man who is going to be President for 4 more years.

Thank you, and God bless you all.

Note: The President spoke at 5:50 p.m. at Acadiana High School. Dud Lastrapes, former Mayor of Lafayette and district chairman, Bush-Quayle '92, served as moderator for the session. A tape was not available for verification of the content of these remarks.

Statement on Signing the Elwha River Ecosystem and Fisheries Restoration Act
October 24, 1992

Today I am signing into law H.R. 4844, the "Elwha River Ecosystem and Fisheries Restoration Act." This Act authorizes the Secretary of the Interior to prepare a detailed report on alternatives for restoring the important Elwha River ecosystem and fisheries in the State of Washington. The ecosystem includes resources inside one of our Nation's premier assets, the Olympic National Park.

I wish to express, however, two concerns that I have with the Act. First, the Secretary of the Interior is given only 15 months to prepare the required report. This report must include a study on the acquisition of the existing Elwha River dams, plans for full restoration of the Elwha River ecosystem, and alternatives to removal of the dams. Considering the amount and the complexity of the information required to be included in the report, this timeframe is very unrealistic.

Second, the Secretary of the Interior is required in the report to identify nonfeder-

al parties, besides Indian tribes, that would directly benefit from restoration of the Elwha River ecosystem, if the Secretary believes that these parties should assume some portion of the costs of restoration. However, the Act does not provide express authority to require restoration cost sharing among the benefitted parties. I am instructing the Secretary of the Interior to prepare alternatives for Elwha River restoration, including potential dam removal, that assume nonfederal cost sharing.

I am also instructing the Department of the Interior to consult with the Department of Energy in the preparation of the report on alternatives to dam removal.

GEORGE BUSH

The White House,
October 24, 1992.

Note: H.R. 4844, approved October 24, was assigned Public Law No. 102–495. This statement was released by the Office of the Press Secretary on October 25.

Statement on Signing the Intelligence Authorization Act for Fiscal Year 1993
October 24, 1992

Today I am signing into law H.R. 5095, the "Intelligence Authorization Act for Fiscal Year 1993." The Act authorizes appropriations for the intelligence and intelli-

gence-related activities of the United States during fiscal year 1993.

Title VII of the Act, separately entitled the "Intelligence Organization Act of

1992," amends the 1947 National Security Act with respect to the organization of the Intelligence Community and the responsibilities and authorities of both the Director of Central Intelligence and the Secretary of Defense. The title allows for further organizational changes, while establishing a legislative framework that accurately reflects the existing relationships between elements of the Intelligence Community.

I am pleased that title VII preserves the authority and flexibility that the President must have to organize the Intelligence Community to conduct effectively U.S. intelligence activities in the post cold-war world. Specifically, title VII preserves the authority of the President to create, abolish, or reorganize the Department of Defense intelligence elements, and the authority of the Secretary of Defense under the President to determine which of these elements will execute Department of Defense intelligence functions. In this, title VII is consistent with Executive Order No. 12333, "United States Intelligence Activities," dated December 4, 1981, which remains in force.

I note that title VII also provides that the positions of Director and Deputy Director of Central Intelligence may not simultaneously be occupied by commissioned officers of the Armed Forces. Although this provision is a restatement of current law, it fails to recognize that the Appointments Clause of the Constitution gives the President the sole power to nominate Federal officers whose appointments are subject to the advice and consent of the Senate. Under that Clause, neither the Senate nor the Congress as a whole has any role in choosing the person who will be nominated for appointment, such as by specifying certain qualifications in legislation. I will accordingly treat this provision as advisory rather than mandatory.

GEORGE BUSH

The White House,
October 24, 1992.

Note: H.R. 5095, approved October 24, was assigned Public Law No. 102–496. This statement was released by the Office of the Press Secretary on October 25.

Statement on Signing the Veterans Compensation Cost-of-Living Adjustment Act of 1992
October 24, 1992

It gives me great pleasure to sign into law S. 2322, the "Veterans Compensation Cost-of-Living Adjustment Act of 1992."

Our Nation provides compensation payments to service-disabled veterans and Dependency and Indemnity Compensation (DIC) benefits to the survivors of those who die as a result of military service to our country. My Administration is committed to ensuring that these payments keep pace with changes in the cost of living.

S. 2322 provides a 3 percent increase in compensation and DIC benefits, which is the same cost-of-living adjustment Social Security beneficiaries and veteran pensioners will receive. Nearly 2.2 million veterans and their dependents and about 313,000 surviving spouses and children will benefit from this increase, which is effective December 1, 1992.

As a Nation, we must always remember the special debt that we owe those veterans who unselfishly give of themselves to assure that the security and honor of this country are maintained. The freedom and liberty that we enjoy as citizens of this great Nation depend on the men and women of our Armed Forces. The measure that I sign today bears witness to our gratitude and continued commitment to those who serve our country. It tangibly demonstrates that the American people will not forget the valuable contribution that veterans have made to this Nation.

GEORGE BUSH

The White House,
October 24, 1992.

Note: S. 2322, approved October 24, was

assigned Public Law No. 102–510. This statement was released by the Office of the Press Secretary on October 25.

Statement on Signing the FREEDOM Support Act
October 24, 1992

Today I have signed into law S. 2532, the "FREEDOM Support Act." This historic legislation authorizes a range of programs to support free market and democratic reforms being undertaken in Russia, Ukraine, Armenia, and the other states of the former Soviet Union. In particular, the bill endorses the $12 billion increase in the U.S. share of the International Monetary Fund (IMF) and authorizes $410 million in U.S. bilateral assistance. In addition, the bill removes a number of outdated Cold War legislative restrictions on U.S. relations with the new independent states.

I am proud that the United States has this historic opportunity to support democracy and free markets in this crucially important part of the world. While it is clear to all that the future of the new independent states of the former Soviet Union is in their own hands, passage of the FREEDOM Support Act demonstrates the commitment of the United States to support this endeavor.

Once again, the American people have united to advance the cause of freedom, to win the peace, to help transform former enemies into peaceful partners. This democratic peace will be built on the solid foundations of political and economic freedom in Russia and the other independent states. We must continue to support reformers in Russia, Ukraine, Armenia, and the other new states.

I am pleased that the bill draws our private sector, as never before, into the delivery of technical assistance to Russia and the other new states. Various provisions of this bill will call upon the specialized skills and expertise of the U.S. private sector. S. 2532 will provide support for the trade and investment activities of U.S. companies to help lay the economic and commercial

foundations upon which the new democracies will rest. This is an investment in our future as well as theirs.

The IMF quota increase will ensure that the IMF has adequate resources to promote free markets in the former Soviet Union and elsewhere throughout the world. By contributing to a more prosperous world economy, the IMF will expand markets for U.S. exporters and increase jobs for American workers.

This bill will allow us to provide humanitarian assistance during the upcoming winter; to support democratic reforms and free market systems; to encourage trade and investment; to support the development of food distribution systems; to assist in health and human services programs; to help overcome problems in energy, civilian nuclear reactor safety, transportation, and telecommunications; to assist in dealing with dire environmental problems in the region; and to establish a broad range of people-to-people exchanges designed to bury forever the distrust and misunderstanding that characterized our previous relations with the former Soviet Union.

The bill also provides additional resources and authorities to support efforts to destroy nuclear and other weapons, and to convert to peaceful purposes the facilities that produce these weapons.

We undertake these programs of assistance out of a commitment to increased security for ourselves, our allies, and the peoples of the new independent states. These programs will enhance our security through demilitarization and humanitarian and technical assistance.

A number of provisions in the bill, however, raise constitutional concerns. Some provisions purport to direct me or my delegates with respect to U.S. participation in international institutions. Under our constitutional system, the President alone is responsible for such matters. I therefore will treat such provisions as advisory.

Furthermore, the bill could interfere with my supervisory power over the executive branch by giving a subordinate official in the Department of State the authority to resolve certain interagency disputes and by regulating how other agencies handle license applications by the National Aeronautics and Space Administration. I will interpret these provisions in the light of my constitutional responsibilities.

The bill also authorizes the creation of supposedly nongovernmental entities—the Democracy Corps and a foundation that will conduct scientific activities and exchanges—that would be subject to Government direction, established to carry out Government policies, and largely dependent on Government funding. As I have said before, entities that are neither clearly governmental nor clearly private undermine the principles of separation of powers and political accountability. In determining whether to exercise the authority granted by this bill, I will consider, and I direct the Director of the National Science Foundation to consider, whether these entities can be established and operate in conformity with those principles.

I also note a concern with the provision under which Freedom of Information Act litigation involving the Democracy Corps would be the "responsibility" of the Agency for International Development. This responsibility should not be understood in any way to detract from the Attorney General's plenary litigating authority. Therefore, I direct the Agency for International Development to refer all such matters to the Attorney General consistent with his current authority.

GEORGE BUSH

The White House,
October 24, 1992.

Note: S. 2532, the Freedom for Russia and Emerging Eurasian Democracies and Open Markets Support Act of 1992, approved October 24, was assigned Public Law No. 102–511. This statement was released by the Office of the Press Secretary on October 25.

Remarks to the International Association of Chiefs of Police in Detroit, Michigan
October 25, 1992

Thank you, Chief Vaughn, and all of you. Thank you very much. Thank you so much. I'm just delighted to be here. Thank you, Chief Vaughn, the president, for that kind introduction. And may I salute Steve Harris, who I understand is the incoming leader of this most distinguished group.

I don't know where you get that enthusiasm. I fell asleep in the 9th inning, and I'm sure some of you stayed up until the 11th. [*Laughter*] But nevertheless, may I salute the distinguished members of the board. And a special welcome to the chiefs of police from around the world. You'll have to excuse me if I'm not talking today about the importance of international cooperation. But don't think I've lost it. I understand. And I hear it from the domestic chiefs, from the local chiefs, how important cooperation is with the international component represented here today. Whether it's in antinarcotics, or whether it's in antiterrorism, we are very, very grateful to those law enforcement officers from overseas who are here today and to your colleagues who may not have made it to this wonderful convention.

I would simply say to you that you're choosing, or you have chosen, a very interesting time to visit our great country. The weather's turning colder, and if you turn on the TV you can't help but notice that there's an election going on in just—and Barbara and I were talking about this a few minutes ago—just 9 days. In fact, some of the U.S. police chiefs here may ask if they can go back with you to your country until all this hectic yelling and shouting is over with.

But we are getting down to the home stretch, and so let me talk this morning about Government's first and foremost domestic responsibility, function, and that is to protect every citizen at home and on the street. Let me start with a story that most of the domestic chiefs have heard about, probably the kind of story you hear about every day but one that just sickened Barbara and me when we saw it on the news. I believe it was almost a month ago. In broad daylight, in a neighborhood near Washington, DC, a woman was forced from her car at a stop sign by two men, who then drove off. But the woman got tangled in her seatbelt outside the car. Or maybe she hung on. What mother wouldn't? You see, her baby was locked inside. And that woman was dragged almost 2 miles before the thieves crushed her to death against a fence. And then they tossed her little baby out by the roadside, like some kind of a piece of trash. And I know that on this special Sunday in this special audience I am preaching to the choir, but this sort of thing must provoke outrage. People who act like animals have no place in decent society, and they should go to jail and stay in jail. I strongly support you and your effort to do just that.

I think when the history of this century is written, it will be clearly seen that America got too soft on crime in the sixties, and for 20 years you and your brothers and sisters in law enforcement paid for it. But we fought back, and for the first time in decades, the overall crime index is actually down. And with your help, your leadership, we've slowed the rate of violent crime the past 12 years. We are turning the tide on drugs. I take heart from the fact that there's 60 percent—use of cocaine by teenagers. But as you can tell by comparing our crime statistics with other nations, we still have a way to go, a long way to go. And that's what I really want to talk to you about today.

There are so many issues in this Presidential campaign where the voters have a clear choice. And crime is one of the most impor-

tant. And I do have big differences with Governor Clinton on crime and law enforcement. I would only ask a simple, objective look at the record. Records reveal it. Here are some of the facts. Under Governor Clinton, Arkansas' violent crime rate went up about 60 percent in the eighties: more than twice the national average. They had the Nation's single-biggest increase in serious crime during the decade. In '83, there were about 300 violent crimes for every 100,000 people in Arkansas. Last year, there were almost 600 violent crimes. It has doubled on the Governor's watch. The average inmate there served less than one-fifth of his sentence last year. But the Federal inmate, as I'm sure most know here, an inmate for which I have responsibility, he served 85 percent of his time.

You can't obviously, and I don't mean to leave that impression, blame the dedicated law enforcement officers from that State. Because you've got to look behind that, at the statistics. Arkansas ranks near the bottom for every important per capita crime dollar that it spends, 46th; for police officers, 49th. Spending on judicial and legal systems, Arkansas ranks 50th. Dead last in the country. And so, no wonder crime goes ballistic there during the eighties. You're supposed to handcuff criminals, not tie the hands of the police.

It's obvious and I firmly believe—and I'll get to the positive aspects of this in a minute—that that crime record, that Clinton record, is wrong for Arkansas, and clearly it would be wrong for America. If you don't believe me, ask the Fraternal Order of Police in Little Rock. They know the Clinton record better than anyone, and they're joining hands with their national organization to endorse me for President of the United States. I think they did take the time to look at the overall record, the good news that you don't hear out there on the network news every night.

Let me just tick off a few of our priorities. Start with money. Since I took office, we've increased the crime budget by almost 50 percent. We've hired more than 1,200 new Federal prosecutors since 1989, assigned 300 FBI agents to help you get the gang members off the streets, and proposed a program to double Federal spending for prison space in the 1990's. We're working to stop the abuse of our appeals process, to enforce the death penalty, and to let your cops use evidence seized in good faith. Since 1989, we've taken more than $400 million from criminals and used it to help the victims of crime. We've also targeted the violent repeat offender, putting over 3,000 of those most dangerous fugitives behind bars in just a couple of months last spring. Finally, we're helping to take back 20 worst inner-city neighborhoods, and again I salute the police chiefs and the law enforcement officers for this, take it back with our acclaimed "Weed and Seed" program. Weed out the criminals and the drugs, and then seed the neighborhood with education and training and hopefully, if we can ever get enterprise zones enacted into law, with jobs in the private sector.

Now, listen to Bernie Edwards, a 70-year-old resident of a tough neighborhood in Fort Worth, Texas, Tarrant County. He saw "Weed and Seed" help to keep the young kids in his neighborhood off drugs and out of gangs. And he says, "For the first time in years I can sit on my porch. It sure feels good." There's example like example all across the country. You know them far better than I do.

We've fought for these initiatives, though, not just tough talk, and we're taking action. But our action would be stronger if it were part of a national crime strategy supported by Congress. That's why, 1,228 days ago, on June 15, 1989—the same day Mikhail Gorbachev first hinted that the Berlin Wall might someday come down—I sent a comprehensive crime bill to Capitol Hill, up to the Congress. I extended my hand in partnership to Congress, and I asked for help fighting crime on a national level.

Since I first sent that bill to the Hill in 1989, 60,000 Americans have been murdered. There have been 260,000 rapes, 1.6 million robberies, and 2.6 million assaults. And 69,000 of those violent crimes took place, regrettably, right here in Detroit. Think about it. Enough Americans to fill Detroit's Cobo Hall four times over were brutalized by assault, rape or murder while that bill languished on Capitol Hill. No wonder Americans stare at every news,

every night, shake their heads, and ask, "Why doesn't somebody do something about this incredible mess? People are dying in the streets."

Well, as frustrating as this crime bill has been for me, it is still my job as President to get results. So we've fought and won a couple of big battles in the past few weeks. And today I'm proud to announce that right after this speech, I'm going to sit down here at Cobo Hall and sign two of the crime initiatives that I've fought for, two tough new Federal laws.

The first one severely punishes carjackers. And we told the Congress that I wanted to make armed carjacking a Federal offense with harsh penalties. Thugs who take cars at gunpoint should sit in a cell so long that when they get out they're going to be too darn old to drive.

And the second one deals with parents, mostly fathers, who refuse to make child-support payments. They're called the deadbeat dads. And right now, a single mother in Detroit can struggle to keep the kids fed on a small salary while their father's on a lark in Chicago. He could be way behind in child support, but no one can touch him across State lines. Well, that's a disgrace, and now the long arm of the law can reach over the border and tell that dad to pay up or go up the river.

Why did these two ideas become law? Because national attention created national outrage that brought pressure on Congress to act. It's a formula I want to use again and again in the next 4 years. You see, there are at least six other initiatives that Congress didn't pass, that I care a great deal about and that I think would benefit your work. So next year, with a new Congress—and there's going to be a new one. You might ask why, and I would say to some of the foreign officials here you have been spared the sight of a Congress controlled by one group for 38 years that can't even run a two-bit bank or a two-bit post office. And so there's going to be a lot of new Members. And those Members, regardless of what party, are going to do what the people want. They'll be listening to the same voters I do. And so, then we're going to go after them, and we're going to be given a new Congress. And with 150 new Members next session, maybe up to that many in the House, we're going to pass those six items into law, too.

And here they are: Number one, I want to strengthen the laws dealing with sexual and domestic violence. It's bad enough when a woman is brutally attacked in the first place. Then she takes the stand for testimony and gets attacked by some clever lawyers. I say that's two attacks too many. So we're going to go after tightening up these laws.

Two, I want repeat armed offenders behind bars until trial. Today, even a repeat rapist can get arrested and be out on bond hours later. I say detain him until the trial, let the prosecution use past behavior against him. Right now, certain little details often can't even be mentioned in court, like the fact that everyone within a country mile knows the guy's done this before. And that's wrong. Let him face what he's done and pay for it.

We've got to—on the second major point here—we've got to crush gang violence. I want the gangs to be treated like the criminal enterprises that they are, so we can go after the leaders with Federal medicine that they deserve. I want to toughen penalties for using juveniles in crimes. I've talked to many chiefs about this, and they tell me that gangs send out these under-age kids, send them out to do the dirty work of the leaders, and because they're minors who will get off easy if they're caught. That's disgraceful. I remember going out to South Central in L.A. and hearing about two that were apprehended by the law enforcement community. I think they were 13 or 14. They had been assigned targets to firebomb during the outbreaks—two little kids. It's a heartbreak. It's disgraceful. We've got to go after the big guys, make the big boys pay, those that would use little kids in this way.

And three, protection for the elderly. It's absurd that the folks who have contributed to society all their lives have to live in terror just because some young punks see them as an easy target. I want to beef up the laws so instead of stalking the streets and mugging grandmothers, they're down at the precinct, mugging for the police camera.

Four, and I've heard from many of you on this one, and we promise you we're going to keep on trying: habeas corpus reform. Habeas corpus? Yes, habeas corpus should protect the innocent, but it's turned into a perversion of the law. Some petitions can drag on for more than a decade, more than 10 years. And criminal lawyers are abusing the law to postpone justice, and it's time we put a stop to it. Let them have one habeas petition and be done with it.

Five—and I know this one's controversial, but I'll tell you exactly how strongly I feel about it—and I'm talking about a Federal death penalty. I think certain acts of violence deserve the ultimate penalty. The sentence should be carried out fairly, but swiftly. Assassinations, murder for hire, terrorism, random drive-by shootings, gang massacres, and certainly and especially the killing of a police officer. All must pay with the death sentence. And there is another collateral point here, and that has to do with Justices. I notice that Governor Clinton is here today with Mario Cuomo. But Governor Clinton has mentioned Cuomo for the Supreme Court. And it is my conviction to get this kind of tough crime legislation through, that we must not go back to appointing judges to the Court who oppose tough anticrime measures, who oppose the death penalty for these most heinous of crimes.

And the sixth one is firearms. This one's short and sweet. I want much tougher penalties for the criminal use of firearms.

So there's a lot of work to be done. But America's worth it. For every hardened criminal you face down, there are countless thousands of good and decent Americans out there with strong values and big hearts. And you don't hear much from them. But I happen to know on good authority that they certainly appreciate you, and I know because so many people tell me this. So in conclusion, let me just pass it on to you: America stands behind you. You should never understand some of these crazy liberal appeals as an attack on our law enforcement officers. I am with you 100 percent, bringing to bear the full weight of the Federal Government. And on behalf of all those unheard but grateful Americans, I really do thank you. I thank your families. I know sometimes it must be a real strain when your chief or your officer goes out there and you're not going to know how he's going to be treated by these thug elements out on the street. So we can identify with that. I really came here to say thank you to every single one of you for putting your lives on the line for us every single day.

Now you pass it on, that support, and go back and tell your brave men and women that we appreciate you, and we need you all. You've done so much already. But let's face it, there is much more to be done. And

to do it, I'd be remiss if I saw this many voters out here if I didn't say to you I need your support, and I ask for your vote on November 3d, because I want to be in Washington for 4 more years.

Thank you. And may God bless our great country on this beautiful fall day. May God bless the United States. Thank you very much.

Note: The President spoke at 10:20 a.m. at the Cobo Arena. In his remarks, he referred to C. Roland Vaughn, president of the association and chief of police, Conyers, GA.

Statement on Signing the Anti Car Theft Act of 1992
October 25, 1992

Today I am pleased to sign into law H.R. 4542, the "Anti Car Theft Act of 1992." This legislation is absolutely critical if we are to strike back against auto thieves and carjackers. These criminals, who show no respect for the lives or property of law-abiding Americans, must be punished in the strongest possible manner.

This bill makes armed carjacking a Federal offense. The recent wave of these carjackings has made the need for action clear.

The bill also seeks to sap the profit motive for auto theft. Last year in the United States, auto thieves stole cars valued at $8 billion. H.R. 4542 creates a second

Federal crime: operating or maintaining a "chop shop" to alter stolen cars for resale or reduce them to parts that can be resold.

It is my sincere hope that this legislation will reduce the level of auto thefts and carjackings. Thugs and criminals will now have to think twice about stealing a car. If not, they will pay a high price for their actions.

GEORGE BUSH

The White House,
October 25, 1992.

Note: H.R. 4542, approved October 25, was assigned Public Law No. 102–519.

Statement on Signing the Child Support Recovery Act of 1992
October 25, 1992

Today I am signing into law S. 1002, the "Child Support Recovery Act of 1992." I am particularly pleased that it includes two of my proposals to improve interstate child support enforcement.

When parents separate, children may suffer. Their suffering is, unfortunately, often made much worse through the deliberate failure of a parent to comply with legally imposed child support obligations.

According to evidence presented to the House Committee on the Judiciary, over $5 billion in child support goes unpaid in the United States each and every year. This outrage—which frequently forces innocent and blameless families onto State welfare rolls—is something that we can, and indeed must, address.

S. 1002 attacks this serious problem in several ways. First, it creates a new Federal criminal offense for failure to make child support payments for more than 1 year or amounting to more than $5,000 with respect to a child who resides in another State. This new Federal offense, which I proposed in both my Project KIDS initiative and my Violent Crime Control Act of 1992, carries a potential prison term of up to 2 years for repeat offenders.

Second, the bill includes the proposal in my Violent Crime Control Act of 1992 to give Federal judges discretion to require full payment of child support obligations as a condition of probation.

Finally, the bill authorizes the Department of Justice to make grants to States to develop, implement, and enforce criminal child support legislation and to coordinate interstate enforcement activities. Up to $10

million could be devoted to these grants for each of fiscal years 1994, 1995, and 1996.

The welfare of our families and our children is a deep and abiding concern of all Americans. This legislation is a positive and significant step in holding irresponsible, deadbeat parents accountable to those who depend on them financially. I congratulate the sponsors and supporters of this important legislation, especially Congressman Henry Hyde, on their leadership in bringing it to a successful conclusion.

GEORGE BUSH

The White House,
October 25, 1992.

Note: S. 1002, approved October 25, was assigned Public Law No. 102–521.

Remarks to the Community in Sioux Falls, South Dakota
October 25, 1992

The President. Thank you, Governor. Thank you, South Dakota. Thanks for that welcome.

Audience members. Four more years! Four more years! Four more years!

The President. Thank you, George. Hey, listen, thank you so very much. I am very proud to be introduced by your great Governor, George Mickelson. Let me salute the others here: Larry Pressler, your Senator; Lieutenant Governor Walt Miller; Bill Janklow, the former Governor, warming up the crowd in more ways than one out here. Jim Abdnor is here, a former Senator. Arlene Ham is here. We've got two from Nebraska, former Governor Charlie Thone and the present Congressman Doug Bereuter, both outstanding servants from nearby. Don Peterson and, of course, Mary McClure, the executive director; and then Baillie and the Boys. You've had a full house here, with great people. And let me just say that I am delighted to be here with them.

I will also say that, you know, everyplace I go in the country, you have signs held up, and they say, "Clean House!" Clean House! Change the United States Congress. Well,

you can do something about it right here. You can help clean out the House of Representatives by sending John Timmer to the United States Congress. And you've got a great chance to make history in the Senate, because we have an outstanding candidate standing here with me in Char Haar. Elect her to the Senate, and let's get this country moving again.

Well, we're going down to the wire in this national election. I come back here to South Dakota fired up. And the reason we're going to win is because the American people have a clear choice. There is a vast difference between experience, difference in philosophy, and yes, character does count, a difference in character.

Governor Clinton—I hate to ruin a lovely rally like this, but I've got to just point out since Clinton's going around the country talking about my record, ill-defining it for 11 months—and I'll talk about the positive things in a minute—but let's just take a quick look at his record in Arkansas. Sorry about that.

He promises health care for America. He's been around there for 12 years; 40

percent of the Arkansas workers have no health insurance. He promises education reform. And 12 years later, 75 percent of Arkansas college students, when they first get to college, have to have remedial education because they're not getting the job done the way you are here in high school education. He promises to get the American economy moving. But 12 years in Arkansas, wages, income, and jobs are trailing the entire Nation. So when he stood up there in that debate the other night and he said, "I want to do for the country what I've done to Arkansas," we must not let him do that.

You know, Bill Clinton made a lot of promises to the people of Arkansas, and he broke most of them. But last year, he told the Arkansas people that he would not assume higher office in 1992. He looked right into the lens and says, "I'm not going to do it." And here he is, one more promise that he has not kept.

He calls this change? Let me tell you something. He says that he is the candidate for change, but let's look at the record. He wants $150 billion in new taxes. He wants $220 billion in new spending. That is not change, that is trickle-down Government. We do not need any more of that.

His numbers don't add up. Anyway, he says he's going to just sock it to the rich. Not so. To pay for all his programs, he's got to get down to everybody making over $36,600. And then, to take care of all the promises, every nurse out here, every teacher, every farmer watch out, he's coming right after your wallet. Mr. and Mrs. America, don't let him do this to us. Tax and spend, tax and spend, tax and spend. George talked about it, your Governor. The last time we had that, had a Democratic President along with this spendthrift Congress that's been controlled by the Democrats for 38 years, we had inflation at 15 percent. We had interest rates at 21.5 percent. And they had a malaise or a "misery index" that's doubled what it is today. We cannot let this man do this to the country. Your hear Clinton and Gore, the Ozone Man, talking about change. That's all you're going to have left in your pocket if you get these guys in there, I'll guarantee you that.

Also, if you haven't detected, I'm a little sore at the national media. Let me tell you something—remember what Harry Truman said? I'd better be careful—well, I'd better not say that. They're mad at me anyway. I love my favorite bumper sticker: "Annoy the Media. Reelect Bush." I love it, absolutely love that sticker. There it is. There it is.

But you know, if you listen to these guys, you'd think everything was wrong with this country. They try to tear down. The only way that Clinton and Gore can win is to make everybody convinced everything is horrible. We forget 93 percent of the people are working in this country. We forget that interest rates are at record lows. We forget that inflation is better. And we forget that ag income is up in the United States, and as long as I'm President it's going to stay up.

Audience members. You tell them, Mr. President.

The President. I will. And besides that, I want to say a word about ethanol. I am the one who worked out the ethanol waiver to spur the use of ethanol. Ethanol use has gone up, way up, since I've become President of the United States, and I'm going to keep it going up. But Governor Clinton's adviser, one of them, says that ethanol might blow a hole in the ozone. Well, heck with that. It's not going to blow any hole in the ozone. It is safe, and we're going to use it more.

And then another adviser gets up—because I did the right thing for the corn growers in fixing that waiver—another one gets up and says, well, we'll review that after Clinton is elected. Two things wrong with that: He ought not to review it because I made the right decision, and two, he ain't going to be elected President. He comes to South Dakota and talks ethanol, and then he goes out and starts talking about reviewing the waiver. We cannot have that flip-flop on every single issue.

Now, on international trade, we are working hard to open markets for our agricultural goods all over the world. And I am proud of our export enhancement program. I am proud that we are fighting against these European subsidies. And this fall, out here in South Dakota at a wonderful farm nearby—farmer is standing right over my right shoulder—we announced a new EEP, a new export program. We're staying with that. We're going to sell billions of tons of U.S. wheat to 28 countries, and we are going to protect South Dakota jobs and sell our products all over the world. We've promoted another $1 billion in ag exports under the so-called GATT triggers, technical but very important to farmers in this State. And we're going to keep on fighting for new markets. This North American free trade agreement is going to be good for American jobs and good for American agriculture. And Governor Clinton is on all sides of that question.

Let me tell you, there was something disturbing, and this is a very serious one, this morning, this Sunday, this very day in the Daily Telegraph in London, the Sunday Telegraph of London. The Clinton campaign worked out a secret agreement, it is alleged in the paper—I have to be fair, it is alleged—they worked out a secret agreement with Jacques Delors of the EC, the President of the European Community, on the Uruguay round of GATT trade. And what the agreement was is that they would delay making an agreement on the GATT round until after the election because apparently this man sides with Governor Clinton's ideology.

Well, let me tell you something: If this report is true, and if the Clinton campaign is going over to Europe interfering with an agreement that would benefit all American agriculture, it is a sorry, pathetic thing to be doing a few days before an election. It is in the national interest to work out a GATT agreement, and it's a sorry thing if somebody would put their own personal political interest—afraid we might get something done for the American people—right now to stand in the way of it. I don't think that's good foreign policy, and I don't think that's very good politics, either, because it's going to blow up right in their face.

Other priorities, South Dakota is doing great. Your business is moving, and you've got a low unemployment. But the rest of the country has been hurting. We don't need more tax and spend. What we need to do is stimulate small business. Small business creates jobs for two-thirds of the American people. And we need relief: relief from regulation, relief from taxation, and yes, we need relief from litigation. We're suing each other too much and caring for each other too little.

These crazy lawsuits by these trial lawyers that are the biggest supporters of Governor Clinton: Doctors don't even dare deliver babies, or they have to have additional tests, running the cost of health care up. Some Little League coaches don't dare coach, afraid of some nutty lawsuit. Along the highway, somebody can be hurt, and the person won't come along and pick them up, afraid that a trial lawyer will get to the victim and say, hey, this guy didn't handle you right when you were in your hour of distress. We cannot continue to sue each other. We're trying to do something about it in the United States Congress. Send us Char Haar and let us help get the job done, and John Timmer as well.

We've got a much better program for education. We literally want to revolutionize K through 12, and our America 2000 program will do that. A part of it is this: I believe in school choice, and I want to help parents choose their schools, public, private, or religious.

Health care: Let's not let the Government get further involved. Let's provide insurance to the poorest of the poor through vouchers. Let's provide that overworked middle class a little bit of a tax relief to get the insurance. Let's pool insurance. Let's correct malpractice. And let's move forward so that those who don't have health care have it. But do not lower the quality by setting some board that the United States Government will run. We've got enough trouble with the post office. Don't give us trouble with health care.

A couple of more subjects here—I'm just getting warmed up, you'll be pleased to know—now, crime. I've just come from a marvelous meeting in Detroit with the police chiefs from all across the country; indeed, an international meeting. And there I spelled out the things I was for on crime. But we have a big difference. Arkansas prisoners spend 20 percent of their sentences in jail. The Feds, Federal ones—that comes under me—85 percent. I have this peculiar feeling that we ought to have a little more sympathy for the victims of crime and a little less for the criminals.

I hope you heard the difference when we had the debate on getting this budget deficit down, because I don't believe you need to spend and tax more. I think we need to control the growth of those mandatory spending programs. And then give me these things: Give me that line-item veto, and let the President try it if the Congress can't do it. Give me a taxpayer check-off, or put it this way, give you a taxpayer check-off so you can check 10 percent of your tax to go to lowering the deficit, and the Congress has to find the spending to go with it. And if they don't, we sequester across the board. It is time to put the power back in the hands of the people as far as this deficit goes. And there's two other things that would help: a balanced budget amendment to the Constitution—we almost got it—and that will discipline the Congress and the executive branch. And I like term limits because that gives power back to the people.

But the last one and the key one, in my view, in this election and what it's going to be determined about is character and trust. You simply cannot be on all sides of all questions. You cannot come to a State that doesn't have right to work and say, "I'm against it," and then in a State that does, say, "I'm for it." You cannot one day be on the North American free trade agreement and saying, "Well, I'm for it," and then go to the big labor unions, "Well, I'm for it, but I'm going to change it." You cannot keep making these waffles. We must not turn the White House into the waffle house. And that is what's happening.

It's not any one thing. It is not any one thing. It is this pattern. It is this pattern of deception, trying to be all things to all people. You can't do that as President. Let me remind you of what it was like at Desert Storm. I had to go out and say, here's what we are going to do. I couldn't say maybe; I couldn't say, on the one hand we'll do this, and on the other hand we'll do that. I made a very difficult decision. And thanks to the sons and daughters of South Dakota and other States, the mission was accomplished. Saddam's army was destroyed, and we kicked him out of Kuwait.

But where was Governor Clinton? He was on both sides of the question. Just when I was trying to mobilize national support in the United States Congress and in the press, just as I was trying to mobilize it, he made this statement about the time of the vote: I favor the position—that is paraphrased—I favor the position of the minority—let sanctions work; don't do any—favor the position of the minority, but I guess I would have voted for the majority.

I'm sorry, as Commander in Chief you cannot have a waffle for a position. You've got to make the tough calls. If they ever put this guy on Mount Rushmore, they'll have to have two faces for him, one on one side of the issue, the other on the other. You cannot do that.

Audience members: Four more years! Four more years! Four more years!

The President. I've told you my view. And some ask that I not discuss it because—I don't know what the politics are, but I said what I think about somebody that goes abroad when his comrades or his peer group are in prison in Hanoi or are drafted out of the ghettos to serve. I know that war was controversial, but I don't believe it is right to go to a foreign country when your country is at war and demonstrate there, mobilize demonstrations against your country.

And the liberal press hate it. The press don't like it. I'll tell you, I feel I owe it to the American people to say what I think on that. The trouble with the draft is not that he didn't serve. A lot of people didn't serve. A lot of people didn't like the war. But on April 17th he said, "I'm going to tell the full record." And he hasn't done it. I think you're entitled to know whether he had a draft notice or whether he didn't, whether he went to England because he wanted to serve or because he didn't. It is not right to play both sides of the issue to protect your own political neck.

Now, I believe we're going to win this election. And it's been about the ugliest political year I can remember. I've never seen anything quite like it. The news media wouldn't know good news if it hit them right in the face. But I'll tell you something, there's something wrong with them; they lost it. No, no, we don't want to be too hostile about the media. But I do remember what Harry Truman said about 50 reporters: They couldn't pound sand in a rat hole if they had to. Well, that was Harry Truman speaking, that wasn't me.

Well, let me tell you, I do believe we're going to win this election. And I'll tell you why I think it's going to happen. First place, I think we've got a first-class First Lady, and that helps, I'll tell me. But here's the reason. I've made mistakes, of course. And I do like you do, say, hey, I messed this one up, I'm sorry. You look into the American people's eyes and you say, I made a mistake. And now you get on about doing the American people's business.

But I have tried very hard as your President to uphold the trust that you have placed in me and in Barbara and in my family, to be living in that most prestigious and most awed house in the entire world, the White House. And I honestly believe that when people look to this country, they look, not as Governor Clinton said, to "the character of the Presidency," but they look to both the character of the President and the Presidency. They are interlocked. You cannot separate them. You cannot separate these two.

Life has been very good to me and to my family and to our 5 kids and to our 12 grandchildren. Life has treated us well. We believe and we've tried to live family, faith, friends, and all of that. But I'll tell you why—and there's other lines of work I'm sure that would be a lot more pleasant every day, day in and day out, than taking the shots one takes in this life. But I want to finish the job I've started.

Tonight these kids here will go to bed at night without the same fear of nuclear war that the generation precedent had. That is something that is significant. Ancient enemies are talking to each other around the world, talking peace in the Middle East. Russia is now democratic and trying to perfect their democracy. To the south of our border you see democracy and freedom on the march. And literally, because of the taxpayer, because of my predecessor staying with strength, peace through strength, we have literally changed the world.

But the job is not done. And it won't be done until we can lift up every family in this country, inspire them that the American dream is still alive, help them with education, make our families more secure in the neighborhood by less crime. Lift up America.

Lastly, Clinton says we are a nation in decline, somewhere south of Germany but just ahead of Sri Lanka. He ought to open his eyes. We are the most fair, the most decent, most honorable country on the face of the Earth. Now help me make it even better. I ask, as we drive down to the close with things moving and the excitement building, I ask for your support. I ask for your vote. Help me change America and make life better for every kid here today.

Thank you. Thank you. And may God bless our great country on this beautiful Sunday in South Dakota. We are fortunate to be here. May God bless us all. Thank you all. Thank you.

Note: The President spoke at 1:20 p.m. at the Sioux Empire Fairgrounds Exposition Center. In his remarks, he referred to Arlene Ham, Republican national committeewoman; Don Peterson, State Republican Party chairman and State Victory '92 chairman; Mary McClure, executive director, South Dakota Bush-Quayle '92; and entertainers Baillie and the Boys.

Remarks and a Question-and-Answer Session in Billings, Montana
October 25, 1992

The President. Thank you. I feel like Phil Donahue, sitting here. Thank you for that great welcome to the Big Sky country. Thank you so much. Please be seated.

Audience members. Four more years! Four more years! Four more years!

The President. Wall to wall people. Thank you so very much. This is a little bit of unique forum here today. But I want to start off by just saying a few words about those with us. You have had a great Governor. You've got a wonderful Governor, a great friend of ours. And he is leaving; he is leaving. And Marc Racicot, who is running, is in another part of the State, out working the trenches as he should. But I strongly urge his reelection.

I needn't tell you what a hit Conrad, the Burnses, plural, have made, but Conrad has made in the United States Senate. You've got strong representation there by a good and decent man. I don't listen to all his jokes; I've got a certain standard I must adhere to as President of the United States. [*Laughter*] Well, some of them, some.

But then there's another one that's been at my side in the political trenches as long as I've been—certainly before I was in the White House and even before I was Vice President. And I'm talking about Congressman Ron Marlenee. We've got to see him reelected. And I want to thank two other friends, Chuck Heringer and Tim Babcock, the former Governor of this State, all good people. And I'll tell you, it makes me wonder how you get along without friends.

But let me start this way. This is an unusual format. We're going to take a few questions. But before I start, I want to tell you, this is the strangest political year I've ever seen. But I swing into the great State of Montana absolutely convinced that I'm going to be reelected for 4 more years. People will say, why is that going to happen? And I'll develop that in the question-and-answer session. But I believe it's going to come about because we literally have changed the world. The kids here today go to bed at night—and I heard Conrad generously mention this—the kids go to bed at night without the same fear of nuclear war. And I am very proud that a lot of that occurred since I've been President of the United States. Communism is dead. Ancient enemies are talking to each other. Democracy is on the move in Russia and south of our border. There's been an enormous change. And now what we've got to do is take that same leadership that changed the world, even though we're now

at an economic international global slowdown, use the leadership to lift these kids up and give them the opportunity that I know exists for them in the days ahead.

And then the last, I think, the other reason I'll win, Barbara and I have tried very hard—I think we've got a great First Lady, and I wish she were here. But we have tried very hard to uphold the public trust. And one reason I'm confident is that in the final analysis, I believe voters are going to really think: Who would you want to look after your family, deal with a crisis that might occur? Who can best keep the public trust and serve with honor? We have tried very hard to do that, and I hope that's going to be one of the reasons that we're reelected when it comes Tuesday, a week from this coming Tuesday.

Now, the program is to take a few questions, and I don't know how we're going to arrange all that. But if anybody—Conrad, are you kind of the Phil Donahue of this thing? [*Laughter*] Get in here. We're in real trouble if he is, I'll tell you. He can't even get his umbilical cord untied. Now, come on.

Senator Conrad Burns. I used to be an old farm broadcaster, you know.

The President. Never mind. No, we don't want any of that.

Senator Burns. Mr. President, welcome to Montana. Okay, do we have a question here? Just pick one out. Got a hand right here from a young man right there, Mr. President.

The President. Shoot. We'll get our act together in a minute here.

The Economy

Q. I wasn't born when Carter was around, and I heard about the high taxes and the bad economy. Would that happen if Clinton was elected?

The President. Good question. That's what we call a slow ball in the trade. You can see the seams on it going across the plate. [*Laughter*] The question was, he just has heard talk—he's a young guy, you couldn't see him—but he's heard talk of what it was like when Jimmy Carter was President, the last time a Democrat controlled the White House and those that Conrad and Ron fight against every day controlled the Congress. And here's what it was like. I'm afraid that the Clinton-Gore spend-and-tax plan would take us back there. The interest rates, 21.5 percent they hit. Inflation was 15 percent. The Democrats, to embarrass Republicans, invented something called the "misery index," unemployment and inflation added together. Under me it's 10, and under them it was 20. We cannot go back to the days when they had both ends of Pennsylvania Avenue. We had grain embargoes. And they talk about malaise. It was right there.

So my view is, our agenda for America's renewal—it stimulates small business, cuts down on the Government spending through putting a cap on the mandatory spending—is the way to go. And hold the taxes down. I have a very big difference with the Clinton-Gore tax-and-spend program. Thanks for the question.

Gun Control

Q. Mr. President, what is your position on gun control, please?

The President. I oppose gun control. It's a good time to point it out in the first day of the big game hunting season out here. I'm surprised there's this many people in here. [*Laughter*] But I'm delighted to see you. I am a hunter, and I'm a fisherman, and I believe I've got a sound record on the environment. But when it comes to guns, the answer is to have tougher anticrime legislation. Go after the criminal and not after the gun owner. And I've always felt that way. I gave a speech on that today to the police chiefs, and I believe we have strong support in the law enforcement community. We need a little more sympathy for the victims of crime, a little less for the criminal.

Taxes

Q. President Bush, throughout this election and elections I've listened to in the past, we've always talked about where the middle class is over-taxed, the wealthy aren't taxed enough. I think the people of America are willing to pay their fair share. Why is it we cannot have a uniform tax where it doesn't matter what your income, we all pay the same?

The President. Well, that would be a flat tax, and it's pretty hard to get because I

think a lot of people would think that's unfair. They think it's unfair that a rich guy would pay the same as the person that's really struggling to make ends meet.

Here's my view on the tax situation: I believe this is where we have perhaps the major difference with the Clinton-Gore program, because I went along with the Democratic tax increase one time and I made a mistake. I said I did the wrong thing. Quite different than Governor Clinton that has to have it both ways on every issue. When you screw something up, you say it. You say, "I was wrong." But now let's move forward and hold the line on the taxes. We don't need to raise taxes at all right now. We just don't need to do it. But what we need to do is control the growth of spending. Two-thirds of the budget, two-thirds of the Federal budget, never comes to the President of the United States. One-third does. We've got caps now, out of that budget agreement that I don't like, but out of it we did get one good thing. That was caps on the discretionary spending. On the mandatory programs, it's just free-flowing. So we've got to control their growth, and then stimulate business.

Here's what I want to do in the way of taxes: I want an investment tax allowance, I want a capital gains cut. It is not a tax for the rich. It will stimulate new business, small business. And I want a credit for the first-time homebuyer so that the guy, a family, young family trying to buy their first home, gets a $5,000 credit. And that will stimulate not only the housing industry but all the other businesses that go with it. The flat tax is a—I don't believe it's even possible to get done, so I think we've got to stay with what we've got, but hold the line on it.

Energy Policy

Q. Mr. President, Montana's a great resource State, and we've been looking for an energy plan that would allow us to reasonably develop those resources and lead our country into a future without having an energy shortage. You just signed a new bill, but can you explain what your plans are for the future?

The President. The new bill we signed yesterday, the day before yesterday—

maybe it was just yesterday—these things blend into each other. I'll tell you, like today we were in Detroit, South Dakota, and here. Yesterday, don't give me a quiz, but I believe I was in Louisiana. And if I was, I signed the energy bill.

It's a brandnew national energy strategy. You've got some independents, independent oil and gas producers here. One of the things that's been like a wet blanket over the domestic search for oil and gas has been the alternative minimum tax. And that has been changed now—see, there's two oilmen up there—that has been changed now. And that will free up a lot more domestic drilling. The IPAA estimates 45,000 new jobs in the domestic oil and gas business. Also, our energy strategy goes for alternative sources. We free up as best we can the use of corn for ethanol. I believe that you can safely use nuclear power. We're trying to cut down in some of the endless ways of holding that up. I believe in that.

So it's a good new energy strategy that goes for alternate sources and freeing up domestic oil and gas so we will not be as dependent on foreign oil. We count our blessings that we have good relationships with Saudi Arabia and other countries today. But we must not become more dependent for our energy needs as a country on foreign sources. And that's what this bill helps do.

Foreign Affairs and Domestic Policy

Q. Mr. President, even the Democrats recognize that you are A-plus in foreign affairs. Can you explain to the people how foreign relations means good domestic policies, such as lower gas prices, grain markets for us, and things like that?

The President. Well, the answer is we're living in an interconnected world. In fact, our economy today—and this may come as a surprise to some, because don't listen to the evening network news if you want to get any good news. You're not going to get it. But it will surprise some to know that our economy is doing better than Japan, and we are doing better than Europe, and we're doing better than Canada. But we're not doing good enough. But we're in something that's—I'll take my share of the blame. But I don't think it's fair for Clinton

and Gore to say it's all George Bush's fault when the whole world is caught up in a slowdown.

What's going to save us is your question, is how we handle international affairs. We've made the world more peaceful. With me today is a guy who was a real leader in that—I don't know whether he's standing around modestly in the background—but our Secretary of State, now with me in the White House, Jim Baker. Where is he? He's out here someplace. Anyway, I say for him and Dick Cheney and Colin Powell and Brent Scowcroft in the White House, we have done something about establishing world leadership. And I took a lot of gas at the time we were trying to mobilize the world to stand up against aggression in the Middle East. But we did it.

I might point out a difference: Governor Clinton said on the war, he said, "Well, I agree with the minority but I guess, I guess I would have voted with the majority." What kind of leadership would that be for the Commander in Chief of the Armed Forces? Now, we made a decision; we made a decision. The sons and daughters of this State and all the rest busted up the fourth largest army in the world, kicked him out, and in the process we established the United States as the only military superpower and the most credible leader for democracy and freedom.

And that means that as we move into this internationally connected economy, that we are going to be the ones to lead on trade. The things that saved us in a slowdown, as I'm sure you know, are exports. And we are fighting to increase our exports by getting a satisfactory solution to this GATT round, the Uruguay round on trade. That is in the interest of American jobs. American agriculture will sell more abroad.

I was annoyed to read a London Daily Telegraph article saying that the Clinton campaign intervened with the leaders of the European Community to say, don't make a deal before the election. What kind of statesmanship is that? We ought to make a deal this minute if it's a good one for American agriculture and a good one for the American interest.

So world leadership is important. World

leadership is important. And let me say one last point on this question: Do not let them tell you that we are a nation in decline or are not respected. Governor Clinton, I believe, or someone around him used the word "mockery," and they say we're something less than Germany and just above Sri Lanka. He ought to open his eyes, open that Little Rock narrow vision, and look at the world. We are the most respected country on the face of the Earth.

Barbara Bush

Q. Where's Barbara?

The President. All right. Well, she was last sighted waving goodbye to me at the White House today. But here's the situation. She's doing a great job, but I find that she can go out there on her own and really talk to the people about literacy, about how you help families.

You know, the liberals don't like it when we talk about family values. We're not trying to say a family has to be any particular size, or if you have a one-parent family, that's not a good family. What we're talking about is values. And Barbara's good at it. Because when she holds an AIDS baby in her arms, why, she's teaching compassion. Or when she reads to those children in the Diplomatic Entrance of the White House, she's trying to say parents ought to read to the kids. We talk about family values, we're talking about choice in child care. Let the parents choose, not just the Government. We're talking about choice in education. Let the parents decide, public, private, or religious school, and then support them.

So I believe all of these things add up: teaching discipline, teaching respect—I just met with some of your law enforcement people here—respect for the law. It's unfair that people in some of these heavily impacted drug areas are scared to death to go down to the corner market. Family values can help, because if your kids can be weaned away from the drugs or whatever it is, you strengthen the American family. And that's what Barbara, I think, exemplifies. She's out doing that every single day. I wish she were here. She'd be overwhelmed by this fantastic turnout.

College Costs

Q. As the number of people who want to attend college has increased while the rise in costs of college have dramatically decreased their chance of going, if you're reelected, what would you do to help the financially burdened students and their parents?

The President. The question is a very good question: How do you help financially burdened students and their parents, because college costs have risen?

The step we have taken so far is to double the amount of money for Pell grants. That's the best way that students can participate. We have doubled it. Education spending is up. But I must tell you, we cannot do all the spending we want. As you know, the Federal Government participation in education is about 6 percent or 7 percent, and then the rest of the '93 is local and State and private and all of that. So the feds will continue to do our part. We will continue to, as this economy grows, to increase our commitment. But I am very proud that we have already raised Pell grants, which is the thing that helps children get to college, more than any previous administration and increased Head Start at the same time, for those who are starting to go to school.

The Character Issue

Q. Mr. President, I have two sons in college. One is 18 and one is 22. First of all, I'd like to say we appreciate your answers. No matter what part of the country you're in, you're consistent, unlike your opponent. My question is this: When we sit at the dinner table and we say grace, and then we have a man running for President who we've read his letters on how he tried to get out of the military. The ROTC is after them both; they are honor students. How do we tell them, if that other guy gets in, how they can be faithful to their country? When Kennedy was in, I was getting ready to be drafted, and I volunteered ahead of time. How do we talk to our kids on this important subject if that other guy gets in?

The President. The gentleman raises a very serious question. I can understand people being opposed to the Vietnam war; I

can understand that. What I think the problem Governor Clinton has is, there's a pattern of not leveling with the American
people. I am old-fashioned. I served my
country in combat. I believe that that has
helped me be a little sensitive when the
decisions come, and twice it's come to me,
of having to send somebody else's son or
daughter into combat. So I believe my own
experience has helped me be a sensitive
and decisive Commander in Chief. But I
don't think everybody has to do that. We've
got new generations who might not have
served. But what you have to do is to level
with the American people.

I've spoken out, and frankly, we've got a
difference in our own group about this.
Some say it's not important; I find it incom-
prehensible that when Americans are being
held prisoner in Hanoi or when kids are
being drafted out of the ghetto, that an
American would mobilize, or "organize"
was the word he used, demonstrations
against his own country in a foreign land. If
you want to demonstrate, do what other
people—come to the White House with
your sign. But don't go to a foreign country
and tear down your own country. So I've
got a fundamental difference, I have a fundamental difference with Governor Clinton
on this question.

But the big question, the bigger question
is, on April 17th he said he was going to
level with the American people and tell the
record about the ROTC and the draft, and
he hasn't done that. But it's not just the
military. He goes to Detroit and says one
thing on fuel efficiency standards, and then
he goes someplace and says something else.
He goes one place and said he's for the
North American free trade agreement, and
then in the debate you heard him, "Yes,
but." You can't have a "yes, but" in the
White House. You can't make it into the
waffle house. You have to say, here's what
I'm for, here's what I'm against. And that is
character. And that is trust.

Gasoline Tax

Q. Mr. President, Montana is a big State,
and we have a lot of our citizens travel
from 50 miles to 150 miles just to go shopping or do their business in their county
seats. As I understand, Governor Clinton is

highly in favor of putting a tax on gasoline
to go to some of the expenses of Government. What are your thoughts on this?

The President. Well, my thoughts on the
subject: I'm not sure. I want to be fair. I'm
not sure he's proposing a gasoline tax. If he
is, I strongly oppose it. We've already got a
lot of Federal tax. There's several reasons.
I'm afraid Mr. Perot is proposing a 50-cent
gasoline tax increase. I mean, for people
that have to drive to work or drive cabs,
whatever it is, I mean, that's pretty steep. I
don't think we need to increase the tax on
gasoline.

There's two reasons. One is it's heavily
taxed at the Federal level anyway. And secondly, we preempt a source for the Governors and for the States if they have to do
that. So I would like to hold the line on this
fuel tax, on the gasoline tax right now. We
don't need to do that. And rather than raise
the tax is control the growth of spending.

And how do you do that? All right, I'll
give you three reasons, three ways. Give us
a balanced budget amendment to the Constitution. That's one, and that will discipline
whoever is President and the executive
branch. Give me a check-off, give the
people, rather, a check-off on their tax
return, a little tin box, and you can check
off 10 percent of your taxes to go to reducing the deficit. And the law would be that
then Congress must make the reductions
that go with that. And the third one is, 43
Governors can take a piece of legislation,
and they can knock out the wasteful parts.
So give me the line-item veto, and let the
President try to get the deficit down.

Native Americans

Q. Mr. President, the Democrats would
have you believe that all Native Americans
are Democrats. But I'd like you to know
that a lot of Native Americans are Republicans also.

The President. Glad to know that.

Q. I am a member of Fort Belmount
Tribal Council, and I'd like to express our
appreciation for all the work you've done
on behalf of Native Americans, especially in
the area of education.

The President. I want to ask how it's
going. I know it's a one-way deal, I'm sup-

posed to answer. But is this approach to education helping?

Q. Yes, it is. We're having more and more Native Americans complete their college education, and that really helps us a lot.

The tribal councils are very active in the area of economic development. We'd like to ask your support and assistance in the area of providing more jobs for our people. Everyone on the reservation would like a job, and we need your assistance in that regard.

The President. You know what would help in this regard is this whole broad concept of enterprise zones. And what it says is to give breaks to businesses to move to areas where you really are adversely impacted by unemployment. I think that concept makes sense.

I'm glad that approach to letting the control of education be closer to the ground is making sense. We have a national program called America 2000. Congress—I hope you don't sound, I'm down on the Democratic-controlled Congress that I am—but I am. We need to change it. We need to clean House. And we need to, but we can get a lot done without it on this program called America 2000, because it bypasses a lot of the bureaucracy and goes right to the communities.

Where are we for the next one?

Q. Well, first of all, Montana's good Bush country because just look—[*applause*]

The President. Amazing.

Defense Cuts

Q. My question was concerning the military cuts. With the military cuts, what do you plan to do with all the military personnel that are going to lose their jobs?

The President. I just signed a defense authorization bill, and in it we have a lot of money for retraining. And that is a very important part of it. But let me explain my view toward defense. Because we have been successful in the cold war and because we have lowered the threat of nuclear war—the deal I worked out with Yeltsin was to eliminate these SS–18's which are the major intercontinental ballistic missiles. It's a good thing. That hasn't been accomplished yet, but the deal is signed. Because we have made a lot of progress, we've been able to reduce defense spending. To reduce

it to where we are, I took the recommendation of Colin Powell and the Chiefs and Dick Cheney, who I think have earned the confidence of the American people. I do not want to cut into the muscle of our defense.

Governor Clinton, to pay for a lot of other domestic spending, is now wanting to cut $50 billion, or $70 billion—I can't remember. He and Perot both want to cut significantly more than I do. My view is there are still wolves out there. The Soviet bear may be dead, but there are a lot of wolves in the woods. You've got antiterrorism; you've got all kinds of people trying to acquire nuclear weapons. And who knows where the next challenge will come to the security of the United States? And so I don't want to cut into the muscle of defense.

But for those that are being dropped out of the military, we must go for the retraining. The Montgomery bill on education is a very important part of all of this, but retraining is the answer. And the bill I've just signed adequately provides funding to really help on that.

Health Care

Q. Mr. President, I'd like to know what could be done about our health insurance? You know, I'm older than my wife, and now I'm having an awful time buying insurance for her because we're about to lose our insurance with the business since I retired.

The President. The gentleman asked about perhaps the most pressing social question that we're all facing today, and that is the question of health care. The health care plan that I proposed and, when reelected, will push as an early objective provides the following: Insurance for all. The poorest of the poor will get vouchers to get the insurance. The next range up the income ladder will get assistance, tax credits to provide, to be sure they can acquire coverage.

We will pool the insurance. The small operators find it very difficult to get insurance as cheap as some of the large operators. And so we've got a whole new system of pooling where you can pool insurance, people, small operators getting in together to make a large pool, thus reducing costs.

And there's another way we've got to get the costs down. Frankly, we've got too many of these suits where doctors are afraid to practice medicine, even deliver babies, because of lawsuits. And so to protect themselves and the hospitals protecting themselves against these reckless lawsuits, they increase the number of tests that are needed or require people to stay longer in the hospital than they might ought to, because they're afraid of getting sued if they get out early or something. So we've got to go after these malpractice suits and stop this crazy lawsuit business because, good heavens, people are afraid to coach Little League. They're afraid to stop along a highway and pick up somebody that's hurt, for fear that person will get a lawyer and come and sue them. We're suing each other too much and caring for each other too little. So we've got to put some caps on these reckless lawsuits. And that's number one priority. Governor Clinton will not do it, because the trial lawyers own him lock, stock, and barrel as far as these campaign contributions go.

Education

Q. Mr. President, we want to thank you for your support of educational choice. And we just want to encourage you on that issue, that you will continue to give parents the opportunity to choose alternative forms of education.

The President. I will continue that choice. It is right. We've got a pilot program called "GI bill" for kids. You know, people say, well, you've got to be careful that you don't undermine the public schools or that you merge this justifiable and proper separation of church and state. But the answer is, in the GI bill after the war, the same charge was made in some quarters. The GI bill went to the soldiers that got out, and then they could choose private, public, or religious colleges. And it did not diminish public education. Indeed, some felt that that was enhanced, that it enhanced public education. So my plan is for school choice, public, private, or religious, and try it. It's working in Milwaukee, Wisconsin, and I believe it will work nationwide. It's going to be very expensive, but we've got to start with a pilot program. And we're going to

stay right on it.

Q. Mr. President, I'm a public school teacher. I have had to live under communism and under Nazi, and I'm proud to be an American. Every time we play the national anthem I have tears. But my question is to you, Mr. President. I'm sick and tired of being bashed. Every morning you and I are being bashed by a Democratic organization that I am forced to belong to. And I would like you to give me a one-liner that tomorrow morning I can go back and give to them.

The President. What is the organization?

Q. The teachers organization, NBEA, NEA, and MEA.

The President. Well, the NEA, that's not my favorite so I have to watch—I have to clean it up for you because, I'll tell you, they oppose us at every turn. And part of our education program is to go around them and get the support for the teachers in the communities. We've tried this bureaucratic layering that they have insisted on, and it doesn't work. And too much of the money goes to overhead, and too little right in there to the classroom. So you can put me down as not their strongest supporter. They attack us all the time, no matter what I propose. It's time to stand up and fight against the power-hungry union like that that have more at interest in themselves in organization and less in the teacher in the classroom. I can't think of one line, though, to get them down.

Patrick Goggins. Mr. President, they tell me it's time for you to move on.

The President. The big sky.

Mr. Goggins. We will take, I think, one more question, and then we're going to have to move. And you get to do the picking because I'm not going to make—I live here.

The President. You guys are in charge. Go ahead.

Health Care

Q. I have another health care question, Mr. President.

The President. Hold it. Hold it. Hold it. He says, he says, "Give 'em hell." You remember what Truman said? He said you just tell the truth, and they think it's hell.

[*Laughter*] Anyway, go ahead.

Q. Some smaller communities in Montana have been forced to close their hospitals. I was wondering what some of your solutions to providing health care for rural Americans would be.

The President. Well, I think I touched on that in our whole health care plan. It does cover that, but the main thing is to provide the insurance. I can't give you a firm answer on what we can do in rural areas with the limited funds we've got. We can assist rural areas. We can assist communities. But we cannot start a new program of building Federal hospitals. We simply have to say we don't have the funds to do that when we're operating at this enormous deficit.

Our health care plan, I think, would help. And it would certainly help the individual get access. But it does not answer the problem of the need for more, like veterans hospitals, higher spending on veterans hospitals now under me. I don't want to mislead you to think that we can go ahead and spend a lot more money to build hospitals in the rural areas. We just don't have the funds to do that.

Let me end on a more positive note. Who's got one? Yes, ma'am.

Q. [*Inaudible*]

Mr. Goggins. I'll interpret for you.

The President. Go ahead.

Q. [*Inaudible*]—I just want you to know, for any of these people that haven't made up their mind yet, that I don't want to see Clinton and Gore riding on your Bush tail, your shirt tails—[*laughter*]—and taking any credit for everything you have been working for. And what the hell am I going on—and you know, taking any of the credit, because these changes are slow to come. If they haven't made up their mind, one of your best campaigners is Rush Limbaugh. And you can listen to him.

The President. Yes. Are you finished? Well, let me, that gives me a——

Q. If you haven't made up your mind, you will make up your mind by the election if you listen to him, tell them on 91–AM from 10 to 1.

[*Inaudible*]

Term Limits

The President. She asked a question at the end. And the question is, what do I think of term limits. I support term limits. That's the way to put power back to the people.

Well, we do have to run. But let me end this way, that this has been a very exhilarating experience for me. I just want to tell you, Barbara and I are very lucky. We're lucky with our family. It has not been a particularly pleasant year for people in politics or serving, trying to serve their country—understatement of the year. But we are very blessed. And it isn't that I just want to be President for being President. I'm President now, and we've had a lot of wonderful things happen. We've got a lot of problems that have not been solved. But I want to be President because I like to finish the job. The job means lifting up every kid here to understand that you've got a bright future ahead. I would hate to do what the Clinton crowd is doing, running around—the only way they can win is to tell everybody everything that's wrong with this country and that we're a country in decline. We are not. So my message is more hopeful and more optimistic.

And yes, we've been through hell. And a lot of families don't know whether the job they got today, if they're going to have it tomorrow. But if we do the things that are outlined in our agenda for America's renewal, and if we continue the worldwide leadership, I am absolutely convinced that in the next 4 years the life is going to be an awful lot brighter for every young person in this country. And that's why I want to be reelected for 4 years. I ask for your support. I've tried to uphold your trust. And I would like to serve and finish the job. And don't let them tell you America's in decline.

God bless this great and free and wonderful country. And thank you all.

Note: The President spoke at 3:55 p.m. at Pioneer Park. Patrick K. Goggins, publisher of Western Livestock Reporter, Inc., publications, served as moderator for the session. In his remarks, the President referred to Chuck Heringer, chairman, Montana Bush-Quayle '92.

Notice on Continuation of Iran Emergency
October 25, 1992

On November 14, 1979, by Executive Order No. 12170, the President declared a national emergency to deal with the threat to the national security, foreign policy, and economy of the United States constituted by the situation in Iran. Notices of the continuation of this national emergency have been transmitted annually by the President to the Congress and the *Federal Register*, most recently on November 12, 1991. Because our relations with Iran have not yet returned to normal, and the process of implementing the January 19, 1981, agreements with Iran is still underway, the national emergency declared on November 14, 1979, must continue in effect beyond November 14, 1992. Therefore, in accordance with section 202(d) of the National Emergencies Act (50 U.S.C. 1622(d)), I am continuing the national emergency with respect to Iran. This notice shall be published in the *Federal Register* and transmitted to the Congress.

GEORGE BUSH

The White House,
October 25, 1992.

[*Filed with the Office of the Federal Register, 4:35 p.m., October 26, 1992*]

Note: This notice was released by the Office of the Press Secretary on October 26, and it was published in the Federal Register on October 28.

Letter to Congressional Leaders on Continuation of the National Emergency With Respect to Iran
October 25, 1992

Dear Mr. Speaker: (Dear Mr. President:)

Section 202(d) of the National Emergencies Act (50 U.S.C. 1622(d)) provides for the automatic termination of a national emergency unless, prior to the anniversary date of its declaration, the President publishes in the *Federal Register* and transmits to the Congress a notice stating that the emergency is to continue in effect beyond the anniversary date. In accordance with this provision, I have sent the enclosed notice, stating that the Iran emergency is to continue in effect beyond November 14, 1992, to the *Federal Register* for publication. Similar notices have been sent annually to the Congress and the *Federal Register* since November 12, 1980, most recently on November 12, 1991.

The crisis between the United States and Iran that began in 1979 has not been fully resolved. The international tribunal established to adjudicate claims of the United States and U.S. nationals against Iran and of the Iranian Government and Iranian nationals against the United States continues to function, and normalization of commercial and diplomatic relations between the United States and Iran has not been achieved. In these circumstances, I have determined that it is necessary to maintain in force the broad authorities that may be needed in the process of implementing the January 1981 agreements with Iran and in the eventual normalization of relations with that country.

Sincerely,

GEORGE BUSH

Note: Identical letters were sent to Thomas S. Foley, Speaker of the House of Representatives, and Dan Quayle, President of the Senate. This letter was released by the Office of the Press Secretary on October 26.

Remarks to the Ace Hardware Convention in Denver, Colorado
October 26, 1992

What a great welcome. Thank you very, very much. Thank you all. That was just first-class. Please be seated. Roger, thank you. My heavens, what a wonderful—I'm kind of glad I'm running against Clinton instead of this guy, I'll tell you. [*Laughter*] No, but when he was citing those values and what you all stand for about hard work, it really resonates. I'm very grateful to Roger Peterson. I want to thank your chairman, who just met me, greeted us out there in the hall, Richard Laskowski; say to your executive vice president, David Hodnick—thank him for, I'm sure, a lot of the arrangements in all of this. And I am just really pleased to be here.

I was accompanied here today by one of Colorado's Congressmen, Congressman Dan Schaefer, doing a great job for our country in the Congress, and also with Terry Considine, a great friend, who I'm convinced is going to be the next Senator from here. So we brought a little political clout to this nonpolitical meeting. Somewhere over here also is one of the unique characters in the whole United States Senate, a legend not only in this time but I expect will live forever as a great down-to-earth American. I'm talking about Wyoming's Al Simpson, who is here, one of the great, great U.S. Senators.

So I'm delighted to be here. And, you know, hardware stores are viewed—I listened carefully to Roger, but I knew it—hardware stores are viewed as the typical small business, literally the foundation of our economy. When you talk hardware, okay, I've heard it, "Ace is the place." So put it down this way: I'm the guy that's honored and I'm the one that's very, very pleased to share a few minutes here with you and to salute those men and women who really are the backbone of small business in this country.

I would say that my friends over there in the national media—we've got a little bit of a thing going here, because I like holding up a bumper sticker. It says "Annoy the Media. Reelect Bush." I say it with total

good humor but great conviction, I might add. [*Laughter*] So I'm sure some of them want to know why I stopped by this convention. And the truth is, I need a few tools. You see—[*laughter*]—I've got some work to do around my house, and I don't plan moving out for another 4 years.

Oh, heavens. But now let me just try to put things in perspective. One week from tomorrow, it's hard to believe that one week from tomorrow American voters are going to choose a President, not just the President of the United States but really the leader of the entire world, given the demise of international communism. In many ways we're going to be choosing a future.

I believe that this election comes down to three fundamental questions. Who has the vision for America's future? Who has the road map to get us to that future? And then, fundamentally, who can you trust when we hit those unexpected bumps, those crises that lie ahead, inevitably?

Let's begin by talking the question of philosophy. Whose vision makes more sense to you? My opponents say that this election is about change, and I agree. But being in favor of change is like being in favor of breathing. The real question is not who is for change, but whose change will make life better for all Americans.

A philosopher once observed that "those who cannot remember the past are condemned to repeat it." And so let's see where we've been over the past 4 years. We won a 50-year cold war because we stood up for ideals, communism versus freedom. Freedom finished first. You know, the cold war was defined for half a century in ways large and small. It claimed literally millions of lives and crushed the spirit of millions of others. And here in America, the cold war defined us, financially, economically, even psychologically. My kids, and many of you out here, grew up crawling under desks in these "duck and cover" drills. In the sixties during the Cuban missile crisis, we stood on the brink of Armageddon. In the eighties, families huddled together in fear to watch a TV movie called "The Day After." And always, the shadow of the cold war lingered right outside our windows.

You talk change, well, all that has changed with our leadership. And because of that change, our children go to sleep tonight without that same fear of nuclear war. We should be proud that we gave this gift to them. But if we were the cold war victors, we have yet to receive the spoils. There's little celebration in America today; instead a nagging anxiety, a feeling that it's time to turn our attention to challenges at home, to creating new industries and better schools and affordable health care. And whose philosophy should we follow to get there?

Well, we've seen in recent years the power of a tank or a gun, but the power of a simple idea is what we've really seen, an idea called freedom. In Asia, in Eastern Europe, South America, Mexico, people are coming to understand that government is neither superior nor savior. It is and must be their servant.

In the midst of a worldwide economic slowdown, our free-market economy remains afloat, while many nations are drowning. We are growing faster than Japan, faster than Germany, faster than Canada. But here's the irony. At the very moment when the rest of the world is moving our way, my opponent, Governor Clinton, wants us to move their way.

Governor Clinton says he is, quote, "different" than the old tax-and-spend liberals. But if you look at the details of what he offers, you see $150 billion in new taxes, more than Mondale and Dukakis combined. You see at least $220 billion already in new spending, just to begin to pay for all the promises.

With each program Governor Clinton puts forth, you see a philosophy where bureaucrats in Washington or some entrenched Members of Congress carve out the exact same programs to try and solve problems facing people in Denver and Dallas, or Dover, or Delaware. I believe Americans understand that these old liberal solutions are not right for our new postwar era.

It does not make sense that hardware store owners will somehow get richer by giving more of your money to the IRS. It doesn't make sense that we will get this terrible deficit down by giving more money to the Government to spend. At a time when every organization is decentralizing power, why turn back to central bureaucracy in Washington?

And yet, saying that is not enough because, of course, we have real problems. Our children won't be able to compete unless our schools are literally reinvented. The cost of health care is skyrocketing. We have to get it down. So Government can't just keep the tanks running. Government must help people.

During this campaign, many have sought to portray the choice between a, quote, "activist" Government and a trickle-down approach to Government. But that is wrong. The real choice is not between activism and passivity. The real choice is between a liberal activist Government that seeks to impose solutions on individuals, families, and the private sector, and a conservative activist Government that gives individuals, businesses, and families the means to make their own choices through competition and economic opportunity.

We know one size does not fit all. We know the American people are individuals, each with their own needs and skills and, yes, dreams. So our activist approach gives more power to individuals, families, and businesses, so you can choose what is best.

Let me give you just a couple of specific examples here. Start with education. Governor Clinton worked with me, and I give him great credit for this, when we set six national education goals, the very first time in history that the Governors came together with the President to set these national education goals. And as I say, Governor Clinton deserves credit for that. But if elected President, Governor Clinton wants to pour more money into the same failed education system, a system where funds are controlled tightly by central bureaucracies, where powerful teachers unions block real reform, and where we spend as much per pupil as any nation but Switzerland, but don't get an adequate return on our investment.

If the system is broken, tinkering around

the margins won't do the job. So I want to use competition to improve our schools. I want to provide scholarships for elementary and high school students so that every parent, rich and poor alike, can choose the best schools for their kids, public, private, or religious. Give the parents a choice, and competition will make all these schools better.

This same principle, you live by this principle in your work. You see the same thing in health care. Governor Clinton has offered three plans in this campaign. One said to all of you, either offer care—small businesses, remember—either offer care on your own or pay a new payroll tax, at least 7 percent. Many experts said it was a backdoor way to get Government directly involved in running health care.

Now he offers a slightly different plan, but he still wants to control the price of health care by setting up a gigantic board in Washington, not unlike what the Government tried to do with gasoline in the 1970's. I say we don't need to sock you with a new tax, and we don't want to tell you what doctor to see, and we don't need to inflict you with any more mandates from Washington, DC.

How about tax incentives for small businesses, so that you can afford to buy health care on your own, or let small businesses pool coverage, to get the advantage, so you can get the same price breaks as the AT&T's and IBM's. Government can't control prices by fiat, but competition can bring prices down. For people who are too poor to pay taxes, we will give vouchers. The poorest of the poor will receive vouchers so that they can choose the care that best suits them.

Freedom, power, choice for people: You see the philosophical difference in every area. I trust you to choose the best child care for your kids. My opponent says trust the Government. I trust you, with the right incentives, to figure out how to give your employees parental leave. My opponent says Government should tell you how to do that. I favor parental leave. I do not favor more mandates on small business. I trust entrepreneurs to place their bets on the growth industries of the future. You've got a big difference here. My opponent thinks

Government can do as good a job, if not better.

Governor Clinton talks about Government, and here's the word he uses, "investing" your money. I talk about cutting capital gains taxes, investment tax allowances to small business, because you know what to do with your money better than any bureaucrat; a big difference between Government investment and investment in the private sector.

Governor Clinton says we need professional politicians in Washington, who won't get anything done. I trust Americans' judgment so much that I want to limit the terms of Members of Congress and give the Government back to the people. The Republic's been able to survive with the Presidents having limited terms. I'd like to try it out on some of these old geezers in Congress; wouldn't hurt them a damn bit.

No, you see, here's my point, there's a conservative agenda for helping people. It's an activist agenda that empowers people, not the bureaucracies. It gives people power to make their own choices, control their own lives, create their own destinies.

I believe that even in these challenging times these ideas make more sense to the American people than the siren song of higher taxes, more spending, bigger Government in Washington. Now, it all sounds great, but how do you translate words into action? After all, people are sick and tired of gridlock, and they want to turn Washington into a "bicker-free" zone.

Well, many of the ideas that I've talked about are already underway. In child care, for example, we succeeded in passing legislation that literally allows parents to choose their kids' care, whether it's a government agency or a church down the street.

But with a new Congress—and it's going to be new not just in the sense of reforming; a new Congress is going to have 150 new Members maybe; certainly over 100— we have a historic opportunity to push this agenda even further, literally to renew America.

In September, I laid out what we call an Agenda for American Renewal. It's a comprehensive, integrated approach to fixing our schools, reforming health care, rightsizing Government, and creating here in America the world's first $10 trillion economy. My agenda includes 13 first-year priorities, but three really dwarf all others.

First, America needs jobs. Not 2 years from now, not next fall, we need them today. I understand what it takes to create jobs. I built a business myself, small business, met a payroll. I have a big difference here because Governor Clinton wants you to send more of your money to Washington, remember, to invest, and say the Government will invest it for you. I say, let's cut out the middle man. We don't need that. We'll put together a package to give you incentives to grow, to further cut—and I've got to do well on this one in the next 4 years; we've made some progress—but further cut redtape and regulation and make more credit available.

Right now, we have $150 billion—one of the things we did get passed in the last Congress, Senator Simpson and Congressman Schaefer taking lead roles in this—$150 billion in money for highways. We'll make sure that that money gets to the States just as soon as possible and get those steamrollers moving quickly, so that your customers will have more money in their pockets.

While we're strengthening our business, we must, and I will, open new markets for our products by winning congressional approval of our free trade treaty with Canada and Mexico. This is the bottom line: More trade creates more American high-paying jobs, jobs for all Americans. It is exports that have saved us in this global slowdown, global recession, and it is exports that are going to lead the way out of this with jobs for American manufacturers and American services.

Our immediate third priority is health care. I already mentioned some of the ideas, but the need for action is urgent. We simply cannot control the deficit, we can't make our companies even more competitive until we make health care more affordable and more accessible for you and for all that work with you.

As we are working on these priorities, we're going to be working on others. We'll take new steps to reform our education and legal system. Our children will not be able to compete unless we reinvent, literally reinvent our schools, K through 12.

Our society will be drained of precious resources unless we start suing each other less and caring for each other more. It is a crying shame that these crazy lawsuits have gotten out of control. I have tried for 3 years to get the Congress to move on tort reform and on limiting some of these outrageous claims. Because when a doctor can't deliver a baby for fear of being sued or has to run the price of your health care up to protect against a suit, or when a Little League coach won't dare coach, or when a guy driving along the highway sees an accident on the side and says, well, I better not stop because somebody might sue me if I move this poor guy off the road, we've got to do something: Stand up to these trial lawyers, and get these lawsuits under control.

My plan includes reducing the deficit, not by raising taxes but by getting control of spending. We need a balanced budget amendment. We need a line-item veto. And we need to cap the growth of these mandatory programs, except Social Security. We need a check-off on your tax return, so you, the taxpayer, can earmark up to 10 percent of your taxes to be used for nothing but to get the debt off our children's shoulders.

Some of you are from urban America, and to you I say we must restore hope to our inner cities. So I will work with the new Congress to get tougher crime laws, to fight the drug problem, to reform the welfare system, and to attract and keep business, all using this principle of putting faith and power not in bureaucracies but in real people.

We will further expand free trade, using our stature as world's number one superpower, to reach new trade agreements with countries in Europe and Asia.

Perhaps most important, we'll reform and right-size the Government, subject it to the same discipline as every other large organization in America. We'll cut the White House staff by a third, and look to Congress to match our action. Until we get all these things under control, at the outset we will take 5 percent off the salary of the best-paid Federal employees. Unfortunately, that includes the President, too, but I'll do my share. We will abolish these political action committees; get rid of them. We will limit the terms of Members of Congress, and we will try in every way to give the Government back to the people.

I know some of you come from communities that have been heavily impacted by defense cuts. One of the great things about our performance in the cold war, yours and ours, has been that we've been able to cut back on some defense. But a critical part of this reorganization will be to help our defense industry adjust now to a peacetime economy. Immediately following the election, I will assemble a defense conversion council. It will include every necessary Cabinet Agency and work closely with key Members of the United States Congress.

We're already directing more weapons research in our great labs, our great national labs, to civilian use and retraining military personnel. To support this plan, this effort, I plan to create in my next budget submission a fund for future generations. That fund would provide seed monies to help defense sector and civilian firms form joint partnerships to use the knowledge we've gained from building weapons to building a stronger economy.

That is my immediate agenda, and it builds on the foundation that we have laid for the last 4 years. It's what I've been talking about on the campaign trail and what I will fight for in my second term.

But I believe each candidate owes you more than his agenda, but what specifically will he do to get it done. As the support for Ross Perot has made clear, there is a strong desire for a new coalition in America, to overcome gridlock, to get the job done. With 150 new Members of Congress from both parties, we will move quickly to respond to the demands of the people. I plan to use the time from November 4th through convening of the new Congress to meet with all the new Members of Congress, regardless of party, and to shape a legislative package in a way that will guarantee swift passage.

You know, the best time to move is when you're reelected. No more elections ahead. No worry about the future politics. Just get the people's business done and do it fast.

A committee has been called a cul-de-sac down which ideas are lured and strangled to death. And if this is true, then the modern Congress has become a giant subdivision. Good ideas go in, and they never come out again. [*Laughter*] So we will seek agreement with the congressional leaders to form a steering group that can help ride herd over Congress, to make sure our legislative package does not get bogged down. We'll set deadlines for decisions, and we'll meet them. We can mobilize for war. We can mobilize for hurricanes. Let's mobilize for our economy, and get this country moving again.

If we need to, we'll go beyond Washington. Already, our American 2000 education reform effort involves parents, teachers, and business leaders in over 1,700 communities. This will be a model for other efforts. America's desire for positive change requires building new coalitions, taking advantage of grassroots power, and we will.

Now, that's the action plan. But what about Governor Clinton? Well, in June, he promised to present his 100-day plan even before the election. It's 8 days away; we have not had a sighting yet. [*Laughter*] No plan has been sighted. And here's why: His plan simply does not add up. He's promised too much. And his new congressional friends want to raise the ante even higher. The result will be much higher spending and taxes and a much bigger deficit or continued gridlock in Washington.

My agenda can break the gridlock without breaking the bank. It is ambitious, but it is doable. With it we can start to make progress on our fundamental challenges and match the peace of mind in the world, with the peace of mind right here at home.

Finally, a word about character. In the final analysis, it is my view that this election is going to be decided on character and trust. Horace Greeley—I mentioned this in the debate out in Michigan—Horace Greeley once said that character is the only thing that endures. I think that's especially true in the Presidency. Character matters, not just because of the plans you make but the crises that you never foresee. A friend of mine says character is real simple. He says it's acting alone the way you would act with a million people watching. As President, you're never more alone than at times of crisis. While nobody may be watching in the Oval Office, millions, literally millions, will feel the impact of your judgment.

It is easy in the aftermath of Desert Storm to portray the decision to go to war as an easy one, but it was not. It was not uniformly popular. The Democratic Congress had spent much of the fall parading experts up there, if you'll remember, to Capitol Hill, who said we'd get into, quote, "another Vietnam." The thing that hurt the most or that made me think the most was the horrible tales of the numbers of body bags that we would be responsible for if we made a commitment to send somebody else's son, somebody else's daughter to war. The critics said a war would kill any hope for peace in the Middle East. And the vote in the Congress, a cliffhanger, not overwhelming. Many said, "Let's give sanctions more time." But I made a decision to go to war because I knew it was right, not because I knew it was popular.

I remember well the cold, rainy February day at Camp David when ground war to liberate Kuwait began, and how fervently I prayed that our plans would work and our young men and women would return home, victorious and alive. This is an awesome responsibility to ask our young people to knock early on death's door. It is a responsibility I have tried to fulfill with honor

and duty and, above all, honesty, integrity to the American people. But that's your call.

That's the wonderful thing about this system. And yes, I confess it's been an ugly year. But that's the wonderful thing, because it is your call on November 3d. Then the polls and all these deadly talking heads we see on these Sunday television shows, each getting 500 bucks to tell us what we think, it doesn't matter anymore. They don't matter anymore. It's up to the American people.

When you enter that voting booth, ask yourself three common sense questions: Who has the right vision for America's future? Who can get us from here to there? Which character has the character? And who would you trust with your family or with the United States of America in a crisis?

Ideas, action, character: I have tried very hard to demonstrate all three. So I came out here to Ace to ask for your support on November 3d.

Thank you, and may God bless our great country, the United States of America. Thank you very, very much.

Note: The President spoke at 10:55 a.m. at the Colorado Convention Center. In his remarks, he referred to Roger Peterson, president and chief executive officer, Ace Hardware.

Remarks to the Community in Albuquerque, New Mexico
October 26, 1992

The President. Thank you, New Mexico. And thank you especially to one of the truly great, decent, honorable, committed United States Senators, Pete Domenici. And, you know, you've got a great Republican delegation to the Congress in Steve Schiff, the local Congressman; Joe Skeen is with us here today. Former Governor Garrey Carruthers is over here. I want to thank our New Mexico State chairman, John Lattauzio, and our special guest, my dear friend Ricky Skaggs, just back from Russia, one of

the great entertainers and a really decent guy.

Let me say I am very, very pleased to be in Albuquerque. And let me tell you this: Ignore the pundits, annoy the media, and let the people decide who's going to win this election. We are going to win the election.

Let me tell you why. There's a clear choice before the American people, a vast difference in experience, a vast difference in philosophy, and a vast difference in character. And character counts when you're talking about the President.

Now, I hate to ruin a beautiful day in this lovely plaza with this magnificent unbelievable turnout. But let me tell you a little bit inasmuch as Clinton has been misrepresenting mine, let me tell you the facts about his record in Arkansas. Sorry, I've got to do it.

Here's what it is. You like your environment? Arkansas is 50th in the quality of environmental initiatives. They are 50th in the percentage of adults with a college degree. They are 50th in per capita spending on criminal justice. They are 49th in per capita spending on police protection. They are 48th, sorry, in percentage of adults with a high school diploma. They are 48th in spending on corrections. They are 46th—they're moving up—46th in teacher salaries. They are 45th in the overall well-being of children. And listen to this one, New Mexico, Governor Clinton signed into law a prejudicial English-only statute for Arkansas.

Audience members. Boo-o-o!

The President. We do not need that kind of leadership in Washington, DC. He calls this change. All you hear out of him and Mr. Ozone, Al Gore—[*laughter*]—I've never seen a guy with such crazy ideas. They'd screech this country to a halt, I'll tell you.

But Governor Clinton talks change, change, change. But let's just take a look at what he wants. He's already proposed $150 billion in new taxes, $220 billion in new spending. You talk about trickle-down Government, that's it. His numbers do not add up, and he is going to sock it to the middle class, and we're not going to let him do that.

Remember what it was when the Democrats controlled the White House and have these silly liberals controlling Congress. Remember how it was. The last time they controlled it, inflation was 15 percent, interest rates were 21 percent, the "misery index" was out through that ozone layer, and the country was in a disaster. And we're not going to let him go back to that.

Watch your wallets, men. You've heard it before: Sock it to the rich. He means sock it to the working man, the nurse, the teacher, the cab driver. And we're not going to let him do that. You listen to this guy, and

change, change is all you're going to have left in your pocket if you hear from him.

You know, Governor Clinton can only win if he tells everybody how bad everything is. Today, employment is at 93 percent; inflation is only 2½ or 3 percent; home mortgages are about 8 percent. Ask yourself this question: Can Bill Clinton do better, or is he going to make it worse? He is going to make it worse.

And maybe some New Mexico issues. On defense, we've got a good defense. I have cut defense where we're able to. But I've accepted the recommendations of the respected Colin Powell and Dick Cheney. We're not going to cut into the muscle of our defense. And Clinton wants $60 billion more, throwing a lot of New Mexicans out of work. We cannot let them cut the muscle of our defense. Clinton is no expert. He has no feeling for foreign affairs or defense. He was the guy that said the Patriot missile was the one that goes down chimneys. Governor, that is Santa Claus. [*Laughter*] That is not the Patriot missile. That shoots down other missiles. I mean, come on. This guy wants to be Commander in Chief, and he doesn't know the difference between a Patriot and Santa Claus. [*Laughter*]

The energy bill, I was proud, with the help of Pete Domenici and the Members of Congress with us here today, to sign an energy bill that's going to get our domestic energy industry moving again. We have changed the alternative minimum tax. And that frees up the independents to go to drill for more oil. We are too dependent on foreign oil. Let's get the domestic industry moving.

And beware of environmental extremists, these crazy people that say that we cannot—you want to protect the owl but throw the timber worker out of business. You want to protect CAFE, car efficiency standards, throw the auto workers out of business. But around here, I favor multiple use of public lands. And I will stop these environmental extremists.

And here's something that New Mexico understands and I'm not sure the Clinton-Gore ticket understand, the thing that has saved us in a global slowdown. And remember, the United States is doing better than

Japan; we are doing better than Germany and the rest of Europe; we are doing better than Canada. And all you hear from these guys, assisted by these talking heads on the news, is how bad everything is. But the way we're going to lead this world actually into recovery is by creating more jobs for Americans as we export more products. And I am proud that we negotiated the North American free trade agreement with Mexico. This is sound and solid. And it will create 175,000 jobs.

Small business, look, small business creates two-thirds of America's jobs. Let's get the regulatory burden off of small business. Let's reduce the tax burden on small business. And let's reform our legal system. We're suing each other too much. We're suing each other too much and, frankly, caring for each other too little. And what we've got to do is put a cap on some of these frivolous lawsuits.

Governor Clinton is in the pocket of the trial lawyers. I am trying to reform this legal system so doctors can practice medicine without raising the cost, Little League people can coach without fear of some crazy lawsuit. And if you drive by and you see somebody hurt on the highway, you don't want to have to worry whether some lawyer's going to come and say you shouldn't have tried to help that person; you did the wrong thing.

I have the best plan for health care reform. It is to keep the Government out of the business and provide insurance for all, the poorest of the poor through vouchers, the over-taxed rest of the people through tax assistance. Get these malpractice suits under control, pool the insurance so you bring the cost down, but do not let the Government get into the business of rationing health care.

On education, my administration has increased spending for education tremendously. But let me tell you this: We need a new approach, and we've got one. Seventeen hundred communities are literally reinventing their schools. One out of two college students gets financial aid. But we've got to do better. And I want to give parents a choice. Parents should choose private, public, or religious schools and get help as they do that.

Those merchants of change, Mr. Clinton and Mr. Gore, aren't even willing to try a new idea. They wouldn't know one if it hit them in the face.

I've got a big difference with those two guys on crime also. You know, the Arkansas prisoners spend 20 percent of their sentences—they serve only 20 percent; the Federal criminals, 85 percent. And my view is we ought to have a little less respect for the criminal and a little more to the victims of crime.

I support our law enforcement people, and they're getting a bum rap. We ought to back them up more. You know, the other day in the White House I had a visit from eight people from the South. They came, and they were real down-to-earth, wonderful family people. They said, "We're supporting you." They were from the Fraternal Order of Police from Little Rock, Arkansas, and they endorsed me for President of the United States.

Governor Clinton says he wants to take more tax money to invest. Since when is the Government able to invest in anything? You can't do it. I want to see private business invest by giving them tax relief and by getting this deficit down.

Do you want to know how we should do that? I'll tell you: We need, right, we need a balanced budget amendment. The Democrats fight us, and we're going to get it done in the new Congress. We need a taxpayer check-off. The taxpayer should say, "Look, I'm going to allocate, if I want to, 10 percent of my income tax to go to reducing the Government debt." That should be enforced by the Congress, and it will if I am reelected.

We need term limits. The President serves limited terms. Let's limit it for these Congressmen.

The last point on getting this deficit down, let's try something new for the Federal Government. Forty-three Governors have it. They can take a pen and wipe out the pork. Give me the line-item veto, and let's get this budget down.

No, we've got a world of difference between the Clinton-Gore ticket and the Bush-Quayle ticket. And may I say I'm very proud of my running mate. I love the equity in the news media. They beat up on Dan Quayle for going into the service, and they apologize for Clinton for staying out of the service. Come on. Where's fairplay out there? Where is fairplay?

Now, I'll tell you what's going to make the difference, though. The newspaper generously referred to it. It really does have to do with character. My argument with Governor Clinton is, as President of the United States you cannot be all things to all people. You cannot say you're for one issue and then flip-flop the next day. When you make a mistake you ought to look to the American people in the eye and say, "I made a mistake, and I'm sorry. And I'm going to go on and lead the American people to greater heights." You cannot cover up. You cannot cover up. I have a big difference, as you know.

But here's a test of leadership. I had to make a tough call, a very difficult call for any President when you have to commit someone else's son or daughter to go into harm's way. I did it. I led, and we brought along the Congress. We formed an international coalition, and we kicked Saddam Hussein out of Kuwait. We busted up the fourth biggest army. And we restored the United States as the one leader in the world.

Now, where was Bill? Here's what he said. Here's what he said about the Persian Gulf: "I was for the minority"—meaning let sanctions work, let Saddam Hussein march into Saudi Arabia—"I was for the minority, but I guess"—this is an exact quote—"I guess I would have voted with the majority." My friends, you cannot do that as the President of the United States.

Audience members. Boo-o-o!

The President. He comes from Arkansas, a right-to-work State, says he's for it there; goes up to the labor leaders in Detroit and says he's against it. He's for term limits one place, against them in another.

The biggest argument I have with him on the draft is this: I have said, and I feel it viscerally, I do not believe that it is proper when your brothers or when the guys out of the ghetto are drafted, to be over in a foreign country leading, organizing demonstrations against your country no matter how strongly you feel. But I recognize that people differ on that question. But I recog-

nize they differ on serving in that war.

But let me tell you something, what I don't think is right is to try to have it both ways on there. He said on April 17th, "I'm going to reveal all my records on the draft"—was he inducted, wasn't he; was he drafted, wasn't he? He has not done that. You cannot equivocate and obfuscate. You've got to tell the truth if you want to be President of the United States of America.

There is a pattern of deception, and you cannot lead America by misleading. You darned sure can't turn the White House into the waffle house. The phone rings over there sometimes in the Oval Office or sometimes upstairs where Barbara and I live in the White House, and you don't have time to equivocate. You have to make up your mind and call them as you see them, as the umpires do, and do your level-best.

Here is why, in conclusion, I believe we are going to win. I believe, in the final analysis, when people go into that booth, I think they're going to say the President has the best agenda for renewing America. I think they're going to say we have the best record because we are saying to these young people here, you don't grow up with that same fear of nuclear war that your mother and dad had. We have led and dramatically changed the world, and I want to take that leadership now and help lift these kids up and give them a better life.

But I'll tell you why I believe it. I believe I will win because I believe in the final analysis that my wonderful wife—and I think we've got a first-class First Lady in that White House, and I am very proud of her. We have tried—the reason I'll win this election is I have tried very hard to keep the public trust. You have placed in me a trust, and we have had a clean, a decent administration. We've made some mistakes, admitted them. We are leading. Don't believe it when Governor Clinton and the Ozone Man tell you, don't believe it when they say we're a nation in decline. They had the nerve to tell the American people that we're less than Germany and a little more than Sri Lanka. Forget it. We are number one in the entire world. We are the fairest, the most decent, the most honorable country in the world. I ask for your support and your vote to lead this country for 4 more years.

Thank you, and may God bless the United States. Thank you very much. Thank you very, very much. Thank you all.

Note: The President spoke at 2:15 p.m. at the Civic Plaza.

Statement by Press Secretary Fitzwater on Sulfur Dioxide Emissions Regulations
October 26, 1992

The President today announced that the administration is issuing final regulations that will remove 10 million tons of sulfur dioxide from our air, cutting acid rain by about one-half. This major environmental achievement was made possible through the use of an innovative, market-based emissions allowance trading program that was proposed and signed into law by the President as part of the Clean Air Act. This trading program will save over $1 billion per year compared to the traditional "command and control" regulatory approach for achieving the same amount of reductions.

Through the President's leadership in passing the Clean Air Act, a decade-long congressional stalemate was broken, and one of the Nation's most important environmental goals was accomplished, significant progress toward cleaner air. Today's action further exemplifies the President's commitment to implementing fully the Clean Air Act, which utilizes the power of the marketplace to improve our environment.

Memorandum of Disapproval for Legislation Requiring an Historical and Cultural Resources Study in Lynn, Massachusetts
October 26, 1992

I am withholding my approval of H.R. 2859, which would require the Secretary of the Interior to conduct a study to identify historic sites in the vicinity of Lynn, Massachusetts, and provide alternatives on the appropriate Federal role in preserving and interpreting these sites.

The National Park Service (NPS) studies many sites to determine if they are nationally significant and therefore suitable for inclusion in the National Park System. A site is nationally significant if it is an outstanding example of a unique natural, historic, or cultural resource with demonstrated importance to the entire Nation.

In many instances, the Congress has used the findings of a congressionally mandated NPS study, regardless of the study's conclusion, to justify authorization of a new unit of the National Park System. To restore credibility and a national focus to its study process, the NPS re-established in 1991 a program to evaluate sites and prioritize candidates for future study. The most promising candidates identified by the NPS experts would be proposed for formal study.

For my fiscal year 1993 Budget request, NPS professionals rated and ranked 41 candidates from criteria established by the Department of the Interior. The fiscal year 1993 Budget proposed $1.2 million to study the seven highest-rated candidates from the list of 41 originally reviewed. The Congress appropriated $848,000 to conduct four of the studies proposed by the NPS.

The NPS experts have not identified the Lynn, Massachusetts, study as a high priority. The effect of this legislation would be to place completion of this study before the completion of other studies that the experts agree are much more important to the Nation.

H.R. 2859 would ignore professional analysis and budget constraints. It would also undermine the critical objective of identifying and evaluating the Nation's most promising natural, historic, and cultural assets for protection as units of the National Park System. I am therefore withholding my approval of H.R. 2859.

GEORGE BUSH

The White House,
October 26, 1992.

Note: This memorandum was released by the Office of the Press Secretary on October 27.

Statement on Signing the International Dolphin Conservation Act of 1992
October 26, 1992

Today I am signing into law H.R. 5419, the "International Dolphin Conservation Act of 1992." I strongly support this Act because it builds upon the efforts of my administration to protect dolphins.

I wish to make clear that the provisions in H.R. 5419 concerning the terms of international agreements to protect dolphins are advisory, and will not be interpreted to interfere with the President's constitutional responsibility to conduct this Nation's foreign affairs. In addition, nothing in this Act will be construed to preempt the President's authority to enter into other international agreements concerning the protection of dolphins.

GEORGE BUSH

The White House,
October 26, 1992.

Note: H.R. 5419, approved October 26, was assigned Public Law No. 102–523. This statement was released by the Office of the Press Secretary on October 27.

Statement on Signing the Native American Languages Act of 1992
October 26, 1992

Today I am signing into law S. 2044, the "Native American Languages Act of 1992," a bill to establish a program to help preserve Native American languages. Traditional languages are an important part of this Nation's culture and history and can help provide Native Americans with a sense of identity and pride in their heritage.

I am concerned, however, about provisions in this bill that provide benefits to "Native Hawaiians" as defined in a race-based fashion. This race-based classification cannot be supported as an exercise of the constitutional authority granted to the Congress to benefit Native Americans as members of tribes. In addition, the terms "Native American Pacific Islanders" and "Indian organizations in urban or rural non-reservation areas" are not defined with sufficient clarity to determine whether they are based on racial classifications. Therefore, I direct the affected Cabinet Secretaries to consult with the Attorney General in order to resolve these issues in a constitutional manner.

GEORGE BUSH

The White House,
October 26, 1992.

Note: S. 2044, approved October 26, was assigned Public Law No. 102–524. This statement was released by the Office of the Press Secretary on October 27.

Statement on Signing Legislation Establishing the Brown v. Board of Education National Historic Site
October 26, 1992

Today I am signing into law S. 2890, a bill to establish the *Brown* v. *Board of Education* National Historic Site in Topeka, Kansas, redesignate the Fort Jefferson National Monument as the Dry Tortugas National Park, and provide for studies of the New River in West Virginia and Boston Harbor Islands in Massachusetts.

Although I have signed S. 2890, I will withhold my approval of H.R. 5021, the "New River Wild and Scenic Study Act of 1992," and H.R. 5061, a bill concerning the

"Dry Tortugas National Park," because S. 2890 contains the identical provisions of both H.R. 5021 and H.R. 5061.

GEORGE BUSH

The White House,
October 26, 1992.

Note: S. 2890, approved October 26, was assigned Public Law No. 102–525. This statement was released by the Office of the Press Secretary on October 27.

Statement on Signing the President John F. Kennedy Assassination Records Collection Act of 1992
October 26, 1992

Today I am signing into law S. 3006, the "President John F. Kennedy Assassination Records Collection Act of 1992." This legislation provides for the review and, wherever possible, the release of records about the assassination of President Kennedy that have not yet been made public. I fully support the goals of this legislation.

In the minds of many Americans, questions about President Kennedy's assassination remain unresolved. Although the Government already has released many thousands of documents, the existence of additional, undisclosed documents has led to speculation that these materials might shed important new light on the assassination. Because of legitimate historical interest in this tragic event, all documents about the assassination should now be disclosed, except where the strongest possible reasons counsel otherwise.

While I am pleased that this legislation avoids the chief constitutional problems

raised by earlier versions of the bill considered by the Congress, it still raises several constitutional questions. First, S. 3006 sets forth the grounds on which the release of documents may be postponed, but this list does not contemplate nondisclosure of executive branch deliberations or law enforcement information of the executive branch (including the entities listed in sections 3(2) (G) through (K)), and it provides only a narrow basis for nondisclosure of national security information. My authority to protect these categories of information comes from the Constitution and cannot be limited by statute. Although only the most extraordinary circumstances would require postponement of the disclosure of documents for reasons other than those recognized in the bill, I cannot abdicate my constitutional responsibility to take such action when necessary. The same applies to the provision purporting to give certain congressional committees "access to any records held or created by the Review Board." This provision will be interpreted consistently with my authority under the Constitution to protect confidential executive branch materials and to supervise and guide executive branch officials.

Second, S. 3006 requires the Board to report to the President and the Congress. If the bill were interpreted to require simultaneous reports, S. 3006 would intrude upon the President's authority to supervise subordinate officials in the executive branch. I will construe the provisions to require that the Board report to the President before it reports to the Congress.

Third, the bill purports to set the qualifications for Board members, to require the President to review lists supplied by specified organizations, and to direct the timing of nominations. These provisions conflict with the constitutional division of responsibility between the President and the Congress. The President has the sole power of nomination; the Senate has the sole power of consent.

I note also that S. 3006 provides that, upon request of the Board, courts may enforce subpoenas that the Attorney General has issued at the Board's urging. I sign this bill on the understanding that this provision does not encroach upon the Attorney General's usual, plenary authority to represent the agencies of the United States, including the Board, whenever they appear in court.

S. 3006 will help put to rest the doubts and suspicions about the assassination of President Kennedy. I sign the bill in the hope that it will assist in healing the wounds inflicted on our Nation almost 3 decades ago.

GEORGE BUSH

The White House,
October 26, 1992.

Note: S. 3006, approved October 26, was assigned Public Law No. 102–526. This statement was released by the Office of the Press Secretary on October 27.

Remarks and a Question-and-Answer Session in Des Moines, Iowa
October 27, 1992

The President. Thank you all. Thank you very, very much. Please be seated. Let's get right about our business. But first, I certainly want to thank our great Governor, Terry Branstad, for being at my side for that warm welcome. And of course, I needn't tell Iowans how important Chuck Grassley's reelection is, I'll tell you. And for Jim Ross Lightfoot and for Jim Leach, two stalwart friends, if we had more like them in the Congress, you wouldn't hear everybody yelling everyplace I go "Clean House!" We need more like him, so send us more like him, and let's get this country moving. I'm delighted to see former Governor Ray here, and I also want to thank "Major Dad," Gerald McRaney, who is—you talk about telling it like it is—he does a great job.

Terry mentioned the ag economy, and I do think that when people get down to the wire in the heartland of America they ought to look at the record. I am very proud that ethanol is up and that we made a tough call. I took on some of the extremes in the environmental movement. I've got a good record on the environment. We took on some of the extremes and said, look, ethanol is a tremendous fuel of the future. Ethanol sales are up. The waiver we gave the other day is appropriate. It is sound conservation, and it is darn good for the American economy, and we're going to keep on.

Similarly, the use of the export program, the Export Enhancement, the EEP, is important. We extended it to pork, and it was the right thing to do. I think that will help. We will continue to fight for opening up our markets. We've got the best producers of agricultural goods in the world. Exports have saved us through tough times, agricultural exports leading the way. And my opponent, Clinton, comes along, Governor Clinton, and says, "Well, I'm for the NAFTA agreement." But he goes to the auto workers and has a very different tale. And my view is, the free trade agreement is good for American jobs, and it's good for American agriculture.

I believe we will keep working for a successful conclusion of the GATT round. And I was very disturbed the other day to read in the Daily Telegraph, the London paper, and again, a report in one of the papers here that some Clinton minion had gone to try to get the EC to postpone consideration of this important agreement. We cannot put politics ahead of the welfare of this Nation. He has denied it. The Governor has denied that, and I think I should give credit for that. But these reports keep persisting. And we will work to get a successful conclusion of the GATT round.

One other thing before I start taking the questions—you know, if you listened to the Clinton-Gore ticket, the only way they can win is to convince America that we're in a deep recession. This morning, 8:30 Eastern this morning, the figures were announced for the third quarter of this growth, the gross domestic product. The third quarter was plus 2.7 percent. It grew twice as much, about twice as much as the quarter before. We have now six straight quarters of growth in the United States, and yet the Democrats keep telling us that everything is going to hell. And they're wrong. They are wrong.

So people are hurting, yes, people are hurting. But the thing to do is to put the whole economy in perspective. You hear them talk, "Well, Japan's doing this." We've got a better economy. We're growing now, with these figures, 4 times as fast as Japan, far better than Germany—had negative growth—better than England and France and Canada. And all they can do is think, "Well, George Bush is to blame." They don't understand the world. It is the United States that's going to lead the world to new prosperity. Mark it down.

Why don't we start right in. This is the latest thing in American politics, the Phil Donahue approach to life. So we'll take a few questions here, and I'll try to—if you give me a short question, I'll try to shorten

the answers up. But I get too enthusiastic.

Expanding the Job Market

Q. I'm going to be graduating from Drake University this May, and I'm obviously pretty nervous about finding a job. What are you planning on doing to increase the job market?

The President. Well, the best thing we can do is stimulate growth in the small business sector. What I have proposed is investment tax allowance, a first-time credit for homebuyers. The Democrats say that a capital gains cut is a break for the rich. It is not. It is a stimulus to small business and entrepreneurship. Those are simply three incentives. Job retraining for those in the defense industries who are going to have to find different work because of our success in the world. I believe that the best answer is to stimulate the growth of the private sector.

Governor Clinton talks about Government investing. Let me tell you something. All the European countries have moved away—Eastern Europe—from this idea that Government should invest. They've moved to what we ought to be doing more, getting the private sector to invest, free up savings, free up investment. That is the way we will create jobs. It won't be from more taxes and more spending.

All right. I've lost control of the questioners. [*Laughter*] I'll leave that to—it's coming along good.

Entitlement Programs

Q. Mr. President, I'm concerned with the growth of entitlements in our Federal budget, and not so much in economic terms but in human terms. Can you outline your plan for reforming the system so that it builds more self-reliance and less dependence on Government?

The President. Well, let me first address it on the economic side. The deficit is clearly too big. The Government taxes too much and spends too much. That is a fundamental difference with the other side.

The President has no control over about two-thirds of the budget—it doesn't come to me—and that is known as the entitlement programs. What we must do to get the deficit down is to control the growth of the entitlement programs. We've got to control it by—let it grow in terms of population, let it grow in terms of inflation, and that's it. Then set Social Security aside. Don't touch it. I am the President that was with Ronald Reagan when it was fixed, and I think we ought to leave Social Security totally alone. Don't mess with it. But on these others, put a cap on the growth.

But in terms of your question, which was only partly economic, it is important that we understand that it is private initiative, that it is savings, that it is investment, and that it's not Government that creates opportunity. It is the private sector of the economy.

Another point that I would emphasize in relation to this question is, we have tried—Barbara's tried, I have tried, support from many Americans—to reiterate the importance of what we call the Points of Light approach, voluntarism. Government can do some things—this is to your question—Government can do a lot of things. Government can show compassion. Government has a responsibility for the national security. But much of helping each other is done in what we call this Points of Light, one American reaching out to another and helping.

You look at the hurricane down in South Florida and over in Louisiana. Government helped. We moved in with troops, and we moved in with Government aid for this and that and the Small Business Administration and FHA and all of that. But when the chapter is written on that, the people that deserve the credit are those caring Americans who reached out from 49 other States to help the people in south Florida. And that, I think, is what you're talking about.

And this idea that everything should be done by Government is not the American way, and yet that's what you're hearing in this campaign out of the Clinton-Gore ticket.

Agricultural Trade

Q. Mr. President, when reelected, what do you intend to do to get tough with the European Community, to force a GATT agreement for the American farmer?

The President. I like that positive premise, "when reelected." Let me tell you

something. Let me tell you—and here we clearly have a nice objective cross section of America, and they seem to agree with me. But nevertheless, no—[*laughter*]—we are working very hard to get a successful conclusion of GATT. I think most people recognize that the Maastricht vote in France held things up. We, I am confident, will get an agreement. We've narrowed the gap on agriculture and on a lot of these other categories.

Right now, to be very candid with you, the common agricultural policy in Europe is a detriment to getting it done, although we're making progress. Right now, some would tell you, well, France seems to be the biggest problem area in this. But I am convinced that we can move forward and get a GATT agreement. We have to do it.

You know, the best answer to helping those in the Third World—I told some interviewers yesterday, I think of Iowa, right out in the middle of America, as a State that has an international perspective. You've always been interested in world peace and in these kinds of things, how the world interacts. But I really believe that in terms of this GATT agreement, the best way to help Third World countries, those countries that are suffering the most, is to open their markets, open markets around the world, whether it's—whatever products we're talking about. And a successful conclusion of the GATT arrangement will do that.

We are caught up in a lot of tough European policies. She asked the right question—EC. We are going to have to insist through a lot of application of the technical provisions of the trade law, that if they don't open up these markets then we are going to have to—I would use a little softer term than retaliate—but we are going to have to insist on our rights, and I think the world knows that, on oilseeds and these other things. And I believe we're going to get the job done.

This stool is perilous here.

Congress

Q. Good morning, Mr. President. The success of your second term will depend to a large extent on how the newly Members of the House will react to your various pro- posals. And I read in the Wall Street Jour- nal, oh, 10 days ago or so, that congressional leaders have been meeting to plan strate- gies in how to squash any reforms that the new Members might propose, changing the status quo. Do you have a counter strategy in how to reach these new Members?

The President. Let me tell you what it is: It's to listen to the people. But here's the problem we've got. We got some things done in our first term, good things, caring things: the Americans for Disabilities Act that lifts up those that are disabled and helps them fit into the mainstream, or the Clean Air Act, or more recently even, a transportation bill that puts $150 billion into the infrastructure. So we've been able to accomplish quite a few good things. As we got near the end of the first term, this gentleman is right, the leadership, not all the Members but the leadership in the Con- gress made a determination: We can win if the economy is bad, and we can win if the President doesn't look good by mistake and try to fix something, do something. So we've been up against what is a gridlocked Congress.

Now, what's going to change? Because they can't even run a two-bit post office or a failed little tiny bank this big, you're going to have a lot of new Members of Congress. Like me, they're listening to the voters. And I will be reelected and not have any politics on the horizon, no more, no more campaigns, no more debates, thank God. [*Laughter*] No more whatever else it is. And we'll say, let's get the people's busi- ness done; Democrats, Republicans, sit down with me now, and let's do what I have told the people I want to do. Health care, make insurance available to all. What- ever it is, education, revolutionize it. Don't go back and patch up, put band-aids on something where our kids are getting short- changed; revolutionize it. Budget deficit, give me the balanced budget amendment, the line-item veto, a check-off for tax re- turns. And they will have to be listening. When I'm elected, it will be because people are listening to these ideas. And I'll say, "Okay, sit down," like Lyndon said, "Come reason together." With a two-by-four in one hand and a very open approach in another.

And I believe we can move this country forward in the first 120 days.

The politics will subside for a while. The best time for a new President is the first days of the second term, because politics is gone, the voters' words are ringing in the ears of all politically elected people, and the country is beginning to move.

You know, I mentioned these growth fig- ures. But interest rates are down. Who wants to go back to the way they were when you had a Democratic President in the White House, at 21.5 percent interest rates and 15 percent inflation and grain em- bargoes. This Congress, if the status quo prevails, will roll over Clinton like a stone steamroller, and we can't have that.

So we're talking about the new ideas that will stimulate the growth in the economy, do more in the private sector. And I really am optimistic about moving the country forward with the new Members of Con- gress. Clean House! It's been done by the voters already.

Taxes

Q. Mr. President, I was curious, I've been listening to Clinton's economic proposals, trying to make it add up in my own mind. But this idea that you can raise $250 billion in taxes just taxing the top 2 percent, how does he do this math? Have you and your people had a chance to look into that?

The President. We don't have anybody dumb enough to figure it out. Here's what they're saying. He is saying he wants to raise $150 billion in new taxes, and then this gentleman is right, because there are a lot of other proposals where you'd have to get the money to pay for it. And he says, "I will tax the top 2 percent." The top 2 per- cent means you go down to $64,000 to start with. Then, to pay for the $220 billion in spending—and that doesn't consider how much his health care plan and these other things would cost—you get down where you're hitting everybody at $36,000.

Then, to do all the spending for all the programs, you nurses, you cab drivers, you guys that are assisting in the field, watch your wallet, because he is not going after just the rich guys. He's doing it the way the Democrats have always done when they control both ends, going right after your pocketbook. So the math does not add up. And it is tax and spend, tax and spend. They kept saying it is not tax and spend, and it is.

When he talks about—he uses the word "investment." And I'll repeat this: He uses the word, the Government "investing." The Government does not create wealth. It's the private sector that does. So free that up and keep the Government constrained.

Now, who is next? Herb.

The Environment

Q. Mr. President, when you're elected, the environment will continue to have high priority in this Nation. Do you have special plans you'd like to tell us about, your plans for the environment?

The President. Well, one thing I'd like to say at the very beginning: One, it's good to see you, but secondly—one of the great Iowans, respected well beyond the borders of Iowa for his knowledge of agriculture and his promoting of great values—but let me simply say this: On the environment, we have a good, sound record. We've done well in forestry. We've done well in assisting in cleaning up the beaches and in the ocean. We've done extraordinarily well in wilderness, setting aside more acres. We've done far better than any previous administration in enforcement of EPA.

But what I've been unwilling to do is go to the extreme. And what we have to do in this country is to say we've got to find—and we're striving to do that every day—the balance between growth and sound environmental practice.

So I think the record is a good one. We will continue to be good stewards of the land. But I am not going to go to the extreme that says to a farmer, if it rains and you've got a little puddle there, a tiny one, that means you can't use your land. We've gone too far under regulation and too far under interpretation on some of these statutes.

So I think of agricultural—we've got a good conservation set-aside program—I think of farmers as conserving. They've got their families coming along. They don't want to ruin, rape, pillage, and plunder on their own land. It's ridiculous to start with

that assumption.

I'll tell you something. Governor Gore—Governor Gore—[*laughter*]—if you read the book on Mr. Gore's proposals, I'll tell you, it would screech this country to a halt. We cannot go to the extreme. He's out there talking about the protection of this feathery little owl. Yes, I love little owls. I think they're wonderful. But we've got to also protect the 30,000 families that are trying to work for a living. The extreme groups will not vote for me; sound environmentalists will vote for me.

Education

Q. President Bush, as a student myself, I was wondering if you could describe certain points of your education plan for the next 4 years that would help the U.S. rank higher in the world in education.

The President. Good question. And education—health care and education. Education. We have a program called America—I don't want to get too programmatic—called America 2000. We have 1,700 communities across this country who are literally sitting down—they're bypassing the teachers union, and they're working with the teachers. They're saying let's reinvent the schools.

In some urban area, the school will have one conformation. In another, in a rural area, it might have an entirely different one. We spend more per capita on education than every country, I believe, except Switzerland, and the results aren't good enough. So when I became President, we worked with the Governors, including Governor Branstad, and set six national education goals. Then this program, America 2000, is designed to meet the goals.

One of the key points is, I believe, that we ought to have parental choice for schools, public, private, or religious. It worked for the GI bill. The money goes to the families, and the public system of education was strengthened under the GI bill. So that's one of the provisions.

Then we've got a lot of programs for adult retraining in the schools which should come under the heading of education. We have more than doubled the money for Head Start, which I still feel is a very important program, to keep up with one of our education goals: every kid starts school ready to learn.

So the program is really good, and the nice thing about it is, you only have to depend on the old thinkers on the Democratic side in Congress for this much. The rest of it is being done by the communities, community leaders, teachers, and parents, and that's where the action has to be. We've gotten away from all of that.

We'll go here, and then we'll come over there.

Foreign Policy

Q. Good morning, Mr. President. Most people have been hearing a lot about the domestic issues, which are very important. But we're not getting anything from the other side on the international side of events. If most people have been watching their TV and reading the newspapers, they see that there's instability again in the Soviet Union. We're not getting anything from the other side of the media on what to do about the instability in the world. Without stability in the world, there will be no good trade, and there will be no growth.

I'd like to know what your plan is, because there is no plan on the other side for stability in this world that we need for growth.

The President. Okay. You're right. I never see it on the programs. Democrats don't want to talk about foreign policy. It's almost like there's no threat anywhere in the world. I noticed your shot at the media. Please be careful. I'm an expert on that. [*Laughter*] But the best-selling bumper sticker is "Annoy the Media. Reelect Bush." But I want to—here it is. By coincidence, there it is.

But I feel I'm going to make—I'll divert for one minute, and then I'll come back to your question. The problem is, there is so much understanding of this that some people are taking it out on those who they should not take it out on. Like the photographers with us today, these guys that struggle around, carrying these boom mikes and the cameras. So put them down as good guys, and leave the traveling press alone. But I hope you share my view about all these talking heads that come on the na-

tional television and tell us how bad everything is and that we don't have a chance to win. They don't understand it.

Why do you not talk about foreign policy? Because they know that is a strength, and they know that we are the leader of the world, and we are not, as Governor Clinton says, a nation in decline. He puts us south of—Clinton and Gore, they've got about as much foreign policy experience as Millie, put together.

Let me tell you something. The world is still dangerous. We have reduced defense spending, and we've been able to reduce it because with bipartisan support we stayed strong. We didn't listen to the freeze movement. We stayed strong. I salute Ronald Reagan: peace through strength. It worked. It worked. But there are still wolves. The Soviet bear may be gone, but there are wolves out there. I have reduced defense spending by many billions of dollars. Now, I see the Democrats coming in, and to pay for all their, quote, "investment," unquote, they want to cut the guts out of the defense. We cannot do that. Who knows where the next crisis will come?

So, I'll say this: I believe that it is exports that have sustained us in the roughest of economic times. I believe it is exports that will lead the world to new heights of prosperity, and I believe that foreign policy is tremendously important in implementing a strong export program. So it's not just defense. It is also international economics. And we've got a good record.

My argument with Governor Clinton on the war is this: Nobody likes to make a tough decision where you commit someone else's son or daughter to war. No one likes to do it. I do believe that having been in combat at least has made me sensitive to all of the ramifications of a decision like that. I made a tough decision. It was the right decision. Your sons and your daughters responded. We stood up against aggression. And as a result, and it wouldn't ever have happened without that, you see ancient enemies talking to each other in the Middle East. You see Russia going down democracy's path. You look south of our border, and you see some trouble spots, but you also see a persistent wave of democracy and freedom there. You see elections in Africa. And you see the Eastern Europeans and the Baltics free. We've had dramatic progress. And the best thing is, the kids here in this wonderful band go to bed at night without the same fear of nuclear war that their predecessors had.

So I believe foreign policy is important. I believe national security policy is important. And I believe that it is an interconnected world; the economies are interconnected. And it is the United States, with the programs I've outlined, that is going to lead us and the world into new levels of prosperity. We're ready. Inflation is down. Interest is down. Business is more lean now. Our productivity in this country is up. And all of this will work towards enhancing not only world peace but world economic progress.

Small Business

Q. Mr. President, thank you for making America proud during Desert Storm.

I'm here today as a small voice representing small business. I have a small business in the Des Moines area here. In an effort to provide to my employees a solid work environment and good benefits, I spend each year about $200,000 in taxes, $25,000 a year for insurance, and substantially a lot of money complying with various Government regulations. Now, I'm here as a proponent for the Bush-Quayle administration. I'm particularly a big fan of Mrs. Bush.

The President. So am I.

Q. My message to you comes today in the form of an appeal rather than a question. Given that the success of the American economy depends on the success of America and small business, we'd really like to have the administration's help in controlling the skyrocketing costs of doing business.

The President. Okay.

Q. When next Tuesday rolls around, you'll be needing our help, and I, for one, intend to support you. After next Tuesday, we'll be needing your help.

The President. All right. You should have been getting it by now. We put a freeze on regulations. He's absolutely right, there's too much redtape. And I'm not saying there's not more to do. There's plenty more to do. I want to see a freeze and a cap on some of these outrageous lawsuits that are

running the cost of business, the small business, in particular, right out of the roof. Governor Clinton refuses to stand up against these trail lawyers who literally are driving the cost of health care and business right out through the roof.

You don't need more mandates. I am for family leave, but I don't think that Government needs to mandate it. Give tax credits to the smallest business of the small, and help them do it. So I think we've got to guard against too many mandates telling a small-business person, man or woman, how they're going to run their lives.

I think that gets back to this gentleman's question, because really freeing up the private sector is the way to offer opportunity to these kids that are asking about where they get a job, but it also is the way we ought to go. We are not going to reverse the trend and go like the failed European policies, where government invests. Government doesn't know how to invest.

Now, she was going to get the next question. Are you nervous?

Q. Yes.

The President. You don't look nervous. Go ahead.

The Arkansas Record

Q. Well, in all these debates I watch, Clinton says that he has rankings in Arkansas that are one, four, four and one. What are those rankings that he has?

The President. Hey, good question. That's what we call a—in the World Series every once in a while you'll see the seams on it when it comes over the plate, the slow ball. You know what I mean.

But, look, Governor Clinton said in the debate, "I want to do for this country what I've done for Arkansas." That is a terrible threat.

Audience members. Boo-o-o!

The President. We cannot let that happen to this country.

And look, I lived near Arkansas, and they are wonderful people. But regrettably, they are at the very bottom on environment. They're on the bottom on job creation. He talks about they led the Nation on job creation. That was the year he was out of the State 85 percent of the time. The rest of the time they are 30 percent below the national averages. The teachers are either 49th or 50th in terms of teacher pay. Twenty percent of the—I've got all these statistics coming at you—20 percent of the criminals—I mean, the criminals serve 20 percent of their time. Under Federal law it's 85 percent. Less spent on corrections than in all but one State. And it is statistic after statistic. Yes, Arkansas starts as a poor State. But in some categories you ought to see, after 10 years as being Governor, some progress that one can point to, instead of that thing that we led in new jobs or wages this last year. As I say, he was out of the State 85 percent of the time.

So the record is not good. I'm saying we've got problems in this country. I believe we've got the answers to solve them. But I think it's fair, since your senior Senator and Governor Clinton and Tsongas and several of these other guys were going around saying what was bad about my record, I think it is fair, as the American people get ready to vote, to take a look at the record in Arkansas. It's a sorry record. And we cannot let him do that to the United States of America.

Health Care

Q. Good morning, Mr. President. Governor Clinton has proposed a 7-percent tax on businesses to pay for his national health care system. I was wondering if you could explain just what that tax in itself—with the other ones that the other gentleman was talking about—would do to businesses in this country?

The President. Well, he says now that he didn't want to—he's had three health plans. Every time one gets knocked down, he comes up with another one. And this gets to the fundamental question of waffling. To coin a phrase: We cannot let the White House be turned into the waffle house. We simply can't do that.

But the one you're talking about, the one he's talking about is an insurance system called "pay or play," and that if these small-business people do not want to go along with the plan, they've got to pay. If they pay, the estimates are it will cost 7-percent payroll tax on every business. Now, businesses at this juncture or at any juncture

don't need a 7-percent payroll tax.

Our plan is better. What it does is provide insurance to the poorest of the poor through vouchers. To those next overtaxed and overworked lower, middle-income people, they get a tax credit. We pool the insurance, thus meaning a small-business person can buy at lower rates and get lower rates provided for his or her business people. We make the health care transportable, so if you move from job to job, and I think the averages are quite high in the numbers of people that change employment, those health benefits go with you. We go after malpractice suits that are driving the cost of doctors right through the roof. We use much more efficient billing. And we get it done without slapping a tax on the small-business people or any business. I believe that's the way we need to go for health care.

Presidential Appointees

Q. Greetings, Mr. President. First, some positive news. I went to college back in the late seventies, when I attended and started as a freshman. And when I came out as a senior, when my younger brother over here attended as a freshman, tuition doubled. That was the years of the high inflation. When your administration and Reagan's administration was in there, I've had a chance to live the American dream. Things have been very, very positive. I have a great job, great family, super company to work for, and things are good out there. The people that are hurting, I think, is going through a purging process. So positive news, I think, from here.

I've got a question for you on administration, if I could. There's been very little talk about administration besides just the President and the Vice President. And I'm really concerned about if a new person came in, who would they bring in. There's been talk of Mario Cuomo on the Supreme Court. Who knows, maybe our own Tom Harkin would be in the Department of Defense or something like that. I think you have some of the most sharpest people out there with Dick Cheney and Jim Baker, Margaret Tutwiler, and I can't name them all here right now. But can you please address that, because I know there's thousands of jobs there.

The President. I do think it's important. I can understand their not wanting to name who they're going to have. But the gentleman raises a very, very important question: Who are the people that are going to come in? What is their philosophy? And from what I've seen, it looks to me—and maybe this is unfair—like a return to the Jimmy Carter days, and I don't think we need that, when that "misery index" was through the roof, you guys had a grain embargo on you, and these interest rates were at 21 percent.

But let me put it this way: In our administration I have been very, very well served by the people you mentioned and many, many more. But to revitalize a new administration, it is traditional and proper that there be a lot of new people in the Cabinet. And there will be in our administration. I think that's good because I think you can bring in fresh new blood, and I think people start in to implement the program.

So I have said there's going to be a lot of change. Then they say, "Well, when you say this, are you trying to blame somebody for the economy?" I've never believed that you can shift blame to somebody. You're the captain of the ship as President of the United States. If things are going well, maybe you'd get credit. But if things are going badly, the buck does stop on that Oval Office. One of the problems I've got— this is off your question a little bit, but it's to—we should and will bring in people. We're right-sizing Government. I have challenged the Congress to reduce their staffs by a third. We can do the White House staff by a third. We'll have to respond to far fewer of these ridiculous queries from a very partisan Congress, and we'll be able to do that. We're going to put a cap on the Federal pay until we get this economy really moving. The only trouble is, the President's pay gets cut a little bit. But never mind. [*Laughter*] That's the way it works, and that's the way it should work. And so I really believe new approach is required.

On the Clinton-Gore ticket, I'm afraid we would see a lot of the same old names that had failed foreign policy and this kind of Government control, more Government intervention, more Government in the domestic side. And I must insist that when the whole world is moving away from Government investing, this is no time for the United States to bring in a bunch of people that think they can figure it out better than the farmers out in Iowa.

Moderator. Mr. President, I think we have time for just one more question.

The President. Time flies when you're having fun here. [*Laughter*]

Russia

Q. Mr. President, I am from Moscow, from Russia. And I have a question for you. Are you planning a visit in Moscow again to continue working with Mr. Yeltsin?

I repeat—you don't understand?

The President. No, I'm hearing. I'm here.

Q. Are you planning a visit in Moscow?

The President. Oh, excuse me, I thought you were just in the middle of it. Planning a visit—well, first place, I support President Yeltsin. I support the move towards democracy. They're having some problems in Russia right now, as we know. But they are problems in a sense of democracy, Yeltsin fighting with the Congress. Have you heard that one before? [*Laughter*]

So I have no specific plans. But let me tell you something that might sound a little self-serving to you: I was very pleased when Boris Yeltsin has said publicly that "George Bush was the first world leader to recognize what we were doing." Do you remember— I'll never forget the sight of Yeltsin standing on top of that tank. And I didn't waffle. Governor Clinton said, "Well, let's wait and see who's going to come out or how it's going to work out," when he was Governor, asked to comment on the democratic change in Moscow. Yeltsin is publicly on record saying, "President Bush supported us. He never wavered. And that support and that consistency was one of the things that guaranteed that our move to democracy would succeed." That is world leadership, if you'll excuse it. And that is important. It gets back to this gentleman's questions. Those things are important.

Closing Statement

Well, look, the Governor tells me we're

out of here. So let me just end this way. You know, in the first place, I wish Barbara Bush were here because I really believe she has been an outstanding First Lady, and she would love to see this marvelous crowd.

Secondly, I wouldn't be standing here as President of the United States if it weren't for Iowa—and I'm thinking back to the seventies, early, the eighties—I would not be here. And we have tried—I say "we" because in a sense it is whoever's living in the White House—we have tried to uphold the trust that has been placed in us by the American people. When I make a mistake, I've—"Look, I made a mistake." Isn't that what families do? Isn't that what your kids do or maybe some of you all do? And go on then and try to lead the country.

When Governor Clinton said it's not the character of the President but "the character of the Presidency," I violently disagree with that because the two are interlocked. Not just in this country but people from all around the world look to the White House and the occupant to the White House for their character and the character that shapes the character of the Presidency. I have tried very hard to uphold the trust. I have not tried to be on all sides of all issues.

And so in the final days, as we wind down to this election, I am confident, not overconfident, but I am very confident of reelection. Because I think what will happen is people will go into the booth; they'll look at all the issues; they'll listen; they'll have in the back of their minds the debates; they'll know the problems we have; and they'll also begin to see some of the good things that are happening in our country. But in the final analysis, they're going to say: Who has the honor, the integrity, that sense of service that merits my trust? Who does have the character? And on that basis, I ask for your support and I ask for your vote.

May God bless our great country. Thank you very, very much. Thank you.

Note: The President spoke at 9 a.m. at the Des Moines Convention Center.

Remarks to the Community in Paducah, Kentucky
October 27, 1992

The President. Thank you very much.

Audience members. Four more years! Four more years! Four more years!

The President. Four more! Thank you. Thank you very much, Gerald McRaney. I am proud to have "Major Dad," Gerald McRaney, at my side. And I am grateful to him for his loyal support. Let me just say at the outset I'm very pleased to be here, back again, back for me in this great part of——

Audience member. Kentucky.

The President. I was going to say, of western Kentucky. But let me point it out this way. Every place I go, every place I go, I see signs that say, "Clean House!" I want to see David Williams elected to the United States Senate, and I want to see Steve Hamrick elected to the United States Congress. Let's clean House!

May I thank your Mayor, Gerry Montgomery; Bob Gable, our State chairman.

And it is great to be in Paducah. You should have seen it, flying in with these fall colors. It makes you agree with the guy who said, "Heaven is a Kentucky kind of place."

Here we come down to the wire with 7 days to go. It's like a close race at Bluegrass Downs, and we're closing the gap. And in 7 days, we are pulling ahead at the finish line to win this election.

You know, I was very pleased today that the figures came out refuting the Clinton-Gore claim of how bad everything is. The figures came out for growth in the third quarter, and the economy of the United States led Europe, led Canada, led Japan, and we grew at 2.7 percent, 2.7 percent. All you get from Clinton and Gore is bad news. That is good growth, and we're going to do even better.

You know, Mac referred to this, and I hate to ruin such a lovely day, but I must do this, because for months the Clinton-Gore crowd have been telling everybody how bad everything is and that he's going to make things better, that Clinton will make things better. Let me just remind you, as a southern State, and a good one at that, and Arkansas has some wonderful people, but let me remind you of just a few statistics on the Arkansas record. They are 50th in the quality of environmental initiatives. They are 50th in the percentage of adults with college degrees. They are 50th in per capita spending on criminal justice. They are 49th—getting better—in per capita spending on police protection; 48th in percentage of adults with a high school diploma; 48th in spending on corrections; 46th in teachers' salaries; 45th in the overall well-being of children. And this man said in a debate, he wants to do for America what he's done for Arkansas. We cannot let him do that.

Imagine trying to bring a record like that. He did point out one thing: In the debate, you may remember, he said that the work had gone up, jobs had gone up in Arkansas one year. That was this year. He's been out of the State 85 percent of the time. That's why it went up. For 10 years, for 10 years they averaged 30 percent of the national average.

So, enough for Arkansas. Now look what he wants to do to this country. He's already said he wants to raise $150 billion in new taxes. He's already said $220 billion in new spending. That is trickle-down Government. The numbers don't add up, and the middle class of America, watch out. He says he'll sock it to the rich, but he's coming after your wallet. He's coming after you. Don't let him do it to America.

He talks about change, change, change. We changed inflation. It was changed when you had a Democrat in the White House and Democrat Congress. You had inflation at 15 percent. You had interest rates at 21.5 percent. He wants change. That's what he'll bring us, and we're not going to let him do it. You listen to that kind of change, and change is all you'll have left in your pocket, believe me. We cannot go back. Here is the economy growing, and we cannot go back to those failed policies that brought us a "misery index" going right out through

Gore's ozone layer.

You know, you hear from the—I'm kind of down. Some of you may have noticed my favorite bumper sticker. I don't see it around here. Is it up there? There it is. And everybody knows what it means. Everyone knows what it means, "Annoy the Media. Reelect Bush." You know and I know that inasmuch as we've got some wonderful people traveling with us, let me say, don't take it out on the photographers. Don't take it out on these guys with the cameras and the boom mikes. They're all good folks. Take it out on those talking heads in the national press that come on and tell us everything that's bad about America.

Harry Truman had it right. Talked about 50 reporters who were talking the same thing about gloom and doom. He said, "They couldn't know enough to pound sand in a rathole." That's true. And we are going to win the election in spite of these mournful polls.

Here is why: Employment is at 93 percent in this country. Inflation is down, only 2.5, 3 percent. Home mortgage rates, as I mentioned to you, interest rates were 21.5; now they're down around 8. The gross domestic figures today: 2.7 percent. We have grown for six straight quarters. And all you hear is gloom and doom from Clinton and Gore. We're moving, and we're going to lead the world to recovery.

We've got a good plan to hold the line on this domestic spending and get that tax base down and lower the deficit by helping small business. Governor Clinton says, "Look, I want to have the Government invest." The Government never made a sound investment in its life. The investment is small business, and that's where we want it to be.

You know how he wants to do it all, is to cut the muscle out of our defense. We have cut defense because we were successful in standing up against aggression around the world, and we must not cut into the muscle of defense. You throw millions of people out of work needlessly, have an adverse effect on where we've landed at Fort Campbell. Look, the Soviet bear may be dead, but there are wolves out there, and we must keep our eyes open and keep America strong.

And here's the way we're going to do it. We're going to create more jobs in America through exports. We make the best product. We have the best workers anywhere in the world. You build cars right in this State that are sold over in the Middle East. We are going to create more jobs through free and fair trade, not by listening to the waffle iron of Clinton and Gore.

Small business creates two-thirds of the new jobs, and they need relief from taxation, they need relief from regulation and, yes, they need relief from litigation. We are suing each other too much and caring for each other too little.

So I propose tax relief for small business. What does Mr. Gore, the Ozone Man, propose? A carbon tax. He suggests it in his book, a carbon tax. That's supposed to do something about the environment, but I'll tell you what it would do to industry in Kentucky: drive it right into the ground. We're not going to let him do that. We have a good record on the environment, a good, sound record. But you do not have to go to the extreme and throw a lot of families out of work to keep the Sierra Club happy.

I mentioned legal reform. One thing we've got to do is make it so that these Little League coaches aren't afraid to coach, that doctors are no longer afraid to deliver babies, that a person going by the highway is not scared to stop and help his fellow American because of a lawsuit. We sue each other too much. Help me get some Congressmen that are willing to put a cap on these outrageous lawsuits.

We've got a great health care plan to make insurance provided to the poorest of the poor through vouchers, through—give tax credits to the next group of overtaxed Americans, to bring insurance to all, to make insurance go from job to job with the person that has the insurance. But we do not do what Clinton and Gore want to do, create some Government board and let Government ration health care. We're not going to do that.

In education, I see these kids, and it is priority. We've got an America 2000 program that bypasses that all-powerful, dictatorial teachers' union and goes to the teach-ers and works with them to strengthen education. God bless our teachers. We are working—college grants for kids are up under my administration by far. Spending for education is up. Now we've got to go with America 2000 and literally reinvent our public schools. And that's another idea. Let's give the parents the right to choose and help them do it, public, private, or religious schools.

You know, everyplace I go we're helped by police officers. And let me be very clear: I don't think we need anybody on the Supreme Court that is going to go on there like Governor Cuomo, one suggested by Mr. Clinton. We need people on there that will interpret the Constitution, not legislate, and those who will have a little more sympathy for the victims of crime and a little less for the criminal elements.

The Democrats talk tough, the liberal Democrats, about crime. But let me tell you something: The other day I had a visit in the Oval Office from eight individuals, grassroots family men, all coming up there. They said, "We are for you for President," and they represented the Fraternal Order of Police of Little Rock, Arkansas. I was proud to have their support.

In the next term we are going to reform Government. We're going to get the deficit down. I ask you to send people to Washington, only those who will do the following: Give us a balanced budget amendment to the Constitution. Give us a taxpayers' check-off so you can check 10 percent of your taxes, and make that money go to lowering the deficit. Give me a line-item veto and let me try to cut the deficit.

You know, in one of our debates Governor Clinton said it's not the character of the President, it is "the character of the Presidency." And I beg to differ. I think they are interlocked. I do not believe you can have a candidate who tries to be on all sides of all issues.

Here's what he said on the Persian Gulf war. That was not an easy decision, to send someone else's son, someone else's daughter into combat. A President has to make it, and he can't say "maybe," or he can't say "but." I made a tough call. But here's what Governor Clinton said. He said, "I agree with the minority," that means those who wanted to let sanctions work; if we'd listened to that, Saddam Hussein would be in Saudi Arabia today. "I agree with the minority, but I guess I would have voted with the majority." You cannot flip-flop and waffle if you want to be President of the United States.

He says one thing about right-to-work laws in right-to-work States and then goes up to the powerful union bosses and said he's against that. He says, "Well, maybe I'll be for term limits," which I support, and then he says he's against term limits. You cannot flip-flop. You cannot do this. It would be like him judging the Hatfield and McCoy feud: "I guess I would have agreed with the arguments that the McCoys made, but I would have sided with the Hatfields." That is not leadership. [*Laughter*]

What is troubling America is a pattern of deception. Everyone's aware of politics, but when you're going for President, you cannot be followed by this pattern of deception. You can't lead the American people by misleading the American people.

I have differed with Governor Clinton on the war and on his own service. My position is clear. And some people differed with me on the Vietnam war. But I'll tell you the thing I do not understand. I simply do not understand a person whose peers are dying in Vietnam, some of whom are held in Hanoi prisons, going to England to organize demonstrations against the United States. We cannot have that. What will he tell a young man or a young woman as Commander in Chief if they said, "Oh, no, we want to go off and organize demonstrations"?

We differ on the draft, on what he did. But the problem is the pattern. He said, "I'll bring out all my records on April 17th," and we haven't seen anything. It isn't his choice about the war. It's the idea that he tried to have it both ways. And you can't do that if you're a leader.

You know, all around America, people look to the United States, and they look to the President of the United States for moral leadership. And so when you go into that booth, I ask this question—we see our economy recovering; we know people are hurting—but you ask the question: Who do you trust and who has the character to lead this great country?

Barbara and I—I know one other good reason to keep me as President. We've got the best First Lady you possibly could have. But she and I have tried very hard to keep the public trust. I think most people by now know that we've been blessed by a strong and wonderful family. We have faith in God. We believe we are one Nation under God. Now it's not a question of needing to be President of the United States. It is a question that we have literally changed the world. These kids go to bed at night without that same fear of nuclear war that their mother and dad had.

Now what I want to do is bring that same leadership and lift these kids up, convince them that the opportunity is bright. Execute our program, the agenda for America's renewal, increase our exports.

Let me end this way: Clinton and Gore say we're a nation in decline. They say we're south of Germany and a little better than Sri Lanka. Let me tell you something: They ought to open their eyes. We are the most respected nation in the whole world. We are the leader of the world. I ask for your support. I ask for your vote to lead us to new prosperity for every American young person here today.

Thank you. Thank you, and God bless you. What a spectacular rally. What a wonderful, wonderful turnout in western Kentucky. This is superb. Thank you.

Note: The President spoke at 12:36 p.m. at Paducah Community College.

Question-and-Answer Session in Paducah
October 27, 1992

Tom Butler. Thank you, and welcome to our program today. Mr. President, welcome to you, sir. We're delighted to have you here. You're helping us to make a little bit of history, because this is the first and only Kentucky statewide town meeting of this campaign. I want you to also know that there are viewers watching today in southern Illinois, southeast Missouri, and west Tennessee, as well as in western Kentucky. And some of our audience are from those other States. So they'll be asking questions today. We have a studio audience today that we've invited here, mainly a group of undecided voters. It's up to you to try to convince them, Mr. President. And so based on what they hear today, it may help them to make a decision about this election.

Also today Jackie Hays is at WAVE–TV in Louisville. She has a group there in her studios. And Tom Kenny has some folks with him at WLEX–TV in Lexington, Kentucky. We're going to be going back to them shortly. So get your questions ready in Louisville and Lexington, and we'll see you in just a few minutes.

The Economy

Mr. President, I'd like to sort of get the ball rolling, if I might. You know, the GDP figures came out today showing a 2.7 increase, surprised some folks, I think, for the last quarter. Given the fact that we've now had this long a positive economic growth, meager though some of it has been, does it not suggest that maybe the Congress and the administration in order to—ought to leave it alone and just let it happen? This is happening since you've had gridlock in Congress for a while. So this thing seems to be correcting itself.

The President. It suggests a lot of things. We've been told as a nation, 92 percent of the news coverage, negative on the economy. The economy has grown for six straight quarters. And yet you hear some of these talking heads come on there, these guys they pay a couple of hundred bucks, on the national news telling everybody how bad things are. We've grown, and this is very

encouraging news. The United States will lead the way out into real recovery. But it's very encouraging.

I still feel we need to give more incentives to small business. I'm for investment tax allowance. The Democrats, the liberals, call it, a capital gains reductions, a break for the rich. It isn't. It will stimulate investment by small business, create new jobs. And I love the idea of a tax credit for the first-time homebuyer.

So yes, 2.7 percent is darned good growth. And it pulls the rug right out from under Mr. Clinton, who is telling everybody how horrible everything is. People are hurting in this country, but they've been told that there's no hope. Here we're growing at 2.7 percent, more than Germany, more than Japan, more than the rest of Europe, and more than Canada. It's very good news. But I still think we need to do things. Not to invest—Clinton says, invest Government, get the Government to invest more—I don't believe it. I think we need to help small business invest more. That means jobs for people, hope for the future.

Entitlement Programs

Q. President Bush, my question for you is why is it that handicapped people who draw SSI/disability do not get an equal amount to today's standard cost of living?

The President. Let me first say that one of my proudest accomplishments—and give credit to the Democrats on this, and I must and I do, but also to us—we passed something called the Americans for Disabilities Act. It's a wonderful piece, the most forward piece of civil rights legislation in the last couple of decades. What it does is enable disabled people to work their way into the mainstream, instead of being pushed off to the side.

On this one, I think most of the benefits have these cost-of-living increases. I don't know technically—I'll have to get from you your own specific case. I'll just take that question to move a little bit off of it. My view is to get this deficit down, we must set aside Social Security, don't touch it. It was fixed back in the mid-eighties. But then we're going to have to control the growth of the other mandatory programs. Let it grow, let them grow to inflation and population, but not increase the spending. Otherwise we won't get the deficit down.

But in this case, you would be exempt and covered. So I'll have to check as to why you're not getting your increases.

Quality of Life for Children

Q. Mr. President, I work in small business development and in economic as well, and done that for the past 9 years. But I also work with a number of women and women's issues. One of the major concerns I keep hearing is in the pro-life position. What guarantee does your administration propose for the quality of life for the individual who would be brought into our society based upon the pro-life stance?

The President. Well, you're right, I do favor life. And I favor adoption. I think the answer is more adoption and fewer abortions. We've had 28 million. You know, this is an issue, Karen, that just divides this country. A lot of people feel differently than I do, and I have respect for their judgment. I hope they have respect for mine. But the answer—I wouldn't say it makes a difference to whether a kid is adopted or brought into the world through a pro-life position, because kids that are born into families or kids that come and don't have parents look after them, we have to have policies that help all of them.

I think my program for getting more emphasis on the private sector is good. We have increased the women and children WIC program, which is the main support from the Federal Government for women, infants, and children. The spending under the Bush administration has reached all-time highs. Therein lies the answer to those kids that are put off in foster homes and all of that.

But I really believe the answer is to—it's not a pro-life or a pro-choice question. It is how do you lift the hopes for all kids in this country. And I think with our emphasis on Head Start, education, we've got all but—all the 4-year-olds are now eligible. Increased spending for Head Start, that's very impor-

tant. My whole program for education, America 2000, which bypasses the powerful teachers union but gets the teachers themselves involved in the community with the parents, is a good program. So I don't discriminate between a child that comes into the world and is put up for adoption, between regular kids that are born into a family that need help.

Welfare Reform

Q. I find that there are lots of problems with Federal assistance. People that would like jobs can't afford to work because they lose their benefits. What will you do to correct that situation?

The President. She raises a very important point. I favor the welfare reform. Let me give you an example of one thing that really troubles me with the existing setup and one of the reasons we're trying to get the Congress to change it.

A mother is on welfare. A kid has a little piddly job somewhere saving for her education or his education. If that kid saves over 1,000 bucks, that mother gets off welfare. We have got to have welfare reform with workfare and learnfare.

This isn't just the Federal Government, ma'am. The way we do it, you give States waivers. Wisconsin's taken a lead. Jersey's taken a lead. All of these States are trying different formulas for working and learning. But I think one of the reforms at the Federal level is the one you're talking about to permit these families to save a little more of what they get through jobs without getting thrown off of the welfare; work their way off. That is going to happen. That's going to happen soon.

Q. By the way, my son said to tell Millie hello. [*Laughter*]

The President. Really? Hey, listen, how would you like to have an author in your family that, like Millie—the dog wrote a book, with a little help from Barbara Bush, and it made over $1 million. It's now in Japan and Russia, and every dime of it has gone for education. It's a wonderful thing. Now the dog's thinking of writing another book. [*Laughter*]

Undecided Voters

Q. Mr. President, in this highly competitive election, recent polls have indicated that many voters are still undecided. As the incumbent, do you consider this to be favorable or unfavorable to your reelection bid?

The President. In the first place, I have trouble understanding the polls. Secondly, I think that's favorable, because it's my view in elections that a lot of people make up their minds, really make them up at the last week, the last few days, actually. I think there's a lot of evidence to support that. So given the hammering that I've taken out there by these Democrats running around saying the economy is in the tank, in recession, now we see it's growing at 2.7 percent for the last quarter and growing for six quarters, I think that's a good thing. I'd much rather have them open-minded.

Here's my view on all of this: Look, when you make mistake as President, you do like you teach your kids. Hey, say I was wrong. Let's move forward. I think we've got by far the best programs for the economic recovery. I think people are beginning to see that, particularly now that they see there's some hope out there for the economy.

I also believe that this one is right on your question. I don't think many people yet have focused on the final decision: Who do you trust; who has the character; and things like foreign policy or the fact that your kids, my grandkids go to bed at night without that same fear of nuclear war. That's not resonating. You don't read that on the front pages. But when people go into the booth, they're going to say, "Hey, let's look at the overall record."

So I think undecided at this point is probably positive for me. We see the polls closing nationally now, dramatically, over where it was just a week ago. These darned Sunday shows they have on television, these guys coming on there telling me that I have no chance, heck with that. There's too many elections to prove that contradictory. So I cannot live and die by the polls. But undecided at this point has got to be positive, given the negative coverage we've been receiving.

North American Free Trade Agreement

Q. Mr. President, my question: With the free trade agreement, big business that has headquarters here in the U.S., they can make their products in Mexico, bring it back here to sell. And by doing this, it's going to reduce some of our tax base. And then when you're comparing the wage to a country with a lower standard of living than ours, competitively how would this benefit us?

The President. Okay, I'll answer your question with a rhetorical question. If wage base is what's required to locate plants, why is not Haiti the industrial capital of the world? You see my point.

Businesses are not going to move overseas, flock overseas because of a fair trade agreement. Exports have saved our economy in a very extraordinarily difficult time. You look at the sales—exports and jobs created in tough economic times; it's been related to exports. So do not believe the argument that exports and fair trade agreements are going to do anything but create jobs. They're going to create jobs. Don't believe the argument that they're going to cost jobs. The evidence is overwhelming.

I come back to the point, if wage rates are the only thing that matters, why today aren't these companies all moved down there to wherever that might be? They're not going to do that. We're going to create more jobs. It's exports that's going to lead the entire world, not just the United States, into new prosperity. I'm absolutely convinced of it. I'm against protection. I am for free trade. I think the NAFTA agreement with Mexico is extraordinarily positive. I think the conclusion of the GATT round that we're working on right now would certainly benefit agriculture. I think it will benefit the entire world.

So my view is, look, it's not going to cost us jobs; it's going to create jobs. Remember, if wages were the thing, Haiti would be booming, and they're having a rough go down there.

The Environment

Q. Mr. President, yesterday the Courier Journal printed questions submitted to your campaign concerning your environmental issues, environmental policies, to which you did not respond. I was wondering if you could clarify your environmental policy, specifically regarding wetlands, and also if you could explain how you intend to strike a balance between protecting the environment and creating new jobs?

The President. Very important question. I don't know the questionnaire you're talking about, but I think we've got a darned good environmental record. It has achieved a balance, because I don't believe you can go to the environmental extreme.

Let me tell you: Since I've become President, we passed a Clean Air Act. We have got a tree-planting program for a billion trees a year, which is a very sound program that will help clean up the environment, help the climate change. We've done well on the oceans. Our enforcement agency, the EPA, has brought more enforcement actions against people that violate the environment than all of them put together, I believe, in the previous administration. So I think we're doing well in getting this balance.

What was the other part of your question? I should have written it down. But you just asked about——

Q. ——specifically on your policies towards wetlands?

The President. Wetlands, yes. We've got a policy of no net loss of wetlands. But let me tell you something. When one of these extreme environmental groups considers all of Alaska, the tundra, a wetland, I say let's find the balance, as your last part of your question said. We cannot go to the extreme.

Farmers are good conservationists for the most part. And yet, some extreme rulings say if you've got a low place on your farm, you can't even farm your own land. We've got a good no-net-loss-of-wetlands policy. I'm implementing it, and I think we should be very proud of it. But you've got a guy coming over here in Ozone Man, Gore, and he'll shut down this country, I'll tell you. And we've got to find the balance.

I mean, it is too much when you go and say that the owl is so important that you're going to throw 30,000 people in the timber business out of work; or go up, as Mr. Gore's book says, and say you want 40- to 45-miles-per-gallon standards, fuel efficien-

cy standards. You've got some auto stuff in this State, and you're going to throw those workers needlessly out of work by setting these strange and too far-out standards.

We've got to find what your last point was, a balance. I think we're striving very hard to do it. We've got a great environmentalist heading our EPA, and I am proud of the record. But I'm not going to go down to Rio, as Mr. Gore suggested, and sign a treaty—I don't care how many countries are for it—if it goes against the interest of the United States. I'm proud of the record, but we're not on the extreme.

Education and Job Training

Q. My question is, Mr. President, if reelected, what is your plan to help the common families with both parents that work and make less than $25,000 a year?

The President. The best answer is education, because we're moving into a new technical era. We're moving into an era where math and science mean something. We have proposed, and indeed, it's operating now under our Job Training 2000, a very vigorous program, a $10 billion program to retrain people for the future. I mean, we've got a lot of defense workers, for example, that are coming out of defense because we've been successful in the cold war.

Incidentally, my opponent, Mr. Gore, wants to cut the muscle of defense. He'll say to Fort Campbell, Kentucky, forget it, we're going to cut many more troops than Colin Powell and Cheney tell me are necessary. I'm in charge of the national security, and I'm going to keep it strong.

But job retraining is the answer to the family you're talking about who aspires up the ladder. Part of our job retraining program says to a guy who is working at a job that you describe, maybe not the most productive: While you're working, you can participate in this apprenticeship program. So I really believe that is the key and only answer. Then along with it comes the fundamentals of education reform for the kids.

Racial Harmony

Q. Good afternoon, Mr. President. It is generally agreed that over the last 12 years race relations in our country has greatly deteriorated. What plans, if you are reelected, do you have to begin to heal our Nation?

The President. I'm not sure I agree with your premise about the last 12 years. I'm old enough to remember some really ugly scenes in this country when the country was really divided on race. And I think the country has come a long, long way over the past 25 years. So we start with a very different premise.

Yes, there is some racism, and yes, I've tried as President to speak out against it. We have passed two major pieces of civil rights legislation, but what you're talking about, respect for each other, is not going to be legislated. But we passed the ADA bill that I mentioned, which is forward-leaning civil rights, and one bill to avoid discrimination in the workplace. So that has happened on my watch. But it's not going to be legislated. It's got to be done through good will. It's got to be done through strengthening families' knowledge, education, so you educate out of the kids any propensity for intolerance. The President must continue to speak out against anti-Semitism or racial bigotry at every time. I think that's the only thing that's going to happen, moral persuasion.

But please look at your history, because I think we would all remember that we've had times which have been uglier than now in terms of race relations. It's not good, but we've got to make it better.

I'll tell you what we've got to do. We've got to strengthen our communities and our families. And the liberals hate it when I say this, but family is vital. When Mayor Bradley of Los Angeles—I'll not filibuster here, but when he came to see me with a lot of other mayors from the National League of Cities, he said, "The biggest concern we've got about urban unrest is the decline of the American family." So let the liberal Democrats scream, but strengthening family, not through legislation but through education, teaching discipline, teaching respect for the law, supporting law enforcement people, choice in child care, choice in education, all of these things will strengthen the family. As that happens, we lower this threshold of discrimination which is terrible, and we've got to make it better.

Education

Q. My question is regarding education. Earlier, you mentioned Millie's book. You have said that you would subsidize families to send their children to private schools. Please explain to me why that's better than putting more money and efforts into the public school system. Because my husband and I would fall in the middle class range; we would not be low-income to receive subsidies, and we're not in the upper end to be able to afford to send children to——

The President. Let me try to explain it to you. I do believe in parental choice for public, private, and religious schools. When I got out of the service, many thousand years ago, I was eligible for the GI bill. And the GI bill said you can go to the college of your choice, religious college, Holy Cross, or go to public State college or go to a private. We're giving—assist the family—separation of church and state, money goes to the family.

In Milwaukee, Wisconsin, the Democratic Mayor and a black Democratic legislator, Polly Williams, came to see me to tell me how successful their choice plan had been. Her child was considered dysfunctional. And that child is now performing because they chose, and were assisted in the choice, a better school. The irony is that the public schools not chosen have found they are improving themselves.

And under the plan, under our "GI bill" for kids, they could have chosen a public school. So the plan is to try, in a model system, the choice to see if it doesn't do what I'm convinced it will, which is elevate the public schools and private. Did you know 46 percent of the public schoolteachers in Chicago send their kids to private school? Now, why is that? It is that some of those public schools are not performing well enough. So I think competition will make them perform better, and that's the basis. I know that the teachers union doesn't like it, but I am convinced that nationwide it will work as it did in Milwaukee.

I don't want to probe into the internal affairs of your family, but it can't happen—there's not enough money in the world to do it for every family. So there is a cutoff point.

Job Retraining

Q. Mr. President, as a dislocated worker, an older worker, what kind of programs do you have in store for an older dislocated worker?

The President. Well, John, the only answer is this retraining program I mentioned here to the gentleman from Illinois. I believe that's what the Federal Government should do. I'm sure your community has some training programs, too. But that's the answer. And we're going to have more of it because you're having a shift to higher technology out of ordinary jobs, jobs that heretofore have been pretty darned good, and you're having this change in defense.

One other thing we're doing, and this isn't of any comfort to you right now, but we're taking the laboratories, the Government labs, and having them cooperate with business to bring new technology to the private sector. That will mean new jobs. But it will mean in your case, sir, job retraining.

Take a look at the programs, because I think you'll find some that might fit your needs. I hope you do, anyway, because I certainly can empathize with somebody who is a good worker, wants to work, and can't find work. I might say unemployment in this country has gone down for the last 3 months. And every time it happens, again back to my talking head friends: Bad news for President Bush, job market shrinks. Come on, it's getting better.

So we've got to keep this recovery going, without doing bad things to it, and helping stimulate it. And then a guy like John, who just mentioned this, will find work because I think we're going to have a much more plentiful job market. We created 15 million new jobs in the eighties, and I think we can do it more now that we're coming out of this long slow period.

Education

Q. Mr. President, you've declared yourself the education President. But why is our country still behind Japan in math and science? And what do you plan to do about it in the next 4 years?

The President. When I came in as President, we convened all the Governors. We did something that's never been done before—and I'll give Bill Clinton credit for

this. He was one of the leaders in it as a Governor—to get educational standards. We adopted six national education standards, and communities now are striving to reach them. One of the standards is math and science. Kids must be proficient in math and science by the year 2000. That's caused a whole array of new teaching methods being used for math and science.

So we've already started on that. And the program I referred to, I just refer you back to it, America 2000, because it really does help us achieve these six education goals. But you're on to something, and we've got to do better in math and science. Do you know we spend more per education per kid than every country except Switzerland? And we're not getting the results. The Federal Government, what, 6 percent of the spending is from the Federal Government, and it's way up. But that's not good enough for this country. So we've got to break the mold in these schools. We've got to challenge the establishment. Education fundamentally hasn't changed in this country for the last 50 years. Now it's got to, to accommodate young kids like this.

The Economy

Q. Mr. President, you mentioned the value of high wages to the entire economy. Recently in Winchester where I live, our once-largest employer, Rockwell International, closed their truck axle plant. Manufacturing jobs are now only 16 percent of our economy. In Germany, manufacturing jobs are fully 32 percent of their economy, and they have the highest wages in the world. America's now 13th in wages and still falling. Governor Clinton favors a more direct partnership between business, labor, and Government, similar to the German approach. Why is this not a good idea to develop new technologies?

The President. I challenge your figures on the wages. Manufacturing in this country is up as a percentage of our gross domestic product, manufacturing is. Some of the reason that manufacturing jobs has sloughed off is because manufacturing has become much more modern and streamlined.

But the answer is not to do what Clinton wants, which is to have the Government invest. He talks about Government investment. Government does not create wealth. And therein I have a—and most of Europe, including Germany, has moved away from this concept of this kind of social fabric of government in terms of business.

You've got to free up through less regulation, less lawsuits. We're killing ourselves with the cost of lawsuits. Less taxation; stimulate—I just said earlier, and I won't repeat them, these ways to stimulate business investment here. But we cannot go back to the failed European model of, you know, it used to be pure socialism. Those countries have all come out of it now.

So I think we've got a little fact difference here as to how Germany is doing. They had a 4 percent negative growth, or 3 this last quarter, when we grew at 2.7. So I'm not about to think of Germany as the great example. They're good on some things, and they make good products, but I notice that Germany is putting a BMW plant in South Carolina. Now, why are they doing that if this gentleman is so right about how swimming everything is going in Germany? Because we've got the best workers, and we're the most productive nation there is.

Sorry I can't debate you eyeball to eyeball. I might come out ahead; I might not. You sound like you know what you're talking about.

Mr. Butler. When the time is over for things like this, Helen Thomas usually says "Thank you, Mr. President," and that's where we are.

The President. I looked at my watch in the debate, and I caught the dickens for it. But time flies when you're having fun. [*Laughter*]

Mr. Butler. We want to thank you. We want to thank my colleagues in Louisville where Jackie Hays had some very good questions from her group; from WLEX–TV in Lexington, where Tom Kenny had a good group to ask questions. And we want to thank all of you in our studio audience. I know that many of you had questions that didn't get asked, but we appreciate those that were. So we thank all of you.

And Mr. President, thank you for joining us today. We were real glad you came and answered the questions.

The President. I'm just delighted to be here. It's a wonderful thing you all do, of public service, I think. I mean, it transcends politics, and it's a very good thing. And I appreciate it.

Mr. Butler. Maybe you won a few votes today out of all this.

The President. Well, I don't know. I hope so. That's what it's all about.

Note: The question-and-answer session began at 1:30 p.m. at the WPSD–TV studios. Tom Butler, WPSD–TV vice president of news, served as moderator for the session.

Remarks at a Miami Valley Rally in Kettering, Ohio
October 27, 1992

The President. Thank you, Mac. Thank you very, very much. Thank you, Gerald McRaney. Thank you for that great Ohio welcome. Thank you very, very much. Thank you.

Audience members. Four more years! Four more years! Four more years!

The President. We are fired up. Thank you. If I ever needed convincing, you have convinced me that we are going to win 4 more years on November 3d. This is fantastic. Wall to wall people. And thank you for that great welcome.

May I salute Congressman John Boehner, who is here with us today. And may I say, you hear a lot of talk around the country, "Clean House!" Change the Congress. Send Mike DeWine to the United States Senate, and let's get on with changing this country for the better. While we're at it, send Pete Davis to the United States Congress. We need a good man there.

It's great to be here at the birthplace of aviation. And the choice before the American people this year is a vast difference in experience, a difference in philosophy, and yes, character counts, a difference in character.

I think it is only fair that we look at the record of the man who wants to become President, because the other night in a debate, Governor Clinton said this: "I want to do for America what I have done for Arkansas." No way!

Audience members. Boo-o-o!

The President. Let me give you just a couple of statistics. Arkansas—and they've got wonderful people there—this man has been Governor for 10 years, I believe. He talks about the fact that they did the most in job creation this year. True, but he was out of the State 85 percent of the time. For the 10 years he's been Governor, they're 30 percent below the national average. They are the 50th in environmental quality. They are 50th in the percentage of adults with college degrees, 50th in the per capita spending on criminal justice, 49th on police protection, 48th on adults with a high school diploma, 48th in spending on corrections, 48th on teachers' salaries. We cannot let him do that to the United States of America.

You know, for months the Democrats have been going around this country telling everybody that we were in a deep recession and that they would change things. Let me tell you something. Today there was some good economic news for America. We have grown in this country for five consecutive quarters. And in the last quarters, growth was 2.7 percent, better than Japan, better than Germany, better than Europe.

So don't let these guys come in there talking about change, and change things back to where they were the last time the Democrats had the White House and the Congress. Do you remember what it was like?

Audience members. Boo-o-o!

The President. Interest rates under the Carter and the Congress was 21 percent, inflation 15. Governor Clinton and Gore, the Ozone Man, want to go ahead—this guy's out of it. Where is he? I mean, come on. They say we're in a deep recession. So what do they want to do? They want to raise your taxes by $150 billion and increase

$220 billion in spending, and we're not going to let them do that to America.

Change, change, change, change, change—all you're going to have left in your pocket if you listen to those guys. We're not going to let it happen. They and their media talk-show people wouldn't know it if good news hit them in the face.

Ninety-three percent of America is working. And, yes, we've got to be concerned about those who aren't. We've got the program to do it. The program isn't to have Government invest. The program is to have small business unleashed from regulation, unleashed from regulation, from taxation, and yes, from litigation. We are suing each other too much and caring for each other too little in this country.

Change, change—they forget that the last time they left office, inflation was wiping out every senior citizen at 15 percent, and we brought it under control. People say, are you better off? Well, ask the homeowner who can refinance that mortgage and save a couple of thousand dollars a year. Ask a senior citizen who's saved all his or her life, saw those savings wiped out by the cruel Democrat Congress inflation. We got that back in the box, and that's saving millions for people.

But here's the good news for America: Unemployment has been down for 3 straight months. And I said the country is growing at 2.7 percent. Let's keep it growing by my plan, not by the Democrats' plan.

Here's the way we're going to do it. Exports have led the recovery at very difficult times. We are going to create more American jobs by opening these foreign markets to the best made-in-America products, the best in the entire world. The free trade agreement will create jobs. Ohio agriculture is moving. It will move better when we complete the GATT round, we complete the fair trade agreement. We can outhustle and outproduce any country in the world. We've got the message of optimism for this country and real growth.

Governor Clinton wants to tax foreign investment, he says. That would threaten 4.5 million jobs, including 150,000 right here in Ohio. The people are investing here because we've got the best workers in the world. Let's not run them off.

Audience members. We want Bush! We want Bush! We want Bush!

The President. We've got a good record on the environment. But I'll be darned if I'm going to go to the extreme. The Ozone Man and Governor Clinton want, listen to this one, they want 40- to 45-miles-per-gallon fuel efficiency standards. That would throw every auto worker in Ohio out of his job. And I'm not going to let that happen.

Audience members. Boo-o-o!

The President. Twenty thousand jobs are at stake if we listen to the extremists that are coming out of that environmental movement. I care about that little spotted owl, but I also care about 30,000 families whose jobs are at stake.

I mentioned the need for small business to have the burden of legal reform lifted, but it's not just small business. People are afraid to coach Little League because of crazy lawsuits. Doctors are afraid to deliver babies because somebody's going to come and sue them for malpractice, or the hospitals have to raise the cost and raise the tests for fear they'll get some crazy lawsuit. A citizen going along the highway is afraid to stop and help his fellow American because he's afraid somebody's going to say, "Oh, you didn't do it just right. We're going to sue you." We've got to put some restrictions on these outrageous lawsuits. We've got to care for each other more.

Health care, health care, we have the best plan for health care. It makes insurance available to the poorest of the poor through vouchers. It gives tax relief to the next income group. It says make insurance available through pooling, bring the cost down, do something about malpractice, but do not get the Government further into the health care business.

On education, the answer in a struggling time is to educate people better, and we've got the best program. America 2000 says to the communities and to the teachers—not to that all-powerful teachers union that tries to dictate to these teachers—it says to them, look, we're going to work with you. We have 1,700 America 2000 communities already in existence, many of them right here with Ohio in the lead. And we've got to revolutionize education. We've got to give these kids every opportunity. One big difference I have with Governor Clinton and Gore is this: I want to see the parents be able to choose public, private, or religious schools and give them a chance.

You know, Barbara and I talk about family values. One family value is that a family ought to be able to grow up in a neighborhood free of crime and drugs. And I back our police officers. I don't want some leftwing judges appointed to the Supreme Court who don't care about the victims of crime and spend all their time worrying about the criminals. Let's turn it around. Let's have more compassion for the victims and less for the criminals.

You know, the Arkansas—I hate to go back to that because we're on a roll here—go back to Arkansas—a guy is sentenced, he spends 20 percent of that sentence under the—that's not enough. Under the Federal prison program, 85 percent. We must support our police.

The other day from Arkansas eight people came to see me, and they endorsed me for President. They were the Fraternal Order of Police of Little Rock, Arkansas.

Here's the big difference. Here's the big difference. Clinton and Gore talk about Government investing in getting jobs. The Government takes your money and does not invest. It is the business sector. It is the mom-and-pop store. It is small business that needs relief. And here's the way we're going to give it to them. Here's the way we're going to get that deficit down and get the mortgage burden off the back of these kids:

One, give me a balanced budget amendment and force the Congress to get this deficit down.

Give us a check-off so the individual taxpayer can check his tax return, she can say—he or she can check it and say 10 percent of my tax must go to reducing the Federal deficit. Make the Congress do it.

Third, give me what 43 Governors have. Congress can't do it. Give me that line-item veto, and let the President have a shot.

Four, the President has a limited number of terms, two terms for a President. Let's limit the terms on the U.S. Congress and hand the power back to the people.

I have a big argument—I talk about trust and character, and I believe they are important. In the debate, Governor Clinton said it's not the character of the President, it is "the character of the Presidency." He's wrong. The two are interlocked. You've got to stand for something as President of the United States.

Let me tell you something. I have learned this as President. You can't please everybody on everything. It's like any normal human being. You make a mistake; you look the American people in the eye and say, "I did it." Then you go on and lead. But you cannot be all things to all people.

My argument with Governor Clinton is, he tries to be on all sides of all questions. On right to work, he's for it in the South, against it when he talks to the labor unions. On free trade, he's for it, and you heard this in the debate, "I'm for it, but." You can't have any "buts" in the White House.

On term limits, he sees the merits of it, but he's opposed to it. And on the Gulf war—how do you like this for leadership from the Commander in Chief—when the going got tough, here's what he said: "I agree with the arguments of the minority"—that's who wanted to stand pat—"I agree with the arguments of the minority, but I guess I would have voted with the majority." You cannot waffle when you're Commander in Chief of the Armed Forces.

Audience members. Boo-o-o!

The President. There is a pattern of deception. And we simply cannot——

Audience members. Give 'em hell, George.

The President. I'm trying to. We cannot have—you know, the guy's got a good point. Do you remember when Harry Truman was campaigning and a guy yells, "Give 'em hell, Harry." "I don't give 'em hell. I just tell the truth, and they think it's hell."

But seriously, you've got to call them as you see them, as the umpires do. You can't just be out there, lead by misleading, and you cannot turn the White House into the waffle house. You've got to stand for something.

No, we now see, America sees clearly that we are not in the recession, as told by the Clinton-Gore ticket and repeated endlessly on that television. We have some difficult problems. But I have the best programs to solve these problems.

Let me tell you this. Here's the end of it, and here is the bottom line as you go to the polls on Tuesday. Barbara—and I think we've got a first-class First Lady, I might add. She and I—I told you I think character and trust matter because people all around the world look to the White House, look to the Oval Office, at least for integrity and honor. I served my country in war, hopefully with duty, honor, and country in the foremost. I had to make very difficult decisions as the Commander in Chief of the Armed Forces. And believe me, it is tough when you have to send someone else's son, someone else's daughter into harm's way. But we did it, and the sons and daughters of Ohio kicked the aggressor out of Kuwait and restored the leadership of the United States to the entire world.

So I ask you to meditate and think on what Mac said. When that Oval Office phone rings or at night the phone at White House rings, my question to the American people is, who do you trust? Who do you trust for the security—[*applause*]—far more important than partisan politics is the honor of the United States of America.

I have tried to uphold the public trust. I believe we have the programs. I am absolutely convinced that Clinton-Gore are wrong when they say we're a nation in decline. Good heavens, we are the leading nation in the entire world. We are not in decline.

Now I ask, on Tuesday, I ask you to go to the polls and get your friends to the polls. I ask for your support. I ask for your vote to let me finish the job of lifting up the young lives here and giving America a prosperous 4 more years.

May God bless the United States. Thank you all very much.

Note: The President spoke at 6:10 p.m. at the Frazee Pavilion. In his remarks, he referred to actor Gerald McRaney.

Memorandum of Disapproval for Legislation To Include Revere Beach, Massachusetts, in the National Park System
October 27, 1992

I am withholding my approval of H.R. 2109, which would require the Secretary of the Interior to conduct a study of Revere Beach, Massachusetts, and provide alternatives on the appropriate Federal role in preserving and interpreting this site.

The National Park Service (NPS) studies many sites to determine if they are nationally significant and therefore suitable for inclusion in the National Park System. A site is nationally significant if it is an outstanding example of a unique natural, historic, or cultural resource with demonstrated importance to the entire Nation.

In many instances, the Congress has used the findings of a congressionally mandated NPS study, regardless of the study's conclusion, to justify authorization of a new unit of the National Park System. To restore credibility and a national focus to its study process, the NPS reestablished in 1991 a program to evaluate sites and prioritize candidates for future study. The most promising candidates identified by the NPS experts would be proposed for formal study.

For my fiscal year 1993 Budget request, NPS professionals rated and ranked 41 candidates from criteria established by the Department of the Interior. The fiscal year 1993 Budget proposed $1.2 million to study the seven highest-rated candidates from the list of 41 originally reviewed. The Congress appropriated $848,000 to conduct four of the studies proposed by the NPS.

The NPS experts have not identified the Revere Beach study as a high priority. The effect of this legislation would be to place completion of this study before the completion of other studies that the experts agree are much more important to the Nation.

H.R. 2109 would ignore professional analysis and budget constraints. It would also undermine the critical objective of identifying and evaluating the Nation's most promising natural, historic, and cultural assets for protection as units of the National Park System. I am therefore withholding my approval of H.R. 2109.

GEORGE BUSH

The White House,
October 27, 1992.

Statement on Signing the Battered Women's Testimony Act of 1992
October 27, 1992

Today I am signing into law H.R. 1252, the "Battered Women's Testimony Act of 1992."

Each year, more than 3 million women are the victims of domestic violence. Of these, between 3,000 and 4,000 are murdered by a spouse or domestic partner. Many of these attacks are witnessed by children.

Some victims of domestic violence are driven to retaliate and even kill their abusive spouses. In some cases these victims may raise as a legal defense "battered woman's syndrome." This syndrome, which some experts believe is brought on by re-

peated physical, mental, or sexual attacks by a spouse or partner, may help to explain or extenuate these retaliatory attacks. Expert testimony regarding the nature and effect of "battered woman's syndrome" is not universally accepted by all the States.

H.R. 1252 addresses the problems associated with the defense of "battered woman's syndrome" in two ways. First, it authorizes a study on the admissibility of expert testimony on the experiences of battered women in the defense of criminal cases under State law. Second, the bill directs the development and dissemination of training materials to assist battered women and their attorneys and advocates in using expert testimony in appropriate cases.

I am pleased to approve this legislation and to commend its sponsor and cosponsors for taking this important step in combatting violence against women.

GEORGE BUSH

The White House,
October 27, 1992.

Note: H.R. 1252, approved October 27, was assigned Public Law No. 102–527.

Statement on Signing Legislation on Child Custody Litigation
October 27, 1992

Today I am signing into law H.R. 1253, a bill that provides for research and training materials to assist State courts in child custody litigation involving domestic violence.

Domestic violence is a serious problem in our Nation. Each year more than 3 million women are the victims of domestic violence. Much of this violence is witnessed by children, often with devastating and far-reaching emotional and psychological consequences.

Many battered women eventually divorce their husbands. But spousal abuse does not always end with divorce. In fact, the abuse can become worse, especially in connection with child custody litigation.

H.R. 1253 takes an important step in addressing this problem. The bill authorizes the funding of up to five projects to investigate and carry out research regarding State

judicial decisions in child custody cases that involve domestic violence. The legislation also authorizes the development and dissemination of training materials to assist State courts in formulating appropriate responses in such cases.

This legislation will help send a strong message about our commitment both to combatting domestic violence and to ensuring that the children of battered women are raised in safe, loving, and nonabusive environments. I am pleased to sign H.R. 1253 and commend its sponsor and cosponsors for their foresight and concern.

GEORGE BUSH

The White House,
October 27, 1992.

Note: H.R. 1253, approved October 27, was assigned Public Law No. 102–528.

Statement on Signing the Preventive Health Amendments of 1992
October 27, 1992

Today I am signing into law H.R. 3635, the "Preventive Health Amendments of 1992." The primary purpose of this legislation is to authorize appropriations for, and make amendments to, the Preventive Health and Health Services Block Grant (Prevention Block Grant) administered by the Department of Health and Human Services (HHS).

My Administration is committed to the importance of preventive health services.

Support of prevention programs is a sound investment in our future. H.R. 3635 authorizes programs that will provide States with funding needed to target their prevention efforts as effectively as possible toward reducing some of the Nation's most pressing health problems.

H.R. 3635 will authorize appropriations through fiscal year 1997 for the Prevention Block Grant. This block grant is important for funding activities intended to achieve the national health objectives for the year 2000. The Prevention Block Grant represents an effective means of financing activities designed to reduce the burden of disease and premature death in this country.

This legislation will also continue HHS programs to prevent lead poisoning in children. Lead poisoning is the most common and societally devastating environmental disease of young children. This program enables us to identify children who have lead levels in their blood high enough to impair

their health and to refer them to the help they need.

I am gratified to see health legislation that focuses on prevention. I applaud the cooperative effort that made it possible.

GEORGE BUSH

The White House,
October 27, 1992.

Note: H.R. 3635, approved October 27, was assigned Public Law No. 102–531.

Statement on Signing the Telecommunications Authorization Act of 1992
October 27, 1992

Today I am signing into law H.R. 6180, the "Telecommunications Authorization Act of 1992." The Act codifies authorities of the National Telecommunications and Information Administration (NTIA) in the Department of Commerce. The Act reflects the importance to the Nation of the development of sound telecommunications and information policies.

In addition to codifying these authorities, however, the Act contains some problematic and unnecessary provisions. I have instructed the Secretary of Commerce to work with the next Congress to amend or delete these troublesome provisions. Among the provisions that are unnecessary or disruptive to the efficient Federal management of telecommunications policy are the following:

—Section 105(d), which restricts the Secretary of Commerce from reassigning any NTIA function without first reporting to specified congressional committees and waiting for 90 legislative days.

This section undermines the Secretary's ability to manage the Department effectively.

—Section 104, which will unnecessarily micromanage NTIA's responsibility for Federal use of the radio frequency spectrum by detailing specific requirements for public participation. NTIA is already meeting the laudable goal of increasing public participation in these activities.

The Act also contains provisions specifying responsibilities for the Department of Commerce in providing advice on telecommunications policies. These will be interpreted in a way that does not restrict my authority to supervise the executive branch.

GEORGE BUSH

The White House,
October 27, 1992.

Note: H.R. 6180, approved October 27, was assigned Public Law No. 102–538.

Statement on Signing the Mammography Quality Standards Act of 1992
October 27, 1992

Today I am signing into law H.R. 6182, the "Mammography Quality Standards Act of 1992." This important legislation will help make mammography screening safer and more accurate.

As National Breast Cancer Awareness Month draws to an end, we are reminded that one woman in eight will develop this devastating disease during her lifetime. Fighting breast cancer has been—and continues to be—one of my health care priorities.

For women with breast cancer, early diagnosis is crucial to successful treatment. We all know that safe and accurate mammography screening, together with monthly self-examinations, are essential to making an early diagnosis. H.R. 6182 will enhance the quality of mammographies performed in the United States. It will require facilities that perform this procedure to meet a set of national standards. The legislation contains an important provision allowing States to have their own certification programs as long as their requirements are no less stringent than the national program.

I wholeheartedly support the very important purpose of this legislation. I applaud Senator Orrin Hatch, who worked to improve the bill and to accommodate Administration concerns about the overly regulatory nature of the initial proposal. Today, I am directing the Secretary of Health and Human Services to ensure, to the maximum extent possible, that no professional group assumes a *de facto* monopoly on the provision of mammography services. In addition, the standards implementing the new program should create no unnecessary burdens on service providers or barriers to women's access to this vital service. This legislation requires studies on cost-effective regulation and related performance measurements of mammography services that my Administration will follow with interest and use in formulating future policy proposals.

I especially applaud Marilyn Quayle, whose own mother died of breast cancer, for being a champion in the fight against this dreadful disease. My Administration is deeply committed to ensuring that every woman in this country has access to affordable, high-quality mammograms. This bill will complement those efforts.

I must note, however, that certain provisions of this legislation must be interpreted so that they are consistent with the Appointments Clause of the Constitution. Specifically, I do not interpret the language of proposed 42 U.S.C. 351(g)(1), pertaining to inspections of facilities performing mammograms, to permit persons other than officers of the United States duly appointed pursuant to the Appointments Clause to exercise significant Government authority. Similarly, I do not view the language of proposed 42 U.S.C. 351(g), pertaining to State enforcement programs, as giving State officers the authority to enforce Federal law. Instead, I view it as giving the Secretary of Health and Human Services the authority to exempt States from the regime of Federal regulation if he determines that a parallel system of State regulation provides a satisfactory alternative to Federal regulation.

I also do not interpret the language of proposed 42 U.S.C. 351(j), giving the Secretary of Health and Human Services the right to bring suit in Court, to impair the authority of the Attorney General to conduct all litigation on behalf of the United States, its agencies, and its officers.

GEORGE BUSH

The White House,
October 27, 1992.

Note: H.R. 6182, approved October 27, was assigned Public Law No. 102–539.

Statement on Signing Legislation Establishing the Keweenaw National Historical Park
October 27, 1992

Today I am signing into law S. 1664, which establishes the Keweenaw National Historical Park. The Act also establishes the Keweenaw National Historical Park Advisory Commission, most of the Members of which are appointed by the Secretary of the Interior from among the nominees submitted by various State and local officials. Because most of the Members are effectively selected by various State and local government officials, and thus are not appointed in conformity with the Appointments Clause of the Constitution, Article II, section 2, clause 2, I sign this bill on the understanding that the Commission will serve only in an advisory capacity and will not exercise executive authority.

GEORGE BUSH

The White House,
October 27, 1992.

Note: S. 1664, approved October 27, was assigned Public Law No. 102–543.

Statement on Signing Delaware River Port Authority Supplemental Compact Legislation
October 27, 1992

Today I am signing into law S. 2964, a bill granting the consent of the Congress to a supplemental compact or agreement between the Commonwealth of Pennsylvania and the State of New Jersey concerning the Delaware River Port Authority.

Although I have signed S. 2964, I will withhold my approval of H.R. 5452 because it is identical to S. 2964.

GEORGE BUSH

The White House,
October 27, 1992.

Note: S. 2964, approved October 27, was assigned Public Law No. 102–544.

Remarks on Departure from Lima, Ohio
October 28, 1992

I understand that Bruce Willis had a few words to you. But let me tell you something. I think this country likes a fighter. I think this country likes somebody who does not let the national media, nor certainly Clinton and Gore get him down, and is going to fight right on and win this election.

I can tell you this. I was just on a television show, and I can repeat here what I said then—I am absolutely convinced because of this kind of turnout of public support, because of what we tried to do in terms of bringing world peace, because of the movement now in this economy where clearly Gore is wrong, Clinton is wrong when they say we're in a recession—yesterday we saw that this economy is growing, and now we've got to keep it growing until every American that is hurting has a better opportunity.

So I am very grateful to you. For you who might be first-time voters, do not take anything for granted. Go to the polls. Get your friends to vote. It is a privilege. It is an

American privilege to vote, and you ought to do that. So be sure to get to the polls.

We only have a handful of days left. I was telling Jim Baker in the car, I can hardly believe it, that we've only got 6 days. But things are moving nationally, good news in the national polls today. We're going to show these critics and these naysayers and these people of voices of gloom and doom that we are going to win because I have confidence in America, because our economic program is right, because the world is indeed more peaceful. I'm going to ask for your support and your trust, based on character, because I believe we have the best economic answers to lead this country and the entire world to new prosperity.

Thank you, and may God bless you all. May God bless each and every one of you on this beautiful day in Ohio.

Note: The President spoke at 9:14 a.m. at Allen County Airport. In his remarks, he referred to actor Bruce Willis.

Remarks at a Rally in Toledo, Ohio
October 28, 1992

The President. Thank you so very much. Let me just thank Bruce Willis, a man of conviction. I'll tell you a little story about Bruce. About 4 months ago, when everyone was declaring us dead and buried politically, we got a phone call at the White House. Somebody came to me and said, "Well, Bruce Willis is calling." I said, "Well, how do you know it's Bruce Willis?" And they said, "Well, it is." So we called back, and when things were really rough, down he came. Barbara and I had dinner with him. And he has been out there, working hard, helping me at every turn, and I am very, very grateful to him.

Let me tell you something that I think Ohioans know, but again, on a very personal basis something I feel strongly about. I know you know you've got a great Governor. But I want you to know that the Voinoviches are close, personal friends of ours to whom we will always be grateful. He is a good and decent and strong leader for this State, and I'm grateful to George Voinovich.

I want to salute Walbridge Mayor Robson; and Donna Owens, the former Mayor of Toledo; Tom Nowe, the Republican Party chairman. Do me a good favor. Do yourselves a favor. Do the country a favor. Clean Senate, and send Mike DeWine to the United States Senate. We don't need any more gridlocked Congress, so help me clean House, and send Ken Brown to the United States Congress.

I love this sign back here, "Six days to victory." Believe me, we are going to win this election. The reason we're going to win is that there is a vast difference in experience, a vast difference in philosophy, and a vast difference in character and trust. Believe me, character and trust matter for President of the United States.

Governor Voinovich kind of put it out there as it is, talking about the Arkansas record. One reason I will win the election is, after 11 months of distorting our record, we begin to put into focus the Arkansas record. I'll repeat just one or two parts of it, because it is 50th in the quality of environmental initiatives in Arkansas, 50th in percentage of adults with college degrees, 50th spending on criminal justice, 49th per capita of police protection, 48th in percentage of adults with a high school diploma, and on and on and on it goes.

Governor Clinton bragged about leading the Nation in jobs. They did it for one year, and he was out of the State for 85 percent of the year. The rest of the time, they were 30 percent behind the national.

You know, there was a scary moment in one of those debates. He said, "I want to do for America what I've done to Arkansas." I said, "No way. Please, no."

No, but, you know, if you listen to Governor Clinton and the Ozone Man, and all they do is talk about—you know who I mean, Mr. Ozone? You know what they'd do to the auto workers right here in Toledo? They want CAFE standards, those are fuel efficiency standards, of 40 to 45 miles per gallon. Talk to the union guys working in the plants here in the auto business. That will put almost every Ohio auto worker out of work, if we went for the extreme on the environment. I have a strong environmental record, but I'm not going to let Mr. Ozone dictate to the American worker.

One of the reasons things are moving—and everybody here knows that it's moving nationally—good news out there today on these national surveys. One reason it's moving is that people do not want $150 billion in new taxes and $220 billion in new spending. We cannot get the deficit going up. We've got to bring it down. Let me tell you how we're going to do it.

We're going to control the growth of spending, and then I'm going to get the American people to insist that we get a balanced budget amendment to force the Congress to do it; that we get a check-off so every person in this country paying income tax can check 10 percent on their income tax and make that go to one thing, and that's one thing alone: reducing the deficit. The Congress is going to have to cut to make that possible. Then the third thing we're going to do is get the American people to insist that the President be given what 43 Governors have. Give me that line-item veto, and let's get that spending under control. Those three things will help enormously.

There's one more that I like. Presidents serve two terms. Let's give the Congress back to the people and have term limits for the Members of the United States Congress.

I had it figured out one day in one of the speeches. I think Governor Clinton and the Ozone Man had about 58 references to change. Change, change, change. Raise the taxes $150 billion, and that's all you'll have left in your pocket is change. We're not going to do that.

Something happened yesterday that's casting fear into the hearts of these talking heads on television, fear into the hearts of the Clinton-Gore team. You know what it was? It came out that our economy had

grown at 2.7 percent for the last quarter, and it puts the lie to the fact that we are in a deep recession. And yes, people are hurting; and yes, a guy has a job today and might not know whether he's going to have it tomorrow. But the answer is, we are not in a recession. We are growing. If you go to their plan, you'll put us back into a Jimmy Carter malaise days, with interest rates at 21——

Audience members. Boo-o-o!

The President. Hey, wait a minute, I don't want to ruin this meeting, but you remember what it was when you had a Democratic President and a liberal—you had 21.5 percent interest rates, and you had inflation at 15 percent. They did it through the same Clinton siren's call of tax or spend. Let's keep this economy growing. Let's reduce the Federal deficit. Let's control spending, and let's control taxes.

Two point seven. The economy——

Audience members. Four more years! Four more years! Four more years!

The President. You know, let me tell you something. Let me tell you something good about this country. You hear plenty that's bad from the Clinton-Gore ticket. Our economy is growing. It's growing too weakly, but we're going to lead the country through increasing jobs that sell the best-made products in the world. That's U.S.A.-made products. Expand our markets abroad through exports. We are leading the world in exports, and that means jobs for America.

Our economy is doing better than Japan, than France, than Germany, than England. You hear them talk about it, Clinton and Gore. The only way they can win is to convince the American people that we're in a deep recession, and we're not. The good news yesterday—even the talking heads on those Sunday television shows are going to find a hard time making bad news out of good news. I'm tired of that.

You know, we landed out here, came in a helicopter and landed next to a factory out here. There was a big sign. And on it, it said, "Annoy the Media. Reelect Bush." Why is it? Why is it that everybody, Democrat, Republican, liberal or conservative, know what that sign means?

Now, I ask your forbearance, and I'll tell

you why. We've got some good people traveling with us in the press. And because they've felt that sign so strongly, some of them started hectoring the cameramen or the photographers. These are the good guys. Leave them alone. They're just doing their job. Take your frustrations out, as I do, on the guys back East in those Sunday talk shows who tell you everything that's wrong, whether they're Republicans or Democrats, because we're going to make them eat their words on November 3d.

No, all I'm asking is that people make a comparison on the plans, and I've told you the fundamental differences. But we've got to keep going forward. I'll tell you a big difference we have. Governor Clinton talks about getting the Government to invest to create jobs. That's what Europe tried, and that's where Europe failed. It is not the Government that does it. It is small business that creates the jobs in this country. They create two-thirds of the jobs.

How do we help them? We give them a little relief for taxation. Give them an investment tax allowance. Give them a capital gains so a new guy will get out there and start a new business. Give that first-time homebuyer a tax credit so he or she can buy a home and live the American dream.

Then we lighten up on regulation. And one other thing where I have a big difference with the Governor from Arkansas, and that is on litigation. We are suing each other too much and caring for each other too little; $200 billion a year go to lawyers; $25 billion to $50 billion are added to your health bills every year because of these crazy malpractice suits. Little League coaches are scared to coach because somebody will come up and sue them. You good Samaritans are afraid to stop along the highway for—afraid if you move the person, then this—"Oh, you did that wrong," and they'll slap a lawsuit on you. We've got to end and cap these crazy lawsuits.

Governor Clinton will not do that, because the trial lawyers are his biggest supporters. The lead trial lawyer in Arkansas sent around a letter: Elect our man, and then we won't have anything to worry about changing the lawsuits.

We've got to help the American people, the doctors, the medical practitioners, by

reducing the fear of nutty lawsuits.

Speaking of health care, we've got an enormous difference on that. Governor Clinton, typical of the way the liberal Democrats work, he wants to set up a board to kind of set the controls and prices. You can't do that. The Bush plan is good. Provide insurance through vouchers to the poorest of the poor, pool the insurance, provide tax credit to the next people—the most overtaxed end of the tax scale on the working men and women in this country—pool the insurance, control malpractice, streamline the efficiency, and get the cost down through this pooling, but keep the Government from rationing health care.

My daughter-in-law Margaret is a teacher. God bless the teachers, because they are out there trying to restore some values to these kids. And we have a good program in education. We have a good program. It bypasses the NEA that tells the teachers how to think and supports the bureaucracy. We have 1,700 communities participating in this program. We have a rather old-fashioned idea. We think that the parents should have the right to choose public, private, or religious schools. Give them a chance to do that.

We have a positive record. One out of two college students has financial aid. We've increased the Pell grants. We've increased dramatically Head Start spending. We've got a good education program, but it puts our confidence with the teachers and with the local community, and not with that educational bureaucracy that's sopping up the money and not letting it get to the classroom.

I have a big difference with the Governor on crime, because I have an old-fashioned idea. We ought to have a little more sympathy for the victims of crime and a little less for the criminal. Governor Clinton wants to put—Governor Clinton—quiet, you guys. [*Laughter*] Governor Clinton wants to put Mario Cuomo on the Supreme Court. How do you like that?

Audience members. Boo-o-o!

The President. And I instead want to back up those police officers that lay their lives on the line for you and for me and for our neighborhoods every day of their lives.

Let's pass the Bush plan, the tough anti-crime, pro-law enforcement, and pass that legislation, and let's help our communities. It just isn't right for a mother afraid to send her kid down to the corner store for fear of some criminal in the neighborhood. We have got to win the fight on drugs. We've got to win the fight on neighborhood crime. We've got to back our police officers with strong legislation, and we've got to restore the family values that teach these children right from wrong.

You know, I see all these signs about trust. Let me tell you, I do have a big difference with Governor Clinton. It was expressed by him. It was expressed by him in one of the debates where he said—he put it this way—he said it isn't the character of the President, he said, it is "the character of the Presidency." My view is this: When you're in that White House and when you are the President of the United States, the character of the President shapes and is interlocked with the character of the Presidency. You can't separate them.

My argument with him is you cannot be on all sides of every issue. You cannot flip-flop. You cannot turn the White House into the waffle house. He'll go to the unions here in Toledo and say he's against right to work, and yet in Arkansas he is for it. In one point he's for term limits, and then he says "oh, no"—when he gets into the hands of the Congressmen that he wants to work with, he says, "Oh, no, I am against it." He is, on the North American free trade agreement—you heard it in the debate. He said, well—first he had some reservations; then he is for it. Then he goes to the labor union leaders, not the rank and file; he finds out he's against it. Then he's for it. And then at the debate you heard him, "Well, I am for it, but." He does. You can't have a lot of "buts" in the White House, believe me.

But the biggest difference, I think the clearest difference in this race will be the responsibility a President has as Commander in Chief of the Armed Forces. The biggest difference I had with him was on the war. I had to organize an international coalition. I had to bring along a reluctant Democratic Congress. I had to make a very tough decision.

I mentioned this the other night. Barbara and I sat up there at Camp David on a Sunday before we knew the war was going to start. We'd given the orders to Colin Powell, who passed them on to Norm Schwartzkopf. Believe me, it isn't any fun to have a decision like that on your hands, because you have to send someone else's son or someone else's daughter maybe to die for their country. But I did what I felt was right. I made the proper decision. We kicked this Saddam Hussein out of Kuwait. We restored the leadership, we restored the U.S. position as the only credible, trusted leader in the whole world.

And where was Bill? Let me tell you. Here's what he said at the time of the war. He said, "I was with"—I've got to paraphrase and try to be accurate on it. I wrote it down, but I don't think—here it is: "I agreed with the minority, but I guess I would have voted with the majority." What kind of decisive Commander in Chief would that be?

Audience members. Boo-o-o!

The President. Somebody asked me about some of the unions protesting here. Let me appeal to those union members and say this. Let me say this. I know of your patriotism. I know of your love for country. I know that many of you served in the Armed Forces. And yes, I do have a difference with some—maybe with some here today. But I found it appalling that when our country was at war in Vietnam and Americans were held hostage and prisoner, that Bill Clinton said, "I went to England to organize demonstrations against the United States." I don't believe that is right. Protest in front of the White House, but when you're abroad stand up for the United States.

It does make a difference. Character and trust matter. I have tried to uphold the public trust in the White House. Let me say this: I've had a wonderful person at my side, but you see, I think, and I know Margaret agrees—we wouldn't dare disagree—I think we've got the best First Lady we possibly could have in Barbara Bush.

You know, we have been privileged. We have been very privileged to serve this country, and we've tried to uphold the public trust. And people know this. We're lucky. We've got 12 grandkids. We've got five kids all happily married now, and we've got a lot going for us in terms of family, got a lot going for us in terms of faith. We've got a lot going for us in terms of friends.

People say, well, you know, this hasn't been a particularly pleasant year. You know, you've taken your fair share of shots from the media and from the Clinton-Gore outfit. Why do you need this? You've got a lot of things going for you. Let me tell you why. Bruce touched on part of it. We have changed the world. The kids today go to

bed at night without the same fear of nuclear war. But the job is unfinished. We've got to lift these kids up through better education. We've got to tell them that America is not in decline, that we are on the move. I want to finish the job. I ask for your support. I ask for your trust. We are going to win this election.

May God bless the United States of America. Thank you very much. Thank you.

Note: The President spoke at 10:26 a.m. at Seagate Center.

Remarks to the Community in Strongsville, Ohio
October 28, 1992

The President. Thank you very, very much.

Audience members. Four more years! Four more years! Four more years!

The President. Thank you very much. Thank you. May I just start off here today by thanking my great friends the Oak Ridge Boys and Bruce Willis for being with us. I'm delighted to be in Strongsville, the crossroads of America. Hey, look, look at it this way. If Bruce Willis can overcome all those terrorists and all those bad guys in those "Die Hard" movies, then we can overcome Clinton-Gore, we can annoy the media, and we can win the election.

May I pay my respects at the outset of this remarks and this fantastic rally to Governor George Voinovich at my side, a true and great leader of this State. I want to thank Mayor Ehrnfelt. I want to thank all the law enforcement people in this community that make a rally like this possible. I want to thank Miss Ohio, Robin Meade. That other beautiful one up here was my daughter-in-law Margaret Bush, and I'm proud to have her with us.

But now before we get into a few remarks about the campaign and why I believe I will win it, let me ask two things of you. I am a little tired of this gridlock Congress, and you all can do something about it. First, elect Mike DeWine to the United States Senate. And then get out a great big

broom and help me clean House and elect Martin Hoke to the United States Congress. And for those from the other districts, Beryl Rothschild, Margaret Mueller, and Bob Gardner for the rest of Ohio. We've got to change that Congress.

But now down to what's going to take place on Tuesday of this coming week. The choice before the American people is a vast difference. A vast difference will be there on that ballot, a difference in experience, a difference in philosophy, and yes, a vast difference in character. I believe I am the one that measures up on all three categories.

You know, for months the Democrats have been tearing us down and telling us everything wrong with America. But let me tell you just a couple of things about Arkansas. Arkansas is the 50th in environmental initiatives; it is the 50th in the percentage of adults with college degrees; the 50th in per capita spending on criminal justice; 49th on police protection; 48th in percentage of adults with a high school diploma; 48th in spending on corrections; 46th in teachers' salaries—moving up a little—46th in the whole Nation; 45th in the overall well-being of the children in that State. And this man got up in the debate the other night and he said, "I want to do for America what I've done for Arkansas." No way. We are not going to let him do that.

You know, you heard him talk in the debate. He said that, number one, they've had the number one growth in jobs in 1991. That might well be true. But ever since he's been Governor, they have 30 percent behind the average for the country. The only way the economy got moving in Arkansas was when it turned out Governor Clinton was out of the State for 85 percent of the time. So I wish the people well. But the only way to keep America moving is to send him back to Arkansas.

You know, I'll get on to the positive things in a minute. But there's a very interesting story in the Associated Press today detailing how Arkansas—man says, "Give 'em hell." Let me tell you what Truman said: "You just tell the truth, and they think it's hell." You know what I mean? Even today, talked about an AP story detailing how the Arkansas Medicaid program has been mismanaged. They have a projected $120 million in the hole, a huge amount in that small State, and the story includes tales of secret meetings between Governor Clinton and the legislature to try and figure out whether to raise taxes after the election. It sounds like Governor Clinton better clean up his mess in Arkansas before he ever thinks about helping the United States.

I have gotten sick and tired of hearing them talk about change, Governor Clinton and the Ozone Man, his running mate. He talks about change, change, change, change. That's all you're going to have left in your pocket if you let this guy be President of the United States. Change? Last time we had a Democratic President and a Democratic Congress, we changed things. Interest rates were 21 percent, inflation 15, and we lost respect around the world. We don't need that kind of change.

I will hold the line on taxes. I will get this deficit down by controlling Federal spending. That's what we need to do.

Audience members. Four more years! Four more years! Four more years!

The President. Let me say a word about Ohio. Let me say a word about Ohio. Governor Clinton wants to say, "Well, I want to put taxes on foreign investment." That would threaten 4.5 million jobs, including 150,000 jobs right here in Ohio. He wants to impose CAFE standards, these are the fuel efficiency standards on the auto business, 40 to 45 miles per gallon. That would cost Ohio 20,000 jobs. We do not need this kind of change. We need our kind of change.

The only way they can try to win is by convincing everybody we're in a deep recession. Yesterday the news came out that our last quarter of the year has grown at 2.7 percent, personal income the highest in 9 months. We can do better, but that is progress. That is not recession. That is economic growth. And now we've got to keep it going so we can help every single American that is hurting, everyone that is afraid they might lose the job.

The way we're going to do that is not by raising taxes and raising Government spending, but my plan, the agenda for America's renewal, will get the job done. And here's how we're going to do it. We are going to open new markets. We are going to create more goods for Ohio agriculture and Ohio products all around the world.

[*At this point, audience members interrupted the President's remarks.*]

The President. Who are these guys? Desperation.

Audience members. Four more years! Four more years! Four more years!

The President. You know what's happening? You know what's happening? These guys feel it slipping away from them. They know we're on the move. They know we're going forward. I feel sorry for them.

Here's the way we're going to do it: We're going to open new markets. Governor Clinton talks about investing, Government investing. Government never created a decent job in its life. Small business creates the jobs. Less regulation, less taxes, less lawsuits, and let's get small business moving.

Audience members. Four more years! Four more years! Four more years!

The President. You know, in this country the biggest supporters for Governor Clinton are the trial lawyers. My view is, we sue each other too much and care for each other too little. Let's cap these crazy lawsuits.

Audience members. Hee, hee, haw, haw, Clinton, stay in Arkansas.

The President. We've got it. That's right. These guys were asking about health care. We've got the best health care plan: provide health care insurance to the poorest of the poor through vouchers, give the people at the lower end of the tax spectrum a little break on tax credits, get after these crazy malpractice lawsuits, and keep health care private. Do not do what Clinton wants to do and get the Government further involved. We can't even run a post office. We'd better not try to run health care. Use incentives and markets making insurance available to all. Make it transportable so when you change jobs you've got it. Let's do better by health care by keeping the Government under control.

On education, we've got a tremendous difference on education. We've got a program called America 2000. We've got the best job retraining program to help those who need work as we move from a defense economy to a more private sector. I am very proud of our record. And I'll tell you one place where I really differ with Governor Clinton. I want to put the strength with the families. I want to give the parents the choice: public, private, or religious schools. Let the parents choose, and let's help them with their choice.

Audience members. Four more years! Four more years! Four more years!

The President. Another point. I speak about family values. One family value is to help families live in a neighborhood free of crime. Make no mistake about it, I think we've been a little too lenient on the criminal, a little less caring about the victims of crime. I support our law enforcement officers. And guess what happened the other day: I had a visit from eight people from Little Rock, Arkansas. They came up to endorse me, and they were from the Fraternal Order of Police in Little Rock. I am proud to have their endorsement.

Governor Clinton talks about spending more and taxing more and having Government invest. Let me tell you what I think we need to do about this deficit. We need a balanced budget amendment. Many States have it. Give it to the Federal Government. Make the Congress and the President get

this budget into balance. We need a taxpayer check-off so a taxpayer can check 10 percent of his income tax designated to one thing, reducing the Federal deficit. And we need a line-item veto to let the President cut out the pork out of this budget. And how about this fourth idea? Let's give the Congress back to the people. Presidents have term limits. Let's have term limits on Members of the Congress.

I'll tell you what's going to decide this election, though. It is going to be character and trust. And here's my point: I will continue to criticize because I don't believe as Commander in Chief or as President you can be all things to all people. You have to make tough decisions. And if you make a mistake, you do what you do: You say, "Hey, listen, I was wrong on that one." And you keep on leading, and you can make the tough calls.

You don't do what Governor Clinton does, waffle and vacillate. We cannot make the White House into the waffle house. In the South he'll talk right-to-work; he'll go to the unions and is against it. Some places he's for free trade; other places, well, he's for it, "but." You can't have a lot of "buts" in the White House. Remember that. Term limits, "Oh, term limits have some good ideas," and then it doesn't.

And here we are in the Persian Gulf war. I had to make a tough call. I had to have some of these men and women here today go in to fight for their country. Let me tell you something. That is not an easy decision. But when I made the decision, I did not waffle. I didn't do what Governor Clinton did, which says one day, "Well, I agree with the minority, but I guess I would have voted with the majority." The Commander in Chief cannot do that. You've got to make a decision and stay with it.

Some disagree with me on this one, but I'll tell you something. When your country is at war, I just happen to think that it is plain wrong to go to a foreign country and organize demonstrations against your own, no matter how strongly you feel. A lot of people differed on the Vietnam war, but you can't have it both ways, protect your viability and then fail to level. On April 17th, Governor Clinton said, "I'm going to make all my records available on the draft." Fine. We haven't heard it yet. You cannot waffle. You've got to tell the truth to the American people. And that is what I've been doing. I guess the bottom line is, you can't lead by misleading.

Let me tell you this: Sometimes in the White House in critical moments the phone rings at night, or over there in the Oval Office. You have to make a tough decision. And you cannot keep every single person happy. Barbara—I wish she were here to see this. She is a great First Lady, and I wish she were here. But we have tried very hard. When we talk about family values or caring about people, I think she's done a first-class job in showing that we care. But my point is this: I have tried to be a decent custodian of the public trust.

We see now that our economy is moving. Let's not set it back. Governor Clinton—the only way they can win is if they convince everybody that we're in an economic recession and things that are worse than we are. They say that we are less than Germany and a little better than Sri Lanka. Well, let me tell you something, Millie knows more about foreign policy than these guys do. They ought to open their eyes. They ought to open their eyes. Yes, we've had a tough time. And yes, some families in Ohio are hurting. But we are not a nation in decline. We are the most respected nation on Earth.

Our economy is better than Japan, better than Germany, better than Western Europe, and better than Canada. I am sick and tired of hearing this Clinton and the Ozone Man saying—the only way that they can win, the only way they can do it, is to convince us we are second rate. We are the United States of America. We are the most respected country on the face of the Earth.

Now I ask for your trust. I ask for your trust. I ask you to take this great Ohio enthusiasm to the polls on Tuesday. We are going to show these crazy media talking heads wrong. We are going to win the election. And then we will lead America and lift these kids up. I don't need the job, but I want to finish the job because I want to help every child here. They're living in a world now far less fearful of nuclear war. We've changed the world. Now let's help us strengthen every family in America and lift America up.

Thank you, and may God bless you on this beautiful day in Ohio. This is fantastic. Thank you. Great rally, Strongsville, fantastic. Thank you very much. Great day. Work now. Go to the polls. Get out and vote. We need you.

Note: The President spoke at 1:33 p.m. at Strongsville Commons. In his remarks, he referred to Walter F. Ehrnfelt, Mayor of Strongsville.

Remarks to the Community in Columbus, Ohio
October 28, 1992

The President. Thank you very much. What a fantastic rally. Thank you. Thank you very much. Thank you. Well, let me first say that I get this wonderful feeling that things are really moving across this country. And you look at this crowd and say, "This is it. It's going to happen. It is going to happen."

May I thank Arnold Schwarzenegger. We all know him and respect him. But let me tell you one thing in all seriousness. A while back I asked him to head our fitness program for the entire Nation. He's been to

every single State, and he is doing a first-class job, all pro bono, for this country. And I am very, very grateful to him.

I am delighted that Bruce Willis—let me tell you about that one. Arnold and I have been together for a long time. In fact, it was 4 years ago that he was at my side, not very far from here, as we were coming down the stretch. Bruce Willis called me up and he said, "I have had it with the United States Congress." The polls weren't so hot then, and he said, "I want to help you." And here he is, and I am very, very grateful to him. As for the Oak Ridge Boys, the same thing. You may remember the convention back in 1988. They have been at my side through thick and thin, and I am delighted that they came all this way to be with us.

Two members of the family are with me, my daughter-in-law Margaret and my sister, Ann Ellis. We're going to put the family push on this thing now as we come down to the wire.

And of course, I am so proud to have heading up our effort here your great Governor, George Voinovich. And speaking of Governors, I was so pleased to see the Caribou Man, Jim Rhodes over here, a former Governor of this State; and Chalmers Wylie, the Congressman; and Bob Taft and so many others. I especially want to say thank you to your Mayor. Greg is doing a great job, Greg Lashutka. I am proud to see him every time I come here.

Now, I want you all to do something: Everyplace we go, we see a lot of signs that reflect changing Congress. How about changing Senate and sending Mike DeWine to the United States Senate? And elect Debbie Pryce to the House of Representatives. Clean House! Clean House! No more gridlock! We are going to sit down with that new Congress and get things done for this country.

And may I thank another one from Columbus, Dewey Stokes, who is the president of the National Fraternal Order of Police. I am very proud to have been endorsed by the National Fraternal Order of Police. We back our law enforcement officers, and we'll continue to do that.

And I want to thank John Fisher and Dick McFerson of Nationwide Insurance for letting us use this fantastic facility and being a part of all of this.

And now to the business at hand: You've got a choice on Tuesday between a vast difference in experience, difference in philosophy, and, yes, character. And on that basis I ask for your support. I don't want to ruin this beautiful rally, but I think it is only fair right down to the wire that we point out the record of the person that would like to have this job. And I'm talking about the Arkansas record of Governor Clinton. Sorry to ruin this upbeat meeting, but let me just

give you a few statistics. We have heard everything that's coming out of Governor Clinton and the Ozone Man. We've heard everything that they think is wrong. Well, let me tell you about Arkansas. They are 50th—and they're good people, we lived right next door to them, good people and they're entitled to something better than this—50th in the quality of environmental initiatives; 50th in the percentage of adults with college degrees; 50th in per capita spending on criminal justice; 49th on police protection; 48th—getting better—on adults with a high school diploma; 48th on spending on corrections; 46th in the whole country on teachers' salaries; and 45th in the overall well-being of children.

And Governor Clinton said in that debate "I want to do for this country what I've done for Arkansas." No way! No way!

And I've got only two more things here, I believe, to say about Arkansas. But you've got to hear them, and then I'll get on to the positive aspects. He talks about Arkansas leading in job growth. They had one good year. That was 1991, when he's out of the State 85 percent of the time. And he's been Governor for 10 years and they were 30 percent of the Nation on that one.

And the other one is there's an AP story today—talk about the Arkansas miracle—AP story today detailing how the Arkansas Medicaid program has been mismanaged, projected now to be $120 million in the hole, a huge amount for a tiny little State. And the story includes tales of secret meetings—go read it—between Governor Clinton and the legislature to try to figure out whether to raise taxes after the election. It sounds like Governor Clinton better clean up his mess in Arkansas before fooling around with the United States of America.

No, we can't have that kind of change. Governor Clinton and Ozone, all they do is talk about change. Well, let me tell you something, what kind of change we get—if you went back to the last time we had one of those Democrats in the White House and a Democrat Congress, you had interest rates at 21.5 percent, and you had inflation at 15 percent, and you had a "misery index" at 20.

Audience members. Boo-o-o!

The President. We are not going to go back to those failed days. You talk about change, you talk about change, that's all you guys will have left in your pocket if we get those people in there.

Now, there's bad news for Governor Clinton, because there is good news for the Nation. If you listen to them, you'd think everything was a recession and disaster. Yesterday it came out that for the sixth straight quarter we have had growth. It grew at 2.7 percent, and personal income is the highest in 9 months. The country's beginning to move. Don't set it back.

A lot of people are hurting in this country. And we care about them and we've got to help them. But the last thing we need is to get the Federal Government further involved. Governor Clinton talks about Government investing. Government never created a decent job in its life. It is small business that needs to be stimulated, and small business that does the investing. He wants to raise taxes and raise spending so the Government can invest. I want to get the taxes down and spending down so the people can invest.

You know, Governor Clinton's got one idea. He wants to tax foreign investment that would threaten here in this State 150,000 jobs. They're bringing jobs here from overseas. Let's not seek retaliation. Let's open markets abroad. Free and fair trade, not protection.

And if there are any auto workers out here—this is a great auto State—if there are any auto workers or any people who work in companies that supply things for the auto industry, Governor Clinton and Ozone want to go for 40- to 45-miles-per-gallon CAFE—that's the fuel efficiency standards—that would cost Ohio 20,000 jobs. We've got a good environmental record, but let's not go to the extreme.

Small business, small business creates two-thirds of the new jobs. And they need relief, they don't need more taxation. They need relief from taxation, relief from regulation, and yes, relief from these crazy lawsuits. You know, we spend too much on this, and we need to put some caps on these crazy lawsuits. When a doctor is afraid to practice medicine and deliver a baby, when a Little League coach is afraid to coach for fear some nutty trial lawyer will come along and sue them, why, that means we are suing each other too much and caring for each other too little in this country. Let's put a cap on these lawsuits.

So in addition to holding the line on spending and taxes, I want to get a good health care program. Governor Clinton wants to set up, of course, a Government board. We don't need the Government to do it. Here's what we need to do. Provide insurance to the poorest of the poor through vouchers; give credits to those, the most overtaxed Americans; get pooling of insurance so we can bring it to every single family. But keep the quality of medical care up by keeping the Government out of the medical business. We've got the best health care plan.

And we've got the best education plan. And it's already working, because the gridlock guys don't get too much of their hands on this one. Seventeen hundred communities have already started revolutionizing education. We spend more than every country per capita than Switzerland, and we're not getting the results. Let's help us put the emphasis, and support the teachers and not the teachers union. Let's give the parents a choice of public, private, and religious schools. That will make public education better. That will make public education better, not worse. It worked for the GI bill after World War II. It will work now if we try it for K through 12.

On crime, let me be very clear where I stand. I am not interested in legislation that shows more sympathy for the criminal than for the victims of crime. Toughen it up. Toughen it up, and back our law enforcement officers. Bring in these good programs like our "Weed and Seed" program that weeds out the criminals and then seeds these tough neighborhoods with hope. That's what we've got to do. Homeownership. Enterprise zones. We've got to encourage the communities, not try to legislate from Washington, DC.

And while we're at it, with this new Congress, we're going to sit down with them right after the election—we're not going to wait for anything to happen—sit down with them. And I'm going to say, all right, we want to get the deficit down. Here's a three-point plan, we'll make it a four-point plan. Here it is: Give us a balanced budget amendment; give us what the States have. Give us a check-off, give us a check-off so every taxpayer—don't have to do this, but you can—check 10 percent of your income tax if you want to, to be applied to lowering the Government deficit and making Congress comply. Three, give us what 43 Governors have. If these big spenders in Congress can't do it, let the President have a shot, a line-item veto. And four, let's give the Congress back to the people. The President's terms are limited. Why not limit the terms of Members of Congress?

As we drive down to the wire here in this wonderfully exciting rally, let me point something else out. I've been talking about it, and I feel very strongly about it. Governor Clinton said in the debate it's not the character of the President, it's "the character of the Presidency." Wrong. They are interlocked. You cannot separate the character of the President from the character of the Presidency. You can't do it. And you cannot be Commander in Chief of the Armed Forces if you flip-flop on every issue. You cannot be all things to all people as President. And if you make a mistake, and yes, I have, you look the people in the eye and say, I blew it, now let's get on about leading this great country.

Governor Clinton will go to the auto guys, and he'll say that he's against CAFE standards. And yet he and Ozone go out and say, well, we've got to have 45 miles per gallon. That will drive auto workers out of business. On the one hand—you heard in the debate—the NAFTA agreement, the free trade agreement, yes, he's for it, "but." You cannot have a lot of "buts" sitting there at that Oval Office, I'll tell you. In one part of the world he's for right-to-work, and then he'll go up and tell Mr. Kirkland and the rest of the labor guys he's against it. You can't do it. You've got to say what you're for.

And when it comes to war and peace, you can't do what he did. Let me tell you, it is not easy when you have to commit somebody else's kid to go into battle. But I was tempered by fire. I believe in honor, duty, and service. I made a tough decision on

that war. And we brought along this country. We did the right thing when we kicked Saddam Hussein out of Kuwait. And where was Governor Clinton? Where was Governor Clinton? Here's what he said. Here is what Governor Clinton said: "I agree with"—I'm not giving him hell. It's like Truman said. Do you remember? He says, give 'em hell. He said, "I'm just telling the truth, and they think it's hell."

Okay. Here's what he said. Here is what the man said. You remember, think back to what it was like then: all the demonstrations; all the press fighting us; all the different struggles going on; Congress dragging its feet; people telling me, well, you haven't sold the American people. Here's what Governor Clinton said when it came to that vote. He said, "I agree with the arguments of the minority, but I guess I would have voted with the majority." You cannot make the White House into the waffle house. You can't do it.

The Arkansas Gazette today said Bill Clinton is a master politician, but what principles, if any, informed his politics. The bottom line is, you cannot lead by misleading. You can't be all things to all people. You've got to do it like the umpire does, call it as you see it, and then go forward and lead this country.

Let me say this. First place, I wish our great First Lady, Barbara Bush, were here. She would be thrilled to see this. And yes, we plan to keep Millie in the White House—I see the sign—because, you see, if I want foreign policy advice, I'd go to Millie before I'd go to Ozone and Governor Clinton.

You know, you haven't read anything about—I haven't attacked the media yet. Stay tuned. Wait a minute. No, I want you to be kinder and gentler to the media traveling with us, especially those guys that are taking the pictures, carrying the mikes, and carrying those cameras all around. And yes, be grateful. Amnesty for the White House press. Take it out on these talking heads, Republicans, Democrats, whoever they are, come on every Sunday, tell you how to think, saying we're dead. We are going to show them they are wrong. We are going to prove them wrong. And here's why.

Audience members. Four more years! Four more years! Four more years!

The President. Here's why, here's how it's going to work. Here's how it's going to work and why all these critics and all these naysayers and all these people telling you that we have no chance are going to be wrong. It's going to boil down to this: First place, I believe that we're not a country in decline. I'm absolutely convinced that we are a rising nation, not a declining nation. Secondly, I know it's been tough out there for families and for kids, but we're moving. And I can say as the President of the United States I take great pride in the fact that these young kids here go to bed at night without the same fear of nuclear war as their mothers and dad did. And that is a significant accomplishment. The world is more peaceful, and the world has changed.

People say to me, "Listen, with Barbara at your side and your 5 kids and your 12 grandkids, you've got it made. Why do you want to do this?" Well, let me tell you, I finish what I start. I want to see us lift up these young people here today and make them understand that if we do what I've told you today I want to do, their lives are going to be better than the lives of their parents. And we are going to lead the entire world into economic recovery, and that means jobs for every American that wants to work.

And so I'm not done yet. I ask you to go to the polls on Tuesday. I ask for your support on the basis of character and trust. And I will do my level-best to lead this country to new heights and new prosperity.

Thank you, and may God bless the United States of America and keep her. Thank you very much.

Note: The President spoke at 4:32 p.m. at Nationwide Plaza. In his remarks, he referred to Bob Taft, Ohio secretary of state.

Question-and-Answer Session in Columbus
October 28, 1992

Moderator. Mr. President, I would like to ask the first question tonight. And first of all, let me just say thanks for joining us. It's a pleasure to have you in Columbus, and welcome to our fine State.

The President. Nice to be back.

Fall of Communism

Moderator. I want to start with a campaign flap that surfaced today, as far as I know. Your opponent, one of your opponents, Bill Clinton, has waved a copy of New Yorker magazine, which claims that you said to former Soviet Premier Gorbachev, "Don't worry about what I might say during the campaign about the fall of communism in the Soviet Union; don't worry about that. I'll explain it to you later." What exactly did you say to Mr. Gorbachev?

The President. I said a lot of things to Mr. Gorbachev—I don't recall exactly that—because I did worry about the fall of communism, and I'm delighted that it happened on our watch. I give great credit to my predecessor, because you've got to go back 12 years. A lot of what it was about then was peace through strength versus the nuclear freeze movement. And some people were so frantic about nuclear war they felt the only way you'll get peace is if you have a nuclear freeze.

We didn't believe that. We stayed strong. We tried to work with the Russians. Communism is—international communism or outreach communism—imperial communism is dead, and I'm very proud that it happened when I've been President. But I don't know what they're talking about. I've had many conversations with Mr. Gorbachev. I still salute him. I am very proud that Mr. Yeltsin has said, "It was George Bush who first stood up for me,"— when he was on that tank—"first world leader, and he never wavered, and that meant more to the failure of the coup and the success of Russia going truly democratic than anything else."

So I don't know. I have great respect for Mikhail Gorbachev and for Yeltsin, but I've learned to have a little question mark about the New Yorker these days. I don't want to start by—in front of all these great press, you know, broadcast people, but I've learned something: You can't believe everything you read. And so, I don't know what he's talking about, but I am very proud of our record and how we handled Eastern Europe. A lot of Americans, a lot of Polish Americans, Hungarian Americans, Baltic State Americans, go to bed at night without worrying about their families the way they used to, saying, thank God this administration stood up for democracy and freedom.

Auto Fuel Economy

Moderator. Mr. Bush, yesterday in Dayton and again in Toledo you were warning that Bill Clinton favors increasing fuel economy levels to 40 miles a gallon, and you were warning that that could cost every Ohio auto worker his job. We've talked with United Auto Workers union in Detroit today; they don't seem to share that same concern or fear of Mr. Clinton, Governor Clinton, and they say that to their knowledge there is no one in the industry who is calling for 40 miles a gallon. How do you get people concerned about that issue when the auto workers themselves don't appear to be that concerned?

The President. Well, I think they should be concerned. You've got to remember the auto unions have endorsed Bill Clinton, for a lot of reasons. But I am convinced that 40- to 45-miles-per-gallon CAFE, fuel efficiency standards, would throw—I hope I didn't say all the auto workers; maybe in a hyperbole or an exaggeration for a campaign I did—but they'll throw a lot of workers out of work, because they cannot meet those standards.

And it is another example, in my view, of where—it's in Gore's book, I believe— where they adopt one position in going to one area, the environmental community, then mute it down. Governor Clinton met with the leaders of the three major auto businesses with the head of the UAW at his side, and said, "Well, I'm studying it; I'm going through the National Academy of Sciences report"—about this thick, all square

roots and stuff. He couldn't possibly have done that. And I just believe that—I am certain that I'm correct that trying to meet those standards would throw a lot of people out of work. Not going to back away from it one single bit.

Government Gridlock

Moderator. Mr. President, your popularity after the Gulf war was at a record high. Why did you not use that clout, that influence to push through aggressively your domestic agenda?

The President. Have you ever tried to work with this nutty Congress? I did try. I'll tell you the difference. When we went to war in Desert Storm, I didn't need to get Mr. Gephardt or Mr. Mitchell to go along. I made decisions. We moved troops. I took a lot of flak from the press and from the Congress, and we shaped public opinion, we put together an international coalition; still didn't need anything out of Congress. Then I said to them this: I said, "I would like you to pass a resolution endorsing the United Nations resolution. I don't need that to commit American forces; there are plenty of precedents in it." They did pass it. That's the one I'm accusing Governor Clinton of waffling on, where he said, "I agreed with the minority, but I guess I would have voted with the majority." We got the vote, and we went ahead.

That is quite different than working with the Congress, this Congress, not the new one but this one, in terms of domestic initiatives. And I think they made a calculation after the war that they were not going to cooperate with the President. The reason I'm convinced we can break the gridlock in the future is because they screwed up a little tiny bank and a lousy little post office on Capitol Hill. We're going to have a lot of new Congressmen, Democrats and Republicans.

And the best time for a President elected to his second term is to go in there and say now, no politics. Don't have to worry about it. No more elections, no more debates. Just do the people's business. A whole bunch of new Congressmen, some Democrat, some Republican. We can get it done.

But I'm telling you, I tried very hard to

get the Congress to move on things that would have helped the economy: investment tax allowance, enterprise zones, capital gains reduction, on and on. And they just dug in and didn't want to do it. Now, maybe I could have been more effective, because I am unhappy with the result. But I'm very pleased that this economy seems to be growing in spite of their—their best chance for me not to win is to have things lousy for the American people. And I'm afraid that's an awfully negative attitude.

So it was a difference. You see, in one area you can just do things. In the other, you have to get the Congress to go along. We saw what it was like when a Democratic President was there and a Democratic Congress. Interest rates were out through the ozone layer at 21 percent, and inflation was 15. And the "misery index," invented by the Democrats—inflation and unemployment—was over 20. I don't want to go back to that. But I do think there's hope here in the new one, because they're going to be listening, the new Members, Democrat and Republican, to the same people I'm listening to. And when I win, it will be because my economic plan, my health care plan, my education plan. So I think it will change.

And the other thing is, on her question, we got a lot done for the American people before politics set in, before the war: the Americans for Disability Act, brandnew child care legislation. Even afterward, we got a highway bill that's going to spend $150 billion. So I'm making the distinction between domestic affairs and national security matters.

Moderator. Mr. President, the voters out here have dozens of questions, so we want to get right to them.

The President. Okay, if I get going too long—I get wound up on the answers. So please, you, whoever's the master of ceremonies say, "Please keep it short, sir," because I know I don't want to abuse the process here.

Infrastructure Funding

Q. This relates to the economy, but why has the administration allowed a buildup in the Highway Trust Fund rather than spending down this fund to build and improve highways and spur on the economy? The

same thing is true of the Air Trust Fund.

The President. We've just passed a—well, some of it has budgetary implications—but we've just passed, you know, a few months ago, a $150 billion transportation bill. It's good, and it's going to get the highways building and the infrastructure built. But I disagree with my opponent that what we ought to do is add to that. I think we ought to get money out, but I think the answer to your question is budgetary.

Urban Initiatives

Q. Mr. President, given the riots in Los Angeles and the continued decay in our urban centers, if elected, what can urban residents expect from you in the way of plans and actions over the next 2 or 3 years of your administration?

The President. I think they can expect a revitalization of the cities, because here's what's going to happen: After South Central—and I went out there and I invited Mayor Bradley, Governor Wilson of California, and Peter Ueberroth, who's working the private sector side, trying to bring businesses into the urban areas, to come back to Washington. We met with the Democratic leadership that I was just assailing here and sat down with them: the Speaker, the leaders in both Houses, Republican and Democrat. And the Mayor and those others said the one thing we need for the cities, or the one thing we all agree on is we need urban enterprise zones. Ueberroth, the other day, decried the fact that we haven't gotten them.

I believe that people want that now. I believe that the Congress, in the new Congress, will move on urban enterprise zones. We've got a good program that is already working, that has bipartisan support, just getting started, called "Weed and Seed": weed out the criminal elements and try to hit this drug thing head-on, and seed the neighborhood with hope. I believe our homeownership and tenant management approach is going to prevail in the next Congress, and the enterprise zones.

And the other point I'll make on the mayors is, they came, the National League of City mayors came—separate meeting— and they said to me, the main cause of urban decay or decline is the decline in the American family. That was Tom Bradley of Los Angeles, it was a Republican Mayor out of Plano, Texas, and all across the spectrum. It wasn't liberals, it wasn't conservatives; it wasn't Democrats, it wasn't Republicans. He was talking about finding ways to strengthen the American family. I insist that we have to find ways. And mine are support for law enforcement, choice in child care and schools and whatever it is.

But I think the agenda that I've just outlined here has a very good chance of getting through the next Congress. Some of it is coming my way in legislation that I won't sign because it's hooked into major tax increases. But I think a new Congress is going to want to do exactly what you're saying: Let's help these cities. And I think they're going to want to help them along the philosophical lines I've outlined here.

Economic Issues

Q. Mr. President, throughout the election, it has been said that you are not in touch with the average American. Tonight I'm considering casting a vote for Mr. Clinton for that and several other reasons. How can you convince me tonight that you do understand the concerns of the average American?

The President. Well, that's a pretty hard sell if you're thinking of voting for Clinton, because I would think you'd look at the whole record, including the Arkansas record. I think you would look at the rhetoric, if you're an accountant. We'd been told that this country—by the Democrats—that we're in a big recession. We have had growth for the last six quarters. And I have been saying we're not in a recession. And people like Governor Clinton are saying I am out of touch, aided and abetted by a lot of, you know, talking heads on the television, some Republicans and some Democrats. I believe I am in touch. I believe I understand what's needed. And I think the philosophy of Government that I have would better help the average working man.

Let me give you an example: Governor Clinton talks about having Government invest, to use his—and he puts that to, exact quote, invest. It is not Government that creates any meaningful job and expands the economy. Government takes your money, and you know this as an accountant, and goes about investing it. Well, it's not investment. It is spending. What we need to do is do what I've suggested to spur small business. As an accountant, try this one on: investment tax allowance, capital gains. It is not a tax break for the rich. It will stimulate, in my view, entrepreneurship. And I like the credit, $5,000 credit for the first-time homebuyer, because I think it would stimulate the housing business and also all the businesses that go into it.

He wants to invest, take $220 billion and let somebody back in Washington invest it, and I don't. I want to free up, through less spending and hopefully less taxation, the private sector.

And so we have a big difference on that. And I would say the fundamental philosophy is different. And if you think that we need more Government and more spending on that level, you may go with Governor Clinton, but I'd ask you to look at the Arkansas record. I'd ask you to look at the rhetoric that's been used against me up until yesterday when people saw that we are growing and that our economy is better than Japan and Germany and Europe, although we were told that we've got to grow more like Japan and Germany. This is no time to move toward European nationalism or whatever you want to call it. They're moving toward us.

So I've got a big philosophical difference with him, and how you decide on these economic issues should consider that. I'm also asking people to look at the overall leadership: who do you trust if a crisis comes up, and is the world more peaceful, and all that kind of thing. So I hope I can win you over. Maybe not. I'll put you down as doubtful at this point. [*Laughter*]

Moderator. Mr. President, going back to his question, though, about being out of touch——

The President. Yes.

Moderator. ——with the American people. You've been in office for 4 years. The campaign has really only been hot and heavy for the last year, even the last 6 months.

The President. Yes.

Moderator. How do you account then for this perception among so many people that you are out of touch?

The President. Propaganda by the enemy—opposition. They keep hammering that. They keep saying that. And it's not true. How do you account for the fact that many people in your business keep telling the country we're in a recession when we've grown for 6 straight months? That's six straight quarters now. I mean, that's not out of touch to say that. And I say it, and people say, "You're out of touch." When I say we've grown at 2.7 percent, that's pretty fair growth. I also add, a lot of people are hurting, and a lot of people are scared about their jobs, so here's what to do to help them.

But I think it is pure rhetoric on the part of the opposition, because I'm in touch all the time. My heavens, I wish you saw all the mail that comes in and the phone calls, and share the anxiety and the concern I feel. But when you hear that, that's part of the Democratic—now, the only way that guy can win is to convince America that we're in decline and that the economy is worse than it is. And I will win because I think I have better economic answers.

Moderator. Mr. President, this is a fifth grader, and she's going to be voting in a few years. But she's got a question I think a lot of parents would like an answer to. Betsy, go ahead.

Education

Q. What do you plan to do about—wait. What are you going to do to make it possible for all children to get a good education?

The President. Improve the existing educational system. This is pretty hard for you to realize. We've got all kinds of change in this country, and one thing that really hasn't changed fundamentally in years is elementary and secondary education. We have a program that you may or may not have heard of called America 2000. There are 1,700 communities already participating in this program. It bypasses the powerful teachers union and says to the local teachers and the parents and the community leaders, literally, help us reinvent the schools. So that's one thing that's going to

happen. In some areas, some urban areas, they say, we only want 8 hours. And others might say, we want year-round schools. Others are going to try more emphasis on math and science.

As President, I put into effect, with the help of the Governors, including Governor Clinton, six national education goals. It's never happened before. They're voluntary, but they set the future for education, kids like you. More emphasis on math and science is one of them. Another one is every kid must start ready to learn. That means Head Start, and we've literally doubled the funding for Head Start in this administration. It means nobody's too old to learn. That's one of them, more job retraining and more adult education and give people credits while they're working to get educated. And so we've got the plan. We've got the ideas to revolutionize education.

And there's one last point: I think parents ought to have the right to choose the schools. When I got out of the service they gave you a GI bill, and they didn't say you can only use this in public institutions. They said you can go wherever you want to college or use this money to help you get to college. I want to see the same thing tried in public education. Forty-six percent of the public school teachers in Chicago send their kids to private school. I want to try this now under our "GI bill" for kids that says to parents: You choose, public, private, or religious. And the schools not chosen will do what's happened in Milwaukee where they've tried it. They'll get better. It won't undermine the public school system; it will make it better.

Moderator. Mr. President, just a followup to Betsy's question. When you ran in 1988 against Mr. Dukakis, you said you wanted to be the education President. Four years later, if you had to grade George Bush's paper, what grade would you give yourself?

The President. I would modestly give myself an A, because of what I just told her. Because here's an area that I didn't have to go to the Congress for much of it. There was an education bill they passed. If it ever lands on my desk, I won't sign it. And why is that? Because all it does is put mandates on local school systems and State school systems. The same old tired thinking from an institution that also hasn't changed, that one for 38 years, Democrats controlling the Congress. All they want to do is send me education bills that dictate exactly what kind of program you have, some old geezer that's been there forever thinking he understands education. We've got education goals, and I've outlined here a brandnew and, I think, really good approach to education. So others may not give me the A, but I'll admit that that's what I think.

Women's Issues

Moderator. Mr. President, a longtime voter back here. Nellie Lent is 96 years of age, and she lives in a nursing home in Worthington. She wants you to know that she first voted for a President, President Harding, back in 1921. Nellie?

Q. This was the first year women were allowed to vote. It is now 1992, the year for women. Why should women vote for you?

The President. That's a good question. I don't know if you all heard it. The year of the woman, why should women vote for me? She remembers the first year that women voted. I believe that we've got good programs: Women, Infants and Children, for example. That's a program that Chalmers Wylie, sitting here, knows about. We have vastly increased funding for that program. It helps families.

I believe they ought to vote for me because I think a lot of women are in business. We are trying to say, don't let Governor Clinton's approach invest Government, grow Government. Get the small business going. Women in there are really starting lots of businesses. I think that's good.

Our Secretary of Labor is vigorously fighting against the "glass ceiling," which is kind of an artificial barrier to women. And we have tried to set the pace. I have three women in the Cabinet. No other President's ever done that. We've appointed women to be head of the National Institute of Health and head of Social Security, and meaningful jobs because they have shown tremendous competence. So I believe on all these reasons that I would be a good and, hopefully, effective President for women, upward mobility of women.

Moderator. Nellie, are you satisfied with

the President's answer?

Q. Yes, I would like to shake the President's hand.

The President. We're going to do that after this. You may be—let's see, you're 90—I don't want to—we're in the historical society here. My dad was born here and grew up here. Maybe he might have taken you to the prom someplace. I'll have to come back and find out.

It's not that I'm nervous. I went running this morning. I'm still pounding the water. Now, go ahead. [*Laughter*]

Racial Harmony

Q. Good evening, Mr. President. I would like to commend you on the wonderful job you did on bringing nations together to address the Persian Gulf crisis and peace talks. I would like to know why you have not used that same energy and seriousness to confront the racial divisions which plague our Nation. This is a very serious matter to me. In reading the letters from the Birmingham jail from Dr. Martin Luther King, Jr., he was facing some of the same crises in his time, and that was in 1962 and 1963. Here is 1992, and we still have cities going up in flames. I still have to look at a white Senate, and it's devastating to me. And I would just like to know your response.

The President. My response is, I have tried to be a President sensitive to the elimination of bigotry and of anti-Semitism. Under my Presidency we have passed two pieces of civil rights legislation. One of them is the Americans for Disabilities Act that is a very good piece of forward-looking civil rights legislation. The other one moves against discrimination in the workplace.

I think you're on to something because I don't believe it's a question of legislation now. It's a question of what you care about in your heart and how you feel. And I hope that my record, dating back to when I was a Member of the Congress from Texas, voting for open housing—that wasn't easy in those days. And I hope it shows a commitment to racial fairplay.

I have spoken out about it over and over again from the White House. But I'm sorry you feel this way, because I really believe I understand. I guess I can't say I really understand totally what it is like to be a person who is discriminated against, but I do understand the hurt. I have worked for—this is maybe just one way of sensitizing one's soul—for the United Negro College Fund that my brother today heads. And I believe that we have to do better in education.

But on your point, I think I can accept some criticism on that. But believe me, I will continue to speak out against racism and anti-Semitism, move against it if further legislation is required. It is a blight on ourselves as a country. I don't want to represent to the country who might be listening tonight that I think things are getting worse in this department. I mean, yes, we had those South Central riots, and yes, we've got a lot of tension, but I don't think it's worse than the sixties and things like that. I hope we're improving. But whether we are or not, we've got to do better, and so I appreciate you expressing your concern. I hope I can demonstrate in a far better way in a second term my concern.

Urban Initiatives

Moderator. There's been a lot of talk in the news lately going back to L.A. and to the site of the riots, and a lot of talk about the fact that the rebuilding is not happening very fast. Are there things that you would do in your second administration that were not accomplished in the first?

The President. I think I've outlined to you some that I'm confident can get done with a new Congress. I believe that the whole approach I've outlined here on urban America is the answer to South Central. And please don't just take it from me, take it from Mayor Bradley. Take it from Governor Wilson and take it from Peter Ueberroth, all of whom are working very hard across party lines to make this happen.

I would suggest that people that feel as strongly as I do support me, trying to get those kinds of legislation through. I believe a new Congress will do it, because there's no more politics, at least for a couple of years. And so I think that that's the way we're going to get the job done for South Central and other areas.

I mentioned this "Weed and Seed" program. This is good, new policy in helping

win the fight against drugs and still help the kids. I also happen to think that what I said about family is true. The liberal elite hates it. But when I talk about family values and strengthening family, I can cite the visit from those mayors. And we've got too many teenage pregnancies. We've got too many kids nobody knows their name. We've got too many that don't have respect for their communities and the law enforcement officers and for their own families, their own mothers and dads. We've got to do better. And law enforcement is one way to do it. The kinds of programs I'm talking are a far more satisfactory way to get it done. But we are going to keep working until the problem is solved.

National Debt

Q. I was just wondering, I've been following the debates and everything, and you turned to the cameras during the debates and, you said, "In case of crisis who do you want in the White House?" And your foreign affairs are great, but we are in the middle of a major domestic crisis.

The President. How would you outline it, so I'm sure we're talking to the same thing?

Q. The debt, the $4 trillion debt. Ross Perot says, "I want to get in there, and I want to get that hood up, and I want to work on this." Bill Clinton says, "I'm going to be the main guy in charge of domestic policy." Why are you pushing this off on James Baker? Why aren't you the guy in there with the hood up, fixing the engine, so to speak?

The President. Well, let me tell you what we're going to do. And I am the guy. Jim Baker did a superb job in foreign affairs. He did a superb job in domestic affairs. You may forget he was Secretary of the Treasury, and a very good one. He was the Chief of Staff of the White House, and a very good one. Here is an extraordinarily able person.

But make no mistake about it, nobody's handing off anything. I've learned something: You don't blame somebody if it goes wrong, you take the blame as President. Once in a while you get a little credit, that's fine, as President. But I'm the captain of that ship. I'm the President of the United

States, and I make the decisions.

Now, Jim Baker is extraordinarily able, and I can't think—you need help, and he's the best. He will bring together a new team to get these programs through the Congress where it's needed and help me in every single way.

But let me try some things on you—not just open the hood, fix it—I mean, you've got to do a little more than that. How about let me give you some ideas. Let me give you a couple of ideas. The biggest part of the budget—and somebody referred to it back here—two-thirds of the budget doesn't come to the President: Mandatory spending programs. Put the cap on them. And if I have my way with this Congress I keep getting asked about, they will take the tough decision. And I'll have to take political heat because it isn't easy. Let the mandatory programs grow to population and to inflation,and that's it. No more. They'll grow; they won't be cut. But that's what has to happen to get the deficit down.

Add to that a balanced budget amendment. That got within six votes or eight votes of passing. And what happened? If you think I'm down on Congress on other things, I'm down on them in this because they got something like 12 people that co-sponsored the resolution to change their votes. We're going to get it in the next Congress. We're going to get a line-item veto. Forty-three Governors have it. And my case to the American people is if they can't do it, let the President have a shot. It's not going to solve the whole problem.

I like term limits. Keep the Congress close to the people. I like the idea that I proposed of a check-off that says to the American taxpayer you can check off up to 10 percent of your income tax and that has to go to one thing, reducing the deficit. And if Congress doesn't bring the spending side down, then you have a sequester across the board. And I believe that kind of medicine is necessary. It is not simply saying, "I'm going to fix it," it is a specific proposal. I believe I'm going to win because people think those ideas are important to get into effect. So that's how I'd cope with the deficit, or try to.

Domestic Issues and Foreign Policy

Moderator. Mr. President, just briefly as a followup, by appointing Mr. Baker as domestic czar, can we interpret that to mean that in your second term you will pay more attention to domestic issues than foreign policy? How would you rank those?

The President. It depends what's happening in the world. A foremost responsibility of the President is the national security of this country. And when the history of my Presidency is written, 5 years from now I hope, I think we'll have every analyst, every—we'll have a library and everybody will go in there, and they'll see how my time was spent. My time, much more of it has been spent on domestic matters. The problem is, and we keep getting the same question, is I'm having to fight with a highly partisan Congress. That is going to change.

So I will do what I have to do as Commander in Chief, as the guarantor of peace. And yes, I take some credit that this little girl knows not the same fear of nuclear war that some of you middle-aged guys out there knew. You don't have any training drills. If we're going to take a hit on the economy being disconnected, how about a little credit for world peace and democracy and ancient enemies talking to each other, ancient enemies talking peace when nobody dreamed that was possible?

So I will do what I have to do to guarantee this little kid's future. But I am going to continue to strive, and I've thrown out some of the ideas, for changing things in a domestic way that helps families. And it's a big challenge, but I'm absolutely confident, with the changes that are going to take place in Congress—there's already 100 new Members, might be 150 coming in there—that we're going to get the job done.

Taxes

Q. Good evening, Mr. President. Mr. President, talking about family values and the economy, nowadays there are a lot of us women that are choosing to stay home to be with our children, to raise them and give them a firm foundation, and therefore providing a job opportunity for someone that's unemployed. There's a lot of tax breaks and incentives for two-family incomes and for child care, but where's the tax break for the family where the mother chooses to stay in the house?

The President. I don't think—you sounded like Barbara Bush. She says what happens in your house is more important than what happens in the White House, and she's absolutely right. And that doesn't mean that she looks down on my daughters-in-law who happen to work for a living, or whatever it is. But I think that you're on to something. But I don't want to, you know, promise things. There isn't enough money in the world, in the United States, when we're operating at a deficit, to subsidize people for doing that which historically many people chose to do, stay and look after their kids at home. So I don't want to mislead you, but I just don't think we can promise any such thing.

We do have flexibility in child care. It used to be, well, you have to look to the Government for the kind of child care you want. Now we work it out so parents can choose and they can get people in the neighborhood together or grandparents to look, whatever it is, and not have—and you still get support from the Government. But I don't want to misrepresent it. I don't believe, given the deficit that this gentleman understandably asked about as a young guy, his future being mortgaged every day, that we have enough money out there to subsidize those people like yourself who have sorted out your priorities to do what I admire. And I think that's fine that you're doing it. But I just can't pledge that we can give you money to do it.

Interest Rates

Moderator. Mr. President, families of all ages need help. And Nellie that we were just talking to, the elderly woman, so many of those people call us every day at the television station and they say that as the interest rates go down, their interest on savings is going down. And they're on fixed incomes. Can you hold out any hope for them?

The President. Well, I can't hold out for any hope for saying I want interest rates to go up. I mean, I am proud that they're down. And families that are overburdened on interest are being able to refinance their homes. So I can't say to you they should do anything other than to invest their savings in something that yields more money. We have got to have a policy of keeping interest rates down. And that is, in the final analysis, going to be one of the major stimulants of jobs and opportunity, jobs for kids.

So to those whose earnings are down because they had their money in CD's who are now paying lower interest rates because we've been able to contain inflation, I would simply say, you know, try to find alternative investments because there's plenty that pay more than a CD did or a Government bond does. But I cannot represent myself as wanting to see some policy that would raise interest rates. I am very proud of the fact we brought them down. And I'm very proud of the fact we brought inflation down so that saver, that senior citizen you're talking about doesn't see his or her savings explode in the cruelest tax of all, inflation.

And I would get a partisan shot in here by reminding people what it was like when we had a Democratic President singing the same song that Governor Clinton is singing and a Democratic Congress. "Misery index," 20; inflation, 15; interest rates, 21. We can't go back.

Supreme Court Appointments

Q. Mr. President, I'd like to change the subject for a moment. I believe that many voters who are undecided or those who perhaps might even support your candidacy are quite concerned about the record that you have exhibited in appointments to the Supreme Court and concerned about who you might appoint to the Supreme Court in a second term. And I think perhaps that fear is enhanced or exacerbated a bit by your allowing Pat Buchanan to speak as he did at your convention. I'm wondering if you would speak a bit as to how you would approach likely appointments to the Supreme Court in a second Bush administration.

The President. I'll do that. And unlike the Democratic convention, we didn't censor what people said, and we didn't keep people that disagreed with that Clinton line off the program. That's one thing that's different.

Secondly, maybe we just have a fundamental difference as to what should happen on the Supreme Court. I have put two people on the Supreme Court who are constructionists, not trying to legislate from the Bench. I am not in the least bit apologetic about Clarence Thomas, nor about David Souter, both extraordinarily well-qualified, both passed by a Democratic Senate. And I don't think the Supreme Court ought to legislate. What worries me is what Governor Clinton has indicated. Barbara sat near him at the Italian-American Foundation, and once again he raised this horrible specter of Mario Cuomo going on the Supreme Court. And you want to get somebody on there to legislate with a liberal point of view, then go that route.

My view is, I don't know where these guys stand on individual, specific social issues, but I have confidence in the fact that they are not going to legislate but they are going to interpret the Constitution. And that's what I look for, and no revisionism is going to make me change my mind about Clarence Thomas, none.

You know, the Anita Hill-Clarence Thomas thing. They say, well, they've changed now. Forty-two percent of the people—we live and die by these polls—42 percent of the people used to think it was Thomas. Now he's a minority, and Anita Hill's a hero. Why? What made people change their mind on that? Is it that they suddenly all studied the issues? No, they got drummed into them by the women's movements and all these people that Anita Hill was a hero and Clarence Thomas is the bad guy. But when the American people saw the hearings, and they listened and passed judgment themselves, two to one they believe him.

And so I am proud of him. I'll stand by him. I do not want to appoint people to the Court that have a sick point of view that they want to impose through the Bench on the people. That's the job of the Legislature, and to some degree it's the job of the President. So that's my philosophy and that's why I've acted the way I have.

I looked at my watch during the debate, and I caught all kinds of hell from the media. But I'm going to look at it again, openly here. It is a Timex, and it now is 16 of—thank you. That's exactly what I did in the debate and he—oh, look at—he doesn't know, he doesn't seem assured of himself. He's looking at the watch again. I mean, come on. I wanted to declare myself. This is the strangest political year I've ever seen. Now things are changing, fast.

Family Values

Moderator. Mr. President, I have a follow-up question. Thanks for looking at your watch so the rest of us could get away with not doing it. [*Laughter*] Mr. Sharp asked you about the role of Pat Buchanan in your convention. That goes to some criticism that you have gotten from people in your own party about so leaning to the religious right of the party that you have alienated a lot of centrist Republicans and Democrats, talking about even William Safire's column a couple of weeks ago that you've done damage not only, he says, to your own Presidency but also to the party in general.

The President. Couldn't disagree more. Can't be guided by New York Times columnists. I've decided to take them on. I used to sit quietly—hey, he's entitled to his opinion. I don't agree with him, and I don't agree about that. And as I indicated, Pat Buchanan ran against me. He flailed me out there in the primaries. You've got a short memory, those who are asking that question. How do you think I felt about that? That's the political process. He's entitled to his opinion, his emphasis. I'm entitled to mine. But if your question is, how do I feel about faith and family values and that, I've tried to tell you how I feel about it. And I'm not retreating from it, because it isn't anything to do about prejudice.

I got a question from Tom Brokaw one night on a nationally televised show not so long ago. And he said, with all respect to NBC, he said—and he did it in a very nice way, and it wasn't pejorative—but he said, "Are you suggesting when you talk about family values that your values, your and Barbara's family is better than Hillary and Bill Clinton's?" I said, "Of course not." Of course not.

What we're talking about, though, is what

these mayors told me about. And I happen to believe that family is still the fabric of society. And when a little kid is born to a 13-year-old mother, some way we've got to find a way to have that kid loved by the parent and teach values and respect. And it isn't happening. So I am not going to move away from that, but I am not going to identify myself with the rhetoric of a man that went out and slammed the heck out of me up there in New Hampshire.

So it's a liberal's nightmare, but I call them as I see them. I'm kind of proud that our convention didn't try to censor what suddenly was the wrath of all the talk shows. But we'll see, we'll see how it comes out on election day.

Health Care

Q. I work for $5.50 an hour. I go to work every day. My boss does not supply health care for us. We cannot afford to purchase health care. What is your plan, if any, to help us get insurance of some kind so we don't have to starve to go to the doctor?

The President. That's the key, get insurance. What we need to do is pass my health care plan that provides insurance to the poorest of the poor. Gives a voucher to the poorest, it gives a tax credit to the next bracket above that so that they can get insurance, make insurance available. It pools insurance, small businesses pooling insurance so they get the benefit that a big company has. If you buy a lot of something, you get it at a cheaper price. If you buy a lot of insurance, you get it at a cheaper price. If you pool small businesses so they represent a lot of purchases, you get insurance at a cheaper price. That is a part of it.

The other part of it is, we've got to go against this malpractice that is driving costs up to $25 billion to $50 billion. Doctors don't dare to deliver babies because of some frivolous suit, or hospitals say, give this guy three tests to protect us against a malicious lawsuit.

My program to control, put lids on these limitless lawsuits is really going to help bring health care costs down. And so will the pooling. And another thing about our plan is, right now people go to the emergency room and the hospital is stuck with the bill. The people don't have insurance. If you have insurance, that takes a burden off the hospitals.

So we do have a good plan, and it really helps small business, I think. I don't know whether your employer is large or small, but whoever you work for, you'll be able to get it as an individual, and it will be portable. You take it with you if you find another job.

Who is in charge of the water here? Anybody? Here's one. Here, I'll just wander down like Phil Donahue and get myself a water. [*Laughter*] There you go. Thank you. That's great.

All right, shoot. I can hear you, sir.

Unemployment

Q. Psychological studies of unemployed people have been viewed as suffering from unemployment neurosis. The most prominent symptom is not depression but apathy. The blacks of America suffer disproportionately from this neurosis, as well as many other Americans. This mental state makes people incapable of grasping the helping hand which may be extended to them. Mr. Bush, for our information, what form has your helping hand taken, and how do you view the American jobless reaction to that hand?

The President. Well, I'm not a psychiatrist, and that's a very—I didn't know that. What I do know is, we're trying very hard with the programs I've outlined to give people jobs, break the cycle of dependency and welfare. And we have indeed given waivers to many States to change the welfare system that just breeds dependency.

You talk about a psychological neurosis. How would a kid feel, born into a, say, third or fourth generation? We've got to break that cycle. Learnfare and workfare—many of the States are trying, and I, through Dr. Lou Sullivan, our black Secretary of HHS who is a superb doctor and a great humanitarian, is trying hard to break that cycle. But the best way to break the cycle is a job with dignity in the private sector. And that's why my small business program that I mentioned—regulation, taxes, lawsuits— plus what we're talking about in enterprise zones is the answer. And we're going to get it done.

Ross Perot

Q. Mr. President, I was wondering which of Ross Perot's ideas on the economy and the deficit do you like? It seemed so often in the debate you and Mr. Clinton both said, "Yes, I agree with you, Ross." And upon your reelection, in your second term, any room for a job for Ross in your administration?

The President. Well, not on the tax side of things, because I don't want to raise the gasoline tax 50 cents a gallon, I mean, 50 cents. I just think that would be bad for working America, and I don't want that. So I differ with him. I don't think we ought to touch Social Security.

What I agree with him on is putting the focus on the need to get the deficit down. At the debates, there wasn't that much time, nor were there many specifics as to how to do that. I don't agree with him that what I've subsequently learned he's proposed, because it will, in my view, screech a fragilely growing economy to a halt. I just don't think it needs that kind of a shock.

I do agree with him on what we're doing about mortgaging the future of various people. I don't agree with him when he says we gave Saddam Hussein permission to take the northern part of Kuwait. That is simply not true. So we agree, I do agree with him on his dedication to trying to get the help on the POW question.

So I have some places I agree, some places I don't. Hey, but listen, I need all the help I can get. So, I don't know about future jobs, but let's get this election over, and then we'll see.

I think this claim the other day, I mean, that thing was strange, and I don't agree with him about that, obviously.

Ronald Reagan

Q. Mr. President, Ronald Reagan ran two of the most successful campaigns that we've ever seen in history. His influence or assistance in your campaign, and I don't mean him personally but maybe his camp of people, seems to be absent. Because I know part of the strategy in a campaign is to reach those voters that may be undecided, there is always a faction that will vote for you no matter what you do, and that faction that won't vote for you no matter what you

do. But why haven't you enlisted his people or him more to assist you in this campaign?

The President. Coincidence. Ronald Reagan will be going either tomorrow or the next day for me to North Carolina and someplace else. He's agreed to do it, and I hope he does. I campaigned at his side in Orange County. He has been more than helpful in everything we've asked him to do. You know, I had a meeting with the former—the Reagan Alumni Association, I think they call themselves, in Washington, headed by Ed Meese, remember, who used to be—very, very supportive.

So if there's a perception that they are not helping, I think that's an unfair perception. I hope that the more recent visits by the President will be focused on, because I can't ask for any more from him than what he's doing to be supportive. And the things he was saying, even my mother would have blushed when she heard the nice things he said about what we're trying to do. So he's with us.

Child Support

Q. Mr. President, I'd like to ask you about your views concerning another national tragedy: the billions of dollars owed single parents in uncollected child support. Presently 20 percent of the children in this county are living at or below the poverty level. As a trial attorney, what can I tell my clients about your future efforts, if you're elected next week, to eliminate this national dilemma?

The President. Tell them I just signed a bill last week, and that bill goes after the deadbeat dads. And it was passed by this Congress, thus demonstrating we can, even with them, get something done. And what it did was, where they needed Federal support, whether it's a passport or anything else, crack down on them and see that Federal support no longer—or any—Federal permission really to do things is not granted to those who are running away and leaving these people.

Because what happens, as you know, I'm sure, far better than I do because of your concern for usually the mother, that spouse, is that these people go across State lines. And until this legislation was passed, they haven't been able to go at them. So I believe that legislation is a good step towards cracking down on these people who you're after, and will be helpful to those mothers, normally, that you're trying to help.

Closing Statement

Moderator. Mr. President, thanks for answering all of our questions in the past hour. And according to my old broken watch, we have about a minute left for you to make a closing statement, sir.

The President. Can it be a direct appeal? I hate to have this many voters—I mean, is there any restriction on it?

Well, let me just say that, one, thank you for everybody that did this, including the Historical Society and the Association of Broadcasters.

But look, this has been a terrible year in a sense. I believe I'm going to win the election. And I'm going to ask for everybody's support here. We have tried very hard to keep the public trust. We've had a clean administration. We've tried to serve with honor. We've literally changed the world through leadership. And what I'm asking people is this: Look, you're going to the polls, consider character. It is important.

Clinton's wrong when you said it's "the character of the Presidency," not the President. The President's character shapes the Presidency. They are interlocked. And I hope I have demonstrated the character. I hope I've earned the trust of the American people. I see this economy moving. I believe that our programs that I've outlined will lift up everyone that's hurting and give them a much better shot at the American dream. So that would be my appeal.

I must say in conclusion, I have never felt such a sea change in politics as I have in the last 2 weeks. It's beginning to happen. And people are looking at it: Who do you trust? Who has the character to serve in the Presidency of the United States? And that's why I'm asking for your vote and your support. And thank you all very, very much.

Moderator. Thank you, Mr. President. We appreciate your visit to Columbus, Ohio. I would like to make some quick thanks.

The President. I think it would be most appropriate if I started walking down to say hello to Nellie before she changes her mind back there at 91. [*Laughter*]

Moderator. I think that's a great idea.

The President. Is that all right?

Moderator. Absolutely.

The President. Okay. Don't move.

Note: The question-and-answer session began at 7 p.m. at the Ohio Historical Society. Moderators for the session were Gary Robinson, president of the Ohio Association of Broadcasters, and Columbus television anchors Doug Adair of WCMH–TV, Deborah Countiss of WSYX–TV, and Bob Orr of WBNS–TV. In his remarks, the President referred to Peter Ueberroth, chairman of the Rebuild L.A. Committee; Representative Chalmers P. Wylie; and Gov. Mario Cuomo of New York.

Statement on Signing the Veterans Home Loan Program Amendments of 1992
October 28, 1992

Today I am signing into law H.R. 939, the "Veterans Home Loan Program Amendments of 1992." On balance, the bill improves the Veterans Home Loan Program by authorizing new programs and expanding or extending existing programs.

I am, however, concerned that certain provisions of this bill raise serious constitutional concerns. For example, the race-based classification of "Native Hawaiian" cannot be supported as an exercise of the constitutional authority granted to the Congress to benefit Native Americans as members of tribes. Therefore, this classification would be subject to the most exacting equal protection standards. I direct the affected Cabinet Secretaries to consult with the Attorney General in order to ensure that the program is implemented in a constitutional manner.

In addition, the bill purports to require the Secretary of Veterans Affairs to recommend future legislation regarding a pilot program for housing loans to Native American veterans. The Constitution grants exclusively to the President the power to recommend to the Congress such measures as he judges necessary and expedient. The Congress may not by law command the President or his subordinates to exercise the power that the Constitution commits to his judgment. Therefore, I will treat this requirement as advisory rather than mandatory.

GEORGE BUSH

The White House,
October 28, 1992.

Note: H.R. 939, approved October 28, was assigned Public Law No. 102–547.

Statement on Signing the Intermodal Safe Container Transportation Act of 1992
October 28, 1992

Today I am signing into law H.R. 3598, the "Intermodal Safe Container Transportation Act of 1992."

This Act will require shippers to certify the cargo weights and contents of intermodal containers and trailers. The Act also authorizes States to impose liability on shippers where citations for violations of State highway weight limits are issued to highway motor carriers as a result of erroneous certifications. The legislation is a progressive step toward reducing the number of overweight vehicles on U.S. highways and the threats that they pose to public safety and highway pavement conditions.

I regret, however, that there are some problems with the bill's approach. I am concerned about the paperwork burden that will be levied on small shippers, the potential for inconsistent application by States, and the fact that the bill would, in effect, establish two enforcement programs: one for shippers in intermodal commerce and another for all other shippers.

The Department of Transportation has been given considerable flexibility to develop the regulations required by H.R. 3598. The Department will use its flexibility to minimize these potential problems.

I urge all States to adopt a similar approach. Failure to do so could complicate, instead of clarify, the intermodal shipping community's understanding of weight regulations for intermodal cargoes.

This legislation is a first step toward a full review of overweight vehicle operations on U.S. highways. My Administration intends to undertake such a review.

One section of the bill purports to require the Secretary of Transportation to submit, to several congressional committees, legislative and other recommendations for improving the collection of certain transportation data. Under Article II, section 3 of the Constitution, the President possesses the exclusive authority to determine what legislative measures he and his subordinates will recommend for the Congress' consideration. To avoid constitutional difficulties, and consistent with established practice, I interpret this section of the bill to be advisory, not mandatory.

GEORGE BUSH

The White House,
October 28, 1992.

Note: H.R. 3598, approved October 28, was assigned Public Law No. 102–548.

Statement on Signing the Land Remote Sensing Policy Act of 1992
October 28, 1992

Today I am signing into law H.R. 6133, the "Land Remote Sensing Policy Act of 1992."

The Act will carry out my proposals for the future of the Landsat satellite program. It will ensure that continuity of Landsat-type data is maintained for the foreseeable future. That data will improve our understanding of the environment, strengthen our ability to manage natural resources, and assist with other activities of scientific, economic, and national security importance.

The Act will also encourage future commercial opportunities in remote sensing by:

—supporting investments in new remote sensing technologies;

—removing unnecessary restrictions on the dissemination of privately gathered data;

—streamlining the licensing process for private remote sensing systems; and

—encouraging growth of the market for remote sensing data by pricing federally provided data at the cost of fulfilling user requests, but no higher.

Finally, I note that section 203(b) of the Act, regarding review of certain agency actions under the Act, cannot be understood to supersede section 554 of title 5, United States Code, which exempts from review such matters as the conduct of military or foreign affairs functions.

GEORGE BUSH

The White House,
October 28, 1992.

Note: H.R. 6133, approved October 28, was assigned Public Law No. 102–555.

Statement on Signing the Small Business Research and Development Enhancement Act of 1992
October 28, 1992

Today I have signed into law S. 2941, the "Small Business Research and Development Enhancement Act of 1992." This measure recognizes the unique contribution of America's small businesses in performing innovative research and thereby creating high skill jobs. It is these entrepreneurs who are leading our private sector into the high technology global markets of the 21st century.

The Act will ensure the continuation of the highly successful Small Business Innovation Research (SBIR) program for another 7 years. Indeed, it will more than double the program's size over the next 5 years to approximately $1 billion annually.

The SBIR program, which is celebrating its 10th anniversary, is coordinated by the Small Business Administration. The program helps small businesses bring cost-effective research and development expertise to Federal agencies. It encourages entrepreneurs to find new commercial uses for Federal technology. The innovative goods and services that these small businesses develop are sold in the domestic and international markets.

Over the history of the program, small businesses have received $2.8 billion in funding from 11 Federal agencies for over 21,000 projects. At least one in four SBIR award winners has achieved commercial sales or expects that commercial sales will occur. SBIR firms have produced new innovations in all areas of high technology, including superconductors and biotechnology. Perhaps the most gratifying are the many new products and services developed in the biological, medical, and educational fields.

S. 2941 will provide expanded opportunities for this Nation's vital asset, its small business entrepreneurs. It will foster their pioneering spirit in inventing, producing, and selling high technology products and services here at home and around the world.

GEORGE BUSH

The White House,
October 28, 1992.

Note: S. 2941, approved October 28, was assigned Public Law No. 102–564.

Statement by Press Secretary Fitzwater on the Baltic-American Enterprise Fund
October 28, 1992

The President announced today that he will seek congressional authorization for the creation of a Baltic-American Enterprise Fund. This new fund, which will serve Estonia, Latvia, and Lithuania, will be capitalized at $45 million over 3 years and will be led by a board of directors composed of American citizens and representatives from the three Baltic countries.

The enterprise fund will be modeled after similar funds established by the administration for Poland, the Czech and Slovak Federal Republic, Hungary, and Bulgaria, which have proven extremely successful in assisting private sector development. The objective of the fund will be to provide capital, in the form of either debt or equity financing, to small and medium-sized private enterprises in the Baltics. Just as the other U.S. enterprise funds have done, the Baltic-American Enterprise Fund may assist in the channeling of certain U.S. technical assistance in the Baltic countries,

as well as financial assistance from other countries.

The U.S. Government will also encourage participation in the fund by the European Bank for Reconstruction and Development, other donor countries, and private investors. Such a partnership would leverage USG funds by augmenting them with outside capital.

This U.S. initiative demonstrates once again strong administration support for the independence of Estonia, Latvia, and Lithuania. Since the three countries regained their independence one year ago, the administration has supported and continues to support the withdrawal of all Russian forces from their territory at the earliest possible time, and has also provided substantial economic assistance. The administration's overriding objective is to help the three countries integrate themselves economically and politically with the West to ensure their future prosperity and their freedom.

Statement on Signing the Futures Trading Practices Act of 1992
October 28, 1992

Today I am signing into law H.R. 707, the "Futures Trading Practices Act of 1992." This forward-looking legislation is good for America's futures exchanges, good for farmers and ranchers who use futures, and good for U.S. financial markets. Indeed, this modernization of our financial laws will benefit everybody who works and invests in the American economy.

The bill contains an important provision sought by the Administration to give the Federal Reserve Board authority to oversee margin levels on stock index futures. The margin provision is crucial to help avoid the kinds of major market disruptions that occurred in October 1987 and October 1989. It is part of my Administration's continuing effort to adapt financial laws to the "one market" of stock and stock derivative products.

The bill also gives the Commodity Futures Trading Commission (CFTC) exemptive authority to remove the cloud of legal uncertainty over the financial instruments known as swap agreements. This uncertainty has threatened to disrupt the huge, global market for these transactions. The bill also will permit exemptions from the Commodity Exchange Act for hybrid financial products that can compete with futures products without the need for futures-style regulation.

The margin and exemptive authority reforms are critical for keeping U.S. financial markets strong and competitive. The Administration first requested them 2 years ago, and I am delighted that they now have been adopted.

The bill strengthens the ability of the CFTC to police the futures markets, impose tougher penalties on wrongdoers, and obtain assistance from foreign futures regulators. These provisions will further enhance the reputation of the United States as the safest and best place in the world to conduct trading.

Two provisions of the Act could be interpreted in a manner that would raise constitutional concerns and will, therefore, be construed so as to avoid those concerns.

Section 215 purports to direct me to appoint persons to the CFTC who meet certain congressionally mandated criteria. This provision raises constitutional concerns by appearing to circumscribe my power under the Appointments Clause to nominate officers of the United States. I shall treat the provision as containing advisory, rather than mandatory, criteria for appointment.

Section 213(a)(2) directs the CFTC to issue regulations specifying the circumstances under which the governing board of a contract market may issue, without prior CFTC approval but subject to CFTC suspension within 10 days, issue a temporary emergency market rule. To avoid any violation of the Appointments Clause of the Constitution, this section will be construed only to permit the CFTC to waive the usual statutory requirement that it approve such private market arrangements. So construed, the section does not vest exercise of significant governmental authority in the governing boards.

GEORGE BUSH

The White House,
October 28, 1992.

Note: H.R. 707, approved October 28, was assigned Public Law No. 102–546. This statement was released by the Office of the Press Secretary on October 29.

Statement on Signing the Housing and Community Development Act of 1992
October 28, 1992

Today I am signing into law H.R. 5334, the "Housing and Community Development Act of 1992." This bill establishes a sound regulatory structure for Government-sponsored enterprises (GSEs), combats money laundering, provides essential regulatory relief to financial institutions, authorizes several key Administration housing initiatives, and reduces the risk of lead-based paint poisoning.

This legislation addresses the problems created by the rapid expansion of certain

GSEs in the last decade. It establishes a means to protect taxpayers from the possible risks posed by GSEs in housing finance. The bill creates a regulator within the Department of Housing and Urban Development (HUD) to ensure that the housing GSEs are adequately capitalized and operated safely.

H.R. 5334 includes many of my Administration's regulatory relief proposals for depository institutions. The regulatory burden that the Congress has placed on our banking system has reached a staggering level that prevents banks from providing the credit that is necessary to assure economic growth. By reducing the regulatory burden, this bill will assist banks, borrowers, and the economy as a whole.

This legislation also improves the Federal Government's ability to combat money laundering. It penalizes financial institutions convicted of money laundering and strengthens Federal law enforcement capabilities significantly. These provisions create important new tools in fighting the war against illegal drugs and other serious criminal activities.

The bill allows Federal prosecutors to obtain orders forfeiting tens of millions of dollars in assets belonging to drug kingpins that have been moved from the United States to foreign lands. It also authorizes the Government to prosecute those who launder the proceeds of corrupt foreign banks in the United States.

The anti money-laundering provisions of the bill include authority to seize funds belonging to foreign banks involved in criminal activities when those funds are located in interbank accounts in the United States. Interbank accounts, of course, are used to facilitate the transactions of innocent third parties. Because of the potential impact on such transactions, it is important that this seizure authority be used judiciously and with attention to the effect such seizures might have on the interbank payment and clearing system. The Attorney General and the Secretary of the Treasury will work together to ensure coordinated review of such cases.

This legislation also advances the Federal Government's efforts to eliminate lead-based paint hazards, especially among those most vulnerable—young children. The bill would focus inspection and hazard reduction efforts by HUD on older housing stock where the incidence of lead paint is greatest. It also supports the development of State programs to certify contractors who engage in lead-based paint activities.

I regret, however, that the Congress chose to attach these important reforms to a housing bill that contains numerous provisions that raise serious concerns. My Administration worked diligently to craft a compromise housing bill that would target assistance where it is needed most, expand homeownership opportunities, ensure fiscal integrity, and empower recipients of Federal housing assistance.

I also note that two provisions of the bill must be narrowly construed to avoid constitutional difficulties. Section 1313 would authorize the Director of the newly established Office of Federal Housing Enterprise Oversight within HUD to submit "reports, recommendations, testimony, or comments" to the Congress without prior approval or review by "any officer or agency of the United States." The bill also provides the Director authority, exclusive of the Secretary of Housing and Urban Development, to promulgate safety and soundness regulations and to formulate an annual budget. When a member of the executive branch acts in an official capacity, the Constitution requires that I have the ultimate authority to supervise that officer in the exercise of his or her duties. In order to avoid constitutional difficulties, and without recognizing the Congress' authority to prevent the Secretary from supervising on my behalf an agency within HUD, I will interpret this provision to permit me to supervise the Director through other means, such as through the Office of Management and Budget.

Section 911 of the bill requires the Secretary of Housing and Urban Development to establish guidelines for housing credit agencies to "implement" section 102(d) of the Department of Housing and Urban Development Reform Act of 1989 (42 U.S.C. 3545(d)). That provision requires the Secretary to certify that HUD assistance to housing projects is not more than necessary to provide affordable housing, after taking other Federal and State assistance into account, and to adjust the amount of HUD assistance to compensate for changes in assistance amounts from other sources. To avoid the constitutional difficulties that would arise if section 911 were understood to vest in housing credit agencies the exercise of significant authority under Federal law, I interpret section 911 to permit the Secretary to formulate guidelines under which he will retain the ultimate authority to make the determinations required by section 102(d).

GEORGE BUSH

The White House,
October 28, 1992.

Note: H.R. 5334, approved October 28, was assigned Public Law No. 102–550. This statement was released by the Office of the Press Secretary on October 29.

Statement on Signing the Agricultural Credit Improvement Act of 1992
October 28, 1992

Today I am signing into law H.R. 6129, the "Agricultural Credit Improvement Act of 1992," which modifies the Farmers Home Administration program.

Although I have signed H.R. 6129, I will withhold my approval of H.R. 6138 because it is identical to section 24 of H.R. 6129.

GEORGE BUSH

The White House,
October 28, 1992.

Note: H.R. 6129, approved October 28, was assigned Public Law No. 102–554. This statement was released by the Office of the Press Secretary on October 29.

Statement on Signing the Defense Production Act Amendments of 1992
October 28, 1992

Today I have signed into law S. 347, the "Defense Production Act Amendments of 1992."

The Defense Production Act (DPA) provides the President with extraordinary authority to establish production and material allocation priorities when the national defense so requires. The DPA expired on March 1, 1992. Enactment of S. 347 restores that authority through September 30, 1995. The availability of these authorities to the President, in the event of unexpected national defense crises, enables him to ensure that the Nation will have the equipment and supplies it needs under all circumstances.

I must, however, note several reservations that I have regarding sections 124, 135, and 163. Section 124 requires the Secretary of Commerce to report to specified congressional committees on the impact of offset agreements between importers and exporters of American-made weapons systems. These agreements stipulate, as a precondition of a sale, that the exporter will partially compensate the importer—through either co-production, countertrade, or barter arrangements—for the purchase. The report is to include alternative findings or recommendations on offsets offered by heads of other departments and agencies to the Secretary. I sign this bill with the understanding that this provision does not detract from my constitutional authority to protect the executive branch deliberative process.

Section 135 requires the Government to keep a new data base on America's businesses. Under section 705 of the DPA, the Government is permitted, for the purpose of collecting information for the data base, to issue subpoenas to America's businesses, issue administrative search warrants to inspect the premises of America's businesses, and require America's businesses to keep records and make reports to the Government. Failure to comply with those Government requirements is punishable by a fine or up to 1 year in jail.

Collecting industrial base data from America's companies through the means provided in section 705 would intrude inappropriately in peacetime into the lives of Americans who own and work in the Nation's businesses. Such intrusion is neither necessary to meet U.S. national defense needs nor would be consistent with the liberties of those who own and work in America's businesses. Accordingly, I direct the affected heads of executive departments and agencies not to use subpoena, search warrant, or other intrusive techniques under the authority of section 705 of the Defense Production Act in implementing section 722 of the Act without the specific approval of the President. They will proceed instead to seek information from America's busi-

nesses on a voluntary basis. However, the provisions of section 705 may be used to support other programs and other provisions of the Defense Production Act, in accordance with current delegations of authority under section 705.

Section 163 requires a study on foreign investment in the United States and the possible motives of foreign investors. While this Administration will prepare such a study, I note again that I remain committed to the historic, open investment policy that I reaffirmed in my statement of December 26, 1991.

GEORGE BUSH

The White House,
October 28, 1992.

Note: S. 347, approved October 28, was assigned Public Law No. 102–558. This statement was released by the Office of the Press Secretary on October 29.

Statement on Signing the Audio Home Recording Act of 1992
October 28, 1992

Today I am signing into law S. 1623, the "Audio Home Recording Act of 1992," which will benefit American consumers, creators, and innovators.

S. 1623 will ensure that American consumers have access to equipment embodying the new digital audio recording technology. It also protects the legitimate rights of our songwriters, performers, and recording companies to be fairly rewarded for their tremendous talent, expertise, and capital investment. This will be accomplished by fairly compensating these artists for the copying of their works and by creating a system that will prevent unfettered copying of digital audio tapes.

This legislation sends an important message to unscrupulous competitors abroad. We will not stand by and allow the creativi-

ty and ingenuity of our people to be unfairly copied. We will vigorously fight attempts to copy the cutting-edge technologies developed by our biotechnology, chemical, and pharmaceutical industries; to copy our sought-after books, movies, and computer programs; and to copy the trademarks that represent the quality of the goods for which we are famous. We will protect the American jobs and exports represented by these American innovations.

GEORGE BUSH

The White House,
October 28, 1992.

Note: S. 1623, approved October 28, was assigned Public Law No. 102–563. This statement was released by the Office of the Press Secretary on October 29.

Remarks to the South Wayne County Chamber of Commerce in Southgate, Michigan
October 29, 1992

Thank you, John. Thank all of you very, very much. Please be seated. May I thank the Governor and say how pleased I am that he is leading our campaign in Michigan. There's no way that you can look at an electoral map or look at a map of this country and put priorities on States without realizing the significance that Michigan has for whoever is running for President. And I'm very encouraged with what John told me when we climbed off the plane. I'm encouraged with the way these polls that we live and die by are shaping up.

But today what I thought I'd do, after thanking Heinz Prechter, my old friend—I tell you, you get nervous just around the guy, he's so energetic. He is too much. He's got a thousand ideas. But I'll tell you something. The longer I've been in politics, the more I understand something that I think is a real verity, and that is, friendships really matter. You can tell them when things are tough, the friends that hang in there with you. Heinz has been at my side for some time, and I'm grateful to him. He is doing, as he modestly pointed out, a very good job on the exports. [*Laughter*] So I thank him for that.

I thank Omer and all the rest of you for being here from so many communities. What I thought I'd do today in hopefully a relaxed way—because we go off to these rallies where it's not particularly relaxed—is just make some comments on the economy and try to fairly, to objectively point out the differences that I have with Governor Clinton on this. I'd point out the differences I have with H. Ross on this, but I'm not sure exactly what they are because all he says is "fix it." Well, we want to fix it, but not by raising the gasoline tax 50 cents, I might add.

So, here we go. Governor Clinton—I honestly believe that they won't—could not win the election unless they convince everybody that the economy is really worse than it is. That led Governor Clinton to say, this is the worst economy in 50 years. It led

a rebuttal from the Wall Street Journal editorial, saying this is talking the biggest economic lies in 50 years.

It isn't the worst economy. You only have to go back to the Jimmy Carter years when you had those interest rates up at 21 percent and inflation that touched 15 percent before you realize that they—and they invented the "misery index," unemployment and inflation—it was double what it is now, even though we've been through extraordinarily difficult times.

Governor Clinton says we have the— wages are 13th in the world. Our total compensation leads the world. Many of you business people know that the cost of doing business is not simply wages, it is the total package, and total compensation leads the world. That is a good point.

On industrial decline: Governor Clinton says we have industrial decline. He says our economy is somewhere less than Germany but more than Sri Lanka. Well, he ought to get around the world a little bit to understand that we, in spite of our economic difficulties, have an economy that's better than Japan, better than Germany, better than Canada, better than Western Europe, and certainly Eastern Europe and the struggling economies that have just come out from behind the Iron Curtain.

Our farmers, our workers are the world's most productive. Productivity is going up in this country. And the U.S. is gaining manufacturing market. We hear about our manufacturing base being shipped overseas; not so. We are gaining manufacturing market. And yes, some of the companies and maybe some of your businesses have had to streamline, be a little more efficient, modernize. But I do believe that because you've done that, we are poised for a vigorous recovery with interest rates and inflation, as John Engler and Heinz both said, moving towards decade-worth lows there.

Clinton talks about the trickle-down policies benefiting the rich. The fact of it is that the rich pay a higher percentage of the total taxes than in 1980 and then in the years before that. The reduction in the capital gains and in the top level, even though I want a greater capital gains reduction, led to a bigger percentage of the tax burden being paid by the rich.

Governor Clinton says we can't compete with Japan and Germany; not so. We are the number one exporter. Exports have saved us in these extraordinarily difficult times of global recession, and now I would say global slowdown. Our exports are up 40 percent. They're going to go up more if I accomplish my aim of more free and fair trade agreements.

Governor Clinton talks about a deep recession, bordering on depression. That is simply not true. For a person out of work, it's depression. I'll admit that, and I'll say, listen, we want to help you with job retraining, better education, stimulating the growth of the small business sector so we can create more jobs. Yes, for a person out of work it doesn't matter what you call it, recession, depression; that family is hurting.

But in terms of the overall economy, it isn't true. We have grown now, albeit anemically, for six straight quarters. The technical definition of recession has always been two quarters of negative growth. We have had growth for six straight quarters. And the worst news in the world for Clinton and Gore—and I will admit it surprised us a little—was when the growth came out at 2.7 for the third quarter. That's pretty darn good turnaround here, beginning. It's not robust growth, but it's far more impressive than obviously all these economists had been predicting. So we are not in a recession. We're fixing to move, and we're moving with some of our fundamentals in far better shape.

He always talks about, "Well, the worst since Herbert Hoover." And that is because they don't want to talk about what it was like when we had a Democratic President and a Democratic Congress. That was when we had the Carter years of malaise. Remember the word? Again, the "misery index," a standard that was invented by the Democrats to try to embarrass us, it is half the "misery index" of what it was when Jimmy Carter went out of office.

We have had six quarters of growth. The last one, as I say, was 2.7. And if you look, and some of you all know this, we are growing much better than Japan and Germany. Germany had negative growth for the last month. Japan was half of our growth when it was 1.7. So it is not fair to try to scare the American people and tell them how bad everything is.

We are in a global economy, and that's one reason I think international affairs and understanding of the world matter. Because I am convinced that if we do what we must do in exports, it's the United States that's going to lead the world, not just for United States economy but for the global economy. So we are doing better than those trading partners that Governor Clinton keeps holding up to us as an image.

We've got another difference. Eastern Europe and certainly Russia and other countries, because of our policies, I think, peace through strength—and I salute my predecessor—are free now, and they're democratic, and they are moving. They're moving away from the very kinds of policy that Governor Clinton's talking about. He talks about Government investing. Government does not create productive jobs. The private sector does. This is perhaps the most major difference I have with him in the economic field. It is not the Government that creates jobs.

He wants to get more money, $220 billion in new spending right off the top. And I want to hold the line, constrain the growth of the mandatory spending programs, get them under control because they're the ones that are increasing this deficit all the time, and then stimulate growth. Invest, if you will, but have the private sector do it through investment tax allowance or first-time homebuyers tax credit or capital gains. The Democrats have called capital gains a break for the rich. It is no such thing. We get a proper level of capital gains, it will spur entrepreneurship and spur creativity in starting new businesses.

Governor Clinton says, "Well, I'm a different kind of Democrat," but his tax increase that he's already proposed of $150 billion that he says he'll get from the rich—no way—is more than Mondale and Dukakis said to start, for openers. You add those two together, and Clinton's approach is higher. And I just don't believe, even if we were not in a very slow economic growth period, I just don't believe that taking more of the GDP in taxes is the answer. So we've got a fundamental difference on that.

Clinton asked the other morning how much things cost. And I would simply remind him what it would have been like if we'd have continued with the Carter rates of inflation. Take milk today, what, $2.70, say. It would have been something like $8.23 if that rate of inflation had continued. Gasoline—I don't even—different prices in different communities. But you can get it for, what, $1.19, $1.25. If you use that math to continue their inflation, you'd be in orbit, 56 bucks. [*Laughter*] So I think that may be a little unfair to project that inflation rate, but that's what we were up against. We forget that as a nation. We simply cannot go back to policies that brought that out.

People have been able to refinance their mortgages because we brought the interest rates down. People say, "Well, are you better off than you were?" Well, it depends who you're talking to. If you can refinance your home and save $600, $700, maybe $2,000 in a year, you're better off, provided you're working. If you're a senior citizen and your interest rates are—your inflation rate is down, you are far better off than if you'd stayed there with anything like the Carter rate of inflation, because you would have had your savings disappear, blow up right in front of your eyes.

Also in a foreign affairs sense, if you're a kid you're better off because you grow up with less fear of nuclear war. And if you're an ethnic American, and there's plenty of them around this State of Michigan, you're better off because your parents and your family are growing up under freedom and democracy and not under the yoke of communism.

So that question that they try to use against me I think should be selectively asked. I think that in totality a lot of people would be better off. Again, that doesn't mean we shouldn't empathize with and feel great compassion for those who are hurting and those who are out of work.

I have a big difference with Governor Clinton on exports. A billion dollars in exports creates 20,000 new jobs. And I hear a lot of talk out of Governor Clinton on the free trade agreement. You heard the debate. He tries to have it both ways.

I've discovered as President, you can't do that. You can't say on the one hand, and then on the other. You can't be for the NAFTA agreement one day and then have caveats the next. You can't be for right-to-work in one State, and then oppose it when you talk to the union leaders in another State. You can't be for the CAFE standards when you're trying to win over the Sierra Club, and then come up here and tell the workers that you don't mean it.

So we have a big difference on exports. And I believe the North American free trade agreement will create jobs. I'm absolutely convinced it will create 200,000 jobs. I want to see that followed with trade agreements with Chile. I want to see it with Eastern Europe. And let's never forget we are a Pacific power as well, and free and fair trade with access to those markets under a much freer basis will mean jobs for the American worker.

So we have a big difference in how we approach the market, how we approach the marketplace. And I know that there's some people that get dislocated, but very few when you look at the totality of new jobs. And for those you have a vigorous retraining program. We've proposed one that I think will take care of the requirements.

I also get asked, particularly in Michigan, about "Well, why won't all the jobs be shipped to Mexico?" Or I get charged by Governor Clinton and the Ozone Man—[*laughter*]—saying that all the jobs will be switched down to Mexico. My rhetorical question is, if labor rates are the basis for shipping companies overseas, how come Haiti isn't the industrial capital of the world, or Mexico, today? It isn't. I read in the paper that General Motors might bring 1,000 jobs back from Mexico. So we should not let them scare the American people by this siren's song of protection. It does not work. It shrinks markets and puts people out of work.

So in all of these areas we have a major difference. I still feel that my idea of stimulating investment for small business that I clicked off a minute ago, with less regulation, less taxes, is a far better way to go than the investing in America through the Government taking your money and trying to invest it.

On health care, I've got a big difference. Governor Clinton wants a payroll tax for health care and training. He says he doesn't, but his program would lead to that. And mine, through tax credits and vouchers to the poorest of the poor, for the vouchers and for relief for the next bracket and pooling of insurance and doing something about these crazy malpractice suits that cost 25 to 50 billion dollars, is the way to go.

He wants to set up a Government board. A Government board ends up in rationing health care. And we've got the best quality of health care in the world. And the way to keep it up is to keep the system as private as possible and not slap a 7 percent payroll tax on small business. So we've got a big difference on that.

I believe that the answer to being competitive in the future is education. But again, Clinton's program is to go for expanding mandated programs. And ours, America 2000 is for getting the teachers and the parents and the community involved in revolutionizing schools through our New American Schools Corporation, but not emphasizing the bureaucracy or catering to the NEA, which is a powerful union which has simply presided over the building up of educational bureaucracy. So I've got a big difference on education.

One of the biggest areas of difference that affects the economy is the area of legal reform. I touched on it, but the Arkansas trial lawyers head says, "Well, the Governor has never stood against us at all." You look at where the funds come from for the campaigns, and they are in his corner 100 percent. The costs in this are just absolutely outrageous. I have sent legislation up after legislation to put a cap on some of these outrageous liability claims, because we are suing each other too much and caring for each other too little in this country. And we've got to do something about it.

I believe on health—well, I mentioned the health care plan.

On CAFE standards, this one I have a very big difference with him. In Lansing,

Governor Clinton said, and I will give you the quote, "I defy anyone to find where we said it should be in legislation." But here is the Bill Clinton national energy strategy, and here is a quote in that, "I support an increase in corporate average fuel economy standards. The 45-miles-per-gallon standard should be incorporated into national legislation."

Now, in my view, that would throw an awful lot of auto workers out of work. Every automotive expert says to meet those 45-mile-per-gallon, say nothing of 40, standards would be a tremendous burden and almost scientifically impossible for tomorrow on the auto industry. And I don't think that's what we need to do in order to get this industry moving again. So I have a very big difference on that one.

I mentioned regulation generally. Some of that is legislative. And very candidly, I must accept some of the responsibility for the executive branch. We have put a freeze on legislation. All I want you to know is we are going to try to do a superb job on lifting the regulatory burden. On the Clean Air Act and on the Americans for Disability Act, we've had to put, understandably, put in a lot of new regulations. But we put the freeze on on a lot of other ones, and I believe that will lift the burden on those of you who are in the small-business sector.

Again, our biggest difference, a biggest difference, is on spending and taxes versus trying to hold the line on both. The mandatory growth programs are the ones that are totally out of control. And our program is to put a cap on them. Let them grow to inflation, and let them grow to population increases, but no more. That does mean that there's going to be some tough decisions as you sort out which of those programs can't grow as rapidly as they'd been growing heretofore. But it is the only way we're going to get it down.

Then with it, I call for the following disciplinary actions. One is a balanced budget amendment to the Constitution. We almost had it done, passed the Senate, passed the House. Then the leadership, who oppose it—those same leaders that have been in charge for 38 years in the Congress—whipped about eight or nine cosponsors of the legislation into changing their vote after they had voted for it. That is simply outrageous. And I believe that we can get that done in the next session of Congress, because you're going to have at least 100, maybe 150 new Members of Congress. Why? Because the crazy guys that are running it out there can't even control a two-bit bank or a two-bit post office. I mean, people have lost confidence in them, and that's why you're going to have such a big turnover. So we've got to get that balanced budget amendment.

I want that check-off where people that are concerned about the deficit can put a check in their box—tax return for 10 percent of their taxes to go for one thing, lowering the deficit. Then Congress, under this proposal, will have to do it. If they can't do it on a priority basis, you have what's known as a sequester, and that goes across the board. Tough medicine, but we're going to have to do something about it.

The third point is the line-item veto. Forty-three Governors have it. It in itself will not permit the budget to get in balance, but along with these other things it would be of enormous, enormous benefit. I have a couple of bills sitting there right now that I have to make a decision on in the next couple of days that could be altered and made satisfactory if I had a line-item veto, and I don't. I think the American people are strongly supportive.

And the last one, point four on all this, is that I do believe it's time for the Congress to have the same limitations a President does, not in length of term, but I'm talking about term limits on the Members of the Congress. It's a way to give it back to the people, and I believe that that time has come to do that. Presidents serve 8 years, and I think Members of Congress should serve 12 and then go on home and let somebody else have a shot at it. Congress was not set up to be a year-round self-perpetuating organization. So we're going to— I'm going to take that case to the American people.

There are many other differences. But I just wanted to dwell a little bit on the economic side.

Let me simply say in conclusion, I agree things have dramatically changed out in the country. Some of it is because I think people now realize that though we have economic difficulties, the economy is not as sick as the opposition would have you believe.

I had a little contretemps with one of the more famous news commentators this morning. He asked about this, and I said, "Well, what do you expect the American people to think when 92 percent of the news on the network news is negative? By accident, you ought to be able to make it up to 10 percent positive." [*Laughter*] The unemployment is down. Unemployment is down for 3 straight months, and the 3d month out comes the headline on the evening news, "Bad news for President Bush: job market shrinks." I mean, come on, unemployment is down for 3 straight months, and that's a good thing. In fact, unemployment claims, even though they ooched up a tiny bit now, are for the last 3 or 4 months at all-time lows, which is encouraging in terms of what it says about the fundamentals of this economy.

So, when you see me holding up that bumper sticker that says "Annoy the Media. Reelect Bush," I hope you'll understand it is not simply out of frustration. It is simply that I think they've lost in this election year all productivity—objectivity—productivity they've always lost—[*laughter*]—but objectivity. And my point on all that is, hey, don't let it get you down. Just say what Harry Truman said: "There's 50 of them covering the White House, and none of them know enough to pound sand in a rat's hole." That was Harry Truman, not George Bush. So I can quote him and be gentle and kind with these guys. [*Laughter*]

I'll tell you, I've had enough. I know you've suffered enough here, but let me just point out, I hold up that bumper sticker, and everybody knows exactly what we're talking about. I'm not asking for sympathy. I'm asking just that it be judged. And you see, the media, the national media now holding little seminars on Ted Koppel at night, "Have we been truly fair? Have we been objective?" Koppel did that down in Houston with a nonpartisan audience, and he said, "Now, if you think we've been unfair to George Bush, please clap."

They're still clapping down there. [*Laughter*] And he sat there very—ooh, and it went on and on and on.

The point is, the good thing about a campaign is, you take your message to the people. What I was going to say is, if you don't get—if you feel the same way as I do about "Annoy the Media. Reelect Bush," don't take it out on the cameramen. Some people get so excited there, they were jabbing the American flag into the back of these poor guys. These are the good guys. The people traveling with us are the good guys. Save your wrath for those faithless Republicans and faithless Democrats who wrote me off about 2 months ago, because we are going to show that rat hole that we're going to win this election. We're going to win it. I'm afraid this was a little boring today, but we're going to win it because there is a reality out there, and the American people understand it.

Then there's a subject that never even comes up anymore, world peace, democracy, freedom, less fear of nuclear war. I believe that those are pretty good things. Then the last ingredient, when people go into the booth, they're going to say, "Look, Bush may have screwed this up. At least he admits it when he does." What we teach my kids to do; make a mistake, admit it, go on about leading the country.

But in the final analysis they're going to ask themselves the question: Who do I trust? Who would I trust with my family? And who would I trust with a crisis coming up, whether it's domestic or international? I've worked hard, and so has Barbara Bush, I might add, to earn the trust of the American people. That's what I think is beginning to happen. I think people are asking themselves that serious question.

And I obviously wouldn't like to see this many people assembled—if I said I need your support, I need your vote. Do it on the basis of economics, character, trust, whatever it is, I don't care. I want you to vote.

Thank you very, very much.

Note: The President spoke at 11:50 a.m. at the Ramada Heritage Center. In his remarks, he referred to Gov. John Engler of Michigan; Heinz Prechter, chairman and chief executive officer, American Sun Corp.; and Omer O'Neil, president, South Wayne County Chamber of Commerce.

Remarks to the Community in Macomb County, Michigan
October 29, 1992

The President. What a great welcome. Thank you very much. Thank you, Governor Engler. You guys are fired up, and that makes me feel like victory is ours.

May I start by singling out my friend Bruce Willis. I'm proud to have this guy at our side here and very grateful. And, of course, if you want to win a race in Michigan, you'd better have Governor John Engler at your side. And may also I salute Congressman Bill Broomfield, who's leaving the Congress, but a great Member of Congress, and I'm very proud of him; thank State Senator Carl; and then say this: Everyplace you go people yell, "Clean House!" Clean House. Do your part now. Send John Pappageorge up there, Doug Carl. Of course, I'm grateful to Senator DiNello for being with us today, a man of conviction, that puts conviction ahead of party.

Hey listen, may I thank these seven high school bands that are with us today, great!

[*At this point, there was a disturbance in the audience.*]

The President. We'll get them. You know, last week—I want to mention the Utah—look at these characters. Kind of sad, isn't it? A little pathetic.

Audience members. Boo-o-o!

The President. A little pathetic. They feel it slipping away from them. They know it's moving away from them. They know we're going to win the election.

I'm delighted to be here. And the decision that people make is going to be a tremendous difference, a vast difference on experience, a difference on philosophy, and yes, a difference on character. Character matters.

You know, I hate to ruin this beautiful rally, but let me just tell you a little bit about the Arkansas record.

Audience members. Boo-o-o!

The President. Yes, I'm sorry. I've got to do it. Here's the way they stand after 10 years of Governor Clinton. They are 50th in the quality of environmental concerns. They are 50th in the percentage of adults with a college degree. That's it. They are 50th in per capita spending on criminal justice. They are 49th in per capita spending on police protection.

Audience members. Boo-o-o!

The President. They are 48th in percentage of adults with a high school diploma.

Audience members. Boo-o-o!

The President. Forty-eighth in backing up their police and spending on corrections.

Audience members. Boo-o-o!

The President. Forty-sixth on teachers' salaries; 45th in the overall well-being of children. And Governor Clinton says, "I want to do for America what I've done for Arkansas." No way!

You know, Governor Clinton said in the debate that they were number one in job growth. That's true for one year, and during that year he was out of the State 85 percent of the time. For the other 10 years, they were 30 percent of the national average. We cannot let him do that to the United States of America.

Governor Clinton says he's the candidate of change. He wants to sock a $150 billion tax increase to the working man, and we're not going to let him do that. He talks about investing, let the Government do it. I want to get small business to create more jobs, not the Government. You remember what it was like before. He wants that trickle-down Government, and we want business to provide jobs in the private sector.

You know, Governor Clinton and the Ozone Man, that's the guy that wants to put a 45-mile-per-gallon gas fuel efficiency standard on the auto business.

Audience members. Boo-o-o!

The President. How would the auto workers like that one? They'd be losing jobs

hand over fist. But the last time we tried the kind of change he's talking about, the last time Democrats had the White House and that spendthrift Congress, inflation was 15 percent and interest rates were 21 percent. We are not going to go back to those kind of standards.

Change, Governor Clinton and Ozone, they just keep talking about change, change, change. That's all you will have left in your pocket if Governor Clinton becomes President of the United States. That's it.

No, the last time we had that kind of inflation rate that Gore and Clinton would take us to, it was up there at there, as I said, inflation 15 percent, interest 20 percent. Now, how would you like that? If we'd stayed at their rate of inflation, milk, which costs, what, $2.70, would be $8.23. That's what would happen.

Audience members. Boo-o-o!

The President. Bread, 84 cents, would be up about $2.50. We cannot go back to that Clinton-Gore inflation by raising taxes and raising spending.

Now, there's been some bad news. There's been some very bad news for Clinton and Gore. It comes out that we are not in a deep recession. We grew 2.7 percent. And these guys are weeping tears.

The only way they can win is to tell everybody everything isn't worth a darn. They criticize our country and say we are less than Germany and slightly better than Sri Lanka. My dog Millie knows more about foreign affairs than these two bozos. It's crazy. Let them tear down the country. Let us all build it up by getting this economy moving.

No, the economy's beginning to move, and we've got to be sure we keep it moving so every American that's hurting has a job with dignity in the private sector. And my plan does just exactly that: control the growth of spending, keep the lid on those taxes, relieve business from regulation.

Let's do something about these crazy lawsuits. Governor Clinton is right in the pocket of the trail lawyers. We ought to put limits on these lawsuits. And it is my view that we ought to care for each other more and sue each other less.

We can do it. We're going to get the

change done, because the Democrats fouled up the Congress. They can't run a two-bit bank, and they can't run a two-bit post office; so, so many of them are going to get kicked out that we can move this country ahead. Clean House! Clean House! Clean them out! Get rid of them all! Bring more guys in like Bill Broomfield, and get this thing moving.

You know, it's small business that creates the jobs. Two-thirds of the new jobs are small business. They need not more regulation. They need relief from regulation, relief from taxation, and relief from lawsuits.

On health care, Governor Clinton wants a board, a Government board to set the prices. I want to free up the private market to provide insurance to the poorest of the poor through vouchers; the next tax bracket, to give them a tax break; and to let it be said that the Government can't run health care, the private insurance can. We want to give everybody insurance. Give them vouchers and give them tax credits, and let's get going, and let's keep the quality of health care up. Don't get the Government trying to set prices.

We'll be able to get it done this time because we're going to have at least 150 new Members of Congress. The gridlock will be gone.

As I look around here one of the main things we've got to do it make our education system—we're going to clean the House, you're right. And I want to bypass the NEA and get the teachers a chance to reform these schools. I want the parents to have the choice and the ability to make that choice, public, private, and religious schools. Give the parents a choice.

Very candidly, on another subject, I've got big differences with Governor Clinton on crime. You know, the other day eight people came up to see me in the Oval Office, and they said, "We are for you." They were the Fraternal Order of Police from Little Rock, Arkansas, endorsing me for President of the United States.

The answer is to back our police officers. Get the gridlock guys in Congress to give us stronger anticrime legislation, and let's have more sympathy for the victim of crime and a little less for the criminal.

Governor Clinton has had about four economic plans, and he's given up on the budget deficit. Let me give you three ideas. How about a balanced budget amendment to the Constitution. How about a check-off for taxpayers, say 10 percent of your taxes must go for reducing that deficit. And how about giving me what 43 Governors have, a line-item veto. They can't do it; let the President do it.

Here's another one for you: Why not give the Congress back to the people. The President's terms are limited to 8 years. Let's limit the Members of Congress' terms.

But I guess the biggest difference of all, the biggest difference of all, relates to character and trust. Let me just say this: You cannot be President if you try to be all things to all people. You cannot say, "On the one hand I'm for this"; "but I am" on the other. You cannot have a lot of "buts" in the Oval Office. You've got to look the American people in the eye and call them as you see them. If you make a mistake, you say so. But you don't waffle. We cannot turn the White House into the waffle house.

Governor Clinton is on all sides of all issues, and there is a pattern of deception. Let me tell you about the decision to go to war. It was not an easy decision. We were fought by a lot of the media. We were fought by a lot in the Congress. And here's what Governor Clinton said, he said, "I agreed with the minority,"—that was the Democrat's—"but I guess I would have voted with the majority." You cannot be a Commander in Chief and waffle around. That is character. That is character.

I heard Governor Clinton raise the character question yesterday. Well, come on in. Let's take it on on character and trust.

I see these veterans here. I see these veterans here, and I welcome their support. Let me tell you one difference. I'll be honest with you. I don't think it is right when your brothers are in a prison in Hanoi or kids are being drafted out of the ghetto, to go over and lead, organize demonstrations in a foreign land against your country when it's in war. That's a big difference. That's a big difference. That is a big, big difference.

I don't think you have to have served in

the service, but I do think it helps if you want to be Commander in Chief, so you can hold your head up and look at these young men and women you have to send into battle.

No, the differences are between night and day. Look, if you listen to Governor Clinton and Ozone Man, if you listen to them—you know why I call him Ozone Man? This guy is so far off in the environmental extreme, we'll be up to our neck in owls and out of work for every American. This guy's crazy. He is way out, far out. Far out, man. Hey, listen, do you think he would save General Motors by slapping more regulation on them? Less regulation. Less taxes. Bring that back.

But you listen, as I say, if you listen to Governor Clinton and Senator Gore, you'd think that foreign affairs don't matter. Let me tell you something. I take great pride in the fact that the young kids go to bed at night without the same fear of nuclear war that their parents had. That is a major accomplishment. Ancient enemies are talking peace. Democracy is on the move. Imperial communism is dead. Now what I want to do is take that same leadership and, with the help of a new Congress, lift up every family in America and give them a shot at the American dream.

So in the final analysis, one of the reasons we're moving is because I think people are focusing now as they get down to the wire on who has the trust and the character to lead. Let me tell you something, let me tell you, Barbara Bush—and I think we've got a great First Lady, as a matter of fact—she and I have tried to uphold the trust. And you know, we're lucky, 12 grandchildren and 5 kids and a good life. But let me tell you something: I want to finish the job I have started. I want to help those young people here today to understand that the American dream is still alive.

So as we drive down the wire, the train rolling, I look you in the eye, and I say, I ask for your support. And I ask for your vote, based on character and trust. Let's lead the world to new heights of prosperity for every single American. Don't let them tear it down.

God bless America. Thank you all very much. Thank you.

Note: The President spoke at 1:42 p.m. in the gymnasium at Macomb Community College. In his remarks, he referred to Douglas Carl and Gilbert J. DiNello, Michigan State senators.

Statement on Signing the National Oceanic and Atmospheric Administration Authorization Act of 1992
October 29, 1992

Today I am signing into law H.R. 2130, the "National Oceanic and Atmospheric Administration Authorization Act of 1992." In signing this bill I must, however, note several concerns.

First, the imposition of procedural obstacles could create delays in efforts to modernize the National Weather Service. Such delays would hamper our efforts to improve the Nation's weather forecasting system, especially with regard to severe storms. The delays could add significantly to the cost and quality of the modernization program. Nonetheless, the Administration will interpret the provisions of this Act to minimize the costs and delay of weather service modernization, and proceed expeditiously with current plans to provide advanced weather service technology.

Second, a number of provisions of the bill raise constitutional concerns. Accordingly, I sign this bill with the following understandings:

(1) Requirements to transmit reports to the Congress or particular congressional committees apply only to final recommendations that have been reviewed and approved by the appropriate officials within the executive branch.

(2) Provisions requiring an executive agency to consult with another executive agency or private group concerning executive policy do not dictate the decision making structure or chain of command of the executive branch deliberative process.

(3) The members of any advisory committee or private group who have not been appointed as officers of the United States in conformity with the Appointments Clause of the Constitution may perform only advisory or ceremonial functions.

Further, I understand that the term "significant subsidy" for a shipyard in section 607 applies only to those subsidies enumerated in section 607(b)(1–8) to the extent that they are significant in value. Without such an interpretation, the provision could be inconsistent with our international trade obligations and practices. It could also have the unintended consequence of interfering with NOAA's purchase of virtually any ship.

GEORGE BUSH

The White House,
October 29, 1992.

Note: H.R. 2130, approved October 29, was assigned Public Law No. 102–567.

Statement on Signing the Rehabilitation Act Amendments of 1992
October 29, 1992

Today I am signing into law H.R. 5482, the "Rehabilitation Act Amendments of 1992." H.R. 5482 extends and improves important programs under the Rehabilitation Act of 1973, a law that directly affects the lives of millions of Americans with disabilities. I am particularly pleased that major provisions contained in the Administration's proposal for reauthorization of the Act are included in the bill.

The scope of the Rehabilitation Act is broad. It provides for partnerships among the Federal, State, and private sectors to help Americans with disabilities participate more fully in the economic and social life of our Nation. Vocational rehabilitation, client assistance, independent living services and centers, and projects with industry are only some of the activities authorized under the Act.

Increased emphasis on program results, provider accountability, and client choice are the hallmarks of H.R. 5482. The Act requires that performance indicators and evaluation standards be developed for the $1.8 billion Basic State Grant program. These requirements are the key to ensuring continuing improvements in services provided under the largest program in the Act. This legislation will further our efforts to make consumer choice a tool for strengthening government services. Additional reforms afford clients a greater voice in their rehabilitation plans and authorize the Secretary of Education to demonstrate other ways in which client choice of services and providers can be increased in vocational rehabilitation. Finally, the Act authorizes model projects that give underemployed workers with disabilities the opportunity to acquire the knowledge and skills they need to advance.

Just over 2 years ago, I signed into law the landmark Americans with Disabilities Act of 1990, which marked the end of the wrongful segregation and exclusion of individuals with disabilities from the mainstream of American life. In signing H.R. 5482, I am pleased once again to emphasize my commitment to ending discrimination against Americans with disabilities and ensuring their full integration into our Nation's workplaces and communities.

GEORGE BUSH

The White House,
October 29, 1992.

Note: H.R. 5482, approved October 29, was assigned Public Law No. 102–569.

Statement on Signing the Indian Health Amendments of 1992
October 29, 1992

Today I am signing into law S. 2481, the "Indian Health Amendments of 1992." S. 2481 reauthorizes appropriations for health services for American Indians and Alaska Natives.

S. 2481 continues Indian scholarship and training programs, thereby assuring an available source of health care professionals to serve American Indian and Alaska Native communities. In addition, the bill expands primary and preventive health programs, emphasizing mental as well as physical health. The bill's other significant new or expanded activities include the encouragement of Native Americans to enroll in Medicare and Medicaid, continued services to urban Native Americans, and expansion of substance abuse programs.

S. 2481 also contains specific health care objectives drawn from the U.S. Public Health Service's "Healthy People 2000" report and ties the allocation of resources to these objectives. This new approach will prove useful in measuring progress toward the goal of raising the health status of American Indians and Alaska Natives to the highest possible level.

Although S. 2481 clearly contains a number of provisions to improve the health of Native Americans and Alaska Natives, it also includes provisions that are problematic. For example, the bill prohibits third-party collections from self-insured health plans for services provided by the Indian Health Service (IHS). This prohibition actually reduces the number of Native Americans and Alaska Natives who can be served and sets an undesirable precedent. In addition, the establishment of yet more categorical authorities in S. 2481, especially grants for specified tribes or tribal organizations, is counterproductive to a rational allocation of limited resources.

Finally, S. 2481 also includes a "Buy American" provision that directs the IHS to comply with the requirements of the Buy American Act with respect to its construction procurements. This provision will not apply to the extent that I determine it would violate the Nation's international obligations under the General Agreement on Tariffs and Trade or any other international agreement to which this country is a party.

GEORGE BUSH

The White House,
October 29, 1992.

Note: H.R. 2481, approved October 29, was assigned Public Law No. 102–573.

Statement on Signing the Hawaii Tropical Forest Recovery Act
October 29, 1992

Today I have signed into law S. 2679, the "Hawaii Tropical Forest Recovery Act." This Act demonstrates our intent as a Nation to conserve and protect irreplaceable tropical forests and to provide world leadership in stemming the decline of these forests. It allows us to meet our obligations to the principles of forest management, conservation, and sustainable development that were established at the recent United Nations Conference on Environment and Development (UNCED).

My Administration's "Forests for the Future" initiative, which I announced on June 1, 1992, has provided the policy framework for the enactment of this legislation. This initiative places conservation of the Earth's forests as a top priority for our country. For this purpose the United States is committed to new funding, partnerships with other governments and interested organizations, and actions to address the needs of our domestic forests.

Expansion of the Institute of Pacific Islands Forestry in Hawaii is a concrete step in meeting the challenge of fulfilling the domestic and international goals of Forests for the Future and tropical forest conservation generally. This Act will permit the Institute to serve as a center for transferring scientific, technical, managerial, and administrative assistance to organizations at home and abroad that seek to improve the management of tropical forests.

Almost two-thirds of Hawaii's original forest cover has been lost over the last three centuries. This loss has severely affected the State's diverse ecosystems, which are among the most fragile and complex in the world. To better understand these changes and to develop means to conserve these forests for human and ecological needs, this Act authorizes the establishment of the Hawaii Experimental Tropical Forest. This experimental forest will serve as a

center for long-term research and a focal point for developing and transferring knowledge and expertise for the management of tropical forests.

This Administration has sponsored many initiatives, such as the "America the Beautiful" and the "Urban and Community Forestry" programs that have resulted in millions of new trees being planted in our country. With our Forests for the Future initiative as a foundation, the Hawaii Tropical Forest Recovery Act is another important aspect of our overall commitment to understanding and wisely using the resources of the world's forests.

GEORGE BUSH

The White House,
October 29, 1992.

Note: S. 2679, approved October 29, was assigned Public Law No. 102–574.

Remarks to the Community in Grand Rapids, Michigan
October 29, 1992

The President. Thank you very much. May I start by paying my respects and giving my profound thanks to Gerald R. Ford, a great President, a wonderful friend, and a terrific guy.

You guys are fired up. Of course, I am very proud that John Engler is running our campaign. I believe I've learned a lesson for John. A couple of years ago, the pollsters, the media, if you'll excuse the expression——

Audience members. Boo-o-o!

The President. No, no, wait a minute. No, they said he had no chance, that he was 10 points back a night before the election. And here he is, Governor of Michigan. And he's a great Governor.

May I also thank Bruce Willis who is with us. I'll tell you, and you know, everywhere I go, everywhere I go I see signs yelling, "Clean House!" Why don't you help by sending Pete Hoekstra to the United States Congress. There's one right there.

I'm delighted to be here with your party

leaders Chuck Yob, Dick and Betsy DeVos, Dave Doyle. We have a great team going. And let me just say this: Michigan is absolutely essential. We must and we will win the State of Michigan.

Audience members. Four more years! Four more years! Four more years!

The President. May I also just ask for a minute. I'd like to just say a word about a man who is not well today, the great Congressman Paul Henry. As many of you know, he's in the hospital recovering from surgery. Barbara and I just wish him a speedy recovery, joining all who love him in that regard. And our prayers are with the entire Henry family.

Now on to the election. The choice before the American people is a vast difference on experience, philosophy, and yes, character. Character matters. I heard Bruce Willis clicking off some of this, but let me just remind you, for 11 months Governor Clinton and the rest of the liberal Democrats have been running around saying what's wrong with my record. Let me just tell you briefly about his record. It is terrible. So you won't like it, but here it is.

They are 50th in environmental quality; 50th in percentage of adults with a college degree; 50th in per capita spending on criminal justice; 49th on police protection; 48th in percentage of adults with a high school diploma; 48th in spending for corrections; 46th on teachers' salaries; and 45th in the overall well-being of children. And in the debate the other night he says, "I want to do for America what I've done for Arkansas." No way! No way!

The President. He brags on the fact that last year, one year, they led the Nation in jobs created. That was the year he was out of the State for 85 percent of the time. And for 10 years, for 10 years they were 30 percent of the national average. We need somebody that's going to stimulate investment in small business, not tax and spend some more.

Governor Clinton—all they do is talk about change, change, change, change. Now, here's his idea of change: $150 billion in new taxes, $220 billion in new spending, trickle-down Government, numbers that don't add up, and a middle class—let me tell you this, if these guys come in, watch your wallet. They're going after the taxpayer. And that deficit will explode. It will blow up right in your face.

The last time we had a liberal Democrat in the White House and a Democrat controlling the Congress, do you remember how things were? We got change, all right. We got interest rates at 21 percent. We got inflation at 15 percent. And we got a "misery index" of 20. We do not need that kind of change.

Audience members. Four more years! Four more years! Four more years!

The President. Change is all you'll have in your pocket if you put that guy into the White House.

Audience members. Four more years! Four more years! Four more years!

The President. Now, here's the bad news for Clinton and the Ozone Man. Here it is. You know who I mean by the Ozone Man. I'll tell you why I call—he and Governor Clinton, Ozone and Clinton—[*laughter*]—they want to put CAFE standards—that's

the fuel efficiency standards—at 40 to 45 miles per gallon on the auto industry. That will throw a lot of Grand Rapids and other people out of work. And we're not going to let it happen.

Audience members. Boo-o-o!

The President. But the bad news for them is this. The bad news for them is there was very good news for this country 2 days ago. And they hate it. They hate it. The only way they can win is to convince America we're in a recession. We had growth of 2.7. We have grown for six quarters. And now let's keep it going.

There's a lot of people hurting. There's a lot of people hurting and worried about jobs. But the last thing we need is to go back to the failed policies of the past. Let's have the United States of America lead the worldwide recovery that will bring jobs to more Americans.

And here's how we're going to do it. We're going to open up new markets. America's the best workers in the world. We can outproduce anyone else. Let's open up new markets through exports and create more jobs here in the United States.

Governor Clinton says that he wants to have Government invest. Government never created any wealth at all. Let's get this, do this: less regulation for small business, less taxation for small business, and less lawsuits for small business.

The trial lawyers are Governor Clinton's biggest supporters. What we need to do on these crazy lawsuits is to put some caps. It's wrong when a doctor is afraid to deliver a baby because of a malpractice suit. It is wrong. It is wrong when a Little League coach is afraid to coach for fear of some crazy lawsuit. And it is wrong if you see an accident along the highway, you're scared to pick up somebody and help them because you're afraid you'll be sued. We must sue each other less and care for each other more.

In health care, we've got the best health care plan for this country. And here's how we're going to get it through. There's going to be a brandnew Congress, at least 100, maybe 150 new Members. And we'll reach out, and we'll say let's do what the people want, make insurance available to every single American and keep the quality of health care up.

Audience members. Clean the House! Clean the House! Clean the House!

The President. We're going to do that. Clean the House! Thirty-eight years, one party. Thirty-eight years they've controlled the House of Representatives. I think it's about time to clean House, I'll tell you. That leadership up there, they can't run a two-bit post office, and they screwed up a little tiny bank. We need to clean House.

You remember that Harry Truman—it's not giving 'em hell, it's just telling them the truth, and they think it's hell. That's what Truman said, and he's right.

Education: We've got the best program to help these kids, America 2000. It's got a lot of great features. It supports the teachers, not that NEA teachers union. Let's help the teachers. Help the teachers. And one thing it says is let's help parents choose the school of their choice, private, public, or religious. It worked for the GI bill after World War II, and it can work to make our public schools better. Let the parents choose.

I've got a big difference with Governor Clinton on crime. You see, I think we don't need a lot of liberal judges on the Supreme Court. He has threatened—he has made a terrible threat. He says he wants to put Mario Cuomo——

Audience members. Boo-o-o!

The President. ——on the Supreme Court. No, we can't let that happen. You talk about a disaster, that would be it. In crime—let me tell you why. We must back up these law enforcement officers who are out there on that street for you and me every single day. The Arkansas prisoners serve only 20 percent of their sentences; Federal, 85 percent. Let's have a little more sympathy for the victims of crime, a little less for the criminals.

And everybody here ought to be worried about the deficit. Let me give you a couple of ways to get that down. One, we almost got it in the last Congress, until that liberal leadership twisted the arms of eight of the cosponsors and made them change their mind.

Audience members. Boo-o-o!

The President. People cosponsoring it. Give us a balanced budget amendment and let's get the job done. Give us a check-off. Give us a check-off so every taxpayer can check off 10 percent of their taxes. And that will have to be applied to lowering the deficit. And third, give me what 43 Governors have: a line-item veto, and cut right through it.

Audience members. Line-item veto! Line-item veto! Line-item veto!

The President. These guys! And fourth, why don't we give the Congress back to the people and have term limits for the Members of Congress. We've got them for the President; let's do that.

But my biggest argument for Governor Clinton—we've got a big difference on the issues, the deficit, on education, and crime and all of these, but the biggest argument is: I do not believe you can be President of the United States and try to be all things to all people. We cannot have the White House turn into the waffle house. He talks one time about, "Oh, term limits, yes," and then he's against them. Talks about a fair trade agreement, says he's for it; then, well, he's not sure. And then in the debate you heard him, he says, "Well, I'm for the NAFTA agreement, but." You can't have a lot of "buts" in the White House. You've got to call it the way you see it.

And what's catching up with him now, what is catching up with him just as we go down to the wire is this pattern of deception. Look, if you make a mistake in the real world, you say, "I made a mistake," and you go on about leading the country or about your business. In the White House you should do the same thing. But you cannot be on all sides of all questions. Let me remind you. Let me remind you about the war. During the war, when we had to mobilize—and President Ford was very generous—we had to mobilize world opinion and then make a very difficult decision to send someone else's son or daughter into combat. And what did Bill Clinton say? He said, "Well, I agree with the minority, but I guess I would have voted with the majority." You cannot waffle. You cannot waffle if you want to lead.

Audience members. Boo-o-o!

The President. And that is character. That is character. And if you keep doing it, you lose trust. Character and trust are important. The thing that bothers me is there is a pattern of deception, being on all sides of these questions. He said on April 17th, "I'm going to reveal my draft records," and we haven't seen them yet. Listen, a lot of people disapproved of the war. But you can't try to have it both ways. You can't say, "I got an induction," and then, "I didn't." You can't say that you wrote the man, that you once—you can't say that you're going to have one position and then another. You've got to stand up and take a position and lead. And that's what being President is about. You cannot lead by misleading.

Audience members. Bush! Bush! Bush!

The President. I'll tell you what's happening out there. Governor Clinton had his transition team moving forward, the same old liberal crowd that was run out of business in 1980. They're all measuring the drapes and getting the carpet ready. And the media said the President has no chance at all.

Audience members. Boo-o-o!

The President. Everyone, hey listen, we've got to get some ground rules on the media. Where's our crowd? Our gang is the good gang. We're giving exemption, we're giving amnesty to the photographers, to those carrying the cameras, and even to those traveling with us. But my ire goes to those talking heads on those Sunday television shows.

Audience members. Boo-o-o!

The President. You're right. There it is. This is the fastest selling bumper sticker in America. There is an enormous demand for this bumper sticker. And all these talk show guys that wrote us off, we're going to show them. Harry Truman said something—and I'm paraphrasing—he said, there's 50 of them out there, and none of them know how to pound sand in a rat hole.

So as this thing gets moving now, as this thing gets moving now—and all the people who were measuring the drapes and all the people that were studying the plans of who they were going to put in office, they're coming up short, because the American people know what the Arkansas record was. They know what waffling and character mean. And I am going to win election on November 3d.

Audience members. Four more years! Four more years! Four more years!

The President. Let me tell you. Let me tell you something. Let me end this way. First place, you've got one good reason to keep me there, and that is that Barbara Bush is a great First Lady, and I wish she were here. But I'll tell you the main one. You're right. You're right, Millie does know more about foreign policy than Clinton and the Ozone Man. Hey, these guys wouldn't know foreign policy it if hit them in the face. We have changed the world. The kids here today in that band go to bed at night without the same fear of nuclear war that their predecessors did. Ancient enemies are talking to each other in the Middle East. Russia is going democratic. South of our border is democracy. And Ozone and Clinton keep talking about change, change, change. We've already done that. We've already made the world safer.

I'll tell you this. We're getting right down to the wire, right down to the wire. And here is my appeal: Barbara and I both, and our family, have tried to uphold the public trust. And character, Bill Clinton—Bruce Willis mentioned this—Clinton said that it is not the character of the President but "the character of the Presidency." Wrong. They're locked in. They are interlocked.

This country is starting to move. And so I ask—they say, why do you want this job? You've got a good life with all the family; you're lucky in life. Yes. But I finish what I start, and I want to lift up every single kid here and make them understand we are not a nation in decline. We are the greatest on the face of the Earth, and your future is bright. Your future is bright.

And so on Tuesday, go to the polls. Take your friends to the polls. I ask for your support. I ask for your trust to lead this great country for 4 more years.

And may God bless the United States of America. Thank you very much. Thank you.

Note: The President spoke at 5:05 p.m. at the Gerald R. Ford Museum. In his remarks, he referred to actor Bruce Willis; Republican national committeeman Chuck Yob; Republican national committeewoman Betsy DeVos and her husband, Dick; David

Doyle, State chairman, Michigan Republican State Committee; and Gov. Mario

Cuomo of New York.

Question-and-Answer Session in Grand Rapids
October 29, 1992

Moderator. Okay, something about the questions that you're going to hear tonight: Contrary to some of the reports that some of you may have heard, TV–13 and Channel 4 in Detroit have selected the questions and selected the audience participants. There was no outside interference or approval from the Bush-Quayle campaign or the White House.

There are a lot of questions, so without further ado, let's get to them. Ladies and gentlemen, I'd like to introduce you to the President of the United States, George Bush.

The President. Thank you very much. Fire away, Mort.

Moderator. Thank you, Mr. President. Thank you for being with us tonight.

The President. Delighted to be here, Mort.

Moderator. We have gotten a lot of questions from people all over this State. And needless to say, a majority of them have concerned themselves with the economy, jobs, the business climate, taxes, things that go directly to the wallet.

Job Retraining

Q. I have a question related to jobs. Despite the recent very minimal increases in growth, our economic crisis has resulted in a recent General Motors loss of more than $750 million. We are told that as many as 40,000 more auto workers will soon be out of work as a result. Aside from your position on modification of CAFE standards, I'd like to know specifically what you plan to do that will assist the working men and women of our great State of Michigan.

The President. In the first place, I'm not sure I agree with your premise on the minimal growth; 2.7 is a fairly good growth. We have grown for six straight quarters. And yet the opposition keeps saying we're in a deep recession. If somebody's out of work, I'm sure he feels we're in a recession or a depression. So what we've got to do is get them back to work.

I favor increasing our exports. Exports are going to lead us out of this global slowdown. I favor job retraining. You asked about people that might be out of a job. We have a vigorous $10 billion job retaining program. I think that's essential. But the main thing is to stimulate the economy, particularly the small business sector, through investment tax allowances, through capital gains reduction. Democrats all say that's a big break for the rich. It isn't. It will help people start businesses. Then, of course, I think that that first-time homebuyers credit—take a family that wants to buy a home for the first time, give them a $5,000 credit, and not only they'll get part of the American dream, but it will stimulate the entire housing industry.

I think those three specifics are good. But the big difference I have with Governor Clinton on this is they want to come in and invest, have Government invest. Government never produced a constructive job in its life. It has to be the private sector. So the big difference I have is when they say they want to raise $220 billion in more spending and raise taxes. I think that would be the most counterproductive thing for an economy that is growing, albeit too slowly. Education, job retraining for the individuals you asked about.

Q. Among minorities, unemployment is a major concern. I'd like to know what specifically you would do to improve the educational and job training opportunities for minority people.

The President. Bernard, good question. We have a program called Job Training 2000. And it's a good one, and as I say, it takes people that are working and gives them a chance to get job training while they're working. That's a new approach, apprenticeship approach.

The best answer has got to be—you asked about education. I can't see where he is—I guess out there—education. We have a bold, new program called America 2000; 1,700 communities are already participating in it. You know, school choice—parents should be able to choose the school of their choice, whether they're religious, public, or private. And say, oh, that will diminish the public schools. No, it won't. It didn't do it when you had the GI bill. It will be a good thing, and it's working in Milwaukee in areas very much like downtown Detroit.

So education is a little longer run; job training is the shorter run, job retraining.

Government Gridlock

Q. Mr. President, if you're reelected, how do you specifically propose to enact your post-cold-war economic agenda through a Democratically controlled Congress?

The President. Oh, that's going to be much better. First place, the time you get something done is the first part of your second term, no politics on the horizon, no more rallies, no more debates, maybe more of these kinds of things, but no more of the politics.

Secondly, because Congress, who has been controlled by one party for 38 years, has been in such disarray, they've disgraced themselves so much by fouling up a little tiny bank and a little tiny post office, you're going to have at least 100 new Members. Might have more than that. So what I'll do is sit down with these new Members, and they'll be listening to the same voters I am, and say, now let's get the people's business done. It's going to be done. I'm getting more confident. When I'm reelected, it's going to be done on the plan that I've been talking about, not the invest-and-grow-Government plan.

He calls our plans for the economy trickle-down. It's trickle-down Government to go back to what Governor Clinton's talking about. We're not going to do that. But the way of getting it through the Congress is to start right in, sit down with them before they even take their seats, and say, now look, you're all brandnew around here; you don't have to do it the way it was—always

been done by your leaders.

Let me give you one example. I favor a balanced budget amendment. That's not going to cure everything, but many States operated under it, including Arkansas. I want that for the Nation. It passed the Senate. We had it down so it's almost passing the House. We needed eight votes. The Speaker and Mr. Gephardt twisted the arms of cosponsors, people that had actually cosponsored the legislation, and we lost it by I think it was four votes, three or four votes. That won't happen in a new Congress.

You know, I want the line-item veto. I want the balanced budget amendment. I want a check-off so taxpayers can say, hey, we're worried about the deficit; make the Congress put this much money into deficit reduction. But the fundamental political science answer is new people get new things done.

The Economy

Q. Mr. President, last evening the ABC News went back to New Hampshire and talked with a lady about, well, about how well she had done over the past 4 years. During that time her employer had had layoffs but has recently hired back, I believe, 17. She has received this year an increase of 4 percent in her wages. She stated that she now has approximately $4 per month deducted from her pay for health insurance, et cetera, that she didn't have 4 years ago. How do you answer people who appear to be living at about the same level as 4 years ago, and what do you feel that you can do for them for the next 4 years?

The President. Well, I'm delighted that somebody found somebody in New Hampshire that had some good news, because every time I see one of these network programs you find somebody that has bad news. The unemployment's gone down for 3 straight months. And yet the minute they say, well, unemployment is down, "Bad news for President Bush: job market shrinks." Here's Joe Schmaltz over here from New Hampshire, and he's having a tough time of it. So first, I'm delighted that somebody is doing a little bit better.

I think the answer—first place, our productivity is way up in this country. We are more productive than any other nation. We are not a nation in decline.

Secondly, we've got interest rates down and inflation down, which poises this country for a real strong growth.

Thirdly, the biggest growth for jobs that will pay better for this woman will be in exports, increasing our sales abroad, creating jobs in America. We've got the best product, the best workers. And you do that through continuing on my approach for a fair trade agreement, free trade agreement with Mexico. I want to do the same thing with Chile. I want to do the same thing in Eastern Europe. And I know some of the labor union leaders don't like that. They try to tell the workers, rank and file, that's going to mean shipping jobs abroad. It is not. And it's exports that's going to lead this world out of this slowdown.

By the way, we are doing better than Japan and Germany and France and Canada. And I think I'd like to get that in perspective tonight because everybody listens to—those who listen to the other side think that the whole thing is in decline, and it's not.

That's what I'd say to her. And more productivity. If you want to challenge up into a higher level kind of job, look at our six national education goals. The first President to ever have the goals adopted for this country. All 50 Governors—and I give Governor Clinton credit for this; he was activist in this. He helped the President, me, get these six education goals set. One of them is you're never too old to learn, which means more job retraining. And the other one, the second one, is more math and science. It's very difficult for a woman who already has a job. But for the future, to get the levels of pay up, we've got to do a better job on education.

So it's a combination of these things, in my view, that will make her life better. But do not believe the American dream is dead. We're going to grow more. We've been told for months we're in a recession, and we're not. We've got growth out there. If we listen, have sound policies, and don't go back to the failed "misery index" days of Jimmy Carter with interest rates at 21 or 19, between 19 and 21 percent, and inflation at 15. Spend and tax, spend and tax got

us there. If we don't do that, I think that this woman has an enormously challenging and bright future.

Capital Gains Tax

Q. Mr. President, you propose a capital gains cut to stimulate the economy. Isn't it likely that this will only increase the bipolarization in the classes, since it traditionally favors the rich?

The President. I don't think so at all. There was a thing called the Steiger amendment in 1978, where capital gains rates were reduced. And it resulted in a splurge of new businesses being started. I realize that if you are just trying to get some facts out there, all you hear from the Democrats is that that helps the rich. It is small business that benefits from that. It is small businesses that get started from a capital gains reduction, particularly in the science and electronic fields.

So I would say it isn't just rich people that benefit at all. And it's going to stimulate the economy. So for those who think it's a break for the rich, I just disagree with them. And I've got evidence on my side through when Bill Steiger of Wisconsin got it passed in '78, it gave a real surge to the economy.

Moderator. President Bush, we thank you. And in a moment we're going to be back to talk about other issues that are obviously of great concern to people around the State of Michigan. One of those, perhaps ranking right up there with the jobs situation, at least for people in the city of Detroit, is the issue of crime. And we'll have a question on that subject when we return.

[At this point, the television station took a commercial break.]

Urban Policy

Q. Mr. President, I see my neighbors locked behind their doors with bars on their windows. I've had two cars stolen. I see crackheads on the street. And I want to know what's your plan to combat the urban crime, the urban problem of crimes, drugs, and guns.

The President. You know, that's a very good question. And some of the areas that are impacted like his, really there's a sense of hopelessness. Mothers don't dare go down to the corner store at night. I'll tell you what I think we need to do. I think we need to get some stronger anticrime legislation. Then I'll tell you what else I think we need to do. By stronger anticrime legislation, I think we need to back our police officers more, people that are risking their lives for his neighbors and anybody's neighbors. By that I mean we've go to pass changes to the exclusionary rule, a little technical, but it says if a police officer arrests a guy and then he has a slight technicality, not malicious, not willful, that that case is not going to be thrown out of court.

I want to see habeas corpus reform. I am not a lawyer. I wear that badge proudly. But I do think that these endless appeals make swift and sure and fair sentencing much less likely. And so we need to change the habeas corpus reform, reform habeas corpus. I happen to believe we need a stricter Federal death penalty for those who kill law enforcement officers.

So I am for much stronger legislation. Again, I've battled with the gridlock guys for a long time on that. But the new Members coming, I think we can get that done.

Now on the hope side. We have a program called "Weed and Seed." And it is an outstanding program. It's already working in Detroit under a program called Reach where a private guy, a minister, I believe it is, works with some Federal money to make it work. "Weed and Seed:" weed out the criminal elements through tough law enforcement and then seed the neighborhood with hope. That means enterprise zones, which we have been battling to get through in the Congress; more homeownership; tenant management, where the tenants manage the property to bring back pride.

But on his point, we must go with tougher law and Federal law enforcement. You know, I can't speak for the locals, but I back the police, and I was very pleased when eight guys from Little Rock, Arkansas, the FOP, the Order of Policemen, came up and endorsed me for President, because I think they know I back them with strong legislation. But I don't think there's any other answer to it.

One other thing. We've got to win the battle on our antidrug fight. We're doing better on interdiction. Sixty percent lower use of cocaine by teenagers, that's good. But where we're not making progress is with these addicts, the addictive age. Crack cocaine is just brutal for them. So we've got to do better in terms of interdiction, and we've got to do better in terms of rehabilitation and treatment. And drug spending, antidrug spending from us is way, way up.

School Choice

Q. President Bush, this question goes back to the issue of education in our society. You have proposed allowing students to attend the schools of their choice, and this would mean that students who have more resources would be able to attend the more affluent schools, leaving those who are socio-economically disadvantaged in the poorer quality schools. How would your proposal help those who are socio-economically disadvantaged, and what do you propose for improving the quality of disadvantaged schools?

The President. The first place, my program for school choice was tried first in Milwaukee, Wisconsin. A Democratic Mayor and a Democratic legislator, a woman named Polly Williams, decided something different had to happen there. Polly was told that her kid was dysfunctional, going to a lousy school. They worked out a choice program at the Milwaukee level. And her kid is now performing well. And the school that wasn't chosen is making itself better.

The GI bill after World War II went to an individual soldier getting out of the armed service. He could choose public, private, or religious. That did not hurt the State universities. The same thing would be true with this plan. The answer to the socio-disadvantaged is to do what my program calls for: give them a stipend to choose whether they want a public school, fine; private school, fine; or religious school, fine. As you do that, you're going to find that the schools not chosen are going to better themselves.

There's plenty of examples. Rochester, New York, has some of that. Milwaukee, I've already mentioned. So we ought to try it. And my program's called the "GI bill" for kids. It helps the kind of person that she properly was identifying with and talking about. I think we ought to try something new. Education and the control of the Congress are two things that haven't changed in years, and we ought to change both.

Moderator. President Bush, as a followup to that, there are those, and you're well aware of it, who claim that this program of yours is flirting dangerously with the separation of church and state.

The President. Uh-uh. No, because it doesn't go to the schools, it goes to the parents. Did anyone make that claim, Mort, after the GI bill? Is anyone saying that violates separation of church and state? It doesn't. It goes to the family. And the families can choose what they want. Does a Pell grant blur the lines between separation of church and state? I don't think so. So I would argue that since it goes to the people, goes to the family, it is not a separation of church and state problem.

Q. Mr. President, I represent many parents in this community that sacrifice greatly to send our children to the Christian schools so they can enjoy the religious freedom that this great country was built on. We also pay property taxes, which go to support the public schools. My question for you is, will your "GI bill" for children go far enough to give us relief from this double payment? And alternatively, what are your views on tax deductions or tax credits for this?

The President. Well, tax credits is a good idea, but I don't want—level with you, there isn't enough money around when we're operating at these enormous deficits to do that. But the school choice will supplement your family income to permit them to go to this school that you've already chosen. But I don't want to mislead you. I don't believe that you can, even though there's—you're choosing, you're choosing the school. I don't think I can offer more than this "GI bill" for people that choose.

I like the concept of tax credits. But I just don't want to mislead you. I don't think that that's going to be enacted in the next few years because of the deficit we're operating at and because of the need to try to live within our means a little more at the Federal level, thus stimulating more jobs in the private sector.

Bosnia

Q. Mr. President, what in your opinion is the main obstacle that hinders the United States from intervening in the killing of innocent people in Croatia and Bosnia?

The President. The main obstacle is that as long as I'm President, I'm not going to put American forces into a troubled situation unless I can see what the mission is, I can see how that mission is going to be achieved, and then I can see how those troops come out. I'm old enough to have learned something from my own experience in uniform. One of it was World War II. We fought and won. Everybody had everything they needed to get the job done. Vietnam, we didn't. And the horrible problems that your loved ones face cannot be solved by putting the 82d Airborne division into Bosnia. It simply can't be done.

He's torn because there's these tremendous historic ethnic rivalries that are now coming to the surface because of the collapse of Soviet communism and thus the iron hand that they once had over all these different, now independent countries. We are helping. The United States is helping with relief. We always do. We always should, as we are here, as we are in Somalia and elsewhere. But I don't want to act like we're going to solve this problem militarily.

We took the lead at the United Nations in passing a no-fly zone, so those Serbian aircraft would not bomb the hapless citizens. And it is working. The question is what do we do in terms of enforcement if it doesn't work, and that's a question that any President will have to face at the appropriate time. But it does not lend itself—I say this to him with great angst—to put American kids on the ground, in these mountains, down into an area that looks like Dien Bien Phu. And I simply won't do that as President, unless my respected military leaders, Colin Powell and Dick Cheney, come and say, "Now, look, here's the way you get them in. Here's their mission. And here's when you get them out." We did it in Desert Storm. We'll do it—but I don't believe that's going to happen.

Somalia

Moderator. Mr. President, a followup to

that. There are those who, having seen the pictures of the enormous tragedy in Somalia, the starving children, the death, the devastation there, feel that the United States with all of its wealth and traditional compassion has reacted too little and too late to assist the people of Somalia. Your response to that?

The President. My response is they're wrong. They're right in the angst and the agony one feels in one's heart when you see those ghastly pictures of those starving kids. But it is the United States that has taken the lead in relief.

And you've got a problem, Mort. Again, you've got almost anarchy over there. You have warlords controlling the ports. They're armed. They go—and they're shooting up the United Nations forces. We were very active in the United Nations to get U.N. forces on the ground. But they're having difficulty separating these warlords one from the other. We're sending our supplies in there. We are helping.

I had quite a positive report the other day, because some of those kids—the pictures, my gosh, they just kill you, the little skinny arms. And it just wrenches the heart of any American. But the good news is a lot of those kids getting any nourishment are coming back. And I think we can take pride that once again we have stepped up to the lick-log and done our share.

So I would argue with those who say that we're not doing our part. We are. And maybe you can say, well you never do enough. But then you've got to look at the situation on the ground. There's anarchy there. It's a terrible thing. Once the Siad government went out, you've got all these factions shooting, fighting, killing. Seventeen-year-olds with weapons from the former Soviet empire just shooting it up on the port, stealing the relief supplies, and taking them for their families and leaving these kids starving. It is tough.

Middle East Peace Talks

Q. How do you plan, Mr. Bush, to keep the Middle East peace talks going in a fair and representative manner? What do you hope that each side will ultimately aspire to, and how will it affect the global community?

The President. Dana, I never thought anybody would ask such an intelligent question, because I've been running this campaign—you might think foreign affairs don't matter. Look—and this gives me a chance to hit it partially out of the park. Because of what we did in Desert Storm, we were able—with the able leadership of a great team, Jim Baker, who's with me here tonight, and Brent Scowcroft in the White House and Larry Eagleburger and many others—to get these parties, historic enemies, talking to each other in the Middle East. If you'd have said when I became President that Arabs would be talking to Israel, nobody would have believed it. And we did it. We did it by defending our own foreign policy interests. We did it by helping kill aggression.

So the talks are going on, and in my view they will continue to go on. There were some cross-border problems in Lebanon and Israel the other day, but I think the talks are going to go on because I think all sides want it. You're seeing progress. You're seeing Syrian Jews permitted to leave, and you're seeing much more in the way of talking.

You asked what do I aspire for, to do: Simply to have peace in the Middle East. It's got to be based on the U.N. Security Resolutions 242, 338, which talks about getting the borders adjusted, safe and secure borders for Israel. And you're going to—have to be compromise. But they're talking. And it is a dramatic accomplishment.

There's so many factions there, the Syrians and the Palestinians and the Lebanese, that I can't give you a formula in 10 seconds about it. But I am convinced that the talks will continue. They want peace. And all the Arab countries are pitching in. We are the first administration to ever bring about that kind of widespread negotiation.

Moderator. Do you think if you were reelected for the next 4 years, it is possible to get some kind of a settlement once and for all?

The President. I would think it's possible. I wouldn't want to hold out a false goal. But I think it's possible, yes. That's a good word for it, possible. But it's very important that it do happen. We have a special relationship with Israel because of the way we've conducted our foreign policy. Again back to the Gulf, we have very strong relations with Saudi Arabia.

I took a little flak for talking to Assad of Syria in some quarters. But it was the right thing to do, and now Syria is having some discussion at these peace talks with Israel. Who would have thought that possible?

So I think it is possible. I certainly hope it's possible.

[*At this point, the television station took a commercial break.*]

Polls

Moderator. And we are back in Grand Rapids for a live statewide town hall meeting with the President of the United States. We're going to talk politics just a minute, oh my goodness. We're going to talk about the polls that have been out in the last couple of days. They've shown a narrowing, no matter how you read them. How do you respond? What do you think is happening?

The President. Well, you're talking to a guy that berated the pollsters when they were looking horrible—[*laughter*]—about a week ago or 2 weeks ago. You're talking to a guy that was written off by the talking heads in the national media. So I think it might be inappropriate to try to analyze the polls when they're looking very, very encouraging, because then the talking heads will come on and say on Sunday morning with the Republicans, Democrats, all of whom have written me off, "Hey, here he is. Said he doesn't count on polls, and he's talking about how great the polls are."

Leave the poll aside; something's happening in the country. There's some change. There's something that's beginning. I'll tell you what I think it is. I think people get serious at the end. And I think they are really saying, who do you trust with your family, in a crisis, to be in that Oval Office? Who has the character? Who do you trust? I honestly believe that's what's beginning to happen out there.

So I'd rather not comment on the polls because I'll get hit in the face with them if they goose up about three points tomorrow, you know. [*Laughter*]

Moderator. You don't still consider them all nutty pollsters, though, now.

The President. Well, I'm less inclined to say that, but—[*laughter*]—but to be very candid with you, but look, how do they jump around? How does one poll have 10 points and the very same day the other one have 2 or 20 points and 3? Something's strange. And I don't know what it is. It's the weirdest political year I've ever seen in my life. And the pollsters can fit right into there. Now they do seem to be coming together in a—you know, but we'll see. I just don't know.

Ross Perot

Moderator. As a good reporter, I have to tell you what I observed. And during our break a while ago, President Bush got a big laugh from this audience when he picked up a magazine and flipped through it and said, "I want to be like Ross Perot and have my flip charts."

Well, we do have a question about Ross Perot.

Q. Good evening, Mr. President. My question is rather brief. If you are reelected, do you have any intentions of putting Ross Perot on any economic committees?

The President. Well, not the one in charge of gas taxes—[*laughter*]—because he wants to raise gasoline taxes 50 cents a gallon over 5 years. I don't want to do that. I think all people that have to drive to work, particularly with long distances, it's a bad thing to do. I don't think we need to raise the taxes. I've got a difference with him on Social Security, where he thinks all mandatory programs must be cut to some degree, and he included at one juncture Social Security. I don't believe we should touch Social Security. It's a sacrosanct trust, and I don't think we ought to do it.

I've already consulted Ross Perot when I was Vice President on the POW thing. I give him credit for having a dedication in that area. But I don't really know on the overall economic—anybody that makes himself $3 billion has got to be pretty bright on some of the economic matters. So I would reach out to a wide array of people. But I've got to be a little vague because we do have some fundamental differences as what we need to do to get the economy going.

AIDS

Q. The 1991 report of the National Commission on AIDS states that the people of the United States must either engage seriously the issues and needs posed by this deadly disease or face relentless, expanding tragedy in the decades ahead. Mr. President, you've been accused of failing to respond to the recommendations of your committee. How do you respond?

The President. One, it's not my committee. And two, I respond by saying we've increased AIDS spending dramatically. I requested in the last year $4.9 billion. That is 10 times as much per AIDS victim as is spent on cancer. We've got a strong program. The NIH researchers, National Institute of Health researchers, are the best in the world.

We get plenty of criticism, but here's my view on it. We must continue with AIDS research at substantial levels. We have sped up the coming to market of AIDS-related drugs, having to stimulate, get that FDA to move those drugs to market. And then I've got to do a better job on education, because AIDS is a disease where behavior matters.

I said that one time, and a bunch of these crazy ACT–UP, the extreme group that hurt their cause, came up to a little town where Barbara and I were and started saying, Bush ought to change his behavior. When you're doing something that is known to cause the disease you ought to stop doing it, whether it's a dirty needle or some kind of a sexual behavior that is known to cause the disease. In addition to being compassionate, in addition to spending money for research, we ought to be sure that everybody knows what causes the disease. People that do things that cause it ought to stop doing them, whether it's dirty needles or what I've just referred to.

I feel uncomfortable talking about it. But the people at NIH asked me to make clear to the American people that AIDS is a disease where some of it is behavioral. So we ought to change behavior if it's going to cause more of the disease.

Moderator. Mr. President, speaking of your Commission on AIDS, in a much-publicized move, Magic Johnson, of course, resigned. Why do you think he did that?

The President. I'll be darned if I know. I had a good meeting with him in the White House, and said, "If you've got any specific suggestions, let me know." I never heard from him after that.

I do have some differences with the Commission. The reason I answered her tersely is that it is not a Presidential commission. It might be Presidential level, but some of the people on there are not appointed by me; some are. And I have respect for them. But they are far out. They want more, more, more. And I have to sort out priorities for all diseases that the Federal Government can help spend money on. How about cancer? How about heart? How about all of these diseases? We're dealing with somewhat limited resources. In spite of that, AIDS—I want to say doubled since I've been President, but it's a major increase. But I have some differences with the Commission.

I've met with the Commission. I've gone to NIH and held a seminar with AIDS victims, young kids whose lives were going away, teenagers and young men, and held AIDS babies in my arms. But somehow the extreme elements in that community refused to say that we care about it.

You know, they had this big quilt ceremony out on the lawn, south of the White House there. It was a very moving thing, because I saw a lot of pictures of it. And one of the AIDS activists said, "Well, why didn't you go?" And I said, "I didn't want to go to take something solemn and sensitive and be a lightning rod for the extremes." That's why I didn't go, and that's why Barbara didn't go. She's a very caring person.

Abortion

Q. Many college students support the freedom of reproductive choice. If you would support your granddaughter's choice to have an abortion, then why would you not want us to have that same choice?

The President. I don't support her choice of having abortion. The question was, if she had an abortion, what would I do? I'd love her. I'd hold her in my arms and comfort her. If she came to me for advice, I'd say,

"Hey, listen, I come down on the side of life." I'm appalled that there's 28 million abortions. So it's a very tough issue. It divides everybody. People get mad at each other. People get hurt on the issue. I happen to opt for life because I—and we have two adopted grandchildren. Thank God they weren't aborted. So I feel that way.

But I'll tell you where I think choice—let me ask you something. I can't—through this television set here. But let me ask you: A 13-year-old can't get her ears pierced or take medicine without getting the parent's approval. Yet a 13-year-old, according to some of these people, ought to be able to have an abortion. I don't think that's right. I think parents should have to have a say in this. There's a big difference I have with some of the women's movement out there.

But I will say this: I do recognize there are strong differences. I have just concluded, after a lot of agony and evolution of position, that we ought to err on the side of life and not on the side of more and more abortions.

Environmental Policy

Moderator. Mr. President, a lot of people believe that the ultimate ability to sustain life on this planet will be directly linked to how well we preserve it and take care of it and clean it up. Environmental issues are big this year with a lot of people, and we have somebody standing by in Holland right now who has such a question on their mind.

Q. Mr. President, 4 years ago you claimed to be an environmentalist. But last summer in Brazil our country failed—and was one of the only countries, if not the only one, that failed to sign on to an agreement to protect biological diversity. And furthermore, our country sought to weaken one on protecting the global environment from increases in global temperature. Repeatedly your administration has also sought to weaken the Clean Air Act and the Endangered Species Act, as well as to permit increased oil exploration in the Arctic National Wildlife Refuge.

The President. We're strongly for that.

Q. And also to decrease the amount of protection to wetlands. My question then is

if you're elected for another 4 year term, are we going to continue along the same path vis-a-vis environmental issues, or are we going to see some change in environmental policy that a lot of folks in the country think is important?

The President. Well, professor, you sound like Ozone Man, Mr. Gore. I am not an extremist. We have a good, good record on the environment. We've done more for the oceans. We passed the Clean Air Act. We've done great things for the forests. But I do not consider it leadership to go down to Rio de Janeiro in front of a bunch of NGO's, non-government organizations, and try to buy their favor by getting in line, buy a lot of other people who want to go after our biodiversity proprieties, our research. We have a strong record in biodiversity. But I simply don't think that just getting in line and signing up for a treaty is a good thing to do. We're the leaders on it, and because of what I did, we will be in a much better position to share our research with other countries.

On climate change, we did change it a little bit, because I don't want to see us burden the automotive industry with the kind of costs that the Europeans wanted us to put on the industry.

What I'm saying—you mentioned the Endangered Species—yes, I came down in favor of a more moderate consideration for this owl out there, the spotted owl, because 30,000 American families—somebody ought to think about them, too.

So I think we've got a good record. But my difference is, when you come up here to the auto industry and suggest we put 40- to 45-miles-per-gallon CAFE standards, these fuel efficiency standards—who's going to think of the auto worker's family? Yes, it would be nice to be able to say that. Who's going to be able to produce cars with that kind of thing right away? Nobody. And so we've got to find some balance.

Moderator. President Bush, on the subject of CAFE standards, you have repeatedly charged that Governor Clinton has set 40 or 45 as something he would like to legislate. We've gone back and listened to the tapes and examined his speeches. He insists that he has set that as a goal, that it's something we ought to aspire to. Would you accept that as a goal?

The President. No. I don't want to set it as a goal until I'm told by good scientists it can be achieved without putting a lot of people out of work. I wish I had my notes here with me, because I read a specific quote from Clinton's energy strategy that had it calling for legislation.

Yes, he's changed his position. But that gets back to a whole other argument I've got with him. You're changing wherever you go, whether it's the free trade agreement, whether it's on your own record on the draft, or whether it's clean air standards. You can't do that.

So if you want to set a goal for way out there, fine. But let's not go to the extreme on these environmental matters. We've got a very good record on the environment. We've got a great environmentalist in Bill Reilly heading EPA. We've got a good record on wetlands. But I'll tell you, with all respect to the professor, maybe he's pretty reasonable, but I couldn't tell it from the way the question came out, because we can't go off to the extremes and still talk about how we're going to help all these people that are looking for jobs.

Leadership

Q. Mr. President, you were elected to provide leadership in the governance of this country. Good leaders get results through working with people and through people. Good leaders are also held accountable for results. My question is why are you constantly blaming Congress for your failures?

The President. Well, I'm not always blaming them. I'm just trying to shift some of the blame where it belongs, to the Congress. They appropriate every dime. They tell me as President how to spend every dime. I have gone up—I'll give you a good example, Larry. It was Larry, wasn't it? I'll give you a good example anyway, whether it was Larry or not. [*Laughter*]

Look, after South Central riots over there in Los Angeles, I sat down with Mayor Bradley, a big Democrat out there; the Governor, a Republican; Peter Ueberroth. They said what we need is enterprise zones. Every one of them agreed on that. I went to the boys club there in the neighborhood

that had been wiped out by these rioters. Everyone said we need enterprise zones. I invited them back. We met with the Democratic leadership, Speaker, Mitchell, Gephardt. I still haven't got the kind of enterprise zones legislation that would have helped South Central and would help Detroit today. It's not my fault that the Congress refuses to go along. Here was a bipartisan appeal. I give you but one example of that.

You talk about leadership. I didn't need Congress in the war, and we forged the coalition. We made a tough decision. We dragged some of the reluctant ones along, and we did what had to be done. And so there is a difference between national security policy, foreign affairs, and some domestic policy. We got some things done early on with Congress. The best piece of civil rights legislation in this decade is the Americans for Disabilities Act. We passed it. We got a good child care bill. We now have a highway bill.

But I'll tell you, they made a decision: The only way we are going to win the White House is by denying the President success on some of this terribly important domestic legislation. That is the fact. And if you want to help change it, clean House. Clean House, and give some new ideas a chance that are just stymied by these old thinkers.

President's Motivation for Reelection

Q. Mr. President, why do you want 4 more years as President? What's your motivation?

The President. Well, I'll tell you something, that is a profound question, because—look, Barbara and I have got a pretty good life. This has been the ugliest year I can ever remember in terms of politics. It has been terrible. Ironically, it's true around the world if you look—have a broad perspective. But I like to finish what I've started. I believe that this country is not in decline. I believe we're a rising nation. I believe we can ameliorate the problems that we're hearing about here tonight with the answers that I've given you here tonight. And I just feel driven to try to help achieve our education goals, to win the battle against narcotics, to do better with the new ideas I've got on housing.

So get in there and finish what you start. And that's what does it. Because, beckoning out there, let's face it—everyone knows everything about my worth or lack thereof, or debt or lack thereof. Life's been pretty good to me. I'm big in the grandchild business now, and someday I'll get a lot bigger in it.

But you set these things aside. I want to finish and try to help people. That's what motivates us. Because otherwise, in this kind of year, why in God's name would anybody in his right mind want to be in this arena, when anybody can take a cheap shot at you. It's the worst. I've never seen the national media, ever, anything like this. I've never seen them having seminars—"Have we been fair to President Bush"—before, a President. They're doing it. Ted Koppel comes on, "Oh, yes, they're wondering whether they've been fair." They know darn well they haven't.

Go around them. Go to the people. Get the job done. But it isn't much fun. But it's going to change after the election. Help me.

Moderator. Speaking of change, Mr.—I'm sorry?

The President. No, no. I'm finished.

Asian Americans

Q. My question is, you've made a concerted effort to hire African Americans and Hispanic Americans to your Cabinet. You often speak of Asian Americans as like a model minority, but very few can be found in your administration. What plans do you have to redress this issue?

The President. Good question. And I think we can do better on that. There's none that I know of in the Cabinet. We have, I think—you know, all these people, "We have appointed more Asian Americans"—I believe I have, at high levels; not in the Cabinet. But I take your point. I think we ought to strive to do better. But I think if I could—I don't know how to get a hold of you—but send you the analysis of Asian Americans in high-level jobs, I think you'll find that it has exceeded the record by any other administration.

But I take your point on Cabinet. I think there's some status and standing to Cabinet that gives groups of all persuasions a certain hope. Maybe we can do better there.

Urban Policy

Moderator. Mr. President, there is a perception, certainly in the city of Detroit—I can't speak for all American cities—that beginning with the election of Ronald Reagan in 1980, nominated in the city of Detroit, as you well know, that the administration simply has ignored the cities; the theory being that inner-city people aren't voting for Republicans, so therefore let's go out and work with the areas where we're getting the most votes. Is that a true perception? If it's not, how do you break it down?

The President. It's not a true perception because I have just cited some things that would in a very likely way lift up and give hope to urban America. And I'm talking about empowerment of people as opposed to Government jobs. I'm talking about enterprise zones. I'm talking about homeownership. Again, I'll cite "Weed and Seed." I believe that those programs and those ideas ought to be tried.

Some say there's no new ideas. They're new until they've been tried. Instead of that, you have a lot of these bosses in these cities that haven't had a new thought in years. They promise the people one thing, tell them to vote the straight lever, and then the people say, "Hey, I didn't get anything out of anything." Why don't they try some new ideas? Why aren't they willing to try what I've said, for example, start out on enterprise zones?

Moderator. Mr. President, time flies when we're having fun. And we do thank you. The hour is up. It's been a pleasure having you in Grand Rapids to address the people of Michigan through this statewide network.

The President. Thank you, Mort.

Note: The question-and-answer session began at 8 p.m. at the West Michigan Public Broadcasting Center. News anchors Lee Van Amede, WZZM–TV, Grand Rapids, and Mort Krim, WDIV–TV, Detroit, served as moderators for the session.

Statement on Signing the Veterans Benefits Act of 1992
October 29, 1992

Today I am signing into law H.R. 5008, the "Veterans Benefits Act of 1992." This bill, which is a landmark in veterans' legislation, reflects America's continuing recognition of the invaluable contributions that veterans and their families have made to our Nation. It includes a major reform of the Dependency and Indemnity Compensation (DIC) program and significant improvements in a variety of other veterans' benefits.

H.R. 5008 brings a new measure of fairness to the DIC program, which provides benefits to the surviving spouses and children of those who die in service or whose deaths after service are related to their service-connected disabilities. Under current law, DIC benefits are based on military rank and length of service. As a result, survivors who have experienced the same misfortune—a service-connected death—receive widely differing payments.

H.R. 5008 replaces this inequitable system with one in which surviving spouses receive the same basic monthly payment of $750. This is $134 more than the current minimum DIC payment. Recognizing the effect that total disability can have on a family's income, the bill provides an additional $165 per month to families of certain service-disabled veterans. For families with children, the current per child benefit is increased, almost tripling by fiscal year 1995.

Education benefits available under the Montgomery GI Bill also increase under H.R. 5008. Our Nation has a proud tradition of assisting veterans in the smooth transition from military to civilian life through educational and training assistance. Indeed, the GI Bill programs have been widely acclaimed as the best investment America has made. These programs have promoted quality education for our country's veterans, providing them the opportunity to be the best that they can be. This Nation remains committed to these programs.

I am also gratified that H.R. 5008 benefits our veterans in many other ways. It improves the Department of Veterans Affairs programs of educational assistance, vocational rehabilitation and training, and insurance. In addition, H.R. 5008 restores eligibility for Veterans Readjustment Appointments with the Federal Government to all Vietnam-era veterans through December 31, 1995.

I have often said that we must remember a statement made by President Kennedy: "A nation reveals itself not only by the men and women it produces, but by the men and women it remembers." On behalf of the American people, I am proud to sign this bill that expresses our Nation's gratitude and continuing commitment to our veterans and their families.

GEORGE BUSH

The White House,
October 29, 1992.

Note: H.R. 5008, approved October 29, was assigned Public Law No. 102–568. This statement was released by the Office of the Press Secretary on October 30.

Statement on Signing the Federal Courts Administration Act of 1992
October 29, 1992

Today I am signing into law S. 1569, the "Federal Courts Administration Act of 1992." I am pleased that the bill explicitly authorizes an American national to file suit in the United States for the recovery of treble damages against the perpetrators of international terrorism. This will ensure that, if needed, a remedy will be available for Americans injured abroad by senseless acts of terrorism.

My approval of this bill also enacts a number of recommendations made by the Federal Courts Study Committee and contains a number of other important provisions for the judicial branch and its personnel. In addition, the bill makes certain important amendments to the Contract Disputes Act—amendments that will serve to provide a more efficient and fair resolution of contract disputes for many of those who do business with the Federal Government.

S. 1569 abolishes the Temporary Emergency Court of Appeals (TECA), which was established in 1970 to rule on appeals of certain oil price control cases. TECA's appellate jurisdiction will be transferred to the U.S. Court of Appeals for the Federal Circuit. I hope and expect that the Federal Circuit will adopt TECA precedent, just as the Federal Circuit earlier adopted Court of Claims precedent when its appellate juris-

diction was transferred to the Federal Circuit. Adoption of TECA precedent would reduce any uncertainty prompted by the change of appellate jurisdiction, reducing delay in resolution of these matters and assisting the Department of Energy's efforts to bring these petroleum cases to a proper conclusion.

Although I have signed S. 1569, I will also withhold my approval of H.R. 6185. While both bills contain many of the same provisions, the amendments to the Contract Disputes Act contained in S. 1569 will better serve the public interest of improving the resolution of contract claim disputes between the Federal Government and its contractors.

GEORGE BUSH

The White House,
October 29, 1992.

Note: S. 1569, approved October 29, was assigned Public Law No. 102–572. This statement was released by the Office of the Press Secretary on October 30.

Remarks to the Kentucky Fried Chicken Convention in Nashville, Tennessee
October 30, 1992

The President. Thank you, John Cranor. Thank you very much. Thank you, John and Kitty, and president Kyle Craig, and John Neal, Charlie Middleton, and all the other franchise leaders. It is, indeed, a pleasure to be here. I want to salute the man that walked in with me, one of the truly great leaders that has ever been in the United States Senate, now in private business, but my dear friend and really a real statesman, Senator Howard Baker, who's with us here today.

Well, we're getting down to the wire. And you know, in this campaign we've been to many States, towns large and small in every corner of this great Nation. Yet I still have one burning question: Where the heck is Lake Edna? [*Laughter*] Just kidding. Steve Provost works with me—and was

with this company—is at my side, and he gave me all the advice, all the hints about this fantastic get-together here.

But my friends over here in the national media, and I use that term advisedly—[*laughter*]—want to know exactly—oh, I love that bumper sticker, "Annoy the Media. Re-elect Bush"—[*laughter*]—and everybody knows what it means. I appeal for amnesty to these guys, particularly the guys that are doing the heavy lifting, you know who you are over here, and the photo dogs and others. If you want to join me in taking out your wrath on the media, which is a little dangerous because they have the last word, I suggest we look at the faceless talking heads on those Sunday morning talk shows, those Republicans and Democrats who have written me off long ago. We're going to show them next Tuesday.

But I do believe that these friends in the media want to know exactly why I stopped by this convention, and I'll tell you the real reason. You see, just last week all the pollsters and pundits said the election was over. The media carried stories about my opponent planning his transition, all but measuring the drapes in the White House. So I came here today because I heard you were experimenting with home delivery and I want to give you my address: 1600 Pennsylvania. [*Laughter*] And when we call for delivery you can reach us there any time because, I don't care what all the pundits say, Barbara and I don't think we'll be moving out until 1996. So you've got our number.

Next Tuesday, in all seriousness—and I appreciate what your president said because this is a serious subject, the election, a privilege really—next Tuesday we will all participate in this great ritual of democracy. The choice that you make that day will cast its shadow forward in history. I came here today to talk with you hard-working businesswomen, businessmen about the choice you face.

My opponent says this election is about change, and with that I agree. But being in favor of change is like being in favor of the Sun coming up tomorrow. Change is going to happen. The real question is not who is for change but whose change will make your life better and make the world safer.

Over the past 4 years, we have seen change of almost Biblical proportion. For 50 years we stood up for freedom; we stood up for a policy of peace through strength. Today, at last, at long last, the cold war is finally over. Our kids grew up crawling under desks in those duck-and-cover drills in the sixties. During the Cuban missile crisis we stood on the brink of armageddon. And in the eighties families huddled together in fear to watch that TV movie, remember, "The Day After." Always the shadow of the cold war lingered right outside our window. You talk change, well, all that has changed. Our children and our grandchildren go to sleep tonight without that same fear of nuclear war.

But do we feel like celebrating? Well, not exactly. There's work to be done right here at home in America, creating new industries and better schools, certainly more affordable health care. Whose philosophy should we follow? Well, the cold war was won not by tanks, not by guns but by this simple idea called freedom. Across the globe people are coming to understand that government is not their superior, not their savior; it is their servant. In the midst of a global economic slowdown, we are proving once again that freedom works. Despite all our challenges, our economy is growing faster than Japan and Germany, faster than Canada, clearly faster than Eastern Europe.

But here's the irony. At the very moment when the rest of the world is moving our way, my opponent Governor Clinton wants us to move the old way, move their way. Governor Clinton likes to say he is, quote, "different." [*Laughter*] Okay. No, different than the old tax-and-spend liberals. But if you look at the details, you see nothing different at all. He talks of the power of the marketplace, but promises $150 billion in new taxes, more than Mondale and Dukakis combined. Most of those taxes will be paid by small business and the middle class. He says he wants to cut the deficit, but he calls for at least $220 billion in new spending. All those billions just begin to pay for all the promises.

Let me give you one timely example. Last night, Governor Clinton was in New Jersey making another promise. He called for a national offensive against AIDS. He called, though, for a massive increase in Federal funding and creation of an AIDS czar in Washington. Well, what Governor Clinton didn't mention is that he has done very little for AIDS at home in Arkansas. He didn't say that this year we spent $4.9 billion on AIDS, a 118-percent increase since I took office. More Federal resources are devoted to research and prevention of AIDS than any other disease including cancer, 10 times as much per victim of AIDS as per victim of cancer, far more than spent on heart disease. Yes, AIDS is a national tragedy. But we don't need a bureaucratic czar in our Nation's Capital. We need more compassion in our hometowns, more education, more caring.

A President has to set priorities because it's your money that we're talking about.

And if you look at Governor Clinton closely, you see a philosophy where bureaucrats in Washington carve out the exact same programs to try and solve problems facing people in Nashville or Nashua or anywhere. You might call this old-fashioned idea trample-down economics: Tramples down business with these deadly new mandates and regulations, tramples down individual initiative with higher taxes, and tramples down the dreams of people with the power of that bureaucracy, the power of bureaucrats. In this age of global transition it will not work, and I think most Americans know it.

It doesn't make sense that restaurant owners will somehow get richer by giving more of your money to the IRS.

Audience members. Boo-o-o!

The President. It doesn't make sense it will get the deficit down by giving Government more money. He uses the word "to invest." The Government doesn't invest. Private business does. Give them more money to spend. At a time when every organization is decentralizing power, why turn back to a central bureaucracy in Washington?

Yet, saying this isn't enough. We've got real problems here in America. You see them every single day in your communities. You hire high school graduates who can't figure out how to run the cash register. You strive to give your people health insurance, but the cost just keeps going through the roof. Those of you who run restaurants in the cities see the problems of crime and drugs and poverty right up close, firsthand. So it's not enough to criticize the old way. Government must find a new way to help.

I'm a conservative, and to me being a conservative means to renew, to reinvigorate what has always made America great, and that is the power of the individual. During this campaign many have sought to portray the choice between, quote, "activist Government" and a trickle-down approach to Government. But the real choice is not between activism and passivity. The real choice is between a liberal bureaucratic Government that seeks to impose solutions on everybody else and a conservative activist Government that gives individuals, businesses, and families the means to make their own choices through competition and economic opportunity.

Let me give you a couple of specific examples. Start with education. Governor Clinton worked with me when we set for the first time in history six national education goals, first time in history. I give him credit for that effort; he was very active in it, deserves credit. But as a candidate for President, Governor Clinton has adopted the agenda of the status quo. He wants to pour more money into the same failed education system, a system where funds are controlled tightly by central bureaucracies, where powerful unions, the teachers union, the NEA, block real reform, and where we spend as much per pupil as any nation but Switzerland. But we don't get an adequate return on our investment.

But tinkering with the system won't do it. It is my view it simply will not get the job done. So I want to put power in the hands of the teachers themselves, not the union. So I want to use competition to improve our schools. Our "GI bill" for kids provides scholarships for elementary and high school students so that every parent, rich and poor, can choose the best schools for their kids, public, private, and religious. Somebody asked me, won't that make the public schools worse? Where it's been tried, in Milwaukee and other places, it doesn't. The public schools that aren't chosen do what you have to do: compete and do better.

And it isn't a violation of church and state. It's like the GI bill; the money goes to the families. It does not violate church and state. It's a good idea. It's a new idea. And we ought to try it.

Now, you see the same differences in health care. Governor Clinton has offered three plans in this campaign. One said to all of you, either offer care on your own or pay a new payroll tax, at least 7 percent. Now, many experts said it was a backdoor way to get Government directly involved in running health care. Now Governor Clinton wants to control the price of health care by setting up a big board in Washington, DC, to set prices. And I say Government cannot lower prices by fiat; only competition can. Government doesn't need to tell you what doctor to see. And we don't need to inflict small business with any more mandates from Washington, DC.

But we've got to do something about health care. So here's my alternative, and I'm convinced with the new Congress we can get it through: Offer tax incentives for small businesses so that you can afford to buy health care on your own. Let small businesses pool the coverage so you can get the same price breaks as AT&T or IBM. For people who are too poor to pay taxes, we will give vouchers so that they can choose the care they want. Freedom, putting people over bureaucracy, these are the principles that we offer.

My opponent trusts Government to choose the best place for child care. I fought for and won a new law that gives low income parents the freedom to use Federal money for child care wherever they want to, whether a government center or a church. And when it comes to deciding where your child spends the day, rich or poor, it doesn't matter, Government should not limit your options. Parents ought to have the freedom to do what they think is right.

My opponent thinks Government can pick the industries of the future with your money. I talk about cutting capital gains and investment tax allowances, giving first-time homebuyers a tax credit, because you know what to do best with your money, better than any bureaucrat.

Governor Clinton says that it's okay that we have Members of Congress who serve decade after decade in Washington. I trust America's judgment, so I want to limit the terms of Members of Congress and give Government back to the people.

Now, when you look at the election in these terms, you see a clear choice. Governor Clinton dreams of expanding the American Government. I want to work to expand the American dream. I offer an agenda for helping people by giving you and your families the power to make your own choices, shape your own destiny. We call it the Agenda for American Renewal. It's a comprehensive, integrated approach to fixing our schools, reforming our health care, right-sizing Government, and creating here in America the world's first $10 trillion economy.

My agenda includes 13 priorities for the first year of my second term, but 3 dwarf all others. First, America needs jobs, not in a while, not tomorrow but now. This week new numbers came out indicating that our economy grew at 2.7 percent last quarter, the sixth straight quarter of growth. It's a long way from the depression that Governor Clinton talks about. But look, we must do better. We don't need higher taxes so that Government can put more people to work. We need incentives to grow, to cut Government redtape and make more credit available so that you can put more people to work.

While we are strengthening small business, we will open new foreign markets for our products by winning congressional approval of our free trade treaty with Canada and Mexico. The bottom line is this: More trade creates more high paying jobs for all Americans. They make the charge that free trade agreements will ship our jobs overseas. My question is: If that's the case, lower labor rates is the determining factor, why isn't Haiti the industrial capital of the world? Decisions are made on other things. We will create more jobs with opening up export markets.

Our third priority is health care. I already mentioned some of my ideas, but the need for action is urgent. We simply cannot control the deficit, we simply cannot make our companies even more competitive until we make health care more affordable and more accessible for you and all your workers.

Those are the three. As we're working on these priorities, we'll be working on others. One special priority is to reform our crazy legal system. It's gotten out of hand. I'm sure many of you fear the customer who will try to rip off the system by sticking you with a frivolous lawsuit. America now spends up to $200 billion every year on direct payments to lawyers. People say, "So what?" As the Wall Street Journal said this week, "If we could devote just some of that money to productive activity, we could do far more for our economy than all the Government investment that Governor Clinton promises." For our economy, for productivity, for our national sanity, we must sue each other less and care for each other more. It is a crying shame when your neighbors can't coach Little League because of a frivolous lawsuit, or someone sees a victim along the side of the highway and doesn't dare stop because he or she remembers a case of where a lawyer came on and said, "Oh, you shouldn't have moved that person, and we're going to sue you." We can't do that. We are a caring country. We've got to put caps on these outrageous liability claims.

We also, obviously, we must reduce this deficit, but not by raising taxes but by getting ahold of spending, cutting spending. We need a balanced budget amendment. We need a line-item veto so the President can cross out frivolous expenditures. This one isn't easy, but we need to cap the growth of the mandatory programs. Set Social Security aside, except Social Security, but get ahold of the growth of those mandatory programs that make up two-thirds of the President's budget. And we need a check-off on your tax return so each taxpayer can earmark up to 10 percent of his taxes to be used for nothing but getting the debt off our children's shoulders.

We have simply got to restore hope to our inner cities. And so I will work with the new Congress to get tougher crime laws, to battle more on this drug problem—we're making some progress there but we've got to do better—to reform the welfare system and to attract and keep business. All using this principle of putting faith and power not in bureaucracies but instead in real people. And perhaps most important, we will reform and right-size Government, subject it to the same discipline as every other large organization in America.

Now, that then is our agenda for America's renewal, and it builds on the foundation we've laid for the last 4 years. But it's what I've been talking about on the campaign trail and what I will fight for in my second term. Obviously you must be thinking, well, it sounds great, but what will be different? After all, today there is a gridlock in Congress, gridlock in Washington. If people want arguments and shouting, they can turn on their TV talk shows, but they expect and deserve better from their elected officials.

I understand this, but I really believe we have an historic, unique opportunity before us. After next week there may be up to as many as 150 new Members of Congress from both parties, all who have heard the same rumble of discontent across our land. So I plan to use the time between November through January to meet with all the new Members of Congress and to shape a legislative package in a way that will guarantee swift passage. The time to move for a new President, with no politics over the horizon, and a reelected President, is early in the first term. Politics aside, sit down with Democrats and Republicans and get the people's business done fast.

We will set deadlines for decisions, and we'll meet them. We'll put aside partisan politics, as I tried to do in the very first term—and we did get some very good things done early in the first term—and we'll abandon this politics as usual. When we confronted Saddam Hussein we saw that when America turns its attention to a problem, we can do literally anything. We can mobilize for war. We can mobilize for hurricanes. Let's mobilize for our economy and get this country moving again.

If we need to, we'll go beyond Washington. Already our America 2000 education reform effort involves parents and teachers and business leaders in over 2,000 communities, and this will be a model for other efforts. America's desire for positive change requires building new coalitions and taking advantage of grassroots power, and we will.

That then is my action plan. But what about Governor Clinton? In June, he promised to present his 100-day plan even before the election. That's 4 days away. No plan, no plan has been sighted yet, and the reason is simple. You're more apt to see a UFO than you are his plan. [*Laughter*] The reason is simple: The numbers, his numbers, just don't add up. He's promised too much. His new congressional friends want to raise the ante even higher, and the result will be more spending, a bigger deficit, continued gridlock.

My agenda offers an alternative. We can break the gridlock without breaking the bank. A vote for our philosophy is a vote for change that really matters; a vote for change that builds on our strengths, not accentuates our weaknesses; a vote for a philosophy that is right for your businesses, right for your families, right for America.

Let me wrap up now with a word about character. Listen to the words of Horace Greeley. He said, "Fame is a vapor, popularity an accident, riches take wing; only character endures." I think that as you look back in history, hopefully now, I think that's especially true in the Presidency. Character matters, not just because of the plans you make but the crisis you never foresee.

A couple of weeks ago my Secretary of Defense, Dick Cheney, gave a speech that didn't get a lot of attention. But he made an objective case that the world is still very uncertain. He said, and I quote, "The next 4 years may be far more challenging, far more difficult, the problems far more complex internationally than the problems we've just come through the past 4 years." We don't know where the next crisis will occur. But we do know this: When the next crisis happens, the entire world will look to the American President. They will look to his experience, and they will count on his character, on his word of honor.

What is character? How do you define it? I'm not sure. But a friend of mine says it's acting alone the way you would act with a million people watching. As President you're never more alone than at times of a crisis. While nobody may be watching in the Oval Office, millions here and abroad will feel the impact of your judgment.

It is easy, in the aftermath of Desert Storm, to portray the decision to go to war as an easy one, but it was not. Think back. It was not uniformly popular. The Democratic Congress had spent much of the fall parading experts who said we'd get into another Vietnam. They said a war would kill any hope for peace in the Middle East. What really got to me was the charge that I didn't care about the numbers of body bags that were coming back from the sands of Kuwait. The vote in the Congress was not overwhelming. Many said, let's give sanctions more time. But I made the tough decision, a decision to go to war, because I knew it was right, not because I knew it was popular.

I remember well the cold, rainy February day at Camp David when the ground war to liberate Kuwait began, and how fervently I prayed that our plans would work and our young men and women would return home victorious and alive. This, then, is an awesome responsibility, to ask our young men and women to knock early on death's dark door—is a responsibility I believe I have fulfilled with honor and duty and, above all, integrity.

That is your call on November 3d. Then the polls and the pundits don't matter any more. God bless them, it's all up to the people. When you enter that voting booth, please ask yourself three commonsense questions: Who has the right vision for America's future? Who can lead us through this global transition? And which candidate has the character? Who would you trust with your kids? Who would you trust in a crisis?

Ideas, action, character. I have tried very hard to demonstrate that I have all three. So I ask for your support on November 3d.

Thank you, and may God bless the United States of America. Thank you very much.

Note: The President spoke at 10:40 a.m. at the Opryland Hotel. In his remarks, he referred to John M. Cranor III, president and chief executive officer, Kentucky Fried Chicken; Kyle T. Craig, president, KFC–USA; John R. Neal, president, JRN, Inc.; Charles W. Middleton, president, KFC of Elizabethton; and Steven D. Provost, Assistant to the President and Chief Speech Writer.

Remarks on Arrival in St. Louis, Missouri
October 30, 1992

Thank you, Don. I just will only say that I am very, very grateful to Governor Schaefer. This is of tremendous support. And yes, we're friends. But I've respected his work for a long, long time. We believe in many of the same objectives. I'm delighted that Maryland is leading the way to America 2000, our education reforms. I've been at his side as we've talked health care, trying to provide better health care for all. I've valued his trust and support during troublesome times of Desert Storm and other matters related to foreign affairs. You heard him talk about international trade.

So it is an honor for me to be endorsed by this outstanding Democratic Governor. And it's just one more reason that I feel that I will, on November 3d, be elected for 4 more years. So, Don, thank you, sir, very much for being with us.

Note: The President spoke at 12:30 p.m. at Lambert/St. Louis Airport. In his remarks, he referred to Gov. William Donald Schaefer of Maryland.

Remarks at a Rally in St. Louis
October 30, 1992

The President. Thank you very much.

Audience members. Four more years! Four more years! Four more years!

The President. Thank you all very, very much. Thank you so much for this great return-to-Missouri reception. May I start by thanking the Democratic Governor of Maryland. It takes a lot of guts to do what he did today, and I'm delighted to have his endorsement.

Of course, the special icing on the cake is to have the support of Jack Buck and have him here today. I would remind Jack of the old saying, when the Atlanta Braves were being—said they couldn't make the World Series—you remember the old saying, "It ain't over 'til Cabrera swings"? It turned out to be coming-back time, and I'm proud to have Jack at my side.

Of course, John Ashcroft, this great Governor of this great State. I'll tell you, he has done a superb job for me, and I know that it'll mean that we'll carry Missouri. May I also thank two great Senators, one of whom is comfortably there now; the other one is comfortably there, but he must be reelected. I'm talking about Kit Bond for the United States Senate, and Jack Danforth, who brings us such quality in that body. If we had more Senators like that, people wouldn't be yelling, "Clean House!" all the time. But we know how to clean House, and so I've got some good ideas for here. Elect Jim Talent to the United States Congress. Provide us new leadership by sending Mack Holekamp to the United States Congress, and add the names Montgomery and Ferguson, and we will clean House.

I know it's going to be hard to fill the shoes of John Ashcroft, but send Bill Webster, elect him Governor. We've got to have a Republican Governor.

May I thank all the students at Maryville and thank everybody involved in this rally. You know what I feel today? The "Spirit of St. Louis." And I've felt that spirit in Ohio and in Michigan and New Jersey and in Florida and all across this country. And that spirit tells me in my soul that on November 3d, we are going to be reelected for 4 more years.

Audience members. Four more years! Four more years! Four more years!

The President. It boils down to experience, to a difference in philosophy, and yes, it boils down to character. Character and trust matter.

I hate to ruin this beautiful rally out here,

but I've got to put in perspective the record of Arkansas. It won't take me long, but you've got to listen. Here's a man who wants to be President of the United States, and here is the Arkansas record. They're good people there. Barbara and I lived next door to them. They're entitled to something better: 50th in the quality of environmental initiatives; 50th in the percentage of adults with a college degree; 50th in per capita spending on criminal justice; 49th in per capita spending on police protection; 48th in percentage of adults with a high school diploma; 48th in spending on corrections; 46th on teachers' salary; 45th in the overall well-being of children. And he said in the last debate, "I want to do for America what I've done for Arkansas." No way! No way!

Audience members. Boo-o-o!

The President. We cannot let that happen. We cannot let him do that to this country. I think people are beginning to focus on that.

For 11 months, Governor Clinton and a bunch of the other liberal Democrats were running around saying everything that was wrong with me and everything that's wrong with America. Now we see the American economy is growing, not shrinking, and we are going to win this election.

No, Governor Clinton and the Ozone Man, all they do—[*laughter*]—all they do is—hey, listen, put Ozone in there and every worker who depends on reasonable balance between the environment and growth and business is going to be out of work. I'm a good environmental President, but we're not going to go to the extreme under Clinton and Ozone.

No, but they both talk about change, change, change. Well, here's what they want to change. They want to bring in, just for openers, $150 billion in new taxes, $220 billion in new spending, trickle-down Government, and the numbers don't add up. So when they say we're going after the rich guys, you cab drivers, you nurses, you teachers, watch your wallet; they're coming right after you. And we're not going to let them do it.

I don't want to ruin this part of the rally either, but we've got to remember what happened when we had a President of the Democratic left, like Bill Clinton, with a Democratic Congress. You remember what it was like? Inflation, 15 percent; interest rates 21.5 percent; the "misery index" twice what it is now, up around 20. And if you put in for that kind of change, change is all you'll have in your pocket. Let's not take a chance with the future of America.

The only way, the only way that Governor Clinton and Senator Gore can win is to convince everybody that everything in this country is wrong. They got the worst news in the world, which happened to be great news for the American working man and woman, because the other day it came out that instead of the recession that they've been talking about, instead of the recession that many of those national talking heads in the media have been talking about, we grew at 2.7 percent.

Now, wait a minute, a word of caution on the media. Please bear with me. The guys with the cameras and the long boom mikes and carrying the burden out there, they're good guys. The traveling press with us, exempt them from the anger. But if you want to know who I really feel strongly about, it's those Republican consultants and those Democratic consultants on those deadly Sunday talk shows saying I don't have a chance. We are going to show them wrong. We're going to prove them wrong. Annoy the media. "Annoy the media. Re-elect Bush." Every American knows what that means. Every American knows what it means. Even the press traveling with me knows what it means.

But I feel like Harry Truman when he talked about 50 reporters. He said not one of them knows enough to pound sand in a rat hole. And that's what we're going to show them on Tuesday. They can't do any more to me, so I'm on the offense.

Now look, yes, there's some good news. Yes, there's some good news, but a lot of people are still hurting. So, here's what we want to do to help them. First place, we've got to control the growth of Federal spending and hold the line on taxes. Secondly, and Governor Schaefer talked on it, we've got to open new markets. It is exports that have saved us through this tough international economic slowdown. It's exports that'll lead the way out. We are going to open up markets for the best products in the world, those that say "Made in America."

We do not need to do, I will say this to the auto workers in this State, what Governor Clinton and Ozone want to do. They said in their energy strategy, Governor Clinton did, that he wanted 45 miles per gallon of these fuel efficiency standards. That would break the auto companies, throw men out of work. We are not going to let them do that extreme to the United States of America.

I'll tell you what to do. Governor Clinton wants to grow Government, have Government invest. Government never invested in a creative job in its life, but small business does. So let's lift the regulation on small business. Let's give them some tax incentives. And let's get rid of these crazy lawsuits, these crazy lawsuits that are driving a lot of small business for cover.

Governor Clinton will not touch the trial lawyers, lawsuit crowd. He's supported by them. The trial lawyers' man down there said, "He's never gone against us yet." Let me tell you something: When a guy can't practice medicine; a woman doctor won't go to deliver a baby because she's afraid of a lawsuit, a malpractice suit; when you don't stop along the highway, afraid some trial lawyer's going to come along and kind of get the person you're trying to help to sue you; when a coach won't coach Little League, it is time that we put a cap on these crazy liability suits, and let's get that burden off the back of small business.

Health care: We've got a good program on health care. Make insurance available to the poorest of the poor through vouchers. Help the overtaxed middle class with tax credits. Keep insurance and pool it so small businesses can get insurance for the same price as these great, big companies. But do not put the Government in charge of health care. You'll ruin the quality of health care.

A guy says, "Give 'em hell." I just tell the truth, and they think it's hell. There's another one from Harry Truman.

Education: Governor Schaefer talked about it. Governor Ashcroft in this State has been right out in the lead on helping the schoolteachers, the community leaders, and the parents revolutionize education. We

spend per capita, it's higher than any country except Switzerland, and we're not getting the results. So what we've got to do is work my program, America 2000, get every community involved, literally reinvent our schools. And while we're at it, let's give parents school choice for public, private, and religious schools. It'll work.

I've got a big difference with Governor Clinton on crime because, you see, I think it's time we have a little more sympathy for the victims of crime and a little less for the criminals themselves. Thus, I'm fighting for stronger anticrime legislation. In Arkansas, the prisoners spend 20 percent of their sentences, that's all, in jail; Federal prisoners, 85 percent. We've got to be tougher on them and back up our law enforcement officers. Guess who endorsed me the other day? The Fraternal Order of Police from Little Rock, Arkansas.

We talk about getting the deficit down. Our plan will do it. But let me just ask for some things for the American people to give the next President. I want to see a balanced budget amendment. Make the Congress get it done. I want to see a taxpayer check-off that says to every taxpayer, check off 10 percent of your income tax, and once that's done, the Congress must make the reductions. If you don't, you have a sequester all across the board. Give the power to the people to tell the Congress what we want. And then third, let's have some term limits for the United States Congress. The President is limited. That ought to be a good one. And the fourth point, give me a line-item veto. Let the President cut out all this extra stuff they throw into the— [*applause*].

You know, we've heard a lot of discussion down the wire here about character, whether it matters or not. Governor Clinton said the other night in debate, he said it's not the character of the President but "the character of the Presidency." Let me tell you something: They're interlocked. What the President does reflects all around the world. People judge our country to a large degree by that. They are interlocked. And I don't believe you can have a person in the White House who's going to try to be on all sides of every issue, flip-flopping. The pattern of deceit is wrong for America.

One day he's for right to work in one State, and then he goes to the union bosses and says he's not. One time he's considering term limits; then he's against it. One time on the war—here's what he said on the war, he said, "I agree with the minority, but I guess I would have voted with the majority." What kind of waffle house is that? Good heavens. Good heavens, you can't be on all sides. If you make a mistake, you look the American people in the eye, "Hey, I messed that one up." Then you go on and lead. But you don't do it through a pattern of deception. And you don't do it through waffling.

No, I believe, I really and truly believe that character does matter. Barbara and I have tried hard to uphold the trust that has been placed in us for 4 years. Frankly yes, I wish she were here. She'd be thrilled by this fantastic—and I think we've got a great First Lady, incidentally. And I think we've got a great First Dog, and that dog knows more about foreign policy than Governor Clinton and Gore.

So let me tell you why I think character matters. You know, Horace Greeley said this: "Fame is a vapor, popularity an accident, riches take wing; only character endures." I really believe that is especially true in the Presidency. It matters not just because of the plans you make, but the crises you never foresee.

You know, Dick Cheney, our great Secretary, said the other day that the world is still very uncertain. And he's right. We don't know where the next crisis will come from. But we do know this: When it happens, the entire world will look to the American President, and they will look to his experience, and they will count on his keeping his word. They will count on his character. Never forget it.

You know, there's a lot of students here. Let me just end with a serious note. You might say, what is character? And a friend of mine says, well, it's acting alone the way you would act with a million people watching. As President you are never more alone than at time of a crisis. While nobody may be watching in the Oval Office, millions will feel the impact of a Presidential decision in time of crisis.

It's an easy aftermath to Desert Storm to portray the decision to go to war as an easy one. But think back to the demonstrations in front of the White House, to the problems in the United States Congress, to the honest men and women who said we don't want to do this because we may end up in another Vietnam. I'll tell you what hurt me the most was the charges that I was uncaring about body bag counts. You heard it from some of the talking heads, and you heard it from some of the protestors. But the Congress had spent much of the fall parading experts up there to the Congress saying, "Well, they're going to have another Vietnam. We must avoid it." And they said that a war would kill any hope of peace in the Middle East.

The vote in the Congress, as you remember, was not overwhelming. Many said, "Let's give sanctions more time." But I had to make a tough decision. And the decision was to go ahead, because I knew it was right, not because I thought it was popular. And I remember, I will never forget it with Barbara at my side in that little chapel at Camp David on a cold day just before the ground war to liberate Kuwait began, and how fervently, frankly, I prayed for our plans that they would work. When you send somebody else's kid, somebody else's son, somebody else's daughter into combat, it is a very difficult decision, and I prayed they'd come back. There is an awesome responsibility here, and it's a responsibility I have tried very, very hard to fulfill as President of the United States. You see, I believe in duty, honor, and country, and I always will.

So I believe character is important. And it's your call. On November 3d then the polls and the pundits don't matter anymore. It's that individual in the booth with his conscience or her conscience. When you enter that voting booth, please ask yourself three commonsense questions: Who has the right vision for America's future to help especially the young people? Who can lead us through this global transition? And which candidate has the character? Who would you trust with your family? Who would you trust with your country in a moment of crisis?

Ideas, action, character, I believe I have demonstrated. I certainly have tried to demonstrate all three. And so I ask you, go to the polls on November 3d, give me your vote, and let us lead America to new heights of prosperity.

Thank you, and God bless our great country. May God bless the United States. And don't let them say we're a nation in decline.

We're a nation on the move. Thank you all. Thank you very much. Thank you for this great day.

Note: The President spoke at 1:12 p.m. at the Maryville Center Executive Park. In his remarks, he referred to Gov. William Donald Schaefer of Maryland and CBS announcer Jack Buck.

Memorandum of Disapproval for the Military Health Care Initiatives Act of 1992
October 30, 1992

I am withholding my approval of S. 3144, the "Military Health Care Initiatives Act of 1992." This legislation would substantially change Federal policy with respect to abortion.

S. 3144 would provide that any eligible member of the Armed Forces or dependent "is entitled" to obtain an abortion "in the same manner as any other type of medical care" at U.S. military facilities overseas. It would thus require these Federal facilities to provide abortion on demand, even as a method of birth control, at least through the sixth month of pregnancy.

Contrary to the claims made by some supporters of this legislation, S. 3144 would establish a rule on the availability of abortions at military facilities overseas more radically pro-abortion than the laws in most parts of the United States. The bill is also broader than the pre-fiscal year 1989 practices of the Armed Services, which had been to provide elective abortions at military facilities with limitations, including restrictions on late-term abortions.

Current DOD policy is to perform abortions only if the life of the mother is threatened. I have repeatedly voiced my strong support for that policy and made clear that any attempt to weaken it would warrant disapproval. Accordingly, I am withholding my approval of S. 3144.

GEORGE BUSH

The White House,
October 30, 1992.

Statement on Signing the Reclamation Projects Authorization and Adjustment Act of 1992
October 30, 1992

Today I am signing into law H.R. 429, the "Reclamation Projects Authorization and Adjustment Act of 1992."

The Act will make a major contribution to the development and reform of water resources in States throughout the West. It is the product of years of debate and compromise in the Congress. This bill will provide substantial economic and environmental benefits throughout the West.

H.R. 429 authorizes numerous water projects in the western States that the Administration has supported. Included among the projects in the bill are the Buffalo Bill Dam and Reservoir in Wyoming; the Central Utah Project; South Dakota water planning studies; the Cedar Bluff Unit in Kansas; the Vermejo and Elephant Butte

Projects in New Mexico; the Glen Canyon Dam affecting the Grand Canyon in Arizona; the Sunnyside Valley Irrigation District in Washington; the Plataro Dam and Reservoir and the Leadville Mine Drainage Tunnel in Colorado; the Mountain Park Project in Oklahoma; and the Central Valley Project in California.

Several of the provisions that substantially reform the operation of the Central Valley Project in California are less flexible and more intrusive on the rights of the State of California and current project beneficiaries than I would have preferred. Nevertheless, the final bill includes several substantial modifications to the original House-passed version. These modifications will ensure that the fish and wildlife objectives of the legislation can be met in a manner that maintains the viability of other important uses to which CVP water is now devoted. Moreover, by establishing a voluntary system of water transfers—on a willing seller basis—H.R. 429 presents an important opportunity to increase the availability of water for uses which will best accommodate California's growth. A market-oriented water policy will create new jobs in the California economy.

I am concerned, however, that a number of provisions, if broadly construed, could violate the basic principle of Federal Western water policy—State primacy. A fundamental principle of my Western water policy is that the Federal Government must respect the primary role that individual States have in shaping and controlling their own policies regarding water use and allocation. An individual State is best positioned to assess its needs and to accommodate competing interests. Except in those instances where an overriding Federal interest or an interstate conflict is present, States should retain primacy in fashioning their policies regarding water. Accordingly, I am directing the Secretary of the Interior, in implementing this legislation, to ensure that its provisions are conducted with due deference to State primacy. In addition, in implementing section 3411(a), I am directing the Secretary of the Interior to consult with the California Water Resources Control Board before reallocating water to implement title XXXIV, even if such reallocation

might be allowable under the current conditions in existing permits or licenses. Lastly, I intend to submit legislation in the coming Congress which is substantially consistent with that introduced by Senator Seymour (S. 2016) in the 102nd Congress. This legislation has as its primary objectives the mitigation and enhancement of fish and wildlife resources in the Central Valley of California and the orderly allocation of available water supplies while maintaining the productivity of the Bureau of Reclamation's Central Valley Project.

H.R. 429 also contains certain provisions that warrant careful construction to avoid constitutional concerns. First, section 301 establishes a Utah Reclamation Mitigation and Conservation Commission that would formulate the policies and objectives for the implementation of certain projects authorized by the Act and administer expenditures of substantial Federal funds. The Commission members are to be appointed by the President from lists submitted by certain members of the Congress, the Central Utah Water Conservancy District, and the Governor of Utah. In order to avoid any conflict with the Appointments Clause of the Constitution, I will interpret the Act to provide for the appointment of members of the Commission after due consideration of the recommendations of those submitting lists, and not to inhibit my discretion to request from those groups and individuals the names of additional potential nominees.

Second, section 301(h)(3) permits the Commission to "secure directly from any department or agency of the United States" information necessary to enable it to carry out the Act, and requires the heads of all agencies and departments to comply with a request for information from the Commission. I will construe this section consistent with my authority to supervise and guide executive branch officials, and to control access to information the disclosure of which might significantly impair the conduct of foreign relations, the national security, or the deliberative processes of the executive branch or the performance of its constitutional duties.

Third, section 3201 establishes the conditions under which a South Dakota Preservation and Restoration Trust may receive and disburse Federal funds. Under the Act, such a trust must be governed by a five-member Board of Trustees, three of whom would be appointed by the members of the South Dakota congressional delegation, and one each of whom would be appointed by the South Dakota Academy of Sciences and the Governor of South Dakota. Under the Supreme Court's decision in *Washington Metropolitan Airports Authority* v. *Citizens for the Abatement of Aircraft Noise, Inc.*, such a board exercises sufficient Federal power to subject it to separation of powers scrutiny. The Board, moreover, performs functions that are executive in nature, and therefore agents of the Congress may not manage its affairs. In addition, all members of the Board appear to exercise significant governmental authority, yet are not appointed in a manner consistent with the Appointments Clause. For all these reasons, I direct the Secretary of the Interior, in consultation with the Attorney General, to propose legislation to remedy these constitutional defects. Such legislation must be effective prior to the expenditure of any appropriated funds.

Fourth, section 3405(a)(1), which purports to give contracting districts or agencies the authority to review and approve certain transfers of water under standards established by the Act, could be construed to permit the exercise of Federal executive power by the districts or agencies, which are not composed of individuals appointed pursuant to the Appointments Clause of the Constitution. To avoid constitutional questions that might otherwise arise, this section must be interpreted so as not to vest such power in those districts or agencies. Accordingly, I will interpret the role of these bodies under this section to be an advisory one.

Notwithstanding the concerns I continue to have with certain provisions of the bill, I am signing H.R. 429 so that the establishment of water markets in California, and the bill's numerous beneficial water projects, can move forward without further delay. On balance, these projects will better enable the citizens in our western States to manage one of their most precious resources.

GEORGE BUSH

The White House,
October 30, 1992.

Note: H.R. 429, approved October 30, was assigned Public Law No. 102-575.

Remarks on Beginning a Whistlestop Tour in Burlington, Wisconsin
October 31, 1992

The President. Well, thank you all. Before we say all aboard, let me thank Tommy Thompson for being at my side through thick and thin. When everything looked a little more difficult than it does today, he stayed right at our side. He has been an outstanding Governor. He has led not just this State but many in the country by the example you all have set, the example he has set. And I am very proud to have the Thompsons as good, close personal friends of the Bush family. Thank you, Tommy.

May I thank Mayor Hefty and our Republican chairman, Dave Opitz; and John MacIver, an old friend, helping so much on our campaign. But there's some real business ahead for next Tuesday. We must keep Bob Kasten in the United States Senate. He is doing a superb job for our country, a real leader up there. So do not gamble with the future. Make sure you've got Bob Kasten returned to the Senate.

And you know, everyplace I go—haven't seen them here today—but you see these signs saying, "Clean House!" Clean House. People are tired of that House of Representatives being controlled by that same body for 38 years, the one institution that hasn't changed. Send Mark Neumann to the United States Congress.

And we Bushes are delighted to be here in Burlington, the Chocolate City, USA. If my opponent were here today he might even inhale, it smells so good. [*Laughter*] Don't take it personally, Bill, please. These guys can dish it out, but they can't take it too well. Well, anyway.

And may I salute the veterans here today from the VFW. And let me just say this: I am proud to have worn the uniform of this country. I believe in honor, duty, and country. And I salute those who served.

Today is Halloween, our opponents' favorite holiday. [*Laughter*] They are literally trying to scare America. The only way that the Clinton-Gore ticket can win is if they convince us that we're a nation in decline. And here's the way they do it. They say we're less than Germany but a little more than Sri Lanka, or if they can convince the hard-working families in this country that we're in a deep recession. Neither is true. We are the most respected nation in the world. And our economy, thank God, is moving forward. So the difference on Tuesday is going to be a difference between experience, a philosophy, and yes, it is very important, character matters.

You know, for months, Governor Clinton has been ill-defining our record and talking very little about his. So on this lovely Saturday, let me just tell you some facts about Arkansas. I won't dwell on it because I don't want to ruin this day. Arkansas: 50th in the quality of environmental initiatives; 50th in the percentage of adults with college degrees; 50th in per capita spending on criminal justice; 49th in spending on police protection; 48th in percentage of adults with a high school diploma; 48th in spending on corrections; 46th on teachers' salaries—getting better—45th on the overall well-being of children. And he said in the debate, "I want to do for America what I've done for Arkansas." No way! We're not going to let him do that.

Audience member. [*Inaudible*]

The President. Please point out I did not invent that expression. [*Laughter*]

Governor Clinton says he's a candidate of change. Let's take a close look, a little look, at what he's talking about. Under him, every day is going to be Halloween: fright and terror. He dreams of—he talks about

Government investing. The answer is not to have Government investing by taking more of your taxes. The answer is for us to stimulate small business by tax relief, less regulation, and less lawsuits that finish off a lot of these small businesses.

The last time we had his kind of change, remember what it was like? He loves to point out—he goes, "Let's go back to Herbert Hoover." Let's not. Let's go back to Jimmy Carter, when you had a Democrat in the White House and that spendthrift Congress, led by those liberal Democrats. And what did you have? Maybe some of the young ones don't remember. Interest rates 21.5 percent; inflation 15 percent; the "misery index" that they invented twice as much as it is now. And you want that kind of change? Change is all you'll have left in your pocket if you put this guy into office.

No, a lot of families are hurting, but the economy is moving. And the worst news in the world—you could see the tears coming down the face of the Governor and the Ozone Man—you could see it when the tears trickled down their face because it came out that our economy grew for the sixth straight quarter, and grew at 2.7 percent. We're going to move. Now let's keep it going, but don't do it by raising taxes and increasing Government spending.

Our plan does just—here's what it does. It controls the growth of spending. It holds the line on taxes. And then I'm saying to the American people, give me these four things:

Give us a balanced budget amendment. Republicans want it. Conservative Democrats want it. Discipline the Congress and the executive branch by a balanced budget amendment.

Give us a check-off. Give you all a check-off, so if you feel strongly about the deficit you check a little box on your tax return, up to 10 percent of your tax, and that must go, under the law, to reducing the Federal deficit. If Congress can't do it, let the people have a say and try to get it done.

Then the next thing—43 Governors have it—give us a line-item veto, and let's stomp out some of the waste out of the spending.

And the fourth one, let's have the Congress, like the Presidency, let's have some term limits on the United States Congress.

You know, small business creates two-thirds of the new jobs. All we hear from Governor Clinton is let's get Government to invest. Government never invested productively a dime in anything. So we want to free up that small business sector, by giving them relief and letting them lead the way to new heights, new recovery, and new opportunity for these kids here today.

I mentioned litigation. We are suing each other too much and caring for each other too little in this country. It is a crying shame when a doctor is afraid to deliver a baby because of a malpractice suit; when a Little League coach is afraid to coach because somebody might bring a nutty lawsuit against them; or when you're driving along the highway, you see somebody hurt, you want to stop but you're afraid to for fear somebody will say, "Oh, they moved the body just wrong," and slap you with one of these ridiculous lawsuits. Let's put a cap on these lawsuits that are finishing off—[applause]—a lot of goodwill and finishing off a lot of small businesses.

Health care: We've got a good plan. Make insurance available to the poorest of the poor; pool insurance so you bring the prices down; and do something about malpractice that costs $20 billion to $25 billion a year. But do not let the Government ration health care or control prices, because we'll fail here like many others who have tried it failed abroad.

Education, education: Wisconsin's in the lead. We've got a good record, and we've got a good program. It says it's not good enough to do it the way the subcommittee chairmen in Washington say. Give the power not to the teachers union but to the teachers. God bless our teachers who are doing so much for our kids. And give parents—Milwaukee has led in this, Milwaukee has led—give parents the choice of public, private, or religious schools. Help them, and that will make all schools better.

Welfare reform: We've got bold new programs. Let me just salute your Governor for leading the Nation with Learnfare and Workfare and trying to break the cycle of welfare. That is a compassionate approach, the strong approach. I salute Tommy Thompson, and I want to see this happen for the entire country.

Crime: we've got a very positive record. Our spending to support our law enforcement officers is way up. The Arkansas record is sorry. The other day, who came to see me in the Oval Office? Eight officers. They were from the Little Rock Fraternal Order of Police. And they endorsed me for President of the United States.

And the point I'm going to make right down to the election is that character counts. You cannot make the White House into the waffle house. You cannot flip-flop on all these issues. Whether it's right to work, whether it's term limits, whether it's free trade, whatever it is, Governor Clinton can be on one side and then heroically on the other side. I am telling you that Harry Truman was right; the buck does stop on that Oval Office desk. It is a question of character if you keep trying to waffle and be on all sides.

Let me give you one key example. I had to mobilize probably the most historic world coalition we've ever seen in order to stand up against aggression in the Middle East. And I had to go against all these talking-head pundits; I had to go against demonstrations; I had to go against a determined Democrat majority in the House until we won them over. And where was Governor Clinton the day I made that fateful decision? He said, "Well, I agree with the arguments of the minority, but I guess I would have voted with the majority." What kind of leadership is that? That is a waffle. There is a pattern of deception here, and we cannot have that in the Oval Office. You cannot lead by misleading.

Finally, let me wrap it up by saying, first place, I'm elated that there's only 3 days more to go. Barbara and I can hardly believe it. I've given you some positive reasons, whether it's crime or education or welfare reform, to vote for me for President. But I'll give you another one. I think we've got the best First Lady we possibly could have.

But let me tell you why I believe that character——

Audience members. Barbara! Barbara! Barbara!

The President. Barbara's a perfect 10, the

man says. Okay.

But let me tell you why, in a serious moment here before we take this exciting train trip, let me tell you why I believe that character really does count. Remember, I cited this in the debate, but Horace Greeley said this: "Fame is a vapor, popularity an accident, riches take wing; only character endures." And I really believe that that's especially true in the Presidency. It matters not just because of the plans you make but because of the crises that you never possibly can foresee.

Yes, the world is much safer today. But as Dick Cheney, our able Secretary of Defense, reminded us the other day, who knows where the next crisis will come? The Soviet bear is dead, but there are a lot of wolves out there in the woods. So imagine, a year from today, if you picked up a newspaper out in front of your house and you read about some upheaval, some unforeseen upheaval, some terrorist getting ahold of a nuclear weapon, and how you would react to that. I believe that you've got to close your eyes, imagine in that dangerous situation an American leader without any experience, completely untested, a leader about whom literally we know very, very little. And what we do know is this troubling pattern that I mentioned, this pattern of being on one side, pattern of indecisiveness.

So I don't believe that we can take this kind of risk, not now, not in this incredibly uncertain time, and not when our children's security is at stake. When that next crisis occurs, and you can bet that somewhere it will, whether it's at home or abroad, the entire world is going to look to the American Presidency.

Bill Clinton says it's not the character of the President, it's "the character of the Presidency." Wrong. They're interconnected; they're locked. So you've got to ask, what is character? A friend said, well, it's acting alone the same way you would act with a million people watching. That's a good description. But while nobody may be watching in the Oval Office, millions will feel the impact of the judgment of the President of the United States.

I've been tested. We've managed world change that I think history will record as almost Biblical proportions. These young kids here go to bed at night without the same fear of nuclear war that their mothers and dads had. That is a major accomplishment, and we as a country can take great pride in it.

But I'll never forget when we were faced with a crisis now known as Desert Storm. I didn't waver. I took a stand. I made the decision to go to war because I knew it was right, not because I felt it was popular. You've got to go back and remember all the predictions of the body bags, and how I hadn't convinced the country, and how the demonstrators were expressing the will of the people, and that I had to make a lonely decision.

I'll never forget being with Barbara up at a little chapel we have there at Camp David, when we had to make a decision, when I had just made a decision. A couple of days later, America's sons and daughters would go into war again. It is not an easy decision. You've got to do it from conviction all the way. It's an awesome responsibility to ask anybody's kid to possibly knock on death's door a little early. It's a responsibility that I've tried very hard to fulfill with honor and decency and, yes, duty; above all, I hope, integrity.

And so that's your call. And now as we go down to the wire on November 3d, and all the polling and all the pundits won't make any difference at all. It's up to the American people. When you enter that voting booth, please ask yourself three common-sense questions: Who has the right vision for America's economic future? Who can lead us through this global transition? And which candidate has the character? Who would you trust with your family? Who would you trust with your country when a crisis arrives?

Ideas, action, and character: I have tried hard to be a proponent of all three. May God bless this country. Go to the polls. We need your support. We are going to win this election for the young people here today.

Thank you, and God bless each and every one of you.

Note: The President spoke at 9 a.m. at the train depot.

Remarks to the Community in Sussex, Wisconsin
October 31, 1992

The President. Thank you, Tommy. Let me return the compliment. In case Wisconsin doesn't know it—I know it; everybody else seems to know it—you have one of the truly great Governors in the United States, Tommy Thompson; great wife, Sue Ann.

Thank heavens for people like Jim Sensenbrenner in the United States Congress. We need more like him. Send us more like him, Tom Petri as well. May I thank Paul Fleischman, thank all of you. We've got a very important election coming up, and one of the key races is to reelect Bob Kasten for the United States Senate.

Audience members. Bobby! Bobby! Bobby!

The President. Well, I'm told that this is the home town of Quad Graphics. They do a lot of printing. One of the things they help with is Newsweek. Well, maybe you saw last week Newsweek had a cover of my opponent. And the caption said, "President Clinton?" with a question mark.

Well, we're about to answer that question. Hold the presses for the next cover. Tell all those Washington—those kind of salon leaders, tell those media talking heads we are going to win this election on November 3d. And here is why. Here is why. There is a vast difference between experience, political philosophy, and yes, a vast difference in character, and on all three of those I believe I will win.

I think we have it in focus now. After 11 months of Governor Clinton bashing us and our record, telling the Nation that we're in decline, the Arkansas record is finally in perspective. Here's a couple of the characteristics that you might want to guard against.

Arkansas is the 50th in the quality of environmental initiatives. Fiftieth—you're going to get worked up when you hear this list—50th in the percentage of adults with a college degree; 50th in per capita spending on criminal justice; moving up now, 49th in per capita spending on police protection; 48th in percentage of adults with a high school diploma; 48th in spending on corrections; 46th on teacher salaries; 45th in the

overall well-being of children. And he said in the debate, "I want to do for the United States what I've done for Arkansas." No way! No way! We're going to not let him do that.

Audience members. We want Bush! We want Bush! We want Bush!

The President. This guy says, the guy says, "Give 'em hell." I'm reminded of what Truman said. He said, "I don't give them hell, I just tell the truth and they think it's hell."

Governor Clinton says he's the candidate of change. Yes, that's the kind of change we need: $150 billion in more taxes, $220 billion more spending. That change would take us right back where we were the last time we had a Democratic President and Congress.

Audience members. Boo-o-o!

The President. You had interest rates at 15 percent, you had the—no, interest rates at 21 percent. You had inflation at 15. You had the "misery index" at 20. We've cut that in half. You had the country going the wrong way. Now we're starting to grow. Let's keep it growing.

You talk about change. All you hear from these two is change, change, change. That is all you will have in your pockets if you put Clinton and Ozone into office.

But look, we've been told that the whole world's going to Hell, and we're in a deep recession. We are growing, but we're not growing enough. It's going to be the United States because of my experience in international affairs that's going to increase the markets for Wisconsin products. We are going to lead the way internationally to new prosperity for the United States and for our workers.

Let me mention something about the farm; let me just mention the farm economy. Income on ag is up, in fact, in the last couple of years at record highs. Ethanol is up. As I drove through on this train through some of that beautiful corn country, I'm thinking, thank heavens we're using more ethanol. Thank heavens I stood up against the extreme environmentalists and said we're going to use more ethanol and try to use it year-round.

They get on me about calling Senator Gore Mr. Ozone. Well, let me tell you what I mean. We've got a good record on the environment. We're the ones that are leading on CFC's, on planting one million trees a year, on climate change, on getting a Clean Air Act. It is our administration that has done all these things. But I believe you can use ethanol, and I believe you do not screech this country to a halt in the name of some extreme environmental position. We've got a good record. But jobs matter. Families matter. Jobs and families ought to take a little priority around here, if you ask me.

Governor Clinton says he wants to have Government invest. Government can't even run a two-bit—Congress can't even run a two-bit bank or a two-bit post office. They can't invest anything. But it's small business that creates the jobs. So, less regulation, less Government spending, less in taxes for small business, and fewer lawsuits that drive small business to the wall.

The trial lawyers are the ones that are supporting Governor Clinton, and the people are supporting me. We're going to put a cap on these outrageous lawsuits that keep doctors from delivering babies or keep Little League coaches from coaching or keep somebody along the highway from helping his fellow man because they're afraid of some crazy lawsuit. Let's sue each other less and care for each other a little more in this country.

Health care: We've got the best program. Provide insurance to the poorest of the poor through vouchers. Help that overtaxed middle class by some tax credits. Get rid of the frivolous malpractice claims. But keep the Government out of the quality of health care. Our plan will work. Our plan will work.

Welfare reform: I salute your Governor. He is leading with Learnfare and Workfare. We've got to break the cycle of dependency, and I am proud that we have supported Tommy. We're going to do the same thing for the entire country: reform it, work and learn; work and learn.

Crime: I think we all ought to recognize that with the neighborhoods and some places being threatened by crime, we owe a great vote of thanks to our law enforcement officers, the police, the sheriffs, whoever they are. We need stronger anticrime legislation that has a little more compassion for the victims of crime and a little less for the criminals themselves. I've worked hard. We just got a bill through the Congress to do something about these deadbeat fathers, speaking of welfare reform, those that leave mothers with paying all the bills. We're cracking down on those people, and we're supporting the law enforcement people that are going after them.

Balanced budget: We've got the best plan to get this crazy deficit off the back of these young people. Here's some ideas for you. Why don't we do what a lot of States have and give us a balanced budget amendment, and make the Congress and the President get it down? Why don't we give you, the taxpayer, a check-off so you can say if you want to, we'll check off 10 percent of your income, and that then will have to be spent by Congress finding the reductions, have to be spent on lowering the deficit. The third one: How about giving me what 43 Governors have, that line-item veto? You're right. Take this, mark it out.

You know, we've had a big discussion in this election about character, and character does count. It is my view that as President you cannot waffle. You cannot be on all sides of every question. If you make a mistake, you do what your kids do. You look the people in the eye as President, and you say, "I made a mistake." Then you get on with leading the American people. But you cannot waffle.

Audience members. We trust Bush! We trust Bush! We trust Bush!

The President. You cannot vacillate and be on one side of an issue one day and one the next. The right-to-work States say, "Oh, I'm for right to work," and then come the labor leaders and say you're against it. Term limits: one day, oh, it makes sense; then in the debate, no, it makes no sense. North American free trade agreement: You heard it in the debate. I am for it, because it will create jobs through exports. He says, "Well, I am for it, but." You cannot have a lot of "buts" in that Oval Office. You've got to call them as you see them, like the umpire does. Call them, and take the consequences. Don't worry about your own popularity; do what is principled and right. You cannot lead America by misleading the American people. That's one of the reasons I am going to be reelected on November 3d.

Audience members. Four more years! Four more years! Four more years!

The President. You know, I had to make a tough call a while back when aggression threatened the entire Middle East and, in my view, would have threatened the United States. If we'd have listened to the critics, I believe Saddam Hussein would be sitting in Saudi Arabia today, and oil prices would be up about $10 a gallon for gas; certainly $5.

But we took some action, and I had to make a decision that was unpopular. And where was Governor Clinton? Here's what he said, I agree with the minority—that's a paraphrase—I agree with the minority, but I guess I would have voted with the majority. You cannot do that as the Commander in Chief of the Armed Forces. I believe because I did serve my country in war and did put on a uniform and do believe in honor, duty, and country that that makes me a better choice for Commander in Chief of the Armed Forces.

But let me tell you in conclusion why I think character counts. Do you remember what I said in the debate? I paraphrased Horace Greeley. And he says, "Fame is a vapor, popularity an accident, riches take wing, and only character endures." I think that is especially true of the Presidency of our great country.

I know that we've made the world safer. The Soviet bear is no longer. International communism, imperial communism, certainly on the wane, if almost nonexistent. But we've got to remember, there are still threats. There are still wolves in the woods. We've reached historic agreements with Boris Yeltsin to eliminate these SS-18's, the most destabilizing of all weapons. I am proud that we have done that. But the world is not free of conflict, and the United States must remain strong. We must not cut the muscle of our defense.

But I ask you to close your eyes and imagine in a crisis situation an American leader totally without experience, completely untested, a leader about whom we know very, very little, if you get down to it. What we do know is a troubling pattern of being on one side and then another, an ingrained habit of trying to lead by misleading and not coming clean. I don't believe we can take this kind of risk.

When that next crisis occurs, whether it is at home or abroad—and you can be certain one will occur—the entire world is going to focus on the American Presidency. And they're going to look to his experience, and they're going to count on his character.

Some say, well, what exactly is character? Well, a friend of mine put it this way, saying it is acting alone the same way you would act with a million people watching. Well, as President, you're never more alone than at times of crisis. While nobody may be watching the Oval Office, millions will feel the impact here and abroad, the impact of your judgment.

I have been tested, and we've managed world change of almost Biblical proportions. Our success can be measured by the headlines never written, the countless crises that never occurred. But when that real event did occur, I did not waver. I took a stand. I made the decision to go to war because I know it was right, not because it was popular.

I remember being at Camp David with Barbara on a cold day, rainy day, when the ground war was about to begin to liberate Kuwait. I remember the agony of having to decide, especially in the face of all the protests, especially in the face of all the criticism from some of the more liberal Members of the Congress saying, Bush will have on his hands the body bags. Do you remember the counts, 20,000, 50,000, whatever it was?

And I remember the agony of having to make that call. And I remember praying—yes, I do, and so does Barbara; we still say our prayers—praying that these young kids, somebody else's sons and daughters, would return home safe and sound. God bless those kids that went. God bless those that went.

What I think I'm trying to tell the American people here on this beautiful day in Wisconsin is, there is an awesome responsibility, to ask our young men and women to knock early on death's door. It's a responsibility that I have tried to fulfill with honor and duty for my country. I hope I brought integrity to it. But that is up to the people now on November 3d. And then the polls, all these pundits, they don't matter anymore. It is up to the American people.

When you enter that voting booth, I ask you to ask yourself three commonsense questions: Who has the right vision for America's economic future? Who can lead us through this global transition? And which candidate has the character to merit the trust of the American people?

Audience members. We want Bush! We want Bush! We want Bush!

The President. So my view is this: Do not listen to the doomsayers. Do not listen to those that say we're a nation in decline. We've got some big problems, but you solve them by leadership. I ask for your support. I ask for your trust to lead this, the greatest country on the face of the Earth, for 4 more years. Thank you.

May God bless the United States of America. May God bless our wonderful country. Thank you very much. Thank you so much. Thank you very, very much.

Now let me just say it is my view, my impartial view, that we've got the best First Lady we could possibly have. I want you to listen to her.

Note: The President spoke at 11:03 a.m. on the observation deck of the Spirit of America train. In his remarks, he referred to Mayor Paul Fleischman of Sussex. A tape was not available for verification of the content of these remarks.

Remarks to the Community in Oshkosh, Wisconsin
October 31, 1992

The President. Thank you. Thank you, Tommy. Thank you, Governor Thompson.

Audience members. Four more years! Four more years! Four more years!

The President. Thanks for that great Oshkosh welcome. Thank you. And may I salute Governor Tommy Thompson, who's doing such a great job for this State and for the whole country. You've got a great leader in Tommy.

And you've got a couple of good races going right here, but we must send Bob Kasten back to the United States Senate. He's doing a great job for Wisconsin and for the country. And I want to suggest that we get Tom Petri going, get him back there. He's looking awful good. We need him in the Congress. There he is over there.

You know, this Spirit of America, this wonderful train, is going all the way across Wisconsin. And we are not going to stop rolling until we win this election on November 3d. We are going to surprise these mournful pundits. We are going to annoy the media, and we are going to finish the job. I love it. And I'll tell you why we're going to do it. It's because the choice before the American people is a vast difference in experience, on philosophy, and yes, a vast difference on character.

I hate to ruin this day by talking about the Arkansas record. But before we go to the polls, let me just put a couple of figures in perspective. Here's the way Arkansas is doing. They are 50th in the quality of environmental initiatives; 50th in the percentage of adults with college degrees; 50th in per capita spending on criminal justice; 49th in per capita spending on police protection; 48th in percentage of adults with a high school diploma; 48th on spending on corrections; 46th on teachers' salaries; 45th in the overall well-being of children. And Governor Clinton said in that debate, "I want to do for America what I've done for Arkansas." No way! We're not going to let him do that. The people who know Governor——

Audience members. We need Bush! We need Bush! We need Bush!

The President. His own hometown newspaper, the Arkansas Gazette, couldn't endorse him for President. And the people that know him best agree that he will be wrong for America. Now, he talks about change. He says he's the candidate of change. We do not need to change by raising taxes and increasing spending. You want to go the Clinton route, every day will seem like Halloween. [*Laughter*] Fright and terror, witches and devils everywhere.

Governor Clinton dreams of expanding the American Government. I want to expand the American dream by stimulating small business.

The last time we tried the change that he wanted, you all remember that, remember what it was like with a Democrat in the White House and these same Democrats controlling Congress? You had interest rates at 21 percent—she remembers—you had inflation at 15, you had the "misery index" at 20, and you had hope and despair. Things are better, and they're going to be even better if you send us more Members of Congress like the ones that are here today.

You talk about change; with this guy's tax plan, that's all you're going to have left in your pocket if you get Clinton and the Ozone Man in there.

The only way that they thought they could win was to tell everybody in America that things were terrible. Some families are hurting, but we have grown for six straight quarters. We grew at 2.7, and we're doing far better than Japan, Germany, and the other countries around the world. It is the United States leadership that is going to lead the world to economic recovery with more jobs for America.

And here's how we're going to do it. In Wisconsin and others, we've got the best workers anywhere in the world. Let's open markets abroad. Let's expand trade with "Buy USA" products, "Made in USA" products going into every market around the world. And we are the ones to lead for that.

The farm economy is at a record high. We're doing better on ethanol. I was so pleased to drive through the corn country and see a good crop. We're doing better on exports. But this environmental extremist of the Ozone Man and Governor Clinton is not the way to go. Somebody ought to care about the working men and women in this country. We've got a strong environmental record, but it is not an extreme. And I do not want fuel efficiency standards of 40 to 45 miles per gallon that says to every auto worker, your job is at stake. Hold the line. Do not let them do that.

Governor Clinton says, "I want to have Government invest more." What I want to do is unleash small business. They create two-thirds of the job. Less regulation, less taxes, and less—these crazy lawsuits that run the cost of business up. Governor Clinton refuses to even try to put the caps on these lawsuits, these crazy malpractice suits, these liability suits. I will stand up to the trial lawyers. With a new Congress, we will get the job done.

We've got the best plan on health care. Governor Clinton wants to set up a board, a Government board for health care. I want to give vouchers to the poorest of the poor. I want to give credits to those overtaxed Americans. I want to make insurance available to all. I want to go after the malpractice suits. I want to pool insurance. But I do not want to let Uncle Sam try to run the health care in this country.

Education: We've got the best plan, America 2000. Governor Thompson and Wisconsin are in the lead on it. And what we say is, let's not worry so much about the National Education Association, let's help the teachers. Let's help the teachers, and God bless them for what they do for our kids. Besides that, one way to make schools better—public, private, and religious—is to give the parents a choice; help them choose public, private or religious schools.

Tommy Thompson has been in the forefront of welfare reform. We've got to break the cycle of dependency. And I am proud that we have been able to work with him by giving him waivers because, you see, I agree with Wisconsin that we need learning and we need work, and we don't need to perpetuate dependency on welfare.

On crime, I have a very radical idea about crime. I think we ought to back up our police officers a little bit more and have less concern for the criminals themselves; a little more concern for the victims, a little less for the criminal element. Back to Arkansas, in Arkansas the prisoners spend 20 percent of their sentence in jail. Under the Federal Government it's 85. I think we need to be a little tougher. Send me more Congressmen like these who will help us back the law enforcement officers and back the communities that are suffering from this outrageous crime. And the other day some guys from Arkansas came up and endorsed me for President, and they represented the Fraternal Order of Police of Little Rock, Arkansas. How about that?

With the new Congress we're going to reform Government. We're going to get the deficit down, and we're going to do it whether the liberals like it or not. We're going to get a balanced budget amendment. We are going to give the taxpayers a check-off so they can check off 10 percent of their income tax to be applied against the debt. We're going to fight for a line-item veto to let me have a shot at cutting the spending. And how about giving the Congress back to the people by term limits? The President's term is limited; how about term limits for Congress? Now we're getting down——

Audience members. Clean the House! Clean the House! Clean the House!

The President. Clean the House! That's a good idea. You've got a good Congressman. Give us more like him, and I wouldn't be reading those signs. But yes, one institution. The liberal Democrats have controlled Congress for 38 years. They wouldn't know change if it hit them in the face. Let's clean House!

Now let's talk about something that is going to be the determining factor. Character and trust, both of them matter. And over the past 24 hours——

Audience members. We want Bush! We want Bush! We want Bush!

The President. Over the past 24 hours, Governor Clinton has become panicked. He uses the word "pathetic." Well, he ought to know a performance like that when he sees one. He's afraid for the power that he's lusted for, the political viability that he wrote about when he was demonstrating against this country over in England, is going to slip away from him. He's afraid it's going to slip away, and he's begun a series of personal attacks on my character, and he has basically called me a liar. And the charges he makes are not new. I have responded to them repeatedly and under oath, under oath in numerous investigations in a 6-year, Democrat-run political fiasco that has cost the taxpayers $40 million. And yet, he has now latched on to these silly little charges, accusations, in a desperate attempt to stop his free fall in the polls. And we're not going to let him do that. We're going to keep on——

Audience members. Bush! Bush! Bush!

The President. You see, I welcome this. I welcome this spotlight on character because it is an essential test of the Presidency. And Governor Clinton, on character, simply cannot pass the test.

Here's a quote. Here's a quote from a paper a couple of days ago. Speaking at a crowd of 8,000, the Presidential nominee, in this instance that was Governor Clinton, said, "President Bush is a liar." Well, frankly, being attacked on character by Governor Clinton is like being called ugly by a frog. Don't worry about it. You want to talk character, Governor? You and Ozone want to talk character? All right, here we go. You can't go to the trade unions one day and say you're against right to work, and then propound that you are for it. You can't say you're for the North American free trade agreement in a debate, and then add "but." You don't need any "buts" in the White House. You've got to call them direct. Truman is right, the buck stops there.

Term limits, oh yes, he thinks that's good. But then he's opposed to it in the debate. He smoked a little, but he didn't inhale. Sure. Who believes that? This guy's wound up. You can't lead, you cannot lead the American people by misleading. And that's the bottom line. And the pumpkin in Arkansas Governor's Mansion has two faces: Whatever side you're on, he's right there. You can't do that as President of the United States.

Let me give you a little example of what I mean. On April 17th he said, "I'm going to come out with all my draft records." Fine. Some people agreed with him on the war; some didn't. But he said he was going to do it; he hasn't done it. Let me remind you about the war. I've already said my position. Frankly, I don't think when your brothers are rotting in a Hanoi jail, or when people that are drafted out of the ghettos are serving and being killed in Vietnam, that you ought to lead demonstrations against your own country in a foreign land. I don't believe that. He differed. But you can't have it both ways, is my point. You can't protect your political viability, and then still try to ask for the trust of the American people.

And let me give you one other example. I'll give you another example. If he wants to talk character and trust, how about this one? I had to make a tough decision on Desert Storm; it wasn't easy. But I'll tell you this. I looked the American people in the eye and said, this is what we're going to do. And where was Bill? He was saying, let me get it right now, he said, "Oh, I agree with the arguments made by the minority, but I guess I would have voted with the majority." What kind of waffling leadership is that? Character, trust—let's make the election on character and trust. That's the way we're going to win it.

And let me sum it up for you.

Audience members. Four more years! Four more years! Four more years!

The President. Four more.

Audience members. Four more years! Four more years! Four more years!

The President. Let me end on a very serious note, because on Tuesday we've got serious business. We have the privilege of going to the polls. And yes, I do believe character matters, not just because of the plans you make but because of the crises that you never foresee.

The world is a much safer place today. And I am very proud that these kids here go to bed at night without the same fear of nuclear war that their parents had. I am very proud that there is democracy and freedom around the world where there used to be imperial communism. But let me tell you this: We've got to stay strong. The Soviet bear may be gone, but there's wolves out there in the woods. And you'd better have a leader who you can trust when it comes to making tough decisions.

We have reached historic decisions to reduce and indeed eliminate nuclear weap-

ons. But they've yet to be implemented. And just yesterday or the day before I talked to Boris Yeltsin, and I was reminded of how uncertain things can be in foreign lands. Imagine a year from today, if you pick up your newspaper in front of you and you see that there is a crisis around the world, imagine reading about an upheaval somewhere, or about a terrorist dictator getting ahold of a nuclear weapon. And then the question of character and trust becomes very, very important. And you have to ask yourself, do you want a leader that has proven himself in mettle, whether in battle or in making tough decisions, or do you want a leader about whose character we don't know near enough and who has no experience? I say choose experience and character.

You know, when the next crisis occurs, whether it's domestic or international, the entire world is going to be looking to the American President. And Governor Clinton said in the debate, he said it's not the character of the President, he said, it's "the character of the Presidency." Wrong. They are interlocked. We are judged by the character of the person in the White House and, to some degree, by the family in the White House. And thank God we have Barbara Bush. And in this one, I think we've got a great First Lady. We've got a great First Lady.

Audience members. Barbara! Barbara! Barbara!

The President. This will go to her head if you keep this up. Now, come on. I've got to live with her.

You know, as President you are never, never more alone than at time of a crisis. And millions will feel the impact of your judgment. I believe I've been tested. We've managed world change of almost, I believe history will write this, of almost Biblical proportions. And our success can be measured by the headlines that were never written, the countless crises that never occurred.

But when a real evil did arise in the sands of the Persian Gulf, I did not waver. I took a stand and I made a decision to go to war, not because it was the popular thing to do but because it was the right thing to do.

And I'll never forget, nor will Barbara, just before the war broke out, actually, praying in our little chapel there at Camp David for the safety of someone else's sons and daughters who had to go into battle. And did they ever perform with courage and did they ever make America proud.

But this showed me that there is indeed in that office an awful, awesome responsibility. It's a responsibility that I have tried to honor. It is a responsibility that I have tried to fulfill with honor and duty and, above all, integrity.

So on November 3d it all boils down to this: All those naysayers, those pundits on those Sunday morning televisions won't be heard anymore, because we're voting on a Tuesday and you don't have to listen to them on election day. All these polls that are all over the field that these people live and die by, we don't have to read those anymore.

But when you enter that voting booth, you have to ask yourself three common-sense questions: Who has the right vision? And I've touched on the positive answers of that today. Who has the right vision for our economic future? Who can lead us through what is a global transition? Which candidate has the character? And who would you trust in a crisis with your family or with the United States of America?

Audience members. Bush! Bush! Bush!

The President. Ideas, action, and character. I have tried very hard to demonstrate all three. And so I came here to this great part of Wisconsin in Oshkosh to ask for your support, to ask for your vote. Do not believe we are a nation in decline. We are the United States of America, the most respected country on the face of the Earth. I ask for your vote for 4 more years to lead this country.

May God bless the United States of America. Thank you very much.

Note: The President spoke at 2:03 p.m. on the observation deck of the Spirit of America train.

Remarks to the Community in Stevens Point, Wisconsin
October 31, 1992

The President. Thank you. Thank you, Tommy. Thank you, Tommy Thompson. What a great Governor Wisconsin has in Tommy Thompson, a leader all across this country. And may I thank Mayor Shultz for the hospitality, and everybody that arranged this outstanding rally. It is first-class. It's good for the soul. It shows that we're moving.

And let's do ourselves a favor. Let's be very sure that Bob Kasten is reelected for the United States Senate. It is an absolute must. And you keep hearing "Clean House! Clean House!" Well, elect Dale Vannes to the United States Congress. Let's try to really do something different here.

Audience member. Clean the House!

The President. That's it, clean the House! That's the one institution that hasn't changed for 38 years. Let's clean it out right.

Well, it's great to be by the hardest working river in America and to talk with some of the hardest working people in America. And I like the kids in these costumes, kind of like a thousand points of fright. [*Laughter*] I saw one of those great big pumpkins back there. It had a face on one side, and they turned it around and it had a face on the other. I thought Bill Clinton was back somewhere else, but here he is.

No, I've got this wonderful feeling that things are on the move. And yes, annoy the media and reelect George Bush for President. Have you ever seen a year with that kind of coverage? I haven't, as long as I've been in politics.

But we're going to show them. We are going to win this election on November 3d. And here's why: It's a difference between experience, philosophy, and yes, a big difference in character. And that's why we're going to win the election.

I have been pointing out all day what many have failed to point out in a year, and that is the sorry record of Governor Clinton in Arkansas. He threatened the other night to do for America what he's done for Arkansas. And we cannot let that happen.

Audience members. Boo-o-o!

The President. Let me just give you a couple of statistics: 50th—here we are in a great outdoor state—50th in environmental initiative for Arkansas; 50th in percentage of adults with college degrees; 50th in per capita spending on criminal justice; 49th in per capita spending on police protection; 48th with adults with high school diplomas; 48th, spending on correction; 46th in teachers' salaries; 45th in overall well-being of children. We cannot let him do that to the United States of America.

His own hometown newspaper, the Arkansas Gazette, said they could not endorse him for President. The people that know him best think he is wrong for America.

Now, he talks about change, change, change. We cannot go back to the spend-and-tax ways that brought us inflation at 15 percent, interest rates at 21 percent, a "misery index" twice what it is today. Let us not go back to that change, because if we did, change is all you'd have left in your pocket. And we're not going to do that to the American people.

I guess one of the biggest differences we've got is on tax and spend. Governor Clinton has already said he wants to spend $220 billion more and he wants to tax you $150 billion, because he wants Government to invest. Government doesn't invest; small business does. So here's my plan: Let's cut the regulation. Got to give the break for investment tax allowances and for capital gains and for first-time homebuyers, tax credit. Let's get small business, the real employer, on the move.

Agriculture is doing well, thank heavens, and we cannot go back. And here's what we're going to do. Thank heavens ag income is up. Thank heavens I believe and have worked for ethanol, and ethanol is up under my administration. And the best answer is to close these trade agreements and open up the world market to the greatest production of agriculture in the world,

the United States of America.

The only way, the only way that Governor Clinton and the Ozone Man can win election, the only way they can do it is by convincing the country that everything is bad. The worst news they had was when it came out this week that growth across the country was 2.7 percent. We must keep it growing until every single American has a job with dignity in the private sector.

Audience members. We want Bush! We want Bush! We want Bush!

The President. I'll tell you, I'm getting to that. I'm getting to that one. I'll tell you something else we need that I'm for and that he's against: legal reform. We are suing each other too much and caring for each other too little in this country. We're spending $200 billion on lawyers and we ought to spend more on helping each other. And so my proposal is to put a cap on these outrageous liability suits that keep people from coaching Little League, keep friends from helping neighbors, keep doctors from practicing medicine. It is time to stand up to the trial lawyers and do something for the people.

Another big area, we've got the best plan for health care. Governor Clinton started off by saying, well, he has a "pay or play" plan. We pointed out to him that would throw a tax on small business of 7 percent. So once again, why, he backs away, the Waffle Man, moving away from it all.

But here's our plan: Make insurance available to all; make vouchers for the poorest of the poor so they can be insured and that insurance can go with them when they get a job, to another job; pool the insurance so you bring to small business, the guys along Main Street here, the same kind of price for insurance that the big companies can buy; go against malpractice suits. But do not do what Governor Clinton wants and then set up a price-fixing board by the Government. Government can't even run a post office, and the Congress can't run a two-bit bank. We don't need to get Government further involved.

Education: Clinton wants to do it the same old way. And we've got a program, America 2000, that gives the power to the communities, to the teachers, and to the parents, and gives school choice to every parent for private, public, or religious schools. It's worked in Milwaukee; it can work all across this country. Let's let Wisconsin lead the way to literally revolutionizing and improving our education.

A big difference on welfare. I salute Tommy Thompson, I salute all of you who have led the way for the Nation in saying this: We've got to break the cycle of dependency. We've got to give people a chance on welfare, some Learnfare, Workfare. It is not fair to the taxpayer unless people work their way off of welfare. And that's what we're doing.

A big difference on crime. We need more Senators there, like Bob Kasten, who stand up and favor the police officer and not the criminal element. Be tough on the criminal and have more compassion for the victims of crime. You know, I had a visit from about eight guys the other day. They came to see me; they were from Arkansas. They were the Fraternal Order of Police of Little Rock, Arkansas, and they endorsed me for President of the United States.

Now, I heard somebody ask about how we get this deficit down. First place, you do it by controlling the growth of mandatory spending. Second, you don't tax and spend. Third, how about this one, give us a balanced budget amendment and make that Congress live within its means. Give us a taxpayer check-off so everybody here that pays taxes, if he wants to or if she decides to, can check off on that tax return 10 percent of the tax to be used for one thing only: reducing the Federal deficit. And Congress must find the spending cuts to go with it. Then give me what 43 Governors have—every day I get legislation down there, every day legislation comes down loaded up with pork—give me the line-item veto. And if they can't do it, give me a shot at it.

And now let's talk about what's going to decide the election in addition to these good programs compared to the old tax-and-spend programs. Let's talk about character and trust. Governor Clinton, over the last 24 hours, has been frantically flopping around like a bass on the side of the Arkansas River, and panicked, afraid that these pollsters may indeed prove to be wrong,

those that had us dead and buried 2 weeks ago and now see us moving. So he's begun a new bunch of assaults on my character. And if Bill Clinton wants to play on the character field, let's go to work right now.

These crazy charges you heard out of him last night are not new. We've responded to them over and over again, you taxpayers have spent about $40 million on this Democratic witch hunt, and I'm sick and tired of it. The only way he can win is some last-minute smoking gun. The guy is not telling the truth about what happened. I am. I have. And I'll continue to.

Here is a guy, as I mentioned, whose hometown newspaper says he is a politician utterly devoid of principle; a guy whose supporters gave him the word "slick." I haven't used that, he has. I say "slippery when wet." I think that's a little better. [*Laughter*] Here's a guy who has waffled and weaseled about the draft. I can understand somebody not serving, but I cannot understand somebody trying to have it both ways, convincing the draft board one thing and then saying something else. He ought to level with the American people.

Here's a guy who actually went out—he doesn't like name-calling. I made a mistake; I won't repeat it today. But the difference is, if I make a mistake I admit it. But here's a guy that called me a liar the other day—I have the clipping here—and very frankly, being attacked by Governor Clinton on character is like being called ugly by a frog. It doesn't matter. He has no credibility in that field.

But here's why character counts. You cannot be on all sides of every issue if you want to serve as President of the United States. You see, Truman was right; the buck stops in the Oval Office. And my view is, if you make a mistake, look the American people in the eye and tell them you made a mistake, and then get on about the business of leading the American people.

But all through this campaign and all through his political career he's trying to be one thing to one group and another thing to another. Somewhere in Arkansas, oh, yes, he's for right to work. He goes to the unions and says he's not. On the North American free trade agreement—you heard it on the debate—first he was, well, he wasn't sure. Then he was for it. Then in the debate he says, "Well, I'm for it, but I'll make some more changes." You can't have a lot of "buts" in the White House. You've got to make up your mind and call them as you see them.

One time he was for the term limits, and then it didn't seem so good. There is this pattern of deception. There is this pattern of deception that is troubling the American people. And you can't lead the American people by misleading them.

Let me remind you of what he said at a critical moment in our history on the war. I had to make a tough call. And here's what Governor Clinton said. He said, "I agree with the arguments of the minority, but I guess I would have voted with the majority." What kind of character, what kind of leadership is that? It is none at all.

Audience members. Boo-o-o!

The President. And when I stood with Boris Yeltsin—and Yeltsin has said, "It was George Bush, the first international leader to stand with me, and that did more for the failure of that coup and the support of democracy than anything else"—where was Governor Clinton? He's saying, "Well, we better wait to see how it works out." You can't do that as President of the United States. So it does matter. Character does matter, and trust matters.

I believe we've got the best program. You see, Governor Clinton's going around telling everybody we're a nation in decline; we're less than Germany and maybe higher than Sri Lanka. Good heavens, he ought to open his eyes. Millie knows more about foreign affairs than he does. If you get out and look around the world, you'd see we have never been more respected. We are the leader. Even our economy is better than Japan and Germany and the rest of Europe and now Canada. We've been caught up in a global slowdown. And it is the United States of America that is going to lead the entire world out of it with more jobs for American workers.

And so in the final analysis, here's what it boils down to. Horace Greeley put it this way: "Fame is a vapor, popularity an accident, riches take wing; only character endures." And I think that's especially true for

the Presidency. Bill Clinton said—you heard it in the debate—it's not the character of the President, it's "the character of the Presidency." I think he's wrong. I think they are interlocked. And I think what both Barbara and I do in that White House is reflective of the character of the Presidency. I am very proud of our First Lady. I am very proud of what she stands for and the way she has conducted herself with dignity and honor and caring and compassion. And that's another good reason for 4 more years.

Audience members. Four more years! Four more years! Four more years!

The President. You know, if you'd have said 4 years ago, this President is going to be the one to see the end of the cold war, this President is going to be the one to have negotiated with the Soviet leader the elimination of all of these deadly ICBM missiles, this President is the one that's going to bring ancient enemies talking to each other in the Middle East and see democracy on the move south of our border, somebody would have said that you'd been inhaling. [*Laughter*] I'm telling you, these are dramatic changes, and I am very proud of them.

But here's the problem: That international communism, that imperial communism may be gone, the bear may be dead, but there are still wolves in the woods. And we'd better have a President who understands you've got to keep America strong to guarantee the national security of these kids, the security of these kids here tonight.

And so I ask you to imagine this. If you go in there, think about it when you go to the booth: Suppose there's a crisis here, domestically, some serious interruption, some crisis—or abroad. The question is: Who has the character and the trust to lead the United States of America? You cannot have a troubling pattern of deception in that Oval Office. It is too special. It is too trusted in itself by people around the world.

And so, let me tell you just a little experience I had. I don't believe that we can take the kind of risks that Governor Clinton is asking us to take. When the next crisis occurs, and you can bet that it will, the entire world is going to be looking to the American President. They're going to look at experience, and they're going to count on character.

And you might say, well, what is character? And I quoted it today. A friend of mine says it's acting alone the same way you would act with a million people watching. As President, you're never more alone than at times of a crisis. And while nobody may be watching the Oval Office, millions will feel the impact of your judgment, millions here and millions around the world.

And I believe I have been tested. We've managed world change of almost Biblical proportions, and our success can be measured by the headlines that were never written, the countless crises that never occurred. But when a real event did occur in the sands of the Persian Gulf, I did not waver. I took a stand. I made the decision to go to war not because it was popular but because it was the right thing to do.

I'll never forget being with Barbara up at Camp David just before our kids were sent into battle in Kuwait. And yes, we attended a little chapel service there; and yes, we prayed for their safety because, I'll tell you something, it's a terrible responsibility to send somebody else's son or somebody else's daughter into combat. I think I was better able to make that decision because I did stand up and serve my country. Honor, duty, and country mean something to me.

But I have tried hard to keep the trust. And so on November 3d, when the pundits don't matter anymore, these instant replay guys come on the television, it doesn't matter what they say when you're alone in that voting booth. And when you enter it, please ask yourself these three common-sense questions: Who has the right vision, the right program to help Americans? Who can lead us through the global transition? And which candidate has the character? Who would you trust with your family? Who would you trust in a crisis?

I believe people will answer those three questions that George Bush is the one to lead. I am confident about America. We are not a nation in decline. We are the greatest, freest and most productive nation on Earth. Now let's join together and help every young person here live the American dream.

May God bless the United States of America. Thank you so much. Thank you.

Note: The President spoke at 5:25 p.m. beside the Spirit of America train.

Remarks on Concluding a Whistlestop Tour in Chippewa Falls, Wisconsin
October 31, 1992

The President. Thank you very much. What a great rally. Thank you very much, Governor. Thank you, thank you very, very much. May I say at the beginning of these brief remarks that I am very, very grateful to your Governor, to my friend Tommy Thompson. You couldn't have a better guy helping you win this State. I want to salute—you know, everywhere we go we see "Clean House!" What we need to do is have more Congressmen like Steve Gunderson there to get the job done. I support him. And then Wisconsin has a major national objective this year, and that is to reelect your great Senator Bob Kasten for another 6 years, 6 more.

I want to thank all of those who made this spectacular rally at the end of a long day in this State of Wisconsin such a tremendous success. It is great for the morale. It convinces me we'll win Wisconsin. It convinces me we will win the election. I'll tell you something. I've got a little less voice but a lot more heart after this crowd, I'll tell you.

Here's what it boils down to between Governor Clinton and me: the vast difference in experience, a vast difference in philosophy, a vast difference in character. And in all three of those, I ask for your vote.

You know, for years, for years, I mean, make this months—[*laughter*]—Governor

Clinton has been going around the country knocking us and saying everything bad not only about me, but he says that we are a nation somewhere less than Germany and a little bit more than Sri Lanka. He ought to open his eyes. We are the greatest, best nation on the face of the Earth.

But while he's knocking our record, I think it's only appropriate to take a quick look at his. Here it is for Arkansas: 50th—I think of Wisconsin as an environmental State—Arkansas, 50th in environmental initiatives; 50th in the percentage of adults with a college degree; and you go on and on and on. Unfortunately, the people of Arkansas deserve better. But here's the problem. Governor Clinton said, "I want to do for the United States what I've done for Arkansas." No way! No way! Happy Halloween. We don't need that for the United States of America.

By the way, if a couple of yuppies dressed as moderates come to your door, bags in hand, give them some candy, but watch your wallet. They're coming after you, Governor Taxes and the Ozone Man. Don't let them in. It's a trick, not a treat.

No, Governor Clinton goes all around the country talking about change. He says he is the candidate of change. That's outrageous. I'll tell you the kind of change we'd get if we'd elected him: the same as we got when we had a Democrat in the White House and the liberal Democrats controlling Congress. We would have inflation—remember how it was in 1980—inflation at 15, interest rates at 21, the "misery index" at 20. And change is all you'd have left in your pocket. We cannot go back. And we're not going to.

Audience members. Four more years! Four more years! Four more years!

The President. Governor Clinton—they say they don't want a tax, but why is he dressed up as Fred Flintstone? He wants to tax America back to the Stone Age, and we're not going to let him do it. He has already proposed $150 billion in new taxes and $220 billion in new spending, a lot more Government programs. The answer is not that. It is to hold the line on taxes, hold the line on spending, and give the taxpayer a break for a change.

The only way that Governor Clinton and Ozone can win, the only way they can win

it, is if they convince America that everything is wrong with our economy. And yes, a lot of people are hurting. But let me tell you something: All around the world our economy, in spite of its slowness, is the envy of the world. We grew at 2.7 percent in the last quarter. And we're going to keep on leading until every American that wants a job gets a job. But we are not going to tax and spend to do it.

Our agenda for America's renewal has a good plan. It's a great plan on long-term issues. The answer to lead us out of this is to open new markets abroad. We'd have the best workers, the most productivity of any country. We are going to open new markets abroad by free and fair trade, and then goods marked "Made in the United States" will have more opportunities around the world, and workers in this country will have more jobs.

Our agricultural economy, thank heavens, is not doing too bad at all. Incomes are at a record high since I've been President. Exports have saved our Nation. One out of every three acres, one way or another, ends up going to foreign markets. We've done well with ethanol, and the other day I made a waiver so that we can use ethanol hopefully around the clock. Governor Clinton's campaign, oh, well, they had great problems with this because Ozone Man didn't like it. But let me tell you something. If I have to come down on an environmental extreme or the side of the American farmer, put me on the side of the farmer. We have a good record. This is a good, sound environmental State, and we've got a good, strong record. But you've got to think of the working man and the working woman and the family. We have found the balance between growth and sound environment, and we must not go to the extreme.

You heard Governor Clinton in the debates talking about Government investing. Government doesn't invest. Small business invests. Individuals invest. Small business creates two-thirds of the jobs in this country. So how about this for a plan: less regulation, less taxes, and fewer lawsuits. Let's get business going again.

The trial lawyers do not want to put caps

on these liability claims, and it is a crime. It is absolutely wrong when an American passes another by on the highway for fear he's going to get sued if you reach out a helping hand, or when a Little League coach doesn't dare coach, or when a doctor doesn't deliver a baby because of a malpractice suit. We've got to sue each other less and care for each other more.

We have the best plan for health care. A new Congress is coming in. The old one has screwed up a tiny little bank and a tiny little post office, so a lot of those bozos are going to be gone. Excuse the expression. No, no, I shouldn't say that. I apologize. A lot of these old fogies are going to be out of there, put it that way. We've got the best health care plan. What it says is provide vouchers to the poorest of the poor so they'll have health insurance; give the next bracket in income a little break on the taxes; go after the malpractice suit; pool insurance so you bring the cost down. But do not do what Governor Clinton wants and get the Government further involved, because that means less quality of health care.

In education, Governor Clinton wants to think the same old way, same old bureaucratic way. We've got a good program, America 2000. It literally revolutionizes American education. It puts the power not in the head of the teachers union but in the head of the teachers and the families and the parents, and that's where it belongs. One thing we're going to do is provide— like it's working in Milwaukee—provide school choice so the parent can decide private, public, or religious schools. We've done well. One out of every two college students has financial aid; Pell grants are up. And we are going to keep fighting until every student has a share of the American dream by a good education.

Another thing we've got to do, and Governor Thompson is in the lead on this one, we've got to have national welfare reform. Your State has led the way, thanks to Tommy Thompson. We've got to break this cycle of welfare. We need more jobfare, more learningfare, and less dependency. We need to get those deadbeat dads to pay up. We need to let kids save a little more money so their parents aren't thrown off of welfare. But we've got to put incentive into the system. And I am proud that we have led with Wisconsin on doing that for the Nation.

Let me be clear on another difference. Make no doubt about it, I support the men and women of the law enforcement community who are risking their lives for us every single day. And I want to back them up with strong anticrime legislation. Let's have a little more legislation that's concerned about the victims of crime with a little less concern for the criminal. And I might say I am very proud that I was endorsed for President by the Fraternal Order of Police in Little Rock, Arkansas. How do you like that?

I see these wonderful kids here, and I'm going to redouble my efforts to do something about this deficit. And here's what we're going to fight for with a new Congress: no more gridlock. There'll be 100 to 150 new Members of Congress, and here's what we're going to get them to do: a balanced budget amendment. A taxpayer check-off so every one of you can have some say in it. You check 10 percent of your income taxes if you want to and have them applied to one thing, bringing down the Federal deficit. And Congress all have to cut accordingly. And then I will ask the new Congress to give me what 43 Governors have. They send all this pork-laden legislation. Give me that line-item veto. If they can't do it, give me a shot at it.

A President's term is limited. Why not limit the term for Members of Congress and give the Congress back to the people?

Slight cold. Well, now let's talk about what's going to decide this election. We've got the best policies. We've got the best programs. But there's a couple of other ingredients, and they are called character and trust. And I believe we have to lead there. Governor Clinton about a week ago called me a liar, but that's all right. Being attacked by Governor Clinton on character is like being called ugly by a frog. I don't worry about it. I don't worry about it one single bit.

I'll tell you, though, in all seriousness, what bothers me. I found out something about being President. You make a mistake, you look the American people in the eye and say, look, I messed that one up. I blew it. Now, let's get on with the people's business. But I also found out this: You cannot be all things to all people. You can't be on every side of every issue. You've got to stand for something. And you cannot lead the American people by misleading the people.

Now, let me give you a few examples of flip-flops. One day he's for the free trade agreement. Then he goes to the labor union leaders in Washington, he's got a few reservations. In the debate the other night, everybody had to say what they were for. He said, "Well, I am for it, but"—then he started to hedge. You cannot have "buts" in the Oval Office. You've got to say yes or no. In one part of the country he's for the right-to-work laws. In another he goes up to Michigan, and he says he's opposed to them. One part of the country he says, well, maybe term limits are okay. Then again he says, well, on the other hand, maybe they're not. Flip-flop, flip-flop. You cannot do that if you want to be President of the United States.

Let me remind you about the Persian Gulf. I had to lead. I had to bring along a reluctant Congress. I had to stand up to the media who said, "Oh, George Bush is inarticulate. He can't defend his policies. He can't lead." I did it. And I brought along the entire world. We had to make a very difficult decision. And at the time I made the Congress stand up and vote, here's what Governor Clinton said. He said, "I agree with the arguments made by the minority, but I guess I would have voted with the majority." What kind of leadership is that for the Commander in Chief of the Armed Forces?

Audience members. Boo-o-o!

The President. And did you read the dispatch out of Baghdad today? Has anybody seen it? I'll paraphrase it. Tonight, Saddam Hussein's government plans to have a rally for 500,000 people in downtown Baghdad if I lose the election. Well, they can put that party on hold, because I'm not going to lose it.

Audience members. Four more years! Four more years! Four more years!

The President. Character and trust. Character and trust. And you know, we've done a lot. I am proud to have been a part of this

part of history so every kid here tonight can say, we go to bed at night without the same fear of nuclear war that our parents had. Ancient enemies are talking peace in the Middle East, and democracy is on the move in Eastern Europe and in Russia and south of our border. It's democracy and freedom are the order of the day. And our foreign policy helped bring this about. And as a result we've been able to reduce defense spending. But let me tell you something. The world is still a dangerous place. We must keep our national security up, and we must not cut into the muscle of our defense. But the times call for a leader who has been tested and who has been experienced by the realities of war and peace.

It is a strange year. I don't believe I've ever seen a stranger year in politics. How would you like to be a talking head on a Washington TV show the day after the election? They are going to be wrong, every single one of them. Annoy the Media. Re-elect Bush. I've never seen anything like it. Have you ever seen these talk shows at night going on asking themselves, "Have we been fair to the President?" I've never seen that before in my life. They know the answer. They don't have to have a show about it. And we're going to show them on November 3d.

But you know, last night, it got a little odd last night, a little strange. A voter in Michigan called in—I think it was a call-in show—and Governor Clinton told him that he planned now to be playing his saxophone in the White House and that he's already planning his inauguration parade. Not so fast there, Bill. Not so fast. He's been declared the prohibitive favorite by the talking heads. Yesterday he said he was the underdog. And today he's got his saxophone warming up to play in the Oval Office. Only Bill Clinton can change his mind that fast.

But let me tell you—let me help him. I know he studied at Oxford, and I know when he studied in Oxford. But let me tell you something. He doesn't understand exactly how this system works. You see, it is the people that choose the leaders, not the pollsters and not some kind of campaign rhetoric.

These pundits, I feel like Harry Truman does about these pundits. And let me be clear: I'm not talking about these guys with the cameras here tonight. People take it out on them. These are the good guys. We've granted them amnesty until November 4th, and we're all for them. But I'm talking about these deadly talking heads that come on these Sunday television—some Republicans, I'm embarrassed to say, and a heck of a lot of Democrats and a lot of others that make you think that they're sent down from heaven. But let me tell you something. I am not giving them hell, I'm doing like Harry Truman says: I tell the truth, and they think it's hell. [*Laughter*] But they are not going to decide this election. The decision is going to be made on who's got the best program to lift this country up, move us out of what has been a global recession, and lead us to new prosperity for the young people here today.

And it's also going to be this: People realize that though the world is more peaceful, it is not totally free and safe. There's going to be a crisis. Someday, sure enough, there will be a crisis. I have found out the hard way that you have to make the decision. And I have tried to keep the trust that you have placed in me as President of the United States.

Let me tell you what it was like. Barbara and I sat up there at Camp David, or attended church a day or two before we had to make this decision, before I made this decision on sending your sons and your daughters to Kuwait. And it is not easy. It is not an easy decision. I'll be very candid with you. We went to church there, a little chapel, and prayed that we do the right thing, that I make the right call, that I make the right decision. And we did that, and we liberated a tiny little land. And in the process we elevated the United States to the most respected leadership role in the entire world.

So I hope I have earned your trust. And so when the American people go into that voting booth on November 3d, I am going to look them in the eye and look at each one of you here in the eye, and I say this: I ask for your support for 4 more years based on trust and character and the ability to lead this, the greatest nation on the face of the Earth.

May God bless the United States. Thank you for a fantastic rally. It is unbelievable. Thank you. Thank you all.

Note: The President spoke at 8:50 p.m. on the observation deck of the Spirit of America train.

Statement on Signing the Airport and Airway Safety, Capacity, Noise Improvement, and Intermodal Transportation Act of 1992
October 31, 1992

Today I am signing into law H.R. 6168, the "Airport and Airway Safety, Capacity, Noise Improvement, and Intermodal Transportation Act of 1992."

This legislation maintains the flow of capital to our Nation's infrastructure, ensuring the preeminent position of American aviation. Airport grants funding alone will provide more than 75,000 jobs to the economy in this fiscal year.

I have instructed the Secretary of Transportation to expedite the review and approval of projects funded by this legislation. We are prepared to put these dollars to

work quickly in communities across America. This Act and the historic Intermodal Surface Transportation Efficiency Act of 1991 that I signed last December together demonstrate my Administration's resolve to improve our Nation's transportation infrastructure.

This bill will authorize substantial funding for the next 3 years to modernize the Federal Aviation Administration's air traffic control system. The bill also adopts several other notable aspects of our proposals. It increases discretionary grants for noise abatement, which will make better neighbors of our airports as they grow with the economy. A small and successful State block grant program, shifting funds and decision-making for small airport development from the Federal to the State level, will be continued and expanded.

Not all of our goals were achieved, but the bill is a substantial gain for the American people. I am disappointed, however, that the legislation intended to accompany ratification of the Montreal Protocols to the Warsaw Convention was dropped from the bill this year, but we will work for enactment of such legislation and ratification of the Protocols in the 103rd Congress.

This is an important bill for our Nation, and I am pleased to sign it into law.

GEORGE BUSH

The White House,
October 31, 1992.

Note: H.R. 6168, approved October 31, was assigned Public Law No. 102-581.

Statement by Press Secretary Fitzwater on Emergency Food Shipments to Armenia
October 31, 1992

The President authorized today the immediate transport of emergency food shipments to Armenia. The President ordered this action in response to an urgent request October 30 from Armenian President Levon Ter-Petrosyan concerning critical shortages of wheat grain in Armenia caused by unstable political and economic conditions in the Caucasus region.

To assist Armenia in this current crisis, the United States will begin to airlift on November 1, employing four U.S. Air Force C–5 aircraft from Kelly Air Force Base in San Antonio, TX. These aircraft will transport 236 metric tons of all purpose flour for delivery to the Armenian capital of Yerevan during the next few days.

In order to address the longer term winter food needs of the Armenian people, the United States has begun the shipment by sea of 66,000 metric tons of wheat grain. The U.S. will also transport 3,000 metric tons of processed commodities from warehouses in Turkey.

Today's action by the President demonstrates anew U.S. commitment to the welfare of the Armenian people and to the independence of Armenia. It is another example of the close bilateral relationship between the United States and the government of Armenian President Levon Ter-Petrosyan.

White House Statement on Disaster Assistance for Florida, Louisiana, Hawaii, and Guam
October 31, 1992

The President today made available emergency appropriations for the Department of Housing and Urban Development (HUD). These funds will provide assistance in Florida, Louisiana, Hawaii, and Guam to victims of Hurricanes Andrew and Iniki and Typhoon Omar.

These funds were appropriated in Public Law 102–368, the Dire Emergency Supplemental Appropriations Act, 1992, which was signed into law on September 23, 1992. These funds were made available contingent upon the President submitting budget requests to the Congress and designating the amounts requested as emergency requirements. Forwarding these requests for

$160 million in budget authority for HUD and $57.3 million in budget authority for the Department of the Interior will automatically make the funds available.

In submitting this request the President said:

> I am disappointed that the Congress has directed that any use of the $60 million provided for HUD's HOME investment partnership program funds by States and localities be conditioned upon a proportional use of public housing funds. Public housing new construction often requires 5 or more years to complete and consequently cannot provide the immediate assistance required by these disaster victims. I am therefore asking the Congress to allow the Secretary of HUD to transfer any of the $100 million provided for public housing new construction to other HUD housing programs that are able to work more quickly and efficiently to meet the immediate housing needs in these disaster areas.

The requested amounts for Interior are as follows:

- $30 million to meet the emergency needs for areas in the western United States stricken by drought;
- $1.3 million to document the extensive erosion to the Louisiana barrier islands caused by Hurricane Andrew;
- $1.5 million for the National Wetlands Research Center to assess and monitor the ecological response of Louisiana wetlands to Hurricane Andrew; and
- $24.5 million for a grant to the Louisiana Department of Wildlife and Fisheries to restore damage to fish and wildlife resources caused by Hurricane Andrew.

Remarks to the Community in Auburn Hills, Michigan
November 1, 1992

The President. Thank you very much. Thank you, thank you, thank you. Bill, hey, listen, thank you, Bill Laimbeer. Thank you all very, very much for the welcome to the Palace. And I am very proud to have Bill Laimbeer at my side. I think that's going to get us in there for victory in Michigan. So, Bill, thank you very much. Let's slam-dunk our opponent, the Governor from Arkansas, on Tuesday.

No, I'm delighted to be here—very proud to have at my side and running our campaign perhaps the most effective leader this State has ever seen, but in any event, the great Governor John Engler. I salute him. I thank him.

Do me a favor. Help me clean House. Clean it out. And here's how we're going to do it. Elect Megan O'Neill; elect Dick Chrysler, John Pappageorge, Joe Knollenberg; elect them and we can help make a big step toward cleaning House. That one institution has not changed for 38 years. And now we can make a big change.

I want to thank Mitch Ryder and the band. I want to thank all these high school bands, just fantastic music. And I want to salute my friend, our emcee, Brooks Patterson; you've got a good one there. And also the party leaders, because here's when we get down to getting out the vote and getting down to the crunch. And Dave Doyle and the rest of them are doing a first-class job. So go the polls, bring your neighbors, and let's carry the State of Michigan.

I am absolutely confident of victory because the American people are going to decide that there is a vast difference in experience, a vast difference in philosophy, and yes, a vast difference in character. You know, I think finally one of the reasons is we're getting in perspective exactly what has happened in Arkansas since this man has been Governor. They don't like it, but it doesn't hurt to tell the truth. And here it is: Arkansas is the 50th in the quality of environmental initiatives, 50th State.

Audience members. Boo-o-o!

The President. How do you environmentalists like that? Fiftieth in the percentage of adults with college degrees.

Audience members. Boo-o-o!

The President. It gets worse; hold your fire. Fiftieth in per capita spending on criminal justice; 49th—wait a minute, they're going up here—49th in per capita spending on police protection; 48th in the percentage of adults with a high school diploma. A little more for you guys here.

Audience members. Boo-o-o!

The President. Forty-eight for spending on corrections; 46th in teachers' salaries; 45th in the overall well-being of children. And Governor Clinton said, "I want to do for the country what I've done for Arkansas." No way!

Audience members. Boo-o-o!

The President. We cannot let that happen to this country. This country's just beginning to move. Governor Clinton says he's the candidate of change. We'll get to Ozone Man in a minute. Let's look closely at what Governor Clinton offers, and this is one thing the American people should focus on now in the last day before this campaign, $150 billion in new taxes——

Audience members. Boo-o-o!

The President. ——$220 billion new spending. You talk about trickle-down, that's trickle-down Government. Take it from the people and have Government spend it. And we're not going to let that happen.

And you hear the same old siren's call: Well, we'll take it from the rich. There aren't enough rich people. So all you cab drivers, all you nurses, all you overworked teachers, watch out, watch out for it. Watch your pocketbook and watch your wallets. They're coming right after you.

You know, they talk about change, change, change. And all you have to do is remember the last time we had a man like Governor Clinton as President and a Democrat-controlled Congress. You had change all right. You had inflation at 15 percent; you had interest rates, 21.5 percent; you had a "misery index" at 20. And we cannot let that happen to the United States. Change, change, change.

Audience members. No way, Bill! No way, Bill! No way, Bill!

The President. No way, that's right. Change, change is all you'll have left in your pocket if you let this guy become President of the United States of America.

And you know the only way, the only way they can win is by scaring America that we're in some deep recession. Look, the economy is growing. We are caught up in a fragile international economy. You hear them talk, Governor Clinton says we're something less than Germany and a little above Sri Lanka. But let me tell you something: Our economy is doing better than Germany, better than Japan, better than Canada. And if we keep going the way we're moving now and get our programs in, we'll be leading the entire world.

Yes, people are hurting. Yes, people are hurting in this country. But we don't need to make it worse for them by going back to tax and spend. We need our program. And let me tell you what it is.

First place, we're going to open new markets. Exports have saved us. We are going to open new markets for American products all around the world. We are not going to go protection. We think we have the best workers in the world. Now let's open those markets.

We're going to continue to have a strong environmental policy. But we are not going to go to the extreme. Governor Clinton and the Ozone Man, here's what they want to do. They're backing off a little now because they're on all sides of every issue. They want to go and put a 40- to 45-mile-per-gallon CAFE standard, fuel efficiency standard, on American autos.

Audience members. Boo-o-o!

The President. And that will throw auto workers out of work. And I'm not going to go the extreme. We are not going to go to the extreme on this environment.

Instead of those crazy Government policies, we are going to inspire and invigorate small business. And here's how we're going to do it. Two-thirds of the jobs created are in small business, so we're going to get relief from taxation, relief from regulation, and yes, relief from litigation. We have got to have legal reform.

These trial lawyers are backing Governor Clinton right up to the hilt. The lead trial lawyer in Arkansas said, "Don't worry. Bill won't go against us on tort reform." Look, we've got Little League coaches that are afraid to coach; we've got doctors that are afraid to bring babies into the world because of a lawsuit; we've got people that are afraid to help people along the highway because they're afraid to be sued. We've got to put an end to these crazy lawsuits. And we're going to do it. Whatever your politics, you should have an interest in that one. And we've got to sue each other less and care for each other more in this country.

Big difference on health care. We've got the great health care program. And we're going to get it through because there is going to be a cleaning of the House, and there's going to be 100 new Members of Congress. And the reason is those guys up there can't even run a two-bit post office or a two-bit bank. So we're going to get 100 or maybe 150 new Members of Congress. And we're going to get this health care program through. We're going to provide health care, insurance to the poorest of the poor through vouchers. We're going to help the overburdened next income bracket and the income tax range there by tax credit. We're going to pool the insurance so the small operator can get the same cost benefits as the larger ones, large companies. And then we're going to do this: We are going to say no to Governor Clinton's want to let the Government ration health care through this board he is proposing. Health care for all. Health care for all, but use market forces to get it done.

On education, I've got a big difference with Governor Clinton on this one. I cited the sorry record in Arkansas. Now we've adopted national education goals for the very first time. And I give Governor Clinton credit for this one, because as a Governor he worked with us on this. The program is this: Renew, literally reinvent American schools and give parents the choice of schools, private, public, or religious. And that competition will make all the public schools better. It works in Wisconsin; it can work right across the country.

On welfare reform, we've got to break the cycle of welfare; too many people, generation after generation, dependent. So what we're going to do is go nationally with the waiver system, give those States the right to put in Workfare. People are going to get the check, let them do a little work and work their way off of the welfare. And Learnfare, help people to learn, these kids. It's a tragedy, generation after generation. Make part of the welfare reform Learnfare so people on welfare will have the privilege of an education in this country and be able to do better.

We've gone after these deadbeat dads; we're going to keep after them. And yes, I don't care what the liberal elite says, family is important. Family values are important. And we need to help all families, single parent, whatever it is. But we need to help them by getting crime out of our areas. We've got to have better crime legislation. We better get some that supports the police and some that has more compassion for the victims of crime and a little less for the criminals.

And I'll tell you what I mean. Arkansas, people that are sentenced there spend 20 percent of their sentence in jail. And under the Federal jurisdiction, which is mine, 85 percent. We must support our local police officers. And awhile back I had a visit from eight guys from Arkansas, and they came up to endorse me for President of the United States. They were the Fraternal Order of Police in Arkansas, in Little Rock. And I was proud to have their endorsement.

We've got to get the deficit down, but Bill Clinton talks about let Government invest. Government never created a job. It is small business and private sector that creates jobs. So if you want to get the deficit down, here's the way to do it: Control the growth of these mandatory spending programs. Give us a balanced budget amendment to the Constitution to discipline Congress. Give every taxpayer the right to check 10 percent of his tax return, and if you want it to go the deficit, make the Congress put it on the deficit. Give the President what 43 Governors have, a line-item veto, and let the President draw a line through this excessive spending. And I'll throw in a fourth measure: I think it's time to give the Congress back to the people. I want term limits for the Members of the United States Congress.

And here's the last point: I mentioned

character and trust. Well——

Audience member. We love you.

The President. Well, I hope so.

There's been a little panic in Little Rock, because I think they see that the goal that Bill Clinton has been eagerly awaiting ever since he was studying in Oxford might be slipping away for him. He's begun attacking my character. And I love to fight this one out in the last couple of days on character and trust. Yes, he is a character. But being attacked on character by Governor Clinton is like being called ugly by a frog. We don't need to worry about it. We didn't invite that term "Slick Willie." We didn't invite it. It's come in from Arkansas. It was all through the Democratic primary. We are not going after his character. We're doing what Harry Truman is: We tell the truth, and they think it's hell. So be it. We're simply telling the truth.

It's difficult for him to level with the American people, and here I'm very serious. You can't have it both ways as President of the United States. You can't tell one story and then another. In April, for example, on the draft, he said he would release all his draft records. And he never has done that to this day. He is waffling and ducking——

Audience members. Boo-o-o!

The President. ——and bobbing and weaving. And you cannot do that as President.

Listen, a lot of people opposed the war, and I understand that. That's not the point here. The point is there is a pattern of deception: on one side of the issue one day, and another side the next. And you cannot do that in the Oval Office.

I think, I know a lot of the media don't like this. I know a lot of our friends in the media don't like this. In fact, I like these hats, "Annoy the Media. Reelect Bush." Let me divert for a minute. Have you ever seen a year where they have their own seminars, "Have we been fair?" They know very well they haven't, but we're going to win without them.

Listen, before you get too angry about this, share my frustration about it, please grant amnesty to the good guys: the photographers, the guys carrying the boom mikes. Somebody stuck them with the American flag the other day. These are our friends. They are good people. Don't harass them. Save your rile for those that aren't here, those Sunday talk show people, those guys that are telling us how we're going to vote.

But you know, I mentioned the draft. Even today we have new evidence, an affidavit that when Governor Clinton first ran for office his friends used special connections to seize his ROTC file and destroy all others. He's got to level with the American people on this kind of thing.

But it's not just the draft. You know my differences with him on organizing demonstrations. Look, people objected to the war. But I make a distinction: When your brothers or your peers are in a jail in Hanoi, or kids are being drafted out of the ghetto to go into that war that was not a popular war, I simply think it is wrong to go to a foreign country and organize demonstrations against the United States of America. And that's what he did. And all his apologists out there, all these talking heads say, oh yes, but it was 23 years ago. Okay, if it was wrong to do that, just say so. If you make a mistake, admit it. I have done it, and that's what you have to do as President of the United States.

But the pattern continues. One time he's for the North American free trade agreement; another he started to be against it, then in the debate say, "Well, I'm for it, but I will make some changes." You cannot have a lot of "buts" in the Oval Office. You've got to call them as you see them.

Term limits, CAFE standards, whatever it is, he's got a position for whatever audience he's talking to. And I really mean this, you lose all credibility as President if you try to do that on every issue. And let me finish this little start, this little beginning here by saying, here's what he said on the war. It was a tough decision, tough time for our country. People were divided. And here's what Governor Clinton courageously said about the time I had to make this decision. He said, "I agree with the arguments the minority made, but I guess I would have voted with the majority." What kind of waffle iron is that?

Audience members. Boo-o-o!

The President. You can't do it. You cannot

be here and there. The bottom line is we simply cannot take the risk on Governor Clinton. Character, inexperience, his experience and character do not meet the criterion of the Oval Office. And the world is still a dangerous place. We've made great progress. And frankly, I take great pride in the fact that, with a very able team, I was President when we greatly reduced the threat of nuclear war to every family here and around the world. Great that we had ancient enemies talking to each other in the Middle East; that the Soviet Union is no longer international communism but democracy on the move. A lot of progress toward world peace.

And I was thrilled the other day, yesterday, as a matter of fact, when an announcement came out of Baghdad. Saddam Hussein's government plan a big party the next day after the election, because they think Governor Clinton is going to win. Hold the phone, Saddam. They are not going to have a demonstration in Baghdad, because they're going to have to contend with me for 4 more years.

Audience members. U.S.A.! U.S.A.! U.S.A.!

The President. Well, actually the other night in Michigan, Governor Clinton told a voter that he's already thought about what he's going to do as President. He said he's going to play his saxophone in the White House. And he's already planning the inauguration parade, you know. Hold the phone, Bill. Hold the phone. We are going to show that you're not going to be in the White House and you're not going to have the parade. And the press are going to be wrong about you. The day before that he said he was an underdog, and then yesterday he was a saxophone player in the White House. He's waffling even on that.

I've got a lesson for him. I know he studied at Oxford, and I know when. But he might not understand how democracy works. It's not the pundits, it's the people that decide these elections. And that's why we're going to do it. You know, I believe it's going to boil down to character and

trust. I think we've already kind of won the debate on taxing and spending. People do not want to tax and spend more. They want a little relief from taxation and a little less Government spending.

But the bottom line is you cannot have this pattern of deception and deceiving. I will tell you this: The toughest decision I had to make did relate to the war. I remember being up there at Camp David with Barbara a day or so before the battle actually began. And it is tough when you have to send somebody else's son or somebody else's daughter into harm's way, into combat. But you can't waffle. You've got to get your judgment made up and then you've got to say, here's what we're going to do. And I did it, and I have no regrets. And as a result of doing it, we lifted the entire world. We smashed aggression, and we restored hope in the United States of America.

And now, you go to the polls. And so I'm going to ask—in the first place, you've got to work hard. You've got to go there and get the vote out. One of the reasons we're going to win, we've got the most committed supporters. We've got people like you all who are going to go to those polls.

Then I'm going to look into the lens the evening of the election, and I say to America: Give me your support based on trust, based on character, based on confidence in the United States of America. I want to lead this country, finish the job, restore hope and opportunity to every young person here. And with your help, we're going to get the job done.

Thank you all. And may God bless the United States of America. Thank you so very much for a great rally.

Note: The President spoke at 2:10 p.m. at the Palace of Auburn Hills. In his remarks he referred to Bill Laimbeer, Detroit Pistons basketball player; entertainer Mitch Ryder; Brooks Patterson, Oakland County executive; and David Doyle, State chairman, Michigan Republican State Committee.

Remarks to the Community in Stratford, Connecticut
November 1, 1992

The President. Thank you. Thank you all. What a fantastic rally. Four more.

Audience members. Four more years! Four more years! Four more years!

The President. Thank you all. Thank you so very much. What a great welcome back to Connecticut. Thank you very much. Thank you very, very much for that warm welcome back. And to all of you inside and the 10,000 outside, thanks for that welcome back.

May I start by saluting our great congressional delegation, the Members of Congress, Chris Shays, Gary Franks, and Nancy Johnson. We've got a great delegation. And now help them clean House by electing more to the United States Congress. We need Brook Johnson, we need Tom Scott, we need Phil Steele, we need Edward Munster all to go to Washington.

I salute John Rowland, our emcee. I thank Paul Overstreet and the Gunsmoke for the great music. And let me thank the others that made this great rally possible, Doc Gunther, Betsy Heminway, Brian Gaffney, Dick Foley, and Fred Biebel—came to Connecticut in late 1988 just before the election. We won then, and we are going to win now and annoy the media.

Audience members. Bush! Bush! Bush!

The President. I am very grateful to all of you, and I thank my brother Pres for the introduction. The choice before the American people this year is very different, a vast difference in experience, a vast difference in philosophy, and a vast difference in character. And we are going to win on all three.

There's another collateral reason, not nearly as important, but people are beginning to take a look or have already looked at the record in Arkansas. And without ruining a fantastically upbeat rally, let me just click off a couple of numbers for you. I think of Connecticut as an environmentally sound State. Arkansas is the 50th in the quality of environmental initiative. They are 50 in the percentage of adults with college degrees.

Audience members. Boo-o-o!

The President. I don't want to ruin the evening, only a few more here. They are 50th in per capita spending on criminal justice. They are 49th in per capita spending on police protection. They are 48th in the percentage of adults with a high school diploma. They are 48th in the spending on corrections. They are 46 on teachers' salaries. They are 45th in the overall well-being of children. And Clinton has said, "I want to do for America what I've done for Arkansas." No way! Governor Clinton, we do not need that kind of change in this country.

Audience members. Four more years! Four more years! Four more years!

The President. We got it.

Audience members. Four more years! Four more years! Four more years!

The President. For a long time, the Governor's been running around talking about change. Well, let's take a look at what he's already proposed: $150 billion in new taxes, $220 billion in new spending. You talk about trickle-down Government, that's it. His numbers don't add up. And as I say to the middle class, he says he's going to sock it to the rich, but everybody that's got a job, every teacher, every cab driver, every farmer, watch your wallet. The guy's coming after you, and we're not going to let him do that.

Change, change, change, change, that's all he talks about. Remember what it was like when we had a Democrat in the White House and a Democratic liberal leadership in the Congress? You had inflation at 15 percent; you had interest rates at 21 percent; you had the "misery index" at 20. And we are not going back to that kind of change. Change, that's all you'll have left in your pocket if we go his route, I'll tell you. [*Laughter*]

You know, the bad news for Governor Clinton is that there's been some good news for our economy. The economy grew at 2.7 percent. It's grown for six quarters. Clinton and the Ozone Man tell you that we are worse off. They tell you that we're worse off than Japan and Germany. We're not.

We've been in an economic international slowdown. It is the United States of America, with knowledgeable leadership on international affairs and increasing our exports, that's going to lead the way to new recovery. And the answer to it is not tax and spend but hold the line on taxes and put a cap on the growth of these mandatory spending programs and then stimulate small business, investment tax allowance, capital gains to get people to start new businesses, a credit for that first-time homebuyer that wants to live the American dream. That's the way to do it, not bigger Government.

I have a responsibility as the Commander in Chief and in charge of the national security to be sure we don't cut into the muscle of the defense. Because we've been successful with world peace and because we've stayed strong and made some tough decisions, I've been able to cut defense. But now along comes Governor Clinton, and he wants to cut the muscle of our defense $60 billion more. We cannot let him do that. And besides that, besides the national security, we don't need to throw an additional 1 million people out of work, including 9,500 right here in Connecticut. So we are going to hold the line and keep this country secure, because who knows where the next threat is coming to. We'd better have a leader that understands international affairs.

You know, Connecticut is a great trading State. We've got some of the best made products in the world right here by Connecticut workers. And what we're going to do is expand our exports. Exports have saved us at a critical time, and we are going to create more American jobs by increasing exports, by increasing free and fair trade.

I mentioned small business. You know, small business creates about two-thirds—has about two-thirds of the jobs. I don't want to slap a tax on them for any reason. What I want to do is give them less taxes, less regulation, and less litigation, fewer of these crazy lawsuits, so we can move small business ahead and create jobs for everyone in Connecticut that needs jobs.

I mentioned legal reform. We're having a big battle in Congress. We must put a cap on some of these outrageous lawsuits. You know, when a Little League coach says,

"Hey, it's not worth it; I don't want to get sued by somebody"; when a person along the highway sees somebody that's been hurt and hesitates to help his or her fellow man because they're afraid of getting sued; and when we've got baby doctors that refuse to deliver them because they're afraid of malpractice, it is time to stand up to Governor Clinton and the trial lawyers and do something about it. I think the bottom line is we ought to sue each other less and care for each other more in the United States.

Health care: we've got the best health care plan. The first thing we don't need is what Governor Clinton wants, is a big Government board to ration health care. What I want to do is provide insurance to the poorest of the poor through vouchers. I want to give the next tax bracket up a break with some tax credits. We want to pool the insurance so everybody can get the benefit of a lower premium for these ever-increasing insurance costs. Then I want to keep the Government from mandating prices. I want to keep the Government out of the business, because we've got the best health care quality in the entire world.

And education: we've got a great program, America 2000. It's beginning to work, 1,700 to 2,000 communities across this country already sitting down, the teachers, the parents, the school boards, to literally revolutionize education in this country. I believe that parents ought to have a right to choose the school of their choice, public, private, or religious, and get some help from the Government. It's been tried, and where it's tried it works. It works. And those schools that aren't chosen do a better job. It worked for the GI bill. It is separation of church and state. Let's try something new in this country. Let's help these young kids have the best education possible.

Welfare reform: we've got to break the back of welfare dependency. We've been working with the States to give them waivers so they can try learnfare or workfare and try to help people get off of welfare. And we can do it. But we've got to do it by giving waivers to the States and reforming our welfare system.

I've got a big difference on Governor Clinton on crime. You know, in Arkansas prisoners spend 20 percent of their sentences and that's all; Federal Government, it is 85 percent of their sentences in jail. It's my firm belief that we need to back up our police officers more. We need to have a little more compassion for the victims of crime and a little less for the criminal element. Thank God for the local police that are out there standing up against these drug and criminal elements. Our police officers are trying to make our neighborhoods safer. And the other day I was endorsed by eight people, came up from Arkansas, and they were the Fraternal Order of Police from Little Rock, to endorse me for President of the United States.

I wish we had more Members of Congress like the ones——

Audience members. Bush! Bush! Bush!

The President. I wish we had more Members of Congress like the ones here who care about the Federal deficit. And here's some ideas for getting it down. Give us a balanced budget amendment to discipline the Congress and the President. Give us a taxpayer check-off so you, the voters, can say—if the thing that concerns you the most is the deficit, you can check off 10 percent of your tax return and compel the Congress to bring that spending down to meet that contribution. Then if the liberal leadership in the Congress can't do it, and they haven't been able to do it, why don't we give the President what 43 Governors have: Give him the line-item veto, and let the President draw a line through these pork barrel projects.

And now let's talk about what people are going to decide on, in addition to who's got the best program and who has the best record on world peace. Let me tell you this: I see these kids here, and I take great pride that our administration did an awful lot to help eliminate the fear of nuclear weapons from the minds of these kids. That is major. That is significant.

But now let's talk about character and trust. Over the past few days you've seen Governor Clinton kind of panic, afraid that the power for which he has lusted—do you remember when he wrote back from Oxford, when he was over there organizing demonstrations against this country when his country was at war? Do you remember

that? In the letter to Colonel Holmes, he said something about protecting his political viability. Well, we are going to give his political viability a chance to mature a little more in Arkansas, because he is not going to win the Presidency.

Do you remember that old expression "Sticks and stones hurt your bones, but names will never hurt you?" He called me a liar the other day, but that doesn't hurt. It's like being called ugly by a frog. It doesn't matter. I didn't invent the word "Slick Willie." He got that long before I started running against him. I have a confession to make. I did say in the convention "slippery when wet," and I refuse to take it back. Because look, he's on one side of an issue and then on the other side of the issue. And as President you simply cannot do that.

A lot of people objected to the war. I've no problem with that. I happen to be proud that I did serve my country in uniform and served with honor. What I object to is trying to have all sides of it. He ought to level with the American people on the draft. In April he said, "I'm going to come up with all my draft records." And we haven't heard a peep out of any record yet. And even today there was new evidence: an affidavit that when he first ran for office, Governor Clinton's friends used special connections to seize his ROTC file and destroy all others. He ought to level on these kinds of things.

He'll talk about term limits one place—may be good; then in the debate says he's against it. He goes to the auto workers and said, oh, he's against the fuel efficiency standards, but then he goes to the environmental group and says he's for them. He says one thing on one place, another thing in another place. And you simply cannot be all things to all people.

All during this campaign Governor Clinton has been talking about, "Let's get Government to invest." I have a different philosophy. I don't think the Government invests anything. I think it's private business and private individuals that invest.

But here are his own words from 4 years ago in Newsweek magazine. Here's what Clinton said. He said, "There's lots of evidence you can sell people on tax"—exact quote. Let me start. "There's lots of evidence you can sell people on tax increases if they think it's an investment." His own words revealed this duplicity. We're talking about investment, and he means tax increase.

Audience members. Boo-o-o!

The President. Hey, listen, this is Halloween, but you can't have a pumpkin with two faces on it. You know what I mean? We simply cannot let the American people fall for this scam. Let me tell you what he said on the Gulf war. It was a tough decision. Let me tell you what he said. When I had to make this very difficult call, a call to which Connecticut's sons and daughters responded with great patriotism, great service, and great pride, Governor Clinton put it this way. He said, "I agree with the arguments the minority made, but I guess I would have voted with the majority." You talk about a waffle iron. You can't have that in the White House. You cannot take a risk for the White House on character, on inexperience. His do not add up and don't meet the demands of this high office that I'm honored to hold.

You know, the world is still a dangerous place, and I think we've got to remember that. Who knows where the next crisis is going to come from? You know, I loved this yesterday, the message out of Baghdad. I don't know if they covered it in the Connecticut papers. Saddam Hussein's government is planning a party for 500,000 people in downtown Baghdad predicated on the fact that I'm going to lose. They're wrong. No party. No loss. A big win. A big win. And we are going to keep the pressure on the Bully of Baghdad. We are going to keep the pressure on him until he lives up to every single United Nations resolution; until we can bring peace and relief to his people, the people of Iraq. Stay strong. Do not vacillate.

And one other thing, I don't mean to be hypercritical of Governor Clinton, but the other night he started—at one point—no, no, I'm not giving him hell. No, no. I don't give him hell. It's like Truman said, you know, you tell the truth, and they think it's hell. That's the difference.

You know, the other night in Michigan he told a voter that he's already thought hard about what he's going to do. He said he'll play his saxophone in the White House. He's already planning an inauguration parade. Recently he said he was the underdog, and yesterday he's got his saxophone hanging in the Oval Office. Only Bill Clinton can change his mind that fast.

I know that he studied at Oxford. He's a very bright fellow. But maybe he doesn't understand exactly how it works. You see, it's not these pollsters, it's not the pundits, it's not these talking heads on television that tell you how to vote. The American people make up their own mind on election day.

I don't know why it is there's been such a hot-selling item as that bumper sticker that says "Annoy the Media. Reelect Bush." There it is. Everyone knows what it means, including the press. But I should caution you, we've granted amnesty to all these that are traveling with us. My ire is not at most of them. It's certainly not at the photo dogs and all these guys with the boom mikes. So grant them amnesty and welcome to Connecticut. But I'll tell you where it is. I'll tell you where it stands. It's with these network know-it-alls and these talking heads. They tell you what to think, and we're going to prove them wrong. I love a good fight, and we're going to take it right to them, right around the media and right to the American people.

No, this has been a strange political year. But we're on the move. And I honestly in my heart of hearts tell you, I believe I am going to win this election on November 3d. I have never wavered, and I never will.

Audience members. Four more years! Four more years! Four more years!

The President. I really believe that the American people want a person with experience, certainly don't want one with a pattern of deception, and they want a leader who's been tested. Let me just take you back into history. I'll never forget a cold and rainy day up at Camp David just before I had to make the toughest decision of my life. Kuwait had been invaded, and it stood to the United States to demonstrate to the entire world that aggression would not stand. And yes, Barbara and I went to our little chapel there and prayed that our young men and women would return alive, victorious, and well.

And let me say this: This town and all the good people of this State responded in a way that brought this country together unlike anything since the end of World War II. We lifted up the country and with it the veterans of Vietnam and every other occasion, all because we stood firm and did what was right.

I learned then the agony of making a really difficult decision, one where you have to send somebody else's son or somebody else's daughter into combat. And it isn't an easy decision. I believe that you have to have the experience. I think you have to have the character. I hope you have to have the strength to be able to make a difficult call like that in the face of all the controversy; in the face of all the press telling you hadn't made your case; in face of all those experts telling us how many body bags would be taken overseas. I made a tough call. I did it not to be popular but because it was right. I know I can do it. I know I can lead this country to 4 more years of prosperity.

So your call is: Who best to lead the United States of America into new prosperity? Who best? Who best to say to these young kids, our best days are ahead of us? Who best to accept the trust, the trust of the American people to be in that Oval Office?

Thank you for all you've done. Thank you in the inside and the 10,000 people outside. Thank you for what you're doing. Now, go to the polls, elect these people here with me. Do something for your country. Keep America on the move. And don't let them tell you we're a nation in decline. We are the freest, the fairest, the greatest nation on the face of the Earth. Now, let's go and win this election.

May God bless you all. May God bless the United States of America. Thank you. Thank you very much.

Note: The President spoke at 7 p.m. at Sikorsky Memorial Airport. In his remarks, he referred to the Paul Overstreet and Gunsmoke bands; George L. (Doc) Gunther, State senator; Betsy Heminway and J. Brian Gaffney, Connecticut Bush-Quayle '92 co-chairmen; Richard Foley, Connecticut Republican State Central Committee chairman; Fred Biebel, former Connecticut Republican Party chairman; and Prescott Bush, his brother.

Remarks to the Community in Madison, New Jersey
November 2, 1992

The President. Thank you very much. Thank you so much. Here we go for the last day. Thank you all. Thank you so very much. Thank you. May I start by thanking Rush Limbaugh. And last night, Governor Clinton was at the Meadowlands with Richard Gere and other Hollywood liberals.

Audience members. Boo-o-o!

The President. Well, here's a good deal for you. Let Governor Clinton have Richard Gere. I'll take Rush Limbaugh any day.

May I salute Governor Tom Kean. There's a great nostalgia in this State wishing they had Tom Kean back because they don't like the tax-and-spend policies of Governor Florio. My friend, Dean Gallo, great Congressman; and Mayor Capen and Jinny Littel; and the Madison High School and Chatam High School bands. It's just great to have them here today.

You know, you see some strange reports. Yesterday or the day before they had Governor Clinton talking about his inaugural parade. My advice is, put the parade on hold, Governor, because I am going to win this election tomorrow.

The pundits don't matter. These national pollsters who have been all over the field, they don't matter. What Governor Clinton doesn't understand, it is the people in that booth tomorrow that matter. They don't want somebody who is going to expand the

American Government. They want somebody like me who is going to expand the American dream and make life better for every young person here today.

You know, the choice tomorrow is based on these points: a vast difference in experience, a vast difference in philosophy, and yes, Rush is right, a vast difference in character. That matters. Don't let them tell you it doesn't matter. I guess it boils down to this when you go into the booth all across this country: Who do you trust? If there's a crisis out there, who do you trust with your family? Who do you trust with the future of this country?

Audience members. Four more years! Four more years! Four more years!

The President. Thank you very much. I had planned to ruin part of this rally by talking about the Arkansas record. I won't do it to you. I won't do it to you. But I will say this: I remember coming to——

Audience member. Give 'em hell, George!

The President. I don't give them hell, I just tell them the truth, and they think it's hell. You know, it's like Truman said. But let me point this out: Governor Clinton has the 50th record, 50 out of 50, at the bottom, in environmental initiatives. I came to this State 4 years ago and said we're going to clean up those beaches, we're going to stop ocean dumping; we're going to get a Clean Air Act. We've got a good record on the environment, and Governor Clinton has the 50th in the entire country down there in Arkansas.

As we approach the environment, we ought not to go to the extreme, like Ozone Man does. He'd throw everyone—he's backtracking so fast he looks like the guy on the unicycle we just saw, going backwards. We've got to have a little more concern about the working man and the working woman in this country and still be good for the environment. And that's what we've been.

You know, 48th in the percentage of adults with high school diplomas, 48th in spending on corrections, 46th on teachers' salaries, 45th on the overall well-being of children. Then Governor Clinton gets up and says, "I will do for America what I've done for Arkansas." No way, Bill! No way! The bad news for Governor Clinton is

that there's good news for this country. We've got a long way to go. We've got to help people. But when the economy is showed to be not in a recession, as he's been telling the country, but growing at 2.7 percent, that came as bad news, because the only way they can win is to convince the people of America that we are in decline and that the economy is awful. Yes, it needs to improve, but the worst thing we could do is put a tax-and-spend liberal back into that White House.

You know, in this campaign Governor Clinton said, "Well, I'm a different kind of a Democrat, especially on the economy." He says he doesn't favor middle class taxes, he wants investment. He's talking about Government investing. Now, remember that, and listen to this. Here's what he said in Newsweek magazine: Bill Clinton says, and this is an exact quote, "There's a lot of evidence you can sell people on tax increases if they think it's an investment." Those were his own words, his own duplicity. When he says "investment," America, watch your wallet. He's talking about taxes.

Now, you got plenty of that message right here in New Jersey, *déjà vu* all over again with Jim Florio, higher taxes, more spending, economic stagnation. We're going to change all that. When Bill Clinton's blowing that "taxophone"—[*laughter*]—middle class America will be singing the blues. We just can't let that happen to the United States.

Governor Clinton says he's the candidate of change. What he means by that is he wants—and this is his numbers—"I want to tax $150 billion more. I want $220 billion more in new spending." You talk about trickle-down, that is trickle-down Government, take it from you and let Government spending. We cannot do that.

And I would remind America what it was like the last time we had a man coming in with exactly the same approach. When Jimmy Carter left office, or just before, we had inflation at 15 percent. We had interest rates at 21 percent, 21 percent. We had the "misery index" at 20. America was then in decline until Ronald Reagan and I came along and straightened it out and gave hope for this country.

The way we're going to do that—New

Jersey is a great export State. We are going to create more American jobs by selling the best product in the world, "Made in America" products, overseas. We're going to open these foreign markets. And it is small business that creates the jobs. Instead of putting the money in Government, how about a little tax relief for the people along Main Street? How about less taxes, less regulation, less lawsuits?

We need legal reform. We are suing each other too much in this country and caring for each other too little. And the trial lawyers won't let the slippery one do anything about it at all. They won't let him do anything about it at all. The head trial lawyer in Arkansas said he's never been for reform. And we are going to reform it so doctors can practice medicine, Little League coaches can coach, good Samaritans along the highway can help their fellow man without fear of a crazy lawsuit.

Health care: We've got the best plan. Make insurance available to all, but do not let the Government screw around with the quality of health care in this country.

In education we've got the new approach: reform. More than that, it is actually revolutionizing education. Bypass the powerful NEA, and let the teachers and the parents and the communities have more say in education without mandates from the Federal Government. And beside that, one way to make all schools better is for parents to have the choice of whatever school they want, private, public, or religious. Given them competition and give those parents a needed break.

Crime: Let me be clear where I stand on that one. I support the men and women who are out there in our neighborhoods every single day, trying to fight against the criminal elements. I'm talking about the police, the local police, the State police, whoever it is. I support the police officers and not the criminals. You know, we need more—I think of Dean Gallo here and what he's doing for the victims of crime. He's been a leader in Congress for that. And I believe we need more sympathy for the victims of crime and a little less, a little less for the criminals themselves.

They talk about getting the deficit down. With the new Congress—and there's going to be over 100, maybe 150. And you know why they're going there? Because the leadership that's controlled the Congress for 38 years has messed it up so bad they can't even run a two-bit bank, say nothing about a tiny little post office. They're going to clean House. And with them will come a lot of new Members of Congress. And when that happens, how about protecting the taxpayers with this: a balanced budget amendment; a taxpayer check-off so the taxpayer gets to allocate 10 percent of his taxes to making the Congress bring that deficit down; a line-item veto so the President can do—[*applause*]. And I like that concept of giving the Congress back to the people and having term limits so these people don't become entrenched over the years.

And now let's talk a little about character, because I really believe that the Presidency is shaped by the—you know, Governor Clinton said it's not the character of the President, it is "the character of the Presidency." Wrong, Bill, wrong. They are interlocked. You have to have the trust of the people through character, and you have to have the trust of the world when you are President of the United States.

You know, I quoted Horace Greeley in one of the debates. And here's what he said. He said, "Fame"—and think about this now—"Fame is a vapor, popularity an accident, riches take wing; only character endures." That is so true. And I think it is especially true of the Presidency. It matters not just because of the plans you make but the crises that you never foresee.

And we simply cannot take a risk on Governor Clinton. He is wrong for America on the issues, and I believe I am better for America on character. He goes after me with a vengeance. And let me tell you something, I'm not the guy who invented the word "slick." I did say "slippery when wet," and I'll stand with that. But I did not say "slick." That came from the primary. That came from his own hometown newspapers. So I am going to say, let them speak for them; I'll speak for me. I am a better, I will be a better President for the young people in this country for 4 more years than Governor Clinton ever would. Here's why. Here's why.

Audience members. Four more years! Four more years! Four more years!

The President. Here is why. You know, as President you cannot be on all sides of every issue. You've got to look people in the eye, call them as you see them, like the umpire. If you make a mistake, say so, and then go on about leading the American people. But Governor Clinton, one day he's for the NAFTA agreement; the next day he's against it. One day he's for term limits, oh yes; in the debate he opposes it. One day he's going to go for these taxes, and then the next day he backs away. One day he's for fuel efficiency standards that would throw a lot of auto workers out of work; the next day he backs away, and he's going to study that one.

Here's what he said, his own words, on the Persian Gulf: "I agree with the arguments the minority made, but I guess I would have voted with the majority." What kind of Commander in Chief would that be?

Audience members. Boo-o-o!

The President. And in spite of the harassing from the media—listen, I've got to define the ground rules on the media. I love these signs, "Annoy the Media. Reelect Bush." And every one of you know what that means. Every one of you know that there has not been objectivity in the coverage. Every one of you know it. And they are having their own debates, all these talking heads: "Have we been fair? Well, this is the way we do it. That's the way we do it." And everyone knows that they're covering up the fact this has been the most biased year in the history of Presidential politics. But we don't need them anymore. We don't need them. I take out as much ire on these Republican talking heads on the talk shows on Sunday as I do on the Democrats. They're all running for cover. And we are going to show them wrong.

I'll tell you who else we're going to show wrong. It was Saddam Hussein's government. A couple of days ago they said they were going to have a celebration, 500,000 people in downtown Baghdad, thinking I was going to lose. And then yesterday they kind of backed away from—well, I've got a message for Saddam Hussein: You're going to have to contend with me. You're going to have to do what the United Nations said. We're going to keep the pressure on you until you take the pressure off your own people.

So here it is. Here is what is going to determine this election. Yes, it is trust, and yes, it is character. Because, look, we've come a long way. These kids in these bands go to bed at night without the same fear of nuclear war as their mothers and dad had. That is dramatic change. It is worldwide change, and we helped bring it about.

But here's the problem. We still have problems out there threatening this country. Who knows where the next crisis will appear? And imagine a dangerous situation; an American leader totally without experience, completely untested; a person who couldn't even call it right when aggression threatened the whole world. And what we see is a troubling pattern of deception, an ingrained habit of trying to lead people by misleading them. And when that crisis occurs, and you can bet it will, the entire world looks to the President of the United States of America, looks to his experience, looks to his determination. And they will. They will count on his character.

I have been tested. We've managed the world change of almost Biblical proportions. And our success can be measured by the headlines that were never written, the countless crises that never occurred. Let's keep a President in that Oval Office who is strong and knows to stand up for America.

Audience members. Four more years! Four more years! Four more years!

The President. And let me give you another reason to reelect me. I've tried very hard to stand for true family values there, respecting all different kinds and sizes of family, but standing for values like safety in the neighborhoods and teachers, supporting them, and discipline in the family, respect for this flag of ours, whatever it may be. I've tried to stand for that all along.

And tomorrow you're going to have a major decision to make on who do you trust to stay in that Oval Office. Let me tell you something. I think we've got one good reason, because every time Barbara Bush holds a little child in her arms, an AIDS baby, or reads to them, she is demonstrating compassion. And believe me, we have the best First Lady we possibly could have.

Audience members. Barbara! Barbara! Barbara!

The President. I know it's unfashionable to talk about faith, but I remember that cold day up in Camp David when we had to make this terrible decision about sending the sons and daughters of New Jersey into Desert Storm, into combat. And my experience in combat, the pride I felt in wearing the uniform of this country made a difference in how I made that decision. On that cold day in Camp David, Barbara and I went to that little chapel, and yes, we prayed that I would do the right thing and that these young men and women would come home safe. And they did. They lifted up the morale of this country. They lifted the burden off the veterans of Vietnam. They raised with pride service to country. And I'll tell you something: It was a proud moment. And the press and the media are not going to distort it. It was decent and noble and made us the leader of the entire world.

So now we go. The last day I will ever campaign for myself for President of the United States or anything else, and I can't tell you what this crowd means. So just take this enthusiasm and go to the polls, take your neighbor, get that Local 172 mobilized. You talk about good, decent, hard-working Americans. Fantastic. Get them to the polls. Vote for trust and character and lifting up this country.

And don't let Governor Clinton win based on the country in decline. Look, we are the United States of America. We are the envy of the world. We are one Nation under God, the world leader. Don't let them forget it. Vote for George Bush.

Thank you all very much. May God bless our great country. Thank you very, very much. What a great send-off. Fantastic. Thank you very, very much.

Note: The President spoke at 8:03 a.m. at the Hartley Dodge Memorial Building. In his remarks, he referred to actor Richard Gere; radio commentator Rush Limbaugh; Mayor Donald R. Capen of Madison; and Virginia Littel, State Republican chair.

Remarks to the Briarcliff Father and Son Athletic Association in Glenolden, Pennsylvania
November 2, 1992

Thank you very, very much. Thanks for coming out in the rain. And let me just say this: I am very grateful to all of you, grateful to Tom Judge. I want to salute Congressmen Curt Weldon and Larry Coughlin, Bob Walker, with us. You know, you see a lot of signs saying "Clean House!" People are tired of the Congress the way it is. So send Larry Hollin and send Craig Snyder to Washington. May I send a special vote of thanks to the Oak Ridge Boys and urge that we send Arlen Specter back to the United States Senate. And let me thank so many people who are working hard to guarantee a Republican victory throughout Pennsylvania.

You know, Governor Clinton has gotten a little premature. He's talking about his in-

augural parade. My advice to him is: Put the parade on hold, Bill; you're not going to win this election.

Tomorrow, you see, it's not the pollsters, and it's not the national press, it is the people that decide these elections. That's what we're going to show them tomorrow. The reason we're going to win is this: Because the choice the American people have is about a difference in experience, a difference in philosophy, and yes, a difference in character. Character matters. Parents are going to say, "Who do I trust our kids with?" And I believe the answer is George Bush.

You know, Governor Clinton made a scary statement in one of the debates. He said, "I want to do for this country what

I've done for Arkansas." No way! We can't let that happen. They are near the bottom in education, on the environment, on the economy. We cannot let that happen to the United States of America.

You've heard all this time about how things are not going. We are improving. The economy moved at 2.7. And the last thing we need is to go back to tax and spend the way the Democrats want to do it.

Bill Clinton offers an economic disaster for this country. You know, in this campaign he said, "I am a different kind of Democrat, especially on the economy." He says he doesn't want middle class tax cuts, he wants investment. But the American people, before they go to the polls, as you hear Governor Clinton talk about investment, ought to listen to this. Here's what he said in Newsweek magazine: "There is a lot of evidence that you can sell people on tax increases if they think it's an investment." Those were his words, and that means he is out to tax the American people. Let's not let him do that.

Governor Clinton says he is a candidate of change. You remember that last time we had a Democrat in the White House and this Congress controlled by the Democrats. You had interest rates at 21 percent. We had inflation at 15 percent. You had the "misery index" at 20. And we simply cannot go back to those days. Let's move this forward with less taxes and less spending.

The way to do that is to stimulate small business. Give them a tax break for investment taxes. Give them a tax break for that first-time homebuyer to let that homebuyer live in the American dream. Let's do something about these crazy lawsuits that are killing this country.

We've got the best agenda for education. You see, I think it's about time we let the parents choose, whether public, private, or religious schools, and give them a chance.

Governor Clinton wants, like all these guys, to expand American Government. I want to expand the American dream.

But let me tell you here, let me tell you what it really is all about. When you go into that booth, the reason we're going to win is it boils down to character and to trust. You know, Horace Greeley said, "Fame is a vapor, popularity an accident, riches take wing; only character endures." I think that is especially true as the President of the United States of America. If you make a mistake, tell the truth about it. But you cannot be on all sides of every issue. You can't do that. You cannot lie to the American people.

Here's a man, Governor Clinton, whose own hometown newspaper says he's a politician utterly without principle, a guy whose supporters gave him that name "Slick." We didn't invent that. It came out of the Democratic primary, out of Arkansas. I say "slippery when wet," a little different but the same thing.

But the pattern of deception is what is troubling the American people. They see it on term limits. They see it on North American free trade agreement. They see it on taxes. They see it on these environmental standards. I think we ought to think about the working man and the working woman and have good environment without going to the extreme like the Ozone Man wants. We've got it. Somebody better think of the families that are working for a living, and we're doing both, a good sound environmental record but not the extreme that's going to throw more Americans out of work.

But you know, being on all sides of the issue, listen to this one about the Gulf war. Here's what he said, when Bob Walker and these other Congressmen here, Curt Weldon and Larry, were standing up and doing what's right, here's what Governor Clinton said. He said, "I agree with the arguments the minority made, but I guess I would have voted with the majority." What kind of leadership is that for the Commander in Chief of the Armed Forces?

You know there was a statement out of Baghdad the other day, said that Saddam Hussein was planning a big rally when Governor Clinton won. Well, Saddam ought to put it on hold. And today he backed away. He's probably listening to the national media, who see us moving now. And here's my point: Saddam Hussein is not going to rejoice, because we're going to win the election and we're going to make him live up to those international resolutions and help the people over there.

So what it boils down to is this, it boils down to character and trust. I ask you to just imagine reading about an upheaval now. We brought peace to the world and way and tremendous quantities. These young people here, even these characters, they go to bed at night without the same fear of nuclear war. That's something big. That is something important for the world, for mankind.

But the world is not without threat. Imagine in a dangerous situation—the question is if a crisis arises, at home or abroad, who do you want to solve the crisis? Who do you want to do it? You cannot do it with a leader that has a pattern of deception. You cannot do it with a leader who went to a foreign country and demonstrated against his own country when his people were at war. Look, a lot of people disagreed on the war, but not many of them went to a foreign land and organized a demonstration when kids were being drafted out of the ghetto and Americans were held prisoner in Hanoi. I don't like that. I think that was wrong.

So in the final analysis, what it boils down to is who has the experience and who has the character to lead the greatest, freest country on the face of the Earth.

I'll give you another reason to reelect me. I think we've got a great First Lady in Barbara Bush, I'll tell you. When she holds those AIDS babies in her arms or when she reads to those children or when she lifts up these families, she's saying family values do matter. Don't let the liberals and the media tell you they don't. They do matter. God bless the American families.

I see these signs saying here, "Annoy the Media. Reelect Bush." Well, let me tell you something. We are going to show the pundits and the pollsters that they are wrong. We are going to win this election.

So now it doesn't matter what they are telling us we think. Now it's up to what the American people think. We are going to pull off one of the biggest surprises in political history. Discard the pundits; discard the pollsters; discard the rhetoric out of Governor Clinton. Vote for me, and we will lead this country to new heights.

Thank you, and God bless you. Thank you and bless you all.

Note: The President spoke at 11:06 a.m. at the association. In his remarks, he referred to Tom Judge, chairman, Delaware County Republican Party, and entertainers the Oak Ridge Boys.

Remarks on Arrival in Akron, Ohio
November 2, 1992

The President. Thank you, thank you. Thank you very much. Thank you so much.

Audience members. Four more years! Four more years! Four more years!

The President. What a terrific Akron welcome. Thank you. Thank you for that great Ohio welcome. Feel good; I feel good. Thank you very much. Thank you very, very much for that welcome. All right. Thank you, Governor.

Let me thank Governor Voinovich. May I start by thanking your great Governor, my great friend, George Voinovich, for being at my side, leading us to victory in Ohio, and salute Congressman Ralph Regula, one of the all-time greats in the Congress, who's with me here today, a great man. You know, I want to thank Alex Arshinkoff, a great political leader who you heard from earlier, and pay my special thanks to four friends who came with us here, traveling with me, the Oak Ridge Boys, great Americans, wonderful musicians.

You know, as you drive down to—there they are. As you drive down to the wire I see these signs saying, "Clean House! Clean House!" Change that one institution, the United States Congress, that hasn't changed in 38 years. So let me tell you what to do. Obviously, we need Ralph Regula there, but send Bob Morgan and Margaret Mueller to Washington as Congresspeople. That's what we need. While we're at it, let's clean Senate and send Mike DeWine to the United States Senate.

Your Governor is a man of total truth, like George Washington. He never told a lie. He just told me we are going to win Ohio, and I believe him. I'm sure it's true.

You know, I got a big kick out of this the other day. I read in the paper that Governor Clinton was already planning his inaugural parade.

Audience members. Boo-o-o!

The President. No problem. Put the parade on hold, Bill. Put it on hold, because it's not the pundits that matter; it's not the media back in Washington, DC, that matters. On Tuesday it is the voter, the American people that matter.

Here's why we're going to win it: Because the choice before the American people is a choice of real differences, difference in experience, difference in philosophy, and yes, difference in character. Character is important. The American people are going to have to decide, and they will. The issue tomorrow is also trust, and they're going to have to decide: Who do you trust with your children? Who do you trust with the United States of America?

We have literally, through our leadership, helped dramatically change the world, bring peace to the world. The young people here today go to bed at night without the same fear of nuclear war that their parents had. That is dramatic change. Now America's economy is recovering. We are going to bring that same leadership, with a brand-new Congress, to help every single family here in the United States of America.

You know, one reason that I believe I'm going to win is that things are getting in focus on what's happened in Arkansas. The press hasn't wanted to talk about it, but I do, because I think it is only fair that the American people know what Governor Clinton's record is. They are near the bottom on education, 45th for teachers' salaries; 50th for environment; terrible on the economy. He's had one good year, and that's the year he was out of town most of the time. And the good people of Arkansas deserve better. But here's what worries me.

Governor Clinton in the debate said, "I want to do for America what I've done for Arkansas." No way!

Audience members. Boo-o-o!

The President. No, Arkansas changed its slogan from "Land of Opportunity" to "Natural State." I want America to be the land of opportunity, and it is. It is.

The worst news for Governor Clinton and the worst news for the liberals that control the United States Congress is they've been telling us all along that we've been in a recession. We have grown for six straight quarters, and this quarter grew at 2.7 percent. They're telling us that we're worse than Japan, Germany, and Europe. We are better than they are, and we're going to make it better still and move this country ahead. Yes, people are hurting. Yes, people are hurting, but now with things beginning to move, let's not go back and take us back to the tax-and-spend days that brought us real ruin.

Governor Clinton—you know, you've been reading he talks about investment, we need more money so we have Government invest. Let me tell you something. Government never made a sound investment in human beings in their life, or in jobs. It's the small business that makes investment. Let's help small business: less taxes, less regulation.

Just so we tell it straight before people go to the polls, talking about investment, here's what Governor Clinton said in 1988 in Newsweek. He said, "There's a lot of evidence you can sell people on tax increases if they think it's an investment." That was what he said 4 years ago. Now we hear that cry, "investment." What he means is, America, watch your wallets. He's coming after you in taxes.

We are not going to let the middle class pay for that scam. It is a scam. Change, change, change, change, change, says Clinton and the Ozone Man. Change, change, change, change, change. That's all you're going to have left if he gets in there with more taxes and more Government spending.

You know why I call him Ozone Man? Let me tell you something, our administration has taken the lead on CFC's internationally, the thing that causes concern for the ozone. We brought you the Clean Air Act. We've done better on forests. We've cleaned up the oceans and the beaches. But we are not going to go to the extremes like Gore and Clinton when they say, "We want Federal fuel efficiency standards at 40 to 45 miles per gallon." You've got some great auto workers in this State. I am going to keep them at work, not throw them out of work.

Change, change, Governor Clinton got in a huddle with the handlers, and they said keep talking about change. Let me remind you of what it was like when we had a Democratic President and a Democratic Congress. We had change. We had interest rates at 21 percent. We had inflation at 15. We had a "misery index" at 20 percent. We don't need that kind of change for America.

What we need instead is a positive agenda. We've got one for rebuilding our schools, for reforming health care, for creating jobs through less spending, less taxation, and more tax breaks for these businesses.

Governor Clinton—I can just feel it, these liberals, they want to expand Government, and I want to expand the American dream.

Now let's talk trust, and let's talk character, because they do matter. I love it when that national talking-head media take me on. I love it, because I like a good fight. There's no reason my holding back anymore.

Audience members. Four more years! Four more years! Four more years!

The President. Hey, wait a minute, before I go any further, we grant amnesty. I want this clearly understood. Grant amnesty to these guys over here. Aim your feelings— and I know you have them because every time somebody holds up one of those bumper stickers, it says, "Annoy the Media. Re-elect Bush," and everybody in this country knows what it means. You know what it means. Everybody knows what it means.

So don't let them tell you that family values don't matter. They do. We want to strengthen the American family by backing up our law enforcement people. Do what Barbara Bush does, reading to those children, get the parents to do that. We have a great First Lady, incidentally.

Give them school choice so the parent can choose private, public, or religious schools. We've already brought choice in child care. Strengthen the American family. Strengthen the American family.

[*At this point, there was an interruption in the audience.*]

I think we need a doctor over here. We'll get it. Somebody will be coming. And now let's finish. And let's be sure we get attention. They've got somebody—all right? Okay. We'll get—is she okay? Now, here we go. We've had a little accident over here.

But let me just say this: It is character and it is trust that is going to determine this election. There's no question about it. Listen to the words of Horace Greeley. You young people particularly, remember this. Here's what he said. He said, "Fame is a vapor, popularity an accident, riches take wing; only character endures." And this is true. This is very true.

Governor Clinton said in the debate, he said it's not the character of the President, it is "the character of the Presidency." Wrong, they're interlocked. The President is forming the character of the Presidency. And that is important.

Audience members. Four more years! Four more years! Four more years!

The President. We cannot have a pattern of deception. It's like any family. A President makes a mistake, he says, "Look, I made a mistake. Now let me help continue to lead this country." You cannot be on all sides of all issues if you're President of the United States.

I'll give you one example. Let me give you one example. When I had to make the toughest decision of my life, whether to send somebody else's son, somebody else's daughter into combat on Desert Storm, I made a decision not because it was popular. We had plenty of people in the media, plenty of people demonstrating, plenty of Congressmen telling me it was wrong. But I made the right decision. And what did Governor Clinton say? He said, "I agree with the arguments of the minority, but I guess I would have voted with the majority." What kind of Commander in Chief will waffle like that?

Audience members. Boo-o-o!

The President. As a result, we crushed

aggression. We lifted the spirits of America. We honored the Vietnam veterans as well as the veterans of Desert Storm.

There was a very interesting announcement out of Baghdad, of all places, the other day, that Saddam Hussein's government is planning a party—they said 500,000 people—if Governor Clinton wins. Well, Saddam, put it on hold, old fellow, because we are going to make you live up to every resolution passed by the United Nations. We're going to make you lighten up on the people of Iraq.

I ask this at the end. We've helped the world become more peaceful by busting up international communism. But let me tell you this: The world is still a dangerous place. I don't want to cut into the muscle of our defense. I feel a responsibility to young people to keep this country strong. We've reduced defense, but we can't do what Clinton and Gore want, cut right into the muscle of the defense. I'm not going to do that. The reason we're not is because it still is a dangerous place, this world of ours. It's still a dangerous place. I believe that we need a Commander in Chief that the

people trust, who has had the experience and hopefully has demonstrated the character to lead this country in peace and to lead it in war.

And so tomorrow——

Audience members. Four more years! Four more years! Four more years!

The President. So tomorrow when you go into that polling booth——

Audience members. Four more years! Four more years! Four more years!

The President. So tomorrow when you go into that polling booth, pollsters be darned, everything else aside, I ask for your support. I ask for your trust to lead this great country for 4 more years.

Thank you, and may God bless the greatest country on the face of the Earth. May God bless the United States of America.

Don't listen to these guys that say we're in decline. We are the United States. God bless you all. Thank you very much. Great rally. Now go to the polls, Ohio.

Note: The President spoke at 1:52 p.m. at Akron-Canton Regional Airport. In his remarks, he referred to Alex Arshinkoff, Summit County Republican chairman.

Remarks on Arrival in Louisville, Kentucky
November 2, 1992

The President. Thank you very much. Thank you so very much. Thank you, thank you, thank you.

Audience members. Four more years! Four more years! Four more years!

The President. Thank you very much. Let me just start by thanking first all of you for this great Kentucky welcome and a great Kentucky sendoff into the final hours of the campaign. Tomorrow, let's do the country a favor and give the country back to the people by sending some new Representatives to the United States Congress. Let's send Dave Williams to the Senate. And you know, you hear a lot about the able women candidates, strong, powerful women. We have one right here in Susan Stokes. I want to see her win. Get her in there. Get her up

there. You talk about cleaning House, we can start right here, I'll tell you. May I thank Mitch McConnell, who has been at my side through thick and thin. We climbed off the plane, and he said, we are going to win Kentucky. What a great Senator you have.

You know, the last couple of days, I don't know whether you saw it here, but Governor Clinton's been talking about his inaugural parade and playing sax—wait a——

Audience members. Boo-o-o!

The President. ——playing his saxophone in the White House. Well, I told him, hold on, Bill, not so fast. Don't believe the pollsters; believe the American people. We are going to win the election.

No, that's the way it works. You go to the

polls, and the people make these decisions. They don't have to have a filter. They don't have to have one of those instant analysts coming across, those people that tell us from Washington every Sunday what's wrong with our country. Let's go and vote for what's right, the reelection of George Bush and more prosperity for this country.

Hey, listen, if we'd do it the way the media wants you, they wouldn't even have—if they were running the races here, they'd just say who the favorite is and let it go. That's not the way it works at Churchill Downs, and that ain't the way it works for American politics, either.

Here's what it's about. The choice before the American people is the vast difference in experience, a vast difference in philosophy, and yes, a vast difference in character. Character matters. The big question the American people ask tomorrow is: Who do we trust? Who do we trust with our kids? Who do we trust with our country?

Governor Clinton talks about change, change, change. That's all we hear about—uses the word about 50 times every minute with gusts up to 250. [*Laughter*] But let's look at what he offers. Change: $150 billion in new taxes before he can get started.

Audience members. Boo-o-o!

The President. And $220 billion in new spending before he even gets started.

Audience members. Boo-o-o!

The President. Bigger Government: He talks about Government investing. Government doesn't invest. It's small business that invests and creates jobs in this country.

Clinton and the Ozone Man don't like to hear this, but—[*applause*]—hey, wait a minute. Wait a minute. That's fair. "Ozone Man" is fair. How about trying a carbon tax on the coal industry here—what he wants to do. We're not going to let him do that.

Audience members. Boo-o-o!

The President. This Ozone Man and Governor Clinton want to put fuel efficiency standards on the auto business of 40 to 45 miles per gallon and throw a lot of auto workers out of work. And we're not going to let them do that.

Audience members. No-o-o!

The President. These guys are my favorites, I'll tell you. These Oak Ridge Boys are just great. And I want to tell you some-

thing, I wish you could have been with us on the plane, every single one of you—might have been a little over baggage there. But nevertheless, I wish you could have heard these guys singing those beautiful gospel songs. It made us—not a dry eye in the house. These are my friends, and I am grateful to all four of them.

Back to the business at hand. The last time we tried the kind of change that Clinton and the Ozone Man are talking about, we had change—exactly. We had interests rates at 21 percent. We had inflation at 15 percent. We had a "misery index" of 20. Now it's 10. We cannot go back in the name of change to those failed policies of the past.

We're going to win not just on character and trust. We're going to win on a positive agenda. We have the best program for rebuilding our schools, putting the faith in the teacher, putting the faith in the family to have a choice. Give the parents the right to choose public, private, or religious schools, and all schools will be better.

We've got the best plan for reforming health care: Make insurance available to the poorest of the poor through vouchers; next income bracket, give them a break through taxes; pool insurance so you get the price down. But do not do what Governor Clinton wants and get the Government in the rationing business. Keep the quality of health care up.

At every turn, every turn, Governor Clinton talks about expanding Government. I want to expand the American dream. There is a difference.

Now let's just talk about character and trust. And let me tell you what this election is about. Here's a quote by Horace Greeley. He said, "Fame is a vapor, popularity an accident, riches take wing; only character endures." And that is true. That is very true.

In the debate, Governor Clinton said it's not the character of the President, it is "the character of the Presidency." Wrong. They're both interlocked. What happens in that White House shapes the character of the Presidency, and make no mistake about it.

We have tried very, very hard to uphold

the trust. Frankly, in Barbara Bush I think we have a first-class First Lady that has held America in her arms and cares about people. She cares. And when she reads to those children in the Diplomatic Entrance of the White House or holds an AIDS baby in her arms, she's saying two things: We should care about each other, and she's saying family matters, family values matter.

So what it boils down to is we simply cannot take a risk on a man who keeps changing his position every single day in order to get votes. You can't do it. You know, Kentucky, Fort Campbell and many other places, rallied around when we faced a very critical moment in our history, on the Persian Gulf. I had to make a tough decision, look the American people in the eye, and say here's what we're going to do. And we did it with the help of the American people. But I would remind you what Governor Clinton said at the time. He said, "I agreed with the arguments the minority made, but I guess I would have voted with the majority." You cannot do that as Commander in Chief of the Armed Forces.

Hey, the good one happened the other day. Maybe you didn't see it in the press; I did. Don't read it too much anymore, but I saw this one—[*laughter*]—this one said that Saddam Hussein's government plans a party of 500,000 people when George Bush loses. Saddam, put it on hold, old friend. We're going to come after you until you lighten up on the people of Iraq. We are going to make you live by the United Nations resolutions. He's not going to get rid of us. We're going to keep to it until he does what's right by his people. Frankly, I couldn't care less whether he's unhappy if I win. That doesn't bother me one single bit.

So here's what it is. Just picture this: We've dramatically changed the world, dramatically. All these kids here go to bed at night without the same fear of nuclear war than they had 4 years ago. Now, that's change. You talk about change, that's change.

But we're not out of it yet. Governor Clinton and the Ozone want to cut defense by $50 billion more. They are still some wolves out there. We have cut defense. We have cut it, but we must not cut the muscle of our defense.

Just imagine if there's a crisis; imagine if we have to face an unforeseen crisis. The question then is this: What American leader will you trust in that kind of a crisis? I do not believe we should put our trust in a man who is all side of every issue. You can't do that in the Oval Office. You have to make the tough decision.

I remember well that very cold and rainy February just before our young men and women from Kentucky and the other States were sent into battle. Barbara and I were at the Camp David chapel. And yes, we prayed, prayed hard to do the right thing. We prayed that these young people would come back. And boy, did they ever do this country proud. They did us proud, and don't let them take it away from us.

But my point is, this is an awesome responsibility, to ask someone else's son or someone else's daughter to put their lives at stake. It's a responsibility that I have tried to fulfill with honor, duty, and above all, integrity. We must serve this country with integrity.

So tomorrow, as we end the long campaign trail in what's got to be one of the most controversial years, certainly probably the most unpleasant year of my life, which is totally unimportant, but I think others know it's been a rather ugly year with this national media just writing us off from day one.

Audience members. Boo-o-o!

The President. Let me tell you something. We're going to show them they're wrong.

So tomorrow is the day of responsibility. I ask you not to take this responsibility lightly. You see, democracy was conceived from liberty, nurtured by freedom, and protected by the blood of those who came before. When you walk alone into that booth tomorrow, you will not spend more than a couple of minutes, but your single voice will echo down the corridor of time. With your vote, you will shape and help shape the entire future of this, the most blessed special nation that the world has ever known and that God has ever created.

Never forget, I don't care what they say, never forget that we are one Nation under God, and we ought to be grateful for that.

So what we do will cast its shadow forward into history. Your vote—look at it this way—it's an act of power, a statement of principle, and a harbinger of possibility. So like all the candidates, I ask only that you think deeply about our Nation and its needs, because tomorrow the polls don't matter. The pundits don't count on election day. Only conscience should be your guide. And never, never let anyone tell you that the United States is a nation in decline. We've got problems, but together we can solve them and lift America up.

May God bless you, and may God bless our great country. Thank you so much. Let's go win it. Go to the polls. Go to the polls and win. Thank you very much. Thank you, Kentucky. Thank you.

Note: The President spoke at 4:33 p.m. in the Signature Flight Support Hangar at Standiford Field.

Remarks at a Rally in Baton Rouge, Louisiana
November 2, 1992

The President. Thank you very much. What a great Louisiana welcome. Unbelievable. Thank you very much. Thank you so very much for this welcome back. And may I at the outset of these remarks say thank you, Louisiana, and thank you, Cheryl Ladd, an old friend, for introducing me here today.

And I want to salute Congressman Richard Baker, Congressman Holloway, Congressman Livingston, all three great guys; former Congressman and your former Governor Dave Treen, who's at my side through thick and thin; another great Louisianian, Henson Moore, who is so important to us in the White House and been working his heart out here; and Fox McKeithen and Chuck McMains and Carl Crane and so many others that are helping us in every single way, but especially all of you here tonight to put us over the top in the State of Louisiana.

I'll tell you, something is happening across this country. Something is happening across this country. And we are going to annoy the media and reelect George Bush. They don't like it; they don't understand it. Something is happening in our great country. Come Monday, we feel things moving. But come Wednesday, there's going to be no joy in Little Rock, believe me. We're going to win this election. And the pollsters, the pollsters are going to be unemployed, and the rest of the country is going to move forward to jobs and opportunity. [*Applause*] No, you guys are too much.

But here's what it's about. Here's what it is about. There is the choice, is a big difference on experience, on philosophy, and yes, on character. Character matters for President of the United States of America. And yes, the issue is, tomorrow when you go into that booth, the question of trust. Who do you trust with your kids? Who do you trust with your country? Who do you trust to lead the free world?

Governor Clinton says he's the candidate of change. But let's look at what he offers: $150 billion of new taxes to start with——

Audience members. Boo-o-o!

The President. ——$220 billion in new spending. That is trickle-down Government. And we do not need to go back to the failed days when you had a Democrat in the White House and Democrats running, the liberals running the Congress. Governor Clinton's numbers don't add up. He says, "Oh, I'm going to sock it to the rich." All you guys driving a cab, being a nurse, teaching school, watch out: He's coming after you. And we're not going to let him do that to the United States of America.

And I would remind the entire country from this fired-up rally right here in Baton Rouge—the one I'm told is the biggest they've ever had here—what it was like when we had another guy sounding just like this in the White House, like Governor Clinton. We had interest rates at 21 percent. We had inflation at 15. We had a "misery index" of 20. And we are not going to go back to those days.

This guy—change—he and Ozone Man, all they do is say, change, change, change. That is all you'll have in your pocket if you put these two guys in office, believe me. We're the ones with the positive program. We want to renew, revolutionize education, K through 12, give the parents a choice of schools, religious, private, and public. Put your faith in the parents and in the teachers and in the community, not in some bureaucracy in Washington, DC.

We've got the best plan for reforming health care: making insurance available to the poorest of the poor through vouchers; tax credits to that next overworked and overtaxed part; get that insurance pooled so you bring the prices down; and then go after these malpractice lawsuits that are driving the cost of health care right up through the roof.

We've got to teach those trial lawyers and Governor Clinton that people want reform of the legal system. It's a shame when people don't dare coach Little League for fear of a crazy lawsuit, don't dare help their fellow man along the highway for afraid of a crazy lawsuit, doctors don't dare deliver babies for fear of a crazy lawsuit. It is time to stand up to the trial lawyers and put some liability limits on this insurance.

And there's another big difference. The other day in southern Louisiana, I signed a brandnew national energy strategy that changes this alternative minimum tax and says, look, we are going to get the oilfields back to work by giving them a tax break.

And we've got a very good record in the environment. But it is Ozone Man—and this is why I call him that—who has said in Santa Barbara, California, "No more offshore drilling anywhere." That is wrong. That is wrong for this country.

Audience members. Boo-o-o!

The President. But typical, one day he makes that statement in California, "No more anywhere"; then he comes here and hedges and said he didn't say it. Then they played the tape to him right in Louisiana where he said, "No more drilling anywhere." And now he said, "Well, yes, I said it, but." You cannot have a lot of "buts" in the Oval Office. And Governor Clinton

keeps going, one side of the issue one day, one side the next.

No, you can't have it all ways. You can't be all things to all people in this job. You call them as you see them. If you make a mistake, you look the American people in the eye, like any family person would, and say, I was wrong. And then you go forward and lead the country. You don't try to waffle. You don't try to be on all sides of every question.

And believe me, Governor Clinton wants to expand the American Government. And I want to expand the American dream for every kid here today.

Now let's talk about character and trust. I happen to believe that they're both important. I happen to believe they are both important, because people look to the United States and to the President for just that kind of leadership. And Governor Clinton said in the debate, he said it's not a question of the character of the President, it is "the character of the Presidency." Wrong. They're interlocked. You can't separate them out for the time that the man is President.

I mentioned Horace Greeley's words in the last debate we had. But here's the full quote. He said, "Fame is a vapor, popularity an accident, riches take wing; only character endures." And that's true, whether it's in a family, whether it's in a business deal, or whether it's as President of the United States of America.

And so, my pitch at the end is that we simply cannot take a risk on Governor Clinton. Neither his experience nor his character, given this position on one side or the other, is what's right for this country at this time.

We are the greatest nation. You know, Governor Clinton and Ozone go around telling everybody that we are a nation in decline, that we're less than Germany, that we are more than Sri Lanka. Wrong. We are the most respected nation on the face of the Earth. And we have made dramatic strides towards world peace. They don't ever like to talk about foreign affairs. But let me tell you something on the eve of going to the polls. I am very proud to have been the President that has greatly reduced, if not eliminated, the threat of nuclear war from the face of the Earth.

Audience members. Four more years! Four more years! Four more years!

The President. You know, let me tell you something——

Audience members. Four more years! Four more years! Four more years!

The President. I honestly believe we're going to get 4 more years tomorrow.

You know, I have another big difference with Governor Clinton. It relates to war and peace. I am very proud that I wore the uniform of this country and fought for my country in combat. And the media elite don't like it, but I still think it is wrong, when your country is fighting, to go to organize demonstrations in a foreign land against the United States of America.

Audience members. Boo-o-o!

The President. And thank God we didn't waffle when Saddam Hussein took over Kuwait. Thank God we stood up and said this aggression will not stand. And thanks to the sons and daughters of Louisiana and others across this country, it did not stand.

And yesterday, a couple of days ago, there's this marvelous dispatch out of Baghdad a couple of days ago, Saddam Hussein's government announcing that they plan a party in downtown Baghdad of 500,000 people if I lose. Well, let me tell Saddam something here tonight: He can put his party on hold. And he'd better live up to all those resolutions of the United Nations and take the pressure off his people. Now, Saddam won't be happy, but I'll be happy that he's not happy. Look at it that way.

Now, let me ask you this. Imagine a year from today picking up a newspaper in your house and seeing that somewhere in the world or somewhere right at home there is a significant domestic crisis, an unforeseen crisis. Imagine that in this dangerous situation an American leader, totally without experience, completely untested, a leader about really whom we know very little still, and what we do know is his troubling pattern of being on one side and then another and bringing this ingrained habit of trying to lead people by misleading them. And when that next crisis comes, and you know darn well it will, the entire world is going to be looking to the American President.

Make no mistake about that. And they will look to his experience, and they will count on his character.

And I have been tested by fire. We have managed world change. It gets of almost Biblical proportions. And our success can be measured by the headlines that were never written, the countless crises that have never taken place, because we stayed firm and strong and never waffled.

Audience members. Four more years! Four more years! Four more years!

Audience members. George Bush! George Bush! George Bush!

The President. The decision that we made on Desert Storm was made not because it was popular. Think back to the demonstrations, to the reluctance of Congress, to the testimony before the Congress, counting millions of body bags that might return. It was not an easy call, and clearly it was not a popular call. But as President you have to make a call when you believe it was right, and that was the right thing to do.

And I will never forget that cold day up there in Camp David at our little chapel when Barbara and I literally prayed for the safety of the young men and women that were about to go to war. And let's never forget, we are one Nation under God, and in the Oval Office or in your families, we should never forget that. And we prayed those kids would come back. And back they came, with their heads high. And they lifted our country up and brought it together and erased the agony of Vietnam and made everybody proud, proud again to be Americans.

And so yes, I do believe in honor, duty, and country. And I ask for you to remember that another crisis may occur, and we better have a Commander in Chief that shares those Louisiana values.

Let me conclude now. We're getting near the end of the trail. This is the second-to-last campaign appearance that I'll ever make on my own behalf after half my adult life in public life—half in the private life right here, much of it in Louisiana; half of it in business, the other half in public life. And this is the end of the road in terms of the campaigning.

And so let me ask you in all seriousness to

think seriously about this and ask that you not take lightly your responsibility that you'll have tomorrow. You see, democracy was conceived from liberty, nurtured by freedom, and protected by the blood of those who came before us. And when you walk alone into that booth tomorrow, you'll not spend more than a couple of minutes. But your single voice will echo down the corridor of time. And with your vote, you will help shape the entire future of this, the most blessed, special nation that man has ever known and that God has ever created. And what we do together tomorrow, what we do together tomorrow will cast its shadow forward into eternity.

And so your vote is an act of power, a statement of principle, and a messenger of possibility. And so like all the candidates, I ask only that you think deeply about our Nation, about those that need help, about our needs, because tomorrow the polls don't matter. The pundits don't count. On election day, it is the American people who speak their mind. And only conscience should be your guide.

And don't let anyone tell you we're a nation in decline. We've come out of some very hard times. We're beginning to move. And I ask for your support for 4 more years to help every young person in this room enjoy the American dream.

May God bless the United States of America. Thank you very much. Thank you and God bless you all. Thank you.

Note: The President spoke at 6:55 p.m. at the Baton Rouge Metropolitan Airport. In his remarks, he referred to actress Cheryl Ladd; Henson Moore, Assistant to the President for Intergovernmental Affairs; Fox McKeithen, Louisiana secretary of state; and Chuck McMains and Carl Crane, Louisiana State representatives.

Remarks at a Rally in Houston, Texas
November 2, 1992

The President. What an awesome array——

Audience members. Four more years! Four more years! Four more years!

The President. What an awesome array. What a great homecoming and a great welcome back.

Audience members. Four more years! Four more years! Four more years!

The President. Thank you very, very much. Thank you, thank you. Thank you so very much. Thank all of you. And may I start by thanking this awesome array of wonderful people, Bob Hope and all the rest of them, for being with us tonight. Thank all of you from the bottom of our grateful hearts.

Texas, that's where it all started for Barbara and me: 44 years ago when we moved out to Texas, west Texas, we voted in our first Presidential election out there; here in Houston, 30 years ago, when I gave my very first speech on my own behalf. And tonight, in Texas, I will give my last speech ever on my own behalf as a candidate for reelection as President of the United States.

Audience members. Four more years! Four more years! Four more years!

The President. You know, when we drove that car out to Odessa 44 years ago, we were tired and we were worn out. Our spirits were high. We knew we had big things in front of us. And tonight we come home from another long, long journey a little tired, a little worn, but fired up because we are going to win this election tomorrow.

We are on the verge of something big. We are on the verge of something very, very big, something historic in American politics: the biggest comeback in American political history. And this guarantees it. I'm not much for predictions. No, I just tell the truth, and they think it's hell. You remember Harry Truman? I'm not very much for predictions, but come Wednesday morning, there's going to be a whole lot of pollsters looking around for something else to do. And America's going to be moving forward.

America will be moving forward again, united, strong, ready to move this country into the end of this century with a lot of power. And the bottom line is this: Yes, we will "Annoy the Media and Reelect Bush."

Audience members. Four more years! Four more years! Four more years!

The President. We came to Texas, as I said, 44 years ago to begin our lives. I got the book-learning back East, but I learned about life right here in Texas, first at Corpus Christi where I got my Navy wings—and yes, I am proud that I served my country in war—and then out west in the Permian Basin and later right here in the Gulf Coast. We come here tonight to begin again, begin the process of American renewal, because we know that we have changed the world. Now let's get together and help change America and lift everybody up.

And so the pundits say our campaign is against the odds. So what. I have a feeling the gods are smiling on us, and I know we're going to win this campaign. And here is why: My confidence stems from a simple fact that even in this time of uncertainty and transition, the American people share our values. And that's one of the reasons we'll do it, some simple, commonsense beliefs that Barbara and I learned right here in the great State of Texas. I learned that the strength of our Nation does not end up on the marble mausoleums along the Potomac but in the souls and the hearts of the hard-working people in places like Tyler and Waco and Corpus and Houston.

And while Governor Clinton dreams, while he dreams——

Audience members. Boo-o-o!

The President. ——while he dreams of expanding the American Government, I know what really matters: I want to expand the American dream.

And in Texas, I learned that family and faith and certainly friends are all there really is, and that America always will be indivisible, undivided, one Nation under God. It was here in west Texas in the oilfield I learned that a person's word is worth a million dollars, just the word of honor, and that if you don't stand for something, you will fall for anything. And it was there that I learned that great nations, like great

men, must keep their word of honor. And I have done that as President of the United States. Great men, like great nations, must also do that.

And I learned about character. Character is what you are when no one's looking and what you say when no one is listening. And I learned that character really is the father of leadership—not money, not fame, not intelligence. It is character. And here in Texas, or in the Oval Office, character counts.

And most of all, right here in Texas at Sunday dinners or at those Friday night football games, I was reminded every single day that there is no place like this great Nation. We are a special land with a special spirit. There is no place like America. And don't let Clinton and Gore tell you we're a nation in decline. We're a rising nation. We can solve any problem. And I want to lead this country to new heights for 4 more years.

Audience members. Four more years! Four more years! Four more years!

The President. And so I offer in this campaign a proven record of leadership, leadership that has literally revolutionized the world. Leadership that has been tested by fire. Leadership that has made our children dream the sweet dreams of peace instead of the nightmare of nuclear war.

And I offer trust, not in Government but in you, the American people. And I offer a deep and abiding faith in the future of our great Nation. Clinton and Gore say we are in decline, something less than Germany but a little more than Sri Lanka. They are wrong. We are the United States of America, the greatest, freest nation on the face of the Earth.

And I learned a lot about life. I learned a lot about life right here. I learned that you fight when your back is up against the wall. You never give up when you're behind. You push on and you fight for what you believe in. And you will win.

There is no way that Barbara and I can ever adequately say thank you—not possible—thank you to the people in this room, thank you to the people of Texas, thank you to our friends here. I will single out one person who is at my side once again in the battle of my life, and that is Jim Baker of Houston, Texas, our great Secretary of State. And I remind you that time and again our political journeys, we've defeated the odds. And time and again we've proved the naysayers wrong. I think America likes a comeback. I think they like somebody that fights for what he believes in. And that's what I am doing, right here, right down to the wire.

Audience members. Four more years! Four more years! Four more years!

The President. Did you see the dispatch out of Baghdad a couple of days ago? Saddam Hussein is said to be planning a party in the streets of Baghdad for 500,000 Iraqis if we lose. But tonight I have a message for my friend Saddam Hussein: Cancel. Cancel the celebration. Cancel the celebration. We are going to win, and we are going to make you adhere to every single resolution passed by the United Nations.

You know, I will readily contend that I've never been too hot with words, and I think you know that. In fact, some of the more elite pundits say I can't finish a sentence. Well, they may be right from time to time. But I'll tell you something, though. I think you also know, I think especially the people here do, that I care very deeply about our Nation. And I believe that we must treat this precious treasure with great care. America is something that has been passed on to us. And we must shape it. We must improve it. We must help people and be kind to people. And then we must pass that on to our kids and to our grandkids.

And tomorrow you participate in a ritual, a sacred ritual of stewardship, a ritual that was conceived by liberty and nurtured by freedom and defended by the blood of those who came before. And when you walk alone into the voting booth, you will not spend more than a couple of minutes, but your voice will echo down the corridors of history. And with your vote, you are going to help shape the future of this, the most blessed, special nation that man has ever known and God has helped create. And so, look at your vote—especially the young people—look at your vote as an act of power, a statement of principle. And tonight I ask only that you think deeply about our Nation and about its needs, because tomorrow the polls don't matter. The pundits don't count. On election day, only conscience should be your guide.

And when America votes their conscience, we will unleash a great power, a power stronger than any tank, faster than any airplane. This power will sweep past the cynics and the pundits and the pollster, and it will sweep us into office. And it will lift America up. It will lift us up to new heights for all. Don't listen to those critics and those pessimists who can only win by telling you how bad things are. We can solve the problems. But we are the greatest, fairest, freest nation on the face of the Earth. And I ask for your trust and your support to lead our great country for 4 more years.

Thank you—a most magnificent welcome home. And may God bless you all. May God bless our great country, the United States of America. Thank you all very much. Now let's go do it.

Note: The President spoke at 9:42 p.m. at the Houston Astro Arena. In his remarks, he referred to entertainer Bob Hope. A tape was not available for verification of the content of these remarks.

Statement on Signing the High Seas Driftnet Fisheries Enforcement Act
November 2, 1992

Today I am signing into law H.R. 2152, the "High Seas Driftnet Fisheries Enforcement Act."

H.R. 2152 calls for a number of measures in support of United Nations General Assembly Resolutions 44/225, 45/197, and 46/

215, which pertain to large-scale driftnet fishing and its impact on the living marine resources of the world's oceans and seas. The Act also calls for measures to address unregulated fishing in the area of the Central Bering Sea that is beyond the jurisdiction of the United States and the Russian Federation.

As a principal cosponsor of all three Resolutions, the United States has demonstrated strong leadership to address the problems of wastefulness and harm to the ecosystem caused by this fishing technique. I am grateful for the cooperation and support of many concerned countries that contributed to the successful adoption of the Resolutions. The United States has a particular interest in the effective implementation of the Resolutions because of the threat that driftnet fishing poses to living marine resources on the high seas.

It was appropriate that the United Nations General Assembly, by its Resolution 46/215, called upon all members of the international community to ensure that a global moratorium on all large-scale driftnet fishing is fully implemented by December 31, 1992. The Resolution is consistent with our treaty commitments under the Wellington Convention done on November 24, 1989.

Through this Act, the United States reinforces its commitment to cooperate with all concerned nations to ensure that the moratorium is implemented on time. The United States urges that all nations take appropriate measures to prohibit their nationals and fishing vessels flying their flags from undertaking any activities contrary to Resolution 46/215, and to impose appropriate penalties for such activities.

For its part, the United States has already taken steps, through the enactment of Public Law 101–627 on November 28, 1990, to prohibit any U.S. national from engaging in large-scale driftnet fishing in areas subject to the jurisdiction of the United States, as well as in areas beyond the 200-nautical mile exclusive economic zone of any nation.

With respect to problems posed by unregulated fishing in the Central Bering Sea, the United States is pleased with the success achieved with other concerned countries, including the Russian Federation, in securing an agreement voluntarily to suspend fishing in the area during 1993 and 1994. The Administration intends to continue actively to pursue a longer term conservation and management regime for this area.

Contrary to long-standing Administration policy, this Act unfortunately requires the Government to charge access fees for maritime freight rate information that exceed the cost of disseminating the information. It also imposes fees on private sector resale of Government information. These provisions impede the flow of public information from the Government. They run counter to Federal information policy and the traditions of the Copyright Act and the Freedom of Information Act.

Some provisions of the Act could be construed to encroach upon the President's authority under the Constitution to conduct foreign relations, including the unfettered conduct of negotiations with foreign nations. To avoid constitutional questions that might otherwise arise, I will construe all of these provisions to be advisory, not mandatory. With respect to section 203, which states the "sense of the Congress" concerning trade negotiations, I note that my Administration has taken the initiative in bringing environmental issues into our overall trade agenda.

Finally, I note that section 101 of the bill will be interpreted in accord with the recognized principles of international law. Those principles recognize the right of innocent passage of ships of all states through the territorial sea, a right that shall not be hampered.

GEORGE BUSH

The White House,
November 2, 1992.

Note: H.R. 2152, approved November 2, was assigned Public Law No. 102–582.

Statement on Signing the Arkansas-Idaho Land Exchange Act of 1992
November 2, 1992

Today I am pleased to sign into law S. 2572, the "Arkansas-Idaho Land Exchange Act of 1992." My approval of this bill enacts the Administration's proposal to benefit our Nation's wetlands through an equal value exchange of lands in the States of Arkansas and Idaho between the United States and the Potlatch Corporation.

This exchange will add nearly 41,000 acres to the Cache River and White River National Wildlife Refuges. The Refuges, together with nearby State conservation areas, protect nearly 185,000 acres of wetlands, one of only ten areas in the Nation recognized internationally as a "Wetland of International Importance." The United States has only a handful of such large wetland conservation areas and few if any opportunities for establishing new ones.

The lands to be protected as part of the National Wildlife Refuge System contain some of the most productive fish and wildlife habitat in North America. The area provides wintering habitat for a variety of migratory waterfowl and is home for a number of threatened or endangered species, including the bald eagle and the least tern.

In exchange for this environmentally sensitive land, the Potlatch Corporation will receive scattered tracts of Federal land in Idaho. The company will then be able to use the land to create jobs and expand the local tax base, making money available for important local tasks, such as education and economic development. This transfer of land to private ownership is crucial in a State like Idaho where much of the land is federally owned.

Protection of such wetland areas has been a high priority of my Administration, and enactment of this proposal clearly demonstrates our commitment to the environment. This Act enhances not only our environment, but also our economy, underscoring my strong belief that we can and must do both.

GEORGE BUSH

The White House,
November 2, 1992.

Note: S. 2572, approved November 2, was assigned Public Law No. 102–584.

Remarks in Houston on the Results of the Presidential Election
November 3, 1992

The President. Thank you. Thank you very, very much. Hey, listen, we've got to get going. Thank you. Thank you very much. Hey, listen, you guys.

Audience members. Thank you, George! Thank you, George! Thank you, George!

The President. Hey, thank you very much. Look, thank you so much. Well, here's the way I see it. Here's the way we see it and the country should see it, that the people have spoken. And we respect the majesty of the democratic system.

I just called Governor Clinton over in Little Rock and offered my congratulations.

He did run a strong campaign. I wish him well in the White House. And I want the country to know that our entire administration will work closely with his team to ensure the smooth transition of power. There is important work to be done, and America must always come first. So we will get behind this new President and wish him well.

To all who voted for us, voted for me here, especially here, but all across the country, thank you for your support. We have fought the good fight, and we've kept the faith. And I believe I have upheld the honor of the Presidency of the United States. Now I ask that we stand behind our new President. Regardless of our differences, all Americans share the same purpose: to make this, the world's greatest nation, more safe and more secure and to guarantee every American a shot at the American dream.

I would like to thank so many of you who have worked beside me to improve America and to literally change the world. Let me thank our great Vice President, Dan Quayle. You know, in the face of a tremendous pounding, he stood for what he believes in. He will always have my profound gratitude and certainly my respect.

I would like to salute so many that did special work: Rich Bond up at the RNC; Bob Teeter, who ran the campaign; Bob Mosbacher; our entire campaign team. They've run a valiant effort in a very, very difficult year. I also want to salute the members of the Cabinet, all of whom who have served this Nation with honor, with integrity, and with great distinction. And I would like to single out two leaders who represent the ideal in public service. Together they've helped lead the world through a period of unprecedented transition. I'm talking, of course, about my National Security Adviser, Brent Scowcroft, and my good friend and fellow Texan, our Secretary of State, Jim Baker.

Finally, of course, I want to thank my entire family, with a special emphasis on a woman named Barbara. She's inspired this entire Nation, and I think the country will always be grateful.

But tonight is really not a night for speeches. But I want to share a special message with the young people of America. You see, I remain absolutely convinced that we are a rising nation. We have been in an extraordinarily difficult period. But do not be deterred, kept away from public service by the smoke and fire of a campaign year or the ugliness of politics. As for me, I'm going to serve and try to find ways to help people. But I plan to get very active in the grandchild business and in finding ways to help others. But I urge you, the young people of this country, to participate in the political process. It needs your idealism. It needs your drive. It needs your conviction.

And again, my thanks, my congratulations to Governor Clinton; to his running mate, Senator Gore. And a special thanks to each and every one of you, many of you who have been at my side in every single political battle.

May God bless the United States of America. Thank you very, very much. Thank you so much. Thank you.

Note: The President spoke at 10:20 p.m. at the Westin Galleria Hotel. In his remarks, he referred to Rich Bond, chairman, Republican National Committee; Robert Teeter, campaign chairman, Bush-Quayle '92; and Robert Mosbacher, general chairman, Bush-Quayle '92. These remarks were released by the Office of the Press Secretary on November 4.

Remarks at a Welcome Home Ceremony
November 4, 1992

Thank you so very much. What a fantastic welcome back. Maybe you didn't read the election returns; it didn't work out quite the way we wanted. This is a fantastic return home, and it gives me a chance to just say thank you all so very much. I know most in one way or another have worked here and contributed to this administration of which I will always be extraordinarily proud.

I see some leaders here from the Congress. I especially want to thank Bob Dole. If you heard him last night, that was a class act. We have a great Cabinet, great top officials, and then everybody else helping out there. It means so much to Barbara and me.

Now we will go inside, start readjusting.

But you have given us a marvelous lift. And let me just say about the guy standing next to me, we are so grateful to Dan Quayle for everything he did. The guy almost killed himself out there, hard work day in and day out, and what he wasn't doing Marilyn was. And so was Barbara Bush. So, I think we owe all of them a great vote.

But I can think of nothing other to say than say let's finish this job with style. Let's get the job done, cooperate fully with the new administration. The Government goes on, as well it should, and we will support the new President and give him every chance to lead this country into greater heights.

So, I am very grateful to all of you. It's been a wonderful 4 years, and nobody can take that away from any of us. It's been good and strong, and I think we've really contributed something to the country. And maybe history will record it that way.

Thank you all very, very much.

Note: The President spoke at 3:03 p.m. on the South Lawn at the White House upon his return from Houston, TX.

Memorandum of Disapproval for the Revenue Act of 1992
November 4, 1992

I am withholding my approval of H.R. 11, the "Revenue Act of 1992," because it includes numerous tax increases, violates fiscal discipline, and would destroy jobs and undermine small business. The urban aid provisions that were once the centerpiece of the bill have been submerged by billions of dollars in giveaways to special interests.

My Administration's agenda for tax legislation has been clear from the outset: a focused measure to encourage economic growth, address the needs of economically deprived urban and rural areas, and make a limited number of significant and broadly supported changes in the tax law. While certain provisions in H.R. 11 meet these objectives, the bill as a whole does not. Its 647 pages contain more than 600 provisions, require more than 25 new studies or reports, set up 4 new commissions and advisory groups, and mandate numerous new demonstration and pilot projects. Most of these provisions are unrelated to the true needs of the economy and the American people.

The original focus of the bill—to help revitalize America's inner cities—has been lost in a blizzard of special interest pleadings. In fact, the enterprise zones provisions in H.R. 11 account for less than 10 percent of the revenue cost of the measure. While the enterprise zones provisions are a step in the right direction, more than 75 percent of all seriously distressed communities are left out in the cold. In addition, the capital incentives are far too limited. My proposal would grant eligibility to all areas that meet objective criteria. My proposal also would provide a complete exclusion from capital gains taxation for all investors in enterprise zone businesses, including gains from goodwill, the principal asset created by small business.

The bill's other major urban aid provision, which authorizes assistance to distressed communities, is also inadequate. My "Weed and Seed" proposal, currently being implemented on a pilot basis, coordinates Federal assistance to drug- and crime-ridden neighborhoods and targets much of the assistance to enterprise zone communities. H.R. 11 falls short of my plan. The bill adopts a business-as-usual approach to dispensing Federal assistance. It ignores the Administration's bottom-up method of combining strong law enforcement with resources to assist residents and neighborhoods in attaining economic self-sufficiency. Finally, communities currently benefiting from the pilot program could be denied continued funding because they may not be located in enterprise zones. It is regrettable that the Congress has not included a "Weed and Seed" program in a bill that I can sign.

The revenue provisions of H.R. 11 include some of my proposals, but omit three major components of my economic growth agenda. These are my proposals to provide a credit for first-time homebuyers; capital gains tax relief for start-up businesses; and incentives for investment in capital equipment. On balance, the revenue provisions of H.R. 11 are unacceptable. They would:

- Raise $33 billion in new taxes over 5 years on a wide array of American families, workers, and small businesses.
- Increase taxes on individuals, including middle-class taxpayers, in numerous ways. For example, the bill limits deductions for moving expenses and for losses resulting from theft, fires, and natural disasters.
- Repeal the 100 percent estimated tax safe harbor for small businesses. This would throw a monkey wrench into the primary engine of job creation.
- Raise numerous taxes on large employers, which will slow the recovery and undermine our competitive position in world markets.
- Lose about $2.5 billion in revenue as a result of more than 50 special relief provisions for limited numbers of taxpayers that have no policy justification.
- Impose needless and costly paperwork and recordkeeping burdens on the private sector.

H.R. 11 goes 180 degrees in the wrong direction in its treatment of expiring provisions of tax law. It would make permanent those expiring measures that are very costly and have negligible long-term benefits according to a broad range of government and private sector analysts. In contrast, the bill fails to make permanent the research and development tax credit and the deduction for 25 percent of health insurance premiums paid by self-employed individuals. It also fails to raise the health insurance deduction to 100 percent, as I have proposed.

The bill's Medicare provisions move in the opposite direction from the consensus view that we need to contain rising health care costs. They would increase Medicare costs by an estimated $3 billion over 5 years. For example, they invite a flood of costly lawsuits to challenge Medicare payments made as long as 6 years ago. These provisions would burden the courts and undermine consistent nationwide application of Medicare rules.

Another costly provision of H.R. 11 would permanently divert income taxes from the general fund of the Treasury to the Railroad Pension Fund. According to the Railroad Retirement Board, by the year 2016 this taxpayer subsidy could add $13 billion to this single industry pension fund. The diversion would set a dangerous precedent for other industry pension plans that may seek Federal taxpayer support in the future.

H.R. 11 abandons all pretense of fiscal discipline. It would increase the deficit in fiscal years 1994, 1995, and 1996. "Mandatory" spending would rise by more than $7 billion over 5 years—at a time of growing consensus that this portion of the budget must be brought under control.

The bill also arbitrarily increases statutory spending limits to allow roughly $600 million in increased payments to Medicare contractors for administrative costs. To benefit these companies, the Senate voted by the narrowest possible margin to waive its own rule requiring compliance with legal spending limits. These limits on discretionary spending were agreed to by bipartisan majorities of both Houses of Congress. It is irresponsible to waive them to benefit one group of companies.

I regret that my disapproval of H.R. 11 will prevent the enactment this year of many provisions that have my full support. However, the bill's benefits are overwhelmed by provisions that would endanger economic growth. I am therefore compelled to withhold my approval.

GEORGE BUSH

The White House,
November 4, 1992.

Statement on Signing the Veterans Health Care Act of 1992
November 4, 1992

Today I am signing into law H.R. 5193, the "Veterans Health Care Act of 1992." This legislation will improve the delivery of health care and other services to our Nation's veterans.

H.R. 5193 implements the Administration's proposal to establish the Persian Gulf War Veterans Health Registry within the Department of Veterans Affairs (VA). This registry is a reflection of our Nation's commitment to the men and women who served in the Persian Gulf War. Iraqi troops retreating from Kuwait maliciously set fire to many Kuwaiti oil wells, blanketing the region in thick black smoke. In the aftermath of the war, many veterans exposed to those oil fire pollutants and other environmental hazards in the area expressed concern for their health. This provision will enable VA to learn more about, and deal effectively with, potential health problems by providing a complete physical examination to any Persian Gulf veteran who requests it. The results of the examinations will be maintained in the registry and will be available if needed for scientific research.

H.R. 5193 also authorizes VA to provide counseling services to women who suffer the trauma of being sexually assaulted or harassed during their military service. Sexual harassment of women in any setting is abhorrent. We must continue working to make certain that such behavior does not occur. Nevertheless, when it does occur, we must be prepared to assist the victims. H.R. 5193 will do exactly that.

A number of other provisions to improve services to veterans are included in this bill. For example, H.R. 5193 implements an Administration proposal to provide a permanent authorization for VA's State home construction program. Through this VA-State partnership, VA helps with the construction and renovation of veterans homes operated by the States. Over the years, these facilities have provided much needed nursing home and domiciliary care to thousands of disabled and elderly veterans. The bill also extends VA's successful respite care program, under which disabled veterans living at home are hospitalized for short periods to give family caregivers a period of "respite." In addition, H.R. 5193 continues a VA scholarship program, used primarily for nurses, which pays for a student's education in exchange for service at VA medical facilities.

I have previously warned of the enormous and extremely costly burden imposed by various congressional reporting requirements. Notwithstanding these concerns, H.R. 5193 includes no less than 12 separate provisions requiring the Secretary of Veterans Affairs to submit reports to the Congress. I must again object to such costly requirements and call on the Congress to end the incessant imposition of onerous reporting requirements.

GEORGE BUSH

The White House,
November 4, 1992.

Note: H.R. 5193, approved November 4, was assigned Public Law No. 102–585.

Statement on Signing the National Aeronautics and Space Administration Authorization Act, Fiscal Year 1993
November 4, 1992

Today I am signing into law H.R. 6135, the "National Aeronautics and Space Administration Authorization Act, Fiscal Year 1993." Our civil space program is a major contributor to this Nation's status as a world leader. H.R. 6135 authorizes the continuation of space research and technology programs that are vital to the future of our country and its ability not only to remain competitive in today's technological world, but also to be the leader. I proposed these programs to the Congress because I was convinced that the United States must not relinquish its leadership role in space. The world continues to look to us in space exploration, and also in global environmental monitoring, aeronautics, materials, propulsion, and life sciences, among other areas. The Congress has endorsed these initiatives by passage of H.R. 6135.

I am particularly pleased that this Act continues Space Station Freedom and the Earth Observing System, at close to the funding level I proposed. The Space Station is absolutely vital to the continued exploration and understanding of our next frontier. The Earth Observing System is of critical importance to the understanding of our home planet and the environmental changes it may be undergoing.

I regret that the Congress chose to reduce substantially the funding for certain important initiatives—a new launch system, the National Aero-Space Plane, and the Space Exploration Initiative.

This Act also authorizes funds for the National Space Council, the Department of Transportation's Office of Commercial Space Transportation, and the Department of Commerce's Office of Space Commerce. These offices provide important guidance

and support in the development and implementation of our space policies.

In connection with the establishment of an Earth Observing System program, the Act requires the Administrator of the National Aeronautics and Space Administration (NASA) to carry out a program of earth observation "that addresses the highest priority international climate change research goals as defined by the Committee on Earth and Environmental Sciences and the Intergovernmental Panel on Climate Change." Because the members of the Intergovernmental Panel on Climate Change—jointly formed by the United Nations Environmental Programme and the World Meteorological Organization—are not appointed in conformity with the Appointments Clause of the Constitution, Article II, section 2, clause 2, they may not exercise significant governmental power under the laws of the United States. Accordingly, I sign this bill with the understanding that any future work of the Intergovernmental Panel on Climate Change shall be treated as advisory and that the Administrator of NASA shall retain authority to determine the scope and content of the Federal program.

GEORGE BUSH

The White House,
November 4, 1992.

Note: H.R. 6135, approved November 4, was assigned Public Law No. 102–588.

Radio Address to the Nation on the Results of the Presidential Election
November 7, 1992

Way back in 1945, Winston Churchill was defeated at the polls. He said, "I have been given the Order of the Boot." That is the exact same position in which I find myself today.

I admit, this is not the position I would have preferred, but it is a judgment I honor. Having known the sweet taste of popular favor, I can more readily accept the sour taste of defeat, because it is seasoned

for me by my deep devotion to the political system under which this Nation has thrived for two centuries.

I realize that defeat can be divisive. I want the Republican Party to be as constructive on the outside of executive power as it has been for 12 years on the inside. There must be no finger pointing, no playing the blame game. New ideas will flourish, and that is good. But as for what has passed, I can only say that it was my administration, my campaign. I captained the team, and I take full responsibility for the loss. No one else is responsible. I am responsible.

I hope history will record the Bush administration has served America well. I am proud of my Cabinet and my staff. America has led the world through an age of global transition. We have made the world safer for our kids. And I believe the real fruits of our global victory are yet to be tasted.

I'm also proud of my campaign team. They put together a tenacious, spirited effort in a difficult year. When you win, your errors are obscured; when you lose, your errors are magnified. I suspect history will take the edge off both interpretations. One thing I know for sure: My supporters should go out with their heads held high.

One final thought. As I campaigned across this Nation, I had the opportunity to talk to many people. I felt the anxiety that accompanies a time of change, but I could also see every day, in ways large and small, the resiliency of the American spirit.

Ours is a nation that has shed the blood of war and cried the tears of depression. We have stretched the limits of human imagination and seen the technologically miraculous become almost mundane.

Always, always, our advantage has been our spirit, a constant confidence, a sense that in America the only things not yet accomplished are the things that have not yet been tried. President-elect Clinton needs all Americans to unite behind him so he can move our Nation forward. But more than that, he will need to draw upon this unique American spirit.

There are no magic outside solutions to our problems. The real answers lie within us. We need more than a philosophy of entitlement. We need to all pitch in, lend a hand, and do our part to help forge a brighter future for this country.

On January 20th, Barbara and I will head back to Texas. For us there will be no more elections, no more politics. But we will rededicate ourselves to serving others because, after all, that is the secret of this unique American spirit. With this spirit, we can realize the golden opportunities before us and make sure that our new day, like every American day, is filled with hope and promise.

Thanks for listening. And God bless the United States of America.

Note: This address was recorded at 3:52 p.m. on November 6 in the conference room at Laurel Lodge, Camp David, MD, for broadcast after 9 a.m. on November 7.

Letter to Congressional Leaders Reporting on the National Emergency With Respect to Iran
November 10, 1992

Dear Mr. Speaker: (Dear Mr. President:)

I hereby report to the Congress on developments since the last Presidential report on May 14, 1992, concerning the national emergency with respect to Iran that was declared in Executive Order No. 12170 of November 14, 1979, and matters relating to Executive Order No. 12613 of October 29, 1987. This report is submitted pursuant to section 204(c) of the International Emergency Economic Powers Act, 50 U.S.C. 1703(c), and section 505(c) of the International Security and Development Coopera-

tion Act of 1985, 22 U.S.C. 2349aa–9(c). This report covers events through October 15, 1992. My last report, dated May 14, 1992, covered events through March 31, 1992.

1. There have been no amendments to the Iranian Transactions Regulations ("ITRs"), 31 CFR Part 560, or to the Iranian Assets Control Regulations ("IACRs"), 31 CFR Part 535, since my last report.

2. The Office of Foreign Assets Control ("FAC") of the Department of the Treasury continues to process applications for import licenses under the ITRs. However, as previ-

ously reported, recent amendments to the ITRs have resulted in a substantial decrease in the number of applications received relating to the importation of nonfungible Iranian-origin goods.

During the reporting period, the Customs Service has continued to effect numerous seizures of Iranian-origin merchandise, primarily carpets, for violation of the import prohibitions of the ITRs. FAC and Customs Service investigations of these violations have resulted in forfeiture actions and the imposition of civil monetary penalties. Additional forfeiture and civil penalty actions are under review.

3. The Iran-United States Claims Tribunal ("the Tribunal"), established at The Hague pursuant to the Algiers Accords, continues to make progress in arbitrating the claims before it. Since my last report, the Tribunal has rendered 5 awards for a total of 533 awards. Of that total, 359 have been awards in favor of American claimants: 217 of these were awards on agreed terms, authorizing and approving payment of settlements negotiated by the parties, and 142 were decisions adjudicated on the merits. The Tribunal has issued 34 decisions dismissing claims on the merits and 81 decisions dismissing claims for jurisdictional reasons. Of the 59 remaining awards, 3 approved the withdrawal of cases, and 56 were in favor of Iranian claimants. As of September 30, 1992, payments on awards to successful American claimants from the Security Account held by the NV Settlement Bank stood at $2,046,090,574.01.

As of September 30, 1992, the Security Account has fallen below the required balance of $500 million 35 times. Iran has periodically replenished the account, as required by the Algiers Accords, by transferring funds from the separate account held by the NV Settlement Bank in which interest on the Security Account is deposited. Iran has also replenished the Security Account with the proceeds from the sale of Iranian-origin oil imported into the United States, pursuant to transactions licensed on a case-by-case basis by FAC. Iran has not, however, replenished the account since the last oil sale deposit on December 3, 1991. The aggregate amount that has been transferred from the interest account to the Security Account is $859,472,986.47. As of September 30, 1992, the total amount in the Security Account was $499,528,936.74, and the total amount in the interest account was $17,301,717.98.

4. The Tribunal continues to make progress in the arbitration of claims of U.S. nationals for $250,000.00 or more. Since the last report, 4 large claims have been decided. More than 85 percent of nonbank claims have now been disposed of through adjudication, settlement, or voluntary withdrawal, leaving 85 such claims on the docket.

5. As anticipated by the May 13, 1990, agreement settling the claims of U.S. nationals against Iran for less than $250,000.00, the Foreign Claims Settlement Commission ("FCSC") has continued its review of 3,112 claims. The FCSC has issued decisions in 849 claims, for total awards of more than $17 million. The FCSC expects to complete its adjudication of the remaining claims in late 1993.

6. In coordination with concerned Government agencies, the Department of State continues to present United States Government claims against Iran, as well as responses by the United States Government to claims brought against it by Iran.

7. As anticipated by my last report, the Tribunal terminated Case No. A/15 (I:G), the case brought by Iran concerning bank syndicate claims against Dollar Account No. 1 at the Federal Reserve Bank of New York, on June 12, 1992, on the joint request of the two governments.

8. Jose Maria Ruda, President of the Tribunal, tendered his resignation on October 2, 1992. His resignation will take effect on March 31, 1993, or on such later date as his successor becomes available to take up his duties.

9. The situation reviewed above continues to involve important diplomatic, financial, and legal interests of the United States and its nationals, and presents an unusual challenge to the national security and foreign policy of the United States. The IACRs issued pursuant to Executive Order No. 12170 continue to play an important role in structuring our relationship with Iran and in enabling the United States to implement

properly the Algiers Accords. Similarly, the ITRs issued pursuant to Executive Order No. 12613 continue to advance important objectives in combating international terrorism. I shall continue to exercise the powers at my disposal to deal with these problems and will continue to report periodically to the Congress on significant developments.

Sincerely,

GEORGE BUSH

Note: Identical letters were sent to Thomas S. Foley, Speaker of the House of Representatives, and Dan Quayle, President of the Senate.

Remarks at a Senate Republican Leadership Dinner Honoring the President
November 10, 1992

Thank you for that wonderful welcome. Dan, thank you for those kind remarks. Please be seated. Well, thank you. I kind of had mixed emotions about this night, whether to—coming to something that would be a wake and something sorrowful and sad, or something like it's turned out to be, at least in my view, something upbeat and very positive. So I'm glad to be here, and Barbara's glad to be here.

I'd like to pick a little fight with the members of the Senate wives, because Barbara has enjoyed that work and being with them so much, you've created a bit of a monster. You've given her a whole new self-confidence which is—[*laughter*]—some of you thought she was never lacking in self-confidence. But nevertheless, now she's getting ready to shift gears. And my advice to those of you who are her friends, and I think you all are: Give her a wide berth, which is what I'm trying to do around the White House there, because she's a bundle of energy, shifting gears from the present into the future. That's the way it ought to be. But tomorrow we head off for a little vacation, get a little rest, and think about what has been and then what's about to be.

But first I want to thank Bob Michel and the House leadership. Newt's here and others, I'm sure, we can't see. But I think the Senate was very broadminded in inviting you all over here tonight. [*Laughter*] But it has been a joy to work with the House leadership. Sometimes you have to do stuff by being negative, and during this

time of being President, why, we've had to accomplish some things by keeping bad things from happening.

Both in the House and the Senate there has been a remarkable show of unity. It put individual Senators and individual Congressmen in a difficult position, because sometimes they had to sublimate their passions a little bit in order to stay with the overall good or stay with the party, and it has not been easy. That is something, though, that I want to just thank everybody for, because the record was superb. And I think by beating back, against tremendous odds, some lousy legislation, we ended up with getting good legislation.

I'm afraid in the campaign, in the process, we were accused of being against people because of having to take a stand for fiscal responsibility. But nevertheless, I think on the bottom line we came out and did the right thing. I am very grateful to the leadership on both sides, the House and the Senate, for all of that.

A word about the Vice President: Nobody could have asked to have a better Vice President at his side than I had with Dan Quayle. He has been absolutely superb. He's worked hard. He's worked with the Senate particularly, but also the House. Then in the campaign, he was tireless; Marilyn, sometimes at his side, sometimes on her own, doing a superb job not just for ourselves, for this ticket, but for some in this room and so many that aren't here that the Quayles worked for and helped. So,

Dan, I will be eternally grateful to you, and I just wish you all the best in the future.

In terms of the Cabinet, I don't think anybody could have been blessed with a better Cabinet. The problem I've got is that I wasn't able in the campaign to get into focus the enormous accomplishments of the men and women that are here tonight in our Cabinet. They have done a superb job. I don't want to start clicking it off, but I know Lou Sullivan is here. What we've done in leadership in preventive medicine, for example, and doing things that really are making a wonderful contribution to mankind are going to be recorded, I believe, in a favorable way. And Lou has been magnificent.

I see Carla here. Heaven's sakes, what we've been able to do in the free trade areas, standing up for free and fair trade, is a remarkable contribution. I just hope that it comes to fruition, certainly on the NAFTA, in the next term. I know we're going to keep working right down to January 20th on the Uruguay round. You want to help Third World countries? Well, the way to help them is through trade, not the aid programs that have failed. That's exactly what she and Nick Brady, who's with us tonight, and Barbara Franklin, who's with us tonight, and a lot of others have been working on in terms of free and fair trade. So we've got an awful lot to be grateful for.

I think we've had a good record of stewardship. Manuel Lujan is here. I think when history is written, why, we're going to have a very proud record in terms of stewardship of the national parks and the great heritage that we want to leave to our kids.

Ed Madigan's here. My heavens, you look at agricultural America, it's done pretty darned well in a very, very difficult time. And yet, for some reason, I wasn't able to get that in the proper focus.

But anyway, I'm omitting many friends that are here in the Cabinet, but I am very grateful to this outstanding group of leaders. I was telling Lamar Alexander, who's with us tonight, one of my real regrets is that somehow, given the hue and cry for change and change, and the hue and cry about how everything is wrong with the country, we never got in focus the fact that we have literally made suggestions as to

how to revolutionize the education in this country, to elevate it to have the same quality for K through 12 that we have for college. And it just didn't connect. But that program and that zeal that Lamar brought to the program certainly will be recognized.

So again, with the fear of omission, I will stop, but just simply say thank you for a fantastic Cabinet and a very sound record and all of that.

I want to tell Bob Kasten and Senator Seymour, both Senators Kasten and Seymour, the regret I feel about their demise. They worked awful hard. They've been great Senators. They were caught up in a whirlwind; they were caught up in both States in something that was beyond their own control. And they worked hard. Many Senators here went out and helped both of them. But I have great regret about that because the Senate is going to be deprived of the committed leadership and stewardship of both those Senators. In fact, we might ought to give them a little round of applause and thank them for what they have done.

I am always going to be grateful to the Senate leadership. The support has been superb. I mentioned earlier, sometimes when you're in the White House, you take a position that you feel strongly about, and you put various leaders in a difficult position. Clearly we did that to various Senators here from time to time. But I want to single out Bob Dole, because this is a remarkable leader, a remarkable—[*applause*]. It's well-known that he and I went head-to-head in tough primary days long ago. But the beautiful thing is—and I think it speaks—anybody that studies government can learn from all this. Here's a guy that took on this role of leader and working with a President with whom he had done combat in the past, but subsequently we became, again, fast friends. But he never ever put his own personal agenda ahead of the agenda of the President, and that's kind of the way it ought to work when you have the White House.

But the lovely thing about it is the way he has conducted himself subsequent to, as Winston Churchill said, receiving "the Order of the Boot" that I have received. I thought the speechwriter that wrote that, that I delivered last Saturday, was a little harsh in his assessment of what happened to me. Then I thought, "Well, listen, being in the company of Churchill ain't all bad." So I gave him a little raise and sent him back to Kentucky Fried Chicken. [*Laughter*]

But nevertheless, I was watching Bob very carefully, and I've watched others, and the tendency when there's a defeat of this magnitude and of this hurtfulness and of this enormity is to criticize, to find somebody to blame. Regrettably some Republicans and certainly many Democrats have fallen into this marvelous second-guessing track, figuring it all out and analyzing to the detriment of somebody else and to tearing down somebody in order to ooch yourself up a little with your wisdom. Not Senator Dole. From the minute the election results were in, he has been courageous in standing up against the common wisdom, saying nice things about the President and Dan and Barbara and all of this.

In addition, he's shown where the leadership really is now in this country in terms of party. It can be in Bob Michel over in the House, but because of the numbers, it's more apt to rest on Bob Dole's shoulders. I think people understand it. I think they respect the way he has assumed, without arrogance, without any kind of bitterness, a significant leadership role to hold our party together so people can look to him and look, of course, to the results that will be coming out of the Senate, and then under Bob's leadership, that will come out of the House.

The idea that this party has seen its demise—and I love these little analysts, these media that I tried to annoy and failed. [*Laughter*] To hear them analyze it all, you'd think that history had been indelibly writ, that the party is out of here. I don't believe it for one single minute.

The thing that I've admired and respected about Bob is the way he has, without arrogance, taken on this mantle of leadership that he has earned through his years as leader up here on the Hill and said, "Look, we're here to do battle. We're here to do what's right for the country. We're going to be with you when we think you're right, and we are going to stand on principle when we think you're wrong." That's exactly the way it should be. And I can tell you, it's made it an awful lot easier for us as we contemplate a future without politics but look over, obviously with some distress and some angst, over what has transpired one week ago tonight.

So, Bob, there is no way that we can ever adequately say thank you to you. But you watch, the country is going to say it in plenty of ways in the troubled and tough days that lie ahead. So I'm grateful to you. I didn't want to come here, but I'm sure glad I did, because it gives me a chance to say thanks to so many friends in this room.

Don't worry about the Bushes. We are looking ahead now. I didn't think we would about a week ago today, but we're doing it. And we'll count our blessings when we get back to Houston on January 20th for all the friends that have supported us so much.

Thank you, and God bless you all.

Note: The President spoke at 7:46 p.m. in the East Hall at Union Station.

Notice on Continuation of Emergency Regarding Chemical and Biological Weapons Proliferation
November 11, 1992

On November 16, 1990, consistent with the authority provided me under the International Emergency Economic Powers Act (50 U.S.C. 1701, *et seq.*), I issued Executive Order No. 12735. In that order, I declared a national emergency with respect to the unusual and extraordinary threat to the national security and foreign policy of the United States posed by the proliferation of chemical and biological weapons. Because the proliferation of these weapons continues to pose an unusual and extraordinary threat to the national security and foreign policy of the United States, the national emergency declared on November 16, 1990, must continue in effect beyond November 16, 1992. Therefore, in accordance with section 202(d) of the National Emergencies Act (50 U.S.C. 1622(d)), I am continuing the national emergency declared in Executive Order No. 12735.

This notice shall be published in the *Federal Register* and transmitted to the Congress.

GEORGE BUSH

The White House,
November 11, 1992.

[Filed with the Office of the Federal Register, 10:19 a.m., November 12, 1992]

Note: This notice was released by the Office of the Press Secretary on November 12, and it was published in the Federal Register on November 13.

Letter to Congressional Leaders on Continuation of the National Emergency Regarding Chemical and Biological Weapons Proliferation
November 11, 1992

Dear Mr. Speaker: (Dear Mr. President:)

On November 16, 1990, in light of the dangers of the proliferation of chemical and biological weapons, I issued Executive Order No. 12735 and declared a national emergency under the International Emergency Economic Powers Act (50 U.S.C. 1701, *et seq.*). Under section 202(d) of the National Emergencies Act (50 U.S.C. 1622(d)), the national emergency terminates on the anniversary date of its declaration unless I publish in the *Federal Register* and transmit to the Congress a notice of its continuation.

The proliferation of chemical and biological weapons continues to pose an unusual and extraordinary threat to the national security and foreign policy of the United States. Therefore, I am hereby advising the Congress that the national emergency declared on November 16, 1990, must continue in effect beyond November 16, 1992. Accordingly, I have extended the national emergency declared in Executive Order No. 12735 and have sent a notice of extension to the *Federal Register* for publication.

Section 204 of the International Emergency Economic Powers Act and section 401(c) of the National Emergencies Act contain periodic reporting requirements regarding activities taken and money spent pursuant to an emergency declaration. The following report is make pursuant to these provisions.

The three export control regulations issued under the Enhanced Proliferation Control Initiative are fully in force and have been used to control the export of items with potential use in chemical or biological weapons or unmanned delivery systems for weapons of mass destruction.

Over the last 6 months, the United States has continued to address actively in its international diplomatic efforts the problem of the proliferation and use of chemical and biological weapons.

In August 1992, the 39 members of the Conference on Disarmament completed work on the Chemical Weapons Convention. In addition to banning chemical weapons among parties, the Convention will also require parties to restrict, and ultimately cut off, trade in certain chemical weapons-related chemicals with non-parties. The Convention will be opened for signature in January 1993, and we expect it to enter into force in January 1995.

The membership of the Australia Group of countries cooperating against chemical and biological weapons proliferation stands at 22. It is anticipated that the group's membership will expand somewhat over the next 6 months.

At the June 1992 Australia Group meeting, all member countries agreed to expand the list of identified chemical weapons precursors subject to Australia Group controls from 50 to 54, and to impose controls on a common list of dual-use chemical equipment that was tentatively agreed at the December 1991 meeting. At the same meeting, the Australia Group agreed, *ad referendum*, to a list of biological organisms, toxins, and equipment to subject to export controls. We expect these lists to be formally adopted at the December 1992 meeting.

Encouraging progress can also be reported in the steps taken by countries outside the Australia Group, including several Eastern European countries and Argentina, to establish effective chemical and biological export controls comparable to those observed by Australia Group members. In December 1992, Hungary will host a seminar on Australia Group practices for non-Australia Group members from Eastern Europe and the former Soviet Union.

Finally, the March 31, 1992, report regarding expenditures under the declaration of a national emergency to deal with the lapse of the Export Administration Act in Executive Order No. 12730 also includes measures related to the Enhanced Proliferation Control Initiative. Pursuant to section 401(c) of the National Emergencies Act, there were no additional expenses directly attributable to the exercise of authorities conferred by the declaration of the national emergency.

Sincerely,

GEORGE BUSH

Note: Identical letters were sent to Thomas S. Foley, Speaker of the House of Representatives, and Dan Quayle, President of the Senate. This letter was released by the Office of the Press Secretary on November 12.

Letter to Congressional Leaders Reporting on Iraq's Compliance With United Nations Security Council Resolutions
November 16, 1992

Dear Mr. Speaker: (Dear Mr. President:)

Consistent with the Authorization for Use of Military Force Against Iraq Resolution (Public Law 102–1), and as part of my continuing effort to keep Congress fully informed, I am again reporting on the status of efforts to obtain Iraq's compliance with the resolutions adopted by the U.N. Security Council.

In my report of September 16, 1992, I described Operation Southern Watch, with its accompanying "no-fly zone." Operation Southern Watch implements Security Council Resolution 688, which requires Iraq to end the repression of its civilian population immediately, allow immediate access by international humanitarian organizations to all parts of Iraq, and make available all facilities for the operation of these organizations. Southern Watch has been working extremely well. Iraq's use of aircraft to repress its civilian population, in particular Iraq's bombing of its citizens in and around the southern marsh areas, has stopped. There have been no major Iraqi military operations south of the 36th parallel since the monitoring zone was announced, nor has there been any major increase in Iraqi forces in the southern region. Some Iraqi repression of the civilian population in the region continues, however. Meanwhile, the Coalition's effort to ensure compliance with Resolution 688 in northern Iraq, Operation Provide Comfort, also continues to discourage major Iraqi military operations against the inhabitants of northern Iraq.

Since my previous report, the Iraqi opposition has held two meetings in northern Iraq to broaden the base of the Iraq National Congress (INC). We support the efforts of the INC to rally Iraqis against the Saddam regime and in favor of a future Iraq based on the principles of political pluralism, territorial unity, and full compliance with all the U.N. Security Council resolutions. We encourage other governments to do the same.

Moreover, the U.N. Special Commission on Iraq (UNSCOM) and the International Atomic Energy Agency (IAEA) have continued to investigate Iraq's weapons of mass destruction program and to verify the destruction of relevant facilities, equipment, and weapons.

The fourteenth ballistic missile inspection team, UNSCOM 45, October 16–29, was the largest and most complex inspection UNSCOM has conducted. It inspected declared and undeclared facilities associated with the manufacture and storage of ballistic missile fuels in an effort to learn whether Iraq is attempting to maintain a clandestine SCUD force. Initial fuel sample analyses were inconclusive. The team found little evidence of SCUD missile activity at any site. Russian cooperation was essential to this inspection, which depended heavily on both information and technical assistance from Russian experts.

A nuclear inspection team, UNSCOM 46/ IAEA 15, was in Iraq in early November. Weather permitting, it will have completed water sampling throughout Iraq. Initial results from the first round of water samples taken in early September (and mentioned in my last report) have not revealed evidence of any facility in Iraq producing fissionable fuel. Some new sites likely will be designated for inspection.

In late September, the Chemical Destruction Group in residence at the Muthanna State Establishment destroyed the following items: 120 122mm rocket warheads; 350 122mm propellant grain; 153 122mm rocket motor tube assembly; 1335 liters of nerve agent (GB/GF); 13 al Hussein warheads; 228 liters of isopropyl alcohol; 4 500 gauge oil-filled bombs; 2 155mm oil-filled projectiles; 4 250 gauge oil-filled bombs; and 14 R400 aerial bombs. Destruction activity will continue for the next twelve months.

The inspectors continue to be subjected to harassment, but harassment subsided to a low level after the strong international protests in response to Iraq's actions in August and September.

UNSCOM continues to face a shortage of funds. As I noted in my previous report, the United States has contributed over $40 million to UNSCOM since its inception. Recent pledges from two other countries exceed $40 million, but the funds have not reached UNSCOM.

On October 2, the U.N. Security Council adopted Resolution 778, which permits the use of a portion of frozen Iraqi oil assets to fund crucial U.N activities concerning Iraq, including UNSCOM, humanitarian relief, and the Compensation Commission. On October 21, I signed Executive Order No. 12817, which implements that Resolution in the United States. We are prepared to transfer up to $200 million in frozen Iraqi oil assets held in U.S. financial institutions, provided that U.S. contributions do not exceed 50% of the total amount contributed. These funds will be repaid, with interest, from Iraqi oil revenues as soon as Iraqi oil exports resume.

The Iraq-Kuwait Boundary Demarcation Commission continues its work, without Iraqi participation. The land boundary is expected to be completely demarcated through the placement of boundary pillars in the ground by the end of the year. During its seventh session October 12–16, the Commission considered the offshore boundary section, which it will take up again at its next meeting, tentatively scheduled for December.

The U.N. Compensation Commission has continued to prepare for the processing of claims from individuals, corporations, other entities, governments, and international organizations that suffered direct loss or damage as a result of Iraq's unlawful invasion and occupation of Kuwait. The next session of the Governing Council of the Commission is scheduled in Geneva December 14–18, with a further meeting in March 1993.

At its latest session September 21–24, the Governing Council adopted decisions on extending the filing deadlines for certain types of claims (including claims for environmental damage) and on protection against multiple recovery. The Council discussed business losses, interest, and costs, without making decisions. The Executive

Secretary reported that the Commission already has received over 150,000 claims and expects many times that number. He noted that the Commission will require at least $9 million in one-time expenditures, plus $1.2 million annually, for a computer system for processing and verifying such a large number of claims.

We plan to meet some of the Commission's needs with funds derived from frozen Iraqi oil assets. Thirty percent of the funds derived from frozen oil assets transferred under U.N. Security Council Resolution 778 are to go to the Compensation Fund. This should generate sufficient funding for the Commission to proceed with its permanent computer system and to begin processing claims.

Meanwhile, the Department of State has distributed the forms for claims by governments (Form F) to federal agencies and state governments. On September 23, the U.S. Government filed its second set of 180 consolidated individual claims with the Commission, bringing the total of U.S. claims filed to 380. The Department is reviewing about 1200 additional claims received from individuals and is now receiving claims from corporations. The next filing is scheduled for December.

In accordance with paragraph 20 of Resolution 687, the Sanctions Committee has received notices of approximately 3.1 million tons of foodstuffs to be shipped to Iraq thus far in 1992. The Sanctions Committee also continues to consider and, when appropriate, approve requests to send to Iraq materials and supplies for essential civilian needs. Iraq, in contrast, has for months maintained a full embargo against its northern provinces. Iraq has also refused to utilize the opportunity under Resolutions 706 and 712 to sell $1.6 billion in oil, proceeds from which could be used by Iraq under U.N. supervision to purchase foodstuffs, medicines, materials, and supplies for essential civilian needs of its population. The Iraqi authorities bear full responsibility for any suffering in Iraq that results from their refusal to implement Resolutions 706 and 712.

Through the International Committee of the Red Cross (ICRC), the United States, Kuwait, and other Coalition members continue to press the Government of Iraq to comply with its obligations under Security Council resolutions to return some 800 detained Kuwaiti and third-country nationals. Likewise, the United States and its allies continue to press the Government of Iraq to return to Kuwait all property and equipment removed from Kuwait by Iraq. Iraq continues to withhold necessary cooperation on these issues and to resist unqualified ICRC access to detention facilities in Iraq.

As I stated in previous reports, in concert with our Coalition partners, we will continue to monitor carefully the treatment of Iraq's citizens, and together we remain prepared to take appropriate steps if the situation requires. To this end, we will continue to maintain an appropriate level of forces in the region for as long as required by the situation in Iraq.

I remain grateful for the support of the Congress for these efforts, and look forward to continued cooperation toward achieving our mutual objectives.

Sincerely,

GEORGE BUSH

Note: Identical letters were sent to Thomas S. Foley, Speaker of the House of Representatives, and Robert C. Byrd, President pro tempore of the Senate.

Statement by Press Secretary Fitzwater on the President's Meeting With President Chaim Herzog of Israel
November 16, 1992

President Bush met today with Israeli President Herzog at his request. The two leaders discussed U.S.-Israeli relations, the ongoing Middle East peace negotiations, and the Middle East generally. It was agreed that the United States must remain engaged if peace is to be achieved in the Middle East.

Statement by Press Secretary Fitzwater on the President's Meeting With Prime Minister Constantine Mitsotakis of Greece
November 17, 1992

The President met for approximately 45 minutes this afternoon in the Oval Office with Prime Minister Constantine Mitsotakis of Greece. The two leaders discussed Cyprus, the situation in the former Yugo-slavia, and other European issues. On the issue of Macedonia, the President reiterated our strong hope that this issue be resolved as soon as possible.

Statement by Press Secretary Fitzwater on the President's Meeting With President-Elect Bill Clinton
November 18, 1992

President Bush and President-elect Clinton had a warm and informative conversation in the Oval Office today which lasted for 1 hour and 45 minutes. President Bush reviewed a number of trouble spots around the world and discussed United States policy in these areas.

At approximately 2:15 p.m., the President and President-elect visited their transition staffs in the Roosevelt Room. President Bush said he wanted a smooth transition and said he appreciated the task that lay ahead of the transition team. The transition meeting was attended by Secretary Andrew Card, Chase Untermeyer, and Bob Zoellick representing the administration; Vernon Jordan, Warren Christopher, Alexis Herman, and Mark Gearan representing President-elect Clinton. The discussion focused on procedures for making appointments, including FBI clearances and financial disclosure forms.

The two transition teams will maintain regular contacts. Secretary Card will maintain a small staff here in the White House and will oversee three transition phases: President Bush's departure and establishment of an office in Houston; the transfer of authority from the Bush administration to the Clinton administration; and the process of transferring Presidential papers to the Archives or Presidential library.

Both President Bush and President-elect Clinton expressed satisfaction with the meeting.

Letter to Congressional Leaders Transmitting a Report on Withdrawal of Russian and Commonwealth of Independent States Armed Forces from the Baltic Countries
November 19, 1992

Dear Mr. Speaker: (Dear Mr. President:)
In accordance with the Foreign Oper-ations, Export Financing, and Related Programs Appropriations Act, 1993 (Public

Law 102–391), I am submitting the attached report on progress being made toward the withdrawal of the armed forces of Russia and the Commonwealth of Independent States (CIS) from the territories of Estonia, Latvia, and Lithuania and on the status of negotiations regarding the establishment of a timetable for total withdrawal.

Sincerely,

GEORGE BUSH

Note: Identical letters were sent to Thomas S. Foley, Speaker of the House of Representatives, and Dan Quayle, President of the Senate.

Letter to Congressional Leaders on the Exclusion of the United States Marshals From the Performance Management and Recognition System
November 19, 1992

Dear Mr. Speaker: (*Mr. President:*)

Supervisors and management officials in GS–13, 14, and 15 positions throughout the Federal Government are covered by the Performance Management and Recognition System as required by chapter 54 of title 5, United States Code, unless otherwise excluded by law or under the President's authority as provided in 5 U.S.C. 5402(b)(1).

Upon proper application from the United States Department of Justice and upon the recommendation of the Acting Director of the Office of Personnel Management, I have excluded the United States Marshals from coverage under the Performance Management and Recognition System, pursuant to 5 U.S.C. 5402(b)(1).

Attached is my report describing the reasons for excluding the U.S. Marshals.

Sincerely,

GEORGE BUSH

Note: Identical letters were sent to Thomas S. Foley, Speaker of the House of Representatives, and Dan Quayle, President of the Senate.

Remarks Announcing the Agreement on Agricultural Trade With the European Community
November 20, 1992

I want to salute Secretary Madigan and Ambassador Carla Hills, and my announcement relates to their work. I am exceptionally pleased to announce that the United States and the European Community's Commission have reached unanimous agreement on an agricultural package that should enable us to press forward the global trade negotiations to a successful conclusion.

These global trade negotiations, the so-called Uruguay round under the GATT, are fundamental to spurring economic growth, creating jobs here at home and indeed all around the world. I am hopeful that the breakthrough that we achieved today will spur movement across-the-board in the ongoing negotiations among all the GATT parties in Geneva so that we can achieve this comprehensive, global, and balanced agreement that we've sought for so long. In addition, by agreeing to solutions to our differences on oilseeds and other agricultural disputes, we've avoided a possible trade war, and that is very, very important.

I am particularly pleased that Ambassador Hills and Secretary Madigan are here with us today because they've done extraordinary work to achieve this historic result—I salute their teammates who are with us here today as well—and also because they will remain with you to answer your questions. Some of this is very, very technical. And they know how proud I am of their work. I've seen them in action both here and abroad, hammering out this agreement. It's taken a long time, but it was sound.

It's been a long and difficult course to the result that we've achieved today. I recall these extensive and frequently vigorous—I've chosen the word carefully—discussions on agriculture and other trade issues at the economic summit that we hosted in Houston in 1990 and at each of the summits that followed. But I am now absolutely convinced that the work was well worth it. I talked to Prime Minister John Major this

morning, had an opportunity to thank him for his key role as the current President of the EC.

The next step then will be for the United States and the EC and all the other parties in the Uruguay round to return to the negotiating table in Geneva prepared to show the flexibility necessary to bring these negotiations to a successful close.

So, once again, I salute our partners in all of this. And I certainly salute our extraordinarily effective team that has been able to bring this about. And with no further ado, I will turn it over to them to take all your questions.

Note: The President spoke at 12:10 p.m. in the Briefing Room at the White House.

Statement on the Death of Roy Acuff
November 23, 1992

Barbara and I mourn the death of our long-time friend and the King of Country Music. Roy Acuff showed that America loves country music because country music loves America. He helped the Grand Ole Opry become America's heirloom of the heart.

Roy made his Opry debut in 1938 and played it nearly every weekend. Often, Barbara and I visited him and heard Roy sing

"Great Speckled Bird" or "Wabash Cannonball." We marveled at his talent. Even more, we cherished his kindness, modesty, love of life, and loyalty to friends.

Roy said, "I want to go down as a gentleman in country music. That's all I care to be." Our great and good friend achieved that goal and more. Roy Acuff leaves what for 89 years he lived, a touch of the American dream.

Remarks at the Thanksgiving Turkey Presentation Ceremony
November 24, 1992

Thank you, kids. Thank you very much. Please be seated. And let me just say I want to welcome all of you. Certainly Mr. Cuddie, who is the president of the National Turkey Federation; Stuart Proctor, the executive vice president. I want to especially welcome all the kids: From Kent Gardens Elementary, now, where are you? Hold up your—there they are, right over—this group, good. Amidon Elementary? Yep.

Holy Cross, and maybe some strays out there from other schools. Anyway, everyone is really welcome.

And of course, the special guest of honor, the bird over here. I hope you guys have seen him. After participating in this ceremony year after year, I've come to learn a little about the turkey. For instance, it's hand fed. It gets lots of personal attention. And it's over-weight and reminds me of

Ranger, who you may have seen running around here, our dog. We're trying to avoid a confrontation between the turkey and our springer.

But I want to set the guests at ease and especially tell the kids something. After all, this turkey represents America's 45 million turkeys who will begin making their irreplaceable contribution to our Thanksgiving celebration. So take it easy, turkey, we're just here to serve you. [*Laughter*]

We all know that Thanksgiving is more than just an occasion to stuff yourself. It's a uniquely American holiday, a time for remembering all the good things that we've been given or asking ourselves what good we can find to do. After all, only America would set aside a special holiday just for the purpose of giving thanks. George Washington, in the first Presidential Thanksgiving Day proclamation, spoke of, and here's the quotation, "the duty . . . to acknowledge the providence of Almighty God, to obey His will, to be grateful for His benefits, and humbly to implore His protection and favor . . . ."

Well, this turkey must have said some prayers of his own. And we're going to grant him a special Presidential pardon. He will be going into early retirement, I'm told, living out his years on a Virginia children's farm.

I want to thank all of you for being here on this special occasion, welcome all our new friends to the White House. God bless you, and may you have a happy Thanksgiving.

Note: The President spoke at 2:05 p.m. in the Rose Garden at the White House. In his remarks, he referred to Bruce Cuddie, president, and Stuart E. Proctor, Jr., executive vice president, National Turkey Federation.

Statement by Press Secretary Fitzwater on the President's Telephone Conversation With President Boris Yeltsin of Russia
November 30, 1992

The President called President Boris Yeltsin of Russia today on the eve of the Congress of People's Deputies meeting in Moscow. They discussed the situation in Russia and U.S.-Russian relations.

The President reaffirmed to President Yeltsin the strong and unequivocal U.S. support for efforts to promote democracy and economic reform in Russia. The President made it clear that the United States will not waver in its firm support for the Russian Government.

The United States and its Western partners have a unique and historic opportunity to construct a democratic peace in Europe as we approach a new century. Russia is pivotal to that opportunity, and the United States has committed itself to building a new partnership with Russia based on a shared commitment to ending the arms race, cooperation in resolving regional disputes, and strong Western economic support for Russia's reforms. The President supports the continuation of concerted and ambitious Western efforts to assist the Russian people in building a democratic society and in integrating their economy and future with the West. The President therefore believes it is imperative for the United States and other countries to do everything possible to support the Russian Government at this critical time.

Memorandum on the Commonwealth of Puerto Rico
November 30, 1992

Memorandum for the Heads of Executive Departments and Agencies

Puerto Rico is a self-governing territory of the United States whose residents have been United States citizens since 1917 and have fought valorously in five wars in the defense of our Nation and the liberty of others.

On July 25, 1952, as a consequence of steps taken by both the United States Government and the people of Puerto Rico voting in a referendum, a new constitution was promulgated establishing the Commonwealth of Puerto Rico. The Commonwealth structure provides for self-government in respect of internal affairs and administration, subject to relevant portions of the Constitution and the laws of the United States. As long as Puerto Rico is a territory, however, the will of its people regarding their political status should be ascertained periodically by means of a general right of referendum or specific referenda sponsored either by the United States Government or the Legislature of Puerto Rico.

Because Puerto Rico's degree of constitutional self-government, population, and size set it apart from other areas also subject to Federal jurisdiction under Article IV, section 3, clause 2 of the Constitution, I hereby direct all Federal departments, agencies, and officials, to the extent consistent with the Constitution and the laws of the United States, henceforward to treat Puerto Rico administratively as if it were a State, except insofar as doing so with respect to an existing Federal program or activity would increase or decrease Federal receipts or expenditures, or would seriously disrupt the operation of such program or activity. With respect to a Federal program or activity for which no fiscal baseline has been established, this memorandum shall not be construed to require that such program or activity be conducted in a way that increases or decreases Federal receipts or expenditures relative to the level that would obtain if Puerto Rico were treated other than as a State.

If any matters arise involving the fundamentals of Puerto Rico's status, they shall be referred to the Office of the President.

This guidance shall remain in effect until Federal legislation is enacted altering the current status of Puerto Rico in accordance with the freely expressed wishes of the people of Puerto Rico.

The memorandum for the heads of executive departments and agencies on this subject, issued July 25, 1961, is hereby rescinded.

This memorandum shall be published in the *Federal Register*.

GEORGE BUSH

[Filed with the Office of the Federal Register, 11:27 a.m., December 1, 1992]

Note: This memorandum was released by the Office of the Press Secretary on December 1.

Remarks at the Presentation Ceremony for the President's Environment and Conservation Challenge Awards
December 2, 1992

Thank you all very much. Barbara and I are just delighted to welcome everyone to the White House. And let me single out a few people. I'll get in trouble on this in this distinguished group, but our Cabinet members here: Jim Watkins, who brought our National Energy Strategy through the Congress; Manuel Lujan, who's helped expand our parks and refuges; Secretary Barbara Franklin, her team's been out there pushing on the economic benefits of environmental protection. Don Atwood was to be here, but I single him out because he and the military brought an environmental ethic, I think, to everything from basic training to the conduct of a successful military operation halfway around the world in Desert Storm. Then our Secretary of Transportation was to be here, Andy Card. He's now Secretary of Transition—[*laughter*]—and as well as Secretary of Transportation.

Let me just say to this distinguished nonpartisan group that I am just determined that this transition goes smoothly and go well. And I'm absolutely convinced under Andy's leadership it is going well and will go well.

Speaking of nonpartisanship, I salute the Governor of Florida, and I'm just delighted that Lawton Chiles is with us, leader in the environmental movement; Senator Domenici was to be here—I don't see him, but nevertheless; and Congressman Gilchrest; Congressman Porter Goss. And I want to reserve a very special thanks for Bill Reilly, our able EPA Administrator, in whom I have great confidence, a confidence that has been well rewarded, I might say, by an outstanding performance; and then for Mike Deland, the key figure here today. He's the Chairman of our Council on Environmental Quality, and I believe he's done an outstanding job. And so I'm just delighted, Barbara and I are delighted to be standing at his side.

Finally, of course, I want to salute the awards partners for making this day possible: Gil Grosvenor of the National Geographic Society, Frank Bennack of Hearst, John Johnstone of the Business Roundtable, and Kathryn Fuller of the World Wildlife Fund. And I want to thank the awards selection committee and especially my old friend Bob Stafford who's back in Washington. I'm just delighted to see him, and Gaylord, Senator Gaylord Nelson, as well. And most of all I want to send a special welcome to the guests of honor, the 9 medal and the 13 citation recipients. Congratulations to all, and I look forward to seeing the presentations.

I am not going to make a long-winded speech, because I take the Clean Air Act very seriously. [*Laughter*] I've had a chance, under a very different schedule, to do a lot of thinking over the past 3 weeks. And let me just share some of your reflections. I hope you'll excuse me if I take pride in talking about certain accomplishments. Over the next few years I reckon I'll be spending a lot of time in what Teddy Roosevelt called the great cathedral of the outdoors, and I can't wait. I'll remember what we've tried to do to conserve it, to preserve it, and I am very proud of our team's efforts.

Everyone is and should be, whatever age, interested in the environment. And my own conviction, or environmental policy, if you will, was born out of the concerns of a President, an outdoorsman, and maybe most of all, a grandfather. Our approach signaled a step beyond command-and-control regulation toward a more market-oriented, decentralized philosophy of environmental action.

Those who said we posed a false choice between a strong economy and a safer environment just didn't get it, just missed the point. We sought to achieve both while sacrificing neither. And we combined a pragmatism about human nature with an idealism about Mother Nature, an ambitious agenda that harnessed the energy of capitalism in the service of the environment.

Now, excuse me, as I say, if I take pride in listing a few accomplishments that we pass on to a new generation. The Clean Air Act, with the help of Democrats and Republicans on the Hill, we broke 10 years of congressional gridlock by pushing through the world's most protective and cost-effective clean air legislation. And we've already proposed or finalized rules that promise to get at 85 percent of the pollution reductions that are targeted in this law. [*Applause*] Reilly's clapping for himself, and I don't blame him. [*Laughter*]

We won major funding—shifting to environmental programs—increasing the EPA's budget, I believe it was almost 50 percent; increasing funding for clean energy research and development by 66 percent. We enlisted the private sector in the voluntary pollution prevention efforts that are reshaping American industries, making us leaner, more efficient, and reducing toxic pollution by hundreds of millions of pounds a year.

On the law enforcement front, we broke new ground and old records, filing more cases, collecting more penalties, and putting more polluters behind bars than every previous administration in history combined. We helped make America's great outdoors even greater, securing over a billion dollars to expand parks and wetlands and wildlife refuges, campgrounds and scenic rivers. We decided to end clear-cutting as a standard practice on Federal land. And our America the Beautiful initiative has gotten off to a good start with several million new trees all across this great country.

We ensured that America's seas would still be shining, ending ocean dumping and sewage sludge, proposing and signing a tough oil pollution bill, and imposing a 10-year moratorium on oil and gas leasing over vast areas of the really sensitive, the ecologically sensitive coasts. We've launched a new generation of clean energy technologies, not only by increasing funding for research and development but also by increasing incentives for their use. And we've pushed through comprehensive national energy legislation—a salute to Jim again—that will guide our country into the next century.

In terms of Federal leadership, we've tripled funding for Federal facility cleanups, secured over 100 enforceable cleanup agreements for Federal facilities, and signed Executive orders spurring the Federal Government to take the lead in increasing energy efficiency, recycling, waste reduction, and converting the Federal fleet to alternative fuels.

Finally, we've insisted that a new world order include a cleaner world environment, and we reached over 20 new international environmental agreements. Just by way of example, we reduced Poland's debt in order to help them fund a new environmental foundation. We also launched the center, the Environmental Center in Budapest, to help countries in Central and Eastern Europe. We made America the world leader in the phaseout of ozone depletion, the ozone-depleting CFC's, and we led the way to global bans on driftnet fishing.

We built environmental cooperation into trade negotiations with Mexico. We've ex-

panded the debt-for-nature swaps to protect the rain forests in Latin America and created networks for cooperation with Asia. And our comprehensive, action-oriented approach to global climate change was ratified by the Senate and adopted by the world community.

At the same time that we renewed our national commitment to the environment, we redoubled our efforts to support and encourage people like you. Everyone in this room, everyone here today, has demonstrated the principles of a new environmentalism. This national environmental awards program was established to honor those who honored the environment.

Some here have forged innovative partnerships, environmental alliances that are protecting our wetlands, preserving our resources, and preparing a new generation of environmental leadership. Others have taken the lead in combining sound business with a safer environment, a smart new merger between profitability and preservation. And still others are pioneers on the frontier of technology, the environmental technology, finding ways to remove CFC production from manufacturing or reduce pollution while recycling metal scrap. And finally we've got recipients here who are cultivating our human resources to conserve our natural ones, leaders like Hazel Johnson, who realize that the greening of America is truly a grassroots operation, or the Environmental Education Program, teaching our children how to care for the great land that they will inherit.

I remember back in July, I was out visiting Sequoia National Park. And there was a camp there for inner-city youngsters. It was called Pyles Boys Camp. And I remember quoting Teddy Roosevelt, talking about the beautiful gifts we received from nature, gifts that we ought, and here's the quote, "ought to hand on as a precious heritage to our children and our children's children." That heritage is the family legacy that all Americans share and share responsibility for. Each of you understand President Roosevelt's challenge, and each of you that we honor has acted on it. And for that you have our admiration, our respect, my own personal gratitude.

That is the end. And I now would like to happily turn this over to Mike Deland, asking that he hand out the medals. Mike.

[*At this point, the awards and citations were presented.*]

Let me just thank you all once again for coming. I don't think it's too early to wish you a Merry Christmas. I wish in a sense it were Monday because this place will come alive with Christmas trees and Christmas lights. And I hope you all have a wonderful one. Thank you.

Note: The President spoke at 2:29 p.m. in the East Room at the White House. In his remarks, he referred to Deputy Secretary of Defense Donald J. Atwood, Jr., and former Senators Robert T. Stafford and Gaylord Nelson.

Statement by Press Secretary Fitzwater on the President's Discussions on Somalia
December 2, 1992

President Bush today called President-elect Clinton to update him on the continuing situation in Somalia. They discussed the status of U.N. consultations. President Bush will continue to stay in touch with the President-elect on this issue.

The President today also is consulting with other world leaders concerning a possible U.N. resolution.

Statement by Press Secretary Fitzwater on the United Nations Vote To Authorize Use of Military Forces in Somalia
December 3, 1992

We are pleased by the U.N. vote to authorize military forces to ensure the delivery of humanitarian aid to alleviate the starvation and human suffering in Somalia. President Bush will meet tomorrow morning with congressional leaders to discuss U.S. participation in a U.N. military action. Since August 14, the United States has airlifted 21,000 tons of food and medicine into Somalia. But the crisis remains urgent.

Address to the Nation on the Situation in Somalia
December 4, 1992

I want to talk to you today about the tragedy in Somalia and about a mission that can ease suffering and save lives. Every American has seen the shocking images from Somalia. The scope of suffering there is hard to imagine. Already, over a quarter-million people, as many people as live in Buffalo, New York, have died in the Somali famine. In the months ahead 5 times that number, 1½ million people, could starve to death.

For many months now, the United States has been actively engaged in the massive international relief effort to ease Somalia's suffering. All told, America has sent Somalia 200,000 tons of food, more than half the world total. This summer, the distribution system broke down. Truck convoys from Somalia's ports were blocked. Sufficient food failed to reach the starving in the interior of Somalia.

So in August, we took additional action. In concert with the United Nations, we sent in the U.S. Air Force to help fly food to the towns. To date, American pilots have flown over 1,400 flights, delivering over 17,000 tons of food aid. And when the U.N. authorized 3,500 U.N. guards to protect the relief operation, we flew in the first of them, 500 soldiers from Pakistan.

But in the months since then, the security situation has grown worse. The U.N. has been prevented from deploying its initial commitment of troops. In many cases, food from relief flights is being looted upon landing; food convoys have been hijacked; aid workers assaulted; ships with food have been subject to artillery attacks that prevented them from docking. There is no government in Somalia. Law and order have broken down. Anarchy prevails.

One image tells the story. Imagine 7,000 tons of food aid literally bursting out of a warehouse on a dock in Mogadishu, while Somalis starve less than a kilometer away because relief workers cannot run the gauntlet of armed gangs roving the city. Confronted with these conditions, relief groups called for outside troops to provide security so they could feed people. It's now clear that military support is necessary to ensure the safe delivery of the food Somalis need to survive.

It was this situation which led us to tell the United Nations that the United States would be willing to provide more help to enable relief to be delivered. Last night the United Nations Security Council, by unanimous vote and after the tireless efforts of Secretary-General Boutros-Ghali, welcomed the United States offer to lead a coalition to get the food through.

After consulting with my advisers, with world leaders, and the congressional leadership, I have today told Secretary-General Boutros-Ghali that America will answer the call. I have given the order to Secretary Cheney to move a substantial American force into Somalia. As I speak, a Marine amphibious ready group, which we maintain at sea, is offshore Mogadishu. These troops will be joined by elements of the 1st Marine Expeditionary Force, based out of Camp Pendleton, California, and by the Army's 10th Mountain Division out of Fort Drum, New York. These and other American forces will assist in Operation Restore Hope. They are America's finest. They will perform this mission with courage and compassion, and they will succeed.

The people of Somalia, especially the children of Somalia, need our help. We're able to ease their suffering. We must help them live. We must give them hope. America must act.

In taking this action, I want to emphasize that I understand the United States alone cannot right the world's wrongs. But we also know that some crises in the world cannot be resolved without American involvement, that American action is often necessary as a catalyst for broader involvement of the community of nations. Only the United States has the global reach to place a large security force on the ground in such a distant place quickly and efficiently and thus save thousands of innocents from death.

We will not, however, be acting alone. I expect forces from about a dozen countries to join us in this mission. When we see Somalia's children starving, all of America hurts. We've tried to help in many ways. And make no mistake about it, now we and our allies will ensure that aid gets through. Here is what we and our coalition partners will do:

First, we will create a secure environment in the hardest hit parts of Somalia, so that food can move from ships over land to the people in the countryside now devastated by starvation.

Second, once we have created that secure environment, we will withdraw our troops, handing the security mission back to a regular U.N. peacekeeping force. Our mission has a limited objective: To open the supply routes, to get the food moving, and to prepare the way for a U.N. peacekeeping force to keep it moving. This operation is not open-ended. We will not stay one day longer than is absolutely necessary.

Let me be very clear: Our mission is humanitarian, but we will not tolerate armed gangs ripping off their own people, condemning them to death by starvation. General Hoar and his troops have the authority to take whatever military action is necessary to safeguard the lives of our troops and the lives of Somalia's people. The outlaw elements in Somalia must understand this is serious business. We will accomplish our mission. We have no intent to remain in Somalia with fighting forces, but we are determined to do it right, to secure an environment that will allow food to get to the starving people of Somalia.

To the people of Somalia I promise this: We do not plan to dictate political outcomes. We respect your sovereignty and independence. Based on my conversations with other coalition leaders, I can state with confidence: We come to your country for one reason only, to enable the starving to be fed.

Let me say to the men and women of our Armed Forces: We are asking you to do a difficult and dangerous job. As Commander in Chief I assure you, you will have our full support to get the job done, and we will bring you home as soon as possible.

Finally, let me close with a message to the families of the men and women who take part in this mission: I understand it is difficult to see your loved ones go, to send them off knowing they will not be home for the holidays, but the humanitarian mission they undertake is in the finest traditions of service. So, to every sailor, soldier, airman, and marine who is involved in this mission, let me say, you're doing God's work. We will not fail.

Thank you, and may God bless the United States of America.

Note: The President spoke at 12:32 p.m. from the Oval Office at the White House. In his remarks, he referred to Gen. Joseph P. Hoar, USMC, commander in chief, U.S. Central Command. The address was broadcast live on nationwide radio and television.

Remarks at a Christmas Greeting for the White House Staff
December 7, 1992

Don't dare move my hands—[*laughter*]—what I wanted to do—[*laughter*]. No, but I am very grateful to Dana and to Paula for being here. And Dana's given me a lot of laughs. He said to me on the phone, "Are you sure you really want me to come there?" [*Laughter*] And I said yes. And he said, "I hope I've never crossed the line." I knew exactly what he meant, and as far as I'm concerned, he never has. The fact that we can laugh at each other is a very fundamental thing. I'm not sure on November 4th that the invitation would have gone out and then had the same enthusiasm. [*Laughter*] But we're shifting gears. And I think he's given us a wonderful kickoff to what I hope will be a joyous, totally friendly, very happy, somewhat nostalgic but merry Christmas for everybody.

In a few minutes, Barbara shows the press through this spectacular house that we've been privileged to live in for 4 years. And we wanted to share with some of you—I wish we could have had everybody—the majesty of this place, which I hope many will get to see in these various receptions and all. But I think there's something special seeing it for the first time when it's just beginning.

So let me take this opportunity once again to thank Dana Carvey for brightening our lives, giving us a little joy, and wish each and every one of you a Merry Christmas. And we can never adequately say thanks for all you've done for us, for your country, and for the Bush family.

Thank you so much, and God bless you.

Note: The President spoke at 9:50 a.m. in the East Room at the White House. In his remarks, he referred to comedian Dana Carvey and his wife, Paula.

Remarks at a Wreath-Laying Ceremony at the United States Navy Memorial
December 7, 1992

Please be seated. May I say to Admiral Thompson, it's a great pleasure to be with you, sir, on this sunny day; Secretary of the Navy Sean O'Keefe; Admiral Frank Kelso; and Admiral Howell. And Captain Bill Perry, thank you, sir, for the invocation. And thank all of you for attending.

Let me say at the very beginning, I am proud to have served in the United States Navy. And I am very proud of those who are serving in the United States Navy, each and every single one of them.

Today we remember the servicemen, the brave and the innocent, who gave their lives to keep us free. The men we honor served a noble cause and made America forever proud. War embodies man's inhumanity to man. And these heroes mirrored man's fidelity to honor.

The men of Pearl Harbor knew the things worth living for were also worth dying for: principle, decency, liberty, truth. So it is in their honor that the two new ships will join the fleet. The first, a new destroyer, will be named U.S.S. *Ross* for Captain Donald Ross, hero and Medal of Honor winner at Pearl Harbor. I met Don Ross at the memorial service commemorating the 50th anniversary of Pearl Harbor just last December. He passed away in May of this year, but the destroyer *Ross*, U.S.S. *Ross*, will pay tribute to Captain Ross in a way that will always live.

The second ship is in a sense named for all who fought at Pearl Harbor, indeed for the entire generation of young men and women who entered the service inspired by the heroism of that day. To commemorate the sacrifice and honor of every sailor, marine, soldier, and airman who fought so valiantly on the 7th day of December in 1941, we will be naming amphibious dock landing ship 52, the U.S.S. *Pearl Harbor.*

On that long ago day of infamy, brave boys became men, and brave men became heroes. And in that spirit, let this wreath that I place at the foot of the memorial serve as a symbol of our gratitude and respect. We can never properly repay these men. What we can and must do is honor them, remember them. Remember, too, the lesson we learned at Pearl Harbor, that America will always stand fast so that human liberty can stand tall.

May God bless all the service people and their families, particularly those who are serving overseas at this minute and those who have served and those who are serving both at home and abroad. And may God bless this great country, the United States of America. Thank you very much.

Note: The President spoke at 3:02 p.m. at the U.S. Navy Memorial. In his remarks, he referred to Rear Adm. William Thompson, USN (Ret.), president, U.S. Navy Memorial Foundation; Adm. Frank B. Kelso II, USN, Chief of Naval Operations; Rear Adm. Paul N. Howell, USNR (Ret.), chairman, U.S. Navy Memorial Foundation; and Capt. Bill Perry, U.S. Navy District Chaplain.

Recess Appointment of Lawrence S. Eagleburger as Secretary of State
December 8, 1992

The President today announced the recess appointment of Lawrence S. Eagleburger, of Florida, a career member of the Senior Foreign Service with the personal rank of Career Ambassador, to be Secretary of State. He would succeed James A. Baker III.

Mr. Eagleburger has served as Acting Secretary of State since August 23, 1992.

Statement by Press Secretary Fitzwater on Operation Restore Hope
December 8, 1992

President Bush is pleased by the success of the initial landing phase of Operation Restore Hope in Somalia. United States forces went ashore at approximately 8:30 p.m. e.s.t., this evening (4:30 a.m. Somali time). This initial phase will focus on establishing secure airport and port facilities. President Bush will be advised of developments in Somalia on a regular basis by his national security staff in the White House Situation Room.

Earlier today the President spoke by telephone with Ambassador Robert Oakley, our special envoy in Somalia. Ambassador Oakley briefed the President on his meetings with relief agency representatives and Somali factional leaders. Ambassador Oakley indicated that the discussions were encouraging. The President also spoke by phone with United Nations Secretary-General Boutros-Ghali and discussed with him the latest developments and plans for the humanitarian effort.

The President met with his national security advisers around 5 p.m. this afternoon for a final update on the status of the coalition preparations. General Colin Powell, Chairman of the Joint Chiefs of Staff, said Operation Restore Hope was on schedule and proceeding well. The response from other nations to join the coalition has been quite positive. Forces from several countries are being integrated into the overall operation.

Message on the Observance of Hanukkah
December 8, 1992

I am delighted to send greetings to members of the Jewish community in the United States and around the world as you celebrate Hanukkah.

As you commemorate the rededication of the Temple in Jerusalem more than 2,000 years ago, you call to mind the many great spiritual and political struggles that have been borne by the Jewish people—a people of faith and resolve. When it burned miraculously for eight days instead of one, the small cruse of oil that was found in the reclaimed Temple by Judah Maccabee and his followers symbolized the power of prayer and the unfailing wisdom of the Almighty.

Now, as you once again light the menorah, in keeping with centuries-old Judaic law and tradition, know that countless others join with you in praying for peace and for the expansion of religious liberty and tolerance around the world. During this time of renewal, we pray especially that the Middle East peace talks will lead to a comprehensive, just, and lasting peace between Israel and her Arab neighbors.

Barbara joins me in sending best wishes for a Happy Hanukkah.

GEORGE BUSH

Note: This message was released by the Office of the Press Secretary on December 9.

Message on the Observance of Christmas
December 8, 1992

During the Christmas season, millions of people around the world gather with family and friends to give thanks for their blessings and to recall the events that took place in Bethlehem almost 2,000 years ago. As we celebrate the birth of Jesus Christ, whose life offers us a model of dignity, compassion, and justice, we renew our commitment to peace and understanding throughout the world. Through His words and example, Christ made clear the redemptive value of giving of oneself for others, and His life proved that love and sacrifice can make a profound difference in the world. Over the years, many Americans have made sacrifices in order to promote freedom and human rights around the globe: the heroic actions of our veterans, the lifesaving work of our scientists and physicians, and generosity of countless individuals who voluntarily give of their time, talents, and energy to help others—all have enriched humankind and affirmed the importance of our Judeo-Christian heritage in shaping our government and values. This Christmas we are especially grateful for the expansion of democracy and hope throughout the former Soviet Union, Eastern Europe, and elsewhere—progress that is being encouraged by the help of many Americans.

In some regions, however, the joy and peace that normally mark the Christmas season are marred this year by violence that is rooted in ethnic hatreds and nationalist rivalries. Our prayers go out especially in behalf of the victims of such fighting—just as our thoughts are with those who are helping to provide humanitarian relief. Their selfless, caring efforts are a wonderful example of the true meaning of Christmas.

Barbara joins me in wishing all of our fellow Americans a Merry Christmas and a Happy New Year.

GEORGE BUSH

Note: This message was released by the Office of the Press Secretary on December 9.

Letter to Congressional Leaders on the Situation in Somalia
December 10, 1992

Dear Mr. Speaker: (Dear Mr. President:)

Beginning in January of this year with the adoption of U.N. Security Council Resolution 733, the United Nations has been actively addressing the humanitarian crisis in Somalia. The United States has been assisting the U.N. effort to deal with a human catastrophe. Over 300,000 Somalis have died of starvation. Five times that number remain at risk, beyond the reach of international relief efforts in large part because of the security situation. As a result, voluntary relief organizations from the United States and other countries have appealed for assistance from outside security forces.

On November 29, 1992, the Secretary General of the United Nations reported to the Security Council that the deteriorating security conditions in Somalia had severely disrupted international relief efforts and that an immediate military operation under U.N. authority was urgently required. On December 3, the Security Council adopted Resolution 794, which determined that the situation in Somalia constituted a threat to international peace and security, and, invoking Chapter VII of the U.N. Charter, authorized Member States to use all necessary means to establish a secure environment for humanitarian relief operations in Somalia. In my judgment, the deployment of U.S. Armed Forces under U.S. command to Somalia as part of this multilateral response to the Resolution is necessary to address a major humanitarian calamity, avert related threats to international peace and security, and protect the safety of Americans and others engaged in relief operations.

In the evening, Eastern Standard Time, on December 8, 1992, U.S. Armed Forces entered Somalia to secure the airfield and port facility of Mogadishu. Other elements of the U.S. Armed Forces and the Armed Forces of other Members of the United Nations are being introduced into Somalia to achieve the objectives of U.N. Security Council Resolution 794. No organized resistance has been encountered to date.

U.S. Armed Forces will remain in Somalia only as long as necessary to establish a secure environment for humanitarian relief operations and will then turn over the responsibility of maintaining this environment to a U.N. peacekeeping force assigned to Somalia. Over 15 nations have already offered to deploy troops. While it is not possible to estimate precisely how long the transfer of responsibility may take, we believe that prolonged operations will not be necessary.

We do not intend that U.S. Armed Forces deployed to Somalia become involved in hostilities. Nonetheless, these forces are equipped and ready to take such measures as may be needed to accomplish their humanitarian mission and defend themselves, if necessary; they also will have the support of any additional U.S. Armed Forces necessary to ensure their safety and the accomplishment of their mission.

I have taken these actions pursuant to my constitutional authority to conduct our foreign relations and as Commander in Chief and Chief Executive, and in accordance with applicable treaties and laws. In doing so, I have taken into account the views expressed in H. Con. Res. 370, S. Con. Res. 132, and the Horn of Africa Recovery and Food Security Act, Public Law 102–274, on the urgent need for action in Somalia.

I am providing this report in accordance with my desire that Congress be fully informed and consistent with the War Powers Resolution. I look forward to cooperating with Congress in the effort to relieve human suffering and to restore peace and stability to the region.

Sincerely,

GEORGE BUSH

Note: Identical letters were sent to Thomas S. Foley, Speaker of the House of Representatives, and Robert C. Byrd, President pro tempore of the Senate.

Letter to Congressional Leaders on the Determination Not To Prohibit Fish Imports From Colombia
December 10, 1992

Dear Mr. Speaker: (Dear Mr. President:)

Pursuant to section 8(b) of the Fishermen's Protective Act of 1967, as amended (22 U.S.C. 1978(b)), generally known as the Pelly Amendment, I am notifying you that on November 3, 1992, in accordance with section 101(a) of the Marine Mammal Protection Act (MMPA), the Secretary of Commerce certified to me that a denial of an affirmative finding and resulting embargo of yellowfin tuna and products derived from yellowfin tuna harvested in the eastern tropical Pacific Ocean (ETP) by Colombian flag vessels has been in effect since April 27, 1992.

By the terms of the MMPA, such certification is deemed to be a certification for the purposes of the Pelly Amendment, which requires that I consider and, at my discretion, order the prohibition of imports into the United States of products from the identified country, to the extent that such prohibition is sanctioned by the General Agreement on Tariffs and Trade. The Pelly Amendment also requires that I report to the Congress any actions taken under this subsection and, if no import prohibitions have been ordered, the reasons for this action.

After thorough review, I have determined that additional sanctions against Colombia under the Pelly Amendment will not be imposed at this time while the Administration continues to implement an international dolphin conservation program in the ETP.

Sincerely,

GEORGE BUSH

Note: Identical letters were sent to Thomas S. Foley, Speaker of the House of Representatives, and Dan Quayle, President of the Senate.

Remarks on Presenting Congressional Gold Medals to General Colin Powell and General H. Norman Schwarzkopf
December 10, 1992

Let me just say this is a very brief but, in my view, significant presentation ceremony. But in April of 1991, the laws were passed authorizing me as President to present gold medals on behalf of the Congress to Generals Powell and Schwarzkopf. The medals were designed and struck by the U.S. Mint to commemorate their exemplary service in liberating the nation of Kuwait pursuant to those United Nations resolutions. And the mint is also producing duplicates of these medals, bronze duplicates, for public sale.

I'm just delighted to be here. I salute the Members of Congress who are with us today, who had an awful lot to do with making this happen.

So we'll start by a presentation to General Schwarzkopf who was, as we know, commander in chief of the United States Central Command. He valiantly directed the United States and coalition in the Operation Desert Storm. And the U.S. and coalition forces under his command met the objectives that we established to counter ruthless aggression and to free Kuwait. He led the men and women of the Armed Forces of the United States in a magnificent achievement in United States military history.

I will now ask the commander to read the citation.

[*At this point, the gold medal was presented to General Schwarzkopf.*]

They tell me you're not supposed to touch it except with a glove. Congratulations, well-deserved honor.

Then General Colin Powell, Chairman of the Joint Chiefs. He displayed an extraordinary degree of leadership, competence, professionalism throughout Operation Desert Shield and Operation Desert Storm. General Powell and his subordinates brilliantly planned and coordinated the rapid mobilization, the deployment of more than one-half million men and women of the Armed Forces to the Persian Gulf. And that resulted in the successful prosecution of the Persian Gulf war. And Congress fittingly honors General Powell.

[*At this point, the gold medal was presented to General Powell.*]

Note: The President spoke at 4:04 p.m. in the Roosevelt Room at the White House. Lt. Comdr. Wayne E. Justice, USCG, Coast Guard Aide to the President, read the citations.

Remarks on Lighting the National Christmas Tree
December 10, 1992

Thank you, Joe, for being the President of the Christmas Pageant of Peace. And may I salute Lucie Arnaz and Lee Greenwood, Keshia Knight Pulliam; the world's greatest weatherman, who missed it tonight, Willard Scott; the Children's Chorus of Maryland; the cast of "A Christmas Carol"—great of them to come down; and of course, the U.S. Coast Guard Band.

Barbara and I are very pleased that all of you could be here tonight. It's wonderful to see so many smiling faces in spite of the adversity. It's especially wonderful to see the children. This is their holiday, an entire season dedicated to the impact of one child on the world. And there's a lesson to be learned from these young people here. Look at what's most important to them, the people they love.

Barbara and I want to dedicate this Christmas tree to the children of America, for they are more than our future; they are our present. And they remind us that we must love one another in order to achieve peace. We must love one another. Our prayers are with them and the ones they cherish.

May I simply say, let us think of the children of Somalia, too, the children everywhere who live in fear and want. Our prayers are with them, and may their families be safe and the sporadic fighting over there end soon.

Let us also say a special prayer for our Armed Forces who are doing their duty, vindicating the values of America and the spirit of Christmas in this far-off land. We salute them and their selfless devotion to country.

For Barbara and me and from our entire family, we wish you all a Merry Christmas, a happy and healthy New Year, and love that will outshine this tree year-round.

God bless you all, and God bless our great country, the United States of America. Merry Christmas.

Note: The President spoke at 5:50 p.m. on the Ellipse during the annual Christmas Pageant of Peace. In his remarks, he referred to Joe Riley, pageant president, and entertainers Lucie Arnaz, Lee Greenwood, and Keshia Knight Pulliam.

Remarks to the President's Drug Advisory Council Leadership Forum
December 11, 1992

What a nice welcome. Thank you very much. Normally I wouldn't say anything bad about Jim Burke, but he's got it backwards. I came over here to thank you people for this fantastic job, voluntarism at its very best. And that's what this is all about.

I am delighted to be here. Of course, I salute Jim. You take a man like that with a fantastic record in business and then in community service and ask him to do a big job, and he's done it as president now of our Drug Advisory Council, as well as chairman of the Partnership for a Drug-Free America. And I salute him. I don't believe a lot of the action we've seen that's resulted in success would have been possible without his steadfast, determined leadership, and I salute him for all of that. I think particularly we owe him a vote of gratitude for what he's been able to do in lining up support in the media for getting this antidrug message out all across the country. Literally hundreds of millions of dollars worth of advertising that's on the air and has been on the air and is making a difference can be attributed to his steadfast leadership.

As for Alvah Chapman, the other man

here, the old theory is if you want to get a job done, get a busy person to do it. And when Miami was devastated by the hurricane, he stepped up, organized a volunteer coalition, and is doing a superb job in actually—an outfit known as Rebuild—rebuilding Miami. He's brought that same dedication to this work as each and every one of you know. And he's chairman of our National Coalition Committee, and he's hard at work rebuilding in the antidrug field just as he is in south Florida. So I'm grateful to him.

I want to salute Father Malloy over here. I'm surprised he's as pleasant to me as he is when I walked in because he's had a terrible time getting here, diverted I'm told, and landing off in some faraway city and ending up here at about 2 in the morning. But again, here he is with a full agenda, running one of our great educational institutions and yet finding time to give to this people's war. And I'm delighted about that.

And of course, I see Bill Moss here. And I think we owe him a vote of thanks as the founding chairman of the PDAC.

I really did come here to give my heartfelt thanks to the members of the Drug Advisory Council for this outstanding work that you've done to rid the Nation of illegal drugs. You've given tireless service and a service to others, and that is deeply appreciated. And to all the drug coalition leaders and members that are with us today, I hear from all across the country, I'm told over 200 cities in 40 States, let me just add a few words to these thanks.

Charles de Gaulle once said that France was not her true self unless she was engaged in a great enterprise. Well, the same is true here. And you have led America in a great enterprise, truly becoming involved in a cause larger than yourselves. And you are part of a growing movement that is sweeping across this Nation.

Today there are more antidrug coalitions than ever, over a thousand, a thousand across the country, because of your efforts. And that means a thousand communities aided by Federal, State, and local governments have accepted the responsibility to work side by side with their neighbors to get drugs out and keep drugs out of their neighborhoods. Block by block, street by

street, home by home, ordinary people are doing absolutely extraordinary things.

You're showing that every citizen has a role to play in eliminating drugs from our neighborhoods. You're enriching our Nation's future. You've got to look at it that way. You are enriching our Nation's future through community-based programs, the very backbone of America's drug policy.

That noted philosopher, who I wish were with me here today, Barbara Bush—[laughter]—said, what happens in your house is more important than what happens in the White House. And as I think back over 12 wonderful years in the Vice Presidency and then in the Presidency, I am absolutely convinced she's right. There are certain things Government can do, but there's things that you can do in your own house and in your own neighborhood, in your own community that Government cannot possibly do. And so she's right when she makes a statement like that. And the people with the most influence are not here in Washington, DC. It's the people back home, the friend, the pastor, the patient, the parent, the teacher, whoever it is, somebody on the team, and the doctor or the daughter, who can stir the soul of somebody that's needing help.

So it's a team effort. And our ability to solve the drug problem in America depends on the extent to which we can convince individuals not to try drugs or use them and to help those individuals addicted to get into treatment. We've got a lot to do in that addicted category, as Jim and Alvah, I'm sure, have shared with you. And perhaps you know it better from your own experience. But this understanding is the very basis for the enormous progress that's been made in reducing illegal drug use and simply must be the foundation of any future drug strategy.

In the span of this administration—and I don't think most people know this across the country, and I bear, obviously, my share of the responsibility for the fact that they don't—but in the span of this administration, we've seen drug use go down. Overall drug use decreased by more than 12 percent between 1988 and 1991; occasional cocaine use went down 25 percent, twice the goal that we all set; adolescent cocaine use, we'd hoped to reduce that by 30 percent, and the facts are clear that it's fallen by more than 60 percent.

When a neighbor's front yard became the front line of a drug war, rather than looking to government for solutions you looked to each other to meet the drug problem in your community head-on. And because you did, today a little girl isn't afraid to ride her bike over to the park, or a senior citizen once again sits on his front porch in the afternoon without fear. We've got to keep going until that is universal. But there's some wonderful examples of how your work has already paid off. And so what you're doing in the workplace and in the school-yard and the corner grocery store is work-ing.

I am very grateful to you because, as I look at this, you are restoring hope, you're saving lives, and you're healing our country one person at a time. And for that you have the gratitude of your community, your country, and certainly your President.

May God bless you all in this wonderful work. And thank you very, very much for what you're doing for the United States. God bless you.

Note: The President spoke at 9:20 a.m. at the Washington Hilton. In his remarks, he referred to Rev. Edward A. Malloy, C.S.C., President's Drug Advisory Council Leadership Forum chairman.

Remarks on Presenting the Presidential Medals of Freedom
December 11, 1992

Barbara and I thank you all very much. Barbara and I are just delighted to have you here on this special occasion. Welcome to the White House. I'm going to keep this relatively short today because afterwards Richard Petty and I are going to take a few laps around the Ellipse in number 43— [*laughter*]—so we've got plenty to do. Mr. Vice President and Mrs. Quayle and members of our Cabinet, a special welcome to all of you.

One of the great privileges of being President is being able to recognize and honor some of our finest Americans. And that's exactly what I'm doing today by awarding the Presidential Medal of Freedom to 10 people who have made extraordinary contributions to our country.

Today, freedom is mankind's North Star. And I am grateful that more people have breathed their first breath of freedom over the last 4 years than at any time in history. And the great question of the cold war was whether people would put their faith in the state or in themselves. Freedom won, and America enjoys the fruits of victory as people around the world join in the great democratic experiment that we began some 216 years ago.

History honors those people who wrest the torch of freedom from the hands of their oppressors. But in America, that torch lies safely in the hands of the people. And the Presidential Medal of Freedom honors those who carry that torch. And our light of freedom is bright enough to light the world.

Today, every man on the street in Moscow realizes what Americans have always understood. It is human nature to be free. And just as nature abhors a vacuum, so does human nature abhor the absence of freedom. So today in essence, by awarding people from these various different pursuits, we celebrate the triumph for freedom, by recognizing these 10 American greats who have set an example for the world.

The Presidential Medal of Freedom was reestablished by President John F. Kennedy who tragically did not live to award it. And when President Johnson awarded the medal to its first recipients, he said that President Kennedy had intended the awards as, and here's the quote, "a means of national thanks and encouragement for the selfless effort and the brilliant task." In a sense he was talking about what we refer to here as Points of Light, as a Point of Light, because the definition of a successful life must include serving others. And America's greatness lies not in its Government but in its people. And it's not enough to be free; we must serve each other.

Each of us, each of today's award winners certainly understands this, and each is a great American. Their names read like a roll call of American heroes:

Harry Schlaudeman, a tireless crusader for democracy, who after a life of public service came out of retirement 2 years ago to ensure Nicaragua's peaceful transition to democracy.

David Brinkley, the elder statesman of broadcast journalism. His record speaks for itself.

Richard Petty, who rose from humble beginnings in Level Cross, North Carolina, to become the king of stock car racing.

General Vessey, who was the ultimate never-say-die soldier, the last four-star combat veteran of World War II to retire. And General Vessey came out of retirement to counsel my predecessor and me and to help us reach full accounting of all our Vietnam veterans, and he's still engaged in this pursuit.

Elie Wiesel is another type of veteran of World War II who survived the Holocaust and still today keeps watch against the forces of hatred.

Isaac Stern, one of the greatest violinists of our time, who has brought music to countless others.

I.M. Pei, the modernist architect whose work graces skylines worldwide.

To much of America, Johnny Carson was late-night TV. And with decency and style, he's made America laugh and think. And Johnny, I don't care what you say, I still think Dana Carvey does a better impersonation of you than he does of me. [*Laughter*]

Finally, two special medal recipients who couldn't be with us today: By doctors' orders, Ella Fitzgerald and Audrey Hepburn are unable to join us. Ella Fitzgerald has changed the face of jazz since she was discovered as a teenager, and she is an American music legend. And Audrey Hepburn, whose acting career put her among our most talented artists but whose work with the International Children's Emergency Fund put her in our hearts. And I wish they could be with us today so that I could recognize them personally on behalf of our Nation.

Today we reward your greatness with America's highest civilian honor, the Presidential Medal of Freedom. And you will join the ranks of our Nation's greatest public servants, scholars, and entertainers.

If you'll please step forward to receive your medal as Commander Joe Walsh reads the citation.

[*At this point, the President and Mrs. Bush presented the medals.*]

Well, I think that concludes our ceremony. And Barbara and I would love to greet you all out here. And it's been a great pleasure to have everybody here, but a special pleasure to be able to honor the 10 so recognized today. Thank you all for coming.

Note: The President spoke at 11:45 a.m. in the East Room at the White House. Comdr. Joseph Walsh, USN, Naval Aide to the President, read the citations.

Remarks on Presenting the Malcolm Baldrige National Quality Awards
December 14, 1992

Thank you, Secretary Franklin. And let me first recognize our Baldrige Foundation trustees, our private sector examiners and judges, and all those who coordinated this year's Baldrige Awards. Distinguished Members of Congress present, welcome. And also it's my special privilege to salute members of the Baldrige family who are with us today.

I really do look forward, Barbara indicated, to these yearly award ceremonies. It is an opportunity to honor the Nation's best and a chance to revisit the legacy of an extraordinary man, Malcolm Baldrige.

I remember a story that President Reagan used to tell about Mac. He phoned him to ask him to join his Cabinet, and he was told by his wife, Midge, that he'd have to call back later. Mac was out on his horse roping and couldn't come to the phone. [*Laughter*]

Well, I think everybody at Commerce who worked with this extraordinary man knows exactly that that's the way he was, a man whose collection of belt buckles was the only thing that could outnumber his many achievements. And in a hand-tooled western belt and a pinstriped suit, he was the Connecticut cowboy, a man whose name is now enshrined in the Cowboy Hall of Fame in Oklahoma and the only guy I know who'd complain of saddle sores from sitting around a desk too long. [*Laughter*]

He used to say that the thing he liked about cowboys was that they didn't talk unless they had something to say, and when they said something, they meant it. And that was true of Mac Baldrige. And when he talked business, he meant business. When he talked of making America's products second to none, you listened. The standards of excellence that Mac embodied are still very much with us today. Fairness, honesty, tenacity: these were his yardsticks and the same yardsticks we use today in looking for the very best that American industry has to offer.

This year we've found them in five exceptional companies. Ninety companies this year decided that they were tough enough to take the Baldrige tests. And it's estimated 175,000 others used these criteria, the Baldrige criteria, as an internal test, as a way to be tough on themselves. And a few of our past winners—and I come to mind Motorola and IBM—have even gone so far as to urge their suppliers to follow the Baldrige criteria. What this tells us is simple: America is number one because it demands not only the best for itself but also from itself.

Now a comment on this year's winners. Some might think the Commerce Department offered a two-for-one deal with

AT&T, but not so. Though both Transmission Systems and Universal Card Services are divisions of AT&T, they are two separate businesses who share one common goal, a commitment to quality. AT&T Chairman Robert Allen said of this commitment, "The real challenge is to define quality not from our own perspective but from the customers'." And this, both divisions have done.

Transmission Systems Business Unit dedicates itself not only to its customers' short-term needs but its long-term needs as well. With the input of more than 7,500 employees at 9 U.S. sites, Transmission Systems has initiated programs to predict what new technologies will be needed to meet their customers' long-term goals. In slightly more than 3 years, Transmission Systems has nearly doubled international sales and now sells systems to more than 50 countries. And that is a lot of satisfied customers.

Universal Card Services hasn't become a benchmark of other companies by accident but by effort, top performances by all of its 2,500 employees. And Universal Card led its charge to excellence by centralizing their business around one key principle: Delight the customer. And it seems they are, indeed, delighted. Ninety-eight percent of their customers rate overall services as better than the competition, 98 percent. That's pretty good for a poll, and I could have used it about a month ago. [*Laughter*]

It's not often that small business means big business. And it's true for the Granite Rock Company, another of our honorees. With the initiation of their total quality program, Granite Rock has exceeded its industry standards for high quality and unmatched service. And rather than follow a well-worn path, Granite Rock chose to chart its own way, a journey that's brought them here today, an award-winning company that defines success in three little words: Another satisfied customer.

Ritz-Carlton: They won 121 quality-related awards in 1991. But ask any employee how they gauge their success, and they'll say, "The Gold Standards," the Ritz-Carlton's bible for premium service. And with almost 12,000 employees, the Ritz-Carlton has implemented a rigorous quality program that seeks a memorable visit for every guest. This luxury hotel business knows that a mint on the pillow isn't enough to keep a customer coming back. It's the principle "Service must be excellent if it is anything" that has earned Ritz-Carlton one of the most loyal followings in the travel and tourism industry.

Now, for Texas Instruments Defense Systems and Electronics Group: Its best product is always surpassed by its next innovation. Mac used to call this kind of inventiveness Yankee ingenuity. I'm not sure this Texas-based company cottons to be called Yankee—[*laughter*]—but ingenious I think they'll accept. And they've earned it. Formed during World War II, this TI subsidiary has grown to become the Nation's eighth largest defense electronics contractor. And we know from the success of Desert Storm that in matters of advanced weaponry, quality is absolutely essential. It's the key. And we know, too, from the success of Desert Storm that TI's contributions

to this effort were absolutely invaluable.

In today's competitive global marketplace, quality of service and quality of goods takes on top priority in American business. And premium standards are no longer lofty goals but vital components of every basic business strategy. This year's Baldrige winners know that quality standards do not impede success, they encourage it. And Mac Baldrige would certainly agree with that.

Each time we revisit our memories of Mac Baldrige at this ceremony, I'm reminded of the wisdom that he used to impart most often: Always, in anything and everything, rise to the highest standard. This year's Malcolm Baldrige Quality Award winners have all done just that.

So I came over here to say congratulations to all of you. And may God bless our great country. Thank you very much.

Note: The President spoke at 11:52 a.m. at the Department of Commerce.

Statement by Press Secretary Fitzwater on Relations With Vietnam
December 14, 1992

The United States is today taking additional steps concerning our policy towards Vietnam. The decision to take these steps is in response to Vietnam's implementation of agreements reached with the President's Special Emissary for POW–MIA Affairs, General John Vessey. It is in keeping with the established "roadmap" policy of a step-by-step process for normalizing relations with Vietnam.

Effective today, the United States will permit U.S. firms to sign contracts to be executed should the embargo with Vietnam be lifted. To assist U.S. firms, we will also begin implementing a decision that permits a liberal licensing policy allowing commercial transactions relating to contracts, in-

cluding opening offices in Vietnam, hiring staff, writing and designing plans, and carrying out preliminary feasibility studies and engineering and technical surveys. Other than these actions, the embargo with Vietnam remains in effect.

We look to Vietnam to intensify efforts to achieve the fullest possible accounting of all our POW–MIA's, including the rapid repatriation of all recovered and readily recoverable American remains. In this context, we have noted Hanoi's recent call for Vietnamese citizens to turn in any American remains they may possess. As further results in accounting for missing Americans are obtained, we are prepared to consider additional "roadmap" steps of our own.

Notice on Continuation of Libyan Emergency
December 14, 1992

On January 7, 1986, by Executive Order No. 12543, President Reagan declared a national emergency to deal with the unusual and extraordinary threat to the national security and foreign policy of the United States constituted by the actions and policies of the Government of Libya. On January 8, 1986, by Executive Order No. 12544, the President took additional measures to block Libyan assets in the United States. The President has transmitted a notice continuing this emergency to the Congress and the *Federal Register* every year since 1986. On April 15, 1992, I barred authorization for aircraft to take off from, land in, or overfly the United States, if the aircraft, as part of the same flight or as a continuation of that flight, is destined to land in or has taken off from Libya. Because the Government of Libya has continued its actions and policies in support of international terrorism, the national emergency declared on January 7, 1986, and the measures adopted on January 7 and January 8, 1986, and April 15, 1992, to deal with that emergency, must continue in effect beyond January 7, 1993. Therefore, in accordance with section 202(d) of the National Emergencies Act (50 U.S.C. 1622(d)), I am continuing the national emergency with respect to Libya.

This notice shall be published in the *Federal Register* and transmitted to the Congress.

GEORGE BUSH

The White House,
December 14, 1992.

[*Filed with the Office of the Federal Register, 2:42 p.m., December 15, 1992*]

Note: This notice was released by the Office of the Press Secretary on December 15, and it was published in the Federal Register on December 17.

Letter to Congressional Leaders on Continuation of the National Emergency With Respect to Libya
December 14, 1992

Dear Mr. Speaker: *(Dear Mr. President:)*

Section 202(d) of the National Emergencies Act (50 U.S.C. 1622(d)) provides for the automatic termination of a national emergency unless, prior to the anniversary date of its declaration, the President publishes in the *Federal Register* and transmits to the Congress a notice stating that the emergency is to continue in effect beyond the anniversary date. In accordance with this provision, I have sent the enclosed notice, stating that the Libyan emergency is to continue in effect beyond January 7, 1993, to the *Federal Register* for publication.

The crisis between the United States and Libya that led to the declaration on January 7, 1986, of a national emergency has not been resolved. The Government of Libya continues to use and support international terrorism, as evidenced by its involvement in the destruction of Pan Am Flight 103, in violation of international law and minimum standards of human behavior. Such Libyan actions and policies pose a continuing unusual and extraordinary threat to the national security and vital foreign policy interests of the United States. For these reasons, I have determined that it is necessary to maintain in force the broad authorities necessary to apply economic pressure to the Government of Libya to reduce its ability to support international terrorism.

Sincerely,

GEORGE BUSH

Note: Identical letters were sent to Thomas S. Foley, Speaker of the House of Represent-

atives, and Dan Quayle, President of the Senate. This letter was released by the Office of the Press Secretary on December 15.

Remarks at Texas A&M University in College Station, Texas
December 15, 1992

Thank you all for that welcome back. Thank you very, very much. Good afternoon, everybody, and thank you all. I knew if I wore this necktie I'd get a nice welcome. But anyway—[*applause*]. Thank you, Dr. Mobley, thank you, Bill, for your kind introduction.

May I salute Congressmen that are with us today, Congressman Joe Barton and Congressman Jack Fields; and Commissioner Rick Perry and Kay Bailey Hutchison and Representative Ogden; my old friend Fred McClure, who served at my side in the White House. And may I thank Chairman Ross Margraves for the wonderful program that he arranged for me today as I heard about this library. And I salute the board of regents members that are here; the members of the library committee; Chancellor Richardson, I think I mentioned, but I salute him.

I want to say thanks to my hosts, the Memorial Student Center Political Forum. When that forum started, I think Congressman Bob Eckhardt and I were the first two speakers to speak at the political forum. I'd hate to tell you how far back that was. But anyway, I'm glad to be back here. And may I send my heartiest thanks to the corps of cadets and the fightin' Texas Aggies band over here.

As I told Bill Mobley and Ross earlier, on a personal note, I am looking forward to spending more time here, to actively participating in our Presidential library that will be built here, to helping with the School of Public Service that will be part of that library. And Barbara and I are both looking forward to being part of the A&M family. Thank you very much.

Now for the business at hand. In 36 days, I'll hand over the stewardship of this great Nation, capping a career in public service that began 50 years ago in wartime skies

over the Pacific. And our country won that great contest but entered an uneasy peace. You see, the fires of World War II cooled into a longer cold war, one that froze the world into two opposing camps: on the one side, America and its allies, and on the other—[*applause*]—the forces of freedom thus against an alien ideology that cast its shadow over every American.

Three years ago when I was honored to address the graduating class here at Texas A&M, I spoke of the need to move beyond containment. And I said, "We seek the integration of the Soviet Union into the community of nations. Ultimately, our objective is to welcome the Soviet Union back into the world order." And was this aim too ambitious? Not for the American people.

Today, by the grit of our people and the grace of God, the cold war is over. Freedom has carried the day. And I leave the White House grateful for what we have achieved together and also exhilarated by the promise of what can come to pass.

This afternoon I would like to just share some of my thoughts on the past few years and on America's purpose in the world. My thesis is a simple one. Amid the triumph and the tumult of the recent past, one truth rings out more clearly than ever: America remains today what Lincoln said it was more than a century ago, "the last best hope of man on Earth." This is a fact, a truth made indelible by the struggles and the agonies of the 20th century and in the sacrifice symbolized by each towering oak on Simpson Drill Field here at Texas A&M University. The leadership, the power, and yes, the conscience of the United States of America, all are essential for a peaceful, prosperous international order, just as such an order is essential for us.

History's lesson is clear: When a war-weary America withdrew from the international stage following World War I, the world spawned militarism, fascism, and aggression unchecked, plunging mankind into another devastating conflict. But in answering the call to lead after World War II, we built from the principles of democracy and the rule of law a new community of free nations, a community whose strength, perseverance, patience, and unity of purpose contained Soviet totalitarianism and kept the peace.

In the end, Soviet communism provided no match for free enterprise beyond its borders or the yearning for liberty within them. And the American leadership that undermined the confidence and capacity of the Communist regimes became a beacon for all the peoples of the world.

Steadfast and sure, generations of Americans stood in the path of the Soviet advance while our adversary probed for weaknesses that were never found. Presidents from both parties led an Atlantic alliance held together by the bonds of principle and love of liberty, facing a Warsaw Pact lashed together by occupation troops and quisling governments and, when all else failed, the use of tanks against its own people. By the 1980's, Kremlin leaders found that our alliance would not crack when they threatened America's allies with the infamous SS–20 nuclear missile. Nor did the alliance shrink from the deployment of countervailing missiles to defend against this menace.

In the Pacific, too, we built a new alliance with Japan, defended Korea, and called hundreds of thousands of Americans to sacrifice in the jungles of Southeast Asia.

The American people demonstrated that they would shoulder whatever defense burden, make whatever sacrifice was needed to assure our freedom and protect our allies and interests. And we made use of this superb technology that our free enterprise system has produced. And having learned that they could not divide our alliance, the Soviets eventually were forced to realize that their command economy simply could not compete. As the Soviet system stalled and crumbled, so too did the ability of its rulers to deny their people the truth, about us and about them.

In the end, Soviet communism was destroyed by its own internal contradictions.

New leaders with new vision faced the hard truths that their predecessors had long denied. *Glasnost, perestroika*: They may have been Russian words, but the concepts at their core were universal.

The Soviet Union did not simply lose the cold war; the Western democracies won it. I say this not to gloat but to make a key point. The qualities that enabled us to triumph in that struggle, faith, strength, unity, and above all, American leadership, are those we must call upon now to win the peace.

In recent years, with the Soviet empire in its death throes, the potential for crisis and conflict was never greater, the demand for American leadership never more compelling. As the peoples of Eastern Europe made their bold move for freedom, we urged them along a peaceful path to liberation. They turned to us. They turned to America, and we did not turn away. And when our German friends took their hammers to tear down that wall, we encouraged a united Germany, safely within the NATO alliance. They looked to America, and we did not look away. And when the people of Russia blocked the tanks that tried to roll back the tide of history, America did not walk away.

I can remember speaking to Boris Yeltsin at that terrible moment of crisis. At times the static on the telephone made it almost impossible to hear him, but there was no mistaking what he wanted to know. He asked where the United States of America stood. And America answered, for all the world to hear, "We stand with you."

Boris Yeltsin to this day hasn't forgotten. Praising our country on his visit to the White House this June, he said George Bush was the first to understand the true scope and meaning of the victory of the Russian people on August 19, 1991. He addressed me, but he was talking about our country, the United States of America.

The free peoples of the world watched; they watched in awe as the Soviet Union collapsed, but they held their breath at what might take its place, wondering who might control its tens of thousands of nuclear weapons. Only America could manage that danger. We acted decisively to help the new leaders reduce their arsenals and gain firm control of those that remain.

Here, then, is the remarkable fact that history will record, a fact that will be studied for years in the library right here at Texas A&M University: The end of a titanic clash of political systems, the collapse of the most heavily armed empire in history, took place without a shot being fired. That should be a source of pride for every American.

From the days after World War II, when fragile European democracies were threatened by Stalin's expansionism, to the last days of the cold war, as our foes became fragile democracies themselves, American leadership has been indispensable. No one person deserves credit for this. America does. It has been achieved because of what we as a people stand for and what we are made of.

Yes, we answered the call, and we triumphed, but today we are summoned again. This time we are called not to wage a war, hot or cold, but to win the democratic peace, not for half a world as before but for people the world over. The end of the cold war, you see, has placed in our hands a unique opportunity to see the principles for which America has stood for two centuries, democracy, free enterprise, and the rule of law, spread more widely than ever before in human history.

For the first time, turning this global vision into a new and better world is, indeed, a realistic possibility. It is a hope that embodies our country's tradition of idealism, which has made us unique among nations and uniquely successful. And our vision is not mere utopianism. The advance of democratic ideals reflects a hard-nosed sense of our own, of American self-interest. For certain truths have, indeed, now become evident: Governments responsive to the will of the people are not likely to commit aggression. They are not likely to sponsor terrorism or to threaten humanity with weapons of mass destruction. Likewise, the global spread of free markets, by encouraging trade, investment, and growth, will sustain the expansion of American prosperity. In short, by helping others, we help ourselves.

Some will dismiss this vision as no more than a dream. I ask them to consider the last 4 years when a dozen dreams were made real: The Berlin Wall demolished and Germany united; the captive nations set free; Russia democratic; whole classes of nuclear weapons eliminated, the rest vastly reduced; many nations united in our historic U.N. coalition to turn back a tyrant in the Persian Gulf; Israel and its Arab neighbors for the first time talking peace, face to face, in a region that has known so much war. Each of these once seemed a dream. Today they're concrete realities, brought about by a common cause: the patient and judicious application of American leadership, American power, and perhaps most of all, American moral force.

Without a doubt, there's going to be serious obstacles and setbacks ahead. You know and I know that we face some already. Violence, poverty, ethnic and religious hatreds will be powerful adversaries. And overcoming them is going to take time, and it's going to take tenacity, courage, and commitment. But I am absolutely convinced that they can be overcome.

Look to Europe, where nations, after centuries of war, transformed themselves into a peaceful, progressive community. No society, no continent should be disqualified from sharing the ideals of human liberty. The community of democratic nations is more robust then ever, and it will gain strength as it grows. By working with our allies, by invigorating our international institutions, America does not have to stand alone.

Yet from some quarters we hear voices sounding the retreat. We've carried the burden too long, they say, and the disappearance of the Soviet challenge means that America can withdraw from international responsibilities. And then others assert that domestic needs preclude an active foreign policy, that we've done our part; now it's someone else's turn. We're warned against entangling ourselves in the troubles that abound in today's world, to name only a few: clan warfare, mass starvation in Somalia; savage violence in Bosnia; instability in the former Soviet Union; the alarming growth of virulent nationalism.

It's true, these problems—some frozen by the cold war, others held in check by Communist repression—seem to have ignited all at once, taxing the world's ability to respond. But let's be clear: The alternative to American leadership is not more security for our citizens but less, not the flourishing of American principles but their isolation in a world actively held hostile to them.

Destiny, it has been said, is not a matter of chance; it's a matter of choice. It's not a thing to be waited for; it's a thing to be achieved. And we can never safely assume that our future will be an improvement over the past. Our choice as a people is simple: We can either shape our times, or we can let the times shape us. And shape us they will, at a price frightening to contemplate, morally, economically, and strategically.

Morally, a failure to respond to massive human catastrophes like that in Somalia would scar the soul of our Nation. There can be no single or simple set of guidelines for foreign policy. We should help. But we should consider using military force only in those situations where the stakes warrant, where it can be effective and its application limited in scope and time. As we seek to save lives, we must always be mindful of the lives that we may have to put at risk.

Economically, a world of escalating instability and hostile nationalism will disrupt global markets, set off trade wars, set us on a path of economic decline. American jobs would be lost, our chance to compete would be blocked, and our very well-being would be undermined.

Strategically, abandonment of the worldwide democratic revolution could be disastrous for American security. The alternative to democracy, I think we would all agree, is authoritarianism: regimes that can be repressive, xenophobic, aggressive, and violent. And in a world where, despite U.S. efforts, weapons of mass destruction are spreading, the collapse of the democratic revolution could pose a direct threat to the safety of every single American.

The new world could, in time, be as menacing as the old. And let me be blunt: A retreat from American leadership, from American involvement, would be a mistake for which future generations, indeed our own children, would pay dearly.

But we can influence the future. We can rededicate ourselves to the hard work of freedom. And this doesn't mean running off on reckless, expensive crusades. It doesn't mean bearing the world's burdens all alone. But it does mean leadership, economic, political, and yes, military, when our interests and values are at risk and where we can make a difference. And when we place our young men and women of the military in harm's way, we must be able to assure them and their families that their mission is defined and that its success can be achieved.

It seems like ages ago that the people of Germany tore down that wall. But it's been only 3 years, and just over a year since the August coup was defeated by brave Russian democrats. And in this brief time, we've embarked on a new course through uncharted waters. The United States and its friends, old and new, have begun to define the post-cold-war reality. And we are already transforming the old network of alliances, institutions, and regimes to face the future. And those challenges must be met with collective action, led by the United States, to protect and promote our political, economic, and security values.

Our foundation must be the democratic community that won the cold war. And we've begun to adapt America's political, economic, and defense relationships with Europe and Japan to ensure their vitality and strength in this new era, for these will continue to be essential partners in addressing the next generation of problems and opportunities.

For example, we've begun to transform the Atlantic alliance, that bulwark against the Soviet threat, into a partnership with a more united Europe, a partnership primed to meet new security challenges in this age of uncertainty. And a new feature of our alliance, the North Atlantic Cooperation Council, enables NATO to reach out to our former adversaries in the Warsaw Pact.

In the Pacific, we've affirmed the importance of the U.S.-Japan security ties to stability in Asia. But we're also exploring ways to work together as global partners to address common interests in economics, development, and regional problems.

Then we've committed ourselves to expanding the democratic community by supporting political and economic freedom in nascent democracies and market economies. And we're sharing this burden with the very nations America helped after World War II.

Look, in Central and Eastern Europe, our enterprise funds and these other programs have helped develop a new political, economic, and civic infrastructure for nations long oppressed by Stalin's legacy. And now the FREEDOM Support Act will provide crucial help for reform in the lands of our former enemies.

In Latin America, the day of the dictator has given way to the dawn of democracy. This very day, our Vice President is taking part in a ceremony in El Salvador that caps the long effort to end the killing and give the people there the opportunity to live in peace.

Throughout the region, economic initiatives are helping a new generation of leaders reform their societies. The Brady plan and our Enterprise for the Americas Initiative have opened up extraordinary possibilities for a new relationship with our hemispheric neighbors. Investment, free trade, debt relief, and environmental protection will nurture the homegrown reforms throughout Latin America.

We're strengthening the ability of the democratic community to deal with the political landmines that the cold war has exposed: aggressive nationalism, earlier I mentioned ethnic conflict, civil war, and humanitarian crises. The United States has led the world in supporting a United Nations more capable with dealing with these crises.

All over the world, Nicaragua, Namibia, Angola, Cambodia, we've promoted elections not only as a goal but as a tool, a device for resolving conflicts and establishing political legitimacy.

One of vital interest to every young person: In the area of security and arms control, we've stepped up patrol against the spread of weapons of mass destruction. The new chemical weapons convention will ban chemical weapons from the arsenals of all participating states. We've strengthened multilateral export controls on nuclear and chemical and biological and missile-related technologies. And in a mission without

precedent, a U.N. inspection team is demolishing Iraq's unconventional weapons capability, and we're going to support them every inch of the way. And once implemented, the agreements we've negotiated will ban new nuclear states on the territory of the former Soviet Union. And above all, we've sought to erase nuclear nightmares from the sleep of future generations.

We underscored one key security principle with a line in the sand: Naked aggression against our vital interests will be answered decisively by American resolve, American leadership, and American might. Our victory in the Gulf, in the Persian Gulf, was more than a blow for justice; it was a reminder to other would-be aggressors that they will pay a price for their outlaw acts.

We've been committed to building the basis for sustained international economic growth for ourselves and for those nations of what were once the so-called second and third worlds. The heart of our efforts has been the creation of a stronger and freer international trading market.

Our recent breakthrough with the European Community clears the way for an early conclusion to the Uruguay round of GATT and a major boost to world economic recovery. This week, Mexico, Canada, and the United States will sign a landmark agreement establishing the largest free trade zone the world has ever seen. And our efforts to forge a new mechanism for Asia-Pacific economic cooperation confirm America's commitment to remain an economic and security power in Asia.

I believe we've taken important steps toward a world in which democracy is the norm, in which private enterprise, free trade, and prosperity enrich every region, a world in which the rule of law prevails. We must not stumble as we travel toward a world without the brutal violence of Bosnia, the deadly anarchy of Somalia, or the squalor that still haunts so much of the globe. We can't rest while a handful of renegade regimes aspire to obtain weapons of mass destruction with which to threaten their neighbors or even America. There is much to be done before we are within reach of the democratic peace. But these first steps have taken us in that right direction.

The challenge ahead, then, is as great as the one we faced at the end of the last great war. But the opportunity is vastly greater. Success will require American vision and resolve, an America secure in its military, moral, and economic strength. Success will require unity of purpose: a commitment on the part of all our people to the proposition that our Nation's destiny lies in the hope of a better world, a new world made better, with our friends and allies, again by American leadership.

History is summoning us once again to lead. Proud of its past, America must once again look forward. And we must live up to the greatness of our forefathers' ideals and in doing so secure our grandchildren's futures. And that is the cause that much of my public life has been dedicated to serving.

Let me just say this—[*applause*]—in 36— hey listen—[*applause*]—come on now, you guys, as Barbara Bush would say—[*ap-*

plause]. But in 36 days we will have a new President. And I am confident, I am very confident that he will do his level-best to serve the cause that I have outlined here today. And he's going to have my support— [*applause*]—and he will have my support, and I'll stay out of his way. And I really mean that. But it is more important than my support, it is more important that he have your support. You are our future.

God bless you, and God bless the United States of America. Thank you all.

Note: The President spoke at 12:08 p.m. at G. Rollie White Coliseum. In his remarks, he referred to William H. Mobley, president, Herbert H. Richardson, chancellor, and Ross Margraves, chairman, board of regents, Texas A&M University; Rick Perry, Texas State commissioner of agriculture; Kay Bailey Hutchison, Texas State treasurer; and Frederick D. McClure, former Assistant to the President for Legislative Affairs.

Letter to Congressional Leaders Transmitting the Report of the Presidential Commission on the Assignment of Women in the Armed Forces
December 15, 1992

Dear Mr. Speaker: *(Dear Mr. President:)*

Pursuant to section 543(c) of the National Defense Authorization Act for Fiscal Years 1992 and 1993 (Public Law 102–190), I have the honor to transmit the Report to the President of the Presidential Commission on the Assignment of Women in the Armed Forces.

Sincerely,

GEORGE BUSH

Note: Identical letters were sent to Thomas S. Foley, Speaker of the House of Representatives, and Dan Quayle, President of the Senate.

Remarks Honoring the World Series Champion Toronto Blue Jays
December 16, 1992

This is about as much fun as I've had since the election, I'll tell you. I am just delighted that the Toronto Blue Jays are here. Ambassador Burney was to be here; I don't know that he is. But he's a good man. He's represented Canada well. And that

brings me to the subject at hand. Is Steve— I can't see—there's Bobby. Hi, Steve. Bobby Brown is here, an oldtime, longtime friend, the American League president, and I appreciate your being here, and Steve Greenberg, who is the deputy commissioner of baseball and doing a superb job in that very tough office. And I want to salute Mike Reilly and Joe West, the umpires. Very little good is said in kind about the umpires, but I'm glad to stand up for them. They do a great job. And our Little League champs are here from Long Beach, California. And behind them, I'm told, the Babe Ruth champs, Babe Ruth League champions from across the Nation. So welcome to all of you.

I wish that Carla Hills were here. You might say, "Why?" She is our Trade Representative. And I thought she understood that our free trade agreement with Canada did not mean that the United States would trade away the world's championship. [*Laughter*] And most of these guys are very loyal to Canada and the Blue Jays, but most of them are Americans. And so we salute them as championship baseball players. I really am pleased that you could come down this festive time of year, and I'm proud to honor a team whose greatness transcends nationality.

The Atlanta Braves—it's like the Dallas Cowboys used to be, America's team, you know—the Atlanta Braves are known as America's team. And beating them, the Blue Jays became a true world championship team.

You know, I'm not sure in the World Series if it's getting more exciting each year or if I'm just enjoying it more. But this year's matchup was a heart-stopper that baseball fans I don't believe will ever forget. Think of it: four one-run ball games, three Toronto victories won in the final time at bat. The Braves and Blue Jays staged a fall classic that even Ripley wouldn't believe.

And your season and this series were punctuated by some great individual efforts: Joe Carter, the man who brought you all home with the RBI's; Mike Timlin and the relief pitching crew who came up with some tight pitching at the end of very close ball games; the MVP effort put in by catcher Pat Borders, who couldn't be with us this morning—you see, his wife is due any day now with their second child; and then pitcher Jack Morris, who is here for the second year in a row. He manages to come no matter what happens. [*Laughter*] He

came here with the Twins last year, and if he comes next year, we're going to give him a guest room—[*laughter*]—or get Governor Clinton to.

But, anyway, it was Old Man River's 11th-inning double in game 6 that put this series in the record books. And that hit, by a 41-year-old veteran, showed that baseball isn't about country; it's about courage and stamina and grit. And after 21 years in the majors, Dave Winfield finally has the World Series ring.

Cito Gaston, his coaching staff, and the entire Blue Jays team showed that America's pastime is becoming the world's pastime. And for that, as a fan, I could not be happier. By winning Canada's first World Series, you all became national heroes as well as cultural ambassadors, and you did it with class. You did it with class all the way. And class, of course, has marked the entire Blue Jays history. In 16 years, you've gone from the doghouse to the penthouse. Millie likes that. [*Laughter*]

Your general manager, Pat Gillick, will tell you those first few seasons were not easy. But in five of the last six seasons, Toronto has either won the American League East or finished second. And your fans have taken notice of your hard work. When you built the world's first convertible stadium, Skydome, who would have expected major league attendance records in 1991 and in 1992? More than 4 million fans each year.

Now, it's no secret that in the series, I had to—it was kind of an international thing; please, don't you guys be sore—I kind of rooted for the Braves, you may remember. [*Laughter*] But I've also got—and I'm not holding it against you all that you beat up my kid's team, the Texas Rangers, like you did. [*Laughter*] About the All Star Game, they were doing pretty well, until they ran into you guys from time to time; down they went. But nevertheless, that's another subject.

But look, I do want to congratulate the Braves also. They had another great season. They fought hard, and they never gave up. But in the end you won it, and you won it fair and square. And both personally and on behalf of the United States, I salute you. As I told Cito from Air Force One the day after the series, America is proud of you.

And in a larger sense I want to salute all of baseball, a game that I've loved since my dad took me to my first game—I think it was in Yankee Stadium—many, many years ago. In that spirit let me recognize the future major leaguers that are here this morning: The world Little League champions, the All Stars from Long Beach, California—you guys stand up for one second. There they are. Welcome, and I'm glad you came all this way. No speeches out of you guys; I'll do that. [*Laughter*] Okay. Special congratulations to the Babe Ruth League champs from Lexington, Kentucky, in the 6-to-12 division—where are they? You guys stand up. Thank you. And then from Phoenix in the 13-to-15-year-old division, big guys—where are they? Well done. And then lastly from Vancouver, Washington, in the 16-to-18-year-old category, we have some of those—there they are.

I hope all of you recall this day and these world's champions from Toronto. I can't think of better role models to follow or better examples of character: Fight clean and fair, and do your best.

Joe McCarthy, the great Yankee manager—Bobby, did you play for Joe?—once said, "Give a boy a bat and a ball, and he'll be a good citizen." And those words are as relevant today as when I was playing baseball some 40 years ago, hitting eighth, second cleanup we called it. [*Laughter*] And to the heroes of baseball, young and old, I congratulate you on behalf of our Nation, and I extend to you a very warm welcome to the White House. You've all excelled in that great American pastime we follow to this day. And so congratulations.

At this very special time of year, may God bless each and every one of you. Thanks for coming to the White House.

And now Cito, as a closing thing, I wish you'd come over here. This is a rookie ball player who needs a job. [*Laughter*] And I'm going to give you this baseball card. Take a look at him. You need a good-fielding first baseman; I'm your man.

Good to see you all, and thanks for coming.

Note: The President spoke at 9:47 a.m. in Room 450 of the Old Executive Office Building.

Statement by Press Secretary Fitzwater on the President's Meeting With King Hussein of Jordan
December 16, 1992

The President today met with King Hussein of Jordan in connection with the King's private visit to the U.S. for a medical checkup. The two leaders had a discussion of the situation in the Gulf, especially the importance of maintaining U.N. sanctions against Iraq, and the Middle East peace process. The President also welcomed Jordan's decision to commit forces to both the peacemaking and peacekeeping phases in Somalia.

Recess Appointment of Sean Charles O'Keefe as Secretary of the Navy
December 16, 1992

The President today announced his intention to recess-appoint Sean Charles O'Keefe, of Virginia, to be Secretary of the Navy. He would succeed H. Lawrence Garrett III.

Since July, Mr. O'Keefe has served as

Acting Secretary of the Navy. Prior to this, Mr. O'Keefe served as Comptroller for the Department of Defense, 1989–92. He has also served on the Defense Subcommittee of the Senate Appropriations Committee as minority counsel, 1987–89; minority staff director, 1986–87; and majority professional staff member, 1981–85. Mr. O'Keefe also served as a budget analyst for Naval Sea Systems at the Department of Defense, 1980–81.

Mr. O'Keefe graduated from Loyola University (B.A., 1977) and Syracuse University (M.P.A., 1978). He was born January 27, 1956, in Monterey, CA. Mr. O'Keefe is married, has three children, and resides in Arlington, VA.

Remarks Prior to Discussions With Ambassador Saud Nasir Al-Sabah of Kuwait
December 17, 1992

The President. I don't think anybody has been more steadfast in their support of a common purpose than you have, and I am very grateful to you. And I hope you'll pay my respects, when you go home, to His Majesty.

But I want to take this opportunity to thank you all. During that Desert Storm you stayed in close touch, and you just did a dramatic and wonderful job for the coalition. And we're going to miss you, darn it.

But best of luck back there.

Q. Going to Somalia?

Q. Mr. President, are you going to Somalia for Christmas?

Ambassador Al-Sabah. I wanted to say a few words to express on behalf of His Highness the Amir and my government and the people of Kuwait our deep sense of gratitude for your support, your leadership, and the liberation of Kuwait. And our relationship with the United States, I assure you, will remain steadfast, strong as you like it to be.

And I wish you all the best in your future endeavors, Mr. President, and tell you the Kuwaiti people hold you in deep respect for your role here. And we're all looking forward to seeing you in Kuwait as soon as your time allows it, Mr. President.

The President. Well, someday I want to do that, I tell you. I really do. It's a wonderful, wonderful invitation.

Q. Will we see you in Somalia soon, Mr. President?

The President. Maybe some of these fellows don't understand that under our new policy that's been in effect now for 2 months, that we have a more rigid policy than we used to. You've been in here many times. But under the new policy, I don't take questions at these, essentially what are photo opportunities. And so I just simply cannot—I understand their interest in whether I might travel someplace, but of course you're welcome to say anything you want.

Q. Are you going?

Q. May we request a news conference then, sir?

The President. We've had 235 news conferences. Isn't that enough?

Thank you all very much.

Q. You mean, you won't answer the question of whether you're considering?

The President. I hope you have a wonderful Christmas.

Q. I hope you——

The President. We will, we will. We're having the family coming here soon and everything.

Note: The President spoke at 9:30 a.m. in the Oval Office at the White House.

Remarks Prior to Discussions With Ambassador Souheil Chammas of the Lebanese Peace Delegation
December 17, 1992

The President. Welcome, and my respects to people at home. And we're just delighted you're here at the White House. I think it's proper and fitting, and I'm very pleased you're here.

Q. Are you happy with the way these talks are going, Mr. President?

The President. You can answer, sure.

Ambassador Chammas. Maybe we would have wished that the peace talks go ahead at a larger pace. But I take this opportunity to express the deep gratitude and recognition of the Lebanese Government on behalf of my President, the Prime Minister, and the political leadership, as well as the people of Lebanon. We think the initiative of President Bush in holding the Madrid conference and initiating the peace process will in the end be an historic landmark. And time will prove that we're right. Those of us who have accepted to come and join the peace process came knowing in the end, regardless of the difficulties, it would reach ultimately its fruitful conclusions. And this would be good for the area, its people,

and all the states there.

The President. A very good statement. A very good statement.

Q. Do you think the deportation of 400 Palestinians will disrupt the talks?

Ambassador Chammas. It will loom largely over the talks. And we expressly hope that President Bush, with his weight in the administration, will do what they think they can in order to have the Israeli Government rescind the decision, because in itself deportation is bad. And under the circumstances it will adversely affect the peace process, I regret to say. And if the news were to be correct that they could be deported to Lebanon, this will further aggravate an already grave situation in Lebanon. And I'm sure I will raise this with the President of the United States if President Bush would be kind enough to listen to me.

The President. And I look forward to— [*inaudible*]—having a good discussion. Thank you all very much.

Note: The President spoke at 10 a.m. in the Oval Office at the White House.

Remarks Prior to Discussions With Ambassador Mowaffak Aloaf of the Syrian Peace Delegation
December 17, 1992

The President. We're glad you're here and look forward to hearing from you how you feel the peace process is going and all of that. We salute you for staying in the game and being at the negotiations. I want to assure you of our determination to try to bring these as far along as we can while we're here. And I'm confident that our successors will want to see this process actively and vigorously continued.

Ambassador Aloaf. Well, we are grateful very much, Mr. President, for receiving us. We consider this, really, as an indication of the great importance you attach to the

peace process, something where our people and our authorities are convinced very deeply of. And they already, I think, have expressed their appreciation for your efforts.

This is your peace initiative. If we are sorry that after 13 months of this peace process we are still without real progress, it is because we know how much effort and how much—especially Secretary Baker— time, I think—has spent a lot of energy and efforts under your leadership in order to make this peace process the hopeful end for a conflict which has lasted for more than half a century—before and after.

The President. Well, we can talk in a little more detail now as to how you see it and what you think we might be doing. But I, again, I say welcome.

Q. Do you believe the process has not succeeded, Mr. President?

The President. He doesn't remember that I don't take questions at these photo opportunities. But I'm glad and appreciate your——

Q. Are you boycotting the talks today, Mr. Ambassador?

Ambassador Aloaf. We are not boycotting the peace process. We are protesting against what's happening today when more than 400 people, human beings, sitting blindfolded, their hands tied behind their back, in buses, waiting for a decision about something which is, to begin with, really not acceptable in neither an international nor in humanitarian roles. So we shall tell our Israeli counterpart how we feel about that. And we believe that this is not really helpful to the peace process.

Q. But you will remain in the peace process.

Ambassador Aloaf. We are in the peace process because we believe in the seriousness of the United States of America. We consider this invitation by President Bush to us as an indication of that importance and also as a message to the successor of President Bush, President-elect Clinton, a message that the peace process is important not only to the parties but also to the United States of America and to the world.

The President. I can assure you it is. And we'll see where we go. But we'll discuss that item here now as soon as we have our private talks.

Note: The President spoke at 10:20 a.m. in the Oval Office at the White House.

Statement by Press Secretary Fitzwater on the Middle East Peace Talks
December 17, 1992

The President met today with Lebanese, Syrian, Jordanian-Palestinian, and Israeli delegations involved in the bilateral negotiations of the Middle East peace process. He did so to emphasize the continuing value of the process begun in Madrid, one that aims at a just, lasting, and comprehensive peace based on United Nations Security Council Resolutions 242 and 338.

The President commended the parties for their sustained commitment to this process and for the progress they have achieved. It is significant that all of the parties have engaged seriously on the key issues of land, peace, and security. Substantial achievements are within reach if the parties make additional efforts to address the legitimate concerns of their negotiating partners.

The actions and statements of the parties away from the table are no less important than the negotiations themselves. Both Arabs and Israelis need to elaborate their visions of peace. This will build public support for the negotiating process. They also need to form a concerted voice calling for an end to all forms of violence and avoid reactions such as deportations that risk complicating the search for peace.

Peace between Israel and its neighbors has never been more achievable. A way has been created whereby the people of the Middle East can escape the wars that have too often defined the region's history. Making peace a reality through these negotiations is the only way to frustrate those who would sabotage the peace process by violence.

The U.S. role as catalyst, honest broker, and driving force was instrumental in achieving the historic breakthrough at Madrid. The United States remains an essential participant in the search for peace, willing to assist actively in making the negotiations succeed.

Remarks on Signing the North American Free Trade Agreement
December 17, 1992

Thank you, Mr. Secretary General. And let me say at the outset how very pleased I am to be here. May I thank you for permitting us to have this ceremony here and welcoming us. I'm delighted to be back here. I've been privileged as Vice President and President over the past 12 years to be here on quite a few occasions, and I am so thrilled that this, the final one, is to sign the NAFTA agreement.

I want to salute so many people here today. I see so many members of our Cabinet that worked diligently on this agreement, whether it was Commerce under Bob Mosbacher; or Labor, Lynn Martin; or the Environmental Protection Agency under Bill Reilly; the Interior with Manuel Lujan. We're all represented here today. And the list should be inclusive, not exclusive, because this has been a massive team effort on the part of the Canadian Government, the Mexican Government, and certainly the U.S. side as well. But I do want to single out Ambassador Jules Katz, who is the Deputy to Carla Hills sitting over here, who worked tirelessly on this agreement, and then, of course, our special representative, the U.S. Trade Representative, Carla Hills, herself, sitting in the middle, who made this a labor of love and put everything she had into it. We owe her a great vote of thanks from the U.S. side.

Many others at the State Department, from Jim Baker on, were extraordinarily interested in this, kept the diplomacy alive and moving forward, and I salute them. Bernie Aronson is with us today. I'm delighted to see him here. He, too, has taken this on as a very special project. Arnold Kanter, our Acting Secretary, today Acting Secretary of State, is with us, and as I say, Bernie Aronson. And of course, I would be remiss if I singled out Americans if I didn't mention one who came in with me here, General Brent Scowcroft, who's done an awful lot to see that the White House was fully involved in these proceedings. So, there we are. And again I salute two more: the Mexican Ambassador to the United States, Gustavo Petricioli, who's over here, and of course, Derek Burney, over here.

I know we have many representatives from other nations here, and I don't want to bore you with how things work in this country, but we have tried since the beginning of these negotiations to keep the various Members of Congress, the key Members of Congress, fully engaged in this, having them understand the gives and the takes that go with any complicated negotiation. And I'm very pleased to see several of the key Members of Congress, Members of the United States Senate here today. So, that's the American side.

Let me just now get on with some comments about this agreement and about the common business that brings us all together, the affairs of this hemisphere. Throughout history, the destiny of nations has often been shaped by change and by chance and by the things—when I say chance, I'm talking about things that happen to them. And then there are those unique nations who shape their destinies by choice, by the things that they make happen.

Three such nations come together today, Mexico, Canada, and the United States. And by signing the North American free trade agreement, we've committed ourselves to a better future for our children and for generations yet unborn. This agreement will remove barriers to trade and investment across the two largest undefended borders of the globe and link the United States in a permanent partnership of growth with our first and third largest trading partners.

The peace and friendship that we've long enjoyed as neighbors will now be strengthened by the explosion of growth and trade let loose by the combined energies of our 360 million citizens trading freely across our borders.

I want to pay a personal tribute to my partners in this endeavor, two rare and gifted leaders, two special and valued friends without whose courage and leadership and vision this day could not have possibly come about. And when the history of our era is written, it will be said that the citizens of all the Americas were truly fortunate that Mexico and Canada, two great nations, two proud people, were led by President Carlos Salinas and Prime Minister Brian Mulroney. For Mexico particularly, especially, the NAFTA is a bold undertaking, made possible by President Salinas' brave reforms to reinvigorate, to invigorate the Mexican economy.

It's especially fitting that an American President sign this agreement in this great Hall of the Americas, the home of the Organization of American States. You see, the NAFTA represents the first giant step towards fulfillment of a dream that has long inspired us all, the dream of a hemisphere united by economic cooperation and free competition. Because of what we have begun here today, I believe the time will soon come when trade is free from Alaska to Argentina; when every citizen of the Americas has the opportunity to share in new growth and expanding prosperity.

I hope and trust that the North American free trade area can be extended to Chile, other worthy partners in South America and Central America and the Caribbean. Free trade throughout the Americas is an idea whose time has come. A new generation of democratic leaders has staked its future on that promise. And under their leadership, a tide of economic reform and trade liberalization is transforming the hemisphere.

Today, as a result, the hemisphere is growing again. For the first time in years, more capital is flowing into the Americas for new investment than is flowing out. Every major debtor nation, from Mexico to Argentina, has negotiated a successful agreement to reduce and restructure its commercial bank debt under the Brady plan.

Let me just offer a brief aside about the Brady plan if I might. I remember telling my good friend Nick Brady, our Secretary of the Treasury, "Okay, we'll call it the Brady plan, but if it's successful we're going to call it the Bush plan." [*Laughter*] And he reluctantly accepted that guidance.

I think history will show that the leadership of our distinguished Secretary of the Treasury did pay off and the plan has been highly successful. And by the way, the name will always be, appropriately, the Brady plan. And that's the way it's going to stay.

Now, under the Enterprise for the Americas, many nations, Jamaica, Bolivia, Chile, Colombia, El Salvador, Uruguay, have reduced or shortly will reduce their official debt with the United States. The Enterprise for the Americas Initiative is working. The initiative allows interest payments on official debt to be channeled into trust funds that protect the environment and support programs for child survival.

To those in other regions struggling to reform statist economies, Latin America shines as a solid example of hope that hyperinflation can be tamed, growth can be revitalized, and new investment and trade can accelerate if developing nations stay the course through the difficult challenge of economic restructuring.

These profound economic changes are a tribute to a courageous group of democratic leaders in Latin America and the Caribbean. Their revolutionary vision has altered forever the face of the Americas. Their friendship and counsel have been enormously gratifying to me as President. But these profound changes, along with the NAFTA itself, reflect a broader and, I believe, a more fundamental change in relations between the United States and the nations of this hemisphere. For many decades, we've proclaimed ambitious goals for ourselves of a good neighbor policy, of an alliance for progress, of a partnership built on mutual respect and shared responsibility. And those goals now are rapidly becoming a reality.

My talks with the hemisphere's leaders in recent weeks show a strong consensus that relations between the United States and its neighbors have never in our history been better, and that this development is working to benefit all of our peoples. And I take great pride in the fact that, working with those leaders, we've been a part of all of that.

I believe that in the future, America's relations with Latin America and the Caribbean will grow even stronger. I was pleased to hear our new President-elect, Bill Clinton, affirm that same goal in his remarks recently, both to the Rio group and to the Caribbean Latin America Action Conference.

This century's epic struggle between totalitarianism and democracy is over. It's dead. Democracy has prevailed. And today, we see unfolding around the world a revolution of hope and courage, propelled by the aspiration of ordinary people for freedom and a better life.

The world will long remember the images of that struggle: a citizen of Berlin, you know, sitting atop of the wall, chipping away with his hammer and chisel; Boris Yeltsin and his followers waving the flag of free Russia and defying the tanks and coup plotters. And here in this hall, it is worth remembering that those images were preceded by a democratic revolution in Latin America. No people struggled for freedom against oppression more bravely than the people of this hemisphere.

And here too, in the Americas, we are constructing a hopeful model of the new post-cold-war world of which we dream. This is the first hemisphere and the OAS is the first regional organization in the world to take on through the Santiago Declaration the formal collective responsibility to defend democracy. And in this hemisphere, the weapons of mass destruction, strategic missiles, as well as nuclear, chemical, and biological weapons, have been rejected voluntarily. And in this hemisphere, we've created new models of multilateral cooperation and success in resolving the conflicts that have tormented Central America.

As recent proof of the progress we've made, just 2 days ago we celebrated—and I'm sure everyone did—celebrated the end of the war in El Salvador. In this hemisphere, we have forged a new partnership to defeat the global menace of narco-trafficking, and we must succeed in that effort. And still we're not satisfied. The birth of democracy has raised expectations throughout the Americas, and now democracy must deliver. The communications revolution has opened the eyes of this hemisphere's citizens to the wider world. We're no longer blind to limits on legitimate political participation, to official corruption, or to economic favoritism.

If democracy is to be consolidated, the gulfs that separate the few who are very rich from the many who are very poor, that divide civilian from military institutions, that split citizens of European heritage from indigenous peoples, these gulfs must be bridged, and economic reform must ensure upward mobility and new opportunities for a better life for all citizens of the Americas.

To fulfill its promise, democratic government must guarantee not only the right to regular elections but human rights and property rights, swift and impartial justice, and the rule of law. Democratic governments must deliver basic services. Their institutions must be strengthened and must be modernized. To defend democracy successfully, the OAS must strengthen the tools at its disposal, and I commend the new steps that you took this week to suspend nondemocratic regimes. Together we must also create new means to end historic border disputes and to control the competition in conventional weaponry.

In all of this, I believe my country, the United States of America, bears a special responsibility. We face a moment of maximum opportunity but also, let's face it, continued risk. And we must remain engaged, for more than ever before our future, our future, is bound up with the future of the Americas.

This is the fastest growing region in the world for U.S. products. And in the struggle to defend democracy our most cherished values are at stake. Travel to Miami or El Paso, Los Angeles or Chicago or New York, and listen to the language of our neighborhoods. We are tied to the Americas not just by geography, not just by history but by who we are as a people. And no one knows that more profoundly than this proud grandfather.

This year marks the 500th anniversary of a voyage of discovery to the New World. And let this also be a time of rediscovery for my country, the United States, of the importance of our own hemisphere. If we are equal to the challenges before us, we can build in the Americas the world's first completely democratic hemisphere. Just think about that. Think of the importance. Think of the significance. Think of the example for the rest of the world.

This hemisphere can be as well a zone of peace, where trade flows freely, prosperity is shared, the rule of law is respected, and the gifts of human knowledge are harnessed for all.

More than 150 years ago, Simon Bolívar, the Liberator, whose statue stands outside this hall, spoke about an America united in heart, subject to one law, and guided by the torch of liberty. My friends, here in this hemisphere we are on the way to realizing Simon Bolívar's dream. And today with the signing of the North American Free Trade Agreement, we take another giant step towards making the dream a reality.

Thank you all very much for coming. And now I have the high honor of signing this agreement. Thank you.

[*At this point, the President signed the North American Free Trade Agreement.*]

Good luck to all of you now in the future. God bless you.

Note: The President spoke at 2:32 p.m. at the Organization of American States. In his remarks, he referred to João Clemente Baena Soares, Secretary General of the Organization of American States; Bernard Aronson, Assistant Secretary of State for Inter-American Affairs; and Derek H. Burney, Canadian Ambassador to the United States.

Remarks Following Discussions With European Community Leaders
December 18, 1992

Today's discussions with Prime Minister Major and President Delors mark our fifth meeting since we agreed to these semiannual consultations with the European Community. And the frequency of these meetings is a sign of their vital importance for the world trading system, for our own economic well-being, and for meeting the challenges of the new world. And this morning we covered a broad agenda reflecting the many interests that we share in global partnership.

On trade, we are of one mind. We agreed that a sound Uruguay round agreement is essential to boost worldwide economic growth. And we all agreed to conclude the GATT agreement in Geneva by mid-January. We've instructed our negotiators to work together to this end. And we're committed not only to resolving the differences remaining among ourselves but also to encouraging Japan and other countries to join us in an energetic effort to bring the negotiations to a successful conclusion.

I continue to believe that for the people of Europe as well as of the United States, free and open trade is the key to expanding prosperity. And a successful Uruguay round could result in over $5 trillion in increased world output over the next 10 years. Our estimate suggests that the European Community's gains would amount to about $1.4 trillion, and the United States would benefit from a boost of $1.1 trillion in that period. Clearly these tremendous gains would promote the well-being of all of our citizens.

Also this morning we discussed the continuing tragedy in what once was Yugoslavia. We reaffirmed our commitment to the unhampered flow of humanitarian aid and to ending the violence there through a sound political solution.

We also reiterated our continued support for the Russian people's brave efforts to create a market economy there. And we believe that reforms must be implemented quickly if external aid is to be effective. Used wisely, western aid can be a catalyst to democratic reform, reforms that are in the interest of all the world. And we agreed to work closely with President Yeltsin to achieve these goals.

Then I took the opportunity to share with the Prime Minister and the President our views of the Middle East peace process. I welcome the continued active role of the EC, particularly in the multilateral side of the talks.

After Prime Minister Major and President Delors briefed me on the results of the EC summit in Edinburgh this week, I reaffirmed our longstanding support for European integration.

So I want to thank the Prime Minister, Prime Minister John Major, and President Delors for their support and friendship, friendship they've shown me personally and most of all shown to the people of the United States. Talks such as these serve as a reminder of their friendship and of our common interests in creating a world of peace and prosperity for all our peoples.

So once again, to both of you my sincere thanks. And Mr. Prime Minister would you take the floor, sir.

Note: The President spoke at 1:35 p.m. on the South Lawn at the White House, following a meeting with European Community Commission President Jacques Delors and Prime Minister John Major of the United Kingdom, President of the European Council.

Presidential Determination No. 93–6—Memorandum on Assistance to Refugees of the Former Yugoslavia
December 18, 1992

Memorandum for the Secretary of State

Subject: Determination Pursuant to Section 2(b)(2) of the Migration and Refugee Assistance Act of 1962, as Amended

Pursuant to section 2(b)(2) of the Migration and Refugee Assistance Act of 1962, as amended, 22 U.S.C. 2601(b)(2), I hereby designate refugees, displaced persons, and victims of conflict from and within the former Yugoslavia as qualifying for assistance under section 2(b)(2) of the Act, and determine that such assistance will contribute to the foreign policy interests of the United States.

You are directed to inform the appropriate committees of the Congress of this determination and the obligation of funds under this authority, and to publish this determination in the *Federal Register*.

GEORGE BUSH

[*Filed with the Office of the Federal Register, 3:13 p.m., December 28, 1992*]

Statement by Press Secretary Fitzwater on the Elections in the Republic of Korea
December 18, 1992

Korean voters went to the polls today and elected Kim Young Sam to succeed President Roh Tae Woo. We welcome the success of the Korean people in expressing their preference in a constitutional process which enables all concerned to support the winner through free and fair elections. The President has sent his personal congratulations and those of the American people to President-elect Kim Young Sam.

We would like to take this opportunity to express our respect and admiration for the many accomplishments of President Roh. We wish President Roh well and look forward to working closely with President-elect Kim Young Sam.

Remarks With Prime Minister John Major of the United Kingdom and an Exchange With Reporters
December 20, 1992

The Former Yugoslavia

The President. Let me just say that we've had a very, once again, had a very good meeting with the Prime Minister up at Camp David. I expect this will be my last such meeting, but I'll tell you it was fruitful. I feel as strongly as I ever have about the strength of the U.K.–U.S. relationship that is vital to our own interests. I know the Prime Minister feels that way, and the talks just couldn't have gone better.

We covered a wide array of subjects, almost every area of the globe. We did it in a relaxed atmosphere. It was a special joy to have Mrs. Major with us at this Christmas season. We inundated him with Christmas carols. And I think it was, as far as I'm concerned, a very wonderful visit with a distinguished world leader.

We did spend a lot of time talking about the former Yugoslavia. We spelled out some objectives for our policy, nothing particularly new in it, but we agreed that working for a peaceful and just settlement in the former Yugoslavia is essential. We agreed that there's a risk and that we must prevent the spread of fighting in particular to Kosovo and Macedonia. And then I saluted the British leadership role on the humanitarian side of things. They have forces on the ground in harm's way, and those forces are doing the Lord's work in terms of bringing relief. So, we talked about maintaining the humanitarian aid effort which includes the British troops and without which, clearly, many more lives would be lost in the winter.

So, we spelled these objectives out. And Prime Minister, I enjoyed the visit. I don't want to monopolize it. Maybe you would care to add something, sir.

The Prime Minister. Mr. President, thank you very much.

Can I just echo what the President's had to say about the discussions we've had over the weekend. But further than that, as the President said, this may be the last meeting we have of this kind, and I've found the last 2 years especially fruitful in those discussions. There's been a lot happening in the last 2 years. I think it's been remarkably good not just for the United Kingdom but for Europe to know we've had such a good friend here in the White House. I think there are many people across the world who will have good cause to say thanks for the work that President Bush has done in the last 4 years. And I believe I speak not just for myself but for many millions when we wish him the best of futures after he leaves the White House in a few days' time.

We had not only a very enjoyable weekend, I think we had a very productive weekend. The President has set out the objectives that we discussed as far as Yugoslavia is concerned. We looked at some of the details to underpin those objectives as well. We did agree to cooperate in a resolution at the United Nations to enforce compliance with the no-fly zone. The aim of the resolution will be to make sure we enforce the resolution previously agreed and to prevent flights taking place other than those that have been specifically authorized to do so.

We looked also at the possible need for measures to prevent the spread of fighting into Kosovo and into Macedonia, and that clearly is a matter of immense importance in the future. With that in mind, we both agreed that it would be wise to press for an early increase in the number of observers in Kosovo.

We also looked at the question of present and future sanctions and the present and future relationship with Serbia. We agreed that our attitude to sanctions would depend on rapid and radical change of policy by Serbia and confirmed that we would be ready, depending on Serbia's response, to impose new sanctions on Serbia. The sort of things we had in mind, of course, were initially cutting postal and telecommunication links but going on, of course, to the closing of borders if necessary. And if it proves necessary, complete and total diplomatic isolation, not just in the short term but making it clear to them that that would apply for a very long time indeed.

Both of us wish to see a political settlement. The President was very sensitive to the work done by the British troops and by the U.N. agencies there. And I'm most grateful for his kind words about that this morning.

Amongst a number of other issues, we also looked at the problems that have arisen in Iraq in the last few days in the delivery of humanitarian aid by the United Nations to the Kurds in northern Iraq. That has come to a halt temporarily as a result of the Iraqis placing bombs in a number of the trucks that were delivering that aid. And we agreed that we were determined to ensure that that aid does get through to northern Iraq. And that is a matter that will have to be developed over the course of the next few days.

So those were some, not an exclusive list but some of the issues that we discussed this morning. And I would just like to end by yet again thanking the President for the nature of these discussions and for the relationship between our two countries.

The President. Marlin, are we going to be passing out a statement that summarizes some of this discussion here?

Q. Mr. President, would U.S. planes be used to enforce the no-fly zone?

The President. This is a little ahead of where we're going. We don't discuss how we are going to do things, especially before we've decided what they're going to be, so I just would have to duck that one right now.

Q. Do you expect a 15-day deadline?

The Prime Minister. I saw those stories in the press this morning about a 15-day deadline. Certainly, that was nothing we discussed this morning, nothing we discussed over the weekend. That's a matter that isn't just for the President and for I, not just for the United States and the United Kingdom. That's something that would have to be agreed in a Security Council resolution. So I don't know where these 15-day stories come from, but they have no credibility at the moment.

Q. Would you be prepared to see British involvement if necessary in enforcing the deadline, Prime Minister?

The Prime Minister. Well, we've got a lot of discussing to do before we determine how the deadline's going to be enforced. We've agreed that it's necessary to enforce the no-fly zone. There's more than one way of doing that, but we have to discuss that with a lot of other interested parties as well before we can agree to the Security Council resolution.

Robin Oakley [British Broadcasting Corporation].

Q. What kind of action would be taken to protect the forces already on the ground protecting humanitarian effort if there were to be retaliation as a result of the enforcement of the no-fly zone?

The Prime Minister. We've always made it clear right from the start that we were concerned about maintaining the humanitarian assistance that's going into Sarajevo and other centers. That clearly is of critical humanitarian importance, and so is the paramount importance of preserving the security of the United Nations agencies and the British and other troops that are assisting in the delivery of that humanitarian aid. So clearly, that has to underpin any resolution and any progress we make. And these are the matters that will be discussed further over the next few days with our colleagues and allies.

The President. And may I add to that, may I simply add to that that on behalf of the United States, we are very sensitive to the fact that the sons and daughters from other countries are serving on the ground in Sarajevo and trying to facilitate the relief in the former Yugoslavia. The United States has done a fair amount, a good amount I'd say, in getting relief supplies in, but when it comes to taking decisions that affect the lives of troops, I would view a British soldier the same as I would if these were United States soldiers there. We must do that. We owe them prudence in making these decisions. And the fact that these are Brits serving there in no way lessens the feeling I have that we must be very careful we don't needlessly put young men and women who are there in harm's way more than they are. And I just want to say that particularly to the parents of the young people that are wearing British uniforms in the former Yugoslavia today. They must know that that's the way the United States views these things.

Yes, Randall [Randall Pinkston, CBS News].

Q. Mr. President, do you anticipate any problems from Russia in terms of getting an enforcement resolution given the reports——

The President. No, we don't anticipate any. As a matter of fact, they have not raised it. I talked to Boris Yeltsin for 35 minutes this morning on other matters, and had that been on his mind I expect he would have raised it. He's a very frank interlocutor, as the Prime Minister knows. So I don't anticipate difficulty. But the way we avoid that is to do exactly what we're doing, the ultimate in consultations at the United Nations. Would you want to add on the Soviets—Russian side?

The Prime Minister. No, I've nothing to add on that.

START II

Q. On to the other matters, Mr. President, START treaty, are you ready to sign? Are you going to go to Anchorage?

The President. Well, we discussed that, and I can tell you it's not agreed totally. We've made some real progress.

The Former Yugoslavia

Q. Mr. President, do you have a trigger of some sort for these other sanctions that you've mentioned down the line? Is it something that the Serbs would do to make these happen, or is it just the passage of time, or what?

The President. Well, I don't want to—the answer to your question is no. The answer to your question is no; we don't have a trigger time.

Q. Do you want the U.N. resolution to stipulate that planes which violate the no-fly zone will be shot down?

The Prime Minister. No, I don't, I don't think that the U.N. resolution will stipulate anything of the sort, not in those terms. But the U.N. resolution is not yet decided. There is a lot of discussion. We need to get the agreement of the Security Council and others. There's some way to go before we get the resolution.

Q. Prime Minister, how long will it take to get that resolution through? Do you feel there's pressure to do it quickly, within a week, 2 weeks?

The Prime Minister. I don't think I want to put a time scale, but I doubt it will be too long.

Q. If Mr. Milosevic is elected, how would that affect things?

The Prime Minister. I think commenting on elections is a dangerous, hazardous business.

The President. So do I.

The Prime Minister. Especially on the day of the election.

The President. That's a good way to end this, I think. Thank you all very much.

Note: The President spoke at 10:38 a.m. on the South Lawn at the White House following his return from Camp David, MD. A reporter referred to President Slobodan Milosevic of Serbia.

Joint Statement With Prime Minister John Major of the United Kingdom on the Former Yugoslavia
December 20, 1992

The President of the United States and the Prime Minister of the United Kingdom have agreed as follows.

The objectives of our policy are:

(a) to work for a peaceful and just settlement in the former Yugoslavia;

(b) to prevent the spread of the fighting in particular to Kosovo and Macedonia;

(c) to maintain the humanitarian aid effort which includes over 2,000 British troops and without which many more lives will be lost this winter.

The President and Prime Minister paid tribute to the work of the United Nations in the former Yugoslavia and to the courage and dedication of the troops who are ensuring that convoys get through. They welcomed the success of the UN and its agencies, despite all the odds, in delivering large quantities of aid to those in need. They agreed on the importance of enabling that effort to go ahead.

The United States and the United Kingdom have agreed to cooperate on a Resolution in the United Nations to enforce compliance with the 'no-fly' zone for Bosnia should violation of the existing ban continue. The aim of the resolution would be to prevent flights taking place other than those specifically authorized by the United Nations.

The President and the Prime Minister:

(a) agreed that steps need to be taken to prevent the spread of fighting into Kosovo and Macedonia;

(b) welcomed the decision to deploy UN troops in Macedonia and hoped that this UN presence would be stepped up over the coming weeks;

(c) agreed also to press for the very early increase in the numbers of observers in Kosovo;

(d) agreed that our attitude to sanctions would depend on a rapid and radical change of policy by Serbia;

(e) confirmed that they would be ready, depending on Serbia's response, to impose new sanctions. They could initially include cutting postal and telecommunication links and could lead to closing the borders and complete diplomatic isolation for years to come.

The President and the Prime Minister paid tribute to the work of Cy Vance and David Owen in trying to negotiate a peaceful settlement in the former Yugoslavia. Both Governments will continue to give the negotiators their full support.

Note: The joint statement was made available by the Office of the White House Press Secretary but was not issued as a White House press release. The statement referred to Cyrus Vance and Lord David Owen, Co-chairmen of the International Conference on the Former Yugoslavia.

Statement by Press Secretary Fitzwater on the President's Discussions With Foreign Ministers of Central European States
December 22, 1992

The President met today with the Foreign Ministers from Austria, Hungary, Poland, and Slovenia, representing members of the Central European initiative, to discuss the crisis in the Balkans. The Foreign Ministers emphasized their concerns over the direction of events in the former Yugoslavia.

The President expressed deep concern over the violence still wracking Bosnia and highlighted the efforts that the United States has taken, along with the EC and other concerned nations, to help alleviate the suffering of innocents. He recognized the importance of stability to the new democracies of the region, including those represented in the meeting, and encouraged them to work in support of the efforts under the auspices of the United Nations and CSCE to help defuse the crisis and contribute to the search for a political settlement.

Remarks on Departure for Camp David, Maryland
December 23, 1992

I just want to wish everybody a very Merry Christmas. I want to say that to everybody that's worked so hard in our administration. I want to say that to Governor Clinton's new team, to wish them all the very best in the new year. I want to say it to all the press. The amnesty extended during the campaign to the photographers, it's been granted to Helen Thomas [United Press International] and all the rest of you guys. So have a wonderful Christmas and a very happy new year. And inasmuch as I've had 268 press conferences, I think it would kind of ruin the spirit of Christmas if I took any questions here. But I really hope you all have a good one.

Note: The President spoke at 11:37 a.m. on the South Lawn at the White House.

Letter to Congressional Leaders Reporting on Sanctions Against the Federal Republic of Yugoslavia (Serbia and Montenegro)
December 23, 1992

Dear Mr. Speaker: (Dear Mr. President:)

On May 30, 1992, in Executive Order No. 12808, I declared a national emergency to deal with the threat to the national security, foreign policy, and economy of the United States arising from actions and policies of the Governments of Serbia and Montenegro, acting under the name of the Socialist Federal Republic of Yugoslavia or the Federal Republic of Yugoslavia, in their involvement in and support for groups attempting to seize territory in Croatia and Bosnia-Hercegovina by force and violence utilizing, in part, the forces of the so-called Yugoslav National Army (57 *FR* 23299). In that order, I ordered the immediate blocking of all property and interests in property of the Government of Serbia and the Government of Montenegro, and all property and interests in property in the name of the Government of the Socialist Federal Republic of Yugoslavia or the Government of the Federal Republic of Yugoslavia, then or thereafter located in the United States or within the possession or control of United States persons, including their overseas branches. Treasury agents immediately carried out these orders and blocked more than $450 million within the first 24 hours, closing down two Serbian-based banks that had been operating in New York City and sealing the offices of Yugoslav subsidiaries across the country.

Subsequently, on June 5, 1992, to implement in the United States the prohibitions of United Nations Security Council Resolution No. 757 of May 30, 1992, I issued Executive Order No. 12810 adding trade and other economic sanctions against the Federal Republic of Yugoslavia (Serbia and Montenegro) (The "FRY(S/M)") to the sanctions imposed on May 30 (57 *FR* 24347). Under this order, I prohibited the importation into the United States of any goods originating in, or services performed in, the FRY(S/M), exported from the FRY(S/M) after May 30, 1992, or any activity that promotes or is intended to promote such importation. The Executive order also prohibits the exportation to the FRY(S/M), or to any entity operated from the FRY(S/M), or owned or controlled by the Government of the FRY(S/M), directly or indirectly, of any goods, technology (including technical data or other information controlled for export pursuant to the Export Administration Regulations, 15 C.F.R. Parts 768 *et seq.*), or services, either (1) from the United States, (2) requiring the issuance of a license by a Federal agency, or (3) involving the use of U.S.-registered vessels or aircraft, or any activity that promotes or is intended to promote such exportation.

Additional economic sanctions contained in Executive Order No. 12810 prohibit (1) any dealing by a United States person related to property originating in the FRY(S/M) exported from the FRY(S/M) after May 30, 1992, or property intended for exportation from the FRY(S/M) to any country, or exportation to the FRY(S/M) from any country, or any activity of any kind that promotes or is intended to promote such dealing; (2) any transaction by a United States person, or involving the use of U.S.-registered vessels or aircraft, relating to transportation to or from the FRY(S/M), the provision of transportation to or from the United States by any person in the FRY(S/M), or any vessel or aircraft registered in the FRY(S/M), or the sale in the United States by any person holding authority under the Federal Aviation Act of 1958, as amended (49 U.S.C. 1301 *et seq.*), of any transportation by air that includes any stop in the FRY(S/M); (3) the granting of permission to any aircraft to take off from, land in, or overfly the United States, if the aircraft, as part of the same flight, is destined to land in or has taken off from the territory of the FRY(S/M); (4) the performance by any United States person of any contract, including a financing contract, in support of an industrial, commercial, public utility, or governmental project in the FRY(S/M); (5) any commitment or transfer, direct or indirect, of funds or other financial or economic resources by any United States person to or for the benefit of the Government of the FRY(S/M) or any other person in the FRY(S/M)—effectively halting all transfers; (6) any transaction in the United States or by a United States person related to participation in sporting events in the United States by persons or groups representing the FRY(S/M); and (7) any transaction in the United States or by a United States person related to scientific and technical cooperation and cultural exchanges involving persons or groups officially sponsored by or representing the FRY(S/M), or related to visits to the United States by such persons or groups other than as authorized for the purpose of participation in the United Nations.

1. The order exempts from trade restrictions (a) the transshipment through the FRY(S/M) of commodities and products originating outside the FRY(S/M) and temporarily present in the territory of the FRY(S/M) only for the purpose of such transshipment, and (b) activities related to the United Nations Protection Force ("UNPROFOR"), the Conference on Yugoslavia, or the European Community Monitor Mission.

2. The declaration of the national emergency on May 30, 1992, was made pursuant to the authority vested in me as President by the Constitution and laws of the United States, including the International Emergency Economic Powers Act (50 U.S.C. 1701 *et seq.*), the National Emergencies Act (50 U.S.C. 1601 *et seq.*), and section 301 of title 3 of the United States Code. I reported the emergency declaration to the Congress on May 30, 1992, pursuant to section 204(b) of the International Emergency Economic Powers Act (50 U.S.C. 1703(b)). The additional sanctions set forth in my order of June 5, 1992, were imposed pursuant to the authority vested in me by the Constitution and laws of the United States, including the statutes cited above, section 1114 of the Federal Aviation Act of 1958, as amended (49 U.S.C. App. 1514), and section 5 of the United Nations Participation Act of 1945, as amended (22 U.S.C. 287c), and implement in the United States provisions of United Nations Security Council Resolution No. 757. The present report is submitted pursuant to 50 U.S.C. 1641(c) and 1703(c), and discusses Administration actions and expenses directly related to the exercise of powers and authorities conferred by the national emergency with respect to the FRY(S/M) declared in Executive Order No. 12808, as implemented pursuant to that order and Executive Order No. 12810 (the "Executive orders").

3. In its implementation of the sanctions program against the FRY(S/M) pursuant to Executive Orders No. 12808 and No. 12810, Foreign Assets Control ("FAC") has issued seven general licenses authorizing various transactions otherwise prohibited by the Executive orders and directing certain implementing measures. Copies of these general licenses are attached. General License No. 1

authorizes transactions incident to the receipt or transmission of mail and informational materials between the United States and the FRY(S/M). General License No. 2 authorizes transactions with respect to telecommunications transmissions involving the FRY(S/M), provided that any funds owed the Government of the FRY(S/M) are placed into a blocked interest-bearing account. General License No. 3 authorizes the importation and exportation of diplomatic pouches.

General License No. 4 authorizes transfers of funds or other financial or economic resources for the benefit of individuals located in the FRY(S/M) in connection with the operation of accounts at U.S. financial institutions, provided that no transfers into the FRY(S/M) occur. This general license also requires that interest be paid on blocked FRY(S/M) Government funds and sets forth certain guidelines for the administration of blocked accounts. General License No. 5 authorizes the importation and exportation of the household and personal effects of persons arriving from or departing to the FRY(S/M), in conjunction with General License No. 6, which authorizes transactions related to nonbusiness travel by U.S. persons to, from, and within the FRY(S/M). Finally, General License No. 7 authorizes transactions involving secondary-market trading in debt obligations originally incurred by banks organized in the Republics of Slovenia, Croatia, Bosnia-Hercegovina, and Macedonia, notwithstanding the joint and several liability on those debts undertaken by the National Bank of Yugoslavia and/or banks organized in Serbia or Montenegro.

In addition to the seven general licenses, FAC issued General Notice No. 1 on July 6, 1992, entitled "Notification of Status of Yugoslav Entities," followed by a list of "Blocked Yugoslav Entities Currently Identified." 57 *Fed. Reg.* 32051 (July 20, 1992). A copy of the notice is attached. The list is composed of government, financial, and commercial entities organized in Serbia or Montenegro and a number of foreign subsidiaries of such entities. The list is illustrative of entities covered by FAC's presumption, stated in the notice, that all entities organized or located in Serbia or Montene-

gro, as well as their foreign branches and subsidiaries, are controlled by the Government of the FRY(S/M) and thus subject to the blocking provisions of the Executive orders. Accordingly, during the first 6 months of the sanctions program, 13 U.S. subsidiaries of entities organized in the FRY(S/M) were blocked as entities owned or controlled by the Government of the FRY(S/M). Similarly, six ships owned indirectly by Montenegrin shipping companies were blocked in U.S. ports as property in which the FRY(S/M) Government has an interest.

FAC's presumption of FRY(S/M) Government control over subsidiaries of firms located or organized in Serbia or Montenegro was challenged in Federal district court by a blocked U.S. subsidiary of a Serbian firm (*IPT Company, Inc.* v. *U.S. Department of the Treasury, et al.,* S.D.N.Y., No. 92 CIV 5542), and by a Maltese subsidiary of a Montenegrin ocean shipping company managing five of the six blocked ships (*Milena Ship Management Co., Ltd.* v. *Newcomb et al.,* E.D. La, No. 92–2535). In both cases, FAC argued through the Department of Justice that its presumption is justified by the unique legal concept of "social capital" in the economic systems of both the prior Socialist Federal Republic of Yugoslavia and the current FRY(S/M), under which, by law, capital assets were, and generally continue to be, owned by the society but managed by the workers. Active state control of such enterprises is also often manifest by a crossover of political leaders between the enterprises and the government. Based upon the administrative record and FAC's denial of a license authorizing the blocked ships in the *Milena* case to conduct normal operations outside the FRY(S/M), the U.S. District Court for the Eastern District of Louisiana ruled in the government's favor and dismissed the suit on October 5, 1992. This decision was appealed by the plaintiffs to the U.S. Court of Appeals for the Fifth Circuit on October 21, 1992. The suite brought by IPT Company, Inc. is still pending in the Southern District of New York.

4. Over the past 6 months, the Departments of State and Treasury have worked closely with European Community ("EC")

member states and other U.N. member nations to coordinate implementation of the sanctions against the FRY(S/M). This has included visits by assessment teams formed under the auspices of the United States, the EC, and the Conference for Security and Cooperation in Europe (the "CSCE") to states bordering on Serbia and Montenegro; deployment of CSCE sanctions assistance missions ("SAMS") to Hungary, Romania, and Bulgaria to assist in monitoring land and Danube River traffic; bilateral contacts between the United States and other countries with the purpose of tightening restrictions on FRY(S/M) financial assets; and establishment of a mechanism to coordinate enforcement efforts and to exchange technical information.

5. In these initial months of the sanctions program against the FRY(S/M), FAC has made extensive use of its authority to specifically license transactions with respect to the FRY(S/M) in an effort to positively influence both the political process within Serbia-Montenegro and negotiations between warring factions in the former Socialist Federal Republic of Yugoslavia. For example, specific licenses have been issued (a) permitting Milan Panic, a naturalized U.S. citizen of Serbian birth, to serve as Prime Minister of the FRY(S/M), (b) authorizing the International Republican Institute to provide support to the opposition political parties in the FRY(S/M), and (c) permitting the Free Trade Union Institute to attend meetings with the independent labor confederation, Nezavisnost, and the trials of union activists in the FRY(S/M).

Since the issuance of Executive Order No. 12808, FAC has worked closely with the Board of Governors of the Federal Reserve Board, the Office of the Comptroller of the Currency, the New York State Banking Department, and the banking industry to assure compliance with the President's blocking order. On June 1, 1992, when FAC directed the closing of two Serbian banking institutions in New York, full-time bank examiners were posted in their offices to ensure that banking records were appropriately safeguarded. The examiners continue on-site compliance monitoring on a full-time basis.

In all, FAC has issued 217 specific li-

censes regarding transactions pertaining to the FRY(S/M) or assets it owns or controls. Specific licenses have been issued for (1) payment to U.S. or third-country secured creditors, under certain narrowly defined circumstances, for pre-embargo import and export transactions; (2) for legal representation or advice to FRY(S/M) or FRY(S/M)-controlled clients; (3) for restricted and closely monitored operations by subsidiaries of FRY(S/M)-controlled firms located in the United States; (4) for limited FRY(S/M) diplomatic representation in Washington and New York; (5) for patent, trademark, and copyright protection and maintenance transactions in the FRY(S/M) not involving payment to the FRY(S/M) Government; (6) for certain communications, news media, and travel-related transactions; (7) for the payment of crews' wages and vessel maintenance of FRY(S/M)-controlled ships blocked in the United States; (8) for the export of certain non-FRY(S/M) manufactured property owned and controlled by U.S. entities; and (9) to assist the United Nations in its UNPROFOR and relief operations. Pursuant to United Nations Security Council Resolution 757, specific licenses have also been issued to authorize exportation of food, medicine, and medical supplies intended for humanitarian purposes in the FRY(S/M).

To ensure compliance with the terms of the licenses that have been issued, stringent reporting requirements have been imposed that are closely monitored. Licensed accounts are regularly audited by FAC compliance personnel and by cooperating auditors from other regulatory agencies.

6. Since the issuance of Executive Order No. 12810, FAC has worked closely with the U.S. Customs Service to ensure both that prohibited imports and exports (including those in which the Government of the FRY(S/M) has an interest) are identified and interdicted, and that permitted imports and exports move to their intended destination without undue delay. Violations and suspected violations of the embargo are being investigated, and appropriate enforcement actions are being taken.

7. The expenses incurred by the Federal Government in the 6-month period from May 30, 1992, through November 30, 1992,

that are directly attributable to the authorities conferred by the declaration of a national emergency with respect to the FRY(S/M) are estimated at $872,155, most of which represent wage and salary costs for Federal personnel. Personnel costs were largely centered in the Department of the Treasury (particularly in FAC, the U.S. Customs Service, and the Office of the General Counsel), the Department of State, the National Security Council, and the Department of Commerce.

8. The actions and policies of the Government of the FRY(S/M), in its involvement in and support for groups attempting to seize territory in Croatia and Bosnia-Hercegovina by force and violence, continue to pose an unusual and extraordinary threat to the national security, foreign policy, and economy of the United States. The United States remains committed to a multilateral resolution of this crisis through its actions implementing the resolutions of the United Nations Security Council with respect to the FRY(S/M). I shall continue to exercise the powers at my disposal to apply economic sanctions against the FRY(S/M) as long as these measures are appropriate, and will continue to report periodically to the Congress on significant developments pursuant to 50 U.S.C. 1703(c).

Sincerely,

GEORGE BUSH

Note: Identical letters were sent to Thomas S. Foley, Speaker of the House of Representatives, and Dan Quayle, President of the Senate.

Letter to Congressional Leaders on Trade With Ethiopia
December 23, 1992

Dear Mr. Speaker: (Dear Mr. President:)

I am writing to inform you of my intent to add Ethiopia to the list of beneficiary developing countries under the Generalized System of Preferences (GSP). The GSP program offers duty-free access to the U.S. market and is authorized by the Trade Act of 1974.

I have carefully considered the criteria identified in sections 501 and 502 of the Trade Act of 1974. In light of these criteria, and particularly Ethiopia's level of development and initiation of economic reforms, I have determined that it is appropriate to extend GSP benefits to Ethiopia.

This notice is submitted in accordance with section 502(a)(1) of the Trade Act of 1974.

Sincerely,

GEORGE BUSH

Note: Identical letters were sent to Thomas S. Foley, Speaker of the House of Representatives, and Dan Quayle, President of the Senate. The related proclamation is listed in Appendix E at the end of this volume.

Letter to Congressional Leaders Reporting on Whaling Activities of Norway
December 23, 1992

Dear Mr. Speaker: (Dear Mr. President:)

On October 26, 1992, Secretary of Commerce Barbara Hackman Franklin certified under section 8 of the Fishermen's Protective Act of 1967, as amended ("Pelly Amendment") (22 U.S.C. 1978(a)), that Norway has conducted whaling activities that diminish the effectiveness of the International Whaling Commission (IWC) conservation program. This letter constitutes my report to the Congress pursuant to subsection (b) of the Pelly Amendment.

The certification of the Secretary of Commerce was based on the issuance by the Government of Norway of permits to its nationals, allowing the killing of North Atlantic minke whales for research purposes. At its 44th Annual Meeting, the IWC adopted a resolution stating that the Norwegian research program did not satisfy all criteria for research involving the take of whales. In particular, concern was expressed that the Government had not adequately structured the research so as to contribute to or materially facilitate the completion of the IWC comprehensive assessment. The IWC was also of the view that the Government of Norway had not established that its research addresses critically important research needs. Research that does not meet all applicable criteria is considered inconsistent with IWC conservation policy. In view of these concerns, the IWC invited Norway to reconsider its program. The Norwegian Government issued permits for the proposed take prior to the IWC meeting, and, on the last day of the meeting, the Norwegian whaling vessels reportedly set sail. Since then, 95 minke whales have been taken.

I am also greatly concerned about the announcement made by the Government of Norway at the beginning of the 44th Annual Meeting of the IWC that Norway would resume commercial whaling in 1993, irrespective of the decisions of the IWC. The moratorium on commercial whaling adopted by the IWC is observed by the entire community of nations, including those that are not members of the IWC. If Norway, a founding member of the IWC, were to disregard the moratorium, it would very likely lead to grave consequences for the effectiveness of the IWC conservation program.

I have carefully considered these developments and concluded that we should continue to give a high priority to working with all IWC members to maintain the integrity of the IWC. I want to ensure that the IWC has the full support of the United States in carrying out its responsibility to conserve the great natural resources represented by whale stocks.

I am not at this time directing the Secretary of the Treasury to impose sanctions on Norwegian products for the whaling activities that led to certification by the Secretary of Commerce. I will ensure, however, that our concerns are communicated to the highest levels of the Norwegian Government. I am also requesting that further senior-level consultations with Norway and our other IWC partners be undertaken to ensure that the IWC's conservation program is upheld. I hope that our actions will encourage all members of the IWC to cooperate in its important mission.

Sincerely,

GEORGE BUSH

Note: Identical letters were sent to Thomas S. Foley, Speaker of the House of Representatives, and Dan Quayle, President of the Senate.

Recess Appointment of Brian C. Griffin as Chairman of the Administrative Conference of the United States
December 29, 1992

The President has recess-appointed Brian C. Griffin, of Oklahoma, to be Chairman of the Administrative Conference of the United States. He would succeed Marshall Jordan Breger.

Since 1989, Mr. Griffin has served as Deputy Assistant Attorney General with the Tax Division at the Department of Justice. Prior to this, he served as a partner with the firm of Griffin & Griffin, 1979–80 and 1985–89. From 1980 to 1985, he served as executive vice president and general counsel for Petroleum Investments, Ltd.

Mr. Griffin graduated from Harvard University (B.A., 1974), Oxford University (M.A., 1976; B.A., 1983), University of Oklahoma (J.D., 1978), and Southern Methodist University (LL.M., 1989). He was born January 11, 1953, in Oklahoma City, OK. Mr. Griffin is married, has two children, and resides in Bethesda, MD.

Remarks on the START II Treaty and the Situation in Somalia and an Exchange With Reporters
December 30, 1992

The President. Well, I have just spoken this morning by telephone with Russian President Boris Yeltsin, and I am very pleased to announce that we have completed agreement on the START II treaty. U.S. and Russian expert teams are remaining in Geneva now to complete the formal work on the treaty text. This historic treaty will reduce by two-thirds current nuclear arsenals and will dramatically lower the numbers of strategic nuclear arms permitted by START I. In my view, this treaty is good for all mankind.

President Yeltsin and I have agreed to meet in Sochi, Russia, on January 2d and 3d, where we will sign the treaty. And I want to take this opportunity to congratulate the team standing here with me today: Larry Eagleburger, Secretary Cheney, Chairman Powell, and others who have done a superb job on this treaty.

We're going to use the occasion of the meeting in Sochi to consider a number of bilateral and regional issues and then to discuss ways to fulfill the promise and the potential of the U.S.-Russia relations.

Let me just say a word about our trip to Somalia. The trip, I hope, will show the concern that all Americans feel for the people of Somalia and for the condition. These are humanitarian concerns, and in my view it is proper that the President show this concern to the people over there.

I also want to make very clear how strongly we support our troops that are over there. They're doing a first-class job. I've had a good briefing from General Powell and Secretary Cheney, and I just can't tell you how proud I am of the young men and women that are serving halfway around the world in this great humanitarian cause.

We've tried to keep Governor Clinton closely advised, informed on the Somalia trip and obviously on the arms control agreement. So I think these are both important events, the trip to Sochi and the trip to Somalia. And I would like to take this occasion, because it'll be the last I see some of you this year, to wish you all a very happy new year.

Serbia

Q. Mr. President, have you warned the Serbs not to widen the war?

The President. Well, I don't want to get into what we're doing in terms of detail there, but we've expressed our concern in a lot of different ways, Helen [Helen Thomas, United Press International]. And I don't want to go into more detail on that one.

Somalia

Q. Sir, is it safe for you to go to Somalia?

The President. Yes, it's perfectly safe. I'm not in the least bit concerned of the security. I have great confidence in our military and in, certainly, as always, in the Secret Service. So no, there's not a worry in the world on that.

START II

Q. Do you worry about whether START II could actually be approved, both in the U.S. Congress and can President Yeltsin get START II approval?

The President. No, I feel confident after talking to Larry Eagleburger, representations having been made by his interlocutors there, both their Defense Secretary and their Foreign Minister, that that will be approved. Boris Yeltsin is quite confident of that. He feels that it is a historic agreement and good for the whole world, as do I. I believe that our Congress will approve it. And of course, I've been appreciative of the words of—without committing him on any way to any details—the general words from Governor Clinton, President-elect Clinton, on this subject.

Q. Mr. President, do you view START II as a vindication of your attention to the foreign account?

The President. No, I view it as a great step for mankind. And it's not—certainly it's not a personal achievement. The people standing here with me have worked hours, endless hours, to bring this about. So it's not personal. But I take great pride in this accomplishment because I think it's a very good treaty, and I'm proud that this team was able to work it out.

POW–MIA's

Q. Are you going to ask Yeltsin to unleash more information about the American POW's situation?

The President. Well, I am confident that Boris Yeltsin will go the extra mile on that. I think he has. But we just have to wait and see on that subject because all of us remain concerned about it. But I should express my confidence in his willingness to cooperate. I don't think anyone would disagree with that at all.

I think I've got to get ready to go to Somalia. Last one.

Executive Clemency

Q. Mr. President, on the Christmas Eve pardons, does it give the appearance that Government officials are above the law?

The President. No, it should not give any such appearance. Nobody is above the law. I believe when people break the law, that's a bad thing. I've read some stupid comment to the contrary. And of course, I feel that way. But the Constitution is quite clear on the powers of the President. And sometimes a President has to make a very difficult call, and that's what I've done.

But I'm glad you asked it, because I've read some rather frivolous reporting that I don't care about the law. I pride myself on 25 or more years of public service, of serving honorably, decently, and with my integrity intact. And certainly I wouldn't feel that way if I had a lack of respect for the law. And I don't think there is one single thing in my career that could lead anybody to look at my record and make a statement of that nature. So thank you for giving me the opportunity to clear it up.

Thank you all.

Note: The President spoke at 9:45 a.m. in the Rose Garden at the White House. The proclamation of December 24 which granted Executive clemency to six former Government officials for their conduct related to the Iran-contra affair is listed in Appendix E at the end of this volume.

Statement by Press Secretary Fitzwater on the Iran-*Contra* Investigation
December 30, 1992

On December 14, President Bush asked the Independent Counsel to supply him with a copy of his deposition of January 11, 1988, given in connection with the Iran-*contra* investigation. On December 18, the Independent Counsel wrote President Bush a letter stating that his office was considering the request. The Independent Counsel assured the President that his office would "try to comply."

Yesterday, however, the Deputy Independent Counsel informed the White House that the Independent Counsel had decided not to provide President Bush with a copy of the deposition at this time. President Bush has therefore asked former Attorney General Griffin Bell to assist him in seeking to obtain for public release a copy of this document. Judge Bell will also assume full responsibility for advising the

President should the Independent Counsel fail to complete his investigation during the President's term in office.

Judge Bell was appointed by President Kennedy to the U.S. Circuit Court of Appeals for the Fifth Circuit, on which he served from 1961 to 1976. He served as President Carter's Attorney General from 1977 to 1979. He also served as Vice Chair-

man of President Bush's Commission on Federal Ethics Law Reform in 1989. Judge Bell is presently a partner in the law firm of King & Spalding.

The President hopes that Judge Bell's efforts will further his goal of putting his sworn testimony about the Iran-*contra* matter before the American people.

Letter to Congressional Leaders Transmitting a Report on Tariff Modifications on Canadian Plywood
December 30, 1992

Dear Mr. Chairman:

Pursuant to section 103 of the United States-Canada Free-Trade Agreement (CFTA) Implementation Act of 1988 (Public Law 100–449), I am pleased to submit the attached report and related documents pertaining to a proposed action to proceed with staged tariff reductions on certain plywood originating in Canada in accordance with the provisions of article 2008 of the CFTA, implementation of which had been delayed pending preparation and imple-

mentation of common performance standards into the building codes in the United States and Canada.

Sincerely,

GEORGE BUSH

Note: Identical letters were sent to Dan Rostenkowski, Chairman, House Committee on Ways and Means, and Lloyd Bentsen, Chairman, Senate Committee on Finance. The related proclamation is listed in Appendix E at the end of this volume.

Letter to Congressional Leaders Transmitting Budget Deferrals
December 30, 1992

Dear Mr. Speaker: (Dear Mr. President:)

In accordance with the Congressional Budget and Impoundment Control Act of 1974, I herewith report three revised and two new deferrals of budget authority, totaling $3.7 billion.

These deferrals affect International Security Assistance programs and the Departments of Agriculture and State. The details of these deferrals are contained in the at-

tached report.

Sincerely,

GEORGE BUSH

Note: Identical letters were sent to Thomas S. Foley, Speaker of the House of Representatives, and Dan Quayle, President of the Senate. The report detailing the deferrals was published in the Federal Register on January 8, 1993.

Letter to Congressional Leaders Reporting on Economic Sanctions Against Libya
December 30, 1992

Dear Mr. Speaker: *(Dear Mr. President:)*

I hereby report to the Congress on the developments since my last report of July 7, 1992, concerning the national emergency with respect to Libya that was declared in Executive Order No. 12543 of January 7, 1986. This report is submitted pursuant to section 401(c) of the National Emergencies Act, 50 U.S.C. 1641(c); section 204(c) of the International Emergency Economic Powers Act ("IEEPA"), 50 U.S.C. 1703(c); and section 505(c) of the International Security and Development Cooperation Act of 1985, 22 U.S.C. 2349aa–9(c).

1. Since my last report on July 7, 1992, the Libyan Sanctions Regulations (the "Regulations"), 31 C.F.R. Part 550, administered by the Office of Foreign Assets Control ("FAC") of the Department of the Treasury have been amended twice. The first amendment, published on September 11, 1992, 57 *Fed. Reg.* 41696, revoked (1) the authority in section 550.511 for transfers between blocked accounts in different domestic banking institutions and (2) section 550.515, which authorized receipt of payments from unblocked sources for obligations of the Government of Libya to persons in the United States. These classes of transactions are now prohibited unless specifically licensed by FAC. In addition, the amendment required banking institutions to pay interest on blocked funds and authorized debits to blocked accounts by U.S. banking institutions for normal service charges. A copy of the amendment is attached to this report.

Section 550.511 of the Regulations previously permitted transfers of funds between blocked accounts in different domestic banking institutions, provided the name or designation of the accounts remained identical. Out of concern for possible abuse of such funds movements, future transfers of this nature may only be authorized by specific license.

Section 550.515 of the Regulations had previously authorized the transfer of fresh funds through or to any banking institution or other person within the United States solely for purposes of payment of obligations owed by the Libyan government to persons within the United States. "Fresh funds" are funds from an unblocked account outside the United States. To ensure that transfers from the Libyan government are received only for obligations lawfully arising within the context of the Libyan Sanctions Regulations, such payments must now be authorized by specific license.

Another amendment, published on November 17, 1992, 57 *Fed. Reg.* 54176, added the names of six companies and banks to Appendix A, the list of organizations determined to be within the term "Government of Libya" (Specially Designated Nationals of Libya), revised the information for one company previously listed at Appendix A, and added the names of five individuals to Appendix B, the list of individuals determined to be Specially Designated Nationals of Libya. A Specially Designated National ("SDN") of Libya is an entity or individual that is owned or controlled by the Government of Libya or that engages in transactions directly or indirectly on behalf of the Libyan government. A copy of the amendment is attached to this report.

The most significant of these designations is the listing of a bank in the United Arab Emirates, the Arab Bank for Investment and Foreign Trade, also known as "ARBIFT," which has been identified by FAC as an institution that engages in U.S. dollar clearing transactions on behalf of the Government of Libya. The ARBIFT is held 42 percent by the Libyan Arab Foreign Bank, another SDN of Libya, while ARBIFT's chairman also serves as the Governor of the Central Bank of Libya. Two other Libyan-controlled banks, two Libyan-owned petroleum marketing firms, and an insurance company controlled by Libya also were added to the Libyan SDN list. All five of the individuals named to the SDN list are senior Libyan banking officials who act on behalf of the Government of Libya.

2. During the current 6-month period, FAC made numerous decisions with respect to applications for licenses to engage in transactions under the Regulations, issuing 81 licensing determinations—both approvals and denials. Consistent with FAC's ongoing scrutiny of banking transactions, the majority of the determinations (70) concerned requests to unblock bank accounts initially blocked because of an apparent Libyan interest. An additional seven determinations involved license applications for export sales transactions from the United States to Libya. Finally, four determinations concerned registration of individuals pursuant to a general license authorizing travel to Libya for the sole purpose of visiting close family members.

FAC has participated actively on the Operating Committee of the Department of Commerce to coordinate review by State, Defense, Energy, and Commerce of certain reexport applications, including those where Libya is the new destination for goods. In addition to providing guidance on such reexport applications, FAC has identified attempted illegal transactions involving exportation of parts to Libyan SDNs and continues to work closely with the Department of Commerce to assure compliance with the Regulations.

3. Various enforcement actions mentioned in previous reports continue to be pursued, and several new investigations of possibly significant violations of the Libyan sanctions were initiated. As a result of such initiatives, the amount of Government of Libya assets blocked in U.S. banking institutions has risen to more than $818,218,440.

During the current reporting period, substantial monetary penalties were assessed against U.S. firms for engaging in prohibited transactions with Libya. Since my last report, FAC has collected nearly $560,000 in civil penalties for violations of U.S. sanctions against Libya. The majority of the violations involved banks' failure to block funds transfers to Libyan-owned or -controlled banks.

Due to aggressive enforcement efforts and increased public awareness, FAC has received numerous voluntary disclosures from U.S. firms concerning their sanctions

violations. Many of these reports continue to be triggered by the periodic amendments to the Regulations listing additional organizations and individuals determined to be Specially Designated Nationals ("SDNs") of Libya. For purposes of the Regulations, all dealings with the organizations and individuals listed will be considered dealings with the Government of Libya. All unlicensed transactions with these persons, or in property in which they have an interest, are prohibited. The listing of Libyan SDNs is not static and will be augmented from time to time as additional organizations or individuals owned or controlled by, or acting on behalf of, the Government of Libya are identified.

In March 1992, FAC announced a new law enforcement initiative, Operation Roadblock, which targets U.S. travellers who violate the U.S. sanctions on Libya. Under this initiative, FAC has issued more than 100 warning letters and demands for information to persons believed to have travelled to and worked in Libya, or made travel-related payments to Libya in violation of U.S. law. FAC's investigation of suspected violations is ongoing, assisted by an interagency task force including the Departments of State and Justice, the Treasury Department's Financial Crimes Enforcement Network (FinCEN), the Federal Bureau of Investigation, and the U.S. Customs Service.

4. The expenses incurred by the Federal Government in the 6-month period from June 15 through December 15, 1992, that are directly attributable to the exercise of powers and authorities conferred by the declaration of the Libyan national emergency are estimated at approximately $1.8 million. Personnel costs were largely centered in the Department of the Treasury (particularly in the Office of Foreign Assets Control, the Office of the General Counsel, and the U.S. Customs Service), the Department of State, and the Department of Commerce.

5. The policies and actions of the Government of Libya continue to pose an unusual and extraordinary threat to the national security and foreign policy of the United States. I shall continue to exercise the powers at my disposal to apply economic

sanctions against Libya fully and effectively, so long as those measures are appropriate, and will continue to report periodically to the Congress on significant developments as required by law.

Sincerely,

GEORGE BUSH

Note: Identical letters were sent to Thomas S. Foley, Speaker of the House of Representatives, and Dan Quayle, President of the Senate.

Memorandum on Delegations of Authority Concerning Former Soviet Republics
December 30, 1992

Memorandum for the Secretary of State, the Secretary of Defense, the Director, Office of Management and Budget

Subject: Delegation of Responsibilities under Title XIV of Public Law 102–484 and Title V of Public Law 102–511

By the authority vested in me by the Constitution and the laws of the United States of America, including section 301 of title 3 of the United States Code, I hereby delegate:

1. to the Secretary of State the authority and duty vested in the President under section 1412(d) of the Former Soviet Union Demilitarization Act of 1992 (title XIV of the National Defense Authorization Act for Fiscal Year 1993, Public Law 102–484) and section 502 of the Freedom Support Act (Public Law 102–511).

2. to the Secretary of Defense the authorities and duties vested in the President under sections 1412(a), 1431, and 1432 of Public Law 102–484 and sections 503 and 508 of Public Law 102–511.

The Secretary of Defense shall not exercise authority delegated by paragraph 2 hereof with respect to any former Soviet republic unless the Secretary of State has exercised his authority and performed the duty delegated by paragraph 1 hereof with respect to that former Soviet Republic. The Secretary of Defense shall not obligate funds in the exercise of authority delegated by paragraph 2 hereof unless the Director of the Office of Management and Budget has determined that expenditures during fiscal year 1993 pursuant to such obligation shall be counted against the defense category of discretionary spending limits for that fiscal year (as defined in section 601(a)(2) of the Congressional Budget Act of 1974) for purposes of Part C of the Balanced Budget and Emergency Deficit Control Act of 1985.

The Secretary of State is directed to publish this memorandum in the *Federal Register.*

GEORGE BUSH

[Filed with the Office of the Federal Register, 4:34 p.m., January 6, 1993]

Recess Appointment of Stephen T. Hart as an Assistant Secretary of Transportation
December 30, 1992

The President has recess-appointed Stephen T. Hart, of Virginia, to be an Assistant Secretary of Transportation for Public Affairs. He would succeed Marion Clifton Blakey.

Currently Mr. Hart serves as Deputy Assistant Secretary for Industry Affairs and Public Liaison at the U.S. Department of Transportation. Prior to this he served as Deputy Assistant to the President and Director of the Office of Legislative Affairs, 1991–92. He has also served as a Special Assistant to the President and Deputy Press Secretary, 1989–91; Assistant to the Vice President for Press Relations, 1987–89; and Assistant Press Secretary for Foreign Affairs for the Vice President's Office, 1985–87.

Mr. Hart graduated from George Washington University (B.A., 1982). He was born September 22, 1957, in Pasadena, CA.

Statement by Press Secretary Fitzwater on Recognition of the Czech and Slovak Republics
January 1, 1993

The President today recognized the new Czech and Slovak Republics and offered to establish full diplomatic relations. In an exchange of letters, Czech Prime Minister Klaus and Slovak Prime Minister Meciar welcomed U.S. recognition and accepted our offer of full diplomatic relations.

Both leaders provided assurances that the new states will fulfill the obligations and commitments of the former Czechoslovakia and will abide by the principles and provisions of the U.N. Charter, the Charter of Paris, the Helsinki Final Act and subsequent CSCE documents. They also pledged to prevent the proliferation of destabilizing military technology, to respect human rights and fundamental freedoms, to uphold international standards concerning national minorities, and to move rapidly to create free-market economies.

The United States looks forward to full and mutually productive relations with the new Czech and Slovak states. We commend both Republics for the peaceful means by which their separation was carried out. In the interest of ensuring stability and prosperity in the region and speeding full integration into the international community, the United States urges continued close regional cooperation among the states of central Europe.

Our Ambassador to Czechoslovakia will remain in Prague as the U.S. Ambassador to the Czech Republic. We look forward to appointing an Ambassador to the Slovak Republic as soon as possible.

Remarks at a State Dinner Hosted by President Boris Yeltsin of Russia in Moscow
January 2, 1993

President Yeltsin and members of the Russian Government, friends, all, Americans and Russians, we are here for an historic occasion. I believe that this is a moment that history will record most positively as we sign that treaty. As I prepare to leave the Presidency, I bid farewell to a man for whom I have enormous respect, a man whose courage captured the imagination of every single American as he stood on a Russian tank and straddled Russian history, steering it toward a democratic future. His voice spoke loudly for freedom through the chaos of change, and it spoke softly of friendship through the static of a long distance telephone line, a patriot who silenced the guns of August, President Boris Yeltsin.

Mr. President, as you so eloquently stated, there is now a new U.S.-Russian partnership built together, affirming our dedication to a democratic peace in Europe and, indeed, to a global peace. The two powers that once divided the world have now come together to make it a better and safer place. Mr. President, we've come together again this weekend amid a Moscow winter to sign the most significant arms reduction treaty ever.

All of us, sir, wish you and your colleagues well on the bold reforms that you've undertaken. Reform is never easy, and this we understand. But your people do not run away from a challenge. And in this challenge, America will stay with you, shoulder to shoulder.

May I simply say a word about my successor, President-elect Clinton. I am confident that what we do tomorrow is of tremendous importance to him, and I am confident that you will find him a 100-percent partner in working for this U.S.-Russian relationship that we treasure so much.

I salute everybody in this room and elsewhere who had a hand in completing this historic treaty. I raise my glass to toast a strong future between Russia and the United States, to toast President and Mrs. Yeltsin, dear friends, and to toast this new year, a new year of hope, freedom, and peace for the Russian people.

Good luck and may God bless you all.

Note: The President spoke at approximately 7:05 p.m. in the Winter Garden Room at the Kremlin. A tape was not available for verification of the content of these remarks.

The President's News Conference With President Boris Yeltsin of Russia in Moscow
January 3, 1993

Mr. Kostikov. Ladies and gentlemen, let us consider that the press conference is open.

First, we'll give the floor to the Presidents of Russia and the United States for brief statements, and then we'll hold our press conference. The first floor is to President Yeltsin.

START II Treaty

President Yeltsin. President George Bush, Mrs. Bush, members of the delegations, representatives of mass media, ladies and gentlemen:

It is not every century that history gives us an opportunity to witness and participate in the event that is so significant in scale and consequences. Today, the Presidents of the two great powers, the United States and Russia, have signed the treaty on further radical cuts in strategic offensive arms of Russia and the United States, START II.

In its scale and importance, the treaty

goes further than all other treaties ever signed in the field of disarmament. This treaty is the triumph for politicians and diplomats of Russia and the United States. It is also an achievement for all mankind and benefits all peoples of the Earth. The START II treaty becomes the core of the system of global security guarantees.

The scale of this treaty is determined by a number of factors. Its historical factor is that in the course of all its previous history, mankind was arming itself and just dreamed of beating the swords into plowshares. The treaty signed today represents a major step towards fulfilling mankind's centuries-old dream of disarmament.

Its political factor is that the treaty we have signed today belongs to a new epoch. This treaty was concluded by two friendly states, by partners who not only trust each other but also assist each other. It testifies to our joint and determined movement towards a new world order.

From the very outset the new democratic Russian state has been pursuing a policy of building equal partnership with the United States. Today, we have every right to say that relations between the two major powers have undergone a genuine revolution. Its political factor lies also in the fact that during the last decade of the 20th century and at the turn of the 21st century, the START II treaty will affect policies not only of the United States and Russia but of other countries of the world as well. The START II treaty established parameters of possible political agreements in other spheres of interaction among states.

Thus, the military factor is determined by the scale of mutual reductions in nuclear arms. By comparison with the START I Treaty, every state will have to reduce and destroy the number of strategic offensive warheads by approximately a threefold magnitude. The deepest cuts will affect those categories of arms which are of greatest concern to the parties and the world. For the United States these are submarine-launched ballistic missiles and heavy bombers, and for Russia, land-based intercontinental ballistic missiles, ICBM's. This reduces drastically the level of danger, military mistrust, and suspicion.

We opened up real prospects for cooperation based on trust between people in military uniform, between people with military discipline and military thinking. Thus, the START II treaty will change and gradually replace the very psychology of confrontation.

At the same time, as President and supreme commander in chief, I can say with absolute certainty the signed treaty strengthens the security of Russia rather than weakens it. I think that President Bush can make a similar statement concerning the security of the United States.

The implementation of the new treaty will not be economically destructive for Russia. We have made most of our calculations, and they show that the proposed reductions would cost us much less than the mere maintenance of nuclear weapon systems in a safe condition. We save seriously on verification and inspections, two of the most expensive, to put it mildly, items of expenditures. The new character of Russian-U.S. relations makes it possible for us to substantially simplify verification procedures while ensuring their reliability.

We expect to cut and to cut considerably the cost of the physical destruction of armaments. We have agreed with the United States to cooperate in developing and applying appropriate technologies. Thus, the expenditures under this then will in fact be shared equally. This will enable us to eliminate our nuclear weapons not with a delay of several years but in parallel with the United States in accordance with the schedule provided for in the treaty. In the context of the present economic crisis, it would be difficult for us to keep the pace without outside assistance. The U.S. Congress has made a decision to support Russia in the destruction of these nuclear warheads.

Its moral factor will manifest itself in the fact that the treaty gives all mankind the hope for a nuclear-weapons-free world. The high moral value of the treaty is that we will be able to hand over to our children, the children of the 21st century, a more secure world. I would call this treaty a treaty of hope.

As to the purely diplomatic aspect of this START II treaty that has just been signed, it will undoubtedly go down into the history of diplomacy as an example of using the potential of the partners who are waiting to overcome the heritage of animosity and confrontation. As you may recall, it took 15 years to prepare the first START Treaty. The elaboration of START II, which is of considerably great magnitude, took several months. But there was absolutely no rush in the process. Naturally this reflects, above all, the high level of confidence and mutual understanding achieved between the United States and Russia, between the Presidents of the two countries. It gives great impetus to the world diplomacy as well.

Today, I would like to express the hope that the diplomatic services of the United States and Russia, diplomats of European countries, will double or even triple their efforts in order to settle conflicts that are of concern to the world.

I would like to focus on another important aspect, the personal stand of President George Bush, who is our guest, being on a working visit with us. I would like to pay tribute to my colleague and friend, George. His remarkable personal and political qualities and competence have contributed to a successful transition from the cold war to a new world order. I am grateful to him for all he has done to establish new relations between Russia and the United States, for his solidarity and support during the push for the FREEDOM Support Act, for the START II treaty. Thank you, George.

I consider it of fundamental importance that the future President of the United States, Mr. Clinton, fully supported the conclusion of the START II treaty. We can without delay proceed to the direct implementation of this instrument and consider further steps to strengthen global stability, the system of global protection, and international security.

President Bush and I have maintained regular contacts with President-elect Clinton. Today's signing ceremony would not have taken place had there been the slightest reason to doubt his solidarity with our endeavors.

I would like to personally thank the most active participants in this process and above all the President of the United States, who personally took part in the elaboration and polishing of the text of the treaty. And I would say we spoke often. And it was a rare week that we did not speak on the phone in the last few weeks.

I am also grateful personally to Mr. Scowcroft, who took an active participation in the consideration of this subject, and to Jimmy Baker, of course, who treated globally the entire subject of the treaty and was mainly responsible for this breakthrough. And finally, I am grateful to Mr. Eagleburger, who on the finishing line darted with boldness and practically initialed the draft treaty there.

I'm thankful also to the experts, to analysts and consultants, and also to the leaders of our delegation, to Mr. Kozyrev and Grachev and the other 48 experts who work very hard for us to come today to the signing of this treaty, the SALT II [1] treaty.

I'm also grateful to all the journalists, press people, who kept their hand constantly on the pulse of this subject and who did not manage to criticize the treaty before it was signed.

I do believe that there is no reasonable alternative to the policy of friendly partnership between Russia and the United States. Strategic partnership relations serve the fundamental national interests of the two countries and of the international community as a whole. I am deeply confident that the signing of the START II treaty opens new, promising prospects for the peoples of our countries. I'm certain that this day will be a milestone in this process.

Thank you.

Mr. Kostikov. I thank you. And now I pass the floor to the President of the United States, George Bush.

President Bush. Mr. President and Mr. Vice President, Mr. Prime Minister, Minister of Justice, Minister of Defense, Minister of Foreign Affairs, representatives of the Russian and American delegations, and distinguished guests:

We meet at the beginning of a new year, at a moment that is also a new era for our two nations and for the world. For half of this century, the Soviet Union and the United States stood locked in a nuclear

_____

[1] START II (White House correction).

standoff. For our two nations and for the world, cold war, hot words, and the constant threat of war seemed imminent, indeed, at times inevitable. The time that we might meet as friends and the time that we might meet in freedom seemed distant, indeed a dream.

Today, the cold war is over, and for the first time in history an American President has set foot in a democratic Russia. And together we're now embarked on what must be the noblest mission of all: to turn an adversarial relationship into one of friendship and partnership.

We stand together today in this great city at the threshold of a new world of hope, a widening circle of freedom for us and for our children. This historic opportunity would simply not have been possible without our combined common effort.

Mr. President, I salute you for your unwavering commitment to democratic reform and for the history you've written since the heroic day in August '91 when you climbed atop that tank to defend Russia's democratic destiny. And I also want to salute the heroism of the Russian people themselves, for it is they who will determine that Russia's democratic course is irreversible.

Today, as we meet on Russian soil, home to 1,000 years of heritage and history, to a people rich in scientific and creative talent, I want to assure the Russian people on behalf of all Americans, we understand that Russia faces a difficult passage. We are with you in your struggle to strengthen and secure democratic rights, to reform your economy, to bring to every Russian city and village a new sense of hope and the prospect of a future forever free.

Let me say clearly, we seek no special advantage from Russia's transformation. Yes, deep arms reductions, broader and deeper economic ties, expanded trade with Russia, all are in the interest of my country. But they're equally in the interest of the Russian people. Our future is one of mutual advantage.

We seek a new relationship of trust between our military forces. They once confronted each other across Europe's great divide, and let them now come together in the cause of peace. We seek full coopera-

tion to employ our collective capabilities to help resolve crises around the world. We seek a new cooperation between the U.S. and Russia and among all states to prevent the spread of nuclear weapons and other weapons of mass destruction.

The world looks to us to consign the cold war to history, to ratify our new relationship by reducing the weapons that concentrate the most destructive power known to man. The treaty we signed today builds on the strong beginning we made with START I, and, together, these treaties will reduce by more than two-thirds the strategic arsenals in place today. And just as important, START II will bring much better stability to remaining forces.

This agreement represents a common effort to overcome the contentious differences and complexities that surround nuclear weapons. In the face of many who doubted Russia and America's intentions and our energy, it vindicates our insistence that arms control must do more than simply freeze the arms race in place.

The START Treaty, START I, reduced a quarter century of growth in our nuclear arsenals and reversed the course that caused many to fear that nuclear conflagration was inevitable. The treaty that we signed today goes much further in a way that few believed possible just one year ago.

May I congratulate Messrs. Kozyrev and Grachev and Eagleburger for their outstanding work to bring this treaty to fruition. And I also want to congratulate former Secretary of State Jim Baker for his important work on the treaty during the spring and summer.

In closing, let me tell you what this treaty means, not for Presidents or Premiers, not for historians or heads of state but for parents and for their children: It means a future far more free from fear.

So, as we sign today this treaty, let us pledge also to move forward together throughout this decade and into the next century toward common aims: for Russia, a democratic peace; for our two nations, a strong partnership between our people and the lasting friendship that springs from a common love of freedom.

And Mr. President, may I wish you and

the Russian people at this critical moment in history a new year rich with hope and peace.

Bosnia

Q. Mr. President, both of you, each of you spoke about moving on to other areas of concern as a result of having achieved this kind of a treaty. Can you give us in some detail what your discussions were with regard to the situation in Bosnia, what you see achievable there and what differences separate you?

President Bush. Well, we discussed that question in some detail. Our prime common objective is to see the suffering stop and see the fighting stop. I can't go into—I certainly wouldn't want to quantify what differences we may have, but I came away with the feeling that we were very close together, these two countries, in wanting to see peace restored to that area.

President Yeltsin. I would like to continue the answer of President Bush, because the question was raised to both Presidents. We discussed a very wide range of issues, and I would say we have cleaned up all of the problems remaining after the conclusion of this important agreement, and the conclusion of this important period which is crowned with an historic event and the visit by President Bush to our country.

We also considered the course of the reforms in Russia and the problems related to the new government, whether it will continue along the road of reforms. And I assured the President that this is not a new government, and it is the old composition government. And the chairman of the government himself will go on the same road of reforms.

We have also considered the problems of bilateral relations and the foreign debt of the former Soviet Union, the grain supplies, international conflicts, including the conflict in the former Yugoslavia, and our positions are close. We previously supported the United States in adopting the U.N. resolution on the subject, and we shall continue this line and try at the same time to continue the line for establishing peace among all parties and to be more active in this area than we have been heretofore.

We have also discussed military issues, in-

cluding the issue of whether the SALT II Treaty is harmful to anyone or at anyone's disadvantage. Then we came to the conclusion that it does not harm either side and does not harm any third party. It is only to the advantage of everyone. Thus, our negotiations were businesslike, respectful, and open, as always.

START II Ratification

Q. Boris Nikolayevich, you have just signed the START II treaty, and you will have to ratify it into Parliament. If in the past there were difficulties mainly in the U.S. Congress, now you may face certain difficulties on the part of certain delegates or a number of Russian deputies. So, what are in your view the prospects for the ratification of the treaty?

President Yeltsin. I am not going to conceal from you that a certain part of the deputies is against the treaty. And they are against anything positive that should take place in Russia. So, complete negation is their position. You could consider what they are, because they support Iraq and its aggression. So you understand who they represent. And finally, I would say that fortunately they do not represent the majority of the Supreme Soviet, as most of the Supreme Soviet deputies believe in reason, and of course, they believe in the significance of this treaty.

Many delegates, deputies, were in Geneva themselves. They took part in the negotiations. And the chairman of the Foreign Relations Committee has always been here with us. So if there are any difficulties with the ratification of this START II treaty, still I am certain that the Supreme Soviet will ratify it.

President-Elect Clinton

Q. Mr. President, how confident are you that the treaty that you're now going to be turning over to a new administration will be—that it will be ratified by the Senate? And Mr. Yeltsin, I'd like to know your thoughts on how awkward is it for you to find yourself suddenly having to deal with a new President in Washington?

President Bush. Clearly, I'm not in a position to commit President-elect Clinton, but

I can confidently predict that this treaty will be quickly ratified by the Congress.

Butting in on the second part of your question, I've talked to President-elect Clinton enough to know that he is most interested in keeping this U.S.-Russia relationship on the high plane at which it stands right now. And I've told President Yeltsin that I think he will enjoy working with Governor Clinton and that I know that Governor Clinton is committed to the general theory of these arms reductions that START II takes on.

President Yeltsin. I met with President-elect Clinton when I was on my official state visit to the United States and when Mr. Clinton at that time was a Presidential candidate. We discussed in our meetings different things. The discussions were normal, interesting, and he voiced his support for Russia, for the democratic reforms in Russia, and for our movement along the democratic road.

Two days ago I sent him a letter where I proposed that there should be no lull in our relations with the new administration, because any lull in bilateral relations between the superpowers would give cause for concern.

I suggested on the phone to President Bush that after the 20th of January, we—that is, myself and President-elect Clinton—should meet somewhere in a neutral place for a working meeting to consider different international problems and bilateral relations. And I hope that he will take over the baton that was given to him with such grace by President Bush.

Russian Nuclear Shield

Q. This is the question to, mainly, the Russian President. I ask you, Boris Nikolayevich, to expand a little bit on that part of your statement where you say that the signing of the treaty will not be harmful to the strategic and military balance existing between the United States and Russia, as certain of our conservatives assert, and that the nuclear shield of Russia will not be weakened. This is a question to you not only to the President of the country but also as to the commander in chief.

President Yeltsin. Shall I give you the numbers? As of January 1st, we have 9,915 strategic nuclear warheads. According to the new START II treaty, there will be 3,000, 3,500 warheads left, 3,000 to 3,500 warheads. This number is not possessed by any other single state, only by the United States and Russia. I express—not a single other state, including nuclear powers like China, Great Britain, and France. This is a powerful shield which is capable of defending Russia in case of an unexpected aggression from any site.

President Bush. May I simply add that we do not view this as a one-sided treaty at all. We view it as balanced, and I think that history will record it as such.

Mr. Fitzwater. Let's have a final question from Ann Compton [ABC News].

U.S. Assistance to Russia

Q. President Bush, do you think that the START II—START I and II can be ratified and implemented if the United States doesn't come forward with or even increase the amount of aid that some of the other countries need to actually dismantle the weapons they've got?

President Bush. I think the ratification will stand on its own two feet. The Congress will look at it, and in my view they'll have hearings, and they'll ratify it. And clearly, we all have a stake at helping and being sure that the materials are properly disposed of, and the United States will be ready to assist to the best of our ability. But I don't see a resolution to that second question being required before this treaty is ratified.

I'm sorry, what was the second question?

Q. Can it be implemented? Doesn't the United States have to come up with more money to actually have the missiles at the silos?

President Bush. The treaty and the protocols speak for themselves. But clearly, I think the new administration will be as interested as we have been in helping Russia in every way we possibly can. I expect that it'll get to that subject as well as it will to ag credits and a lot of other things. So I think that the treaty will be ratified, and I think it will be implemented. And to the degree the United States can be of assistance when times are tough for Russia, that will demonstrate our interest in this partnership when we help.

Note: The President's 141st news conference began at 12:15 p.m. in Vladimir's Hall at the Kremlin. President Yeltsin spoke in Russian, and his remarks were translated by an interpreter. Vyacheslav Kostikov, Presidential Press Spokesman for President Yeltsin, *served as moderator. During the news conference, the following persons were referred to: Andrey Kozyrev, Russian Minister of Foreign Affairs, and Pavel Grachev, Russian Minister of Defense. The question-and-answer portion of this news conference could not be verified because the tape was incomplete.*

Recess Appointment of Gregory Stewart Walden as a Member of the Interstate Commerce Commission
January 4, 1993

The President today announced the recess appointment of Gregory Stewart Walden, of California, to be a member of the Interstate Commerce Commission. Mr. Walden would succeed Edward Martin Emmett.

Since 1990 Mr. Walden has served as an Associate Counsel to the President at the White House. Prior to this, he was Chief Counsel of the Federal Aviation Administration at the Department of Transportation,

1988–90. Mr. Walden has served in various capacities at the Department of Justice including: Associate Deputy Attorney General, 1987–88; Deputy Associate Attorney General, 1986–87; Special Assistant to the Assistant Attorney General in the Civil Division.

Mr. Walden graduated from Washington and Lee University (B.A., 1977) and the University of San Diego (J.D., 1980). He currently resides in Alexandria, VA.

Remarks at the United States Military Academy in West Point, New York
January 5, 1993

Thank you all very much. Good luck. Please be seated. Thank you, General Graves, for that very kind introduction. Barbara and I are just delighted to be here and honored that we could be joined by our able Secretary of the Army, Mike Stone; of course, the man well-known here that heads our Army, General Sullivan, General Gordon Sullivan; and Gracie Graves, General Robert Foley, General Galloway; Shawn Daniel, well-known to everybody here, been our host, in a sense; and a West Point alum who has been at my side for 4 years, over here somewhere, General Scowcroft, graduate of this great institution who served his country with such distinction. May I salute the members of the Board of

Visitors. I see another I have to single out, General Galvin, who served his country with such honor. And, of course, save the best for last, the Corps of Cadets, thank you for that welcome.

Let me begin with the hard part: It is difficult for a Navy person to come up to West Point after that game a month ago. Go ahead, rub it in. [*Laughter*] But I watched it. Amazing things can happen in sports. Look at the Oilers, my other team that took it on the chin the other day. [*Laughter*]

But I guess the moral of all of this is that losing is never easy. Trust me, I know something about that. [*Laughter*] But if you have to lose, that's the way to do it: Fight with all you have. Give it your best shot. And win or lose, learn from it, and get on with life.

I am about to get on with the rest of my life. But before I do, I want to share with you at this institution of leadership some of my thinking, both about the world you will soon be called upon to enter and the life that you have chosen.

Any President has several functions. He speaks for and to the Nation. He must faithfully execute the law. And he must lead. But no function, none of the President's hats, in my view, is more important than his role as Commander in Chief. For it is as Commander in Chief that the President confronts and makes decisions that one way or another affects the lives of everyone in this country as well as many others around the world.

I have had many occasions to don this most important of hats. Over the past 4 years, the men and women who proudly and bravely wear the uniforms of the U.S. armed services have been called upon to go in harm's way and have discharged their duty with honor and professionalism.

I wish I could say that such demands were a thing of the past, that with the end of the cold war the calls upon the United States would diminish. I cannot. Yes, the end of the cold war, we would all concede, is a blessing. It is a time of great promise. Democratic governments have never been so numerous. What happened 2 or 3 days ago in Moscow would not have been possible in the cold war days. Thanks to historic treaties such as that START II pact just reached with Russia, the likelihood of nuclear holocaust is vastly diminished.

But this does not mean that there is no specter of war, no threats to be reckoned with. And already, we see disturbing signs of what this new world could become if we are passive and aloof. We would risk the emergence of a world characterized by violence, characterized by chaos, one in which dictators and tyrants threaten their neighbors, build arsenals brimming with weapons of mass destruction, and ignore the welfare of their own men, women, and children. And we could see a horrible increase in international terrorism, with American citizens more at risk than ever before.

We cannot and we need not allow this to happen. Our objective must be to exploit the unparalleled opportunity presented by the cold war's end to work toward transforming this new world into a new world order, one of governments that are democratic, tolerant, and economically free at home and committed abroad to settling inevitable differences peacefully, without the threat or use of force.

Unfortunately, not everyone subscribes to these principles. We continue to see leaders bent on denying fundamental human rights and seizing territory regardless of the human cost. No, an international society, one more attuned to the enduring principles that have made this country a beacon of hope for so many for so long, will not just emerge on its own. It's got to be built.

Two hundred years ago, another departing President warned of the dangers of what he described as "entangling alliances." His was the right course for a new nation at that point in history. But what was "entangling" in Washington's day is now essential. This is why, at Texas A&M a few weeks ago, I spoke of the folly of isolationism and of the importance, morally, economically, and strategically, of the United States remaining involved in world affairs. We must engage ourselves if a new world order, one more compatible with our values and congenial to our interest, is to emerge. But even more, we must lead.

Leadership, well, it takes many forms. It can be political or diplomatic. It can be economic or military. It can be moral or spiritual leadership. Leadership can take any one of these forms, or it can be a combination of them.

Leadership should not be confused with either unilateralism or universalism. We need not respond by ourselves to each and every outrage of violence. The fact that America can act does not mean that it must. A nation's sense of idealism need not be at odds with its interests, nor does principle displace prudence.

No, the United States should not seek to be the world's policeman. There is no support abroad or at home for us to play this role, nor should there be. We would exhaust ourselves in the process, wasting precious resources needed to address those problems at home and abroad that we cannot afford to ignore.

But in the wake of the cold war, in a world where we are the only remaining superpower, it is the role of the United States to marshal its moral and material resources to promote a democratic peace. It is our responsibility, it is our opportunity to lead. There is no one else.

Leadership cannot be simply asserted or demanded. It must be demonstrated. Leadership requires formulating worthy goals, persuading others of their virtue, and contributing one's share of the common effort and then some. Leadership takes time. It takes patience. It takes work.

Some of this work must take place here at home. Congress does have a constitutional role to play. Leadership therefore also involves working with the Congress and the American people to provide the essential domestic underpinning if U.S. military commitments are to be sustainable.

This is what our administration, the Bush administration, has tried to do. When Saddam Hussein invaded Kuwait, it was the United States that galvanized the U.N. Security Council to act and then mobilized the successful coalition on the battlefield. The pattern not exactly the same but similar in Somalia: First the United States underscored the importance of alleviating the growing tragedy, and then we organized humanitarian efforts designed to bring hope, food, and peace.

At times, real leadership requires a willingness to use military force. And force can be a useful backdrop to diplomacy, a complement to it, or, if need be, a temporary alternative.

As Commander in Chief, I have made the difficult choice to use military force. I determined we could not allow Saddam's forces to ravage Kuwait and hold this critical region at gunpoint. I thought then, and I think now, that using military force to implement the resolutions of the U.N. Security Council was in the interest of the United States and the world community. The need to use force arose as well in the wake of the Gulf war, when we came to the aid of the peoples of both northern and

southern Iraq. And more recently, as I'm sure you know, I determined that only the use of force could stem this human tragedy of Somalia.

The United States should not stand by with so many lives at stake and when a limited deployment of U.S. forces, buttressed by the forces of other countries and acting under the full authority of the United Nations, could make an immediate and dramatic difference, and do so without excessive levels of risk and cost. Operations Provide Comfort and Southern Watch in Iraq and then Operation Restore Hope in Somalia all bear witness to the wisdom of selected use of force for selective purposes.

Sometimes the decision not to use force, to stay our hand, I can tell you, it's just as difficult as the decision to send our soldiers into battle. The former Yugoslavia, well, it's been such a situation. There are, we all know, important humanitarian and strategic interests at stake there. But up to now it's not been clear that the application of limited amounts of force by the United States and its traditional friends and allies would have had the desired effect, given the nature and complexity of that situation.

Our assessment of the situation in the former Yugoslavia could well change if and as the situation changes. The stakes could grow; the conflict could threaten to spread. Indeed, we are constantly reassessing our options and are actively consulting with others about steps that might be taken to contain the fighting, protect the humanitarian effort, and deny Serbia the fruits of aggression.

Military force is never a tool to be used lightly or universally. In some circumstances it may be essential, in others counterproductive. I know that many people would like to find some formula, some easy formula to apply, to tell us with precision when and where to intervene with force. Anyone looking for scientific certitude is in for a disappointment. In the complex new world we are entering, there can be no single or simple set of fixed rules for using force. Inevitably, the question of military intervention requires judgment. Each and every case is unique. To adopt rigid criteria would guarantee mistakes involving American interests and American lives. And it would give would-be troublemakers a blueprint for determining their own actions. It could signal U.S. friends and allies that our support was not to be counted on.

Similarly, we cannot always decide in advance which interests will require our using military force to protect them. The relative importance of an interest is not a guide: Military force may not be the best way of safeguarding something vital, while using force might be the best way to protect an interest that qualifies as important but less than vital.

But to warn against a futile quest for a set of hard-and-fast rules to govern the use of military force is not to say there cannot be some principles to inform our decisions. Such guidelines can prove useful in sizing and, indeed, shaping our forces and in helping us to think our way through this key question.

Using military force makes sense as a policy where the stakes warrant, where and when force can be effective, where no other policies are likely to prove effective, where its application can be limited in scope and time, and where the potential benefits justify the potential costs and sacrifice.

Once we are satisfied that force makes sense, we must act with the maximum possible support. The United States can and should lead, but we will want to act in concert, where possible involving the United Nations or other multinational grouping. The United States can and should contribute to the common undertaking in a manner commensurate with our wealth, with our strength. But others should also contribute militarily, be it by providing combat or support forces, access to facilities or bases, or overflight rights. And similarly, others should contribute economically. It is unreasonable to expect the United States to bear the full financial burden of intervention when other nations have a stake in the outcome.

A desire for international support must not become a prerequisite for acting, though. Sometimes a great power has to act alone. I made a tough decision—I might say, on advice of our outstanding military leaders who are so well known to every-

body here—to use military force in Panama when American lives and the security of the Canal appeared to be threatened by outlaws who stole power in the face of free elections. And similarly, we moved swiftly to safeguard democracy in the Philippines.

But in every case involving the use of force, it will be essential to have a clear and achievable mission, a realistic plan for accomplishing the mission, and criteria no less realistic for withdrawing U.S. forces once the mission is complete. Only if we keep these principles in mind will the potential sacrifice be one that can be explained and justified. We must never forget that using force is not some political abstraction but a real commitment of our fathers and mothers and sons and daughters, brothers and sisters, friends and neighbors. You've got to look at it in human terms.

In order even to have the choice, we must have available adequate military forces tailored for a wide range of contingencies, including peacekeeping. Indeed, leading the effort toward a new world order will require a modern, capable military, in some areas necessitating more rather than less defense spending. As President, I have said that my ability to deploy force on behalf of U.S. interests abroad was made possible because past Presidents, and I would single out in particular my predecessor, Ronald Reagan, and past Secretaries of Defense sustained a strong military. Consistent with this sacred trust, I am proud to pass on to my successor, President-elect Clinton, a military second to none. We have the very best.

Yet, it is essential to recognize that as important as such factors are, any military is more than simply the sum of its weapons or the state of its technology. What makes any armed force truly effective is the quality of its leadership, the quality of its training, the quality of its people.

We have succeeded abroad in no small part because of our people in uniform. The men and women in our Armed Forces have demonstrated their ability to master the challenges of modern warfare. And at the same time, and whether on the battlefield of Iraq or in some tiny little village in Somalia, America's soldiers have always brought a quality of caring and kindness to their mission. Who will ever forget—I know I won't—those terrified Iraqi soldiers surrendering to American troops? And who will forget the way the American soldier held out his arms and said, "It's okay. You're all right now." Or in Somalia, the young marine, eyes filled with tears, holding the fragile arm of an emaciated child. There can be no doubt about it: The All Volunteer Force is one of the true success stories of modern day America.

It is instructive to look at just why this is so. At its heart, a voluntary military is based upon choice—you all know that—the decision freely taken by young men and women to join, the decision by more mature men and women to remain. And the institution of the Armed Forces has thrived on its commitment to developing and promoting excellence. It is meritocracy in action. Race, religion, wealth, background count not. Indeed, the military offers many examples for the rest of society, showing what can be done to eradicate the scourge of drugs, to break down the barriers of racial discrimination, to offer equal opportunity to women.

This is not just a result of self-selection. It also reflects the military's commitment to education and training. You know, people speak of defense conversion, the process by which the defense firms retool for civilian tasks. Well, defense conversion within the military has been going on for years. It is the constant process of training and retraining, which the military does so well, that allows individuals to keep up with the latest technology, take on more challenging assignments, and prepare for life on the outside.

Out of this culture of merit and competition have emerged hundreds of thousands of highly skilled men and women brimming with real self-confidence. What they possess is a special mix of discipline, a willingness to accept direction, and the confidence, a willingness to accept responsibility. Together, discipline and confidence provide the basis for winning, for getting the job done.

There is no higher calling, no more honorable choice than the one that you here today have made. To join the Armed Forces is to be prepared to make the ultimate sacrifice for your country and for your fellow man.

What you have done, what you are doing, sends an important message, one that I fear sometimes gets lost amidst today's often materialist, self-interested culture. It is important to remember, it is important to demonstrate that there is a higher purpose to life beyond one's self. Now, I speak of family, of community, of ideals. I speak of duty, honor, country.

There are many forms of contributing to this country, of public service. Yes, there is government. There is voluntarism. I love to talk about the thousand Points of Light, one American helping another. The daily tasks that require doing in our classrooms, in our hospitals, our cities, our farms, all can and do represent a form of service. In whatever form, service benefits our society, and it ennobles the giver. It is a cherished American concept, one we should continue to practice and pass on to our children.

This was what I wanted to share on this occasion. You are beginning your service to country, and I am nearing the end of mine. Exactly half a century ago, in June of 1942, as General Graves mentioned, we were at war, and I was graduating from school. The speaker that day at Andover was the then-Secretary of War, Henry Stimson. And his message was one of public service, but with a twist—on the importance of finishing one's schooling before going off to fight for one's country. I listened closely to what he had to say, but I didn't take his advice. And that day was my 18th birthday. And when the commencement ceremony ended, I went on into Boston and enlisted in the Navy as a seaman 2d class. And I never regretted it.

You, too, have signed up. You, too, will never regret it. And I salute you for it. Fortunately, because of the sacrifices made in years before and still being made, you should be able to complete this phase of your education.

A half century has passed since I left school to go into the service. A half century has passed since that day when Stimson spoke of the challenge of creating a new world. You will also be entering a new world, one far better than the one I came to know, a world with the potential to be far better yet. This is the challenge. This is the opportunity of your lifetimes. I envy you for it, and I wish you Godspeed. And while I'm at it, as your Commander in Chief, I hereby grant amnesty to the Corps of Cadets.

Thank you all very much. Thank you. Thank you very, very much. Good luck to all of you. Warm up here. Good luck to you guys. Thank you.

Note: The President spoke at 1:22 p.m. in

the Washington Mess Hall at the U.S. Military Academy. In his remarks, he referred to Lt. Gen. Howard D. Graves, USA, Superintendent of the Academy, and his wife, Gracie; Gen. Gordon R. Sullivan, USA, Chief of Staff of the Army; Brig. Gen. Robert Foley, USA, Commandant of the Academy; Brig. Gen. Gerald R. Galloway, USA, Dean of the Academy; Cadet Shawn Daniel, 1st Capt., U.S. Corps of Cadets; and Gen. John R. Galvin, USA, Ret., visiting professor in the Academy's department of social science.

Letter to Congressional Leaders Reporting on the Cyprus Conflict
January 5, 1993

Dear Mr. Speaker: (Dear Mr. Chairman:)

In accordance with Public Law 95–384 (22 U.S.C. 2373(c)), I am submitting to you this bimonthly report on progress toward a negotiated settlement of the Cyprus question. This report covers the months of September and October and, for the sake of continuity and completeness, the first 12 days of November 1992. Also, included with this report are the U.N. Secretary General's report on the October-November negotiating round and U.N. Security Council Resolution 789, which endorsed that report, both of which were issued in the latter half of November 1992.

Most of the September-October reporting period was taken up with preparations for the resumption of U.N.-sponsored Cyprus negotiations scheduled for October 26. During the second and third weeks of September, Ambassador Nelson Ledsky made his last trip to Cyprus, Greece, and Turkey before retiring September 30 and relinquishing his position as Special Cyprus Coordinator to Ambassador John Maresca. During his visit to the area, Ambassador Ledsky discussed the status and future of the negotiations with President Vassiliou of Cyprus, Turkish Cypriot Leader Rauf Denktash, Prime Minister Demirel of Turkey, and Prime Minister Mitsotakis of Greece.

During the third week of September, the first week of the 1992 Session of the United

Nations General Assembly, then Acting Secretary of State Lawrence Eagleburger met in New York with President Vassiliou, Greek Foreign Minister Papakonstantinou, and Turkish Foreign Minister Cetin. Ambassador Ledsky, accompanied by his designated successor, Ambassador John Maresca, had additional separate meetings with President Vassiliou, Foreign Ministers Papakonstantinou and Cetin, and representatives of the Turkish Cypriot community.

Ambassador Maresca traveled to Cyprus, Greece, and Turkey during the second and third weeks of October to do more preparatory work for the talks in New York that were scheduled to resume on October 26. During the same period, the U.N. Secretary General's representatives traveled to Cyprus, Greece, and Turkey to prepare for the talks.

Face-to-face meetings between President Vassiliou and Mr. Denktash under the chairmanship of the U.N. Secretary General resumed on October 28 in New York, a 2-day delay having been caused by problems related to the way titles of the two leaders were listed in the U.N. Secretariat daily agenda. Between October 28 and November 11, there were 10 joint meetings, during which the Secretary General recorded in detail the positions of the two parties on the U.N. "set of ideas" for a framework for a Cyprus settlement. (A copy of the "set of ideas" was appended to the Secretary General's report of August 21, 1992, which was provided with my last letter on this subject.)

Having noted the positions of the parties, the Secretary General prepared a "non-paper" setting out the essential elements of the positions of both sides, along with relevant parts of the "set of ideas" and U.N. resolutions. Both sides confirmed that their respective positions were accurately reflected in the Secretary General's "non-paper."

The Secretary General's report to the Security Council of November 19, 1992, on his good offices mission in Cyprus, which is attached, went into some detail on the positions of the two parties, and noted that in some areas the Turkish Cypriot side deviated from the U.N. "set of ideas." The Secretary General also noted that, although the Greek Cypriot side declared it accepted provisions of the "set of ideas," such declarations were frequently accompanied by provisos. He stated that these questions should be cleared up in a manner that does not deviate from the "set of ideas."

The Secretary General, in paragraph 59 of his report, indicated that intensive efforts had failed to produce an overall agreement, and he concluded that the lack of political will mentioned in his previous report "continues to block the conclusion of an agreement that is otherwise within reach." He noted in the following paragraph that the Security Council had asked in its Resolution 774 (provided with my last letter) that, should an agreement not be reached, the Secretary General should recommend alternative courses of action to resolve the Cyprus problem. Subsequent paragraphs outline his proposals, including a number of measures to help create a new climate of confidence between the two parties, which would contribute to the success of the negotiating process. These confidence-building measures are outlined in paragraph 63 of the Secretary General's report.

On November 25, the U.N. Security Council adopted its Resolution 789, which endorsed the U.N. Secretary General's report of November 19, and urged both sides to commit themselves to the Secretary General's series of confidence-building measures, including initiating a significant reduction of foreign troops and defense spending on the island.

I am happy to note that, before departing New York in November, the parties agreed to resume their face-to-face negotiations in March 1993, which will be after the presidential elections in the Republic of Cyprus scheduled for February 7, 1993. We would have preferred, of course, that the October-November round of negotiations would have proceeded beyond the point of defining positions and differences and would have entered the phase of bridging gaps between the positions of the parties and the U.N. "set of ideas," including the Secretary General's map, which remains the basis for negotiations for a fair and permanent resolution that would benefit all Cypriots.

I continue to believe and to agree with the statement in Security Council Resolution 789 that the present status quo is not acceptable. An overall agreement in line with the U.N. "set of ideas" should be achieved without further delay. I also urge all concerned to commit themselves to the implementation of the confidence-building measures set out in Resolution 789 and to come to the next round of talks prepared to make the difficult decisions that will bring about a speedy agreement.

Sincerely,

GEORGE BUSH

Note: Identical letters were sent to Thomas S. Foley, Speaker of the House of Representatives, and Claiborne Pell, Chairman of the Senate Committee on Foreign Relations.

Letter to Congressional Leaders Transmitting Forest Service Reports
January 7, 1993

Dear Mr. Speaker: (Dear Mr. President:)

I am pleased to transmit to the Congress three study reports prepared by the Department of Agriculture's Forest Service. I support the recommendations provided by the Secretary of Agriculture in each of these reports. The three reports are:

(1) Wild and Scenic River study and draft legislation to designate 19.4 miles of the Red River in Kentucky as part of the National Wild and Scenic Rivers System.

(2) Wild and Scenic River study and recommendation for designation of 133 miles of the Greenbrier River in West Virginia as a component of the National Wild and Scenic Rivers System under State administration and jurisdiction.

(3) Wilderness study report for the Pyramid Peak Wilderness Study Area in California with a recommendation that this area be released from further consideration for wilderness designation. Current management will emphasize nonmotorized, dispersed recreation, essentially maintaining the area in an undeveloped state.

Red River:

I am particularly pleased to transmit legislation to designate 19.4 miles of the Red River as a component of the National Wild and Scenic Rivers System. Designation of the Red River received strong public support during the study, and this would be the first Wild and Scenic River designated in the State of Kentucky.

The natural, scenic, and recreational qualities of the Red River are unique and irreplaceable resources. The majority of the river corridor is within the Red River National Geologic Area, a "geological wonderland" of sedimentary rock formations unique to that area and the United States. The Red River also flows through the scenic Clifty Wilderness for a distance of 4.5 miles.

Recreational use of the Red River and adjacent lands totaled over 200,000 visitor days in 1990. This figure is expected to increase in the future, as approximately 94 million people presently live within a day's drive of the Red River.

Greenbrier River:

The Greenbrier River in West Virginia was studied by the Forest Service, in cooperation with the State of West Virginia and local communities. The Secretary recommends that 133 miles of the river be added to the System through local and State initiatives.

Outstanding outdoor recreation values are associated with the Greenbrier River and its corridor lands. Recreation activities include boating, whitewater canoeing, primitive and developed site camping, hiking, fishing, hunting, spelunking, and cross-country skiing. In recognition of these values, the State of West Virginia has already included the main stem of the Greenbrier River below Knapps Creek under the West Virginia Natural Streams Preservation Act. This Act maintains the free-flowing character of that portion of the river. This indicates the considerable support by local residents and interest groups for protection of the values of the river corridor, provided such protection is under local management control.

Under the approach recommended by the Secretary, the decision to seek designation as a Wild and Scenic River would be the prerogative of the State. First, the West Virginia State legislature would include the remainder of the upper Greenbrier River under the West Virginia Natural Streams Preservation Act. Second, a group would be formed locally to develop a proposed management plan for the river, which would be reviewed and approved by the Governor. The Governor would then recommend to the Secretary of the Interior that the Greenbrier River be federally designated under section 2(a)(ii) of the Wild and Scenic Rivers Act. If the Secretary approves, the river would be so designated, and the State would have the primary responsibility for administration of the river according to the management plan. I am hopeful that the State of West Virginia will assume this responsibility.

This emphasis on local control is recommend over Federal administration of the river because the State of West Virginia already manages a significant portion of the river corridor lands and the recreational activities associated with the river. In addition, the corridor includes a significant acreage of private lands that can be most effectively managed through local land-use controls and landowner participation. Landowners are particularly concerned that Federal administration would impact management and use of their private lands. I believe that the Secretary's recommendation provides for protection of the river's natural values, while maintaining control at the local level.

Pyramid Peak:

The third report addresses the Pyramid Peak Planning Area in the San Bernardino National Forest in California. The Congress directed that this area be studied as a potential Wilderness Area in the California Wilderness Act of 1984. The suitability of this area for inclusion in the National Wilderness Preservation System was analyzed in the San Bernardino National Forest Plan, which was implemented in 1989. The Forest Plan decision was to allocate this area to a management prescription that emphasizes nonmotorized, dispersed recrea-

tion management, essentially maintaining the area in an undeveloped state. This management direction has advantages over wilderness designation because it provides for development of habitat improvement projects, both for the bighorn sheep and other wildlife species in the area. Nonwilderness management will also allow treatment of vegetation to enhance resources such as water yield and to reduce fuel accumulations. I support the Secretary's recommendation and request that the Pyramid Peak Planning Area be released from further consideration for wilderness designation.

Transmittal of these recommendations to the Congress fulfills the requirements of section 5(b) of the Wild and Scenic Rivers Act and section 102 of the California Wilderness Act of 1984. I urge the Congress to pass legislation designating the Red River as a component of the National Wild and Scenic Rivers System. I also request that the Congress take no action at this time to designate the Greenbrier River as a Wild and Scenic River or include the Pyramid Peak Planning Area in the National Wilderness Preservation System.

Sincerely,

GEORGE BUSH

Note: Identical letters were sent to Thomas S. Foley, Speaker of the House of Representatives, and Dan Quayle, President of the Senate.

Letter to Congressional Leaders Transmitting Proposed Legislation on Colorado Public Lands Wilderness Designation
January 7, 1993

Dear Mr. Speaker: (Dear Mr. President:)

I am pleased to submit for congressional consideration and passage the "Colorado Public Lands Wilderness Act".

The Federal Land Policy and Management Act of 1976 (FLPMA), (43 U.S.C. 1701 *et seq.*), directs the Secretary of the Interior to review the wilderness potential of the public lands.

The review of the areas identified in Col-

orado began immediately after the enactment of FLPMA and has now been completed. Approximately 771,822 acres of public lands in 54 areas in Colorado met the minimum wilderness criteria and were designated as wilderness study areas (WSAs). These WSAs were studied and analyzed during the review process and the results documented in eight environmental impact statements and five instant study area reports. The wilderness studies and reviews have now been completed except for four areas that are contiguous to the Sangre de Cristo Study Area administered by the U.S. Forest Service and were studied under section 202 of FLPMA. They will remain under wilderness review pending resolution of the Sangre de Cristo study.

Based on the studies and reviews of the WSAs, the Secretary of the Interior recommends that all or part of 20 of the WSAs, totaling 395,792 acres of public lands, be designated as part of the National Wilderness Preservation System.

I concur with the Secretary of the Interior's recommendations and am pleased to recommend designation of the 18 areas (395,792 acres) identified in the enclosed bill as additions to the National Wilderness Preservation System.

The proposed additions represent the diversity of wilderness values in the State of Colorado. These range from the 14,000-foot Redcloud Peak to the canyons of the Dolores, Gunnison, and Yampa Rivers, to the 13 natural arches of the Black Ridge Canyons. These areas span a wide variety of Colorado landforms, ecosystems, and other natural systems and features. Their inclusion in the wilderness system will improve the geographic distribution of wilderness areas in Colorado, and will complement existing areas of congressionally designated wilderness. They will provide new and outstanding opportunities for solitude and unconfined recreation.

The enclosed draft legislation provides that designation as wilderness shall not constitute a reservation of water or water rights for wilderness purposes. This is consistent with the fact that the Congress did not establish a Federal reserved water right for wilderness purposes. The Administration has established the policy that, where it is necessary to obtain water rights for wilderness purposes in a specific wilderness area, water rights would be sought from the State by filing under State water laws. Furthermore, it is the policy of the Administration that the designation of wilderness areas should not interfere with the use of water rights, State water administration, or the use of a State's interstate water allocation.

The draft legislation also provides for access to wilderness areas by Indian people for traditional cultural and religious purposes. Access by the general public may be limited in order to protect the privacy of religious cultural activities taking place in specific wilderness areas. In addition, to the fullest extent practicable, the Department of the Interior will coordinate with the Department of Defense to minimize the impact of any overflights during these religious cultural activities.

I further concur with the Secretary of the Interior that all or part of 46 of the WSAs encompassing 376,030 acres are not suitable for preservation as wilderness.

Also enclosed are a letter and report from the Secretary of the Interior concerning the WSAs discussed above and a section-by-section analysis of the draft legislation. I urge the Congress to act expeditiously and favorably on the proposed legislation so that the natural resources of these WSAs in Colorado may be protected and preserved.

Sincerely,

GEORGE BUSH

Note: Identical letters were sent to Thomas S. Foley, Speaker of the House of Representatives, and Dan Quayle, President of the Senate.

Letter to Congressional Leaders Transmitting Proposed Legislation on Montana Public Lands Wilderness Designation
January 7, 1993

Dear Mr. Speaker: (Dear Mr. President:)
I am pleased to submit for congressional consideration and passage the "Montana Public Lands Wilderness Act".

The Federal Land Policy and Management Act of 1976 (FLPMA), (43 U.S.C. 1701 *et seq.*), directs the Secretary of the Interior to review the wilderness potential of the public lands.

The review of the areas identified in Montana began immediately after the enactment of FLPMA and has now been completed. Approximately 470,443 acres of public lands in 46 areas in Montana met the minimum wilderness criteria and were designated as wilderness study areas (WSAs). Six WSAs containing 17,880 acres were subsequently released from further wilderness review through the Bureau of Land Management's land use planning process, and four other small areas containing approximately 5,236 acres will be studied in future land use plans and are not included in the recommendations. The remaining 36 areas were studied and analyzed during the review process and the results documented in nine environmental impact statements and two instant study area reports.

Based on the studies and reviews of the WSAs, the Secretary of the Interior recommends that all or part of 15 of the WSAs, totaling 173,499 acres of public lands, be designated as part of the National Wilderness Preservation System.

I concur with the Secretary of the Interior's recommendations and am pleased to recommend designation of the 15 areas identified in the enclosed bill as additions to the National Wilderness Preservation System.

The proposed additions represent the diversity of wilderness values in the State of Montana. These range from the badlands and prairie areas of eastern Montana to the peaks of the Rocky Mountains in the western part of the State. These areas span a wide variety of Montana landforms, ecosystems, and other natural systems and features. Their inclusion in the wilderness system will improve the geographic distribution of wilderness areas in Montana, and will complement existing areas of congressionally designated wilderness. They will provide new and outstanding opportunities for solitude and unconfined recreation.

The enclosed draft legislation provides that designation as wilderness shall not constitute a reservation of water or water rights for wilderness purposes. This is consistent with the fact that the Congress did not establish a Federal reserved water right for wilderness purposes. The Administration has established the policy that, where it is necessary to obtain water rights for wilderness purposes in a specific wilderness area, water rights would be sought from the State by filing under State water laws. Furthermore, it is the policy of the Administration that the designation of wilderness areas should not interfere with the use of water rights, State water administration, or the use of a State's interstate water allocation.

The draft legislation also provides for access to wilderness areas by Indian people for traditional cultural and religious purposes. Access by the general public may be limited in order to protect the privacy of religious cultural activities taking place in specific wilderness areas. In addition, to the fullest extent practicable, the Department of the Interior will coordinate with the Department of Defense to minimize the impact of any overflights during these religious cultural activities.

I further concur with the Secretary of the Interior that all or part of 30 of the WSAs encompassing 273,828 acres are not suitable for preservation as wilderness.

Also enclosed are a letter and report from the Secretary of the Interior concerning the WSAs discussed above and a section-by-section analysis of the draft legislation. I urge the Congress to act expeditiously and favorably on the proposed legislation so that the natural resources of these WSAs in Montana may be protected and preserved.

Sincerely,

GEORGE BUSH

Note: Identical letters were sent to Thomas S. Foley, Speaker of the House of Representatives, and Dan Quayle, President of the Senate.

Remarks to Central Intelligence Agency Employees in Langley, Virginia
January 8, 1993

Anything to keep from having to go back to work. I know how it is. [*Laughter*] But listen, it's the other way around. I came out here to thank you all for fantastic support for your country in so many ways. And of course, I want to thank Bob Gates, my right-hand person and trusted adviser when at the White House, and then thank him for the superb job he's done out here.

It's great to be back at Langley. I guess the last time I was out here was when Bob Gates was sworn in as DCI. I have loved this warm welcome back, wandering through the halls out there, and now this. I just can't get over it. I feel very welcome. And I want to thank each and every one of you.

Last November when Bob became Director, I noted that the men and women of the intelligence community faced a new mission in a dramatically different world. I stated then, and I'd like to just repeat it now, that we must not diminish our intelligence. There are big changes. I think the world may be perceived to be more peaceful, but in my view, the need for intelligence is as great as ever. You're doing a great job. And I will try to be a voice after I leave in a few more days for keeping this intelligence community the strongest, the best in the entire world, which it is now.

I do think there have been dramatic changes. I had a chance to visit with some of the analysts and operators upstairs. We talked about the visit that Barbara and I had to the Soviet Union—what used to be the Soviet Union; I've got to learn to say Russia now—but with Yeltsin. And I think that the work of this Agency and of the intelligence community through the years really probably will never get the credit that it deserves for effecting these changes, for your role in bringing about these changes and having Presidents hopefully make informed decisions on the world we face. But we did manage to work out with Yeltsin a treaty over there, finalize a treaty that many here in one way or another contributed to that does provide great hope for a better and safer world. So I'm very happy that we were able to conclude that treaty before I go back to Houston, Texas, on January 20th.

But we can't fool ourselves. Those who would challenge us, and we're seeing it right now as we try to decide what we should do over in Iraq, those who would challenge freedom's gains are many. We continue to face threats in the world of terrorism where a lot of good work has been the antiterrorist work. And the intelligence contributing to that out here has been fantastic. Many here are concerned about and have worked on weapons proliferation. And of course, I remain very much concerned about that. I had a little briefing on just a corner of the world on narcotics trafficking. And here the Agency and the community is doing a superb job on the intelligence for that. Economic security—I salute those who are involved in the economic side of our intelligence. And all of these things must continue, and all of these accounts must be strongly serviced.

So I come back to the point that the threats we face are real. We need more intelligence, not less, if we're to meet the challenge. We've got to have the best possible intelligence as we work for peace and decency and respect for the rule of law.

I wish all of you could have been with me on this visit to Somalia. It was very moving. And we are doing the right thing. But I'll tell you, when you say respect for the law, there isn't any there. We've got to conduct ourselves in such a way in the last days of our administration, and I'm sure the new President will feel the same way, to demonstrate America's lasting respect for law. And again, this Agency and the people, all the people here in one way or another, I think, point out the fact that we must work for peace, for decency, and respect for the rule of law.

So this is not a time to claim victory and turn our backs on the intelligence needs of the future. And as we face a more turbulent and unpredictable world, and as our military forces are being reduced, I just don't think that we ought to be contemplating significant reductions in the intelligence budget. I'm going to be glad to convey that on to those who follow General Scowcroft and Bob Gates and me.

So let me just say that the work you've done has always been hard. There's no question about that. I think of the operations side, particularly, but it's true on the intelligence side, everything. The dangers that we face as a country are real. I still get emotionally convinced of that when I see the stars out in the hall of this building. I just think that the Nation is very fortunate to have the service of everybody here. You don't get to sit at the head table quite as much as I have in my last incarnations, and you don't get saluted as much as perhaps others in different Departments, but you deserve a great deal of credit. So I came to say, thank you.

And now before I depart, I have one last matter that I want to do. And I would like to—I don't know—Bob, is Becky out here?

Where is she? Right in front. Becky, come on up here, and the kids as well. I want to get the Gates family here. And it gives me great pleasure, particularly surrounded by people who have worked with Bob, to honor him here as a distinguished public servant by awarding him the National Security Medal. This is the highest medal that a President can give for national security.

I have a long list here that some very thorough speechwriter wrote out about Bob Gates' accomplishments, his record, his service to his country, but I expect people here know this better than most. But you ought to know how much I trust him, admire him, and respect him. I will ask—— [*applause*]

So this is the National Security Medal. And if there's ever been one that's been well deserved or well earned, it's the one I present now with great pride to Bob Gates, Director of Central Intelligence.

Is that it? We're out of here. Thank you all very much. Thanks a lot.

Note: The President spoke at 1:15 p.m. at the Central Intelligence Agency headquarters.

Letter to Congressional Leaders Transmitting a Report on Alaska's Mineral Resources
January 8, 1993

Dear Mr. Speaker: (Dear Mr. President:)
I transmit herewith the 1992 Annual Report on Alaska's Mineral Resources, as required by section 1011 of the Alaska National Interest Lands Conservation Act (Public Law 96–487; 16 U.S.C. 3151). This report contains pertinent public information relating to minerals in Alaska gathered by the U.S. Geological Survey, the Bureau of Mines, and other Federal agencies. This report is significant because of the impor-

tance of the mineral and energy resources of Alaska to the future well-being of the Nation.

Sincerely,

GEORGE BUSH

Note: Identical letters were sent to Thomas S. Foley, Speaker of the House of Representatives, and Dan Quayle, President of the Senate.

Statement by Press Secretary Fitzwater on the Situation in Iraq
January 8, 1993

We continue to keep the situation in Iraq under close scrutiny. We have observed no penetrations by Iraqi aircraft of the no-fly zone below 32 degrees north latitude since Wednesday's coalition warning. The disposition of surface-to-air missiles specified in the January 6 warning is less clear. There has been a good deal of movement involving these missiles, but we are still in the process of determining whether Iraq is in compliance with the terms of the coalition démarche.

Letter to Congressional Leaders Transmitting the Report on Federal Advisory Committees
January 11, 1993

Dear Mr. Speaker: (Dear Mr. President:)

In accordance with the requirements of section 6(c) of the Federal Advisory Committee Act, as amended (Public Law 92–463; 5 U.S.C. App. 2, sec. 6(c)), I hereby transmit the Twenty-first Annual Report on Federal Advisory Committees for fiscal year 1992.

Sincerely,

GEORGE BUSH

Note: Identical letters were sent to Thomas S. Foley, Speaker of the House of Representatives, and Dan Quayle, President of the Senate.

Letter to Congressional Leaders Transmitting the Report of the Commodity Credit Corporation
January 11, 1993

Dear Mr. Speaker: (Dear Mr. President:)

In accordance with the provisions of section 13, Public Law 806, 80th Congress (15 U.S.C. 714k), I transmit herewith the report of the Commodity Credit Corporation for fiscal year 1989.

Sincerely,

GEORGE BUSH

Note: Identical letters were sent to Thomas S. Foley, Speaker of the House of Representatives, and Dan Quayle, President of the Senate.

Remarks at a Disability Community Tribute to the President
January 12, 1993

Thank you all for this honor. You talk about a sea of friendly faces. I'll get in trouble for singling some out and leaving out others, but certainly Evan Kemp and Justin, Justin Dart; Dick and Ginny Thornburgh here; Pat Wright; Judi Chamberlin; Tom

McKeithan; Doro, my daughter; King Jordan, Dr. I. King; and of course, Senator Bob Dole and other Members of Congress here. I think of my receiving this, and I think of all Bob has done over the years. I pale by comparison, my efforts. I see Steny Hoyer over here, who's committed and has worked very hard as a Member of Congress; Tony Coelho, the same thing, as a leader in the Congress; Norm Mineta here with us today; had a lovely letter from Tom Harkin—I can't remember ever agreeing with Tom Harkin on anything other than this, and he points that out to me in the letter. [*Laughter*] I think it bespeaks the breadth of the interest in the Americans with Disabilities Act, and I appreciate it very much. Of course, I'd be remiss if I didn't single out Boyden Gray, who was working very hard. And she and Pat going steady for a while as even she admitted. You talk about the odd couple, that's it. But nevertheless—[*laughter*].

But I make this point because this cause or this legislation really moved across all barriers. Whether it's liberal or conservative or Democrat or Republican, it was wonderful the way the people in this room and people all across this country came together to do something good.

And so I am very grateful to be over here. Doro is right; Barbara wanted to be here. And I wish she were here, because the more she packs boxes over there, the more irritable she gets. [*Laughter*] But serious—no, Bar, if you're listening—[*laughter*]. I know her.

But the irony is that so many people here today, because of their dedication and, yes, their hard work that led to the passage of the ADA, deserve to receive this honor. I really feel this way. Some of you have been fighting for that act for year after year after year. And on the eve of my departure from the Office of Presidency, I am just delighted to have this opportunity to meet again with those who shared in one of its finest moments, this country's finest moments: the proposal, the passage, and the signing of the most comprehensive civil rights bill in the history of this country and indeed the history of the world, the Americans with Disabilities Act.

ADA runs deep in the vein of the Ameri-

can tradition, and that is, a belief in equal opportunity—we heard it over here from Ms. Chamberlin—devotion to individual rights, the ethic really of inclusion. Resisting the extremes of either negligence or patronization, the act reflects a conservative way of helping people, one that helps others help themselves.

At the beginning of this century, one African American bishop described his aspiration for civil rights saying, we ask not that others bear our burdens, but don't obstruct our pathway, and we'll throw them off, throw off those burdens as we run. In the same spirit, the 43 millions with disabilities have asked, to paraphrase President Kennedy, not that their country can do for them but only that they be allowed to do for themselves, and thereby their country. I believe that the economic challenges of the next century cannot, simply cannot, be met without the energy and the intelligence of, the industry of every citizen. ADA broadens our economic mainstream so that all Americans can share in the responsibilities and rewards of hard work worth doing.

A few critics—Bob knows this well from his leadership role in the Congress—have complained about the costs of ADA, as if some rights were simply too expensive. But when you add together Federal, State, local, and private funds, it's been costing almost $200 billion annually to support our disabled in artificial isolation. And this legislation takes an economic inefficiency and reinvents it then as opportunity and enterprise.

Indeed, I believe that the costs of forgotten citizens is greater than any that can be factored into some Government budget. And when we neglect the rights of some, we simply degrade the rights of all. The quest for civil rights is not a zero sum game, as if there were only so many rights to go around. Our founders thought of rights not as privileges granted by man but as self-evident truths ordained by God.

But just as our Constitution pledges equality under law, so we must strive for legal equality, one that broadens opportunity, increases access, and gives each citizen a fair shot at the American dream. And the beautiful thing is this legislation does just that, not by setting up new institutions but by tearing down old walls. And you see, I believe that in the end it will take more than better regulations and bigger bureaucracies to make this land the land of opportunity for all.

Government can certainly make good laws; it can't make men good. It can ban unfair acts; it can't banish unkind thoughts. And so it's up to us to reach out to those Americans disabled by ignorance or handicapped by prejudice and teach them a better way. Each American shares a responsibility for a kinder, gentler America, to follow the example that so many of you in this room have led with your lives.

I'm not sure I know exactly what I'll be doing a few months from now, but I want to say this: I want to stay involved. I want to help. I'll be a private citizen, not sitting at the head table, out of the Government limelight, but I want to help. I want to stay involved in this kind of important work.

I'm not sure how historians will record

the fact that the first George Bush Medal was given to George Bush. [*Laughter*] There seems something a little contradictory perhaps on that. But you've made me very happy. And I admire you. I respect you. I love you, and I wish you all well.

Thank you, and may God bless you all.

Note: The President spoke at 2:20 p.m. at the Capital Hilton. In his remarks, he referred to Evan Kemp, Chairman, Equal Employment Opportunity Commission; Justin Dart, Chairman, President's Committee on Employment of People with Disabilities; former Attorney General Dick Thornburgh and his wife, Ginny; Patrisha Wright, government affairs director, Disability Rights Education and Defense Fund, Inc.; Judi Chamberlin, coordinating committee member, National Association of Psychiatric Survivors; Thomas McKeithan II, Benjamin Banneker High School student; and Dr. I. King Jordan, president, Gallaudet University.

Remarks on Presenting the Presidential Medal of Freedom to President Ronald Reagan
January 13, 1993

President Reagan, you can see from that welcome how we all feel about your and Nancy's return to this house that you graced. We're delighted to welcome you back here. And of course, I want to send my special greetings to those who served in the Reagan Cabinet and to the Reagan family. And it's a pleasure to welcome all of you back here to the White House.

Being President has its privileges. And this morning I have the privilege to present America's highest civilian award, the Presidential Medal of Freedom, with distinction, to my predecessor, the 40th President of the United States. Today we honor the American life of an American original. We all remember the movie in which he once said, "Win one for the Gipper." Well, as President, Ronald Reagan helped win one for freedom, both at home and abroad. And I consider him my friend and mentor, and

so he is. And he's also a true American hero.

Just think of the whistlestops that ring unsummoned, like a postcard from the past: Dixon, Tampico, Eureka College, WHO radio in Des Moines. Always Ronald Reagan embodied the heart of the American people. And once he described it as "hopeful, big-hearted, idealistic, daring, decent, and fair."

Ronald Reagan didn't just make the world believe in America; he made Americans believe in themselves. And I remember Inauguration Day in 1981 and how the clouds—maybe you remember it—of a gloomy morning gave way as he began his speech. He turned that winter of discontent into a springtime of possibility.

President Reagan believed in the American people, so he helped the private sector create 19 million new jobs. He knew that

Government was too big and spent too much, and so he lowered taxes and spending, cut redtape, and began a peacetime boom, the longest in American history.

Some men reflect their times. Ronald Reagan changed his times. And nowhere was that more true than abroad where he championed the holy grail of liberty. Mr. President, you helped make ours not only a safer but far better world in which to live. And you yourself said it best. In fact, you saw it coming. We recall your stirring words to the British Parliament. Here were the words: "the march of freedom and democracy . . . will leave Marxist-Leninism on the ashheap of history."

Few people believe more in liberty's inevitable triumph than Ronald Reagan. None, none was more a prophet in his time. Ronald Reagan rebuilt our military; not only that, he restored its morale. And when I became President, President Reagan passed on to me the most dedicated and best equipped fighting force that the world has ever seen.

He signed also the INF treaty, the first agreement to eliminate a whole category of nuclear weapons. And it was a treaty that lay the foundation then for START I and the historic START II agreement that President Yeltsin and I signed 2 weeks ago.

Ronald Reagan sought a world where nations could talk, not die, over differences and a world of prosperity, peaceful competition, and freedom without war. And he helped achieve it, helped end the cold war.

When Ronald Reagan's favorite President died in 1945, the New York Times wrote, "Men will thank God on their knees a hundred years from now that Franklin D. Roosevelt was in the White House." Well, Mr. President, it will not take a hundred years; millions thank God today that you were in the White House.

You loved America, blessed America, and with your leadership certainly helped make America that shining city on a hill. All this explains why today Ronald Reagan becomes only the third President to receive the Medal of Freedom, the first to receive it in his own lifetime. He's a man whose life embodies freedom, who nurtured freedom as few Presidents ever have.

And so now, Mr. President, let me invite you, sir, to join me as Major Wissler reads the citation for the Medal of Freedom. Please come up.

Note: The President spoke at 10:20 a.m. in the East Room at the White House. Maj. John Wissler, USMC, was Marine Corps Aide to the President.

Remarks on Presenting the National Security Medal to Admiral Jonathan T. Howe and an Exchange With Reporters
January 13, 1993

The President. John, welcome. This is a surprise. *[Laughter]* *[Inaudible]*—are very proud to award you the National Security Medal. And I would ask Bill Sittmann to read a very quick citation. We're sorry to blindside you like this, but the only way we knew that you'd show up is if you didn't know about it. *[Laughter]*

[At this point, William F. Sittmann, Executive Secretary, National Security Council, read the citation, and the President presented the medal.]

The President. Well, that is the under-

statement of the year, but we are very, very proud of you. And it is well-deserved, and great, honorable service to your country. Particularly, I want to thank you for all you've done here.

[Inaudible]—this, that goes with it. I thought you looked good sitting over there at that desk—*[laughter]*. I hardly got him out of there, I'll tell you. *[Laughter]*

Allied Action in Iraq

Now, you wanted to ask a question on the military action. Let me simply say that once again the American military, in coalition with strong allies, has performed in a superb fashion. Our planes are all accounted for. I've not yet seen a damage assessment or results of the strike. But they did the right thing, and the coalition did the right thing. I have said before that we are determined that Saddam Hussein will abide by the United Nations resolutions, and we're very serious about that.

I can say with confidence here, and I think it's important, that I'm confident Governor Clinton, the President-elect of the United States, feels that way too. I have talked to him before these strikes hit, and he as much as told me that, and then I've heard statements out of Little Rock. But I think that's a very important message to go not just to our coalition forces, that we have every intention of working together in the future as we have in the past, but to Saddam Hussein who has violated the resolutions.

Q. Do you think it will work?

The President. Well, I don't know what "work" means, but I am confident that when I—I will continue to insist that he abide by these resolutions. We've taken action, and I hope that will convince him he must do that. And I'm as confident that President Clinton will do this and feel the same way after the 20th.

Q. Did you have any reservations, sir, doing it so close to the end of your term in office?

The President. No, absolutely not. I'm President until the 20th, and I will run foreign policy and make these kinds of decisions as long as I'm President. We will keep the new team fully informed. And I believe they've been very generous and gracious in saying that we have done that. General Scowcroft is in almost daily contact with the transition people from the national security field, and then I know Dick Cheney's had good visits with, as has Larry Eagleburger, with the people coming in. So we'll just keep it closely informed. But I have no reservations at all. You've got to do what you have to do. And there should be no ques-

tion about that.

Q. Sir, was there any particular action by Saddam that triggered the strike?

The President. Just his failure to live up to the resolutions and then his moving around of these missiles in a way that was unacceptable to the coalition of the United Nations.

Q. Are you prepared to order additional sites to be—[*inaudible*]——

The President. I will conduct myself until the 20th just as I have in the almost 4 years gone by, and that is, I don't say what we might or might not do. But I would think that soon Saddam Hussein would understand that we mean what we say and that we back it up. And I have no intention of changing that approach to life in the last 6 or 7 days of my Presidency.

Thank you very much. I should say I'm very proud of the pilots and those who supported the pilots. Once again, we see what superb training we have and what dedicated young people are out there. I must say I worried when I heard premature stories of this because I hesitate ever—I would never put a young flyer in harm's way because of leaked information. Fortunately the leaks that occurred on this did not result in the loss of life for any of our pilots. But I will always—I would just urge everybody to guard against that, whatever administration is here, now or in the future.

Q. Did they encounter any kind of resistance?

The President. We'll have more to say about that when we do a fuller briefing on the mission itself. But any time you divulge plans when somebody's life is at stake, it is not a good thing to do. I just never understood it. I don't like it. I saw it happen today. But that's history now. But we ought to have more responsibility when you risk the life of a single U.S. pilot.

Thank you all very much.

Note: The President spoke at 4:05 p.m. in the Oval Office at the White House.

Statement on Completion of the Chemical Weapons Convention
January 13, 1993

For more than 20 years the United States and many other countries have labored to achieve a ban on chemical weapons. The long-awaited Chemical Weapons Convention is now completed and open for signature.

I have had a deep and abiding personal interest in the success of the effort to ban these terrible weapons. As Vice President, I had the honor on two occasions to address the Conference on Disarmament and to present United States proposals to give impetus to the negotiations. As President, I directed the United States to take new initiatives to advance and conclude the negotiations. The United States is profoundly gratified that these talks have now been successfully concluded.

The countries that participated in the negotiations at the conference on disarmament deserve special congratulations. The Chemical Weapons Convention is uniquely important in the field of arms control agreements. It will improve the security of all nations by eliminating a class of weapons of mass destruction that exists in all quarters of the world and that has been used in recent conflicts. It is a truly stabilizing and nondiscriminatory agreement.

The United States strongly supports the Chemical Weapons Convention and is proud to be an original signatory. We are encouraged that so many other states have also decided to take this step. This clearly demonstrates global international endorsement of the convention and the new norm of international conduct that it establishes. However, we must not cease our efforts until the norm becomes truly universal, with all countries becoming not only signatories but also parties to the convention.

Much work remains to make the convention fully effective. The United States will cooperate closely with other countries to bring the convention into force as soon as possible and to ensure that it is faithfully implemented. Only then will we be able to say that the risk of chemical warfare is no longer a threat to people anywhere in the world.

Letter to Congressional Leaders on the National Strategy on the Environment
January 13, 1993

Dear Mr. Speaker: (Dear Mr. President:)

During the past 4 years, the world has witnessed major changes in the political profile of nations. The Earth Summit, sponsored by the United Nations in Brazil in June 1992, signaled the next era in world history—one characterized by the recognition that environmental protection, economic development, and public participation in decision-making are interrelated and crucial to our future quality of life.

In these last 4 years, the United States charted an ambitious agenda to remain in the vanguard of environmental protection by harnessing the energy of capitalism in service of the environment. Those who said that we posed a false choice between a strong economy and a healthy environment disregarded our words and our deeds. We worked to achieve both while sacrificing neither—as must all nations in the coming century.

Economic development and environmental protection go hand in hand. Economic growth supplies the financial and technological resources necessary for environmental enhancement; while its opposite, the struggle for bare survival, places strains on natural protection. We have seen this phenomenon in America as our economy grew in the 1980s and waters and skies became cleaner, just as we have seen it in the degraded forests and rivers of Eastern Europe and in the faces of Africa's starving children. The challenge for leaders in all parts of the world is to ensure both economic growth and environmental progress at the same time.

A Strategy That Produced Results

The pioneer American conservationist, Gifford Pinchot, once remarked, "There are just two things on this material earth—people and natural resources." Human beings are not intruders in nature but an essential species with a responsibility to sustain other species.

The Bush Administration combined an understanding of human nature with an idealism about Mother Nature in developing a National Strategy for Environmental Quality, based on six goals:

- Harnessing the power of the marketplace;
- Managing natural resources as responsible stewards;
- Promoting creative partnerships;
- Developing cooperative international solutions;
- Preventing pollution before it starts;
- Enforcing environmental laws firmly and fairly.

And the strategy worked. In just 4 years, consider what has been accomplished:

Clean Air Act Amendments of 1990: We broke 10 years of congressional gridlock to enact the world's most protective and cost-effective clean air legislation. At its heart is an innovative, market-based, emission-allowance trading system. During the past 2 years, we proposed and finalized rules that promise to achieve 85 percent of the anticipated pollution reductions.

Budgets: By shifting Federal funds from other programs to environmental programs, we were able to increase the operating budget of the Environmental Protection Agency by more than 50 percent and increase funding for clean energy research and development by 66 percent.

Pollution Prevention: Market-driven pollution prevention efforts by the private sector are reshaping American industries, making us leaner and more efficient. For example, under just one Administration initiative, the EPA 33/50 program, more than

900 companies have reduced releases and transfers of toxic chemicals by 347 million pounds—25 percent below the 1988 baseline, with enormous savings in operating costs.

Enforcement: We broke new ground and old records, filing more cases, collecting more penalties, and putting more polluters behind bars than every previous administration in history combined.

Public Lands: We helped make America's great outdoors even greater by investing over a billion dollars to acquire wetlands, improve campgrounds, and add half a million acres to our national parks and 1,200 miles to our Wild and Scenic Rivers System. We created 57 new wildlife refuges—more than any administration in history. We adopted a philosophy of ecosystem management and ended clear-cutting as a standard practice on Federal land. The America the Beautiful initiative got off to a good start with the planting of more than 225 million new trees in rural and urban areas across the Nation.

Coasts and Oceans: To ensure that America's seas always will shine, we ended the ocean dumping of sewage sludge. We proposed and won passage of the Oil Pollution Act of 1990, a vigorous antipollution measure. To protect our ecologically sensitive coastal areas, we imposed a 10-year moratorium on oil and gas leasing and added six national marine sanctuaries, including the Monterey Bay sanctuary off California—which is second only to Australia's Great Barrier Reef as the largest marine protected area in the world.

Energy: We launched a new generation of clean energy technologies, not only by increasing funding for research and development but also by increasing incentives for the application of new technologies. We proposed and won passage of comprehensive national energy legislation with the Energy Policy Act of 1992, an act that will guide the United States into the next century.

Federal Leadership: We tripled funding for Federal facility cleanups, especially at nuclear weapons manufacturing sites, and secured more than 100 enforceable cleanup agreements at Federal facilities. Executive orders spurred the Federal Government to speed improvements in energy efficiency, recycling, waste reduction, and conversion of the Federal fleet to alternative fuels.

International Leadership: We insisted that a new world order include a cleaner world environment and reached 27 new international environmental agreements. We made America the world leader in phasing out ozone-depleting chlorofluorocarbons (CFCs) and led the way to a global ban on driftnet fishing. We launched a Forests for the Future initiative that proposed doubling international aid for forest conservation as a step toward halting global deforestation and dieback. We reduced Poland's debt to help that nation fund a new environmental foundation, and we launched the East-West Environmental Center in Budapest, Hungary, to help countries in Central and Eastern Europe. We addressed environmental protection in trade negotiations with Mexico, expanded debt-for-nature swaps to protect rainforests in Latin America, and created a network for environmental cooperation with Asia.

Global Climate Change: Our comprehensive action-oriented approach to global climate change was adopted by the world community at the United Nations Conference on Environment and Development in Brazil and ratified unanimously by the United States Senate. The United States was the first industrialized nation to ratify the treaty and the first nation to set forth its action plan to reduce greenhouse gas emissions.

President's Commission on Environmental Quality (PCEQ): This Presidential commission was unique because it was not created to provide advice but rather to demonstrate innovative ideas through action. Over the last 18 months, PCEQ built a network of more than 200 organizations to design and carry out 10 voluntary initiatives on such issues as biodiversity, energy efficiency, education and training, and environmental management.

President's Environment and Conservation Challenge Awards: We established a Presidential medal to honor those who honor the environment. Medal recipients have forged innovative solutions across the environmental spectrum from agriculture

to manufacturing to small business, from the classroom to the great outdoors and back to the inner city. Their good deeds have improved our Nation's air, water, and lands.

Why the Strategy Worked

Too often, the Federal Government has adopted goals with little regard to costs, practicality, or actual degree of risk. At times our environmental laws and regulations have been unnecessarily costly and punitive, especially for small businesses and communities.

That is why our environmental strategy was based on concepts that will make environmental protection a practical goal, consistent with economic growth. In an era of large Federal deficits and intense international economic competition, our country cannot afford policies that ignore costs.

A free society needs sensible regulation; our emphasis on market incentives and voluntary collaboration was credible because of its link to vigorous law enforcement, which motivated businesses to be innovative. But we cannot rely solely on the legislate-regulate-litigate pattern of the past. That approach will waste more time and money than it saves, hurting our economy and environment in the process.

Looking Forward

Our national environmental strategy has produced lasting benefits that prepare the stage for additional progress in the future. These and many other accomplishments in environmental quality are possible within the coming decades:

I look forward to a time when our natural vistas and urban skylines are never obscured by smog.

I look forward to the day when all industrial corporations can improve their energy efficiency and eliminate toxic discharges into the environment, at a profit.

I look forward to a less contentious era when ecologists, business people, and community leaders collaborate in finding ways to protect species and ecosystems without sacrificing an area's long-term economic development potential.

I look forward to the day when our scientists can tell us how to reorient regulations toward problems that pose the greatest risks to human health and the environment. A more scientific approach to setting priorities could save the country many billions of dollars while focusing on the greatest risks.

I look forward to the day when trade agreements are routinely matched by closer environmental cooperation. Trade liberalization is crucial to the growth of America and every nation in the 21st century, and growth is the key to greater environmental protection. Trade-environmental linkages are a practical way to realize sustainable development, especially for the developing nations that need it so desperately.

In the years ahead, we can take pride in what the American people helped us accomplish to protect our environment. We can be comforted by the knowledge that the next generation will continue the work we started to leave a better world.

Sincerely,

GEORGE BUSH

Note: Identical letters were sent to Thomas S. Foley, Speaker of the House of Representatives, and Dan Quayle, President of the Senate.

Remarks at a Celebration of the Points of Light
January 14, 1993

Thank you all very, very much. And I'm just delighted to be with you today to celebrate the work of those wonderful Americans we call Points of Light. And I think our First Lady is a Point of Light. So I salute her for what she's done in literacy and helping this country understand the importance of reading.

There's another guy here who's been a personal Point of Light to me, and that's Gregg Petersmeyer, who many of you know. In a sense it was his dream and his dedication that made all this possible. And Joe and Jenny, your witnessing, your testimony really makes this speech superfluous. I don't need to do it, but I will anyway. [*Laughter*] But thank you. You said it all with your own lives.

I also want to thank the leaders of three new institutions that have been established in the last 4 years: Tom Ehrlich of the Commission on National and Community Service, Dick Munro of the Points of Light Foundation, and Solon Cousins of the National Center for Community Risk Management and Insurance. And I also want to thank my friends: Ray Chambers, what an inspiration he has been in this whole voluntarism concept; Pete McCloskey; also George Romney, who I hope is here with us today. But we're grateful.

What an honor it is to have Larnelle here, Larnelle Harris, for helping make this event so very special. Anybody that can get up without a pitch pipe or a band and do what he did, we've got to look them over and see what makes him tick. [*Laughter*] But I'll tell you, his song said it all; his song got right to the heart. And I understand that he's just been nominated for his seventh Grammy Award. And Presidents ought not to do this, but I know who I'm rooting for. So there we are.

But above all, Barbara and I wanted to come over and thank the Points of Light that we're honoring today. I know that many of them have gone to great efforts to get here. And lots of folks ask me about the phrase, Points of Light. And some say it's religion; others say, well, it's a patriotic theme, like the flag; and others think it's an image of hope. But I think that Points of Light are all of these things and yet still something more. It's what happens when ordinary people claim the problems of their community as their own. And it's the inspiration and awakening to the God-given light from within, lit from within, and it's the promise of America.

We've got Points of Light here today from all 50 States, shining all the way from Anchorage to Harlem, Miami to Maine. And never before has there been so much light in this marvelous house. Each of you here today knows what I mean by that. Each of you found within yourselves your own special genius for helping others. And each discovered the imagination to see things that others could not: the human dignity in the eyes of a homeless man; the musicians and business leaders in an inner-city gang; the light and laughter in the shadows of a shattered life.

I've always believed that in each individual, there's a Point of Light waiting to be revealed; in each community, a thousand miracles waiting to happen. And when I assumed this great office, I pledged to do all I could to honor, encourage, and increase volunteer efforts until their light filled every dark corner of our country.

We began with a national strategy. And if you'll bear with me, I'd like to remind you of what that strategy is: first, changing attitudes so that all Americans define a successful life as one that includes serving others; and second, identifying what is already working so that those efforts can be enlarged and multiplied; and third, encouraging leaders to help others become Points of Light; and fourth, reducing volunteer liability, because I believe that it's time that we ought to care for each other more and sue each other less; and fifth and finally, within every community, linking people to ways that they can help.

Everything I've done as President has tried to support this strategy. And that's why we've worked together to create the Points of Light Foundation, the Commission on National and Community Service, and then the National Center for Community Risk Management and Insurance.

We envision national service not as a Government program, not even as a White House initiative but as a grassroots movement, a movement that makes full use of the many different ways that Americans want to help. This strategy is significant not because it indicates Washington's role but because it illuminates yours. And this is something where it's easy to miss the constellation for the stars.

You see, it's not just Points of Light that are important. It's the idea that every community in America could be filled with light. America could become like this room. You're only a fraction of the stories that we've told. And those stories are only a fraction of those that could be told.

You know, look around this room and then picture what would happen throughout America if every former gang member discovered the Rodney Dailey within and offered young people good alternatives to life on the streets. Imagine if every member, every member of a club, like the Rotary Readers, filled someone's life with the wonder of reading. Or what if every little girl found the imagination to follow Isis Johnson to clothe the cold and feed the hungry in her little corner of America. Imagine what America would look like.

Regardless of what we believe Government should do, all of us agree that no serious social problem in this country is going to be solved without the active engagement of millions of citizens in tens of thousands of institutions, schools and businesses, churches and clubs, armies of ordinary people doing extraordinary things.

Government has a critical role in helping people and so does solid, sustainable economic growth. But people, people, not programs, solve problems. And somewhere in America, every serious social problem is being solved through voluntary service, for therein lies the greatest national resource of all. It doesn't matter who you are. Everybody's got something to give: a job skill, a free hour, a pair of strong arms. And that's what I mean when I say that from now on, any definition of a successful life must include serving others.

Let me tell you another story about success. Today, I've recognized the 1,014th Daily Point of Light, the Lakeland Middle School eighth grade volunteers. These remarkable young people from Baltimore have overcome their own challenges to become tutors and role models for younger students in special education. Their special courage reminds me of the words of a poet who said, "The generosity is not in giving me that which I need more than you do, but in giving me that which you need more than I do." That courage has made the Lakeland eighth graders into the wonderful and confident young people who grace our lives today.

Because I know that America is filled with young people who want to help, I signed an Executive order last October that created the President's Youth Service Award. And as with the President's Physical Fitness Award, young people in voluntary service will be able to receive Presidential recognition in their local communities.

I want to thank the boards of the commission, the foundation, and the American Institute for Public Service for their help in implementing this program. What all of us seek in our life is meaning and adventure. And it's through service that all of us can find both.

Barbara and I will soon be making our way back to Texas, and I'd like to leave you with one thought: If I could leave but one legacy to this country, it would not be found in policy papers or even in treaties signed or even wars won; it would be return to the moral compass that must guide America through the next century, the changeless values that can and must guide change. And I'm talking about a respect for the goodness that made this country great, a rekindling of that light lit from within to reveal America as it truly is, a country with strong families, a country of millions of Points of Light.

I want to thank the Points of Light in this room and everywhere across this country, those that we have recognized and the millions more that have found no recognition but are doing the Lord's work.

Thank you and God bless you all. And God bless the U.S.A.

Note: The President spoke at 1:40 p.m. in the East Room at the White House. In his remarks, he referred to Ray Chambers, founding chairman, Points of Light Foundation; Paul N. (Pete) McCloskey and George Romney, members of the board of directors, Commission on National and Community Service; gospel singer Larnelle Harris; and the following Points of Light: Joe Thompson, Jenny Richardson, Rodney Dailey of Gang Peace, and Isis Johnson. The Executive order of October 28, 1992, which established a Presidential Youth Award for Community Service is listed in Appendix E at the end of this volume.

Remarks at an Armed Forces Salute to the President in Arlington, Virginia
January 14, 1993

Thank you very, very much, Secretary Cheney, Dick, my dear friend. I am honored by this salute; very, very grateful to all who participated in it, these same troops, many of whom have done so much to welcome distinguished visitors to the United States and in every way served their country with distinction.

But you guys have got it backwards. I came over here to thank all of you and to salute the members, past and present, of our Armed Forces: those who have given their lives, those who have served so honorably and so well, and those who serve today around the globe to keep the vigil of peace and to hold out the loving arms of the United States to those who are hurting.

Secretary Cheney has served with great distinction. I asked him to leave the United States Congress to take on this tremendous responsibility, and he's performed with great, great service to his country. He's done it all with excellence, dedication, and commitment.

As to General Powell, I just can't think of words to describe how strongly I feel about his service to his country and his leadership. And I am grateful to you, Colin. And may I single out the Secretaries, the Service Secretaries; and of course, the Joint Chiefs with whom I've worked very, very closely. I am grateful to all of you for your leadership and for your sound advice. And each of you should be proud because you were the key to the success of our military missions in Panama, in the Persian Gulf, in Somalia, and then in so many other places around the world. So, thank you all very, very much.

Just yesterday, we showed Saddam Hussein once again that he cannot violate international law with impunity. And people asked me about the mission. And I said the skies are safer and the message is clearer today because of the courage of those young air crews that did the Lord's work yesterday. We are grateful to each and every one of them. I congratulate General Hoar, all the commanders involved, all who laid their lives on the line. And once again, our military proved what we all know: They are absolutely the finest in the entire world.

America must always be mindful of the fact that our military is not simply the sum of our weapons or the state of our technology. What makes our military truly outstanding is the quality of its leadership, the quality of its training, the quality of its people, from the youngest soldier to the most decorated fighter.

As we enter the 1990's, we can be proud of what we've done to shape a new world. But while we're safer and certainly more secure with the end of the cold war, this new world will almost surely have its share of uncertainties and dangers. It is essential that we keep a strong defense. We must not make reckless cuts in defense.

We owe our victory in the cold war in no small part to our people in uniform. The men and women in our Armed Forces have demonstrated their ability to master the challenges of modern warfare, humanitarian aid, and peacekeeping, to do the hard work of freedom.

There is no doubt that the All Volunteer Force is one of the true success stories of modern day America. This did not simply happen; it is the result of the military's commitment to education and training. Out of the military's culture of merit and competition have emerged hundreds of thousands of highly skilled men and women brimming with justifiable self-confidence. And what they possess is a special kind of discipline: a willingness to accept direction, a willingness to accept responsibility. And together, discipline and confidence provide the basis for winning, for getting the job done.

And finally, let me speak not as President and not as Commander in Chief, but as a citizen, as an American. I look back on my service to this great Nation with pride. I think my 3 years in the Navy did more to shape my life than anything that's followed on. And I'm very proud to stand with you all here today, honored that we share this sacred bond of duty, honor, country.

Thank you for this salute, and may God bless the United States of America. Thank you very much.

Note: The President spoke at 3:36 p.m. at Fort Myer. In his remarks, he referred to Gen. Joseph P. Hoar, USMC, commander in chief, U.S. Central Command.

Letter to Congressional Leaders Transmitting the National Nutrition Monitoring and Research Plan
January 14, 1993

Dear Mr. Speaker: (Dear Mr. President:)

As required by the provisions of section 103 of the National Nutrition Monitoring and Related Research Act of 1990 (Public Law 101–445; 7 U.S.C. 5313(d)(2)), I hereby submit to the Congress the Ten-Year Comprehensive Plan for the National Nutrition Monitoring and Related Research Program.

This report was developed under the joint auspices of the Departments of Agriculture and Health and Human Services. It identifies activities to be conducted by the Federal Government over the next decade to strengthen the National Nutrition Monitoring and Related Research Program.

Sincerely,

GEORGE BUSH

Note: Identical letters were sent to Thomas S. Foley, Speaker of the House of Represent- *atives, and Dan Quayle, President of the Senate.*

Letter to Congressional Leaders Transmitting the Report of the Department of Energy
January 14, 1993

Dear Mr. Speaker: *(Dear Mr. President:)*
In accordance with the requirements of section 657 of the Department of Energy Organization Act (Public Law 95–91; 42 U.S.C. 7267), I transmit herewith the 12th Annual Report of the Department of Energy, which covers the year 1991.
Sincerely,

GEORGE BUSH

Note: Identical letters were sent to Thomas S. Foley, Speaker of the House of Representatives, and Dan Quayle, President of the Senate.

Remarks on the Forests for the Future Initiative
January 15, 1993

Welcome to the White House, and thank you all for coming. I'm delighted to see so many people here who care so deeply about the forests. And first I want to greet and welcome the representatives from Belize and Brazil, Ghana, Guatemala, Indonesia, Mexico, Papua New Guinea, and Russia. And I congratulate you on the progress that your countries are making on forest management. We're delighted to be able to work with you on this important effort.

It's good to see the cochairs of the effort, Bill Reilly, our EPA Administrator, and then Boyden Gray, my General Counsel here, and the officials from all the U.S. Agencies who have worked to make Forests for the Future a reality. And welcome also to the representatives of the NGO, the nongovernmental groups, working alongside: Kathryn Fuller of World Wildlife, Dan Dudek of the Environmental Defense Fund.

Today I'm announcing a significant step forward in the effort to conserve and sustainably manage the Earth's forests. Last June on the way to the Earth summit in Rio, I announced our Forests for the Future

initiative. And I said then it was about achieving results through cooperative partnerships. If we work together in mutual cooperation instead of trying to force painful concessions, we can make progress. And that's what FFI is about.

Today we're celebrating the beginning of eight initial partnership activities that will make this effort a reality. These new partnerships will mean economic incentives for forest conservation, better information for communities to practice sustainable management, better cooperation among government researchers and conservation groups.

I also promised last June to ask the Congress for $150 million in additional forest conservation assistance next year. And that is what we recommended in our budget statement of January 6th. And I hope the Congress will come through. I believe there's good support in the Congress for this approach.

These partnership approaches show that with effort and insight, we can truly conserve healthy, productive, and successful forests for our future. I will obviously be

2253

recommending to my successor that he continue this approach.

I just wish all of you the best. And now I'm going to turn the meeting over to Boyden and Bill Reilly. And thank you all

very much for coming.

Note: The President spoke at 10:34 a.m. in the Roosevelt Room at the White House.

Remarks and an Exchange With Reporters on the Situation in Iraq
January 15, 1993

The President. I have a brief statement that I want to make before heading up to Camp David. It relates to Iraq. And I just wanted to let you know that we continue to monitor Iraq's behavior for compliance with the United Nations resolutions.

Yesterday's mission was a success. It seriously depleted Iraq's air defense system, the one south of the 32d parallel. And nevertheless, we continue to examine the residual aspects of that mission.

In addition, we continue to demand access by United Nations aircraft for inspections in Iraq. And the United Nations has made it clear to the Iraqis that the United Nations inspection teams are prepared to resume their work and have the right to fly U.N. aircraft into that country at any time. The flight scheduled for today did not receive clearance to enter Iraqi airspace. And the United Nations has informed Saddam Hussein that if flight clearance is not granted by 4 p.m. Eastern Standard Time today,

Iraq will be in noncompliance. And the coalition partners are firm in demanding compliance with United Nations resolutions.

Q. Does that mean you would bomb again?

The President. Helen [Helen Thomas, United Press International], you've been covering things around here ever since I've been President, and I'll never say what we do do or don't do in terms of compelling compliance.

Q. But you don't intend to give any further warnings, is that correct?

The President. I think sufficient warnings have been granted. And they know what they must do. And this is not just the United States. This is the United Nations. It's a strong coalition whose determination has not diminished in any single way.

So, we'll see you all.

Note: The President spoke at 12:35 p.m. on the South Lawn at the White House prior to his departure for Camp David, MD.

Message to the Senate Transmitting the Russia-United States Treaty on Further Reduction and Limitation of Strategic Offensive Arms
January 15, 1993

To the Senate of the United States:

I am transmitting herewith, for the advice and consent of the Senate to ratification, the Treaty Between the United States of America and the Russian Federation on Further Reduction and Limitation of Strategic Offensive Arms (the START II Treaty) signed at Moscow on January 3, 1993. The Treaty includes the following documents,

which are integral parts thereof:

—the Protocol on Procedures Governing Elimination of Heavy ICBMs and on Procedures Governing Conversion of Silo Launchers of Heavy ICBMs Relating to the Treaty Between the United States of America and the Russian Federation on Further Reduction and Limitation of Strategic Offensive Arms (the Elimination and Conversion Protocol);

—the Protocol on Exhibitions and Inspections of Heavy Bombers Relating to the Treaty Between the United States of America and the Russian Federation on Further Reduction and Limitation of Strategic Offensive Arms (the Exhibitions and Inspections Protocol); and

—the Memorandum of Understanding on Warhead Attribution and Heavy Bomber Data Relating to the Treaty Between the United States of America and the Russian Federation on Further Reduction and Limitation of Strategic Offensive Arms (the Memorandum on Attribution).

In addition, I transmit herewith, for the information of the Senate, the report of the Department of State and letters exchanged by representatives of the Parties. The letters are associated with, but not integral parts of, the START II Treaty. Although not submitted for the advice and consent of the Senate to ratification, these letters are provided because they are relevant to the consideration of the Treaty by the Senate.

The START II Treaty is a milestone in the continuing effort by the United States and the Russian Federation to address the threat posed by strategic offensive nuclear weapons, especially multiple-warhead ICBMs. It builds upon and relies on the Treaty Between the United States of America and the Union of Soviet Socialist Republics on the Reduction and Limitation of Strategic Offensive Arms (the START Treaty) signed at Moscow on July 31, 1991. At the same time, the START II Treaty goes even further than the START Treaty.

The START Treaty was the first treaty actually to reduce strategic offensive arms of both countries, with overall reductions of 30–40 percent and reductions of up to 50 percent in the most threatening systems. It enhances stability in times of crisis. It not only limits strategic arms but also reduces them significantly below current levels. In addition, the START Treaty allows equality of forces and is effectively verifiable. Finally, commitments associated with the START Treaty will result in the elimination of nuclear weapons and deployed strategic offensive arms from the territories of Belarus, Kazakhstan, and Ukraine within 7 years after entry into force, and accession of these

three states to the Treaty on the Non-Proliferation of Nuclear Weapons (NPT) as non-nuclear-weapon States Parties. As a result, after 7 years, only Russia and the United States will retain any deployed strategic offensive arms under the START Treaty.

The START II Treaty builds upon and surpasses the accomplishments of the START Treaty by further reducing strategic offensive arms in such a way that further increases the stability of the strategic nuclear balance. It bans deployment of the most destabilizing type of nuclear weapons system—land-based intercontinental ballistic missiles with multiple independently targetable nuclear warheads. At the same time, the START II Treaty permits the United States to maintain a stabilizing sea-based force.

The central limits of the START II Treaty require reductions by January 1, 2003, to 3000–3500 warheads. Within this, there are sublimits of between 1700–1750 warheads on deployed SLBMs for each Party, or such lower number as each Party shall decide for itself; zero for warheads on deployed multiple-warhead ICBMs; and zero for warheads on deployed heavy ICBMs. Thus, the Treaty reduces the current overall deployments of strategic nuclear weapons on each side by more than two-thirds from current levels. These limits will be reached by the end of the year 2000 if both Parties reach agreement on a program of assistance to the Russian Federation with regard to dismantling strategic offensive arms within a year after entry into force of the Treaty. Acceptance of these reductions serves as a clear indication of the ending of the Cold War.

In a major accomplishment, START II will result in the complete elimination of heavy ICBMs (the SS–18s) and the elimination or conversion of their launchers. All heavy ICBMs and launch canisters will be destroyed. All but 90 heavy ICBM silos will likewise be destroyed and these 90 silos will be modified to be incapable of launching SS–18s. To address the Russians' stated concern over the cost of implementing the transition to a single-warhead ICBM force, the START II Treaty provides for the conversion of up to 90 of the 154 Russian SS–18 heavy ICBM silos that will remain after the

START Treaty reductions. The Russians have unilaterally undertaken to use the converted silos only for the smaller, SS–25 type single-warhead ICBMs. When implemented, the Treaty's conversion provisions, which include extensive on-site inspection rights, will preclude the use of these silos to launch heavy ICBMs. Together with the elimination of SS–18 missiles, these provisions are intended to ensure that the strategic capability of the SS–18 system is eliminated.

START II allows some reductions to be taken by downloading, i.e., reducing the number of warheads attributed to existing missiles. This will allow the United States to achieve the reductions required by the Treaty in a cost-effective way by downloading some or all of our sea-based Trident SLBMs and land-based Minuteman III ICBMs. The Treaty also allows downloading, in Russia, of 105 of the 170 SS–19 multiple-warhead missiles in existing silos to a single-warhead missile. All other Russian launchers of multiple-warhead ICBMs—including the remaining 65 SS–19s—must be converted for single-warhead ICBMs or eliminated in accordance with START procedures.

START II can be implemented in a fashion that is fully consistent with U.S. national security. To ensure that we have the ability to respond to worldwide conventional contingencies, it allows for the reorientation, without any conversion procedures, of 100 START-accountable heavy bombers to a conventional role. These heavy bombers will not count against START II warhead limits.

The START Treaty and the START II Treaty remain in force concurrently and have the same duration. Except as explicitly modified by the START II Treaty, the provisions of the START Treaty will be used to implement START II.

The START II Treaty provides for inspections in addition to those of the START Treaty. These additional inspections will be carried out according to the provisions of the START Treaty unless otherwise specified in the Elimination and Conversion Protocol or in the Exhibitions and Inspections Protocol. As I was convinced that the START Treaty is effectively verifiable, I am equally confident that the START II Treaty is effectively verifiable.

The START Treaty was an historic achievement in our long-term effort to enhance the stability of the strategic balance through arms control. The START II Treaty represents the capstone of that effort. Elimination of heavy ICBMs and the effective elimination of all other multiple-warhead ICBMs will put an end to the most dangerous weapons of the Cold War.

In sum, the START II Treaty is clearly in the interest of the United States and represents a watershed in our efforts to stabilize the nuclear balance and further reduce strategic offensive arms. I therefore urge the Senate to give prompt and favorable consideration to the Treaty, including its Protocols and Memorandum on Attribution, and to give its advice and consent to ratification.

GEORGE BUSH

The White House,
January 15, 1993.

Statement by Press Secretary Fitzwater on the START II Treaty
January 15, 1993

I am pleased to announce that today the President submitted the START II treaty to the Senate for its advice and consent to ratification. This treaty marks an achievement of fundamental importance not only to the United States and Russia but to the whole world. START II is the capstone of a process over the past 2 years that has set back the hands on the nuclear doomsday clock.

The President urges the Senate to act promptly and approve the START II treaty. He also looks forward to prompt ratification of this treaty by Russia, as well as the ratification of START I and accession to the Non-Proliferation Treaty by Belarus, Ukraine, and Kazakhstan. Once these ac- tions are completed the historic reductions can begin without delay.

Letter to Congressional Leaders on Science and Technology Policy
January 15, 1993

Dear Mr. Speaker: (Dear Mr. President:)

My Administration has accelerated our national investment in America's future through increased support for science and technology. Had the Congress fully enacted my FY 1993 budget, investments in applied civilian R&D would have increased by 49 percent over the past 4 years. My Administration also has revitalized the Federal Government's ability to deal with science and technology. These actions included establishing the President's Council of Advisors on Science and Technology to insure high-level input from the private sector and restructuring the Federal Coordinating Council for Science, Engineering, and Technology to facilitate crosscutting multiagency R&D programs. Among these programs intended to harness science and technology to meet 21st century needs are Presidential initiatives on biotechnology, advanced materials, information technologies, and manufacturing.

To strengthen the educational foundations for growth, I convened the 1989 Education Summit and in 1991 transmitted to the Congress the AMERICA 2000 Excellence in Education Act to facilitate the educational reform needed to reach the National Education Goals set forth by the Summit. As part of this reform, my Administration has developed a strategic plan for education in mathematics, science, engineering, and technology that involves the coordinated efforts of 16 Federal agencies.

A particular strength of America's science and technology effort in my Administration has been its international leadership. The superiority of U.S. science and technology was manifested in the weapons systems that performed so admirably in Desert Storm, allowing us to win the war with minimal loss of life. As we restructure our military systems to face the greatly altered national security threats of the future, we must maintain an active and inventive program of defense R&D. Through our Global Change research program and a vigorous program of domestic initiatives, ranging from the revised Clean Air Act to my decision to accelerate the phaseout of the chemicals that degrade the Earth's ozone layer, we also have been an international leader in confronting the problems of the global environment. Under my Administration, the United States has provided more support for research on Global Change than all other countries put together—research that is providing a scientific basis for environmentally and economically sound stewardship of the Earth. Finally, my Administration has extended the hand of cooperation in science and technology to many nations, forging new bilateral and multilateral agreements and seeking a truly international basis for proceeding with increasingly large and complex megaprojects in science that have the potential to produce fundamental knowledge of benefit to all humanity.

Despite the strength and overall health of our American science and technology enterprise, I must call the attention of the Congress to a number of areas of concern for the future. My Council of Advisors on Science and Technology has recently reported on signs of stress in our universities. Our precollege educational system still has far to go to meet our National Education Goals and to adequately prepare our work force and our citizens for the 21st century. Private sector investment in R&D is stagnating even as the competitive pressures of a global economy accelerate. In addition, the relationships between the critical elements of our science and technology enterprise—universities, private industry, and the Federal Government—are changing rapidly, even as the nature of science and technology itself is changing.

These considerations suggest that it is time to rethink our national policies for science and technology: to reexamine the role and the rationale for Federal support, to reconsider the structure of the Nation's R&D capacity, and to revitalize the mechanisms and educational institutions that support that capacity. These ideas as well as a

review of selected science and technology policy initiatives in my Administration are described in the Biennial Report of the Office of Science and Technology Policy, which accompanies this Report.

Sincerely,

GEORGE BUSH

Note: Identical letters were sent to Thomas S. Foley, Speaker of the House of Representatives, and Dan Quayle, President of the Senate.

Letter to Congressional Leaders Transmitting a Report on Federal Regulatory Policy
January 15, 1993

Dear Mr. Speaker: (Dear Mr. President:)

This *Regulatory Program of the United States Government* compiles, under one cover, my Administration's regulatory programs, goals, and objectives for the year 1992–93. By providing a preview of significant regulatory activities, we reaffirm our unwavering commitment to agency accountability for improved regulation, intragovernmental coordination, and public and congressional access to our regulatory agenda and priorities. Our regulatory program constitutes a coherent, consistent, and constructive program with unity of purpose. Our purpose is to promote economic growth while maintaining this Administration's strong tradition of upholding health, safety, and environmental quality as top priority.

Federal regulations to implement the laws that safeguard the Nation's health and safety, environment, and economic well-being are essential to maintain and improve the public welfare. Excessively burdensome regulation, however, hampers the creativity and energy of the American people. Regulation should instead channel this creativity and energy to maximize social and economic benefits. The concepts of "efficiency" and "maximized net benefits" guide our regulatory program in promoting a strong economy and protecting our citizenry.

In my State of the Union Address, I called

for a "top-to-bottom" review of Federal regulation. This occurred during our 90-day regulatory review and moratorium. That period was followed by a 120-day extension to implement significant reforms. During this 7-month period, we strove to eliminate many overly burdensome Federal regulations and have promulgated new regulations that will save American consumers and workers billions of dollars. We also extended the review and moratorium for an additional year.

The Federal regulatory environment must be dynamic and changing to reflect a changing world. It must be lean and focused on specific areas where Federal regulation contributes to the public good. An excessive or static regulatory system loses its ability to solve problems and instead creates them by forcing individuals, businesses, and State and local governments into expensive compliance exercises. We have "cleaned house" by scrapping obsolete and unduly burdensome regulations; by modifying and updating current rules; and by implementing new rules to release American capital and the Nation's competitive spirit.

Everyone pays for overly burdensome regulation. Regulatory costs must be reduced. This report embodies our efforts to aid in that quest.

Sincerely,

GEORGE BUSH

S. Foley, Speaker of the House of Representatives, and Dan Quayle, President of the Senate.

Note: Identical letters were sent to Thomas

Letter to Congressional Leaders Transmitting the Report of the Tourism Policy Council
January 15, 1993

Dear Mr. Speaker: (Dear Mr. President:)
In accordance with section 302 of the International Travel Act of 1961, as amended (22 U.S.C. 2124a(f)), I transmit herewith the annual report of the Tourism Policy Council, which covers fiscal years 1991 and 1992.
Sincerely,

GEORGE BUSH

Note: Identical letters were sent to Thomas S. Foley, Speaker of the House of Representatives, and Dan Quayle, President of the Senate.

Letter to the United States Trade Representative on Rubber Thread Imports
January 15, 1993

Dear Ambassador Hills:
Pursuant to section 201 of the Trade Act of 1974 (Public Law 93–618, 19 U.S.C. 2252), I have reviewed the Report of the United States International Trade Commission (USITC) dated December 21, 1992, concerning the results of its investigation of a petition for import relief filed by domestic producers of extruded rubber thread.
I have accepted the findings of Vice Chairman Watson and Commissioners Brunsdale and Crawford that extruded rubber thread was not being imported into the United States in such increased quantities as to be a substantial cause of serious injury, or the threat thereof, to the industry in the United States producing an article like or directly competitive with the imported articles.
This decision is to be published in the *Federal Register*.
Sincerely,

GEORGE BUSH

Note: The notice of the President's decision was published in the Federal Register on January 27.

The President's News Conference With Prime Minister Brian Mulroney of Canada at Camp David, Maryland
January 16, 1993

The President. May I just say how wonderful it is to have the Prime Minister of Canada here with us today, great friend of the United States. The relationship between Canada and the United States is strong; tremendous trading partner. Prime Minister Mulroney has done an awful lot in all ways in cooperating and working with us. Their leadership in many areas of peacekeeping is one that we respect and admire. He was the one that prodded me to do more on environmental legislation.

And so for me and for Barbara, this is a fond farewell as we leave this job. And it's most fitting, in our way of looking at things, that Prime Minister Mulroney and his wonderful family are with us here today. So we're going to talk some business, and then we're going to look around and have a little R&R.

The floor is yours, sir. Welcome.

Prime Minister Mulroney. Thank you, George.

Well, we're delighted to be here. The President has pointed out the strength of the Canadian-American relationship. It's, as you know, a huge and a complicated one and not always an easy one. But it indicates the extent to which neighbors can become friends and mutually assisting partners.

Canada is the largest trading partner that the United States has, and you are ours. And so President Bush's visionary initiative in respect to free trade throughout the hemisphere is one part of a very important legacy that he will be leaving.

The Clean Air Act that gave rise to the Canadian-American treaty on acid rain is another very important matter that people in both countries had fought for for literally decades.

And I can tell you that, because I happened to be there, that his remarkable assembling of the coalition in terms of the Gulf war——

Q. What do you think ought to be done on the Gulf——

Prime Minister Mulroney. ——is probably without precedent, certainly in recent decades.

So I'm delighted to have a chance to come by and say hello to the President and the family before he leaves office. And of course, he'll always have the friendship and the respect of Canadians.

Iraq

Q. Are you with him now in this current standoff with Iraq?

Prime Minister Mulroney. Yes, I am.

Canada-U.S. Trade

Q. Prime Minister, you said there would be structural changes in the relationship between Canada and the U.S. to avoid some of the trade irritants when you were last here and met with the President. Do you think they'll survive the new administration, or will you have to work to put them in place again?

Prime Minister Mulroney. Well, I think we have to work hard at trade at all times. It's a difficult matter because it affects jobs sometimes in both countries, and so it's not easy. And we're going to have to work hard to maintain this relationship, as we did in the past. Fortunately, in the past we had a friend in the White House, and I suspect that will be the case in the future. Governor Clinton understands and has told the President——

The President. That's right.

Prime Minister Mulroney. ——and told me of his recognition of the great importance of Canada as a trading partner and a friend to the United States.

The President. No question about that. No question about that.

Iraq

Q. Mr. President, what's your response to 'Aziz, Mr. President? Are there any more warnings?

The President. We have no response now. We're interested in knowing what the United Nations response is. It's the United

Nations going on with this; it's the United Nations, Dr. Ekeus, that we'll be talking to. And we'll all be talking about that a little later. But his move just was announced, and we'll just have to wait and see how it's regarded. We don't do these things unilaterally. We consult. We'll be able to talk now with the Prime Minister. We'll be talking with others as well, I think, during the course of this afternoon.

Q. Mr. Prime Minister——

[*At this point, a question was asked and answered in French, and a translation was not provided.*]

Canadian Elections

Q. Mr. Prime Minister, after a week of reflection, have you decided that you will definitely lead your party into the next election?

Prime Minister Mulroney. I've already spoken to that issue in the year-enders in Canada, and I've got nothing further to add.

Canadian Ambassador

Q. What signal did you hope to send to the Americans with the appointment of General de Chastelain? Was there a message in it in terms of the role and expanded relationship we want with the United States?

Prime Minister Mulroney. No. He's just an outstanding Canadian, a remarkably talented man who can do a very good job for Canada in Washington at a crucial moment. And he's held in very high regard. In fact, he'll be here this afternoon at Camp David.

The President. Yes, I'm looking forward to that.

Q.——push them on the U.N. or other matters?

Prime Minister Mulroney. Well, we're not pushing anybody. He'll be there to defend our interests.

President's Diary

Q. Mr. President, on your diary, do you think you got a fair shake?

The President. I don't like any stuff about that.

Prime Minister Mulroney. Helen [Helen Thomas, United Press International], what

we want to do is read your diaries. [*Laughter*] That's what I'm waiting for.

[*At this point, a remark was made in French, and a translation was not provided.*]

Prime Minister Mulroney. I'm going to read them, Helen, I tell you.

Haiti

Q.——tighten the net around Haiti as a favor to Clinton?

The President. I don't think of that as a favor to Clinton. I will say this for the Clinton security team, and I'm sure General Scowcroft would agree with this: There's been extraordinarily good cooperation. I determined early on that from our end the transition would go well on these important issues. I think he made the same determination. And so there's nothing being done to kind of look like we're doing something, that wouldn't be done as if it were one team running the show.

Q. But do you resent the fact that he insulted your Haiti policy during the campaign, and now he's adopted it?

The President. No, I don't resent anything. It's a funny thing. I'm in a mood where I don't have any resentment in my heart. [*Laughter*] It's not ever been thus, I can tell you guys. [*Laughter*]

Transition

Q. He doesn't think the transition's going well because you're not leaving anyone to hold over for a few weeks to——

The President. I think we're following what they want. They want to have the decks cleared. Remember all the stories you people wrote about, what was it? Calling—it wasn't rat-holing, but it had a lovely term like, kind of, people wedging their way into the bureaucracy so they could be employed. What we've done is follow the agreement, so to clear the decks with those people who were not civil service. And that's what an outgoing administration should do. So if they want somebody to stay, they're welcome to ask them, of course.

Canada-U.S. Relations

Q. President Bush, what is your assessment of Canada-U.S. relations as you leave office? Have they improved?

The President. Thumbs up.

Q. Still any problems that have to be worked out?

The President. None. Well, once in a while you can run into a little hiccup, a little bump in the road. Once in a while we've had some differences on trading problems. But look, you've got to look at the big picture. And the relationship is outstanding. It's important. I mean, it is vitally important to the United States. It's important today, was yesterday, will be tomorrow. And so it really is fundamentally sound and good and strong.

[*At this point, a question was asked and answered in French, and a translation was not provided.*]

Iraq

Q. Sir, have we moved back from the brink of military action that you hinted at yesterday?

The President. We're not on the brink or moved back from anything. We're just going to be consulting, and we'll see where we go from there. I wasn't trying to be belligerent. I'm just simply saying they're going to comply with these resolutions, period. And so we'll see.

Q. Well, was it more conciliatory, their response today? Was there any movement?

The President. Well, we're going to talk about it. I mean, I've learned something about this. You don't jump to conclusions until you know all the facts, get all the translation. I heard him. What I heard in English sounded—that he was going to let these people in, but we've got to wait and see. I don't know about these conditions and all of that. But those are the things you consult about. He's thrown some conditions on it.

Thank you all.

Prime Minister Mulroney. Thank you very much.

Camp David

Q. How do you feel about leaving Camp David?

The President. Leaving Camp David? Well, I'm not leaving until—[*laughter*]— Monday night. But Monday night if you ask me, I expect I'd feel sad about that. This has been a wonderful retreat here, and I've sure enjoyed sharing it with friends, domestic and from overseas. And this weekend is going to be pure joy because we've got some good friends here.

Q. What have you got in store for the Prime Minister and his family?

The President. A lot of exercise. A lot of exercise. [*Laughter*]

Q. Are you flying back to Houston without us, sir?

The President. Look for deer.

Q. Are you going to take a press pool to Houston?

The President. No. Oh, I forgot to tell you. On January 20th at noon, I'm through with press pools. We're shifting. It shifts over to the new President. And I'm going back to private life. And it's going to be low key. And it's going to be—there's no point in trying to continue something that isn't. And I'm trying to conduct myself with dignity and hopefully in a spirit of total cooperation with Governor Clinton. No bitterness in my heart. But look, January 20th when I walk out of that Capitol, I'm a private citizen. And I hope I'll be treated as a private citizen by my neighbors in Houston. And I'm not looking to sit at the head table. I'm not looking to have press conferences. I love you guys, especially the photo dogs. [*Laughter*] But we're not going to—we're going to really shift gears like that. It's going to be interesting.

Q. ——on that last ride in the big Government plane?

The President. No, no, no. January 20th it ends at noon. It ends.

Q. I bet you won't be able to do it.

The President. I'm going to try. I'm going to sure try.

Note: The President's 142d news conference began at 12:15 p.m. at Camp David.

Letter to Congressional Leaders Transmitting the Report on the National Security Strategy
January 19, 1993

Dear Mr. Speaker: *(Dear Mr. President:)*

In accordance with section 603 of the Goldwater-Nichols Department of Defense Reorganization Act of 1986 (Public Law 99–433; 50 U.S.C. 404a), I hereby transmit the annual report on the National Security Strategy of the United States.

Sincerely,

GEORGE BUSH

Note: Identical letters were sent to Thomas S. Foley, Speaker of the House of Representatives, and Dan Quayle, President of the Senate.

Statement on the National Security Strategy Report
January 19, 1993

Today, as required by the Goldwater-Nichols Defense Reform Act of 1986, I signed and forwarded to the Congress the National Security Strategy Report. This report comes at a particularly important time, when the international security environment is in the midst of a turbulent transition and when the continuity of America's engagement and leadership is perhaps more important than ever before. No other nation can provide the same combination of moral, cultural, political, economic, and military leadership. No other has won such confidence, respect, and trust. If we are to seize the opportunities that will be offered and reduce the dangers that will surely confront us in the future, America must lead. We must lead because we simply cannot hope to achieve a more democratic and peaceful future in a world still rife with turmoil and conflict and political or economic isolation. This does not mean we aspire to be the world's policeman or that we can postpone addressing our own domestic imperatives while we devote attention and resources to international demands. It is not an either/or choice. We cannot be strong abroad if we are not strong at home. We cannot be strong at home if we are not strong and engaged abroad.

The National Security Strategy Report acknowledges the diverse political, economic, and military challenges that America faces, as well as the domestic imperatives that define our overall national health. It identifies our enduring national security interests and objectives: the security of the United States as a free and independent nation; global and regional stability; open, democratic, and representative political systems worldwide; an open international trading and economic system; and an enduring global faith in America.

The report acknowledges our political achievements over recent years and outlines both short- and long-term approaches to promote peace and democracy worldwide. It specifically addresses priorities of our bilateral efforts as well as initiatives in multinational and regional organizations designed to influence the future. Emphasizing the now-diminishing distinction between domestic and international economic policy, it identifies the steps necessary for domestic economic renewal, as well as prioritized initiatives to strengthen our international economic competitiveness. It also emphasizes the need to reform U.S. economic institutions and our bilateral development assistance and to expand considerably our efforts in the environment and in space.

Stressing the continued mandate for security through strength, the report defines four enduring and mutually supportive strategic goals: deterrence and the capability to defeat aggression should deterrence fail; strengthening our alliance arrangements and our preference for multilateral action; maintaining stability through forward presence and force projection; and helping to preclude conflict and keep the peace. Most important, the report identifies a strategy for near-term leadership and outlines ways the United States can help influence the future through the United Nations, regional organizations, and alliances.

America has always stood for much more than the sum of its political and economic goals and aspirations. We do care about the world around us, and our contributions are written in history for all to see. We inspire others because of what we have achieved and because of what we represent. We have a vision for the future. We seek a world of cooperation and progress, not confrontation; a world no longer divided but a community of independent and interdependent nations joined together by shared values; a world in which the U.S. role is defined by what we stand for, freedom, human rights, economic prosperity, the rule of law and peace, rather than what we stand against.

To succeed, our strategy must be more than words on a piece of paper. We must have faith, courage, hard work, and inspiration. We must continue the dialog and the debate, for that too is what democracy is all about. As a nation, let us work together to lead the world toward the 21st century, the age of democratic peace. There is no more important goal to which we would aspire.

Letter to Congressional Leaders Reporting on Nuclear Nonproliferation
January 19, 1993

Dear Mr. Speaker: (Dear Mr. President:)

I have reviewed the activities of the United States Government departments and agencies during calendar year 1992 relating to preventing nuclear proliferation, and I am pleased to submit my annual report pursuant to section 601(a) of the Nuclear Non-Proliferation Act of 1978 (Public Law 95–242, 22 U.S.C. 3281(a)).

The accomplishments of the past year provide a fitting capstone to this Administration's efforts to stem the spread of nuclear weapons. These efforts were provided additional focus on July 13, when I issued a statement setting forth a number of initiatives as well as a clear framework of guiding principles for our nonproliferation policy.

Global norms and institutions have strengthened this year. Membership in the Nuclear Non-Proliferation Treaty has grown to 155, including the last declared two nuclear weapon states: France and China. The three Baltic states as well as two of the newly-independent states have also joined the Treaty, while three others—Ukraine, Belarus, and Kazakhstan—committed to do so "in the shortest possible time." The United States increased its support for the International Atomic Energy Agency, which sought to strengthen its safeguards system in response to its experience in Iraq.

In addressing regional dangers, the United States also joined with the international community to continue to support efforts to destroy Iraq's nuclear weapons program under U.N. Security Council resolutions and to press North Korea to honor its nonproliferation commitments. Focusing on the Middle East, the five permanent members of the U.N. Security Council agreed to interim guidelines to restrain destabilizing transfers of arms and technologies related to weapons of mass destruction, while the arms control and regional security talks provided an unprecedented forum for countries in that troubled region to address these issues face to face. The United States held talks separately with India and Pakistan in the hope of stemming a nuclear arms race in South Asia. Meanwhile, the United States has been gratified by steps taken by countries such as Argentina, Brazil, and South Africa to join international nonproliferation regimes.

We have worked hard to address the proliferation concerns arising from the breakup of the Soviet Union and its domination of Eastern Europe. With the firm support of the Congress, we are developing assistance to Russia, Ukraine, Belarus and Kazakhstan to support the safety and security of the dismantlement of nuclear weapons in the former Soviet Union. The U.S. has also provided assistance to Russia and Ukraine in developing systems for physical protection and material accounting and control for materials removed from nuclear warheads. In August, U.S. negotiators initialed an agreement to seek recovery of highly-enriched uranium from the former Soviet nuclear arsenal and dilute it to commercial reactor fuel with no military implications. In collaboration with our allies, we fostered the creation of science and technology centers in Moscow and Kiev to prevent the outflow of nuclear weapons expertise from the former Soviet Union, and provided export control and reactor safety assistance to the states of Eastern Europe and the former Soviet Union.

These accomplishments constitute a solid contribution to continuing international efforts to stem nuclear proliferation and to promote the peace and security of all nations. Nevertheless, proliferation remains a significant and growing concern that will require even more attention, energy, and resources in the years ahead.

Sincerely,

GEORGE BUSH

Note: Identical letters were sent to Thomas S. Foley, Speaker of the House of Representatives, and Dan Quayle, President of the Senate.

Letter to Congressional Leaders Transmitting a Report on Arms Control Treaty Compliance
January 19, 1993

Dear Mr. Speaker: (Dear Mr. President:)

Pursuant to Public Law 99–145; 22 U.S.C. 2592a as amended, and section 52 of the Arms Control and Disarmament Act, I am transmitting to the Congress a classified and unclassified report on arms control treaty compliance by the successor states to the Soviet Union and other nations that are parties to arms control agreements with the United States, as well as by the United States itself.

Sincerely,

GEORGE BUSH

Note: Identical letters were sent to Thomas S. Foley, Speaker of the House of Representatives, and Dan Quayle, President of the Senate.

Letter to Congressional Leaders Transmitting the Report on Science, Technology, and American Diplomacy
January 19, 1993

Dear Mr. Speaker: (Dear Mr. Chairman:)

In accordance with Title V of the Foreign Relations Act of Fiscal Year 1979, as amended (Public Law 95–426; 22 U.S.C. 2656c(b)), I am pleased to transmit this annual report on Science, Technology and American Diplomacy for fiscal year 1992.

This is the first Title V report in which the entire period of coverage falls within the post-Cold War era, and a number of trends important to international science and technology (S&T) have become evident. As traditional Cold War concerns fade, the character and impact of S&T in U.S. foreign policy are also changing significantly. The importance of S&T in addressing problems such as environmental degradation and international economic and technological competitiveness will grow. At the same time, S&T will continue to be important to traditional military concerns and in areas of increasing importance following the demise of the Soviet Union, such as proliferation of weapons of mass destruction.

The material presented in this report illustrates the significant role of S&T in American diplomacy and the tremendous changes in its character and impact following the end of the Cold War. This year's report focuses on three topical areas: S&T interactions with the Newly Independent States and the Baltics; the United Nations Conference on Environment and Development (UNCED); and a number of very big ("megascience") programs, including illustrative space activities. The report also features narratives on 22 selected countries and 3 international organizations (the European Community, NATO, and the OECD).

As the definitive annual official reference on U.S. Government international S&T agreements and activities, this Title V report:

- Reviews a number of salient international S&T themes and issues, chosen by consensus in the executive branch;
- Illustrates by means of both narratives and an extensive data base an in-depth review of U.S. Government activities in the chosen thematic areas; and
- Provides, via the data base, a comprehensive overview of official U.S. Government international S&T activities in all areas.

In early 1991, I enunciated five major interrelated foreign policy challenges and objectives in the post-Cold War era:

1) promoting and consolidating democratic values;
2) promoting market principles and strengthening U.S. competitiveness;
3) promoting peace;
4) protecting against transnational threats such as environmental degradation; and
5) meeting urgent humanitarian needs.

The importance of S&T to achieving all five goals is seen clearly in the thematic areas that are the focus of this report.

Science and Technology Interactions with the Newly Independent States and the Baltics: U.S. S&T efforts in the former Soviet Union and Baltics have focused on forging new S&T links, assisting in military S&T conversion and the meeting environmental, health, energy and other needs, and helping to maintain a sound S&T infrastructure. A collapse of the former Soviet scientific community would greatly endanger sustainable progress toward open societies and market economics and would increase the risk of weapons proliferation. Building a strong S&T infrastructure will help provide a solid foundation for a stable transition away from Communist rule and centrally planned economies.

United Nations Conference on Environment and Development: Science and technology are critical tools in protecting against transnational threats such as global change, ozone depletion, and loss of biological diversity. Communication and cooperation in the international S&T community provided the basis for UNCED preparations and the three principal documents it produced, the Rio Declaration on Environment and Development, Agenda 21, and a statement of principles for the management, conservation, and sustainable use of forests. The convention on global change, opened at UNCED for signature, is based on the results of an extensive international S&T effort.

Megascience Programs: The scientific facilities needed to pursue ever more fundamental questions about the nature of the universe are growing larger and more complex. As the costs associated with scientific research rise, maintaining national intellectual and technological competence in forefront areas requiring large facilities or global-scope research will increasingly require international collaboration. By sharing the burdens of supporting megascience projects, nations produce fundamental knowledge not possible to attain unilaterally.

The thematic focus of this report illustrates the critical role of S&T in meeting our major foreign policy challenges. These challenges transcend partisan political differences and will, I believe, continue to permeate U.S. foreign policy into the next century.

Sincerely,

GEORGE BUSH

Note: Identical letters were sent to Thomas S. Foley, Speaker of the House of Representatives; Claiborne Pell, chairman, Senate Committee on Foreign Relations; and John Glenn, chairman, Senate Committee on Governmental Affairs.

Letter to Congressional Leaders on Additional Measures With Respect to the Federal Republic of Yugoslavia (Serbia and Montenegro)
January 19, 1993

Dear Mr. Speaker: (Dear Mr. President:)

On June 1, 1992, pursuant to section 204(b) of the International Emergency Economic Powers Act (50 U.S.C. 1703(b)) and section 301 of the National Emergencies Act (50 U.S.C. 1631), I reported to the Congress by letters to the President of the Senate and the Speaker of the House, dated May 30, 1992, that I had exercised my statutory authority to issue Executive Order No. 12808 of May 30, 1992, declaring a national emergency and blocking "Yugoslav Government" property and property of the Governments of Serbia and Montenegro.

On June 5, 1992, pursuant to the above authorities as well as section 1114 of the Federal Aviation Act of 1958, as amended (49 U.S.C. App. 1514), and section 5 of the United Nations Participation Act of 1945, as amended (22 U.S.C. 287c), I reported to the Congress by letters to the President of the Senate and the Speaker of the House, that I had exercised my statutory authority to issue Executive Order No. 12810 of June 5, 1992, blocking property of and prohibiting transactions with the Federal Republic of Yugoslavia (Serbia and Montenegro). This latter action was taken to ensure that the economic measures that we are taking with respect to the Federal Republic of Yugoslavia (Serbia and Montenegro) conform to U.N. Security Council Resolution No. 757 (May 30, 1992).

On November 16, 1992, the U.N. Security Council adopted Resolution No. 787, calling on member states to take additional measures to tighten the embargo against the Federal Republic of Yugoslavia (Serbia and Montenegro). On January 15, 1993, I took additional steps pursuant to the above statutory authorities to enhance the implementation of this international embargo and to conform to U.N. Security Council Resolution 787 (November 16, 1992).

The order that I signed on January 15, 1993:

—prohibits any transaction within the United States or by a United States person related to the transshipment of commodities or products through the

Federal Republic of Yugoslavia (Serbia and Montenegro) and revokes the previous exception for such transshipment contained in Executive Order No. 12810;

—prohibits any transaction within the United States or by a United States person relating to any vessel, regardless of the flag under which it sails, in which a majority or controlling interest is held by a person or entity in the Federal Republic of Yugoslavia (Serbia and Montenegro); and

—requires for purposes of Executive Order No. 12810 that any such vessel be considered as a vessel of the Federal Republic of Yugoslavia (Serbia and Montenegro).

The order that I signed on January 15, 1993, authorizes the Secretary of the Treasury in consultation with the Secretary of State to take such actions as may be necessary to carry out the purposes of this order. Such actions may include the prohibition and regulation of trade and financial transactions involving any areas of the territory of the former Socialist Federal Republic of Yugoslavia as to which there is no adequate assurance that such transactions will not be diverted to the benefit of the Federal Republic of Yugoslavia (Serbia and Montenegro).

The declaration of the national emergency made by Executive Order No. 12808 and the controls imposed under Executive Order No. 12810 and any other provisions of that order and of Executive Order No. 12810 not modified by or inconsistent with the January 15, 1993, order, remain in force and are unaffected by that order.

Sincerely,

GEORGE BUSH

Note: Identical letters were sent to Thomas S. Foley, Speaker of the House of Representatives, and Dan Quayle, President of the Senate. The Executive order of January 15 is listed in Appendix E at the end of this volume.

Presidential Determination No. 93–14—Memorandum on Assistance to Refugees of Tajikistan
January 19, 1993

Memorandum for the Secretary of State

Subject: Determination Pursuant to Section 2(c)(1) of the Migration and Refugee Assistance Act of 1962, as Amended

Pursuant to section 2(c)(1) of the Migration and Refugee Assistance Act of 1962, as amended, 22 U.S.C. 2601(c)(1), I hereby determine that it is important to the national interest that up to $5,000,000 be made available from the U.S. Emergency Refugee and Migration Assistance Fund to meet the urgent and unexpected needs of refugees, displaced persons, and victims of conflict from Tajikistan. These funds may be contributed on a multilateral or bilateral basis as appropriate to international organizations, private voluntary organizations, and other governmental and nongovernmental organizations engaged in this relief effort.

You are directed to inform the appropriate committees of the Congress of this determination and the obligation of funds under this authority, and to publish this memorandum in the *Federal Register*.

GEORGE BUSH

[*Filed with the Office of the Federal Register, 10:59 a.m., January 26, 1993*]

Letter to Congressional Leaders Reporting on Iraq's Compliance With United Nations Security Council Resolutions
January 19, 1993

Dear Mr. Speaker: (Dear Mr. President:)

Consistent with the Authorization for Use of Military Force Against Iraq Resolution (Public Law 102–1) and as part of my continuing effort to keep Congress fully informed, I am again reporting on the status of efforts to obtain Iraq's compliance with the resolutions adopted by the U.N. Security Council.

Since my last report on November 16, 1992, Iraq has repeatedly ignored and violated its international obligations under U.N. Security Council Resolutions. Iraq's actions include the harassment of humanitarian relief operations in northern Iraq contrary to U.N. Security Council Resolution 688, violations of the Iraq-Kuwait demilitarized zone, interference with U.N. operations in violation of Security Council Resolution 687, repeated violations by Iraqi aircraft of the southern and northern no-fly zones, and threats by Iraq's air defense forces against Coalition aircraft enforcing the no-fly zones.

The southern no-fly zone and Operation Southern Watch were established in August 1992 to assist the monitoring of Iraq's compliance with Security Council Resolution 688. Since that time, Iraq has stopped aerial bombardments of its citizens in and around the southern marsh areas and ceased large-scale military operations south of the 32nd parallel. Operation Southern Watch cannot detect lower-level acts of oppression, however.

In December 1992, Iraqi aircraft on several occasions entered the southern no-fly zone and demonstrated hostile intent, including by firing a missile at a U.S. aircraft. On December 27, 1992, a U.S. aircraft shot down an Iraqi aircraft that entered the no-fly zone. Beginning in late December, Iraq moved surface-to-air missiles into the zone, threatening Coalition aircraft operating south of the 32nd parallel. On January 6, 1993, the United States and its Coalition partners issued an ultimatum to Iraq to disperse and render non-threatening its surface-to-air missiles deployed in the zone and to cease aircraft activities in the area. Iraq initially acceded to this demarche. The United States then announced that it would scrutinize Iraqi activity and that "[n]o further warning will be issued if Iraq violates the requirements of the January 6 demarche."

By January 11, 1993, it had become clear that Iraq had stopped complying with the requirements of the January 6 demarche and that missiles once again threaten Coalition aircraft. Accordingly, U.S. and Coalition aircraft attacked and destroyed surface-to-air missile sites and related facilities in southern Iraq on January 13. There were no losses to the aircraft taking part in the mission. In this connection, I note the statement of U.N. Secretary General Boutros-Ghali on January 14, 1993, that "the raid and the forces that carried out the raid, have received a mandate from the Security Council, according to Resolution 687, and the cause of the raid was the violation by Iraq of Resolution 687 concerning the cease-fire. So, as Secretary General of the United Nations, I can say this action was taken and conforms to the resolutions of the Security Council and conformed to the Charter of the United Nations." On January 18, 1993, Coalition aircraft again struck air defense sites and related infrastructure to ensure the safety of Coalition flight operations in the area. There were no losses to Coalition aircraft.

On January 7, 1993, the Iraqi Government refused permission for certain U.N. aircraft to land in Baghdad, thereby interfering with the missions of the U.N. Special Commission on Iraq (UNSCOM) and the U.N. Iraq-Kuwait Observer Mission (UNIKOM). On January 8, and again on January 11, 1993, the U.N. Security Council formally found this Iraqi action to "constitute an unacceptable and material breach of the relevant provisions of Resolution 687 (1991), which established the cease-fire and provided the conditions essential to the restoration of peace and security in the region." The Council also warned Iraq of the "serious consequences which would ensue from failure to comply with its obligations."

On January 13, 1993, we underscored our full support for the Council's statements. On January 15, 1993, UNSCOM found Iraq's refusal to guarantee the safety of flights constituted an abdication of Iraq's responsibilities to ensure the safety of UNSCOM personnel. On January 16, 1993, UNSCOM found that Iraq's decision to condition ensuring the safety of flights on entry of Iraqi airspace from Jordan to be an unacceptable attempt to restrict UNSCOM's freedom of movement. If accepted, such a condition would prevent the Special Commission from effectively carrying out its mission.

On January 17, 1993, at my direction, U.S. Tomahawk missiles destroyed the Zaafaraniyah nuclear fabrication facility near Baghdad. This facility was selected because of its role in Iraq's electromagnetic isotope separation (EMIS) program. The Coalition attack was designed to help achieve the goals of U.N. Security Council Resolutions 687, 707, and 715 requiring Iraq to accept the inspection and elimination of its weapons of mass destruction and ballistic missiles. Zaafariniyah had been inspected a number of times, and some equipment used for the production of EMIS components for Iraq's nuclear weapons program was removed. The facility nonetheless contained precision machine tools used to fabricate items for military and civilian customers and could again be used to support Iraq's nuclear weapons program.

In early January 1993, Iraq sent personnel into Kuwait and the demilitarized zone (DMZ) to seize military equipment and other valuable goods. These actions violated the DMZ, the recently demarcated Iraqi-Kuwait boundary, and agreements with the United Nations. On January 8, the U.N. Security Council declared that, "the presence of Iraqi military personnel in the demilitarized zone was a serious violation of Resolution 687." It also said that "the removal of the Iraqi property and assets from Kuwaiti territory should be undertaken only after prior clearance by UNIKOM and by the

Kuwaiti authorities through UNIKOM."

On January 10, 1993, Coalition representatives notified the Iraqi Government that additional Iraqi intrusions into Kuwait and the DMZ would not be tolerated. On January 11, the Security Council condemned the Iraqi actions as "further material breaches of Resolution 687" and warned Iraq again of serious consequences that would flow from continued defiance. Nevertheless, each day from January 10 to 13, Iraq continued to send personnel to retrieve material in violation of the DMZ, the boundary, and its agreements with the United Nations. In these circumstances, I ordered the deployment of a task force to Kuwait to reemphasize our commitment to Kuwaiti independence and security.

Meanwhile, Operation Provide Comfort, the Coalition's effort to monitor compliance with U.N. Security Council Resolution 688 and to provide humanitarian relief in northern Iraq, discourages significant Iraqi military operations against the inhabitants there. On the other hand, the Iraqi Government has maintained an embargo of food, fuel, and medicine on northern Iraq. It has made every effort to frustrate U.N. humanitarian relief efforts by planting bombs on relief convoys, using violence against relief workers, and creating bureaucratic delays. We are determined to assist the humanitarian effort and have repeatedly warned Iraq to cease its harassment.

As in southern Iraq, Saddam Hussein has sought to interfere with the operations of Coalition aircraft in the north since early January. On January 17, 18, and 19, 1993, Coalition aircraft encountered hostile Iraqi activity and took limited defensive actions to suppress Iraqi air defenses. On January 17, 1993, Coalition aircraft shot down an Iraqi aircraft after it entered the no-fly zone.

We continue to support the efforts of the Iraq National Congress to develop a broad-based alternative to the Saddam regime. We encourage other governments to do the same. The Congress espouses a future Iraq based on the principles of political pluralism, territorial unity, and full compliance with all the U.N. Security Council resolutions.

Until Iraq's recent violations of its obligations, UNSCOM and the International Atomic Energy Agency (IAEA) continued to investigate Iraq's weapons of mass destruction programs and to verify the destruction of relevant facilities, equipment, and weapons. UNSCOM 45, the fourteenth ballistic missile team (October 16 to 29, 1992), with significant Russian cooperation, did not find evidence of a clandestine Iraqi SCUD force. Fuel and oxidizer samples were analyzed and tested negative for substances of interest.

Two nuclear inspections were carried out. UNSCOM 46/IAEA #15 (November 8 to 18, 1992) completed water sampling at 37 additional sites throughout Iraq. Analysis of more than 550 water and sediment samples is underway, although evidence of any major facility in Iraq that is producing fissionable fuel has not yet been found. The team also destroyed 100 tons of steel which Iraq declared had been procured for its centrifuge program. IAEA #16 was part of UNSCOM 47 (December 5 to 8, 1992). The team reinspected the former headquarters of the PC–3 project (where important documents had been seized) and carried out inspections at Tuwaitha and al Atheer.

The third combined chemical and biological weapons inspection, UNSCOM 47 (December 5 to 14, 1992), focused on question-and-answer sessions with Iraqi scientists to close gaps in Iraqi disclosures about its CBW programs and short-notice inspections to pressure Iraq to reveal more details about those programs.

Since my last report, the Chemical Destruction Group in residence at the Muthanna State Establishment destroyed the following items: 300 122mm rocket warheads; propellant for 750 122mm rockets; 82 122mm rocket motors; and 2830 liters nerve agent (GB/GF).

The Iraq-Kuwait Boundary Demarcation Commission continues its work, without Iraqi participation. The land boundary has been demarcated through the placement of boundary pillars in the ground. At its last meeting, the Boundary Commission agreed to begin the demarcation of the offshore boundary section.

Since my last report, the U.N. Compensation Commission has continued to prepare for the processing of claims from individuals, corporations, other entities, governments, and international organizations that suffered direct loss or damage as a result of Iraq's unlawful invasion and occupation of Kuwait. The next session of the Governing Council of the Commission is scheduled to be held in Geneva from March 29 to April 2, 1993, with another meeting in July 1993.

At its most recent session, December 14 to 18, 1992, the Governing Council took decisions on trade embargo losses, interest, and a committee on administrative matters. The Council discussed the issues of priority of payments, costs, and attorney fees. The Executive Secretary reported that the Commission has now received about 380,000 claims and expects many times that number. He noted that the Commission hopes to be able to present to panels of Commissioners the first claims for fixed amounts for departure and personal injury by the middle of 1993 and the first claims for individuals' actual losses up to $100,000 later in the year.

The U.S. Government is prepared to file its third set of 170 consolidated individual claims with the Commission, bringing the total of U.S. claims filed to 550. The Department of State is reviewing about 1,000 additional claims received from individuals and corporations. The next filing is scheduled for March.

In accordance with U.N. Security Council Resolution 687, the Sanctions Committee received notices of 13.5 million tons of foodstuffs to be shipped to Iraq through November 22, 1992. The Sanctions Committee also continues to consider and, when appropriate, approve requests to send to Iraq materials and supplies for essential civilian needs. Iraq has also refused to use the opportunity under U.N. Security Council Resolutions 706 and 712 to sell up to $1.6 billion in oil, proceeds from which could be used to purchase foodstuffs, medicines, materials, and supplies for essential civilian needs, as well as to fund essential U.N. activities concerning Iraq. The Iraqi authorities bear full responsibility for any suffering in Iraq that results from their refusal to implement Resolutions 706 and 712.

Since my last report, important progress

has been made in addressing U.N. financial difficulties in conducting a number of activities in Iraq as a result of Iraq's refusal to implement Resolutions 706 and 712. In December, Kuwait and Saudi Arabia made total voluntary contributions of $50 million to the U.N. escrow account established under Resolution 778. Pursuant to Executive Order No. 12817, the United States has transferred a matching amount from certain frozen Iraqi oil proceeds, making a total of $100 million transferred to the escrow account.

Of this total, $21 million has been transferred to the U.N. Compensation Fund under the terms of Resolution 778; this should be sufficient to allow it to proceed with the acquisition of the computer system and staff needed to begin full-scale adjudication of claims against Iraq. In addition, $30 million has been earmarked for UNSCOM, and most of the remainder will provide humanitarian relief in Iraq.

As I noted in my last report, we are prepared to transfer up to $200 million in frozen Iraqi oil proceeds to the escrow account to match transfers by others, and we are actively encouraging others to do so. These funds will be repaid, with interest, from Iraqi oil revenues as soon as Iraqi oil exports resume.

Through the International Commission of the Red Cross (ICRC), the United States, Kuwait, and our allies continue to press the Government of Iraq to comply with its obligations to repatriate or account for some 800 detained Kuwaiti and third-country nationals. An emissary of the Arab League has also undertaken to elicit Iraqi cooperation on the issue of detainees. The United States and its allies continue to press the Government of Iraq to return to Kuwait all property and equipment removed from Kuwait by Iraq. Iraq continues to withhold necessary cooperation on these issues and to resist unqualified ICRC access to detention facilities in Iraq.

In this my last report under the joint resolution, let me again note how grateful I am for the support and cooperation Congress provided during my Administration toward achieving our mutual objectives in the Persian Gulf region.

Sincerely,

GEORGE BUSH

Note: Identical letters were sent to Thomas S. Foley, Speaker of the House of Representatives, and Dan Quayle, President of the Senate. This letter was released by the Office of the Press Secretary on January 20.

Letter to Congressional Leaders Transmitting Reports on Occupational Safety and Health
January 19, 1993

Dear Mr. Speaker: (Dear Mr. President:)

In accordance with section 26 of the Occupational Safety and Health Act of 1970 (Public Law 91–596; 29 U.S.C. 675), I transmit herewith the 1990 annual reports on activities of the Department of Labor, the Department of Health and Human Services, and the Occupational Safety and Health Review Commission.

Sincerely,

GEORGE BUSH

Note: Identical letters were sent to Thomas S. Foley, Speaker of the House of Representatives, and Dan Quayle, President of the Senate. This letter was released by the Office of the Press Secretary on January 20.

Letter to Congressional Leaders Transmitting the Report of the National Critical Technologies Panel
January 19, 1993

Dear Mr. Speaker: (Dear Mr. President:)

In accordance with Title VI of the National Science and Technology Policy, Organization, and Priorities Act of 1976 (Public Law 94–282), as amended by section 841 of the National Defense Authorization Act for Fiscal Years 1990 and 1991 (Public Law 101–189; 42 U.S.C. 6683(d)), I transmit herewith the second biennial report of the National Critical Technologies Panel.

Sincerely,

GEORGE BUSH

Note: Identical letters were sent to Thomas S. Foley, Speaker of the House of Representatives, and Dan Quayle, President of the Senate. This letter was released by the Office of the Press Secretary on January 20.

Letter to Congressional Leaders Transmitting the Lithuania-United States Fishery Agreement
January 19, 1993

Dear Mr. Speaker: (Dear Mr. President:)

In accordance with the Magnuson Fishery Conservation and Management Act of 1976 (Public Law 94–265; 16 U.S.C. 1801 *et seq.*), I transmit herewith an Agreement between the Government of the United States of America and the Government of the Republic of Lithuania Concerning Fisheries off the Coasts of the United States, with annex, signed at Washington on November 12, 1992. The agreement constitutes a governing international fishery agreement within the requirements of section 201(c) of the Act.

U.S. fishing industry interests have urged prompt consideration of this agreement to take advantage of opportunities for seasonal cooperative fishing ventures. I recommend that the Congress give favorable consideration to this agreement at an early date.

Sincerely,

GEORGE BUSH

Note: Identical letters were sent to Thomas S. Foley, Speaker of the House of Representatives, and Dan Quayle, President of the Senate. This letter was released by the Office of the Press Secretary on January 20.

Message to the Senate Transmitting the Argentina-United States Investment Treaty
January 19, 1993

To the Senate of the United States:

With a view to receiving the advice and consent of the Senate to ratification, I transmit herewith the Treaty Between the United States of America and the Argentine Republic Concerning the Reciprocal Encouragement and Protection of Investment, with Protocol, signed at Washington on November 14, 1991; and an amendment to the Protocol effected by exchange of notes at Buenos Aires on August 24 and November 6, 1992. I transmit also, for the information of the Senate, the report of the Department of State with respect to this treaty.

This is the first bilateral investment treaty with a Latin American country to be transmitted to the Senate since the announcement of my Enterprise for the Americas Initiative in June 1990. The treaty is designed to protect U.S. investment and encourage private sector development in Argentina and to support the economic reforms taking place there. The treaty's standstill and roll-back of Argentina's trade-distorting performance requirements are precedent-setting steps in opening markets for U.S. exports. In this regard, as well as in its approach to dispute settlement, the treaty will serve as a model for our negotiations with other South American countries.

The treaty is fully consistent with U.S. policy toward international investment. A specific tenet, reflected in this treaty, is that U.S. investment abroad and foreign investment in the United States should receive fair, equitable, and nondiscriminatory treatment. Under this treaty, the Parties also agree to international law standards for expropriation and expropriation compensation; free transfers of funds associated with investments; and the option of the investor to resolve disputes with the host government through international arbitration.

I recommend that the Senate consider this treaty as soon as possible, and give its advice and consent to ratification of the treaty, with protocol, as amended, at an early date.

GEORGE BUSH

The White House,
January 19, 1993.

Note: This message was released by the Office of the Press Secretary on January 20.

Message to the Senate Transmitting the Bulgaria-United States Investment Treaty
January 19, 1993

To the Senate of the United States:

With a view to receiving the advice and consent of the Senate to ratification, I transmit herewith the Treaty Between the United States of America and the Republic of Bulgaria Concerning the Encouragement and Reciprocal Protection of Investment, with Protocol and related exchange of letters, signed at Washington on September 23, 1992. I transmit also, for the information of the Senate, the report of the Department of State with respect to this Treaty.

The Treaty will help to encourage U.S. private sector involvement in the Bulgarian economy by establishing a favorable legal framework for U.S. investment in Bulgaria. The Treaty is fully consistent with U.S. policy toward international investment. A specific tenet, reflected in this Treaty, is that U.S. investment abroad and foreign investment in the United States should receive fair, equitable, and nondiscriminatory treatment. Under this Treaty, the Parties also agree to international law standards for expropriation and expropriation compensation; free transfers of funds associated with investments; and the option of the investor to resolve disputes with the host government through international arbitration.

I recommend that the Senate consider this Treaty as soon as possible, and give its advice and consent to ratification of the Treaty, with Protocol and related exchange of letters, at an early date.

GEORGE BUSH,

The White House,
January 19, 1993.

Note: This message was released by the Office of the Press Secretary on January 20.

Letter to Congressional Leaders Transmitting the Report on the Recommendations of the United Nations Secretary-General
January 19, 1993

Dear Mr. Speaker: *(Dear Mr. President:)*

Consistent with section 1341 of the National Defense Authorization Act for Fiscal Year 1993 (Public Law 102–484), I hereby transmit my report on the proposals of the Secretary General of the United Nations contained in his report to the Security Council entitled "Preventive Diplomacy, Peacemaking and Peacekeeping", dated June 19, 1992.

Sincerely,

GEORGE BUSH

Note: Identical letters were sent to Thomas S. Foley, Speaker of the House of Representatives, and Dan Quayle, President of the Senate. This letter was released by the Office of the Press Secretary on January 20.

Appendix A—Digest of Other White House Announcements

The following list includes the President's public schedule and other items of general interest announced by the Office of the Press Secretary and not included elsewhere in this book.

August 2

In the morning, the President traveled from Camp David, MD, to Andrews Air Force Base and on to Chicago, IL, where he held a telephone interview with radio station WGN-AM. He then traveled to Rosemont and Elk Grove, IL, and returned to Washington, DC, in the late afternoon.

August 3

In the morning, the President traveled to Dalton, GA, where he attended a Georgia Victory '92 leadership meeting at the Multitex Corp. The President then traveled to Jacksonville, FL. In the afternoon, he attended a Victory '92 reception at the Omni Hotel in Jacksonville and then returned to Washington, DC.

The President selected the following individuals to represent him at the 50th anniversary commemoration of the U.S. landings on the Island of Guadalcanal, August 7–8:

Head of Delegation:

Gen. Raymond Davis, of Georgia.

Delegates:

Leo Nadeau, of California.
Jack Guy, of Georgia.

August 4

In the morning, the President met at the White House with:
—domestic advisers;
—the Vice President; Samuel K. Skinner, Chief of Staff to the President; Brent Scowcroft, Assistant to the President for National Security Affairs; and members of the CIA briefing staff;
—leaders of veterans service organizations.

The President then met with the Senate Republican conference at the Capitol.

In the afternoon, the President met at the White House with:
—the Vice President, for lunch;
—members of the House of Representatives;
—Samuel K. Skinner.

The President declared a major disaster existed in the State of Ohio and ordered Federal aid to supplement State and local recovery efforts in the area struck by severe storms, tornadoes, and flooding that began on July 12.

August 5

In the morning, the President met at the White House with domestic advisers. He then traveled to New York City, where he met with John Cardinal O'Connor at the Marriott Marquis Hotel.

In the afternoon, the President traveled to Reno, NV, where he attended a Victory '92 leadership meeting at the Cannon International Airport.

In the evening, the President traveled to Colorado Springs, CO.

August 6

In the morning, the President addressed the Colorado Republican State leadership at the Broadmoor Hotel in Colorado Springs. The President then held a telephone interview with radio station KOA–AM at the Broadmoor Hotel International Center. Later in the morning, the President held a radio interview with James Dobson at the Focus on the Family Building and then returned to Washington, DC.

August 7

In the morning, the President met at the White House with:
—domestic advisers;
—the Vice President; Samuel K. Skinner, Chief of Staff to the President; Brent Scowcroft, Assistant to the President for National Security Affairs; and members of the CIA briefing staff.

In the afternoon, the President met at the White House with:
—energy and natural resources industry leaders;
—agricultural industry leaders.

Later, the President traveled to Kennebunkport, ME.

August 8

In Kennebunkport, ME, the President met in the afternoon with Deputy U.S. Permanent Representative to the United Nations Alexander Watson, Secretary of Defense Dick Cheney, Deputy Secretary of State Lawrence S. Eagleburger, and Assistant to the President for National Security Affairs Brent Scowcroft to review the situation in Bosnia.

August 10

In Kennebunkport, ME, the President held meetings with Prime Minister Yitzhak Rabin of Israel.

August 11

In the morning, the President met with Prime Minister Rabin. Following the meeting, the President and Mrs. Bush and Prime Minister and Mrs. Rabin returned to Washington, DC.

In the afternoon, the President met with Jewish media representatives and then with congressional leaders.

August 12

In the morning, the President met at the White House with:
—members of Congress;
—domestic advisers;
—the Vice President; Samuel K. Skinner, Chief of Staff to the President; Brent Scowcroft, Assistant to the President for National Security Affairs; and members of the CIA briefing staff.

In the afternoon, the President met with:
—Secretary of State James A. Baker III;
—economists;
—Samuel K. Skinner.

August 13

In the morning, the President met at the White House with:
—domestic advisers;
—the Vice President; Samuel K. Skinner, Chief of Staff to the President; Brent Scowcroft, Assistant to the President for National Security Affairs; and members of the CIA briefing staff;
—Secretary of Health and Human Services Louis W. Sullivan.

In the afternoon, the President and Mrs. Bush went to Camp David, MD.

August 14

The President declared a major disaster existed in the State of Florida and ordered Federal aid to supplement State and local recovery efforts in the area struck by severe storms and flooding on June 23–30.

August 16

In the afternoon, the President and Mrs. Bush returned to the White House from a weekend stay at Camp David, MD.

August 17

In the morning, the President met at the White House with:
—domestic advisers;
—the Vice President; Samuel K. Skinner, Chief of Staff to the President; Brent Scowcroft, Assistant to the President for National Security Affairs; and members of the CIA briefing staff.

Later in the morning, the President and Mrs. Bush traveled to Indianapolis, IN, where the President attended a fundraising reception for Senator Dan Coats of Indiana at the Westin Hotel.

In the afternoon, the President held interviews with CNN and NBC network television, after which he and Mrs. Bush traveled to Houston, TX, for the Republican National Convention. In the evening, they went to their residence at the Houstonian Hotel.

The President declared a major disaster existed in the State of Indiana and ordered Federal aid to supplement State and local recovery efforts in the area struck by severe weather, torrential rains, and flash flooding on August 8–9.

August 18

In the afternoon, the President held media interviews in the Magnolia Room at the Houstonian Hotel.

In the early evening, the President and Mrs. Bush attended a reception for family and friends at the Museum of Fine Arts.

August 19

In the morning, the President and Mrs. Bush attended a reception with the sponsors of the Republican National Committee luncheon at the George R. Brown Center.

In the afternoon, the President held media interviews at the Houstonian Hotel.

The President declared a major disaster existed in the State of Nebraska and ordered Federal aid to supplement State and local recovery in the areas struck by severe storms and flooding on July 11–29.

The President selected Senator Jake Garn of Utah to be his personal representative at the Farnborough International Air Show in Farnborough, England, September 4–9.

August 21

In the morning, the President and Mrs. Bush traveled from Houston, TX, to Gulfport, MS, where they attended a Victory '92 fundraiser.

In the afternoon, the President and Mrs. Bush traveled to Springfield Regional Airport, MO, for a Victory '92 fundraiser and then to Branson,

MO, where they attended an evening performance at the Americana Theatre.

August 22

In the morning, the President and Mrs. Bush
traveled from Branson, MO, to Woodstock, GA.
While en route, the President held a telephone
interview with radio station WGST–AM of Atlanta, GA. In the early afternoon, the President and
Mrs. Bush attended a Victory '92 fundraiser on
Main Street in Woodstock. They then traveled to
Hoover, AL, where they attended a Victory '92
fundraiser at the Wynfrey Hotel.

Later in the afternoon, the President and Mrs.
Bush traveled to Dallas, TX. While en route, the
President held a telephone interview with radio
station WBAP–AM of Fort Worth, TX.

August 23

In the morning, the President and Mrs. Bush
traveled from Dallas, TX, to Springfield, IL,
where in the afternoon they toured the farm exposition at the Illinois State Fairgrounds.

Upon returning to the Springfield Capital Airport, President and Mrs. Bush attended a Victory
'92 fundraiser. They then returned to Washington, DC.

August 24

In the morning, the President traveled to
Union, NJ, where he attended a Victory '92 fundraiser at a private residence and toured the Lincoln Technical Institute.

In the late morning, the President traveled to
Ansonia, CT, where he attended a Victory '92
fundraiser at a private residence.

In the afternoon, the President traveled to Opa
Locka, FL, to inspect the damage caused by Hurricane Andrew.

In the evening, the President returned to
Washington, DC.

The President declared a major disaster existed
in the State of Florida and ordered Federal aid to
supplement State and local recovery efforts in
the area struck by Hurricane Andrew on August
23.

The President announced his intention to appoint the following individuals to be members of
the Architectural and Transportation Barriers
Compliance Board for terms expiring December
3, 1994:

Fritz Edmunds, Jr., of Kansas.
Tracy James Mueller, of Colorado.
Peggy Pinder, of Iowa.
R. Jack Powell, of Maryland.

August 25

In the morning, the President traveled to Chicago, IL, and then to Canton, MI, where he held

a roundtable discussion with Michigan business
people in the afternoon.

Later in the afternoon, the President returned
to Washington, DC.

August 26

In the morning, the President met at the
White House with:
—James A. Baker III, Chief of Staff to the
President;
—the Vice President; James A. Baker III, Chief
of Staff to the President; Brent Scowcroft,
Assistant to the President for National Security Affairs; and members of the CIA briefing
staff;
—the Vice President, for lunch.

In the afternoon, the President traveled to Lafayette, LA, to inspect the damage caused by
Hurricane Andrew.

In the evening, the President returned to
Washington, DC.

The President declared a major disaster existed
in the State of Louisiana and ordered Federal aid
to supplement State and local recovery efforts in
the areas struck by Hurricane Andrew on August
25.

August 27

In the morning, the President traveled to St.
Louis, MO, where he attended a Victory '92 supporters meeting at the Stouffer Concourse Hotel.

In midmorning, the President traveled to Cincinnati, OH. While en route, he held a telephone
interview with radio station WLW–AM of Cincinnati.

In the afternoon, the President traveled to
Findlay, OH, and returned to Washington, DC,
in the evening.

The White House announced that David Bates
will return to the White House as Assistant to the
President and Special Assistant to the Chief of
Staff.

August 28

In the morning, the President met at the
White House with:
—James A. Baker III, Chief of Staff to the
President;
—the Vice President; James A. Baker III, Chief
of Staff to the President; Brent Scowcroft,
Assistant to the President for National Securi-
ty Affairs; and members of the CIA briefing
staff;
—Deputy Secretary of Defense Donald J.
Atwood, Jr.;
—Acting Secretary of State Lawrence S. Eagle-
burger.

In the afternoon, the President went to Camp
David, MD.

The President announced his intention to appoint Siggi B. Wilzig, of New Jersey, to be a member of the U.S. Holocaust Memorial Council for a term expiring January 15, 1995. This is a reappointment.

August 29

In the afternoon, after returning to the White House from Camp David, MD, the President met with Secretary of Transportation Andrew H. Card, Jr., Deputy Secretary of Defense Donald J. Atwood, Jr., and Director of the Federal Emergency Management Agency Wallace E. Stickney.

In the evening, the President went to Camp David, MD.

The President declared a major disaster existed in the State of California and ordered Federal aid to supplement State and local recovery efforts in the area struck by fires commencing on August 16 and August 20.

August 31

In the morning, after returning to the White House from Camp David, MD, the President met with:

—James A. Baker III, Chief of Staff to the President;

—the Vice President; James A. Baker III; Brent Scowcroft, Assistant to the President for National Security Affairs; and members of the CIA briefing staff.

The President then met with Secretary of Housing and Urban Development Jack Kemp, Secretary of Education Lamar Alexander, Secretary of Health and Human Services Louis W. Sullivan, and Small Business Administrator Patricia F. Saiki.

In the afternoon, the President met with Secretary of Health and Human Services Louis W. Sullivan, Postmaster General Marvin T. Runyon, and Social Security Commissioner Gwendolyn S. King.

The President then met with:

—representatives of housing and homebuilding associations;

—representatives of volunteer organizations involved in Hurricane Andrew relief efforts;

—Secretary of the Treasury Nicholas F. Brady;

—representatives of insurance associations and small-business groups.

September 1

In the morning, the President and Mrs. Bush traveled to Homestead, FL, and Lafayette, LA, to inspect the Hurricane Andrew relief efforts. In the evening, they returned to Washington, DC.

September 2

In the morning, the President traveled to Humboldt, SD, and Shallowater, TX. In the after-noon, the President traveled to Fort Worth, TX, and returned to Washington, DC, in the evening.

The President declared a major disaster existed in the State of Wisconsin and ordered Federal aid to supplement State and local recovery efforts in the area struck by severe storms and tornadoes on August 29.

September 3

In the morning, the President met at the White House with:

—James A. Baker III, Chief of Staff to the President;

—the Vice President; James A. Baker III; Brent Scowcroft, Assistant to the President for National Security Affairs; and members of the CIA briefing staff;

—Small Business Administrator Patricia F. Saiki;

—the Vice President, for lunch.

The President announced his intention to appoint the following individuals to be members of the Glass Ceiling Commission, for which Secretary of Labor Lynn Martin will serve as Chairperson:

Patricia V. Asip, of Texas.

J. Alphonso Brown, of Kentucky.

Joanne M. Collins, of Missouri.

Delia M. Reyes, of Texas.

Henry Tang, of New York.

Carol Cox Wait, of the District of Columbia.

The President recess-appointed the following individuals:

James H. Grossman, of California, to be Chairman of the Foreign Claims Settlement Commission of the United States, Department of Justice.

David J. Ryder, of Virginia, to be Director of the U.S. Mint, Department of the Treasury.

The President recess-appointed the following persons to be Commissioners of the Copyright Royalty Tribunal:

Edward J. Damich, of Virginia.

Bruce D. Goodman, of Pennsylvania.

September 4

In the morning, the President met at the White House with:

—James A. Baker III, Chief of Staff to the President;

—the Vice President; James A. Baker III; Brent Scowcroft, Assistant to the President for National Security Affairs; and members of the CIA briefing staff.

Later in the morning, the President traveled to Fredericksburg, VA, where he visited the Fredericksburg Hardware store.

After returning to the White House in the afternoon, the President met with Acting Secretary of State Lawrence S. Eagleburger. The President then held an interview with radio station WWWE of Cleveland, OH.

September 5

In the morning, the President and Mrs. Bush traveled to Painesville, OH, where they attended a Victory '92 supporters reception at the Grange Food Hall.

In the afternoon, the President and Mrs. Bush traveled to Greenville, SC, where they participated in an arrival ceremony at the Greenville-Spartanburg Airport. They then traveled to Asheville and Hendersonville, NC, and Louisville, KY.

September 6

In the morning, the President and Mrs. Bush attended a Victory '92 supporters meeting at the Executive Inn in Louisville, KY. In the afternoon, they traveled to Chicago, IL, and on to Sault Sainte Marie, MI. In the evening, the President held a satellite television interview with Tom Brokaw of NBC News from the lobby of the Ojibway Hotel.

September 7

In the morning, the President and Mrs. Bush traveled to Mackinac City, MI, and then to Waukesha, WI, where they attended a Victory '92 supporters meeting at the Waukesha County Exposition Grounds.

In the afternoon, the President and Mrs. Bush traveled to Hamtramck, MI, and returned to Washington, DC, in the evening.

September 8

In the morning, the President met at the White House with:
—James A. Baker III, Chief of Staff to the President;
—the Vice President; James A. Baker III; Brent Scowcroft, Assistant to the President for National Security Affairs; and members of the CIA briefing staff;
—congressional leaders.

In an afternoon ceremony at the White House, the President received diplomatic credentials from Ambassadors Mohammad Bin Hussein Al-Shaali, United Arab Emirates; Simon Massoud Karam, Lebanon; El-Hadj Boubacar Barry, Republic of Guinea; Ahmed Maher El Sayed, Arab Republic of Egypt; Dunstan Weston Kamana, Republic of Zambia; and Sione Kite, Tonga.

September 9

In the morning, the President met at the White House with:

—James A. Baker III, Chief of Staff to the President;
—Republican congressional leaders.

Later in the morning, the President traveled to Norristown and Collegeville, PA. In the afternoon, he traveled to Middletown, NJ, and then returned to Washington, DC.

September 10

In the morning, the President met at the White House with:
—domestic advisers;
—James A. Baker III, Chief of Staff to the President; and Brent Scowcroft, Assistant to the President for National Security Affairs;
—the Vice President; James A. Baker III; and Brent Scowcroft.

Later in the morning, the President traveled to Detroit, MI. In the afternoon, following a Victory '92 supporters meeting at the Detroit Annex of Cobo Hall, he returned to Washington, DC.

The President announced his intention to appoint Mark A. Shiffrin, of Connecticut, to be a member of the President's Committee on Mental Retardation for a term expiring May 11, 1994. He would succeed B. Dean Owens.

The President announced his intention to appoint Charles J. Heringer, Jr., of Montana, to be a U.S. Commissioner on the Bear River Commission. This is a noncompensated position. He would succeed Kenneth T. Wright.

The President announced his intention to nominate the following individuals to be members of the Board of Directors of the Commission on National and Community Service for terms of 3 years. These are reappointments:

William J. Byron, of the District of Columbia.
George W. Romney, of Michigan.
Glen W. White, of Kansas.
Thomas H. Ehrlich, of Indiana.
Johnnie M. Smith, of South Carolina.

September 11

In the morning, the President traveled to Joplin, MO, where he met with employees of Contract Freighters, Inc. He then traveled to Excelsior Springs, MO, where he toured the carpentry shop of the Job Corps center.

In the afternoon, the President traveled to Kansas City, MO, where he attended a Victory '92 luncheon and a Victory '92 supporters meeting at the Kansas City Airport Hilton Inn. He then traveled to St. Louis, MO.

In the evening, the President traveled to Virginia Beach, VA, where he attended a Victory '92 supporters meeting. Later, he traveled to Hagerstown, MD, and then on to Camp David, MD, for the weekend.

September 12

The President declared a major disaster existed in the State of Hawaii and ordered Federal aid to supplement State and local recovery efforts in the area struck by Hurricane Iniki on September 11.

September 13

In the morning, the President traveled to Andrews Air Force Base from Camp David, MD, and then on to Anaheim, CA.

In the afternoon, the President traveled to San Diego, CA, where he held interviews with the news media and attended a Victory '92 supporters meeting at the U.S. Grant Hotel.

September 14

In the morning, the President traveled to Colville, WA, where he met with the Jobs Coalition for Washington State at Vaagen Brothers Lumber, Inc.

In the afternoon, the President traveled to Spokane, WA, where he attended a Victory '92 supporters meeting at the Spokane International Airport fire station. He then traveled to Medford, OR, where he attended a Victory '92 supporters meeting at Erickson Air-Crane Co.

In the evening, the President traveled to Salt Lake City, UT.

September 15

In the morning, the President attended a Victory '92 supporters meeting at the Salt Palace Convention Center in Salt Lake City, UT. He then traveled to Englewood, CO, where he attended a Victory '92 supporters meeting at the Scanticon Hotel in the afternoon. The President then traveled to Albuquerque, NM, where he toured the robotics laboratory at Sandia National Laboratories and attended a Victory '92 supporters meeting at Cutter Aviation. In the evening, the President returned to Washington, DC.

The President appointed the following individuals to be members of the National Commission for Employment Policy:

John Charles Gartland, of Maryland. He will also be designated Chairman.

Eduardo Aguirre, Jr., of Texas.

Mark D. Cowan, of the District of Columbia.

Melanie Mitchell Lackland, of Ohio.

Margot E. Machol, of the District of Columbia.

The President announced his intention to nominate the following individuals to be:

Representatives of the United States of America to the Forty-seventh Session of the General Assembly of the United Nations:

Edward Joseph Perkins, of Oregon.

Alexander Fletcher Watson, of Massachusetts.

Larry Pressler, of South Dakota.

Gloria Estefan, of Florida.

Alternate Representatives of the United States of America to the Forty-seventh Session of the General Assembly of the United Nations:

Irvin Hicks, of Maryland.

Shirin R. Tahir-Kheli, of Pennsylvania.

Parker G. Montgomery, of New York.

Prezell Russell Robinson, of North Carolina.

Margaretta F. Rockefeller, of New York.

September 16

In the morning, the President met at the White House with:

—congressional leaders;

—James A. Baker III, Chief of Staff to the President; Brent Scowcroft, Assistant to the President for National Security Affairs;

—James A. Baker III.

Later in the morning the President held an interview with the AARP Bulletin and St. Louis television affiliates.

In the afternoon, the President met at the White House with:

—Acting Secretary of State Lawrence S. Eagleburger;

—John Cardinal O'Connor.

The President declared an emergency existed in the State of Rhode Island and ordered Federal aid to supplement State and local recovery efforts in the areas affected by water contamination on August 3.

September 17

In the morning, the President traveled to Enid, OK, where he attended a Victory '92 supporters meeting and met with Oklahoma independent oil and gas producers at the Best Western Inn.

In the late morning, the President traveled to Jonesboro, GA. In the afternoon, he traveled to Atlanta, GA, where he attended a November Victory Committee fundraiser at the Hyatt Regency Atlanta, after which he was joined by Mrs. Bush.

In the evening, the President and Mrs. Bush returned to Washington, DC.

The President appointed Kay Bailey Hutchison, of Texas, to be a member of the Commission to Promote Investment in America's Infrastructure. This is a new position.

September 18

In the morning, the President met at the White House with:

—James A. Baker III, Chief of Staff to the President;

—the Vice President; James A. Baker III; Brent Scowcroft, Assistant to the President for National Security Affairs; and members of the CIA briefing staff;

—Acting Secretary of State Lawrence S. Eagleburger.

In the afternoon, the President traveled to Basking Ridge, NJ, where he attended a Victory '92 supporters meeting at the AT&T corporate headquarters. In the late afternoon, the President traveled to Hagerstown, MD, and then on to Camp David, MD, for the weekend.

The President declared a major disaster existed in the State of Wisconsin and ordered Federal aid to supplement State and local recovery efforts in the area struck by severe storms and tornadoes on June 17.

The President declared a major disaster existed in the State of Indiana and ordered Federal aid to supplement State and local recovery efforts in the area struck by severe storms, tornadoes, and flooding during the period of June 16–July 23.

September 20
In the afternoon, the President returned to the White House from a weekend stay at Camp David, MD.

September 21
In the morning, the President and Mrs. Bush traveled to the United Nations in New York City, where the President met with Secretary-General Boutros Boutros-Ghali and General Assembly President Stoyan Ganev.

In the afternoon, the President held an interview with Rush Limbaugh at radio station WABC–AM. The President and Mrs. Bush then met with supporters and attended Victory '92 and Presidential Trust dinners at the Waldorf-Astoria Hotel before returning to Washington, DC.

The President accorded the personal rank of Ambassador to Robert L. Hutchings, of Virginia, in his capacity as Special Adviser for East European Assistance.

September 22
In the morning, the President traveled to Springfield, MO, and Tulsa, OK, and in the afternoon to Longview, TX, Shreveport, LA, and Greenville, MS. In the evening, he traveled to Memphis, TN, and then returned to Washington, DC.

The President selected the following individual to head the U.S. delegation to the International Telecommunications Union Conference, December 7–22:

Ambassador Bradley P. Holmes, of Virginia.

The President selected the following individual as his special representative to the Congress of the American Woman in the Dominican Republic, October 10–11:

Ambassador Holly Coors, of Colorado.

September 23
In the morning, the President traveled to Greensboro, NC, where he met with business leaders and Victory '92 supporters at the Joseph S. Koury Convention Center. He then traveled to State College, PA, where he met with Victory '92 supporters at the Nittany Lion Inn before traveling to Hagerstown, MD, and on to Camp David, MD.

The President designated Edward L. Hennessy, Jr., of New Jersey, to be a member of the Board of Governors of the United Service Organizations, Inc., for a term of 3 years. He would succeed Gavin de Becker.

The President accorded the personal rank of Ambassador to Richard Lee Armitage, of Virginia, in his capacity as Deputy to the Coordinator for Assistance to the Commonwealth of Independent States.

September 24
In the afternoon, the President returned to the White House from Camp David, MD.

September 25
In the morning, the President met at the White House with:
—James A. Baker III, Chief of Staff to the President;
—the Vice President; James A. Baker III; Brent Scowcroft, Assistant to the President for National Security Affairs; and members of the CIA briefing staff.

Later in the morning, President traveled to Schaumburg, IL, where he toured the Motorola plant.

In the afternoon, the President traveled to Chicago, IL. In the evening, he attended a Victory '92 supporters reception and a Presidential Trust dinner at the Chicago Hilton Hotel. He then traveled to Columbus, OH, where he was joined by Mrs. Bush.

September 26
The President and Mrs. Bush traveled from Columbus, OH, aboard the Spirit of America train through Ohio and Michigan. They stopped at Marysville, Arlington, Findlay, and Bowling Green, OH, and at Plymouth, MI. They then traveled by motorcade to Livonia, MI, where they stayed overnight at the Marriott Hotel.

September 27
The President and Mrs. Bush traveled from Livonia to Plymouth, MI, where they reboarded the Spirit of America train and continued on to Wixom, Milford, Holly, and Grand Blanc, MI. They then traveled by motorcade to Flint, MI, and later returned to Washington, DC.

September 28

In the morning, the President held an interview with ABC–TV's "Good Morning America" at the White House. He then traveled to St. Louis, MO, where he met with Victory '92 supporters at the Stouffer Concourse Hotel.

In the afternoon, the President traveled to Dallas, TX, where he met with the U.S. Hispanic Chamber of Commerce at the Loews Anatole Hotel. In the evening, he attended a Victory '92 fundraising reception and a Presidential Trust dinner at private residences.

The White House announced that President Bush, President Salinas of Mexico, and Prime Minister Mulroney of Canada will witness the initialing of the North American free trade agreement (NAFTA) by trade ministers of the three Governments in San Antonio, TX, on October 7.

The President announced his intention to appoint the following individuals to be members of the National Cancer Advisory Board for terms expiring March 9, 1998:

Zora Kramer Brown, of the District of Columbia.
Pelayo Correa, of Louisiana.
Robert Winsor Day, of Washington.
Barbara P. Gimbel, of New York.
Ellen V. Sigal, of the District of Columbia.

September 29

In the morning, the President traveled from Dallas, TX, to Tennessee, making stops in Blountville, Knoxville, Chattanooga, Clarksville, and Nashville, TN. In the late evening, the President returned to Washington, DC.

September 30

In the morning, the President traveled to Oshkosh, WI, and on to Fond du Lac, WI, where he met with families of Children First at the city/county government center and with Victory '92 supporters at the National Exchange Bank. He then traveled to Newark, NJ.

In the evening, the President traveled to Hagerstown, MD, and on to Camp David, MD.

The President selected the following individuals to serve on the Board of Directors of the Eurasia Foundation:

William Frenzel, of Minnesota. He will serve as Chairman.
William Bader, of the District of Columbia.
McGeorge Bundy, New York.
Andrew Falkiewicz, of the District of Columbia.
Gordon Humphrey, of New Hampshire.
Vernon Jordan, of the District of Columbia.
Max Kampelman, of the District of Columbia.
Thomas Kemp, of California.
Susan King, of New York.
Peter McPherson, of California.
Arnold Weber, of Illinois.
Marina Von Neumann Whitman, of Michigan.

The President declared a major disaster existed in the State of Wisconsin and ordered Federal aid to supplement State and local recovery efforts in the area struck by severe storms and floods, September 14–24.

October 1

In the afternoon, the President returned to the White House from Camp David, MD.

The President announced his intention to nominate the following individuals to be members of the National Advisory Council on Educational Research and Improvement:

John K. Andrews, Jr., of Colorado.
Dale P. Gold, of Virginia.
Eugene L. Madeira, of Pennsylvania.
Eunice N. Sato, of California.

October 2

In the morning, the President met with:
—James A. Baker III, Chief of Staff to the President;
—the Vice President; James A. Baker III; Brent Scowcroft, Assistant to the President for National Security Affairs; and members of the CIA briefing staff.

In the afternoon, the President traveled to Boston, MA, where he received a law enforcement endorsement at Florian Hall and attended a Victory '92 reception and Presidential Trust dinner at the Boston Park Plaza Hotel.

In the evening, the President traveled to Clearwater, FL.

The President declared a major disaster existed in the State of Iowa and ordered Federal aid to supplement State and local recovery efforts in the area struck by severe storms and flooding, September 14–15.

October 3

In the morning, the President addressed a Seniors for Bush-Quayle Coalition meeting at the On Top of the World retirement community in Clearwater, FL. Later in the morning, he traveled to Homestead, FL, to assess the Hurricane Andrew relief efforts. There he visited the Campbell temporary housing unit and Campbell Drive Middle School and toured the FEMA disaster assistance center. He then went to Florida City, where he visited a FEMA temporary housing unit and met with residents.

In the afternoon, the President traveled to Fort Lauderdale, FL, where he attended a Fort Lauderdale Historical Association ceremony at the naval air station and held an interview with Telemundo at the AMR COMBS Executive Terminal. He then traveled to Orlando, FL, where he met with Victory '92 supporters at the Church Street

Station. In the evening, he returned to Washington, DC.

October 5

In the afternoon, the President traveled to Dover, DE, where he met with Victory '92 supporters at the Dinner Bell Inn before returning to Washington, DC.

The President announced his intention to appoint Donald E. Vinson, of California, to be the Representative of the United States of America on the South Pacific Commission for a term of 2 years. He would succeed Admiral James L. Holloway III.

The President announced his intention to appoint Roland I. Perusse, of the District of Columbia, to be Deputy Commissioner of the United States of America on the Commission for the Study of Alternatives to the Panama Canal. He would succeed Prieur J. Leary, Jr.

October 6

In the morning, the President met at the White House with:
—James A. Baker III, Chief of Staff to the President;
—the Vice President; James A. Baker III; Brent Scowcroft, Assistant to the President for National Security Affairs; and members of the CIA briefing staff.

In the afternoon, the President attended a ceremony for the West Side Light Rail Project in the Oval Office at the White House.

October 7

In the morning, the President traveled to San Antonio, TX, where he met with President Carlos Salinas of Mexico and Prime Minister Brian Mulroney of Canada at the Plaza San Antonio Hotel.

In the evening, the President held an interview with Larry King of CNN–TV at the Arneson River Theater.

The President appointed Mary D. Fisher, of Florida, to be a member of the National Commission on Acquired Immune Deficiency Syndrome. She would succeed Earvin (Magic) Johnson.

October 8

In the morning, the President traveled from San Antonio, TX, to New Orleans, LA, where he met with Victory '92 supporters at the World Trade Center. In the afternoon, the President traveled to Houston, TX. In the evening, he returned to Washington, DC.

The President announced his intention to appoint the following individuals to be members of the President's Council on Physical Fitness and Sports:

Harris John Frank, of Missouri.
Kevin Vaughn Saunders, of Texas.

The President announced his intention to appoint David M. Mulcahy, of New Jersey, to be a member of the President's Export Council. He would succeed Jerry Douglas Geist.

The President announced his intention to appoint Charles R. Lee, of Connecticut, to be a member of the President's National Security Telecommunications Advisory Committee. He would succeed James L. Johnson.

The President announced his intention to nominate Ray E. Witter, of Missouri, to be a member of the Chemical Safety and Hazard Investigation Board for a term of 5 years. This is a new position.

The President announced his intention to appoint James C. Lin, of Illinois, to be a member of the President's Committee on the National Medal of Science for a term expiring December 31, 1993. He would succeed Y.W. Kan.

The President announced his intention to nominate David M. Brewer, of New Jersey, to be a member of the board of directors of the Federal Agricultural Mortgage Corporation. He would succeed Gordon Clyde Southern.

The President declared a major disaster existed in the State of Florida and ordered Federal aid to supplement State and local recovery efforts in the area struck by severe storms, tornadoes, and flooding on October 3.

October 9

In the afternoon, the President traveled to Cincinnati and Columbus, OH, where he attended a Victory '92 reception and dinner at a private residence before returning to Washington, DC.

October 11

In the afternoon, the President and Mrs. Bush traveled to St. Louis, MO, where the President toured the site for the Presidential debate in the Field House at Washington University.

In the evening after the debate, President and Mrs. Bush went to Forest Park and then returned to St. Louis.

October 12

In the morning, the President and Mrs. Bush traveled from St. Louis, MO, to Springfield, PA, where they met with Victory '92 supporters at a private residence.

In the afternoon, the President and Mrs. Bush traveled to Grand Rapids and Holland, MI. In the evening, they attended a Victory '92 reception and dinner at private residences in Grand Rapids before returning to Washington, DC.

October 13

In the morning, the President met at the White House with:

—James A. Baker III, Chief of Staff to the President;
—the Vice President; James A. Baker III; Brent Scowcroft, Assistant to the President for National Security Affairs; and members of the CIA briefing staff;
—James A. Baker III.

The President recess-appointed Evan J. Kemp, Jr., of the District of Columbia, to be a member of the Equal Employment Opportunity Commission. He also redesignated him Chairperson. Since 1987, Mr. Kemp has served as Chairman of the U.S. Equal Employment Opportunity Commission.

The President announced his intention to appoint the following individuals to serve as members of the National Commission on Measured Responses to Achieve a Drug-Free America by 1995.

Chairman:

Bob Martinez

Commissioners:

Kent B. Amos, of Washington, DC.
Ramona L. Barnes, of Alaska.
Ralph R. Brown, of Iowa.
Keith A. Butler, of Michigan.
Ronald D. Castille, of Pennsylvania.
Kay B. Cobb, of Mississippi.
Shirley D. Coletti, of Florida.
Sylvester Daughtry, of North Carolina.
David A. Dean, of Texas.
Steven Goldsmith, of Indiana.
Daniel S. Heit, of Pennsylvania.
Rose Hom, of California.
Richard P. Ieyoub, of Louisiana.
Vincent Lane, of Illinois.
Daniel E. Lungren, of California.
Robert H. Macy, of Oklahoma.
N. Hector McGeachy, Jr., of North Carolina.
Edwin L. Miller, Jr., of California.
John D. O'Hair, of Michigan.
Jack M. O'Malley, of Illinois.
Ruben B. Ortega, of Arizona.
Robert T. Thompson, Jr., of Georgia.

October 14

In the morning, the President met at the White House with:
—James A. Baker III, Chief of Staff to the President;
—the Vice President; James A. Baker III; Brent Scowcroft, Assistant to the President for National Security Affairs; and members of the CIA briefing staff.

The President announced his intention to appoint the following individuals to be members of the President's Advisory Commission on Educa-

tional Excellence for Hispanic Americans. These are initial appointments:

Juana Dainis, of New York.
Robert D. Segura, of California.

The President announced his intention to appoint Eugene F. Yeates, of Maryland, to be Executive Director of the President's Foreign Intelligence Advisory Board. He would succeed Nina J. Stewart.

October 15

In the morning, the President met at the White House with:
—James A. Baker III, Chief of Staff to the President;
—the Vice President; James A. Baker III; Brent Scowcroft, Assistant to the President for National Security Affairs; and members of the CIA briefing staff.

In the afternoon, the President and Mrs. Bush traveled to Richmond, VA, where the President toured the site for the Presidential debate in Robins Center at the University of Richmond. In the evening after the debate, the President and Mrs. Bush attended a reception at Richmond Center before returning to Washington, DC.

The President announced his intention to appoint Harold T. Shapiro, of New Jersey, to be a member of the President's Council of Advisors on Science and Technology.

The President announced his intention to appoint the following individuals to be members of the Board for International Food and Agricultural Development for terms expiring July 18, 1996:

Paul Findley, of Illinois.
Christopher Hicks, of Maryland.
William Hodges Mobley, of Texas.

October 16

In the morning, the President met at the White House with:
—James A. Baker III, Chief of Staff to the President;
—the Vice President; James A. Baker III; Brent Scowcroft, Assistant to the President for National Security Affairs; and members of the CIA briefing staff.

In the afternoon, the President traveled to Edison, NJ. In the evening, he traveled to Somerset, NJ, where he attended a private reception and dinner at the Garden State Convention Center before traveling to Camp David, MD, for the weekend.

The President named the following individuals to represent him at the Federal Republic of Germany's state funeral for Willy Brandt, October 17:

Ambassador Vernon Walters, of Virginia.
Senator Claiborne Pell, of Rhode Island.

October 17

The President declared a major disaster existed in the State of Mississippi and ordered Federal aid to supplement State and local recovery efforts in the area struck by tornadoes, high winds, hail, and severe storms on October 10.

October 18

In the afternoon, the President returned to the White House from a weekend stay at Camp David, MD.

October 19

In the morning, the President met at the White House with:
—James A. Baker III, Chief of Staff to the President;
—the Vice President; James A. Baker III, Chief of Staff to the President; Brent Scowcroft, Assistant to the President for National Security Affairs; and members of the CIA briefing staff.

In the afternoon, the President and Mrs. Bush traveled to East Lansing, MI, where the President toured the site for the Presidential debate in Wharton Center at Michigan State University.

In the evening after the debate, the President and Mrs. Bush traveled to Atlanta, GA.

October 20

In the morning, the President and Mrs. Bush boarded the Spirit of America train at Armour Drive train yard in Atlanta for a trip through Georgia, South Carolina, and North Carolina, making their first stop in Norcross, GA. In the afternoon, the President continued on to Gainesville and Cornelia, GA, and Spartanburg, SC, where he stayed overnight.

October 21

In the morning, the President continued on to Gastonia, Kannapolis, Thomasville, Burlington, and Raleigh, NC, where he stayed overnight.

The President announced his intention to appoint Huda Bingham Jones, of Kentucky, to be a member of the Commission on Presidential Scholars.

The President announced his intention to appoint John H. Harriman, of California, to be a public member of the National Advisory Council on the Public Service. This is a new position.

October 22

In the morning, the President held a television interview with "CBS This Morning" in the Governor Kerr Scott Building at the North Carolina State Fairgrounds in Raleigh, NC.

The President then traveled to Vineland, Robbinsville, Ridgewood, and Secaucus, NJ, and returned to Washington, DC, in the evening.

October 23

In the morning, the President met at the White House with Gen. John W. Vessey, Special Presidential Emissary to Hanoi for POW–MIA Affairs. The President then traveled to London, KY.

In the afternoon, the President traveled to Fort Lauderdale, FL, where he attended a Presidential Trust reception at a private residence, and then to Miami.

In the evening, the President traveled to Montgomery, AL.

The President announced his intention to appoint Richard J. Wall, of California, to be a member of the Board of Visitors to the U.S. Military Academy for a term expiring December 30, 1994. He would succeed Rhett B. Dawson.

The President made available emergency appropriations for the Departments of Agriculture, Commerce, Housing and Urban Development, the Interior, and Labor, to provide assistance in Florida, Louisiana, Hawaii, and Guam to victims of Hurricanes Andrew and Iniki and Typhoon Omar.

The President announced his intention to accord the personal rank of Ambassador to Edward L. Lacey, of Virginia, in his capacity as head of delegation to the Biological and Toxic Weapons Convention Verification Conference.

October 24

In the morning, the President held media interviews at the Atlanta Crossing Shopping Center in Montgomery, AL. He then traveled to Houston, TX, where he attended a private memorial service at the First Presbyterian Church.

In the afternoon, the President traveled to Maurice and Lafayette, LA, before returning to Washington, DC, in the evening.

October 25

In the morning, the President traveled to Detroit, MI, and Sioux Falls, SD, where he held media interviews at the Kiwanis Club Pancake House. In the afternoon, he traveled to Billings, MT, where he held a taped interview with David French of CNN–TV at Billings Senior High School.

October 26

In the morning, the President traveled to Denver, CO, and in the afternoon, to Albuquerque, NM.

In the evening, he traveled to Des Moines, IA, where he held a taped interview with David Frost at the Iowa Republican headquarters.

The President announced his intention to appoint Barbara Hackman Franklin, Secretary of Commerce, to be a member of the Competitiveness Policy Council for a term expiring October 16, 1994. This is a reappointment.

The President appointed Stuart A. Bernstein, of the District of Columbia, to be a member of the Board of Trustees of the John F. Kennedy Center for the Performing Arts for a term expiring September 1, 2002. He would succeed Dina Merrill.

October 27

In the morning, the President held an interview with NBC–TV's "Today Show" at the State capitol in Des Moines, IA, before traveling to Paducah, KY. In the afternoon, he traveled to Kettering and Lima, OH.

The President announced his intention to designate Harold T. Shapiro, of New Jersey, to be Vice Chairman of the President's Council of Advisors on Science and Technology. He would succeed Bernadine P. Healy.

The President announced his intention to appoint J. Michael Farrell, of the District of Columbia, to be Commissioner of the United States of America on the Commission for the Study of Alternatives to the Panama Canal. He would succeed John A. Svahn.

October 28

In the morning, the President held an interview with ABC–TV's "Good Morning America" at the Civic Center in Lima, OH, before traveling to Toledo, Strongsville, and Columbus, OH. In the evening, he traveled to Warren, MI.

October 29

In the morning, the President traveled from Warren, MI, to the Henry Ford Museum in Detroit, MI, where he held a television interview with "CBS This Morning" and taped an interview for "Prime Time Live" with Sam Donaldson of ABC–TV.

In the afternoon, the President returned to Warren, MI, and then traveled on to Grand Rapids, MI. In the evening, he traveled to Nashville, TN.

The White House announced that the President had a telephone conversation with President Boris Yeltsin of Russia to discuss the situation in Moscow.

The President announced his intention to designate Paul Calabresi, of Rhode Island, to be Chairman of the National Cancer Advisory Board for the term expiring March 9, 1994.

October 30

In the morning, the President traveled from Nashville, TN, to St. Louis, MO, where he held several local media interviews.

In the afternoon, he traveled to Racine, WI, where he addressed the community and held an interview with Larry King of CNN–TV in the evening.

October 31

In the morning, the President and Mrs. Bush traveled from Racine to Burlington, WI, where they boarded the Spirit of America train for a trip through Wisconsin. They stopped at Sussex, Oshkosh, Stevens Point, and Chippewa Falls, where the whistlestop tour ended. In the evening, they traveled to La Crosse, WI.

November 1

In the morning, the President held an interview for "Newsmaker Sunday" with Frank Sesno of CNN–TV at the La Crosse County Republican Headquarters. The President then traveled to Auburn Hills, MI, where he held interviews with the local media in the afternoon.

In the evening, the President traveled to Stratford, CT, and Short Hills, NJ.

November 2

In the morning, the President traveled to Madison, NJ, Glenolden, PA, and in the afternoon to Akron, OH, and Louisville, KY.

In the evening, the President traveled to Baton Rouge, LA, and Houston, TX, where he was joined by Mrs. Bush.

November 3

In the morning, the President and Mrs. Bush voted at St. Mary's Seminary in Houston. In the afternoon, they attended a reception at the Manor House of the Houstonian Hotel, and in the evening, they went to the Westin Galleria Hotel.

November 4

In the afternoon, the President and Mrs. Bush returned to Washington, DC.

November 5

In the morning, the President met at the White House with:

—the Vice President; James A. Baker III, Chief of Staff to the President; Brent Scowcroft, Assistant to the President for National Security Affairs; and members of the CIA briefing staff;

—members of the Cabinet.

In the afternoon, President and Mrs. Bush went to Camp David, MD, for the weekend.

November 6

The President selected the following individuals to represent him during the ceremonies commemorating the 50th anniversary of the arrival of General MacArthur's headquarters on November 6, 1942:

Head of Delegation:

Ambassador Everett Bierman, of Virginia.

Delegates:

Reynaldo Maduro, of Maryland.
Rear Admiral James Carey, of Virginia.

November 8

In the afternoon, the President and Mrs. Bush returned to the White House from a weekend stay at Camp David, MD.

November 9

In the morning, the President met at the White House with the Vice President; James A. Baker III, Chief of Staff to the President; Brent Scowcroft, Assistant to the President for National Security Affairs; and members of the CIA briefing staff.

The President announced his intention to accord the personal rank of Ambassador to Michael K. Young, of Virginia, in his capacity as Special Negotiator for Trade and Environment.

November 10

In the morning, the President met at the White House with the Vice President; James A. Baker III, Chief of Staff to the President; Brent Scowcroft, Assistant to the President for National Security Affairs; and members of the CIA briefing staff.

In the evening, the President and Mrs. Bush attended a reception for Senate Republican leaders in the Columbus Club at Union Station prior to the Senate Republican leadership dinner. At midnight, they visited the Vietnam Veterans Memorial.

November 11

In the morning, the President and Mrs. Bush traveled to Boca Grande, FL, for a vacation.

November 15

In the afternoon, the President returned to Washington, DC, from a vacation trip to Boca Grande, FL.

November 16

In the morning, the President met at the White House with the Vice President; James A. Baker III, Chief of Staff to the President; Brent Scowcroft, Assistant to the President for National Security Affairs; and members of the CIA briefing staff.

In the evening, the President went to Blair House where he received the Benjamin Franklin Award from the Council of American Ambassadors.

The President appointed Thomas Neal Tripp, of Ohio, to be a member of the Board of Directors of the Federal Prison Industries, Inc. He would succeed Joseph Lane Kirkland.

The President appointed the following persons as members of the National Commission on Measured Responses to Achieve a Drug-Free America by 1995. These are new positions:

Mike Moore, of Mississippi.
Keith M. Kaneshiro, of Hawaii.

November 17

The President met at the White House with:
—the Vice President; James A. Baker III, Chief of Staff to the President; Brent Scowcroft, Assistant to the President for National Security Affairs; and members of the CIA briefing staff;
—the Vice President, for lunch.

November 18

The President met at the White House with:
—the Vice President; James A. Baker III, Chief of Staff to the President; Brent Scowcroft, Assistant to the President for National Security Affairs; and members of the CIA briefing staff;
—Secretary of Transportation Andrew H. Card, Jr.

In an afternoon ceremony at the White House, the President received diplomatic credentials from Ambassadors Roza Otunbayeva, Republic of Kyrgyzstan; Roland Bimo, Republic of Albania; Adamou Seydou, Republic of Niger; Rene Arturo Bendana, Honduras; Corinne Averille McKnight, Republic of Trinidad and Tobago; Immo Stabreit, Federal Republic of Germany; Ananda Guruge, Democratic Socialist Republic of Sri Lanka; and Hiem Phommachanh, Lao People's Democratic Republic.

The President announced his intention to appoint Patricia Diaz Dennis, Assistant Secretary of State for Human Rights and Humanitarian Affairs, to be an executive branch Commissioner-Observer on the Commission on Security and Cooperation in Europe. She would succeed Richard Schifter.

November 19

The President met at the White House with the Vice President; James A. Baker III, Chief of Staff to the President; Brent Scowcroft, Assistant to the President for National Security Affairs; and members of the CIA briefing staff.

The President traveled to Greenwich, CT, to visit his mother, Mrs. Prescott Bush, and returned to Washington, DC, in the afternoon.

In an afternoon ceremony at the White House, the President received diplomatic credentials from Ambassadors Ernest Petric, Republic of Slovenia; Michael Zantovsky, Czech and Slovak Federal Republic; Petar A. Sarcevic, Republic of Croatia; Siddhartha Shankar Ray, India; Alim Shakirovich Djambourchine, Republic of Kazakhstan; Edgar Teran Teran, Ecuador; and Timothy Baswell Donaldson, Commonwealth of the Bahamas.

The White House announced that the President's mother died late in the afternoon and that the President and Mrs. Bush will attend the funeral services in Greenwich, CT, on November 23d.

November 20

The President met at the White House with the Vice President; James A. Baker III, Chief of Staff to the President; Brent Scowcroft, Assistant to the President for National Security Affairs; and members of the CIA briefing staff.

In the afternoon, the President and Mrs. Bush went to Camp David, MD, for the weekend.

The President announced his intention to appoint the following individuals to be members of the President's National Security Telecommunications Advisory Committee:

C. Michael Armstrong, of California.
Bruce L. Crockett, of Virginia.
Roy A. Wilkens, of Oklahoma.

November 22

In the afternoon, the President and Mrs. Bush returned to the White House from a weekend stay at Camp David, MD. Later in the afternoon, the President presented the 1992 National Literacy Honors on the State Floor.

November 23

In the morning, the President and Mrs. Bush traveled to Greenwich, CT, to attend funeral services for the President's mother, Mrs. Prescott Bush, and returned to Washington, DC, in the evening.

November 24

The President met at the White House with:
—the Vice President; James A. Baker III, Chief of Staff to the President; Brent Scowcroft, Assistant to the President for National Security Affairs; and members of the CIA briefing staff;
—the Vice President, for lunch;
—the President's Foreign Intelligence Advisory Board.

November 25

In the morning, the President met at the White House with the Vice President; James A. Baker III, Chief of Staff to the President; Brent Scowcroft, Assistant to the President for National Security Affairs; and members of the CIA briefing staff.

In the afternoon, the President and Mrs. Bush traveled to Kennebunkport, ME, for the Thanksgiving holiday weekend.

November 29

In the afternoon, the President and Mrs. Bush returned to Washington, DC, from a holiday weekend stay in Kennebunkport, ME.

November 30

The President met at the White House with the Vice President; James A. Baker III, Chief of Staff to the President; Brent Scowcroft, Assistant to the President for National Security Affairs; and members of the CIA briefing staff.

December 1

The President met at the White House with:
—the Vice President; James A. Baker III, Chief of Staff to the President; Brent Scowcroft, Assistant to the President for National Security Affairs; and members of the CIA briefing staff;
—Gov. Fife Symington of Arizona.

The President declared a major disaster existed in the State of Georgia and ordered Federal aid to supplement State and local recovery efforts in the area struck by tornadoes, high wind, and heavy rain that began on November 22.

December 2

The President met at the White House with:
—the Vice President; James A. Baker III, Chief of Staff to the President; Brent Scowcroft, Assistant to the President for National Security Affairs; and members of the CIA briefing staff;
—Acting Secretary of State Lawrence S. Eagleburger;
—Senators Hank Brown, Thomas A. Daschle, and John F. Kerry.

December 3

The President met at the White House with:
—James A. Baker III, Chief of Staff to the President;
—the Vice President; James A. Baker III; Brent Scowcroft, Assistant to the President for National Security Affairs; and members of the CIA briefing staff;
—the President's Council of Advisors on Science and Technology;
—the Vice President, for lunch.

In the evening, the President and Mrs. Bush attended a performance of "A Tuna Christmas" at the National Theatre.

The White House announced that the President will sign the North American free trade agreement in Washington, DC, on December 17.

December 4

The President held morning meetings at the White House with:
—the Vice President; James A. Baker III, Chief of Staff to the President; Brent Scowcroft, Assistant to the President for National Security Affairs; and members of the CIA briefing staff;
—congressional leaders.

In the afternoon, the President and Mrs. Bush went to Camp David, MD, for the weekend.

The President transmitted to the Speaker of the House and the President pro tempore of the Senate a report on Federal Agencies implementation of the Privacy Act of 1974.

December 6

In the afternoon, the President and Mrs. Bush returned to the White House from a weekend stay at Camp David, MD.

In the evening, the President and Mrs. Bush hosted a reception for the John F. Kennedy honorees on the State Floor at the White House before attending the honors ceremony at the John F. Kennedy Center for the Performing Arts.

December 7

In the morning, the President met at the White House with:
—the Vice President; James A. Baker III, Chief of Staff to the President; Brent Scowcroft, Assistant to the President for National Security Affairs; and members of the CIA briefing staff;
—Gov. Walter J. Hickel of Alaska.

In the afternoon, the President toured the U.S. Navy Memorial.

In the evening, the President and Mrs. Bush hosted the congressional Christmas ball on the State Floor.

December 8

The President met at the White House with:
—the Vice President; James A. Baker III, Chief of Staff to the President; Brent Scowcroft, Assistant to the President for National Security Affairs; and members of the CIA briefing staff;
—the 1992–93 Duck Stamp Design Award winner.

In the evening, the President and Mrs. Bush hosted a Christmas reception on the State Floor.

The President announced his intention to recess-appoint Pauline Crowe Naftzger, of California, to be the Alternate Representative of the United States of America on the Executive Board of the United Nations Children's Fund. She would succeed Mrs. Potter Stewart.

December 9

The President met at the White House with the Vice President; James A. Baker III, Chief of Staff to the President; Brent Scowcroft, Assistant to the President for National Security Affairs; and members of the CIA briefing staff.

In the late morning, the President signed the Religious Freedom Day proclamation in an Oval Office ceremony.

In the evening, the President and Mrs. Bush hosted a Christmas reception on the State Floor.

December 10

The President met at the White House with:
—the Vice President; James A. Baker III, Chief of Staff to the President; Brent Scowcroft, Assistant to the President for National Security Affairs; and members of the CIA briefing staff;
—the Vice President, for lunch.

In the afternoon, the President received the 1992 Christmas Seals from Kristi Yamaguchi, American Lung Association chairperson, in an Oval Office ceremony.

In the evening, the President and Mrs. Bush hosted a Christmas reception on the State Floor.

December 11

The President met at the White House with the Vice President; James A. Baker III, Chief of Staff to the President; Brent Scowcroft, Assistant to the President for National Security Affairs; and members of the CIA briefing staff.

In the evening, the President and Mrs. Bush went to Camp David, MD, for the weekend.

December 13

In the afternoon, the President and Mrs. Bush returned to the White House from a weekend stay at Camp David, MD.

In the evening, the President and Mrs. Bush attended the "Christmas in Washington" show at the National Building Museum.

December 14

The President met at the White House with the Vice President; James A. Baker III, Chief of Staff to the President; Brent Scowcroft, Assistant to the President for National Security Affairs; and members of the CIA briefing staff.

In the afternoon, the President attended the White House Military Office farewell ceremony at Anacostia Naval Base.

December 15

In the morning, the President traveled to College Station, TX, where he attended a Presidential library board meeting at Texas A&M University. In the afternoon, he returned to Washington, DC.

In the evening, the President and Mrs. Bush hosted a Christmas reception on the State Floor.

December 16

The President met at the White House with the Vice President; James A. Baker III, Chief of Staff to the President; Brent Scowcroft, Assistant to the President for National Security Affairs; and members of the CIA briefing staff.

In the evening, the President and Mrs. Bush hosted a Christmas reception on the State Floor.

The President announced his intention to appoint the following individuals to be members of the Advisory Committee for Trade Policy and Negotiations for terms of 2 years:

Robert E. Allen, of New Jersey.
Remedios Diaz-Oliver, of Florida.
John A. Rollwagen, of Minnesota.
Gordon B. Zacks, of Ohio.

The White House announced that on January 13, 1993, the President will award the Presidential Medal of Freedom to former President Ronald Reagan.

December 17

The President met at the White House with the Vice President; James A. Baker III, Chief of Staff to the President; Brent Scowcroft, Assistant to the President for National Security Affairs; and members of the CIA briefing staff.

In the afternoon, the President attended a reception at the Organization of American States building.

In the evening, the President and Mrs. Bush hosted a Christmas reception on the State Floor.

The President declared a major disaster existed in the Republic of the Marshall Islands and ordered Federal aid to supplement State and local recovery efforts in the area struck by Typhoon Gay on November 17–18.

The President declared a major disaster existed in the State of Connecticut and ordered Federal aid to supplement State and local recovery efforts in the area struck by a winter storm and coastal flooding on December 10–13.

December 18

The President met at the White House with:
—the Vice President; James A. Baker III, Chief of Staff to the President; Brent Scowcroft, Assistant to the President for National Security Affairs; and members of the CIA briefing staff;
—Philip Johnston, president of CARE;
—Palestinian peace delegation members;
—Cyrus Vance, Special Negotiator for the United Nations on Yugoslavia.

The President hosted a working lunch with European Commission representatives in the Residence.

In the afternoon, the President and Mrs. Bush went to Camp David, MD, for the weekend.

The President declared a major disaster existed in the State of New Jersey and ordered Federal aid to supplement State and local recovery efforts in the area struck by a severe coastal storm, unusual high tides, heavy rain, and riverine flooding that began on December 10.

The President announced the reappointment of David Q. Bates, Jr., of Texas, to be a member of the Board of Directors of the Student Loan Marketing Association. Mr. Bates currently serves as Assistant to the President and Special Assistant to the Chief of Staff.

The President announced his intention to designate Charles G. Untermeyer, of Texas, and Bobbie G. Kilberg, of Virginia, to be members of the Board of Visitors to the United States Naval Academy. Mr. Untermeyer currently serves as Director of Voice of America. Ms. Kilberg currently serves as Deputy Assistant to the President and Director of Intergovernmental Affairs.

December 19

The President and Mrs. Bush hosted a visit by British Prime Minister and Mrs. John Major at Camp David, MD.

December 20

In the morning, the President and Mrs. Bush and Prime Minister and Mrs. Major returned to the White House from a weekend stay at Camp David, MD.

December 21

The President met at the White House with the Vice President; James A. Baker III, Chief of Staff to the President; Brent Scowcroft, Assistant to the President for National Security Affairs; and members of the CIA briefing staff.

In the afternoon, the President and his family viewed the film "The Fires of Kuwait" at the National Air and Space Museum.

In the evening, the President and Mrs. Bush hosted a Christmas party on the State Floor.

The President declared a major disaster existed in the State of New York and ordered Federal aid to supplement State and local recovery efforts in the area struck by the coastal storm, high tides, heavy rain, and riverine flooding that began on December 10.

December 22

The President met at the White House with the Vice President; James A. Baker III, Chief of Staff to the President; Brent Scowcroft, Assistant to the President for National Security Affairs; and members of the CIA briefing staff.

The President declared a major disaster existed in the Commonwealth of Massachusetts and ordered Federal aid to supplement State and local recovery efforts in the area struck by a winter storm and coastal storm on December 11–13.

The President announced his intention to appoint Susan Porter Rose, of Virginia, to be a member of the Commission of Fine Arts for a term of 4 years. She would succeed Neil H. Porterfield.

The President announced his intention to appoint the following individuals to serve in an advisory capacity to the James Madison Memorial Fellowship Foundation Board of Trustees for a term of 6 years. These are reappointments:

Orrin G. Hatch, of Utah.
Edward M. Kennedy, of Massachusetts.

The President announced the recess appointment of John N. Raudabaugh, of Georgia, to be a member of the National Labor Relations Board. This is a reappointment.

The White House announced that the President will travel to Somalia to spend New Year's Eve with U.S. troops and then will visit relief operations on New Year's Day before returning to the United States.

December 23
The President met at the White House with the Vice President; James A. Baker III, Chief of Staff to the President; Brent Scowcroft, Assistant to the President for National Security Affairs; and members of the CIA briefing staff.

Later in the morning, the President and Mrs. Bush went to Camp David, MD, for the Christmas holiday.

The President appointed Albert V. Casey, of Texas, to be a member of the National Commission to Ensure a Strong Competitive Airline Industry. This is a new position.

December 24
Throughout the day, the President placed telephone calls to U.S. military personnel stationed overseas.

December 27
In the morning, the President returned to Andrews Air Force Base from Camp David, MD. He then traveled to Houston and Beeville, TX, where he visited Will Farish's ranch.

December 29
In the evening, the President returned to Washington, DC, from Beeville, TX.

December 30
The President met at the White House with the Vice President; James A. Baker III, Chief of Staff to the President; Brent Scowcroft, Assistant to the President for National Security Affairs; and members of the CIA briefing staff.

Later in the morning, the President departed for Saudi Arabia.

The President made available $10.5 million in previously appropriated funds to provide assistance in Florida, Louisiana, Hawaii, and Guam to victims of Hurricanes Andrew and Iniki and Typhoon Omar.

The President recess-appointed Robert F. Goodwin, of Maryland, to be a Commissioner on the part of the United States on the International Joint Commission, United States and Canada. This is a reappointment.

The President recess-appointed Norman D. Shumway, of California, to be a member of the Board of Directors of the Legal Services Corporation. This is a reappointment.

December 31
In the morning, the President arrived in Riyadh, Saudi Arabia, where he met with King Fahd before traveling on to Somalia.

In the afternoon, after arriving in Mogadishu, Somalia, the President went to the American Embassy compound where he held a Joint Task Force briefing and addressed the staff and troops. He then toured the International Red Cross/Somali camp near Afgooye. Later in the afternoon, the President traveled to the U.S.S. *Tripoli* where he greeted the ship's company and officers and spent the night.

The President recess-appointed David P. Prosperi, of Illinois, to be a member of the Board of Directors of the Corporation for Public Broadcasting. He would succeed Marshall Turner, Jr.

The President announced his intention to appoint Jeannette Louise Naylor, of Texas, to be a member of the Board of Directors of the Pennsylvania Avenue Development Corporation for a term expiring October 26, 1998.

The President announced his intention to appoint the following individuals to the Advisory Council on Unemployment Compensation:

Janet L. Norwood, of Maryland.
Mitchell E. Daniels, Jr., of Indiana.
Gov. Tommy G. Thompson, of Wisconsin.

January 1
In the morning, the President traveled from the U.S.S. *Tripoli* to Baidoa Airfield, where he visited the Marine forces, toured the airfield, visited foxholes, and met an incoming patrol. He then went to the Bonka Orphanage Center to tour the facility and returned to the Baidoa Air-

field where he addressed the Marine forces before departing for a visit to a helicopter maintenance facility near Baledogle.

After having lunch with Army and Marine troops near Baledogle, the President attended the sendoff of an Army platoon on patrol and visited the Marine tent city. He then traveled to Mogadishu Airport where he addressed members of the coalition forces.

Later in the afternoon, the President returned to the U.S.S. *Tripoli* where he spent the night.

January 2

In the morning, the President traveled from the U.S.S. *Tripoli,* located off the coast of Somalia, to Mogadishu. He then traveled to Riyadh, Saudi Arabia, and to Moscow, Russia, where he joined Mrs. Bush. They then went to Spaso House, residence of the U.S. Ambassador.

January 3

In the morning, the President and Mrs. Bush toured the Kremlin. President Bush then met with President Boris Yeltsin, and they signed the START II treaty.

In the afternoon, the President and Mrs. Bush traveled to Paris, France. Following an arrival ceremony at Orly International Airport, they went to the Elysee Palace, where President Bush and President François Mitterrand held a meeting and a joint press conference.

In the evening, the President and Mrs. Bush attended a dinner hosted by President Mitterrand at the palace before returning to Washington, DC.

January 4

The President met at the White House with the Vice President; James A. Baker III, Chief of Staff to the President; Brent Scowcroft, Assistant to the President for National Security Affairs; and members of the CIA briefing staff.

The President transmitted to the Congress the 27th annual report of the Department of Housing and Urban Development for calendar year 1991 and the 25th annual report of the United States-Japan Cooperative Medical Science Program for the period of July 1990 to July 1991.

January 5

In the morning, the President met at the White House with the Vice President; James A. Baker III, Chief of Staff to the President; Brent Scowcroft, Assistant to the President for National Security Affairs; and members of the CIA briefing staff.

Later the President and Mrs. Bush traveled to the U.S. Military Academy at West Point, NY, where he had lunch with the Corps of Cadets at Washington Mess Hall and attended a private reception at the Superintendent's residence. They returned to Washington, DC, in the late afternoon.

January 6

The President met at the White House with:
—the Vice President; James A. Baker III, Chief of Staff to the President; Brent Scowcroft, Assistant to the President for National Security Affairs; and members of the CIA briefing staff;
—congressional leaders;
—Secretary of State Lawrence S. Eagleburger.

In the late afternoon, the President and Mrs. Bush hosted a Presidential Trust and Eagles reception on the State Floor.

The President recess-appointed the following individuals to be members of the National Security Education Board for terms of 4 years. These are new positions:

Steven Muller, of Maryland.
S. William Pattis, of Illinois.
John P. Roche, of Massachusetts.
Richard F. Stolz, of Maryland.

January 7

The President held morning meetings at the White House with:
—the Vice President; James A. Baker III, Chief of Staff to the President; Brent Scowcroft, Assistant to the President for National Security Affairs; and members of the CIA briefing staff;
—freshman Republican Congressmen.

In the late morning, the President attended a reception hosted by the U.S. Trade Representative in the Indian Treaty Room of the Old Executive Office Building.

In the late afternoon, the President and Mrs. Bush hosted a Presidential Trust and Eagles reception on the State Floor.

The President announced his intention to appoint Margaret DeBardeleben Tutwiler, of Alabama, to be an Alternate Representative of the United States of America on the South Pacific Commission for a term of 2 years. She will succeed Lois L. Evans.

The President nominated John P. Roche, of Massachusetts, to be a member of the National Security Education Board for a term of 4 years. This is a new position.

January 8

The President met at the White House with:
—the Vice President; James A. Baker III, Chief of Staff to the President; Brent Scowcroft, Assistant to the President for National Security Affairs; and members of the CIA briefing staff;

—Deputy Foreign Minister Boris Tarrasuik of Ukraine.

In the late morning, the President went to the CIA headquarters in Langley, VA, for a working luncheon and briefing. In the afternoon, he was joined there by Mrs. Bush, and they went to Camp David, MD, for the weekend.

The President appointed Vincent H. Dreeszen, of Nebraska, to be the U.S. Representative on the Kansas-Nebraska Big River Compact Administration. He would suceed Maurice A. Kremer.

The President announced his intention to appoint the following individuals to be members of the National Commission on Independent Higher Education:

William J. Keating, of Ohio.
Carolynn Reid-Wallace, of the District of Columbia.

The President appointed the following individuals to be members of the National Commission on Intermodal Transportation:

Phillip D. Brady, of California.
Thomas J. Donohue, of Maryland.
Edmund S. Hawley, of Nebraska.

The President recess-appointed the following individuals to be members of the Defense Base Closure and Realignment Commission for terms expiring at the end of the first session of the 103d Congress:

James A. Courter, of New Jersey. He will be designated Chairman.
Peter B. Bowman, of Maine.
Beverly Butcher Byron, of Maryland.
Rebecca Gernhardt Cox, of the District of Columbia.
Hansford T. Johnson, of Texas.
Arthur Levitt, Jr., of New York.
Harry C. McPherson, Jr., of Maryland.
Robert D. Stuart, Jr., of Illinois.

The President recess-appointed Thomas Ludlow Ashley, of the District of Columbia, to be a Governor of the U.S. Postal Service. He would succeed Crocker Nevin.

The President announced his intention to appoint the following individuals to be members of the J. William Fulbright Foreign Scholarship Board:

Mark N. Blitz, of Virginia.
Charles E. Horner, of the District of Columbia.
Ewell E. Murphy, Jr., of Texas.
Katherine L. Super, of Virginia.
Margarita B. Tonkinson, of Florida.
Rose M. Zamaria, of Virginia.

The President recess-appointed Marion G. Chambers, of New Mexico, to be a member of the Board of Trustees of the Institute of American Indian and Alaska Native Culture and Arts

Development for a term expiring May 19, 1998. She would succeed James Courtney Jennings.

The President announced his intention to appoint the following individuals to be members of the U.S. Holocaust Memorial Council for terms expiring January 15, 1998:

Jack Africk, of Florida.
Louis Gonda, of California.
Cecile Kremer, of Maryland.
Ronald Lauder, of New York.
Miles Lerman, of New Jersey.
Simcha Lyons, of Missouri.
Murray Pantirer, of New Jersey.
Dennis Ross, of Maryland.
Samuel Rothberg, of Illinois.
Arnold Thaler, of Illinois.

January 10
In the afternoon, the President and Mrs. Bush returned to the White House from a weekend stay at Camp David, MD.

January 11
The President met at the White House with the Vice President; James A. Baker III, Chief of Staff to the President; Brent Scowcroft, Assistant to the President for National Security Affairs; and members of the CIA briefing staff.

The President announced his intention to appoint the following individuals to be members of the Board of Trustees of the Woodrow Wilson International Center for Scholars for terms expiring October 23, 1998:

James Addison Baker III, of Texas.
Max Marlin Fitzwater, of Kansas.
Roger B. Porter, of Utah.

The President announced his intention to appoint C. Boyden Gray, of North Carolina, to be a public member of the Council of the Administrative Conference of the United States for a term of 3 years. Mr. Gray currently serves as Counsel to the President.

The President designated Paul A. Vander Myde, of Virginia, to be Vice Chairman of the Administrative Conference of the United States.

January 12
In the morning, the President went to the National Naval Medical Center in Bethesda, MD, for a checkup and then returned to the White House.

In the afternoon, the President signed the economic report and met with Michael J. Boskin, Chairman of the Council of Economic Advisers.

In the evening, the President hosted the Team 100 dinner on the State Floor.

The White House announced that on Saturday, January 16, the President will meet with Prime

Minister Brian Mulroney of Canada at Camp David, MD.

The President announced his intention to appoint Richard A. Hauser, of the District of Columbia, to be a member of the Board of Directors of the Pennsylvania Avenue Development Corporation for a term expiring October 26, 1998. This is a reappointment.

The President announced his intention to appoint the following individuals to be Commissioners on the White House Conference on Small Business Commission. These are new positions:

Andrew P. Ireland, of Florida.
James H.K. Bruner, of New York.
Janet Harris-Lange, of Florida.
James S. Herr, of Pennsylvania.
Anita Lugo King, of California.
Carmen Munoz, of Michigan.
Jose F. Nino, of Illinois.
JoAnn H. Price, of Maryland.
Ella D. Williams, of California.

The President announced his intention to designate the following individuals to be members of the Board of Visitors to the U.S. Military Academy:

John H. Lindsey, of Texas.
Sally Freeman McKenzie, of Texas.
Edwin Meese III, of California.

January 13

The President met at the White House with the Vice President; James A. Baker III, Chief of Staff to the President; Brent Scowcroft, Assistant to the President for National Security Affairs; and members of the CIA briefing staff.

Later in the morning, the President received the Ellis Island Congressional Medal of Honor in an Oval Office ceremony.

The President announced his intention to appoint the following individuals to be members of the Advisory Commission on Intergovernmental Relations for terms of 2 years:

Paul Bud Burke, president of the Kansas State Senate.
Robert Michael Isaac, Mayor of Colorado Springs, CO.
Edward G. Rendell, Mayor of the City of Philadelphia, PA.

The President announced his intention to appoint the following individuals to be members of the Architectural and Transportation Barriers Compliance Board:

Porfirio C. Diaz, Jr., of California.
Scott Moore Duncan, of Texas.
Margaret Chase Hagar, of Virginia.
Anne Marcia Harding, of New York.
S. Craig Kiser, of Florida.

The President announced his intention to appoint the following individuals to be members of the National Capital Planning Commission:

Thaddeus A. Garrett, of Ohio.
Melvyn J. Estrin, of Maryland.
Glen T. Urquhart, of Virginia.

The President announced his intention to appoint Ronald Carlin Kaufman, of Massachusetts, to be a member of the Commission for the Preservation of America's Heritage Abroad. Mr. Kaufman will serve the remainder of the 3-year term expiring February 27, 1995.

The President announced his intention to appoint the following individuals to be members of the Board of Governors of the United Service Organizations for 3-year terms:

Suzanne Marx, of California.
John J. Tedesco, of New Jersey.

The President announced his intention to appoint Jean Stein, of New York, to be a member of the U.S. Holocaust Memorial Council for a term expiring January 15, 1998.

The President announced his intention to appoint Daphne Wood Murray, of Texas, to be a member of the Cultural Property Advisory Committee for a term expiring April 25, 1993.

The President announced his intention to appoint Bill Dickinson, of Alabama, to be a member of the National Commission on Defense and National Security. This is a new position. He will be designated Chairman.

January 14

In the morning, the President met at the White House with:
—the Vice President; James A. Baker III, Chief of Staff to the President; Brent Scowcroft, Assistant to the President for National Security Affairs; and members of the CIA briefing staff;
—Ambassador Malcolm Toon;
—families of the KAL flight 007 victims.

In the evening, the President and Mrs. Bush attended a dinner hosted by Cabinet members at the Blair House.

The President announced his intention to appoint the following individuals to be members of the Board of Visitors to the U.S. Air Force Academy:

Andrew H. Card, Jr., of Massachusetts.
Barry M. Goldwater, Sr., of Arizona.
Brent Scowcroft, of Maryland.
Fred M. Zeder II, of New York.

The President announced his intention to appoint the following individuals to be members of the Board of Trustees of the John F. Kennedy Center for the Performing Arts for terms expiring September 1, 2002:

Phyllis C. Draper, of New York.
Craig L. Fuller, of Virginia.

Mary Galvin, of Illinois.
Alma Johnson Powell, of Virginia.
Joshua I. Smith, of Maryland.

The President announced his intention to appoint the following individuals to be members of the Advisory Committee for Trade Policy and Negotiations for terms of 2 years:

Roger J. Baccigaluppi, of California.
Alberto R. Cardenas, of Florida.
Donald G. Fisher, of California.
Donald V. Fites, of Illinois.
Kathryn S. Fuller, of the District of Columbia.
John A. Georges, of Connecticut.
D. George Harris, of Connecticut.
David S. Lee, of California.
Rudolph A. Oswald, of Maryland.
William F. Pickard, of Michigan.
C.J. Silas, of Oklahoma.
Jack Valenti, of California.
Robert Van Dine, of California.

January 15

The President met at the White House with:
—the Vice President; James A. Baker III, Chief of Staff to the President; Brent Scowcroft, Assistant to the President for National Security Affairs; and members of the CIA briefing staff.
—Secretary of State Lawrence Eagleburger.

Later in the morning, the President attended the National Republican Campaign Committee President's Forum luncheon at the Willard Hotel before departing for Camp David, MD, for the weekend.

The President transmitted to the Congress requests for FY 1993 appropriations language for the Department of Defense, to provide authority to transfer available appropriations to cover the incremental costs arising from Operation Restore Hope in Somalia.

The President declared a major disaster existed in the State of Delaware and ordered Federal aid to supplement State and local recovery efforts in the area struck by a severe coastal storm and flooding on December 11–14.

The President announced his intention to appoint William D. Novelli, of New Jersey, to be a member of the Enterprise for the Americas Board. This is a new position.

The President announced his intention to appoint Robert Zoellick, of the District of Columbia, to be a member of the Board of Directors of the Federal Home Loan Mortgage Corporation.

The President announced his intention to appoint Lester H. Lee, of California, to be a Commissioner of the 1994 White House Conference on Small Business Commission. This is a new position.

The President announced his intention to appoint the following individuals to be members of the President's Commission on White House Fellowships:

Roger Porter, of Utah.
Jose Manuel Casanova, of Florida.

The President announced his intention to appoint the following individuals to be Alternate Representatives of the United States to the South Pacific Commission for terms of 2 years:

Edith Elizabeth Holiday, of Georgia.
Timothy J. McBride, of Michigan.

The President announced his intention to appoint the following individuals to be members of the U.S. Commission on Civil Rights for terms expiring December 5, 1998:

Constance Horner, of the District of Columbia.
Robert George, of New Jersey.

The President announced his intention to appoint Theresa Neese, of Oklahoma, to be a member of the National Advisory Council on Indian Education for a term expiring September 29, 1995. This is a reappointment.

The President announced his intention to appoint the following individuals to be members of the Thomas Jefferson Commemoration Commission. These are new positions:

Charles L. Bartlett, of the District of Columbia.
Daniel J. Boorstin, of the District of Columbia.
Pamela K. Jensen, of Ohio.
Roger G. Kennedy, of Virginia.
Merrill D. Peterson, of Virginia.

The President announced his intention to appoint John Robert Longenecker, of California, to be Transition Manager of the United States Enrichment Corporation. This is a new position.

The President announced his intention to appoint Samuel B. Nunez, Jr., president of the Louisiana State Senate, to be a member of the Advisory Commission on Intergovernmental Relations for a term of 2 years. This is a reappointment.

The President announced his intention to appoint the following individuals to be members of the President's National Security Telecommunications Advisory Committee:

Lester M. Alberthal, Jr., of Texas.
Royce J. Holland, of Nebraska.
Bert C. Roberts, Jr., of Maryland.

The President announced his intention to appoint Clifford M. Sobel, of New Jersey, to be a member of the U.S. Holocaust Memorial Council for a term expiring January 15, 1998. He will succeed Herbert Katz.

The President announced his intention to appoint the following individuals to be members of the National Council on Surface Transportation Research:

John P. Browning, Jr., of Florida.
Frederic Vincent Malek, of Virginia.

The President announced his intention to appoint the following individuals to be members of the Permanent Committee for the Oliver Wendell Holmes Devise for terms of 8 years:

Harold M. Hyman, of Texas.
Vincent Lee McKusick, of Maine.

January 18

In the afternoon, the President and Mrs. Bush returned to the White House from a weekend stay at Camp David, MD.

January 19

The President met at the White House with:
—the Vice President; James A. Baker III, Chief of Staff to the President; Brent Scowcroft, Assistant to the President for National Security Affairs; and members of the CIA briefing staff;
—the Vice President, for lunch.

The President announced his intention to appoint David Abshire, of Virginia, to be a member of the National Commission on Defense and National Security.

The President announced his intention to appoint the following individuals to be members of the High Resolution Information Systems Advisory Board. These are new positions:

Roy L. Beasly, of Maryland.
John L. Doyle, of California.
Kenneth R. Edwards, of the District of Columbia.
Kyupin Philip Hwang, of California.
James R. Loomis, of Indiana.
Robert D. Pavey, of Ohio.
Leigh Mitchell Rothschild, of Florida.
Laurence C. Seifert, of New Jersey.

The President announced his intention to appoint the following individuals to be members of the Board of Trustees of the Christopher Columbus Fellowship Foundation. These are new positions:

John Harper, of the District of Columbia. He will be designated Chairman.
William A. Seavey, of California. He will be designated Vice Chairman.
Frank Annunzio, of Illinois.
Howard G. Buffett, of Illinois.
Nicholas E. Calio, of Ohio.
Salvador Diaz-Versaon, Jr., of Georgia.
M. Joyce Van Schaak, of California.

The President announced his intention to appoint the following individuals to be members of the Board of Governors of the United Service Organizations for terms of 3 years:

Sigmund A. Rogich, of Nevada.
Phillip S. Bradley, of Florida.

The President announced his intention to appoint the following individuals to be members of the Advisory Commission (Western Water Resources). These are new positions:

Thomas Lawrence Sansonetti, of Wyoming. He will be appointed Chairman.
Robert N. Broadbent, of Nevada.
Garry Carruthers, of New Mexico.
Gale Norton, of Colorado.
Jack Robertson, of Oregon.
Ralph William Tarr, of California.

The President announced his intention to appoint John Patrick Schmitz, of California, to be a Representative of the United States of America on the Joint Commission on the Environment between the United States and the Republic of Panama, established by the Panama Canal Treaty of 1977, for a term of 3 years. He would succeed Norman C. Roberts.

The President declared a major disaster existed in the State of Arizona and ordered Federal aid to supplement State and local recovery efforts in the area struck by flooding on January 5, 1993.

January 20

In the morning, the President and Mrs. Bush welcomed President-elect William J. Clinton and Hillary Clinton to the White House for coffee before leaving together for the Capitol and the Inauguration.

Appendix B—Nominations Submitted to the Senate

The following list does not include promotions of members of the Uniformed Services, nominations to the Service Academies, or nominations of Foreign Service officers.

Submitted August 4

Marion Clifton Blakey,
of Mississippi, to be Administrator of the National Highway Traffic Safety Administration, vice Jerry Ralph Curry, resigned.

Gerald Paul Regier,
of Virginia, to be Administrator of the Office of Juvenile Justice and Delinquency Prevention, vice Robert W. Sweet, Jr., resigned.

Charles A. Felton,
of Florida, to be U.S. Marshal for the Middle District of Florida for the term of 4 years, vice Richard L. Cox, resigned.

J. Keith Gary,
of Texas, to be U.S. Marshal for the Eastern District of Texas for the term of 4 years (reappointment).

Submitted August 5

Roland Karl Kuchel,
of Florida, a career member of the Senior Foreign Service, class of Minister-Counselor, to be Ambassador Extraordinary and Plenipotentiary of the United States of America to the Republic of Haiti.

Edward S. Walker, Jr.,
of Maryland, a career member of the Senior Foreign Service, class of Minister-Counselor, to be the Deputy Representative of the United States of America to the United Nations, with the rank and status of Ambassador Extraordinary and Plenipotentiary.

Submitted August 7

Robert W. Kostelka,
of Louisiana, to be U.S. District Judge for the Western District of Louisiana, vice Thomas E. Stagg, Jr., retired.

The following named persons to be members of the Railroad Retirement Board:

Glen L. Bower, of Illinois, for the term of 5 years from August 29, 1992 (reappointment).
Jerome F. Kever, of Illinois, for the remainder of the term expiring August 28, 1993, vice Andrew F. Reardon, resigned.
Virgil M. Speakman, Jr., of Ohio, for the remainder of the term expiring August 28, 1994, vice Charles J. Chamberlain, resigned.

Submitted August 10

Harry J. Gilmore,
of Virginia, a career member of the Senior Foreign Service, class of Minister-Counselor, to be Ambassador Extraordinary and Plenipotentiary of the United States of America to the Republic of Armenia.

Submitted August 12

Lois L. Evans,
of New York, to be the Representative of the United States of America on the Economic and Social Council of the United Nations, with the rank of Ambassador.

John J. Maresca,
a career member of the Senior Foreign Service, class of Minister-Counselor, for the rank of Ambassador during his tenure of service as Special Cyprus Coordinator.

Brian C. Griffin,
of Oklahoma, to be Chairman of the Administrative Conference of the United States for the term of 5 years, vice Marshall Jordan Breger.

Submitted September 9

Alvin P. Adams, Jr.,
of Virginia, a career member of the Senior Foreign Service, class of Minister-Counselor, to be Ambassador Extraordinary and Plenipotentiary of the United States of America to the Republic of Peru.

Paul J. Barbadoro,
of New Hampshire, to be U.S. District Judge for the District of New Hampshire, vice Shane Devine, retired.

Richard E. Dorr,
of Missouri, to be U.S. District Judge for the Western District of Missouri, vice Howard F. Sachs, retired.

Steven J. McAuliffe,
of New Hampshire, to be U.S. District Judge for the District of New Hampshire, vice Norman H. Stahl, elevated.

Randall Harvey Erben,
of Texas, to be an Assistant Secretary of Housing and Urban Development, vice Skirma Anna Kondratas.

James Michael Reum,
of Illinois, to be a member of the Securities and Exchange Commission for the term expiring June 5, 1997, vice Edward H. Fleischman, resigned.

Nancy A. Nord,
of the District of Columbia, to be a Commissioner of the Consumer Product Safety Commission for a term of 7 years from October 27, 1992, vice Carol Gene Dawson, term expired.

Badi G. Foster,
of Illinois, to be a member of the National Institute Board for the National Institute for Literacy for a term of 3 years (new position).

The following named persons to be members of the Chemical Safety and Hazard Investigation Board for terms of 5 years (new positions):

Lewis S.W. Crampton, of the District of Columbia.
Robert B. Taylor, of Tennessee.
Jack Robert Witz, of California.

Lewis S.W. Crampton,
of the District of Columbia, to be Chairperson of the Chemical Safety and Hazard Investigation Board for a term of 5 years (new position).

James H. Grossman,
of California, to be Chairman of the Foreign Claims Settlement Commission of the United States for the term expiring September 30, 1994, vice Stanley L. Glod, term expired, to which position he was appointed during the last recess of the Senate.

David J. Ryder,
of Virginia, to be Director of the Mint for a term of 5 years, vice Donna Pope, term expired, to which position he was appointed during the last recess of the Senate.

The following named persons to be Commissioners of the Copyright Royalty Tribunal for terms of 7 years, to which positions they were appointed during the last recess of the Senate:

Edward J. Damich, of Virginia, vice J.C. Argetsinger, term expired.
Bruce D. Goodman, of Pennsylvania, vice Mario F. Aguero, term expired.

Submitted September 10

Robert E. Wallace,
of New Jersey, to be Assistant Secretary of Labor for Veterans' Employment and Training, vice Thomas E. Collins III.

The following named persons to be members of the Board of Directors of the Commission on National and Community Service for terms of 3 years (reappointments):

William J. Byron, of the District of Columbia.
Thomas Ehrlich, of Indiana.
George W. Romney, of Michigan.
Johnnie M. Smith, of South Carolina.
Glen W. White, of Kansas.

Submitted September 15

Annette L. Kent,
of Hawaii, to be U.S. Marshal for the District of Hawaii for the term of 4 years, vice Faith P. Evans, resigned.

Submitted September 17

Timothy K. Lewis,
of Pennsylvania, to be U.S. Circuit Judge for the Third Circuit (new position).

James H. Payne,
of Oklahoma, to be U.S. District Judge for the Northern, Eastern, and Western Districts of Oklahoma, vice H. Dale Cook, retired.

Walter B. Prince,
of Massachusetts, to be U.S. District Judge for the District of Massachusetts, vice John Joseph McNaught, retired.

Joe L. Heaton,
of Oklahoma, to be U.S. Attorney for the Western District of Oklahoma for the term of 4 years, vice Timothy D. Leonard, resigned.

Submitted September 18

The following named persons to be the Representative and Alternate Representatives of the United States of America to the Thirty-sixth Session of the General Conference of the International Atomic Energy Agency:

Representative:

Ivan Selin, of the District of Columbia.

Alternate Representatives:

Richard T. Kennedy, of the District of Columbia.

Jane E. Becker, of the District of Columbia.

Submitted September 21

Mark Johnson,
of Montana, a career member of the Senior Foreign Service, class of Minister-Counselor, to be Ambassador Extraordinary and Plenipotentiary of the United States of America to the Republic of Senegal.

Marshall Fletcher McCallie,
of Tennessee, a career member of the Senior Foreign Service, class of Counselor, to be Ambassador Extraordinary and Plenipotentiary of the United States of America to the Republic of Namibia.

Robert Gregory Joseph,
of Virginia, to be an Assistant Director of the U.S. Arms Control and Disarmament Agency, vice Manfred Eimer.

Mark McCampbell Collins, Jr.,
of the District of Columbia, to be U.S. Executive Director of the International Bank for Reconstruction and Development for a term of 2 years, vice E. Patrick Coady, term expired.

Blaine B. Goff,
of Iowa, to be U.S. Marshal for the Southern District of Iowa for the term of 4 years, vice Warren D. Stump, resigned.

Charles F. Little,
of West Virginia, to be U.S. Marshal for the Northern District of West Virginia for the term of 4 years, vice Ronald A. Donell, resigned.

The following named persons to be Members of the Peace Corps National Advisory Council:

Frank B. Hower, Jr., of Kentucky, for a term of one year expiring October 6, 1992 (new position).

Frank B. Hower, Jr., of Kentucky, for a term expiring October 6, 1994 (reappointment).

Craig R. Stapleton, of Connecticut, for a term expiring October 6, 1993 (reappointment).

Submitted September 24

George A. O'Toole, Jr.,
of Massachusetts, to be U.S. District Judge for the District of Massachusetts, vice David Sutherland Nelson, retired.

Barry M. Goldwater, Sr.,
of Arizona, to be a member of the Board of Directors of the Communications Satellite Corporation until the date of the annual meeting of the corporation in 1995 (reappointment).

Randall Brooks,
of the District of Columbia, to be a member of the Board of Directors of the Commission on National and Community Service for the remainder of the term expiring August 4, 1994, vice Joyce M. Black.

Withdrawn September 24

Joseph Gerard Sullivan,
of Virginia, to be Ambassador Extraordinary and Plenipotentiary of the United States of America to the Republic of Nicaragua, which was sent to the Senate on February 27, 1992.

Submitted September 25

Eric James Boswell,
of California, a career member of the Senior Foreign Service, class of Minister-Counselor, to be Director of the Office of Foreign Missions, with the rank of Ambassador.

John W. Gillis,
of California, to be a member of the United States Sentencing Commission for a term expiring October 31, 1997, vice Helen Corrothers, term expired.

William Lucas,
of Michigan, to be Director, Community Relations Service, for a term of 4 years, vice Grace Flores-Hughes, term expired.

Victor Jackovich,
of Iowa, a career member of the Senior Foreign Service, class of Counselor, to be Ambassador Extraordinary and Plenipotentiary of the United States of America to the Republic of Bosnia and Hercegovina.

Mara M. Letica,
of Michigan, to be Ambassador Extraordinary and Plenipotentiary of the United States of America to Croatia.

E. Allan Wendt,
of California, career member of the Senior Foreign Service, class of Minister-Counselor, to be Ambassador Extraordinary and Plenipotentiary of the United States of America to the Republic of Slovenia.

Submitted September 30

The following named persons to be Representatives and Alternate Representatives of the United States of America to the Forty-seventh Session of the General Assembly of the United Nations:

Representatives:

Edward Joseph Perkins, of Oregon.
Alexander Fletcher Watson, of Massachusetts.
Larry Pressler, of South Dakota.
Paul S. Sarbanes, of Maryland.
Gloria Estefan, of Florida.

Alternate Representatives:

Irvin Hicks, of Maryland.
Shirin R. Tahir-Kheli, of Pennsylvania.
Parker G. Montgomery, of New York.
Prezell Russell Robinson, of North Carolina.
Margaretta F. Rockefeller, of New York.

Wayne Arthur Schley,
of Alaska, to be Commissioner of the Postal Rate Commission for the remainder of the term expiring October 14, 1994, vice Henry R. Folsom, resigned.

Thomas J. Tauke,
of Iowa, to be a member of the Board of Directors of the Federal Agricultural Mortgage Corporation, vice John R. Dahl.

The following named persons to be members of the National Advisory Council on Educational Research and Improvement:

For terms expiring September 30, 1994:

John K. Andrews, Jr., of Colorado, vice Carl M. Kuttler, Jr.
Eugene L. Madeira, of Pennsylvania (reappointment).
Eunice N. Sato, of California (reappointment).

For a term expiring September 30, 1995:

Dale P. Gold, of Virginia (reappointment).

Submitted October 2

Sean Charles O'Keefe,
of Virginia, to be Secretary of the Navy, vice H. Lawrence Garrett III, resigned.

William P. Dimitrouleas,
of Florida, to be U.S. District Judge for the Southern District of Florida, vice James C. Paine, retired.

Henry W. Saad,
of Michigan, to be U.S. District Judge for the Eastern District of Michigan, vice Horace W. Gilmore, retired.

Jeni Brown Norris,
of Virginia, to be an Assistant Secretary of Housing and Urban Development, vice Mary Shannon Brunette.

Submitted October 5

Geraldine R. Gennet,
of the District of Columbia, to be an Associate Judge of the Superior Court of the District of Columbia for a term of 15 years, vice Ronald P. Wertheim, retired.

Gerald R. Riso,
of Virginia, to be Chief Financial Officer, Department of Housing and Urban Development (new position).

Submitted October 6

Douglas Alan Brook,
of Virginia, to be Director of the Office of Personnel Management for a term of 4 years, vice Constance Berry Newman, resigned.

Submitted October 7

John J. McKenna,
of Pennsylvania, to be U.S. Marshal for the Eastern District of Pennsylvania for a term of 4 years, vice Thomas C. Rapone, retired.

David M. Brewer,
of New Jersey, to be a member of the Board of Directors of the Federal Agricultural Mortgage Corp., vice Gordon Clyde Southern.

Submitted October 8

Ray E. Witter,
of Missouri, to be a member of the Chemical Safety and Hazard Investigation Board for a term of 5 years (new position).

Submitted January 5

The following named persons to be members of the Defense Base Closure and Realignment Commission for terms expiring at the end of the first session of the 103d Congress:

James A. Courter, of New Jersey, to be Chairman (reappointment).
Peter B. Bowman, of Maine, vice Duane H. Cassidy, term expired.
Beverly Butcher Byron, of Maryland, vice Alexander B. Trowbridge, term expired.
Rebecca Gernhardt Cox, of the District of Columbia, vice James C. Smith II, term expired.
Hansford T. Johnson, of Texas, vice William L. Ball III, term expired.
Arthur Levitt, Jr., of New York (reappointment).
Harry C. McPherson, Jr., of Maryland, vice Howard H. Callaway, term expired.
Robert D. Stuart, Jr., of Illinois (reappointment).

The following named persons to be members of the National Security Education Board for terms of 4 years (new positions):

Steven Muller, of Maryland.
S. William Pattis, of Illinois.
Richard F. Stolz, of Maryland.

Marion G. Chambers,
of New Mexico, to be a member of the Board of Trustees of the Institute of American Indian and Alaska Native Culture and Arts Development for a term expiring May 19, 1998, vice James Courtney Jennings, term expired.

The following named persons to be commissioners of the Copyright Royalty Tribunal for terms of 7 years:

Edward J. Damich, of Virginia.
Bruce D. Goodman, of Pennsylvania.

The following named persons who were appointed during the last recess of the Senate:

Brian C. Griffin, of Oklahoma, to be Chairman of the Administrative Conference of the United States for the term of 5 years, vice Marshall Jordan Breger.

Robert F. Goodwin, of Maryland, to be a Commissioner on the part of the United States on the International Joint Commission, United States and Canada (reappointment).

Stephen T. Hart, of Virginia, to be an Assistant Secretary of Transportation, vice Marion Clifton Blakey.

David P. Prosperi, of Illinois, to be a member of the Board of Directors of the Corporation for Public Broadcasting for a term expiring January 31, 1998, vice Marshall Turner, Jr., term expired.

Norman D. Shumway, of California, to be a member of the Board of Directors of the Legal Services Corporation for the remainder of the term expiring July 13, 1993.

Appendix C—Checklist of White House Press Releases

The following list contains releases of the Office of the Press Secretary which are not included in this book.

Released August 4

Transcript:
Press briefing on the President's health care plan—by Gail R. Wilensky, Deputy Assistant to the President for Policy Development, and Kevin E. Moley, Deputy Secretary of Health and Human Services

Released August 5

Announcement:
Nomination of Robert W. Kostelka to be U.S. District Judge for the Western District of Louisiana

Released August 6

Transcript:
Remarks by Press Secretary Marlin Fitzwater in an exchange with reporters

Released August 7

Announcement:
Nomination of members of the Railroad Retirement Board

Released August 8

Announcement:
President's meeting on the situation in Bosnia

Released August 10

Transcript:
Press briefing on Governor Clinton's economic plan—by Clayton Yeutter, Counselor to the President for Domestic Affairs

Released August 12

Statement by the President:
Completion of negotiations on the North American free trade agreement

Transcript:
Press briefing on the North American free trade agreement—by Carla A. Hills, U.S. Trade Representative

Released August 13

Transcript:
Remarks to State Department employees—by Secretary of State James A. Baker III

Transcript:
Press briefing on AIDS research, prevention, and treatment efforts—by Secretary of Health and Human Services Louis W. Sullivan

Statement:
Resignation from White House staff and acceptance of position as general chairman of the Republican National Committee—by Samuel K. Skinner, Chief of Staff to the President

Released August 27

Announcement:
Appointment of Robert Mosbacher as general chairman of finance for the Republican Party

Released August 31

Fact sheet:
U.S.-Russian agreement on highly enriched uranium

Released September 1

Announcement:
President's address to the Nation

Released September 3

Fact sheet:
"Nevada Public Lands Wilderness Act"

Fact sheet:
Small Business Administration—Hurricane Andrew disaster assistance

Released September 4

Fact sheet:
"Idaho Public Lands Wilderness Act"

Advance text:
Remarks to the community in Fredericksburg, VA

Released September 7

Fact sheet:
"Product Liability Fairness Act"

Released September 8

Announcement:
Nomination of Paul J. Barbadoro to be U.S. District Judge for the District of New Hampshire

Announcement:
Nomination of Steven J. McAuliffe to be U.S. District Judge for the District of New Hampshire

Announcement:
Nomination of Richard E. Dorr to be U.S. District Judge for the Western District of Missouri

Advance text:
Remarks to the B'nai B'rith International convention

Released September 10

Announcement:
Appointment of Mark A. Shiffrin as a member of the President's Committee on Mental Retardation

Announcement:
Nomination of Charles J. Heringer, Jr., to be U.S. Commissioner on the Bear River Commission

Released September 11

Fact sheet:
Saudi F–15XP

Released September 14

Advance text:
Remarks to Vaagen Brothers Lumber employees in Colville, WA

Announcement:
Nomination of Annette L. Kent to be U.S. Marshal for the District of Hawaii

Fact sheet:
Caring for America's forests

Fact sheet:
The spotted owl/timber supply crisis: a chronology

Released September 15

Transcript:
Press briefing on DOE support of the President's nonproliferation initiative—by Secretary of Energy James Watkins

Released September 16

Announcement:
Nomination of Joe L. Heaton to be U.S. Attorney for the Western District of Oklahoma

Fact sheet:
"Family Leave Tax Credit Act of 1992"

Released September 17

Announcement:
Nomination of James H. Payne to be U.S. District Judge for the Northern, Eastern, and Western Districts of Oklahoma

Announcement:
Nomination of Walter B. Prince to be U.S. District Judge for the District of Massachusetts

Announcement:
Nomination of Timothy K. Lewis to be U.S. Circuit Judge for the Third Circuit

Announcement:
Nomination of Kay Bailey Hutchison to be a member of the Commission to Promote Investment in America's Infrastructure

Fact sheet:
President Bush's record on women appointees

Released September 18

Announcement:
Nomination of Ivan Selin to be a Representative and Richard T. Kennedy and Jane E. Becker to be Alternate Representatives of the United States of America to the 36th session of the General Conference of the International Atomic Energy Agency

Fact sheet:
North American free trade agreement: official notification of Congress

Released September 21

Announcement:
According the personal rank of Ambassador to Robert L. Hutchings in his capacity as Special Adviser for East European Assistance

Announcement:
Nomination of Mark McCampbell Collins, Jr., to be U.S. Executive Director of the International Bank for Reconstruction and Development

Announcement:
Nomination of Blaine B. Goff to be U.S. Marshal for the Southern District of Iowa

Announcement:
Nomination of Charles F. Little to be U.S. Marshal for the Northern District of West Virginia

Fact sheet:
The challenges of our age: peacekeeping, proliferation, and prosperity

Released September 22

Announcement:
Nomination of Frank B. Hower, Jr., to be a member of the Peace Corps National Advisory Council

Announcement:
Nomination of Craig B. Stapleton to be a member of the Peace Corps National Advisory Council

Released September 23

Fact sheet:
Encouraging entrepreneurial capitalism: strengthening small businesses

Announcement:
According the personal rank of Ambassador to Richard Lee Armitage in his capacity as Deputy to the Coordinator for Assistance to the Commonwealth of Independent States

Announcement:
Nomination of Edward L. Hennessey, Jr., to be a member of the Board of Governors of the United Service Organizations, Inc.

Released September 25

Announcement:
Nomination of George A. O'Toole, Jr., to be U.S. District Judge for the District of Massachusetts

Announcement:
Nomination of Barry M. Goldwater, Sr., to be a member of the Board of Directors of the Communications Satellite Corporation

Announcement:
Nomination of Randall Brooks to be a member of the Board of Directors of the Commission on National and Community Service

Announcement:
Nomination of John W. Gillis to be a member of the United States Sentencing Commission

Fact sheet:
"Federal Pay Reduction Act of 1992"

Released September 28

Fact sheet:
The President's Agenda for American Renewal: combating violent crime

Statement:
Ceremony for initialing the North American free trade agreement—by Press Secretary Fitzwater

Released September 30

Announcement:
Nomination of Wayne Arthur Schley to be a Commissioner on the Postal Rate Commission

Fact sheet:
Child support enforcement initiative: Project KIDS

Announcement:
Nomination of Paul S. Sarbanes to be United States Representative to the General Assembly of the United Nations

Released October 1

Announcement:
Nomination of Thomas J. Tauke to be a member of the Board of Directors of the Federal Agricultural Mortgage Corp.

Fact sheet:
The President's program to encourage ethanol use in meeting the environmental goals of the Clean Air Act

Released October 2

Announcement:
Nomination of William P. Dimitrouleas to be U.S. District Judge for the Southern District of Florida

Announcement:
Nomination of Henry W. Saad to be U.S. District Judge for the Eastern District of Michigan

Released October 5

Announcement:
Nomination of Donald E. Vinson to be U.S. Representative on the South Pacific Commission

Announcement:
Nomination of Roland I. Perusse to be U.S. Deputy Commissioner on the Commission for the Study of Alternatives to the Panama Canal

Announcement:
Nomination of Geraldine R. Gennet to be an Associate Judge of the Superior Court of the District of Columbia

Released October 6

Announcement:
The President's 1993 annual Points of Light awards program

Released October 7

Transcript:
Remarks of Prime Minister Carlos Salinas of Mexico at the initialing ceremony for the North American free trade agreement in San Antonio, TX

Transcript:
Remarks of Prime Minister Brian Mulroney of Canada at the initialing ceremony for the North American free trade agreement in San Antonio, TX

Transcript:
Press briefing on the North American free trade agreement—by U.S. Trade Representative Carla A. Hills

Fact sheet:
San Antonio meeting and the initialing of the North American free trade agreement

Statement:
Disaster assistance for the State of Florida as a result of tornadoes which struck on October 3— by Press Secretary Fitzwater

Announcement:
Nomination of John J. McKenna to be U.S. Marshal for the Eastern District of Pennsylvania

Announcement:
Appointment of Mary D. Fisher as a member of the National Commission on Acquired Immune Deficiency Syndrome

Released October 8

Announcement:
Nomination of James C. Lin to be a member of the President's Committee on the National Medal of Science

Announcement:
Nomination of David M. Mulcahy to be a member of the President's Export Council

Announcement:
Nomination of Charles R. Lee to be a member of the President's National Security Telecommunications Advisory Committee

Announcement:
Nomination of Ray E. Witter to be a member of the Chemical Safety and Hazard Investigation Board

Announcement:
Nomination of David M. Brewer to be a member of the Board of Directors of the Federal Agricultural Mortgage Corporation

Released October 13

Announcement:
Nomination of 22 individuals to be members of the National Commission on Measured Responses to Achieve a Drug-Free America by 1995

Released October 14

Announcement:
Appointment of Juana Dainis and Robert D. Segura as members of the President's Advisory Commission on Educational Excellence for Hispanic Americans

Fact sheet:
Emergency suspension of the Davis-Bacon Act

Announcement:
Appointment of Eugene F. Yeates as Executive Director of the President's Foreign Intelligence Advisory Board

Released October 15

Announcement:
Appointment of Paul Findley, Christopher Hicks, and William Hodges Mobley as members of the Board for International Food and Agricultural Development

Announcement:
Appointment of Harold T. Shapiro as a member of the President's Council of Advisors on Science and Technology

Released October 19

Fact sheet:
President Bush's record on Hispanic appointments

Released October 21

Announcement:
Appointment of Huda Bingham Jones as a member of the Commission on Presidential Scholars

Announcement:
Nomination of John H. Harriman to be a member of the National Advisory Board on Public Service

Released October 23

Announcement:
Nomination of Richard J. Wall to be a member of the Board of Visitors to the U.S. Military Academy

Announcement:
Emergency appropriations for Departments of Agriculture, Commerce, Housing and Urban Development, the Interior, and Labor

Fact sheet:
Executive order to promote open bidding on Federal and federally funded construction projects

Announcement:
According the rank of Ambassador to Edward L. Lacey as head of delegation to the Biological and Toxic Weapons Convention Verification Conference

Released October 25

Transcript:
Press briefing on availability of Vietnamese records relating to POW–MIA's—by Gen. John W. Vessey, USA ret., Presidential Emissary to Hanoi for POW–MIA Affairs, and Senators John McCain and John Kerry

Released October 26

Transcript:
Remarks on poll results at Stapleton Airport in Denver, CO—by Press Secretary Fitzwater

Released October 30

Announcement:
Signing of H.R. 429, the Reclamation Projects Authorization and Adjustment Act of 1992

Transcript:
Remarks and question-and-answer session in St. Louis, MO—by Gov. William Donald Schaefer of Maryland

Released November 6

Statement:
White House staff's transition cooperation

Released November 16

Announcement:
Appointment of Keith M. Kaneshiro as a member of the National Commission on Measured Responses to Achieve a Drug-Free America by 1995

Announcement:
Appointment of Mike Moore as a member of the National Commission on Measured Responses to Achieve a Drug-Free America by 1995

Announcement:
Appointment of Thomas Neal Tripp as a member of the Board of Directors of the Federal Prison Industries, Inc.

Released November 18

Announcement:
Appointment of Patricia Diaz Dennis as Commissioner-Observer on the Commission on Security and Cooperation in Europe

Released November 19

Statement:
President's visit to his mother in Greenwich, CT—by Press Secretary Fitzwater

Statement:
Death of the President's mother, Mrs. Prescott Bush—by Press Secretary Fitzwater

Released November 20

Transcript:
Press briefing on the agreement on trade with the European Community Commission—by U.S. Trade Representative Carla A. Hills and Secretary of Agriculture Edward R. Madigan

Released November 24

Statement:
Foreign access to U.S. ports—by Press Secretary Fitzwater

Released December 2

Announcement:
President's Environment and Conservation Challenge Awards

Released December 3

Statement:
Signing ceremony for the North American free trade agreement—by Press Secretary Fitzwater

Released December 8

Announcement:
Recess appointment of Pauline Crowe Naftzger as Alternate Representative of the United States of America on the Executive Board of the United Nations Children's Fund

Released December 9

Announcement:
Presidential Medal of Freedom recipients

Released December 11

Announcement:
Presidential Medal of Freedom citations

Released December 22

Statement:
President's trip to Somalia—by Press Secretary Fitzwater

Announcement:
Appointment of Susan Porter Rose as a member of the Commission of Fine Arts

Released December 23

Announcement:
Appointment of Albert V. Casey as a member of the National Commission to Ensure a Strong Competitive Airline Industry

Released December 30

Fact sheet:
START II treaty

Announcement:
Recess appointment of Robert F. Goodwin as a Commissioner on the International Joint Commission, United States and Canada

Announcement:
Recess appointment of Norman D. Shumway as a member of the Board of Directors of the Legal Services Corporation

Released December 31

Announcement:
Recess appointment of David P. Prosperi as a member of the Corporation for Public Broadcasting

Announcement:
Recess appointment of Jeannette Louise Naylor as a member of the Board of Directors of the Pennsylvania Avenue Development Corporation

Released January 1

Fact sheet:
START II treaty

Fact sheet:
Treaty Between the United States of America and the Russian Federation on Further Reduction and Limitation of Strategic Offensive Arms

Fact sheet:
Update on the START treaty

Released January 6

Transcript:
Press briefing on the budget—by Richard G. Darman, Director, Office of Management and Budget

Released January 7

Fact sheet:
Forest Service study reports: Red River, KY; Greenbrier River, WV; and Pyramid Peak Planning Area, CA

Fact sheet:
"Colorado Public Lands Wilderness Act"

Fact sheet:
"Montana Public Lands Wilderness Act"

Released January 8

Announcement:
Appointment of Vincent H. Dreeszen as the U.S. Representative on the Kansas-Nebraska Big Blue River Compact Administration

Released January 11

Announcement:
Designation of Paul A. Vander Myde as Vice Chairman of the Administrative Conference of the United States

Released January 12

Announcement:
Appointment of Richard A. Hauser as a member of the Board of Directors of the Pennsylvania Avenue Development Corporation

Statement:
President's physical examination—by Burton J. Lee III, Physician to the President

Released January 15

Announcement:
Appointment of Robert Zoellick as a member of the Board of Directors of the Federal Home Loan Mortgage Corporation

Announcement:
Appointment of William D. Novelli as a member of the Enterprise for the Americas Board

Announcement:
Appointment of John Robert Longenecker as Transition Manager of the United States Enrichment Corporation

Released January 19

Announcement:
Appointment of John Patrick Schmitz as a U.S. Representative on the Joint Committee on the Environment between the United States and the Republic of Panama

Announcement:
Appointment of David Abshire as a member of the National Commission on Defense and National Security

Appendix D—Acts Approved by the President

H.R. 479 / Public Law 102–328
To amend the National Trails System Act to designate the California National Historic Trail and Pony Express National Historic Trail as components of the National Trails System

H.R. 5343 / Public Law 102–329
To make technical amendments to the Fair Packaging and Labeling Act with respect to its treatment of the SI metric system, and for other purposes

S. 2938 / Public Law 102–330
To authorize the Architect of the Capitol to acquire certain property

S.J. Res. 92 / Public Law 102–331
To designate July 28, 1992, as "Buffalo Soldiers Day"

S.J. Res. 295 / Public Law 102–332
Designating September 10, 1992, as "National D.A.R.E. Day"

S. 992 / Private Law 102–4
To provide for the reimbursement of certain travel and relocation expenses under title 5, United States Code, for Jane E. Denne of Henderson, Nevada

Approved August 4

S.J. Res. 310 / Public Law 102–333
To designate August 1, 1992, as "Helsinki Human Rights Day"

S. 249 / Private Law 102–5
For the relief of Trevor Henderson

Approved August 6

S. 2641 / Public Law 102–334
To partially restore obligation authority authorized in the Intermodal Surface Transportation Efficiency Act of 1991

H.R. 3289 / Private Law 102–6
For the relief of Carmen Victoria Parini, Felix Juan Parini, and Sergio Manuel Parini

Approved August 7

H.R. 3836 / Public Law 102–335
Pacific Yew Act

H.R. 5059 / Public Law 102–336
To extend the boundaries of the grounds of the National Gallery of Art to include the National Sculpture Garden

S. 2917 / Public Law 102–337
To amend the National School Lunch Act to authorize the Secretary of Agriculture to provide financial and other assistance to the University of Mississippi, in cooperation with the University of Southern Mississippi, to establish and maintain a food service management institute, and for other purposes

S. 295 / Private Law 102–7
For the relief of Mary P. Carlton and Lee Alan Tan

Approved August 11

H.R. 4026 / Public Law 102–338
Zuni River Watershed Act of 1992

H.R. 5566 / Public Law 102–339
To provide additional time to negotiate settlement of a land dispute in South Carolina

Approved August 12

S.J. Res. 270 / Public Law 102–340
To designate August 15, 1992, as "82d Airborne Division 50th Anniversary Recognition Day"

Approved August 14

H.R. 5487 / Public Law 102–341
Agriculture, Rural Development, Food and Drug Administration, and Related Agencies Appropriations Act, 1993

S. 2759 / Public Law 102–342
Child Nutrition Amendments of 1992

Approved August 17

S. 959 / Public Law 102–343
Thomas Jefferson Commemoration Commission Act

Approved August 26

H.R. 4312 / Public Law 102–344
Voting Rights Language Assistance Act of 1992

H.R. 5481 / Public Law 102–345
FAA Civil Penalty Administrative Assessment Act of 1992

S. 544 / Public Law 102–346
Animal Enterprise Protection Act of 1992

S. 807 / Public Law 102–347
To permit Mount Olivet Cemetery Association of Salt Lake City, Utah, to lease a certain tract of land for a period of not more than 70 years

S. 1770 / Public Law 102–348
To convey certain surplus real property located in the Black Hills National Forest to the Black Hills Workshop and Training Center, and for other purposes

S. 1963 / Public Law 102–349
To amend section 992 of title 28, United States Code, to provide a member of the United States Sentencing Commission whose term has expired may continue to serve until a successor is appointed or until the expiration of the next session of Congress

S. 2079 / Public Law 102–350
Marsh-Billings National Historical Park Establishment Act

S. 3001 / Public Law 102–351
To amend the Food Stamp Act of 1977 to prevent a reduction in the adjusted cost of the thrifty food plan during fiscal year 1993, and for other purposes

S. 3112 / Public Law 102–352
Public Health Service Act Technical Amendments Act

S. 3163 / Public Law 102–353
Prescription Drug Amendments of 1992

H.R. 2549 / Public Law 102–354
Administrative Procedure Technical Amendments Act of 1991

H.R. 2926 / Public Law 102–355
To amend the Act of May 17, 1954, relating to the Jefferson National Expansion Memorial to authorize increased funding for the East Saint Louis portion of the Memorial, and for other purposes

H.R. 2977 / Public Law 102–356
Public Telecommunications Act of 1992

H.R. 3795 / Public Law 102–357
To amend title 28, United States Code, to establish 3 divisions in the Central Judicial District of California

H.R. 4437 / Public Law 102–358
To authorize funds for the implementation of the settlement agreement reached between the Pueblo de Cochiti and the United States Army Corps of Engineers under the authority of Public Law 100–202

H.R. 5560 / Public Law 102–359
To extend for one year the National Commission on Time and Learning, and for other purposes

H.R. 5623 / Public Law 102–360
To waive the period of congressional review for certain District of Columbia Acts

H.R. 5688 / Public Law 102–361
Bankruptcy Judgeship Act of 1992

H.J. Res. 411 / Public Law 102–362
To designate the week of September 13, 1992, through September 19, 1992, as "National Rehabilitation Week"

H.J. Res. 507 / Public Law 102–363
To approve the extension of nondiscriminatory treatment with respect to the products of the Republic of Albania

Approved September 2

H.J. Res. 492 / Public Law 102–364
Designating September 1992 as "Childhood Cancer Month"

Approved September 3

H.R. 2607 / Public Law 102–365
Rail Safety Enforcement and Review Act

Approved September 4

H.R. 4111 / Public Law 102–366
Small Business Credit and Business Opportunity Enhancement Act of 1992

Approved September 7

H.R. 3033 / Public Law 102–367
Job Training Reform Amendments of 1992

Approved September 23

H.R. 5620 / Public Law 102–368
Dire Emergency Supplemental Appropriations Act, 1992, Including Disaster Assistance To Meet the Present Emergencies Arising From the Consequences of Hurricane Andrew, Typhoon Omar,

Hurricane Iniki, and Other Natural Disasters, and Additional Assistance to Distressed Communities

Approved September 24

H.J. Res. 413 / Public Law 102–369
To designate September 13, 1992, as "Commodore John Barry Day "

S.J. Res. 303 / Public Law 102–370
To designate October 1992 as "National Breast Cancer Awareness Month"

Approved September 27

H.R. 4551 / Public Law 102–371
Civil Liberties Act Amendments of 1992

Approved September 30

S. 680 / Public Law 102–372
Tourism Policy and Export Promotion Act of 1992

S.J. Res. 337 / Public Law 102–373
Designating September 18, 1992, as "National POW/MIA Recognition Day", and authorizing display of the National League of Families POW/MIA flag

S. 1607 / Public Law 102–374
Northern Cheyenne Indian Reserved Water Rights Settlement Act of 1992

H.R. 2967 / Public Law 102–375
Older Americans Act Amendments of 1992

H.R. 238 / Private Law 102–8
For the relief of Craig A. Klein

H.R. 454 / Private Law 102–9
For the relief of Bruce C. Veit

H.R. 478 / Private Law 102–10
For the relief of Norman R. Ricks

H.R. 712 / Private Law 102–11
For the relief of Patricia A. McNamara

Approved October 1

H.J. Res. 553 / Public Law 102–376
Making continuing appropriations for the fiscal year 1993, and for other purposes

Approved October 2

H.R. 5373 / Public Law 102–377
Energy and Water Development Appropriations Act, 1993

H.R. 2850 / Public Law 102–378
Technical and Miscellaneous Civil Service Amendments Act of 1992

Approved October 5

H.R. 5126 / Public Law 102–379
Civil War Battlefield Commemorative Coin Act of 1992

H.R. 5428 / Public Law 102–380
Military Construction Appropriations Act, 1993

H.R. 5503 / Public Law 102–381
Department of the Interior and Related Agencies Appropriations Act, 1993

H.R. 6056 / Public Law 102–382
District of Columbia Supplemental Appropriations and Rescissions Act

S. 1731 / Public Law 102–383
United States-Hong Kong Policy Act of 1992

S. 3175 / Public Law 102–384
National and Community Service Technical Amendment Act of 1992

Passed October 5, over the President's veto

S. 12 / Public Law 102–385
Cable Television Consumer Protection and Competition Act of 1992

Approved October 6

H.R. 2194 / Public Law 102–386
To amend the Solid Waste Disposal Act to clarify provisions concerning the application of certain requirements and sanctions to Federal facilities

H.J. Res. 560 / Public Law 102–387
Waiving certain enrollment requirements with respect to any appropriations bill for the remainder of the One Hundred Second Congress

H.R. 5518 / Public Law 102–388
Department of Transportation and Related Agencies Appropriations Act, 1993

H.R. 5679 / Public Law 102–389
Departments of Veterans Affairs and Housing and Urban Development, and Independent Agencies Appropriations Act, 1993

H.R. 3654 / Public Law 102–390
To provide for the minting of commemorative coins to support the 1996 Atlanta Centennial Olympic Games and the programs of the United States Olympic Committee, to reauthorize and reform the United States Mint, and for other purposes

H.R. 5368 / Public Law 102–391
Foreign Operations, Export Financing, and Related Programs Appropriations Act, 1993

H.R. 5427 / Public Law 102–392
Legislative Branch Appropriations Act, 1993

H.R. 5488 / Public Law 102–393
Treasury, Postal Service, and General Government Appropriations Act, 1993

H.R. 5677 / Public Law 102–394
Departments of Labor, Health and Human Services, and Education, and Related Agencies Appropriations Act, 1993

H.R. 5678 / Public Law 102–395
Departments of Commerce, Justice, and State, the Judiciary, and Related Agencies Appropriations Act, 1993

H.R. 5504 / Public Law 102–396
Department of Defense Appropriations Act, 1993

S. 1766 / Public Law 102–397
To add to the area in which the Capitol Police have law enforcement authority, and for other purposes

S.J. Res. 23 / Public Law 102–398
To consent to certain amendments enacted by the legislature of the State of Hawaii to the Hawaiian Homes Commission Act, 1920

Approved October 7

H.R. 5058 / Public Law 102–399
To authorize appropriations for the American Folklife Center for fiscal year 1993

H.R. 5399 / Public Law 102–400
United States Commission on Civil Rights Authorization Act of 1992

H.R. 5630 / Public Law 102–401
Head Start Improvement Act of 1992

Approved October 9

H.R. 1435 / Public Law 102–402
Rocky Mountain Arsenal National Wildlife Refuge Act of 1992

H.R. 3379 / Public Law 102–403
To amend section 574 of title 5, United States Code, relating to the authorities of the Administrative Conference

S. 1216 / Public Law 102–404
Chinese Student Protection Act of 1992

S. 2344 / Public Law 102–405
Veterans' Medical Programs Amendments of 1992

Approved October 12

H.R. 2448 / Public Law 102–406
Benjamin Franklin National Memorial Commemorative Medal and Fire Service Bill of Rights Act

Approved October 13

H.R. 1628 / Public Law 102–407
To authorize the construction of a monument in the District of Columbia or its environs to honor Thomas Paine, and for other purposes

H.R. 3508 / Public Law 102–408
Health Professions Education Extension Amendments of 1992

H.R. 4178 / Public Law 102–409
DES Education and Research Amendments of 1992

H.R. 5673 / Public Law 102–410
Agency for Health Care Policy and Research Reauthorization Act of 1992

Approved October 14

H.R. 5925 / Public Law 102–411
EEOC Education, Technical Assistance, and Training Revolving Fund Act of 1992

H.J. Res. 320 / Public Law 102–412
Authorizing the government of the District of Columbia to establish, in the District of Columbia or its environs, a memorial to African-Americans who served with Union forces during the Civil War

H.J. Res. 542 / Public Law 102–413
Designating the week beginning November 8, 1992, as "Hire a Veteran Week"

S. 3195 / Public Law 102–414
World War II 50th Anniversary Commemorative Coins Act

H.R. 3157 / Public Law 102–415
Alaska Land Status Technical Corrections Act of 1992

H.R. 2144 / Public Law 102–416
Advisory Council on California Indian Policy Act of 1992

H.R. 2324 / Public Law 102–417
Incarcerated Witness Fees Act of 1991

S.J. Res. 287 / Public Law 102–418
To designate the week of October 4, through October 10, as "Mental Illness Awareness Week"

Approved October 16

H.R. 2321 / Public Law 102–419
Dayton Aviation Heritage Preservation Act of 1992

H.R. 5258 / Public Law 102–420
An act to provide for the withdrawal of most favored nation status from Serbia and Montenegro and to provide for the restoration of such status if certain conditions are fulfilled

H.R. 5483 / Public Law 102–421
Education of the Deaf Act Amendments of 1992

S. 1880 / Public Law 102–422
To amend the District of Columbia Spouse Equity Act of 1988

S. 3007 / Public Law 102–423
To authorize financial assistance for the construction and maintenance of the Mary McLeod Bethune Memorial Fine Arts Center

S.J. Res. 305 / Public Law 102–424
To designate October 1992 as "Polish-American Heritage Month"

S.J. Res. 319 / Public Law 102–425
To designate the second Sunday in October of 1992 as "National Children's Day"

Approved October 19

H.R. 4016 / Public Law 102–426
Community Environmental Response Facilitation Act

Approved October 21

H.R. 3665 / Public Law 102–427
Little River Canyon National Preserve Act of 1992

H.R. 5237 / Public Law 102–428
Rural Electrification Administration Improvement Act of 1992

H.R. 5739 / Public Law 102–429
Export Enhancement Act of 1992

Approved October 23

H.R. 1216 / Public Law 102–430
Indiana Dunes National Lakeshore Access and Enhancement Act

H.R. 2181 / Public Law 102–431
To permit the Secretary of the Interior to acquire by exchange lands in the Cuyahoga National Recreation Area that are owned by the State of Ohio

H.R. 2431 / Public Law 102–432
To amend the Wild and Scenic Rivers Act by designating a segment of the Lower Merced River in California as a component of the National Wild and Scenic Rivers System

H.R. 3118 / Public Law 102–433
To designate Federal Office Building Number 9 located at 1900 E Street, Northwest, in the District of Columbia, as the "Theodore Roosevelt Federal Building"

H.R. 3818 / Public Law 102–434
To designate the building located at 80 North Hughey Avenue in Orlando, Florida, as the "George C. Young United States Courthouse and Federal Building"

H.R. 4281 / Public Law 102–435
To designate the Federal building and courthouse to be constructed at 5th and Ross Streets in Santa Ana, California, as the "Ronald Reagan Federal Building and Courthouse"

H.R. 4489 / Public Law 102–436
To provide for a land exchange with the city of Tacoma, Washington

H.R. 4539 / Public Law 102–437
To designate the general mail facility of the United States Postal Service in Gulfport, Mississippi, as the "Larkin I. Smith General Mail Facility" and the building of the United States Postal Service in Poplarville, Mississippi, as the "Larkin I. Smith Post Office Building"

H.R. 4771 / Public Law 102–438
To designate the facility under construction for use by the United States Postal Service at FM 1098 Loop in Prairie View, Texas, as the "Esel D. Bell Post Office Building"

H.R. 4999 / Public Law 102–439
To authorize additional appropriations for implementation of the development plan for Pennsylvania Avenue between the Capitol and the White House

H.R. 5013 / Public Law 102–440
To promote the conservation of wild exotic birds, to provide for the Great Lakes Fish and Wildlife Tissue Bank, to reauthorize the Fish and Wildlife Conservation Act of 1980, to reauthorize the African Elephant Conservation Act, and for other purposes

H.R. 5122 / Public Law 102–441
Jicarilla Apache Tribe Water Rights Settlement Act

H.R. 5222 / Public Law 102–442
To designate the Federal building and United States courthouse located at 204 South Main Street in South Bend, Indiana, as the "Robert A. Grant Federal Building and United States Courthouse"

H.R. 5291 / Public Law 102–443
To provide for the temporary use of certain lands in the city of South Gate, California, for elementary school purposes

H.R. 5328 / Public Law 102–444
To amend title 35, United States Code, with respect to the late payment of maintenance fees

H.R. 5431 / Public Law 102–445
To designate the Federal building located at 200 Federal Plaza in Paterson, New Jersey, as the "Robert A. Roe Federal Building"

H.R. 5432 / Public Law 102–446
To designate the Federal building and United States courthouse located at the corner of College Avenue and Mountain Street in Fayetteville, Arkansas, as the "John Paul Hammerschmidt Federal Building and United States Courthouse"

H.R. 5453 / Public Law 102–447
To designate the Central Square facility of the United States Postal Service in Cambridge, Massachusetts, as the "Clifton Merriman Post Office Building"

H.R. 5479 / Public Law 102–448
To designate the facility of the United States Postal Service located at 1100 Wythe Street in Alexandria, Virginia, as the "Helen Day United States Post Office Building"

H.R. 5491 / Public Law 102–449
To designate the Department of Veterans Affairs medical center in Marlin, Texas, as the "Thomas T. Connally Department of Veterans Affairs Medical Center"

H.R. 5572 / Public Law 102–450
To designate May of each year as "Asian/Pacific American Heritage Month"

H.R. 5575 / Public Law 102–451
To authorize certain additional uses of the Library of Congress Special Facilities Center, and for other purposes

H.R. 5602 / Public Law 102–452
Granting the consent of the Congress to the Interstate Rail Passenger Network Compact

H.R. 5605 / Public Law 102–453
Cedar River Watershed Land Exchange Act of 1992

H.R. 5751 / Public Law 102–454
To provide for the distribution within the United States of certain materials prepared by the United States Information Agency

H.R. 5831 / Public Law 102–455
To designate the Federal Building located at Main and Church Streets in Victoria, Texas, as the "Martin Luther King, Jr. Federal Building"

H.R. 6000 / Public Law 102–456
To redesignate Springer Mountain National Recreation Area as "Ed Jenkins National Recreation Area"

H.R. 6049 / Public Law 102–457
Congressional Award Act Amendments of 1992

H.R. 6072 / Public Law 102–458
To direct expedited negotiated settlement of the land rights of the Kenai Natives Association, Inc., under section 14(h)(3) of the Alaska Native Claims Settlement Act, by directing land acquisition and exchange negotiations by the Secretary of the Interior and certain Alaska Native corporations involving lands and interests in lands held by the United States and such corporations

H.R. 6165 / Public Law 102–459
To amend certain provisions of law relating to establishment, in the District of Columbia or its environs, of a memorial to honor Thomas Paine

H.R. 6179 / Public Law 102–460
To amend the Wild and Scenic Rivers Act

H.R. 6184 / Public Law 102–461
To amend the National Trails System Act to designate the American Discovery Trail for study to determine the feasibility and desirability of its designation as a national trail

H.J. Res. 353 / Public Law 102–462
Designating the week beginning January 3, 1993, as "Braille Literacy Week"

H.J. Res. 399 / Public Law 102–463
Designating the week beginning November 1, 1992, as "National Medical Staff Services Awareness Week"

H.J. Res. 457 / Public Law 102–464
Designating January 16, 1993, as "Religious Freedom Day"

H.J. Res. 467 / Public Law 102–465
Designating October 24, 1992, through November 1, 1992, as "National Red Ribbon Week for a Drug-Free America"

H.J. Res. 471 / Public Law 102–466
Designating October 14, 1992, as "National Occupational Therapy Day"

H.J. Res. 484 / Public Law 102–467
Designating the week beginning February 14, 1993, "National Visiting Nurse Association Week"

H.J. Res. 489 / Public Law 102–468
Designating February 21, 1993, through February 27, 1993, as "American Wine Appreciation Week", and for other purposes

H.J. Res. 500 / Public Law 102–469
Designating March 1993 as "Irish-American Heritage Month"

H.J. Res. 520 / Public Law 102–470
To designate the month of October 1992 as "Country Music Month"

H.J. Res. 523 / Public Law 102–471
Designating October 8, 1992, as "National Firefighters Day"

H.J. Res. 529 / Public Law 102–472
Supporting the planting of 500 redwood trees from California in Spain in commemoration of the quincentenary of the voyage of Christopher Columbus and designating the trees as a gift to the people of Spain

H.J. Res. 543 / Public Law 102–473
Designating November 30, 1992, through December 6, 1992, as "National Education First Week"

H.J. Res. 547 / Public Law 102–474
Designating May 2, 1993, through May 8, 1993, as "National Walking Week"

H.J. Res. 563 / Public Law 102–475
Providing for the convening of the first session of the One Hundred Third Congress

S. 1146 / Public Law 102–476
Scientific and Advanced-Technology Act of 1992

S. 1530 / Public Law 102–477
Indian Employment, Training and Related Services Demonstration Act of 1992

S. 2625 / Public Law 102–478
To designate the United States courthouse being constructed at 400 Cooper Street in Camden, New Jersey, as the "Mitchell H. Cohen United States Courthouse"

S. 2661 / Public Law 102–479
To authorize the striking of a medal commemorating the 250th anniversary of the founding of the American Philosophical Society and the birth of Thomas Jefferson.

S. 2834 / Public Law 102–480
To designate the United States Post Office Building located at 100 Main Street, Millsboro, Delaware, as the "John J. Williams Post Office Building"

S.J. Res. 166 / Public Law 102–481
Designating the week of October 4 through 10, 1992, as "National Customer Service Week"

S.J. Res. 218 / Public Law 102–482
Designating the calendar year, 1993, as the "Year of American Craft: A Celebration of the Creative Work of the Hand"

S.J. Res. 252 / Public Law 102–483
Designating the week of April 18 through 24, 1993, as "National Credit Education Week"

H.R. 5006 / Public Law 102–484
National Defense Authorization Act for Fiscal Year 1993

H.R. 6050 / Public Law 102–485
Depository Institutions Disaster Relief Act of 1992

H.R. 240 / Private Law 102–12
For the relief of Rodgito Keller

H.R. 1101 / Private Law 102–13
For the relief of William A. Cassity

H.R. 2156 / Private Law 102–14
For the relief of William A. Proffitt

H.R. 5164 / Private Law 102–15
For the relief of Craig B. Sorensen and Nita M. Sorensen

H.R. 5749 / Private Law 102–16
For the relief of Krishanthi Sava Kopp

H.R. 5923 / Private Law 102–17
For the relief of Anna C. Massari

H.R. 5998 / Private Law 102–18
For the relief of the Wilkinson County School District, in the State of Mississippi

S. 1181 / Private Law 102–19
For the relief of Christy Carl Hallien of Arlington, Texas

Approved October 24

H.R. 776 / Public Law 102–486
Energy Policy Act of 1992

H.R. 2263 / Public Law 102–487
To amend chapter 45 of title 5, United States Code, to authorize awards for cost savings disclosures

H.R. 2896 / Public Law 102–488
Minute Man National Historical Park Amendments of 1991

H.R. 3638 / Public Law 102–489
Koniag Lands Conveyance Amendments of 1991

H.R. 3673 / Public Law 102–490
Membrane Processes Research Act of 1992

H.R. 4398 / Public Law 102–491
Federal Reserve Bank Branch Modernization Act

H.R. 4412 / Public Law 102–492
To amend title 17, United States Code, relating to fair use of copyrighted works

H.R. 4773 / Public Law 102–493
Fertility Clinic Success Rate and Certification Act of 1992

H.R. 4841 / Public Law 102–494
Granting the consent of the Congress to the New Hampshire-Maine Interstate School Compact

H.R. 4844 / Public Law 102–495
Elwha River Ecosystem and Fisheries Restoration Act

H.R. 5095 / Public Law 102–496
Intelligence Authorization Act for Fiscal Year 1993

H.R. 5686 / Public Law 102–497
To make technical amendments to certain Federal Indian statutes

H.R. 6014 / Public Law 102–498
To designate certain land in the State of Missouri owned by the United States and administered by the Secretary of Agriculture as part of the Mark Twain National Forest

H.R. 6047 / Public Law 102–499
To amend the United States Information and Educational Exchange Act of 1948, the Foreign Service Act of 1980, and other provisions of law to make certain changes in administrative authorities

H.R. 6164 / Public Law 102–500
To amend the John F. Kennedy Center Act to authorize appropriations for maintenance, repair, alteration, and other services necessary for the John F. Kennedy Center for the Performing Arts

H.R. 6183 / Public Law 102–501
Federally Supported Health Centers Assistance Act of 1992

H.J. Res. 271 / Public Law 102–502
Authorizing the Go For Broke National Veterans Association Foundation to establish a memorial in the District of Columbia or its environs to honor Japanese American patriotism in World War II

H.J. Res. 409 / Public Law 102–503
Designating January 16, 1993, as "National Good Teen Day"

H.J. Res. 429 / Public Law 102–504
Designating May 2, 1993, through May 8, 1993, as "Be Kind to Animals and National Pet Week"

H.J. Res. 458 / Public Law 102–505
Designating the week beginning October 25, 1992, as "World Population Awareness Week"

S. 1145 / Public Law 102–506
Office of Government Ethics Amendments of 1992

S. 1577 / Public Law 102–507
Alzheimer's Disease Research, Training, and Education Amendments of 1992

S. 1583 / Public Law 102–508
Pipeline Safety Act of 1992

S. 2201 / Public Law 102–509
Soviet Scientists Immigration Act of 1992

S. 2322 / Public Law 102–510
Veterans' Compensation Cost-of-Living Adjustment Act of 1992

S. 2532 / Public Law 102–511
Freedom for Russia and Emerging Eurasian Democracies and Open Markets Support Act of 1992 (FREEDOM Support Act)

S. 2875 / Public Law 102–512
Children's Nutrition Assistance Act of 1992

S. 3224 / Public Law 102–513
To designate the United States Courthouse to be constructed in Fargo, North Dakota, as the "Quentin N. Burdick United States Courthouse"

S. 3279 / Public Law 102–514
To extend the authorization of use of official mail in the location and recovery of missing children, and for other purposes

S. 3312 / Public Law 102–515
Cancer Registries Amendment Act

S.J. Res. 304 / Public Law 102–516
Designating January 3, 1993, through January 9, 1993, as "National Law Enforcement Training Week"

S.J. Res. 309 / Public Law 102–517
Designating the week beginning November 8, 1992, as "National Women Veterans Recognition Week"

S.J. Res. 318 / Public Law 102–518
Designating November 13, 1992, as "Vietnam Veterans Memorial 10th Anniversary Day"

H.R. 3336 / Private Law 102–20
For the relief of Florence Adeboyeku

Approved October 25

H.R. 4542 / Public Law 102–519
Anti Car Theft Act of 1992

H.R. 5862 / Public Law 102–520
To amend title I of the Omnibus Crime Control and Safe Streets Act of 1968 to ensure an equitable and timely distribution of benefits to public safety officers

S. 1002 / Public Law 102–521
Child Support Recovery Act of 1992

Approved October 26

H.R. 2042 / Public Law 102–522
Fire Administration Authorization Act of 1992

H.R. 5419 / Public Law 102–523
International Dolphin Conservation Act of 1992

S. 2044 / Public Law 102–524
Native American Languages Act of 1992

S. 2890 / Public Law 102–525
To provide for the establishment of the Brown v. Board of Education National Historical Site in the State of Kansas, and for other purposes

S. 3006 / Public Law 102–526
President John F. Kennedy Assassination Records Collection Act of 1992

Approved October 27

H.R. 1252 / Public Law 102–527
Battered Women's Testimony Act of 1992

H.R. 1253 / Public Law 102–528
To amend the State Justice Institute Act of 1984 to carry out research, and develop judicial training curricula, relating to child custody litigation

H.R. 2660 / Public Law 102–529
To authorize appropriations for the United States Holocaust Memorial Council, and for other purposes

H.R. 3475 / Public Law 102–530
Women in Apprenticeship and Nontraditional Occupations Act

H.R. 3635 / Public Law 102–531
Preventive Health Amendments of 1992

H.R. 4059 / Public Law 102–532
Enterprise for the Americas Initiative Act of 1992

H.R. 4250 / Public Law 102–533
Amtrak Authorization and Development Act

H.R. 5716 / Public Law 102–534
To extend for two years the authorizations of appropriations for certain programs under title I of the Omnibus Crime Control and Safe Streets Act of 1968

H.R. 5763 / Public Law 102–535
To provide equitable treatment to producers of sugarcane subject to proportionate shares

H.R. 5853 / Public Law 102–536
To designate segments of the Great Egg Harbor River and its tributaries in the State of New Jersey as components of the National Wild and Scenic Rivers System

H.R. 6022 / Public Law 102–537
Ted Weiss Child Support Enforcement Act of 1992

H.R. 6180 / Public Law 102–538
Telecommunications Authorization Act of 1992

H.R. 6182 / Public Law 102–539
Mammography Quality Standards Act of 1992

H.J. Res. 503 / Public Law 102–540
Acknowledging the sacrifices that military families have made on behalf of the Nation and designating November 23, 1992, as "National Military Families Recognition Day"

S. 225 / Public Law 102–541
To expand the boundaries of the Fredericksburg and Spotsylvania County Battlefields Memorial National Military Park, Virginia

S. 759 / Public Law 102–542
Trademark Remedy Clarification Act

S. 1664 / Public Law 102–543
To establish the Keweenaw National Historical Park, and for other purposes

S. 2964 / Public Law 102–544
Granting the consent of the Congress to a supplemental compact or agreement between the Commonwealth of Pennsylvania and the State of New Jersey concerning the Delaware River Port Authority

S. 3134 / Public Law 102–545
Ready to Learn Act

Approved October 28

H.R. 707 / Public Law 102–546
Futures Trading Practices Act of 1992

H.R. 939 / Public Law 102–547
Veterans Home Loan Program Amendments of 1992

H.R. 3598 / Public Law 102–548
Intermodal Safe Container Transportation Act of 1992

H.R. 4996 / Public Law 102–549
Jobs Through Exports Act of 1992

H.R. 5334 / Public Law 102–550
Housing and Community Development Act of 1992

H.R. 5954 / Public Law 102–551
An Act to amend the Food, Agriculture, Conservation, and Trade Act of 1990 to improve health care services and educational services through telecommunications, and for other purposes

H.R. 6125 / Public Law 102–552
Farm Credit Banks and Associations Safety and Soundness Act of 1992

H.R. 6128 / Public Law 102–553
To amend the United States Warehouse Act to provide for the use of electronic cotton warehouse receipts, and for other purposes

H.R. 6129 / Public Law 102–554
Agricultural Credit Improvement Act of 1992

H.R. 6133 / Public Law 102–555
Land Remote Sensing Policy Act of 1992

H.R. 6191 / Public Law 102–556
Telephone Disclosure and Dispute Resolution Act

H.J. Res. 546 / Public Law 102–557
Designating February 4, 1993, and February 3, 1994, as "National Women and Girls in Sports Day"

S. 347 / Public Law 102–558
Defense Production Act Amendments of 1992

S. 474 / Public Law 102–559
Professional and Amateur Sports Protection Act

S. 758 / Public Law 102–560
Patent and Plant Variety Protection Remedy Clarification Act

S. 893 / Public Law 102–561
To amend title 18, United States Code, with respect to the criminal penalties for copyright infringement

S. 1439 / Public Law 102–562
To authorize and direct the Secretary of the Interior to convey certain lands in Livingston Parish, Louisiana, and for other purposes

S. 1623 / Public Law 102–563
Audio Home Recording Act of 1992

S. 2941 / Public Law 102–564
Small Business Research and Development Enhancement Act of 1992

S. 3309 / Public Law 102–565
To amend the Peace Corps Act to authorize appropriations for the Peace Corps for fiscal year 1993 and to establish a Peace Corps foreign exchange fluctuations account, and for other purposes

S. 3327 / Public Law 102–566
To amend the Agricultural Adjustment Act of 1938 to permit the acre-for-acre transfer of an acreage allotment or quota for certain commodities, and for other purposes

Approved October 29

H.R. 2130 / Public Law 102–567
National Oceanic and Atmospheric Administration Authorization Act of 1992

H.R. 5008 / Public Law 102–568
Veterans' Benefits Act of 1992

H.R. 5482 / Public Law 102–569
Rehabilitation Act Amendments of 1992

H.R. 5809 / Public Law 102–570
To authorize the Secretary of the Interior to construct and operate an interpretive center for the Ridgefield National Wildlife Refuge in Clark County, Washington

H.R. 6181 / Public Law 102–571
To amend the Federal Food, Drug, and Cosmetic Act to authorize human drug application, prescription drug establishment, and prescription drug product fees and for other purposes

S. 1569 / Public Law 102–572
Federal Courts Administration Act of 1992

S. 2481 / Public Law 102–573
Indian Health Amendments of 1992

S. 2679 / Public Law 102–574
Hawaii Tropical Forest Recovery Act

Approved October 30

H.R. 429 / Public Law 102–575
Reclamation Projects Authorization and Adjustment Act of 1992

H.R. 2032 / Public Law 102–576
Nez Perce National Historical Park Additions Act of 1991

H.J. Res. 422 / Public Law 102–577
Designating November 1992 as "Neuro-fibromatosis Awareness Month"

S. 775 / Public Law 102–578
Veterans' Radiation Exposure Amendments of 1992

S. 1671 / Public Law 102–579
Waste Isolation Pilot Plant Land Withdrawal Act

Approved October 31

H.R. 6167 / Public Law 102–580
Water Resources Development Act of 1992

H.R. 6168 / Public Law 102–581
Airport and Airway Safety, Capacity, Noise Improvement, and Intermodal Transportation Act of 1992

Approved November 2

H.R. 2152 / Public Law 102–582
High Seas Driftnet Fisheries Enforcement Act

H.R. 6187 / Public Law 102–583
International Narcotics Control Act of 1992

S. 2572 / Public Law 102–584
Arkansas-Idaho Land Exchange Act of 1992

Approved November 4

H.R. 5193 / Public Law 102–585
Veterans Health Care Act of 1992

H.R. 5194 / Public Law 102–586
To amend the Juvenile Justice and Delinquency Prevention Act of 1974 to authorize appropriations for fiscal years 1993, 1994, 1995, and 1996, and for other purposes

H.R. 5617 / Public Law 102–587
Oceans Act of 1992

H.R. 6135 / Public Law 102–588
National Aeronautics and Space Administration Authorization Act, Fiscal Year 1993

Approved November 10

H.R. 5377 / Public Law 102–589
Cash Management Improvement Act Amendments of 1992

H.R. 5400 / Public Law 102–590
Homeless Veterans Comprehensive Service Programs Act of 1992

Approved January 15

S.J. Res. 2 / Public Law 103–1
To authorize the United States Secret Service to continue to furnish protection to the former Vice President or his spouse

Approved January 19

S.J. Res. 1 / Public Law 103–2
To ensure that the compensation and other emoluments attached to the Office of Secretary of the Treasury are those which were in effect on January 1, 1989

Appendix E—Proclamations and Executive Orders

The texts of the proclamations and Executive orders are printed in the Federal Register (F.R.) at the citations listed below. The documents are also printed in title 3 of the Code of Federal Regulations and in the Weekly Compilation of Presidential Documents.

PROCLAMATIONS

EXECUTIVE ORDERS

Appendix F—Points of Light Recognition Program

The President named the following individuals and institutions as exemplars of his commitment to making community service central to the life and work of every American. The daily recognition program, which began on November 22, 1989, was a national tribute to voluntarism. The recipients for the period covered by this volume are listed in chronological order.

Emily Dutro, of Rochester, NY

Volunteers of A Safe Place, of Waukegan, IL

James Trammell III, of Greenville, SC

Volunteer counselors of the Rape Crisis Center, of Mobile, AL

Volunteers of St. Vincent's Center, of Timonium, MD

Vera McCoy, of McAlester, OK

Connie Maultsby and the Junior Kapps, of Sarasota, FL

Diana Gail Mills, of Means, KY

Fanniedell Peeples, of Detroit, MI

Father Jim Scholz and the volunteers of Sacred Heart Elementary School, of Omaha, NE

Volunteers of Kids With Character, of Columbus, MS

Ethletta Charles, of Danville, PA

Volunteers of Caldwell Care Network, of Caldwell, KS

Volunteers of Steamer Company No. 5, of Richmond, VA

Volunteers of the Vigo County School Corp. Adult Literacy Program, of Terre Haute, IN

Ivy Olson and the volunteers of the Angel Network, of Honolulu, HI

Volunteers of the Susquehanna County Volunteer Literacy Council, of Montrose, PA

Volunteers of Bethlehem House Project, Inc., of Redlands, CA

Carol and Hurt Porter and the volunteers of We Care About Kids, Kid Care, Inc., of Houston, TX

Jerry and Elouise Lee, of Page, AZ

Community Caring Volunteers, of Billings, MT

Volunteers of Rainbow House, of Trenton, NJ

Volunteers of the Committee Against Domestic Abuse, of Mankato, MN

Volunteers of One-to-One, of Ithaca, NY

Kenneth MacKenzie, of Gulf Breeze, FL

Volunteers of the Margaret Hudson Program, of Tulsa, OK

Volunteers of the Jersey Battered Women's Service, of Morris County, NJ

Volunteers of Students Against Violence Everywhere (S.A.V.E), of West Charlotte, NC

Loretta Warsow, of McMurray, PA

Volunteers of Turning Point, of Roanoke, VA

Volunteers of the St. Vincent DePaul Society, of Meriden, CT

Kay Dyer Arrillaga, of Carmel, CA

Walter Yurcik, of Wharton, NJ

Volunteers of McCurdy School, of Espanola, NM

James S. Burton, of Nashville, TN

Volunteers of Rainbow Home, of Wernersville, PA

Queen Mims, of Bridgeport, CT

Cletus Lyday, of Milwaukee, WI

Volunteers of the Enterprise Helping Hands Network, of Newport News, VA

Volunteers of Seniors Actively Volunteering in Education (SAVE), of Honolulu, HI

Volunteers of Created for Caring, of Bay City, MI

Volunteers of the Greater Gulf Literacy Council, of Mobile, AL

Heather Brown, of Dayton, OH

Volunteers of Project Understanding, of Ventura, CA

Volunteers of Winthrop's Involvement in Nurturing and Graduating Students (WINGS), of Rockhill, SC

Volunteers of Groveport Madison LINK, of Groveport, OH

Ann Jackson, of Freeport, NY

Volunteers and staff of PROJECT MENTOR, of Wye Mills, MD

Volunteers of the Early Gang Learning Experience (EAGLE), of Sacramento, CA

Shawn Huff, of Colorado Springs, CO

Volunteers of the Society of St. Vincent de Paul, of Portland, OR

Volunteers of the Southern Mutual Help Association, of New Iberia, LA

SuEllen Fried, of Prairie Village, KS

Volunteers of Because We Care II, of Dover, DE

Volunteers of the Rochester Toy Library, of Rochester, NY

Volunteers of the Lehman Community Service Council, of Williamstown, MA

Volunteers of Adjacent Generational Exchange (A.G.E.), of Royal Oak, MI

Volunteers of Feed My Sheep, of Gulfport, MS

Volunteers of Winners On Wheels (WOW), of Fresno, CA

Volunteers of Holy Angels of Belmont, of Belmont, NC

Yvonne Pointer, of Cleveland, OH

Volunteers of the Friends Program, of Orlando, FL

Lloyd Porter, of Great Falls, MT

Volunteers of Interval House Crisis Shelters, of Orange County and Long Beach, CA

Volunteers of the Ronald McDonald House, of Philadelphia, PA

Betty Simon, of Olean, NY

Volunteers of the 36th Avenue Task Force, of Omaha, NE

Gwynette Hatcher, of North Charleston, SC

Robert Williams and Dwayne Claassen, of Lakewood, CO

Volunteers of Kinship of Greater Minneapolis, of Minneapolis, MN

Grace Hiddleson, of Woodland, CA

Mary Dell Robinson, of Lumberton, MS

Dorothy and William Pahl, of Bridgeport, OH

Volunteers of Habitat of Evansville, of Evansville, IN

Volunteers of the Center for Parenting Excellence, of La Grande, OR

Service Company Midshipmen Battalion Naval ROTC Unit of Vanderbilt University, of Nashville, TN

Volunteers of the Full Circle Student Support Program, of San Rafael, CA

Volunteers of Youth to Youth, of Columbus, OH

Myra Arnold, of Shalimar, FL

Doris Frank, of Lake Waukomis, MO

Volunteers of Mobile AIDS Support Services, of Mobile, AL

Volunteers of Genesis Women's Shelter, of Dallas, TX

Andrew Bales, of Des Moines, IA

Volunteers of the Hidenwood Tutoring Team, of Newport News, VA

Helen Shapiro, of Cleveland Heights, OH

Lydia Flores Perkins, of Pharr, TX

Volunteers of Safe Place, of Raleigh, NC

Volunteers of San Diego Rescue Mission, Inc., of San Diego, CA

Jesse Chambers, of Las Vegas, NV

Volunteers of City Mission Society, of Buffalo, NY

Ahmed Dahir, of Los Angeles, CA

Volunteers in Corrections, Inc., of St. Paul, MN

Volunteers of the Burnet County Library System, of Burnet, TX

Volunteers of the Johns Hopkins University Tutorial Project, of Baltimore, MD

Loi Van Nguyen, of Grand Rapids, MI

Col. Victor Ferrari, of San Antonio, TX

Joe Anna Caldwell, of Jacksonville, IL

Volunteers of Our Kids, of Sacramento, CA

Volunteers of the Visiting Nurses Association Mobile Meals Program, of Dayton, OH

Volunteers of the Hunger Coalition Community Gardens of Interfaith Ministries for Greater Houston, of Houston, TX

Volunteers of Save the Seed, of Charlotte, NC

Volunteers of the Kansas City, Kansas (KCK) Rebound Center, Inc., of Kansas City, KS

Jenny and Joseph Tranfaglia, of Farmingville, NY

Richard Olango Abuka, of San Diego, CA

Volunteers of the Literacy Council of Bowie and Miller Counties, of Texas and Arkansas

Volunteers of Child Abuse Prevention Services, of Lansing, MI

Volunteers of Youth Competency in Math and Science, of Boulder, CO

Volunteers of Partners in Progress of the Agricultural Research Service of the U.S. Department of Agriculture, of Mississippi State, MS

Volunteers of Vietnamese Social Services' Elders Program, of St. Paul, MN

Volunteers of The A+ Coalition, of Austin, TX

Heather Vultee and the volunteers of Colby Friends, of Waterville, ME

Volunteers of Long Island Youth Guidance, of Dix Hills, NY

Volunteers of Casa de los Niños, of Tucson, AZ

Jane Rozett, of Macon, GA

Richard Cushman, of Auburn, CA

Volunteers of the Oregon Human Development Teen Parent Special Friends Program, of Hillsboro, OR

Volunteers of the Service Guild Early Intervention Program, of Homewood, AL

Jacquelyn Meadors, of New Market, VA

Vernon Shive, of Phillipsburg, NJ

Harry Vines, of North Little Rock, AR

Literacy Volunteers of America, Maine, Dover-Foxcroft Affiliate, of Dover and Foxcroft, ME

Volunteers of the Bates Buddy Program, of Tacoma, WA

Ellen Bigger, of Key Largo, FL

Volunteers of Edgehill Community Center, of Nashville, TN

Mary Schermerhorn, of San Antonio, TX

Volunteers of the Senior Victim Assistance Team, of Colorado Springs, CO

Volunteers of Union Gospel Mission, of Spokane, WA

Volunteers of the California Grey Bears, Inc., of Santa Cruz, CA

Volunteers of the Burn Intensive Care Volunteer Program, of Cleveland, OH

Margie Sumlin, of Mobile, AL

Volunteers of Students Engaged in Rewarding Volunteer Experiences (S.E.R.V.E.), University of Minnesota-Duluth, of Duluth, MN

Volunteers of Oregon Outreach, Inc., of Portland, OR

Volunteers of Bootstraps of America, Inc., of Anchorage, AK

Volunteers of the Saturday Academy, of Dover, DE

James and Sharon Ferrari, of Kalamazoo, MI

Henry Huffman, of Santa Clara, CA

Volunteers of Campus Coalition for Literacy, of Columbia, SC

Volunteers of the COMSAT Corp.-Jefferson Junior High School Education Alliance, of Washington, DC

Eileen Ayvazian, of Virginia Beach, VA

Volunteers of TeenAdvisors, of Columbus, GA

Volunteers of the Youth Service Bridge Builders Program, of Memphis, TN

Volunteers of Hot Springs Village, of Hot Springs, AR

Volunteers of the ARCO-Bakersfield High School Partnership, of Bakersfield, CA

Mathog & Moniello Team Volunteers, of East Haven, CT

Volunteers of the El Paso Shelter for Battered Women, of El Paso, TX

Kate Porter, of Columbus, OH

Bob Richie, of Philadelphia, PA

Theresa Orzechowski, of Newburgh, NY

Volunteers of the Tutoring Team, of Livonia, MI

Stamford Women's Mentoring Program, of Stamford, CT

Kathryn "Babe" Weiller, of Sarasota, FL

Volunteers of the Harlem Junior Tennis Program, of New York, NY

Volunteers of Gang Peace, of Dorchester, MA

Dale Huffman, of Miamisburg, OH

Waymon Logan and the volunteers of Dayspring Outreach, of Sacramento, CA

YES! Atlanta's Rising Star Program, of Atlanta, GA

Volunteers Involved for the Emotional Well-Being of Seniors (VIEWS), of Gresham, OR

Volunteers of CityTeam Ministries, of San Jose, CA

Camille Germain, of Huntington, NY

Dorothy Veasey, of Newark, DE

Volunteers of MacMagic Classroom, of San Rafael, CA

Eugene Crawford, of Uniontown, PA

Ron and Melinda Cowart, of Dallas, TX

Iva Kaufman, of Hemet, CA

Volunteers of the Community Involvement Program of Barnett Bank, of Jacksonville, FL

Melodee Lazaruk, of Memphis, TN

Volunteers of the Lakeland Middle School Eighth Grade, of Baltimore, MD

Volunteers of Mary House, of Washington, DC

Volunteers of Rape Victim Services, of Paducah, KY

Phyliss Fishleder and the volunteers of Fabulous Finds, of San Diego, CA

Robert Thompson, of St. Joseph, MO

Jennifer Trigg, of San Jose, CA

Volunteers of Mariucci Inner City Hockey Starter Association, of St. Paul, MN

Subject Index

Name Index

Document Categories List